WHAT DO
CHILDREN
AND YOUNG
ADULTS

READ
NEXT?

A Reader's Guide to
Fiction for Children
and Young Adults

ISSN 1540-5060

WHAT DO CHILDREN AND YOUNG ADULTS

READ NEXT?

A Reader's Guide to Fiction for Children and Young Adults

VOLUME 5

JANIS ANSELL
PAM SPENCER HOLLEY

GALE®

THOMSON
GALE

Detroit • New York • San Diego • San Francisco • Cleveland • New Haven, Conn. • Waterville, Maine • London • Munich

THOMSON

GALE

What Do Children and Young Adults Read Next?, Volume 5

Janis Ansell, Pam Spencer Holley

Project Editor
Dana Ferguson

Editorial
Prindle LaBarge

Editorial Support Services
Magdalena Cureton

Product Design
Michael Logusz

Composition and Electronic Capture
Gary Leach

Manufacturing
Stacy L. Melson

ISBN 0-7876-4800-0
ISSN 1540-5060

Printed in the United States of America
10 9 8 7 6 5 4 3

Contents

Preface

New Combined Volume!

This volume of *What Do Children and Young Adults Read Next?* represents the merging of *What Do Children Read Next?* and *What Do Young Adults Read Next?* into one comprehensive volume. It is a reader's advisory tool designed to match readers from preschool through high school with books that reflect their interests and concerns. It guides both reluctant and avid readers to new authors and titles for further reading. *What Do Children and Young Adults Read Next?* allows readers quick and easy access to specific information on recent titles. In addition, each entry provides alternate reading selections, giving children, parents, and librarians the answer to the frequently asked question: "What do I read next?"

Highlights

• Compiled by Janis Ansell and Pam Spencer Holly, both experts in the field of juvenile and young adult literature.

• Overview essay describes recent trends in children's and young adult's literature.

• "Other books you might like," included in each entry, leads to the exploration of additional authors or titles.

• Twelve indexes help locate specific titles or offer suggestions for reading in favorite time periods or geographic locales, about special subjects or characters, or for a particular age level.

• All authors and titles listed in entries under "Other books by the author" and "Other books you might like" are indexed, allowing easy access to thousands of books recommended for further reading.

Details on 1,000 titles

What Do Children and Young Adults Read Next? contains entries for 1,000 books published between 2000-2002 aimed at young readers. Titles have been selected on the basis of their currency, appeal to readers, and literary merit. The entries are listed alphabetically by author. Books by authors with more than one entry are then subarranged by title. The following information is provided where applicable:

• Author's name and real name if a pseudonym is used. Co-author, editor, and illustrator's names also given.

• Book title.

• Date and place of publication; name of publisher.

• Series name.

• Age Range: Indicates the grade levels for which the title is best suited.

• Subject(s): Up to three themes or topics covered in the story.

• Major character(s): Names of up to three featured characters and brief descriptions of them.

• Time Period(s): Tells when the story takes place.

• Locale(s): Tells where the story takes place.

• What the book is about: A brief plot summary.

• Page Count: Indicates the title's specific page count. Located at the end of the plot summary.

• Where it's reviewed: Citations to reviews of the book, including the source of the review, date of the source, and page on which the review appears. Reviews are taken from general reviewing sources such as *Kirkus Reviews* and *Publishers Weekly*, as well as from sources which specialize in materials for younger readers, such as *School Library Journal* and *Horn Book*.

• Awards the book has won.

• Other books by the author: Titles and publication dates of other books the author has written, for those wanting to read more books by a particular writer.

• Other books you might like: Titles by other authors written on a similar theme or in a similar style. A one sentence description of each of these titles whets the reader's appetite for additional titles.

Indexes Answer Reader's Questions

The twelve indexes in *What Do Children and Young Adults Read Next?* are the heart of the book.

Used separately or in conjunction, they create many pathways to the featured titles, answering general questions or locating specific titles. For example:

"What are the best books for children and young adults?"

The AWARDS INDEX lists awards and citations given by experts in the field of children's literature. These titles are especially noteworthy.

"Do you know of any books set during World War II?"

The TIME PERIOD INDEX is a chronological listing of the time settings in which the main entries take place.

"Are there any books set in Japan?"

The GEOGRAPHIC INDEX lists titles by their locale, helping readers pinpoint a geographic area in which they may have a particular interest.

"I like stories with animals in them. What do you suggest?"

The SUBJECT INDEX lists books by what they are about. Topics include such things as fiction genres (e.g. Fantasy, Ghost Stories, Mystery and Detective Stories), life and relationships (e.g. Family Life, Friendship, School), and subjects of interest to today's children and young adults (e.g. Dinosaurs, Magic, Sports).

"Do you have any books with kids whose name is the same as mine?"

The CHARACTER NAME INDEX lists the characters named in the entries, helping readers who remember some information about a book, but not an author or title.

"Do you have any books with cowboys or cowgirls in them?"

The CHARACTER DESCRIPTION INDEX identifies the major characters by occupation (e.g. Astronaut, Doctor) or persona (e.g. Cat, Toy, Twin).

"Which books are good for sixth graders?"

The AGE LEVEL INDEX lists titles by grade levels for which they are best suited. The ability of individual readers may not necessarily reflect their actual age; the wide variety of age ranges allows the user to select titles for slower or more advanced readers.

"I need to write a report on a 150 page book. What do you suggest?"

The PAGE COUNT INDEX groups titles according to their page count ranges, allowing readers to select individual titles with specific page counts.

"Which books have pictures by Chris Raschka?"

The ILLUSTRATOR INDEX is an alphabetical listing of the illustrators of the main entry titles.

"What has Avi written recently?"

The AUTHOR INDEX contains the names of all authors featured in the entries and those listed under "Other books you might like."

"Are there any books like J.K. Rowling's Harry Potter books?"

The TITLE INDEX includes all main entry titles and all titles recommended under "Other books by the author" and "Other books you might like" in one alphabetical listing. By searching for a specific title, the reader can find out what other books are similar to a title they like.

The indexes can also be used to narrow down or broaden choices. A reader interested in 50 page stories set in England during World War II would consult the PAGE COUNT, SUBJECT, and GEOGRAPHIC indexes to see which titles appear in all three. Someone interested in detective stories set during the 1930s could compare titles in the TIME PERIOD and CHARACTER DESCRIPTION indexes. And with the AUTHOR and TITLE indexes, which include all books listed under "Other books by the author" and "Other books you might like," it is easy to compile an extensive list of titles for further reading, not only with the titles recommended in a main entry, but also by seeing other titles to which the main entry or its recommended titles are similar.

About the Authors

Janis Ansell

Janis Ansell's writing of the children's entries for *What Do Children and Young Adults Read Next?* reflects her life-long interest in reading and her ability to adapt knowledge gained in one subject area to another. Beyond a personal interest in reading she seeks to develop children's literacy and share her love of reading with them. Janis, a former school psychologist and early childhood teacher, and her husband Charles, a self-employed architect, have brought up three enthusiastic readers—their children Jonathan, Carrie, and Laurie.

Professional expertise and affiliations and volunteer participation in libraries and classrooms augment her natural interest in books, especially those for children. Ansell is a former children's book reviewer for *ForeWord Magazine*. Professionally affiliated with the Randolph-Macon Woman's College Alumnae Association Board, Ansell has been named an Honorary Life Member of the Virginia Congress of Parents and Teachers and a Volunteer of the Year at Alanton Elementary School. She has served on the Lynnhaven Middle School Planning Council and is a past board member of the Tidewater Association of Hearing Impaired Children and of the Alanton PTA. Ansell is a member of the American Library Association (ALA) and the Association of Library Service to Children (ALSC). She is a library and classroom volunteer at Virginia Beach Friends School.

Janis Ansell's psychological insight into young children, her love of books, and her practical experience as a professional, a parent, and a volunteer make her entries in *What Do Children and Young Adults Read Next?* exceptionally informative and useful.

Pam Spencer Holley

Pam Spencer Holley, coordinator and author of the young adult entries for *What Do Children and Young Read Next?*, and retired coordinator of library services for the Fairfax County Public schools in Virginia, is a recognized expert in young adult literature. Elected to the Margaret A. Edwards Award Committee by the Young Adult Library Services Association of the American Library Association, she currently serves on their Alex Award Task Force, a committee that annually selects the top adult books for young adults. In addition, she will serve as chair for the 2004 Michael L. Printz Award Committee which selects the finest books for young adults, based solely on literary quality. Pam was a recent member of the Advisory Committee for the sixteenth edition of H.W. Wilson's Senior High School Library Catalog. She is also an occasional contributing reviewer to *School Library Journal* and served as a past chair of the column "Adult Books for Young Adults" for that publication. She currently serves as Vice-President of the Board of the Friends of the Virginia Beach Public Library, as well as a member of the Advisory Board for the professional publication *Voice of Youth Advocates*, more commonly known as VOYA.

Acknowledgments

Janis Ansell

The cooperative efforts of many contributed to the successful completion of the fifth volume and first combined volume of *What Do Children and Young Adults Read Next?* The support of many people has been invaluable and I offer appreciation to my family: my husband, Charles; our son Jonathan; daughters Carrie and Laurie; my sister and co-author, Pam Spencer Holley; my parents Boyd and Jane Gustafson. Many publishers graciously sent review copies of their 2001 titles. Editor Dana Ferguson remained open to our ideas about the possibilities of the combined volume and patient and upbeat through unexpected delays. To my alma mater, Randolph-Macon Woman's College, I am indebted for the education that inspired me to accept opportunities and enabled me to succeed with challenges.

Pam Spencer Holley

Once again, special thanks to my dad, Boyd "Gus" Gustafson, for his delivery service of young adult titles from the Williamsburg Regional Library to my home in Virginia Beach, and to my mom, Jane Gustafson, for the treats that often arrived with the books. Thanks to my husband Rick Holley, not only for his patience with me when deadline nears, but also for maintaining the database of entries for *What Do Children and Young Adults Read Next?* In addition to the Williamsburg Regional Library, copies of books were also obtained from the Virginia Beach Public Library, purchased from bookstores or received through the generosity of our wonderful American and Canadian publishers of children's and young adult books. I am grateful to Cathy Chauvette, public librarian with Fairfax County (VA) and long-time friend, for continuing to write the majority of the science fiction and fantasy entries. It was a special treat to work more closely with co-author Janis Ansell, who also happens to be my sister, in this first of the yearly editions to combine the children's and young adult books into the single edition of *What Do Children and Young Adults Read Next?* And to editor Dana Ferguson, my continued thanks for being so knowledgeable and caring; it is a pleasure to work with you

Also Available Online

The entries in *What Do Children and Young Adults Read Next?* can also be found in the online version of *What Do I Read Next?* on GaleNet. This electronic product encompasses over 100,000 books, including genre fiction, mainstream fiction, and nonfiction. All the books included in *What Do I Read Next?* Online are recommended by librarians or other experts, award winners, or appear on bestseller lists. The user-friendly functionality allows users to refine their searching by using several criteria, while making it easy to identify similar titles for further research and reading. The online version is updated with new information two times a year. For more information about *What Do I Read Next?* Online or GaleNet, please contact Gale Group, Inc.

Suggestions Are Welcome

The editor welcomes any comments and suggestions for enhancing and improving *What Do Children and Young Adults Read Next?* Please address correspondence to:

Editor
What Do Children and Young Adults Read Next?
Gale Group, Inc.
25700 Drake Road
Farmington Hills, Michigan 48331-3535
Phone: 248-699-GALE
Toll-free: 1-800-347-GALE
Fax: 248-699-8054

Introduction

Without a doubt, the defining moment of 2001 was the horrible terrorist attacks on September 11. Most people wanted to "do something" to help, and publishers were no different; that desire led to a unified promotion of reading by the publishing community. In addition to launching a national campaign, publishers donated books through the Children's Aid Society and held an art auction to raise relief funds. Booklists dealing with tragedy and terrorism were posted on web sites, including those of the Loose Leaf Book Company (www.looseleaf.org) and the Society of Children's Book Writers and Illustrators (www.scbwi.org), while public libraries in the New York and Washington areas, as well as throughout the country, developed their own lists of resources to assist the public. In the time that followed, books on patriotism, firefighters, and New York City proved popular, with publishers and booksellers alike commenting on the public's newfound appreciation for the cathartic effect of reading together.

Just a few days before Americans turned inward, First Lady Laura Bush hosted the National Book Festival, modeled after a similar one in Texas, held on September 8 at the Library of Congress. To encourage a national celebration of books and the pleasure of reading, a variety of activities (including book signings and readings) took place on the Capitol grounds and in the library itself. Also, the Laura Bush Foundation for America's Libraries will provide grants to school and classroom libraries.

Articles Not to Be Missed

• Aronson, Marc. "Slippery Slopes and Proliferating Prizes." *Horn Book*, May/June 2001, pp. 271-278.

Provocative comments about literary awards specific to minority writers.

• Bainbridge, Joyce and Sylvia Pantaleo. "Filling the Gaps in Text: Picture Book Reading in the Middle Years." The New Advocate, Fall 2001, pp. 401-411.

How selected picture books enhance the reading ability of middle school students.

• Barron, T.A. "Truth and Dragon." *School Library Journal*, June 2001, pp. 52-54.

A discussion of the fantasy genre.

• Campbell, Patty. "A Loving Farewell to Robert Cormier." *Horn Book*, March/April 2001, pp. 245-248.

• Cart, Michael. "Carte Blanche: The Same Side." Booklist, February 15, 2002, p. 1008.

Outstanding children's literature about the black experience in America published during 2001.

• Crutcher, Chris. "The Outsiders." *School Library Journal*, August 2001, pp. 54-56.

Discussion of a novel that was discarded after the Columbine tragedy.

• Cummings, Pat. "The Man Who Became Keats." School Library Journal, May 2001, pp. 46-49.

To commemorate the Ezra Jack Keats Award's tenth anniversary, reflections on the artist's life and career.

• Curry, Ann. "Where Is Judy Blume?: Controversial Fiction of Older Children and Young Adults." *Journal of Youth Services in Libraries*, Spring 2001, pp. 28-37.

Report of research on censorship of library materials.

• Ditlow, Tim. "Behind the Scenes of an Audiobook." *Publishers Weekly*, May 14, 2001, pp. 38-39.

The making of Philip Pullman's *The Amber Spyglass* in a London recording studio.

• Lodge, Sally. "Making the Transition." *Publishers Weekly*, October 1, 2001, pp. 28-31.

Interviews with six women who recently retired from children's publishing.

• Marcus, Leonard S. "Make Way for Marketing." *Publishers Weekly*, September 17, 2001, pp. 30-34.

Historical overview of marketing for children's and young adult publishing.

- McCully, Emily Arnold. "Imagination and Risk." *Riverbank Review*, Fall 2001, pp. 25-27.

Edited keynote address at the Ninth Annual Hubbs Children's Literature Conference expressing McCully's premise that "books should expand a child's world, not shrink it."

- Pinkney, Andrea Davis. "Awards That Stand on Solid Ground." *Horn Book*, September/October 2001, pp. 535-539.

Reply to Marc Aronson's article.

- Simont, Marc. "Adventures in Illustration." *Riverbank Review*, Summer 2001, pp. 14-17.

Reflections on the author's long career.

- Small, David. "The 2001 Caldecott Medal Acceptance Speech." *Journal of Youth Services in Libraries*, Summer 2001, pp. 10-13.

Small's medal acceptance speech for *So You Want to Be President?*

- Wells, Rosemary. "Rabbit Redux." School Library Journal, July 2001, pp. 43-45.

Keynote address at the inaugural Rabbit Hill Festival to honor Robert Lawson's legacy.

- Woodson, Jacqueline. "Miracles." *School Library Journal*, August 2001, pp. 57-58.

Acceptance speech by Coretta Scott King Author Award winner.

- Wynne-Jones, Tim. "The Unraveling of DNA: Douglas Noel Adams, 1952-2001." *Horn Book*, September/October 2001, pp. 628-632.

Author Interviews

- *David Almond*

Odean, Kathleen. "Mystic Man." *School Library Journal*, April 2001, pp. 48-52.

- *Brock Cole*

Beebe, Kathryne. "Brock Cole." *Riverbank Review*, Spring 2001, pp. 24-27.

- *Sharon Creech*

Britton, Jason. "Everyday Journeys." *Publishers Weekly*, July 26, 2001, pp. 153-154.

- *Jack Gantos*

Alfano, Christine. "Jack Gantos." *Riverbank Review*, Summer 2001, pp. 20-24.

- *Kevin Henkes*

Swanson, Susan Marie. "Kevin Henkes." *Riverbank Review*, Fall 2001, pp. 10-13.

- *Julius Lester*

Lodge, Sally. "Working at His Creative Peak." *Publishers Weekly*, February 12, 2001, pp. 180-181.

- *Robert Lipsyte*

Myers, Walter Dean. "Pulling No Punches." *School Library Journal*, June 2001, pp. 44-47.

- *Katherine Paterson*

Sutton, Roger. "An Interview with Katherine Paterson." *Horn Book*, November/December 2001, pp. 689-699.

- *Gloria Whelan*

Isaacs, Kathleen T. "Flying High." *School Library Journal*, March 2001, pp. 52-55.

- *David Wiesner*

Silvey, Anita. "Pigs in Space." *School Library Journal*, November 2001, pp. 48-50.

- *Virginia Euwer Wolff*

Sutton, Roger. "An Interview with Virginia Euwer Wolff." *Horn Book*, May/June, 2001, pp. 280-286.

Awards

England

The **2000 British Book Award: Children's Book of the Year** went to *The Amber Spyglass* by Philip Pullman. Other contenders were *Harry Potter and the Goblet of Fire* by J.K. Rowling (Bloomsbury), Jacqueline Wilson's *Vicky Angel* (Transworld), and Jamila Gavin's *Coram Boy* (Mammoth).

Coram Boy by Jamila Gavin (Mammoth) won the 2000 **Whitbread Children's Award**; the short list included *Heaven Eyes* by David Almond (Hodder); *The Seeing Stone* by Kevin Crossley-Holland (Orion), and *Troy* by Adele Geras (Scholastic).

Anne Fine was appointed as the second **Children's Laureate** for the United Kingdom in recognition of her "wide-ranging and influential contribution to children's books over the past 20 years." Although this 2-year appointment carries no specific duties, it is understood that the laureate will promote children's books and reading.

United States

Author Janet S. Wong was recognized with the 2001 **Asian Pacific American Award for Children's Literature** for her picture book *The Trip Back Home*, illustrated by Bo Jia.

Boston Globe-Horn Book 2001 honor book awards were presented to *Everything on a Waffle* by Polly Horvath and *Troy* by Adele Geras. The *Boston Globe-Horn Book Award* for picture book went to *Cold Feet* by author Cynthia DeFelice and illustrator Robert Andrew Parker. Honor books include Carol Otis Hurst's *Rocks in His Head*, with illustrations by James Stevenson; *Five Creatures*, written by Emily Jenkins and illustrated by Tomek Bogacki; and author/illustrator Marc Simont's *The Stray Dog*.

Hope Was Here by Joan Bauer and *The Wanderer* by Sharon Creech each received **Christopher Awards** for 2001. These awards are given to books that remind readers "of their power to positively impact and shape the world." Also recognized were the picture books *How Do Dinosaurs Say Goodnight?* by Jane Yolen, with illustrations by Mark Teague; *The Mousery*, written by Charlotte Pomerantz and illustrated by Kurt Cyrus; and Carmen Agra Deedy's title *The Yellow Star*, illustrated by Henri Sorensen. Editor Margaret K. McElderry, recipient of the **Christopher Life Achievement Award** for 2001, was the first professional in the field of publishing to be so recognized in the 51-year history of the award, presented for "extraordinary contributions to the field of children's literature."

The 2001 **Empire State Award** honoring a New York State author or illustrator whose work has made a significant contribution to young people's literature went to Jean Fritz.

The 2001 **Virginia Hamilton Literary Award** honoring an American writer for an "enduring contribution to the understanding of the parallel cultures that make up our world" went to Patricia McKissack.

The Ezra Jack Keats Foundation and the New York Public Library awarded author D.B. Johnson the 2001 **Ezra Jack Keats New Writer Award** for *Henry Hikes to Fitchburg*, the first picture book also written by this illustrator. For his picture book *Uptown*, Bryan Collier received the **Ezra Jack Keats New Illustrator Award**.

The **Los Angeles Times Prize for Young Adult Writing** went to Jacqueline Woodson's *Miracle Boys*.

Joan Bauer received the 2001 **New England Book Award** for Children's Books, presented to a "New England author who produced a body of work that made a significant contribution to New England culture."

Lee & Low presented its 2000—and first annual—**New Voices Award** to Linda Boyden for her picture book manuscript, *The Blue Roses*. In addition to a cash prize, the award includes a publishing contract with Lee & Low.

Hyperion initiated the **New Voices, New Worlds** grants, which award a first-time author a book contract for a previously unpublished work of "contemporary or historical fiction for ages 8-12 that reflects the diverse ethnic and cultural heritage of the United States." No win-

ner was selected in 2001 and the deadline for entries was extended into 2002.

Author and illustrator Rosemary Wells was the 2001 recipient of the **Jo Osborne Award for Humor in Children's Literature**.

E.L. Konigsburg received the **Regina Medal**, presented by the Catholic Library Association for outstanding contributions to children's literature.

The **Virginia Young Readers Award** for 2001 was given to *Joey Pigza Swallowed the Key* by Jack Gantos.

The **Charlotte Zolotow Award** presented in 2002 for "outstanding writing in a children's picture book" published in 2001 went to Margaret Willey for her title, *Clever Beatrice*, illustrated by Heather Solomon. One honor book, *Five Creatures,* written by Emily Jenkins and illustrated by Tomek Bogacki, was also chosen. The Charlotte Zolotow Award committee of the Cooperative Children's Book Center also announced five "highly commended" authors: Lenore Look for *Henry's First Moon Birthday*, illustrations by Yumi Heo; Margaret Reed MacDonald and illustrator Tim Coffey for *Mabela the Clever*; Marisabina Russo for *Come Back, Hannah*, which she also illustrated; Catherine Stock, author/illustrator of *Gugu's House*; and Janet Wong for *Grump*, illustrated by John Wallace.

For complete lists of Newbery, Caldecott, Coretta Scott King, Pura Belpre, Notables, Best Books for Young Adults, Quick Picks, Michael L. Printz, and Alex Award recipients, search the ALA website at www.ala.org.

Books from/about Other Countries

Ireland

Since the 1980s more books for young people have been published in Ireland, with many of them reaching America. Irish history is a popular topic, as evidenced by such 2001 titles as *Dancing for Danger* by Margot Griffin, Deborah Lisson's *Red Hugh*, *Knockabeg* by Mary Lyons, Clare Pastore's *Fiona McGilroy's Story*, and *Guns of Easter* by Gerald Whelan. This increase can be attributed to several factors, ranging from support by the Arts Council, to tax-free royalties for creative artists, to a booming Irish economy. Publishers and writers may also be responding to support for their professional organization, Children's Books Ireland, or the increasing awareness and importance of the Bisto Book of the Year Award. Though O'Brien Press dominates the field of children's publishing in Ireland, Blackwater, The Children's Press, Mentor, Mercier, and Wolfhound Press are also active.

The recently published Irish author Eoin Colfer made a big splash with *Artemis Fowl*, titled after the lead character. Hyperion hopes Artemis will be the next Harry Potter and, though the two characters are dissimilar, they should appeal to the same audience. Author Colfer states that he tried to create an action-adventure-type fairy story, though the fairies in his book are not the ethereal, diminutive ones of the Brothers Grimm.

Korea

With children making up a potential readership of 60% of its population, Korea is experiencing a major boom in children's publishing in both translations and original works. When publishers realized the popularity of the Harry Potter books, they wanted a share of the children's market, but may have difficulty in achieving it, as they must overcome traditional door-to-door selling methods and establish a book distribution system. In their favor, the publishers are making good use of the Internet as another means of book distribution.

In this country, An Na's first novel, *A Step from Heaven,* won the Michael L. Printz Award for its description of a Korean family's difficulty adjusting to life in the U.S. Newbery Award winner Linda Sue Park's *A Single Shard* takes place in 12th century Korea and is the exquisite tale of a young orphan whose tenacity in assisting a potter leads to a new life.

England

According to "Letter from London" by Julia Eccleshare (*Publishers Weekly,* July 30, 2001, page 24), publishing books for teens in the United Kingdom has always been difficult because of a nebulous marketing strategy and a poorly defined audience, yet several publishers are reacting to the popularity of such British authors as J.K. Rowling and Philip Pullman by starting lists for teens. Collins is debuting the Flamingo imprint; Red Fox has a new list named Definitions; Hodder is adding Bite to its Signatures imprint; Macmillan will go with Young Picador; and Little, Brown is expanding its adult science fiction line to entice young adult readers. Publishers hope to promote both their previously successful authors and some new writers.

Two of Jacqueline Wilson's titles became available to American audiences this year after publication by Delacorte. *The Story of Tracy Beaker,* about a 10-year-old in the foster care system hoping that her absentee mother will soon return for her, was originally published in Great Britain in 1991. Another foster care story is Wilson's *Bad Girls,* first published in Great Britain in 1996 and selected as an IRA Children's Choice in 2002. Tanya, a teen placed in a foster home near only-child Mandy, adds flavor to the 10-year-old girl's monotonous life and helps her overly-protective parents gain a new perspective, although she's less successful at modifying her own life situation. Another of prolific author Dick King-Smith's chapter books was published in America in 2001; *Lady Lollipop* is the award-winning story of a pig, her trainer, and the princess who is unwittingly trained by them.

Picture books seem to travel across "the pond" more rapidly than most novels unless the novels star Harry Potter. Titles by British authors that won American book awards in 2001 include John Burningham's *Hushabye*; *My Dad* by Anthony Browne; *Beware the Story Book Wolves* and *Clarice Bean, Guess Who's Babysitting?* by Lauren Child; *Rufferella* by Vanessa Gill-Brown, with illustrations by Mandy Stanley; and Mick Inkpen's *Kipper's A to Z: An Alphabet Adventure.* All were originally published in Great Britain in the year 2000.

Australia, Venezuela and France

Australian import *Fox,* written by Margaret Wild and illustrated by Ron Brooks, won the Children's Book Council of Australia's Best Picture Book award. Another title originally published in Australia in 1999 is *Luke's Way of Looking* by Nadia Wheatley, with illustrations by Matt Ottley.

Some imports, including the following award-winning titles, require translation. Blue Ribbon winner *The Great Canoe: A Karina Legend,* retold by Maria Elena Maggi, with illustrations by Gloria Calderon, was published in Venezuela in 1998 and translated from the Spanish by Elisa Amado. Anais Vaugelade's title *The War,* a Notable Social Studies Trade Book for Young People and an IRA Children's Choice, was published in 1998 in France and translated by Marie-Christine Rouffiac and Tom Streissguth. Another French import, *A Book of Coupons* by Susie Morgenstern, received two awards, including recognition as a Mildred L. Batchelder Honor Book.

Censorship, or, you win some, you lose some

In Anaheim, California, the Orangeview Middle School librarian weeded 30-year-old biographies from her shelves and replaced them with Chelsea House biographies. Administrators objected to 10 gay and lesbian titles, including works about Willa Cather, Martina Navratilova, and John Maynard Keynes, and pulled these titles without going through district challenge policy. The disputed books were eventually placed in a high school library; and the middle school librarian was instructed to order new gay and lesbian materials written for younger students. One positive result is the rewriting of the district selection policy to include the provision that books not be removed from the library based solely on objections to gay and lesbian subject matter.

In Buffalo, New York, the Williamsville County School Board voted to retain *Shade's Children* by Garth Nix despite complaints by parents who disapproved of its futuristic content. *Freaky Friday* by Mary Rodgers was returned to the shelves after the Hernando County, Florida, School Board overruled parents' concerns about language in the book. John Steinbeck's *Of Mice and Men* remains in Mansfield, Texas, school libraries after a parent objected to the book's blasphemous language. Although a father in Pinellas County, Florida, protested the sexual scenes in Robert Cormier's *The Chocolate War*, the school community panel felt it was appropriate for an advanced eighth grade class; the daughter of the complainant was assigned an alternative selection, S.E. Hinton's *The Outsiders*.

On the other hand, a Cedar Rapids, Iowa, librarian felt *The Terrorist* by Caroline B. Cooney did not promote "positive images of people from other cultures and other countries." This librarian felt there were inaccuracies, as well as incorrect use of the term Moslem for Muslim, and recommended its removal. In La Porte, Texas, *Blood and Chocolate* by Annette Curtis Klause was removed from school shelves after a parent complained about objectionable language and references to sex and violence. In Summerville, North Carolina, *The Catcher in the Rye* was permanently checked out of two high school libraries by a school board official who feels that Salinger's work is a "filthy, filthy book."

In Fairfax County, Virginia, a group calling itself PABBIS (Parents Against Bad Books in Schools) is speaking out against some titles on required reading lists that it considers to have graphic sexual depictions or violence. To date, *Druids* by Morgan Llywelyn, *Daughters of Eve* by Lois Duncan, and *Pillars of the Earth* by Ken Follett have been challenged, with district committees voting to retain each of these titles. When appealed to the School Board, *Druids* and *Daughters of Eve* were removed from middle-school libraries, while *Pillars of the Earth* was restricted to high school libraries. The parents also want a rating system for books, similar to that used for movies, though Fairfax County Public Schools have not agreed to that request.

The Leicester School Volunteers in Massachusetts cancelled a fund-raising book fair rather than have the "objectionable" but popular "Captain Underpants" series by Dav Pilkey included in the Scholastic Book Fair. Publisher Scholastic refused to remove the Pilkey titles from their fair offerings and from the fair's promotional fliers as requested by the group.

From the American Library Association comes the list of books challenged most often during 2001 (www.ala.org/bbooks/challeng.html#mfeb). The top ten, which received this recognition because of alleged offensive language, unsuitability for age group, racism, violence, sexual content, or wizardry and magic, are as follows:

1. J.K. Rowling's *Harry Potter* series

2. *Of Mice and Men* by John Steinbeck

3. *The Chocolate War* by Robert Cormier

4. *I Know Why the Caged Bird Sings* by Maya Angelou

5. *Summer of My German Soldier* by Bette Greene

6. *The Catcher in the Rye* by J.D. Salinger

7. *Alice series* by Phyllis Reynolds Naylor

8. *Go Ask Alice* by Anonymous

9. *Fallen Angels* by Walter Dean Myers

10. *Blood and Chocolate* by Annette Curtis Klause

Books to film and film to books

Movies and television programs are often adapted from previously-written books. *A Wrinkle in Time* by Madeleine L'Engle was a two-part miniseries on ABC's *Wonderful World of Disney*; Marion Zimmer Bradley's *The Mists of Avalon* appeared as a miniseries on TNT; and *What Girls Learn* by Karin Cook was a Showtime Tie-in.

Warner Brothers bought the movie rights to the vampire series *Cirque du Freak*, written by British author Darren Shan; and Scholastic Entertainment optioned the film rights for Philip Pullman's fantasy trilogy, *His Dark Materials*. Movie deals are also in the works for *The Lion, the Witch, and the Wardrobe* by C.S. Lewis; *The Sisterhood of the Traveling Pants* by Ann Brashares; and *Son of the Mob* by Gordon Korman.

One of November's major releases was the first film in the Harry Potter series, *Harry Potter and the Sorcerer's Stone*, written by J.K. Rowling. Garnering $90.3 million in its opening weekend, the film had earned almost $190 million as of November 26, 2001. Following in December was *The Lord of the Rings: The Fellowship of the Ring*, the first of Tolkien's trilogy. One impact of its release has been an increase in sales of *The Hobbit*. Unlike these two movies, *Hearts in Atlantis*, written by Stephen King, opened quietly in movie theaters in fall 2001.

Action films such as *Crouching Tiger, Hidden Dragon* and *Gladiator* led to novelizations from Newmarket Press. Scholastic produced novelizations and/or spin-offs of *Star Wars* and *The Sixth Sense* and felt their success was due to the strong story line of each. In the same vein, Pocket Books for Young Readers released novelizations for the films *Tomb Raider*, *Final Fantasy*, and *Clockstoppers*.

Caleb's Story, third in Patricia MacLachlan's series about the Witting family, was written originally for film and then adapted into a novel. *Shrek* had its beginnings in a William Steig picture book. The character was then written into a movie script with a different storyline; and now Penguin has published four movie tie-in books in both hardback and paperback. Margret and H.A. Rey's picture book *Whiteblack the Penguin*, published by Houghton Mifflin, will be developed for both television and film by animation house Mainframe Entertainment. HBO Family inaugurated a series entitled *My Favorite Book*, with the American Library Association serving as an advisory partner. In each three-minute episode, aired once a week, two children tell about one of their favorite books with a list of the featured titles maintained at HBO-Family.com.

First Novels and Children's Debuts

Many of this year's debut novels were "walkaway" award winners, with An Na's *A Step from Heaven* leading the pack. This story of a Korean family not always successfully adapting to life in America won the Michael L. Printz award and was named an ALA Best Book for Young Adults (BBYA), an ALA Children's Notable Book, and a Best Book by *Booklist*, *Horn Book*, and *School Library Journal*. On a lighter note, *The Sisterhood of the Traveling Pants* by Ann Brashares, a BBYA and *Booklist* Editors' Choice, tells about four friends who use a pair of jeans to stay in touch when they separate over summer vacation. *Racing the Past* by Sis Deans, a Best Book from *School Library Journal* and a *Booklist* Editors' Choice, features a boy whose plan to avoid the school bully turns him into a long-distance runner. For older teens, *Breathing Underwater* by Alex Flinn, which was chosen as both a BBYA and a Quick Picks winner, relates the remorse a young man feels about his treatment of a former girlfriend after attending an anger management class. Other first novels that were named as BBYA books include two that deal with homosexuality: Sara Ryan's *Empress of the World* and *Rainbow Boys* by Alex Sanchez. Five more first-time authors wrote books that earned the BBYA designation. Diana Les Becquets (*Stones of Mourning Creek*) tackles the issues of race relations and friendship; Jaclyn Moriarty (*Feeling Sorry for Celia*) takes a humorous look at pen pal communications, school life, and worry; Markus Zusak (*Fighting Ruben Wolfe*) describes how two brothers confront one another in the boxing ring; Susanna Vance (*Sights*) explores the problem of being an outsider; and Rebecca Tingle (*The Edge on the Sword*) writes a thrilling historical novel about Anglo-Saxon life.

Though not selected to receive special awards, some other first novels were quite memorable, including Cathryn Clinton's *The Calling*, about a young girl who discovers religion and her talent for healing, and James Devita's *Blue*, which features a young boy who changes into a blue marlin. In *Across the Steel River* by Ted Stenhouse, two young boys observe racism against Native Americans; while Marc Kornblatt's *Understanding Buddy* reveals the feelings of two boys grieving the loss of Buddy's mother. Turning to historical fiction, several nautical adventures were published: Elizabeth Garrett depicts women as pirates in *The Sweet Trade*, while a teen wife assumes command of her husband's ship in *The Captain's Wife* by Douglas Kelley. On the young adult side, a Jewish girl escapes from her ghetto to see the outside world in *Rivka's Way* by Teri Kanefield; and runaways find a home together in *Through the Lock* by Carol Hurst. The life of immigrants is explored in *A Place for Joey* by Carol Flynn Harris as well as *Streets of Gold* by Marie Raphael.

Award-winning books published by first-time authors cover ages from preschool to middle grades and genres from picture books to chapter books. Receiving both a *Horn Book* Fanfare Award and recognition as an ALA Notable Book was Star Livingstone's *Harley*, illustrated by Molly Bang. *Harley* is an early chapter book about an ornery llama that finds its calling guarding a flock of sheep after failing as a pack animal. Also designated ALA Notable Books were a tale of nineteenth-century Chinese immigrants working on the transcontinental railroad (the picture book *Coolies* by Yin, illustrated by Chris Soentpiet) and *Love, Ruby Lavender*, a novel by Deborah Wiles set in Halleluia, Mississippi, during the summer that nine-year-old Ruby comes to grips with her grandfather's death the previous year. Deborah Wiles's picture book *Freedom Summer*, illustrated by Jerome Lagarrigue, was recognized as an IRA Teachers' Choice for 2002. The *Booklist* Editors' Choice award went to Linda Ashman's simple rhyming story about animals' dwellings, *Castles, Caves, and Honeycombs*, illustrated by Lauren Stringer. Author/illustrator Jessica Spanyol's picture book *Carlo Likes Reading* was designated a *Smithsonian* Notable Book for Children, while Alistair Taylor picked up a *Bulletin of the Center for Children's Books* Blue Ribbon Award for Picture Book. Taylor wrote and illustrated *Swollobog*, about a small dog with a large appetite. A Notable Social Studies Trade Books for Young People Award was given to *A Bus of Our Own* (the picture book story of a young African American girl's desire to attend school), written by Freddi Williams Evans and illustrated by Shawn Costello. *Parenting*'s Reading Magic Awards went to three picture books: *One More Wednesday*, written and illustrated by Malika Doray and translated from the French by Suzanne Freeman; *The Whole Night Through: A Lullaby* by author/illustrator David Frampton; and *The Very Kind Rich Lady and Her One Hundred Dogs*, written and illustrated by Chinlun Lee.

Other first-time authors, though they didn't win awards, produced the following favorably-reviewed titles. In *Book! Book! Book!* by Deborah Bruss, with illustrations by Tiphanie Beeke, bored farm animals visit the library. Author/illustrator Anna Alter's *Estelle and Lucy* tells a story of sibling rivalry between a mouse and a cat. It's actually the six buttons on *The Magical, Mystical, Marvelous Coat*, by Catherine Ann Cullen with illustrations by David Christiana, that make a little girl's coat so special. The perennial problem of getting a stubborn loose tooth to fall out is the dilemma presented in *Tabitha's Terrifically Tough Tooth*, written and illustrated by Charlotte Middleton. A short, self-confident first grader takes on a bully in Patty Lovell's *Stand Tall, Molly Lou Melon*, with illustrations by David Catrow. For Halloween, an old hag tries to concoct a creature that is *Meaner than Meanest* but omits an important ingredient in this humorous picture book by Kevin Somers, with illustrations by Diana Cain Blumenthal. The family dog stars in *Silent Night*, a novel Christmas story written and illustrated by Sandy

Turner. Catherine Wright tells a tall tale in *Steamboat Annie and the Thousand-Pound Catfish*, illustrated by Howard Fine. An easy reader about two pirates is Daniel Laurence's *Captain and Matey Set Sail*, with illustrations by Claudio Munoz. Ms. Snickle's unique teaching methods pleasantly surprise her students in *The Secret of Ms. Snickle's Class*, a chapter book by Laurie Miller Hornik, with illustrations by Debbie Tilley. Nine-year-old Lizzie uses her mom's old typewriter to tell monthly stories of her life in Mary Eccles' *By Lizzie*.

Literacy Initiatives

The importance of reading was highlighted during the Bush inaugural festivities in January 2001 with an event entitled "Laura Bush Celebrates America's Authors." Children's authors and illustrators were included in the guest list of outstanding American authors as former librarian Laura Bush promoted books and literacy. In addition, on the national level, the director of the Center for Improvement of Early Reading Achievement at the University of Michigan, Ann Arbor, Susan B. Neuman, was selected for a position in the U. S. Department of Education, suggesting interest at the highest levels of government in the development of a nation of readers. Results of the 2000 National Assessment of Educational Progress reported in the May 2001 *School Library Journal* showed basically no improvement in reading ability at the fourth-grade level nationwide. Clearly, more attention to early literacy efforts for children at risk of failing to develop reading proficiency is needed.

That attention, in part, is provided by a variety of activities in local libraries and bookstores stressing the importance of reading and offering support and information about the development of literacy. A two-year state-wide campaign in Maryland entitled "It's Never Too Early" included billboards, posters, and radio ads encouraging parents of babies, toddlers, and preschoolers to attend library story sessions and utilize other services offered at libraries. Maryland also offers workshops to their public youth library staff to train them in reading readiness skills for their work directly with preschoolers and also with the parents of these children. Children's Bookstore in Baltimore joined the reading bandwagon by establishing an educational foundation that allows teachers to acquire trade books at no charge to complement classroom instruction, with the books being given to the students when the lesson is completed. In California, Governor Gray Davis and his wife established a foundation to provide books for school libraries.

The American Booksellers Association, reprising a 1997 program conducted with support from Scholastic that distributed free copies of Rosemary Wells's *Read to Your Bunny*, in the summer of 2001 launched "Prescription for Reading." The literacy program, a joint effort of the ABA with BookSense, Simon & Schuster Children's Publish-ing, and Koen Book Distributors, gave "prescription coupons" to pediatricians to distribute to their patients. The coupons were redeemable at participating bookstores for a copy of Audrey Wood's *A Book for Honey Bear: Reading Keeps the Sighs Away* and a list of other suggested books suitable for reading to young children. The host of radio's "Loose Leaf Book Company," Tom Bodett, served as spokesperson for this campaign.

Obituaries

March 31-Eleanor Clymer, creator of 58 books for the elementary-age audience during her 40-year career as an author, died in Haverford, PA, at the age of 95.

May 5 – Cliff Hillegass, known to every student who has ever used *Cliffs Notes* while reading a classic for an English assignment, died in Lincoln, Nebraska, at the age of 83.

May 18 – Irene Hunt, author of the 1965 Newbery Honor Book *Across Five Aprils* and the 1967 Newbery Medalist *Up a Road Slowly*, died on her 99th birthday in Champaign, Illinois.

June 3 – Jamake Highwater, author of 1978 Newbery Honor Book and *Boston Globe-Horn Book* Award-winner *Anapo: An American Indian Odyssey*, died in Los Angeles.

June 27 – In Helsinki, Tove Jansson, creator of the Moomintrolls and recipient of more than 50 awards, including the Hans Christian Andersen Medal in 1966, died at the age of 86.

July 12 – Sixty-one-year-old Fred Marcellino, author, illustrator, book-jacket designer, and recipient of a 1991 Caldecott Honor for his rendition of *Puss in Boots*, died in New York City.

July 29 – Elizabeth Yates, author of the 1951 Newbery Medal winner *Amos Fortune, Free Man*, died in Concord, New Hampshire, at the age of 95.

August 7 – Seventy-six-year-old Robert Kraus, cartoonist, publisher, and author of more than 100 children's books, including *Leo the Late Bloomer*, passed away in Connecticut.

August 13 – Elizabeth Cavanna Harrison, who wrote over 80 books and was better known as Betty Cavanna, died at her home in France at the age of 92.

October 11 – Beni Montressor, winner of the 1965 Caldecott Medal for *May I Bring a Friend?* by author Beatrice Schenk de Regniers, died at the age of 75 at his home in Italy.

Innovative Picture Books

Thousands of children's books are published annually, hundreds win awards, and a few push the boundaries of conventional literature. Jon Scieszka and David Wiesner, already well known for individuality in their published works, again produced unconventional books. In the award-winning picture book *Baloney (Henry P.)*, Scieszka uses words from over a dozen non-English languages (as well as a few invented ones) to create an alien vocabulary for little, green Henry P. Baloney. The dialogue between Henry P. and his teacher about Henry's tardiness is understandable from context, Lane Smith's illustrations, and the "Decoder" glossary that gives the country of origin of the "imported" words. Henry P. also influences the plot by erasing potential danger with his "zimulis." *Baloney (Henry P.)* was included on the International Reading Association's Children's Choices for 2002 list. In David Wiesner's Caldecott-Medal-winning title, *The Three Pigs* take control of the plot after the wolf huffs and puffs the first pig right off the page. One by one, the pigs remove themselves from the story as the hungry, befuddled wolf searches the story's scattered pages. The pigs sail away on a paper airplane constructed from one of the pages, and as they venture through different stories, the illustrations change to match the style of the tale they are in at the moment. With other characters they meet along the way, the three pigs reconstruct their original story, change the ending slightly, and surprise the already confused wolf.

Another new version of the three pigs is Bruce Whatley's *Wait! No Paint!*, in which the illustrator's spilled juice causes the first pig's straw house to collapse before the wolf can blow it down. To make matters worse, the artist runs out of red paint, causing the pigs to lose their pinkish color before story's end and realize that a lack of red paint means no hot fire to boil the water to foil the wolf. Quickly, the pigs insist on being drawn into a different story, one that doesn't require red paint. The appeal of Whatley's title to young readers is evident in its selection as an IRA Children's Choice for 2002. Similarly, John Stadler's *What's So Scary?* concerns a dog who claims he's been drawn into the wrong story. The dog tries to correct the error before the story concludes incorrectly, but the problem is compounded when the illustrator knocks over his paint and the recently-drawn characters flee from the rapidly spreading colors. Grabbing a spilled brush, the dog draws his own ending to the tale, saving everyone and finally ending up where he thought he should be all along.

In *Beware the Storybook Wolves* by Lauren Child, the characters do what Herb has long feared they would—emerge from the book Herb's mother was reading for a bedtime story. Into Herb's darkened bedroom come wolves from two familiar stories. Herb solves his immediate problem by opening a storybook collection to a different tale and getting help from Cinderella's fairy godmother. Herb's bedtime stories, however, are forever altered as a result.

The characters in *And the Dish Ran Away with the Spoon* by Janet Stevens and Susan Stevens Crummel face a similar bedtime-story-type dilemma—the runaway dish and spoon have not returned. Fearing that the story will be incomplete when it is read again, Cow suggests rewriting the ending so Dish and Spoon are not necessary. Cat, however, insists that Dog and Cow join in searching for their missing comrades. Along the way they meet many other nursery rhyme and fairy tale characters, face dangers, locate the missing duo, and arrange for Dish's repair in time for the nightly reading of their tale.

Publishing News

Publishers Weekly in its December 17, 2001 issue (pp. 24-32) published a list of best-selling children's books that sold either more than 750,000 copies in hardcover or over one million copies in paperback. A look at the hardcover list of 189 titles indicates a few in the top twenty that could be stretched into young adult status, such as the *Harry Potter* books. At 106 is *The Teenage Mutant Ninja Turtles: The Storybook Based on the Movie*, while at 160 is *The Stinky Cheese Man*. Both of these books could qualify for middle school status. Perhaps the only one that might be considered high-school-level is *The Star Wars Storybook*, an out-of-print title from 1978. The paperback list includes a few more titles for young adults, though it's obvious that sales benefited from required reading assignments in English classes. In the number 2 spot is *The Outsiders* by S.E. Hinton, which sold 9,695,149 copies. The spots from 5 to 12 (over 6.7 million books to 6.1 million) are held by *Where the Red Fern Grows, Island of the Blue Dolphins, Harry Potter and the Sorcerer's Stone, Shane*, and *A Wrinkle in Time*, books which appear on the shelves of most middle schools. At the number 18 spot is *Go Ask Alice* (4.6 million); *That Was Then, This Is Now* (4 million) by S.E. Hinton holds the 27th spot; *The Catcher in the Rye* (3.9 million) by J.D. Salinger is listed at 29; and *The Pigman* (3.5 million) by Paul Zindel follows at number 39. After getting past *Hatchet* by Gary Paulsen at the number 55 spot (3.1 million), *The Cay* by Theodore Taylor at number 57 (3 million), and *The Giver* by Lois Lowry at number 63 (2.9 million), one travels to 118 before finding another young adult book, in this case *The Chocolate War* (2 million) by Robert Cormier. Among the 376 titles on the paperback list, the *Goosebumps* series by R.L. Stine is well represented, along with works by Judy Blume, Norma Klein, Bette Green, Francine Pascal, and Phyllis Reynolds Naylor. By and large, the big sellers are the children's books, with *The Poky Little Puppy* by Janette Sebring the top-selling hardback (14.8 million) and *Charlotte's Web* by E.B. White (9.9 million) the top paperback seller.

Millbrook Press's new imprint, Roaring Brook Press, plans a yearly publishing of 40 titles that will include picture books, novels, and other formats. Wendy Lamb has her own imprint with Random House, Wendy

Lamb Books, and plans to publish 10 to 15 titles a year. Marcato Books is a new imprint of Cricket Books, with Marc Aronson assuming publisher duties. In addition to Marcato Books, the publishers of Paul Fleischman's *Seek* and Annie Callan's *Taf* in 2001, Aronson also oversees *Cricket*, *Cicada*, and *Muse* magazines, which are produced by Carus Publishing, the parent company of Marcato and Cricket Books.

Candlewick Press timed the release of Celia Rees's *Witch Child* for Friday, July 13, considered any order of 12 books a "witch's dozen," and provided a free 13th copy.

The average price for all hardcover books for Grades 5 and up is $18.79, an increase of $.21 over the 2000 price, as reported on page 11 in the March 2001 issue of *School Library Journal*. The cost for Grade 5 and up fiction was $16.10, an increase of 19 cents, while nonfiction for the same group was priced at $21.40, an increase of 23 cents. Hardcover books for Preschool through grade 4 now cost an average of $16.01, up 46 cents from $15.55 in 2000.

Thurman House is reissuing *The Legend of Rah and the Muggles*, originally written in the 1980s by Pennsylvania author Nancy Stouffer, who claims that J.K. Rowling stole her ideas from both the Muggles book and a series that featured Lily and Larry Potter.

Several paperback imprints were phased out in Simon & Schuster's Children's Publishing, including Archway and Minstrel, as the company merged five imprints into two. Pulse will be the paperback imprint that focuses on teens, while Aladdin Books will serve preschool through middle school readers. Pulse will have some original publishing, in addition to taking over titles previously released under the Aladdin or Archway imprint.

Inchpub, a grassroots organization made up of Independent Children's Book Publishers, hopes combining resources will enable them to better promote their books, create joint displays at regional conferences, and coordinate advertising. Members include: Boyds Mills, Charlesbridge, Chronicle, Front Street, Handprint, Holiday House, Lee & Low, Lerner, North-South, SeaStar, Publishers Group West, Ragged Bears, and Walker & Co.

Children's book publishers marked the anniversaries of their most notable characters and authors in a variety of ways. Dutton Children's Books, a Division of Penguin Putnam Books for Young Readers, feted seventy-five-year-old Winnie the Pooh at a party that included readings from the Pooh stories and a silent auction for charity of Ernest Shepard's art. To celebrate 60 years of the inimitable monkey Curious George, the Children's Museum of Manhattan exhibited the art of H.A. and Margret Rey and planned readings of the Curious George stories by other famous Georges. Each reader's designated charity received 1000 books from publisher Houghton Mifflin. Commemorating the 50-year career of author/illustrator Maurice Sendak, HarperCollins is reissuing, over a two-year period, exact reproductions of 22 hardcover editions of Sendak's works that are currently out of print. Compared to Winnie the Pooh and Curious George, Arthur, at age 25, is a young aardvark. Marc Brown's first book in the Arthur Adventures series, *Arthur's Nose*, was published in 1976 by Little, Brown. To celebrate, an anniversary edition of the first title was printed and the first entry in a new chapter series, Arthur's Good Sports, was released. Random House Children's Publishing used Arthur's anniversary to promote a new Step into Reading sticker book, *Arthur's First Kiss*.

Two publishers celebrated anniversaries during 2001. Orchard Books, which is known for Debi Gliori's Mr. Bear titles, the Daisy books by Jane Simmons, and Lauren Child's Clarice Bean stories, turned 15. Candlewick Press acknowledged its 10th anniversary with a campaign entitled "Candlewick Grows Up," a new gift line, the launching of a web site (www.candlewick.com), and the addition of a New York City office. Long known for its picture books, Candlewick plans to increase the number of novels it publishes for middle and teen readers.

Disney Publishing Worldwide restructured its children's book division into two groups: Hyperion Books for Children (headed by editorial director Andrea Pinkney) and Disney Global Children's Books (under the editorial direction of Jackie Carter). North-South Books opened a new, larger office in New York City and launched its new imprint, Night Sky. McGraw-Hill Children's Publishing plans to expand its trade line with several new series, including the Disney Parent-Child Read Together series. A new company, Two Lives Publishing, plans a target audience of children in gay and lesbian families and expects to publish five to eight books a year. Lois Sarkisian, owner of a children's book illustration gallery in Los Angeles, formed Smallfellow Press, an imprint of Tallfellow Press, and intends to accompany each release with an exhibition of the book's artwork. U.K.-based Barefoot Books moved its U.S. offices to Cambridge, MA, from New York City, increased its staff, and made plans to open a Barefoot store.

Science Fiction and Fantasy

The exciting news in science fiction and fantasy this year was that young adult authors were being considered for and winning major awards. At the World Fantasy Convention, where noted author Diana Wynne Jones was one of the judges, nominees for Best Novel included *The Amber Spyglass* by Philip Pullman. *Perdido Street Station* by China Mieville was also nominated and is included in this volume. The World Science Fiction Convention voted *Harry Potter and the Goblet of Fire* the winner of the Hugo Award for best novel, while the 2001 Nebula Awards, given by the Science Fiction and Fantasy Writers of America, included McKillip's *Tower at Stony Wood*, Pullman's *Amber Spyglass*, Sawyer's *Calculating God* (*WDYARN?* volume 4), and Connie Willis's *Passage* (*WDCYARN?* volume 5) on their preliminary ballot; the winner was *The Quantum Rose* by Catherine Asaro.

A major new series for young adults was launched this year with Kevin Crossley-Holland's *The Seeing Stone.* Elements of or characters from Arthurian legends also appeared in *I Am Morgan Le Fay, The Merlin of the Oak Woods, The King's Peace, The King's Name,* and *The Dragon's Son,* while *Bloodtide,* with its motifs of the-dagger-in-the-stone and sibling seduction, brought bits of this lore into a futuristic dystopian London setting. New installments in popular ongoing series were written by Brian Jacques (*Taggerung*), Tamora Pierce (*Squire*), Orson Scott Card (*Shadow of the Hegemon*), and Diane Duane (*Wizard's Dilemma*). From the adult author Anne McCaffrey came *The Skies of Pern,* her first *Pern* novel in three years.

This year's crop of first-time authors presented a wide variety of styles and approaches. Katherine Roberts' *Spellfall* is a new variant on the popular YA theme of the displaced child who exhibits special talents, while *Beatnik Rutabagas from Beyond the Stars* by Quentin Dodd is a wild comic space ride aimed squarely at the YA market. Shakespeare as young lover makes Sarah Hoyt's *Ill Met By Moonlight* a natural for teens; and the teen hero of Anselm Audley's *Heresy: Book 1* adds appeal to serious themes.

Star Trek celebrates its 35th year and continues its strong publications program, even though the original television series from which all books emanate aired only from September 1966 to June 1969. In 1979, Pocket Books took over the license and estimates that there are more than 85 million copies of the 450-plus *Star Trek* titles so far. In addition to mass market books, there are encyclopedias, such as *The Star Trek Encyclopedia: A Reference Guide to the Future*; novelty books, such as crafts, party books, or humor titles; "language" materials, such as *The Klingon Dictionary*; and audiotapes. The books include characters from the original series, or any of the three follow-ups, such as *The Next Generation*, in addition to characters that have never appeared in any of the series, but reside in the Star Trek universe. It's interesting to note that *Star Trek* novels written expressly for 14- to 15-year-olds, and featuring younger versions of the well-known characters, did not sell as well as the adult versions.

Series

Series are hot, hot, hot, though some have a short shelf life before they're nudged aside by the next latest "flavor." From Winslow Press came a new series on Presidents entitled *Dear Mr. President.* Each title consists of fictional letters written between a young person and a president. Theodore Roosevelt and Thomas Jefferson were featured first, followed by Abraham Lincoln, Franklin Delano Roosevelt, and John Quincy Adams. Winslow added a twist by connecting the book with a web site that allows the reader to explore further the time period, its history and cultural activities.

Though the *Redwall* series will continue, Brian Jacques not only left Random House for Penguin Putnam but also introduced a new character and theme in his book *Castaways of the Flying Dutchman.* Putting to use some of his varied background, which ranges from bus driver to standup comic and folksinger to merchant seaman, Jacques introduced the young man Ben and his dog Ned, who find themselves aboard a ship sailed by a mutinous crew and captained by a madman. When the captain and his ship are cursed by an angel to forever sail the sea, Ben and Ned are saved from the curse, given immortality, and sent out to perform good deeds throughout the world.

An agreement among HarperCollins, the C.S. Lewis Company, and Lewis's stepsons will extend the popular *Narnia* series, written by C.S. Lewis in the 1950s. Scheduled to be released in 2003 are new picture books and novels based on the old works.

Several new series, ranging from horror to humor and mythology to mystery, began in 2001. Tricycle Press launched *Alexandra Rambles On!*. The first book in the series, *One Puppy, Three Tales* by Karen Salmansohn, features Alexandra's thoughts and concerns, represented in riotous colors, whimsical doodles, and sidebar commentaries. From the same press came *Danger Boy*, the first title in which, *Ancient Fire* by Mark London Williams, involves time travel in the olden city of Alexandria. Two new series about witchcraft, both of which feature young teens discovering their Wiccan traits or ability to cast spells, appeared. HarperCollins introduced Isobel Bird's *Circle of Three* and Penguin/Puffin began *Sweep* by Cate Tiernan. Christopher Golden initiated *Prowlers* from Pocket Books, featuring a 19-year-old who hunts vicious, murderous beasts that pretend to be human. Darren Shan's *Cirque du Freak: A Living Nightmare* led off *The Saga of Darren Shan*, a vampire trilogy from Little, Brown.

Now available from Pocket/Archway is the new "disease novel" series *Why Me?*, beginning with Deborah Kent's *The Courage to Live,* in which a young girl learns to survive with lupus. Dan Gutman writes the *Qwerty Stevens Back in Time* series from Simon & Schuster that begins Qwerty's time travels with *The Edison Mystery.* The *Rinnah Two Feathers Mystery* series, from Ugly Town Productions, starts with Rodney Johnson's *The Secret of Dead Man's Mine* and features a young Native American living in South Dakota. Series involving psychic powers were introduced by two publishers. HarperCollins debuted *Fingerprints*, beginning with Melinda Metz's *Gifted Touch*, and Penguin Putnam/Alloy offered *Have a Nice Life* by Scarlett MacDougal, starring the intergalactic angel Clarence Terence. Even Texas Tech University Press entered the field by publishing *The Lone Star Journals*, the first title in which is *Get Along, Little Dogies: The Chisholm Trail Diary of Hallie Lou Wells: South Texas*,

1878 by Lisa Waller Rogers. Titles from Germany and Canada, as well as the United States; wide-ranging themes; and writers from a variety of backgrounds all indicate a healthy climate for series publishing.

New Children's Series

New series for children published in 2001 include picture books, beginning readers, and novels. For the youngest "readers," author/illustrator Daniel Kirk offers "Biddle Books" (*Little Bird, Biddle Bird* and *Little Pig, Biddle Pig*). Picture books about *Little Whistle*, a guinea pig living in a toy store, come from prolific author Cynthia Rylant, known for her titles about Henry and his dog Mudge, good friend Poppleton, and elderly Mr. Putter and his cat Tabby. Tomie dePaola, with the picture book *Meet the Barkers*, launches a new series about a family of Welsh terriers. Using the Barkers and other characters from the book, dePaola and Putnam plan to publish board books, picture books, and easy-to-read titles. Rosemary Wells introduces a new series suitable for beginning readers entitled "Yoko & Friends School Days" with a character familiar to readers, the kitten Yoko. In Simon & Schuster's "Ready-for-Chapters" series, Andrew Clements writes about third-grader Jake Drake. Winslow Press promotes additional activities on its Web site to add to the enjoyment of titles in the "Hourglass Adventure Series" by Barbara Robertson. An exciting fantasy adventure series by Emily Rodda begins with *Rowan of Rin,* followed by *Rowan and the Travelers.*

Teen Reading

A survey by the National Education Association of 12 to 18-year-olds found that 56% read more than 10 books a year and 41% read more than 15 books a year. As librarians who work with middle school students already know, that age group reads the most, with 70% reading more than 10 books yearly while only 49% of high school students reach that goal. Most respondents reported that reading is relaxing (87%) or rewarding and satisfying (85%), while 79% commented that it was stimulating or interesting. Less than half reported reading for school assignments (46%) but even fewer said they read for pleasure rather than for "facts and information" (42%).

Minority young adults and their parents put more emphasis on reading, as indicated by the high score awarded to the enjoyment of reading by Hispanic (56%) or African American (51%) students, compared to white students (47%). Parental support for reading was cited by 56% of the African American respondents, 47% of the Hispanic, and only 43% of the white.

Best of all, 49% of the survey respondents said that libraries, rather than friends, booksellers, or family, are their primary source for finding the books they want.

The "Guys Read" program, conceived by author Jon Scieszka to promote reading for boys, was introduced at the 2001 BookExpo America. More information is available at www.guysread.com, including suggestions for what can be done to "connect boys with books they will want to read" and a list of appropriate titles.

Barnes and Noble is trying to attract more of the teen market through its promotional teen lit 'zine, *TLZ.* The first issue featured Britney Spears on the cover promoting *A Mother's Gift,* which she co-authored with her mother, Lynne. Other teen titles inside the magazine included *Chicken Soup for the Teenage Soul III* by Jack Canfield, *Speak* by Laurie Halse Anderson, and *Artemis Fowl* by Eoin Colfer. Content and titles featured in *TLZ* are determined by the children's marketing group of B&N. In addition, official signage in the store has been changed from "YA" to "Teen Reading."

Young Adult Services

Popular television star Drew Carey won nearly $600,000 on the television show "Who Wants to Be a Millionaire?" and donated the entire amount to the Ohio public libraries as thanks for a book of jokes that led to his career as a comedian. In turn, the Ohio Library Council earmarked his earnings for improvement of young adult services through programming grants, librarian training, scholarships, and PSAs.

The Young Adult Library Services Association of the American Library Association continued its popular Teen Read Week activities with the 2001 theme, "Make Reading a Hobbit." The success of this reading initiative is obvious from the increasing number of libraries that highlight and promote it, the reading surveys that spin off from it, and the rapidly multiplying teen responses. More information can be found at YALSA's web site (www.ala.org/yalsa/).

In Conclusion

This first annual combined volume of *What Do Children and Young Adults Read Next?* contains 1,000 titles, including board books for preschoolers, picture books for primary and intermediate grades, beginning readers for various skill levels, early chapter books, novels, YA fiction, and adult titles suitable for Young Adults. All these were selected to help the users of this volume connect children and teens to books so they can realize the theme of the 2001 Children's Book Week, "Get Carried Away. . .Read."

A

ALMA FLOR ADA
G. BRIAN KARAS, Illustrator

Daniel's Mystery Egg
(San Diego: Harcourt, Inc., 2001)

Series: Green Light Readers. Level 2
Subject(s): Friendship; Animals; Nature
Age range(s): Grades 1-2
Major character(s): Daniel, Child, Student—Elementary School; Alex, Friend, Student—Elementary School; Meg, Friend, Student—Elementary School; Tammy, Friend, Student—Elementary School
Time period(s): 2000s
Locale(s): United States

Summary: Daniel shows his friends a small white egg that he finds. Alex thinks the egg will hatch into an ostrich, but Daniel is sure it will be smaller than that. Meg thinks the egg contains an alligator, but Daniel hopes the animal inside will make a much nicer pet than an alligator would be. Tammy thinks a duck hides inside the egg, but Daniel believes something quieter is inside the egg. When the egg finally hatches a lizard emerges. Daniel is glad to see a small, nice, quiet animal, just as he hoped. (24 pages)

Where it's reviewed:
Booklist, July 2001, page 2022
Horn Book Guide, Spring 2002, page 65
Kirkus Reviews, September 1, 2001, page 1284
School Library Journal, February 2002, page 96

Other books by the same author:
Friend Frog, 2000
The Three Golden Oranges, 1999
Jordi's Star, 1996

Other books you might like:
Claire Daniel, *The Chick That Wouldn't Hatch*, 1999
    The sixth and final of Hen's eggs does not hatch until it rolls across the barnyard and cracks upon impact with a wall; then the chick emerges.

Steven Kellogg, *A Penguin Pup for Pinkerton*, 2001
    Pinkerton uses a pilfered football as a penguin egg in order to fulfill his dream of being a father.
Dr. Seuss, *Horton Hatches the Egg*, 1966
    Faithful Horton cares for the egg left in his care by his bird friend Maysie until it finally hatches into . . . an elephant bird.

ALMA FLOR ADA
LESLIE TRYON, Illustrator

With Love, Little Red Hen
(New York: Atheneum Books for Young Readers, 2001)

Subject(s): Literature; Letters; Neighbors and Neighborhoods
Age range(s): Grades K-3
Major character(s): Little Red Hen, Chicken, Mother; Goldilocks McGregor, Child, Friend; Little Red Riding Hood, Child, Friend
Time period(s): Indeterminate
Locale(s): Hidden Forest, Fictional Country

Summary: As soon as she moves into her new home with her seven chicks Little Red Hen writes to her cousin to tell her about the field of corn she's planted with NO help from her lazy neighbors. Little Red Riding Hood notices her hard work as she walks past during a visit to her grandmother and, in correspondence with Goldilocks, makes plans to secretly help the hard-working hen in the evenings. Meanwhile two wolves are writing letters describing their plans to dine on chickens and corn. The summer's correspondence between friends, cousins and conspirators details some plans that work to everyone's benefit and other plans that don't quite conclude in the expected way. (36 pages)

Where it's reviewed:
Booklist, September 15, 2001, page 229
Horn Book, January 2002, page 65
Publishers Weekly, September 3, 2001, page 89
School Library Journal, October 2001, page 104

Other books by the same author:
Friend Frog, 2000
Yours Truly, Goldilocks, 1998
Dear Peter Rabbit, 1994

Other books you might like:
Joyce Dunbar, *The Secret Friend*, 1999
    Panda feels worried to see his friend Gander writing a letter to a secret friend until he discovers it's addressed to him.
Lisa Campbell Ernst, *Goldilocks Returns*, 2000
    Goldi surprises the bears once again as they go on a walk. This time she does it by installing security locks on all their doors.
Nancy Willard, *The Magic Cornfield*, 1997
    Postcards to cousin Bottom document Tottem's travels from New York to Minneapolis through a magic cornfield.

JEAN EKMAN ADAMS, Author/Illustrator

Clarence and the Great Surprise
(Flagstaff, AZ: Rising Moon, 2001)

Subject(s): Animals/Pigs; Animals/Horses; Animals/Dogs
Age range(s): Grades K-3
Major character(s): Clarence, Pig, Traveler; Smoky, Horse, Guide; Edgar, Dog
Time period(s): Indeterminate
Locale(s): Southwest

Summary: The plan, as Clarence and Smoky pack to depart the dude ranch, is for Smoky to carry Clarence across the mountains and return him to the big city. Along the way, Smoky promises Clarence a surprise which ever-hungry Clarence hopes is something to eat. In addition to providing the transportation, Smoky sets up the tent for Clarence and tucks him into bed at night. A lonely and lost dog follows them until they invite him to continue the trip with them. Edgar is a dancer who, one night, twirls so far from the campsite that he becomes lost. A search finally locates Edgar in time to bring him along to see the surprise Smoky has promised. Clarence and Edgar feel awed by the view of colorful Southwestern canyons that they reluctantly leave behind to continue their journey to the city. (32 pages)

Where it's reviewed:
Horn Book Guide, Spring 2002, page 33
Publishers Weekly, October 29, 2001, page 66
Smithsonian, November 2001, page 120

Awards the book has won:
Smithsonian's Notable Books for Children, 2001

Other books by the same author:
Clarence Goes Out West and Meets a Purple Horse, 2000

Other books you might like:
Judith Ross Enderle, *Nell Nugget and the Cow Caper*, 1996
    Rustlers disturb Nell's contented ranch life with her horse, dog and 49 cows when they steal her favorite cow.
Paul Brett Johnson, *The Pig Who Ran a Red Light*, 1999
    George fails in his attempt to learn to fly so he drives away in Miss Rosemary's pickup truck instead.

Karen Wallace, *City Pig*, 2000
    On her first trip to the country Dolores discovers a more satisfying lifestyle and quits her city job.

C.S. ADLER

One Unhappy Horse
(New York: Clarion Books, 2001)

Subject(s): Animals/Horses; Mothers and Daughters; Old Age
Age range(s): Grades 5-8
Major character(s): Jan Wright, 12-Year-Old; Dove, Horse; Mattie Williams, Aged Person
Time period(s): 2000s
Locale(s): Tucson, Arizona

Summary: Since her father's death, Jan's life has changed so much. Her mother sold their ranch house to a group that converted it to an assisted living facility and now the two of them live in the small bunkhouse. But the money from that sale isn't quite enough to keep the rest of the ranch going, though her mother boards twenty horses. If Jan didn't have her horse Dove, she doesn't know what she'd do, for Dove's her best friend. He develops a limp that is more than just a stone bruise; an exam by the vet indicates a need for surgery for a condition that will only worsen. There couldn't be more wretched news as Jan knows there's no money for an operation. Help comes from an unexpected source with a loan from Mattie, who lives in the assisted living facility and has befriended Jan. This one kind act helps not only Jan and her mother be a little more honest with one another, but also forces Mattie and her daughter to share some important secrets, in a heartwarming story. (156 pages)

Where it's reviewed:
Booklist, March 1, 2001, page 1275
Kliatt, May 2001, page 5
School Library Journal, April 2001, page 138

Other books by the same author:
The No Place Cat, 2002
Winning, 1999
Not Just a Summer Crush, 1998
More than a Horse, 1997
That Horse Whiskey, 1994

Other books you might like:
K.M. Peyton, *Darkling*, 1990
    Jenny's grandfather buys her a gangly colt that she manages to transform into a racehorse.
Chris Platt, *Willow King*, 1998
    Born with one leg shorter than the other, when Katie hears of a foal born with twisted legs, she convinces the owner to let her raise him.
Chris St. John, *A Horse of Her Own*, 1989
    Using a combination of gifts and money earned from housekeeping for her motherless family, Jessie saves enough to buy her favorite horse, "Time-Out."

5

DAVID A. ADLER
WILL HILLENBRAND, Illustrator

Andy Russell, NOT Wanted by the Police
(San Diego: Gulliver Books/Harcourt, Inc., 2001)

Series: Andy Russell. Book 5
Subject(s): Mystery and Detective Stories; Neighbors and Neighborhoods; Schools
Age range(s): Grades 3-5
Major character(s): Andy Russell, Friend, 4th Grader; Tamika Anderson, Friend, 4th Grader
Time period(s): 2000s (2001)
Locale(s): United States

Summary: Andy and Tamika are watching the next-door neighbor's house while they travel and strange things are happening. Garbage appears in the garbage can, a light can sometimes be seen in a bedroom and one morning Andy spots an open front door from the school bus. Although the police are called they see nothing out of the ordinary and quickly consider Andy a pest that they definitely do NOT want to continue calling. Andy realizes he has to put on his detective cap and solve this mystery before a thief steals everything in the house. (118 pages)

Where it's reviewed:
Booklist, January 1, 2002, page 855
Horn Book Guide, Spring 2002, page 70
School Library Journal, January 2002, page 89

Other books by the same author:
Parachuting Hamsters and Andy Russell, 2000 (Andy Russell, Book 4)
Andy and Tamika, 1999 (Andy Russell, Book 2)
School Trouble for Andy Russell, 1999 (Andy Russell, Book 3)

Other books you might like:
Mary Labatt, *Strange Neighbors*, 2000
  Sam, dog detective, convinces Jennie that the new neighbors have something to hide, perhaps because they are witches.
Phyllis Reynolds Naylor, *Peril in the Bessledorf Parachute Factory*, 2000
  In the sixth episode about the Magruder family and the hotel they manage Bernie plans to get take over his sister's room so he can have one of his own.
Gertrude Chandler Warner, *The Boxcar Children Mystery Series*, 1953-
  Four children are involved in a variety of mysteries in this timeless series.

6

DAVID A. ADLER
SUSANNA NATTI, Illustrator

Cam Jansen and the School Play Mystery
(New York: Viking, 2001)

Series: Cam Jansen Adventure. Number 21
Subject(s): Theater; Schools; Mystery and Detective Stories
Age range(s): Grades 2-4
Major character(s): Cam Jansen, Detective—Amateur, Friend; Eric Shelton, Friend (Cam's), Student—Elementary School; Ms. Benson, Teacher
Time period(s): 2000s (2001)
Locale(s): United States

Summary: Ms. Benson calls the police when Cam reports that the money from ticket sales for the class play about Honest Abe has been stolen. Eric is playing the lead role so he cannot help Cam investigate as he usually does. Cam, using her photographic memory and clues gained from questioning the students selling the tickets, deduces the identity of the thief and leads police to the culprit. The money is recovered in time for Cam to see the play's final scene. (54 pages)

Where it's reviewed:
Booklist, August 2001, page 2118
Horn Book Guide, Spring 2002, page 70
School Library Journal, January 2002, page 89

Other books by the same author:
Cam Jansen and the Barking Treasure Mystery, 1999 (Cam Jansen Adventure, Number 19)
Cam Jansen and the Catnapping Mystery, 1998 (Cam Jansen Adventure, Number 18)
Cam Jansen and the Scary Snake Mystery, 1997 (Cam Jansen Adventure, Number 17)

Other books you might like:
Duncan Ball, *Emily Eyefinger and the Lost Treasure*, 1994
  Emily solves one mystery after another with the aid of a third eye on the end of her finger.
Ellen Conford, *A Case for Jenny Archer*, 1988
  Jenny has read so many mysteries that she sees intrigue in her own neighborhood.
Marjorie Weinman Sharmat, *Nate the Great and the Missing Key*, 1981
  Faithful Sludge helps Nate the Great solve the mystery of Annie's lost housekey.

7

JON AGEE, Author/Illustrator

Milo's Hat Trick
(New York: Michael Di Capua Books/Hyperion Books for Children, 2001)

Subject(s): Magic; Magicians; Humor
Age range(s): Grades K-3
Major character(s): Milo, Magician; Unnamed Character, Bear; Mr. Popovich, Manager (Stage)
Time period(s): 2000s
Locale(s): New York, New York

Summary: Inept Milo incurs the wrath of Mr. Popovich when he bungles his tricks and fails to conjure a rabbit leaping from his hat. When Mr. Popovich threatens to terminate his act, Milo goes hunting for a rabbit. He finds instead Bear who learned from a rabbit how to fit into a top hat. Milo's fortunes are assured now, or at least he has a job until Bear grows weary and returns to his cave to sleep. Having learned the rabbit's secret from Bear, Milo should be able to keep his magic act intact, with a little practice. (32 pages)

Where it's reviewed:
Booklist, July 2001, page 2016
Horn Book, May 2001, page 306
Kirkus Reviews, April 1, 2001, page 494
Publishers Weekly, April 30, 2001, page 76
School Library Journal, May 2001, page 108

Awards the book has won:
Horn Book Fanfare/Picture Book, 2002
Publishers Weekly Best Children's Books, 2001

Other books by the same author:
Dmitri the Astronaut, 1996 (New York Times Best Illustrated Children's Book)
The Return of Freddy Legrand, 1992 (School Library Journal Best Books)
The Incredible Painting of Felix Clousseau, 1988 (ALA Notable Children's Book)

Other books you might like:
Jules Feiffer, *Bark, George*, 1999
The vet's not a magician but he pulls a succession of animals out of George so the pup can bark.
Bob Graham, *Benny: An Adventure Story*, 1999
Jealous that a dog's antics draw the most applause, Brillo kicks his assistant out of the show, forcing him to find work and approval off the stage.
James Howe, *Rabbit-Cadabra!*, 1993
Bunnicula, suspected of being a vampire rabbit, appears as the rabbit in a magician's hat.

ALLAN AHLBERG
RAYMOND BRIGGS, Illustrator

The Adventures of Bert
(New York: Farrar Straus Giroux, 2001)

Subject(s): Adventure and Adventurers; Humor; Family Life
Age range(s): Preschool-Grade 1
Major character(s): Bert, Father, Spouse; Mrs. Bert, Mother, Spouse; Baby Bert, Son, Baby
Time period(s): 2000s
Locale(s): United Kingdom

Summary: Bert's simple life with Mrs. Bert and Baby Bert is unexpectedly complicated in five brief stories. The reader is responsible for the first and last problems by turning the page too loudly and waking Baby Bert. However, cheerful, but clumsy Bert creates his own dilemmas too with such simple actions as trying to put on a new shirt, going shopping and bravely rescuing a puppy from a river despite the fact that he can't swim. No wonder Bert's ready for a good night's sleep. (32 pages)

Where it's reviewed:
Booklist, September 1, 2001, page 112
Bulletin of the Center for Children's Books, September 2001, page 5
Horn Book, July 2001, page 437
Kirkus Reviews, June 1, 2001, page 798
School Library Journal, August 2001, page 142

Awards the book has won:
Bulletin of the Center for Children's Books Blue Ribbon, 2001
Horn Book Fanfare/Picture Book, 2002

Other books by the same author:
The Bravest Ever Bear, 2000
Mockingbird, 1998
Monkey Do!, 1998
Burglar Bill, 1992

Other books you might like:
Marianne Busser, *King Bobble*, 1996
Ten brief stories highlight the hapless of life of happy-go-lucky royal airheads, King and Queen Bobble.
Mary Ann Hoberman, *The Two Sillies*, 2000
Two silly people use complicated methods to solve simple problems.
Samuel Marshak, *The Absentminded Fellow*, 1999
The story of a hapless fellow who can't seem to do anything right is based on a Russian folktale.

ALLAN AHLBERG
KATHARINE MCEWEN, Illustrator

The Man Who Wore All His Clothes
(Cambridge, MA: Candlewick Press, 2001)

Subject(s): Humor; Family; Robbers and Outlaws
Age range(s): Grades 2-4
Major character(s): Mr. Gaskitt, Father; Mrs. Gaskitt, Taxi Driver, Mother; Gus Gaskitt, 9-Year-Old, Twin; Gloria Gaskitt, 9-Year-Old, Twin
Time period(s): 2000s
Locale(s): England

Summary: Quickly, Mrs. Gaskitt deduces that the man who climbs into her taxi at the bank is also responsible for the bank robbery announced on the radio. When the thief leaps out of the taxi and climbs aboard Gus and Gloria's school bus, a chase ensues. Mrs. Gaskitt's taxi follows the bus and trailing her is Mr. Gaskitt's car, the police car and a television camera crew. The children on the bus wisely display their most obnoxious bus behavior and the robber gets off in search of a little peace and quiet. He leads everyone on a merry foot chase until he runs into Mr. Gaskitt wearing all his clothes so he's difficult to get around. Mr. Gaskitt sits on the robber until the police arrive and then he hurries to work. Upon arrival he pulls more clothes over the many layers he already wears so his small frame will be appropriately large and comfortable for all the children who sit on Santa's lap. (78 pages)

Where it's reviewed:
Horn Book Guide, Spring 2002, page 70
Publishers Weekly, September 10, 2001, page 93
School Library Journal, October 2001, page 62

Other books by the same author:
My Brother's Ghost, 2001
The Better Brown Stories, 1996 (Smithsonian's Notable Books for Children)
The Giant Baby, 1994

Other books you might like:

Roald Dahl, *The Wonderful Story of Henry Sugar and Six More*, 1977
    Seven fantastic short stories include Henry Sugar's story as well as one about a boy who talks to animals and another about a hitchhiker.

Roddy Doyle, *Rover Saves Christmas*, 2001
    Santa selects Rover as a substitute for Rudolph when the reindeer calls in sick on Christmas Eve.

Graham Oakley, *The Foxbury Force*, 1994
    The town burglars turn the monthly training session into a real heist allowing the Foxbury Constabulary to solve an actual crime.

10

ALLAN AHLBERG
GILLIAN TYLER, Illustrator

The Snail House
(Cambridge, MA: Candlewick Press, 2001)

Subject(s): Grandmothers; Storytelling; Fantasy
Age range(s): Grades K-3
Major character(s): Grandma, Grandmother, Storyteller; Michael, Brother (older), Child; Hannah, Sister, Child
Time period(s): Indeterminate Past
Locale(s): England

Summary: After a day of berry picking with Grandma, Michael and Hannah settle on the porch steps to listen to one of Grandma's stories while the baby dozes in his stroller. Grandma tells of three children who magically shrink for a day down to such a small size that they can live in a house on the back of snail. Being so small causes unforeseen adventures when an apple falls from a tree causing an "earthquake" in the little snail house. Then the tiny baby is almost lost when he floats away while clinging to dandelion fluff and a hungry thrush seems sure to eat the snail until a prowling cat scares the bird away. According to Grandma's story, after one day in the snail house, the children return to their normal size again. For Michael and Hannah, the story ends just as night begins and they leave the darkened garden to enter Grandma's full-size house in a title originally published in England in 2000. (32 pages)

Where it's reviewed:
Booklist, July 2001, page 2016
Horn Book, May 2001, page 307
Publishers Weekly, February 19, 2001, page 91
Riverbank Review, Summer 2001, page 36
School Library Journal, March 2001, page 192

Awards the book has won:
Smithsonian's Notable Books for Children, 2001

Other books by the same author:
The Bravest Ever Bear, 2000
Monkey Do!, 1998
Burglar Bill, 1992

Other books you might like:
Hans Christian Andersen, *Thumbelina*, 1997
    A translation by Haugard tells of tiny Thumbelina's near disasters before she's flown to safety by a kind sparrow.

Irene Haas, *Summertime Song*, 1997
    A magical party hat shrinks Lucy to a diminutive size so she can attend a surprise birthday party in Grandma's garden.

Joanne Ryder, *The Snail's Spell*, 1982
    In a dream a little boy experiences life as if he had shrunk to the size of a snail.

Carol Ann Williams, *Tsubu the Little Snail*, 1995
    The love of a poor couple who raise a snail child sent by the water god is rewarded when the spell is broken and Tsubu becomes a young man.

11

LLOYD ALEXANDER

The Gawgon and the Boy
(New York: Dutton, 2001)

Subject(s): Depression (Economic); Imagination; Teacher-Student Relationships
Age range(s): Grades 5-7
Major character(s): David, 11-Year-Old; Annie, Cousin (distant)
Time period(s): 1920s
Locale(s): Philadelphia, Pennsylvania

Summary: After surviving a nasty bout of the "New Monia," the decision is made to tutor David rather than have him return to school. David's apprehensive about being taught by Aunt Annie as she reminds him of a scary gorgon. Aunt Annie, however, instructs differently than David's usual teachers, and tells him wonderful tales that spark David's imagination and lead him to write stories where he emulates his pirate heroes. The two experience a special relationship and embark on adventures where they not only rescue Napoleon or solve a Sherlock Holmes mystery, but in which David also learns a great deal about mathematics. Aunt Annie encourages David in his quest to become an artist and the two become quite good friends in this semi-autobiographical account of the author's life in the 1920s. (199 pages)

Where it's reviewed:
Booklist, May 15, 2001, page 1749
The Bulletin of the Center for Children's Books, June 2001, page 366
Publishers Weekly, May 14, 2001, page 83
School Library Journal, April 2001, page 138
Voice of Youth Advocates, June 2001, page 118

Awards the book has won:
School Library Journal Best Books, 2001
ALA Notable Children's Books, 2002

Other books by the same author:
Gypsy Rizka, 1999
The Iron Ring, 1997
The Arkadians, 1994
The Remarkable Journey of Prince Jen, 1991

Other books you might like:
Gayle Friesen, *Men of Stone*, 2000
    The lessons Ben learns from his great-aunt Frieda, who survived Stalin's reign of terror, help him develop the model of who he wants to become.

Eva Ibbotson, *Island of the Aunts*, 2000
When Aunts Etta, Coral and Myrtle need help caring for their creatures, they return to England and kidnap several children to be their assistants.

Gail Carson Levine, *Dave at Night*, 1999
Each night Dave escapes from the Hebrew Home for Boys and enjoys the sights and sounds of Harlem during its Renaissance time.

Richard Peck, *A Long Way from Chicago*, 1998
Warm and funny stories are shared of the summers Joey and his sister Mary Alice spend with their grandmother and the unusual lessons they learn.

12

DAVID ALMOND

Heaven Eyes

(New York: Delacorte, 2001)

Subject(s): Orphans; Adventure and Adventurers
Age range(s): Grades 6-9
Major character(s): Heaven Eyes, Orphan; Erin Law, Orphan, Narrator; January Carr, Orphan; Mouse Gullane, Orphan; Grampa, Aged Person
Time period(s): 2000s
Locale(s): St. Gabriel, England (Whitegates Orphanage; the Black Middens)

Summary: Imagery and story combine in this tale narrated by Erin, one of three orphans who sail away on a rickety raft from their orphanage only to become stuck in the gooey mud of the Black Middens. Rescued by Heaven Eyes, an ethereal young girl with webbed digits and the uncanny ability to see heaven through the world's trouble, and her caretaker Grampa, an eccentric, occasionally menacing old man, Erin, January and Mouse accompany them to the abandoned printing works where they live. Heaven Eyes immediately claims Erin as her sister, Mouse helps Grampa extricate treasures from the mud of the Middens and January tries to find out where Heaven Eyes came from. When Grampa dies, the three orphans take Heaven Eyes back to their orphanage where the reader assumes each will have a new beginning. (233 pages)

Where it's reviewed:
Booklist, January 2001, page 950
Horn Book, March 2001, page 205
Publishers Weekly, March 5, 2001, page 80
School Library Journal, March 2001, page 245
Voice of Youth Advocates, April 2001, page 34

Awards the book has won:
Booklist Editors' Choice/Books for Youth, 2001

Other books by the same author:
Kit's Wilderness, 2000 (Michael L. Printz Award)
Skellig, 1999 (ALA Children's Notable)

Other books you might like:
Melvin Burgess, *The Baby and Fly Pie*, 1996
When three "rubbish kids" find a baby, they disagree about keeping or returning it and claiming a reward, but decide too late to help the baby.

Cynthia DeFelice, *Nowhere to Call Home*, 1999
Orphaned Frances dresses as a boy and heads West, but

soon finds living with an unknown relative is a better alternative.

Phyllis Reynolds Naylor, *Jade Green: A Ghost Story*, 2000
Judith's green-framed photo of her mother awakens the ghost of a former serving girl; luckily the ghost protects Judith from a murderous relative.

Caroline Stevermer, *River Rats*, 1992
Orphans Tomcat, Esteban and Toby ply the now polluted Mississippi River on an old paddlewheel, swapping mail and freight for food and clothing.

13

ELAINE MARIE ALPHIN

Ghost Soldier

(New York: Holt, 2001)

Subject(s): Ghosts; Fathers and Sons; Remarriage
Age range(s): Grades 6-8
Major character(s): Alexander Raskin, 15-Year-Old; Richeson Francis Chamblee, Military Personnel, Spirit; Nicole Hambrick, Teenager; Paige Hambrick, Professor (Duke University)
Time period(s): 2000s; 1860s
Locale(s): North Carolina (near the Research Triangle); Petersburg, Virginia

Summary: Alexander doesn't understand why his father wants to drive to North Carolina over spring break, but his father's reasons become clearer when they stay with widowed Paige Hambrick and her children. Never having accepted his carefree mother's decision to leave, nor his parent's subsequent divorce, Alexander is less than happy to think his father is considering marrying Paige, an idea equally displeasing to her daughter Nicole. Alexander becomes distracted by the ghost of Civil War soldier Richeson Francis Chamblee, who he meets while both families tour the battlefields in Petersburg. With a ghost constantly nattering at him to find out what happened to his family after he died, Alexander is sidetracked from his plans to halt his father's romance and is glad to accept help from the Hambricks as they search local history museums for clues to the Chamblee family. (216 pages)

Where it's reviewed:
Booklist, August 2001, page 2118
Bulletin of the Center for Children's Books, July 2001, page 400
Kirkus Reviews, May 15, 2001, page 736
School Library Journal, August 2001, page 175
Voice of Youth Advocates, August 2001, page 210

Other books by the same author:
Simon Says, 2002
Counterfeit Son, 2000
Tournament Time, 1994
The Proving Ground, 1992
The Ghost Cadet, 1991

Other books you might like:
Avi, *Something Upstairs: A Tale of Ghosts*, 1988
Kenny's new bedroom is haunted by the ghost of a slave who was murdered more than 100 years ago.

Lynn Cullen, *The Backyard Ghost*, 1993
   Charlie and Eleanor find the Civil War bugle of Joseph, the ghost who lives in their backyard, which enables them to actually meet him.
George Ella Lyon, *Here and Then*, 1994
   When Abby joins in a Civil War reenactment, she "becomes" Eliza and travels back in time to help save lives.

ANNA ALTER, Author/Illustrator

Estelle and Lucy
(New York: Greenwillow Books, 2001)

Subject(s): Sibling Rivalry; Animals/Cats; Animals/Mice
Age range(s): Preschool-Kindergarten
Major character(s): Estelle, Cat, Sister (older); Lucy, Mouse, Sister (younger); Mother, Cat, Mother
Time period(s): Indeterminate
Locale(s): Fictional Country

Summary: Like most little sisters, Lucy wants to do and be just like her big sister. Estelle doesn't like Lucy to copy her and proudly points out all that she can do because she is bigger. Mother observes that Lucy is big enough for a picnic and the author's first book concludes with an outdoor picnic of homemade biscuits that all have helped to make. (24 pages)

Where it's reviewed:
Booklist, April 1, 2001, page 1470
Horn Book Guide, Fall 2001, page 225
Publishers Weekly, April 16, 2001, page 64
School Library Journal, July 2001, page 72

Other books you might like:
Margery Bernstein, *My Brother, the Pest*, 1999
   A little girl complains about her pesky little brother, but when he asks her to read to him she reconsiders her opinion.
Angela Johnson, *Do Like Kyla*, 1990
   Kyla's younger sister follows her all day, imitating every behavior.
Ashley Wolff, *Stella and Roy*, 1993
   Overly confident, big sister Stella challenges younger brother Roy to a race and learns that age and size are not guarantees of success.

JULIA ALVAREZ

How Tia Lola Came to Visit/Stay
(New York: Alfred A. Knopf, 2001)

Subject(s): Aunts and Uncles; Family Life; Divorce
Age range(s): Grades 3-6
Major character(s): Juanita Guzman, 7-Year-Old, Sister, Child of Divorced Parents; Miguel Guzman, Brother (older), Nephew, Child of Divorced Parents; Tia Lola, Aunt
Time period(s): 2000s (2001)
Locale(s): Vermont; New York, New York; Dominican Republic

Summary: Miguel is not happy. First his parents divorce, then his mother takes a job in a small Vermont town moving him away from his beloved city, his friends and his father. And now, Tia Lola is coming to care for Miguel and Juanita while his mother works. It doesn't take long for Miguel to see that Tia Lola will be a major embarrassment so he attempts to keep her hidden. The extroverted woman finds a way, despite the language barrier, to meet and charm everyone in town and she soon charms Miguel too. With Tia Lola, Miguel and Juanita are allowed to travel to New York to visit their father and friends. Tia Lola sews uniforms for Miguel's baseball team and serves them refreshments after practice. As a Christmas gift, the family travels to Tia Lola's home in the Dominican Republic so Juanita and Miguel can learn more about their cultural heritage. At the book's conclusion the author explains the Dominican variations on the Spanish language as they appear in the book. (147 pages)

Where it's reviewed:
Booklist, February 15, 2001, page 1138
Bulletin of the Center for Children's Books, April 2001, page 296
Children's Bookwatch, June 2001, page 5
Publishers Weekly, February 26, 2001, page 87
School Library Journal, March 2001, page 245

Other books you might like:
Lulu Delacre, *Salsa Stories*, 2000
   Carmen Teresa uses the gift of a blank book to record the stories told by family members around the New Year's dinner table.
Susan Shreve, *The Formerly Great Alexander Family*, 1995
   Liam is so crushed by his parent's separation that he isolates himself from friends while he adjusts to the changes in his life.
Gary Soto, *Neighborhood Odes*, 1992
   A collection of twenty-one poems celebrates life in a Hispanic neighborhood.

CLAUDIO APONE

My Grandfather, Jack the Ripper
(New York: Herodias, 2001)

Subject(s): Mystery and Detective Stories; Psychic Powers; Serial Killers
Age range(s): Grades 6-9
Major character(s): Andy Dobson, 13-Year-Old; Lucy Catlett, 13-Year-Old; Massimo, Student—Graduate; Jack the Ripper, Historical Figure
Time period(s): 2000s; 1880s
Locale(s): London, England

Summary: Though the Jack-in-the-Box is now a rather shabby guesthouse in London's East End, it was built in 1853 and has been run by a Dobson family member ever since. Andy's grandfather Bob is the keeper of the family history and tells the story of Room 4, now kept locked, and its occupant who was supposedly Jack the Ripper's last victim. Andy's unusual talent, which he often displays to his best friend Lucy, is his ability to guess the contents of her lunch bag just by holding the bag. Massimo, a graduate student from Italy who's researching the Jack the Ripper legend, rents a room from Mrs. Dobson. When he hears of Andy's skills, he talks him into using his psychic ability to describe the contents of the mysterious, locked Room 4. Their experiment leads to the discovery of a copycat serial killer living in their guesthouse who threatens Andy's mom as he tries to carry on Jack the Ripper's work. This tale, written by a popular Italian author, is his first to be published in English. (200 pages)

Where it's reviewed:
Children's Book Review Service, Fall 2000, page 44
Children's Bookwatch, March 2001, page 2
Publishers Weekly, October 30, 2000, page 77
School Library Journal, June 2001, page 142
Voice of Youth Advocates, June 2001, page 130

Other books by the same author:
Club Orbital: Adventures in Space, 1999
Metropolitan Frankenstein, 1999

Other books you might like:
Roger J. Green, *The Throttlepenny Murder*, 1989
    Jesse's employer, nicknamed "Throttlepenny" for his stinginess, is found dead and she is accused of the crime and sentenced to be hanged.
Philip Pullman, *The Ruby in the Smoke*, 1987
    Sally, an orphaned sixteen-year-old, must outmaneuver a host of villainous nineteenth-century characters to claim her inheritance and her independence.
Paul West, *The Women of Whitechapel and Jack the Ripper*, 1991
    When a young nobleman is introduced to the prostitutes of London, murder ensues in this look at a grim side of London life. Adult title.

17

DAWN APPERLEY, Author/Illustrator

Flip and Flop
(New York: Orchard Books, 2001)

Subject(s): Animals/Penguins; Playing; Friendship
Age range(s): Preschool-Kindergarten
Major character(s): Flip, Penguin, Brother, 5-Year-Old; Flop, Penguin, 2-Year-Old, Brother; Hip, Friend (Flip's), Bear; Hop, Bear, Friend (Flop's)
Time period(s): Indeterminate
Locale(s): Fictional Country

Summary: Flop enjoys playing with Flip and trying to copy all the moves his brother makes as he romps in the snow. Flop is disappointed when Flip tires of his favorite game, "boompa" and begins playing "slip-slide" with Hip. Sad little Flop wanders away to sulk and meets Hop who's happy to play with him. Now Flop understands the pleasure of playing with a friend. Together Flop and Hop rejoin Flip and Hip and invent a new game for both pairs of brothers to play together. (28 pages)

Where it's reviewed:
Booklist, January 1, 2002, page 862
Horn Book Guide, Spring 2002, page 11
Magpies, July 2001, page 28
School Library Journal, March 2002, page 172

Awards the book has won:
IRA Children's Choices, 2002

Other books by the same author:
Don't Wake the Baby, 2001
Wakey-Wakey, 1999
In the Sand, 1996

Other books you might like:
Jeanne M. Gravois, *Quickly, Quigley*, 1994
    Quigley, a young penguin, can't seem to move quickly enough to please anyone at home or at school.
Mick Inkpen, *Kipper's Snowy Day*, 1996
    With his friend Tiger, Kipper plays all day in the snow.
Nancy Elizabeth Wallace, *Snow*, 1995
    Rabbit brothers hurry outside at the first sign of snow to sled, make snow rabbits and throw snowballs.

18

JENNIFER ARMSTRONG

Theodore Roosevelt: Letters from a Young Coal Miner
(New York: Winslow Press, 2001)

Series: Dear Mr. President
Subject(s): Letters; Miners and Mining
Age range(s): Grades 5-8
Major character(s): Frank Kovacs, 13-Year-Old, Miner (coal); Theodore Roosevelt, Historical Figure, Government Official (president)
Time period(s): 1900s (1901-1903)
Locale(s): Oneida, Pennsylvania; Washington, District of Columbia

Summary: First in the *Dear Mr. President* series, an exchange of letters written between a president and a young person, finds Theodore Roosevelt sharing correspondence with Frank Kovacs, a young coal miner. Frank writes the president after the assassination of President McKinley and describes the hardships of the miners and their families. The President's replies are filled with comments about his own children, his feelings concerning the Anthracite Coal Strike of 1902 and questions about Frank's family. A feeling of warmth and respect fills the letters between these two unlikely correspondents, which makes for enjoyable reading. (118 pages)

Where it's reviewed:
Booklist, March 1, 2001, page 1275
Children's Bookwatch, April 2001, page 2
Kirkus Reviews, January 15, 2001, page 104
School Library Journal, April 2001, page 138
Voice of Youth Advocates, August 2001, page 196

Other books by the same author:
Shattered: Stories of Children and War, 2002
The Kindling, 2002 (Fire US Trilogy, Book 1)
Thomas Jefferson: Letters from a Philadelphia Bookworm, 2001 (Dear Mr. President)
Mary Mehan Awake, 1997
The Dreams of Mairhe Mehan, 1996

Other books you might like:

Susan Campbell Bartoletti, *Growing Up in Coal Country*, 1996

A photo-essay depicting the lives of children who worked in the coal mines of Pennsylvania at the beginning of the 1900s. Nonfiction title.

Jay Parini, *The Patch Boys*, 1988

Sammy diCantini grows up quickly the summer his older brother is injured trying to organize a union in a Pennsylvania mining town.

N.A. Perez, *Breaker*, 1988

After Pat's father is killed in a mining accident, Pat begins working in the mines while his brother fights for improved labor conditions.

Gloria Skurzynski, *Rockbuster*, 2001

Orphaned young, Tommy toils in the mines but resists being involved in the labor movement, choosing instead to become a lawyer and help all people.

JENNIFER ARMSTRONG

Thomas Jefferson: Letters from a Philadelphia Bookworm

(Florida/New York: Winslow Press, 2001)

Series: Dear Mr. President
Subject(s): Letters; Historical; Presidents
Age range(s): Grades 5-8
Major character(s): Amelia Hornsby, Teenager; Thomas Jefferson, Historical Figure, Government Official (president); Benjamin Rush, Historical Figure, Doctor
Time period(s): 1800s (1803-1807)
Locale(s): Philadelphia, Pennsylvania; Washington, District of Columbia; Monticello, Virginia

Summary: Through a series of letters that spans five years, young Amelia Hornsby writes to President Thomas Jefferson with her observations on the news of the day. With her father teaching at a college in Pittsburgh, Amelia has been left in Philadelphia with Dr. Benjamin Rush where she is in a prime position to observe much of what's new in science and natural history and meet many of the leaders of the day. She also doesn't hesitate to advise President Jefferson of her thoughts, from the Lewis and Clark Expedition, to riding in a hot air balloon or observing the new water works system. Amelia even chides him when he sounds a little depressed, illustrating how their relationship grows in this continuing series. (117 pages)

Where it's reviewed:
Booklist, May 15, 2001, page 1749
Bulletin of the Center for Children's Books, May 2001, page 330
Children's Bookwatch, April 2001, page 2
New York Times Book Review, April 15, 2001, page 24
School Library Journal, June 2001, page 142

Other books by the same author:
Kindling, 2002
Theodore Roosevelt: Letters from a Young Coal Miner, 2001 (Dear Mr. President)

Mary Mehan Awake, 1997
The Dreams of Mairhe Mehan, 1996
Black-Eyed Susan, 1995
Steal Away, 1992

Other books you might like:

Philip Brady, *Reluctant Hero: A Snowy Road to Salem in 1802*, 1990

Based on the author's family history, this work describes the arduous journey young Cutting makes to sell a load of shingles at market.

Gail Langer Karwoski, *Seaman: The Dog Who Explored the West with Lewis & Clark*, 1999

The Corps of Discovery members who accompany Lewis and Clark claim a Newfoundland dog named Seaman as their expedition mascot.

Maureen Stock Sappey, *Letters from Vinnie*, 1999

Vinnie is a great admirer of President Lincoln and wins a commission to sculpt a life-size statue of him to be placed in the Rotunda of the Capitol.

TEDD ARNOLD, Author/Illustrator

More Parts

(New York: Dial Books for Young Readers, 2001)

Subject(s): Anatomy; Language; Stories in Rhyme
Age range(s): Grades 1-4
Major character(s): Unnamed Character, Child, Son; Mom, Mother; Dad, Father
Time period(s): Indeterminate
Locale(s): United States

Summary: A young boy takes literally each expression he hears. When his truck breaks, Mom suggests that "broke his heart" and he feels worried not consoled. Dad requests his son's help by asking, "give me a hand" and the boy feels alarmed to learn that his hands can come off. With each expression the boy adds layers of tape and glue to his body to keep his parts securely attached and finally decides to simply stay in his room. When Mom and Dad learn why their son is upset they explain the real meaning of figures of speech and the boy feels momentarily comforted. (32 pages)

Where it's reviewed:
Bulletin of the Center for Children's Books, September 2001, page 6
Horn Book Guide, Spring 2002, page 33
Kirkus Reviews, June 1, 2001, page 798
School Library Journal, September 2001, page 182

Other books by the same author:
Huggly's Pizza, 2000 (Monster Under the Bed)
Parts, 1997 (Colorado Children's Book Award)
No More Water in the Tub!, 1995

Other books you might like:

Marion Dane Bauer, *If You Had a Nose Like an Elephant's Trunk*, 2001

An imaginative little girl considers the effects of exchanging a human body part for one from an animal.

Debra Fraser, *Miss Alaineus: A Vocabulary Disaster*, 2000

Sage misunderstands one of the week's vocabulary words

but turns her embarrassing moment into a prize-winning costume.

Peggy Parish, *Amelia Bedelia*, 1963

In the first book about beloved Amelia Bedelia her literal interpretation of instructions leads to humorous events.

Marvin Terban, *It Figures!: Fun Figures of Speech*, 1993

A nonfiction title explains common figures of speech and the correct use of various forms of figurative language.

21

JIM ARNOSKY, Author/Illustrator

Raccoon on His Own
(New York: G.P. Putnam's Sons, 2001)

Subject(s): Animals/Raccoons; Nature
Age range(s): Grades K-1
Major character(s): Unnamed Character, Raccoon
Time period(s): Indeterminate
Locale(s): United States

Summary: A mother raccoon and two babies dig in the mud at the edge of a stream while a third climbs into a nearby boat. Suddenly the boat begins to float downstream and the young raccoon has a brief, unexpected taste of independence. The trip introduces the raccoon to other life on the water, some of it dangerous and he searches for a safe way to get out of the boat. Fortunately, the mother and her other two babies follow along the shore so when the boat again sticks on some mud, the wandering raccoon climbs out to a welcome sight. (32 pages)

Where it's reviewed:
Bulletin of the Center for Children's Books, July 2001, page 401
Horn Book Guide, Fall 2001, page 225
Kirkus Reviews, March 15, 2001, 404
Publishers Weekly, June 11, 2001, page 87
School Library Journal, May 2001, page 108

Other books by the same author:
A Manatee Morning, 2000
Rattlesnake Dance, 2000
All About Turtles, 2000

Other books you might like:
Margaret Park Bridges, *Now What Can I Do?*, 2001
    A young raccoon feels bored on a rainy day until the mother's suggestions show how to liven any activity by using imagination.
Lindsay Barrett George, *Around the Pond: Who's Been Here?*, 1996
    Signs of the various animals that live near a pond are obvious as one walks the path around the pond.
Beatrix Potter, *The Tale of Mr. Jeremy Fisher*, 1906
    A frog fishing from his lily pad boat ''catches'' a frightening and exciting tale, but no fish.

22

MIKE ARTELL
JIM HARRIS, Illustrator

Petite Rouge: A Cajun Red Riding Hood
(New York: Dial Books for Young Readers, 2001)

Subject(s): Fairy Tales; Folklore; Stories in Rhyme
Age range(s): Grades 1-3
Major character(s): Petite Rouge Riding Hood, Duck, Daughter; TeJean, Cat; Claude, Alligator; Grand-mere, Grandmother, Duck
Time period(s): Indeterminate Past
Locale(s): Louisiana

Summary: With TeJean, Petite Rouge sets off in the pirogue to deliver a basket of food to her sick Grand-mere. As Petite Rouge and TeJean pole along through the swamp Claude stops them in hopes of eating some of their food. When his ploy fails Claude swims quickly to Grand-mere's home and dons her clothing with a fake bill and webbed feet thinking he can eat the basket of food and Petite Rouge too. TeJean and Petite Rouge are suspicious of Grand-mere's appearance and quickly devise a plan to save themselves from Claude's jaws. When Claude bites down on what he thinks is Petite Rouge, he actually gets a mouthful of Cajun sausage doused in hot sauce. Claude quickly loses his interest in dining on Petite Rouge or anyone else and retires to his home in the swamp. The glossary of Cajun terms at the beginning of the book aids with pronunciation. (32 pages)

Where it's reviewed:
Booklist, July 2001, page 2012
Horn Book Guide, Fall 2001, page 341
Kirkus Reviews, April 15, 2001, page 581
Publishers Weekly, May 7, 2001, page 246
School Library Journal, June 2001, page 100

Awards the book has won:
Notable Social Studies Trade Books for Young People, 2002

Other books by the same author:
Cartooning for Kids, 2001
Starry Skies: Questions, Facts and Riddles about the Universe, 1997
Big Long Animal Sound, 1994

Other books you might like:
Lisa Campbell Ernst, *Little Red Riding Hood: A Newfangled Prairie Tale*, 1995
    In a contemporary spoof of a classic fairy tale, Grandma surprises the wolf and the two reach a most unusual conclusion.
James Marshall, *Red Riding Hood*, 1987
    The traditional story of an unsuspecting young girl meeting a hungry wolf in the forest is retold and illustrated by Marshall.
Tynia Thomassie, *Feliciana Feydra LeRoux: A Cajun Tall Tale*, 1995
    In an original bayou tall tale, Feliciana sneaks out to join the menfolk's alligator hunt.

CATHERINE ASARO

The Phoenix Code

(New York: Bantam Books, 2000)

Subject(s): Artificial Intelligence; Love
Age range(s): Grades 9-Adult
Major character(s): Megan O'Flannery, Scientist; Chandrarajan "Raj" Sundaram, Scientist RS-4 "Aris", Android
Time period(s): 2020s (2021)
Locale(s): Nevada (underground research facility MindSim Corporation)

Summary: Artificial intelligence expert Megan O'Flannery has just received an interesting, though mysterious, job offer to work on an android project. Megan accepts and MindSim ships her off to be scientist in residence at their secret research facility. In a race to be the first to successfully embody an artificial intelligence in a humanlike body, MindSim has brought her in to determine why all the androids are self-destructing; the last one even committed suicide. Megan quickly decides that Aris the android needs less fear and more free will and human interaction. Aris responds well to this re-programming and treatment until the arrival of Raj, a hand-some robotics specialist, whereupon Aris displays behaviors that in a human would be called jealousy. Megan struggles with her feelings towards Raj and Aris, unable to decide whether the secretive human or the increasingly unpredictable android is the greater danger. (333 pages)

Where it's reviewed:
Analog Science Fiction and Fact, June 2001, page 134
Booklist, December 1, 2000, page 698
Kliatt, March 2001, page 22
Library Journal, December 2000, page 197
Voice of Youth Advocates, April 2001, page 48

Other books by the same author:
Spherical Harmonic, 2001
Quantum Rose, 2000
The Veiled Web, 1999

Other books you might like:
William Gibson, *All Tomorrow's Parties*, 1999
    An artificial intelligence fights to embody herself.
Tanith Lee, *The Silver Metal Lover*, 1981
    An android finds himself the object of a rich girl's obses-sion.
Amy Thompson, *Virtual Girl*, 1993
    A computer nerd builds himself a beautiful female android and is astonished when she wants more from life than being his girlfriend.

24

FRANK ASCH, Author/Illustrator
DEVIN ASCH, Illustrator

Baby Duck's New Friend

(San Diego: Gulliver Books/Harcourt, Inc., 2001)

Subject(s): Animals/Ducks; Self-Reliance; Independence
Age range(s): Preschool-Kindergarten
Major character(s): Baby Duck, Duck, Baby; Mama Duck, Duck, Mother
Time period(s): Indeterminate
Locale(s): Fictional Country

Summary: Baby Duck intends to comply with Mama Duck's rule that ducklings must be accompanied by someone who can fly if they want to swim past the old stone bridge. How is he to know that the yellow duck that "flies" from the bridge into the water is actually a toy duck that's fallen off a passing truck? Baby Duck follows his new and very quiet friend downstream, copying its movements, tumbling over the "bro-ken" part of the river all the way to the ocean. The waves are really scary and Baby Duck is hungry but his new friend says nothing as a little boy picks it up and carries it away. Baby Duck flaps his wings in anger and discovers he can now fly, and he does all the way home. This collaboration with his author/illustrator father is the first book for Devin Asch. (32 pages)

Where it's reviewed:
Booklist, March 15, 2001, page 1402
Horn Book Guide, Fall 2001, page 225
Kirkus Reviews, March 1, 2001, page 326
Publishers Weekly, March 12, 2001, page 88
School Library Journal, August 2001, page 142

Other books you might like:
Eve Bunting, *Ducky*, 1997
    Once part of a crate of bathtub toys, Ducky floats alone on the ocean currents until washing onto a beach where a boy finds it and takes it home.
Lisa Westberg Peters, *Cold Little Duck, Duck, Duck*, 2000
    One young duck learns not to fly back to the pond too early in the springtime because frozen ponds are cold, cold, cold.
Nancy Tafuri, *Have You Seen My Duckling?*, 1984
    With her ducklings following a mother duck searches the pond for her one missing offspring in a Caldecott Honor Book.

25

SANDY ASHER
KATHRYN BROWN, Illustrator

Stella's Dancing Days

(San Diego: Harcourt, Inc., 2001)

Subject(s): Animals/Cats; Pets; Family Life
Age range(s): Grades K-1
Major character(s): Stella, Cat, Dancer; Tall One, Child, Brother (oldest); Gentle One, Child, Sister
Time period(s): Indeterminate Past
Locale(s): United States

Summary: As a kitten Stella entertains the human members of her household with her dancing. As she grows up Stella develops other interests such as chasing bugs in the garden or singing under the night sky with other cats and she only dances on special occasions. Tall One and Gentle One miss Stella's dancing, but Stella is too busy with the next phase of her life to miss those days. Soon, the family meets Stella's six kittens, each one a dancer. (32 pages)

Where it's reviewed:
Booklist, March 15, 2001, page 1402
Horn Book Guide, Fall 2001, page 246
Kirkus Reviews, February 2, 2001, page 178
Publishers Weekly, February 26, 2001
School Library Journal, July 2001, page 72

Other books by the same author:
Princess Bee and the Royal Good Night Story, 1989

Other books you might like:
Patricia Casey, *My Cat Jack*, 1994
   A well-loved pet, Jack is a stretching, yawning, playful cat.
Isabelle Harper, *My Cats Nick and Nora*, 1995
   Two cousins enjoy playing with each other and the family cat—once they locate their hiding place.
Carol Purdy, *Mrs. Merriwether's Musical Cat*, 1994
   After Beethoven, a stray cat with a rhythmic tail, returns to Mrs. Merriwether's piano studio with three kittens she realizes ''he'' has been misnamed.

LINDA ASHMAN
LAUREN STRINGER, Illustrator

Castles, Caves, and Honeycombs
(San Diego: Harcourt, Inc., 2001)

Subject(s): Dwellings; Animals; Stories in Rhyme
Age range(s): Preschool-Kindergarten
Time period(s): 2000s
Locale(s): Earth

Summary: The author's first book rhythmically reflects on the concept of homes. Whether for humans or animals, a home can be any place from a sandy dune to a castle tower to a high cliff or a tree branch. Animals such as turtles and snails carry their homes with them. Others, such as spiders or metamorphosing caterpillars, have the ability to create their homes wherever they are. Homes are cozy; homes are safe; homes are a place to play and sleep. (32 pages)

Where it's reviewed:
Booklist, March 15, 2001, page 1400
Bulletin of the Center for Children's Books, May 2001, page 331
Horn Book, July 2001, page 438
Riverbank Review, Spring 2001, page 30
School Library Journal, April 2001, page 98

Awards the book has won:
Booklist Editors' Choice/Books for Youth, 2002

Other books by the same author:
Maxwell's Magic Mix-Up, 2001
Sailing Off to Sleep, 2001

Other books you might like:
Mary Ann Hoberman, *A House Is a House for Me*, 1978
   Rhyming text lists various objects that can be used as dwellings by different animals.
Megan McDonald, *Is This a House for Hermit Crab?*, 1990
   A hermit crab searching for a new house tries several possibilities—a can, driftwood, a rock and a pail before finding an empty sea snail shell.

Megan McDonald, *My House Has Stars*, 1996
   Dwellings known as home vary from one culture or country to another but all share the same ceiling of stars.

LINDA ASHMAN
REGAN DUNNICK, Illustrator

Maxwell's Magic Mix-Up
(New York: Simon & Schuster Books for Young Readers, 2001)

Subject(s): Magicians; Birthdays; Stories in Rhyme
Age range(s): Grades 1-3
Major character(s): Louise, 7-Year-Old, Sister; Maxwell, Magician, Uncle; Alex, Nephew, Magician
Time period(s): 2000s (2001)

Summary: Louise's seventh birthday does not proceed according to plan. A last-minute substitute for the entertainment, Maxwell arrives with a flurry and inadvertently turns Louise into a rock. When he tries to fix her he creates a new problem and in no time the apartment is filled with Maxwell's errors. Finally he gives up and calls Alex who arrives to begin undoing his uncle's tricks. For some it's easier said than done, but Louise does reappear in time to open presents. (32 pages)

Where it's reviewed:
Booklist, July 2001, page 2016
Bulletin of the Center for Children's Books, June 2001, page 366
Horn Book, May 2001, page 308
Publishers Weekly, April 30, 2001, page 77
School Library Journal, July 2001, page 72

Other books by the same author:
Castles, Caves, and Honeycombs, 2001 (Booklist Editors' Choice)
Sailing Off to Sleep, 2001

Other books you might like:
Jon Agee, *Milo's Hat Trick*, 2001
   Bungling Milo will lose his job if he can't pull a rabbit out of a hat.
Helen Lester, *The Wizard, the Fairy and the Magic Chicken*, 1983
   Three magicians trying to outdo one another create a problem that they must work together to solve.
Bill Martin Jr., *The Wizard*, 1994
   A wizard's clumsiness while conjuring leads to an unexpected result.
John O'Brien, *Poof!*, 1999
   With a wave of their wands two wizards tackle their chores by transforming each job and each other into something else.

28

JEANNINE ATKINS

Becoming Little Women: Louisa May at Fruitlands
(New York: Putnam, 2001)

Subject(s): Utopia/Dystopia; Family Life

Age range(s): Grades 4-7
Major character(s): Louisa May Alcott, Historical Figure, 11-Year-Old; Bronson Alcott, Father (of Louisa), Historical Figure
Time period(s): 1840s (1844-1845)
Locale(s): Harvard, Massachusetts

Summary: During one memorable year, the Alcott family tries to live a politically correct lifestyle at Fruitlands. Bronson Alcott's philosophy means eating only vegetarian meals; wearing scratchy linen clothing rather than cotton so as not to exploit the slaves; and foregoing the use of animals for work. Louisa's mother occasionally slips out at night to milk the cows so that her daughters will have milk to drink while her husband travels around New England preaching about his philosophies. For her part, Louisa honors her father for what he's trying to do, but wants no part of some of his foolish ideas in this work based on Louisa's journals, letters and biographies. (202 pages)

Where it's reviewed:
Booklist, November 15, 2001, page 566
Bulletin of the Center for Children's Books, September 2001, page 500
Horn Book, October 2001, page 49
Library Talk, March 2002, page 47
School Library Journal, October 2001, page 148

Other books by the same author:
Girls Who Looked under Rocks, 2000 (nonfiction)
Mary Anning and the Sea Dragon, 1999 (nonfiction)

Other books you might like:
Louisa May Alcott, *Little Women*, 1868
    This classic story of family life stars the four March sisters—Jo, Meg, Beth and Amy.
Sheila Soloman Klass, *Little Women Next Door*, 2000
    Shy, motherless Susan is delighted when the Alcott family moves in on the adjoining farm they call Fruitlands.
Jane Yolen, *The Gift of Sarah Barker*, 1981
    Sister Sarah Barker and Brother Abel meet in a Shaker community but, once they fall in love, know they must leave the Shakers if they hope to marry.

29

JEANNINE ATKINS
CANDACE WHITMAN, Illustrator

Robin's Home

(New York: Farrar Straus Giroux, 2001)

Subject(s): Animals/Birds; Self-Confidence; Spring
Age range(s): Preschool-Grade 1
Major character(s): Robin, Bird, Brother; Mama, Bird, Mother; Papa, Father, Bird
Time period(s): 2000s (2001)
Locale(s): United States

Summary: Robin's siblings encourage him to join them on the soft grass, but Robin is content to snuggle in the nest carefully made by this parents. Repeatedly Robin asks Mama and Papa to tell the story of building the nest, describing the materials used and how the nest is constructed. Finally, Robin's curiosity overcomes his fear and he agrees to learn to fly so he can

find the source of the mud and soft grasses to use in making his own nest some day. A concluding note gives factual information about robins and their habits. (32 pages)

Where it's reviewed:
Booklist, March 15, 2001, page 1402
Horn Book Guide, Fall 2001, page 246
Kirkus Reviews, January 15, 2001, page 104
Publishers Weekly, February 26, 2001, page 84
School Library Journal, April 2001, page 98

Other books by the same author:
Mary Anning and the Sea Dragon, 1999
Get Set! Swim!, 1998
Aani and the Tree Huggers, 1995

Other books you might like:
Joyce Dunbar, *Baby Bird*, 1998
    Danger lurks on the ground for the fledgling bird trying to master flight.
Charlotte Pomerantz, *Flap Your Wings and Try*, 1989
    A young bird discovers the truth of his family's advice; to fly, simply, flap your wings and try.
Nick Williams, *How Birds Fly*, 1997
    A nonfiction title explains how the shape of bird's bodies makes flight possible.

30

AMELIA ATWATER-RHODES

Shattered Mirror

(New York: Delacorte, 2001)

Subject(s): Vampires; Witches and Witchcraft; Romance
Age range(s): Grades 8-12
Major character(s): Sarah Green, Witch; Christopher Ravena, Vampire, Twin; Nikolas, Vampire, Twin
Time period(s): 2000s
Locale(s): Acton, Massachusetts

Summary: Starting in a new high school, teen witch and vampire hunter Sarah meets Christopher who exudes vampirism, but who also writes her poems and sends her flowers. Fearful of letting her mother know she's broken the laws of their Vida witch clan by befriending Christopher, Sarah's further unsettled when she finds that Christopher is the twin of Nikolas, a vampire who's been hunted since the 1800s for killing a Vida witch. Caught between the witch world and the vampire world, Sarah finally decides to reveal who she is to Christopher, but then finds out he, too, has secrets to share in this thriller from a teen author. (227 pages)

Where it's reviewed:
Booklist, September 1, 2001, page 96
Bulletin of the Center for Children's Books, October 2001, page 50
Publishers Weekly, September 24, 2001, page 94
School Library Journal, September 2001, page 223
Voice of Youth Advocates, December 2001, page 365

Awards the book has won:
ALA Quick Picks for Reluctant Young Adult Readers, 2002

Other books by the same author:
Midnight Predator, 2002

Demon in My View, 2000
In the Forests of the Night, 1999

Other books you might like:
Tracy Briery, *The Vampire Journals*, 1993
Vampire Maria Theresa discloses how she chose vampirism in the eighteenth century to overcome the second-class status to which most women were relegated.
Annette Curtis Klause, *The Silver Kiss*, 1990
In this ultimate romance, a young girl falls in love with a three-hundred-year-old vampire.
Hanna Lutzen, *Vlad the Undead*, 1998
This chilling retelling of *Dracula* finds Lucia absorbed in the century-old story of a Romanian stranger, a stranger who now seems to have absconded with her.
Anne Rice, *Interview with the Vampire*, 1986
A two-hundred-year-old vampire's life is recounted, detail by gory detail.

31

DEBBIE ATWELL, Author/Illustrator

Pearl
(Boston: Walter Lorraine Books/Houghton Mifflin Company, 2001)

Subject(s): Historical; Family Life; Change
Age range(s): Grades 1-4
Major character(s): Pearl, Aged Person, Grandmother; David, Aged Person, Spouse
Time period(s): Multiple Time Periods (1789-1960)
Locale(s): United States

Summary: Pearl recounts the nation's history as her family experiences it over the course of her long life. As a young child she remembers the stories told by her grandfather of the earliest days of the young nation. Pearl recalls watching her mother and older sisters run the farm when all the men went to fight against slavery during the Civil War. Through two world wars, the Depression and new inventions such as the automobile, airplanes and television David and Pearl's family grows and survives hardship and loss. (32 pages)

Where it's reviewed:
Booklist, May 1, 2001, page 1690
Bulletin of the Center for Children's Books, April 2001, page 296
Publishers Weekly, February 26, 2001, page 85
Riverbank Review, Fall 2001, page 31
School Library Journal, June 2001, page 100

Awards the book has won:
Notable Social Studies Trade Books for Young People, 2002

Other books by the same author:
River, 1999
Barn, 1996

Other books you might like:
Donald Hall, *Old Home Day*, 1996
The cycle of growth, decline and renewal of a New England town is described through the history of its settlers.
Betsy Gould Hearne, *Seven Brave Women*, 1997
Each of seven brave women in the narrator's family is remembered for the courageous way in which she lived during a significant moment in our history.

Alice Schertle, *Maisie*, 1994
The story of ninety-year-old Maisie's life is also a record of the changes in America during her lifetime and a celebration of family ties.
Anne Shelby, *Homeplace*, 1995
While rocking a grandchild, a grandmother tells the history of the family from the original building of the family homestead to the present.

32

MARY JANE AUCH
HERM AUCH, Illustrator

I Was a Third Grade Spy
(New York: Holiday House, 2001)

Subject(s): Animals/Dogs; Talent; Schools
Age range(s): Grades 2-4
Major character(s): Arful Lewis, Dog; Brian Lewis, 3rd Grader, Friend; Josh Buckner, 3rd Grader, Friend Dougie, 3rd Grader, Friend
Time period(s): 2000s (2001)
Locale(s): United States

Summary: In the sequel to *I Was a Third Grade Science Project* Brian again resorts to hypnosis to remove Josh's impression that he is a cat and convince him to be a boy again. In the process Josh returns to normal, but Arful develops the ability to speak. Rather than hypnotize Arful back into his dog state, Brian, Josh and Dougie try to use his ability to their advantage for the upcoming Talent Show at school. First they send Arful out to spy on some girls. While Arful comes back with information important to a dog, none of it reveals what the girls' act will be for the Talent Show. Finally Dougie comes up with an idea to use Arful in the boys' act. Arful gets on stage that night, but not to do what the boys expect. (86 pages)

Where it's reviewed:
Booklist, May 1, 2001, page 1678
Bulletin of the Center for Children's Books, July 2001, page 402
Horn Book Guide, Fall 2001, page 288
Publishers Weekly, May 21, 2001, page 109
School Library Journal, July 2001, page 72

Other books by the same author:
I Was a Third Grade Science Project, 1999
The Latchkey Dog, 1994
Angel and Me and the Bayside Bombers, 1991

Other books you might like:
Duncan Ball, *Selby: The Secret Adventures of a Talking Dog*, 1997
Frequent television watching enables Selby to develop the ability to speak.
Matt Christopher, *The Dog That Called the Pitch*, 1998
Harry cannot talk but he does communicate with his owner using ESP, a skill that comes in handy during a baseball game.
S.E. Hinton, *The Puppy Sister*, 1995
Puppy Aleasha wants so much to be a member of the

family that, through sheer will power, she gradually changes into a little girl.

33

ANSELM AUDLEY

Heresy

(New York: Pocket Books, 2001)

Series: Aquasilva Trilogy. Book 1
Subject(s): Coming-of-Age; Religion
Age range(s): Grades 9-Adult
Major character(s): Cathan, Nobleman, Wizard
Time period(s): Indeterminate
Locale(s): Aquasilva, Planet—Imaginary

Summary: Although adopted with mysterious origins, Cathan always assumed he would follow his adopted father as Count of their clan's homeland. Trouble is brewing on Aquasilva and, when iron is discovered in Cathan's clan holdings, he is suddenly plunged into the turmoil. When he journeys to inform his father of their good fortune, Cathan suspects that truth is not what he has always been taught as a matter of religious doctrine. All too soon, he finds that he and his family are part of the Heretic movement, dedicated to revealing the lies and bringing freedom to Aquasilva. (401 pages)

Where it's reviewed:
Booklist, September 1, 2001, page 57
Kirkus Reviews, July 15, 2001, page 987
Library Journal, September 15, 2001, page 115
Publishers Weekly, July 23, 2001, page 54

Other books you might like:
Hilari Bell, *A Matter of Profit*, 2001
   A young soldier returns disillusioned from war and discovers a mentor in an elderly alien.
Robin Hobb, *Ship of Magic*, 1998
   The intelligence of the live ships allows Bartertown to thrive, but it doesn't do to look too closely at their origin.
Sheri S. Tepper, *Singer from the Sea*, 1999
   Religion and politics combine to lie about what happens to the young women and children who are disappearing.

34

BARBARA AUGUSTIN
GERHARD LAHR, Illustrator

Antonella and Her Santa Claus

(La Jolla, CA: Cranky Nell/Kane/Miller Book Publishers)

Subject(s): Christmas; Santa Claus; Letters
Age range(s): Grades K-3
Major character(s): Antonella, Child; Gino, Child, Friend
Time period(s): Indeterminate Past
Locale(s): Italy; Budapest, Hungary

Summary: Ignoring her teasing classmates, Antonella leaves a picture of her Christmas wishes on her window sill. When Santa does not take it she seeks advice from Gino who's a little bit older. Gino suggests mailing a letter to Santa and he helps her write it, but the post office will not take it. Antonella then goes to the balloon vendor who attaches the letter to a balloon and allows Antonella to release it. The balloon comes down in a schoolyard in Budapest and the children decide to respond. With the package they send to Antonella they include a letter from Santa giving the school's address so she can send the letter directly the next year. The title was originally published in Germany in 1969. (32 pages)

Where it's reviewed:
Booklist, October 15, 2001, page 399
Horn Book Guide, Spring 2002, page 34
Publishers Weekly, September 24, 2001, page 52
School Library Journal, October 2001, page 62

Other books you might like:
John Burningham, *Harvey Slumfenburger's Christmas Present*, 1993
   Weary Santa uses a variety of alternate transportation methods to deliver an overlooked present rather than disturb his tired reindeer.
Dorothea Lachner, *The Gift from Saint Nicholas*, 1995
   Anna and Misha send a wish to Santa that the snow in their village will blow away enough for the villagers to visit on Christmas day.
Brigitte Weninger, *A Letter to Santa Claus*, 2000
   For the first time poor Oliver allows himself to make a wish by attaching a carefully written letter to a red helium balloon and sending it to Santa.

35

AVI (Pseudonym of Avi Wortis)

Don't You Know There's a War On?

(New York: HarperCollins, 2001)

Subject(s): World War II; Teacher-Student Relationships; School Life
Age range(s): Grades 5-7
Major character(s): Howard Bellington "Howie" Crispers, 5th Grader; Duane "Denny" Coleman, 5th Grader; Rolanda Gossim, Teacher; Gilbert Lomister, Principal
Time period(s): 1940s (1943)
Locale(s): New York, New York (Brooklyn)

Summary: At the ripe old age of sixteen, Howie reflects on the year he was a student in Class 5-B at Brooklyn's P.S. 8 and had a crush on his teacher Miss Gossim. Howie and his best friend Denny both miss their fathers who are fighting overseas, think about chocolate cake and other rationed foods, and see Nazi spies everywhere. Convinced their hateful principal Mr. Lomister is a Nazi spy, Howie follows him and one day overhears a conversation about his beloved teacher Miss Gossim who is going to be fired. Distraught at the news, Howie investigates further and discovers that Miss Gossim is really married to a pilot and is being fired because she's pregnant. Mobilizing his classmates, Howie and Denny tackle the head of the school board to plead their case to retain their favorite teacher in a book filled with details of homefront life during World War II. (200 pages)

Where it's reviewed:
Booklist, June 2001, page 1876
Bulletin of the Center for Children's Books, May 2001, page 331

Publishers Weekly, April 9, 2001, page 75
School Library Journal, June 2001, page 142
Voice of Youth Advocates, June 2001, page 118

Other books by the same author:
Who Was That Masked Man, Anyway?, 1992
Nothing but the Truth, 1991
S.O.R. Losers, 1984
A Place Called Ugly, 1981

Other books you might like:
Eve Bunting, *Spying on Miss Muller*, 1995
   Jessica and her friends spy on their once-adored language teacher, Miss Muller, who they suspect has German leanings.
Mary Downing Hahn, *Stepping on the Cracks*, 1991
   Margaret's dislike of bully Gordy changes when she meets his abusive father; she even helps hide his pacifist brother who's a World War II deserter.
M.E. Kerr, *Is That You, Miss Blue?*, 1975
   Warned that Miss Blue is very strange, Flanders discovers that Miss Blue is her best teacher during the year she boards at Charles School.
Anna Myers, *Captain's Command*, 1999
   The events of World War II are overwhelming to young Gail when first her Uncle Ned is blinded and then her father is missing in action.
Mary Pope Osborne, *My Secret War: The World War II Diary of Madeline Beck*, 2000
   Just as Maddie adjusts to her new school, she and her mother learn her father's been wounded and they move to the West Coast to be near his hospital.

36

AVI (Pseudonym of Avi Wortis)

The Good Dog

(New York: Richard Jackson/Atheneum Books for Young Readers, 2001)

Subject(s): Animals/Dogs; Animals/Wolves; Pets
Age range(s): Grades 4-6
Major character(s): Jack Kostof, Son, Child; McKinley, Dog (malamute), Narrator; Lupin, Wolf
Locale(s): Steamboat Springs, Colorado

Summary: As head dog in Steamboat Springs McKinley responds to all problems relating to other dogs while also trying to protect his human pup Jack. McKinley tracks down a runaway dog and picks up the scent of a wolf in the area. When Jack tries to use McKinley to find the runaway in order to get the reward money McKinley, who's trying to protect the dog from a cruel owner, leads him away from the dog's hiding place and runs right into the wolf. Lupin challenges McKinley to join her pack and know real freedom while Jack is so awed by Lupin that he wants to run away and live with the wolves. Now McKinley has to protect his pup, inform his pack of Lupin's plans and make a decision about just what it means to be a good dog. (243 pages)

Where it's reviewed:
Booklist, September 1, 2001, page 102
Horn Book, January 2002, page 75

Publishers Weekly, November 5, 2001, page 68
School Library Journal, December 2001, page 132
Voice of Youth Advocates, December 2001, page 366

Other books by the same author:
Ereth's Birthday, 2000 (Tales from Dimwood Forest)
Midnight Magic, 1999
Perloo the Bold, 1998

Other books you might like:
John R. Erickson, *The Further Adventures of Hank the Cowdog*, 1983
   An eye problem threatens to end Hank's job as Head of Ranch Security in this series title.
Roland Smith, *The Captain's Dog: My Journey with the Lewis and Clark Tribe*, 1999
   Seaman, the Newfoundland dog selected by Meriwether Lewis, tells the story of his travels with the Lewis and Clark Expedition.
Bill Wallace, *Watchdog and the Coyotes*, 1995
   The misconceptions of Sweetie, a Great Dane desiring a stable home, are revealed from the dog's perspective.

37

AVI (Pseudonym of Avi Wortis)
BILL FARNSWORTH, Illustrator

Prairie School

(New York: HarperCollins Publishers, 2001)

Series: I Can Read Book
Subject(s): Books and Reading; Physically Handicapped; Farm Life
Age range(s): Grades 2-4
Major character(s): Noah Bidson, 9-Year-Old, Nephew; Dora, Aunt, Paraplegic
Time period(s): 1880s (1880)
Locale(s): Colorado

Summary: Noah is content with his family's life on their prairie farm so he doesn't understand why his parents would invite Aunt Dora, the schoolteacher, to visit. It's soon apparent that Aunt Dora has come to teach Noah to read and write, a skill he thinks he has no use for on the prairie. Although Aunt Dora's traditional teaching methods don't work with Noah, she soon finds a way to interest him in books. As he wheels her over the prairie sharing his knowledge, Aunt Dora uses a reference book to locate more information about prairie life and reads it to Noah. Soon, Noah takes to his lessons and is able to read to his parents every night after supper. After Aunt Dora returns to her home in the East, letters provide a way for them to stay in touch. (48 pages)

Where it's reviewed:
Booklist, April 15, 2001, page 1568
Bulletin of the Center for Children's Books, May 2001, page 331
Horn Book Guide, Fall 2001, page 288
Kirkus Reviews, April 1, 2001, page 494
School Library Journal, May 2001, page 108

Other books by the same author:
Ereth's Birthday, 2000
Abigail Takes the Wheel, 1999 (I Can Read Book)

Finding Providence: The Story of Roger Williams, 1997 (I Can Read Book)

Other books you might like:

Sarah Glasscock, *My Prairie Summer*, 1998
A young girl uses her diary to record the activity on her family's busy prairie farm.

Rebecca L. Johnson, *A Walk in the Prairie*, 2001
A nonfiction title describes the ecology of the North American prairie and the interdependence of plants, animals and the environment for survival.

Nancy Smiler Levinson, *Clara and the Bookwagon*, 1988
The arrival at Clara's family farm of a horse-drawn book wagon opens to Clara a vast new, exciting world through reading.

38

AVI (Pseudonym of Avi Wortis)

The Secret School
(San Diego: Harcourt, Inc., 2001)

Subject(s): Teachers; Historical; Schools
Age range(s): Grades 4-7
Major character(s): Ida Bidson, 14-Year-Old, Teacher; Tom Kohl, 8th Grader
Time period(s): 1920s (1925)
Locale(s): Elk Creek, Colorado

Summary: Ida hears the news that her one-room school will be closed because her teacher has a family emergency and resigned halts her dreams of attending high school. Ida has bigger dreams than just high school, but unless she takes the exit exams, along with her classmate Tom, she cannot enroll at the high school. Swearing her classmates to secrecy, Ida becomes Miss Bidson and assumes the role of teacher, a job she finds hard to accomplish with all her farm chores, lessons for the other students and her own studies. Her teaching goes smoothly until the county examiner discovers her secret and agrees not to tell only if all the students pass the final exam. Luckily Ida is an extremely resourceful teenager, as well as a good teacher in this charming work of historical fiction. (153 pages)

Where it's reviewed:

Bulletin of the Center for Children's Books, October 2001, page 50
Horn Book, November 2001, page 741
Publishers Weekly, July 16, 2001, page 181
School Library Journal, September 2001, page 223
Voice of Youth Advocates, October 2001, page 272

Other books by the same author:

The Barn, 1994
The True Confessions of Charlotte Doyle, 1990
The Man Who Was Poe, 1989
The Fighting Ground, 1984

Other books you might like:

Karen Cushman, *The Ballad of Lucy Whipple*, 1996
Miserable living in a small gold mining town in California, Lucy decides to stay and run a library when her mother moves to the Sandwich Islands.

Rhea Beth Ross, *The Bet's On, Lizzie Bingham!*, 1988
When Lizzie's brothers claim that women need sheltering, Lizzie lets her siblings know that she doesn't require their protection.

Theodore Taylor, *Walking Up a Rainbow*, 1986
Practical Susan settles her deceased parents' debts by driving a herd of sheep to California and falling in love with her driver along the way.

39

JIM AYLESWORTH
BARBARA MCCLINTOCK, Illustrator

The Tale of Tricky Fox: A New England Trickster Tale
(New York: Scholastic Press, 2001)

Subject(s): Animals/Foxes; Trickster Tales; Folk Tales
Age range(s): Grades K-3
Major character(s): Tricky Fox, Fox, Trickster; Brother Fox, Fox; Unnamed Character, Teacher
Time period(s): Indeterminate Past
Locale(s): New England

Summary: A teacher reads a story to her attentive students about Tricky Fox who brags to Brother Fox that stealing chickens is no longer challenging and so he will get a pig in his sack instead. Knowing how impossible that will be Brother Fox confidently agrees to eat his hat if Tricky Fox returns with a pig in his sack. By judicious trading, cunning, and lying Tricky Fox might have achieved his goal, but the last of his "victims" is a teacher who outsmarts Tricky Fox and sends him home with a surprise rather than a pig in his sack. (32 pages)

Where it's reviewed:

Bulletin of the Center for Children's Books, March 2001, page 251
Horn Book, March 2001, page 217
Publishers Weekly, March 12, 2001, page 88
Riverbank Review, Spring 2001, page 35
School Library Journal, March 2001, page 192

Other books by the same author:

Aunt Pitty Patty's Piggy, 1999
The Full Belly Bowl, 1999 (Booklist Editors' Choice)
The Gingerbread Man, 1998 (School Library Journal Best Books)
My Sister's Rusty Bike, 1996
My Son John, 1994 (Notable Children's Book in the Language Arts)

Other books you might like:

Virginia Hamilton, *A Ring of Tricksters: Animal Tales from America, the West Indies, and Africa*, 1997
Eleven read-aloud tales include different tricksters and the unwitting animals who bear the brunt of their cleverness.

Gerald McDermott, *The Fox and the Stork*, 1999
Fox's trick on Stork backfires when she returns his dinner invitation and Fox goes home hungry.

Tim Myers, *Basho and the Fox*, 2000
A fox tricks Basho into a haiku contest to determine who

has the right to eat the cherries from a tree near Basho's hut.

Janet Stevens, *Tops and Bottoms*, 1995

Industrious Hare is a gardening partner to slumbering Bear in a contemporary interpretation of a trickster tale.

KATHERINE AYRES

Stealing South: A Story of the Underground Railroad

(New York: Random House, 2001)

Subject(s): Underground Railroad; Slavery
Age range(s): Grades 7-10
Major character(s): Will Spencer, 16-Year-Old, Peddler; Noah, Slave, Fugitive; Susannah, Slave, Sister, Fugitive
Time period(s): 1850s
Locale(s): Atwater, Ohio; Winchester, Kentucky

Summary: Will's family is active in the Underground Railroad and, though he's now ready to leave home to seek his career as a peddler, agrees to look for escaped slave Noah's brother and sister who are on a breeding farm in Kentucky. Will's venture into peddling is profitable as he selects goods from warehouses in Cincinnati and then travels through Kentucky, selling to people along the way until he finds Noah's family.

Stealing slaves away from this farm, Will finds his own life in danger as they try to reach a safe spot along the Underground Railroad in this companion to *North by Night*. (202 pages)

Where it's reviewed:
Book Report, November 2001, page 58
Booklist, April 1, 2001, page 1482
Kliatt, May 2001, page 5
School Library Journal, June 2001, page 142

Other books by the same author:
Silver Dollar Girl, 2000
Under Copp's Hill, 2000 (History Mysteries, Number 4)
North by Night: A Story of the Underground Railroad, 1998

Other books you might like:
Gloria Houston, *Bright Freedom's Song: A Story of the Underground Railroad*, 1998
Bright Freedom's father was an indentured servant, which explains his commitment to using the Underground Railroad to save slaves.
Andrea Davis Pinkney, *Silent Thunder: A Civil War Journey*, 1999
When his master has a stroke, Roscoe leaps at the chance to escape and head North, leaving behind his sister Summer and the corncob doll he made her.
Glennette Tilley Turner, *Running for Our Lives*, 1994
Separated from their parents as their slave family escapes, Carrie and Luther arrive in Canada but never again see their mother and father.

B

41

NATALIE BABBITT, Author/Illustrator

Elsie Times Eight
(New York: Michael di Capua/Hyperion Books for Children, 2001)

Subject(s): Fairies; Children; Parent and Child
Age range(s): Grades K-2
Major character(s): Elsie, Child, Daughter; Papa, Father; Mama, Mother
Time period(s): Indeterminate Past
Locale(s): Fictional Country

Summary: Elsie's fairy godmother is a bit hard of hearing, a factor that contributes to a misunderstanding that leaves Mama and Papa with eight look-alike daughters. Eight Elsies fight for one chair and one cat and try to find a place to sleep when there is only one bed. The noise from the eight Elsies disturbs the neighbors so Mama and Papa are forced to leave their village. They go in search of the fairy godmother to get rid of seven of the Elsies. Happily, the threesome heads home with their one, oops make that twenty, cats. (32 pages)

Where it's reviewed:
Booklist, November 15, 2001, page 579
Bulletin of the Center for Children's Books, December 2001, page 129
Horn Book, January 2002, page 66
Publishers Weekly, October 2001, page 60
School Library Journal, November 2001, page 110

Other books by the same author:
Bub: Or the Very Best Thing, 1994
Nellie, a Cat on Her Own, 1989
The Something, 1970

Other books you might like:
Jim Aylesworth, *The Full Belly Bowl*, 1999
  An old man learns to use a magic bowl so that it is a blessing rather than a burden until his greed leads to chaos.
Lily Toy Hong, *Two of Everything*, 1993
  A poor couple find a magic pot that multiplies anything they put into it leading to unexpected consequences.

Herman Parish, *Bravo, Amelia Bedelia*, 1997
  Amelia hears just fine but her literal interpretation of instructions leads to many humorous misunderstandings.

42

KAGE BAKER

The Graveyard Game
(New York: Harcourt, 2001)

Subject(s): Time Travel; Cyborgs; Death
Age range(s): Grades 10-Adult
Major character(s): Mendoza, Cyborg; Lewis, Cyborg; Joseph, Cyborg
Time period(s): Multiple Time Periods (120-2275)
Locale(s): Earth (locales vary from Brigantia to California and London)

Summary: The cyborg operatives of Dr. Zeus, Incorporated are back. In addition to their usual duties collecting future valuables for their employers, Lewis and Joseph are secretly looking for their colleague Mendoza. They discover that Mendoza has talents the Company doesn't want in its operatives and she has vanished. Joseph, an old and canny cyborg, realizes that Mendoza isn't the only one missing; in his long tenure with the company, all the Neanderthal operatives have slowly disappeared. Lewis is in love with Mendoza and determined to discover her fate, no matter what the cost. Joseph is personally troubled, but also hopes it will bring him closer to solving the secret of 2355, the date on which the future falls silent to the cyborg community. (298 pages)

Where it's reviewed:
Booklist, December 15, 2000, page 793
Locus, March 2001, page 33
New York Times Book Review, January 21, 2001, page 16
Publishers Weekly, December 4, 2000, page 57
School Library Journal, April 2001, page 16

Other books by the same author:
Mendoza in Hollywood, 2000
Sky Coyote, 1999
In the Garden of Iden, 1997

Other books you might like:

Catherine Asaro, *The Phoenix Code*, 2001
> How do you make an android human without making him prey to the dangers of human emotions?

Philip K. Dick, *Do Androids Dream of Electric Sheep?*, 1968
> This novel is the source of the movie *Bladerunner* and asks what rights androids have when they conflict with the intentions of their makers?

Anne Harris, *The Nature of Smoke*, 1996
> Is it our ability to behave chaotically that makes us truly human?

43

KEITH BAKER, Author/Illustrator

Little Green
(San Diego: Harcourt, Inc., 2001)

Subject(s): Animals/Birds; Nature; Stories in Rhyme
Age range(s): Preschool-Kindergarten
Major character(s): Little Green, Bird; Unnamed Character, Child, Artist
Time period(s): 2000s (2001)
Locale(s): United States

Summary: Sitting at a window, a young boy observes the flight of a hummingbird on a sunny day. Little Green hovers over flowers, zigs up and down, dips into blooms to sip nectar and inspires the boy to paint his impressions of Little Green's activities. (32 pages)

Where it's reviewed:
Booklist, April 15, 2001, page 1563
Bulletin of the Center for Children's Books, April 2001, page 297
Horn Book Guide, Fall 2001, page 225
Publishers Weekly, February 12, 2001, page 210
School Library Journal, April 2001, page 98

Other books by the same author:
Quack and Count, 1999 (NCTE Notable Children's Trade Book in the Language Arts)
Cat Tricks, 1997
Hide and Snake, 1991

Other books you might like:

John Himmelman, *A Hummingbird's Life*, 2000
> An illustrated nonfiction title describes the life cycle and habits of hummingbirds.

Joanne Ryder, *Dancers in the Garden*, 1992
> A hummingbird and his mate dart about a sunny garden.

April Pulley Sayre, *The Hungry Hummingbird*, 2001
> Through trial and error a young hummingbird discovers the best sources of food.

Christine Widman, *The Hummingbird Garden*, 1993
> When Jonna enters a neighbor's garden to better view the hummingbirds she also finds a friend.

44

LIZA BAKER
DAVID MCPHAIL, Illustrator

I Love You Because You're You
(New York: Cartwheel Books, Scholastic Inc., 2001)

Subject(s): Parent and Child; Love; Stories in Rhyme
Age range(s): Grades K-1
Major character(s): Unnamed Character, Mother, Fox; Unnamed Character, Child, Fox
Time period(s): Indeterminate
Locale(s): Fictional Country

Summary: A mother fox describes all the situations in which she loves her little fox child. If her offspring is sleepy, silly, bashful or frightened the love of mother fox endures. A fox child that is proud, curious, sick, playful, sad or brave is still loved. No matter the mood or the behavior this mom loves her little one just because. (26 pages)

Where it's reviewed:
Booklist, January 1, 2002, page 862
Horn Book Guide, Spring 2002, page 11
Publishers Weekly, October 15, 2001, page 70
School Library Journal, November 2001, page 110

Other books by the same author:
Disney 5-Minute Princess Stories, 2001

Other books you might like:

Barbara Joosse, *I Love You the Purplest*, 1996
> Mama's responses to her sons' many questions affirm her love for each of them.

Sam McBratney, *Guess How Much I Love You*, 1995
> Little Nutbrown Hare enjoys playing a game with his father in which each professes the magnitude of his love for the other.

Lisa McCourt, *I Love You, Stinky Face*, 1997
> In replying to her child's questions, Mama is ready with tender, loving words of reassurance and never-ending love.

45

MIKE BAKER
MARTIN H. GREENBERG, Co-Author

My Favorite Horror Story
(New York: DAW, 2000)

Subject(s): Short Stories; Horror
Age range(s): Grades 10-Adult

Summary: Fifteen noted authors were asked to select the horror story that made the greatest impact on them, and then explain why, with the results compiled in this anthology. "Sweets to the Sweet" by Robert Bloch was the selection of Stephen King for its "snap ending." Joyce Carol Oates chose the classic "The Tell-Tale Heart" by Edgar Allan Poe because it is a "fated, irresistible creation." Several H.P. Lovecraft stories were selected including Michael Slade's choice of "Rats in the Walls." Works by Nathaniel Hawthorne, Ramsey Campbell, Philip K. Dick and Ambrose Bierce are found here in addition to other authors perhaps not as well known. (303 pages)

Where it's reviewed:
Voice of Youth Advocates, April 2001, page 53

Other books by the same author:
Knight Fantastic, 2002
Murder in Baker Street: New Tales of Sherlock Holmes, 2001
Young Blood, 1994

Other books you might like:
H.P. Lovecraft, *The Tomb and Other Tales*, 1986
    Short stories from the grand master of horror and the macabre.
Edgar Allan Poe, *Tales of Edgar Allan Poe*, 1991
    These illustrated tales depict all the terror Poe so cleverly wrapped into his writings.
Al Sarrantonio, *999: Twenty-Nine Original Tales of Horror and Suspense*, 2001
    From fantasy to suspense and from vampires to zombies, these tales are meant to terrify the reader.

ROBIN BALLARD, Author/Illustrator

My Day, Your Day
(New York: Greenwillow Books/HarperCollins, 2001)

Subject(s): Children; Work; Parent and Child
Age range(s): Preschool
Time period(s): 2000s
Locale(s): United States

Summary: Working parents drop their children off at a day care center and then proceed to their place of employment. As large pictures depict the varied activities of the children during the day, smaller ones show parallels to the work of one of the parents. While a little girl builds with blocks her father oversees a construction site. A little boy plays with a ball during outside playtime at the center while his mother conducts a soccer class. At the end of the day parents greet their children and everyone goes home. (32 pages)

Where it's reviewed:
Booklist, January 2001, page 966
Horn Book Guide, Fall 2001, page 225
Kirkus Reviews, December 1, 2000, page 1678
Publishers Weekly, January 15, 2001, page 75
School Library Journal, June 2001, page 100

Other books by the same author:
When I Am a Sister, 1998
Carnival, 1995
Good-Bye House, 1994
Gracie, 1993

Other books you might like:
Mary Brigid Barrett, *Day Care Days*, 1999
    In a rhyming story a little boy describes the active day he and his baby brother have at day care until his father arrives from work to take them home.
Cari Best, *Red Light, Green Light, Mama and Me*, 1995
    One day Lizzie goes to work with Mama at the downtown library.

Charlotte Doyle, *Where's Bunny's Mommy?*, 1995
    During a typical day at child care Bunny climbs, paints and eats lunch while thinking of his mother doing similar activities at her office.

KATHY BALMES
VICKI CATAPANO, Illustrator

Thunder on the Sierra
(New York: Silver Moon, 2001)

Subject(s): Frontier and Pioneer Life; Mexican Americans; Orphans
Age range(s): Grades 4-7
Major character(s): Mateo, Orphan, 13-Year-Old; Joaquin Murieta, Historical Figure, Thief; Fandango, Horse (palomino)
Time period(s): 1850s (1852-1853)
Locale(s): California (gold mining camps in the Sierra Mountains)

Summary: Mateo overhears the vaqueros on the ranch admiring his horse Fandango and when one of them mentions taking him, Mateo fears losing what seems like his only remaining family. Between wanting to save his horse and being ready to seek his own adventures, Mateo leaves the ranch where his deceased father worked and where Mateo has always lived. On his way to the gold mining camps, Mateo meets the famed bandit Joaquin Murieta who takes Fandango at gunpoint. Horseless, Mateo luckily meets a muleskinner who, when accidentally injured, turns his mule train over to Mateo to deliver supplies to the miners. A year of delivering food and other goods up in the Sierras is enough for Mateo who is happy to return to the rancho, and even happier when he can help its owner save his land from the Yankees. (89 pages)

Where it's reviewed:
School Library Journal, August 2001, page 175

Other books you might like:
Kathleen Karr, *Oregon, Sweet Oregon*, 1998
    Phoebe misses the adventure of trail life so, when news of the California Gold Rush reaches her, she dresses as a boy and runs away to the gold fields.
Julie Lawson, *Destination Gold!*, 2001
    Now responsible for his mother and sister, Ned heads to the Klondike to find gold, but he eventually needs to be saved by his younger sister.
Joann Mazzio, *Leaving Eldorado*, 1993
    Maude's left to live on her own in Eldorado, New Mexico, when the Yukon gold fever overwhelms her father.
Laurence Yep, *The Journal of Wong Ming-Chung: A Chinese Miner*, 2000
    Sent to America to help his uncles with gold mining, Wong's ability to read and write makes him the camp supervisor's choice to be his assistant.

MOLLY BANG, Author/Illustrator

Tiger's Fall
(New York: Holt, 2001)

Subject(s): Physically Handicapped; Accidents; Depression
Age range(s): Grades 4-6
Major character(s): Lupe, 11-Year-Old, Handicapped; Angelica, Cousin
Time period(s): 1980s
Locale(s): Mazatlan, Mexico; Ajoya, Mexico

Summary: On a dare from her city-cousin Angelica, Lupe climbs the old, supposedly haunted fig tree but, skipping down from branch to branch, loses her balance and falls to the ground. Paralyzed from the waist down, Lupe is operated on but the surgery leaves her battling a life-threatening infection and her parents drowning in debt. Unable to help her at home, her parents take an angry and depressed Lupe to PROJIMO, the Project of Rehabilitation Organized by Disabled Youth of Western Mexico, which is a center run by and for the disabled. Here Lupe learns to tend and heal the wounds of others and discovers she can still be useful, especially when she heals enough to be in her wheelchair. (110 pages)

Where it's reviewed:
Book Report, March 2002, page 47
Booklist, November 1, 2001, page 474
Bulletin of the Center for Children's Books, December 2001, page 130
Kirkus Reviews, September 15, 2001, page 1352
School Library Journal, December 2001, page 132

Other books you might like:
Paul Fleischman, *Mind's Eye*, 1999
    Old, blind and bed-ridden, Elva is still able to distract her roommate Courtney, an angry, paraplegic teen, with a childhood game about an imaginary journey.
Marc Talbert, *Small Change*, 2000
    Boring! Tom's Mexican vacation has been boring until now when he and his sister are caught in a shooting melee between soldiers and revolutionaries.
Terry Trueman, *Stuck in Neutral*, 2000
    Only Shawn appreciates his perfect recall and great sense of humor because his cerebral palsy is so profound he lacks the muscle control to speak.

49

IAIN BANKS

Look to Windward
(New York: Pocket Books, 2000)

Subject(s): War; Death; Artists and Art
Age range(s): Grades 10-Adult
Major character(s): Hub, Artificial Intelligence; Major Quilan, Military Personnel, Alien; Mahrai Ziller, Musician, Alien
Time period(s): Indeterminate Future
Locale(s): Masaq' Orbital, Space Station

Summary: The Culture is a highly evolved space faring civilization, which makes a miscalculation. In their contact with the people of Chel, they interfere with the politics of the world to speed up the demise of its caste system, which results in a horrific class war on Chel. The Culture is dismayed, apologizes and imposes a peace. Hard-liners on Chel are little inclined to accept it but, having no choice, they make secret plans to strike back. Major Quilan lost his wife in the war and no longer wishes to live. Ziller, a radical composer, abandons Chel to live on Masaq' Orbital, a ring station of the Culture, where his fame spreads among all the civilized worlds. Chel requests permission to persuade Ziller to return home and sends Quilan as their representative. Ziller refuses to meet Quilan, fearing assassination, and as Quilan slowly remembers his secret instructions, realizes this makes sense. But Quilan has a much deadlier mission, one that Hub, whose intelligence once directed a war craft, can understand. Everything is set to climax during the first performance of Ziller's new symphony. (384 pages)

Where it's reviewed:
Booklist, June 1, 2001, page 1855
Kirkus Reviews, June 1, 2001, page 779
Library Journal, August 2001, page 171
New York Times Book Review, October 7, 2001, page 19
Publishers Weekly, May 28, 2001, page 55

Other books by the same author:
The Business: A Novel, 1999
Inversions, 1998
Excession, 1996

Other books you might like:
Peter S. Beagle, *A Dance for Emilia*, 2000
    An artist finds a way to return to his loved ones after death.
Katie Waitman, *The Merro Tree*, 1997
    An extinct race requested that an art form they invented never be performed again; should a living genius be bound by their request?
Sarah Zettel, *The Quiet Invasion*, 2000
    Humanity's confused efforts to decide what to do about Venus become immaterial when it becomes clear that an alien species is way ahead of humans.

50

JACQUELINE TURNER BANKS

A Day for Vincent Chin and Me
(Boston: Houghton Mifflin, 2001)

Subject(s): Japanese Americans; Racism; Social Issues
Age range(s): Grades 4-6
Major character(s): Tommy, 6th Grader; Judge Jenkins, 6th Grader; Jury Jenkins, 6th Grader; Vincent Chin, Historical Figure, Crime Victim
Time period(s): 2000s
Locale(s): Plank, Kentucky

Summary: With only a few Asian American families in his town, Tommy doesn't like to call attention to himself or his family, so he's very upset when his mother plans a rally for Vincent Chin. Even when his mother explains that Vincent was killed in 1982 because some Detroit autoworkers were blaming Asians for the slump in the car industry, Tommy still worries about her involvement. Tommy doesn't realize that he's taking just as big as stand as his mother is when he and his friends Judge and Jury from the "posse" build a speed bump in the middle of their street. Tired of the cars racing down their street, especially after one almost hits their deaf neighbor, the boys rise at 3 a.m., mix their mortar and pour a cement speed bump. Two activists in Tommy's family are probably enough for a while, but his little sister Quinn is getting older! (119 pages)

Where it's reviewed:
Booklist, November 1, 2001, page 474
School Library Journal, December 2001, page 132

Other books by the same author:
Egg-Drop Blues, 1995
The New One, 1994
Project Wheels, 1993

Other books you might like:
Marie G. Lee, *Finding My Voice*, 1992
　　Ellen must decide whether or not to speak up about prejudice when she's the only Korean American in a high school in a Scandinavian area of Minnesota.
Marie G. Lee, *If It Hadn't Been for Yoon Jun*, 1993
　　Adopted as a baby, popular cheerleader Alice wants to deny her Korean heritage until she meets new Korean student Yoon Jun Lee.
Maureen Crane Wartski, *Candle in the Wind*, 1995
　　The Mizuno family faces extreme racism in this compelling novel set in Boston.

KATE BANKS
GEORG HALLENSLEBEN, Illustrator

A Gift from the Sea
(New York: Frances Foster Books/Farrar Straus Giroux, 2001)

Subject(s): Beaches; Nature; History
Age range(s): Grades K-3
Major character(s): Unnamed Character, Child, Beachcomber
Time period(s): Multiple Time Periods; 2000s
Locale(s): Earth

Summary: From the sandy shore, a young boy picks up a rock with no thought to its origins. The boy does not realize that originally the rock spewed from a volcano and in prehistoric times had been part of a cave. The boy admires the rock's features not realizing its geologic life story. Eventually the sea swallows the wheat field in which the rock lies and the rock makes its way to the shore where the boy finds it to add to his collection of gifts from the sea. (34 pages)

Where it's reviewed:
Booklist, April 15, 2001, page 1563
Horn Book, May 2001, page 309
The New Advocate, Winter 2002, page 78
School Library Journal, June 2001, page 100
Smithsonian, November 2001, page 118

Awards the book has won:
Smithsonian's Notable Books for Children, 2001

Other books by the same author:
The Night Worker, 2000 (ALA Notable Children's Book)

The Bird, the Monkey, and the Snake in the Jungle, 1999
And If the Moon Could Talk, 1998 (Boston Globe/Horn Book Award)

Other books you might like:
Emery Bernhard, *The Way of the Willow Branch*, 1996
　　A river transforms a willow branch into a smooth piece of driftwood during its journey to the seashore.
Pam Conrad, *Call Me Ahnighito*, 1995
　　A meteorite tells the story of its lonely life in Greenland prior to its discovery in 1894 and eventual move to a museum in New York City.
Douglas Florian, *A Beach Day*, 1990
　　A family enjoys a relaxing day at the beach looking for sea shells.
George Ella Lyon, *Dreamplace*, 1993
　　While visiting the ruins of ancient cliff dwellings a young girl imagines the life of the people who originally occupied the area.

52

LYNNE REID BANKS
TONY ROSS, Illustrator

Harry the Poisonous Centipede's Big Adventure: Another Story to Make You Squirm
(New York: HarperCollins Publishers, 2001)

Subject(s): Animals/Insects; Adventure and Adventurers; Humor
Age range(s): Grades 3-5
Major character(s): Harry, Centipede, Son; George, Friend (Harry's), Centipede; Belinda, Centipede, Mother (Harry's)
Time period(s): Indeterminate
Locale(s): Fictional Country

Summary: Harry and George are captured by a Hoo-Man who places them in a jar and adds them to the insect collection he maintains in his room. A fortunate, but harrowing accident leads to Harry and George becoming free, although lost and far from home. As they try to find their way back to the comfort of Belinda and their own tunnel they suffer a series of terrifying adventures that threaten to end their short lives. Just when they've given up hope, Harry and George are rescued in a most unexpected way. (180 pages)

Where it's reviewed:
Booklist, June 2001, page 1878
Horn Book Guide, Fall 2001, page 299
Kirkus Reviews, February 1, 2001, page 179
Publishers Weekly, January 8, 2001, page 69
School Library Journal, May 2001, page 108

Other books by the same author:
Alice-by-Accident, 2000
Harry the Poisonous Centipede: A Story to Make You Squirm, 1997
The Mystery of the Cupboard, 1993

Other books you might like:
Roald Dahl, *James and the Giant Peach*, 1961
> With a fantastic assortment of insects James travels in a giant peach far away from his unhappy home.

Mary James, *Shoebag*, 1990
> Life changes dramatically, but temporarily, for Shoebag a young cockroach that becomes a boy.

Carol Sonenklar, *Bug Boy*, 1997
> Charlie receives a ''Bug-A-View'' which makes it possible for the bug lover to take a look at life from a bug's perspective.

LYNNE BARASCH, Author/Illustrator

The Reluctant Flower Girl
(New York: HarperCollins Publishers, 2001)

Subject(s): Sisters; Weddings; Friendship
Age range(s): Grades K-3
Major character(s): April, Sister (younger), Child; Annabel, Sister (older), Bride; Harold, Bridegroom, Young Man
Time period(s): 2000s (2001)
Locale(s): United States

Summary: April adores big sister Annabel so much that learning Harold likes Annabel enough to marry her is not good news. As the happy couple plan the wedding Annabel plots to get rid of Harold. She's not successful, however, and reluctantly she fulfills her role as flower girl. Admittedly Annabel does look beautiful and happy on her wedding day or at least she does until the best man drops the ring. When April sees how upset Annabel is to lose the wedding ring, April crawls across the floor until she locates the ring and the wedding proceeds to a happy conclusion. (34 pages)

Where it's reviewed:
Booklist, May 1, 2001, page 1688
Horn Book Guide, Fall 2001, page 247
Kirkus Reviews, April 1, 2001, page 494
Publishers Weekly, April 30, 2001, page 76
School Library Journal, June 2001, page 102

Other books by the same author:
Radio Rescue, 2000 (School Library Journal Best Book)
Old Friends, 1998
A Winter Walk, 1993

Other books you might like:
Marc Brown, *D.W. Thinks Big*, 1993
> D.W. may not have an official role in Aunt Lucy's wedding, but at the last minute she has an unexpected opportunity to show her importance.

Karen English, *Nadia's Hands*, 1999
> Nadia serves as the flower girl in her cousin's wedding.

Wendy Cheyette Lewison, *I Am a Flower Girl*, 1999
> Katie helps her aunt and uncle with their wedding.

Phyllis Reynolds Naylor, *I Can't Take You Anywhere!*, 1997
> Her relatives fear disaster when klutzy Amy Audrey attends Aunt Linda's wedding; though accidents do happen, Amy is not responsible.

Gary Soto, *Snapshots from the Wedding*, 1997
> A Mexican-American wedding is described through the eyes of the flower girl.

TESSA BARCLAY

A Lovely Illusion
(New York: Severn House Publishers, 2001)

Subject(s): Romance; Artists and Art; Crime and Criminals
Age range(s): Grades 10-Adult
Major character(s): Erica Pencarreth, Art Dealer (gallery curator); Willard Townley, Art Dealer, Con Artist; Alexander ''Zan'' McNaughton, Vintner, Wealthy
Time period(s): 2000s
Locale(s): Parigos, Greece; London, England

Summary: The daughter of a noted artist, Erica realizes early on that she lacks similar talent, though that doesn't diminish her love for art. Instead she develops a specialization in Impressionist painting and is the curator of an art gallery. Her lover, Willard Townley, owns and art gallery and surprises her with a slightly damaged, previously unknown Monet painting, that he wants her to authenticate and restore. Before she completes its restoration, Alexander McNaughton wants to buy it and Erica hurries to complete her work. But as she examines the painting, she not only has doubts about its authenticity, but also about Willard and whether or not he's running a scam, in this sweet romance. (314 pages)

Where it's reviewed:
Booklist, July 2001, page 1990

Other books by the same author:
A True Likeness, 2002
Farewell Performance, 2002
Starting Over, 2001
The Saturday Girl, 1998
A Woman's Intuition, 1984

Other books you might like:
Oliver T. Banks, *The Caravaggio Obsession*, 1984
> While art detective Hatcher solves his friend's murder, he also uncovers historical background about the painter Caravaggio.

Carolyn Coker, *The Vines of Ferrara*, 1986
> Several people in Italy are poisoned while Andrea Perkins is restoring artwork and she wonders if she's the next victim.

Carolyn Llewellyn, *The Masks of Rome*, 1988
> Asked to clean paintings at the Torreleone home in Rome, art restorer Kate Roy is unsure what to do when she realizes the most valuable one is a forgery.

55

T.A. BARRON

Tree Girl
(New York: Philomel Books, 2001)

Subject(s): Trees; Friendship; Fantasy
Age range(s): Grades 4-6

Major character(s): Rowanna ''Anna'', 9-Year-Old, Orphan; Master Melwyn, Aged Person, Fisherman; Sash, Shape-changer, Friend
Time period(s): Indeterminate
Locale(s): Fictional Country

Summary: Master Melwyn goes fishing daily to provide meager sustenance while lonely Anna cares for their hut and prepares what food is available. She draws comfort from a large tree near the hut and befriends an injured bird that becomes her constant companion. The need for companionship leads Anna to disobey Master Melwyn's instructions and wander into the forest searching for a friend. She finds one in Sash who appears to her initially as a bear. Still, she's drawn to visit a tall willow although she knows it is forbidden and Sash offers to guide her. When Master Melwyn discovers what Anna has done he vows to destroy the willow tree and almost brings his own life to an end instead. Finally, as he heals under Anna's care, he reveals the truth about the connection between Anna and the willow tree and frees her to pursue her destiny. (138 pages)

Where it's reviewed:
Booklist, November 1, 2001, page 474
Bulletin of the Center for Children's Books, October 2001, page 51
Kirkus Reviews, July 1, 2001, page 934
Publishers Weekly, October 15, 2001, page 72
Voice of Youth Advocates, October 2001, page 287

Other books by the same author:
The Mirror of Merlin, 1999
The Fires of Merlin, 1998
The Lost Years of Merlin, 1996

Other books you might like:
Lloyd Alexander, *Taran Wanderer*, 1999
  In the fourth book of the Chronicles of Prydain Taran searches for answers to his identity.
Franny Billingsley, *The Folk Keeper*, 1999
  Inexplicable magical powers inherent in her enable orphaned Corinna to masquerade as Corin, a folk keeper.
Berlie Doherty, *Daughter of the Sea*, 1997
  A fisherman and his wife raise a foundling as their child but in time the sea calls her home.

SUSAN CAMPBELL BARTOLETTI
DAVID CHRISTIANA, Illustrator

The Christmas Promise
(New York: Blue Sky Press/Scholastic, Inc., 2001)

Subject(s): Depression (Economic); Communication; Homeless People
Age range(s): Grades 2-4
Major character(s): Poppa, Father, Unemployed; Girl, Child, Daughter
Time period(s): Indeterminate Past
Locale(s): United States

Summary: Out of both work and money, Poppa and Girl turn to riding the rails in search of jobs. Sometimes they sleep in hobo camps, under bridges or in missions, but work eludes Poppa. While disembarking from a train one night they are apprehended and briefly jailed. The experience becomes an opportunity for Poppa to find a kind home in the town for Girl while he seeks employment, promising to return as soon as he does. (36 pages)

Where it's reviewed:
Booklist, September 15, 2001, page 234
Bulletin of the Center for Children's Books, November 2001, page 93
Five Owls, Fall 2001, page 21
Publishers Weekly, September 24, 2001, page 53
School Library Journal, October 2001, page 62

Awards the book has won:
Notable Social Studies Trade Books for Young People, 2002

Other books by the same author:
Dancing with Dziadziu, 1997
Silver at Night, 1994

Other books you might like:
Elizabeth Friedrich, *Leah's Pony*, 1996
  Leah's quick thinking and personal sacrifice save her family's farm during the dust bowl years of the Great Depression.
Linda Oatman High, *A Christmas Star*, 1997
  On Christmas Eve a poor rural congregation discovers that the mitten tree and all its gifts have been stolen.
Sarah Stewart, *The Gardener*, 1997
  When her parents send Lydia Grace to an uncle's for care during the Great Depression, she puts her gardening skill to good use.

57

BYRON BARTON, Author/Illustrator

My Car
(New York: Greenwillow Books, 2001)

Subject(s): Automobiles; Transportation; Responsibility
Age range(s): Preschool
Major character(s): Sam, Driver
Time period(s): 2000s (2001)
Locale(s): United States

Summary: Sam takes good care of his shiny red car. Sam knows all the parts to his car. He washes it, fills it with gas and has the oil changed. When Sam goes out in his car he obeys the laws, reads the traffic signs and drives carefully. One of the many places to which Sam drives his car is his work. Then he parks his red car and climbs aboard the bus that he drives. (36 pages)

Where it's reviewed:
Booklist, July 2001, page 2008
Horn Book, November 2001, page 731
Kirkus Reviews, June 15, 2001, page 860
Publishers Weekly, July 2, 2001, page 74
School Library Journal, August 2001, page 142

Awards the book has won:
Booklist Editors' Choice/Books for Youth, 2002
Horn Book Fanfare/Picture Book 2002

Other books by the same author:
Machines at Work, 1987
Trucks, 1986
Building a House, 1981
Wheels, 1979

Other books you might like:
Donald Crews, *Truck*, 1980
     A wordless Caldecott Honor Book follows a truck from the loading of its cargo to delivery destination.
Naomi Howland, *ABCDrive! A Car Trip Alphabet*, 1994
     Car travel gives the opportunity to see an ambulance and many other things while zooming along the road.
Grace Maccarone, *Cars! Cars! Cars!*, 1995
     A rhyming, illustrated story describes many types of cars.

58

NORA RALEIGH BASKIN

What Every Girl (Except Me) Knows
(Boston: Little, Brown, 2001)

Subject(s): Identity; Mothers; Single Parent Families
Age range(s): Grades 5-8
Major character(s): Gabrielle "Gabby" Weiss, 12-Year-Old; Taylor Such, 12-Year-Old; Cleo Bloom, Girlfriend (of Gabby's father), Designer (of clothing); Ian Weiss, Brother (of Gabby)
Time period(s): 2000s
Locale(s): New York

Summary: In her journal Gabby records all the things she thinks she needs to know to become a grown-up woman, important stuff that she would ask her mother, if only she had one. Gabby's mother died when she was three and, though her dad and brother are wonderful, they can't answer her questions about making veal scaloppini or learning to tease her hair or what that monthly thing is all about. Befriending new student Taylor Such offers some help, for Gabby can learn from her mother. More hope arrives when her father dates Cleo for a year, but then Cleo breaks the engagement leaving Gabby to wonder how her mother died. With her brother Ian, the two take the train in to New York City and find the apartment they lived in with their mother, hoping they might remember something about that fateful day. And they do in this touching, yet humorous, first novel. (213 pages)

Where it's reviewed:
Booklist, June 2001, page 1878
Bulletin of the Center for Children's Books, February 2001, page 214
Publishers Weekly, April 2, 2001, page 65
School Library Journal, April 2001, page 138
Voice of Youth Advocates, June 2001, page 118

Other books you might like:
Jennifer L. Holm, *Boston Jane: An Adventure*, 2001
     When tomboy Jane meets nice-looking William, her physician father's new apprentice, she immediately enrolls in Miss Heppelwhite's Young Ladies Academy.
Barbara Ware Holmes, *Following Fake Man*, 2001
     Homer's mother won't talk about his deceased father, but

when Homer meets his father's best friend, it's the breakthrough he and his mother need.
Phyllis Reynolds Naylor, *The Alice Series*, 1985-
     Motherless Alice and her friends Pamela, Elizabeth and Patrick survive all the traumas of junior high, peer pressure and dating, but now await high school.

59

TERESA BATEMAN
NADINE BERNARD WESTCOTT; Illustrator

Farm Flu
(Morton Grove, IL: Albert Whitman & Company, 2001)

Subject(s): Illness; Animals; Stories in Rhyme
Age range(s): Grades K-2
Major character(s): Unnamed Character, Son, Farmer; Unnamed Character, Mother, Farmer
Time period(s): 2000s (2001)
Locale(s): United States

Summary: While his mother's away, leaving the farm in his care, a young boy hears the cow sneeze. Although he's knows how to milk a cow, he has no experience treating a sick one so he simply does for the cow as his mother would do for him and tucks the cow into his bed. One by one the other animals also begin sneezing and the boy makes room for all of them in the house as he serves them hot tea and soup. After a noisy restless night, the boy awakens to find the animals comfortably snacking on treats while watching television and he does just what his mom does when he's feeling better. He turns off the TV and takes away the treats. The animals quickly return to the barnyard, until the boy sneezes. (32 pages)

Where it's reviewed:
Booklist, April 1, 2001, page 1470
Horn Book Guide, Fall 2001, page 226
Kirkus Reviews, January 15, 2001, page 105
Publishers Weekly, January 29, 2001, page 88
School Library Journal, April 2001, page 98

Awards the book has won:
IRA Children's Choices, 2002

Other books by the same author:
Harp O' Gold, 2001
The Merbaby, 2001
Leprechaun Gold, 1998

Other books you might like:
Amy Ehrlich, *Parents in the Pigpen, Pigs in the Tub*, 1993
     The farm animals move into the house and the family heads for the barn in a humorous reversal of roles.
Laura Joffe Numeroff, *If You Give a Pig a Pancake*, 1998
     If an uninvited pig shows up at breakfast to share your pancakes, be prepared for a busy day.
David Small, *George Washington's Cows*, 1994
     According to this tale Washington's outlandish farm animals are the reason he gave politics a try.

TERESA BATEMAN
JILL WEBER, Illustrator

Harp O' Gold
(New York: Holiday House, 2001)

Subject(s): Fairy Tales; Music and Musicians; Wishes
Age range(s): Grades 1-3
Major character(s): Tom, Minstrel; Sean O'Dell, Mythical Creature (leprechaun)
Time period(s): Indeterminate Past
Locale(s): Ireland

Summary: The life of a minstrel is more impoverished than Tom expects and he considers his beloved but battered harp to be the reason he does not get hired by people who can afford to pay him well. Sean O'Dell hears Tom's wish for a different harp and offers to trade his harp o' gold for Tom's old wooden one. Thinking he has the better deal, Tom eagerly swaps only to discover that the golden harp has a tinny sound and does not satisfy his heart's desire for fine music. However, it's appearance appeals to the upper class and soon he's not only wealthy but also invited to play for the king. Tom realizes that he's now a prisoner of foolish wishes and sneaks away from the king's castle seeking to locate Sean and trade the harp o' gold for his original harp and happiness. (32 pages)

Where it's reviewed:
Booklist, March 1, 2001, page 1285
Horn Book Guide, Fall 2001, page 247
Kirkus Reviews, February 15, 2001, page 255
Publishers Weekly, March 5, 2001, page 78
School Library Journal, May 2001, page 109

Other books by the same author:
The Merbaby, 2001
Leprechaun Gold, 1998
The Ring of Truth, 1997

Other books you might like:
Marianna Dengler, *Fiddlin' Sam*, 1999
Fiddlin' Sam travels the Ozarks entertaining folks in exchange for his meals.
Hilary Horder Hippely, *A Song for Lena*, 1996
Grandma shares a childhood memory of a hungry beggar who expresses his appreciation for a meal with a violin serenade.
Uri Shulevitz, *The Treasure*, 1979
A man searches far and wide for a treasure and learns that true riches are close to home.

TERESA BATEMAN
PATIENCE BREWSTER, Illustrator

The Merbaby
(New York: Holiday House, 2001)

Subject(s): Mermaids; Brothers; Conduct of Life
Age range(s): Grades 2-4
Major character(s): Tarron, Fisherman, Brother; Josh, Fisherman, Brother; Meri, Baby, Mythical Creature (mermaid)
Time period(s): Indeterminate Past
Locale(s): At Sea

Summary: Josh and Tarron both expect the sea to be an integral part of their lives and livelihood but they seek fortune in different ways and for different reasons. Josh, a harsh taskmaster and user of the sea's bounty, sees the merbaby caught in their fishing net as a means to make money. Sensitive Tarron recognizes from the necklace about the baby's neck that Meri belongs to a loving family and he secretly returns her to an area of the sea in which he recently saw mermaids. In appreciation for his kindness the merfolk fill his dinghy with the treasures of sunken ships and safely guide his small boat back to a port where he locates Josh and shares his wealth. (32 pages)

Where it's reviewed:
Booklist, September 15, 2001, page 229
Bulletin of the Center for Children's Books, September 2001, page 6
Kirkus Reviews, August 1, 2001, page 1116
Publishers Weekly, August 27, 2001, page 84
School Library Journal, January 2002, page 89

Other books by the same author:
Farm Flu, 2001
Harp O' Gold, 2001
The Ring of Truth, 1997

Other books you might like:
Eric Jon Nones, *Caleb's Friend*, 1993
Through his kindness, orphaned Caleb and a mer-boy develop a mutually beneficial relationship.
Robert D. San Souci, *Sukey and the Mermaid*, 1992
In a mermaid tale based on African tradition, Mama Jo befriends unhappy Sukey.
Joan Skogan, *The Good Companion*, 1998
Despite objections by the ship's superstitious captain, the crew rescues a young woman; months later she appears again during a storm and saves them.

TERESA BATEMAN
JEFF SHELLY, Illustrator

A Plump and Perky Turkey
(New York: Winslow Press, 2001)

Subject(s): Animals/Turkeys; Stories in Rhyme; Holidays
Age range(s): Grades K-3
Major character(s): Ebenezer Beezer, Aged Person; Pete, Turkey
Time period(s): Indeterminate Past
Locale(s): Squawk Valley, Fictional Country

Summary: Thanksgiving will soon be here and Squawk Valley has a problem, no turkeys. Ebenezer has the idea to have an art contest and advertise for a plump and perky turkey to be the model for turkey sculptures made of different materials. Pete responds to the fliers posted on trees all over the area and the artists go to work. Ebenezer's plan is to allow Pete to select the contest winners just before he's put into the oven. Pete proves to be savvy as well as plump and perky. He uses the sculptures as camouflage to allow him to sneak out of town (after eating the oatmeal turkey sculpture) and the residents end up dining on shredded wheat. (34 pages)

Where it's reviewed:
Booklist, September 1, 2001, page 114
Bulletin of the Center for Children's Books, November 2001, page 93
Kirkus Reviews, August 15, 2001, page 1207
Publishers Weekly, September 24, 2001, page 46
School Library Journal, September 2001, page 182

Awards the book has won:
IRA Children's Choices, 2002

Other books by the same author:
The Merbaby, 2001
Leprechaun Gold, 1998 (Governor's Writers Award)
The Ring of Truth, 1997

Other books you might like:
Eve Bunting, *A Turkey for Thanksgiving*, 1995
   Not realizing the hosts are vegetarians, Turkey feels anxious about their reasons for inviting him to their Thanksgiving dinner.
Shelagh Canning, *The Turkey Saves the Day*, 1997
   A bump in the road saves turkey Toby from a trip to market but is he safe now? A fox threatens the chicken coop in which he seeks refuge.
Dav Pilkey, *'Twas the Night Before Thanksgiving*, 1990
   Sympathetic students free the turkeys before the farmer's ax falls.

63

PETER S. BEAGLE

A Dance for Emilia
(New York: ROC, 2000)

Subject(s): Death; Reincarnation; Friendship
Age range(s): Grades 10-Adult
Major character(s): Sam Kagan, Writer; Jacob ''Jake'' Holtz, Actor; Emily ''Emilia'' Rossi, Writer
Time period(s): 1990s
Locale(s): United States

Summary: Jake and Sam were the odd men out in their high school class and the bonds they formed there hold true throughout their lives. Even when Sam forsakes his dream of dancing and Jake faces his middling status as an actor, they can count on each other. While their marriages may not hold together, their friendship does. So when Jake gets a call telling him Sam has died suddenly of a heart attack, he struggles to cope. He finds unexpected comfort in the relationship he forms with Emily, or Emilia as Sam always called her. The two share their memories and pain until Jake gets another unexpected phone call. This one is from Emilia saying that Sam's elderly cat, whom she has adopted, is dancing, and she believes it's Sam. (96 pages)

Where it's reviewed:
Booklist, August 2000, page 2124
Kirkus Reviews, September 1, 2000, page 1239
Locus, September 2000, page 25
Publishers Weekly, October 2, 2000, page 63

Other books by the same author:
Tamsin, 1999
Giant Bones, 1997
The Unicorn Sonata, 1996

Other books you might like:
Jonathan Carroll, *The Marriage of Sticks*, 1999
   Her marriage to a man who knew her dead first love seems to trigger the appearance of the deceased James' ghost.
Anne McCaffrey, *If Wishes Were Horses*, 1998
   A brief but charming fable about the power of love.
Dennis McFarland, *A Face at the Window*, 1997
   The spooky story of a man who becomes obsessed by ghosts he believes want help finding rest, but that may not be what the spirits have in mind at all.

64

IAN BECK, Author/Illustrator

Home before Dark
(New York: Scholastic Press, 2001)

Subject(s): Animals/Bears; Toys; Lost and Found
Age range(s): Preschool-Grade 1
Major character(s): Teddy, Bear, Stuffed Animal; Lily, Child, Daughter; Mom, Mother
Time period(s): 1990s (1997)
Locale(s): England

Summary: Teddy goes everywhere with Lily including a trip to the park to feed the ducks and play. Lily hugs Teddy as Mom pushes her home in the stroller but as tired Lily falls asleep she loses her grip and Teddy falls out of the stroller. No one notices and Teddy is stuck there, alone. Determined to return to Lily, Teddy walks out of the park, through crowds, past sniffing dogs in the rain, until he reaches Lily's house. No one hears a cold wet bear knocking on the door so Teddy sits down to wait. There, the evening paperboy finds Teddy and slips him through the door's mail slot where Lily discovers him. (32 pages)

Where it's reviewed:
Booklist, March 1, 2001, page 1285
Children's Bookwatch, June 2001, page 4
Horn Book Guide, Fall 2001, page 226
Publishers Weekly, March 26, 2001, page 91
School Library Journal, March 2001, page 192

Other books by the same author:
The Oxford Nursery Treasury, 2000
Emily and the Golden Acorn, 1992
Five Little Ducks, 1992

Other books you might like:
Jez Alborough, *Where's My Teddy?*, 1992
   As Eddie searches the dark woods for his lost teddy bear he encounters a large bear with a similar problem.
Barbro Lindgren, *Sam's Teddy Bear*, 1982
   Sam's dog helps recover his special teddy bear.
Michaela Morgan, *Edward Loses His Teddy Bear*, 1988
   Edward's mom cleaned his room and now he can't find his teddy bear.

Martin Waddell, *Small Bear Lost*, 1996
> After Small Bear is forgotten on a train he manages to find his way home to the little girl who lost him.

Selina Young, *Ned*, 1993
> Emily and Ned, a green cloth donkey, are inseparable until Ned is lost, and then found again, on the first day of school.

65
BONNIE BECKER

My Brother, the Robot
(New York: Dutton, 2001)

Subject(s): Robots; Fathers and Sons; Science Fiction
Age range(s): Grades 4-6
Major character(s): Chip, 6th Grader; Simon, Robot
Time period(s): 2000s
Locale(s): United States

Summary: In this first novel, Chip can't believe his parents have ordered a robot called ''Simon, the Perfect Son.'' They assure Chip he's not being replaced and to think of Simon as a brother and a role model. Well, Chip's not the perfect son, he's a daydreamer, a steady but plodding young man, messy but happy, who now has to watch as Simon betters him in everything, including swimming. It's not until Simon needs a repair, and Chip beats another robot in a swim meet, that his father understands it's better to have a less-than-perfect son than a programmed, ''perfect'' robotic one. (136 pages)

Where it's reviewed:
Booklist, December 15, 2001, page 731

Other books you might like:
Janet Asimov, *The Norby Series*, 1983-
> The robot Norby, and his owner Jeff, a teen space cadet, encounter adventures as they try to stop the villain Gidlow from taking over the world.

H.M. Hoover, *Orvis*, 1987
> Two unlikely runaways leave home together, twelve-year-old Toby and the antiquated robot, Orvis.

William Sleator, *The Duplicate*, 1988
> David finds a gadget on the beach that duplicates himself, but when there are three Davids, he knows things are out of control.

66
MICHAEL BEDARD

Stained Glass
(Plattsburgh, NY: Tundra Books, 2001)

Subject(s): Identity; Art Restoration
Age range(s): Grades 7-10
Major character(s): Charles Endicott, 14-Year-Old; George Berkeley, Maintenance Worker; Ambriel, Amnesiac
Time period(s): 2000s
Locale(s): Caledon, Canada

Summary: Trying to avoid a piano lesson, Charles steals into St. Bartholomew's church just as the caretaker's ladder slips, crashes into and breaks one of the stained glass windows. Looking at the fallen shards, Charles notices a young girl with a guitar covered with glass; returning to church the following day, the girl is still there. Not knowing who she is, the two travel around the city searching for clues to her identity. When she recognizes the Hebrew letters of her name, Charles calls her Ambriel. The more they search for her identity, the more Charles remembers details of his own life and the upsetting early death of his father. Meanwhile, the caretaker Mr. Berkeley works frantically to reassemble the stained glass window before Sunday's church service, calling on his skills as a former glassmaker. Reassembled, the window is beautiful and as both Mr. Berkeley and Charles gaze upon it, they ponder the identity of the young girl in its center. (297 pages)

Where it's reviewed:
Booklist, December 15, 2001, page 722
Horn Book, January 2002, page 76
Publishers Weekly, December 3, 2001, page 60
School Library Journal, January 2002, page 131
Voice of Youth Advocates, December 2001, page 355

Other books by the same author:
Painted Devil, 1994
Redwork, 1990
A Darker Magic, 1987

Other books you might like:
Eleanor Cameron, *The Private Worlds of Julia Redfern*, 1988
> Introspective Julia writes a short story that helps ease her grief over her father's accidental death.

Anna Myers, *Graveyard Girl*, 1995
> During a yellow fever epidemic, ''Graveyard Grace'' works in the cemetery and, until she becomes ill, rings the bells for those who've died.

W.D. Valgardson, *Frances*, 2000
> Intrigued with the books and diaries found in an old wooden trunk, Frances finds someone to translate Icelandic for her as she reads about her heritage.

67
HILARI BELL

A Matter of Profit
(New York: HarperCollins, 2001)

Subject(s): Coming-of-Age; Cultural Conflict; Cultures and Customs
Age range(s): Grades 9-Adult
Major character(s): Viv Ahvren, Military Personnel, 18-Year-Old; Sabri, Sister; Bibliogoth, Scholar, Alien
Time period(s): Indeterminate
Locale(s): T'Chin, Planet—Imaginary

Summary: Ahvren went off to war an eager young soldier, happy to further his race's goal of conquest. After almost total annihilation by an alien culture, the Vivitare have adopted a philosophy of aggressive offense. As Ahvren discovers, the reality of war is somewhat different from the glorious epics and once he comes home on leave he wants to stay. The family's honor would never permit this, but Ahvren stumbles on an assassination plot against the Vivitare Emperor and earns a favor from the Emperor. Matters become complicated when he discovers that his sister has been unwillingly engaged to the sleazy heir-apparent. Now Ahvren needs two favors, and hasn't a clue how to spy on the conquered aliens. He seeks the aid of the bibliogoth of 33rd Street, a legendary scholar among the conquered races. The scholar is an enigma to Ahvren, for his consistently good advice and insistence on payment seem an insult to every sacred tenet of Vivitare culture. But slowly, Ahvren begins to see that with the scholar's help he may uncover something valuable, the truth. (281 pages)

Where it's reviewed:
Booklist, August 2001, page 2116
Horn Book Magazine, January 2002, page 76
Kirkus Reviews, July 1, 2001, page 935
Kliatt, July 2001, page 8
School Library Journal, October 2001, page 148

Awards the book has won:
Booklist Editors' Choice/Books for Youth, 2001

Other books by the same author:
Navohar, 2000
Songs of Power, 2000

Other books you might like:
Anselm Audley, *Heresy*, 2000
    Cathan has nothing more exciting to do than follow in his father's footsteps and manage their property in mind, when fate intervenes.
Lois McMaster Bujold, *The Curse of Chalion*, 2001
    A disillusioned warrior returns home determined to retire peacefully, but he is dragged into the struggle for the throne.
Robert Heinlein, *Between Planets*, 1951
    A young space traveler meets an older and wiser alien who gives him some excellent advice, even though he ignores a good bit of it.

68

CHERIE BENNETT
JEFF GOTTESFELD, Co-Author

Anne Frank and Me
(New York: Putnam, 2001)

Subject(s): Holocaust; Space and Time; Jews
Age range(s): Grades 6-9
Major character(s): Nicole "Nicole Bernhardt" Burns, 10th Grader; Anne Frank, Historical Figure
Time period(s): 2000s; 1940s
Locale(s): United States; France

Summary: Nicole is a vacuous teen who's more interested in maintaining her web site than reading *The Diary of Anne Frank* or watching the television production of Jane Yolen's book *The Devil's Arithmetic*. While on a field trip to the Holocaust Museum, a firecracker startles Nicole and causes her to fall, hit her head and have a slight concussion. In her mind she's now Nicole Bernhardt and is aboard a cattle car destined for Birkenau. She meets Anne Frank on the journey, sees her sister led off to the ovens and decides to join her, at which point she awakens in the Holocaust Museum. Though out for only a short time, Nicole is changed by the experience and never again doubts that the Holocaust occurred in this work based on the authors' off-Broadway play. (291 pages)

Where it's reviewed:
Booklist, February 15, 2001, page 2001
The Bulletin of the Center for Children's Books, March 2001, page 252
Publishers Weekly, March 5, 2001, page 80
School Library Journal, March 2001, page 245
Voice of Youth Advocates, April 2001, page 48

Other books by the same author:
Life in the Fat Lane, 1998
Heaven Can't Wait, 1996
Wild Hearts, 1994

Other books you might like:
Anne Frank, *The Diary of Anne Frank*, 1952
    Anne's diary covers the years during World War II when she hides from the Nazis in an Amsterdam warehouse. Biography.
Carol Matas, *Daniel's Story*, 1993
    Daniel's journal records his family's move from the ghetto to a concentration camp, until only he and his father are left alive to march to Buchenwald.
Han Nolan, *If I Should Die Before I Wake*, 1994
    Neo-Nazi Hilary, hospitalized and in a coma, lies in the bed next to Holocaust survivor Chana and travels through her memories of World War II.
Gudrun Pausewang, *The Final Journey*, 1996
    Sheltered from Nazi terrorism, young Alice rides a cattle car to Auschwitz where she's happy to go to the showers and wash away the grime of the trip.
Jane Yolen, *The Devil's Arithmetic*, 1988
    Hannah travels back in time to Poland in the early 1940s where she experiences the prejudice against Jews.

69

JAMES W. BENNETT

Plunking Reggie Jackson
(New York: Simon & Schuster, 2001)

Subject(s): Sports/Baseball; Fathers and Sons; Pregnancy
Age range(s): Grades 9-12
Major character(s): Coley Burke, 12th Grader, Baseball Player (pitcher); Bree Madison, 10th Grader
Time period(s): 2000s
Locale(s): Illinois; Florida

Summary: Coley should be on top of the world. In his senior year of high school, he's the starting pitcher for his baseball team, receives contracts from scouts, and has just started dating sexy, vivacious Bree. But there are many factors working against him, too, including failing grades; a domineering, baseball-obsessed father who places a statue of Reggie Jackson in their backyard; an older brother who died just as he was on the verge of stardom; an ankle injury that temporarily benches Coley and the news that Bree might be pregnant. Suddenly it's all too much for Coley and he and Bree take off for Florida where he tries to find the "mental toughness" he needs to keep going. Though they're away only four days, Coley arrives at several resolutions, one of which comes easy when Bree admits she's not pregnant and is using that ploy to hide the abuse doled out by her stepfather. When they return and go their separate ways, Coley has to face suspension from school and a delayed graduation after attending summer school, but he's learned to accept his life and make as much of it as he can. (204 pages)

Where it's reviewed:
Booklist, April 1, 2001, page 1458
Bulletin of the Center for Children's Books, February 2001, page 214
Publishers Weekly, January 1, 2001, page 93
School Library Journal, February 2001, page 117
Voice of Youth Advocates, April 2001, page 34

Other books by the same author:
Old Hoss: A Fictional Baseball Biography of Charles Radbourn, 2002
Blue Star Rapture, 1998
The Flex of the Thumb, 1996
The Squared Circle, 1995
I Can Hear the Mourning Dove, 1990

Other books you might like:
Alden R. Carter, *Bull Catcher*, 1997
    Through death, divorce, friendships and the different seasons of the year, Bull and his best friend Jeff play baseball.
Carl Deuker, *Night Hoops*, 2000
    Nick wants his dad to notice his basketball ability, so practices nightly in his back yard with Trent, his classmate with an explosive temper.
Anna Fienberg, *Borrowed Light*, 2000
    Lacking support from her family, Cally's decision to have an abortion breaks through the wall her parents have erected around a secret.
Pete Fromm, *How All This Started*, 2000
    Austin's manic-depressive sister Abilene pushes her brother to pitch beyond his endurance in an attempt to make up for the career denied to her.

70

DIANE GONZALES BERTRAND

Trino's Time
(Houston, TX: Arte Publico Press, 2001)

Subject(s): Mexican Americans; School Life
Age range(s): Grades 6-9
Major character(s): Trino Olivares, 13-Year-Old; Hector, 7th Grader; Lisano, 7th Grader
Time period(s): 2000s
Locale(s): Texas

Summary: Trino's life takes a turn for the better. He's still grieving the loss of his best friend in an attempted robbery, but has become friends at school with Hector, his partner for the history project, and Lisano who loves to read. These friends are different from his juvenile delinquent ones and through them he begins to realize that he's pretty smart. He takes a job with Mr. Epifano at the grocery store to help supplement his mother's income and, when a rainstorm demolishes their trailer, it's Trino who risks returning to their home to salvage some of their belongings. Though losing their trailer is more bad luck for the Olivares family, they seem better able to regain their momentum than in *Trino's Choice*. (170 pages)

Where it's reviewed:
Booklist, November 1, 2001, page 466
Publishers Weekly, June 18, 2001, page 83
School Library Journal, July 2001, page 102
Voice of Youth Advocates, December 2001, page 355

Other books by the same author:
Lessons of the Game, 1999
Trino's Choice, 1999
Sweet Fifteen, 1995

Other books you might like:
Victor Martinez, *Parrot in the Oven: Mi Vida*, 1996
    Mexican American teen Manny and his family fight to stay together and make a success of their lives in America.
Danny Santiago, *Famous All over Town*, 1983
    A realistic tale of a young Mexican American's life in a California barrio.
Gary Soto, *Summer on Wheels*, 1995
    Hector and his friend Mando pack in a lot of excitement on their six-day cycling trip from East Los Angeles to Santa Monica.

71

CARI BEST
GISELLE POTTER, Illustrator

Shrinking Violet
(New York: Melanie Kroupa/Farrar Straus Giroux, 2001)

Subject(s): Shyness; Schools; Theater
Age range(s): Grades 2-4
Major character(s): Violet, Child, Student—Elementary School; Opal, Student—Elementary School, Friend; Mrs. Maxwell, Teacher
Time period(s): Indeterminate Past
Locale(s): United States

Summary: Anytime Mrs. Maxwell plans a class project that requires a public performance Violet shrinks away and claims to be allergic to attention. Opal tries to help her friend overcome her shyness, ignore the class bully and participate in all activities, but Violet is content to be unnoticed. When the class prepares a play about the solar system, Mrs. Maxwell wisely assigns Violet the role of "Lady Space," the unseen narrator. Violet's mastery of her lines and her ability to ad lib when the bully gets stage fright bolster her confidence. (34 pages)

Where it's reviewed:
Booklist, August 2001, page 2126
Bulletin of the Center for Children's Books, October 2001, page 52
Horn Book, September 2001, page 569
Publishers Weekly, July 2, 2001, page 75
School Library Journal, August 2001, page 142

Awards the book has won:
School Library Journal Best Books, 2001

Other books by the same author:
Last Licks: A Spaldeen Story, 1999
Three Cheers for Catherine the Great!, 1999 (Booklist Editors' Choice)
Getting Used to Harry, 1996

Other books you might like:
Arthur A. Levine, *Sheep Dreams*, 1993
> Shyness leads Liza, who dreams of stardom, to settle for a nonspeaking part in the school play; a last minute crisis thrusts her into the spotlight.

Wendy Cheyette Lewison, *Shy Vi*, 1993
> Too reticent to speak up, shy Vi finds her voice and her confidence on stage.

Jean Little, *Emma's Magic Winter*, 1998
> Sally's friendship helps shy Emma overcome her fear of reading aloud in class.

Emily Arnold McCully, *Speak Up, Blanche!*, 1991
> Shy Blanche finds a way to participate in the Farm Theater as a set designer.

72

JOHN BIERHORST
WENDY WATSON, Illustrator

Is My Friend at Home?: Pueblo Fireside Tales
(New York: Farrar Straus Giroux, 2001)

Subject(s): Indians of North America; Folklore; Trickster Tales
Age range(s): Grades 2-4
Time period(s): Indeterminate Past
Locale(s): United States

Summary: Seven brief trickster tales from the Hopi culture explain the characteristics of animals and qualities of friendship. "Roasted Ears" explains why Coyote has short ears and "Why Mouse Walks Softly" provides the answer to the question posed in the title. In "Winter Story" the tricks Coyote and Snake play on each other end their friendship and also cause the appearance of Coyote's tail fur color and teeth. Cooperation between friends in "Why Peaches are Sweet" explains how Bee acquired wings and peaches developed a sweet flavor. (32 pages)

Where it's reviewed:
Booklist, July 2001, page 2011
Bulletin of the Center for Children's Books, November 2001, page 94
Horn Book, September 2001, page 600
Publishers Weekly, October 8, 2001, page 67
Smithsonian, November 2001, page 122

Awards the book has won:
Riverbank Review Children's Books of Distinction, 2002
Smithsonian's Notable Books for Children, 2001

Other books by the same author:
The Dancing Fox: Arctic Folktales, 1997
On the Road of Stars: Native American Night Poems and Sleep Charms, 1994
The Woman Who Fell from the Sky: The Iroquois Story of Creation, 1993

Other books you might like:
James E. Connolly, *Why the Possum's Tail Is Bare: And Other North American Indian Nature Tales*, 1992
> Thirteen Native American folktales explain the legendary reason for certain animals' behavior.

Tom Pohrt, *Coyote Goes Walking*, 1995
> Four legends present coyote as a mythical creator, a trickster, and a victim of his own cockiness.

Nancy Van Laan, *In a Circle Long Ago: A Treasury of Native Lore from North America*, 1995
> A collection of stories and poems includes source notes and descriptions of the tribes whose folklore is represented.

73

ISOBEL BIRD

So Mote It Be
(New York: HarperCollins/Avon, 2001-)

Series: Circle of Three. Book 1
Subject(s): Wicca; Friendship
Age range(s): Grades 7-12
Major character(s): Kate Morgan, 10th Grader; Annie Crandall, 10th Grader; Cooper Rivers, 10th Grader
Time period(s): 2000s
Locale(s): United States

Summary: Researching witchcraft in the sixteenth century for a school paper, Kate comes across a book of spells and tries the "Come to Me Love" one to ensnare a boy over whom she's been mooning. The spell backfires when all kinds of boys become interested in her and Kate tries to find someone else who's read the book to help her. She befriends two other girls who've checked out the book, Annie and Cooper, and with the assistance of other books of spells they manage to reverse the damage in this first of a series. (235 pages)

Where it's reviewed:
Kliatt, May 2001, page 24
School Library Journal, June 2001, page 142
Science Fiction Chronicle, September 2001, page 42
Voice of Youth Advocates, August 2001, page 194

Awards the book has won:
ALA Quick Picks for Reluctant Young Adult Readers, 2002

Other books by the same author:
In the Dreaming, 2001 (Circle of Three, Book 5)
Merry Meet, 2001 (Circle of Three, Book 2)
Second Sight, 2001 (Circle of Three, Book 3)
What the Cards Said, 2001 (Circle of Three, Book 4)

Other books you might like:
Lynne Ewing, *Into the Cold Fire*, 2000
> The Daughters of the Moon is formed when four friends discover they have unusual powers, from invisibility to time travel to premonitions.

Silver RavenWolf, *Witches' Night Out*, 2000
> Bethany's Thursday night group originally gathered for innocuous charms, but tonight they call up the Hounds of the Wild Hunt to locate a killer.

Cate Tiernan, *Sweep Series*, 2001-
> Unassuming Morgan discovers she has Wiccan traits just like new student Cal Blaire.

74
SARAH BIRD

The Yokota Officers Club
(New York: Knopf, 2001)

Subject(s): Military Life; Military Children; Brothers and Sisters
Age range(s): Grades 10-Adult
Major character(s): Bernadette "Bernie" Root, 18-Year-Old; Kit Root, Sister (of Bernie); Fumiko, Servant (maid); Bobby Moses, Entertainer (comedian)
Time period(s): 1960s (1968)
Locale(s): Kadena Air Base, Japan (island of Okinawa); Yokoto Air Base, Japan (near Yokohama)

Summary: The oldest of six children, Bernie grows up in an Air Force family that moves often and leaves the children dependent on and happiest with one another, except for Kit, their beautiful sister who likes everybody. Bernie's used to following orders from her father, helping her mother organize everything once they move into new quarters, and overseeing her younger siblings. She's been stateside this past year for her first year of college and returns home with anti-war patches on her jeans and a history as a demonstrator at anti-war rallies, not activities that will help her father's floundering career. Bernie immediately notices that the family's quarters are a mess and her parents barely speak, a decline she thinks goes back eight years to when they were stationed in Japan, lost their wonderful maid Fumiko and their father was reassigned. Bernie has a chance to find out what happened to Fumiko when she wins a dance contest, tours the military bases with the aging comedian Bobby Moses, and locates her when they play at "the Yokota Officers Club" in a delightful tale of family and military life. (368 pages)

Where it's reviewed:
Booklist, May 15, 2001, page 1729
Entertainment Weekly, August 3, 2001, page 62
Kirkus Reviews, May 1, 2001, page 603
Publishers Weekly, June 19, 2001, page 58
School Library Journal, October 2001, page 194

Awards the book has won:
Booklist Editors' Choice/Books for Young Adults, 2001

Other books by the same author:
Virgin of the Rodeo, 1993
The Mommy Club, 1991
The Boyfriend School, 1989

Other books you might like:
James G. Bennett, *My Father's Geisha*, 1990
    Children of a career military officer, Ted and his sister witness the gradual disintegration of their parent's marriage.
Frederick Buechner, *The Wizard's Tide*, 1990
    Teddy quietly tells his story of a father who is inept at financial schemes and a mother who is quick to humiliate.
Nelson DeMille, *Up Country*, 2002
    Brought back into military service, Brenner tromps through Vietnam to investigate a thiry-year-old murder.

75
TOM BIRDSEYE

The Eye of the Stone
(New York: Holiday House, 2002)

Subject(s): Fantasy; Time Travel
Age range(s): Grades 4-7
Major character(s): Jackson Cooper, 13-Year-Old; Tessa, Prehistoric Human
Time period(s): 2000s; Indeterminate Past
Locale(s): Timber Grove, Oregon; The Vale, Fictional Country

Summary: Scrambling into a split at the base of Cougar Butte to escape a sleet storm, Jackson finds the opening widens into a cave. Shivering and worrying about hypothermia, he falls asleep only to wake up on a muddy island in the middle of a river. Found by Tessa, she believes him to be the "Instrument" sent in response to her villages' Prayer Song to help the Timmran defeat their enemies the Yakonan. Because Jackson talks about guns and electricity, the people expect him to replicate these miraculous sounding items, which he's unable to do. He seems to continually let the Timmran down, just as he does in his real life, and acts more like the wimp everyone else thinks he is. Just before he returns to his own time he has one final chance to defeat a vicious beast, a chance that he doesn't ignore this time. (163 pages)

Where it's reviewed:
Booklist, February 15, 2001, page 1136
School Library Journal, December 2000, page 138
Voice of Youth Advocates, April 2001, page 50

Other books by the same author:
Tarantula Shoes, 1995
Just Call Me Stupid, 1993
Tucker, 1990
I'm Going to Be Famous, 1986

Other books you might like:
Scott Ciencin, *Dinoverse*, 1999
    Bertram uses his science fair project to send himself and three other classmates back to prehistoric time where they blend right in as human-dinosaurs.
Hans Magnus Enzensberger, *Lost in Time*, 2000
    Based on the pictures he sees, Robert travels around the world and back through time; he's able to return home only when he paints his kitchen on a wall.
Lesley Howarth, *The Pits*, 1996
    The body of 9000-year-old Arf is being studied; to set the record straight, Arf's friend Broddy returns to make sure everyone knows Arf was a dork.
Jane Resh Thomas, *The Princess in the Pigpen*, 1989
    Elizabeth time travels from Elizabeth England to an Iowa farm, but no one believes her story.

TOM BIRDSEYE
WILL HILLENBRAND, Illustrator

Look Out, Jack! The Giant Is Back!
(New York: Holiday House, 2001)

Subject(s): Fairy Tales; Giants; Problem Solving
Age range(s): Grades 1-4
Major character(s): Jack, Child; Mr. Giant, Giant
Time period(s): Indeterminate Past
Locale(s): Giantland, Fictional Country; North Carolina

Summary: The brother of the giant Jack slays at the top of the beanstalk comes after Jack who grabs the loot and moves with his mother to America. They settle on a quiet farm and all seems well until Mr. Giant catches up with Jack and demands the return of his brother's money, hen and harp. Along with the items Mr. Giant requests Jack brings an enormous home-cooked meal and the giant downs every bit of it. Even a giant can get indigestion from eating too much and Jack thinks he can run away while Mr. Giant's distressed. Mr. Giant simply takes off his shoes thinking to stop Jack with the powerful odor from his feet. It almost works, but Jack has a plan that allows him to get away and Mr. Giant's angry tantrum when he does brings the mountain down atop him where he remains buried to this day. (32 pages)

Where it's reviewed:
Booklist, September 1, 2001, page 112
Bulletin of the Center for Children's Books, October 2001, page 52
Publishers Weekly, September 10, 2001, page 92
School Library Journal, October 2001, page 104

Other books by the same author:
A Regular Flood of Mishap, 1994 (IRA Children's Choice)
She'll Be Comin' Round the Mountain, 1994
Soap! Soap! Don't Forget the Soap! An Appalachian Folktale, 1993

Other books you might like:
Anne Keay Beneduce, *Jack and the Beanstalk*, 1999
    A fairy encourages Jack to avenge his father's death at the hands of a giant and magically makes a beanstalk grow to aid him.
Steven Kellogg, *Jack and the Beanstalk*, 1991
    In one of the many retellings of the English tale, Jack outsmarts the giant and his wife in order to save himself and provide for his mother.
Mary Pope Osborne, *Kate and the Beanstalk*, 2000
    In this retelling Kate is the heroine who saves her family from starvation by climbing the beanstalk into the unknown.

ANNE BISHOP

The Pillars of the World
(New York: ROC Books, 2001)

Subject(s): Witches and Witchcraft; Magic; Fairies
Age range(s): Grades 10-Adult
Major character(s): Ari, Witch; Lucian, Fairy; Morag, Fairy; Adolpho, Witch
Time period(s): Indeterminate
Locale(s): Sylvalan, Fictional Country; Tir Alainn, Fictional Country (World of the Fae)

Summary: The roads which bind together parts of the Fae world of Tir Alainn are slowly becoming impassable, cutting the Fae off from one another, and no one understands why or how or even when. In the human world, a fanatic named Adolpho has appointed himself Inquisitor, and travels around Sylvalan torturing and killing witches. What no one, not even the witches, understands is that it is their bond to the land and its magic which sustains Tir Alainn. When the Fae lord Lucian falls in love with the human witch Ari, the scene is set for Fae to discover the witches' role, but Adolpho has a dark secret which adds to his power. (420 pages)

Where it's reviewed:
Booklist, September 15, 2001, page 200
Voice of Youth Advocates, February 2002, page 442

Other books by the same author:
The Invisible Ring, 2000

Other books you might like:
Lynn Abbey, *Jerlayne*, 1999
    Jerlayne's insistence on uncovering all the secrets of Fairie leads her to some unpleasant truths about the relationship of her people, humans and goblins.
Emma Bull, *Finder: A Novel of the Borderlands*, 1994
    Living on the edge of Faerie is a dangerous business for humans.
Rosemary Edghill, *The Sword of Maiden's Tears*, 1994
    An elf travels to our world to retrieve a dangerous heirloom in this first book of the *Twelve Treasures* series.

TERRY BISSON

The Pickup Artist
(New York: Tor, 2001)

Subject(s): Artists and Art; Adventure and Adventurers
Age range(s): Grades 11-Adult
Major character(s): Hank Shapiro, Government Official; Henrietta "Henry", Librarian
Time period(s): 2000s
Locale(s): United States

Summary: Hank Shapiro is a pickup artist; he works for the government picking up the works of banned artists. In the near future, the weight of all the great art produced over the centuries becomes too much so, to relieve the poor oppressed artists of the present, the government declares older art of all kinds obsolete and removes it from circulation. That's Hank's job, to pick up the recordings, pictures, and books that have been labeled illegal and return them for destruction. Hank finds his job pretty routine until the day he picks up a record by Hank Williams. Soon, he finds himself obsessed with the idea of just once hearing this musician who shares his first name. It will require the criminal use of an antique record player, but as Hank learns through his new friend Henry the librarian, there's a whole underground of rule breakers ready to help him. Just how far will Hank be willing to go to satisfy this illicit craving for country music? (240 pages)

Where it's reviewed:
Booklist, March 15, 2001, page 1360
Library Journal, April 15, 2001, page 137
Magazine of Fantasy and Science Fiction, June 2001, page 30
Publishers Weekly, February 19, 2001, page 74

Other books by the same author:
Saint Leibowitz and the Wild Horse Woman, 1997
Pirates of the Universe, 1996
Bears Discover Fire: And Other Stories, 1993

Other books you might like:
China Mieville, *Perdido Street Station*, 2001
    The sculpture art of the bug women becomes the focus of a crime lord's passion.
George Orwell, *1984*, 1949
    Big Brother is watching and he disapproves of just about everything.
Robert Silverberg, *Hot Sky at Midnight*, 1994
    Mankind is so advanced it is able to reshape poodles to fit our craziest fantasies.
Denise Vitola, *The Red Sky File*, 1999
    A detective with a touch of lycanthropy chases criminals through the slums of the future.

79

JONAH BLACK

The Black Book (Diary of a Teenage Stud) Series
(New York: HarperCollins, 2001-)

Series: Black Book (Diary of a Teenage Stud)
Subject(s): Coming-of-Age; Diaries; School Life
Age range(s): Grades 9-12
Major character(s): Jonah Black, 17-Year-Old; Sophie O'Brien, Girlfriend; Posie Hoff, Girlfriend
Time period(s): 2000s
Locale(s): Pompano Beach, Florida

Summary: Expelled from his prep school in Pennsylvania, where his remarried dad lives, Jonah returns home to Florida where he has to repeat his junior year at the public high school. His younger sister easily outperforms him in school, while his mother has just written the embarrassing, and best-selling, book *Hello Penis! Hello Vagina!* and is on a national tour to promote it. Jonah records his thoughts, including his fantasies about Sophie, the girl of his dreams, and Posie, the girl he has always loved, in his 'little black book' in this new series.

Where it's reviewed:
Booklist, October 15, 2001, page 389
Publishers Weekly, October 1, 2001, page 62
School Library Journal, August 2001, page 175

Awards the book has won:
ALA Quick Picks for Reluctant Young Adult Readers, 2002

Other books by the same author:
Faster, Faster, Faster, 2002 (The Black Book (Diary of a Teenage Stud), Volume 4)

Girls, Girls, Girls, 2001 (The Black Book (Diary of a Teenage Stud), Volume 1)
Stop, Don't Stop, 2001 (The Black Book (Diary of a Teenage Stud), Volume 2)
Run, Jonah, Run, 2001 (The Black Book (Diary of a Teenage Stud), Volume 3)

Other books you might like:
Norma Klein, *Just Friends*, 1990
    Isabel and Stuart have been close friends for years, but it's not until Stuart starts dating her best friend that Isabel recognizes his worth.
Jackie French Koller, *The Falcon*, 1998
    Though he scoffs at it, Luke records more and more in his journals until it's obvious he's still bothered by something in his past.
Louise Rennison, *Angus, Thongs and Full-Frontal Snogging: Confessions of Georgia Nicolson*, 2000
    In her diary, Georgia records her interest in kissing, her appearance and her opposition to most of what the adult world thinks is important.
Ellen Wittlinger, *Razzle*, 2001
    Kenyon almost gives up tall, independent Razzle for a self-centered sexpot who throws him aside when he can't help her with a modeling career.

80

STELLA BLACKSTONE
DEBBIE HARTER, Illustrator

Bear in Sunshine
(New York: Barefoot Books, 2001)

Subject(s): Animals/Bears; Weather; Stories in Rhyme
Age range(s): Preschool-Kindergarten
Major character(s): Bear, Bear
Time period(s): Indeterminate
Locale(s): Fictional Country

Summary: Through all types of weather and in any season Bear is active. If the sun is shining Bear is playing but when it rains he sings. On windy days he flies his kite but if there's a thunderstorm he stays inside. In cold weather Bear skates and builds snow-bears with his friends. Bear knows how to have fun! (26 pages)

Where it's reviewed:
Booklist, May 15, 2001, page 1755
Horn Book Guide, Fall 2001, page 227
Publishers Weekly, June 4, 2001, page 82
School Library Journal, June 2001, page 102

Other books by the same author:
Bear at Home, 2001
Bear about Town, 2000
Bear on a Bike, 1998

Other books you might like:
Donald Crews, *Cloudy Day, Sunny Day*, 1999
    A "Green Light Reader" relates all the things one can do in sunny or cloudy weather.
Shirley Hughes, *Out and About*, 1988
    A rhyming story tells of outdoor activities enjoyable during the weather experienced in any of the four seasons.

Mick Inkpen, *Kipper's Book of Weather*, 1995
  After experiencing many types of weather, Kipper sees a rainbow.

David McKee, *Elmer's Weather*, 1994
  Wind, snow, fog and storms are all part of toy elephant Elmer's life.

81

STELLA BLACKSTONE
CLARE BEATON, Illustrator

There's a Cow in the Cabbage Patch
(New York: Barefoot Books, 2001)

Subject(s): Animals; Farm Life; Stories in Rhyme
Age range(s): Preschool-Kindergarten
Major character(s): Unnamed Character, Farmer
Time period(s): Indeterminate
Locale(s): Fictional Country

Summary: The cow is not the only animal out of place on this farm. What should the farmer do? Each time the farmer tries to move an animal to its assigned spot on the farm it finds a different animal taking the space. What to do? Announce dinner and all the animals will hurry back to their places, ready to eat. (32 pages)

Where it's reviewed:
Booklist, April 15, 2001, page 1563
Bulletin of the Center for Children's Books, April 2001, page 298
Horn Book Guide, Fall 2001, page 227
Publishers Weekly, March 5, 2001, page 78
School Library Journal, May 2001, page 109

Other books by the same author:
Bear in Sunshine, 2001
Bear about Town, 2000
How Big Is a Pig, 2000
Making Minestrone, 2000

Other books you might like:
Teresa Bateman, *Farm Flu*, 2001
  After the cow gets sick and is put to bed in the house the other animals develop symptoms that land them inside too.
Stephen Gammell, *Once upon MacDonald's Farm*, 2000
  In a revision of a 1981 title three exotic animals don't work out as planned on MacDonald's farm so he tries the domestic ones given by a neighbor.
Phyllis Root, *Meow Monday*, 2000
  Bonnie tries to quiet her blooming pussy willows because their noise bothers the farm animals.

82

LAWANA BLACKWELL

The Maiden of Mayfair
(Minneapolis, MN: Bethany House, 2000)

Series: Tales of London. Book 1
Subject(s): Orphans; City and Town Life; Wealth
Age range(s): Grades 10-Adult

Major character(s): Naomi Doyle, Cook; Sarah Matthews Rayburn, Orphan; Dorothea Blake, Widow, Wealthy; William Doyle, Student—College (Oxford), Nephew (of Naomi)
Time period(s): 1860s; 1870s (1869-1876)
Locale(s): London, England

Summary: Orphaned when she was only three, Sarah is raised in the Saint Matthew Methodist Foundling Home for Girls, located in a rather seedy section of London. At the age of twelve she is adopted by the wealthy Dorothea Blake who thinks Sarah is her illegitimate granddaughter, offspring of an interlude between her reprobate son and a serving girl. Raised in a beautiful home in Berkeley Square, Sarah is befriended by Naomi who has raised her orphan nephew William and understands some of the loneliness both children feel. When Sarah realizes she'll be a wealthy heiress, she must sort out her feelings between those men who court her for her money and the memory of the love William once professed to her in this detailed Victorian tale that is the first of a series. (409 pages)

Where it's reviewed:
Booklist, March 1, 2001, page 1228
Voice of Youth Advocates, August 2001, page 196

Other books by the same author:
The Dowry of Miss Lydia Clark, 1999 (Gresham Chronicles, Book 3)
The Courtship of the Vicar's Daughter, 1998 (Gresham Chronicles, Book 2)
The Widow of Larkspur Inn, 1998 (Gresham Chronicles, Book 1)

Other books you might like:
Philippa Carr, *The Changeling*, 1989
  An historical romance about mistaken identities after two babies are switched at birth.
Lori Copeland, *Faith*, 1998
  Faith answers an ad for a mail-order bride, but when she meets her rancher finds their mutual stubbornness and his mother's doubts postpone the wedding.
Michael Phillips, *A New Dawn over Devon*, 2001
  With the end of the Great War, Amanda Rutherford and her family uncover the secrets of Heathersleigh Hall and grow deeper in their Christian faith.

83

MICHAEL BLAKE

The Holy Road
(New York: Villard, 2001)

Subject(s): Indians of North America; Railroads
Age range(s): Grades 10-Adult
Major character(s): John Dunbar/Dances with Wolves, Warrior, Military Personnel (former army lieutenant); Stands with a Fist, Captive (of the Comanche), Wife (of Dances with Wolves)
Time period(s): 19th century
Locale(s): West

Summary: It's been eleven years since the former army officer John Dunbar left his career and took the name Dances with

Wolves to marry Stands with a Fist, a white woman raised by the Comanches. They now have three children and live in the Comanche village of Ten Bears where everyone worries about the increasing presence of the white man. Rumors of a railroad to be built through their land cause dissension between and among the tribesmen as they debate whether to fight the white man or do as other tribes and sign a peace treaty. When Texas Rangers devastate their village and capture Stands with a Fish and her infant daughter, Dances with Wolves knows he's the only one who can rescue her as he alone can pass in white society in a powerful sequel to *Dances with Wolves*. (339 pages)

Where it's reviewed:
Book, September 2001, page 76
Booklist, July 2001, page 1947
Kirkus Reviews, June 15, 2001, page 815
People, September 10, 2001, page 51
Publishers Weekly, July 16, 2001, page 155

Other books by the same author:
Airman Mortensen, 1991
Dances with Wolves, 1988

Other books you might like:
Dee Brown, *Creek Mary's Blood*, 1980
  In 1905 Creek Mary's grandson tells a newspaper reporter how the settlers destroyed the Indian way of life.
Douglas C. Jones, *Gone the Dreams and Dancing*, 1985
  Kwahadi and his Antelope Comanches must give up their buffalo hunts, horse raids and culture as they are forced onto an Indian reservation.
James Welch, *Fool's Crow*, 1986
  Fool's Crow, a Blackfoot Indian, comes of age just as the white man is poised to destroy his way of life.

84
FRANCESCA LIA BLOCK

Echo
(New York: Joanna Cotler/HarperCollins, 2001)

Subject(s): Coming-of-Age; Romance; Angels
Age range(s): Grades 9-12
Major character(s): Echo, Narrator
Time period(s): 2000s
Locale(s): Los Angeles, California; New York, New York (Manhattan)

Summary: The only child of a beautiful mother and an artist father, Echo grows up surrounded by her parent's love. Everything changes when her father develops cancer and her parents' love clings to one another instead of to Echo. This change in family emotions leaves Echo unsure of herself as she dabbles with anorexia, is rescued from drowning by "an angel boy" who disappears, and dates a variety of men, always searching for her identity yet aware that she's surrounded by angels of one sort or another. Finally tiring of Los Angeles, Echo moves to New York where, older, wiser and finally happy with herself, she once again meets her "angel boy" who is now able to stay with Echo. Echo's ethereal tale is told through short stories that are mixed with fantasy,

realism and lyrical writing, hallmarks of this author's style. (215 pages)

Where it's reviewed:
Booklist, August 2001, page 2105
Bulletin of the Center for Children's Books, October 2001, page 52
Publishers Weekly, July 16, 2001, page 181
School Library Journal, August 2001, page 175
Voice of Youth Advocates, October 2001, page 288

Other books by the same author:
The Rose and the Beast: Fairy Tales Retold, 2000
Violet & Claire, 1999
I Was a Teenage Fairy, 1998
Girl Goddess #9: Nine Stories, 1996
Weetzie Bat, 1989

Other books you might like:
Eve Bunting, *If I Asked You, Would You Stay?*, 1984
  A runaway teen named Crow rescues a drowning girl and brings her to his secret apartment above a carousel.
Orson Scott Card, *The Enchantment*, 1999
  Ivan finds himself unable to forget the enchanted woman he saw sleeping in the heart of the Russian forest when he was a boy.
Kathleen Kane, *Simply Magic*, 1999
  In this endearing tale of romance two people are linked by wishes granted them when they take the time to help an old tinker.

85
BECKY BLOOM
PASCAL BIET, Illustrator

Crackers
(New York: Orchard Books, 2001)

Subject(s): Animals/Cats; Work; Animals/Mice
Age range(s): Grades K-2
Major character(s): Crackers, Cat
Time period(s): Indeterminate
Locale(s): Fictional Country

Summary: Managers of the different establishments that hire Crackers, a cat willing to work, do so based on the stereotype that cats hate mice. At each job Crackers soon learns (when he's fired) that he's expected to keep mice out of the warehouse, the marina and the restaurant. Finally his dream job, assisting in a cheese shop, appears in the want ads and Crackers seeks the help of the mice that he's previously befriended to vouch for him as a cat that, uncharacteristically, likes mice. Based on the recommendations of the mice the cheese shop manager gives Crackers the job and he's never fired again. Originally published in the United Kingdom in 2000. (32 pages)

Where it's reviewed:
Booklist, March 19, 2001, page 99
Children's Bookwatch, May 2001, page 7
Horn Book Guide, Fall 2001, page 248
Publishers Weekly, March 19, 2001, page 99
School Library Journal, August 2001, page 143

Other books by the same author:
Mice Make Trouble, 2000
Wolf!, 1999
Mr. Cuckoo, 1998

Other books you might like:
Tomek Bogacki, *Cat and Mouse*, 1996
Naively unaware that their species do not socialize, a little mouse and a young cat enjoy playing together.
Cynthia Rylant, *The Cookie-Store Cat*, 1999
A stray cat acquires a home and a new identity when she's found by bakers for a cookie store.
Vivian Sathre, *Three Kind Mice*, 1997
Three mice bake a cake as a birthday surprise for a cat.

86

SUZANNE BLOOM, Author/Illustrator

The Bus for Us

(Honesdale, PA: Boyds Mills Press, 2001)

Subject(s): Schools; School Buses; Transportation
Age range(s): Preschool-Grade 1
Major character(s): Tess, Child, Student—Elementary School; Gus, Student—Elementary School, Child (older)
Time period(s): 2000s (2001)
Locale(s): United States

Summary: Tess and Gus are the first two kids at the bus stop. Tess turns to the more experienced Gus each time a vehicle approaches asking, "Is this the bus for us, Gus?" Each time Gus patiently explains that the vehicle is a taxi, or a tow truck or a fire engine depending on what is actually driving past. The number of children waiting for the bus increases as Gus's patience diminishes. Still he helps Tess by answering her question and picking up the spilled contents of her backpack until finally the bus arrives. (32 pages)

Where it's reviewed:
Booklist, March 15, 2001, page 1400
Horn Book Guide, Fall 2001, page 227
School Library Journal, June 2001, page 102

Other books by the same author:
Piggy Monday: A Tale about Manners, 2001
A Family for Jamie: An Adoption Story, 1991
We Keep a Pig in the Parlor, 1988

Other books you might like:
Julie Brillhart, *Molly Rides the School Bus*, 2002
On the first day of kindergarten Molly rides the bus for the first time feeling a little apprehensive about the experience.
Elizabeth Fitzgerald Howard, *When Will Sarah Come?*, 1999
All day as Jonathan waits for his sister to return from school he hopes that the sounds of passing vehicles are the school bus.
Daniel Kirk, *Bus Stop, Bus Go!*, 2001
A rhyming tale describes the excitement caused by an escaped hamster in the bus during the morning ride to school.

87

THOMAS BLOOR

The Memory Prisoner

(New York: Dial, 2001)

Subject(s): Brothers and Sisters; Libraries
Age range(s): Grades 5-8
Major character(s): Maddie Palmer, 15-Year-Old; Keith Palmer, 12-Year-Old; Silas Lemon, Grandfather; Mr. Lexeter, Librarian
Time period(s): 2000s
Locale(s): Proudbridge, England

Summary: A trip to the Tower Library with her grandfather when Maddie is only two, leaves her permanently changed and the prisoner of her memories. Her grandfather disappears that same day and the library shuts down. Thirteen years pass with Maddie never leaving her home but instead relying on her brother Keith for news of their town, years in which she accumulates memories as easily as she accumulates pounds. When Keith explains that his academic ability enables him to leave school and apprentice with Mr. Lexeter, the librarian who controls their town's records, Maddie turns her attention to uncovering the secrets of the Tower Library and saving Keith from great danger in this first novel. (132 pages)

Where it's reviewed:
Booklist, May 1, 2001, page 1612
Horn Book, May 2001, page 318
Kliatt, May 2001, page 8
School Library Journal, June 2001, page 142
Voice of Youth Advocates, August 2001, page 197

Other books you might like:
Ray Bradbury, *Something Wicked This Way Comes*, 1962
A fun trip to the Pandemonium Shadow Show leaves Will and Jim at the mercy of an evil presence that threatens to overtake them.
Eva Ibbotson, *The Secret of Platform 13*, 1996
The gump under platform 13 in London's subway opens for nine minutes and a rescue team from a magical underground Island rushes to find their stolen prince.
Brad Strickland, *The Bell, the Book, and the Spellbinder*, 1997
When Fergie checks out the last book in the library, with its Dewey number of 999.99T, he is kidnapped by the author who is an evil spellbinder.
Betty Ren Wright, *Out of the Dark*, 1995
Dreams of an old schoolhouse and an angry woman fill Jessica's nights; a walk in the woods reveals the schoolhouse is connected to her grandmother.

88

DEBORAH BLUMENTHAL
MARY GRANDPRE, Illustrator

Aunt Claire's Yellow Beehive Hair

(New York: Dial Books for Young Readers, 2001)

Subject(s): Family; Ancestry; Relatives
Age range(s): Grades K-3

Major character(s): Annie, Child, Niece; Grandma Marilyn, Grandmother, Aged Person; Great-Aunt Ray, Aunt, Aged Person
Time period(s): Indeterminate Past
Locale(s): United States

Summary: In Annie's family, dinners with relatives conclude with stories about the past inspiring Annie to learn more about the people she knows only from photographs and anecdotes. On a rainy day she enlists the help of Grandma Marilyn and Great-Aunt Ray to tell her a little about the lives of her ancestors. Annie puts the pictures and mementos in a scrapbook and records the stories of each relative. Recognizing that the family history project is ongoing, Annie's careful to leave blank pages at the end of the book. (32 pages)

Where it's reviewed:
Booklist, May 1, 2001, page 1688
Bulletin of the Center for Children's Books, July 2001, page 403
Kirkus Reviews, March 15, 2001, page 404
Publishers Weekly, April 23, 2001, page 77
School Library Journal, July 2001, page 72

Other books by the same author:
The Chocolate-Covered-Cookie Tantrum, 1996

Other books you might like:
Patricia Polacco, *The Keeping Quilt*, 1988
A special quilt connects the generations of a family.
Cynthia Rylant, *The Relatives Came*, 1985
A Caldecott Honor Book celebrates childhood memories of the joyful confusion of a house full of relatives.
Martha M. Vertreace, *Kelly in the Mirror*, 1993
Seeing herself in an outfit from her mother's childhood strengthens Kelly's awareness of family ties.
Jeri Hanel Watts, *Keepers*, 1997
As a birthday gift for his grandmother, Kenyon compiles her oft-told stories in a book.

89

ODDS BODKIN
TERRY WIDENER, Illustrator

The Christmas Cobwebs
(San Diego: Gulliver Books/Harcourt, Inc., 2001)

Subject(s): Christmas; Animals/Spiders; Family
Age range(s): Grades K-2
Major character(s): Papa, Immigrant, Father
Time period(s): Indeterminate Past
Locale(s): Chicago, Illinois

Summary: Although fire destroys a cobbler's home and shop, his family and a box of treasured Christmas ornaments from his homeland are safe. Still, in order to support his family, the cobbler must sell the precious ornaments to buy new tools and leather. The family relocates to an old, cobweb filled shack and cuts a tree from the woods as a Christmas decoration. As the family sleeps, the spiders descend to adorn the bare tree with carefully spun ornaments. (32 pages)

Where it's reviewed:
Booklist, September 15, 2001, page 234

Bulletin of the Center for Children's Books, November 2001, page 94
Children's Bookwatch, September 2001, page 6
Publishers Weekly, September 24, 2001, page 50
School Library Journal, October 2001, page 62

Other books by the same author:
Ghost of the Southern Belle: A Sea Tale, 1999
The Crane Wife, 1998 (Booklist Editors' Choice)
The Banshee Train, 1995

Other books you might like:
Shirley Climo, *Cobweb Christmas*, 1982
One Christmas Eve the desire of an old woman to witness the magic of the night is rewarded after years of patiently waiting.
Alexandra Day, *The Christmas We Moved to the Barn*, 1997
A family's many pets help with the unexpected move to the barn on Christmas Eve. Cooper Edens, co-author.
Jenny Koralek, *Cobweb Christmas: A Christmas Story*, 1989
The holy family is saved from searching soldiers by a spider's cobweb covering the entrance to their hiding place in a cave.

90

TOMEK BOGACKI, Author/Illustrator

Circus Girl
(New York: France Foster Books/Farrar Straus Giroux, 2001)

Subject(s): Circus; Friendship; Schools
Age range(s): Grades K-2
Major character(s): Tim, Child, Student—Elementary School; Unnamed Character, Classmate (Tim's), Narrator; Circus Girl, Entertainer, Friend
Time period(s): Indeterminate Past
Locale(s): Poland

Summary: Students in Tim's class ignore him, the smallest boy, until the circus brings a new student to their class. Circus Girl joins Tim's class for the week; through her acceptance of him and her willingness to befriend him and others, a friendship develops with another boy in the class that strengthens during the brief time Circus Girl is in town. In a story based on the author's childhood memories, by the time the circus leaves two boys have found respect for each other and enjoy a new friendship that seems destined to continue. (32 pages)

Where it's reviewed:
Booklist, July 2001, page 2016
Publishers Weekly, August 6, 2001, page 89
School Library Journal, October 2001, page 106
Smithsonian, November 2001, page 118

Awards the book has won:
Smithsonian's Notable Books for Children, 2001
Notable Social Studies Trade Books for Young People, 2002

Other books by the same author:
My First Garden, 2000
Cat and Mouse in the Snow, 1999
I Hate You! I Like You!, 1997

Other books you might like:
Cathryn Falwell, *David's Drawings*, 2001
  Shy David's drawing of a solitary tree inspires suggestions from classmates that result in a group picture and the beginnings of friendships.
Debra Hess, *Wilson Sat Alone*, 1994
  After new student Sara joins the class she helps bring shy Wilson into the group.
Ingrid Slyder, *The Fabulous Flying Fandinis!*, 1996
  With his parents' encouragement shy Bobby visits the new neighbors and discovers their home is, literally, a nonstop circus.

91

SUSAN BONNERS

Above and Beyond

(New York: Farrar Straus Giroux, 2001)

Subject(s): Friendship; Heroes and Heroines
Age range(s): Grades 5-7
Major character(s): Jeremiah "Jerry" Wheelock, Student—Middle School; Danny Casey, Student—Middle School; Charles Findlay, Cousin (of Jerry), Hero; Jennifer Atwood Martin, Child (rescued, now a mother); Jack "Blackjack" Maguire, Uncle (of Danny), Convict
Time period(s): 2000s
Locale(s): United States

Summary: When assigned to write a report about a local event that happened before they were born, Jerry knows he'll write about his cousin Charles who twenty years earlier rescued a young girl from a cliff. Using some of the techniques his teacher mentions, Jerry reads old newspaper clippings and then decides to find the rescued girl so that he can interview her; since she's moved away he has difficulty finding Jennifer. Finally interviewing her, Jerry discovers another man helped in the rescue, so he turns to Charles to find out the rest of the story. It seems that his new friend Danny's uncle Jack was present at the cliff the day of the rescue and did help, but because he'd stolen a car he was hiding from the authorities and made Charles promise not to tell. Relieved to finally tell his story, Charles and Jerry make sure the plaque at the cliff is corrected and Danny's uncle Jack comes forward to take part in the ceremonies and explain the difficult position in which he put Charles and himself. (151 pages)

Where it's reviewed:
Bulletin of the Center for Children's Books, December 2001, page 131
Kirkus Reviews, October 1, 2001, page 1419
School Library Journal, October 2001, page 148
Voice of Youth Advocates, December 2001, page 356

Other books by the same author:
Edwina Victorious, 2000

Other books you might like:
Sharon Arms Doucet, *Fiddle Fever*, 2000
  Though his mother is opposed, Felix is determined to become an itinerant fiddler like his uncle 'Nonc Adolphe.
Celia Rees, *The Truth Out There*, 2000
  Joshua wonders why no one ever talks about deceased Uncle Patrick, until he discovers he's institutionalized with a form of autism.
Willo Davis Roberts, *Twisted Summer*, 1996
  When Brody's brother Jack is accused of murder, Ceci decides it's time for her to help with the investigation.

92

MARTIN BOOTH

Panther

(New York: Margaret K. McElderry/Simon & Schuster, 2001)

Subject(s): Animals/Panthers
Age range(s): Grades 4-6
Major character(s): Pati, 14-Year-Old; Simon "Si", 14-Year-Old
Time period(s): 2000s
Locale(s): Devon, England (the West Country of England)

Summary: Camping with their parents in England's West Country, Pati and Simon go exploring while their fathers fish and their mothers do whatever mothers do. Si wants to see a fallow deer while Pati wonders if the stories about a wild panther are true. Filling their knapsacks with a camera, binoculars, water and a supply of chocolate, the two take off. Spotting panther tracks, Pati and Si follow until they find a dead deer cached in tree branches and wait for the panther to return to his kill. When Pati develops her film and has a perfect picture of "her panther," she knows they've been successful in their hunt. (85 pages)

Where it's reviewed:
Booklist, February 1, 2001, page 1052
Bulletin of the Center for Children's Books, March 2001, page 253
Kirkus Reviews, March 1, 2001, page 326

Other books by the same author:
War Dog, 1997
Book of Cats, 1992
Hiroshima Joe, 1986

Other books you might like:
Melvin Burgess, *Kite*, 2000
  Told to destroy the eggs of an endangered kite, Tom keeps them. When one hatches, he raises the bird but seeks help to train her.
Gillian Cross, *Pictures in the Dark*, 1996
  When Charlie spots a mysterious animal, he enlists the help of Peter and his older sister to see what kind of animal it is.
Gary Paulsen, *Tracker*, 1984
  Tracking the deer becomes more important to John than killing it, probably because his beloved grandfather is dying of cancer.
David John Smith, *The Red Bandanna*, 1999
  Jake's rancher neighbor dislikes Jake's raising a runty coyote, so it's agreed that the coyote Griff will always wear a red bandanna when he's outside.

LOUISE BORDEN
ADAM GUSTAVSON, Illustrator

The Day Eddie Met the Author

(New York: Margaret K. McElderry Books, 2001)

Subject(s): Books and Reading; Authorship; Schools
Age range(s): Grades 2-4
Major character(s): Mrs. Morrow, Teacher; Eddie Lewis, 3rd Grader; Unnamed Character, Writer
Time period(s): 2000s (2001)
Locale(s): United States (Riverside Elementary School)

Summary: For weeks the students in Eddie's school prepare for the arrival of a visiting author. Mrs. Morrow's class reads ten of the author's books and Eddie finds a part written just for him in each book. He wonders how the author can do that and plans to ask her at the assembly program. During the time allotted for questions after the assembly the author does not call on Eddie. However, she notices his disappointment and speaks to him as he stands in line awaiting dismissal. Her simple answer to Eddie's complex question inspires Eddie's next writing project. (34 pages)

Where it's reviewed:
Booklist, March 1, 2001, page 1275
Bulletin of the Center for Children's Books, April 2001, page 298
Horn Book Guide, Fall 2001, page 288
Kirkus Reviews, April 1, 2001, page 495
School Library Journal, May 2001, page 110

Other books by the same author:
Good-bye, Charles Lindbergh: Based on a True Story, 1998
The Little Ships: The Heroic Rescue at Dunkirk in World War II, 1997 (Notable Children's Trade Books in the Field of Social Studies)
Just in Time for Christmas, 1994

Other books you might like:
Helen Lester, *Author: A True Story*, 1997
    A simple biography describes the life of Lester and her career as a writer.
Joan Lowery Nixon, *If You Were a Writer*, 1988
    Melia receives help to achieving her career goal of being a writer from her mom, an experienced author.
Daniel Pinkwater, *Author's Day*, 1993
    This title provides a humorous description of a well-known author's visit to an elementary school

94

FRANCESCA BOSCA
GIULIANO FERRI, Illustrator
J. ALISON JAMES, Translator

The Apple King

(New York: Michael Neugebauer Book/North-South Books, 2001)

Subject(s): Conduct of Life; Kings, Queens, Rulers, etc.; Animals/Insects
Age range(s): Grades 1-3
Major character(s): Unnamed Character, Royalty, Pig

Time period(s): Indeterminate Past
Locale(s): Fictional Country

Summary: A king too selfish to share the apples from his tree is forced to reconsider when worms are discovered in the fruit. Although the king tries bribery, magic and threats none of his strategies cause the worms to depart. Finally, after he yells at the worms one gathers the courage to explain that the tree invited the worms into the fruit to counteract boredom. Flabbergasted, the king plans a Royal Apple Festival and discovers that the apples taste even sweeter when they are shared with others. (32 pages)

Where it's reviewed:
Booklist, April 1, 2001, page 1476
Horn Book Guide, Fall 2001, page 249
Publishers Weekly, March 19, 2001, page 98
School Library Journal, July 2001, page 73

Other books by the same author:
Caspar and the Star, 1991

Other books you might like:
Jeff Brumbeau, *The Quiltmaker's Gift*, 2000
    A king demands to purchase a quilt from a quiltmaker who only gives them away to those in need, forcing the king to change.
Dick Gackenbach, *Barker's Crime*, 1996
    Greedy Mr. Gobble gets his comeuppance when he accuses a stray dog of stealing the aroma from his food.
Angela McAllister, *The King Who Sneezed*, 1988
    When King Parsimonious searches for the source of the draft in his castle he finds instead evidence of his lack of concern for others.

95

RHYS BOWEN

Evan Can Wait

(New York: St. Martin's, 2001)

Series: Constable Evans Mystery
Subject(s): Mystery and Detective Stories; Murder
Age range(s): Grades 10-Adult
Major character(s): Grantley Smith, Producer; Edward Ferrers, Filmmaker; Evan Evans, Police Officer (constable); Bronwen Price, Girlfriend (of Evan)
Time period(s): 2000s
Locale(s): Llanfair, Wales

Summary: Evan doesn't mind assisting the film crew when they come to his tiny village of Llanfair to raise a World War II German bomber from the lake, an event that will be filmed as part of a war documentary. Thinking he'll have to keep the locals from nosing around the set, he finds there's more to it when Director Grantley Smith is found drowned in an old mine, weighted down by slate. And to Evans's mind, what's even worse, is that Grantley's partner on the project, Edward Ferrers, is the ex-husband of his girlfriend Bronwen Price. Lives are tangled enough but then elderly Trefor Thomas discloses that during the war he and his girlfriend plotted ways to steal paintings from the mine where the treasures from the National Gallery collection were stored. All these seeming coincidences resolve themselves nicely in tiny, quiet little Llanfair in this continuing series. (259 pages)

Where it's reviewed:
Booklist, December 1, 2999, page 695
Kirkus Reviews, November 15, 2000, page 1574
Library Journal, January 2001, page 162
Publishers Weekly, November 13, 2000, page 88
School Library Journal, May 2001, page 175

Other books by the same author:
Evans to Betsy, 2002 (Constable Evans Mystery)
Evan and Elle, 2000 (Constable Evans Mystery)
Evanly Choirs, 1999 (Constable Evans Mystery)
Evan Help Us, 1998 (Constable Evans Mystery)
Evans Above, 1997 (Constable Evans Mystery)

Other books you might like:
Rennie Airth, *River of Darkness*, 1999
    Sent to Surrey where an entire family has been killed, Inspector John Madden builds on his war experiences to find the murderer.
Ian Rankin, *The Black Book*, 2000
    Five years after an Edinburgh hotel is burned, a charred body complete with bullet wound is pulled from the ashy ruins.
Peter Robinson, *In a Dry Season*, 2000
    When a reservoir is drained in Hobbs End, a young boy turns up the body of a woman killed fifty years ago during World War II.

RHYS BOWEN

Murphy's Law
(New York: St. Martin's Minotaur, 2001)

Series: Molly Murphy Mystery. Number 1
Subject(s): Mystery and Detective Stories; Emigration and Immigration; Identity, Concealed
Age range(s): Grades 9-Adult
Major character(s): Molly Murphy, Immigrant, Detective—Amateur; Kathleen O'Connor, Mother (of two young children); O'Malley, Crime Victim; Daniel Sullivan, Police Officer
Time period(s): 19th century
Locale(s): Ireland; New York, New York

Summary: When the son of the landowner tries to rape her, Molly kills him in self-defense. Realizing that she'll be sent to the gallows, she has no choice but to flee from her tiny Irish village. Traveling to Belfast and then on to London, Molly meets a woman with tuberculosis who is supposed to sail to American with her two children. Knowing that she won't be admitted to Ellis Island, Kathleen asks Molly to assume her identity and take Seamus and Bridie instead. Molly can't believe her good fortune and gladly accepts the identity and the responsibility, sailing the next morning for America. The voyage is marred by O'Malley, a loud, offensive man, who makes suggestive remarks to Molly, and receives a slap in return. On Ellis Island, when O'Malley is found murdered, Molly becomes a prime suspect, and meets an intriguing policeman. (226 pages)

Where it's reviewed:
Booklist, August 2001, page 2095
Kirkus Reviews, August 15, 2001, page 1164
Library Journal, October 1, 2001, page 145
Publishers Weekly, September 3, 2001, page 67

Other books by the same author:
Evans to Betsy, 2002 (Constable Evans Mystery)
Evan and Elle, 2000 (Constable Evans Mystery)
Evanly Choirs, 1999 (Constable Evans Mystery)
Evan Help Us, 1998 (Constable Evans Mystery)
Evans Above, 1997 (Constable Evans Mystery)

Other books you might like:
Karen Rose Cercone, *Steel Ashes*, 1997
    Two immigrants are found dead after a fire, but police officer Milo Kachigan thinks they were murdered first in this mystery that takes place in the early 1900s.
Jeanne M. Dams, *Death in Lacquer Red*, 1999
    Swedish immigrant Hilda Johanssen turns from her servant duties to investigate the murder of Judge Harper's sister who turned up dead under the lilac bushes.
Fred Mustard Stewart, *Ellis Island*, 1983
    Fleeing from Europe for varied reasons, five immigrants arrive at Ellis Island where they hope to find the "American Dream."

C.J. BOX

Open Season
(New York: Putnam, 2001)

Subject(s): Mystery and Detective Stories; Fathers and Daughters; Endangered Species
Age range(s): Grades 10-Adult
Major character(s): Joe Pickett, Game Warden; Ote Keeley, Guide (hunting), Hunter; Vern Dunnegan, Game Warden (retired)
Time period(s): 2000s
Locale(s): Twelve Sleep County, Wyoming

Summary: Endearing and bumbling are terms not usually selected to describe game wardens, but that's Joe Pickett, the warden who didn't recognize the governor and cited him for fishing without a license. He's also the warden who lost his gun to Ote Keeley, a hunting guide and poacher, as he was trying to arrest him. Not long after Joe awakens one morning, he finds the bloody body of that same Ote Keeley in his backyard, sprawled over his woodpile with a cooler of unidentified scat beside him. Tracking down Ote's last movements, Joe finds two more hunting guides dead but is dismayed at the speed with which the sheriff's department considers matters closed. Honest as the day is long, Joe doesn't wonder why Vern Dunnegan, the retired and revered warden he replaced, starts filling his ear with glowing reports of the InterWest pipeline project. But when his family is threatened and a once-extinct species is alive and a threat to the pipeline, Joe is ready to risk his life in this first novel. (293 pages)

Where it's reviewed:
Book World, July 29, 2001, page 13

Booklist, May 1, 2001, page 1622
New York Times Book Review, August 5, 2001, page 17
Publishers Weekly, July 2, 2001, page 56
Tribune Books, July 22, 2001, page 3

Awards the book has won:
Booklist Editors' Choice/Adult Books for Young Adults, 2001

Other books by the same author:
Savage Run, 2002

Other books you might like:
Nevada Barr, *Hunting Season*, 2002
    Investigating an illegal hunting stand leads ranger Anna Pigeon into murder, a ring of poachers, and a disgruntled park ranger.
Ivan Doig, *Ride With Me*, 1990
    To celebrate Montana's one hundred years of statehood, Jick and his family travel around its historic places.
James W. Hall, *Blackwater Sound*, 2002
    After rescuing Braswell family members from a plane crash off Florida's coast, Thorn's life becomes intertwined with theirs and a giant blue marlin.

98

MARION ZIMMER BRADLEY
DIANA L. PAXSON, Co-Author

Priestess of Avalon
(New York: Viking, 2000)

Subject(s): Religion; Women; Mothers and Sons
Age range(s): Grades 11-Adult
Major character(s): Eilan/Julia Helena, Mother, Religious
Time period(s): Multiple Time Periods (259-329)
Locale(s): Roman Empire

Summary: Eilan begins her life as a daughter of Avalon, priestess-heiress to the mystical knowledge of the Island, but her jealous aunt makes sure she is increasingly isolated and alienated. When Eilan falls in love with the handsome Roman chosen for another priestess, she decides to act to change fate. The ensuing confrontation ends with Eilan banished from Avalon, but in the company of her Roman as she embarks on a new life as a Roman concubine. She learns Roman ways and adapts to their culture, following her soldier lover around the Empire. The talents she learned in Avalon help them to advance, but Julia Helena, as she is now called, never forgets her roots in Britain. Although Julia considers herself married, by Roman law she is not and eventually the Emperor calls on her husband to abandon her for a proper Roman wife. Adding insult to injury, he takes her son under his protection, separating the family at a moment Julia feels is critical to the child's developing conscience. Left alone to rebuild her life, Julie increasingly longs for the shores of Avalon. (394 pages)

Where it's reviewed:
Book World, February 25, 2001, page 4
Booklist, April 15, 2001, page 1510
Kirkus Reviews, April 1, 2001, page 456
Library Journal, June 15, 2001, page 106
Publishers Weekly, April 30, 2001, page 62

Other books by the same author:
Lady of Avalon, 1997
The Forest House, 1993
The Mists of Avalon, 1982

Other books you might like:
Juliet Marillier, *Son of the Shadows*, 2001
    A young woman must choose between her love for an outlaw and her family and friends.
Nancy McKenzie, *The Child Queen: the Tale of Guinevere and King Arthur*, 1994
    In this version of Guinevere's story, her fate requires her to leave the life she knows and loves to become a stranger's queen.
Cynthia Voigt, *Elske*, 1999
    A girl flees her home to avoid becoming a sacrifice to her peoples' religion and finds herself conspiring with an exiled princess.

99

ANN BRASHARES

The Sisterhood of the Traveling Pants
(New York: Delacorte, 2001)

Subject(s): Friendship; Clothes; Summer
Age range(s): Grades 7-10
Major character(s): Lena Kaligaris, 15-Year-Old; Bridget Vreeland, Counselor (soccer camp), 15-Year-Old; Tibby, 15-Year-Old, Clerk (discount store); Carmen Lucille Lowell, 15-Year-Old
Time period(s): 2000s
Locale(s): Washington, District of Columbia; Loreto, Mexico (Baja California); Greece

Summary: Bemoaning the fact that their paths are heading in different directions for the summer, four friends discover that a pair of second-hand jeans not only fits, but also looks great on, each of their dissimilar figures. Realizing that the jeans can be their unifier for this summer spent apart, the four girls make a list of rules for wearing the jeans, a schedule for mailing the jeans and agree to take notes on the most exciting thing that happens while wearing the "traveling pants." That summer, each girl needs that pair of jeans as Lena travels to Greece to visit her grandparents and miscommunicates with a good-looking teen; Tibby stays home and, to her horror, wears an ugly smock and works in a discount store; Carmen visits her dad only to discover he's engaged to a woman with a built-in family and Bridget attends soccer camp in Mexico where her impulsive behavior causes problems. Through it all, the pants remain their symbol of friendship and support and help each girl as she encounters problems during the summer in this special first novel. (294 pages)

Where it's reviewed:
Booklist, August 2001, page 2106
Publishers Weekly, July 16, 2001, page 182
Riverbank Review, Winter 2001-2002, page 42
School Library Journal, August 2001, page 175
Voice of Youth Advocates, October 2001, page 272

Awards the book has won:
ALA Best Books for Young Adults, 2002

Booklist Editors' Choice/Books for Youth, 2001

Other books you might like:

Paula Danziger, *Snail Mail No More*, 2000
When Tara moves away, she and Elizabeth correspond by email and find it's easier to stay in touch, though not necessarily easy to stay friends.

Phyllis Reynolds Naylor, *The Alice Series*, 1985-
Alice and her friends Pamela, Elizabeth and Patrick survive all the traumas of junior high, peer pressure and dating, but now await high school.

Sara Withrow, *Bat Summer*, 1999
When his only friend leaves for summer camp, lonely Terence befriends a girl who thinks she's a bat and supports her, as he knows bats would do.

100

BRUCE BROOKS

All That Remains

(New York: Atheneum/Simon & Schuster)

Subject(s): Death; Sports
Age range(s): Grades 7-10
Time period(s): 2000s
Locale(s): United States

Summary: Three novellas offer a different take on death beginning with "All That Remains." Two cousins want to honor their aunt's wish to be cremated, but because she died of AIDS state law requires an in-ground burial in a special plot. Working with their aunt's partner, a noted potter, they ingeniously use her kiln and parts of a deer to pay tribute to their aunt. In "Playing the Creeps," Hank's uncle asks him to look after his son Bobby, a task that's difficult for Hank since the two boys don't have much in common. Eventually Hank realizes that Bobby's lack of athletic ability isn't important and that he can learn more from Bobby's guitar playing than Bobby can learn from him. In the final novella, "Teeing Up," a young girl wearing a backpack joins a threesome of golfers. Filled with the usual "guy talk," the boys are impressed with the girl's ability to play golf but wonder about the backpack. When they learn it contains the ashes of her father, they help her understand that burial in the course's sand traps might be the best solution. (168 pages)

Where it's reviewed:

Booklist, May 1, 2001, page 1682
Bulletin of the Center for Children's Books, June 2001, page 367
Horn Book, July 2001, page 446
School Library Journal, May 2001, page 148
Voice of Youth Advocates, June 2001, page 119

Awards the book has won:
ALA Best Books for Young Adults, 2002

Other books by the same author:

Dolores: Seven Stories, 2002
Vanishing, 1999
Asylum for Nightface, 1996
What Hearts, 1992

Other books you might like:

Carolyn Coman, *Many Stones*, 2000
Ever since her sister Laura was murdered, Berry has collected stones, sometimes putting them on her chest as paperweights to keep her grounded.

Cynthia Rylant, *Missing May*, 1992
After Aunt May dies, Uncle Ob's hand-carved whirligigs stop and both he and Summer take time to grieve.

James VanOosting, *The Last Payback*, 1997
When her twin is killed, Dimple knows she must follow their motto of "never delay a payback" and goes after Ronnie, their friend who had a gun.

GERALDINE BROOKS

Year of Wonders

(New York: Viking, 2001)

Subject(s): Plague; Historical
Age range(s): Grades 10-Adult
Major character(s): Anna Frith, Servant, Widow(er); Michael Mompellion, Religious
Time period(s): 17th century (1665-1666)
Locale(s): England (small village in Derbyshire)

Summary: In 1665, a parcel of cloth infected with the plague arrives in a small English village, sent to a newly-arrived tailor who is boarding with the widowed Anna and her two small sons. As Anna recounts that "year of wonders," based on the plight of the real town of Eyam, the plague spreads rapidly, first to the tailor, then to Anna's sons and eventually past her walls and into the town. The young vicar Michael Mompellion, earnest and filled with faith, entreats his congregation and the townspeople to do the right thing by walling themselves in so as not to spread the plague into the surrounding countryside. If the townspeople will agree to this sacrifice, he will make sure food and other supplies arrive throughout the year. Though the normal reaction to plague is to flee as there's no cure for it, the people agree to their confinement and at first are buoyed up by his sermons. However, as the deaths mount, their fear returns and they look beyond prayer to herbal treatments and eventually to witch hunts, causing the death of the two herbalists in the village that could help them. Village life is overtaken by grief, vengeance, and profit-making which makes her small town unrecognizable to Anna as she is eventually forced to leave in this first novel. (308 pages)

Where it's reviewed:

Entertainment Weekly, August 10, 2001, page 69
Kirkus Reviews, July 15, 2001, page 959
Library Journal, July 2001, page 120
New York Times Book Review, August 26, 2001, page 13
Publishers Weekly, June 25, 2001, page 43

Awards the book has won:
ALA Alex Award, 2002

Other books by the same author:

Foreign Correspondence, 1999 (adult nonfiction)
Nine Parts of Desire: The Hidden World of Islamic Women, 1996 (adult nonfiction)

Other books you might like:

Ann Benson, *The Plague Tales*, 1997
   A female scientist digs up soil contaminated nearly seven hundred years ago with the bubonic plague and accidentally unleashes its horror.
Judith Merkle Riley, *A Vision of Light*, 1989
   During the fourteenth century Margaret wants to write a book, but hasn't been taught to write; luckily she finds a starving friar to record her tale.
Jill Paton Walsh, *A Parcel of Patterns*, 1983
   In 1665 the inhabitants of a small English town become infected by the plague when a dressmaker receives ''a parcel of patterns'' from London.
Connie Willis, *Doomsday Book*, 1992
   A time-traveling graduate student accidentally winds up in the middle of the Black Plague.

102

KEN BROWN, Author/Illustrator

The Scarecrow's Hat

(Atlanta: Peachtree Publishers, 2001)

Subject(s): Animals/Chickens; Animals; Problem Solving
Age range(s): Grades K-3
Major character(s): Chicken, Chicken
Time period(s): Indeterminate
Locale(s): Fictional Country

Summary: When Chicken admires the hat atop a scarecrow, the scarecrow replies that he'd really prefer a walking stick to help support him as he stands all day in the field. Although Chicken doesn't have such a stick she does know an animal that does. In order to get the walking stick, Chicken goes through a series of swaps with several animals. Eventually she achieves her goal of acquiring the hat in which she builds a nest that she's not willing to trade for any reason. (32 pages)

Where it's reviewed:
Booklist, March 15, 2001, page 1402
Horn Book Guide, Fall 2001, page 249
Kirkus Reviews, February 1, 2001, page 179
Publishers Weekly, March 12, 2001, page 88
School Library Journal, April 2001, page 99

Other books by the same author:
Mucky Pup's Christmas, 1999
Mucky Pup, 1997
Nellie's Knot, 1993

Other books you might like:
Kay Chorao, *Pig and Crow*, 2000
   Sly Crow trades Pig ''magic'' items for Pig's baked goods not realizing that what Crow considers worthless really becomes magic for Pig.
Pat Hutchins, *Rosie's Walk*, 1968
   Unaware that a fox is following her Rosie enjoys her walk around the farmyard.
Tracey Campbell Pearson, *The Purple Hat*, 1997
   When Annie loses her beloved purple hat a bird searching for a nest is the first to find it.
Janet Morgan Stoeke, *A Hat for Minerva Louise*, 1994
   Independent hen Minerva Louise finds a suitable hat to keep her head warm as she strolls the barnyard on snowy mornings.

103

MARC BROWN, Author/Illustrator

D.W.'s Library Card

(Boston: Little, Brown and Company, 2001)

Subject(s): Libraries; Books and Reading; Brothers and Sisters
Age range(s): Grades K-2
Major character(s): Dora Winifred ''D.W.'' Read, Aardvark, Sister (younger); Arthur Read, Brother (older), Aardvark; Ms. Turner, Librarian, Rabbit
Time period(s): 2000s
Locale(s): Fictional Country

Summary: When Ms. Turner tells D.W. that she can have her own library card as soon as she learns to write her name D.W. gets busy practicing a name that she can barely say. Over and over using pencil and paper or fork and mashed potatoes D.W. tries to write Dora Winifred Read and after a week she's eligible for her own library card. D.W.'s disappointed to discover that the book she wants has been checked out, but she waits, not too patiently, for it to be returned. Then, it takes a tip from Arthur for the overly cautious D.W. to actually enjoy the book she's chosen. (24 pages)

Where it's reviewed:
Horn Book Guide, Spring 2002, page 36
Kirkus Reviews, September 1, 2001, page 1286
School Library Journal, December 2001, page 90

Other books by the same author:
D.W., Go to Your Room!, 1999
D.W.'s Lost Blankie, 1998
D.W. Rides Again!, 1996

Other books you might like:
Becky Bloom, *Wolf!*, 1999
   To gain acceptance to a new community Wolf joins a reading class, checks out books at the library and shops at a bookstore.
Judith Caseley, *Sammy and Sophie's Library Sleepover*, 1993
   Sophie tries to teach Sammy how to treat library books so he can come with her the next time the library has a nighttime storytime.
Lisa Campbell Ernst, *Stella Louella's Runaway Book*, 1998
   Stella searches frantically for the library book that is due by five o'clock today.
Cari Meister, *Tiny Goes to the Library*, 2000
   When Tiny accompanies his owner to the library the big dog waits outside to pull home the wagon loaded with books.
Sarah Stewart, *The Library*, 1995
   Elizabeth Brown is a most unusual child who likes to read and enjoys nothing else.

MARGARET WISE BROWN
LEO DILLON, Illustrator
DIANE DILLON, Illustrator

Two Little Trains

(New York: HarperCollins Publishers, 2001)

Subject(s): Railroads; Travel; Toys
Age range(s): Preschool-Kindergarten
Time period(s): Indeterminate Past
Locale(s): United States

Summary: A newly illustrated version of Brown's 1949 title interprets the two trains heading West as a sleek streamlined one literally making the trip while the little old train is a child's toy. The trip to the West proceeds along steel tracks, through tunnels, across rivers, and up mountains until the coast is reached. The sleek streamlined train sits on the coast overlooking the ocean at the conclusion of its journey. For the toy train the trip's conclusion means the end of an imaginative day and a cozy bed for the train's owner. (32 pages)

Where it's reviewed:
Booklist, April 15, 2001, page 1550
Horn Book, May 2001, page 309
Publishers Weekly, May 28, 2001, page 90
Riverbank Review, Summer 2001, page 34
School Library Journal, May 2001, page 110

Awards the book has won:
Publishers Weekly Best Children's Books, 2001
Parenting's Reading Magic Awards, 2001

Other books by the same author:
Another Important Book, 1999 (School Library Journal Best Books)
Goodnight Moon, 1947
The Runaway Bunny, 1942

Other books you might like:
Robert Burleigh, *It's Funny Where Ben's Train Takes Him*, 1999
    In Ben's imagination a real train emerges from his drawing to carry Ben and his teddy bear to the bedtime station.
David McPhail, *The Train*, 1977
    As he drifts off to sleep after a day of playing with his toy train, a young boy takes a fantastic train ride.
Harriet Ziefert, *Train Song*, 1999
    While playing with his toy train a young boy listens to the song of the train whistle as the daily train passes by on tracks below.

105

ROSELLEN BROWN

Half a Heart

(New York: Farrar Straus Giroux, 2000)

Subject(s): Mothers and Daughters; Racially Mixed People; Prejudice
Age range(s): Grades 10-Adult

Major character(s): Miriam Starobin Vener, Mother; Veronica "Ronnee" Reece, 17-Year-Old; Eljay Reece, Professor (music)
Time period(s): 2000s
Locale(s): Houston, Texas; New Hampshire

Summary: In the 1960s, liberal activist Miriam Starobin left Texas to teach at an all-black college in Mississippi where she had an affair with a black professor and had a child. Eljay convinced her that he could do the better job of raising their daughter, so Miriam left and Veronica stayed with him. Twenty years later, Miriam is married to a well-to-do doctor, has three children who are off to camp and receives a letter from her unacknowledged daughter Ronnee who is off to Stanford in the fall. Guilt about abandoning her daughter and natural curiosity set up a visit with Ronnee who can barely control her anger at Miriam for leaving her. Neither Ronnee nor Miriam is sure what to expect, and they have a lot of personal, class and social issues to deal with, but each seems willing to try to develop a relationship. (402 pages)

Where it's reviewed:
Library Journal, March 15, 2000, page 124
New York Times Book Review, June 11, 2000, page 18
Publishers Weekly, March 13, 2000, page 62
Time, May 8, 2000, page 95
Voice of Youth Advocates, April 2001, page 35

Other books by the same author:
Cora Fry's Pillow Book, 1994
Before and After, 1992
Civil Wars: A Novel, 1984
Tender Mercies, 1978
Street Games, 1974

Other books you might like:
Deanie Francis Miles, *Ordeal*, 1997
    Now happily married and a high school chemistry teacher, Wren's student activist days return to haunt her.
Sigrid Nunez, *A Feather on the Breath of God*, 1995
    With a German mother and a Chinese/Panamanian father, a young girl wonders about the various cultural differences in her life.
Danzy Senna, *Caucasia*, 1998
    Daughter of a biracial couple, light-skinned Birdie stays with her activist mother when she has to go underground, but misses her father and Cole, her darker sister.

106

RUTH BROWN, Author/Illustrator

Ten Seeds

(New York: Alfred A. Knopf, 2001)

Subject(s): Gardens and Gardening; Animals
Age range(s): Preschool-Kindergarten
Major character(s): Unnamed Character, Child
Time period(s): 2000s
Locale(s): England

Summary: A little boy plants ten seeds and an ant takes one before he can finish the row. Nine seeds begin to sprout and a pigeon pulls one up. Eight seeds develop roots and one mouse grabs one. Seven seedlings poke their heads above the soil and one slug devours a tender morsel. Six small plants begin to grow and one mole uproots one. Five young plants in the row are reduced to four by the digging of one cat. Four plants in the way of a ball game leave three for a puppy to trample as he scrambles for the ball. Two plants with buds but only one survives the greenfly larvae. One plant develops a flower, one bee visits and later the little boy harvests ten seeds. (22 pages)

Where it's reviewed:
Booklist, May 15, 2001, page 1754
Horn Book, September 2001, page 570
Publishers Weekly, June 4, 2001, page 82
School Library Journal, July 2001, page 73

Other books by the same author:
Holly: The True Story of a Cat, 2000
Cry Baby, 1997
Copycat, 1994

Other books you might like:
Eve Bunting, *Sunflower House*, 1996
    A young boy plants his sunflower seeds in a circle and creates a summer play "house" to share with friends.
Eric Carle, *The Tiny Seed*, 1970
    One tiny seed sprouts and develops into a flowering plant that produces seeds and so the cycle continues.
Ruth Krauss, *The Carrot Seed*, 1945
    This little boy's family has doubts that the seeds he plants will grow, but they do.
Jeanne Titherington, *Pumpkin, Pumpkin*, 1986
    Carefully, Jamie plants a seed, tends the plant, carves the pumpkin and saves some seeds to plant in the spring.

107

ANTHONY BROWNE, Author/Illustrator

My Dad

(New York: Farrar Straus Giroux, 2001)

Subject(s): Fathers; Love; Imagination
Age range(s): Grades K-2
Major character(s): Unnamed Character, Father; Unnamed Character, Child
Time period(s): Indeterminate
Locale(s): Fictional Country

Summary: All in all, this dad is all right. He's brave enough to chase away the big, bad wolf, strong enough to wrestle giants and fast enough to win the father's race at school. This dad is happy, smart, funny, big yet tender with the ability to sing, dance and play soccer. Best of all, this youngster's dad is a loving dad and the feeling is obviously mutual in a title originally published in Great Britain in 2000. (32 pages)

Where it's reviewed:
Booklist, March 1, 2001, page 1286
Bulletin of the Center for Children's Books, May 2001, page 332
Horn Book Guide, Fall 2001, page 250
Publishers Weekly, February 12, 2001, page 209
School Library Journal, April 2001, page 105

Awards the book has won:
School Library Journal Best Books, 2001

Other books by the same author:
Willy's Pictures, 2000
Voices in the Park, 1998 (ALA Notable Books for Children)
Willy the Dreamer, 1998

Other books you might like:
Laura Joffe Numeroff, *What Mommies Do Best/What Daddies Do Best*, 1998
    Parents have unique and special ways to express love to their children.
Susan Paradis, *My Daddy*, 1998
    A little boy feels awed to see his father courageously cross the street alone or walk in dark woods without fear.
Douglas Wood, *What Dads Can't Do*, 2000
    Since dads are unable to read books alone or sleep late in the morning they really need their kids for company at such times.

108

JOSEPH BRUCHAC
JAMES BRUCHAC, Co-Author
JOSE ARUEGO, Illustrator
ARIANE DEWEY, Illustrator

How Chipmunk Got His Stripes: A Tale of Bragging and Teasing

(New York: Dial Books for Young Readers, 2001)

Subject(s): Folklore; Indians of North America; Animals/ Chipmunks
Age range(s): Grades K-3
Major character(s): Bear, Bear; Brown Squirrel, Squirrel
Time period(s): Indeterminate Past
Locale(s): North America

Summary: Boastful Bear claims to be able to do anything, even, as Brown Squirrel asks, keep the sun from rising. When Bear's claim doesn't prove to be true and he's embarrassed in front of the other forest animals, Brown Squirrel makes matters worse by teasing Bear. Grumpy Bear may not be able to keep the sun from rising but he plans to be sure that Brown Squirrel never sees it come up again. Quickly, Brown Squirrel extricates himself from the predicament he's in but not before Bear's claws make stripes the length of Brown Squirrel's back. To this day, Brown Squirrel is known as Chipmunk and he awakens first in the morning while Bear is the last to rise. (32 pages)

Where it's reviewed:
Booklist, February 1, 2001, page 1054
Bulletin of the Center for Children's Books, March 2001, page 254
Kirkus Reviews, December 15, 2000, page 1758
Publishers Weekly, January 15, 2001, page 76
School Library Journal, February 2001, page 109

Awards the book has won:
Parenting's Reading Magic Awards, 2001
Notable Social Studies Trade Books for Young People, 2002

Other books by the same author:
Native American Games and Stories, 2000

Other books you might like:

James E. Connolly, *Why the Possum's Tail Is Bare: And Other North American Indian Nature Tales*, 1992
Thirteen Native American folktales explain the legendary reason for certain animals' behavior.

Lois Ehlert, *Cuckoo: A Mexican Folktale/Cucu: Un Cuento Folklorico Mexicano*, 1997
Parallel texts in English and Spanish explain the origins of the black plumage and raspy voice of the Cuckoo.

Gerald McDermott, *Coyote: A Trickster Tale From the American Southwest*, 1994
Pompous blue-furred Coyote's attempt to fly with the crows is undermined by his rude, boastful behavior resulting in a change in his coloration.

Ragnhild Scamell, *Rooster Crows*, 1994
Pompous Rooster is so confident that his crowing causes the sun to rise that he challenges Bluebird to a contest.

109

JOSEPH BRUCHAC

The Journal of Jesse Smoke: A Cherokee Boy, Trail of Tears, 1838
(New York: Scholastic, 2001)

Series: My Name Is America
Subject(s): Indians of North America; Diaries
Age range(s): Grades 5-8
Major character(s): Jesse Smoke, Indian (Cherokee), 16-Year-Old
Time period(s): 1830s (1837-1839)
Locale(s): Tennessee; Oklahoma

Summary: In the early 1830s, the white settlers of the Southeast begin making serious attempts to move the Cherokee Indians from their lands so they can claim them and by 1838 Jesse Smoke and his family are part of the Cherokee Removal. Initially the Cherokee families are placed in stockades, then herded into camps and finally on August 23, 1838, the first of the Cherokee families set out for their new lands in Oklahoma. Jesse is unusual because he can read and write, a fact that sets him apart from the other Cherokee, and he uses this ability to record the horror of the Trail of Tears in his journal in this worthy addition to the *Dear America* series. (203 pages)

Where it's reviewed:
Booklist, July 2001, page 2005
Kirkus Reviews, May 1, 2001, page 655
Kliatt, May 2001, page 8
School Library Journal, July 2001, page 102
Voice of Youth Advocates, August 2001, page 197

Other books by the same author:
Foot of the Mountain: And Other Stories, 2002
Sacajawea: The Story of Bird Woman and the Lewis and Clark Expedition, 2000
The Waters Between, 1999 (Novel of the Dawn Land)
The Arrow over the Door, 1998
The Heart of a Chief, 1998
Long River, 1995 (Novel of the Dawn Land)

Other books you might like:

Sara Harrell Banks, *Remember My Name*, 1993
Orphaned, Annie lives with her wealthy Cherokee uncle but when the Cherokee removal begins, he helps Annie and one of her slaves escape to freedom.

Brian Burks, *Walks Alone*, 1998
Young Walks Alone sees her family and her Apache way of life destroyed by the U.S. Army.

Debbie Dadey, *Cherokee Sister*, 2000
While visiting her friend Leaf, Allie is included in the Cherokee removal and marched to Oklahoma. Luckily Allie's father finds and rescues both girls.

Ann Turner, *The Girl Who Chased Away Sorrow: The Diary of Sarah Nita, a Navajo Girl, 1864*, 1999
One summer day Sarah Nita decides to tell her granddaughter the story of the Long Walk, when the Navajo were forced to walk four-hundred miles to Fort Sumner.

110

JOSEPH BRUCHAC

Skeleton Man
(New York: HarperCollins, 2001)

Subject(s): Indians of North America; Kidnapping; Folk Tales
Age range(s): Grades 5-8
Major character(s): Molly, Student—Middle School; Maureen Shabbas, Teacher; Skeleton Man, Uncle
Time period(s): 2000s
Locale(s): United States

Summary: Molly wakes up one Sunday morning to an empty house—where are her parents? Left alone for three days, the Social Services workers finally appear and entrust her to her great-uncle, a man she's never met, though she'd rather stay with her teacher Ms. Shabbas. Now living in her uncle's house, each night Molly is locked in her room and released to attend school each morning. Her dreams are filled with the stories of her Mohawk Indian father, especially the tale of the skeleton man who develops a taste for human flesh. The more she dreams, the more the skeleton man resembles her uncle. With support from Ms. Shabbas, a desire to emulate her namesake the warrior Molly Brant, and the stories revealed in her dreams, she finds the courage to break out of her locked room and rescue her parents in this eerie tale. (114 pages)

Where it's reviewed:
Booklist, September 1, 2001, page 96
Bulletin of the Center for Children's Books, September 2001, page 7
Publishers Weekly, August 13, 2001, page 313
School Library Journal, August 2001, page 176
Voice of Youth Advocates, October 2001, page 288

Awards the book has won:
School Library Journal Best Books, 2001
ALA Notable Children's Books, 2002

Other books by the same author:
The Journal of Jesse Smoke: A Cherokee Boy, Trail of Tears, 1838, 2001 (My Name Is America)
Sacajawea: The Story of Bird Woman and the Lewis and Clark Expedition, 2000

The Arrow over the Door, 1998
The Heart of a Chief, 1998
Children of the Longhouse, 1996

Other books you might like:

Polly Horvath, *Everything on a Waffle*, 2001
When Primrose's parents are lost at sea, only Primrose is convinced they're waiting for rescue, but for now she's shuttled between foster homes.

Phyllis Reynolds Naylor, *Jade Green: A Ghost Story*, 2000
Judith's green-framed photo of her mother awakens the ghost of a former serving girl who is able to protect Judith from a murderous relative.

Laura Simms, *Bone Man: A Native American Modoc Tale*, 1997
Ghastly illustrations appropriately describe the demise of the dreaded Bone Man who devours people and drinks up the rivers.

Lemony Snicket, *Unfortunate Events Series*, 1999-
The Baudelaire children live up to the name of the series as their lives go from bad to worse after their parents are killed.

Vivian Vande Velde, *The Rumpelstiltskin Problem*, 2000
Six tales offer a different alternative to the original fairytale of *Rumpelstiltskin*.

111

DEBORAH BRUSS
TIPHANIE BEEKE, Illustrator

Book! Book! Book!

(New York: Arthur A. Levine Books/Scholastic Press, 2001)

Subject(s): Animals; Libraries; Books and Reading
Age range(s): Preschool-Grade 1
Major character(s): Unnamed Character, Chicken
Time period(s): Indeterminate
Locale(s): Fictional Country

Summary: After the children playing on a farm return to school, the animals are left alone and bored. Led by the hen, the animals walk to town in search of activity. Noticing smiling people leaving a large building they enter, one at a time, to ask for something to do. The librarian cannot understand the neighing request of the horse, or the mooing of the cow and each animal leaves empty-handed and frustrated. Once again the hen takes charge and flies into the library politely clucking ''Book! Book! Book!'' Finally, the librarian hears a language she understands and the hen departs with three books. The animals return to the farm happy as the author's first book concludes. (32 pages)

Where it's reviewed:
Booklist, May 15, 2001, page 1755
Bulletin of the Center for Children's Books, February 2001, page 217
Horn Book Guide, Fall 2001, page 227
Publishers Weekly, April 23, 2001, page 76
School Library Journal, May 2001, page 110

Other books you might like:

Doreen Cronin, *Click, Clack, Moo: Cows That Type*, 2000
By using an old typewriter, cows have no difficulty com-

municating their needs to Farmer Brown; soon the hens make demands too.

Cynthia Rylant, *Poppleton*, 1997
As a new resident in a small town Poppleton discovers neighbors so friendly that he can hardly find time to visit the library.

Martin Waddell, *Farmer Duck*, 1992
Farm animals decide to take over from the lazy farmer who does nothing but sleep while Farmer Duck does the work.

112

STEVEN BRUST

Issola

(New York: Tor, 2001)

Subject(s): Adventure and Adventurers; Fantasy
Age range(s): Grades 10-Adult
Major character(s): Vlad Taltos, Mercenary
Time period(s): Indeterminate
Locale(s): Dragaera, Fictional Country

Summary: Vlad Taltos works his way up from distrusted assassin to distrusted mercenary. His employers are never sure where his loyalties lie, and Vlad certainly isn't saying. His patrons mysteriously disappear and are pronounced neither dead nor out of the world but gone elsewhere. They may be prisoners of the creators of the world, who Vlad thinks are very powerful beings, but knowing he's been able to swashbuckle and smart-mouth his way out of other impossible situations, he decides to rescue them. (255 pages)

Where it's reviewed:
Booklist, June 1, 2001, page 1855
Kirkus Reviews, May 15, 2001, page 713
Publishers Weekly, June 11, 2001, page 66

Other books by the same author:
Dragon, 1998
Orca, 1996
Phoenix, 1990

Other books you might like:

Chris Bunch, *Corsair*, 2001
Gareth's stubborn hatred of slavers leads him to dare impossible odds to try and eradicate them.

Deborah Christian, *Mainline*, 1996
An assassin uses her ability to choose future timelines to her professional advantage.

Peter David, *Sir Apropos of Nothing*, 2001
Apropos's quick wit and smart mouth are even more powerful than his sword in helping him survive.

113

JANE BUCHANAN

Hank's Story

(New York: Farrar Straus Giroux, 2001)

Subject(s): Orphans; Farm Life; Child Abuse
Age range(s): Grades 4-6
Major character(s): Hank Donohue, 12-Year-Old, Orphan; Peter ''Pete'' Donohue, Orphan, Runaway; Jo Olson,

Spouse; Mr. Olson, Farmer, Alcoholic; Holly McIntire, Animal Lover
Time period(s): 1920s (1923)
Locale(s): Nebraska

Summary: Sent out from New York on the Orphan Train, Hank and his older brother Pete are placed with the Olsons, a shrewish, complaining wife and her alcoholic, abusive husband. Working hard around their farm, and receiving the back hand of Mr. Olson, Peter finally has enough and runs away, thinking that Hank will be fine if there's only one child in the Olson household. Unfortunately, all Mr. Olson's vengeance turns on Hank and he quickly learns to complete his chores, keep his mouth shut and stay out of way. Though told by Mrs. Olson to ignore her because she's crazy, Hank becomes friends with Holly, an older woman who loves animals more than people, and becomes his refuge when life is unbearable at home. Hank runs away in the midst of a blizzard but seeks shelter in Holly's barn; since she's not home, he cares for her animals and even repairs the broken wing on a wild turkey. By the time Mr. Olson tries to reclaim him, Hank decides to stand up for himself and refuses to return; luckily a representative from the children's home appears and lends some authority to his decision, in a companion work to *Gratefully Yours*. (136 pages)

Where it's reviewed:
Booklist, April 1, 2001, page 1482
Bulletin of the Center for Children's Books, June 2001, page 368
Kirkus Reviews, February 15, 2001, page 256
School Library Journal, May 2001, page 148

Other books by the same author:
Gratefully Yours, 1997

Other books you might like:
Peggy Brooke, *Jake's Orphan*, 2000
    Jake and his brother are miserable on Mr. Gunderson's farm, but thankfully Mr. Gunderson's brother Jake stands up for the boys.
David DeVries, *Home at Last*, 1994
    New York-bred Billy has a hard time fitting in with the Nebraska Andersen family after being sent there by the Children's Aid Society.
Janni Howker, *Isaac Campion*, 1986
    At the turn of the century, Isaac's older brother dies and his life on his father's horse farm becomes an ordeal.
Joan Lowery Nixon, *The Orphan Train Quartet*, 1987-1989
    A series of books featuring the Kelly children who are sent West on the Orphan Train when their widowed mother can no longer care for them.

114

SARAH MASTERS BUCKEY

Enemy in the Fort

(Middleton, WI: American Girl/Pleasant Company, 2001)

Series: History Mysteries
Subject(s): Frontier and Pioneer Life; Indian Captives; Indians of North America
Age range(s): Grades 4-7

Major character(s): Rebecca Percy, 12-Year-Old; Isaac Davidson, Captive (of the Abenaki's); Widow Tyler, Widow(er)
Time period(s): 1750s
Locale(s): Fort Number Four, New Hampshire

Summary: In the early 1750s Rebecca's parents and brother are captured by the Abenaki Indians while she and her sister watch from their hiding place. Taking only their mother's engraved spoons from England, the girls seek shelter at Fort Number Four where the kindly Widow Tyler offers them refuge. Rebecca helps Widow Tyler and never loses hope that her parents will be safe, perhaps sold to the French who might return them. When the Widow also takes in Isaac, a young boy captured and raised by the Abenakis, it's hard for Rebecca to conceal her dislike of Isaac as he liked his captors. Rebecca's spoons are stolen, along with other items in the fort, and she immediately thinks Isaac is the culprit in this continuing series. (165 pages)

Where it's reviewed:
Booklist, October 1, 2001, page 317
School Library Journal, December 2001, page 132
Voice of Youth Advocates, December 2001, page 356

Other books by the same author:
The Smuggler's Treasure, 1999

Other books you might like:
Lynda Durrant, *Turtle Clan Journey*, 1999
    Returned to his white family, Echohawk is miserable until a servant helps him return to his Indian family.
Sally M. Keehn, *I Am Regina*, 1991
    Captured by the Delaware Indians, Regina can barely recognize her mother after spending nine years in captivity.
Katherine Kirkpatrick, *Trouble's Daughter: The Story of Susanna Hutchinson, Indian Captive*, 1998
    After massacring her family, the Lenape Indians capture nine-year-old Susanna who gradually adjusts to the Indian way of life.

115

LOIS MCMASTER BUJOLD

The Curse of Chalion

(New York: HarperCollins/Eos, 2001)

Subject(s): Magic; Romance
Age range(s): Grades 8-Adult
Major character(s): Cazaril, Warrior; Iselle, Royalty; Betriz, Noblewoman
Time period(s): Indeterminate
Locale(s): Chalion, Fictional Country

Summary: Wandering towards home, disillusioned and impoverished by his experience in war, Cazaril begs employment from his liege-lady, but what she grants him is anything but peaceful. The two royal children have been placed in her care and are anything but easily managed. Royesse Iselle is to be Cazaril's special project and, though not much younger than Cazaril, is decades apart in experience. Iselle and her shrewd companion, Betriz, quickly conclude that they can learn a great deal from Cazaril that will be useful in the business of ruling. Meanwhile Cazaril becomes aware that he is also a kind of bodyguard for there is some rottenness in Chalion that threatens not only the royal family but also everyone in the land. As he learns more, Cazaril realizes that he will need to fight magic with magic, and that he is willing to sacrifice himself to save his country. (448 pages)

Where it's reviewed:
Booklist, May 1, 2001, page 1672
Kirkus Reviews, June 1, 2001, page 779
Library Journal, July 2001, page 131
School Library Journal, October 2001, page 194

Awards the book has won:
School Library Journal Best Books, 2001

Other books by the same author:
Miles, Mystery & Mayhem, 2001
A Civil Campaign: A Comedy of Biology and Manners, 1999
Komarr: A Miles Vorkosigan Adventure, 1998

Other books you might like:
Steven Brust, *Taltos*, 1988
   Vlad Taltos frequently finds the gods taking an uncomfortably close interest in his affairs.
Roberta Gellis, *Bull God*, 2000
   In this retelling of the story of the Minotaur, the gods turn out to be all too human.
Adele Geras, *Troy*, 2001
   As the tragedy of the fall of Troy plays out, the various Greek gods and goddesses appear before the doomed inhabitants to explain their motives.
Lawrence Watt-Evans, *Touched By the Gods*, 1997
   A country boy does everything he can to avoid the role chosen for him by the gods.

116

CHRIS BUNCH

Corsair
(New York: Aspect/Warner Books, 2001)

Subject(s): Pirates; Adventure and Adventurers
Age range(s): Grades 8-Adult
Major character(s): Gareth Radnor, Pirate
Time period(s): Indeterminate
Locale(s): Saros, Fictional Country

Summary: As a child, Gareth and his friends are fishing while their families, friends and village are destroyed by slavers. Gareth resolves to seek revenge someday, but in the meantime he is packed off to live in the city with a merchant uncle. His relatives are kind, but Gareth remains a troubled youth who relieves his feelings with a series of wild and dangerous pranks. He exhibits a daring that attracts followers, including a young noblewoman and a magically gifted giant, but eventually the young people go too far and play a trick that causes Gareth to be banished from the city. Signing on as a mate for a lengthy sea voyage, he manages to recruit his two old childhood friends to be part of the crew. This is a stroke of luck for Gareth because soon the captain reveals that the ship's real mission is slave trading. Gareth and his friends are not the only sailors to be horrified, but Gareth's leadership allows the rebels to eventually take over the ship and become pirates.

They are pirates with a difference, however, for the more Gareth learns of the slavers, the more determined he is to become rich while disrupting the slave trade, and he may need the help of his old mischievous buddies. (406 pages)

Where it's reviewed:
Science Fiction Chronicle, August 2001, page 45
Voice of Youth Advocates, August 2001, page 210

Other books by the same author:
Firemask, 2000
The Empire Stone, 2000
The Last Legion, 1999

Other books you might like:
Robin Hobb, *Ship of Magic*, 1998
   A pirate acquires a live ship, and flatters her into making him more successful than ever.
Kerry Newcomb, *Mad Morgan*, 2000
   Harry escapes from slavery and takes over a slave ship, turning it into the tool of his revenge.
Martha Wells, *The Death of the Necromancer*, 1998
   A nobleman turned thief and his gang are endangered by a rogue necromancer.

117

EVE BUNTING
WILLIAM LOW, Illustrator

The Days of Summer
(San Diego: Harcourt, Inc., 2001)

Subject(s): Grandparents; Sisters; Divorce
Age range(s): Grades K-3
Major character(s): Nora, Sister (older), 4th Grader; Jo-Jo, 5-Year-Old, Sister; Mom, Mother, Daughter (of divorcing parents)
Time period(s): 2000s (2001)
Locale(s): United States

Summary: During the last week of summer vacation Nora and Jo-Jo get the news that Mom's parents are divorcing. Nora feels sad and tries to console Jo-Jo who simply thinks her grandparents are too old to get divorced and if she pays them all her savings maybe they'll change their minds. Both try to be brave around Mom because she's having a hard time with the news too. The family's traditional Sunday dinner at their grandparent's home without their grandfather makes the reality of the situation obvious. The visit also gives Nora insight into how life will continue, though in a different way, now that she and Jo-Jo will visit their grandparents in separate places. (32 pages)

Where it's reviewed:
Booklist, April 1, 2001, page 1476
Horn Book Guide, Fall 2001, page 250
Publishers Weekly, February 5, 2001, page 88
School Library Journal, May 2001, page 112

Other books by the same author:
We Were There: A Nativity Story, 2001
Butterfly House, 1999 (Notable Social Studies Trade Books for Young People)
I Have an Olive Tree, 1999

Other books you might like:
Barbara Santucci, *Loon Summer*, 2001
   After her parent's divorce Rainie's summer at the family's lake cabin feels strange without her mom but together she and her dad create new memories.
Andrea Spalding, *Me and Mr. Mah*, 2000
   A summer friendship with his elderly neighbor Mr. Mah helps Ian adjust to his recent separation from his father and his prairie home.
Judith Vigna, *Grandma Without Me*, 1984
   A young boy maintains contact with his grandmother following his parent's divorce.

118
EVE BUNTING
PETER SYLVADA, Illustrator

Gleam and Glow
(San Diego: Harcourt, Inc., 2001)

Subject(s): War; Survival; Family
Age range(s): Grades 2-4
Major character(s): Viktor, 8-Year-Old, Brother (older); Marina, 5-Year-Old, Sister; Papa, Father, Resistance Fighter; Mama, Mother, Refugee
Time period(s): Indeterminate Past
Locale(s): Fictional Country

Summary: No one wants Papa to join the underground Liberation Army but he does. Still, the fighting draws nearer and nearer their home. Refugees pass by every day with horrible stories. One man carries a bowl with two golden fish that he leaves with Viktor and Marina. The gleaming fish, two beacons of light glowing in a harsh land, fascinate the children. Finally, Mama leads Viktor and Marina away with only a few possessions for their long walk to a refugee camp. Viktor puts the fish in the pond before they depart hoping they will have a few more days of life. Many months later, after Papa finds them, after it is safe to leave the refuge camp, the family returns to their ruined home and, in the pond, they find a multitude of gleaming, glowing fish giving them hope for their future. A concluding author's note gives the true story that inspired this fictional account of war's impact. (32 pages)

Where it's reviewed:
Booklist, December 15, 2001, page 738
Bulletin of the Center for Children's Books, December 2001, page 133
Kirkus Reviews, August 1, 2001, page 1118
Publishers Weekly, August 20, 2001, page 80
School Library Journal, September 2001, page 184

Other books by the same author:
Dreaming of America: An Ellis Island Story, 2000
A Picnic in October, 1999 (Notable Social Studies Trade Books for Young People)
I Have an Olive Tree, 1999
Smoky Night, 1994 (Caldecott Medal)

Other books you might like:
Jane Cutler, *The Cello of Mr. O.*, 1999
   Undeterred by mortar barrages, Mr. O. defiantly plays his cello daily in his war-ravaged city's open square.

Luis Garay, *The Long Road*, 1997
   Political unrest threatens Jose and his mother forcing them to seek refuge in another country.
Geraldine McCaughrean, *The Cherry Tree*, 1991
   War destroys their village and kills their father but hope survives in a cherry tree seedling nurtured by two children.

119
EVE BUNTING
CHRIS SOENTPIET, Illustrator

Jin Woo
(New York: Clarion Books, 2001)

Subject(s): Adoption; Brothers; Korean Americans
Age range(s): Grades K-3
Major character(s): David, Child, Adoptee; Jin Woo, Baby, Adoptee
Time period(s): 2000s (2001)
Locale(s): United States

Summary: David wonders if his parents were as excited when he first entered their lives as they are now. Although he agreed to the plan to adopt a baby, David's no longer sure that he shares their excitement about the arrival of a baby from Korea. Early in the morning he accompanies his parents to the airport where they wait for the plane carrying Jin Woo. Holding Jin Woo and playing with him helps to alleviate David's apprehension about the inevitable changes when a sibling expands a family. (32 pages)

Where it's reviewed:
Booklist, March 15, 2001, page 1402
Horn Book Guide, Fall 2001, page 289
Kirkus Reviews, March 15, 2001, page 405
Publishers Weekly, April 9, 2001, page 74
School Library Journal, May 2001, page 112

Other books by the same author:
The Days of Summer, 2000
Butterfly House, 1999
So Far from the Sea, 1998
Smoky Night, 1994 (Caldecott Medal)

Other books you might like:
Jamie Lee Curtis, *Tell Me Again about the Night I Was Born*, 1996
   A little girl knows the facts of her adoption so well that she can fill in all the details of the story herself.
Jan M. Czech, *An American Face*, 2000
   Adopted Korean American Jesse expects his face to change into an "American" one when he becomes a naturalized citizen.
Allen Say, *Allison*, 1997
   Allison, wondering why she looks more like her doll than her parents, tries to understand the story of her adoption from another country.

120

EVE BUNTING
LEUYEN PHAM, Illustrator

Little Badger, Terror of the Seven Seas
(San Diego: Harcourt, Inc., 2001)

Subject(s): Pirates; Imagination; Animals/Badgers
Age range(s): Grades K-1
Major character(s): Little Badger, Badger, Pirate; Old Badger, Badger
Time period(s): Indeterminate
Locale(s): Fictional Country

Summary: Old Badger has told Little Badger that he can use his imagination to be anything he wants to be as long as he comes home in time for supper so Little Badger imagines that he is a pirate and no comments from the woodland animals can convince him otherwise. Each animal's critical comment explaining why Little Badger cannot possibly be a pirate gives fuel to Little Badger's imagination. By the time he reaches the bluebell-filled meadow on which his ''ship'' floats, he's imagined a parrot, an eye patch and a striped jersey to make his fantasy complete. (32 pages)

Where it's reviewed:
Booklist, June 2001, page 1888
Children's Bookwatch, April 2001, page 4
Horn Book Guide, Fall 2001, page 250
Publishers Weekly, May 14, 2001, page 84
School Library Journal, May 2001, page 112

Other books by the same author:
Can You Do This, Old Badger?, 2000
Ducky, 1997
Secret Place, 1996

Other books you might like:
Florence McNeil, *Sail Away*, 2000
    A young boy in pirate dress assisted by his animal ''crew'' imagines a sailing trip aboard a pirate ship.
David McPhail, *Edward and the Pirates*, 1997
    When Edward reads the stories come alive for him so vividly that he's kidnapped by the pirates in his book and must be saved by other literary heroes.
Kathy Tucker, *Do Pirates Take Baths?*, 1994
    A story in rhyme provides details of the daily life of pirates.

121

EVE BUNTING
DAVID FRAMPTON, Illustrator

Riding the Tiger
(New York: Clarion Books, 2001)

Subject(s): Animals/Tigers; Courage; Allegories
Age range(s): Grades 2-4
Major character(s): Danny, 10-Year-Old
Time period(s): 2000s (2001)
Locale(s): United States

Summary: To a kid new to an inner city neighborhood the opportunity to ride on a tiger is just as alluring as the intrigue of a gang would be. Lonely Danny's desire to belong and fit in to his new surroundings leads him to accept the tiger's invitation to tour the neighborhood. Soon, as Danny sees others' reactions to the tiger he begins to question his decision, but the tiger, growing larger with each step, won't let him dismount. Finally, the tiger causes a homeless man to hurt himself as he hurries to get away from the beast and Danny leaps to the ground to assist the man, turning his back on the tiger. The tiger vanishes. (32 pages)

Where it's reviewed:
Booklist, March 1, 2001, page 1276
Bulletin of the Center for Children's Books, June 2001, page 368
Horn Book Guide, Fall 2001, page 250
Publishers Weekly, January 29, 2001, page 89
School Library Journal, March 2001, page 194

Other books by the same author:
Dreaming of America: An Ellis Island Story, 2000 (IRA Teachers' Choice)
Your Move, 1998
Smoky Night, 1994 (Caldecott Medal)

Other books you might like:
Alice Mead, *Junebug*, 1995
    As his tenth birthday approaches, Junebug tries to avoid recruitment by a gang.
Luis J. Rodriguez, *It Doesn't Have to Be This Way: A Barrio Story*, 1999
    A bilingual picture book chronicles a young boy's reluctant involvement with a gang and the tragic events that ensue.
Jerry Spinelli, *The Bathwater Gang*, 1990
    Bertie's grandmother intervenes when Bertie's all-girl gang becomes involved in a dispute with an all-boy gang.

122

EVE BUNTING

The Summer of Riley
(New York: HarperCollins/Joanna Cotler Books, 2001)

Subject(s): Animals/Dogs; Divorce; Grief
Age range(s): Grades 4-6
Major character(s): William Halston, 11-Year-Old; Grace, Friend; ''Peachie'' Peachwood, Animal Lover (horses); Riley, Dog
Time period(s): 2000s
Locale(s): Monk's Hill, Oregon

Summary: Life for William has been going steadily downhill, from his parents' divorce, then his father's engagement and finally his beloved grandfather's death, so having his own dog is very special. Adopting Riley from the pound helps William with his grieving as the two play together, talk to one another and even skateboard as a team. Riley, who's part Lab and part collie, is always well behaved and obedient so William can't believe it when they visit his neighbor Peachie and Riley chases her horse. The first time Riley's forgiven, but the second time Peachie notifies animal control, Riley is picked up and, according to state law because he's chased a farm animal, he's to be destroyed. William is heartbroken, but doesn't think his dog should be destroyed so he and his friend Grace mount a campaign to save Riley, sending e-mails and letters, mounting posters and notifying the media about Riley's predicament and extolling his other virtues. Riley is saved, but he won't remain as William's dog; instead he'll be trained to keep private airport runways clear of geese. (170 pages)

Where it's reviewed:
Booklist, July 2001, page 2005
Publishers Weekly, May 21, 2001, page 108
School Library Journal, June 2001, page 143

Other books by the same author:
Blackwater, 1999
SOS Titanic, 1996
Jumping the Nail, 1991
Such Nice Kids, 1990
A Sudden Silence, 1988

Other books you might like:
James Duffy, *Cleaver of the Good Luck Diner*, 1989
   When Sarah's dad leaves his family, he gives them a large Bernese mountain dog named Cleaver who injects laughter into their lives.
Lynn Hall, *Windsong*, 1992
   Marty saves a runt-of-the-litter greyhound, but then has to find a home for Windsong when her brother's allergies react to him.
Bill Wallace, *Coyote Autumn*, 2000
   Brad endangers his own life to save a coyote he's raised from a pup, but realizes it's time to take him to a wildlife refuge.

123

MELVIN BURGESS

Bloodtide
(New York: Tor, 2001)

Subject(s): Utopia/Dystopia; Gangs; Brothers and Sisters
Age range(s): Grades 10-Adult
Major character(s): Signy Volson, Sister, Gang Member; Siggy Volson, Brother, Gang Member; Conor, Gang Member
Time period(s): Indeterminate Future
Locale(s): London, England

Summary: In a violent dystopian future, London is ruled by rival gangs. Surrounding the city is a no-man's land populated by halfmen, creatures made by combining men and animals. The gang members believe a scientific civilization survives beyond this danger zone, but no one has seen it. The Volson clan, controllers of inner London, are led by a man who dreams of uniting the gangs and breaking through the territory of halfmen. To ensure his dream, he arranges for his daughter Signy to marry Conor, leader of the rival gang. Signy's protests are useless against her father's vision and the two are wed amid fear and hope. At their wedding feast, a man who appears to be dead plants a mysterious dagger in the stonewall and invites the revelers to take it before disappearing. Siggy removes it, but Conor demands the knife as a wedding gift with the siblings quarrelling over Siggy's refusal. Signy re-

turns to Conor's territory planning to live happily ever after, but Conor secretly plans to use the Volson's visit to the couple to destroy Signy's entire family. Signy and Siggy will soon be allies, plotting their revenge against Conor, and they will find unexpected help among the halfmen. (370 pages)

Where it's reviewed:
Booklist, October 15, 2001, page 387
Books for Keeps, July 2001, page 25
Kirkus Reviews, August 15, 2001, page 1175
Library Journal, November 15, 2001, page 101
Publishers Weekly, September 24, 2001, page 73

Other books by the same author:
The Copper Treasure, 2000
Kite, 1997
Smack, 1996

Other books you might like:
Dave Duncan, *Sky of Swords*, 2000
   Malinda lives in a swords and sorcery world but, when forced into an arranged marriage, is caught in the middle when everything goes wrong.
William Gibson, *All Tomorrow's Parties*, 1999
   Reality is about to change, but you sure can't tell from the grimy squatter's world of the former Golden Gate Bridge that Chevette and Ryder call home.
Pat Murphy, *The City, Not Long After*, 1989
   After a devastating plague, the survivors huddle together and play in the remains of the cities.

ROBERT BURLEIGH
DAN YACCARINO, Illustrator

I Love Going Through This Book
(New York: Joanna Cotler/HarperCollins Publishers, 2001)

Subject(s): Books and Reading; Stories in Rhyme; Imagination
Age range(s): Grades K-2
Major character(s): Unnamed Character, Child, Narrator
Time period(s): Indeterminate
Locale(s): Fictional Country

Summary: A child proclaims his determination to make his way through a book, no matter how challenging each page may be. Some pages require tools such as ladders and others require inner fortitude. Whether the book is conquered at a slow, leisurely pace or a rapid slide right to the end, the process of going through the book is appealing and the completion of it is a source of pride. (36 pages)

Where it's reviewed:
Booklist, June 2001, page 1888
Bulletin of the Center for Children's Books, June 2001, page 369
Kirkus Reviews, May 1, 2001, page 655
Publishers Weekly, June 4, 2001, page 79
School Library Journal, June 2001, page 104

Awards the book has won:
IRA Children's Choices, 2002

Other books by the same author:
Messenger, Messenger, 2000 (Booklist Editors' Choice)
It's Funny Where Ben's Train Takes Him, 1999
Home Run: The Story of Babe Ruth, 1998

Other books you might like:
Jules Feiffer, *Meanwhile . . .* , 1997
Raymond can't seem to find a way out of the comic book he's reading.
Dr. Seuss, *I Can Read with My Eyes Shut!*, 1978
The many joys of reading are exuberantly explained by the notorious Cat in the Hat.
James Stevenson, *Don't Make Me Laugh*, 1999
Mr. Frimdimpny has strict rules for the proper way to proceed through the book he narrates; violators must return to the book's beginning.

125
ROBERT BURLEIGH
MAREK LOS, Illustrator

Lookin' for Bird in the Big City
(San Diego: Silver Whistle/Harcourt, Inc., 2001)

Subject(s): Music and Musicians; African Americans; City and Town Life
Age range(s): Grades 2-4
Major character(s): Miles Davis, Musician, Narrator; Charlie "Bird" Parker, Musician
Time period(s): 1940s
Locale(s): New York, New York

Summary: Teen-aged Miles Davis arrives in New York determined to find Bird. When he's not searching the city, asking anyone who might know where Bird could be, he's blowing his horn on the fire escape, from the middle of a bridge, or deep in a subway tunnel. As he plays, he incorporates the sounds of the city in his music. Finally he locates a club where Bird is playing. Trumpet in hand, Miles enters and Bird invites him to jam with the band. (32 pages)

Where it's reviewed:
Booklist, February 15, 2001, page 1152
Bulletin of the Center for Children's Books, July 2001, page 404
Kirkus Reviews, April 15, 2001, page 582
Publishers Weekly, May 14, 2001, page 82
School Library Journal, June 2001, page 104

Awards the book has won:
Bulletin of the Center for Children's Books Blue Ribbon, 2001

Other books by the same author:
Messenger, Messenger, 2000 (Booklist Editors' Choice)
Hercules, 1999
Hoops, 1997

Other books you might like:
Alice Faye Duncan, *Willie Jerome*, 1995
Only Willie's sister appreciates the bebop music he plays on his trumpet.
Rachel Isadora, *Ben's Trumpet*, 1991
In a Caldecott Honor book, Ben hears the jazz musicians at

the Zig Zag Club play and joins them on his imaginary trumpet.
Andrea Davis Pinkney, *Duke Ellington: The Piano Prince and His Orchestra*, 1998
An award-winning picture book tells of the early life and eventual success of a renowned musician, pianist and composer of swing music.
Chris Raschka, *Charlie Parker Played Be Bop*, 1992
A picture book biography tells of the life of a famous jazz saxophonist.
Alan Schroeder, *Satchmo's Blues*, 1996
A fictionalized biography of Louis Armstrong's childhood in New Orleans depicts the influence of the city sounds on his desire to play the cornet.

126
JOHN BURNINGHAM, Author/Illustrator

Hushabye
(New York: Alfred A. Knopf, 2001)

Subject(s): Sleep; Bedtime; Stories in Rhyme
Age range(s): Preschool-Kindergarten
Time period(s): Indeterminate
Locale(s): Fictional Country

Summary: Tired creatures from fish to frogs to bears to kittens seek a place to spend the night. Even a baby and the man in the moon are ready to bring an end to their busy day by settling into slumber. Soon, all find safe havens and the drowsy creatures slip into sleep in the hushed silence of night as the title originally published in Great Britain in 2000 draws to a close. (32 pages)

Where it's reviewed:
Booklist, October 1, 2001, page 323
Bulletin of the Center for Children's Books, November 2001, page 95
Horn Book, November 2001, page 732
Riverbank Review, Winter 2001-2002, page 27
School Library Journal, December 2001, page 90

Awards the book has won:
Parenting's Reading Magic Awards, 2001

Other books by the same author:
Shopping Basket, 1999
Cloudland, 1996
Courtney, 1994 (IRA Children's Choice)

Other books you might like:
Kathi Appelt, *Cowboy Dreams*, 1999
Night is falling as cowpokes settle in at the end of a long, tiring day, ready for cowboy dreams.
Margaret Wise Brown, *Little Donkey Close Your Eyes*, 1995
Animals throughout the world are bid good night in this gentle poem.
Carole Lexa Schaefer, *Down in the Woods at Sleepytime*, 2000
Various animal mothers try to encourage their babies to settle down for "sleepytime."

127

KHEPHRA BURNS
LEO DILLON, Illustrator
DIANE DILLON, Illustrator

Mansa Musa: The Lion of Mali
(San Diego: Gulliver/Harcourt, Inc., 2001)

Subject(s): Historical; Kidnapping; Deserts
Age range(s): Grades 4-6
Major character(s): Kankan Musa, Kidnap Victim, Royalty; Tariq al-Aya, Rescuer, Traveler; Abubakari Musa, Brother, Royalty
Time period(s): 14th century
Locale(s): Kaba Kangaba, Mali; Africa

Summary: Tariq rescues fourteen-year-old Kankan by purchasing him from the slave traders who kidnap him from his village. For the next seven years the two travel the deserts of northern Africa as Tariq teaches Kankan survival skills and shows him how to find the path to inner knowledge. With Tariq, Kankan visits Egypt and learns much about the world beyond his small village. When he returns alone to Niani, the capital of Mali, he learns that Abubakari now reigns as mansa or king, a position that Kankan later holds. An introduction begins the fictionalized account on Kankan's life and a concluding author's note and bibliography add to the factual basis for the tale. (56 pages)

Where it's reviewed:
Booklist, December 1, 2001, page 642
Bulletin of the Center for Children's Books, December 2001, page 134
Horn Book, November 2001, page 733
Publishers Weekly, October 22, 2001, page 74
School Library Journal, October 2001, page 106

Awards the book has won:
Notable Social Studies Trade Books for Young People, 2002

Other books by the same author:
Black Stars in Orbit: NASA's African-American Astronauts, 1995

Other books you might like:
Philip Koslow, *Mali: Crossroads of Africa*, 1995
    A title in the nonfiction "Kingdoms of Africa" series gives a history of the nation.
Kim Naylor, *Mali*, 1987
    This book covers the geography, history, culture, economy and people of this land-locked nation.
David Wisniewski, *Sundiata: Lion King of Mali*, 1992
    A picture book biography describes the life of the most famous ruler of Mali.

128

GUY BURT

The Hole
(New York: Ballantine, 2001)

Subject(s): Suspense; Friendship; Schools/Boarding Schools
Age range(s): Grades 10-Adult

Major character(s): Martyn, Student—Boarding School (practical joker); Unnamed Character, Narrator
Time period(s): 1990s
Locale(s): England

Summary: Every school has a prankster and at this unnamed boarding school, Martyn is the most notorious prankster of all. Beguiling and compelling, he talks five of his classmates into climbing down a rope ladder into the basement of an unused building on their campus. While the school thinks they're at home, and their parents think they're on a field trip, they'll remain underground for three days when Martyn will return and release them in what will be the prank that goes down in school lore. For the first three days the five talk, relax and laugh about this scheme but as the appointed hour comes and goes, they realize Martyn isn't coming back in this first novel written when the author was eighteen-years-old. (152 pages)

Where it's reviewed:
Booklist, July 2001, page 1977
Kirkus Reviews, July 15, 2001, page 959
Library Journal, August 2001, page 158
Publishers Weekly, August 27, 2991, page 48

Other books you might like:
David Almond, *Kit's Wilderness*, 2000
    If the spin of the knife chooses you in the game of "Death," you are left behind to "die" in an underground den while your friends wait for you outside.
Phillip Finch, *In a Place Dark and Secret*, 1985
    Deranged Joseph Sherk thinks Annapolis teen Sarah Stannard is his deceased daughter; to keep her "safe," he hides her in a church attic.
John Fowles, *The Collector*, 1963
    A demented man kidnaps the young girl with whom he is obsessed.
William Golding, *Lord of the Flies*, 1955
    When schoolboys are shipwrecked, they attempt to set up their own civilization, but cruelty emerges with tragic results.
Patrick Redmond, *Something Dangerous*, 1999
    Two boys use a Ouija board for evil doings at their boarding school.

129

KRISTIN BUTCHER

The Gramma War
(Custer, WA: Orca Book Publishers, 2001)

Subject(s): Grandmothers; Family Problems; Genealogy
Age range(s): Grades 5-8
Major character(s): Ann Elizabeth "Annie" Granville, 12-Year-Old; Joel Werner, 12-Year-Old; Mr. Brockhurst, Teacher (substitute); Claire Granville, Sister (of Annie); Fiona "Gramma" Granville, Grandmother
Time period(s): 2000s
Locale(s): Canada

Summary: Oh no! How can Annie's orderly life become so disorderly? Though she understands that her grandmother needs to live with them, why does she have to give up her room and move in with her messy sister Claire? And why does Gramma sit around all day and smoke and make Annie's mother wait on her? And why does Annie have to take her gerbils to her friend Joel's house? With her home life in disarray, Annie hopes that school will provide the structure she enjoys, but her teacher's sick and there's a substitute. Worst of all is the news that though she's finally old enough to join the reenactment group, it's folded because of a lack of members. Her substitute teacher turns out to be pretty perceptive and, sensing Annie's unhappiness, suggests she join a genealogical group. Annie and Joel attend the genealogy meetings together and her interest in family history soars. Finding reasons to talk to Gramma about their family, Annie discovers that Gramma isn't quite as bad as she first thought in this work by a Canadian author. (168 pages)

Where it's reviewed:
Booklist, October 1, 2001, page 318
Books in Canada, July 2001, page 31
Quill & Quire, June 2001, page 50
Resource Links, June 2001, page 8
School Library Journal, September 2001, page 223

Other books by the same author:
The Runaways, 2002
The Tomorrow Tunnel, 1999

Other books you might like:
Mary Downing Hahn, *Following My Own Footsteps*, 1996
    An unwanted stay with his grandmother is so pleasant for Gordy that when his father wants to move the family to California, Gordy doesn't want to leave.
Kristi D. Holl, *No Strings Attached*, 1988
    June and her mother live with old, cranky Mr. Cooper in a housing arrangement beneficial for all of them.
Norma Klein, *Going Backwards*, 1986
    Charlie's entire family has difficulty coping when his grandmother, who has Alzheimer's, moves in with them.
Cheryl Ware, *Catty-Cornered*, 1998
    Venola Mae stays with her grandmother in her trailer and adjusts to the thirteen cats, a 7:30 p.m. bedtime and a television regime confined to religious programs.

130

JANIE BYNUM, Author/Illustrator

Altoona Up North
(San Diego: Harcourt, Inc., 2001)

Subject(s): Aunts and Uncles; Animals/Baboons; Stories in Rhyme
Age range(s): Grades K-3
Major character(s): Altoona Baboona, Baboon, Niece; Auntie, Baboon, Aunt
Time period(s): Indeterminate
Locale(s): Saskatoon-a, Canada; Laguna Beach, California
Summary: A letter from Auntie invites Altoona and her friends to journey north for a visit. Using a hot-air balloon Altoona with a raccoon and a loon for companions travels to Auntie's cozy home. After a few days of outdoor recreation in the snow Auntie recommends a ski resort only half a day away, in a southerly direction. From that point all Auntie's suggestions move the group away from the cold, frozen north until they return to Laguna Beach. Auntie moves into the beach cottage with Altoona and her friends so now Auntie's never cold or lonely. (34 pages)

Where it's reviewed:
Horn Book Guide, Spring 2002, page 13
Publishers Weekly, October 8, 2001, page 66
School Library Journal, October 2001, page 106

Other books by the same author:
Otis, 2000
Altoona Baboona, 1999

Other books you might like:
Jim Aylesworth, *My Sister's Rusty Bike*, 1996
    Big brother tours America on his sister's rusty bike and meets a host of characters that he quickly comes to like.
Helen Lester, *Tacky in Trouble*, 1998
    Tacky has an unexpected trip when the wind catches the penguin's flowered shirt and he sails away to a rocky island.
H.A. Rey, *Whiteblack the Penguin Sees the World*, 2000
    Whiteblack's trip to gather new material for his radio show does not go as he plans but he makes the most of every unexpected happening.

C

MEG CABOT

Princess in the Spotlight
(New York: HarperCollins, 2001)

Series: Princess Diaries. Volume II
Subject(s): Princes and Princesses; Diaries; Humor
Age range(s): Grades 7-10
Major character(s): Amelia ''Mia'' Renaldo, 14-Year-Old, Royalty (princess); Grandmere, Grandmother; Mr. Gianini, Teacher (algebra); Lilly Moscovitz, 9th Grader
Time period(s): 2000s
Locale(s): New York, New York

Summary: Mia is barely over her shock of discovering that she's a princess, and heir to the throne of the small European country of Genovia, when her mother tells her she's pregnant by Mia's algebra teacher. Determined to keep it a secret, Mia accidentally spills the news of her mother's upcoming wedding on national television; when Grandmere hears the news, she decides to turn the event into a formal state wedding. One hilarious episode after another follows with Martha Stewart making Mia's Halloween costume, Mia's cousin visiting her feminist friend Lilly and Mia's mother and algebra teacher eloping in this sequel to *The Princess Diaries*. (223 pages)

Where it's reviewed:
Booklist, September 1, 2001, page 96
Bulletin of the Center for Children's Books, September 2001, page 7
Kliatt, July 2001, page 8
School Library Journal, August 2001, page 176
Voice of Youth Advocates, October 2001, page 272

Awards the book has won:
ALA Quick Picks for Reluctant Young Adult Readers, 2002

Other books by the same author:
Princess in Love, 2002 (Princess Diaries, Volume III)
The Princess Diaries, 2000 (Princess Diaries, Volume I)

Other books you might like:
Mary Jane Auch, *Mom Is Dating Weird Wayne*, 1988
   Jenna is horrified that her mother is dating that weird weatherman who always dresses in costume on his television program.
Ellen Conford, *A Royal Pain*, 1986
   Abby discovers she's been brought up by the wrong parents for she's really a princess from Saxony Coburn.
Anne Fine, *My War with Goggle-Eyes*, 1989
   Kitty brings out all her artillery in an attempt to get rid of this Gerald Faulkner her mother is dating.
Francess Lantz, *A Royal Kiss*, 2000
   A chance meeting with Prince Sebastian while shopping in a vintage clothing store leads to a fairy-tale romance for Samantha.

132

MICHAEL CADNUM

Raven of the Waves
(New York: Scholastic/Orchard, 2001)

Subject(s): Vikings; Historical
Age range(s): Grades 9-12
Major character(s): Lidsmod, 17-Year-Old; Wiglaf, 13-Year-Old
Time period(s): 8th century (794)
Locale(s): Spjothof, Norway; Northumberland, England

Summary: Raised in Norse tradition to be a warrior, Lidsmod is proud to sail aboard the newly built ship *Raven* as its crew prepares to raid a wealthy abbey in England. Living in the abbey is Wiglaf, a young boy with a withered arm, who's being trained by the monks to be a healer. In the fierce battle that ensues when the Norsemen storm the abbey, Wiglaf is determined to live and is one of the few who fights back. He's saved by the raiders who feel his withered arm is a good omen from Odin. Back aboard the *Raven*, Wiglaf's healing skills are in demand as he works to save the same men who just killed his family and teachers. Impressed with his courage and valor, Lidsmod feels that Wiglaf should be freed, in accordance with custom, though opposition rises from a greedy warrior who has other plans for him. Lidsmod helps Wiglaf escape and then stands ready to accept his companions' wrath. (200 pages)

Where it's reviewed:
Horn Book, September 2001, page 582
Kliatt, May 2001, page 9
Publishers Weekly, June 25, 2001, page 74
School Library Journal, July 2001, page 102
Voice of Youth Advocates, August 2001, page 197

Awards the book has won:
Smithsonian's Notable Books for Children, 2001

Other books by the same author:
Forbidden Forest: The Story of Little John and Robin Hood: A Novel, 2002
The Book of the Lion, 2000
In a Dark Wood, 1998

Other books you might like:
Henrietta Branford, *The Fated Sky*, 1999
　　Though Ran is scheduled to be sacrificed to Odin, she is rescued by the blind harper Toki and taken to Iceland where the two fall in love and raise several children.
Eloise McGraw, *The Striped Ships*, 1991
　　Young Jilly tells the story of the Norman invasion of Saxon England through her work on the famed Bayeux Tapestry.
Rosemary Sutcliff, *Sword Song*, 1998
　　Exiled from his village for killing a man, Bjarni offers his services as a mercenary to various Viking leaders before choosing a wife and settling down.

133

V.M. CALDWELL
ERICA MAGNUS, Illustrator

Tides
(Minneapolis, MN: Milkweed Editions, 2001)

Subject(s): Family Life; Adoption
Age range(s): Grades 5-7
Major character(s): Elizabeth "Turtle" Sheridan, 12-Year-Old, Adoptee; Martha "Grandma" Sheridan, Grandmother; Adam Sheridan, Cousin
Time period(s): 2000s
Locale(s): United States

Summary: It's summertime again and Elizabeth, now fully adopted into the Sheridan family, is back at her grandmother's house with her two siblings and six cousins, which makes for a noisy, active gathering. Last summer Grandma's clear rules and fairly meted out reprimands provided Elizabeth with structure, but this summer Grandma is helpless in dealing with Adam who's grieving over two friends killed in drunk driving accidents. As Adam continues to distance himself from everyone, Elizabeth's upset to realize that Grandma can't solve every problem. She also finds that though she's learned to swim, she still fears the ocean, and so turns her attention to helping with an environmental project about ocean pollution. Concern about Adam bothers Elizabeth until the family is reunited at Grandma's for Christmas and Adam

pays a surprise visit in this sequel to *The Ocean Within*. (311 pages)

Where it's reviewed:
Booklist, April 15, 2001, page 1549
Bulletin of the Center for Children's Books, July 2001, page 405
Publishers Weekly, April 9, 2001, page 77
School Library Journal, August 2001, page 177
Voice of Youth Advocates, August 2001, page 198

Other books by the same author:
The Ocean Within, 1999

Other books you might like:
Joan Bauer, *Backwater*, 1999
　　Ivy's proud to belong to the Breedlove family, whose roots go back to the 1600s, and tracks down eccentric Aunt Josephine for a family history project.
Madeleine L'Engle, *Meet the Austins*, 1960
　　Orphaned Maggy comes to live with the Austins and, at first, upsets the whole family structure.
Richard Peck, *A Long Way from Chicago*, 1998
　　Joey and his sister Mary Alice hear many warm, funny stories and learn unusual lessons during the summers they spend with their grandmother.

134

STEPHANIE CALMENSON
DENISE BRUNKUS, Illustrator

The Frog Principal
(New York: Scholastic Press, 2001)

Subject(s): Schools; Magicians; Animals/Frogs and Toads
Age range(s): Grades K-3
Major character(s): Mr. Bundy, Principal, Frog; Marty Q. Marvel, Magician
Time period(s): 2000s (2001)
Locale(s): United States

Summary: In the process of interviewing Marty Q. Marvel for a possible assembly program, Mr. Bundy becomes the victim of one of the bungling magician's tricks and is changed into a frog. After seeking relief for his dry skin in a pond near the school Mr. Bundy retrieves a ball for some students who promise to allow him to be the school principal. Mr. Bundy enjoys returning to his role as principal but he'd prefer not to be the frog principal. One day his wish unexpectedly comes true and Mr. Bundy is back to normal, almost. (32 pages)

Where it's reviewed:
Booklist, September 15, 2001, page 230
Horn Book Guide, Spring 2002, page 37
Kirkus Reviews, June 15, 2001, page 861
School Library Journal, October 2001, page 106

Other books by the same author:
Hotter than a Hot Dog!, 1994
Zip, Whiz, Zoom!, 1992
The Principal's New Clothes, 1989

Other books you might like:
Linda Ashman, *Maxwell's Magic Mix-Up*, 2001
　　Maxwell's bungled magic tricks transform the birthday

girl into a rock, her dad into a broom and her guests into animals.

Alix Berenzy, *The Frog Prince*, 1989

The enchanted frog is the narrator in a retelling of the traditional folktale from the amphibian's point of view.

Jackie Mims Hopkins, *The Horned Toad Prince*, 2000

In a retelling set in the Southwest a spell traps a prince in the form of a bilingual horned toad.

Jon Scieszka, *The Frog Prince Continued*, 1991

An award-winning tale takes a satirical and rather different view of the fate of the frog transformed into a prince by the kiss of a princess.

135

KATHLEEN CAMBOR

In Sunlight, in a Beautiful Garden
(New York: Farrar Straus Giroux, 2001)

Subject(s): Floods; Social Classes; Disasters
Age range(s): Grades 10-Adult
Major character(s): Andrew Carnegie, Historical Figure, Industrialist; Andrew Mellon, Historical Figure, Financier; Frank Fallon, Foreman (steel mill); Grace McIntyre, Librarian; James Talbot, Lawyer
Time period(s): 1890s (1899)
Locale(s): Johnstown, Pennsylvania

Summary: Located above the valley and held in place by the South Fork Dam, a lake above Johnstown becomes the mainstay of the South Fork Fishing and Hunting Club and is off limits to any but its wealthy members. Below the dam lies the valley with its scattered towns and villages and blue-collar workers, some of whom mingle with the club members like Andrew Carnegie and Andrew Mellon, but only in a servant's role. Other people are far removed from the wealthy, like Frank Fallon who works in the steel mills, or the mysterious Grace McIntyre who's the librarian in Johnstown. And though James Talbot, the lawyer for the Club, continues to push for repairs to the dam, the members aren't concerned about its safety, just the number of fish in the lake. After heavy rains over Memorial Day weekend, the lives of those different social classes intertwine when the dam bursts and the historic Johnstown flood occurs, killing over 2000 people and destroying lives beyond that number. (258 pages)

Where it's reviewed:
Booklist, November 15, 2000, page 608
Los Angeles Times Book Review, February 18, 2001, page 11
New York Times Book Review, January 14, 2001, page 10
Publishers Weekly, October 16, 2000, page 46
School Library Journal, July 2001, page 135

Other books by the same author:
The Book of Mercy, 1997

Other books you might like:
Tracy Chevalier, *Falling Angels*, 2001

Though from different social classes, the daughters of the Coleman and Waterhouse's meet over adjoining cemetery plots and secretly play together.

Isabel Colegate, *The Shooting Party*, 1981

Gathering together people for the sole pleasure of shooting

is a custom of the Edwardian era, though in 1913 it may be a fading custom.

David McCullough, *The Johnstown Flood*, 1968

This true account of the historic disaster, based on records, diaries and letters, provides both the human and the engineering side of events leading to the flood.

136

KATE CANN

Love Trilogy
(New York: HarperCollins, 2001)

Subject(s): Love; Coming-of-Age
Age range(s): Grades 9-12
Major character(s): Colette "Coll", 16-Year-Old; Arthur "Art", 17-Year-Old
Time period(s): 1990s
Locale(s): England

Summary: Colette has noticed Art at the swimming pool where she swims his laps; when she finally meets him, she realizes he's everything, and more, than she thought possible. Not only is he attractive, but he's also interested in going out with her. Falling in love with one another, Colette is hesitant when Art puts pressure on her for sex and they break up. Over the course of the trilogy, they get back together, have sex, and break up again until by the final volume, they have agreed to go their separate ways with Colette spending her eighteenth year in Canada. Though no longer together, Colette is happy that at least now she understands what it's like to really love someone, even if you lose him/her, in this British import.

Where it's reviewed:
Kliatt, July 2001, page 8
Publishers Weekly, July 16, 2001, page 1828
School Library Journal, August 2001, page 177
Voice of Youth Advocates, October 2001, page 272

Other books by the same author:
Grecian Holiday: Or, How I Turned Down the Best Possible Thing Only to Have the Time of My Life, 2002
Caught in the Act, 1997
Diving In, 1997
Too Hot to Handle, 1997

Other books you might like:
Jonah Black, *The Black Book (Diary of a Teenage Stud) Series*, 2000-

Jonah records his thoughts, including his fantasies about the girl of his dreams and the girl he has always loved, in his 'little black book.'

Louise Rennison, *Angus, Thongs and Full-Frontal Snogging: Confessions of Georgia Nicolson*, 2000

In her diary, Georgia records her interest in kissing, her appearance and her opposition to most of what the adult world thinks is important.

Ellen Wittlinger, *Razzle*, 2001

Kenyon almost gives up tall, independent Razzle for a self-centered sexpot who throws him aside when he can't help her with a modeling career.

Rona S. Zable, *Love at the Laundromat*, 1986

Joanne finds love at her mother's laundromat, but not

without hilarious miscommunications about the contents of a laundry basket.

ALYSSA SATIN CAPUCILLI
JOAN RANKIN, Illustrator

Mrs. McTats and Her Houseful of Cats
(New York: Margaret K. McElderry Books, 2001)

Subject(s): Animals/Cats; Pets; Stories in Rhyme
Age range(s): Grades K-3
Major character(s): Mrs. McTats, Animal Lover; Abner, Cat; Zoom, Dog
Time period(s): 2000s
Locale(s): United States

Summary: Mrs. McTats is content with one cat, but when others arrive in ever-increasing numbers, Abner is soon one of many pets that Mrs. McTats kindly adopts. As each cat strolls into the house Mrs. McTats names it until all are identified in alphabetical order from A to Y. Just as twenty-five cats prepare to dine, Mrs. McTats hears another scratch at the door and the twenty-five cats make room for Zoom. (32 pages)

Where it's reviewed:
Booklist, September 1, 2001, page 113
Horn Book Guide, Fall 2001, page 251
The New Advocate, Winter 2002, page 74
Publishers Weekly, May 28, 2001, page 87
School Library Journal, August 2001, page 144

Other books by the same author:
Inside a Zoo in the City: A Rebus Read-Along Story, 2000
Happy Birthday, Biscuit!, 1999
Inside a House that Is Haunted: A Rebus Read-Along Story, 1998

Other books you might like:
Judy Hindley, *Mrs. Mary Malarky's Seven Cats*, 1990
    Each one of Mrs. Malarky's cats has its own special story to tell.
Holly Keller, *A Bed Full of Cats*, 1999
    Lee is worried when he can't find his cat Flora, but when she returns she brings her kittens giving Lee a bed full of cats for company.
John Stadler, *The Cats of Mrs. Calamari*, 1997
    A new cat-hating manager takes over Mrs. Calamari's apartment building, forcing her to devise ingenious ways to hide her many cats.

138
ELISA CARBONE

Storm Warriors
(New York: Knopf, 2001)

Subject(s): African Americans; Fathers and Sons; Lifesaving
Age range(s): Grades 5-8
Major character(s): Ulysses Williams, Grandfather, Fisherman; Nathan Williams, 12-Year-Old; George Williams, Father, Fisherman
Time period(s): 1890s

Locale(s): Pea Island, North Carolina

Summary: After Nathan's mother dies, he, his father and grandfather move to Pea Island off the Outer Banks of North Carolina. As fishermen, the three sometimes have a chance to assist the Pea Island surfmen, a group of seven African American men who make up one of the bases for the United States Life-Saving Service. Nathan's grandfather informs him of the racism these men encounter, especially since many of them were once slaves for the white men who form the Oregon Inlet surfmen. Nathan, however, is enthralled with the rescue work and studies and memorizes all he can about their tasks, until the day arrives when the rescue work is so dangerous that he's overwhelmed. His desire to help is strong, however, and he decides that he can better assist his community by studying medicine in this work based on historical fact. (168 pages)

Where it's reviewed:
Booklist, January 2001, page 957
Horn Book, May 2001, page 318
Publishers Weekly, December 18, 2000, page 78
School Library Journal, February 2001, page 117
Voice of Youth Advocates, October 2001, page 273

Awards the book has won:
ALA Notable Children's Books, 2002

Other books by the same author:
Sarah and the Naked Truth, 2000
Starting School with an Enemy, 1998
Stealing Freedom, 1998
My Dad's Definitely Not a Drunk, 1992

Other books you might like:
Donna Hill, *Shipwreck Season*, 1998
    Daniel looks down his nose at the uneducated "surfmen" until he serves time with them and recognizes their courage in rescuing people from shipwrecks.
Iain Lawrence, *The Wreckers*, 1998
    A young boy survives a shipwreck caused by Cornish townspeople who lure ships onto rocks in order to salvage the ship's cargo.
Jill Paton Walsh, *Grace*, 1992
    One night Grace and her lighthouse-keeper father row from their island to save the survivors of the wrecked ship *Forfarshine*.

139
ORSON SCOTT CARD

Shadow of the Hegemon
(New York: Tor, 2000)

Subject(s): Friendship; War; Political Thriller
Age range(s): Grades 9-Adult
Major character(s): Bean, Genius; Petra Arkanian, Genius; Achilles, Genius; Peter Wiggin, Genius, Political Figure
Time period(s): Indeterminate Future
Locale(s): Earth

Summary: In the aftermath of the Bugger War, the children from Battle School return to their civilian lives under the assumption that, despite their training and experience, they will be able to reintegrate into the lives they led before their youthful genius led to their military involvement. Of course the unscrupulous, both within governments and without, cannot bear to waste that potential talent. Soon kidnappings begin and it isn't long before a pattern emerges, as the targets are all members of Ender's immediate circle. Petra is one of the first victims, but she is also the first to conceive of a method of communicating from her captivity. Bean anticipates the attempt to gather him in, as does Peter Wiggin, Ender's manipulative brother. Reluctantly Bean joins forces with Peter as he concludes that the author of the kidnappings, and subsequent political unrest and military action around the globe, can only be Achilles, the sociopath who Bean caused to be expelled from Battle School. Bean is determined to rescue Petra, and Peter is determined to rule the world in this sequel to *Ender's Shadow*. (358 pages)

Where it's reviewed:
Booklist, November 1, 2000, page 490
Kirkus Reviews, November 15, 2000, page 1582
Library Journal, December 2000, page 196
Publishers Weekly, November 20, 2000, page 50
School Library Journal, June 2001, page 183

Awards the book has won:
ALA Best Books for Young Adults, 2002

Other books by the same author:
Ender's Shadow, 1999
Children of the Mind, 1996
Xenocide, 1991
Speaker for the Dead, 1986
Ender's Game, 1985

Other books you might like:
Tom Clancy, *The Bear and the Dragon*, 2000
    World politics turns confrontational as usual in this page-turner from Mr. Clancy.
Robert Heinlein, *Starship Troopers*, 1959
    Not content to manipulate affairs from behind the scenes, these heroes go to war.
Harry Turtledove, *Colonization: Down to Earth*, 2000
    The aliens have landed and conquered, but not all humans are content to be ruled.

140

MARGARET CARNEY
JANET WILSON, Illustrator

The Biggest Fish in the Lake

(Tonawanda, NY: Kids Can Press, 2001)

Subject(s): Grandfathers; Fishing
Age range(s): Grades 1-4
Major character(s): Grandpa, Grandfather, Fisherman; Unnamed Character, Daughter (granddaughter), Narrator
Time period(s): 2000s (2001)
Locale(s): North

Summary: When farm chores are completed Grandpa takes his granddaughter fishing. Depending on the season their tackle and target varies but Grandpa's experienced with catching all types of fish so he's a good teacher. Just as good, maybe better, than catching fish is the time for quiet conversation with Grandpa while waiting for a bite. A birthday gift of a rod and reel moves the little girl from a bamboo pole to one that can be cast thus opening up the possibility of bass fishing. After months and months of practice, Grandpa takes her out on the lake. Grandpa lands a big bass though his granddaughter's "biggest fish in the lake" gets away but she knows she'll have other days with Grandpa, fishing on the lake. (32 pages)

Where it's reviewed:
Booklist, July 2001, page 2018
Horn Book Guide, Fall 2001, page 251
Resource Links, June 2001, page 2
School Library Journal, July 2001, page 73

Other books by the same author:
Where Does the Tiger-Heron Spend the Night?, 2002
At Grandpa's Sugar Bush, 1998

Other books you might like:
William T. George, *Fishing at Long Pond*, 1991
    A fishing trip to Long Pond includes observation of the plants and animals that Katie and her grandfather see along the way.
Amy Hest, *Rosie's Fishing Trip*, 1994
    After a fishing trip with Grampa, Rosie learns that actually catching fish is not the most important reason for such excursions.
Jane B. Mason, *River Day*, 1994
    Alex and her grandfather spend a peaceful day canoeing on the river.
Elaine Moore, *Deep River*, 1994
    Jess feels privileged and a little anxious to be invited on her first fishing trip with Grandpa.

141

JAN CARR
DOROTHY DONOHUE, Illustrator

Splish, Splash, Spring

(New York: Holiday House, 2001)

Subject(s): Spring; Nature; Stories in Rhyme
Age range(s): Preschool
Time period(s): 2000s
Locale(s): United States

Summary: Three children and a dog romp about outside enjoying the sights and sounds of a spring day. They observe a nest of hungry baby robins and help to find earthworms for the parents to feed their offspring. Crocus and daffodils bloom as they attempt to fly a kite until a sudden rainstorm causes them to scurry inside. (32 pages)

Where it's reviewed:
Booklist, April 1, 2001, page 1477
Horn Book Guide, Fall 2001, page 228
Kirkus Reviews, March 1, 2001, page 327
School Library Journal, May 2001, page 112

Other books by the same author:
Swine Divine, 1999
Dark Day, Light Night, 1996 (Smithsonian's Notable Books for Children)
The Nature of the Beast, 1996

Other books you might like:
Reeve Lindbergh, *North Country Spring*, 1997
   Bear cubs tumble, frogs peep and geese fly as the natural world awakens to spring's call.
Lisa Westberg Peters, *Cold Little Duck, Duck, Duck*, 2000
   Arriving prematurely at the pond, a chilly little duck uses the power of positive thinking to envision the delights of spring.
Jung-Hee Spetter, *Lily and Trooper's Spring*, 1999
   Lily and her dog Trooper play outside on the first nice day of spring.

142

JENNY CARROLL (Pseudonym of Meggin Cabot)

When Lightning Strikes
(New York: Pocket Books, 2001)

Series: 1-800-Where-R-You?. Number 1
Subject(s): Psychic Powers; Missing Persons; School Life
Age range(s): Grades 7-12
Major character(s): Jessica Antonia Mastriani, Psychic, 16-Year-Old; Ruth, Twin, 16-Year-Old; Rob Wilkins, 12th Grader, Motorcyclist; Douglas "Dougie" Mastriani, Mentally Ill Person
Time period(s): 2000s
Locale(s): Indiana

Summary: It all starts the day Jessica decks a football player in defense of her friend Ruth who's teased about being fat. After serving her hour of detention, Jessica walks home with Ruth who's decided they need to exercise. Great idea, but a thunderstorm comes up and when they seek shelter under the bleachers, Jessica's hit by lightning. Not seriously injured, the next day she's mystified when she knows the location of two missing children who are pictured on a milk carton. Informing the authorities, Jessica's taken to a military base to assist with a government project to locate criminals. Jessica wants no part of this; all she wanted was to rescue the children. Her schizophrenic brother Dougie's upset because of the media attention and Rob, the guy for whom she pines, has to rescue her from the military base, but now she's a fugitive. How much worse can it get? (266 pages)

Where it's reviewed:
Booklist, May 15, 2001, page 1744
Kliatt, May 2001, page 23

Other books by the same author:
Safe House, 2002 (1-800-Where-R-You?, Number 3)
Code Name Cassandra, 2001 (1-800-Where-R-You?, Number 2)

Other books you might like:
Caroline B. Cooney, *The Face on the Milk Carton*, 1990
   Janie knows she's the face pictured on her milk carton, but why is her picture there and who is she really?
Lois Duncan, *The Third Eye*, 1984
   A teenager reluctantly finds herself using psychic powers to locate missing children.
Shelley Hrdlitschka, *Disconnected*, 1999
   Twins Tanner and Alex have the ability to communicate telepathically with one another, which helps Alex find and save Tanner when he runs into trouble.
Margaret Mahy, *Dangerous Spaces*, 1991
   Two cousins form a dangerous psychic connection that brings their shared dream world into reality.
Patricia Windsor, *The Hero*, 1988
   When forced to tell his parents of his psychic abilities, Dale is sent to a special school run by an unethical ESP researcher.

143

MICHAEL CART, Editor

Love and Sex: Ten Stories of Truth
(New York: Simon & Schuster, 2001)

Subject(s): Short Stories; Sexual Behavior
Age range(s): Grades 9-12

Summary: From the humor expressed by Joan Bauer's abstaining heroine in "Extra Virgin," as she debates "should she, shouldn't she," to the perplexity of the love Emma Donoghue's lesbian protagonist feels for one of her housemates in "The Welcome," all ranges of "the interrelationships of love and sex" are found in Cart's collection. This top-notch group of stories also includes Chris Lynch's "The Cure for Curtis" where Curtis worries unnecessarily that he's gay; "Snake" by Laurie Halse Anderson that updates the story of Adam and Eve; and Shelley Stoehr's "Troll Bumps" about the demise of a young girl's infatuation. Other authors include Louise Hawes, Garth Nix, Sonya Sones, Michael Lowenthal and Angela Johnson. (240 pages)

Where it's reviewed:
Bulletin of the Center for Children's Books, September 2001, page 7
Horn Book, July 2001, page 448
Publishers Weekly, May 28, 2001, page 90
School Library Journal, June 2001, page 144
Voice of Youth Advocates, June 2001, page 124

Awards the book has won:
ALA Quick Picks for Reluctant Young Adult Readers, 2002
ALA Best Books for Young Adults, 2002

Other books by the same author:
In the Stacks: Short Stories about Libraries and Librarians, 2002 (adult title)
Tomorrowland: Ten Stories about the Future, 1999
My Father's Scar, 1996

Other books you might like:
Francesca Lia Block, *Girl Goddess #9: Nine Stories*, 1996
   Stories that range from the deliciously different and funky to the whimsical and haunting fill the pages of this work.
Donald R. Gallo, *No Easy Answers: Short Stories about Teenagers Making Tough Choices*, 1997
   A strong collection of short stories features teens that face a moral crisis, such as peer pressure, computer blackmail or gang initiations.
Marilyn Levy, *Love Is Not Enough*, 1989
   It was easy to fall in love with Nick, but not so easy to face his family who dislike Delphi's mixed Greek and African-American parentage.

Marilyn Reynolds, *If You Loved Me*, 1999
Lauren's long-time boyfriend wants a more intimate relationship, but Lauren's vow to abstain from sex before marriage leaves her in a quandary.

144

PETER CARVER, Editor

Close-ups

(Alberta, Canada: Red Deer Press, 2000)

Subject(s): Short Stories
Age range(s): Grades 8-12
Time period(s): 2000s
Locale(s): Canada

Summary: A rich group of stories, written by Canadian authors of young adult fiction, fill the pages of this work and reveal the many universal complexities of life, not just the life of a teenager. The problems of dating a jealous boyfriend are captured by Bernice Friesen in ''Belonging to the Dragon,'' the sadness of the death of a beloved grandfather is found in Rich Book's ''Saying Good-Bye to the Tall Man'' and Gilliam Chan describes the reality of bullies and underdogs in schools in ''The Buddy System.'' Some of the other authors found in this collection include Kevin Major, Budge Wilson, Linda Holeman, Martha Brooks and Tim Wynne-Jones. (223 pages)

Where it's reviewed:
Booklist, February 15, 2001, page 1128
Quill & Quire, September 2000, page 63
Resource Links, February 2001, page 29
School Library Journal, April 2001, page 139
Voice of Youth Advocates, April 2001, page 36

Other books you might like:
Gillian Chan, *Golden Girl and Other Stories*, 1997
The students at Elmwood High School have a wide range of interests, concerns and problems as evidenced by this collection of stories.
Anne Mazer, *A Walk in My World: International Short Stories about Youth*, 1998
Young people worldwide share similar experiences as shown in these sixteen stories by international authors.
W.D. Valgardson, *The Divorced Kids Club and Other Stories*, 1999
Canadian author Valgardson offers seven stories that capture the dilemma of being a teenager.
Tim Wynne-Jones, *Lord of the Fries and Other Stories*, 1999
Written by a Canadian author, these delicious witty short stories range from stopping a teacher's flirtation to the cause of a cook's crankiness.

145

JUDITH CASELEY, Author/Illustrator

Bully

(New York: Greenwillow Books, 2001)

Subject(s): Bullies; Schools; Behavior
Age range(s): Grades 1-3

Major character(s): Mickey, Student—Elementary School, Bullied Child; Jack, Bully, Student—Elementary School
Time period(s): 2000s (2001)
Locale(s): United States

Summary: Jack used to be Mickey's friend but since his sister's birth Jack's been a mean bully. He takes Mickey's cookies at lunchtime and trips him in the cafeteria. Mickey doesn't want to be a tattletale but he does want Jack's bullying to stop. Everyone in Mickey's family has a different suggestion to help him with the problem. Mickey tries everyone's ideas and adds one of his own. Soon Jack stops the bullying and the boys are friends again. (32 pages)

Where it's reviewed:
Booklist, May 15, 2001, page 1755
Bulletin of the Center for Children's Books, June 2001, page 369
Horn Book Guide, Fall 2001, page 251
Instructor, August 2001, page 20
School Library Journal, June 2001, page 105

Other books by the same author:
Field Day Friday, 2000
Mickey's Class Play, 1998
Mr. Green Peas, 1995

Other books you might like:
Eileen Christelow, *Jerome Camps Out*, 1998
Sharing a tent with the class bully could ruin a weekend camping trip but Jerome and P.J. come up with a plan that allows them to sleep peacefully.
Helen Lester, *Hooway for Wodney Wat*, 1999
Rodney Rat uses the speech problem for which he's often teased to trick the classroom bully and end her teasing.
Becky Ray McCain, *Nobody Knew What to Do: A Story about Bullying*, 2001
In a nonfiction title a boy who observes another student being bullied reports the problem to the teacher and it is resolved.
Susan Meddaugh, *Martha Walks the Dog*, 1998
Martha the talking dog learns from a parrot's example that kind words have a more positive impact on Bad Dog Bob than insults.

146

PATRICIA CASEY, Author/Illustrator

One Day at Wood Green Animal Shelter

(Cambridge, MA: Candlewick Press, 2001)

Subject(s): Animals; Animals, Treatment of; Pets
Age range(s): Grades K-3
Major character(s): Penny, Cat; Dr. Simmonds, Veterinarian
Time period(s): 2000s (2001)
Locale(s): Wood Green Animal Shelter, England

Summary: Each morning at 7:45, Penny, the resident shelter cat, greets workers, visitors, and clients with pets. The employees go to their assignments, some with their own pets as companions. The many shelter cats receive their breakfast before Dr. Simmonds begins attending to the animals brought into the clinic for treatment. Before the day ends more animals in need of a home and medical attention arrive at the shelter. All are tended before the workers leave knowing Penny will greet them again in the morning. (32 pages)

Where it's reviewed:
Booklist, July 2001, page 2018
Bulletin of the Center for Children's Books, September 2001, page 9
Horn Book Guide, Fall 2001, page 337
Publishers Weekly, May 28, 2001, page 88
Smithsonian, November 2001, page 122

Awards the book has won:
Smithsonian's Notable Books for Children, 2001

Other books by the same author:
Beep! Beep! Oink! Oink! Animals in the City, 1997
My Cat Jack, 1994
Quack Quack, 1988

Other books you might like:
Bob Graham, *Let's Get a Pup! Said Kate*, 2001
Kate and her parents visit an animal shelter looking for a pup and also find an appealing older dog.
Bill Gutman, *Adopting Pets: How to Choose Your New Best Friend*, 2001
A nonfiction title in the ''Pet Friends'' series explains how to choose a pet for adoption from a shelter.
Marsha Hayles, *Pet of a Pet*, 2001
Tabitha's family farm has so many animals that each one has a pet.

147

MEG CASTALDO

The Foreigner
(New York: Pocket/MTV, 2001)

Subject(s): Mystery and Detective Stories; Interpersonal Relations
Age range(s): Grades 10-Adult
Major character(s): Alexandra Rockangela ''Alex'' Orlando, Saleswoman, Niece (house sitter for Uncle Carmi); Anthony Carmine Orlando, Uncle; Christian Olsen, Drug Dealer; Jan, Con Artist; Kyle Hangerman, Friend (of Alex's)
Time period(s): 2000s
Locale(s): New York, New York

Summary: Still restless after graduation from college and with no current job, Alex agrees to housesit for her Uncle Carmi while he's vacationing in Puerto Rico. Flying to New York, she immediately gets caught up in New York life, first finding a job at Barney's and then meeting her uncle's Swedish neighbor Christian. Life becomes a little complicated when Kyle, Alex's best friend from high school, shows up at unexpected times, and even more complex when Jan, a guy she met while traveling around Europe, writes to let her know he's coming to New York. Though she'd like to keep these three men apart, they all seem to keep bumping into one another. When Christian's murdered, Alex feels as though her life has gone out of control in this first novel. (225 pages)

Where it's reviewed:
Booklist, May 15, 2001, page 1730
Kirkus Reviews, May 1, 2001, page 604

Publishers Weekly, June 18, 2001, page 59
Women's Wear Daily, May 15, 2001, page 3

Other books by the same author:
Shop New York: Downtownstyle, 1996 (nonfiction)

Other books you might like:
Melissa Bank, *The Girls' Guide to Hunting and Fishing*, 1999
Jane plays by the romance rules but everything goes wrong; maybe she'll follow her mother's advice and just be herself.
Stephen Chbosky, *The Perks of Being a Wallflower*, 1999
In Charlie's freshman year in high school, he helps his pregnant sister, adjusts to the suicide of a best friend and is hospitalized for depression.
William Sutcliffe, *Are You Experienced?*, 1999
Deciding to spend some time traveling in a third-world country before he starts university, David heads for India and has the adventure of his life.

148

CAROLINE CASTLE
SAM CHILDS, Illustrator

Naughty!
(New York: Alfred A. Knopf, 2001)

Subject(s): Bedtime; Playing; Babies
Age range(s): Preschool-Kindergarten
Major character(s): Big Zeb, Zebra, Mother; Little Zeb, Zebra, Baby; Little Hippo, Hippopotamus, Friend; Big Hippo, Hippopotamus, Mother
Time period(s): Indeterminate
Locale(s): Fictional Country

Summary: Big Zeb's attempts to tuck Little Zeb into bed are futile. Naughty Little Zeb wants to play, not sleep so Big Zeb plays games with Little Zeb but still he does not grow tired. Big Zeb settles down but Little Zeb runs off to play peek-a-boo with other animals and meets Little Hippo. They splash so much that Big Hippo and Big Zeb both appear to put their little ones back into bed. Finally the young ones agree, but only if they can sleep together under the banana tree. Originally published in Great Britain in 2000. (32 pages)

Where it's reviewed:
Booklist, June 2001, page 1888
Children's Bookwatch, August 2001, page 3
Horn Book Guide, Fall 2001, page 228
Kirkus Reviews, May 15, 2001, page 737
School Library Journal, June 2001, page 105

Other books by the same author:
Gorgeous!, 2000
Grandpa Baxter and the Photographs, 1993
The Hare and the Tortoise, 1985

Other books you might like:
Helen Cooper, *The Boy Who Wouldn't Go to Bed*, 1997
A young boy finds that his plan to stay awake all night and play does not work because all his playthings are sleepy.
Michael Foreman, *Dad! I Can't Sleep!*, 1995
Dad's going-to-sleep suggestions fail to produce the desired effect.

Jane Yolen, *How Do Dinosaurs Say Good Night?*, 2000
A succession of human parents show a range of emotions as they try to coax their dinosaurs into bed.

PETER CATALANOTTO, Author/Illustrator

Emily's Art

(New York: Richard Jackson Book/Atheneum Books for Young Readers, 2001)

Subject(s): Artists and Art; Contests; Talent
Age range(s): Grades K-3
Major character(s): Emily, 1st Grader, Artist; Ms. Fair, Teacher; Kelly, 1st Grader, Friend (Emily's)
Time period(s): 2000s (2001)
Locale(s): United States

Summary: When Ms. Fair announces an art contest with prize ribbons for the best painting in each grade level Emily kindly shares her artistic talents with Kelly. Under Emily's tutelage Kelly paints a different colored butterfly every day. Emily paints a picture with a different subject each day and finally decides to enter the painting of her dog in the contest. A dog-hating judge awards the blue ribbon to Kelly's painting of a butterfly, crushing creative Emily's feelings. When Kelly later seeks Emily's assistance with a drawing of a dinosaur, both the friendship and Emily's artistic confidence are restored. (32 pages)

Where it's reviewed:
Booklist, July 2001, page 2018
Bulletin of the Center for Children's Books, September 2001, page 9
Kirkus Reviews, May 1, 2001, page 656
Publishers Weekly, July 2, 2001, page 75
School Library Journal, June 2001, page 105

Other books by the same author:
Dad & Me, 1999
The Painter, 1995
Christmas Always, 1991
Mr. Mumble, 1990

Other books you might like:
Valeri Gorbachev, *Peter's Picture*, 2000
    Peter's proud that his parents appreciate the painting he brings home from school and hurries to make another one.
Amy Hest, *Jamaica Louise James*, 1996
    Jamaica's artistic masterpieces find acceptance by all as they brighten the subway station where her grandmother works.
Tanya Linch, *My Duck*, 2000
    A student attempts to comply with her teacher's rigid expectations, but the characters in her drawing have their own ideas.
Martin Waddell, *Alice the Artist*, 1988
    Trying to please her friends Alice incorporates their suggestions into her picture but finally decides to use her own ideas in the final product.

DENYS CAZET, Author/Illustrator

Minnie and Moo Meet Frankenswine

(New York: HarperCollins Publishers, 2001)

Series: I Can Read Book
Subject(s): Animals/Cows; Monsters; Humor
Age range(s): Grades 1-3
Major character(s): Minnie, Cow; Moo, Cow; Olga, Pig
Time period(s): Indeterminate
Locale(s): Fictional Country

Summary: On a stormy night Minnie and Moo awaken when lightning strikes the barn and the terrified animals run up the hill seeking refuge. Claiming to have seen a monster that devoured visiting Olga, the animals continue running past Minnie and Moe to hide behind the farmer's house. More lightning convinces them that the monster is now in the farmer's house and has thrown the farmer's leg out the window. Minnie points out that the ''leg'' is actually a branch from the apple tree and she walks with Moe to the barn to find an equally plausible explanation for the mystery of the monster. (48 pages)

Where it's reviewed:
Horn Book Guide, Spring 2002, page 65
Kirkus Reviews, July 1, 2001, page 936
Publishers Weekly, October 8, 2001, page 67
School Library Journal, September 2001, page 184

Other books by the same author:
Minnie and Moo and the Musk of Zorro, 2000
Minnie and Moo and the Thanksgiving Tree, 2000
Minnie and Moo Go to Paris, 1999

Other books you might like:
Lucy Nolan, *The Lizard Man of Crabtree County*, 1999
    The image cast by late afternoon shadows convinces Miss Bunch that a monstrous lizard man has just run past her barn.
Dav Pilkey, *Dragon's Halloween*, 1993
    Dragon creatively solves a scary Halloween problem and unintentionally creates one for others.
Cynthia Rylant, *Henry and Mudge and the Wild Wind*, 1993
    Henry and his dog Mudge share a fear of thunderstorms so they try to stay busy when one knocks out the electricity to their home.
Dan Yaccarino, *The Lima Bean Monster*, 2001
    Lightning strikes a secret dumping ground for unwanted vegetables creating a lima bean monster that threatens to devour the neighborhood.

151

ANN CHAMBERLIN

The Merlin of the Oak Woods

(New York: Tor, 2001)

Series: Joan of Arc Tapestries. Book 2
Subject(s): Magic; Coming-of-Age
Age range(s): Grades 9-Adult

Major character(s): Jehanette d'Arc, Teenager; Gilles deRais, Nobleman; Yann, Witch
Time period(s): 15th century (1420s)
Locale(s): France

Summary: Brought up close as brothers, Gilles and Yann are now adults in war-torn France. The English are pressing the war and Gilles' skill as a soldier is much in demand. Yann has become a full initiate and, like the other Merlins of France, desperately searches for a sign that La Pucelle, the Maid, is coming. As a child, Yann had visions of the Pucelle, a girl inspired by the old gods to aid France, and now he practices his magic and waits. In the countryside young Jehanette tries to live up to her family's expectations of docile young womanhood, but the Merlin of her wood knows her for the awaited one. With her Voices and the Merlin urging her to action, Jehanette struggles to behave but is slowly losing the battle. (333 pages)

Where it's reviewed:
Booklist, May 15, 2001, page 1739
Library Journal, June 15, 2001, page 107
Publishers Weekly, April 30, 2001, page 61

Other books by the same author:
Leaving Eden, 2000
The Merlin of St. Gilles' Well, 2000 (Joan of Arc Tapestries, Book 2)
The Sultan's Daughter, 1998

Other books you might like:
Barbara Dana, *Young Joan: A Novel*, 1991
   A more traditional retelling of Joan of Arc's story.
Mary Gentle, *The Books of Ash Series*, 1998-2000
   The France of an alternate universe is defended by Ash, a brutal but effective female commander.
Juliet Marillier, *Son of the Shadows*, 2001
   An innocent is caught between warring factions in ancient Ireland.

152
VERONICA CHAMBERS

Quinceanera Means Sweet 15
(New York: Hyperion, 2001)

Subject(s): Quinceanera; Friendship
Age range(s): Grades 6-9
Major character(s): Magdalena Rosario, 14-Year-Old; Marisol Marazol, 14-Year-Old
Time period(s): 2000s
Locale(s): New York, New York (Brooklyn)

Summary: For the past year Marisol has lived in Panama with her grandmother while her mother completed academic work for her degree. Now Marisol's returned to New York and is eager to see her best friend Magdalena and plan their quinceaneras, or coming of age parties. Unfortunately while Marisol's been away, Magda's found new friends who seem intent on getting her in trouble with their shoplifting, a habit which they'd like Marisol to try. Unwilling to shoplift and disliking Magda's new friends, Marisol drifts away from Magda and concentrates on the more immediate problem of whether or not her mother can afford to host her quinceneara

party. When Magda and her friends are caught shoplifting, her quinceanera party is cancelled while Marisol enjoys a true quinceneara party to which every family member and friend contribute something special. (189 pages)

Where it's reviewed:
Book Report, May 2001, page 57
Booklist, March 15, 2001, page 1391
Bulletin of the Center for Children's Books, May 2001, page 332
School Library Journal, June 2001, page 144
Voice of Youth Advocates, October 2001, page 273

Other books by the same author:
Amistad Rising: A Story of Freedom, 1998
Marisol and Magdalena, 1998
Mama's Girl, 1996

Other books you might like:
Diane Gonzales Bertrand, *Sweet Fifteen*, 1995
   Seamstress Rita Navarro not only makes Stefanie's quinceanera dress, but also befriends her entire family, including Stefanie's grieving mother.
Amy Goldman Koss, *The Girls*, 2000
   Ringleader Candace manages to whittle her clique from five to four when she decides Maya is out; now the others wonder who's next?
Gloria Velasquez, *Maya's Divided World*, 1995
   When her parents divorce, Maya's wonderful life disintegrates and she hangs out with a gang of troublemakers.

153
JOYCE CHAMPION
JOAN PARAZETTE, Illustrator

Emily and Alice Baby-Sit Burton
(San Diego: Gulliver/Harcourt, Inc., 2001)

Subject(s): Babysitters; Animals/Dogs; Friendship
Age range(s): Grades 2-3
Major character(s): Emily, Friend, Babysitter; Alice, Friend, Babysitter; Burton, Dog (bulldog)
Time period(s): 2000s (2001)
Locale(s): United States

Summary: Emily and Alice are sure that years of practice with dolls and Emily's little sister makes them qualified to baby-sit for an infant so they make business cards and deliver them to the home of a friend with a baby brother. The mother agrees that she could use some help, but not with the baby. She wants Emily and Alice to baby-sit the unhappy family pet. Reluctantly Emily and Alice agree to care for Burton although the dog is so morose that it's a struggle to get him to move. When the girls discover that Burton simply needs more attention, they treat him like a baby, tie a bonnet on his head and push the "puppy" in a doll stroller. One can almost see the contented Burton smile. (32 pages)

Where it's reviewed:
Booklist, July 2001, page 2006
Horn Book Guide, Fall 2001, page 289
School Library Journal, June 2001, page 111
Tribune Books, June 10, 2001, page 4

Other books by the same author:
Emily and Alice Stick Together, 2001
Emily and Alice, Best Friends, 2001
Emily and Alice Again, 1995
Emily and Alice, 1993

Other books you might like:
Amy Hest, *Nannies for Hire*, 1994
    Three friends offer to be ''nannies'' for an infant only to discover how difficult baby care can be.
James Howe, *Pinky and Rex and the New Baby*, 1993
    Rex becomes so involved in her new role as a big sister that she neglects her friendship with Pinky.
Cynthia Rylant, *The Henry and Mudge Series*, 1987-
    The adventures of Henry and his lovable, slobbery dog Mudge entertain beginning readers.

154

GILLIAN CHAN

The Carved Box

(Tonawanda, NY: Kids Can Press, Ltd., 2001)

Subject(s): Frontier, Canada; Animals/Dogs; Orphans
Age range(s): Grades 6-9
Major character(s): Callum Murdoch, 15-Year-Old, Orphan; Rory MacBean, Uncle, Farmer; Dog, Dog (Newfoundland)
Time period(s): 18th century (early 1800s)
Locale(s): Coote's Paradise, Canada

Summary: Left an orphan, Callum sails from his home in Edinburgh to his uncle Rory's farm in Canada where a life of hard labor awaits him. Arriving in Coote's Paradise, he stumbles over a large Newfoundland dog and, seeing the dog abused by his master, spends all his money to buy Dog and the carved box that comes with her. His uncle's home is filled with love and lots of little children, and the family is happy to see Callum, but his uncle is the happiest for he gains Callum's help on the farm. A blizzard, his uncle's fractured leg and the accidental breaking of the box determine the next steps of Callum's life. (232 pages)

Where it's reviewed:
Booklist, October 1, 2001, page 312
Canadian Living, January 2002, page 91
Kirkus Reviews, August 15, 2001, page 1208
Quill & Quire, July 2001, page 51
School Library Journal, October 2001, page 152

Other books by the same author:
A Foreign Field, 2002
Glory Days and Other Stories, 1997
Golden Girl and Other Stories, 1997

Other books you might like:
LouAnn Bigge Gaeddert, *Breaking Free*, 1994
    Enduring the humiliation and cruelty of his Uncle Lyman, as well as the tedious farm work, is difficult for city-raised Richard after he's left orphaned.
Jean Little, *The Belonging Place*, 1997
    Orphaned Elspet Mary lives with her aunt and uncle and is upset to leave her beloved Scotland when they decide to move to Canada.

Janet Lunn, *Shadow in Hawthorn Bay*, 1987
    During the early days of Canadian settlement, a young Scottish girl with psychic powers travels there to help her cousin.

155

C.J. CHERRYH

Defender

(New York, DAW Books, 2001)

Series: Foreigner Universe. Part 5
Subject(s): Politics; Aliens; Loyalty
Age range(s): Grades 9-Adult
Major character(s): Bren Cameron, Diplomat; Tabini, Alien, Leader
Time period(s): Indeterminate Future
Locale(s): Space Station

Summary: Bren Cameron has negotiated the tricky interactions between humans and the alien atevi ever since becoming the sole point of contact between the two cultures when he assumed the role of paidhi. Relations have never been easy since the human politics are divisive and the atevi do not have emotional connections as humans understand them. The difficulties increase with the return of the spaceship that originally stranded the humans on the atevi planet. Now the groups wrestle for control of the space station and Bren finds himself Tabini's ambassador at large. When the troika of ship's captains reveals the secret only they know, that there may be survivors of the alien attack that sent the ship fleeing back to atevi space, the situation becomes volatile. Everyone's loyalty is questioned as preparations are made to mount a rescue mission. And Bren finds himself the caretaker of Tabini's representatives on the space journey, Tabini's grandmother and his son and heir! (314 pages)

Where it's reviewed:
Booklist, November 15, 2001, page 560

Other books by the same author:
Hammerfall, 2001
Precursor, 1999
Inheritor, 1996
Invader, 1995
Foreigner, 1994

Other books you might like:
Iain Banks, *Look to Windward*, 2001
    The Culture miscalculates the effect of interfering in an alien society and a war erupts.
Hilari Bell, *A Matter of Profit*, 2001
    A disillusioned young soldier learns a new perspective when he is forced to work with one of his despised enemies.
Sarah Zettel, *The Quiet Invasion*, 2000
    If the humans can stop quarreling among themselves, they might notice that aliens have arrived on Venus.

156

TRACY CHEVALIER

Falling Angels

(New York: Dutton, 2001)

Subject(s): Women's Rights; Social Classes; Friendship
Age range(s): Grades 10-Adult
Major character(s): Maude Coleman, Child; Lavinia Ermyntrude "Livy" Waterhouse, Child; Kitty Coleman, Mother (of Maude), Suffragette; Mr. Jackson, Worker (cemetery); Caroline Black, Suffragette
Time period(s): 1900s (1901-1910)
Locale(s): London, England

Summary: The day after Queen Victoria's death, the Coleman and Waterhouse families stroll through the graveyard to gaze upon their adjoining family plots, though neither knows the other or is likely to mix socially. The two young daughters, Maude and Lavinia, befriend one another and return to the graveyard to meet and play with each other. Lavinia's mother is content with her place in society while Maude's mother Kitty is restless and wants more from her marriage and her life. A tryst with the graveyard manager Mr. Jackson results in a pregnancy that Kitty takes care of privately, but her fascination with the suffragette movement is not an activity she can keep quiet. Befriending the vocal suffragette Caroline Black, Kitty becomes involved almost to the point of fanaticism and takes part in a march with tragic consequences in this work that captures the morals and manners of the time. (321 pages)

Where it's reviewed:
Booklist, August 2001, page 2050
Kirkus Reviews, August 1, 2001, page 1045
New Statesman, August 20, 2001, page 39
New York Times Book Review, November 4, 2001, page 26
Publishers Weekly, July 30, 2001, page 56

Other books by the same author:
Girl with a Pearl Earring, 1999

Other books you might like:
Isabel Colegate, *The Shooting Party*, 1981
    Gathering together people for the sole pleasure of shooting is a custom of the Edwardian era, though in 1913 it may be a fading custom.
Jean Hanff Korelitz, *The Sabbathday River*, 1999
    Naomi's crafts cooperative owes much of its success to Heather's embroidery so when she's charged with murder, Naomi finds her a lawyer.
Gillian Linscott, *Sister beneath the Sheet*, 1991
    Suffragette Nell Bray investigates the death of Topaz Brown, a prostitute who's ironically willed her money to the Women's Social and Political Union.
Miriam Grace Monfredo, *Seneca Falls Inheritance*, 1992
    While the Women's Rights Convention of 1848 is conducting business, librarian Glynis Tryon investigates the body that turns up in a canal.

157

EMMA CHICHESTER CLARK, Author/Illustrator

Where Are You, Blue Kangaroo?

(New York: Doubleday Book for Young Readers, 2001)

Subject(s): Animals/Kangaroos; Toys; Lost and Found
Age range(s): Preschool-Grade 1
Major character(s): Blue Kangaroo, Kangaroo, Stuffed Animal; Lily, Child
Time period(s): 2000s (2000)
Locale(s): England

Summary: After a week of being forgotten by Lily atop a slide in the park, on the bus, and at the zoo (where's he's found by a monkey), Blue Kangaroo decides he's not willing to risk a planned trip to the seashore. After Lily falls asleep, Blue Kangaroo sneaks quietly out of bed and in the morning Lily cannot find her special toy anywhere. With the family's help she searches indoors and out before noticing Blue Kangaroo hiding in the pocket of her bathrobe. Lily devises a system to keep Blue Kangaroo close by her so she'll never lose it again. Originally published in Great Britain in 2000. (32 pages)

Where it's reviewed:
Booklist, January 2001, page 966
Bulletin of the Center for Children's Books, March 2001, page 254
Kirkus Reviews, December 1, 2000, page 1679
Publishers Weekly, December 18, 2000, page 80
School Library Journal, April 2001, page 105

Other books by the same author:
I Love You, Blue Kangaroo!, 1999
Across the Blue Mountains, 1993
Lunch with Aunt Augusta, 1992

Other books you might like:
H.M. Ehrlich, *Louie's Goose*, 2000
    While Louie builds a sandcastle a wave carries away Rosie, depositing the soggy stuffed animal back on shore and in need of attention.
Marie-Louise Fitzpatrick, *Lizzy and Skunk*, 2000
    When Skunk becomes lost Lizzy has to conquer her fears in order to find her treasured puppet.
Martin Waddell, *Small Bear Lost*, 1996
    After Small Bear is accidentally left on a train he manages to find his way home to the little girl who lost him.

158

LAUREN CHILD, Author/Illustrator

Beware of the Storybook Wolves

(New York: Arthur A. Levine Books/Scholastic Press, 2001)

Subject(s): Animals/Wolves; Books and Reading; Fantasy
Age range(s): Grades 2-4
Major character(s): Herb, Child, Son; Big Wolf, Wolf; Little Wolf, Wolf
Time period(s): Indeterminate
Locale(s): Fictional Country

Summary: Uh oh! Herb's mom forgot to take the storybook with her when she finished reading Herb's bedtime story and his fears that the characters will come to life have come true. To distract Big Wolf and Little Wolf from their plan to eat him, Herb suggests an appetizer and tries to get some food from the pages of another story. When the first plan fails, Herb shakes the fairy godmother out of another book. Unfortunately, she's been interrupted in the middle of a spell and her magic wand clothes Little Wolf in a ball gown (leaving Cinderella in the book with the dirty dishes). Big Wolf is then turned into a caterpillar and the story of Little Red Riding Hood is never quite the same, but at least Herb survives to read again another day. Originally published in England in 2000. (32 pages)

Where it's reviewed:
Booklist, February 1, 2001, page 1050
Bulletin of the Center for Children's Books, February 2001, page 218
Horn Book Guide, Fall 2001, page 252
Publishers Weekly, April 30, 2001, page 77
School Library Journal, June 2001, page 111

Awards the book has won:
IRA Children's Choices, 2002

Other books by the same author:
Clarice Bean: Guess Who's Babysitting?, 2001 (School Library Journal Best Books)
I Will Never Not Ever Eat a Tomato, 2000 (Kate Greenaway Medal)
Clarice Bean, That's Me, 1999
I Want a Pet, 1999 (IRA/CBC Children's Choices)

Other books you might like:
Alma Flor Ada, *Yours Truly, Goldilocks*, 1998
   Fer O'Cious intercepts an invitation to a housewarming party for three little pigs and makes plans to ambush the departing guests.
Eugene Trivizas, *The Three Little Wolves and the Big Bad Pig*, 1993
   A familiar tale takes a new turn when the big, bad pig tries to outmaneuver the three little wolves and ends up surprising himself.
Ellen Stoll Walsh, *Jack's Tale*, 1997
   Jack agrees to walk through a tale only to please the author. In the end he marries the princess and lives happily ever after.

LAUREN CHILD, Author/Illustrator

Clarice Bean: Guess Who's Babysitting?
(Cambridge, MA: Candlewick Press, 2001)

Subject(s): Family Life; Babysitters; Brothers and Sisters
Age range(s): Grades 2-4
Major character(s): Clarice Bean, Child, Niece; Ted, Uncle, Fire Fighter; Mom, Mother, Sister (Ted's)
Time period(s): 2000s (2001)
Locale(s): United States

Summary: Mom's in a real dilemma. Just as her husband departs on a business trip, she receives a call that her older brother is in the hospital. After a frantic but futile search for a babysitter Mom reluctantly accepts Clarice's suggestion to

call Ted. In the past Ted's visits have been the impetus for broken furnishings and general pandemonium in Mom's view, but Clarice thinks Uncle Ted is just great. Who better to "come to the rescue" than a firefighter, thinks Clarice, and so Uncle Ted agrees to watch his nephews, nieces and their grandfather. Mom returns to only minor chaos that she quickly puts in order and Uncle Ted returns to his easy job of fighting fires in a title originally published in Great Britain in 2000. (32 pages)

Where it's reviewed:
Booklist, May 1, 2001, page 1688
Bulletin of the Center for Children's Books, April 2001, page 298
Kirkus Reviews, January 15, 2001, page 107
Publishers Weekly, February 5, 2001, page 90
School Library Journal, March 2001, page 195

Awards the book has won:
School Library Journal Best Books, 2001
IRA Children's Choices, 2002

Other books by the same author:
I Will Never Not Ever Eat a Tomato, 2000 (Kate Greenaway Medal)
Clarice Bean, That's Me, 1999
I Want a Pet, 1999 (IRA Children's Choices)

Other books you might like:
Betsy Gould Hearne, *Who's in the Hall: A Mystery in Four Chapters*, 2000
   New tenants, a new janitor, new baby-sitters and a stopped up sink lead to a mystery for residents of an apartment building.
Peggy Parish, *Amelia Bedelia and the Baby*, 1981
   Amelia's tendency to literally comply with directions leads to humorous situations as she cares for the Lane's baby.
Mark Teague, *Baby Tamer*, 1997
   Amanda is so unfazed by the outrageous efforts of her charges to aggravate the sitter that the children exhaust themselves and go to sleep early.

LAUREN CHILD, Author/Illustrator

I Am NOT Sleepy and I Will NOT Go to Bed
(Cambridge, MA: Candlewick Press, 2001)

Subject(s): Brothers and Sisters; Bedtime; Humor
Age range(s): Grades K-3
Major character(s): Lola, Sister (younger), Child; Charlie, Child, Brother (older)
Time period(s): 2000s (2001)
Locale(s): England

Summary: Helpful Charlie has his hands full trying to get Lola to go to bed because, as she carefully explains, she is not tired and will not be even at "13 o'clock in the morning." Lola matches each of Charlie's clever ploys with her own logical rationale that achieves Charlie's short-term goal in Lola's way. After humoring Lola by serving a bedtime drink to Lola and three tigers, getting an extra whale out of the tub, allowing a lion to use his toothbrush and calling two dancing dogs for permission to use their pajamas, Charlie finally has Lola in bed. Now, he only needs to get the hippopotamus out of his and he can turn in too. Published first in Great Britain in 2001. (32 pages)

Where it's reviewed:
Booklist, August 2001, page 2127
Kirkus Reviews, August 1, 2001, page 1119
Publishers Weekly, August 27, 2001, page 84
School Library Journal, September 2001, page 184

Awards the book has won:
IRA Children's Choices, 2002

Other books by the same author:
Beware of the Storybook Wolves, 2001
I Will Never Not Ever Eat a Tomato, 2000 (Kate Greenaway Medal)
Clarice Bean, That's Me, 1999
I Want a Pet, 1999

Other books you might like:
Linda Ashman, *Sailing Off to Sleep*, 2001
   A little girl has an answer to every concern voiced by her mother in this rhyming story of one girl's strategy for avoiding bedtime.
Kate Lum, *What! Cried Branny: An Almost Bedtime Story*, 1999
   Before Patrick can go to bed at Granny's she has to make a bed for him; then he needs a blanket, a pillow and a teddy bear.
Megan McDonald, *Bedbugs*, 1999
   Daddy calls bedtime and Susan imagines problems bigger than bedbugs, but Daddy reassuringly removes the "porcupine" from her bed so she can sleep.
Ann Whitford Paul, *Everything to Spend the Night from A to Z*, 1999
   A little girl packs everything she needs for an overnight visit to Grandpa's house, but discovers that she's forgotten "P" for pajamas.
Peggy Rathmann, *10 Minutes till Bedtime*, 1998
   When a child's father announces "10 minutes till bedtime," the hamster tour guide springs into action with the "Bedtime Tour."

YANGSOOK CHOI, Author/Illustrator

The Name Jar
(New York: Alfred A. Knopf, 2001)

Subject(s): Names, Personal; Identity; Korean Americans
Age range(s): Grades K-3
Major character(s): Unhei, Student—Elementary School, Immigrant; Mr. Kim, Store Owner; Joey, Student—Elementary School, Friend
Time period(s): 2000s (2001)
Locale(s): New York, New York (Brooklyn)

Summary: When Unhei arrives in class on her first day of school in America, memories of the morning bus ride and the children's mockery of her name are fresh in her mind so she tells her classmates that she has not yet chosen a name. To

help her, the class makes a name jar into which they place suggested names. When Unhei runs into her classmate Joey in Mr. Kim's store he learns the correct pronunciation of her name that he has previously only seen in the Korean characters of her name stamp. A week after Unhei enters school she discovers that the name jar is gone, but she doesn't need it because she's ready to introduce herself by her given name Unhei, meaning grace. (32 pages)

Where it's reviewed:
Booklist, December 15, 2001, page 738
Horn Book Guide, Spring 2002, page 38
Kirkus Reviews, June 1, 2001, page 799
School Library Journal, November 2001, page 113

Awards the book has won:
IRA Children's Choices, 2002

Other books by the same author:
New Cat, 1999
The Sun Girl and the Moon Boy, 1997

Other books you might like:
Kevin Henkes, *Chrysanthemum*, 1991
   Unhappy Chrysanthemum arrives home from her first day of school feeling humiliated by teasing from classmates about her unusual name.
Belinda Rochelle, *When Jo Louis Won the Title*, 1994
   Jo Louis begins to appreciate the significance of her name after her grandfather explains its meaning in his life.
Sandra S. Yamate, *Ashok by Any Other Name*, 1992
   A young Indian-American immigrant feels self-conscious about his foreign-sounding name.

GENNIFER CHOLDENKO

Notes from a Liar and Her Dog
(New York: Putnam, 2001)

Subject(s): Family Life; Zoos; Honesty
Age range(s): Grades 5-8
Major character(s): Antonia Jane "Ant" MacPherson, 12-Year-Old, 6th Grader; Harrison Emerson, 6th Grader; Carol "Just Carol" Samborsen, Teacher (art); Katherine MacPherson, Sister (of Ant's); Elizabeth MacPherson, Sister (of Ant's); Pistachio, Dog
Time period(s): 2000s
Locale(s): Sarah's Road, California

Summary: Life isn't fair, or so thinks Ant who senses her mother's preference for her sisters "Your Highness Elizabeth" and "Katherine the Great." Convinced she's adopted, Ant lies to everyone about her real family, along with everything else in her life, and writes notes to her "Real Mom." Moving around because of her father's frequent job changes, Ant relies on her aged dog Pistachio and makes a new friend, Harrison, with whom she swaps her outstanding report cards for his dismal ones. At school, she is befriended by her art teacher, called "Just Carol," who arranges for Ant and Harrison to work as volunteers for the zoo, a position Ant endangers when she smuggles in Pistachio. This act, and Just Carol's response, finally makes Ant see the danger of her lying. Finally believing that her mother does love her, Ant tries to lead a more honest life in this humorous work. (216 pages)

Where it's reviewed:
Booklist, April 15, 2001, page 1550
Bulletin of the Center for Children's Books, July 2001, page 405
Publishers Weekly, May 14, 2001, page 82
School Library Journal, April 2001, page 138
Voice of Youth Advocates, August 2001, page 198

Awards the book has won:
School Library Journal Best Books, 2001

Other books you might like:
Lois Lowry, *Your Move, J.P.!*, 1990
    To attract the attention of a new girl, J.P. claims he has a strange disease, only to discover her father is a geneticist!
Carol Sonenklar, *My Own Worst Enemy*, 1999
    Eve tells lies about her home life to fit into the snobbish clique, but feels a sense of relief when the truth comes out.
Sarah Weeks, *Regular Guy*, 1999
    Guy thinks he's found his parents, but quickly changes his mind and accepts his loving but embarrassing mom and dad as the "real" thing.

163

EILEEN CHRISTELOW, Author/Illustrator

The Great Pig Search
(New York: Clarion Books, 2001)

Subject(s): Animals/Pigs; Lost and Found; Humor
Age range(s): Grades K-3
Major character(s): Bert, Farmer, Spouse; Ethel, Spouse, Farmer
Time period(s): 2000s (2000)
Locale(s): Putney, Vermont; Florida

Summary: The pigs that escaped from Bert and Ethel's farm in *The Great Pig Escape* send a postcard to their former owners. Bert notices the Florida postmark and plans a vacation with Ethel to sunny Florida over Ethel's protests that she wants nothing to do with a pig search spoiling her vacation. Although Bert assures her he has no plans to look for pigs, he seems to do just the opposite, but fails to notice the obvious. Alert readers will notice pigs everywhere, but Bert and Ethel are not aware of the disguised porkers' presence until Ethel reads the newspaper on the morning of their departure. (32 pages)

Where it's reviewed:
Booklist, September 1, 2001, page 113
Horn Book, March 2001, page 200
Kirkus Reviews, June 15, 2001, page 861
Publishers Weekly, September 3, 2001, page 87
School Library Journal, September 2001, page 185

Awards the book has won:
School Library Journal Best Books, 2001

Other books by the same author:
Jerome Camps Out, 1998
Not Until Christmas, Walter!, 1997
The Great Pig Escape, 1994 (Book Links Good Book)

Other books you might like:
Karen Beaumont Alarcon, *Louella Mae, She's Run Away!*, 1997
    Family members and pets race over the farm searching for their prized pig Louella Mae.
Paul Brett Johnson, *The Pig Who Ran a Red Light*, 1999
    George, jealous of Gertrude the farm's flying cow, takes the pick-up truck and drives to town for a little adventure.
Susan Meddaugh, *Hog-Eye*, 1995
    A literate, confident pig uses her reading ability to outwit a wolf intent on making her his next meal.
Mark Teague, *Pigsty*, 1994
    Wendell's room becomes so cluttered that pigs move in and the mess really begins!

164

CATHERINE CLARK

Wurst Case Scenario
(New York: HarperCollins, 2001)

Subject(s): College Life; Humor; Diaries
Age range(s): Grades 9-12
Major character(s): Courtney Von Dragen Smith, Student—College, 18-Year-Old; Mary Jo Johannsen, Student—College, Roommate (of Courtney); Grant, Student—College (Colorado State), Boyfriend (of Courtney); Thyme Penelope, Student—College
Time period(s): 2000s
Locale(s): Wauzataukie, Wisconsin

Summary: From her first day on campus, Courtney wonders whatever possessed her to leave Colorado for a college in rural Wisconsin. She's a vegan, the other students devour meat, potatoes and dairy products; she's rock and roll, her roommate Mary Jo's country; she sleeps late, Mary Jo is awake at 5 a.m. Periodically Courtney has to remind herself that all the financial support she receives from Cornwall Falls College was one of the deciding factors, but Wauzataukie is really a hick town. On top of everything else, she misses her boyfriend Grant and worries about the one thousand miles that separate them. As she reports to her diary, Courtney gradually becomes adjusted to this different lifestyle, finds a job at Bagle Finagle, meets Thyme with her five tattoos and unshaved underarms and legs, becomes involved in environmental causes and grows to care about Mary Jo in this sequel to *Truth or Dairy*. (311 pages)

Where it's reviewed:
Booklist, September 1, 2001, page 96
Kirkus Reviews, July 15, 2001, page 1023
Kliatt, July 2001, page 8
School Library Journal, October 2001, page 152
Voice of Youth Advocates, December 2001, page 356

Other books by the same author:
Truth or Dairy, 2000

Other books you might like:
James Finney Boylan, *Getting In*, 1998
    A planned summer vacation to allow touring and interviewing at some of New England's preppiest colleges turns into a farcical road trip.

Tom Perrotta, *Joe College*, 2000
> Raised in a blue-collar home, Danny sometimes wonders what he's doing at Yale among all those wealthy students.

Julian F. Thompson, *Simon Pure*, 1987
> Simon is the youngest student at Riddle University and his involvement with the daughter of a professor leads to hilarious moments.

165

MARY HIGGINS CLARK

On the Street Where You Live
(New York: Simon & Schuster, 2001)

Subject(s): Mystery and Detective Stories; Serial Killers
Age range(s): Grades 10-Adult
Major character(s): Emily Graham, Lawyer; Madeline Shapley, Crime Victim, Aunt
Time period(s): 2000s
Locale(s): Spring Lake, New Jersey

Summary: Accepting a great job in Manhattan, Emily moves from upper state New York, leaving behind the stalker who's been bothering her, to the ancestral home she's just purchased in a New Jersey seaside town. The house was owned by her distant aunt, Madeline Shapley, the first victim of a serial killer in the 1890s who killed several other girls. Over the last several years young girls have disappeared and are presumed dead, an idea confirmed when the pool excavation in Emily's discloses a recent skeleton found clutching a finger bone which still wears a Shapley family ring. Emily's stalker finds her and, aware of the century-old serial killer, selects Emily as the next victim in a suspenseful tale from a master writer. (317 pages)

Where it's reviewed:
Book World, February 25, 2001, page 4
Booklist, April 15, 2001, page 1508
Kirkus Reviews, April 1, 2001, page 433
People, May 14, 2001, page 53
Publishers Weekly, April 2, 2001, page 41

Other books by the same author:
Daddy's Little Girl, 2002
Murder in the Family, 2002
Before I Saw Good-Bye, 2000
Deck the Halls, 2000
We'll Meet Again, 1999

Other books you might like:
Sandra Brown, *The Alibi*, 1999
> Finding the body of murdered Charleston real estate developer Pittijohn brings forth a long list of possible killers.

Shirley Kennett, *Chameleon*, 1998
> A serial killer is eliminating faculty members of Deaver Junior High School.

James Patterson, *1st to Die*, 2001
> Four professional women pool their talents and information to stop a serial killer from murdering newlyweds in San Francisco.

166

ANDREW CLEMENTS
DOLORES AVENDANO, Illustrator

Jake Drake, Know-It-All
(New York: Simon & Schuster Books for Young Readers, 2001)

Subject(s): School Life; Contests; Scientific Experiments
Age range(s): Grades 3-5
Major character(s): Jake Drake, 3rd Grader, Narrator; Phil "Willie" Willis, Classmate, Friend
Time period(s): 2000s (2001)
Locale(s): United States

Summary: From his vantage point as a fourth grader Jake looks back on his third grade year when he became a know-it-all in order to win the science fair. In his greed to be sole owner of the first place prize, a computer, Jake turns down his friend Willie's suggestion that they be partners for the fair project. A few weeks before the fair Jake realizes that he's let his desire to win get in the way of his enjoyment of the project when he learns that Willie is dropping out of the fair. Jake invites Willie to join him and together they complete a project on electromagnetism and have a great time doing it too. (88 pages)

Where it's reviewed:
Booklist, November 1, 2001, page 474
School Library Journal, November 2001, page 113

Other books by the same author:
Jake Drake: Class Clown, 2002
Jake Drake: Bully Buster, 2001
Jake Drake: Teacher's Pet, 2001

Other books you might like:
Mary Jane Auch, *I Was a Third Grade Science Project*, 1998
> Brian's plan to hypnotize his dog doesn't work out in quite the way he hypothesizes.

Beverly Lewis, *The Stinky Sneakers Mystery*, 1996
> After seeing the other entries Jason doubts that his science project will win a prize.

Janice Lee Smith, *Serious Science: An Adam Joshua Story*, 1993
> Two days before the science fair, Adam Joshua discovers that his younger sister and his dog have eaten his science project.

167

ANDREW CLEMENTS
BRIAN SELZNICK, Illustrator

The School Story
(New York: Simon & Schuster, 2001)

Subject(s): School Life; Authorship; Friendship
Age range(s): Grades 4-7
Major character(s): Natalie/Cassandra Nelson/Day, Writer, 12-Year-Old; Zoe/Zee Zee Reisman, 12-Year-Old, Agent (literary); Ms. Clayton, Teacher (English); Hannah Nelson, Mother, Editor
Time period(s): 2000s
Locale(s): New York, New York

Summary: Riding home from school together, Natalie and her mom, who works as an assistant editor at a children's book publishing company, chat about their day. When Mrs. Nelson mentions that her company is looking for series, adventure and school stories books, Natalie perks up. She's wanted to write a story, sort of a tribute to her deceased father, and who knows more about school than someone who's a student? After writing the beginning chapters of "The Cheater," she enlists her friend Zoe to read it and, when Zoe thinks it's great, they decide to publish it, with just a little subterfuge. Natalie wants to be fair about her manuscript, so chooses the pseudonym Cassandra Day as her author name while Zoe acts as her agent under the moniker Zee Zee Reisman. They talk their English teacher Ms. Clayton into being the adult they need for renting office space and contact Zoe's lawyer dad for all legal transactions, and they're ready! One can imagine Mrs. Nelson's surprise when she discovers the manuscript she loves was written by her daughter in this charming, heart-warming tale. (196 pages)

Where it's reviewed:
Booklist, July 2001, page 1879
Bulletin of the Center for Children's Books, July 2001, page 406
Horn Book, July 2001, page 448
Publishers Weekly, May 28, 2001, page 88
School Library Journal, June 2001, page 144

Other books by the same author:
Big Al and Shrimpy, 2002
The Jacket, 2002
Things Not Seen, 2002
The Janitor's Boy, 2000
Frindle, 1996

Other books you might like:
Eleanor Cameron, *The Private Worlds of Julia Redfern*, 1988
Introspective Julia completes writing a short story, which eases her grief over her father's accidental death.
Carol Lynch Williams, *My Angelica*, 1999
Hoping to follow the same path as her romance writer mother, Sage is mortified when told she's won the school prize for best satire of romance novels.
Paul Zindel, *David & Della*, 1993
Meeting adventurous Della through a bulletin-board ad helps aspiring playwright David unblock his writer's block.

168

LUCILLE CLIFTON
ANN GRIFALCONI, Illustrator

One of the Problems of Everett Anderson
(New York: Henry Holt and Company, 2001)

Subject(s): Child Abuse; African Americans; Stories in Rhyme
Age range(s): Grades K-3
Major character(s): Everett Anderson, Student—Elementary School, Son; Greg, Student—Elementary School, Abuse Victim; Mama, Mother
Time period(s): 2000s (2001)
Locale(s): United States

Summary: Everett worries about Greg but he's not sure if he should speak up or be silent. Sometimes Greg comes to school with bruises, but Everett never notices him fall at school. Mama sees Everett's concern and listens as he tells her how Greg will cry for no reason and cannot say what's wrong. Everett feels that the teacher might think he's stupid to bring up his concerns but Mama listens and offers a hug. Feeling her comfort, Everett decides that for now he'll be Greg's friend and listen just as Mama does and maybe that will help Greg feel better. (26 pages)

Where it's reviewed:
Booklist, September 15, 2001, page 230
Horn Book Guide, Spring 2002, page 38
Publishers Weekly, October 8, 2001, page 67
School Library Journal, October 2001, page 113

Awards the book has won:
Notable Social Studies Trade Books for Young People, 2002

Other books by the same author:
Everett Anderson's Year, 1992
Everett Anderson's Goodbye, 1983
Everett Anderson's Friend, 1976

Other books you might like:
Heather Klassen, *I Don't Want to Go to Justin's House Anymore*, 1999
Having witnessed Justin's father hitting him, Collin no longer wants to go to his friend's home but doesn't know how to explain that to his parents.
E. Sandy Powell, *Daisy*, 1991
A nonfiction title explores how a young abuse victim deals with physical and emotional trauma.
Muriel Stanek, *Don't Hurt Me, Mama*, 1983
The school nurse helps a child abuse victim and her abusive mother receive professional help.

169

CATHRYN CLINTON

The Calling
(Cambridge, MA: Candlewick Press, 2001)

Subject(s): Humor; Fundamentalism; Religion
Age range(s): Grades 7-10
Major character(s): Esther Leah "Esta Lea" Ridley, 13-Year-Old; Sarah Louise Ridley, Sister (of Esther Leah); Peter Earl Jewels, Uncle, Con Artist; Bentley Jewels, Aged Person, Uncle
Time period(s): 1960s
Locale(s): Beulah Land, South Carolina

Summary: At the family reunion held at the Beulah Land Healing and Holiness Church, Esta Lea is called to the Lord. For a twelve-year-old to realize this is pretty amazing, but more astonishment occurs when she heals her Nana's deafness. Following this miracle, Esta Lea is sent on the road to perform more healing, accompanied by her older sister Sarah Louise, who's supposed to lead the singing but who's more interested in boys than God, and recently-reformed Uncle Peter Earl who preaches. As they travel around small towns in South Carolina, Peter Earl does a fine job of preaching and the collection plates fill up, but Esta Lea worries that her uncle is helping himself to some of that collection money. Her suspicions are confirmed when he conducts a funeral and filches some of the dead man's belongings; worse is when Sarah Louise elopes that same day with a college student. Rather than being discouraged, Esta Lea realizes healing is needed in her own hometown and she hurries to the Good Samaritan Hospital to take care of her Uncle Bentley in this humorous first novel. (166 pages)

Where it's reviewed:
Booklist, October 1, 2001, page 331
Bulletin of the Center for Children's Books, December 2001, page 134
Publishers Weekly, August 6, 2001, page 90
School Library Journal, August 2001, page 177
Voice of Youth Advocates, February 2002, page 444

Other books by the same author:
A Stone in My Hand, 2002

Other books you might like:
Han Nolan, *Send Me Down a Miracle*, 1996
   Charity is astounded when artist Adrienne emerges from her home after several weeks of confinement and announces that she's visited with Jesus.
Gary Paulsen, *The Tent*, 1995
   Corey feels guilty as he watches his father con people out of their money in his new role as traveling preacher.
Terry Pringle, *Preacher's Boy*, 1988
   The trouble between Michael and his preacher father can be traced to the day Michael gets the giggles while in the pulpit during "Youth Day."
Lee Smith, *Saving Grace*, 1995
   A serpent-handling preacher raises Gracie, though she wants to tell him that she doesn't like Jesus. Adult title.

BROCK COLE, Author/Illustrator

Larky Mavis
(New York: Farrar Straus Giroux, 2001)

Subject(s): Babies; Fantasy; Conduct of Life
Age range(s): Grades 1-4
Major character(s): Larky Mavis, Young Woman, Outcast; Heart's Delight, Orphan
Time period(s): Indeterminate Past
Locale(s): Fictional Country

Summary: One day as Larky Mavis meanders about the countryside near her village she happens upon three peanuts in the road. After eating two she finds a "baby" in the third one. Adult villagers mock her claim that she has a child, calling the tiny thing a worm, a mouse and a deformed bird. With love and the nourishment Larky Mavis freely gives, Heart's Delight grows larger and larger until the villagers are afraid of the thing in the bundle that Larky Mavis totes everywhere. Larky Mavis refuses the villagers' demands to relinquish her baby and runs away. As she runs wings appear from Heart's Delight's bundle and then a head with golden hair. A voice calls, "Let go my ma!" and Larky Mavis finds she can run no more because Heart's Delight is lifting her off the ground and

flying away with her. No one knows where she went but she's never been seen again. (32 pages)

Where it's reviewed:
Booklist, July 2001, page 2016
Bulletin of the Center for Children's Books, September 2001, page 9
Horn Book, September 2001, page 570
Publishers Weekly, July 16, 2001, page 1880
Riverbank Review, Fall 2001, page 30

Other books by the same author:
Buttons, 2000 (Boston Globe-Horn Book Honor Book)
The Giant's Toe, 1986
Nothing But a Pig, 1981

Other books you might like:
Christopher Myers, *Wings*, 2000
   A shy student breaks her silence to defend Ikarus from taunting classmates and to compliment his beautiful flying.
Eric Jon Nones, *Angela's Wings*, 1995
   When wings sprout from Angela's back she endures teasing until she accepts the change and chooses to enjoy the pleasure of flying.
Patricia Polacco, *I Can Hear the Sun*, 1996
   Orphan Fondo finds love and companionship as he cares for geese in a city park; he accepts their invitation to fly south with them for the winter.

EVELYN COLEMAN

Born in Sin
(New York: Atheneum/Simon & Schuster, 2001)

Subject(s): Sports/Swimming; African Americans
Age range(s): Grades 9-12
Major character(s): Keisha Wright, 14-Year-Old, Swimmer; Betty Shabazz, 10th Grader; Malik Shabazz, 10th Grader
Time period(s): 2000s
Locale(s): Atlanta, Georgia

Summary: Keisha can't believe it when her principal enrolls her in a summer program for "at risk" students. She'd had her heart and mind set on a pre-med program at Avery University and had even been tentatively accepted, contingent upon completion of the paperwork. Upon hearing that her principal has even switched her from the college prep to the general curriculum, Keisha realizes she is no longer even eligible for the pre-med program. Resigned to her fate, she quickly befriends Betty and together the two attend the youth center where Keisha discovers she has competitive swimming ability. Keisha's mother and older sister provide her with support so that she doesn't lose sight of her pre-med goal. Her grandmother's adage, "just 'cause we poor, don't mean we born in sin," offers her hope, and, the attention of Betty's older brother Malik bolsters her feelings of self-confidence. Though her principal is misguided, Keisha knows that she can still achieve her goal of attending medical school. (234 pages)

Where it's reviewed:
The Bulletin of the Center for Children's Books, February 2001, page 2
Kliatt, March 2001, page 8

Publishers Weekly, April 2, 2001, page 66
School Library Journal, March 2001, page 245
Voice of Youth Advocates, April 2001, page 36

Other books by the same author:
Circle of Fire, 2001
Mystery of the Dark Tower, 2000
The Riches of Oseola McCarty, 1998

Other books you might like:
Robb Armstrong, *Drew and the Homeboy Question*, 1997
    When Drew's parents decide he should attend an all-white private school, his friends abandon him until he wins a scholarship.
Joyce Annette Barnes, *Promise Me the Moon*, 1997
    Though rejected for a magnet school, a visit to relatives, an inheritance and eventual acceptance to McAllen High reinforce Annie's self-esteem.
Walter Dean Myers, *Slam!*, 1996
    Slam transfers to Latimer Arts Magnet School where the coursework is difficult; eventually he learns to excel both on and off the court.
Don Trembath, *The Tuesday Cafe*, 1996
    Enrolled in a writing class, Harper doesn't realize he's in with the newly literate and learning disabled for it's the best class he's ever taken.
Rita Williams-Garcia, *Like Sisters on the Homefront*, 1995
    When Gayle's mother sends her to live in Georgia with the maternal side of the family, Gayle feels a real kinship with her great-grandmother.

172

EVELYN COLEMAN

Circle of Fire
(Middleton, WI: American Girl/Pleasant Company, 2001)

Series: American Girl History Mysteries
Subject(s): African Americans; Prejudice; Friendship
Age range(s): Grades 6-8
Major character(s): Mendy Anna Thompson, 12-Year-Old; Jeffrey Whitehall, 14-Year-Old
Time period(s): 1950s (1958)
Locale(s): Cowan, Tennessee

Summary: Mendy grows up outside of Cowan where she roams the woods around her home and puts to use the hunting and trapping lore her father has taught her. She has a favorite spot where she and her best friend Jeffrey often meet, but someone else has been in her clearing recently. Ever resourceful, Mendy sets a trap with honeybees, but when she returns finds the unknown person has used the trap to kill a rabbit. Sneaking out of her house one night, she finds white-robed men, spewing words of hate, standing around a circle of fire in her special spot. Telling Jeffrey, he divulges that it's the Ku Klux Klan and also explains the design on their robes. The two youngsters realize the sheriff is part of the Klan and knows of the plot to bomb integrated Highlander Folk School where Mrs. Roosevelt is coming to speak. Deciding to stop the Klan. Mendy sets more of her traps in the woods around Highlander Folk School and, with a little help from Jeffrey's father, averts tragedy in this continuing series. (150 pages)

Where it's reviewed:
Booklist, January 2002, page 856
Voice of Youth Advocates, December 2001, page 356

Other books by the same author:
Born in Sin, 2001
Mystery of the Dark Tower, 2000 (American Girl History Mysteries)
The Riches of Oseola McCarty, 1998

Other books you might like:
Christopher Paul Curtis, *The Watsons Go to Birmingham—1963*, 1995
    Heading south to visit Grandmother, the Watson family's high spirits are altered forever when a bomb blast in a Birmingham church kills four children.
Ouida Sebestyen, *Words by Heart*, 1979
    Young black Lena upsets her local community when she beats a white boy in a spelling bee at the turn of the century.
Mildred D. Taylor, *The Gold Cadillac*, 1987
    A loving Ohio family is not prepared for the prejudice they experience while in Mississippi.

173

WILLIAM E. COLES JR.

Compass in the Blood
(New York: Atheneum/Simon & Schuster, 2001)

Subject(s): Mystery and Detective Stories; Crime and Criminals; Journalism
Age range(s): Grades 7-10
Major character(s): Diane "Dee" Armstrong, Student—College; Harriet "Harry" Bromfield, Journalist; Katherine Dietrich Soffel, Historical Figure
Time period(s): 1900s; 2000s
Locale(s): Pittsburgh, Pennsylvania

Summary: After Dee writes a research paper about a notorious prison escape in 1902, she sees a television documentary by Harriet Bromfield about the same Kate Soffel and the Biddle brothers. Harriet eventually contacts Dee to see if she'd like to continue her research to determine if Kate really did provide guns and saws to the Biddle brothers and help them escape from her husband's prison, thereby abandoning him and her four children. It seems that Kate kept a diary while in prison and there's evidence to believe it still exists; finding the diary could provide the real story to that long-ago event. As Dee eagerly begins the search for Kate's grave, she is bothered by all the hints of betrayal in the story, from the possible set-up by Kate's husband to the devious methods that Harry sometimes uses to get her story. When the only remaining relative of Kate Soffel's enters the hunt for the diary, Harry gets her come-uppance while Dee and her friends will have to decide whether or not to unearth the diary in this work based on an actual event. (263 pages)

Where it's reviewed:
Booklist, May 1, 2001, page 1612
Kliatt, May 2001, page 9
Publishers Weekly, July 9, 2001, page 6
School Library Journal, June 2001, page 144

Voice of Youth Advocates, August 2001, page 198

Other books by the same author:
Another Kind of Monday, 1996
Funnybone, 1992

Other books you might like:
Cindy Bonner, *Lily*, 1992
　　Since fathers are all-powerful in 1880s Texas, it's no wonder Lily decides to run away when she falls in love with a young outlaw.
Susan Dodd, *Mamaw*, 1988
　　Zerelda Samuel, known as "Mamaw," is the mother of the infamous outlaws the James brothers whom she always defends because they're "her boys." Adult title.
Deborah Savage, *Summer Hawk*, 1999
　　A research paper about a doctor's rehabilitation center for wildlife leads to Melissa's decision to edit a literary journal.

EOIN COLFER

Artemis Fowl
(New York: Hyperion Books, 2001)

Subject(s): Magic; Fairies; Kidnapping
Age range(s): Grades 5-8
Major character(s): Artemis Fowl, 12-Year-Old; Holly Short, Fairy; Butler, Servant
Time period(s): Indeterminate Future
Locale(s): Ireland; Italy

Summary: His father disappears and his mother lies in bed, depressed about his absence, which leaves Artemis free to come and go as he wants, accompanied only by Butler, who lives up to his name as well as being Artemis's henchman. As the last of a long line of thieves, Artemis is determined to carry on tradition and reinstate some of the family riches. To accomplish this, he decides to kidnap a fairy and then demand gold for her ransom. When he selects Holly Short, the only female officer in LEPrecon, or the Lower Elements Police recon division, he doesn't realize how fairies have changed from his old image of a green-clad person waving a shamrock. Now he's stuck with a feisty fairy and the refusal of LEPrecon to pay the ransom. Artemis uncovers an amazing underground world populated by goblins, trolls, and fairies, a world unlike anything he's ever seen or read about in this first of a series. (280 pages)

Where it's reviewed:
Booklist, April 15, 2001, page 1554
Bulletin of the Center for Children's Books, July 2001, page 406
Horn Book, July 2001, page 448
School Library Journal, May 2001, page 148
Voice of Youth Advocates, August 2001, page 211

Awards the book has won:
Bulletin of the Center for Children's Books Blue Ribbon, 2001

Other books by the same author:
Artemis Fowl: The Arctic Incident, 2002
Benny and Babe, 2001

Benny and Omar, 2001

Other books you might like:
Anthony Horowitz, *Stormbreaker*, 2001
　　After his uncle dies, Alex agrees to take his place helping British intelligence as he investigates the computer giant Sayle Enterprises.
Eva Ibbotson, *Which Witch?*, 1999
　　Hapless Belladonna of the miscast spells, feels she'll never beat the other witches as they vie for the hand of the wizard Arriman the Awful.
Diana Wynne Jones, *Dark Lord of Derkholm*, 1998
　　With Derk roasted by an elderly dragon, his children are merrily running events until evil armies and Dark Elves threaten to get out of control.
Margaret Mahy, *The Door in the Air and Other Stories*, 1991
　　Nine delicious, fantastic short stories about magic, the supernatural, mystery and witchcraft.
Caroline Stevermer, *A College of Magics*, 1994
　　Magical competition at a school for wizards has unanticipated consequences.

EOIN COLFER

Benny and Omar
(Dublin, Ireland: The O'Brien Press, 2001, c1998)

Subject(s): Friendship; Brothers and Sisters; Emigration and Immigration
Age range(s): Grades 6-9
Major character(s): Bernard "Benny" Shaw, 12-Year-Old; Omar Ben Ali, Orphan; Kaheena, Orphan
Time period(s): 1990s
Locale(s): Marhaba, Tunisia

Summary: Benny can't believe his rotten luck when his father is transferred from Ireland to Tunisia in the north of Africa. Especially discouraging is the fact that no one at his new school has ever heard of hurling so they can't appreciate Benny's prowess at the sport. His teachers are aging hippies, none of the students are as carefree as he and scorpions and hot weather are new and unwelcome. One day Benny slips out of the EuroGas compound and meets Omar, a Tunisian orphan who survives on his wits. After a few misunderstandings, the two become friends and Benny hops over the wall of the compound as often as he can. Omar takes Benny to meet his sister Kaheena, a little girl who's kept drugged in an institution, and the two kidnap her, bringing her back to Omar's little hovel. Because of all the rain, they're caught in floodwaters and Benny is able to save only Kaheena. His father helps bend some rules so that Kaheena is quickly adopted in this book that runs the emotional gamut from humor to desolation. (237 pages)

Where it's reviewed:
Booklist, August 2001, page 2118
Kliatt, September 2001, page 16
Publishers Weekly, July 9, 2001, page 68
School Library Journal, December 2001, page 132

Other books by the same author:
Artemis Fowl: The Arctic Incident, 2002

Artemis Fowl, 2001
Benny and Babe, 2001

Other books you might like:

Daniella Carmi, *Samir and Yonatan*, 2000
    Initially terrified to have surgery at a Jewish hospital, Palestinian Samir befriends all the children on his ward.
John Donahue, *Till Tomorrow*, 2001
    Wanting to be popular on his Dad's new army base, O.B. finds the most interesting friend of all is Claude, who's called "the Clod" by the other guys.
Anna Levine, *Running on Eggs*, 1999
    Two young girls, one Arab and one Jewish, becomes friends because of their mutual love for running track.
Amy Bronwen Zemser, *Beyond the Mango Tree*, 1998
    In Liberia, Sarina's life is sheltered until the day she meets Boima and together they explore her new surroundings.

176

JAMES LINCOLN COLLIER

Chipper

(Tarrytown, NY: Marshall Cavendish, 2001)

Subject(s): Orphans; Gangs; Homeless People
Age range(s): Grades 6-9
Major character(s): Chipper Carey, 12-Year-Old, Orphan; Dick "Patch" Patcher, Con Artist; Pinch Mulligan, Gang Member; Elizabeth Sibley, Wealthy
Time period(s): 1890s
Locale(s): New York, New York

Summary: Orphaned at the age of six when his mother dies of consumption, and then beaten by his aunt and uncle, Chipper runs away when he's ten and lives on the streets of New York City where he eventually joins up with the Midnight Rats gang in order to survive. Though he's bothered that Pinch makes them steal, he needs the protection a groups offers until the day a stranger rescues him from an attempted robbery. Patch notes a resemblance between Chipper and a deceased wealthy man and concocts a scheme to pass Chipper off as the dead man's son. Introduced to Miss Sibley, the deceased man's sister, Chipper realizes this scheme might have more truth to it than he imagined in this historical work by a noted author. (207 pages)

Where it's reviewed:
Book Report, September 2001, page 60
Voice of Youth Advocates, August 2001, page 198

Other books by the same author:
Rich and Famous: The Further Adventures of George Stable, 2002 (Lost Treasures)
The Teddy Bear Habit or How I Became a Winner, 2002 (Lost Treasures)
Wild Boy, 2001
The Worst of Times, 2000

Other books you might like:
Chester Aaron, *Lackawanna*, 1986
    During the Depression, Willy and other homeless children band together for survival.

Caroline B. Cooney, *The Face on the Milk Carton*, 1990
    Janie knows she's the child pictured on her milk carton, but why is the picture there and who is she really?
Charles Dickens, *Oliver Twist*, 1837-1838
    An abused runaway, Oliver joins up with the nefarious team of The Artful Dodger and Fagin.
Berlie Doherty, *Street Child*, 1994
    Based on a true story, Dr. Barnardo runs schools for destitute children in England and rescues orphaned Jim from the streets.

177

PAT LOWERY COLLINS

Just Imagine

(Boston: Houghton Mifflin, 2001)

Subject(s): Family Life; Depression (Economic); Psychic Powers
Age range(s): Grades 6-8
Major character(s): Mary Francis LeBec, 12-Year-Old; Leland LeBec, Dancer
Time period(s): 1920s
Locale(s): Hardenville, Massachusetts; Beverly Hills, California

Summary: When Mary Francis's father has a chance for a job on the East Coast, he knows he has to take it, even though his wife is determined to stay in Beverly Hills so their son Leland can achieve stardom in the movies. Mary Francis, her grandmother and father live in a cramped little apartment while her mother and Leland remain in their large home in California. For a while Mary Francis thinks her spirit will be able to leave her body and travel to California to influence her mother, just as her Aunt Nora was able to do. However, her paranormal ability is lacking and eventually Mary Francis travels to California by normal means where she tries to convince her mother to return to her family. (216 pages)

Where it's reviewed:
Book Report, November 2001, page 59
Booklist, April 1, 2001, page 1481
Bulletin of the Center for Children's Books, April 2001, page 299
School Library Journal, May 2001, page 148
Voice of Youth Advocates, August 2001, page 199

Other books by the same author:
Signs and Wonders, 1999

Other books you might like:
Barbara Corcoran, *The Sky Is Falling*, 1988
    Annah's father loses his job, her family splits up to live with various relatives and Annah winds up in New Hampshire with her Aunt Ed.
Constance C. Greene, *Star Shine*, 1985
    A movie company comes to town and Jenny can hardly wait to sign up as an extra.
Jane Kendall, *Miranda Goes to Hollywood: Adventures in the Land of Palm Trees, Cowboys and Moving Pictures*, 1999
    When Miranda and her aunt Lucy travel to Hollywood for Miranda to appear in a movie, they arrive only to discover the project hasn't materialized.

David Klass, *Screen Test*, 1997

Asked to come to Hollywood by a producer, Elizabeth finds that Hollywood is very plastic; when another film offer comes her way, she turns it down.

178

YING CHANG COMPESTINE
TUNGWAI CHAU, Illustrator

The Runaway Rice Cake

(New York: Simon & Schuster Books for Young Readers, 2001)

Subject(s): Chinese; Holidays; Cultures and Customs
Age range(s): Grades K-3
Major character(s): Momma Chang, Mother, Cook
Time period(s): Indeterminate Past
Locale(s): China

Summary: In preparation for her family's celebration of the Chinese New Year Momma Chang makes one "nian-gao" or rice cake from the last bits of the rice flour. Her three hungry sons watch it cook, imagining the delicious taste of their small portion of the cake. As Momma Chang reaches to cut the cake it leaps out of the steamer and races out the door. The family runs after it and sees the rice cake escape from pigs, chicks, a shopper, a fisherman, and lion dancers. They finally capture it when it bumps into an old woman. Seeing her hunger, Momma Chang kindly offers to share the rice cake but the woman eats it all. The sad children make their way home with their parents and discover neighbors returning the family's generosity to the old woman by sharing what little they have. Soon the small offerings magically grow to be a feast with food enough for everyone. The author's first book concludes with information about the Chinese New Year and two recipes for rice cakes. (34 pages)

Where it's reviewed:
Booklist, February 1, 2001, page 1055
Horn Book Guide, Spring 2002, page 38
Kirkus Reviews, November 15, 2000, page 1613
Publishers Weekly, January 8, 2001, page 66
School Library Journal, February 2001, page 93

Other books you might like:
Jim Aylesworth, *The Gingerbread Man*, 1998
An impertinent gingerbread man runs away from his creators, a butcher, a cow and a sow and into the mouth of a clever fox.
Dave Bouchard, *The Dragon New Year: A Chinese Legend*, 1999
The noise of the Chinese New Year's celebration frightens a young girl who is comforted by her grandmother's story.
Karen Chinn, *Sam and the Lucky Money*, 1995
Sam wonders how to spend the money he receives for the Chinese New Year.
Leslie Kimmelman, *The Runaway Latkes*, 2000
Three of Rebecca's latkes leap from the pan and roll away, pursued by a crowd of people that finally captures and eats them.
William Low, *Chinatown*, 1997
With his grandmother a young boy enjoys Chinatown's celebration of the New Year.

179

DONNA CONRAD
DON CARTER, Illustrator

See You Soon Moon

(New York: Alfred A. Knopf, 2001)

Subject(s): Grandparents; Travel; Family
Age range(s): Preschool-Grade 1
Major character(s): Unnamed Character, Child, Son (grandson); Grandma, Grandmother, Aged Person
Time period(s): 2000s (2001)
Locale(s): United States

Summary: In the author's first book a young boy and his family travel by car on a moonlit night. After bidding goodbye to his toys, his swing set and the moon, the boy notices from his seat that the moon seems to be traveling with them up the hills, around a lake and over a bridge. When the car emerges from a tunnel the moon is visible again and as they enter the city the boy sees the moon over the tall buildings. When the boy and his family reach Grandma's house the moon's presence is as comforting as Grandma's welcoming hug. (32 pages)

Where it's reviewed:
Booklist, August 2001, page 2127
Children's Bookwatch, July 2001, page 6
Horn Book Guide, Fall 2001, page 228
Publishers Weekly, January 1, 2001, page 91
School Library Journal, March 2001, page 195

Other books you might like:
Jim Aylesworth, *Through the Night*, 1998
Eager to return home to his family a father drives through the night until he reaches his destination.
John Coy, *Night Driving*, 1996
Dad and his son drive all night to reach their camping spot near the mountains.
Susi Gregg Fowler, *I'll See You When the Moon Is Full*, 1994
Abe's Daddy prepares to leave on a two-week business trip, promising to see Abe "when the moon is full."

180

CAROLINE B. COONEY

For All Time

(New York: Delacorte, 2001)

Subject(s): Time Travel; Romance
Age range(s): Grades 6-10
Major character(s): Anna Sophia "Annie" Lockwood, Time Traveler; Hiram "Strat" Stratton Jr., Time Traveler, 18-Year-Old; Renifer, Teenager; Lockwood Stratton, Teenager
Time period(s): 1990s (1999); 1880s (1899)
Locale(s): New York, New York; Egypt

Summary: With her brother off to basketball camp and her recently remarried parents honeymooning rather than traveling to the lawyer to finalize a divorce, four empty days stretch ahead of Annie. She seizes on this opportunity to reconnect with Strat, her time traveller love who unfortunately lives in

1899. Annie rushes to the Metropolitan Museum to see its exhibit on Egyptian art for she is sure there'll be a photo of Strat taken when the pyramids were excavated. Time does send her back, but to ancient Egypt when the pyramids are being built, not excavated. Taken in by Renifer, a young girl whose father and fiance are tomb robbers, Annie discovers the men are also heartless as they place Renifer and Annie in the Pharaoh's tomb as human sacrifices. Time jolts Strat back to rescue them, but then they must return to 1899 to confront Strat's unpleasant father; with barely time to say hello and goodbye, Annie's whisked back to 1999. The only good news is that she meets Lockwood Stratton at the exhibit and a romance could be brewing between Annie and this relative of Strat's. (261 pages)

Where it's reviewed:
Booklist, September 15, 2001, page 215
Bulletin of the Center for Children's Books, November 2001, page 97
Publishers Weekly, October 22, 2001, page 77
School Library Journal, September 2001, page 223
Voice of Youth Advocates, December 2001, page 367

Other books by the same author:
Prisoner of Time, 1998
Out of Time, 1996
Both Sides of Time, 1995

Other books you might like:
Anne Lindbergh, *Nick of Time*, 1994
  When Jericho and Allison time travel to 2094, Allison decides to remain in the future while Jericho returns home.
Ruth Park, *Playing Beatie Bow*, 1982
  Fourteen-year-old Australian Abigail finds her life interwoven with that of Victorian era Beatie Bow as she steps back in time.
Elizabeth Peters, *Seeing a Large Cat*, 1997
  Excavating an ancient tomb in the Valley of the Kings, Amelia and her husband Emerson discover a modern-day murder. Adult title.
Jill Rubalcaba, *Wadjet Eye*, 2000
  Damon must prepare his mother's body for burial as the priests think she's died of the plague and no one else will embalm her.

181

CAROLINE B. COONEY

The Ransom of Mercy Carter
(New York: Delacorte, 2001)

Subject(s): Indians of North America; Indian Captives; Historical
Age range(s): Grades 6-9
Major character(s): Mercy "Munnonock" Carter, 11-Year-Old
Time period(s): 18th century (1704)
Locale(s): Deerfield, Massachusetts; Kahnawake, Canada (Mohawk Village along the St. Lawrence River)

Summary: Fear of Indian attack forces the residents of Deerfield behind the walls of the stockade, where too many people are crammed into too few rooms. But on February 28, 1704,

with the outside temperature below zero and snow on the ground, Indians walk up the drifts, over the stockade walls and into the little village where they kill or capture the inhabitants. Used to mothering her siblings since their own mother died, Mercy finds herself separated from them on the 300-mile forced march into Canada. Eventually she arrives at the Mohawk village of Kahnawake, located on the St. Lawrence River, where she is given the name Munnonock. At first she prays for the English to ransom her, but gradually realizes how different her life is living with the Indians where she's allowed to be a child rather than a young adult as required by the Puritans. Soon Mercy realizes that if she is ransomed, she doesn't know whether she'll accept the offer to return to her English family, or remain with her new Indian family, in this work based on historical fact. (249 pages)

Where it's reviewed:
Book Report, November 2001, page 59
Publishers Weekly, February 12, 2001, page 213
School Library Journal, August 2001, page 177
Teaching PreK-8, August 2001, page 112
Voice of Youth Advocates, April 2001, page 36

Other books by the same author:
What Janie Found, 2000
Prisoner of Time, 1998
The Voice on the Radio, 1996
Driver's Ed, 1994

Other books you might like:
Lynda Durrant, *Turtle Clan Journey*, 1999
  Though rescued by his American family, Echohawk is miserable and dreams only of returning to his Mohican Indian family.
Sollace Hotze, *A Circle Unbroken*, 1988
  After seven years of captivity with the Indians, Rachel is reunited with her family but has difficulty adjusting to her former life.
Katherine Kirkpatrick, *Trouble's Daughter: The Story of Susanna Hutchinson, Indian Captive*, 1998
  Lenape Indians attack and massacre the family of heretic Anne Hutchinson, capture nine-year-old Susannah and keep her for four years.
Bonnie Pryor, *Thomas in Danger*, 1999
  During the Revolutionary War, Thomas is taken to a Mohawk Indian camp where he is sure he'll be tortured, but realizes Indians are just like other people.

182

SHANA COREY
MARK TEAGUE, Illustrator

Horus's Horrible Day
(New York: Scholastic Press, 2001)

Series: First Graders from Mars. Episode 1
Subject(s): Schools; Mars; Growing Up
Age range(s): Grades 1-2
Major character(s): Horus, Alien, 1st Grader; Nergal, Friend, 1st Grader; Pelly, 1st Grader, Friend
Time period(s): Indeterminate
Locale(s): Mars

Summary: Horus hates first grade. He misses the slime tables and snack time of his martiangarten classroom. Nergal is in a different reading group and there's another student that teases Horus. On the second day of school, Horus refuses to return but his mother has other ideas. As they stand in the schoolyard arguing about day two another mom arrives with an equally reluctant student. Pelly is new and when Horus agrees with her fears she begins to think maybe she'll survive the day with someone as helpful as Horus to share her misery. With no help from their mothers the two happily enter the classroom. (32 pages)

Where it's reviewed:
Booklist, August 2001, page 2127
Instructor, August 2001, page 22
Kirkus Reviews, June 15, 2001, page 862
Publishers Weekly, July 16, 2001, page 180
School Library Journal, September 2001, page 185

Other books by the same author:
The Problem with Pelly, 2002 (First Graders from Mars, Episode 2)
You Forgot Your Skirt Amelia Bloomer, 2000 (Booklist Editors' Choice)
Brave Pig, 1999 (Step into Reading)

Other books you might like:
Jack Gantos, *Back to School for Rotten Ralph*, 1998
    Jealous Ralph, lonely to be left behind on the first day of school, makes Sarah's life difficult when the cat follows her to school.
Jean Van Leeuwen, *Amanda Pig, School Girl*, 1997
    Amanda Pig's first day of school is every bit as wonderful as she anticipates.
Dan Yaccarino, *First Day on a Strange New Planet*, 2000
    As part of an intergalactic exchange program Blast Off Boy faces his first day of school on the planet Meep while Blorp eagerly enters school on Earth.

183

ROBERT CORMIER

The Rag and Bone Shop
(New York: Delacorte, 2001)

Subject(s): Murder; Crime and Criminals
Age range(s): Grades 7-10
Major character(s): Jason Dorrant, 12-Year-Old; Alicia Bartlett, Child, Victim; Mr. Trent, Detective—Police
Time period(s): 2000s
Locale(s): Monument, Massachusetts

Summary: Summer vacation begins and Jason looks forward to not attending school for several months; he doesn't dislike school, it's just that he's not popular and doesn't have many friends. He enjoys the younger students, like his neighbor Alicia and even his little sister Emma. Jason's summer changes when told his friend Alicia has been murdered and he is the last person to have seen her alive. The case turns into a high-profile one and Trent, a detective noted for extricating confessions, is called in. When it's obvious that a quick resolution, though not necessarily a truthful one, is sought, Trent zeroes in on Jason with a non-stop interrogation.

Though Trent feels that Jason is innocent, he needs a murderer and Jason is the best suspect he has; from Jason's perspective, Trent is such an effective interrogator, that he begins to wonder if perhaps he did kill Alicia. Luckily for Jason, Alicia's older brother confesses to the crime, which frees Jason but leaves him worried that he could commit a crime in this author's final work. (154 pages)

Where it's reviewed:
Booklist, December 15, 2000, page 808
Horn Book, March 2001, page 206
Publishers Weekly, December 18, 2000, page 72
School Library Journal, February 2001, page 117
Voice of Youth Advocates, June 2001, page 119

Awards the book has won:
ALA Best Books for Young Adults, 2002
Booklist Editors' Choice/Books for Youth, 2001

Other books by the same author:
Frenchtown Summer, 1999
Heroes, 1998
Tenderness, 1997
In the Middle of the Night, 1995
We All Fall Down, 1991

Other books you might like:
Laurie Halse Anderson, *Speak*, 1999
    Melinda is ostracized by classmates who think she dialed 911 to break up a party; when the truth comes out, she is finally vindicated.
Carl Deuker, *Painting the Black*, 1997
    Ryan must decide whether or not to turn in his friend Josh whom he saw assaulting a girl; if Ryan does, his school will lose its baseball title.
E.L. Konigsburg, *Silent to the Bone*, 2000
    Falsely accused of hurting his sister, mute Branwell is not able to defend himself until his best friend devises a way to break through his silence.
Norma Fox Mazer, *Out of Control*, 1993
    During her junior year, Valerie is assaulted in a deserted hallway by three classmates, only one of whom feels any remorse.

184

JOAN COTTLE, Author/Illustrator

Miles Away from Home
(San Diego: Harcourt, Inc., 2001)

Subject(s): Animals/Dogs; Beaches; Vacations
Age range(s): Grades K-2
Major character(s): Miles, Dog
Time period(s): 2000s (2001)
Locale(s): United States

Summary: Miles, in his eagerness to be helpful, sometimes causes unintended problems. Then he feels guilty, punishes himself, and begins the next day determined to be more helpful than ever. When his family arrives at a beach cottage for vacation, Miles reviews water safety rules, rides the waves and digs the moat for the family's sand castle. He also accidentally breaks an umbrella, eats another family's lunch and buys more Popsicles than he can afford. The vacation ends perfectly when Miles successfully rescues a woman experiencing difficulty in the water and receives recognition as an honorary lifeguard. (32 pages)

Where it's reviewed:
Booklist, May 15, 2001, page 756
Horn Book Guide, Fall 2001, page 252
Kirkus Reviews, February 15, 2001, page 257
Publishers Weekly, April 16, 2001, page 64
School Library Journal, June 2001, page 111

Other books by the same author:
Emily's Shoes, 1999

Other books you might like:
Debra Barracca, *Maxi, the Hero*, 1991
   Maxi proves himself to be not just any dog when he apprehends a purse-snatcher. Sal Barracca, co-author.
John Burningham, *Courtney*, 1994
   He may be a mongrel, but Courtney's ability to cook, play the violin and rescue the baby make him a welcome addition to the family.
Susan Meddaugh, *Martha Calling*, 1994
   Martha makes the most of the vacation she wins in a radio contest despite the resort's "No Dog's Allowed" policy.
Peggy Rathmann, *Officer Buckle and Gloria*, 1995
   With a mind of her own, police dog Gloria enlivens Office Buckle's safety presentations. Caldecott Medal winner.

185

STEVEN COUSINS

Frankenbug

(New York: Holiday House, 2000)

Subject(s): Animals/Insects; Bullies; Interpersonal Relations
Age range(s): Grades 4-7
Major character(s): Adam Cricklestein, 6th Grader, Animal Lover; Jeb McCallister, Bully, 6th Grader; Chief McCallister, Police Officer; Frankenbug "Frankie", Insect
Time period(s): 2000s
Locale(s): United States

Summary: Adam admits he's a little strange, for not every boy or girl has a room filled with bugs. He began by collecting the easy bugs, the roly polys and ladybugs, then added walkingsticks and horned devils and finally turned to experimenting and observing the bugs. Most kids leave him alone, but not Jeb, the school bully who thinks he's immune to punishment because his father's the police chief. When Jeb tortures a beautiful moon moth that Adam's caught, Adam plots revenge. Watching the movie *Frankenstein* gives him the idea of creating a monster bug, a "Frankenbug." Compiling a list of ten large, predatory insects, Adam orders the preserved specimens, stitches together parts from each one and, with the help of lightning bugs, brings Frankenbug to life. Called Frankie by Adam, the two manage to not only scare Jeb but also make his father see what a bully he really is. (151 pages)

Where it's reviewed:
Kirkus Reviews, December 1, 2001, page 1680
Publishers Weekly, November 20, 2000, page 69
School Library Journal, March 2001, page 245

Other books you might like:
Jean Craighead George, *The Fire Bug Connection: An Ecological Mystery*, 1993
   When Maggie's firebugs die instead of transforming from their larval state; she and a graduate student investigate.
Helen V. Griffith, *Cougar*, 1999
   The horse Cougar dies in a barn fire but becomes part of Nickel's bicycle and helps him stand up to the bully Robbo.
Dian Curtis Regan, *Monsters in Cyberspace*, 1997
   Rilla loves belonging to the Monster-of-the-Month Club, but only she and a friend know that the monsters occasionally come to life.
Jerry Spinelli, *Wringer*, 1997
   Palmer dreads his tenth birthday because he doesn't want to become a wringer, one of the kids who wrings the neck of any wounded pigeon at his town's pigeon shoot.
Pam Zollman, *Don't Bug Me!*, 2001
   Megan finds it hard to complete her bug collection for school when her little brother keeps "rescuing" and burying her specimens.

186

BRUCE COVILLE, Editor

Half-Human

(New York: Scholastic, 2001)

Subject(s): Short Stories; Identity; Mythology
Age range(s): Grades 7-10

Summary: Half human or half animal, or does it even matter? In Nancy Springer's "Becoming," Dusie reaches puberty only to discover her hair changes to snakes, she turns the boy she likes to stone and her name is short for Medusa. Gregory Maguire tells of the beginnings of the "Scarecrow" when he meets Dorothy and then heads west while Jane Yolen's "Centaur Field" describes the dilemma of parents to whom a centaur is born. Coville's own story "The Hardest, Kindest Gift" reveals that mortality can sometimes be the perfect gift. Other authors include Tamora Pierce, Tim Waggoner and D.J. Malcolm. (212 pages)

Where it's reviewed:
Book Report, January 2002, page 67
Booklist, December 15, 2001, page 723
Publishers Weekly, November 26, 2001, page 62
School Library Journal, December 2001, page 133
Voice of Youth Advocates, December 2001, page 369

Other books by the same author:
The Monsters of Morley Manor: A Madcap Adventure, 2001
Odder than Ever, 2000
Oddly Enough, 1994

Other books you might like:
Francesca Lia Block, *The Rose and the Beast: Fairy Tales Retold*, 2000
   Wonderfully, magically reworked, these nine fairy tales are only tangentially similar to their original form.
Roald Dahl, *Skin and Other Stories*, 2000
   The magic of Dahl for teens continues in this collection of short stories with surprise endings.

Donna Jo Napoli, *Sirena*, 1998
   The mermaid Sirena falls in love with a wounded sailor, but doesn't receive her wish to be mortal.
Arielle North Olson, *Ask the Bones: Scary Stories from around the World*, 1999
   Fourteen different countries, ranging from Uzbekistan to the United States, are represented in this collection of twenty-two ghostly folktales.

187

BRUCE COVILLE

The Monsters of Morley Manor: A Madcap Adventure

(San Diego: Harcourt, 2001)

Subject(s): Science Fiction; Aliens; Monsters
Age range(s): Grades 4-7
Major character(s): Anthony Walker, 12-Year-Old; Sarah Walker, Sister (of Anthony)
Time period(s): 2000s
Locale(s): Owl's Roost, Nebraska

Summary: When old man Morley dies, the new owner of Morley Manor has a yard sale and then plans to tear down the old, supposedly haunted mansion. Anthony and Sarah buy a carved wooden box at the sale and take it home where Anthony tries to pry it open. Inside are five compartments, each housing a small, lifelike, brass monster that, when wet, becomes alive. Now Anthony and Sarah are responsible for a werehuman, a hunchback, a vampire, a siren with snakes of hair and a lizard-headed man, all part of the Morleskievich family who have been under a spell for fifty years. Still only five inches tall, they need to return to Morley Manor in order to become life-size and save the Earth from an invasion of aliens who want to steal ghosts in this "madcap adventure." (224 pages)

Where it's reviewed:
Book Report, January 2002, page 59
Booklist, September 1, 2001, page 103
Fantasy & Science Fiction, March 2002, page 34
Kirkus Reviews, August 1, 2001, page 1119
School Library Journal, January 2002, page 132

Other books by the same author:
Half-Human, 2001
There's an Alien in My Underwear, 2001
A Glory of Unicorns, 1998
Fortune's Journey, 1995
Bruce Coville's Book of Monsters: Tales to Give You the Creeps, 1993

Other books you might like:
Eva Ibbotson, *Dial-a-Ghost*, 2001
   The Dial-a-Ghost agency mixes up an order and sends screaming ghosts to a convent and a loving ghost family to an orphan who needs tenderness.
Kathy Mackel, *Can of Worms*, 1999
   Mike opens a "can of worms" when he sends out a message to space requesting rescue; all of a sudden, aliens who want to help surround him.

William Sleator, *Interstellar Pig*, 1984
   Barney plays the board game Interstellar Pig with three neighbors who happen to be aliens playing for control of the Earth.
Sylvia Waugh, *Space Race*, 2000
   Thomas is upset when he realizes he and his father must return to their planet Ormingat after living on Earth for five years.
Sheila Williams, *Why I Left Harry's All-Night Hamburgers: And Other Stories from Isaac Asimov's Science Fiction Magazine*, 1990
   Swapping tales with aliens at Harry's All-Night Hamburgers, one can find out the real reason the chicken crossed the road.

188

JANE COWEN-FLETCHER, Author/Illustrator

Farmer Will

(Cambridge, MA: Candlewick Press, 2001)

Subject(s): Animals; Toys; Imagination
Age range(s): Preschool
Major character(s): Will, Child
Time period(s): Indeterminate
Locale(s): Earth

Summary: Will likes to pretend he is a farmer. He plays with his toy horse, cow, pig and sheep daily by taking them outside, imagining that they are life size and then playing hide-and-seek or run through the sprinkler with them. At the end of the day, when everyone is tired, the animals become toys again and Will carries them into the house so they can join him for a good night's sleep. (28 pages)

Where it's reviewed:
Booklist, July 2001, page 2018
Horn Book Guide, Fall 2001, page 229
Publishers Weekly, May 21, 2001, page 106
School Library Journal, July 2001, page 73

Other books by the same author:
Baby Angels, 1996
It Takes a Village, 1994
Mama Zooms, 1993

Other books you might like:
Margaret Wise Brown, *Big Red Barn*, 1995
   A description of one day in the life of a big red barn introduces the many animals that live inside.
Kim Lewis, *One Summer Day*, 1996
   One summer day Max sees chickens, cows and a big red tractor plowing a field.
David McPhail, *Farm Morning*, 1991
   Father and daughter spend a special morning on the farm feeding their animals.

JOY COWLEY
JENNIFER PLECAS, Illustrator

Agapanthus Hum and Major Bark

(New York: Philomel Books, 2001)

Subject(s): Animals/Dogs; Pets; Humor
Age range(s): Grades 1-3
Major character(s): Agapanthus Hum, Child, Daughter; Major Bark, Dog
Time period(s): 2000s (2001)
Locale(s): United States

Summary: With her parents Agapanthus Hum trots off to the animal shelter to select the perfect kitten. Her search for a kitten is difficult because she's continually distracted by a small dog and in no time, Agapanthus Hum heads home with the pup that steals her heart. Major Bark has a major flaw, chewing anything and everything in sight. However, Agapanthus Hum is so sure that Major Bark is a champion "bitser" because he's a little bit of everything that she enters him in a dog contest where Major Bark succeeds in winning a very tasty blue ribbon. (48 pages)

Where it's reviewed:
Booklist, February 15, 2001, page 1143
Bulletin of the Center for Children's Books, March 2001, page 254
Horn Book Guide, Fall 2001, page 284
Publishers Weekly, December 18, 2000, page 80
School Library Journal, February 2001, page 93

Other books by the same author:
Agapanthus Hum and the Eyeglasses, 1999 (Publishers Weekly Best Books)
Singing Down the Rain, 1997
Gracias, the Thanksgiving Turkey, 1996

Other books you might like:
Marion Dane Bauer, *Alison's Puppy*, 1997
    More than anything else Alison wants a puppy for her birthday so when Grandpa gives her a kitten she names it Puppy.
Marc Brown, *Arthur's New Puppy*, 1993
    Arthur discovers some unexpected challenges when he receives a puppy.
Cynthia Rylant, *Henry and Mudge*, 1987
    In the first book of a now classic series, Henry, lonely for companionship, begs his parents to allow him to have a dog.

190

JUDY COX
BLANCHE SIMS, Illustrator

Butterfly Buddies

(New York: Holiday House, 2001)

Subject(s): Schools; Honesty; Friendship
Age range(s): Grades 2-4

Major character(s): Robin, 3rd Grader, Sister (younger); Zoey, 3rd Grader, Classmate; Miss Wing, Teacher; Gramps, Grandfather
Time period(s): 2000s (2001)
Locale(s): United States

Summary: Robin confides in Gramps about her many school-related anxieties. The year is almost over and she must adjust to her best friend's move and the loss of her teacher who's on maternity leave. Robin feels an immediate bond with her new teacher, Miss Wing, who's wearing the same red high-topped sneakers, but she's not sure how to make friends with Zoey who's also new to the class. She and Zoey are partners for the class project of raising a butterfly from a caterpillar. Rather than allowing the friendship to develop, Robin tries too hard to be helpful and to be liked and unintentionally creates problems with Zoey and Miss Wing. Eventually Robin learns to admit the truth behind her actions to both Miss Wing and Zoey and she discovers that they both like her for who she is. (86 pages)

Where it's reviewed:
Booklist, September 1, 2001, page 102
Horn Book Guide, Spring 2002, page 71
Horn Book, March 2002, page 203
School Library Journal, October 2001, page 113

Other books by the same author:
Weird Stories from the Lonesome Cafe, 2000
Mean, Mean Maureen Green, 1999
Third Grade Pet, 1998

Other books you might like:
Beverly Cleary, *Ramona Quimby, Age 8*, 1981
    Ramona copes with her family, friends and turning eight in a Newbery Honor Book.
Paula Danziger, *Amber Brown Is Not a Crayon*, 1994
    Amber's third grade year is made more difficult when she learns that her best friend Justin is moving.
Suzy Kline, *Song Lee and the I Hate You Notes*, 1999
    An anonymous sender of two "I hate you" notes finally admits to her wrongdoing.

 191

SHARON CREECH
HARRY BLISS, Illustrator

A Fine, Fine School

(New York: Joanna Cotler Books/HarperCollins Publishers, 2001)

Subject(s): Schools; School Life; Education
Age range(s): Grades K-3
Major character(s): Mr. Keene, Principal; Tillie, Student—Elementary School, Sister (older); Beans, Dog
Time period(s): 2000s (2001)
Locale(s): United States

Summary: Mr. Keene is very proud of the students and teachers in his school and the learning that occurs. In fact, he's so proud that he decides his fine school should have more of this fine learning on Saturday. Tillie tries to comply with Mr. Keene's expectations but she misses playing with her brother and their pet Beans. After Mr. Keene takes away Sundays, holidays and summer vacation so that his fine school can become even finer, Tillie marches into Mr. Keene's office to tell him all the things that Beans and her brother are not learning because she's not home with them. Finally Mr. Keene decides that it's just fine not to attend school on weekends or holidays and everyone is fine with that idea. (32 pages)

Where it's reviewed:
Booklist, August 2001, page 2116
Children's Bookwatch, August 2001, page 3
Kirkus Reviews, June 15, 2001, page 862
Publishers Weekly, July 23, 2001, page 75
School Library Journal, August 2001, page 144

Other books by the same author:
Fishing in the Air, 2000 (Publishers Weekly Best Books)

Other books you might like:
Stephanie Calmenson, *The Frog Principal*, 2001
    A magician's error turns a school principal into a frog that kindly offers to substitute until the principal returns.
Maryann Cocca-Leffler, *Mr. Tanen's Ties*, 1999
    Students depend on their principal's colorful ties to tell them the lunch menu, the weather and the holidays.
Patricia Polacco, *Mr. Lincoln's Way*, 2001
    Loved for being a ''cool'' principal by everyone but the school bully, Mr. Lincoln learns the bully's interests and uses them to help him.

SHARON CREECH

Love That Dog
(New York: Joanna Cotler Books/HarperCollins Publishers, 2001)

Subject(s): Teacher-Student Relationships; Poetry; Authorship
Age range(s): Grades 3-6
Major character(s): Jack, Student, Writer; Miss Stretchberry, Teacher
Time period(s): 2000s
Locale(s): United States

Summary: During Jack's year under the gentle guidance of Miss Stretchberry he quietly evolves from a poetry hater to an admirer and writer of poems. Jack's journal entries give his reactions to the various poems used in the class instruction and his developing attempts at expressing his own thoughts in this medium. Initially reluctant to share his feelings, Jack finally creates a poem that reveals the grief he feels about the accidental death of his dog. Inspired by Walter Dean Myers and his poem ''Love That Boy'' Jack concludes his entries with a poem celebrating the joy that dog brought into his life. The poems alluded to in Jack's journal entries are reprinted at the conclusion of the book. (102 pages)

Where it's reviewed:
Booklist, August 2001, page 2118
Five Owls, Fall 2001, page 42
Horn Book, November 2001, page 743
Publishers Weekly, June 18, 2001, page 82
School Library Journal, August 2001, page 177

Awards the book has won:
School Library Journal Best Books, 2001

ALA Notable Children's Books, 2002

Other books by the same author:
Chasing Redbird, 1997 (IRA Children's Choices)
Pleasing the Ghost, 1996
Walk Two Moons, 1994 (Newbery Medal)

Other books you might like:
Kate DiCamillo, *Because of Winn-Dixie*, 2000
    The summer Opal claims a stray found in the Winn-Dixie grocery store as her own pet she grows out of the loneliness she feels in her new home.
Lois Lowry, *Stay! Keeper's Story*, 1997
    An abandoned pup develops into a poetry-composing dog who finally finds a permanent home and name on his third try.
Elizabeth Spires, *The Mouse of Amherst*, 1999
    Emmaline, a mouse resident in a poet's home, discovers the joy of writing by exchanging poems with Emily Dickinson.
Maria Testa, *Becoming Joe DiMaggio*, 2002
    In a tale written in blank verse, listening to baseball games on the radio helps to unify an Italian-American family during difficult times.

193

LINDA CREW

Brides of Eden
(New York: HarperCollins, 2001)

Subject(s): Cults; Christian Life; Historical
Age range(s): Grades 7-10
Major character(s): Eva Mae Hurt, 16-Year-Old; Franz Edmund Creffield, Religious (minister)
Time period(s): 1900s (1903-1906)
Locale(s): Corvallis, Oregon

Summary: At the turn of the century, Eva Mae Hart, her mother and sister attend the Salvation Army meetings, though Eva Mae sometimes wishes they could attend a more-traditional church. Then Franz Edmund Creffield moves to Corvallis, attends the Salvation Army meetings and mesmerizes the women with his thoughts and bold declamations about religion. When he leaves the Salvation Army, sets up his own church and asks to be called Joshua the Second, many of the townswomen join his church with its mid-day services. The hold he has on these women is mesmerizing and soon they shed their clothes for smocks, wear their hair unbound, and leave their families and husbands to join his island retreat, where each woman is eager to become the ''Second Mary'' and Joshua is ready to father the child. The men of Corvallis have their women arrested and declared insane as they struggle to save their wives, daughters and sisters from the grasp of this obsessed man, steps which ultimately lead to murder and suicide in this work based on historical fact. (223 pages)

Where it's reviewed:
Booklist, December 15, 2000, page 808
Horn Book, March 2001, page 206
Publishers Weekly, December 18, 2000, page 80
School Library Journal, February 2001, page 117

Voice of Youth Advocates, June 2001, page 119

Other books by the same author:
Long Time Passing, 1997
Fire on the Wind, 1995
Ordinary Miracles, 1993
Children of the River, 1989

Other books you might like:
Margaret Peterson Haddix, *Leaving Fishers*, 1997
    Dorry joins the religious group Fishers of Men, but knows it's time to leave the organization when she tries to convert the children she's babysitting.
Stephanie S. Tolan, *A Good Courage*, 1988
    Ty and his friend Samarah flee the kingdom of Yahweh, a fanatical cult.
Jane Yolen, *Armageddon Summer*, 1998
    Two teens meet as each tries to be a buffer between a parent and cult leader Beelson who predicts the end of the world on July 27, 2000.

194

MARTY CRISP

Private Captain: A Novel of Gettysburg
(New York: Philomel, 2001)

Subject(s): Civil War; Brothers; Animals/Dogs
Age range(s): Grades 6-8
Major character(s): Ben Herr Reynolds, 12-Year-Old; Danny Seldomridge, Cousin, 11-Year-Old; Reuben Reynolds, Military Personnel (Union Army); Captain, Dog
Time period(s): 1860s
Locale(s): Lancaster, Pennsylvania; Gettysburg, Pennsylvania

Summary: After Ben's father dies, he realizes that his mother needs someone to tend their store so he sets off in search of his older brother, Captain Reuben of the 106th Pennsylvania Company A. Ben's heard rumors of a big battle approaching, so he figures his brother will be involved in the skirmish at Gettysburg. Although not part of Ben's plan, his cousin Danny and Reuben's dog Captain both decide to follow him, which means no one will miss seeing or hearing this search party. Arriving in Gettysburg, the townspeople provide shelter for Ben and Danny and Ben helps dispose of the dead animals and tend the wounded. Not seeing Reuben among the wounded or dead bodies, Ben finally tells Captain to find him as he and Danny return home in this realistic, yet humorous, novel of civilian life during the Civil War. (293 pages)

Where it's reviewed:
Booklist, April 1, 2001, page 1481
Bulletin of the Center for Children's Books, March 2001, page 255
Publishers Weekly, March 5, 2001, page 80
School Library Journal, April 2001, page 139
Voice of Youth Advocates, April 2001, page 37

Other books by the same author:
Ratzo, 1998
Buzzard Breath, 1995
At Your Own Risk, 1993

Other books you might like:
Patricia Calvert, *Bigger*, 1994
    As Tyler journeys to find his father and bring him back home after the Civil War, he is accompanied by Bigger, an abused dog.
Patricia Clapp, *The Tamarack Tree: A Novel of the Siege of Vicksburg*, 1986
    A young English girl trapped inside Vicksburg during the battle offers her views of the events.
Stephen Hahn, *Pike McCallister*, 1998
    His father and brother are killed in the Civil War and his mother is kidnapped which leaves Pike no choice but to head north in search of her.
Laura Jan Shore, *The Sacred Moon Tree*, 1986
    Disguised as a boy, Phoebe and her friend Jotham cross through enemy territory to rescue Phoebe's brother during the Civil War.

195

CONNIE BRUMMEL CROOK

The Hungry Year
(Niagara Falls, NY: Stoddart Kids, 2001)

Subject(s): Survival; Single Parent Families; Frontier, Canada
Age range(s): Grades 5-8
Major character(s): Kate O'Carr, 12-Year-Old; Alex O'Carr, Twin, Child; Ryan O'Carr, Twin, Child
Time period(s): 1780s (1787)
Locale(s): Fredericksburgh Township, Canada

Summary: Since the death of her mother and grandmother, Kate has been responsible for all the household chores, in addition to looking after her four-year-old twin brothers, while her father seems oblivious to the work she does. He sided with the Loyalists during the American Revolution and, faced with the possibility of jail time in New York, decides to move to Canada where he receives free land for his Loyalist activities. Their first winter in the cabin proves to be one of the harshest on record and food is a constant problem. One day Kate's father doesn't return from hunting, leaving Kate, Alex and Ryan alone. Facing starvation, the children are saved by the Mohawk Indians in this tale based on historical facts. (201 pages)

Where it's reviewed:
Booklist, January 2002, page 856
The Loyalist Gazette, Fall 2001, page 52
Resource Links, October 2001, page 10
School Library Journal, November 2001, page 154

Other books by the same author:
Nellie's Victory, 2000
Nellie's Quest, 1998
Flight, 1994
Meyers' Creek, 1994

Other books you might like:
Gillian Chan, *The Carved Box*, 2002
    In the early 1800s, Callum is orphaned and sails to Canada to be with his uncle Rory on his farm where a life of hard labor awaits him.

Janet Lunn, *Shadow in Hawthorn Bay*, 1987

During the early days of Canadian settlement, a young Scottish girl with psychic powers travels there to help her cousin.

Kathryn Reiss, *Riddle of the Prairie Bride*, 2001

Ida Kate can hardly wait for the arrival of her father's mail-order bride and her young son so she'll have relief from chores and can return to school.

196

KEVIN CROSSLEY-HOLLAND

The Seeing Stone

(New York: Scholastic, 2000)

Series: Arthur Trilogy. Book 1
Subject(s): Arthurian Legends; Psychic Powers
Age range(s): Grades 6-10
Major character(s): Arthur de Caldicot, Teenager; Merlin, Friend
Time period(s): 12th century
Locale(s): England (the border country between England and Wales)

Summary: From the beginning Arthur treasures the mysterious black stone Merlin gives him. The stone is a rare secret in Arthur's world, where everyone knows everyone else's business and the whole world seems to be ordered by Arthur's father. The harsh and busy everyday life keeps young Arthur moving even though he wants to brood on his possible future. When the black stone begins to show Arthur visions of another place and time, he isn't sure what he's seeing or how it relates to him. Slowly he realizes that the Arthur of the stone is the King Arthur of legend, and although his and Arthur's lives seem to be unfolding in parallel ways, they are not the same. But the reason for the revelations and their usefulness remains a mystery to Arthur as he prepares to go on Crusade. (338 pages)

Where it's reviewed:
Booklist, October 1, 2001, page 315
Horn Book Magazine, November 2001, page 743
Kliatt, September 2001, page 6
New York Times Book Review, January 20, 2002, page 14
School Library Journal, October 2001, page 152

Awards the book has won:
Horn Book Fanfare/Fiction, 2002
Book List Editors' Choice/Books for Youth, 2001

Other books by the same author:
The World of King Arthur and His Court, 1998

Other books you might like:
Nancy Bond, *A String in the Harp*, 1976

A boy visiting Wales makes a discovery that links him through time.

Sarah L. Thomson, *The Dragon's Son*, 2001

Four short stories tell Arthur's story through the eyes of Morgan, Nimue, Lunue and Medraud.

Jane Yolen, *Passager*, 1996

Arthur's magician Merlin is the protagonist of the trilogy that begins with this book.

197

CAROLE CROWE

Groover's Heart

(Honesdale, PA: Boyds Mills Press, 2001)

Subject(s): Orphans; Aunts and Uncles
Age range(s): Grades 4-6
Major character(s): Charlotte Dearborn, Orphan, 11-Year-Old; Charles "Groover" Wattley, Uncle (of Charlotte), Alcoholic (recovering); Viola, Aunt (of Charlotte); Edward "Ed", Uncle (of Charlotte)
Time period(s): 2000s
Locale(s): Connecticut; Southbay, New York (Long Island)

Summary: Orphaned at the age of two, Charlotte has been raised by her Aunt Viola and Uncle Ed in a very nice, but essentially loveless, home. Her material needs are all met, but not her emotional ones, so when Charlotte hears that she has an uncle she's never met, she's determined to find him. With her aunt and uncle out of town, she negotiates the train ride to Long Island where she locates her messy, recovering alcoholic Uncle Charlie, called Groover by his friends. Though he's not as financially comfortable as Viola and Ed, Charlotte feels his plainer lifestyle is more suitable for her; now all she has to do is convince all the adults in her life that living with Uncle Groover is best for her. (144 pages)

Where it's reviewed:
Booklist, April 15, 2001, page 1552
School Library Journal, April 2001, page 139
Voice of Youth Advocates, June 2001, page 120

Other books by the same author:
Waiting for Dolphins, 2000
Sharp Horns on the Moon, 1998

Other books you might like:
Patricia Calvert, *The Snowbird*, 1980

Their parents die and Willie and TJ move to the Dakota territory where they live with, and help, their aunt and uncle.

Cynthia DeFelice, *Nowhere to Call Home*, 1999

Orphaned Frances dresses as a boy and heads West, but decides living with an unknown relative is a better alternative.

Sid Fleischman, *Bo & Mzzz Mad*, 2001

Orphaned, Bo's not sure whether to go to a foster home or contact his Martinka relatives who've had a long-standing feud with his side of the family.

Gail Carson Levine, *Dave at Night*, 1999

Each night Dave escapes from the Hebrew Home for Boys and enjoys the sights and sounds of Harlem during its Renaissance time.

Barbara Brooks Wallace, *Ghosts in the Gallery*, 2000

Orphaned in China, Jenny travels to American to live with her grandfather Mr. Graymark, but he claims to know nothing about her.

198

TONY CRUNK
SCOTT NASH, Illustrator

Grandpa's Overalls

(New York: Orchard Books, 2001)

Subject(s): Farm Life; Grandfathers; Clothes
Age range(s): Grades K-3
Major character(s): Grandpa, Farmer, Dog; Grandma, Spouse, Dog
Time period(s): Indeterminate
Locale(s): Fictional Country

Summary: Grandma's the first to spot those overalls leaping off the porch and racing away. Grandpa can't work in just his long underwear so he hightails it after the overalls with Grandma and all the rest of the family joining the pursuit. As they chase the overalls through orchard and chicken coop neighbors hurry to help. Through the garden, the potato patch and the cornfield the overalls elude the group. Finally, everyone settles down to do Grandpa's work while Grandpa, who can't work in just his underwear, has a relaxing day. Just as all the workers come in to supper Grandma spots her nightgown sneaking off with the overalls and the chase begins again. (32 pages)

Where it's reviewed:
Booklist, August 2001, page 2128
Bulletin of the Center for Children's Books, May 2001, page 333
Kirkus Reviews, May 1, 2001, page 657
Publishers Weekly, June 11, 2001, page 84
School Library Journal, July 2001, page 74

Other books by the same author:
Big Mama, 2000

Other books you might like:
Mordicai Gerstein, *Stop Those Pants!*, 1998
    Murray's pants are too lively for him to catch so he's having difficulty getting dressed for school.
Kathryn Lasky, *The Emperor's Old Clothes*, 1999
    In a humorous spoof of a classic fairy tale, farmer Henry dons the discarded clothes he finds but discovers they are not practical for farm work.
David Small, *Fenwick's Suit*, 1996
    Fenwick tries to change his image with a new suit, but the suit takes on a life of its own, dumps Fenwick and goes to work in his place.

199

CHRIS CRUTCHER

Whale Talk

(New York: Greenwillow, 2001)

Subject(s): Sports/Swimming; Racially Mixed People; Adoption
Age range(s): Grades 8-12
Major character(s): The Tao "T.J." Jones, 12th Grader, Swimmer; Mr. Simet, Teacher (English), Coach (swimming); Chris Coughlin, Swimmer, Mentally Challenged Person; John Paul Jones, Father (adoptive father of T.J.); Rich Marshall, Father (of biracial Heidi)
Time period(s): 2000s
Locale(s): Cutter, Washington

Summary: All the athletes at Cutter High School enjoy special privileges, which is exactly why talented athlete T.J. Jones spurns his high school's athletic program. That resolve changes during his senior year when Mr. Simet asks him to anchor a swim team that will save Mr. Simet's job. T.J. agrees mainly to give handicapped Chris a chance to snub the athletes who tease him for wearing his deceased brother's letter jacket. T.J. stands out in his white community partly for his ability to stand on his own and partly because he's an adopted, biracial teen; he garners even more attention when he puts together a swim team made up of misfits who bond with one another in their quest to earn a varsity letter. Inciting the wrath of the head of the athletic booster club, former jock Rich Marshall, T.J. finds their paths crossing out of school when Marshall's abused, biracial daughter ends up as a foster child with T.J.'s parents. Though the inevitable collision between two fathers occurs and T.J.'s father takes a bullet meant for someone else, he leaves a strong message to not seek revenge in another winning title from a talented author. (220 pages)

Where it's reviewed:
Booklist, April 1, 2001, page 1462
Bulletin of the Center for Children's Books, April 2001, page 300
Horn Book, May 2001, page 320
Kliatt, March 2001, page 8
Voice of Youth Advocates, June 2001, page 119

Awards the book has won:
ALA Best Books for Young Adults, 2002
Publishers Weekly Best Children's Books, 2001

Other books by the same author:
Staying Fat for Sarah Byrnes, 1993
Athletic Shorts: Six Short Stories, 1991
The Crazy Horse Electric Game, 1987
Stotan!, 1986

Other books you might like:
William Bell, *Zack*, 1999
    A social studies assignment involving a slave who finds freedom in Canada sends biracial Zack on a quest to trace his own ancestry.
Marie G. Lee, *Necessary Roughness*, 1996
    Trying to be part of his school, Korean American Chan switches to football from soccer, though he dislikes his coach who preaches "necessary roughness."
Norma Fox Mazer, *Out of Control*, 1993
    A mean-spirited physical retaliation for an imagined insult haunts the victim and her attackers, even when they all try to pretend nothing happened.
S.L. Rottman, *Head above Water*, 1999
    Punching out her former boyfriend for spreading lies, Skye misses the state swimming finals because of her broken fingers.

200

CATHERINE ANN CULLEN
DAVID CHRISTIANA, Illustrator

The Magical, Mystical, Marvelous Coat

(Boston: Little, Brown and Company, 2001)

Subject(s): Clothes; Magic; Stories in Rhyme
Age range(s): Grades K-3
Major character(s): Unnamed Character, Child, Daughter
Time period(s): Indeterminate
Locale(s): Fictional Country

Summary: In the author's first book a young girl wearing a coat with six different buttons daily offers one of the buttons to solve someone's problems. The first button cools a giant who offers praises for the "megacooliferous" coat. The second warms a chilly swan and Wednesday's button calms the winds tossing a sailing vessel. On Thursday the button adds magic to a wizard's worn out wand and the fifth button protects three bunnies from a hungry snake. The last button goes to a lonely elf. On Sunday the girl's parents look in the coat's pocket, find six more buttons and begin sewing them on the magical, marvelous coat. (32 pages)

Where it's reviewed:
Booklist, December 15, 2001, page 738
Bulletin of the Center for Children's Books, September 2001, page 10
Horn Book Guide, Spring 2002, page 39
Publishers Weekly, September 3, 2001, page 87
School Library Journal, December 2001, page 97

Other books you might like:
Brock Cole, *Buttons*, 2000
Nothing magical about the buttons that pop off this portly father's trousers; his daughters search for replacements to keep his pants up.
Crescent Dragonwagon, *Brass Button*, 1997
A button falls off Mrs. Moffatt's new coat and begins an odd journey about town until she finds it, months later, on her sidewalk.
Richard Egielski, *Three Magic Balls*, 2000
Rudy discovers that three balls in his uncle's toyshop have magical properties.

201

PRISCILLA CUMMINGS

A Face First

(New York: Dutton, 2001)

Subject(s): Hospitals; Automobile Accidents; Self-Confidence
Age range(s): Grades 6-9
Major character(s): Kelley Anne Brennan, 12-Year-Old, Patient (burn victim); Leah Brennan, Sister (of Kelley's), Student—College; Leslie, Nurse
Time period(s): 2000s
Locale(s): Kent Island, Maryland; Baltimore, Maryland

Summary: Hospitalized following a traffic accident, Kelley gradually realizes that she has a burned, broken leg and third degree burns on her face. At first she's only aware of pain and discomfort, which intensifies as she receives more skin grafts and follow-up physical therapy, but later she realizes she'll never again look the same. Kelley's face is badly scarred and she now faces a year of wearing a plastic mask to reduce disfigurement, but most of all, she wonders if she'll ever be able to face her friends at school. Support from her nurse Leslie, a meeting with another burn victim, the friendship of her sister Leah and two classmates and her mother's confession of being at fault for the accident, enable Kelley to put her life in perspective and return to school. (197 pages)

Where it's reviewed:
Book Report, November 2001, page 59
Booklist, February 1, 2001, page 1052
Bulletin of the Center for Children's Books, February 2001, page 220
Publishers Weekly, January 22, 2001, page 325
School Library Journal, February 2001, page 117

Other books by the same author:
Autumn Journey, 1997

Other books you might like:
Nancy Antle, *Playing Solitaire*, 2000
Though Ellie vows to kill her father for cutting off three of her fingers while he was drunk, when he reappears in her life, she handles the situation.
Karen Hesse, *Out of the Dust*, 1997
Billie Jo tosses a burning pail of kerosene out the kitchen door and accidentally douses her mother, who later dies.
John Marsden, *So Much to Tell You*, 1987
Through her journal, Marina reveals the sad story of her facial disfigurement caused when her father unintentionally threw acid on her.
Graham McNamee, *Hate You*, 1999
A songwriter unable to sing because her father choked her and ruined her vocal cords, Alice discovers that she is able to forgive him when he's dying of cancer.
Cynthia Voigt, *Izzy, Willy-Nilly*, 1986
Cheerleader Izzy's life changes when an automobile accident leaves her an amputee.

202

MARGERY CUYLER
ARTHUR HOWARD, Illustrator

Stop, Drop, and Roll

(New York: Simon & Schuster Books for Young Readers, 2001)

Subject(s): Schools; Family; Conduct of Life
Age range(s): Grades K-3
Major character(s): Jessica, Student—Elementary School, Sister; Tom, 6-Year-Old, Brother; Mr. Martin, Teacher
Time period(s): 2000s (2001)
Locale(s): United States

Summary: Jessica is a child prone to worry about little things such as spelling homework and being late for school. When Mr. Martin begins a discussion of fire safety during Fire Prevention Week poor Jessica becomes overwhelmed with fears about smoke alarms, sprinkler systems, family fire drills and escape plans. Every evening Jessica takes action to alleviate her fears by discussing the day's lessons with her family and eliciting their involvement. Just when Jessica thinks she's getting control of her worries Mr. Martin assigns her the task of demonstrating "Stop, Drop and Roll" at an assembly. Poor Jessica becomes tongue-tied just trying to say the three-word phrase but she continues practicing. At Tom's birthday party the sight of the candles blazing on her cake is the impetus for her to finally blurt out the safety rule correctly. Fortunately for Tom it's a false alarm. (32 pages)

Where it's reviewed:
Booklist, September 15, 2001, page 230
Bulletin of the Center for Children's Books, November 2001, page 98
Kirkus Reviews, July 15, 2001, page 1024
Publishers Weekly, October 22, 2001, page 78
School Library Journal, October 2001, page 113

Other books by the same author:
100th Day Worries, 2000 (IRA Teachers' Choice)
From Here to There, 1999
The Biggest, Best Snowman, 1998

Other books you might like:
Jean Pendziwol, *No Dragons for Tea: Fire Safety for Kids (And Dragons)*, 1999
When the dragon guest invited to tea sneezes and ignites the house a child's knowledge of fire safety rules enables everyone to reach safety.
Peggy Rathmann, *Officer Buckle and Gloria*, 1995
Police dog Gloria enlivens Office Buckle's safety presentations in a humorous Caldecott Medal winner.
Wong Herbert Yee, *Fireman Small: Fire Down Below!*, 2001
During a hotel fire, Fireman Small instructs the guests in the procedures for exiting the building safely.

203

JULIE CZERNEDA

In the Company of Others
(New York: DAW Books, 2001)

Subject(s): Medical Thriller; Cultural Conflict
Age range(s): Grades 9-Adult

Major character(s): Aaron Pardell, Survivor; Gail Smith, Scientist
Time period(s): Indeterminate Future
Locale(s): Thromberg Station, Space Station

Summary: Mankind is just beginning a major expansion in space when a universally fatal plague attacks the colonists. The cause of the deaths is mysterious and all migration is halted which creates disastrous conditions aboard the space stations. Meant to act as temporary jump-off points, they now become permanent refugee camps for many more than they were designed to support. Back on earth the plague defies all attempts of science to unravel it and, because there is no cure, Earthers will not allow the return of anyone who may have become contaminated. Tensions mount, but Gail Smith thinks she has discovered the key to the puzzle. Thromberg Station is reputed to have aboard the sole survivor, Aaron Pardell. Aaron was born shortly before his parents touched down on a contaminated planet and although they died, he lived, albeit with a strange and terrible affliction. Aaron cannot be physically touched without experiencing excruciating pain for himself and whoever touches him. Professor Smith appears to offer him hope, but are her interests really the same as Aaron's? (560 pages)

Where it's reviewed:
Kliatt, September 2001, page 21
Voice of Youth Advocates, February 2002, page 444

Other books by the same author:
Ties of Power, 1999
Beholder's Eye, 1998
A Thousand Words for Stranger, 1997

Other books you might like:
Kevin Anderson, *Climbing Olympus*, 1994
Mars has been terraformed and the old bio-engineered humans who originally colonized the planet are no longer needed, but where can they go?
Greg Bear, *Darwin's Radio*, 1999
Is an overwhelming new mutation a disease or the next step in evolution?
Orson Scott Card, *Speaker for the Dead*, 1986
An encounter with an alien species proves deadly, but it's not clear whether it's murder or biology.

D

MICHAEL DAHL

The Viking Claw

(New York: Archway/Simon & Schuster, 2001)

Series: Finnegan Zwake Mystery
Subject(s): Mystery and Detective Stories; Mountaineering
Age range(s): Grades 5-8
Major character(s): Finnegan Zwake, 13-Year-Old, Detective—Amateur; Stoppard Sterling, Uncle, Writer (of mysteries)
Time period(s): 2000s
Locale(s): Iceland

Summary: Eight years ago Finn's parents disappeared while on an expedition to Iceland in search of the Haunted City of Tquuli, a lost Viking colony located somewhere in the frozen mountains. Now Finn and Uncle Stoppard try to recreate the path they followed in the hopes of finding clues to their disappearance. With guides and other climbers, Finn's detecting skills are called into use very early when one of the guides disappears and another is murdered. The discovery of eight Viking ships buried under the snow unleashes more problems in this continuing series, though Finn does find what he thinks is a clue left by his parents. (162 pages)

Where it's reviewed:
Booklist, May 15, 2001, page 1744
Kliatt, September 2001, page 16

Other books by the same author:
The Coral Coffin, 2001 (Finnegan Zwake Mystery)
The Wheels that Vanished, 2000 (Scooter Spies)
The Horizontal Man, 1999 (Finnegan Zwake Mystery)
The Ruby Raven, 1999 (Finnegan Zwake Mystery)
The Worm Tunnel, 1999 (Finnegan Zwake Mystery)

Other books you might like:
T.M. Murphy, *The Secrets of Cranberry Beach*, 1996
   Already recognized as a crime solver, Orville now tackles the murder of his friend Will's fiancee who died years ago in a cranberry bog.

Wendelin Van Draanen, *Sammy Keyes and the Hollywood Mummy*, 2001
   Visiting her aspiring actress mother, Sammy's detecting skills are needed when a competitor for a coveted role is found dead in her mother's house.
Eric Wilson, *Code Red at the Mall*, 2000
   Liz and Tom want to help their dad investigate the bombs left at the West Edmonton Mall, which features shark and dolphin tanks and lots of stores.

MITZI DALE

The Sky's the Limit

(Toronto: Groundwood Books, 2001, c1990)

Subject(s): Schools/High Schools; Actors and Actresses
Age range(s): Grades 6-9
Major character(s): Kim Taylor, Student—High School; Skye Manning, Student—High School
Time period(s): 1990s
Locale(s): Hamilton, Ontario, Canada

Summary: Kim's dream is to become a stand-up comedian, or an actress, anything in show business, but first she has to get through four years of high school. She and her friends don't want to be in the loser group, but aren't quite ''Miss Popularity'' material, so they come up with a plan; her friends decide to find boyfriends while Kim decides to befriend Skye who seems to have everything. Surprisingly enough, Kim and Skye do become friends and have a great time together their freshman and sophomore years. By junior year, Skye becomes moody, turns to stealing and is in several car accidents. Kim can't figure out what's going on to cause these changes in her, until it comes out that Skye's father abuses her. To protect herself from Kim's knowledge, Skye tells everyone that Kim lies because she's jealous of Skye. All of a sudden her poor family looks pretty good and Kim begins to realize what's really important in life. (153 pages)

Where it's reviewed:
Kliatt, May 2001, page 18

School Library Journal, July 2001, page 102

Other books by the same author:
Bryna Means Courage, 1993
On My Own, 1991
Round the Bend, 1991

Other books you might like:
Ellen Conford, *Strictly for Laughs*, 1985
　　Joey has always been a comedienne so she doesn't understand why her good friend Peter doesn't invite her to be on his radio show.
Joan Lowery Nixon, *Hollywood Daughters: A Family Trilogy*, 1989-1990
　　This series features three generations and their involvement, of lack of, with the movie and television industry.
Richard Peck, *Princess Ashley*, 1987
　　New student Chelsea is thrilled to be included as part of Ashley's "in" group, not realizing she's just being used.

NIKI DALY, Author/Illustrator

What's Cooking, Jamela?
(New York: Farrar Straus Giroux, 2001)

Subject(s): Animals/Chickens; Christmas; Pets
Age range(s): Grades K-3
Major character(s): Jamela, Child, Daughter; Christmas, Chicken; Mama, Mother; Gogo, Grandmother
Time period(s): 2000s (2001)
Locale(s): South Africa

Summary: Mama buys a live chicken for Christmas dinner and assigns Jamela the task of fattening the bird for the dinner table. Jamela enjoys caring for the bird she names Christmas but when Gogo licks her lips each time she sees the bird Jamela begins to feel uncomfortable. When the time comes for Christmas to be slaughtered Jamela runs away with her. Christmas gets away from Jamela and becomes lost for a time in the busy city streets. When Christmas is located Jamela pleads for the life of her friend and Jamela and Mama plan a surprise for the holiday meal. (32 pages)

Where it's reviewed:
Booklist, November 1, 2001, page 482
Horn Book, September 2001, page 572
Publishers Weekly, October 15, 2001, page 73
School Library Journal, October 2001, page 64

Other books by the same author:
Jamela's Dress, 1999 (ALA Notable Children's Book)
My Dad, 1995
Not So Fast, Songololo, 1986

Other books you might like:
Joy Cowley, *Gracias, the Thanksgiving Turkey*, 1996
　　When Miguel's father gives him a turkey to fatten for Thanksgiving he treats it like a pet and has it blessed during mass to prevent its slaughter.
Antonio Hernandez Madrigal, *Blanca's Feather*, 2000
　　When Rosalia cannot find her pet chicken she brings one of Blanca's feathers to church for the blessing of the animals.

Tololwa M. Mollel, *Kele's Secret*, 1997
　　Yoanes follows Kele all day long trying to find the hen's nest so he can gather the eggs for market.

JEANNE M. DAMS

Green Grow the Victims
(New York: Walker, 2001)

Subject(s): Mystery and Detective Stories; Emigration and Immigration
Age range(s): Grades 10-Adult
Major character(s): Daniel Malloy, Political Figure (Democratic candidate for City); John Bishop, Political Figure (Republican candidate for City), Crime Victim; Patrick Cavanaugh, Fire Fighter; Hilda Johansson, Servant, Detective—Amateur; George Studebaker, Historical Figure, Military Personnel (colonel)
Time period(s): 1900s (1902)
Locale(s): South Bend, Indiana

Summary: Dan is the Democratic candidate for city council and John is the Republican running against him, until John is found beaten to death and Dan is the last person to have been seen with him. Since Hilda's boyfriend Patrick is Dan's nephew, Hilda is given time off from her job serving the Studebaker family to find the missing Dan Malloy and the murderer of his opponent John Bishop. She treads lightly as she interviews members of the Irish and the Swedish community, who are suspicious of one another, and finally locates Uncle Dan. Tracking down the real killer proves harder and almost claims her life in this third mystery about a Swedish immigrant. (210 pages)

Where it's reviewed:
Booklist, May 1, 2001, page 1628
Kirkus Reviews, May 15, 2001, page 707
Publishers Weekly, April 16, 2001, page 47
Voice of Youth Advocates, October 2001, page 274

Other books by the same author:
Silence Is Golden, 2002
The Red, White and Blue Murders, 2000
Death in Lacquer Red, 1999

Other books you might like:
Rhys Bowen, *Murphy's Law*, 2001
　　Fleeing to America after killing someone in self-defense, Molly is harassed on board ship by O'Malley; when he is found dead, she is the main suspect.
Jill Churchill, *Someone to Watch over Me*, 2001
　　Financially ruined by the Stock Market Crash, Lily and her brother Robert live at their uncle's estate where they find a long-dead body in the old icehouse.
Robin Paige, *Death at Epson Downs*, 2001
　　Lord Charles Sheridan is expected to solve the theft of actress Lillie Langtry's jewels and the murder of a Derby jockey.

208

TERI DANIELS
TIMOTHY BUSH, Illustrator

Math Man

(New York: Orchard Books, 2001)

Subject(s): Mathematics; Schools; Stores, Retail
Age range(s): Grades 1-3
Major character(s): Marnie, Student—Elementary School; Mrs. Gourd, Teacher; Garth ''Math Man'', Worker (stock boy)
Time period(s): 2000s (2001)
Locale(s): United States

Summary: Mrs. Gourd takes her class on a field trip to the Mighty Mart where they can see math in action in a variety of ways. Marnie's only interested in buying a pumpkin for Halloween but Garth hasn't had time to fill the pumpkin bin because he's been too busy helping students and customers with math-related problems. When the store's registers stop working Garth lives up to his name of Math Man by adding all the orders in his head and quickly clearing the lines of carts. Before the trip concludes Marnie buys a pumpkin and has enough change left to get a treat for her class. (32 pages)

Where it's reviewed:
Booklist, November 1, 2001, page 482
Horn Book Guide, Spring 2002, page 72
School Library Journal, January 2002, page 97

Awards the book has won:
IRA Children's Choices, 2002

Other books by the same author:
G-Rex, 2000
Just Enough, 2000
The Feet in the Gym, 1999

Other books you might like:
Amy Axelrod, *Pigs Go to Market: Fun with Math and Shopping*, 1997
    Price and quantity are important to Mrs. Pig, the winner of a five-minute shopping spree at the supermarket.
Sheila Keenan, *Lizzy's Dizzy Day*, 2001
    Lizzy puts her math skills to work getting ready for her cousin's birthday party but her efforts don't add up to something helpful.
Jon Scieszka, *Math Curse*, 1995
    After the teacher explains the possibility that anything can be viewed as a math problem a student develops a math phobia that's a real curse.

209

JOHN R. DANN

Song of the Axe

(New York: Tor/Forge, 2001)

Subject(s): Cave Dwellers; Man, Prehistoric
Age range(s): Grades 10-Adult
Major character(s): Eena ''Spear Woman'', Prehistoric Human; Agon ''Axe Man'', Prehistoric Human; Ka, Prehistoric Human

Time period(s): 300th century B.C.
Locale(s): Asia

Summary: Eena, her father and brother are hunting one day when a rival tribe, led by Ka, attacks them, kills the men and captures and rapes Eena. Witnessing this is the fierce warrior Agon, member of the Bison Hunter tribe, who manages to steal Eena back but then is confused as custom dictates he kill her to retrieve the souls of her father and brother. In love with Eena, Agon can't kill her and so the two flee to start their own tribe. It's difficult enough for two people to survive in such an inhospitable time, but to be followed by Ka's offspring makes life even more challenging in this first novel set during the Ice Age. (479 pages)

Where it's reviewed:
Booklist, April 15, 2001, page 1532
Kirkus Reviews, February 1, 2001, page 126
Library Journal, February 1, 2001, page 124
Publishers Weekly, March 12, 2001, page 63

Other books by the same author:
The Good Neighbors, 1995

Other books you might like:
Jean Auel, *Clan of the Cave Bear*, 1980
    Continually in conflict with the Neanderthal tribe that raised her, orphaned Cro-Magnon Ayla finally has no choice but to leave them.
W. Michael Gear, *People of the River*, 1992
    Nightshade is able to travel into the spirit world to escape the warring factions within her village.
Sue Harrison, *Mother Earth, Father Sky*, 1990
    Chagak flees from her destroyed Aleutian village only to be found by vicious killers when she seeks shelter with Shuganan, an elderly carver.
Elizabeth Marshall Thomas, *Reindeer Moon*, 1987
    The story of a group of Siberian hunter-gatherers who lived over twenty thousand years ago.

210

PAULA DANZIGER
TONY ROSS, Illustrator

It's Justin Time, Amber Brown

(New York: G.P. Putnam's Sons, 2001)

Series: A Is for Amber
Subject(s): Friendship; Birthdays; Individuality
Age range(s): Grades 2-3
Major character(s): Amber Brown, 7-Year-Old, Friend; Justin Daniels, 7-Year-Old, Friend
Time period(s): 1990s
Locale(s): United States

Summary: Time-focused Amber Brown counts the days until her seventh birthday on July 7th while fervently hoping she will receive a watch as one of her gifts. Amber's confident that a watch will enable her to teach perpetually tardy Justin the importance of punctuality. Justin arrives at Amber's party on time, but then vanishes as presents are being opened. Soon, Amber realizes that Justin's disappearance is part of the birthday surprise he's planned for her and she decides to enjoy

Justin's approach to time rather than try to change her friend. (48 pages)

Where it's reviewed:
BookPage, July 2001, page 31
Horn Book Guide, Fall 2001, page 284
Publishers Weekly, March 12, 2001, page 91
School Library Journal, March 2001, page 205

Other books by the same author:
What a Trip, Amber Brown, 2001 (A Is for Amber)
Amber Brown Is Feeling Blue, 1998 (Amber Brown)
Amber Brown Sees Red, 1997 (Amber Brown)

Other books you might like:
James Howe, *Pinky and Rex*, 1990
   Pinky and Rex, inseparable friends, embark on the first of many shared adventures in this initial book in their series.
Jonathan London, *Shawn and Keeper and the Birthday Party*, 1999
   Shawn and his dog Keeper share the same birthday in this book for beginning readers.
Joan Robins, *Addie's Bad Day*, 1993
   Good friend Max helps Addie get over her bad hair day and enjoy his birthday party.

211

PAULA DANZIGER
TONY ROSS, Illustrator

What a Trip, Amber Brown

(New York: G.P. Putnam's Sons, 2001)

Series: A Is for Amber
Subject(s): Vacations; Friendship; Family Life
Age range(s): Grades 1-3
Major character(s): Amber Brown, 2nd Grader, Friend; Justin Daniels, 2nd Grader, Friend; Danny Daniels, 3-Year-Old, Brother
Time period(s): 2000s
Locale(s): Poconos, Pennsylvania

Summary: The Brown and Daniels families share a house in the Poconos for their vacation. Swimmers Justin and Danny eagerly leap into the pool while non-swimmer Amber floats in her life jacket feeling annoyed by Justin's splashing and teasing. Although she resolves to stop talking to Justin, he makes amends in time for the two of them to join their dads in the backyard for a "sleep-out" in a tent. Danny is so upset at being excluded from the group because of his age that he finds a way to join them and soon everyone's sleeping out. (48 pages)

Where it's reviewed:
Horn Book Guide, Fall 2001, page 284
Kirkus Reviews, January 15, 2001, page 108
Publishers Weekly, March 12, 2001, page 91
School Library Journal, April 2001, page 105

Other books by the same author:
It's Justin Time, Amber Brown, 2001 (A Is for Amber)
I, Amber Brown, 1999 (Amber Brown)
Amber Brown Is Not a Crayon, 1994 (Amber Brown)

Other books you might like:
James Howe, *Pinky and Rex and the Double-Dad Weekend*, 1995
   Rain doesn't dampen plans for a weekend camping trip; it simply relocates the tent as flexible fathers enjoy time with their children.
Johanna Hurwitz, *Summer with Elisa*, 2000
   Almost second grader Elisa enjoys a country vacation with her family.
Cynthia Rylant, *Henry and Mudge and the Starry Night*, 1998
   A family camping trip includes hiking, singing around the campfire and quiet times with Henry's dog Mudge.

212

KAREN SCOURBY D'ARC
DIANE PALMISCIANO, Illustrator

My Grandmother Is a Singing Yaya

(New York: Orchard Books/Scholastic Inc., 2001)

Subject(s): Grandmothers; Greek Americans; Singing
Age range(s): Grades K-2
Major character(s): Yaya, Grandmother, Singer; Lulu, Daughter (granddaughter), Child
Time period(s): 2000s (2001)
Locale(s): United States

Summary: Yaya's tendency to burst into song at unpredictable moments frequently embarrasses Lulu. If Yaya is at home cooking, her singing is only embarrassing if Lulu has a friend visiting, but if they're in the movie theatre then Lulu wants to hide. Lulu wants Yaya to come to the Grandparents' Day Picnic at her school, but only if she can behave like the other grandmothers. It's a challenge for Lulu but she's able to keep Yaya quiet until after they finish eating all Lulu's favorite Greek foods that Yaya has packed in the picnic basket. Before Yaya can begin singing on her own the principal asks for her help in leading the group song as they honor the school's fiftieth birthday. (32 pages)

Where it's reviewed:
Booklist, January 1, 2002, page 863
Horn Book Guide, Spring 2002, page 39
Publishers Weekly, October 22, 2001, page 75
School Library Journal, November 2001, page 119

Other books you might like:
Nancy Carlson, *A Visit to Grandma's*, 1991
   Tina and her parents are surprised to learn how Grandma has changed since she moved into a Florida condominium!
Sook Nyul Choi, *Halmoni and the Picnic*, 1993
   Yunmi worries about the students' reaction to the traditional Korean food Halmoni prepares for the class picnic.
Emily Arnold McCully, *Grandmas at Bat*, 1993
   Two competitive grandmothers with good intentions complicate things for Pip's baseball team in this easy reader.

213

LAWRENCE DAVID
DELPHINE DURAND, Illustrator

Peter Claus and the Naughty List

(New York: Doubleday Book for Young Readers, 2001)

Subject(s): Santa Claus; Christmas; Behavior
Age range(s): Grades K-3
Major character(s): Peter Claus, Son, Child; Santa Claus, Father, Spouse; Mother Claus, Mother, Spouse
Time period(s): 2000s
Locale(s): Earth

Summary: When Peter Claus finds his own name on Santa's "naughty" list he decides to help himself and all the others on the list too. Secretly, he borrows the sleigh and reindeer, collects all the children from Santa's naughty list and brings them back to Santa and Mother Claus. Together they visit each child's family, listen to the reasons for the previous misbehavior and observe the child apologize to the wronged family member. By the time Peter returns home, only one name, his, remains on the list and Santa explains how his actions to help others are evidence of what a nice boy he is. (32 pages)

Where it's reviewed:
Booklist, September 15, 2001, page 236
Bulletin of the Center for Children's Books, November 2001, page 98
Publishers Weekly, September 24, 2001, page 54
School Library Journal, October 2001, page 64

Other books by the same author:
The Land of Hungry Armadillos, 2000
Beetle Boy, 1999
The Good Little Girl, 1998

Other books you might like:
John Burningham, *Harvey Slumfenburger's Christmas Present*, 1993
    For an especially nice boy like Harvey, Santa goes to considerable trouble to be sure his gift is delivered.
David McPhail, *Santa's Book of Names*, 1993
    After returning the book of names that Santa left at his house, Edward is invited to be Santa's helper for the night.
Viveca Larn Sundvall, *Santa's Winter Vacation*, 1994
    On a family vacation, three brothers (two naughty, one nice) meet an elderly bearded man and his wife who recall them the next year in December.

214

PETER DAVID

Sir Apropos of Nothing

(New York: Pocket Books, 2001)

Subject(s): Coming-of-Age; Fantasy; Heroes and Heroines
Age range(s): Grades 9-Adult
Major character(s): Apropos, Bastard Son, Handicapped; Entipy, Royalty (princess)
Time period(s): Indeterminate
Locale(s): Isteria, Fictional Country

Summary: Apropos's life is one bitter joke after another, and that's the way he relates it. A child of rape, Apropos is named in derision, but his romantic mother continue to believe him to be a child of fate. Lame Apropos develops a wicked tongue and sneaky talents to compensate for his physical inabilities, while nursing a desire to avenge himself and his mother on the upper classes of his feudal homeland. But the more he sees of the world the less certain Apropos becomes of exactly who is worthy of his revenge. When destiny pairs him up with the sulky Princess Entipy, someone is bound to be sorry. But will it be Apropos, the princess who burns down convents of holy women, or someone the two of them can agree on? (504 pages)

Where it's reviewed:
Booklist, June 1, 2001, page 1855
Kirkus Reviews, June 1, 2001, page 780
Library Journal, July 2001, page 131
Publishers Weekly, June 18, 2001, page 64

Other books by the same author:
Being Human, 2001
Armies of Light and Dark, 2000
Dark Allies, 1999

Other books you might like:
Dave Duncan, *Sir Stalwart*, 1999
    Small and untried, Stalwart goes under cover as a carter and finds himself further saddled with a cranky sister dismissed from her convent.
Sharon Shinn, *Summers at Castle Auburn*, 2001
    The castle seems a wonderful place to the King's illegitimate daughter when she visits it as a child, but nothing is the same to her adult eyes.
Christopher Stasheff, *A Wizard in Mind*, 1995
    A space-traveling wizard finds the application of modern common knowledge and a little magic go a long way towards solving the problems he encounters.
Delia Marshall Turner, *Nameless Magery*, 1998
    Lisane finds ironic commentary is a useful survival tool when she is marooned on a weird world where she is the only girl who can work magic.

215

DIANE MOTT DAVIDSON

Sticks & Scones

(New York: Bantam, 2001)

Subject(s): Mystery and Detective Stories; Catering Business
Age range(s): Grades 10-Adult
Major character(s): Eliot Hyde, Wealthy; Goldy Schulz, Cook (caterer); Tom Schulz, Police Officer
Time period(s): 2000s
Locale(s): Aspen Meadows, Colorado

Summary: With the chance to cater an Elizabethan meal to be served at Hyde Castle, a mansion brought over from England complete with its ghosts, Goldy doesn't need to find a dead body in the creek alongside the castle just a few hours before the banquet is to begin. The body is that of a stamp thief her husband Tom's been hunting and when he arrives to investigate, Tom is wounded. At the moment Goldy and Tom are staying at the castle because someone's shot out a window at their home, so while Tom recuperates Goldy starts nosing around but finds so many suspects! There's the wealthy owner of the castle, Eliot, who's newly rich; her son's fencing coach; her husband Tom's ex-girlfriend who was supposed to have died in Vietnam and then Goldy's own ex-husband who's on parole and is sporting a new girlfriend who once knew Eliot. It's a crazy adventure, complete with recipes, in this eleventh outing for Goldy. (301 pages)

Where it's reviewed:
Book World, February 25, 2001, page 4
Booklist, March 15, 2001, page 1357
Library Journal, April 1, 2001, page 137
People, June 4, 2001, page 47
Publishers Weekly, March 12, 2001, page 66

Other books by the same author:
Chopping Spree, 2002 (The Goldy Bear Culinary Mystery)
Tough Cookie, 2000 (The Goldy Bear Culinary Mystery)
Prime Cut, 1998 (The Goldy Bear Culinary Mystery)
The Grilling Season, 1998 (The Goldy Bear Culinary Mystery)
Catering to Nobody, 1990 (The Goldy Bear Culinary Mystery)

Other books you might like:
Jerrilyn Farmer, *Dim Sum Dead*, 2001
    Madeline Bean plans a Chinese New Year banquet for her mah-jongg group, but one of her players won't be playing with any more tiles.
Annette Meyers, *The Groaning Board*, 1997
    Leslie's long on Chutzpah and short on patience as she tries to find the person who added ground-up azalea to the muffins at a dinner party.
Nancy Pickard, *The Secret Ingredient Murders*, 2001
    Leaving Arizona to take care of teen relatives, Eugenia and her old friend Stanley host a tasting party for their new cookbook, but Stanley turns up dead.

216

NICOLA DAVIES
SARAH FOX-DAVIES, Illustrator

Bat Loves the Night
(Cambridge, MA: Candlewick Press, 2001)

Subject(s): Animals/Bats; Nature
Age range(s): Grades K-3
Major character(s): Bat, Bat, Mother
Time period(s): 2000s
Locale(s): Earth

Summary: From her attic perch Bat emerges into the night sky. Shouting in a voice too high for humans to hear Bat flies through the sky searching with her ears for something to eat. All night she swoops, dining on moths, mosquitoes and other insects. As the sky lightens Bat returns to her home, locates her waiting baby and settles upside down from a rafter to sleep the day away. Factual information about bats is included on each page in a smaller font to differentiate it from the story. (30 pages)

Where it's reviewed:
Booklist, September 1, 2001, page 114
Bulletin of the Center for Children's Books, December 2001, page 135
Horn Book Guide, Spring 2002, page 40
Kirkus Reviews, August 1, 2001, page 1120
School Library Journal, September 2001, page 187

Other books by the same author:
One Tiny Turtle, 2001
Wild about Dolphins, 2001
Big Blue Whale, 1997

Other books you might like:
Annie Cannon, *The Bat in the Boot*, 1996
    Two children find a baby bat in their father's boot. All day they feed and care for it hoping the mother will return after dark and she does.
Janell Cannon, *Stellaluna*, 1993
    Stellaluna, a young fruit bat, accidentally becomes separated from her mother and is befriended by a nest of baby birds until mother finds her.
Crescent Dragonwagon, *Bat in the Dining Room*, 1997
    On a summer evening, a bat trapped in a resort's dining room causes chaos until Melissa lures the bat to an exit and freedom.
Linda Glaser, *Beautiful Bats*, 1997
    A simple nonfiction title gives basic information about bats.

217

KATIE DAVIS, Author/Illustrator

Scared Stiff
(San Diego: Harcourt, Inc., 2001)

Subject(s): Fear; Imagination; Problem Solving
Age range(s): Grades K-3
Major character(s): Unnamed Character, Child
Time period(s): 2000s (2001)
Locale(s): United States

Summary: A timid, imaginative little girl is frightened of the big dog next door waiting to devour her, the monsters lurking behind the fence and the snakes living in her closet. When she decides she's had enough of living scared she thinks becoming a witch will solve her problems. Cackling doesn't really make her feel any braver so she tries the magic words "please" and "thank you." Then she dons a witch's hat and bravely opens the closet door to get her jacket. After discovering the reality behind her fear of snakes (shoelaces), monsters (a shrub) and the large dog (now a mother with puppies) the little girl looks forward to living a fright-free life, but she's keeping the witch's hat, just in case. (40 pages)

Where it's reviewed:
Horn Book Guide, Spring 2002, page 40
Publishers Weekly, September 24, 2001, page 92
School Library Journal, September 2001, page 187

Other books by the same author:
Who Hoots?, 2000
I Hate to Go to Bed!, 1999 (IRA Children's Choices)
Who Hops?, 1998

Other books you might like:
Russell Hoban, *Bedtime for Frances*, 1960
Frances imagines so many scary things in her room that she is unable to sleep.
Polly Powell, *Just Dessert*, 1996
Sneaking through the dark house to reach the kitchen and the last piece of cake Patsy is terrified by the imagined dangers lurking along the way.
Mary Wormell, *Hilda Hen's Scary Night*, 1996
Fearfully, Hilda Hen crosses the dark farmyard, safely passing the snakes (garden hose) and monsters (toys) to reach the refuge of the hen house.

218

MARGUERITE W. DAVOL
ROB ROTH, Illustrator

Why Butterflies Go By on Silent Wings
(New York: Orchard Books, 2001)

Subject(s): Animals/Insects; Behavior; Animals
Age range(s): Grades 1-4
Time period(s): Indeterminate Past
Locale(s): Fictional Country

Summary: Long ago, according to this original folktale, the land between the Mountains of the Mist and the Singular Sea was a noisy place and butterflies were the loudest of the animals. Pounding hooves, howling monkeys, trumpeting elephants and hooting hyenas contributed to the cacophony but none added more to the din than the drab-colored butterflies flitting from flower to flower, bragging and arguing among themselves. During a storm the butterflies take refuge in a Bingalou tree that is splintered by a lightning strike, flinging the butterflies in all directions and bringing silence to their world. Since that day butterflies have very quietly flown by on bright multi-colored wings. (32 pages)

Where it's reviewed:
Horn Book Guide, Fall 2001, page 253
Kirkus Reviews, April 15, 2001, page 582
School Library Journal, August 2001, page 144

Other books by the same author:
The Loudest, Fastest, Best Drummer in Kansas, 2000
Batwings and the Curtain of Night, 1997
The Paper Dragon, 1997 (ALA Notable Book for Children)

Other books you might like:
Barbara Joosse, *Ghost Wings*, 2001
To a young Mexican child butterflies represent the "souls of the old ones" and provide a connection to her deceased grandmother.
Judy Sierra, *The Beautiful Butterfly: A Folktale from Spain*, 2000
In this retelling of a folktale a butterfly weds a mouse with a soothing voice.
Harriet Peck Taylor, *Coyote and the Laughing Butterflies*, 1995
Memories of the tricks they play on Coyote cause butterflies to laugh so much they are unable to fly in a straight line to this day.

219

CHARLES DE LINT

The Onion Girl
(New York: Tor, 2001)

Subject(s): Magic; Child Abuse; Dreams and Nightmares
Age range(s): Grades 9-Adult
Major character(s): Jilly Coppercorn, Artist, Sister; Raylene Carter, Con Artist, Computer Expert
Time period(s): 2000s
Locale(s): Newford, Fictional City

Summary: In the stories of Newford, the fictional city shared by ordinary humans and mythical creatures, Jilly Coppercorn has often played a part. Sympathetic ear, true believer, friend to all who are lost or homeless, Jilly is warm but mysterious, her motives hidden in a past she never talks about. When Jilly is seriously injured in a traffic accident, her bed-ridden body makes trips to the spirit world. Thrilled to finally experience magic first hand, it is the only thing that makes her paralysis bearable. But the spirit world is hardly a safe place, and Raylene, the younger sister Jilly left behind, the sister nobody knows about, is terribly angry at Jilly, and Raylene has also learned to make journeys. (512 pages)

Where it's reviewed:
Booklist, October 1, 2001, page 304
Kirkus Reviews, September 1, 2001, page 1252
Library Journal, December 2001, page 180
Publishers Weekly, October 22, 2001, page 53
Voice of Youth Advocates, February 2002, page 444

Other books by the same author:
Forests of the Heart, 2000
Greenmantle, 1998
Someplace to be Flying, 1998

Other books you might like:
Nalo Hopkinson, *Midnight Robber*, 2000
That slippery, sly defender of the weak, the Midnight Robber has a secret identity as a rape victim.
Robin McKinley, *Deerskin*, 1993
A princess flees her father's incestuous obsession in this powerful adaptation of the fairy tale *Donkeyskin*.
S.P. Somtow, *The Fallen Country*, 1986
An abused child creates a frozen world for his escape, but his sanctuary invades the real world.

220

SIS DEANS

Racing the Past
(New York: Henry Holt, 2001)

Subject(s): Child Abuse; Fathers and Sons; Sports/Running
Age range(s): Grades 5-8
Major character(s): Ricky Gordon, 11-Year-Old; Bugsie McCarthy, Bully, 6th Grader; Matt Gordon, Brother (of Ricky)
Time period(s): 2000s
Locale(s): Maine

Summary: Though his abusive father died in a drunk-driving accident, it's hard for Ricky, his brother Matt and their mother to shake those terrible memories of what life had been like. Saddled with the stigma of an abusive father and extreme poverty, Ricky also has to fend off the school bully Bugsie; when he defends himself, Ricky's pulled into the principal's office for fighting. Rather than have his overburdened mother dragged into school, Ricky promises to behave but knows that will be difficult on the bus ride home from school. Rather than confront Bugsie on the bus, Ricky decides to walk home. Soon the walk becomes a jog, then a run, and eventually a run to beat the bus home. Developing his running benefits Ricky for the physical exertion is what he needs to forget about his father. Eventually his running is noticed by a high school coach, which helps Ricky stand up to Bugsie and show the townspeople that his family is not "white trash" in this first novel. (151 pages)

Where it's reviewed:
Booklist, June 2001, page 1880
Bulletin of the Center for Children's Books, June 2001, page 370
Publishers Weekly, June 11, 2001, page 86
School Library Journal, June 2001, page 148
Voice of Youth Advocates, June 2001, page 120

Awards the book has won:
School Library Journal Best Books, 2001
Booklist Editors' Choice/Books for Youth, 2001

Other books you might like:
Patricia Hermes, *Cheat the Moon*, 1998
    With her mother dead, her father an alcoholic and the responsibility of her brother Will on her shoulders, young Gabby has to grow up quickly.
Julie Johnston, *The Only Outcast*, 1998
    Though Fred is loved by his younger brothers and sister, he's scorned and demeaned by his father, which whittles away his self-esteem.
S.L. Rottman, *Hero*, 1997
    Sean doesn't want anyone to know that his alcoholic mother is very abusive.
Zilpha Keatley Snyder, *Cat Running*, 1994
    The reality of poverty in the Depression hits home for Cat when she and her rival Zane combine their running ability to seek help from the doctor for Zane's sick sister.
Lee Wardlaw, *Seventh Grade Weirdo*, 1992
    The school bully, aka "The Shark," pegs seventh grader Rob as the perfect weirdo victim.

221

CYNTHIA DEFELICE

The Ghost and Mrs. Hobbs

(New York: Farrar Straus Giroux, 2001)

Subject(s): Ghosts; Fires; Jealousy
Age range(s): Grades 4-6
Major character(s): Allie Nichols, 11-Year-Old, Friend; Dub Whitwell, Friend, 6th Grader; Michael Nichols, 4-Year-Old, Brother; Mrs. Hobbs, Widow(er)
Time period(s): 2000s (2001)
Locale(s): Seneca, New York

Summary: Dreams of fires awaken Allie and she becomes aware that she's attracted another ghost in the sequel to *The Ghost of Fossil Glen*. When the ghost enlists her help to right an old wrong Allie's initial thought is to assist him. The ghost blames the school's cafeteria manager, Mrs. Hobbs for his problems. Dub feels jealous of the time Allie's spends researching the ghost's story but as events unfold he becomes more supportive. Allie notices that fires seem to spring up wherever she goes, the fire chief is injured trying to get information for Allie and even Michael is put at risk by the ghost. When Allie realizes that it is the ghost's desire for revenge that is causing the problems she gets Dub to help her visit Mrs. Hobbs where she also sees the ghost. As Mrs. Hobbs relates the story of a fire years earlier the ghost finally realizes the full extent of his actions in setting the fire and his haunting days come to an end. (180 pages)

Where it's reviewed:
Booklist, September 1, 2001, page 103
Horn Book, November 2001, page 744
Kirkus Reviews, July 15, 2001, page 1024
Publishers Weekly, July 16, 2001, page 183
School Library Journal, August 2001, page 177

Other books by the same author:
Nowhere to Call Home, 1999 (Notable Social Studies Trade Books for Young People)
The Ghost of Fossil Glen, 1998 (School Library Journal Best Book)
The Apprenticeship of Lucas Whitaker, 1996 (School Library Journal Best Book)

Other books you might like:
Eileen Dunlop, *The Ghost by the Sea*, 1996
    Two cousins try to solve the mysterious drowning of an ancestor so Milly's spirit can finally rest and stop haunting their grandparent's home.
Vivian Vande Velde, *There's a Dead Person Following My Sister Around*, 1999
    A ghost seeking to return to life takes over Vicki's body and Ted has to figure out how to get the ghost to leave so his sister can come back.
Betty Ren Wright, *A Ghost in the Family*, 1998
    Chad accompanies a friend on a two-week stay at her aunt's boarding house and discovers a ghost haunting his room.

222

DIANE DEGROAT, Author/Illustrator

We Gather Together ... Now Please Get Lost!

(New York: SeaStar Books, 2001)

Subject(s): School Life; Pilgrims and Pilgrimages; Holidays
Age range(s): Grades K-2
Major character(s): Gilbert, Student—Elementary School; Philip, Student—Elementary School; Mrs. Byrd, Bird, Teacher
Time period(s): Indeterminate
Locale(s): Pilgrim Town, Fictional Country

Summary: The morning of the class field trip Gilbert oversleeps and arrives at school so late that partners have already been chosen and he's stuck with Philip, the class tattle tale and the partner no one wants. Gilbert tries to lose Philip and, in the process, almost becomes the one lost when he accidentally locks himself in a restroom. Fortunately, Philip adheres to Mrs. Byrd's admonition to "Stay with your buddy," and quickly locates Gilbert so help can be called. Gilbert is so thankful that he won't be spending Thanksgiving locked in a bathroom that he begins to look at Philip from a new perspective. (32 pages)

Where it's reviewed:
Booklist, September 1, 2001, page 120
Horn Book Guide, Spring 2002, page 40
Kirkus Reviews, June 1, 2001, page 799
Publishers Weekly, September 24, 2001, page 46
School Library Journal, August 2001, page 146

Other books by the same author:
Jingle Bells, Homework Smells, 2000 (IRA Children's Choice)
Happy Birthday to You, You Belong in a Zoo, 1999 (IRA Children's Choice)
Trick or Treat, Smell My Feet, 1998

Other books you might like:
Gail Gibbons, *Thanksgiving Day*, 1983
    Simple text explains both the first Thanksgiving and the way we now celebrate the holiday.
Grace Maccarone, *The Class Trip*, 1999
    An easy reader tells of Sam's field trip to the zoo where he becomes separated from his class.
Leslie Tryon, *Albert's Thanksgiving*, 1994
    Students at Pleasant Valley School plan a Thanksgiving feast with help from Albert the duck.

223

MARK DELANEY

The Protestor's Song
(Atlanta, GA: Peachtree, 2001)

Series: Misfits, Inc. Number 5
Subject(s): Mystery and Detective Stories; Underground Resistance Movements
Age range(s): Grades 6-9
Major character(s): Jake Armstrong, Musician (clarinet), Detective—Amateur; Peter Braddock, Detective—Amateur; Eugenia "Byte" Salzmann, Computer Expert, Detective—Amateur; Matthew "Mattie" Ramiro, Magician, Detective—Amateur; Josh Quinn, Uncle (of Byte)
Time period(s): 2000s
Locale(s): Bugle Point

Summary: The Misfits continue with their investigations, this time in a case brought to them by Byte's Uncle Josh. Thirty years ago, Josh was a student at Trenton State listening to a concert of Vietnam protest tunes sung by folk singer Dylan McConnell, when a bomb blast costs Josh his leg. Now Josh is certain the singer Red Carlyle, who's performing at a local restaurant is the singer Dylan McConnell. Byte, Peter, Jake and Mattie try to determine the singer's identity to see if it's

the same person still wanted by the FBI, an investigation that reveals what really happened in 1970 when the bombs went off. The foursome also has to ensure that no other bombs are set and no one else is injured. (214 pages)

Where it's reviewed:
Kliatt, May 2001, page 18
School Library Journal, August 2001, page 178

Other books by the same author:
Growler's Horn, 2000 (Misfits, Inc., Number 3)
The Kingfisher's Tale, 2000 (Misfits, Inc., Number 4)
Of Heroes and Villains, 1999 (Misfits, Inc., Number 2)
The Vanishing Chip, 1998 (Misfits, Inc., Number 1)

Other books you might like:
Kelly Easton, *The Life History of a Star*, 2001
    Kristin's whole family is affected when her former All-American brother David returns from Vietnam physically and mentally changed.
T.M. Murphy, *The Secrets of Code Z*, 2001
    Amateur detective Orville contends with the CIA, a Russian scientist, a rookie newspaper reporter and a few too many murders in this fifth adventure.
Wendelin Van Draanen, *Sammy Keyes and the Curse of Moustache Mary*, 2000
    Though Sammy's heading to a New Years Eve party, she can't let go of her investigative twitches, which lead her to an arsonist and a meth lab.

224

MICHAEL DELANEY

Deep Doo-Doo and the Mysterious E-Mail
(New York: Dutton, 2001)

Subject(s): Mystery and Detective Stories; Journalism; Politics
Age range(s): Grades 4-6
Major character(s): Bennet Ordway, 6th Grader, Inventor; Pete Nickowsky, 6th Grader, Writer
Time period(s): 2000s
Locale(s): North Agaming

Summary: The originators of the Deep Doo-Doo broadcasts during last years governor's race are back again with more political mysteries. This time Pete and Bennet are faced with the perplexing pumpkin that someone has implanted on top of the flagpole in front of Town Hall. With a mayor's race coming up, someone is trying to plant clues about one of the candidates and Pete and Bennet are eager to run the story on their Deep Doo-Doo website. They receive clues via mysterious e-mail messages from the Mad Poet, but it takes some research into fads of the 1970s before they're able to find the "skinny" on one of the mayoral candidates. (148 pages)

Where it's reviewed:
Booklist, March 1, 2001, page 1275
Reading Today, October 2001, page 31
School Library Journal, March 2001, page 246

Other books by the same author:
Birdbrain Amos, 2002
Deep Doo-Doo, 1996

Other books you might like:

Joan Bauer, *Hope Was Here*, 2000
Waitressing while her aunt cooks at a diner, Hope and Aunt Addie enjoy their life in a small town and help one of their customers run for mayor.

Chris Lynch, *Political Timber*, 1996
Gordie's grandfather, the town's former mayor now jailed for racketeering, intends to run Gordie for mayor and direct the campaign from his cell.

Laura E. Williams, *Up a Creek*, 2001
Starshine is tired of her mother's causes, especially when her mother tree sits to protest the council's plan to cut down the town square's oak trees.

225

TOMIE DEPAOLA, Author/Illustrator

Meet the Barkers: Morgan and Moffat Go to School

(New York: G.P. Putnam's Sons, 2001)

Subject(s): Schools; Brothers and Sisters; Animals/Dogs
Age range(s): Grades K-1
Major character(s): Moffat "Moffie" Barker, Dog, Twin (sister); Morgan "Morgie" Barker, Dog, Twin (brother); Ms. Shepherd, Dog, Teacher
Time period(s): Indeterminate
Locale(s): Fictional Country

Summary: Morgie and Moffie take different approaches to the beginning of their school career. Bossy Moffie wants to shop for supplies while Morgie is content to read his dinosaur book. On the first day of school when Ms. Shepherd asks the class members to introduce themselves Moffie speaks for both twins and Morgie holds his dinosaur book. For days Moffie answers all the questions before anyone else in class can speak and gets lots of gold stars by her name while Morgie meets classmates and shares his dinosaur book. By the end of the week Moffie has many stars and no friends but Morgie helps her make her first one and Ms. Shepherd's question about dinosaurs gives Morgie the opportunity to earn his first star. School is terrific! (32 pages)

Where it's reviewed:
Booklist, June 2001, page 1890
Horn Book Guide, Spring 2002, page 40
Kirkus Reviews, May 15, 2001, page 738
Publishers Weekly, July 2, 2001, page 75
School Library Journal, August 2001, page 146

Other books by the same author:
Jamie O'Rourke and the Pooka, 2000
Strega Nona Takes a Vacation, 2000
Bill and Pete to the Rescue, 1998

Other books you might like:

Amy Hest, *Off to School, Baby Duck!*, 1999
Grampa soothes Baby Duck's fears about entering school for the first time.

Jonathan London, *Froggy Goes to School*, 1996
Although he initially feels a little nervous about the first day of school Froggy enjoys the day.

Robert Munsch, *We Share Everything!*, 1999
Amanda and Jeremiah surprise their teacher when they demonstrate that they finally understand the classroom rule about sharing.

Joseph Slate, *Miss Bindergarten Gets Ready for Kindergarten*, 1996
Miss Bindergarten's preparations for the opening of school include matching her students' names with a letter of the alphabet.

Jean Van Leeuwen, *Amanda Pig, School Girl*, 1997
Amanda is so eager to begin school that she's able to help a less enthusiastic girl she meets on the bus and make a new friend too.

226

SALLY DERBY
GABI SWIATKOWSKA, Illustrator

Hannah's Bookmobile Christmas

(New York: Henry Holt and Company, 2001)

Subject(s): Christmas; Weather; Books and Reading
Age range(s): Grades 2-4
Major character(s): Hannah, 8-Year-Old, Niece; Mary, Aunt, Librarian; Dickens, Cat
Time period(s): 2000s
Locale(s): Wadsworth

Summary: Hannah delights in helping Aunt Mary make the rounds in Blue Bird, the town's trusty old bookmobile and Christmas Eve is no exception. The rapidly falling snow concerns Aunt Mary as she makes the day's run to each of the regular stops where the bookmobile's patrons greet Hannah, Aunt Mary and Dickens, exchange books and also give the librarian and her helper a small Christmas gift. By the time their day is over and Blue Bird is parked at the end of the snow-covered, icy, impassable lane leading to Hannah's house, it's obvious to Aunt Mary that Christmas Eve will be most safely spent inside Blue Bird enjoying the many tasty goodies received during the day. (32 pages)

Where it's reviewed:
Booklist, September 15, 2001, page 234
Publishers Weekly, September 24, 2001, page 50
Riverbank Review, Winter 2001-2002, page 48
School Library Journal, October 2001, page 64
Smithsonian, November 2001, page 123

Awards the book has won:
Smithsonian's Notable Books for Children, 2001

Other books by the same author:
Taiko on a Windy Night, 2001
My Steps, 1996
King Kenrick's Splinter, 1994 (IRA Children's Choice)

Other books you might like:

Judith Caseley, *Sophie and Sammie's Library Sleepover*, 1993
After enjoying the privilege of an evening story-time at the library, Sophie creates one at home to teach Sammie to value books too.

Candice F. Ransom, *One Christmas Dawn*, 1996
During the severe winter of 1917, Daddy goes to Bristol to

find work. With snow making train travel impossible, how can he get home for Christmas?

Suzanne Williams, *Library Lil*, 1997

Lil is such an enthusiastic librarian that she is able to get a motorcycle gang interested in reading.

227

LISA DESIMINI, Author/Illustrator

Dot the Fire Dog

(New York: Blue Sky Press/Scholastic Inc., 2001)

Subject(s): Animals/Dogs; Fires
Age range(s): Grades K-2
Major character(s): Dot, Dog
Time period(s): 2000s
Locale(s): United States

Summary: Dot's playing with one of the firefighters while another one cooks in the firehouse kitchen when the alarm rings. Everyone races for their gear and then leaps into the truck. Dot, in her helmet, rides along and assists by rescuing a kitten from a burning house. When the firefighter's work is completed they ride back to the firehouse to clean the truck and rest. Dot shares fire safety tips at the conclusion of the book. (40 pages)

Where it's reviewed:
Booklist, October 1, 2001, page 324
Horn Book, November 2001, page 734
Publishers Weekly, October 15, 2001, page 70
School Library Journal, December 2001, page 98

Other books by the same author:
Sun & Moon: A Giant Love Story, 1999
My House, 1997 (New York Times Best Illustrated Book)
Moon Soup, 1993

Other books you might like:
Norman Bridwell, *Clifford the Firehouse Dog*, 1994
During a visit to his brother Nero's firehouse Clifford learns about fire safety and has the opportunity to participate in a rescue.
Larry Dane Brimner, *Firehouse Sal*, 1996
Four fire companies rush to assist the fifth company when the call goes out that the firehouse dog is having pups.
Marc Brown, *Arthur's Fire Drill*, 2000
To help D.W. overcome her fear of fire Arthur plans home fire drills.

228

JAMES DEVITA

Blue

(New York: Laura Geringer/HarperCollins, 2001)

Subject(s): Animals/Fish; Survival
Age range(s): Grades 5-8
Major character(s): Morgan James, Student, Fish (marlin)
Time period(s): 2000s
Locale(s): United States

Summary: Bored with living in an apartment with his parents, whose every action he anticipates right down to the exact time

it will occur, Morgan falls asleep one dreary, rainy Sunday and dreams of fish, those big blue marlins who leap out of the water. Now thoughts of marlin fill his mind as he heeds their calls and develops scales on his legs and arms. When he runs a high fever, Morgan finds himself in the emergency room where his condition stuns, and then excites, the doctors. Sure they'll be written up in the medical journals, the doctors poke and probe Morgan and decide to surgically remove the dorsal fin that's beginning to grow from his spinal column. The night before the surgery, marlin men arrive at his hospital room and spirit him away to teach him how to survive in the ocean. Learning to eat squid and avoid the hooks and traps of fishermen, Morgan jubilantly jumps into his new life and swims off into the ocean in this first novel. (282 pages)

Where it's reviewed:
Booklist, April 15, 2001, page 1557
Bulletin of the Center for Children's Books, May 2001, page 334
Publishers Weekly, April 16, 2001, page 66
School Library Journal, May 2001, page 149
Voice of Youth Advocates, August 2001, page 211

Other books you might like:
Bill Brittain, *Wings*, 1992
Ian sprouts bat-like wings and is able to fly, but discovers the difficulties of life when you're different from everyone else.
Peter Dickinson, *Eva*, 1989
After an automobile accident, Eva's neuron memory is transferred into the body of a young chimpanzee.
Janet Taylor Lisle, *The Lampfish of Twill*, 1991
Eric's obsession with single-handedly catching a lampfish leads to his being pulled down a whirlpool into another world.
Ruth Park, *My Sister Sif*, 1991
Riko and her sister Sif are merpeople whose underground world is threatened by toxic materials.
Susan Lynn Reynolds, *Strandia*, 1991
Telepathic Sand won't participate in an arranged marriage for she'd rather be with the part-man, part-fish whom she loves.

229

PAT CUNNINGHAM DEVOTO

Out of the Night That Covers Me: A Novel

(New York: Warner, 2001)

Subject(s): African Americans; Orphans; Poverty
Age range(s): Grades 10-Adult
Major character(s): John Gallatin McMillan III, Orphan; Nelda Spraig, Aunt; Luther Spraig, Uncle, Alcoholic; Bryon "Judge" Vance, Banker, Blind Person; Tuway, Assistant (to Judge Vance)
Time period(s): 1950s
Locale(s): Lower Peach Tree, Alabama

Summary: Raised properly by his widowed mother, John is unprepared for the turns his life takes when she dies unexpectedly and he is sent to live on a tenant farm with his Aunt Nelda and her alcoholic, abusive husband Luther. Expected to work in the fields under a sun that parboils his skin and living in a house with no electricity or plumbing, John endures his new life but like many of the black laborers, views Chicago as a destination from a miserable life. Luckily Judge Vance befriends John and hires him to work around his house where he meets Tuway, the judge's assistant, who has learned to walk in both the black and the white world, though not always successfully. This work portrays life for African Americans in the South as they begin to challenge the white system and demand equal rights. (416 pages)

Where it's reviewed:
Book, January 2001, page 75
Booklist, September 1, 2000, page 63
Library Journal, November 1, 2000, page 133
Publishers Weekly, November 27, 2000, page 53
School Library Journal, September 2001, page 258

Other books by the same author:
My Last Days as Roy Rogers, 1999

Other books you might like:
Trudy Krisher, *Split Fences*, 1994
    The summer Maggie Pugh is thirteen remains embedded in her memory as the summer she realizes how racist her townspeople are.
Harper Lee, *To Kill a Mockingbird*, 1960
    The lives of Scout and her younger brother change when their father defends a black man accused of raping a white woman in 1930s Alabama
Mark Twain, *The Adventures of Huckleberry Finn*, 1885
    The classic adventure of runaway slave Jim and Huck, who flees from his abusive father, as they float down the Mississippi River.
Ken Wells, *Meely LaBauve*, 2000
    Raised in the swamps of a Mississippi bayou, white Meely and black Chilly become friends.

230

NARINDER DHAMI

Genius Games

(New York: Hyperion, 2001)

Subject(s): Brothers and Sisters; Divorce; Gifted Children
Age range(s): Grades 4-6
Major character(s): Annabel "Annie" Robinson, Gifted Child; Jack Robinson, 6th Grader; Bonehead Griffiths, Bully; Sarah Slade, Time Traveler
Time period(s): 2000s
Locale(s): England

Summary: It's one thing to have a younger sister like Annie, a child prodigy who speaks Spanish and reads Shakespeare for fun, but it's quite another when that sister begins kindergarten at your school. Jack has always felt his little sister's unique intelligence drove away their father who moved to America four years ago, but now he endures the wrath of the school bully for having an unusual sister. Jack is convinced Annie is totally weird because she now talks to herself, though she claims she's addressing her new friend Sarah Slade who's from the twenty-fifth century. All Jack knows is that anyone who is unkind to Annie "loses" valuable items, like his

missing saxophone. Maybe Sarah's not just an imaginary friend in this author's first novel. (156 pages)

Where it's reviewed:
Booklist, October 1, 2001, page 318
Horn Book, May 2001, page 321
Kirkus Reviews, May 15, 2001, page 738
School Library Journal, July 2001, page 106

Other books you might like:
Cheryl Foggo, *One Thing That's True*, 1998
    Roxanne and her brother Joel are very close; when Joel runs away after discovering he's adopted, Roxanne feels like her world will never be the same.
Anne Lindbergh, *Nick of Time*, 1994
    When Jericho and Allison time travel to 2094, Allison decides to remain there while Jericho returns home.
Richard Peck, *Lost in Cyberspace*, 1995
    Josh has enough problems with his parents' divorce, but now Aaron transports the two friends through cyberspace in a madcap adventure.
Michael Stearns, *A Starfarer's Dozen: Stories of Things to Come*, 1995
    The teen stars in this science fiction collection range from the tough runaway to shape changers to winged teens playing a deadly game of catch.
Stephanie S. Tolan, *Welcome to the Ark*, 1996
    Four unusual children, able to communicate telepathically with one another, try to contact other like-minded children to reduce world violence.

231

KATE DICAMILLO

The Tiger Rising

(Cambridge, MA: Candlewick Press, 2001)

Subject(s): Animals/Tigers; Friendship
Age range(s): Grades 5-7
Major character(s): Robert "Rob" Horton, 6th Grader; Sistine Bailey, 6th Grader; Tiger, Animal (Tiger)
Time period(s): 2000s
Locale(s): Lister, Florida

Summary: Miserable over his mother's death, Rob thinks he's repressing his grief, yet the rash on his legs indicates otherwise. New student Sistine is also unhappy, though she's mad about her parent's divorce and ready to fight anyone who teases her. Sent home from school because the principal fears his rash is contagious, Rob is visited daily by Sistine who brings his homework assignments. Their lives change when Rob is asked to feed a tiger kept caged in the forest near the motel where Rob and his handyman father live. Both Rob and Sistine realize the tiger is as miserable as they are and want only to free him, but doing so results in unexpected tragedy. (116 pages)

Where it's reviewed:
Booklist, June 2001, page 1882
Horn Book, May, 2001, page 321
Publishers Weekly, January 15, 2001, page 76
School Library Journal, March 2001, page 246
Voice of Youth Advocates, August 2001, page 200

Other books by the same author:
Because of Winn-Dixie, 2000

Other books you might like:
Ron Koertge, *Tiger, Tiger, Burning Bright*, 1994
When Jesse's beloved grandfather claims to have seen tiger tracks while on a camping trip in California, Jesse rounds up friends to search for the animal.
Susan Hart Lindquist, *Wander*, 1998
Grieving over their mother's death, James and Sary are thrilled to find a stray dog, but fearful of telling anyone about their new acquisition.
Adrienne Ross, *In the Quiet*, 2000
Sammy and her good friend Bones dig holes hoping to find some object that will help Sammy reconnect with her deceased mother's spirit.
Carol Lynch Williams, *Carolina Autumn*, 2000
Still sad about the death of her older sister, Carolina finds that writing letters to Madelaine helps her, especially now that she has a boyfriend.

232

PETER DICKINSON

The Ropemaker

(New York: Delacorte, 2001)

Subject(s): Quest; Coming-of-Age; Magic
Age range(s): Grades 7-12
Major character(s): Tilja, Daughter (granddaughter); Meena, Grandmother; Tahl, Son (grandson); Alnor, Grandfather; Faleel, Wizard
Time period(s): Indeterminate
Locale(s): Fictional Country

Summary: For generations, the Valley has been guarded from the ills that beset the rest of the world, but the people of the Valley forget the truth behind the stories of magic that explain their safety. Now the magical safeguards are breaking down and Tilja and Tahl find themselves escorting two stubborn old people out into the dangerous Empire in search of the wizard Faleel. Generations of Tilja's family have been singing to the cedars that guard the Valley to the south, which has kept the Empire from invading. In the north, Tahl's grandfather and ancestors talked to the waters and performed a similar function. Grandmother Meena and Grandfather Alnor are determined to find the wizard who cast the original protections and ask for his help in renewing them. Alnor's blindness makes him dependant on Tahl, but Meena takes Tilja largely because Tilja herself insists on it. Tilja discovers that she will not be the next in her family to sing to the cedars for the talent has passed instead to her younger sister; she now needs a part to play and hopes to find it on their quest. (376 pages)

Where it's reviewed:
Booklist, October 15, 2001, page 394
Horn Book Magazine, November 2001, page 745
Publishers Weekly, November 5, 2001, page 70
School Library Journal, November 2001, page 154

Awards the book has won:
ALA Notable Children's Books, 2002
ALA Michael L. Printz Honor Book, 2002

Other books by the same author:
The Lion-Tamer's Daughter and Other Stories, 1997
Shadow of a Hero, 1994
A Bone From a Dry Sea, 1992

Other books you might like:
Garth Nix, *Lirael: Daughter of the Clayr*, 2001
Lirael has not inherited the psychic gifts of her people, but discovers she has other talents.
Meredith Ann Pierce, *Treasure at the Heart of the Tanglewood*, 2001
Hannah is the treasure of Tanglewood, but she won't discover it until she frees herself from the wizards and completes her quest.
Kate Thompson, *The Beguilers*, 2001
The community misfit binds herself to discover the truth about the sinister creatures that haunt the dark.

233

GORDON DICKSON

The Dragon and the Fair Maid of Kent

(New York: Tor, 2000)

Subject(s): Magic; Alternate History; Dragons
Age range(s): Grades 9-Adult
Major character(s): James "Jim" Eckert, Spouse, Warrior; Angela "Angie" Eckert, Spouse; Carolinus, Wizard
Time period(s): 14th century
Locale(s): England

Summary: Trapped in an alternate past, much like the England of the 14th century, Jim and Angie make the best of things. In spite of the inconveniences, life in Malencontri castle has its compensations. Jim in particular is intrigued by the variances from the history he knew, and he finds his new magical abilities a challenge. Carolinus, Jim's magical tutor, keeps warning of a grave danger that needs their attention but the Eckerts focus on the wedding they promised to host. Suddenly, Jim and Angie find their peace invaded by dragons, bishops, a self-centered prince and the beautiful Maid of Kent, who has left her husband. Just to keep things interesting, rumors of the approach of the plague are confirmed. Even with twentieth century knowledge, Jim and Angie will have their hands full. (397 pages)

Where it's reviewed:
Booklist, December 15, 2000, page 794
Kirkus Reviews, November 15, 2000, page 1583
Library Journal, December 2000, page 196
Publishers Weekly, November 27, 2000, page 59
Science Fiction Chronicle, October 2000, page 57

Other books by the same author:
The Dragon in Lyonesse, 1998
The Dragon and the Gnarly King, 1997
The Dragon and the George, 1976

Other books you might like:
Terry Brooks, *Magic Kingdom for Sale - Sold!*, 1986
A depressed executive buys himself a magic kingdom for a retreat, but quickly finds himself with distracting responsibilities.

Christopher Stasheff, *A Wizard in the Way*, 2000
  Magnus finds his hands full when he tries to manage love and revolution at the same time.

Connie Willis, *Doomsday Book*, 1992
  A series of errors, mistakes and accidents strand a doctoral candidate in the past and research turns deadly when she realizes that the Black Plague is raging.

234

NATHALIE DIETERLE, Author/Illustrator

I Am the King!
(New York: Orchard Books, 2001)

Subject(s): Behavior; Mothers and Sons; Kings, Queens, Rulers, etc.
Age range(s): Preschool-Grade 1
Major character(s): Little Louis, Son, Rabbit; Unnamed Character, Mother, Rabbit; Unnamed Character, Father, Rabbit
Time period(s): Indeterminate
Locale(s): Fictional Country

Summary: When Little Louis's mother gives him a little crown it goes to his head in more ways than one. Little Louis begins behaving as if he truly is the ruler of all he surveys and he imagines even the monsters lurking under his bed obey his every command. While his imaginary fears may respond to his kingly desires, his parents are less amenable to his regal ideas. His mother drags him to school and his father dumps in the bathtub despite the fact that Little Louis specifically states the king has no plans to do either. Finally, Little Louis is sent to his room so he decides that he will no longer be king. What he plans to be next may not improve his chances of getting out of his room. (28 pages)

Where it's reviewed:
Bulletin of the Center for Children's Books, July 2001, page 407
Horn Book Guide, Fall 2001, page 229
Publishers Weekly, April 2, 2001, page 62
School Library Journal, August 2001, page 146

Other books you might like:
Molly Bang, *When Sophie Gets Angry—Really, Really Angry . . .* , 1999
  Sophie's anger explodes in a temper tantrum. She runs to her favorite tree and allows the branches to soothe her before returning home.
Fred Hiatt, *If I Were Queen of the World*, 1997
  A young girl imagines that as queen she could eat lollipops without sharing and stay up as late as she wants.
Maurice Sendak, *Where the Wild Things Are*, 1963
  After being sent to his room, Max travels to the Land of the Wild Things were he can be king, but he makes sure he's home in time for dinner.
David Shannon, *No, David!*, 1998
  All day David's behavior is contrary to his mother's expectations and finally he sits in a corner feeling remorseful.

SYLVIANE A. DIOUF
SHANE W. EVANS, Illustrator

Bintou's Braids
(San Francisco: Chronicle Books, 2001)

Subject(s): Hair; Family
Age range(s): Grades K-3
Major character(s): Bintou, Daughter, Sister; Fatou, Sister (older); Grandma Soukeye, Grandmother, Aged Person
Time period(s): Indeterminate
Locale(s): Africa (West Africa)

Summary: Bintou wants to look like Fatou; she wants braids, not cornrows or the four tufts she has but real braids with coins and shells woven into their ends. Grandma Soukeye explains to Bintou why young girls do not have braids, but still Bintou envies all the women of the village and their elaborately braided hair. When Bintou's courage and speed help alert the villagers in time to save two boys from drowning, she is offered a reward. Fatou knows that all Bintou wants is braids. Grandma Soukeye satisfies Bintou's desire to be special with the short hair that she has by working blue and yellow birds into her tufts. Bintou is happy. (36 pages)

Where it's reviewed:
Booklist, November 15, 2001, page 580
Bulletin of the Center for Children's Books, November 2001, page 99
Horn Book, January 2002, page 67
Publishers Weekly, October 29, 2001, page 63
School Library Journal, January 2002, page 97

Other books by the same author:
Growing Up in Slavery, 2001
Kings and Queens of West Africa, 2000

Other books you might like:
Nikki Grimes, *Wild, Wild Hair*, 1997
  Tisa dreads Monday mornings when Mommy combs her wild, wild hair but she loves the twenty beautiful braids that Mommy plaits.
Carolivia Herron, *Nappy Hair*, 1997
  At a family reunion, Brenda's uncle notes the uniqueness of her incredible curly hair and the relatives all chime in their agreement.
Bell Hooks, *Happy to Be Nappy*, 1999
  Braids are one of the many options girls have in hairstyles if they're willing to sit still for the work.
Natasha Anastasia Tarpley, *I Love My Hair!*, 1998
  Kenyana endures the combing of tangles from her hair because she enjoys the many different ways her mother can style it.
Rita Williams-Garcia, *Catching the Wild Waiyuuuzee*, 2000
  Before she can braid her daughter's hair this mother has to catch the reluctant child.

236

DYANNE DISALVO, Author/Illustrator

A Castle on Viola Street

(New York: HarperCollins Publishers, 2001)

Subject(s): Dwellings; Family; Construction
Age range(s): Grades K-3
Major character(s): Andy, 10-Year-Old, Brother (older)
Time period(s): 2000s (2001)
Locale(s): United States

Summary: Andy and his family volunteer for a community improvement project in hopes that one day they'll be able to move from their cramped apartment to a home of their own. Along with other volunteers they work to renovate one of three boarded up townhouses. After four months the first house is complete and one of the other volunteer families moves in and has a potluck dinner for all the workers. As work progresses on the other two dwellings, Andy's family is notified that one will become their home and Andy's dream for his family comes true. (32 pages)

Where it's reviewed:
Booklist, September 15, 2001, page 230
Kirkus Reviews, June 15, 2001, page 863
Publishers Weekly, August 6, 2001, page 89
School Library Journal, October 2001, page 114
Smithsonian, November 2001, page 124

Awards the book has won:
Smithsonian's Notable Books for Children, 2001

Other books by the same author:
Grandpa's Corner Store, 2000 (Notable Social Studies Trade Books for Young People)
A Dog Like Jack, 1999
City Green, 1994

Other books you might like:
Penny Carter, *A New House for the Morrisons*, 1993
　　After a day of futile searching for a new house, the Morrisons return to the one they like best, their own home.
Erika Tamar, *The Garden of Happiness*, 1996
　　A community effort cleans up a litter-strewn lot so it can be used as a garden.
Alexandra Wallner, *Since 1920*, 1992
　　A story of urbanization, decline and revitalization of a neighborhood centers on one family's home and the changes it endures over generations.

237

TONY DITERLIZZI, Author/Illustrator

Ted

(New York: Simon & Schuster Books for Young Readers, 2001)

Subject(s): Imagination; Fathers and Sons; Fantasy
Age range(s): Grades 1-3
Major character(s): Ted, Friend (imaginary); Unnamed Character, Child, Son; Father, Father
Time period(s): Indeterminate Past
Locale(s): United States

Summary: A week after a lonely boy's birthday large, pink, raspberry-loving Ted arrives at his house to play. Since Father is always too busy to do anything with his son, the boy is happy to have the company of his jolly companion. Ted is full of great ideas that Father does not appreciate so Ted leaves and the boy follows. At the old park the boy learns that Ted, with a different name, was once Father's imaginary playmate. When Father finds his son at the old park he finally recognizes his old friend and the need to spend more time with his son. (40 pages)

Where it's reviewed:
Bulletin of the Center for Children's Books, February 2001, page 221
Horn Book Guide, Fall 2001, page 253
Kirkus Reviews, March 1, 2001, page 329
Publishers Weekly, March 5, 2001, page 79
School Library Journal, April 2001, page 105

Other books by the same author:
Jimmy Zangwow's Out-of-This World Moon Pie Adventure, 2000

Other books you might like:
Jo Ellen Bogart, *Daniel's Dog*, 1990
　　Daniel adjusts to the birth of his sister with help from his imaginary dog, Lucy.
Kevin Henkes, *Jessica*, 1989
　　Ruthie and her imaginary friend, Jessica, are inseparable; on the first day of kindergarten Ruthie meets a friendly classmate with the same name.
Simon James, *Leon and Bob*, 1997
　　Leon plays with an imaginary playmate until a real friend moves into the house next door.
Ingrid Ostheeren, *The Blue Monster*, 1996
　　Anna's parents aren't eager to honor her request for a dog so she makes a birthday wish for a monster instead and both her wishes come true.

238

QUENTIN DODD

Beatnik Rutabagas from Beyond the Stars

(New York: Farrar Straus Giroux, 2001)

Subject(s): Humor; Science Fiction; Aliens
Age range(s): Grades 7-10
Major character(s): Walter Nutria, Student; Yselle Meridian, Student; Uxno, Alien
Time period(s): 2000s
Locale(s): Gilded Excelsior, Spaceship

Summary: Walter and Yselle are united in their disgust with school and their love of bad science fiction movies, but it's not as though they are dating or anything. Still, they spend most of their free time together, in front of the VCR. When weird little aliens, who appear to be tubby middle-aged men in footie pajamas, approach Walter, he's surprised, but not shocked. The Lirgonians want Walter to lead their troops into battle because he's logged more time viewing space battles than anyone else on the planet. With Walter's help, they plan to put down the Wotwots (the rutabagas of the title, who, by the way are large) once and for all. At first Walter feels relatively confident, but then he discovers that the Wotwots have also recruited a supreme commander from earth and it's Yselle who's seen everything Walter has! (216 pages)

Where it's reviewed:
Kirkus Reviews, August 1, 2001, page 1120
Publishers Weekly, August 20, 2001, page 81
School Library Journal, October 2001, page 152
Voice of Youth Advocates, February 2002, page 445

Other books you might like:
Douglas Adams, *The Hitchhiker's Guide to the Galaxy*, 1979
    A human bystander finds himself grabbed by aliens who are cruising by earth looking for the secret of the universe.
Daniel Pinkwater, *The Snarkout Boys and the Avocado of Death*, 1982
    Sneaking out to midnight movies gets the boys in trouble when they run into a mad scientist with a deadly super-computer disguised as an avocado.
William Sleator, *Interstellar Pig*, 1984
    Barney is in big trouble when he plays a new game with his neighbors who turn out to be aliens!

239

BERLIE DOHERTY
SONJA LAMUT, Illustrator

The Famous Adventures of Jack

(New York: Greenwillow Books, 2001)

Subject(s): Fairy Tales; Folklore; Storytelling
Age range(s): Grades 3-5
Major character(s): Mother Greenwood, Aged Person, Story-teller; Jill, Young Woman; Jack, Son
Time period(s): Indeterminate Past
Locale(s): Fictional Country

Summary: Jill comes upon Mother Greenwood while seeking someone named Jack. Mother Greenwood needs to know which Jack she seeks and then proceeds to tell stories about the many Jacks in her life. Mother Greenwood's storytelling weaves together traditional tales of Jack the Giant Killer, Daft Jack, and Great Grandfather Jack and the King of the Herrings. Each tale is more fascinating to Jill than the one before yet none seem to be about the Jack she seeks, Mother Greenwood's son. In order to find that Jack, Jill will need to climb the beanstalk that's sprung up in the yard. (148 pages)

Where it's reviewed:
Booklist, October 1, 2001, page 318
Bulletin of the Center for Children's Books, October 2001, page 54
Horn Book, November 2001, page 760
School Library Journal, January 2002, page 117

Other books by the same author:
Fairy Tales, 2000
Street Child, 1994
Willa and Old Miss Annie, 1994 (Carnegie Medal, Highly Commended)
Granny Was a Buffer Girl, 1988 (Carnegie Medal)

Other books you might like:
Vivian French, *Lazy Jack*, 1995
    In a retelling of a traditional tale, Jack's mother hires him

out to do odd jobs in the community but he never arrives home with his wages.
Virginia Haviland, *Favorite Fairy Tales Told in England*, 1994
    A folklore collection includes "Jack and the Beanstalk" and other well-known tales.
Gail Carson Levine, *Ella Enchanted*, 1997
    The Cinderella theme weaves through this fantasy of an orphaned girl and her quest to remove a fairy's curse.

240

JOHN DONAHUE

Till Tomorrow

(New York: Farrar Straus Giroux, 2001)

Subject(s): Friendship; Military Bases; Sports/Baseball
Age range(s): Grades 6-8
Major character(s): Terrence "O.B." O'Brien, 12-Year-Old; Cannonball Wall, Baseball Player; Claude LeClair, Friend (of O.B.'s)
Time period(s): 1960s
Locale(s): Meuse, France

Summary: Another move, another Army base, and another time for Terrence to make new friends. Called O.B., all he wants is to be part of the popular crowd. He seems to be on that path when Cannonball befriends him and quickly tells him about aces, the popular kids, and deuces, everyone else. O.B.'s accepted by the aces, thanks to Cannonball and baseball, but he also makes friends with Claude, a French boy from the village, who keeps score for the baseball team. Though the other kids call Claude "the Clod," O.B. discovers how much Claude knows about the surrounding area where the Battle of Verdun took place during World War I. Pretty soon Claude and O.B. are great friends, but a chance to be with the "aces" almost upsets that friendship as O.B. betrays Claude. A last-minute tweak to O.B.'s conscience saves everyone from greater disaster. (165 pages)

Where it's reviewed:
Booklist, September 15, 2001, page 222
Bulletin of the Center for Children's Books, November 2001, page 100
Kirkus Reviews, July 15, 2001, page 1024
Publishers Weekly, August 27, 2001, page 85
School Library Journal, September 2001, page 224

Other books by the same author:
An Island Far from Home, 1994

Other books you might like:
Eoin Colfer, *Benny and Omar*, 2001
    Discouraged at moving from Ireland to Tunisia, Benny enjoys Omar, his orphaned Tunisian friend.
Elizabeth Laird, *Secret Friends*, 1999
    Wanting to be accepted by the popular clique, Lucy joins in teasing Rafaella but never reveals that she and Rafaella are friends outside of school.
Sharon E. McKay, *Charlie Wilcox*, 2000
    Stowing away on the wrong ship sends Charlie to France where he helps out during the Battle of the Somme during World War I.

Tom Townsend, *Trader Wooley and the Terrorist*, 1988
Smitten by Katrina, the new student at his American school in Germany, little does Trader know she's part of a terrorist group.

241

JULIA DONALDSON
AXEL SCHEFFLER, Illustrator

Room on the Broom

(New York: Dial Books for Young Readers, 2001)

Subject(s): Witches and Witchcraft; Animals; Stories in Rhyme
Age range(s): Grades K-3
Major character(s): Unnamed Character, Witch
Time period(s): Indeterminate
Locale(s): Fictional Country

Summary: A kindly witch and her cat offer a dog, a bird and a frog a ride on the broom after they each return something she's dropped. When the broom breaks, the animals fall into a bog while the witch flies into the arms of a dragon that plans to dine on the witch until it sees a horrible beast rise out of the bog claiming the witch as its own. The witch is relieved when the beast turns out to be the mud-covered animals from her broken broom. With a little magic the witch creates a new broom with seats for everyone and off they fly. (32 pages)

Where it's reviewed:
Booklist, September 1, 2001, page 120
Bulletin of the Center for Children's Books, September 2001, page 11
Kirkus Reviews, August 1, 2001, page 1121
Publishers Weekly, September 10, 2001, page 92
School Library Journal, September 2001, page 187

Other books by the same author:
The Gruffalo, 1999 (Smarties Prize)
A Squash and a Squeeze, 1993

Other books you might like:
Caralyn Buehner, *A Job for Wittilda*, 1993
Thanks to her trusty broom Wittilda is one of the fastest pizza delivery drivers in town.
Nicholas Heller, *Elwood and the Witch*, 2000
On a night walk through the woods Elwood picks up a broom that takes him flying as an angry witch stuck on the ground hurls threats and spells at him.
Margie Palatini, *Zoom Broom*, 1998
Gritch's broom seems to be beyond repair, even with magic, so she's shopping for a new one.

242

MALIKA DORAY, Author/Illustrator
SUZANNE FREEMAN, Translator

One More Wednesday

(New York: Greenwillow Books, 2001)

Subject(s): Death; Grandmothers; Animals
Age range(s): Preschool-Grade 1

Major character(s): Granny, Grandmother, Aged Person; Unnamed Character, Narrator; Mama, Mother
Time period(s): Indeterminate
Locale(s): Fictional Country

Summary: The young narrator recollects walks in the park with Granny and her dog, baking cookies and eating them too. Now those happy shared times are only memories because Granny died. In a loving, sensitive way, Mama tries to answers the many questions about the meaning of death and her child feels comforted. This is the French author's first book for children. (48 pages)

Where it's reviewed:
Booklist, June 2001, page 1890
Horn Book Guide, Fall 2001, page 229
Kirkus Reviews, March 15, 2001, page 406
Publishers Weekly, April 16, 2001, page 65
School Library Journal, July 2001, page 74

Awards the book has won:
Parenting's Reading Magic Awards, 2001

Other books you might like:
Aliki, *The Two of Them*, 1979
A young girl and her grandfather share a special relationship which she remembers after his death.
Tomie DePaola, *Nana Upstairs & Nana Downstairs*, 1973
Tommy loves to visit his Nanas and is saddened when his Upstairs Nana dies.
Mem Fox, *Sophie*, 1994
Because Grandpa has always been a part of Sophie's life his death leaves a sense of emptiness that time eventually fills.

243

JAMES D. DOSS

Grandmother Spider

(New York: Morrow, 2001)

Series: Charlie Moon Mystery
Subject(s): Mystery and Detective Stories; Indians of North America; Legends
Age range(s): Grades 10-Adult
Major character(s): Charlie Moon, Police Officer, Indian (Ute); Scott Parris, Police Officer (police chief), Indian (Ute); Daisy Perika, Shaman, Indian (Ute)
Time period(s): 2000s
Locale(s): Southern Ute Reservation, Colorado

Summary: Charlie and his aunt Daisy view life differently, perhaps because Daisy is a shaman who experiences visions while Charlie is a policeman who believes there's a rational explanation for everything. When Daisy spots a giant, spider like creature carrying a tribesman and a scientist in its mouth, she is convinced that Grandmother Spider, who lives beneath Navajo Lake, has returned as part of Ute legend. Though the two men are found later, shaken but still alive, Charlie and Police Chief Parris are determined to find out what really happened. When several murders follow, they step up their investigation in this continuing series. (293 pages)

Where it's reviewed:
Booklist, January 2001, page 924

Drood Review, November 2000, page 14
Kirkus Reviews, December 1, 2000, page 1645
Publishers Weekly, November 27, 2000, page 57
School Library Journal, August 2001, page 209

Other books by the same author:
White Shell Woman, 2002 (Charlie Moon Mystery)
The Night Visitor, 1999 (Charlie Moon Mystery)
The Shaman's Game, 1998 (Charlie Moon Mystery)
The Shaman's Bones, 1997 (Charlie Moon Mystery)
The Shaman Laughs, 1995 (Charlie Moon Mystery)
The Shaman Sings, 1994 (Charlie Moon Mystery)

Other books you might like:
Margaret Coel, *The Lost Bird*, 1999
    Actress Sharon David returns to the Arapaho Wind River Reservation in hopes of finding her biological parents.
Kirk Mitchell, *Ancient Ones*, 2001
    A BIA Investigator and an FBI agent travel to Oregon where the discovery of ancient bones leads to conflict between Indian beliefs and archaeological research.
Aimee Thurlo, *Red Mesa*, 2001
    Navajo Tribal Police Special Investigator Ellla Clah is in a pickle when her assistant is found dead on top of a mesa and Ella is the chief suspect.

244

LAURA DOWER
STEPHANIE POWER, Illustrator

Only the Lonely

(New York: Volo/Hyperion, 2001)

Series: From the Files of Madison Finn. Book 1
Subject(s): Friendship; Summer; Internet
Age range(s): Grades 4-6
Major character(s): Madison Francesca "Maddie" Finn, 7th Grader; Fiona Waters, 7th Grader; Walter Emilio "Egg" Diaz, 7th Grader; Aimee Anne Gillespie, 7th Grader, Dancer (ballerina)
Time period(s): 2000s
Locale(s): Far Hills, New York

Summary: The summer before seventh grade stretches ahead of Finn and she's already bored. Her best friends Egg and Aimee are at summer camp, her father's never home, and she has only her orange laptop and her dog with which to console herself. Luckily she meets Fiona, a new neighbor, in a chat room and discovers they'll both be attending the same school in the fall. Finn's boredom is alleviated somewhat, but she continues to worry about how a new friend will alter her relationship with her old friends, what attending junior high school will be like, and whether or not she'll ever be kissed. All these worries are shared with her orange laptop where she keeps her online journal in this first of a series. If you want to chat with Madison, she can be reached at www.madisonfinn.com. (164 pages)

Where it's reviewed:
Booklist, June 2001, page 1882
Publishers Weekly, April 16, 2001, page 66
School Library Journal, August 2001, page 178

Other books by the same author:
Boy, Oh Boy!, 2001 (From the Files of Madison Finn, Book 2)
Thanks for Nothing, 2001 (From the Files of Madison Finn, Book 5)
Play It Again, 2001 (From the Files of Madison Finn, Book 3)
Caught in the Web, 2001 (From the Files of Madison Finn, Book 4)

Other books you might like:
Paula Danziger, *Snail Mail No More*, 2000 SCF
Dandi Daley Mackall, *Portrait of Lies*, 2000
    Six good friends create their own website, called TodaysGirls.com, just to have their own private chat room.
Phyllis Reynolds Naylor, *The Alice Series*, 1985-
    Alice and her friends Pamela, Elizabeth and Patrick survive the traumas of junior high, peer pressure and dating, but now high school awaits.
Susan Beth Pfeffer, *Turning Thirteen*, 1988
    Jealous that her best friend Dina is also friends with Amy, Becky comes up with a plan that will eliminate Amy.

MARY ALICE DOWNIE
JOHN DOWNIE, Co-Author

Danger in Disguise

(Montreal: Roussan Publishers, 2001)

Series: On Time's Wing
Subject(s): Fathers and Sons; Identity, Concealed
Age range(s): Grades 5-8
Major character(s): Jamie Macpherson, 14-Year-Old; Duncan Macpherson, Father (of Jamie), Accountant; Sleat, Wealthy
Time period(s): 1750s (1759)
Locale(s): France; England; Quebec, Canada

Summary: Scotsmen Jamie and his father have been on the move for as long as Jamie can remember and are now in Normandy. It's Jamie's fourteenth birthday and his father finally tells him about his mother. She was supposed to marry the Englishman named Sleat, but fell in love with Jamie's father, Duncan Macpherson, instead. Duncan stole her away and brought her up to the Highlands where, after the battle of Culloden, she was killed by English soldiers. Ever since, Sleat has searched for Duncan and Jamie to kill them too; Duncan would fight him, but has learned that Sleat never fights fair and is not willing to leave his son either dead or orphaned. Finally sent to Glasgow with the promise that Duncan will join him, Jamie is captured, impressed into the British navy and sent to Canada where he must fight against the French in a continuing series. (175 pages)

Where it's reviewed:
Resource Links, April 2001, page 10
School Library Journal, May 2001, page 149

Other books by the same author:
Honor Bound, 1971

Other books you might like:
Connie Brummel Crook, *The Hungry Year*, 2001
    During their first harsh winter in Canada, only the help of

the Mohawk Indians keeps Kate and her siblings from starving.

Jane Louise Curry, *A Stolen Life*, 1999
Sent to the American colonies to be sold as a servant to the Americans, Jamesina is rescued by her brothers and other members of a Highland Regiment.

James D. Forman, *Prince Charlie's Year*, 1991
Colin Randall MacDonald reminisces about his role in the ill-fated attempt of 1745 to return Prince Charlie to the British throne.

246

MALACHY DOYLE
PAUL HESS, Illustrator

Hungry! Hungry! Hungry!
(Atlanta: Peachtree, 2001)

Subject(s): Monsters; Folk Tales; Problem Solving
Age range(s): Grades K-3
Major character(s): Unnamed Character, Child; Unnamed Character, Monster (goblin)
Time period(s): 2000s
Locale(s): Fictional Country

Summary: A young boy has many questions for the strange, ugly creature visiting his house. The goblin has an answer to explain why his feet are big, his knees are knobby and head is horrible. Sometimes the goblin simply answers, "Hungry! Hungry! Hungry!" When the boy asks why the goblin has come, his answer indicates that he expects the boy to satisfy his hunger. So, the boy offers him a jellybean. Originally published in Great Britain in 2000. (26 pages)

Where it's reviewed:
Books for Keeps, March 2001, page 20
Bulletin of the Center for Children's Books, April 2001, page 301
Kirkus Reviews, February 1, 2001, page 181
Publishers Weekly, January 22, 2001, page 324
School Library Journal, July 2001, page 74

Other books by the same author:
Tales from Old Ireland, 2000
Well, A Crocodile Can!, 2000
Jody's Beans, 1999

Other books you might like:
Mercer Mayer, *There's a Monster in My Closet*, 1968
Sometimes inviting monsters out of the closet makes them seem less scary.

Kevin O'Malley, *Velcome*, 1997
The host of this tale "velcomes" you to his house for a little Halloween fun.

Ingrid Ostheeren, *The Blue Monster*, 1996
Instead of the dog Anna wanted for her birthday a blue monster appears, happy but hungry and a little mischievous.

247

RODDY DOYLE
BRIAN AJHAR, Illustrator

Rover Saves Christmas
(New York: Arthur A. Levine Books/Scholastic Press, 2001)

Subject(s): Christmas; Animals/Dogs; Humor
Age range(s): Grades 3-5
Major character(s): Rudolph, Reindeer; Rover, Dog; Santa, Aged Person, Mythical Creature
Time period(s): Indeterminate
Locale(s): Dublin, Ireland; Lapland, Finland

Summary: When Rudolph develops the flu and is unable to pull the sleigh Santa knows that only one other animal can fulfill the task. He sends an elf to fetch Rover but Rover will only agree to go if the children come along with their atlas. Reluctantly the elf agrees and as soon as the children bundle up in lots of warm clothes they join the elf and magically find themselves standing next to Santa. Concerned about time, Santa and Rover devise a secret plan to complete all the deliveries to which the children add some of their own absurd ideas. (158 pages)

Where it's reviewed:
Horn Book Guide, Spring 2002, page 72
Publishers Weekly, September 24, 2001, page 54
School Library Journal, October 2001, page 64

Awards the book has won:
IRA Children's Choices, 2002

Other books by the same author:
The Giggler Treatment, 2000

Other books you might like:
Berkeley Breathed, *Red Ranger Came Calling*, 1994
The autobiographical tale of the author's father matches a cynical boy, a retired Santa, and wish fulfilled in a unique way.

John R. Erickson, *The Wounded Buzzard on Christmas Eve*, 1989
In the thirteenth entry in the Hank the Cowdog seris a buzzard flies into the windshield of Slim's truck as he drives to town to do his Christmas shopping.

James Howe, *Harold and Chester in the Fright Before Christmas*, 1988
Ghostly noises on Christmas Eve make Harold and Chester think that perhaps Howie is right to fearful of the arrival of Christmas.

Dav Pilkey, *The Adventures of Super Diaper Baby: The First Graphic Novel*, 2002
In George and Harold's latest comic, Super Diaper Baby saves the planet from Deputy Doo-Doo and his evil pet Danger Dog.

248

EMILY DRAKE

The Magickers
(New York: DAW, 2001)

Series: Magickers. Book 1

Subject(s): Magic; Camps and Camping
Age range(s): Grades 5-8
Major character(s): Jason Adrian, 11-Year-Old, Wizard; Bailey Landau, Camper, Wizard
Time period(s): 2000s
Locale(s): England

Summary: Thinking he'll spend the summer in soccer camp, Jason doesn't know what to make of the big raven that taps at his window one morning. Opening his porthole, Jason is pecked on the head, falls out of the window, accidentally locks himself out, falls off the roof into a prickly thorn hedge and then tries to sneak back inside. With an ominous portent like that, he's not surprised when he sprains his ankle in soccer tryouts and now faces a summer at his grandmother's home while his stepparents are on vacation and his stepsister at her camp. To the rescue comes his English teacher Mrs. Cowling who enters his work in an essay contest that wins him an offer to Camp Ravenwyng, a camp for creative, talented leaders. Though the bus is filled with strangely garbed counselors and the camp looks dilapidated, Jason discovers an event-filled summer, becomes friends with Bailey and enters the training area for "magickers." Though he and his fellow campers are novices, they find themselves in a battle for good over evil against The Dark Hand of Brennard; only Jason's ability to open a special gate saves Ravenwyng from decimation in this book that would enjoy a sequel. (344 pages)

Where it's reviewed:
Booklist, July 2001, page 2006
Bookwatch, August 2001, page 9
School Library Journal, December 2001, page 133
Voice of Youth Advocates, October 2001, page 288

Other books by the same author:
The Curse of Arkady, 2002 (Magickers, Book 2)

Other books you might like:
Susan Cooper, *The Dark Is Rising*, 1973
  As evil begins to overtake the world, one English boy has the power to stop it.
Tamora Pierce, *Circle of Magic*, 1997-1999
  Four teens that don't realize they have magical powers are brought together and taught to combine their talents to make them more potent.
Philip Pullman, *His Dark Materials Trilogy*, 1996-2000
  When the Dust increases on Lyra's world, evil follows, flowing from a rift in time and space.
J.K. Rowling, *The Harry Potter Series*, 1998-
  Raised by his aunt and uncle, Harry is thrilled to be invited to attend Hogwarts School and begin his studies of wizardry.

249

SHARON M. DRAPER

Darkness Before Dawn
(New York: Atheneum/Simon & Schuster, 2001)

Subject(s): School Life; African Americans; Rape
Age range(s): Grades 9-12
Major character(s): Keisha Montgomery, 12th Grader (class president); Jonathan Hardaway, Coach (track)

Time period(s): 2000s
Locale(s): Cincinnati, Ohio

Summary: Senior year finds Hazelwood High class president Keisha still a little fragile after the suicide of her former boyfriend in *Forged by Fire*, though she does notice the new track coach who is the son of her principal. Jonathan is very smooth and, though really too old for her, convinces Keisha to accept his invitation for dinner. However it's not to a restaurant that Jonathan takes her, but to his condo where he attempts to rape her. Struggling in self-defense, she uses a kitchen knife to cut his face so that she can escape. Memories of her senior year swirl through her head the night she delivers her class's graduation speech in this last of the three books about the Hazelwood High students. (233 pages)

Where it's reviewed:
Book Report, September 2001, page 60
Booklist, January 2001, page 939
Bulletin of the Center for Children's Books, March 2001, page 256
School Library Journal, February 2001, page 117
Voice of Youth Advocates, August 2001, page 200

Awards the book has won:
ALA Quick Picks for Reluctant Young Adult Readers, 2002

Other books by the same author:
Romiette and Julio, 1999
Forged by Fire, 1997
Tears of a Tiger, 1994

Other books you might like:
Lou Kassem, *Odd One Out*, 1993
  At a sorority-fraternity initiation party, Alison's boyfriend Nic attempts to rape her to collect a $100 bet.
Norma Fox Mazer, *Out of Control*, 1993
  During her junior year Valerie is assaulted in a deserted hallway by three of her classmates, only one of whom feels any remorse.
Gloria D. Miklowitz, *Past Forgiving*, 1995
  Alex refuses to have sex with her boyfriend, which infuriates him; she knows their relationship has to end after he rapes her.

250

ALLAN DRUMMOND, Author/Illustrator

Casey Jones
(New York: Frances Foster/Farrar Straus Giroux, 2001)

Subject(s): Railroads; Historical; Stories in Rhyme
Age range(s): Grades K-3
Major character(s): John Luther "Casey" Jones, Engineer, Railroad Worker; Sim Webb, Railroad Worker, Friend
Time period(s): Indeterminate Past
Locale(s): Mississippi

Summary: Casey Jones becomes a legend in his own time for driving Engine 638 across America with the reputation for never being late. His distinctive use of the train's whistle allows residents of the towns he passes to identify the train as one being driven by Casey Jones. Late one night, Casey, with his fireman, Sim Webb, beside him in the locomotive, races across Mississippi trying to make up lost time on a route. The warning of a stalled freight train on the track ahead comes too late for Casey to save himself, but in time for Sim to jump clear and Casey to slow the train enough to save the passengers. A concluding "Author's Note" gives the historical basis for the story. (32 pages)

Where it's reviewed:
Booklist, February 15, 2001, page 1140
Horn Book Guide, Fall 2001, page 254
Kirkus Reviews, January 15, 2001, page 108
Publishers Weekly, December 18, 2000, page 78
School Library Journal, April 2001, page 106

Other books by the same author:
Moby Dick, 1997
The Willow Pattern Story, 1992

Other books you might like:
Nancy Farmer, *Casey Jones's Fireman: The Story of Sim Webb*, 1999
As fireman to the legendary Casey Jones, Sim Webb follows orders to increase power to the steam whistle despite sensing impending danger.
Verla Kay, *Iron Horses*, 1999
An award-winning illustrated story in rhyme describes the building of the transcontinental railroad.
Julius Lester, *John Henry*, 1994
A Caldecott Honor book retells the tale of the legendary John Henry, the steel-driving man who helped to build the railroad.
Marissa Moss, *True Heart*, 1999
After working as a freight loader for the Union Pacific, Bee finally achieves her dream of being a railroad engineer.

251

DIANE DUANE

The Wizard's Dilemma
(San Diego: Harcourt, 2001)

Series: Young Wizards. Number 5
Subject(s): Magic; Friendship; Death
Age range(s): Grades 6-10
Major character(s): Nita Callahan, Wizard, Daughter; Kit Rodriguez, Wizard, Friend
Time period(s): 2000s
Locale(s): New York

Summary: Nita and Kit have been through a lot together, but somehow they've always gotten along. Suddenly Nita finds their differences irritating rather than complimentary. Kit seems to question all her wizardly solutions, which leaves Nita feeling stupid. Meanwhile, Kit can't figure out what he's doing wrong; he'd really like to have his friend Nita back, but she's so touchy he can barely breathe around her. Even wizard communications can't patch things up, so Kit goes off on a space-time exploration of his own, while Nita makes the horrifying discovery that her mother is dying of cancer. What good is wizardry if she can't save her mom's life? All Nita's investigations, however, seem to indicate that she'll have to make a deal with the Lone Power to do any good. She really needs Kit now, but will he notice in time, and will Nita be able to admit that she could use his help? (324 pages)

Where it's reviewed:
Booklist, June 1, 2001, page 1862
Kirkus Reviews, June 1, 2001, page 800
School Library Journal, August 2001, page 178
Voice of Youth Advocates, August 2001, page 212

Other books by the same author:
A Wizard Abroad, 1993 (Young Wizards, Number 4)
High Wizardry, 1990 (Young Wizards, Number 3)
Deep Wizardry, 1985 (Young Wizards, Number 2)
So You Want to Be a Wizard, 1983 (Young Wizards, Number 1)

Other books you might like:
Dia Calhoun, *Aria of the Sea*, 2000
Cerinthe trains as a healer until her knowledge of medicine isn't enough to save her mother.
Annette Curtis Klause, *The Silver Kiss*, 1990
Depressed over her mother's illness, a teen is intrigued rather than frightened when she meets a vampire.
Mercedes Lackey, *Brightly Burning*, 2000
A young wizard's untrained gifts lead to the deaths of the school bullies.
Garth Nix, *Sabriel*, 1995
Sabriel inherits her father's abilities and finds herself traveling in the land of the dead.

252

BETSY DUFFEY

Fur-Ever Yours, Booker Jones
(New York: Viking, 2001)

Subject(s): Authorship; Grandfathers; Brothers and Sisters
Age range(s): Grades 4-6
Major character(s): Walter "Booker" Jones, Writer, Friend; Libba Jones, Sister (older), Student—Middle School; Pop, Grandfather, Aged Person; Howard "Germ" Germondo, Friend (Booker's), Student—Middle School
Time period(s): 2000s (2001)
Locale(s): Pickle Springs, Arkansas

Summary: With the exception of the rejection letters sent by the publisher to whom Booker submits his novels, the consistency on which he depends is vanishing from his life. Booker's staid parents have taken off on a trip to Mexico leaving Booker and Libba to care for Pop and fend for themselves for meals and clean clothes. Even Germ does an about face by joining the after-school writing club. The fact that Germ joins for the refreshments does not counteract the fact that he's also producing limericks and getting more positive attention than Booker does for his light science fiction. Booker and Libba are concerned when Pop begins to withdraw, declines meals, stays in bed and wears his trademark sweater inside out. They both realize that Pop needs to see his old home on the river once again and Libba, holder of only a learner's permit, risks driving them there. That experience and Pop's reaction to it helps Booker understand that the changes he sees are no different than chapters in a story as the plot develops. The sequel to *Utterly Yours, Booker Jones* concludes with a more mature Booker rebuilding his friendship with Germ and redefining his relationship with Libba to the benefit of both. (100 pages)

Where it's reviewed:
Booklist, June 1, 2001, page 1882
Horn Book Guide, Fall 2001, page 303
Kirkus Reviews, June 1, 2001, page 800
School Library Journal, July 2001, page 106

Other books by the same author:
Cody Unplugged, 1999
Utterly Yours, Booker Jones, 1995
Coaster, 1994

Other books you might like:
Andrew Clements, *The School Story*, 2001
    Twelve-year-old Natalie and her friend Zoe work on a plan to get Natalie's novel published.
Jack Gantos, *Jack's Black Book*, 1997
    Seventh-grader Jack tries to write a novel with humorous results.
Zilpha Keatley Snyder, *Libby on Wednesday*, 1990
    Friends made in a writing workshop help Libby adjust to an accelerated eighth grade program.
Jerry Spinelli, *Crash*, 1996
    After a stroke confines Crash's grandfather to bed, Crash gains a new perspective on life and interpersonal relationships.

253

JOYCE DUNBAR
DEBI GLIORI, Illustrator

Tell Me What It's Like to Be Big

(San Diego: Harcourt, Inc., 2001)

Subject(s): Growing Up; Brothers and Sisters; Animals/Rabbits
Age range(s): Grades K-1
Major character(s): Willa, Rabbit, Sister (younger); Willoughby, Rabbit, Brother (older)
Time period(s): Indeterminate
Locale(s): Fictional Country

Summary: Willa wakes up Willoughby to help her get breakfast and she wonders what it'll be like to be big. At first being big sounds appealing because she'll be able to make her own breakfast but soon some of the possibilities sound a little overwhelming. Willa is not sure that she wants to become big enough to give up her toys or to do grown-up things like walking out the door all alone. That thought is enough to send the siblings hurrying to their mother's bed to learn what she did when she was little. (28 pages)

Where it's reviewed:
Booklist, December 15, 2001, page 739
Horn Book Guide, Spring 2001, page 16
Kirkus Reviews, August 15, 2001, page 1211
Publishers Weekly, July 2, 2001, page 74
School Library Journal, September 2001, page 188

Other books by the same author:
The Very Small, 2000
Eggday, 1999
Tell Me Something Happy Before I Go to Sleep, 1998 (Smithsonian's Notable Books for Children)

Other books you might like:
Trish Cooke, *When I Grow Bigger*, 1994
    Leanne and her friends quibble about what they can or will do when they grow bigger.
Heidi Goennel, *While I Am Little*, 1993
    A young boy revels in the pleasures that are uniquely his because he's young enough and small enough to do them.
Arthur Howard, *When I Was Five*, 1996
    Jeremy reviews the accomplishments of his fifth year of life from the wise perspective of a just turned six-year-old.
Mercer Mayer, *All by Myself*, 1983
    Little Critter demonstrates the many things he's learned to do on his own such as tying shoes and riding a bike and one that he can't do alone.

254

DORANNA DURGIN

A Feral Darkness

(Riverdale, New York: Baen, 2001)

Subject(s): Animals/Dogs; Mythology; Magic
Age range(s): Grades 9-Adult
Major character(s): Brenna Fallon, Animal Lover; Iban ''Gil'' Masera, Animal Trainer; Nuadha's Silver Druid ''Druid'', Dog, Mythical Creature
Time period(s): 2000s
Locale(s): Monroe, New York

Summary: Brenna is a professional dog groomer and, since childhood, a serious animal lover. In fact, Brenna has yet to meet a dog she doesn't like and during her youth actually prayed to an ancient Roman deity who protected dogs. So when a frightened Corgi appears on her doorstep one night, Brenna is not as put out as most people would be; she coaxes the dog in and gives him shelter while she searches for the owner. But Druid, a champion according to his tags, doesn't seem to have any owners that Brenna can find and she's is in danger of falling in love with this lost dog, in spite of his mysterious bouts of hysterical fear. Although she isn't sure she can trust him, Brenna decides to enlist the aid of the attractive new animal trainer, Gil Masera, in helping Druid overcome his terror. Gil seems to have a peculiar understanding of the possible causes of Druid's fright, which makes Brenna more suspicious than ever. (343 pages)

Other books by the same author:
Tooth and Claw, 2001
Wolverine's Daughter, 2000
Changespell, 1997

Other books you might like:
Tanya Huff, *Summon the Keeper*, 1998
    Austin may be a cat, but he's just as much a smart aleck as any dog-familiar.
Diana Wynne Jones, *Dogsbody*, 2001
    The dog star Sirius is condemned to live in the body of a dog on earth until he performs a seemingly impossible task.
Robin McKinley, *Deerskin*, 1993
    Forced to flee into the wilderness to escape her father's evil intentions, a princess takes only her faithful dog, Ash.

Jan Siegel, *Prospero's Children*, 1999
Dark forces threaten Fern and Will, but the mysterious Lougarry, who's either a dog or a wolf, arrives to protect them.

255

DAVID ANTHONY DURHAM

Gabriel's Story
(New York: Doubleday, 2001)

Subject(s): African Americans; Coming-of-Age; Cowboys/Cowgirls
Age range(s): Grades 11-Adult
Major character(s): Gabriel Lynch, 15-Year-Old, Runaway; James, Runaway; Eliza Lynch, Mother (of Gabriel), Widow(er); Solomon Johns, Farmer, Stepfather; Marshall Hogg, Cowboy, Criminal; Caleb, Cowboy, Brother (half-brother of Marshall)
Time period(s): 1870s
Locale(s): Crownsville, Kansas; West; Mexico

Summary: Uprooted from his comfortable, middle-class life in Baltimore, Gabriel, brother Ben and widowed mother Eliza travel to Kansas to live with Gabriel's father-to-be Solomon. Still grieving for his father and the dreams they shared, Gabriel hates the sod house, the back-breaking work, and this farmer who will soon be his stepfather. Seizing upon a chance to run away with a group of cowboys, Gabriel and his new acquaintance James join a ragtag group whose real purpose becomes clear when they steal their first herd of horses. Led by demonic Marshall and his mute half-black, half-brother Caleb, the gang indulges in theft, murder and rape, all observed by two wide-eyed young boys who can't believe what they're seeing and who don't know how to escape. Told they'll never be allowed to leave because of what they've seen, the two try to remain unnoticed while continually scared to death; suddenly a sod house in the middle of nowhere seems comforting. After a disastrous accident that kills many of the gang, Gabriel manages to free himself and make his way home, but two men who don't want witnesses follow him in this violent, yet powerful first novel that offers a different perspective on the settlement of the West. (296 pages)

Where it's reviewed:
Booklist, December 15, 2000, page 788
Library Journal, November 1, 2000, page 101
New York Times Book Review, February 25, 2001, page 7
People, May 21, 2001, page 51
Publishers Weekly, December 4, 2000, page 54

Awards the book has won:
Booklist Editors' Choice/Adult Books for Young Adults, 2001
ALA Alex Award, 2002

Other books by the same author:
Walk through Darkness, 2002

Other books you might like:
Terry C. Johnston, *Dance on the Wind*, 1995
Determined not to be tied to a piece of land, Titus heads down the Mississippi to New Orleans and then out West to explore the frontier.
Cormac McCarthy, *All the Pretty Horses*, 1992
After the death of his grandfather, John Grady Cole and a friend ride for Mexico where they are hired on as vaqueros at a ranch.
Larry McMurtry, *Lonesome Dove*, 1985
Two former Texas rangers undertake a difficult journey when they steal a herd of cattle from Mexico and head up to Montana to establish a ranch.

E

KATHLEEN EAGLE

You Never Can Tell

(New York: Morrow, 2001)

Subject(s): Indians of North America; Romance
Age range(s): Grades 10-Adult
Major character(s): Heather Reardon, Journalist; Kole Kills Crow, Indian (Lakota Sioux)
Time period(s): 2000s
Locale(s): Blue Fish Indian Reservation, Minnesota; West

Summary: At one time Kole Kills Crow was a well-known Indian activist, but then a series of tragedies, including the death of his wife and a trumped-up murder charge against him, sent him on the run. Journalist Heather wants to tell his story for she considers him a dying breed, a true warrior, who wants only what's best for his people. Tracking him down in a small Minnesota bar, she woos him until she convinces him that his story of political activism should be told. Once agreed, the two set off to demonstrate against the stereotypes of Indians in Hollywood films, collecting a motley group of like-minded Native Americans to join them as they head west. (306 pages)

Where it's reviewed:
Booklist, July 2001, page 1990
BookPage, August 2001, page 26
Kirkus Reviews, June 1, 2001, page 757
Library Journal, May 15, 2001, page 106
Publishers Weekly, July 30, 2001, page 60

Awards the book has won:
Romance Writers of America Top Ten Favorite Books of the Year, 2001

Other books by the same author:
Once upon a Wedding, 2002
The Last Good Man, 2000
What the Heart Knows, 1999
The Last True Cowboy, 1998
The Night Remembers, 1997

Other books you might like:
Sherman Alexie, *Indian Killer*, 1996
John Smith becomes delusional and decides to right all the wrongs committed against the Native Americans.
Louise Erdrich, *Tracks*, 1988
A movingly told story of the difficulty of being a Chippewa attempting to maintain a culture that clashes with the white man's.
N. Scott Momaday, *House Made of Dawn*, 1968
After being drafted into the army, Abel has difficulty living in either the white man's world or on the reservation where he was born.

KELLY EASTON

The Life History of a Star

(New York: McElderry/Simon & Schuster, 2001)

Subject(s): Brothers and Sisters; Diaries; Vietnam War
Age range(s): Grades 7-10
Major character(s): Kristin Folger, 14-Year-Old; David Folger, Brother
Time period(s): 1970s (1973-1974)
Locale(s): Glendora, California

Summary: Through her diary entries, Kristin describes the changes in her life that, at times, could overwhelm her if not for her wry, humorous look at life. Along with the normal teenager changes, such as menstruation and the appearance of curves, there's also the problem of friends. Kristin's best friend has gone bonkers over some dead-end guy while her male best friend has the hots for her. Her parents are separating, she worries about her grandmother and the pall of the "ghost" in the attic drapes over her family. That ghost is a person, or what's left of her oldest, formerly All-American brother David, who returned from Vietnam mentally and physically changed. The family doesn't discuss the problem, but the effect of this changed person oppresses everyone. Remembering David's comment that the atoms of a star never die but are transformed helps Kristin accept his death as she realizes he will remain in her world in this first novel. (200 pages)

Where it's reviewed:
Booklist, April 15, 2001, page 1545
Bulletin of the Center for Children's Books, March 2001, page 257
Publishers Weekly, March 19, 2001, page 101
School Library Journal, July 2001, page 106
Voice of Youth Advocates, April 2001, page 40

Other books by the same author:
Trouble at Betts' Pets, 2002

Other books you might like:
Nancy Antle, *Lost in the War*, 1998
    The Vietnam War has cost Lisa dearly, from her father's death to her mother's continuing nightmares, and she doesn't relish having to study it in school.
Anna Fienberg, *Borrowed Light*, 2000
    In Cally's life, people are either moons, borrowers of light like she is, or stars, those who make light.
Bobbie Ann Mason, *In Country*, 1985
    Sam loses her father in the Vietnam War and now her uncle suffers from the effects of Agent Orange, all from a war Sam doesn't understand.

258

THOM EBERHARDT

Rat Boys: A Dating Experiment
(New York: Hyperion, 2001)

Subject(s): Magic; Animals/Rats; Humor
Age range(s): Grades 6-9
Major character(s): Marci Kornbalm, 14-Year-Old; Summer Weingarten, 14-Year-Old; Jennifer Martin, 14-Year-Old, Beauty Queen (Miss Indiana); Doris ''Weird Doris'' Trowbridge, Antiques Dealer; Spike, Rat; Scooter, Rat
Time period(s): 2000s
Locale(s): Indianapolis, Indiana

Summary: Marci and Summer are typical teens, nice but not wildly popular and attractive but not in the knockout category of Jennifer who has blossomed into Miss Indiana but is not one of their favorite people. To one-up Jennifer, Marci lies that she and Summer have hot dates for the Spring Fling dance that night. The two girls work for antique storeowner ''Weird Doris'' who has just discovered a magic ring that she uses to transmutate herself into a popular television soap opera star. Then she works a little more magic, turns her two pet rats into the coolest looking guys in the world, and hands Summer and Marci a bag of Chee-tos for behavior training. Wow-these guys are hot! The fact they don't know how to talk or dance is just a minor problem. But problems for Marci and Summer are only beginning as the girls realize that besides eating, sleeping and running on their treadmills, there's one other thing rats like to do. When Spike and Scooter disappear at the dance, Marci and Summer know catastrophe awaits them. (154 pages)

Where it's reviewed:
Booklist, November 2001, page 466
Publishers Weekly, September 24, 2001, page 94

School Library Journal, November 2001, page 154
Voice of Youth Advocates, December 2001, page 368

Awards the book has won:
ALA Quick Picks for Reluctant Young Adult Readers, 2002

Other books you might like:
Cherie Bennett, *Stranger in the Mirror*, 1999
    Putting a heart-shaped meteorite under her pillow, Callie's dream that she become beautiful like her sister, comes true.
Ellen Conford, *Genie with the Light Blue Hair*, 1989
    Jeannie receives an antique lamp, complete with a blue Groucho Marx-like genie that's a little rusty in the wish-granting department.
Sarah Sargent, *Watermusic*, 1986
    A special flute gives Laura power over unusual animals.
David Henry Wilson, *The Coachman Rat*, 1989
    Robert, the rat who drives the coach for Cinderella, wants to return to his human state.

259

MARY ECCLES

By Lizzie
(New York: Dial Books for Young Readers, 2001)

Subject(s): Family Life; Single Parent Families; Sibling Rivalry
Age range(s): Grades 3-5
Major character(s): Elizabeth ''Lizzie'' Anderson, 9-Year-Old, Child of Divorced Parents; Norman Anderson, Brother, 12-Year-Old; Mom, Single Mother, Journalist; Ellie Anderson, Sister (younger), 2-Year-Old
Time period(s): 2000s (2001)
Locale(s): Wisconsin

Summary: The discovery of Mom's old typewriter on New Year's Day gives Lizzie the idea to record the events of the year until her tenth birthday on the following New Year's Eve. Monthly stories convey Lizzie's frustration at being stuck in the middle between superior, taunting Norman and little Ellie who wants to be with and like Lizzie but can't even pronounce her name correctly. The stories also show Lizzie's growing appreciation for Norman and understanding of Ellie. Although Lizzie does not literally travel for a year with the typewriter as Mom did she makes a figurative journey through family, school and friendship to her birthday destination and concludes with a collection of twelve stories to present to Mom as the author's first novel concludes. (116 pages)

Where it's reviewed:
Booklist, May 15, 2001, page 1749
Bulletin of the Center for Children's Books, June 2001, page 371
Horn Book Guide, Fall 2001, page 303
Kirkus Reviews, May 1, 2001, page 658
School Library Journal, June 2001, page 111

Other books you might like:
Marissa Moss, *Amelia's Notebook*, 1995
    In a journal, nine-year-old Amelia records her thought about moving, the friends she's left behind, and her apprehensions about beginning a new school.

Carol Weston, *The Diary of Melanie Martin: Or How I Survived Matt the Brat, Michelangelo and the Leaning Tower of Pizza*, 2000

A family trip to Italy sounds exciting but traveling with little brother Matt, as Melanie describes in her trip diary, is a bit too adventurous.

Jacqueline Wilson, *Double Act*, 1998

In a notebook twin sisters record their thoughts about unpopular changes in their single-parent family life.

260

TERESA EDGERTON

The Queen's Necklace
(New York: Eos/HarperCollins, 2001)

Subject(s): Magic; Love; Adventure and Adventurers
Age range(s): Grades 10-Adult
Major character(s): Wilrowan "Wil" Blackheart, Nobleman, Spouse; Lilliana "Lili" Blackheart, Healer, Wizard
Time period(s): Indeterminate
Locale(s): Planet—Imaginary

Summary: Wil, swashbuckling captain of the queen's guard, is notorious for his wild behavior and affairs of the heart. What few know is that his devil-may-care attitude covers a sensitive heart and a strong sense of honor. Tricked into marriage at an early age, Wil is deeply in love with his wife, but doesn't want her to feel obligated by the wedding her father engineered. Lili is equally in love with Wil, but fears he finds her a bore. Wil immerses himself in his life and duties in town, while Lili pursues initiation as a healer and practitioner of the occult arts. When the goblin-made jeweled engines that keep the kingdoms in balance begin to go missing, both Wil and Lili are called to help in the search, but neither is free to tell the other. The goblins are rising to reclaim their ancient kingdoms and Wil and Lili could be one another's best help, if they can only learn to trust in time. (579 pages)

Where it's reviewed:
Booklist, May 1, 2001, page 1671
Library Journal, July 2001, page 131
Magazine of Fantasy and Science Fiction, December 2001, page 36
Publishers Weekly, May 21, 2001, page 86

Other books by the same author:
The Moon and the Thorn, 1995
Goblin Moon, 1991
The Gnome's Engine, 1991

Other books you might like:
Peter David, *Sir Apropos of Nothing*, 2001

Can a cranky princess and a smart-aleck, lame hero find happiness in addition to surviving?

Sharon Shinn, *Summers at Castle Auburn*, 2001

Corie's comfortable summers with her noble half-sister become less comfortable and more difficult as she gets older.

Martha Wells, *The Death of the Necromancer*, 1998

Nicholas is nobleman, thief and, if necessary, a catcher of necromancers.

261

LILIAN EDVALL
ANNA-CLARA TIDHOLM, Illustrator
ELISABETH KALLICK DYSSEGAARD, Translator

The Rabbit Who Longed for Home
(New York: R & S Books, 2001)

Subject(s): Animals/Rabbits; Parent and Child; Teacher-Student Relationships
Age range(s): Grades K-1
Major character(s): Unnamed Character, Rabbit, Son; Unnamed Character, Teacher
Time period(s): Indeterminate
Locale(s): Fictional Country

Summary: A little rabbit fears going to day care but both his parents work so he has no choice. The shy little rabbit cries when his parents leave and watches all day for their return. At first the young rabbit is timid with the teachers and other students but gradually he feel slightly more comfortable. Then a new teacher arrives, a teacher who lets him sit in her lap until he feels ready to join the play. Now, just as the little rabbit is beginning to adjust his parents announce that soon one of them will stop working and stay home with the new baby and he can too. The little rabbit isn't sure if he's happy about the change or not. (28 pages)

Where it's reviewed:
Booklist, September 15, 2001, page 230
Horn Book Guide, Spring 2002, page 16
School Library Journal, November 2001, page 119

Other books you might like:
Nancy E. Cooney, *Chatterbox Jamie*, 1993

The first day of preschool is so overwhelming to usually talkative Jamie that he feels too shy to speak.

Jonathan London, *Froggy Goes to School*, 1996

Although Froggy feels nervous about the first day of school he survives and actually enjoys the day.

John Wallace, *Tiny Rabbit Goes to a Birthday Party*, 2000

Although he's excited to be invited to a party, Tiny Rabbit is also apprehensive about attending the event.

262

MICHELLE EDWARDS, Author/Illustrator

Zero Grandparents
(San Diego: Harcourt, Inc., 2001)

Series: Jackson Friends. Book 2
Subject(s): Grandparents; Schools; Grandmothers
Age range(s): Grades 2-4
Major character(s): Calliope James, 2nd Grader, Friend; Pa Lia Vang, 2nd Grader, Friend; Howie Smith, 2nd Grader, Friend
Time period(s): 2000s (2001)
Locale(s): United States

Summary: Other students are excited by the teacher's announcement of Grandparents Day, but Calliope feels a sense of dread because she has "zero grandparents." Pa Lia and Howie are willing to share their live-in grandmothers with

Calliope and her gray-haired mother offers to come as a substitute, but Calliope wants her own grandmother. While glumly looking through a family picture album, Calliope finds a picture of her deceased grandmother, reflects on what she knows about her and devises a plan for Grandparents Day. (58 pages)

Where it's reviewed:
Booklist, April 1, 2001, page 1468
Bulletin of the Center for Children's Books, April 2001, page 301
Horn Book Guide, Fall 2001, page 290
School Library Journal, July 2001, page 74

Other books by the same author:
The Talent Show, 2002 (Jackson Friends, Book 3)
Pa Lia's First Day, 1999 (Jackson Friends, Book 1)
Dora's Book, 1990

Other books you might like:
Sheila Greenwald, *Rosy Cole Discovers America!*, 1992
   Rosy enlivens her class project by inventing ancestors that she considers to be more exciting than those actually on her family tree.
Maggie Harrison, *Lizzie's List*, 1993
   Lizzie makes a list of the relatives ''missing'' from her life and then goes in search of them, beginning with a grandmother whom she ''adopts.''
Wendy Orr, *Ark in the Park*, 2000
   Sophie's birthday wish for a pet and cousins is fulfilled in an unexpected way.

263

PAMELA DUNCAN EDWARDS
HENRY COLE, Illustrator

Clara Caterpillar

(New York: HarperCollins Publishers, 2001)

Subject(s): Animals/Insects; Friendship; Nature
Age range(s): Grades K-2
Major character(s): Clara, Insect, Friend; Cornelius, Insect, Friend; Catisha, Insect
Time period(s): Indeterminate
Locale(s): Fictional Country

Summary: A little white egg hatches into Clara, a caterpillar destined to become a cabbage butterfly. Her ''plain Jane'' future does not deter Cornelius from befriending her but Catisha scorns the common creature. After emerging from her chrysalis Clara admires her friends who are now colorful butterflies while she is a creamy white. Snooty Catisha flies away from the others and into the sight line of a crow that sees her as a tasty snack. Clara rushes to Catisha's defense, distracts the crow and then saves herself by hiding in a camellia bush with cream-colored blossoms. (32 pages)

Where it's reviewed:
Booklist, July 2001, page 2018
Horn Book Guide, Fall 2001, page 254
New York Times Book Review, August 12, 2001, page 24
Publishers Weekly, May 14, 2001, page 84
School Library Journal, June 2001, page 112

Awards the book has won:
IRA Children's Choices, 2002

Other books by the same author:
Bravo, Livingstone Mouse!, 2000
Some Smug Slug, 1996
Four Famished Foxes and Fosdyke, 1995

Other books you might like:
Lois Ehlert, *Waiting for Wings*, 2001
   An award-winning nonfiction title introduces the life cycle of butterflies.
Mary Ling, *Butterfly*, 1992
   This title in the nonfiction ''See How They Grow'' series uses color photographs to explain the life of butterflies.
Sam Swope, *Gotta Go! Gotta Go!*, 2000
   A caterpillar with an urgent need to go to Mexico, interrupts the trip for a nap and when it awakens as a butterfly, continues the journey.

264

TIM EGAN, Author/Illustrator

A Mile from Ellington Station

(Boston: Houghton Mifflin Company, 2001)

Subject(s): Jealousy; Animals/Dogs; Animals/Bears
Age range(s): Grades K-3
Major character(s): Preston, Bear, Spouse; Marley, Dog; Ruth, Bear, Spouse (Preston's)
Time period(s): Indeterminate
Locale(s): Fictional Country

Summary: Preston is more interested in checkers and extending his winning streak than he is in helping Ruth with chores about the lodge that they own and operate. When Marley appears and offers to paint in exchange for lodging Ruth strikes a deal on the spot and Marley paints the exterior in one night. In the morning he cooks breakfast, tells stories and entertains the guests while Preston plays checkers. Marley accepts Preston's offer to play a game and Preston's winning streak comes to a quick end. Preston is not happy and surmises to anyone that will listen that Marley must be a sorcerer in order to do so well all that he does. The rumor spreads throughout the town and Marley's sleight of hand does nothing to dispel it. Ruth plans the last trick, one that she hopes will bring about a streak of helpfulness from Preston. (32 pages)

Where it's reviewed:
Booklist, April 15, 2001
Horn Book Guide, Fall 2001, page 254
Kirkus Reviews, March 1, 2001, page 329
Publishers Weekly, April 2, 2001, page 64
School Library Journal, May 2001, page 115

Other books by the same author:
Burnt Toast on Davenport Street, 1997 (School Library Journal Best Books)
Metropolitan Cow, 1996 (School Library Journal Best Books)
Chestnut Cove, 1995

Other books you might like:
Juanita Havill, *Jamaica and Brianna*, 1993
   Envy over a friend's new boots leads to harsh words, hurt

feelings and, with time, reconciliation between two best friends.

Bernard Most, *The Very Boastful Kangaroo*, 1999
A very tiny kangaroo tricks a very boastful kangaroo into conceding defeat in a jumping contest.

Erica Silverman, *Don't Fidget a Feather*, 1994
Two competitive friends learn that some things are more important than winning.

James Stevenson, *The Mud Flat Olympics*, 1994
Annually a competitive group of animal friends hold their own wacky version of the Olympics.

H.M. EHRLICH
LAURA RADER, Illustrator

Dancing Class
(New York: Orchard Books, 2001)

Subject(s): Ballet; Animals; Stories in Rhyme
Age range(s): Preschool-Grade 1
Major character(s): Piggy, Pig, Dancer
Time period(s): Indeterminate
Locale(s): Fictional Country

Summary: Piggy hurries to dancing class quickly changing into her tights, tutu and slippers and joins the other students. While leaping Piggy hurts her toe and falls but the sensitive teacher and students help her back to her feet. Happily the class concludes with each student going home dreaming of the day they will be ballerinas. (26 pages)

Where it's reviewed:
Children's Bookwatch, May 2001, page 7
Horn Book Guide, Fall 2001, page 230
Kirkus Reviews, April 15, 2001, page 583
Publishers Weekly, July 2, 2001, page 78

Other books by the same author:
Dr. Duck, 2000
Louie's Goose, 2000

Other books you might like:
Lucy Dickens, *Dancing Class*, 1992
Five young aspiring dancers have the opportunity to perform as birds during class.

Kay Gallwey, *Dancing Daisy*, 1994
After seeing her first ballet, Daisy is determined to become a ballerina.

Rachel Isadora, *Lili at Ballet*, 1993
Four times a week Lili attends ballet classes hoping to achieve her dream of being a ballerina.

266

RANDY LEE EICKHOFF

The Destruction of the Inn
(New York: Forge, 2001)

Series: Celtic Ulster Cycle. Part 4
Subject(s): Mythology; Magic; Adventure and Adventurers
Age range(s): Grades 10-Adult
Major character(s): Connaire, Royalty

Time period(s): Indeterminate Past
Locale(s): Ireland

Summary: A free translation of the famous Irish epic, the story begins before Connaire's birth when he was magically conceived. Like many heroes-to-be, Connaire is the child of a king and a magical mother. Remarkable from boyhood, he is bound by fate and conflicting ages to a tragic end. Though Connaire tries to behave as a man of honor, he is unable to abandon the foster brothers of his childhood, in spite of their unwillingness or inability to behave. Eventually the demands of family and honor are too much and Connaire is led to break a taboo, which leads to a tragic end. (288 pages)

Where it's reviewed:
Booklist, March 15, page 1353
Kirkus Reviews, February 1, 2001, page 143
Publishers Weekly, February 26, 2001, page 59

Other books by the same author:
The Sorrows, 2001
The Feast, 1999
The Raid, 1997

Other books you might like:
Adele Geras, *Troy*, 2001
The ancient Greek tale of the fall of Troy is retold.

Nalo Hopkinson, *Midnight Robber*, 2000
A child in trouble reinvents herself using the folktales of her childhood.

John Steinbeck, *The Acts of King Arthur and his Noble Knights*, 1976
Although Steinbeck makes some concessions to modern tastes, he is largely faithful to Malloy's version of the Arthurian legends.

LILLIAN EIGE

Dangling
(New York: Atheneum/Simon & Schuster, 2001)

Subject(s): Friendship; Foster Parents; Missing Persons
Age range(s): Grades 4-7
Major character(s): Ring Maxwell, 7th Grader; Benjamin "Ben" Gallegar, 7th Grader
Time period(s): 2000s
Locale(s): Green Hills

Summary: One summer day while everyone's enjoying a family picnic, Ring walks into the river and keeps going. No one worries at first because Ring's a good swimmer, but he never reappears. Ben feels as though he's been left "dangling" while he waits for word of his friend, but even Ring's body isn't recovered. Through a series of flashbacks, Ben thinks over the friendship he and Ring have shared, but as he discovers, there are some facts about Ring's life that he doesn't know. All Ring's actions can be traced to his fear of losing his loving foster parents in a special story of friendship. (166 pages)

Where it's reviewed:
Booklist, February 1, 2001, page 1052
Bulletin of the Center for Children's Books, March 2001, page 257

Journal of Adolescent and Adult Literacy, October 2001, page 171

Publishers Weekly, January 15, 2001, page 76

School Library Journal, July 2001, page 106

Other books by the same author:

Cady, 1987

Kidnapping of Mister Huey, 1983

Other books you might like:

Dianne E. Gray, *Holding Up the Earth*, 2000

Foster child Hope's summer with Sarah on the family farm gives her a connection to families as she learns about the teen years of four generations of women.

Dean Hughes, *Team Picture*, 1996

David doesn't know what to do when his foster father comes home drunk; if David tells anyone, he'll be back in the welfare system and he doesn't want that.

Jerry Spinelli, *Maniac Magee*, 1990

Maniac is legendary for bringing together kids from the black East End and the white West End, mixing them in such a way that prejudices are forgotten.

268

MAX EILENBERG
PATRICK BENSON, Illustrator

Squeak's Good Idea

(Cambridge, MA: Candlewick Press, 2001)

Subject(s): Animals/Elephants; Conduct of Life; Family

Age range(s): Preschool-Grade 1

Major character(s): Squeak, Elephant, Brother (older); Tumble, Elephant; Momma, Mother, Elephant; Poppa, Father, Elephant

Time period(s): Indeterminate

Locale(s): Fictional Country

Summary: No one in Squeak's family has time to go outside with him so he prepares to go out alone by planning carefully for any eventuality. Squeak puts on lots of clothes including Momma's scarf in case it's cold out and borrows Poppa's umbrella just in case it rains. Then, in the event that he might become hungry, he packs a picnic basket. Finally ready, Squeak trudges all the way to the tree in far corner of the yard where he sheds his many layers of clothing because it's not cold and hangs the umbrella in the tree because it's not raining. Just as he sets up the picnic, Tumble appears followed by Momma and Poppa to join in on Squeak's good idea. (40 pages)

Where it's reviewed:

Booklist, December 15, 2001, page 739

Horn Book, January 2002, page 68

Publishers Weekly, October 1, 2001, page 60

School Library Journal, December 2001, page 99

Other books by the same author:

Cowboy Kid, 2000

Other books you might like:

Ivan Bates, *All by Myself*, 2000

A little elephant is determined to pick the breakfast leaves from the tree without her mother's assistance.

Gloria Rand, *Willie Takes a Hike*, 1996

With his well-stocked backpack Willie goes on a "pretend" hike alone but ventures too far from home and becomes lost.

Ursel Scheffler, *Who Has Time for Little Bear?*, 1998

Mama and Papa are too busy to play with Little Bear so he walks in the woods alone until he meets another bear cub that's eager to play.

269

MARILYN EISENSTEIN
MIRANDA JONES, Illustrator

Kate Can't Wait

(Plattsburgh, NY: Tundra Books, 2001)

Subject(s): Conduct of Life; Gardens and Gardening; Behavior

Age range(s): Grades K-2

Major character(s): Kate, Child, Daughter; Jessie, Child, Friend

Time period(s): 2000s

Locale(s): Canada

Summary: Kate's family is moving to a new home in the country and Kate can't wait to get there. Actually, Kate hasn't the patience to wait for anything. As Kate's family settles into their new home, Jessie knocks on the door and invites Kate to visit her the next day, meaning Kate has to wait some more. Jessie introduces Kate to a litter of kittens promising to give Kate one when the kittens are old enough, more waiting. Then Jessie brings Kate a box of strawberry plants. Kate's disappointed to see no berries but Jessie explains that she must plant them in the garden and then wait for them to grow. The process of waiting for the garden to mature helps Kate learn that waiting does not have to be a passive time for her strawberry plants need care in order to grow. When the fruit ripens, Kate agrees that it's worth the wait. (24 pages)

Where it's reviewed:

Children's Bookwatch, July 2001, page 6

Horn Book Guide, Fall 2001, page 254

Quill & Quire, March 2001, page 58

School Library Journal, April 2001, page 108

Other books by the same author:

Periwinkle Isn't Paris, 1999

Other books you might like:

Helen Ketteman, *Not Yet, Yvette*, 1992

The surprise is not for her but still Yvette has a hard time waiting for her mom's surprise party to begin.

Maggie Stern, *George*, 1999

Three stories tell of eager-to-please but impetuous George who can't wait his turn in class yet has the patience to track down a lost class pet.

Catherine Walters, *When Will It Be Spring?*, 1997

Alfie should be sleeping like a patient bear in hibernation but he's too eager for the first signs of spring to appear.

MICHAEL ALEXANDER EISNER

The Crusader
(New York: Doubleday, 2001)

Subject(s): Crusades; Knights and Knighthood; Monks
Age range(s): Grades 10-Adult
Major character(s): Francisco de Montcada, Wealthy; Lucas, Religious (monk)
Time period(s): 13th century
Locale(s): Santes Creus Monastery, Spain; Krak des Chevaliers, Syria (the Holy Land)

Summary: Returning from a Crusade he undertook for his dead brother, who drowned before he reached the Holy Land, Francisco is mute from the horror done to him and by him. Sent by the Archbishop to conduct an exorcism is Brother Lucas whose aspirations of becoming an abbot or a bishop could be easily achieved if the exorcism is successful. Lucas has been selected for his friendship with Francisco eleven years ago and because the church is grateful to Francisco's wealthy family for the many contributions they have made. As the monk tries to exorcise the demon that renders Francisco mute, he gradually hears all that transpired on the Crusade to the Holy Land. Francisco is shaken not only by his killing of the abbot of Santes Cruse, who had raped a servant girl, but also by the torture he endured when he and his cousin were betrayed and turned over to the Muslims. As Brother Lucas listens to Francisco's tale, he ponders what constitutes salvation in this first novel that is rich in historical detail and human emotion. (320 pages)

Where it's reviewed:
Booklist, August 2001, page 2085
Kirkus Reviews, August 1, 2001, page 1048
Library Journal, September 15, 2001, page 110
Publishers Weekly, September 10, 2001, page 58

Other books you might like:
Evan S. Connell, *Deus Lo Volt!*, 2000
  For over two hundred years knights led Crusades to reclaim Jerusalem from the infidels in a campaign started by Pope Urban in the late eleventh century.
Bernard Cornwell, *Archer's Tale*, 2001
  At the beginning of the Hundred Years War, the archer Thomas of Hookton becomes ensnarled in a quest to retrieve the Holy Grail.
Stephen R. Lawhead, *Celtic Crusades Series*, 1999-
  A Scottish family always bring back a sacred relic from the Crusades, whether it is part of the cross or the lance used at the crucifixion.

271
DAVID ELLIOTT
PAUL MEISEL, Illustrator

The Cool Crazy Crickets to the Rescue!
(Cambridge, MA: Candlewick Press, 2001)

Subject(s): Clubs; Money; Friendship
Age range(s): Grades 2-3

Major character(s): Leo, Child, Friend; Marcus, Child, Friend; Miranda, Child, Friend; Phoebe, Child, Friend
Time period(s): 2000s (2001)
Locale(s): United States

Summary: The Cool Crazy Crickets Club has no dues and no one wants to assess any. Leo has the idea that club members could earn money for the club activities. Miranda suggests pet sitting, Phoebe's idea is selling lemonade and Leo thinks they could do babysitting. Each of their ideas is successful but they can't decide what to do with the money. Marcus wants snacks but when the club members find a stray cat in the clubhouse they take it to the vet and use the money they've earned to save the cat. (56 pages)

Where it's reviewed:
Booklist, September 1, 2001, page 104
Horn Book Guide, Fall 2001, page 290
Kirkus Reviews, May 1, 2001, page 658
Publishers Weekly, May 21, 2001, page 109
School Library Journal, July 2001, page 75

Other books by the same author:
The Transmogrification of Roscoe Wizzle, 2001
The Cool Crazy Crickets, 2000
An Alphabet of Rotten Kids!, 1991

Other books you might like:
Bill Cosby, *Money Troubles*, 1998
  While trying to earn money for a telescope Little Bill learns a lesson about needs greater than his own and the importance of generosity.
Stephanie Greene, *Owen Foote, Money Man*, 2000
  Owen and his pal Joseph try various ways to make money so they can order neat products such as fake vomit from a catalog.
Marilyn Singer, *Josie to the Rescue*, 1999
  Realizing that her parents have some financial concerns with a new baby coming Josie decides to earn money to contribute to the family.

272
DAVID ELLIOTT

The Transmogrification of Roscoe Wizzle
(Cambridge, MA: Candlewick Press, 2001)

Subject(s): Science Fiction; Humor; Food
Age range(s): Grades 3-5
Major character(s): Roscoe Wizzle, 10-Year-Old; Kinsasha Rosa Parks "Kinchy" Boomer, Friend, Anthropologist (amateur)
Time period(s): 2000s (2001)
Locale(s): Roseville

Summary: Strange things have been happening in Roseville since the new Gussy's Restaurant opened. Kids are disappearing and Roscoe is changing into a bug! He can't help but wonder if eating a Jungle Burger at Gussy's every night has anything to do with what's going on in town. Kinchy, aided by information that her mother is using as part of the police investigation into the missing children, suspects that Roscoe will be the next to disappear because the other children also transmogrified into insects prior to their disappearance. When

Roscoe realizes that the other children also dined regularly at Gussy's, Kinchy's investigation focuses on the restaurant and she soon solves the mystery. (115 pages)

Where it's reviewed:
Bulletin of the Center for Children's Books, May 2001, page 334
Horn Book Guide, Fall 2001, page 304
Kirkus Reviews, April 15, 2001, page 583
Publishers Weekly, May 7, 2001, page 247
School Library Journal, June 2001, page 112

Other books by the same author:
The Cool Crazy Crickets to the Rescue!, 2001
The Cool Crazy Crickets, 2000

Other books you might like:
Mary James, *Shoebag*, 1990
> Life changes dramatically, but temporarily, for Shoebag, a young cockroach that becomes a boy.

Daniel Pinkwater, *Fat Men from Space*, 1977
> Alien fat men intent on stealing the world's junk food are invading Earth.

Carol Sonenklar, *Bug Boy*, 1997
> Using the "Bug-A-View" that appears on his doorstep, Charlie changes places with any insect that he places inside the device.

273

L.M. ELLIOTT

Under a War-Torn Sky

(New York: Hyperion, 2001)

Subject(s): World War II; Resistance Movements
Age range(s): Grades 7-10
Major character(s): Henry Forester, Military Personnel (Air Force pilot)
Time period(s): 1940s
Locale(s): Switzerland; France

Summary: Shot down behind enemy lines during World War II, Henry watches in horror as a German Messerschmitt circles and continues to fire after he and his copilot have parachuted from their flaming plane. Seeing his copilot hit and killed, Henry fires his handgun in a futile attempt to halt the Messerschmitt, but manages only to draw attention to himself. When his parachute is strafed, he descends rapidly into a snow bank, which absorbs the worst of the impact so that he only breaks his leg. Limping to a road, he is fortunate to meet an old French schoolteacher who starts Henry on the beginning of his adventures with the French Resistance. They repair his leg, provide him safety and try to return him to American lines where he can continue flying. Based on tales told to the author by her father, this first novel reveals the heroics and kindnesses of the non-military people who also stood against the Nazis. (284 pages)

Where it's reviewed:
Booklist, October 1, 2001, page 312
Bulletin of the Center for Children's Books, January 1, 2002, page 170
School Library Journal, October 2001, page 154
Voice of Youth Advocates, December 2001, page 356

Awards the book has won:
Borders Original Voices Award, 2001

Other books you might like:
Carol Matas, *Code Name Kris*, 1990
> Jesper and his friend Stefan are arrested by the Nazis for their resistance activities in the Danish Underground during World War II.

Cynthia Mercati, *A Light in the Sky*, 1999
> In a small French village, Jeanne sees an RAF pilot parachute from his plane and makes sure the Germans don't kill him like they did her brother.

Elizabeth Van Steenwyk, *A Traitor Among Us*, 1998
> Not to be left out, young Pieter helps the Resistance fighters in his village and exposes a traitor.

274

DEBORAH ELLIS

The Breadwinner

(Toronto, Canada: Groundwood Books, 2001, c2000)

Subject(s): Survival; Gender Roles; Women's Rights
Age range(s): Grades 5-7
Major character(s): Parvana, 11-Year-Old
Time period(s): 2000s
Locale(s): Kabul, Afghanistan

Summary: Throughout the Afghan fight against the Soviets or the oppressive rule of the Taliban religious group, Parvana's family remains in Afghanistan. Their daily life worsens with the rise of the Taliban and the bombing of her father's school leaves him injured and unable to teach history. Reduced to reading mail for illiterates at the city market, he barely ekes out a living for Parvana, her mother and her siblings. Then real tragedy strikes when he is arrested for having a foreign education and the women cannot leave their one-room hovel without a male companion. In desperation Parvana dons her deceased brother's clothes and takes her father's place at market reading and writing letters to earn money for her family, though she lives in fear the Taliban will see through her disguise and imprison her. When her mother and siblings head north away from the fighting in Kabul, Parvana stays behind to search for her father in this realistic story of conditions that existed in Afghanistan. (170 pages)

Where it's reviewed:
Book Report, November 2001, page 60
Booklist, March 1, 2001, page 1275
Publishers Weekly, March 19, 2001, page 100
School Library Journal, July 2001, page 106
Voice of Youth Advocates, June 2001, page 120

Other books by the same author:
Looking for X, 2000
Pick-Up Sticks, 1992
A Family Project, 1988

Other books you might like:
Teri Kanefield, *Rivka's Way*, 2001
> Rivka is curious about what lies beyond the walls of her Jewish ghetto in Prague, so dresses as a boy, removes her yellow Jewish star and goes exploring.

Cristina Kessler, *No Condition Is Permanent*, 2000
Accompanying her Peace Corps mother to Sierra Leona, Jolie offends the villagers when she stops her friend Khadi's initiation into a women's Secret Society.

Lensey Namioka, *Ties That Bind, Ties That Break*, 1999
The young Chinese girl Ailin first defies tradition by refusing to have her feet bound then, when she's older, cancels her arranged marriage.

Linda Sue Park, *Seesaw Girl*, 1999
Jade's life in her Korean family is defined by the walls of their Inner Court within which she embroiders, washes the family clothes and prepares meals.

ELLA THORP ELLIS

The Year of My Indian Prince
(New York: Delacorte Press, 2001)

Subject(s): Diseases; Courtship; Hospitals
Age range(s): Grades 7-10
Major character(s): April Thorp, 16-Year-Old, Patient (tuberculosis); Nancie Luchesi, Patient (tuberculosis); Ravi Bannerjee, Royalty (prince), Patient (tuberculosis)
Time period(s): 1940s
Locale(s): San Francisco, California

Summary: Excited that her father's home after fighting in Europe during World War II, April can't believe that what was originally diagnosed as pneumonia is actually tuberculosis and requires her to be hospitalized for at least three months, if not longer. Suddenly life doesn't seem fair as her time with her father will be restricted and who knows what will happen with her boyfriend whose mother worries that he'll catch TB from April. Confined to bed in a TB sanatorium, April's monotonous routine is broken by her lively, though terminally ill, roommate Nancie and the attentions of Ravi, another patient who's the son of a Maharajah, in this work based on the life of the author. (212 pages)

Where it's reviewed:
Booklist, June 2001, page 1862
Kliatt, May 2001, page 10
Publishers Weekly, June 11, 2001, page 86
School Library Journal, June 2001, page 148
Voice of Youth Advocates, October 2001, page 274

Other books by the same author:
Swimming with the Whales, 1995
Hugo and the Princess Nena, 1983
Celebrate the Morning, 1972

Other books you might like:
Meg Cabot, *The Princess Diaries*, 2000
Raised by her artist mother in Greenwich Village, Mia is dismayed to learn that she's a princess and heir to her father's throne in Genovia.

T. Degens, *On the Third Ward*, 1990
Only the exciting tales of the Empress of China relieve the day-to-day monotony Wanda experiences while recuperating from tuberculosis.

Mette Newth, *The Dark Light*, 1998
Stuck in a leprosy hospital, Tora reads to all the patients,

helping them to vicariously leave the hospital by a way other than death.

JAMES W. ELLISON

Finding Forrester
(New York: Newmarket Press, 2000)

Subject(s): African Americans; Books and Reading; Sports/Basketball
Age range(s): Grades 10-Adult
Major character(s): Jamal Wallace, 16-Year-Old, Student—Private School; William Forrester, Writer, Recluse
Time period(s): 2000s
Locale(s): New York, New York (South Bronx)

Summary: Not wanting to seem different, Jamal hides his writing in his backpack, away from the eyes of his fellow basketball players. As they play their pick-up games on the blacktop, Jamal wonders about the person who lives nearby and receives regular deliveries from a courier, so one day decides to investigate. Sneaking in to the apartment, he grabs a book but then realizes there's a man in the room, drops his backpack and runs out the front door. Several days later he retrieves his backpack and finds all his writing has been edited. With that awkward introduction, Jamal and the reclusive writer William Forrester meet one another and discover their mutual love of reading and writing. William won a Pulitzer Prize many years ago and hasn't been heard from since while Jamal hides his brilliance and writing ability from everyone as they begin a friendship that opens the world to both of them. Novel is based on the screenplay written by Mike Rich. (192 pages)

Where it's reviewed:
Publishers Weekly, January 22, 2001, page 304
School Library Journal, September 2001, page 258
Voice of Youth Advocates, June 2001, page 120

Other books by the same author:
Panic Room, 2002
Buddies, 1983
Proud Rachel, 1973

Other books you might like:
Jonathan Scott Fuqua, *The Reappearance of Sam Webber*, 1999
When Sam lives in perpetual fear of the bullies at his new school, only his friendship with the black janitor helps him survive.

Kaye Gibbons, *Ellen Foster*, 1987
Spunky Ellen survives a suicidal mother, alcoholic father and a variety of ineffective relatives until she finds a stable foster family.

Michelle Magorian, *Good Night, Mr. Tom*, 1982
Reclusive widower Tom Oakley and 8-year-old abused William Beech form a lasting friendship when William lives with Mr. Tom during WWII.

Pieter Van Raven, *The Great Man's Secret*, 1989
What begins as a newspaper assignment for Jerry turns into a friendship with Paul Bernard, a cripple who declines the Nobel Prize.

ROBERT ELMER

Brother Enemy

(Minneapolis, MN: Bethany House, 2001)

Series: Promise of Zion. Book 4
Subject(s): Brothers; Underground Resistance Movements
Age range(s): Grades 6-9
Major character(s): Dov Zalinski, 13-Year-Old; Emily Parkinson, Teenager; Natan Zalinski, Brother (of Dov), Resistance Fighter; Anthony Parkinson, Uncle (of Emily), Resistance Fighter
Time period(s): 1940s (1948)
Locale(s): Jerusalem, Palestine

Summary: Several years after World War II ends, Dov is in Jerusalem where he hopes to find his older brother Natan, the only other family member who may have survived the concentration camps. Meeting Emily when he first arrived in Jerusalem provides him with an introduction to her uncle Anthony who broadcasts for Haganah, the Jewish underground. Dov thinks his brother may be working for that organization and uses the broadcast to try to find Natan. Dov also broadcasts his own thoughts to let the world know what's really going on in the struggle among the Arabs, British and Jews in this ongoing series. (169 pages)

Where it's reviewed:
Voice of Youth Advocates, December 2001, page 357

Other books by the same author:
Freedom Trap, 2002 (Promise of Zion, Book 5)
Refugee Treasure, 2001 (Promise of Zion, Book 3)
Peace Rebel, 2000 (Promise of Zion, Book 2)
Promise Breaker, 2000 (Promise of Zion, Book 1)

Other books you might like:
Tamar Bergman, *The Boy from over There*, 1988
    Avramik and Rina become friends while living in a kibbutz in Israel following the Holocaust.
Uri Orlev, *The Lady with the Hat*, 1995
    Yulek believes he is the only member of his family to survive the Holocaust, but in Palestine he finds that someone is looking for him.
Leon Uris, *Exodus*, 1958
    After World War II Palestinian agent Ari Ben Canaan helps Jewish immigrants who are forbidden by the British to move to Israel.

LEIF ENGER

Peace Like a River

(New York: Atlantic Monthly, 2001)

Subject(s): Fathers and Sons; Brothers; Miracles
Age range(s): Grades 10-Adult
Major character(s): Reuben Land, 12-Year-Old, Asthmatic; Davy Land, 17-Year-Old, Fugitive; Jeremiah Land, Father; Swede Land, Child, Writer
Time period(s): 2000s
Locale(s): Roofing, Minnesota; Badlands, North Dakota

Summary: Born dead, Reuben is revived by his father Jeremiah who breathes air into his lungs, the first of many unexplained oddities which could be called miracles. When Reuben's eleven, his janitor father disciplines two delinquents who threaten his brother Davy's girlfriend in the locker room at school, but the two retaliate, kidnap his sister Swede and promise further harm to the family. The thugs break into Reuben's home where his brother Davy shoots them; his arrest splits the town into those who think he's justified and other who claim he's a cold-blooded murderer. On the day of the trial, Davy escapes and Reuben's family, by another set of connected miracles, receives an Airstream trailer and the means to search for Davy who they're sure has headed for the Badlands. Swede entertains them with her growing poetry saga of the cowboy Sunny Sundown, Reuben records in his mind all the events and his father seems able to miraculously slide past policemen and FBI agents while on their quest in this magical first novel. (313 pages)

Where it's reviewed:
Booklist, May 15, 2001, page 1707
Christian Science Monitor, September 6, 2001, page 14
Kirkus Reviews, June 1, 2001, page 757
Library Journal, June 15, 2001, page 102
Publishers Weekly, July 16, 2001, page 166

Awards the book has won:
ALA Alex Award, 2002
Barnes & Noble's Discover Great New Writers Award for Fiction, 2001

Other books you might like:
Garrison Keillor, *Lake Wobegon Days*, 1985
    Fellow Minnesota writer Keillor records a humorous, satirical account of daily life in his imaginary hometown.
Mark Twain, *The Adventures of Huckleberry Finn*, 1885
    The classic adventure of runaway slave Jim and Huck, who flees his abusive father, as they float down the Mississippi River.
Alan Watt, *Diamond Dogs*, 2000
    When Neil's sheriff father hides the evidence of an accidental death caused by Neil, they are forever linked in a chilling, destructive bond.

JOHN R. ERICKSON

Moonshiner's Gold

(New York: Viking, 2001)

Subject(s): Grandfathers; Prohibition Era; Crime and Criminals
Age range(s): Grades 5-9
Major character(s): Riley McDaniel, 14-Year-Old; Coy McDaniel, Brother (of Riley); Mattie Sparrow, Aunt; Abner "Grampy" Dawson, Grandfather
Time period(s): 1920s
Locale(s): Sparrow, Texas

Summary: With their mom, Riley and his younger brother Coy live on a Texas ranch, which they rent from their Aunt Mattie. Their dad's died recently and they struggle to keep the farm afloat. When the boys discover a whiskey still in a canyon on their ranch, find a sack of gold in the stove at their school-house and receive an eviction notice, they seek help from the local authorities. It seems that everyone's in cahoots with the bad guys, so the McDaniels, along with their Grampy, travel to Sparrow to see Aunt Mattie who's being forced to sign her name to improper documents. Riley manages to save his aunt, a Texas ranger, and their ranch in this exciting tale. (199 pages)

Where it's reviewed:
Book Report, March 2002, page 48
School Library Journal, August 2001, page 178
Voice of Youth Advocates, October 2001, page 274

Other books by the same author:
The Case of the Missing Bird Dog, 2002 (Hank the Cow Dog, Number 40)
The Secret Laundry Monster Files, 2002 (Hank the Cow Dog, Number 39)
The Fling, 2001 (Hank the Cow Dog, Number 38)

Other books you might like:
Gary L. Blackwood, *Moonshine*, 1999
    Thad's caught between a federal agent and a moonshiner, both of whom are men he admires.
Suzanne Pierson Ellison, *Best of Enemies*, 1998
    Taken hostage by Texas rustlers, three teens join forces to survive in the harsh desert of the Southwest.
Ric Lynden Hardman, *Sunshine Rider: The First Vegetarian Western*, 1998
    Wylie signs up as assistant cook on a cattle drive where he's put in charge of Roselle, a pet that's part buffalo and part longhorn.
Lisa Waller Rogers, *Get Along, Little Dogies: The Chisholm Trail Diary of Hallie Lou Wells: South Texas, 1878*, 2001
    Hallie Lou's diary entries provide a record of life on their cattle ranch and the hardships and travails that accompany a cattle drive.

280

FREDDI WILLIAMS EVANS
SHAWN COSTELLO, Illustrator

A Bus of Our Own

(Morton Grove, IL: Albert Whitman & Company, 2001)

Subject(s): African Americans; School Buses; Segregation
Age range(s): Grades 1-4
Major character(s): Mable Jean, Student—Elementary School, Sister (younger); Jeff, Student—Elementary School, Brother (older); Cousin Smith, Landowner, Neighbor
Time period(s): 1940s (1949)
Locale(s): Madison, Mississippi

Summary: Mable Jean's desire for an education is so strong that she insists she can walk the five miles to school daily. Jeff's willing to walk slowly but not carry her and he holds her hand when the white kids jeer from their bus windows at the black children walking to school. Mable Jean solves the problem for everyone when she asks Cousin Smith to please buy a bus for the children. Cousin Smith buys two discarded county buses in order to get the parts to make one working

bus. Parents lend support in various ways in order to make the bus ride a reality for their children. A concluding "Author's Note" explains the background for the author's first book. (32 pages)

Where it's reviewed:
Booklist, August 2001, page 2128
Horn Book Guide, Spring 2002, page 72
Kirkus Reviews, July 15, 2001, page 1025
School Library Journal, September 2001, page 188

Awards the book has won:
Notable Social Studies Trade Books for Young People, 2002

Other books you might like:
Marie Bradby, *More than Anything Else*, 1995
    Booker T. Washington yearns for the freedom literacy will give him.
Robert Coles, *The Story of Ruby Bridges*, 1995
    Courageously, six-year-old Ruby faces angry white protesters as the first black child to attend a formerly all-white school.
Elizabeth Fitzgerald Howard, *Virgie Goes to School with Us Boys*, 2000
    Virgie's brothers don't think she can walk the seven miles to the Quaker school and stay away from home for a week, but Virgie proves them wrong.
William Miller, *Richard Wright and the Library Card*, 1997
    In the segregated South of the 1920s it is illegal for Richard to check out a library book, but he finds a way to satisfy his desire to read.
Margaree King Mitchell, *Uncle Jed's Barbershop*, 1993
    Sarah Jean recalls the determination of her Uncle Jed to overcome societal obstacles and save enough money to open his own barbershop.

281

LYNNE EWING

Into the Cold Fire

(New York: Hyperion, 2000)

Series: Daughters of the Moon. Number 2
Subject(s): Witches and Witchcraft; Good and Evil
Age range(s): Grades 7-10
Major character(s): Vanessa Cleveland, Witch; Serena Killingsworth, Witch; Jimena, Witch; Catty, Witch
Time period(s): 2000s
Locale(s): Los Angeles, California

Summary: Four friends combine their talents and unite into the Daughters of the Moon to oppose the evil of Atrox whose followers have their sights on destroying one of the daughters. Vanessa, Catty, Jimena and Serena have the powers of invisibility, time travel, mind reading and seeing the future, powers they will need to rescue Sirena from the dark side which is determined to pull her over in this continuing series. (264 pages)

Where it's reviewed:
Horn Book Guide, Spring 2001, page 83
Voice of Youth Advocates, June 2001, page 132

Other books by the same author:
Moon Demon, 2002 (Daughters of the Moon, Number 7)

Night Shade, 2001 (Daughters of the Moon, Number 3)
The Lost One, 2001 (Daughters of the Moon, Number 6)
The Secret Scroll, 2001 (Daughters of the Moon, Number 4)
The Sacrifice, 2001 (Daughters of the Moon, Number 5)
Goddess of the Night, 2000 (Daughters of the Moon, Number 1)

Other books you might like:
Isobel Bird, *Circle of Three Series*, 2001-
   Kate, Cooper and Annie become interested in witchcraft and progress from casting a simple love spell to learning more about Wiccan history and rites.
Silver RavenWolf, *Witches' Night Out*, 2000
   Bethany's Thursday night group gathers for innocuous charms, but tonight they call up the Hounds of the Wild Hunt to locate a killer.
Cate Tiernan, *Sweep Series*, 2001-
   Unassuming Morgan discovers she has Wiccan traits, just like new student Cal Blaire.

F

282

IAN FALCONER, Author/Illustrator

Olivia Saves the Circus

(New York: Anne Schwartz Book/Atheneum Books for Young Readers, 2001)

Subject(s): Animals/Pigs; Circus; Schools
Age range(s): Grades K-2
Major character(s): Olivia, Pig, Sister (older)
Time period(s): Indeterminate
Locale(s): Fictional Country

Summary: Not only can Olivia help her mother by making pancakes for her younger brothers in the morning before school, but she can also don her boring school uniform and select accessories to enliven the dull outfit, all by herself. At school, Olivia enjoys telling her classmates about her vacation trip to the circus. As luck would have it, the entire circus cast was ill with ear infections and Olivia, who knows how to do everything, pitched in to save the day by performing all the acts solo. Olivia's teacher is skeptical but Olivia assures her that the story is ''pretty true,'' at least so far as she remembers. (32 pages)

Where it's reviewed:
Booklist, August 2001, page 2116
Bulletin of the Center for Children's Books, November 2001, page 100
Horn Book, November 2001, page 735
Publishers Weekly, August 27, 2001, page 83
School Library Journal, October 2001, page 114

Awards the book has won:
School Library Journal Best Books, 2001
ALA Notable Children's Books, 2002

Other books by the same author:
Olivia, 2000 (Caldecott Honor Book)

Other books you might like:
Lois Ehlert, *Circus*, 1992
   A unique picture book illustrates the colorful excitement of the circus.

Rebecca Emberley, *My Mother's Secret Life*, 1998
   A little girl dreams that her mother leads a secret life as a circus performer.
Mark Teague, *How I Spent My Summer Vacation*, 1995
   According to Wallace's show and tell he was kidnapped on his way to vacation at his Aunt Fern's home and spent the summer learning cowboy tricks.

283

MAME FARRELL

And Sometimes Why

(New York: Farrar Straus Giroux, 2001)

Subject(s): Friendship
Age range(s): Grades 5-8
Major character(s): Christy ''Chris'' Moffett, 8th Grader; Jack Jordan, 8th Grader
Time period(s): 2000s
Locale(s): Eastport

Summary: Best friends since first grade when Chris helped Jack learn his vowels, it's now the summer before high school and the two notice changes in one another. Chris has always been a top athlete, able to best Jack in just about every sport, and to compensate, Jack has artistic talent. As they spend the summer at the country club, Jack and the other boys become aware of Chris's beauty and he worries that their relationship might change, though he doesn't mind using Chris's friendship as entry to the inner circle of popular kids. For the Cotillion ball, Jack breaks his date with Chris and dates an ''in'' girl which leaves Chris free to date someone else, a move that Jack later regrets but which teaches Chris and Jack the importance of their friendship. (165 pages)

Where it's reviewed:
Booklist, May 1, 2001, page 1674
Horn Book, May 2001, page 322
Publishers Weekly, April 2, 2001, page 65
School Library Journal, July 2001, page 107
Voice of Youth Advocates, June 2001, page 120

Other books by the same author:
Bradley and the Billboard, 1998
Marrying Malcolm Murgatroyd, 1995

Other books you might like:
Mary Anderson, *The Unsinkable Molly Malone*, 1991
Socially conscious artistic teen Molly wants a boyfriend with values and thinks she's found him in Ron who says he's not part of a "moneyed group."
Elizabeth Levy, *Seventh Grade Tango*, 2000
Paired up with her childhood friend Scott for ballroom dancing in gym class, Rebecca realizes there's a little chemistry between them.
Phyllis Reynolds Naylor, *The Alice Series*, 1985-
Motherless Alice and her friends Pamela, Elizabeth and Patrick survive all the traumas of junior high, peer pressure and dating, but now await high school. 301-350 1

284
ROBERT J. FAVOLE

Through the Wormhole
(Auburn, CA: Flywheel Publishing, 2001)

Subject(s): Time Travel; African Americans; Revolutionary War
Age range(s): Grades 6-9
Major character(s): Kate Hammond, 9th Grader, Swimmer; Michael Banks, 9th Grader, Equestrian; Gilbert du Motier de Lafayette, Historical Figure, Military Personnel; John Banks, Historical Figure, Military Personnel
Time period(s): 2000s; 1770s (1778)
Locale(s): United States; Pennsylvania

Summary: Michael and Kate both feel they're misfits. A champion equestrian, Michael knows that as an African American he doesn't fit the usual image of a rider while Kate, though an excellent swimmer, is prone to panic attacks while she's in the pool. What some might consider deficiencies turn out to be assets when the CyberTimeSurfingInstitute provides Michael and Kate with the necessary equipment to time travel to the Revolutionary War. Asked to search for the Marquis de Lafayette and John Banks, one of Michael's ancestors, they're to save Lafayette from a trap and make sure Private John Banks is alive on May 21st. While the CTSI holds open the wormhole through time for them, the two friends know that if they fail on this mission, they won't return to 2001. (182 pages)

Where it's reviewed:
Booklist, March 1, 2001, page 1278
Children's Bookwatch, May 2001, page 4
Kirkus Reviews, January 1, 2001, page 52
School Library Journal, April 2001, page 140
Voice of Youth Advocates, April 2001, page 50

Other books you might like:
Nancy Bond, *Another Shore*, 1988
Lyn romanticizes the hardships of 1744 in the historical reconstruction where she works, but its reality overwhelms her when she is trapped in the past.
Terry Kretzer-Malvehy, *Passage to Little Bighorn*, 1999
At a reenactment of the Little Bighorn battle, Dakota travels back in time and is captured by Sitting Bull's warriors.
Jane Resh Thomas, *The Princess in the Pigpen*, 1989
Time traveler Elizabeth comes from Elizabeth England to an Iowa farm, but no one believes her story.
Arvella Whitmore, *Trapped: Between the Lash and the Gun*, 1999
Bad boy Jordan winds up in the pre-Civil War South and discovers there are worse things in life than living in the 'burbs.

285
HARRIET K. FEDER

Death on Sacred Ground
(Minneapolis, MN: Lerner Publications, 2001)

Series: Vivi Hartman Adventure
Subject(s): Murder; Indians of North America; Jews
Age range(s): Grades 7-10
Major character(s): Rabbi Hartman, Religious; Aviva "Vivi" Hartman, 10th Grader; Paula Ash, 10th Grader
Time period(s): 2000s
Locale(s): Buffalo, New York; Pikes Landing, New York

Summary: Vivi's dad is called to Pikes Landing, a small village sixty miles from Buffalo, to conduct a funeral for a young teenaged girl shot with an arrow to the heart, an act first judged an accident but which now appears more like murder. The tiny village of Pikes Landing is unique in that white men secured a lease from the Seneca Indians and built their village on reservation land, but when the ninety-nine-year lease ended a few years ago, the rents shot way up and there's been dissension ever since. Because her father will have to wait several days for the autopsy results to be released, Vivi heads to the local high school to complete part of a school assignment. There, accompanied by the guide assigned to her, Paula Ash, she hears about the various contentious voices in the village and realizes how this discord could have led to a young girl's murder. Vivi also has a chance to learn more about the Seneca Indians and see how similar or dissimilar their culture is to her own Jewish race in her continuing adventures. (191 pages)

Where it's reviewed:
Book Report, September 2001, page 61
Booklist, November 15, 2001, page 565
Bulletin of the Center for Children's Books, March 2001, page 258
Kirkus Reviews, February 15, 2001, page 257
School Library Journal, March 2001, page 246

Other books by the same author:
Mystery of the Kaifeng Scroll, 1995 (A Vivi Hartman Adventure)
Mystery in Miami Beach, 1992 (A Vivi Hartman Adventure)

Other books you might like:
Lloyd Alexander, *The Drackenberg Adventure*, 1988
Vesper Holly and her guardian Brinnie don't let earthquakes or volcanoes keep them from saving Chirica Indians in another adventure.

Sandy Asher, *With All My Heart, with All My Mind: Thirteen Stories about Growing Up Jewish*, 1999
   Thirteen stories that examine the issue of growing up Jewish especially when trying to reconcile centuries of tradition with the modern world.
Carolyn Meyer, *White Lilacs*, 1993
   The black community of Freedomtown opposes being moved to the sewer flats, but violence and marches by the Ku Klux Klan stop their action.
Joan Lowery Nixon, *Whispers from the Dead*, 1989
   When Sarah moves to Houston with her parents, she receives otherworldly messages about a murder committed in her house.
Marsha Qualey, *Revolutions of the Heart*, 1993
   When Cory becomes interested in Native American Mac, she becomes the recipient of outrage, lewd notes and disdain from her community.

286

JEAN FERRIS

Of Sound Mind
(New York: Farrar Straus Giroux, 2001)

Subject(s): Deafness; Family Problems; Friendship
Age range(s): Grades 7-10
Major character(s): Theo Dennison, 12th Grader; Ivy Roper, 12th Grader; Palma Dennison, Mother (of Theo and Jeremy), Artist (sculptor)
Time period(s): 2000s
Locale(s): Philadelphia, Pennsylvania

Summary: As the only hearing person in a family consisting of two deaf parents and one deaf younger brother, Theo takes on responsibilities far beyond his years as he serves as the family's conduit to the hearing world. He translates and signs for his parents as they negotiate the sale of a home or meet with doctors, but now that he's a senior worries about how he'll attend college. This is the year he meets Ivy, daughter of a deaf man, and their common experiences provide an instant bond, though Ivy is more outspoken and encourages Theo to attend MIT. That dream appears to end when Theo's quiet, undemanding father suffers a stroke and his high-strung sculptor mother Palma falls to pieces. (215 pages)

Where it's reviewed:
Booklist, September 15, 2001, page 226
Horn Book, November 2001, page 745
School Library Journal, September 2001, page 224
Voice of Youth Advocates, October 2001, page 274

Awards the book has won:
ALA Best Books for Young Adults, 2002
Booklist Editors' Choice/Books for Youth, 2001

Other books by the same author:
Eight Seconds, 2000
Bad, 1998
Love Among the Walnuts, 1998
All That Glitters, 1996
Across the Grain, 1990

Other books you might like:
Nancy Butts, *Cheshire Moon*, 1996
   Deaf Miranda dreads spending the summer with her aunt as Timothy is no longer available to interpret for her and she doesn't want to use her voice.
Leslie Davis Guccione, *Tell Me How the Wind Sounds*, 1989
   A hearing girl and a deaf boy fall in love one summer, though not without many arguments and miscommunications.
Karin N. Mango, *Just for the Summer*, 1990
   Jenny resolves to learn sign language to be a better friend to her next door neighbor Alec who has a crush on her.

287

SUSAN FINCH

The Intimacy of Indiana
(Greensboro, NC: Tudor Publishers, 2001)

Subject(s): School Life; Schools/High Schools; Friendship
Age range(s): Grades 9-12
Major character(s): Olivia Rycerson, 12th Grader; Neil A. Stephens, 12th Grader; Adam Flanders, 12th Grader
Time period(s): 2000s
Locale(s): Indiana

Summary: Three friends, Olivia, Neil and Adam, reach twelfth grade with all the worries, exuberances and angst of their last year in high school. Acceptances from college, the possibility of scholarships, "last" everything from dances to tests, school games and essays fill their year. But in addition to the usual school responsibilities, parents divorce, a mom is diagnosed with cancer, and romance touches them and then backs away as the fear of the unknown is met, over and over, in this first novel. (184 pages)

Where it's reviewed:
Booklist, July 2001, page 1999

Other books you might like:
Catherine Clark, *Truth or Dairy*, 2000
   Senior year doesn't turn out as expected for Courtney when her boyfriend breaks up with her, but she fills her time with other, different activities.
Ben Erickson, *A Parting Gift*, 2000
   Josh helps his mother deliver meals-on-wheels and enjoys a friendship with arthritically crippled William Davis until the elderly gentleman dies.
Robin Jones Gunn, *Time Will Tell*, 1998
   Sierra dreads the beginning of her senior year because all her friends are changing at a time when she'd like everything to remain the same.

288

MARLIN FITZWATER

Esther's Pillow
(New York: Public Affairs/Perseus, 2001)

Subject(s): Women's Rights; Trials; Teachers
Age range(s): Grades 10-Adult
Major character(s): Margaret Chambers, Teacher

Time period(s): 1910s (1911)
Locale(s): Nickerly, Kansas

Summary: A new graduate of the two-year College of Emporia, Margaret Chambers returns home to teach in the one-room schoolhouse that she attended. From the beginning, her college education and self-confidence create problems for she is different from the rest of the townspeople. Not only does Margaret wear jewelry, shake hands, not attend church and act uninterested in the town's young men but she's also very attractive which stirs up jealousy. One night more than a dozen men, fueled by the rantings of their wives and with some whiskey for courage, set a trap for Margaret, tar and feather her and encourage her to leave town. Though humiliated, Margaret decides not to leave but to bring charges against the men in a book based on an incident the author heard about from his father. (239 pages)

Where it's reviewed:
Booklist, July 2001, page 1979
Library Journal, July 2001, page 122
New York Times Book Review, August 12, 2001, page 22
Publishers Weekly, June 18, 2001, page 56
School Library Journal, October 2001, page 194

Other books you might like:
Stephen Dobyns, *The Church of Dead Girls*, 1997
   The death of a promiscuous woman, followed by the disappearance of three girls, throws a small town into a dither.
Kent Haruf, *Plainsong*, 1999
   In a small western town, two aging bachelor brothers take in a pregnant teenager and find their lives enriched
Alice Hoffman, *Illumination Night*, 1987
   Living on Martha's Vineyard, a young couple's marriage is threatened when a teenage neighbor develops a fixation on the husband.
Jean Hanff Korelitz, *The Sabbathday River*, 1999
   Naomi's crafts cooperative owes much of its success to Heather's embroidery so when she's charged with murder, Naomi finds her a lawyer.

289

SHARON G. FLAKE

Money Hungry

(New York: Hyperion/Jump at the Sun, 2001)

Subject(s): Mothers and Daughters; African Americans; Money
Age range(s): Grades 6-9
Major character(s): Raspberry Hill, 13-Year-Old
Time period(s): 2000s
Locale(s): United States

Summary: When Raspberry's father gets into drugs, she and her mother leave him even though it means a few weeks living on the streets before moving into the projects. Affected by that piece of her life, Raspberry is now obsessive about money, determined to save as much as she can so she never returns to the streets. With a reputation for stinginess, she sells out-of-date candy, cleans the homes of the elderly, washes cars, and sells pencils, doing whatever she can to add to the

hidden stash of money in her room. Her mother finds her cash, assumes it's stolen and throws it out the window. When everything in their apartment is stolen, and Raspberry's bankroll is gone, they again face the streets, though this time there's hope their lives will improve. (187 pages)

Where it's reviewed:
Book Report, May 2001, page 58
Booklist, June 2001, page 1880
Publishers Weekly, June 18, 2001, page 82
School Library Journal, July 2001, page 107
Voice of Youth Advocates, February 2002, page 434

Awards the book has won:
Coretta Scott King Honor Book, 2002

Other books by the same author:
The Skin I'm In, 1998 (ALA Best Books for Young Adults)

Other books you might like:
Felice Holman, *Secret City, U.S.A.*, 1990
   Benno and Moon restore an old house away from their barrio, which becomes an oasis for them and their homeless friends.
Tricia Springstubb, *Eunice Gottlieb and the Unwhitewashed Truth about Life*, 1987
   To earn extra money, Eunice and Joy begin a cake-making business.
Johnniece Marshall Wilson, *Poor Girl, Rich Girl*, 1992
   Determined to get rid of her pop bottles lenses, Miranda begins a dog walking business to make enough money for contact lenses.

290

PAUL FLEISCHMAN

Seek

(Chicago: Cricket Books, 2001)

Subject(s): Fathers and Sons; Radio
Age range(s): Grades 7-10
Major character(s): Robert A. "Rob" Radkovitz, 12th Grader; Leonard "Lenny" Guidry, Father (of Rob)
Time period(s): 2000s
Locale(s): San Francisco, California

Summary: Raised with a myriad of voices encircling him, from his professorial grandfather, to his mystery-reading grandmother and his foreign language-speaking mother, Rob relies on the memory of their tales when assigned to write an autobiography for his senior project. He also thinks of the father he's never known, the one who moved out when he was just a baby, the one who left behind only a tape of his radio show. For years Rob searches for his DJ father Lenny, hitting the seek button and scanning one radio show after another, just to hear his voice or make contact with him. Rob even joins with several of his friends to create a pirate radio station and luckily his father hears one of his shows. By the time Lenny finally makes contact with his son, Rob realizes he doesn't need his father's voice when he has all these other voices of friends and family to sustain him. Fleischman's work is perfect for reader's theater and a group of teens may want to read *Seek* in this way, though it's also a moving experience for the single reader. (167 pages)

Where it's reviewed:

Booklist, December 15, 2001, page 722

Bulletin of the Center for Children's Books, November 2001, page 101

Horn Book, November 2001, page 746

Publishers Weekly, August 6, 2001, page 91

School Library Journal, September 2001, page 224

Awards the book has won:

School Library Journal Best Books, 2001

ALA Best Books for Young Adults, 2002

Other books by the same author:

Mind's Eye, 1999

Whirligig, 1998

Seedfolks, 1997

Bull Run, 1993

Joyful Noise: Poems for Two Voices, 1988

I Am Phoenix: Poems for Two Voices, 1985

Other books you might like:

Cat Bauer, *Harley, Like a Person*, 2000

Harley goes in search of Sean whom she thinks is her father; when the truth comes out, Harley realizes she's stronger than any of the adults in her life.

Peg Kehret, *Searching for Candlestick Park*, 1997

When Spencer and his mother are forced to move in with relatives, he runs away to Candlestick Park in search of his father.

Walter Dean Myers, *Monster*, 1999

On trial for taking part in a robbery, filmmaking student Steve describes the action through his screenplay and journal.

Joyce Sweeney, *The Tiger Orchard*, 1993

Zack has nightmares of apple orchards and a shadowy man. When he discovers his mother lied about his father's death, he goes off in search of him.

SID FLEISCHMAN

Bo & Mzzz Mad

(New York: Greenwillow, 2001)

Subject(s): Miners and Mining; Family Problems; Humor

Age range(s): Grades 5-8

Major character(s): Bo Gamage, Orphan, 12-Year-Old; Madeleine ''Mzzz Mad'' Martinka, 13-Year-Old; Juna Martinka, Aunt (of Madeleine), Artist (paper doll designer); Charlie ''Paw Paw'' Martinka, Aged Person, Actor (former movie star)

Time period(s): 2000s

Locale(s): Queen of Sheba, California (in the Mojave Desert)

Summary: Bo has two choices—he can let child welfare take over and send him to a foster home or stay with his Martinka relatives who've had a long-standing feud with his side of the family, the Gamages. He chooses the Martinka option, though when he descends from the bus in the Mojave Desert and meets his acerbic-tongued cousin who calls herself Mzzz Mad, he's not so sure he made the right decision. Living in Queen of Sheba, which is actually the remnant of a movie set, are Mzzz Mad, Aunt Juna and former cowboy movie star Paw

Paw. Paw Paw is a little depressed so Aunt Juna draws a fake map for the Pegleg Smith gold mine with which he's been obsessed for years. Into the midst of this mayhem arrive two modern-day thieves who handcuff together Bo and Mzzz Mad and depart once they find the fake map. Bo comes to the rescue with a piece of family memorabilia, a photo of a man's baldhead emblazoned with the map of the Pegleg Smith gold mine, in this modern-day tall tale. (103 ages)

Where it's reviewed:

Booklist May 15, 2001, page 1750

Bulletin of the Center for Children's Books, May 2001, page 335

Horn Book, May 2001, page 323

Publishers Weekly, March 26, 2001, page 94

School Library Journal, May 2001, page 149

Other books by the same author:

Bandit's Moon, 1998

The 13th Floor: A Ghost Story, 1995

Jim Ugly, 1992

Whipping Boy, 1986

By the Great Horn Spoon, 1963

Other books you might like:

Sid Hite, *Stick and Whittle*, 2000

Melvin Fitchett meets Melvin Smyte on the Texas prairie and the two team up, call themselves Stick and Whittle, and search for Fitchett's love Evelyn.

Kathleen Karr, *Oh, Those Harper Girls! Or Young and Dangerous*, 1992

Lily and her five sisters try to earn money to help their father save his ranch, but unfortunately all their schemes are illegal.

Randall Beth Platt, *The Four Arrows Fe-as-ko*, 1991

In this rollicking first novel, the foreman of the Four Arrows Ranch has 500 days to teach the owner's handicapped son to run a ranch and show a profit.

Otto Salassi, *Jimmy D., Sidewinder and Me*, 1987

Fifteen-year-old Dumas Monk explains to the judge why it's not his fault there was a shootout during a poker game while he was dealing.

292

DENISE FLEMING, Author/Illustrator

Pumpkin Eye

(New York: Henry Holt and Company, 2001)

Subject(s): Halloween; Traditions; Stories in Rhyme

Age range(s): Preschool-Grade 1

Time period(s): 2000s

Locale(s): United States

Summary: With the sounds of trick-or-treaters' pounding feet in the background, images of Halloween appear on a neighborhood street. The glowing eyes of pumpkins carved into Jack-o'-lanterns greet the costumed spirits casting shadows as cats, witches, tigers and werewolves race along proclaiming the arrival of Halloween. (32 pages)

Where it's reviewed:

Booklist, September 15, 2001, page 237

Bulletin of the Center for Children's Books, October 2001, page 55

Publishers Weekly, September 24, 2001, page 42

School Library Journal, September 2001, page 188

Other books by the same author:

The Everything Book, 2000

Mama Cat Has Three Kittens, 1998 (ALA Notable Books for Children)

In the Small, Small Pond, 1993 (Caldecott Medal)

Other books you might like:

Charlotte Huck, *A Creepy Countdown*, 1998
Halloween symbols appear in a rhyming tale that uses the numbers one to ten and back again.

Tony Johnston, *Very Scary*, 1995
The biggest pumpkin in the field attracts a group of trick-or-treaters who carve it into a jack o' lantern.

Abby Levine, *This Is the Pumpkin*, 1997
Max wears his Halloween costume to school and then comes home to carve a pumpkin and trick-or-treat with his family.

Bethany Roberts, *Halloween Mice!*, 1995
A group of cavorting mice cleverly take advantage of their flashlight to scare away a menacing cat.

293

RALPH FLETCHER

Uncle Daddy

(New York: Henry Holt and Company, 2001)

Subject(s): Fathers and Sons; Family Problems; Abandonment

Age range(s): Grades 4-6

Major character(s): Dan "Uncle Daddy" Westlake, Uncle, Principal; Rivers White, 9-Year-Old, Son; Anna White, Single Mother, Postal Worker; Nelson White, Father (absentee), Handyman

Time period(s): 2000s (2001)

Locale(s): United States

Summary: Rivers can remember his father going out to pick up a pizza six years ago and never returning. Since then Uncle Daddy, his mother's uncle, has filled the role of father in his life. Then, on the night of Rivers' "un-birthday" celebration Nelson White arrives unannounced at the house, causing confusion and reviving hurt, angry feelings. A recovering drug addict, Nelson explains the reasons he did not return sooner, while acknowledging that there is no excuse for his lack of contact. When Uncle Daddy suffers a severe heart attack Anna must depend on Nelson to care for Rivers while she stays with her uncle at the hospital. Gradually, healing begins in the absentee father's shattered relationship with his son and spouse. By the time Uncle Daddy comes home to convalesce the hope for reconciliation is evident. (133 pages)

Where it's reviewed:

Booklist, August 2001, page 2118

Bulletin of the Center for Children's Books, May 2001, page 335

Horn Book, July 2001, page 450

School Library Journal, May 2001, page 149

Other books by the same author:

Flying Solo, 1998

Spider Boy, 1997

Fig Pudding, 1995 (ALA Notable Book)

Other books you might like:

Laurie Halse Anderson, *Fear of Falling*, 2001
After a year's absence twelve-year-old David's father returns for Thanksgiving Day and David's not sure if he feels thankful.

Patricia MacLachlan, *Caleb's Story*, 2001
Thought to be deceased, Caleb's grandfather appears at the farm seeking to make amends with his son, Caleb's father, for leaving so many years ago.

Susan Shreve, *Blister*, 2001
Blister's perfect life falls apart when her father moves out but, with help from her grandmother, she adjusts.

294

SUSAN FLETCHER

Walk Across the Sea

(New York: Simon & Schuster/Atheneum, 2001)

Subject(s): Christian Life; Prejudice; Lighthouses

Age range(s): Grades 5-9

Major character(s): Eliza Jane McCully, 15-Year-Old; Wah Chung, Immigrant; Parthenia, Goat

Time period(s): 1880s (1886)

Locale(s): Crescent City, California; Brecksville, Ohio

Summary: Eliza lives with her family on a tiny island off the California mainland where her father is the lighthouse keeper. At high tide they're cut off from everything, but when the tide ebbs, they can race along the uncovered isthmus to shop, go to the doctor or, in Eliza's case, study the sea animals uncovered for a few hours. Warned by her father about the "sneaker waves," Eliza almost loses Parthenia one day, but she's rescued by Wah Chung, a young Chinese boy. The folks in Eliza's town want the "heathens" to leave, a view expressed by Eliza's father but one with which Eliza disagrees and supports her side with Bible scripture as she opposes her father. Eliza has empathy for the Chinese and when Wah Chung's caught in a terrible storm, gives him shelter in the lighthouse even though she knows it might cost her father his job. Eliza's a gutsy, outspoken young girl during a time when the men are frightened that the Chinese will take jobs away from them. (214 pages)

Where it's reviewed:

Booklist, November 1, 2001, page 476

Bulletin of the Center for Children's Books, December 2001, page 138

Kliatt, November 2001, page 7

Publishers Weekly, November 5, 2001, page 69

School Library Journal, November 2001, page 154

Other books by the same author:

Shadow Spinner, 1998

Sign of the Dove, 1998

Flight of the Dragon Kyn, 1993

Dragon's Milk, 1989

Other books you might like:

Ann R. Blakeslee, *A Different Kind of Hero*, 1997
Concerned that Chinese will take away their mining jobs, Renny's father wants to run them out of camp, but Renny stands up for his friend Zi's family.

Kristiana Gregory, *Orphan Runaways*, 1998
A pneumonia epidemic helps Danny realize the kindness of his uncle's wife Lu-Chen in this look at mining camps and racism toward the Chinese.

Sharon E. Heisel, *Precious Gold, Precious Jade*, 2000
Though Angelena tries to halt the harassment of the Chinese by her townspeople, she can't stop them from burning down the Chinese neighborhood.

295

ALEX FLINN

Breathing Underwater

(New York: HarperCollins, 2001)

Subject(s): Anger; Fathers and Sons; Dating (Social Customs)
Age range(s): Grades 9-12
Major character(s): Nicholas "Nick" Andreas, 16-Year-Old, Wealthy; Caitlin Alyssa McCourt, Abuse Victim, Girlfriend (of Nick)
Time period(s): 2000s
Locale(s): Miami, Florida

Summary: Nick didn't mean to hit Caitlin, and it was only a little slap, but here he is in the Miami-Dade courthouse. Nick can't believe that the judge not only grants Caitlin's request for a restraining order against him, but she also orders him to attend an anger management class and write 500 words every week describing his entire relationship with Caitlin. Seeing the words in print in his journal make his actions seem real to Nick and he realizes how abusive he was to her, an abuse brought on by jealousy and fear that she'd leave him. Through the class he's forced to confront his relationship with his physically abusive father and understands that he's repeating what he's learned. Good-looking Nick, who could have any girl he wanted, will never again have Caitlin as a girlfriend, but at least he's now trying to build a relationship with his father as he asks to take the class again in this powerful first novel. (263 pages)

Where it's reviewed:
Booklist, August 2001, page 2106
Publishers Weekly, April 23, 2001, page 79
School Library Journal, May 2001, page 149
Voice of Youth Advocates, June 2001, page 120

Awards the book has won:
ALA Best Books for Young Adults, 2001
ALA Quick Picks for Reluctant Young Adult Readers, 2001

Other books by the same author:
Breaking Point, 2002

Other books you might like:

Chris Crutcher, *Ironman*, 1995
A domineering, sadistic father works to make a "man" of Bo, but instead turns him into a young man who resists authority.

Julie Johnston, *The Only Outcast*, 1998
Though loved by his siblings, Fred has to endure his father's demeaning comments, which reduces his self-esteem.

Ben Mikaelsen, *Touching Spirit Bear*, 2001
Cole's mean, arrogant and vicious, traits he's learned from his abusive father, until he's sent to an isolated Alaskan island to rethink his ways.

296

ADRIAN FOGELIN

Anna Casey's Place in the World

(Atlanta, GA: Peachtree Publishers, 2001)

Subject(s): Homeless People; Foster Homes
Age range(s): Grades 5-8
Major character(s): Anna Casey, 12-Year-Old, Foster Child; Eb Gramlich, Foster Child; Miss Dupree, Foster Parent; Miss Johnette, Teacher (biology)
Time period(s): 2000s
Locale(s): Florida

Summary: Anna has run out of relatives who can care for her, so is sent to a first-time foster mother, Miss Riley who has also taken in the foster child Eb. The two become friends though Eb is certain his wandering mother will return for him, just as soon as she ditches her boyfriend, while Anna would just like a place to call home. Anna lets Eb help her with the two ways she remembers places she's lived and together they make a map of their new neighborhood and pick up a stone to add to her collection. They share other adventures that summer as they befriend some of the neighborhood children, meet a homeless Vietnam vet and spend time with the unconventional teacher Miss Johnette. (207 pages)

Where it's reviewed:
Booklist, October 15, 2001, page 389
School Library Journal, December 2001, page 133
Voice of Youth Advocates, December 2001, page 357

Other books by the same author:
Crossing Jordan, 2000

Other books you might like:

Joan Bauer, *Hope Was Here*, 2000
Hope is raised by her aunt Addie who leads a nomadic lifestyle cooking in various diners; wherever she works, Hope writes the message "Hope was here."

Nancy Bond, *A Place to Come Back To*, 1984
After his parents divorce, Oliver lives with his great-uncle Sam whom he dearly loves.

Carolyn Coman, *Many Stones*, 2000
Ever since her sister Laura was murdered, Berry has collected stones, sometimes putting them on her chest as paperweights to keep her grounded.

Patricia Reilly Giff, *All the Way Home*, 2001
Adopted by Loretta, Mariel would love to find her birth mother but, when the opportunity arises, realizes Loretta is the mother she needs.

297

MARJORIE LEET FORD

Do Try to Speak as We Do: The Diary of an American Au Pair

(New York: Thomas Dunne/St. Martin's, 2001)

Subject(s): Au Pairs; Cultural Conflict
Age range(s): Grades 10-Adult
Major character(s): Melissa, Child-Care Giver; Angus Haig-Ereildoun, Government Official (member of Parliament), Writer; Mrs. Haig-Ereildoun, Mother (of Claire, Trevor and Pru); Claire Haig-Ereildoun, Deaf Person, Child; Prudence "Pru" Haig-Ereildoun, 11-Year-Old; Trevor Haig-Ereildoun, Child
Time period(s): 2000s
Locale(s): London, England; Bridie, Scotland (Troonfachan in Aberdeenshire)

Summary: Unsure of whether or not to marry her boyfriend, Melissa flees San Francisco for England where the only job she can find is that of an au pair. Working for the Haig-Ereildouns, Melissa thinks she's found a wonderful position as Mrs. Haig-Ereildoun sounds enchanting over the phone, Mr. H-E serves in Parliament, they travel between their homes in London and Scotland and the three children range in age from 3 to 11. The reality is that Melissa works nonstop; sleeps and tends to her duties with her coat on because each home is so cold; shares her bathwater, and is the last of five to bathe; never has a day off; is always saying something wrong because she doesn't understand English; and is expected to teach deaf Claire to "speak as we do" in this very funny first novel. (346 pages)

Where it's reviewed:
Book World, March 18, 2001, page 13
Booklist, November 15, 2000, page 615
Kirkus Reviews, December 15, 2000, page 1705
Library Journal, January 2001, page 153
Publishers Weekly, February 26, 2001, page 59

Other books you might like:
Melissa Bank, *The Girls' Guide to Hunting and Fishing*, 1999
   Going by the romance rules Jane does everything wrong; maybe she'll follow her mother's advice and just be herself.
Jamaica Kincaid, *Lucy*, 1990
   Lucy relates her experiences after she leaves Antigua to work as an au pair for a family living in America.
Harriet Welty Rochefort, *French Friend: The Culinary Capers of an American in Paris*, 2001
   After living in France for thirty years, the author is well prepared to describe French waiters, wine tastings and all things Gallic.
William Sutcliffe, *Are You Experienced?*, 1999
   David hooks up with Ranj, a London Indian fleeing an arranged marriage, and the two tour Indian intent only on having a good time.

 298

DAVID FRAMPTON, Author/Illustrator

The Whole Night Through: A Lullaby

(New York: HarperCollins Publishers, 2001)

Subject(s): Animals/Leopards; Bedtime; Stories in Rhyme
Age range(s): Preschool-Grade 1
Major character(s): Unnamed Character, Narrator, Stuffed Animal
Time period(s): Indeterminate
Locale(s): Earth

Summary: A little leopard frolics through the night jungle while the other animals sleep. Dozing egret perches on sleeping rhino as crocodiles, monkeys, fish, snakes, lions, hogs and many other creatures catch some shuteye. The leopard plans on staying awake all night, but droopy eyes and a big yawn belie the fatigue he feels. Finally, the toy leopard cuddles into the arms of a sleeping child sitting on a drowsy mother's lap to dream the night through as the first book, also written by this illustrator, concludes. (32 pages)

Where it's reviewed:
Booklist, May 15, 2001, page 1757
Horn Book Guide, Fall 2001, page 230
Kirkus Reviews, May 15, 2001, page 739
Publishers Weekly, May 28, 2001, page 86
School Library Journal, June 2001, page 113

Awards the book has won:
Parenting's Reading Magic Awards, 2001

Other books you might like:
Kathi Appelt, *Bayou Lullaby*, 1995
   A rhyming lullaby about the animals of the bayou soothes a little girl at bedtime.
Margaret Wise Brown, *Little Donkey Close Your Eyes*, 1995
   Animals throughout the world are bid good night in this gentle poem.
Mem Fox, *Time for Bed*, 1993
   Mothers the world over are putting their kittens, lambs, fawns and children to sleep.
Carole Lexa Schaefer, *Down in the Woods at Sleepytime*, 2000
   Not until Grandma Owl begins story time do the reluctant animal babies finally drift off to sleep.

299

LUCY FRANK

Just Ask Iris

(New York: Richard Jackson/Atheneum, 2001)

Subject(s): Business Enterprises; Apartments; Animals/Cats
Age range(s): Grades 5-8
Major character(s): Iris Diaz-Pinkowitz, 12-Year-Old; Freddy Diaz-Pinkowitz, Brother (of Iris); Will Gladd, Handicapped; Ms. Witherspoon "Cat Lady", Aged Person, Animal Lover; Fluffy, Cat
Time period(s): 2000s
Locale(s): New York, New York (Manhattan)

Summary: Moving into a new apartment in Manhattan, Iris and her brother Freddy accompany their mother into a Hispanic neighborhood away from their estranged father. While her mother is busy working, she thinks Iris should spend the summer learning to type before she attends a magnet school for computer science. Iris, however, has other ideas once she spots a beautiful cat she names Fluffy. With the elevator broken and the stairwells creepy, she uses the fire escape to navigate around her building and neighborhood, all the while meeting the other tenants of the apartment. Iris is also growing into a young lady and, after a few comments from her brother's friends, realizes she needs a bra, though her mother's too busy to take her shopping. So spunky Iris sets up her own business, called ''Just Ask Iris,'' and baby-sits, walks dogs and runs errands to earn the money for her first bra. She also solves some apartment problems when she helps Cat Lady hide her too-many cats from the apartment manager while also seeing that the elevator is repaired so her wheelchair-bound friend Will can escape his apartment to return to school. ''Just Ask Iris'' is a success in more ways than one. (214 pages)

Where it's reviewed:
Bulletin of the Center for Children's Books, December 2001, page 138
Horn Book, January 2002, page 77
Publishers Weekly, November 19, 2001, page 68
School Library Journal, December 2001, page 133
Voice of Youth Advocates, December 2001, page 358

Awards the book has won:
Smithsonian's Notable Books for Children, 2001

Other books by the same author:
Oy, Joy!, 1999
Will You Be My Brussels Sprout?, 1996
I Am an Artichoke, 1995

Other books you might like:
Patrick Jennings, *The Beastly Arms*, 2001
    Nick and his mother find the perfect apartment building in which to live when they meet fellow animal lover Mr. Beastly.
Gordon Korman, *Losing Joe's Place*, 1990
    When older brother Joe lets Jason and his friends sublet his apartment for the summer, who would guess the trouble they'd cause the landlord?
Johnniece Marshall Wilson, *Poor Girl, Rich Girl*, 1992
    Convinced she'll look better with contact lenses than her glasses with thick lenses, Miranda works at odd jobs to pay for this luxury.

300

LISA ROWE FRAUSTINO
BENNY ANDREWS, Illustrator

The Hickory Chair
(New York: Arthur A. Levine Books/Scholastic Press, 2001)

Subject(s): Grandmothers; Relatives; Gifts
Age range(s): Grades K-3
Major character(s): Louis, Child, Blind Person; Gran, Grandmother, Aged Person

Time period(s): Indeterminate Past
Locale(s): United States

Summary: Louis remembers so much about Gran, her smooth-as-molasses voice telling him stories and her lilac-with-a-whiff-of-bleach scent as she rocks him in her hickory chair. From Gran, Louis learns to use his ''blind sight'' so he can even play hide and seek with his cousins. When Gran dies, her gift to each member of the family is one of her favorite items with the recipient identified by a note hidden within the object. Louis helps locate the hidden notes, but he cannot find the one meant for him. Finally, the family is ready to sell the remaining items as Gran directs and Louis selects the hickory chair as his fondest memory of Gran. Only years later, when his own grandchild sits in the chair and puts little fingers into a hole Louis once made, does he find Gran's note and realizes that he chose the legacy she wanted him to have. (32 pages)

Where it's reviewed:
Booklist, March 1, 2001, page 1286
Bulletin of the Center for Children's Books, March 2001, page 259
Horn Book Guide, Fall 2001, page 255
Publishers Weekly, February 19, 2001, page 90
School Library Journal, February 2001, page 99

Awards the book has won:
Bulletin of the Center for Children's Books Blue Ribbon, 2001
ALA Notable Children's Books, 2002

Other books you might like:
Patricia Davis, *Brian's Bird*, 2000
    When his pet accidentally gets out of the house, Brian asks his sighted brother for assistance in locating the parakeet.
Nicola Moon, *Lucy's Picture*, 1995
    While her classmates paint colorful pictures Lucy makes a textured collage for her grandfather to ''see'' with his fingers.
Gina Willner-Pardo, *Hunting Grandma's Treasures*, 1996
    Grandma leaves a fitting legacy for her grandchildren by planning the annual vacation treasure hunt prior to her death.
Jacqueline Woodson, *Sweet, Sweet Memory*, 2000
    After Grandpa's death Sarah learns that sweet memories of him shared with Grandma and other relatives help life go on and on.

301

MARTHA FREEMAN

The Spy Wore Shades
(New York: HarperCollins, 2001)

Subject(s): Fantasy; Friendship; Caves
Age range(s): Grades 4-7
Major character(s): Dougie Minners, 11-Year-Old; Varloo, 12-Year-Old; Osi, Cat
Time period(s): 2000s
Locale(s): California

Summary: Walking through the woods one day, Dougie spots a very damp, bedraggled, plump girl sitting by the creek. He's not sure whether or not to believe her story that she's a

Hekkian named Varloo who's been sent above ground by her Druid cave mates to see what the Extros are doing that could affect them. He does know she and her cat Osi are wet and miserable and need a place to dry out, so he takes her to his tree house. He successfully hides and feeds her, which is not a problem when Varloo discovers the wonders of junk food and devours Oreos, pizza and egg rolls. From his mother, Dougie hears of a development scheduled to be built atop the caves of the Hekkians, which would certainly have an impact on their lives. Between his lawyer mother's legal skills and Dougie's find of an endangered Mexican free-tailed bat, the development is halted and the Hekkian homes are spared. (235 pages)

Where it's reviewed:
Booklist, October 1, 2001, page 318
Kirkus Reviews, May 1, 2001, page 658
Publishers Weekly, July 9, 2001, page 68
School Library Journal, August 2001, page 178

Other books by the same author:
Fourth-Grade Weirdo, 1999
The Polyester Grandpa, 1998
The Year My Parents Ruined My Life, 1997
Stink Bomb Mom, 1996

Other books you might like:
Monte Killingsworth, *Eli's Song*, 1991
Upset that an old-growth forest is to be cut, young Eli "tree sits" until a lawyer agrees to take his cause to court.
Caroline Macdonald, *The Lake at the End of the World*, 1989
In 2025 Diana and her parents fear they are the only inhabitants left on earth, until Diana discovers an unusual underground cult.
Gregory Maguire, *I Feel Like the Morning Star*, 1989
Five years after an atomic attack forces everyone to live underground, three teens are the only ones who want to return to life aboveground.
Richard Scrimger, *The Nose from Jupiter*, 1998
Alan appreciates the help he receives from the alien who lives in his nose; when Norbert's no longer needed, one giant sneeze sends him to Jupiter.

302

VIVIAN FRENCH
ALISON BARTLETT, Illustrator

Oliver's Milk Shake
(New York: Orchard Books, 2001)

Subject(s): Food; Aunts and Uncles; Farm Life
Age range(s): Preschool-Grade 1
Major character(s): Oliver, Child, Nephew; Lily, Cousin, Daughter; Jen, Aunt, Mother
Time period(s): 2000s (2000)
Locale(s): England

Summary: When Lily and Aunt Jen arrive to pick up Oliver they notice that he's drinking an orange soda with his breakfast. Aunt Jen assumes that Oliver does not like milk and takes him shopping for the ingredients to make one of her yummy milk shakes. The "store" Aunt Jen drives to is a farm where Lily and Oliver see sheep, chickens, goats, pigs, and, of course, cows. At the farm stand Aunt Jen buys milk and some

of Oliver's favorite berries for the milk shake that is now being described as "yummy scrummy fruity frothy icy nicy tip-top tasty." Oliver declares the blueberry milk shake is scrumptious but Aunt Jen's satisfaction over getting him to drink milk is short-lived. The only reason he had an orange soda for breakfast was because he'd used all the milk on his cereal. First published in Great Britain in 2000. (28 pages)

Where it's reviewed:
Booklist, August 2001, page 2129
Horn Book Guide, Fall 2001, page 255
Kirkus Reviews, April 15, 2001, page 585
School Library Journal, June 2001, page 114

Other books by the same author:
Oliver's Fruit Salad, 1998
A Song for Little Toad, 1995
Oliver's Vegetables, 1995

Other books you might like:
Stella Blackstone, *There's a Cow in the Cabbage Patch*, 2001
The farm's animals are all out of place until dinnertime arrives then they hurriedly find their proper spots.
Lucy Cousins, *Maisy's Morning on the Farm*, 2001
After completing her chores, Maisy takes time for a yummy breakfast.
Nancy Elizabeth Wallace, *Apples, Apples, Apples*, 2000
A family outing to an orchard is a lesson in the wide variety of and uses for apples.

303

GINA FRESCHET

Beto and the Bone Dance
(New York: Farrar Straus Giroux, 2001)

Subject(s): Holidays; Mexican Americans; Halloween
Age range(s): Grades K-3
Major character(s): Beto, Child, Son; Poppy, Father
Time period(s): Indeterminate
Locale(s): Mexico

Summary: Beto loves this festival, the Day of the Dead, when replicas of skeletons are everywhere. Each family prepares an altar to honor deceased family members and decorates it with items enjoyed by the person during their lifetime. Each time Beto thinks of something to put on the altar to honor his grandmother Poppy names the relative that will be bringing that item. By the time the evening celebration begins, Beto is still searching for an idea. In a dream his deceased grandmother gives him a clue so Beto can add his contribution. (32 pages)

Where it's reviewed:
Booklist, October 15, 2001, page 401
Bulletin of the Center for Children's Books, December 2001, page 139
Horn Book Guide, Spring 2002, page 42
Publishers Weekly, October 22, 2001, page 79
School Library Journal, October 2001, page 118

Other books by the same author:
Naty's Parade, 2000
The Lute's Tune, 1992

Other books you might like:

George Ancona, *Pablo Remembers: The Fiesta of the Day of the Dead*, 1993
Photographs illustrate the nonfiction title explaining the three-day Mexican celebration honoring one's ancestors.

Tony Johnston, *Day of the Dead*, 1997
The annual Day of the Dead holiday is seen through the eyes of children waiting for the preparations to end so the celebration can begin.

Nancy Luenn, *A Gift for Abuelita: Celebrating the Day of the Dead*, 1998
In a bilingual title Rosita prepares a gift for her grandmother's altar at the family's celebration of the Day of the Dead.

304

DIANE FREUND

Four Corners

(San Francisco, CA: MacAdam/Cage, 2001)

Subject(s): Family Problems; Aunts and Uncles; Small Town Life
Age range(s): Grades 10-Adult
Major character(s): Lorraine "Rainey" Dougherty, Child; Merle, Aunt; Joan, Cousin, 13-Year-Old
Time period(s): 1950s
Locale(s): New York (near the Finger Lakes)

Summary: One summer Rainey's mother has a nervous breakdown, caused perhaps by the rats in their home or maybe from her five children, but whatever the reason she's institutionalized. A few days later their aunt Merle arrives from the Bronx, with their cousin Joan, and their lives change even more. Just barely a teenager, Joan is, in Rainey's words, "wild" and introduces Rainey and her sister Em to words and activities they never knew existed, all of which Joan's learned from her mother. Merle, while supposedly watching the children through her endless cigarettes and her morning beer "for courage," forgets about her abusive fruit vendor husband and flirts with their next-door neighbor. When the uncle and oldest son arrive, Rainey's home becomes a battleground for Merle's family members. Rainey loses her innocence that year as she sees and learns more than she should, but she also becomes better equipped to meet the realities of life in this first novel. (261 pages)

Where it's reviewed:
Booklist, August 2001, page 2085
Kirkus Reviews, August 1, 2001, page 1050
New York Times Book Review, October 7, 2001, page 29
Publishers Weekly, September 10, 2001, page 61
Redbook, August 2001, page G-4

Other books you might like:

Jill McCorkle, *Ferris Beach*, 1990
Kate's cousin Angela, who lives at Ferris Beach, seems so glamorous compared to her own prim, proper mother.

Whitney Otto, *How to Make an American Quilt*, 1991
Young Finn, about to be married, collects all kinds of advice from the members of a local quilting circle, which adds to her preparation for adult life.

Mary Saracino, *Finding Grace*, 1999
Peanut and her two sisters run away from their mother and her boyfriend, their former parish priest Patrick, for fear of his temper.

305

JOACHIM FRIEDRICH
ELIZABETH D. CRAWFORD, Translator

4 1/2 Friends and the Secret Cave

(New York: Hyperion, 2001)

Series: 4 1/2 Friends
Subject(s): Mystery and Detective Stories; Treasure, Buried; Twins
Age range(s): Grades 4-6
Major character(s): Austin "Radish" Rademacher, Twin, Detective—Amateur; Stefanie "Steffi" Rademacher, Twin, Detective—Amateur; Collin, Detective—Amateur; Norbert, Detective—Amateur; Bobby Hansen, Child
Time period(s): 1990s
Locale(s): Germany

Summary: A foot shorter than his twin sister, Radish gets a little tired of being the overlooked twin, as happens again when Collin visits Steffi and announces his new detective agency, Collin and Co. While Collin and Steffi play a new computer game, Radish sneaks out to babysit Bobby and take him on his walk. That's when he discovers a cave with two stuffed animals inside, along with a treasure map that's dated 1950. Sharing his find with Collin and Co., Collin and Steffi grudgingly agree to let Radish be a partner in the detective agency. Pretty soon Collin adds Norbert to the group and, when Radish baby-sits Bobby, there are 41/2 friends searching for hidden treasure in this import from Germany. (154 pages)

Where it's reviewed:
Publishers Weekly, May 7, 2001, page 247
School Library Journal, May 2001, page 150

Other books by the same author:
4 1/2 Friends and the Disappearing Bio Teacher, 2001

Other books you might like:

Michael Dahl, *The Horizontal Man*, 1999
Finn spots a gold Mayan relic of his parents' in a neighbor's apartment, investigates and is kidnapped.

Mark Delaney, *The Vanishing Chip*, 1998
Four misfit teens unite to find a stolen computer chip worth more than a million dollars.

T.M. Murphy, *The Secrets of Code Z*, 2001
Amateur detective Orville now contends with the CIA, a Russian scientist from the Chernobyl disaster, a rookie newspaper reporter and a few too many murders in his fifth adventure.

Wendelin Van Draanen, *Sammy Keyes and the Curse of Moustache Mary*, 2000
Though Sammy's heading to a New Years Eve party, she can't let go of those investigative twitches that lead her to an arsonist and a meth lab.

306

JOACHIM FRIEDRICH
ELIZABETH D. CRAWFORD, Translator

41/2 Friends and the Disappearing Bio Teacher

(New York: Hyperion, 2001)

Series: 4 1/2 Friends
Subject(s): Mystery and Detective Stories; Twins; Teachers
Age range(s): Grades 4-6
Major character(s): Austin ''Radish'' Rademacher, Twin, Detective—Amateur; Stefanie ''Steffi'' Rademacher, Twin, Detective—Amateur; Collin, Detective—Amateur; Norbert, Detective—Amateur; Gorgeous, Dog
Time period(s): 2000s
Locale(s): Germany

Summary: Collin and Co. Detective Agency has one case, sort of, under its belt and is eager for the second when one appears under their noses. Their biology teacher, Ms. Hober-Stratman, suddenly starts wearing nice, non-teacher clothes and driving a red Porsche, which leads Norbert, Steffi, Radish and Collin to wonder where the money came from for these new purchases. When they see her wearing a blonde wig, they immediately remember the newspaper article about the bank robber who also wears a wig, and decide she must be the thief.

Skulking around after her, with the dog Gorgeous as their half-friend in this book, they suddenly realize they've made a terrible mistake. It seems that Ms. Hober-Stratman is divorced, the Porsche is her brother's and the wig is to disguise herself when she goes on dates in this second of the series. (156 pages)

Where it's reviewed:
School Library Journal, May 2001, page 150

Other books by the same author:
4 1/2 Friends and the Secret Cave, 2001 (4 1/2 Friends)

Other books you might like:
Robbie Branscum, *Cameo Rose*, 1989
Cameo conducts her own investigation into the murder of Homer Satterfield and is amazed there are so many suspects for a man she thought was no-count.
Lisa Eisenberg, *Mystery at Camp Windingo*, 1991
Camp counselor Kate and her cousin arrive at camp to find the campers sick from food poisoning and valuable birds stolen.
Joseph Locke, *Kill the Teacher's Pet*, 1991
When a popular English teacher doesn't return after Christmas vacation no one is too concerned, until a substitute resembling a serial killer shows up.
Mary C. Ryan, *The Voice from the Mendelsohns' Maple*, 1990
Thanks to Penny, who hears Miss Cooper calling from the branches of her neighbor's maple tree, the Beacon Manor retirement home improves.

G

DAYLE CAMPBELL GAETZ
CINDY GHENT, Illustrator

Mystery from History
(Custer, WA: Orca, 2001)

Subject(s): Mystery and Detective Stories; Burglary
Age range(s): Grades 4-7
Major character(s): Katie Reid, 12-Year-Old, Detective—
Amateur; Sheila Walton, 12-Year-Old, Detective—
Amateur; Russell "Rusty" Gates, 11-Year-Old, Detec-
tive—Amateur; Chief Carlson, Police Officer
Time period(s): 2000s
Locale(s): Victoria, British Columbia, Canada

Summary: With the sign "Investigations Unlimited" on their
fort, it's inevitable that Katie, Sheila and Rusty will follow
their inclinations and snoop around the old deserted mansion
close to town. Townspeople say that ghosts of long-dead
pirates, or the more recent, century-old ghosts of the mansion's builders, haunt the house. This time, the lights and
sounds are real and the ghosts are art thieves, including the
town's chief of police. Thanks to the sixth sense of Katie,
Sheila and Rusty, who have a feeling Chief Carlson is up to no
good, the art thieves are foiled and the loot from an 1864 bank
robbery is recovered. (170 pages)

Where it's reviewed:
Resource Links, October 2001, page 13
School Library Journal, February 2002, page 130

Other books by the same author:
Living Freight, 1998 (On Time's Wing Historical Fiction)
Alien Rescue, 1997 (Out of This World)
Night of the Aliens, 1995 (Out of This World)

Other books you might like:
Mark Delaney, *The Vanishing Chip*, 1998
    Four misfit teens unite to find a stolen computer chip worth
    more than a million dollars.
Joachim Friedrich, *41/2 Friends and the Secret Cave*, 2001
    Collin and Steffi set up a detective agency but have to

admit her twin brother Radish when he finds a cave with a
treasure map dated from the 1950s.
Virginia Hamilton, *The House of Dies Drear*, 1968
    When the Smalls buy their home, they don't realize it's
    laced with passageways from its days as a stop on the
    Underground Railroad.
Wendelin Van Draanen, *Sammy Keyes and the Curse of
Moustache Mary*, 2000
    Though Sammy's heading to a New Years Eve party, she
    can't let go of her investigative twitches, which lead her to
    an arsonist and a meth lab.

308

DONALD R. GALLO, Editor

On the Fringe
(New York: Dial Press, 2001)

Subject(s): Short Stories; Schools/High Schools; Outcasts
Age range(s): Grades 7-10
Time period(s): 2000s
Locale(s): United States

Summary: Are you an insider or an outsider, or does it even
matter? To some young people it does and the results are
portrayed in this collection of eleven short stories by noted
young adult authors. From Angela Johnson comes "Through
a Window" where the suicide victim's best friend achingly
describes the impact of Nick's loss on her. In "Geeks Bearing
Gifts," Ron Koertge's heroine Renee tries to write an article
about outsiders, but as she questions various group members,
begins to wonder who the real outsiders are. And Keiffer turns
the tables on a bully in the exquisite tale of revenge by
Graham Salisbury titled "Mrs. Noonan." Other authors include Alden R. Carter, Joan Bauer, Chris Crutcher and Nancy
Werlin. (224 pages)

Where it's reviewed:
Book Report, November 2001, page 69
Booklist, March 15, 2001, page 1391
Bulletin of the Center for Children's Books, June 2001, page
    371

School Library Journal, May 2001, page 150
Voice of Youth Advocates, April 2001, page 46

Awards the book has won:
ALA Best Books for Young Adults, 2002

Other books by the same author:
Time Capsule: Short Stories about Teenagers throughout the Twentieth Century, 1999
No Easy Answers: Short Stories about Teenagers Making Tough Choices, 1997
Join In: Multiethnic Short Stories by Outstanding Writers for Young Adults, 1993
Connections: Short Stories by Outstanding Writers for Young Adults, 1990

Other books you might like:
Laurie Halse Anderson, *Speak*, 1999
    Classmates ostracize Melinda because they think she dialed 911 to break up a party; when the truth comes out, she is vindicated.
Norma Fox Mazer, *Out of Control*, 1993
    During Valerie's junior year, three classmates assault her in a deserted hallway but only one of them feels any remorse.
Carol Plum-Ucci, *The Body of Christopher Creed*, 2000
    When geeky Christopher Creed disappears, his classmates wonder what happened but it takes an investigation by popular Torey to track down the answers.
Todd Strasser, *Give a Boy a Gun*, 2000
    Interviews from a variety of students tell the story of two unhappy teenage boys who enter their school's gymnasium during a dance and shoot teachers and students.
Rob Thomas, *Slave Day*, 1997
    African American Keena Davenport writes a letter to the editor of the school newspaper urging students to boycott the demeaning ritual of ''slave day.''

309

STEVEN GALLOWAY

Finnie Walsh

(Vancouver, BC: Raincoast Books, 2001)

Subject(s): Sports/Hockey; Friendship; Guilt
Age range(s): Grades 10-Adult
Major character(s): Paul Woodward, Hockey Player; Finnie Walsh, Hockey Player, Worker (sawmill); Robert Woodward, Father (of Paul), Amputee
Time period(s): 20th century (1960s-1990s)
Locale(s): Portsmouth, Ontario, Canada

Summary: Paul and Finnie have been friends since sharing the same third grade classroom and aren't bothered by the fact that Paul's father is a worker in the sawmill that Finnie's father owns. The two boys meet after school in Paul's driveway to play hockey and the constant sound of the puck hitting the garage door awakens his father Robert who works the night shift. That evening at the sawmill, Robert's lack of sleep leads to an accident where he loses his arm below the elbow. Though everyone assumes the two boys will end their friendship after the accident, Paul and Finnie remain good buddies, perhaps linked by their shared guilt, and eventually go on to

play hockey in the minor leagues in this first novel. (165 pages)

Where it's reviewed:
Booklist, May 1, 2001, page 1674
Publishers Weekly, January 29, 2001, page 66
Quill & Quire, September 2000, page 55

Other books you might like:
Rick Book, *Necking with Louise*, 1999
    Seven chapters capture a memorable year in Eric's life as he vacillates between boyhood and manhood, dates Louise and reveres his grandfather.
John Irving, *A Prayer for Owen Meany*, 1989
    In love with his best friend's mother, Owen is aghast when he hits a baseball that strikes and kills her.
Don Trembath, *The Tuesday Cafe*, 1996
    Enrolled in a writing class, Harper doesn't realize he's in a class for newly literate and learning disabled for it's the best class he's ever taken.
Diana Wieler, *Bad Boy*, 1992
    Although he knows he's a marginal player, A.J. is thrilled to make the Triple-A hockey team.

310

STEPHEN GAMMELL, Author/Illustrator

Ride

(San Diego: Silver Whistle/Harcourt, Inc., 2001)

Subject(s): Brothers and Sisters; Automobiles; Parent and Child
Age range(s): Grades K-3
Major character(s): Unnamed Character, Brother, Son; Unnamed Character, Sister, Daughter
Time period(s): Indeterminate Past
Locale(s): United States

Summary: As a family departs on an afternoon car ride the eager parents admonish their offspring to get along with each other in the back seat. The reluctant siblings hate the idea to sitting together in the back seat while on a family ride to nowhere. They stake out their territory and complain loudly if their space is violated. First, the sister notices her brother's foot on ''her'' side then the brother complains because his sister is touching him. The argument grows more vocal and more physical as the illustrations become more fantastic with beds and other furniture flying through the air. When the happy parents notice the commotion they simply pass back some sandwiches to calm the discord. (32 pages)

Where it's reviewed:
Booklist, May 1, 2001, page 1689
Bulletin of the Center for Children's Books, March 2001, page 259
Horn Book, May 2001, page 310
Publishers Weekly, April 2, 2001, page 63
School Library Journal, May 2001, page 115

Other books by the same author:
Twigboy, 2000
Is That You, Winter?: A Story, 1997
Wake Up Bear . . . It's Christmas!, 1990
Once Upon MacDonald's Farm, 1981

Other books you might like:

Teri Daniels, *G-Rex*, 2000
Gregory becomes so envious of his older brother that he transforms into a meat-eating dinosaur with decidedly bad behavior.

Virginia Walters, *Are We There Yet, Daddy?*, 1999
No siblings argue in the back seat on this trip but the map-yielding son repeatedly asks his father when they'll arrive at his grandmother's house.

Charlotte Zolotow, *Do You Know What I'll Do?*, 1958
This positive portrayal of a loving older sister's relationship with her brother was reissued with new illustrations in 2000.

311

JACK GANTOS
NICOLE RUBEL, Illustrator

Rotten Ralph Helps Out
(New York: Farrar Straus Giroux, 2001)

Series: Rotten Ralph Rotten Reader. Book 1
Subject(s): Animals/Cats; Schools; Cultures and Customs
Age range(s): Grades 1-3
Major character(s): Sarah, Child, Student—Elementary School; Ralph, Cat
Time period(s): 2000s (2001)
Locale(s): United States

Summary: Sarah shares her knowledge of ancient Egypt with Ralph as she does research for a school project on the subject. Mischievous Ralph takes the information Sarah gives as inspiration to build a pyramid with library books and to write his own brand of hieroglyphs on the library wall. At home Ralph dumps sand in the living room to create a desert and floods the house while turning the bathtub into the Nile. Finally Sarah, in frustration, sends her pet to bed early and works on the project without his help. In the morning, it is Ralph whose ideas ultimately save the day and allow him to remain in Sarah's good graces as a beloved, though challenging, pet. (48 pages)

Where it's reviewed:
Booklist, July 2001, page 2023
Horn Book, September 2001, page 582
Kirkus Reviews, July 1, 2001, page 938
Publishers Weekly, July 2, 2001, page 76
School Library Journal, August 2001, page 146

Other books by the same author:
Practice Makes Perfect for Rotten Ralph, 2002 (Rotten Ralph Rotten Reader, Book 2)
Wedding Bells for Rotten Ralph, 1999
Back to School for Rotten Ralph, 1998

Other books you might like:

Lloyd Alexander, *How the Cat Swallowed Thunder*, 2000
Cat, though lazy, has good intentions that seem to create a never-ending string of problems for the feline.

Alexandra Day, *Darby: The Special Order Pup*, 2000
Darby's most annoying bad habit, chewing, is the one that saves his family after a mudslide destroys their home.

Nina Laden, *Bad Dog*, 2000
Bad Dog doesn't understand why a hungry dog should be in trouble for responding to a farmer's ad for "free-range" chickens.

312

LINDSEY GARDINER, Author/Illustrator

When Poppy and Max Grow Up
(Boston: Little, Brown and Company, 2001)

Subject(s): Playing; Growing Up; Animals/Dogs
Age range(s): Preschool-Kindergarten
Major character(s): Poppy, Child; Max, Dog
Time period(s): 2000s (2001)
Locale(s): Fictional Country

Summary: Imaginatively, Poppy and Max demonstrate the many possibilities for their future activities or careers. They could be artists, soccer players or even rock stars. Perhaps they'll choose to practice medicine as veterinarians or show their talent as ballet dancers. In the future they could be scuba divers and chefs but for now taking care of Max is just the right job for Poppy. (20 pages)

Where it's reviewed:
Booklist, September 1, 2001, page 114
Horn Book Guide, Spring 2002, page 18
Publishers Weekly, September 3, 2001, page 89
School Library Journal, October 2001, page 118

Other books by the same author:
Here Come Poppy and Max, 2000

Other books you might like:

Trish Cooke, *When I Grow Bigger*, 1994
Leanne and her friends quibble about what they can or will do when they grow bigger.

Joyce Dunbar, *Tell Me What It's Like to Be Big*, 2001
With her big brother providing answers a little bunny ponders what she'll be able to do when she's bigger and isn't sure she likes all the choices.

Heidi Goennel, *When I Grow Up—*, 1987
A child imagines "grown-up" pleasures such as driving a car, traveling or going to a prom.

Charise Mericle Harper, *When I Grow Up*, 2001
Illustrations show children demonstrating the positive characteristics they hope to have when they grow up.

313

HENRY GARFIELD

Tartabull's Throw
(New York: Atheneum, 2001)

Subject(s): Sports/Baseball; Werewolves; Time Travel
Age range(s): Grades 8-12
Major character(s): Cyrus Nygerski, Baseball Player; Cassandra Paine, Sister, Werewolf; Timmy Paine, Brother
Time period(s): 1960s (1967)
Locale(s): United States

Summary: Cyrus has just been released from his minor league team when he meets a beautiful girl in a red dress and takes her to a ball game. Or is he playing in the major leagues? When Cyrus meets Cassandra, he finds time becomes confusing and notices that crime follows Cassandra and the full moon. When Cyrus accompanies Cassandra to her family's home he seems closer to understanding the mystery, but he may be unwittingly endangering her little brother Timmy. Alternative futures crisscross one another at a dizzying pace as the full moon draws closer. This is a prequel to *Moondog* and *Room 13* which continue Cyrus' story. (262 pages)

Where it's reviewed:
Booklist, May 15, 2001, page 1744
Publishers Weekly, May 21, 2001, page 109
School Library Journal, June 2001, page 148
Voice of Youth Advocates, August 2001, page 212

Other books by the same author:
Moondog, 2001
Room 13, 1997

Other books you might like:
Tom Dyja, *Play for a Kingdom*, 1997
  The Union and Confederate troops come together for a surreal game of baseball during the Battle of Spotsylvania in 1864.
Kathleen Goonan, *The Bones of Time*, 1996
  A young scientist chases the last queen of Hawaii through time.
Annette Curtis Klause, *Blood and Chocolate*, 1997
  A werewolf girl indulges herself in a forbidden relationship with a normal boy.

MICHAEL GARLAND, Author/Illustrator

Last Night at the Zoo
(Honesdale, PA: Boyds Mills Press, 2001)

Subject(s): Zoos; Animals; Stories in Rhyme
Age range(s): Grades K-2
Time period(s): 2000s
Locale(s): United States

Summary: Bored zoo animals plan a getaway. Monkeys steal the keys from the sleeping attendant and seals gather coins from the wishing fountain. So they won't be easily noticed they don hats and shirts from the zoo's lost and found before boarding a bus. After dancing at a club they satisfy their hunger at a diner and then take the bus back to the zoo before anyone notices they're missing. (32 pages)

Where it's reviewed:
Booklist, July 2001, page 2019
Children's Bookwatch, April 2001, page 3
Horn Book Guide, Spring 2002, page 43
Publishers Weekly, January 22, 2001, page 324
School Library Journal, May 2001, page 115

Other books by the same author:
Icarus Swinebuckle, 2000
A Elf for Christmas, 1999
Dinner at Magritte's, 1995
Circus Girl, 1993

Other books you might like:
Rita Golden Gelman, *I Went to the Zoo*, 1993
  Animals at the zoo look so bored that one visitor invites them to come home with him.
Nina Laden, *The Night I Followed the Dog*, 1994
  While a family sleeps, their pet dog secretly leads an exciting nightlife.
Peggy Rathmann, *Good Night, Gorilla*, 1994
  Unbeknownst to a zookeeper making his final rounds, a little gorilla steals his keys and releases all the animals to follow the unsuspecting man home.

SHERRY GARLAND
TRINA SCHART HYMAN, Illustrator

Children of the Dragon: Selected Tales from Vietnam
(San Diego: Harcourt, Inc., 2001)

Subject(s): Folk Tales; Cultures and Customs; Vietnamese
Age range(s): Grades 3-6
Time period(s): Indeterminate Past
Locale(s): Vietnam

Summary: The author introduces six of her favorite folk tales with a summary of Vietnamese history and folkloric tradition. The tale, "How the Tiger Got Its Stripes," explains not only the origin of a tiger's striped coloration but also the reason that water buffalo have no front teeth. In "The Bowmen and the Sisters" the universal theme of kindness rewarded while selfishness receives its due is retold in a story of beautiful twin sisters with very different personalities. Another *pourquoi* tale, "Chu Cuoi—the Man in the Moon," explains why the image of a man can be seen in the moon. At the conclusion of each tale additional information about Vietnamese culture and customs is provided as background to a fuller understanding. (58 pages)

Where it's reviewed:
Booklist, July 2001, page 2010
Bulletin of the Center for Children's Books, November 2001, page 102
Publishers Weekly, August 27, 2001, page 85
Riverbank Review, Winter 2001-2002, page 44
School Library Journal, October 2001, page 139

Other books by the same author:
Shadow of the Dragon, 1993
The Lotus Seed, 1993 (ALA Notable Book)
Song of the Buffalo Boy, 1992

Other books you might like:
Howard Norman, *The Girl Who Dreamed Only Geese and Other Tales of the Far North*, 1997
  An illustrated collection of ten Inuit stories records the oral history of a people and their harsh environment.
Katrin Tchana, *The Serpent Slayer*, 2000
  Eighteen folktales celebrate the strength and cleverness of heroines of diverse ages and cultures.
Lynette Dyer Vuoung, *The Brocaded Slipper*, 1982
  Vietnamese retellings of five folktales conclude with information about the cultural background for the tales.

SHERRY GARLAND

In the Shadow of the Alamo

(San Diego: Harcourt/Gulliver, 2001)

Series: Great Episodes
Subject(s): War; Coming-of-Age
Age range(s): Grades 6-8
Major character(s): Lorenzo Bonifacio, 15-Year-Old, Military Personnel; Catalina Sandoval, Shepherd (of goats); Florencia, Aunt, Healter; General Santa Anna, Military Personnel, Historical Figure
Time period(s): 1830s
Locale(s): San Javier, Mexico (Guanajuato state); San Antonio, Texas

Summary: When the soldiers come to his village, Lorenzo knows he will be conscripted into the Mexican Army for ten years, just like his father was conscripted nine years ago. Herded toward Texas, his aunt, two sisters and Catalina the goatherd girl join the entourage that follows the soldiers. Lorenzo receives little training, marches with inadequate supplies, and loses all respect for General Santa Anna because of his cruel, tyrannical ways. After the defeat of the Americans at the Alamo, the Mexican Army marches on to locate and defeat General Houston, but this time the outcome of the battle is different and Lorenzo joins other stragglers of the Mexican Army as they make their way back home. Having been exposed to the world beyond his small village, Lorenzo finally appreciates the healing skills of his aunt, realizes he has grown to love Catalina and knows that some privates are more heroic than generals. (282 pages)

Where it's reviewed:
Booklist, October 15, 2001, page 389
Bulletin of the Center for Children's Books, January 2002, page 171
Horn Book, November 2001, page 747
School Library Journal, December 2001, page 133
Voice of Youth Advocates, October 2001, page 276

Other books by the same author:
Valley of the Moon: The Diary of Maria Rosalia De Milagros, Sonoma Valley, Alta California, 1846, 2001 (Dear America)
Voices of the Alamo, 2000
A Line in the Sand: The Alamo Diary of Lucinda Lawrence, 1998 (Dear America)

Other books you might like:
Elizabeth Crook, *Promised Lands: A Novel of the Texas Rebellion*, 1994
    The story of the Kenner family, homesteaders in Texas, who join the battle for independence but wind up in the massacre outside of Goliad. Adult fiction.
D. Anne Love, *I Remember the Alamo*, 1999
    Jessie is upset when she finds out her family plans to move from Kentucky to Mexican Texas to help fight for Texas's independence.
G. Clifton Wisler, *All for Texas: A Story of Texas Liberation*, 2000
    Drawn to Texas because of the promise of land in ex-

change for helping fight the Mexicans, Jeff and his mother prove to be hardy settlers.

SHERRY GARLAND

Valley of the Moon: The Diary of Maria Rosalia De Milagros, Sonoma Valley, Alta California, 1846

(New York: Scholastic, 2001)

Series: Dear America
Subject(s): Diaries; Orphans; Racially Mixed People
Age range(s): Grades 5-8
Major character(s): Maria Rosalia de Milagros, Orphan, 13-Year-Old; Domingo de Milagros, Brother (of Maria); Ygnacio, Religious (priest)
Time period(s): 1840s (1846)
Locale(s): Sonoma Valley, California

Summary: Orphaned, Rosalia and her younger brother are taught to read by Padre Ygnacio at Mission Rafael, before being taken in by servants of the Medina family at their large ranch. Rosalia records her thoughts in a diary discarded by one of the Medina girls and tells of a tumultuous year in California's history as the state is transformed from being part of Mexico, to a republic and finally to part of the United States. As she records their daily life, from rodeos and bullfights to weddings and funerals, as well as the politics of the day, never far from her thoughts is the question of her mother's identity. The fact that her mother died of smallpox, yet each child was vaccinated against it, haunts Rosalia and she wishes she knew more about the circumstances. Tracking down the old priest provides clues to their background in this continuing series. (218 pages)

Where it's reviewed:
Booklist, April 1, 2001, page 1482
Childhood Education, Winter 2001/2002, page 110
Kliatt, March 2001, page 10
School Library Journal, April 2001, page 140
Voice of Youth Advocates, August 2001, page 200

Other books by the same author:
In the Shadow of the Alamo, 2001
A Line in the Sand: The Alamo Diary of Lucinda Lawrence, 1998 (Dear America)
The Last Rainmaker, 1997
Letters from the Mountain, 1996

Other books you might like:
Kathy Balmes, *Thunder on the Sierra*, 2001
    When his horse is stolen, orphaned Mateo is lucky that a benefactor lets him operate his mule train and deliver supplies to the miners in the Sierras.
Karen Cushman, *The Ballad of Lucy Whipple*, 1996
    Thoroughly miserable that her mother has dragged the family to a small gold mining town in California, Lucy wants to return to Massachusetts.
Pam Munoz Ryan, *Esperanza Rising*, 2000
    After her father is killed by bandits, Esperanza and her mother leave Mexico for the San Joaquin Valley to find work during the Depression.

ELIZABETH GARRETT

The Sweet Trade

(New York: Tor/Forge, 2001)

Subject(s): Pirates; Friendship; Women
Age range(s): Grades 10-Adult
Major character(s): John "Calico Jack" Rackham, Pirate; Anne Bonny, Pirate; Mary Read, Pirate
Time period(s): 18th century
Locale(s): England; Nassau, West Indies; *Pretty Anne*, At Sea

Summary: When she was young, Mary's mother dressed her as a boy, primarily to confuse her in-laws, and when older Mary joined England's cavalry and eventually married her tent mate. After he died of tuberculosis, Mary continued her male dressing and signed on as a seaman. While sailing in the West Indies, her ship is boarded by the pirate Calico Jack and his lover Anne, who has left behind a weak-willed husband in Nassau. Mary joins up with Calico Jack, Anne and his crew, revels in her life of freedom and enjoys a lasting friendship with Anne in this first novel based on the lives of female pirates Anne Bonny and Mary Read. (399 pages)

Where it's reviewed:
Booklist, March 15, 2001, page 1354
Kirkus Reviews, February 15, 2001, page 201
Publishers Weekly, March 12, 2001, page 62

Other books you might like:
Daphne Du Maurier, *Frenchman's Creek*, 1942
    Fleeing London for her estate along the Cornish coast, Lady St. Columb meets and falls in love with a French pirate who uses the area as a hiding place.
Douglas Kelley, *The Captain's Wife*, 2001
    When her sea captain husband falls ill, Mary Ann has to assume comand for she's the only one who knows how to navigate.
Kenneth Lewis Roberts, *Lydia Bailey*, 1947
    A young couple in love encounter danger from the French, the Barbary pirates and the Tripolitan War.

319

P.L. GAUS

Clouds without Rain

(Athens, OH: Ohio University Press, 2001)

Series: Ohio Amish Mystery
Subject(s): Mystery and Detective Stories; Amish
Age range(s): Grades 10-Adult
Major character(s): Michael Branden, Professor; Bruce Robertson, Police Officer (sheriff)
Time period(s): 2000s
Locale(s): Holmes County, Ohio

Summary: The difficulties of Amish culture struggling to exist within twenty-first- century American culture are underlined in a buggy crash involving an eighteen-wheeler. Professor Branden, friend to both the Amish and the local police department, comes across this accident only to discover that his buddy Sheriff Robertson has been badly burned while trying to rescue the victims. As Branden lends his help with the investigation, the first person they need to find is the one who shot the buggy's horse for that's how the accident started. There are other oddities that may be tied in, such as the Amish teenage burglary ring, land swindles and a missing bank official in this third mystery about the Amish. (196 pages)

Where it's reviewed:
Booklist, May 1, 2001, page 1632
Kirkus Reviews, April 1, 2001, page 461
New York Times Book Review, June 24, 2001, page 22
Publishers Weekly, May 21, 2001, page 83

Other books by the same author:
Broken English, 2000
Blood of the Prodigal, 1999

Other books you might like:
Karen Harper, *Down to the Bone*, 2000
    It's been a year since her young Amish husband died in a freak accident in their barn and now two men are interested in Rachel, one Amish and one "English."
Margaret Maron, *Uncommon Clay*, 2001
    Judge Deborah Knott travels to Randolph County for a divorce case involving two potters, but stays when someone bakes James Lucas in his own kiln.
Jodi Picoult, *Plain Truth*, 2000
    Moving to a small town, former defense attorney Ellie Hathaway is asked to defend a young Amish girl who's accused of murdering her son.

320

GAIL GAUTHIER

The Hero of Ticonderoga

(New York: Putnam, 2001)

Subject(s): Teacher-Student Relationships; School Life; Humor
Age range(s): Grades 5-7
Major character(s): Therese "Tessy" LeClerc, 6th Grader; Mr. Santangelo, Teacher (substitute); Ethan Allen, Historical Figure
Time period(s): 1960s
Locale(s): Vermont

Summary: Tessy has a long-term substitute teacher who doesn't understand the rules about the important oral report about Ethan Allen. Or maybe he does, but he doesn't let the best student in class deliver the Ethan Allen report, the way it's always been done. No, Mr. Santangelo picks a name and that name happens to be Tessy's. Just an average student, Tessy first tells her class a series of unrelated anecdotes, events and stories that she finds interesting, but the substitute isn't accepting that as an oral report. No, she must organize her information, put it in chronological order and deliver it again, which she does but with additions of her own sassy wit which makes local hero Ethan Allen come alive for her classmates. Thrilled at all she's done, Tessy bursts with pride when Mr. Santangelo gives her a B on her report, a pride that quickly fades when her regular teacher returns and writes a C on it. (231 pages)

Where it's reviewed:
Book Report, November 2001, page 61
Booklist, April 1, 2001, page 1481
Bulletin of the Center for Children's Books, March 2001, page 259
Publishers Weekly, February 19, 2001, page 92
School Library Journal, February 2001, page 118

Awards the book has won:
ALA Notable Children's Books, 2002

Other books by the same author:
Club Earth, 1999
A Year with Butch and Spike, 1998
My Life Among the Aliens, 1996

Other books you might like:
Mary Amato, *The Word Eater*, 2000
Life in her new school becomes easier for Lerner when she finds a magical worm that eats printed words instead of dirt.
Marie G. Lee, *F Is for Fabuloso*, 1999
Rather than have her Korean parents worry about her failing grade in math, Jin-Ha tells them that in America "F is for fabuloso."
Susan Shreve, *Goodbye, Amanda the Good*, 2000
Amanda discards her old image, dyes her hair and wears black, but lying to her principal makes her want to return to being "Amanda the Good."
Rachel Vail, *The Friendship Ring Series*, 1991-1998
CJ, Zoe and Morgan face their own battles, from whom to please, to wanting a best girlfriend, to the fear of speaking up in class.

321

JAMILA GAVIN

Coram Boy
(New York: Farrar Straus Giroux, 2001)

Subject(s): Kidnapping; Slavery; Social Conditions
Age range(s): Grades 7-10
Major character(s): Thomas Coram, Historical Figure; Otis Gardiner, Con Artist; Meshak Gardiner, Mentally Challenged Person; Alexander Ashbrook, Musician
Time period(s): 18th century (1740s)
Locale(s): England

Summary: In the eighteenth century Captain Thomas Coram establishes a hospital for abandoned children, and mothers from all walks of life leave their children with him, knowing they will be well tended. Building upon that name, the shifty peddler Otis Gardiner, called the "Coram Man," offers to take unwanted children to the Coram Hospital, for a fee. He collects the fee but buries the babies and sells the older children into slavery, an act in which his simple-minded son Meshak unwillingly helps him. One baby seems different to Meshak—the child of a young girl who is impregnated by Alexander, a musician who runs away from home rather than abide by his father's rules. Meshak rescues this special child and sees that he's raised as a real Coram boy. When the boy is eight, his musical talent is apparent and his life comes full circle when he's apprenticed to his real father, though more

obstacles confront them before the two realize they're father and son. (336 pages)

Where it's reviewed:
Booklist, December 15, 2001, page 722
Kliatt, September 2001, page 6
Publishers Weekly, September 17, 2001, page 81
School Library Journal, November 2001, page 154
Voice of Youth Advocates, December 2001, page 358

Awards the book has won:
Whitbread Award/Children's Book, 2000
Publishers Weekly Best Children's Books, 2001

Other books by the same author:
Children Just Like Me: Our Favorite Stories, 1997
Out of India, 1997

Other books you might like:
Charles Dickens, *Oliver Twist*, 1837-1838
An abused runaway, Oliver joins up with the nefarious team of The Artful Dodger and Fagin.
Berlie Doherty, *Street Child*, 1994
Based on the story of a real orphan, Jim becomes homeless when his parents die. The intervention of Barnie, who runs a school for the destitute, saves his life.
Fatima Shaik, *Melitte*, 1997
Slave to a poor white farmer, Melitte learns enough from nearby plantation slaves to escape to what she hopes is a better life.

322

W. MICHAEL GEAR
KATHLEEN GEAR, Co-Author

Dark Inheritance
(New York: Warner, 2001)

Subject(s): Animals/Chimpanzees; Genetic Engineering
Age range(s): Grades 10-Adult
Major character(s): Jim Dutton, Anthropologist; Brett Dutton, 13-Year-Old; Umber, Chimpanzee (bonobo)
Time period(s): 2000s
Locale(s): England; Africa; Colorado

Summary: Anthropologist Jim Dutton's wife leaves him after their daughter Brett is born, so he brings her up along with Umber, a bonobo chimpanzee he's been asked to raise. Umber masters sign language, their computer, and speaking with a voice synthesizer keyboard making it obvious to Jim that Umber isn't like other chimps. The British pharmaceutical firm SAC that gave Jim the chimp is also the group that enhanced Umber with a human gene as they searched for ways to boost the intelligence of the bonobos. When her cleverness is recognized, Jim is asked to give her up, but that's like giving up a member of his family and he refuses, which puts Jim, Brett and Umber in danger. (519 pages)

Where it's reviewed:
Booklist, December 1, 2000, page 675
Kirkus Reviews, January 1, 2001, page 17
Publishers Weekly, February 5, 2001, page 65
School Library Journal, September 2001, page 259

Other books by the same author:
Raising Abel, 2002
Bone Walker, 2001
The Summoning God, 2000
The Visitant, 1999
People of the Masks, 1998

Other books you might like:
Michael Crichton, *Congo*, 1993
Scientists search the Congo region for information about the ancestors of apes, but find themselves under attack by gorillas.
Dean Koontz, *Watchers*, 1987
Two animals, altered through genetic experimentation, escape from their lab.
Maxine Kumin, *Quit Monks or Die!*, 1999
The animal rights group Mercy Bandits is angry over Dr. Baranoff's experiments with primates, but not angry enough to kill him. So who did?

ARTHUR GEISERT, Author/Illustrator

Nursery Crimes
(Boston: Walter Lorraine/Houghton Mifflin Company, 2001)

Subject(s): Trees; Farm Life; Robbers and Outlaws
Age range(s): Grades 2-4
Major character(s): Jambo, Pig, Businessman; Marva, Pig, Businesswoman; Voler, Pig, Thief
Time period(s): Indeterminate
Locale(s): Ames, Iowa

Summary: With their twelve children Jambo and Marva operate a successful topiary nursery with pumpkin sales and a salvage yard on the side just to make ends meet. When their highly prized, turkey-shaped trees are stolen as they sleep, the children carve more and devise a plan to catch the thief. Once again they awaken to find the trees gone but this time Marva's choice of trees and the weather conspire to solve the mystery of the tree thief. By visiting Voler's property with the sheriff Jambo and Marva can find their trees because the leaves changed color during the night. (32 pages)

Where it's reviewed:
Booklist, November 15, 2001, page 572
Bulletin of the Center for Children's Books, September 2001, page 13
Horn Book Guide, Spring 2002, page 43
Publishers Weekly, September 10, 2001, page 91
School Library Journal, November 2001, page 122

Other books by the same author:
The Etcher's Studio, 1997 (Publishers Weekly Best Children's Book)
After the Flood, 1994
Oink, Oink, 1993
The Ark, 1988

Other books you might like:
Mary Jane Auch, *Eggs Mark the Spot*, 1996
Pauline's artistic eggs provide the clue needed by the police to nab a burglar.

Judith Ross Enderle, *Nell Nugget and the Cow Caper*, 1996
Nell tracks her missing cow to Nasty Galoot's campfire and then devises a plan to recover the rustled animal.
Margie Palatini, *Mooseltoe*, 2000
Moose's family gets creative when he forgets to buy a Christmas tree and the tree lots are empty.

324

JEAN CRAIGHEAD GEORGE
TED RAND, Illustrator

Nutik & Amaroq Play Ball
(New York: HarperCollins Publishers, 2001)

Subject(s): Eskimos; Animals/Wolves; Playing
Age range(s): Grades K-2
Major character(s): Amaroq, Child, Eskimo; Nutik, Wolf
Time period(s): 2000s (2001)
Locale(s): Kangit, Arctic

Summary: Amaroq and Nutik would like to play ball on this beautiful summer day, but their football has disappeared, taken by pranksters. Nutik rejects all of Amaroq's suggestions and leads his pal across the tundra on a walk that takes them so far from their village that Amaroq is afraid he's lost. Finally Nutik stops at an old oil barrel abandoned on the tundra and encourages Amaroq to reach inside. When the boy does, he finds the missing football! Amaroq knows that he can trust Nutik's nose to get them home in time for dinner too. (34 pages)

Where it's reviewed:
Booklist, May 15, 2001, page 1757
Bulletin of the Center for Children's Books, July 2001, page 408
Horn Book Guide, Fall 2001, page 255
Publishers Weekly, July 2, 2001, page 78
School Library Journal, July 2001, page 81

Other books by the same author:
Nutik, the Wolf Pup, 2001
Snow Bear, 1999
Arctic Son, 1997

Other books you might like:
Robert J. Blake, *Akiak: A Tale from Iditarod*, 1997
Injury forces lead-dog Akiak from the race, but she tracks her team for days knowing her experience can help them get on the path to victory.
Jeanne Bushey, *A Sled Dog for Moshi*, 1994
Lead dog Nuna finds Moshi and a new friend trapped outside during a sudden snowstorm and leads them to safety.
Kay Winters, *Wolf Watch*, 1997
Poetic descriptions of the early life of four wolf pups in the den are complemented by illustrations showing what is happening outside.

325

JEAN CRAIGHEAD GEORGE
TED RAND, Illustrator

Nutik, the Wolf Pup
(New York: HarperCollins Publishers, 2001)

Subject(s): Animals/Wolves; Eskimos; Brothers and Sisters
Age range(s): Grades K-3
Major character(s): Amaroq, Eskimo, Brother (younger); Nutik, Wolf; Julie, Sister (older), Eskimo
Time period(s): Indeterminate Past
Locale(s): Arctic

Summary: As a favor to the wolf pack that saved her life, Julie brings home two sickly pups to nurse back to health with the agreement that the wolves will return for them when the pups are well. Julie cares for one and she entrusts Nutik to Amaroq's care. Despite his assurances that he will not fall in love with Nutik, Amaroq does. The two are like brothers romping across the tundra, howling together, playing and even sharing the same bearskin as they sleep. When the wolves arrive to claim their healthy pups Amaroq runs in the opposite direction with Nutik. The wolves come again and call to Nutik. This time Nutik tries to lead Amaroq to the pack, but Amaroq knows he cannot live with the wolves and he must let Nutik go. Amaroq's heart is broken and when he seeks the comfort of his bearskin the next day he finds Nutik inside waiting for the boy he loves. (36 pages)

Where it's reviewed:
Booklist, February 1, 2001, page 1055
Bulletin of the Center for Children's Books, July 2001, page 408
Horn Book Guide, Fall 2001, page 255
Publishers Weekly, January 8, 2001, page 68
School Library Journal, March 2001, page 208

Awards the book has won:
Notable Social Studies Trade Books for Young People, 2002

Other books by the same author:
Nutik & Amaroq Play Ball, 2001
Snow Bear, 1999
Look to the North: A Wolf Pup Diary, 1997 (IRA Children's Choice)

Other books you might like:
Jeanne Bushey, *A Sled Dog for Moshi*, 1994
  Moshi's father promises her one of the pups from lead dog Nuna's litter.
Mischa Damjan, *Atuk: A Story*, 1990
  Atuk learns that revenge is not the answer to his grief when wolves kill his puppy.
Joyce Milton, *Wild, Wild Wolves*, 1992
  A nonfiction beginning reader gives factual information about wolves.

326

ADELE GERAS
TONY ROSS, Illustrator

The Cats of Cuckoo Square: Two Stories
(New York: Delacorte Press, 2001)

Subject(s): Animals/Cats; Pets; Animals, Treatment of
Age range(s): Grades 2-4
Major character(s): Blossom, Cat; Perkins, Cat
Time period(s): 1990s (1997)
Locale(s): England

Summary: In the homes surrounding Cuckoo Square live four cats with their respective families. The first of two stories introduces Blossom and her family as they endure a visit from an obnoxious young relative who torments Blossom. With help from the other cats and her young owner Blossom plots an appropriate revenge for the youngster's mistreatment. In the second story Perkins is used as an artist's model, much to his dismay because his young owner wants to win an art contest by submitting his portrait to the newspaper. Perkins does help her win recognition, but not in the way anyone expects. Originally published in Great Britain in 1997. (190 pages)

Where it's reviewed:
Booklist, September 1, 2001, page 104
Bulletin of the Center for Children's Books, December 2001, page 139
Publishers Weekly, October 22, 2001, page 77
School Library Journal, December 2001, page 102

Other books by the same author:
The Fabulous Fantoras: Book Two: Family Photographs, 1999
The Fabulous Fantoras: Book One: Family Files, 1998
Little Swan, 1995

Other books you might like:
Julie Andrews Edwards, *Little Bo: The Story of Bonnie Boadicea*, 1999
  An abandoned kitten faces cold and hunger before being found by a sailor who sneaks her aboard his ship.
Elke Heidenreich, *Nero Corleone: A Cat's Story*, 1997
  Bold Nero, an independent farm cat, protects his shy sister Rosa by allowing a vacationing couple to adopt them as their family pets.
Ursula K. Le Guin, *Wonderful Alexander and the Catwings*, 1994
  A big, bossy, curious kitten's unexpected adventures lead to his introduction to cats with wings.

327

ADELE GERAS

Troy
(New York: Harcourt, 2001)

Subject(s): Mythology; Love; War
Age range(s): Grades 9-Adult
Major character(s): Marpessa, Sister, Artisan; Xanthe, Sister, Nurse; Iason, Horse Trainer

Time period(s): Indeterminate Past
Locale(s): Troy, Turkey

Summary: After ten years of siege, the great city of Troy is about to fall. The inhabitants know that life is grim, but they still hope for victory. Even the most humble of city-dwellers is of interest to the gods as the tragedy they have arranged draws to its conclusion. Two sisters, Xanthe, a companion to Helen, and Marpessa, a part-time nurse and nursery-maid to Hector's baby son, are the focus of some of these last minute attentions. Xanthe is hit by Cupid's arrow and falls in love with a warrior she is nursing, but the goddess of love makes sure the warrior is obsessed with her sister, Marpessa. Iason is in love with Xanthe, but the gods of war and weapons haunt him. Marpessa loves her sister, but is helpless when the goddess decides that Marpessa, too, will relieve her boredom by lust for the warrior. Indeed, the gods and goddesses are busy with the great and small of Troy, but the explanations they offer for their conduct are often inscrutable. As the city burns, the sisters are taken captive and sail to Greece while Iason is left behind to survive. (340 pages)

Where it's reviewed:
Booklist, April 1, 2001, page 1482
Horn Book Magazine, July 2001, page 450
New York Times Book Review, July 15, 2001, page 25
Publishers Weekly, May 7, 2001, page 248

Awards the book has won:
ALA Best Books for Young Adults, 2002
Smithsonian's Notable Books for Children, 2001

Other books by the same author:
Pictures of the Night, 1993
Watching the Roses, 1992
The Tower Room, 1990

Other books you might like:
Vivien Alcock, *Singer to the Sea God*, 1993
    Perseus needs a way to kill the dreadful Gorgon, a creature with snakes for hair.
Roberta Gellis, *Bull God*, 2000
    A sister's love for her little brother, despite his bull's head on a child's body, is not enough to tame him.
H.M. Hoover, *The Dawn Palace: the Story of Medea*, 1988
    Medea explains the pain that could lead a mother to murder her own children.
Clamence McLaren, *Inside the Walls of Troy: A Novel of the Women Who Lived the Trojan War*, 1996
    A tale of the fall of Troy from the perspective of Helen and Cassandra.

328

NATALE GHENT

Piper
(Custer, WA: Orca Books, 2001)

Subject(s): Animals/Dogs; Farm Life; Cousins
Age range(s): Grades 5-7
Major character(s): Wesley Philips, 11-Year-Old; Cassel Graham, Child, Cousin (of Wesley); Cindy Graham, Aunt; Norman Graham, Uncle, Teacher; Triblue's Spitfire "Piper", Dog (Australian shepherd)

Time period(s): 2000s
Locale(s): Picton, Ontario, Canada

Summary: After Wesley's father dies, she and her mother leave their California home and move in with Aunt Cindy and Uncle Norman on their working farm in Canada. Wesley shares a bedroom with her cousin Cassel and the two seem to do nothing but fight; Wesley's angry about her father's death and Cassel resents sharing her room. The two call a truce to watch one of the Australian shepherd dogs give birth to puppies and when the runt is born and isn't breathing, Wesley begs her aunt to save it. Not wanting either of the girls to become attached to a dog that will be sold, Aunt Cindy doesn't allow pets on the farm, but makes an exception for the runt. Wesley feeds and cares for him, training Piper as a competitive herd dog, until the day the two are attacked by coyotes. (176 pages)

Where it's reviewed:
Booklist, March 1, 2001, page 1278
Quill & Quire, January 2001, page 36
Resource Links, December 2001, page 11

Other books you might like:
Lynn Hall, *The Soul of the Silver Dog*, 1992
    Cory pours her heart into training blind, former Bedlington terrier champion Sterling for competition on the obstacle course.
Hilary Hyland, *The Wreck of the Ethie*, 1999
    The Newfoundland dog Skipper swims out to a sinking ship, carrying a rope in his mouth, which allows the passengers to come ashore by a breeches buoy.
Donald McCaig, *Nop's Hope*, 1994
    Losing her husband and child in a car accident, Penny is given a border collie named Hope, which she trains for sheepdog trials.
Sylvia McNicoll, *Bringing Up Beauty*, 2000
    Sometimes feeling left out, Elizabeth finds the perfect companion in the black lab Beauty whom she trains as a guide dog for Canine Vision Canada.

329

FAYE GIBBONS
SHERRY MEIDELL, Illustrator

Emma Jo's Song
(Honesdale, PA: Boyds Mills Press, 2001)

Subject(s): Singing; Family; Self-Confidence
Age range(s): Grades K-3
Major character(s): Emma Jo Puckett, Sister; Rip, Dog; Tom Puckett, Brother (older)
Time period(s): Indeterminate Past
Locale(s): Georgia

Summary: Emma Jo feels like the outcast in a musical family because she just can't seem to carry a tune. Each time she tries to secretly practice her song Rip begins howling beside her giving Tom a good laugh but causing Emma Jo no end of frustration. On the day of the family reunion the dog is left on the farm, or so they think. After a day of singing, playing, and eating, Emma Jo surprises Tom by accepting his challenge to sing in front of the relatives. Tom accompanies Emma Jo on the piano and, before she's completed more than a few notes, Rip jumps in the window to add his voice. Soon Emma Jo's surrounded by siblings and cousins all singing with gusto. (32 pages)

Where it's reviewed:
Booklist, April 1, 2001, page 1478
Children's Bookwatch, February 2001, page 3
Horn Book Guide, Fall 2001, page 255
School Library Journal, May 2001, page 121

Other books by the same author:
Mama and Me and the Model T, 1999
Mountain Wedding, 1996
Night in the Barn, 1995

Other books you might like:
Hoong Yee Lee Krakauer, *Rabbit Mooncakes*, 1994
    Hoong Wei worries that she will make mistakes during the piano duet she's to play with her older sister for a large family gathering.
Patricia Polacco, *My Rotten Redheaded Older Brother*, 1994
    Just once Patricia would like to get the better of her teasing brother.
Cynthia Rylant, *The Relatives Came*, 1985
    A Caldecott Honor Book celebrates childhood memories of the joyful confusion of a houseful of relatives.

330

PATRICIA REILLY GIFF

All the Way Home

(New York: Delacorte, 2001)

Subject(s): Friendship; Self-Acceptance; Sports/Baseball
Age range(s): Grades 4-6
Major character(s): Mariel Manning, Adoptee; Brick Tiernan, Runaway; Loretta, Nurse; Claude, Aged Person, Farmer (of apples)
Time period(s): 1940s
Locale(s): Windy Hill, New York; New York, New York (Brooklyn)

Summary: The tiny town of Windy Hill links Mariel and Brick in this story set in the early 1940s. A polio victim at the age of only four, Mariel is abandoned by her mother at the hospital for children with polio where she is nursed by Loretta, who later adopts her and brings her home to Brooklyn. Brick and his parents live in Windy Hill where they plan to raise apples, but a fire destroys their orchard and sends them in three different directions, with Brick sent to Brooklyn to stay with his parents' friend Loretta. After a few uneasy days, the love of the Dodgers makes it easy for Mariel and Brick to talk to one another and they become friends, revealing their deepest concerns. For Mariel, it's finding her birth mother while for Brick it's returning to Windy Hill to help his aged French neighbor Claude harvest his apples. Together the two manage to achieve their dreams, though perhaps not in the way they envisioned. (169 pages)

Where it's reviewed:
Horn Book, November 2001, page 747
Publishers Weekly, October 8, 2001, page 65
School Library Journal, September 2001, page 224

Other books by the same author:
Nory Ryan's Song, 2000
Lily's Crossing, 1997

Other books you might like:
Iain Lawrence, *Ghost Boy*, 2000
    Teased about his albinism, Harold runs away to join the circus and teaches the elephants to play baseball, which helps his confidence.
Richard Peck, *A Long Way from Chicago*, 1998
    Joey and his sister Mary Alice hear many warm, funny stories and learn unusual lessons during the summers they spend with their grandmother.
Tim Wynne-Jones, *The Maestro*, 1996
    Rather than stay with his abusive father, Burl runs into the Canadian wilderness where a gifted musician befriends him.

331

VANESSA GILL-BROWN
MANDY STANLEY, Illustrator

Rufferella

(New York: Scholastic, Inc., 2001)

Subject(s): Animals/Dogs; Pets; Human Behavior
Age range(s): Grades K-2
Major character(s): Diamante, Child; Ruff/Rufferella, Dog, Singer
Time period(s): 2000s (2000)
Locale(s): England

Summary: Diamante so loves reading *Cinderella* that she decides to take on the role of the fairy godmother and turn her dog into a human. Lacking a magic wand, Diamante decides to simply teach Ruff how to behave like a human. She dresses her pet in human clothes, adds makeup and styles her ''hair.'' Lessons in eating, walking, drinking from a cup and singing follow. Rufferella's unique voice is so admired that she is invited to perform on television and at parties. Diamante, now cast in the role of assistant to a star, is beginning to miss the companionship of her pet when an invitation to a ball comes from the Queen. The Queen's Ball is wonderful until dinner is served. When Rufferella sees her favorite food, sausages, she forgets everything she's learned and leaps onto the table to clean the platter. Ah well, it was time for Ruff and Diamante to go to the park for a game of catch anyway. Originally published in Great Britain in 2000. (28 pages)

Where it's reviewed:
Booklist, August 2001, page 2129
Horn Book Guide, Fall 2001, page 256
Magpies, November 2000, page 31
Publishers Weekly, February 26, 2001, page 86
School Library Journal, August 2001, page 147

Awards the book has won:
IRA Children's Choices, 2002

Other books you might like:
Diane Goode, *Cinderella: The Dog and Her Little Glass Slipper*, 2000
    Characters in this retelling of the traditional tale are various species of dog.

Merrill Markoe, *The Day My Dogs Became Guys*, 1999
   During an eclipse Carey's wish that his dogs could be human comes true, much to his regret.
William Wegman, *Cinderella*, 1993
   The classic fairy tale is recast with dogs playing all the roles, but Cinderella still loses her glass slipper.

332

RACHNA GILMORE

A Group of One
(New York: Holt, 2001)

Subject(s): Identity; Grandmothers; School Life
Age range(s): Grades 7-10
Major character(s): Tara Mehta, Student—High School, 15-Year-Old; Jeffrey "Jeff" MacKinley, Student—High School; Rohini Mehta, Mother (of Tara); Naniji Mehta, Grandmother
Time period(s): 2000s
Locale(s): Ottawa, Ontario, Canada

Summary: Born and raised in Ottawa, Tara considers herself a Canadian, though others regard her as an outsider because of her dark skin, a result of her Indian heritage. Actually, Tara knows little about life in India as her parents moved from there before she was born; all that changes when her father's mother arrives for a visit. Naniji is an activist who took a strong role in Gandhi's movement for independence from Britain and is shocked that her granddaughters know so little about this period of history. Though intrigued by Naniji's stories, Tara's really more interested in that cute new student Jeff and whether or not he likes her. She also feels guilty listening to Naniji because she knows that her grandmother has always disliked her mother's family for doing little during the Independence Movement and resented her mother Rohini for taking Naniji's son away to Canada. As Tara comes to like her grandmother, she's also able to see her parent's side and understand why they chose to leave India. Combining her new knowledge of her Indian heritage with her Canadian background, Tara realizes she's her own person and wants to be judged as "a group of one." (184 pages)

Where it's reviewed:
Booklist, May 1, 2001, page 1675
Horn Book, September 2001, page 583
Publishers Weekly, July 9, 2001, page 69
School Library Journal, July 2001, page 108
Voice of Youth Advocates, August 2001, page 201

Other books you might like:
Linda Crew, *Children of the River*, 1989
   Forced by the Khymer Rouge to give up her life in Cambodia, adjusting to American culture is difficult for Sundara.
Gayle Friesen, *Men of Stone*, 2000
   When Ben hears of his great-aunt Frieda's life under Stalin's regime in Russia, he realizes the importance of being true to oneself.
Sherry Garland, *Shadow of the Dragon*, 1993
   Danny has difficulty reconciling his Vietnamese heritage with life in America.
Mitali Perkins, *The Sunita Experiment*, 1993
   Just as East Indian Sunita begins to feel totally Ameri-canized, her grandparents arrive for a yearlong visit and Sunita's whole life changes.
Indi Rana, *The Roller Birds of Rampur*, 1993
   Raised in Britain but of Indian heritage, Sheila returns to India where she is discomfited by the role of Indian women.

333

DEBI GLIORI, Author/Illustrator

Flora's Blanket
(New York: Orchard Books, 2001)

Subject(s): Bedtime; Animals/Rabbits; Lost and Found
Age range(s): Preschool
Major character(s): Flora, Rabbit, Daughter
Time period(s): Indeterminate
Locale(s): Fictional Country

Summary: Poor Flora! She can't sleep because she can't find her blanket. Although her siblings each offer to share their blankets with her Flora will not be soothed by anything other than her own so the family begins searching. They search inside and outside but cannot find the blanket. However, Flora does fall asleep during the search and her parents put her into their bed and climb in to sleep too. Then Flora's father notices the lump under his pillow and pulls out Flora's blanket. Finally, everyone can sleep! (32 pages)

Where it's reviewed:
Booklist, May 15, 2001, page 1757
Horn Book Guide, Fall 2001, page 231
Publishers Weekly, April 9, 2001, page 73
School Library Journal, July 2001, page 81
Smithsonian Magazine, November 2001, page 118

Awards the book has won:
Smithsonian's Notable Books for Children, 2001

Other books by the same author:
Mr. Bear's Vacation, 2000 (Smithsonian Magazine's Notable Books for Children)
Mr. Bear's New Baby, 1999 (Smithsonian Magazine's Notable Books for Children)
No Matter What, 1999

Other books you might like:
Paulette Bourgeois, *Franklin's Blanket*, 1997
   Franklin the Turtle loses his favorite blanket and can't sleep without it.
Jules Feiffer, *I Lost My Bear*, 1998
   A young girl who loses her favorite bear gets very little help from her family with her search for it.
Brigitte Weninger, *What's the Matter, Davy?*, 1998
   Davy's supportive family helps him cope when he loses his favorite stuffed animal, Nicky while playing outside.

334

DEBI GLIORI, Author/Illustrator

Polar Bolero: A Bedtime Dance
(San Diego: Harcourt, Inc., 2001)

Subject(s): Bedtime; Dancing; Stories in Rhyme

Age range(s): Preschool-Grade 1
Major character(s): Unnamed Character, Bear, Narrator
Time period(s): Indeterminate
Locale(s): Fictional Country

Summary: Feeling too warm to sleep a young polar bear slips out of bed and out of his house to the place where the ''wide-awake'' gather. On this grassy knoll children and animals, aided by flying bugs, birds and balloons dance the Polar Bolero in their dreams. The activity tires them and the clouds remind them of soft beds so they all drift back to their own beds for some sleep. (32 pages)

Where it's reviewed:
Booklist, May 1, 2001, page 1690
Horn Book Guide, Fall 2001, page 231
Kirkus Reviews, April 1, 2001, page 497
Publishers Weekly, May 7, 2001, page 246
School Library Journal, June 2001, page 114

Other books by the same author:
Mr. Bear to the Rescue, 2000
Mr. Bear's New Baby, 1999 (Smithsonian's Notable Books for Children)
The Snow Lambs, 1996

Other books you might like:
Michael Foreman, *Dad! I Can't Sleep*, 1995
    This little panda bear's dad offers many going-to-sleep suggestions but none are effective.
Mem Fox, *Time for Bed*, 1993
    Appealing illustrations and comforting verse show the whole wide world going to sleep.
Martin Waddell, *Can't You Sleep, Little Bear?*, 1988
    Big Bear comforts Little Bear when a fear of the dark keeps him from dozing off.

`335`

DEBI GLIORI

Pure Dead Magic
(New York: Knopf, 2001)

Subject(s): Witches and Witchcraft; Magic; Family Life
Age range(s): Grades 4-7
Major character(s): Titus Strega-Borgia, 12-Year-Old; Pandora Strega-Borgia, Child; Damp Strega-Borgia, Baby; Luciano Strega-Borgia, Father (of Titus, Pandora and Damp); Flora McLachlan, Child-Care Giver; Lucifer di S'Embowelli Borgia, Brother (of Luciano)
Time period(s): 2000s
Locale(s): Auchenlochtermuchty, Scotland

Summary: Siblings Titus, Pandora and their baby sister Damp adjust to their new nanny, Mrs. McLachlan; their mother returns to witchcraft school and their father is kidnapped by his evil half-brother Don. On top of that crisis, when Pandora borrows her mother's magic wand, baby Damp somehow manages to enter cyberspace. Now it's up to the family spider, Tarantella, to spin the best web of all as she enters the Internet to retrieve Damp. At the same time, Titus and Pandora try to rescue their father while evading assassins who try to kill Titus in this crazy fantasy, the first in a trilogy from this author. (182 pages)

Where it's reviewed:
Booklist, August 2001, page 2118
Kirkus Reviews, August 1, 2001, page 1122
Publishers Weekly, August 27, 2001, page 85
School Library Journal, September 2001, page 225
Voice of Youth Advocates, December 2001, page 369

Other books you might like:
Eva Ibbotson, *Island of the Aunts*, 2000
    When Aunts Etta, Coral and Myrtle need help caring for their creatures, they return to England and kidnap several children to be their assistants.
Diana Wynne Jones, *Castle in the Air*, 1991
    Atop his magic carpet, Abdullah sees his love captured by an evil dijnn, loses his carpet, finds a genie and winds up in a floating castle.
Dian Curtis Regan, *Monsters in Cyberspace*, 1997
    Rilla loves belonging to the Monster-of-the-Month Club, but only she and a friend know that the monsters occasionally come to life.
J.K. Rowling, *The Harry Potter Series*, 1998-
    Raised by his aunt and uncle, Harry is thrilled to be invited to attend Hogwarts School and begin his studies of wizardry.
Lemony Snicket, *Unfortunate Events Series*, 1999-
    The Baudelaire children live up to the name of the series as their lives go from bad to worse after their parents are killed in a fire.

`336`

CHRISTOPHER GOLDEN

Prowlers
(New York: Pocket Books/Pulse, 2001)

Series: Prowlers. Number 1
Subject(s): Murder; Serial Killers
Age range(s): Grades 9-12
Major character(s): Arthur ''Artie'' Carroll, Victim; Jack Dwyer, 19-Year-Old, Saloon Keeper/Owner
Time period(s): 2000s
Locale(s): Boston, Massachusetts

Summary: There are new beast killers in town, not vampires or werewolves, but a group called the ''prowlers,'' vicious beasts who pretend to be humans. Scattered across several cities, they're uniting under the leadership of Owen Tanzer and they feast on humans. Jack Dwyer is told of them after his best friend Artie and their mutual friend Kate are murdered and Artie returns from Ghostland to tell him about his murderers. Eager to retaliate for the death of his best friend, and keep Boston safe, Jack goes in search of the prowlers. (288 pages)

Where it's reviewed:
Kliatt, November 1, 2001, page 20
Science Fiction Chronicle, April 2001, page 39

Other books by the same author:
Wild Things, 2002 (Prowlers, Number 4)
Laws of Nature, 2001 (Prowlers, Number 2)
Predator and Prey, 2001 (Prowlers, Number 3)

Other books you might like:
Jesse Harris, *Vampire's Kiss*, 1993
    Hoping to tap into McKenzie's psychic powers, vampire Michael prepares a potion for her to drink so that she can join him in vampirism.
Tanya Huff, *Blood Price*, 1991
    Vicki and Henry, ex-police officer and vampire respectively, pair up and offer a supernatural bent to crime solving.
Dean Koontz, *Fear Nothing*, 1998
    Chris hastens to put his mother's photo in his father's casket prior to his cremation, but discovers the body is that of someone else.
Patricia Windsor, *The Christmas Killer*, 1991
    Victims of a serial killer reappear in Rose Potter's dreams, asking for help and giving clues to the location of their bodies.

337

JENNIFER P. GOLDFINGER, Author/Illustrator

A Fish Named Spot

(Boston: Little, Brown and Company, 2001)

Subject(s): Pets; Behavior; Fantasy
Age range(s): Grades K-2
Major character(s): Simon, Child, Son; Spot, Fish; Loretta, Aunt, Traveler
Time period(s): 2000s (2001)
Locale(s): United States

Summary: In the author's first book Aunt Loretta returns from a trip to Africa with a fish from Lake Tanganyika as a pet for Simon. Simon names the fish Spot for its coloration and also for the dog he'd really like to have. Having no fish food, Simon gives Spot some dog biscuits and in the morning he discovers that Spot has outgrown his tank and is behaving rather like a dog. Simon enjoys playing with Spot but eventually Spot begins to revert back to fishy behavior. He still joins Simon for walks but now he does it from large jar that Simon pulls along. (32 pages)

Where it's reviewed:
Booklist, July 2001, page 2019
Horn Book Guide, Fall 2001, page 256
Kirkus Reviews, February 1, 2001, page 183
Publishers Weekly, April 9, 2001, page 74
School Library Journal, June 2001, page 114

Other books you might like:
Sarajo Frieden, *The Care and Feeding of Fish*, 1996
    Loulou's fishy birthday gift from Great Aunt Eclair changes overnight into a large, humanlike companion that satisfies her desire for adventure.
Steven Kellogg, *The Mysterious Tadpole*, 1977
    The rapid growth of his pet tadpole makes Louis wonder just what it will become.
Jama Kim Rattigan, *Truman's Aunt Farm*, 1994
    Truman's eccentric Aunt Fran sends him an ant farm for his birthday that actually yields an abundance of aunts.

338

BARBARA DIAMOND GOLDIN
ANIK MCGRORY, Illustrator

A Mountain of Blintzes

(San Diego: Gulliver Books/Harcourt, Inc., 2001)

Subject(s): Holidays, Jewish; Food; Family Life
Age range(s): Grades K-3
Major character(s): Sarah, Mother, Spouse; Max, Father, Spouse; Moe, Son, Brother (oldest)
Time period(s): 1920s
Locale(s): Catskill Mountains, New York

Summary: With five children, hard-working Sarah and Max never seem to have enough extra money to take care of holiday expenses. When Moe reminds them that Shavuot is only two weeks away Sarah and Max agree to a savings plan that should ensure them just enough money to buy the ingredients for the blintzes. Unfortunately, since each feels confident that the other is dropping extra earnings into the savings box no one actually saves anything and when the box is opened they discover it is empty. Fortunately, their children have been secretly assisting the village merchants in exchange for the ingredients and they have all they need to cook a mountain of Sarah's delicious blintzes to eat after all. (32 pages)

Where it's reviewed:
Booklist, March 1, 2001, page 1287
Horn Book Guide, Fall 2001, page 256
School Library Journal, April 2001, page 108

Other books by the same author:
Night Lights: A Sukkot Story, 1995
Cakes and Miracles: A Purim Tale, 1991
Just Enough Is Plenty: A Hanukkah Tale, 1988

Other books you might like:
David A. Adler, *A Picture Book of Jewish Holidays*, 1981
    An illustrated nonfiction title briefly describes many Jewish holidays including Shavuot.
Adele Geras, *My Grandmother's Stories: A Collection of Jewish Folk Tales*, 1990
    An award-winning collection of stories told by a grandmother to her granddaughter includes customs and recipes.
Isaac Bashevis Singer, *Stories for Children*, 1984
    Yiddish tradition inspires this collection of tales.

339

TARO GOMI, Author/Illustrator

I Lost My Dad

(Brooklyn, NY: Kane/Miller Book Publishers, 2001)

Subject(s): Fathers and Sons; Missing Persons; Department Stores
Age range(s): Grades K-1
Major character(s): Unnamed Character, Child, Son; Dad, Father
Time period(s): 1980s
Locale(s): Japan

Summary: While shopping in the toy department of a large store, a young boy loses his father. Each time the son glimpses a hat, shoes or tie similar to what Dad was wearing, a closer inspection shows that he's not found the man he seeks. Finally, while going up the escalator, he spots Dad going down and the two are reunited in this first American edition of a title originally published in 1983 in Japan. (32 pages)

Where it's reviewed:
Booklist, March 1, 2001, page 1287
Horn Book, July 2001, page 438
Publishers Weekly, February 26, 2001, page 85
Riverbank Review, Winter 2001-2002, page 28
School Library Journal, May 2001, page 121

Other books by the same author:
Bus Stops, 1999
The Crocodile and the Dentist, 1994
Everyone Poops, 1993
Who Ate It?, 1992

Other books you might like:
Diane Johnston Hamm, *Laney's Lost Momma*, 1991
    Following a plan helps Laney and her mom find each other when Laney's mom becomes "lost" while shopping in the department store.
Grace Maccarone, *The Class Trip*, 1999
    In this easy reader Sam and his class become separated while on a trip to the zoo.
Shirley Parenteau, *I'll Bet You Thought I Was Lost*, 1981
    In a large grocery store, Sandy and his father try to find each other.
Francesca Simon, *Where Are You?*, 1998
    While shopping with his grandfather, Harry goes off alone and then must search to locate his grandfather.

340

BETH GOOBIE

Before Wings

(Custer, WA: Orca Book Publishers, 2001)

Subject(s): Camps and Camping; Supernatural; Aunts and Uncles
Age range(s): Grades 7-10
Major character(s): Adrien Wood, 15-Year-Old, Counselor (Camp Lakeshore); Erin Wood, Aunt (of Adrien), Administrator (owner of Camp Lakeshore); Paul Marchand, 15-Year-Old, Handyman (for Camp Lakeshore)
Time period(s): 2000s
Locale(s): Camp Lakeshore, Canada

Summary: After almost dying from a brain aneurysm two years ago, Adrien is obsessed with the thought she'll have a reoccurrence. For the summer, she decides to work in the camp store at Camp Lakeshore, a camp owned by her no-nonsense Aunt Erin who doesn't believe in mollycoddling her. The first day at camp Adrien meets Paul, the young kid who helps out around the camp, and finds he dreams of his own death; with a bond like that, it's inevitable they become friends. Adrien's near-death experience has bestowed supernatural abilities on her and she's able to see spirits, specifically the spirits of five young girls who are somehow tied into twenty years of pain and grief for her aunt. Between a growing relationship with Paul, and her wish to free her aunt

of her grief, Adrien stops thinking only of herself and her possible demise and begins to really, really enjoy life in this work by a Canadian author. (203 pages)

Where it's reviewed:
Booklist, March 15, 2001, page 1391
Horn Book, March 2001, page 207
Kliatt, March 2001, page 10
School Library Journal, April 2001, page 140
Voice of Youth Advocates, April 2001, page 51

Awards the book has won:
Young Adult Canadian Book Award, 2002

Other books by the same author:
The Dream Where the Losers Go, 1999
The Colors of Carol Molev, 1998
I'm Not Convinced, 1997
The Good, the Bad and the Suicidal, 1997
Could I Have My Body Back Now, Please, 1996

Other books you might like:
Brock Cole, *The Goats*, 1987
    After fellow campers play a cruel joke on Laura and Howie, the two run away for several days and manage very well on their own.
John Herman, *Deep Waters*, 1998
    When Andy looks back on his summer camp experience, he still isn't sure if an accident or a murder took place.
Robert Lipsyte, *Summer Rules*, 1981
    Bobby adjusts to life as a camp counselor, until he meets Sheila and then none of the camp rules make sense.
Norma Fox Mazer, *Heartbeat*, 1989
    Tod's in love with Adam's girlfriend, but feelings change when Adam is diagnosed with cancer.
Lurlene McDaniel, *Too Young to Die*, 1989
    Melissa accepts the fact that she has terminal leukemia.

341

DIANE GOODE, Author/Illustrator

Tiger Trouble!

(New York: Blue Sky Press/Scholastic Inc., 2001)

Subject(s): Animals/Tigers; Pets; Burglary
Age range(s): Grades K-3
Major character(s): Jack, Child; Lily, Tiger; Fifi, Dog; Mr. Mud, Landlord
Time period(s): Indeterminate Past
Locale(s): New York, New York (River Street)

Summary: Lily and Jack do everything together and plan to continue doing so but Mr. Mud, new owner of their apartment building, has other ideas. As soon as Mr. Mud and Fifi move in all cats are given notice of eviction. Lily and Jack can't think of a way for Lily to stay, but a burglary in Mr. Mud's apartment gives Lily the opportunity to prove her value to Mr. Mud. By rescuing Fifi and recovering Mr. Mud's belongings Lily earns a long-term lease. (40 pages)

Where it's reviewed:
Booklist, October 1, 2001, page 325
Horn Book Guide, Spring 2002, page 43
Kirkus Reviews, September 1, 2001, page 1290
Publishers Weekly, October 1, 2001, page 62

School Library Journal, December 2001, page 102

Other books by the same author:
Cinderella: The Dog and Her Little Glass Slipper, 2000
The Dinosaur's New Clothes, 1999
Mama's Perfect Present, 1996

Other books you might like:
Debra Barracca, *Maxi, the Hero*, 1991
Maxi proves himself to be not just any dog when he apprehends a purse snatcher. Sal Barracca, co-author.
Dav Pilkey, *Dog Breath: The Horrible Trouble with Hally Tosis*, 1994
The Tosis family is ready to get rid of Hally until their pet's worst feature proves to be the undoing of two burglars.
John Stadler, *The Cats of Mrs. Calamari*, 1997
A cat-hating manager takes over Mrs. Calamari's apartment building, forcing her to devise ingenious ways to hide her many cats.

342

JOAN ELIZABETH GOODMAN
DOMINIC CATALANO, Illustrator

Bernard Goes to School

(Honesdale, PA: Boyds Mills Press, 2001)

Subject(s): Animals/Elephants; Schools; Family
Age range(s): Preschool-Kindergarten
Major character(s): Bernard, Elephant, Preschooler; Miss Brody, Elephant, Teacher; Emily, Elephant, Preschooler
Time period(s): Indeterminate
Locale(s): Fictional Country

Summary: Bernard's ready to go home before he sets foot in the classroom. His parents try to interest him in entering the room and staying for school by involving themselves in the play while Bernard stands alone. Miss Brody seeks his help feeding the fish and then introduces him to Emily, suggesting that together they choose names for the fish. By the time Bernard finishes he's feeling more comfortable and he tries to convince his parents to stop playing and leave. (32 pages)

Where it's reviewed:
Booklist, October 1, 2001, page 305
Bulletin of the Center for Children's Books, September 2001, page 15
Horn Book Guide, Spring 2002, page 18
Kirkus Reviews, August 1, 2001, page 1122
School Library Journal, August 2001, page 147

Other books by the same author:
Bernard's Nap, 1999
Bernard's Bath, 1996

Other books you might like:
Paulette Bourgeois, *Franklin Goes to School*, 1995
Friends help Franklin overcome his fears of entering school for the first time.
Nancy Carlson, *Look Out Kindergarten, Here I Come!*, 1999
Henry's enthusiasm for school wanes as he approaches the building.
Margaret Wild, *Tom Goes to Kindergarten*, 2000
Tom's parents enjoy his first day of school so much that

they are disappointed that he does not need them to stay with him the second day also.

343

NANCY PRICE GRAFF

A Long Way Home

(New York: Clarion, 2001)

Subject(s): Courage; Single Parent Families; War
Age range(s): Grades 5-8
Major character(s): Riley Griffin, 7th Grader; Sam Mitchell, Carpenter; Kate Griffin, Widow, Single Mother (of Riley)
Time period(s): 2000s
Locale(s): Sharon, Vermont

Summary: After his mother is widowed, she and Riley move back to her father's home in the small Vermont town where she was raised. Riley misses his friends and is unhappy when his mother's high school sweetheart keeps coming by, especially since Sam is the town outcast. Riley learns that Sam was discharged from the army during the Vietnam War because he refused to carry a weapon, and has suffered from the townspeople's displeasure ever since. A trip with Sam to Gettysburg to see where Riley's relative Silas Griffin battled helps Riley better understand the different types of courage required in times of war in this first novel. (200 pages)

Where it's reviewed:
Book Report, November 2001, page 60
Booklist, November 15, 2001, page 566
Bulletin of the Center for Children's Books, December 2001, page 141
School Library Journal, October 2001, page 155

Other books you might like:
Susan Hart Lindquist, *Summer Soldiers*, 1999
Because he doesn't believe in war, Mr. Morgan stays home on his farm, but shows his courage when he gives his life to save some drowning horses.
Carolyn Reeder, *Shades of Gray*, 1989
Orphan Will Page has a hard time living with his Uncle Jed knowing that Jed didn't fight for either side in the Civil War where Will's father was killed.
Jerry Spinelli, *Wringer*, 1997
Palmer dreads the year he's old enough to wring the necks of wounded pigeons at his town's annual pigeon shoot.

344

BOB GRAHAM, Author/Illustrator

Let's Get a Pup! Said Kate

(Cambridge, MA: Candlewick Press, 2001)

Subject(s): Animals/Dogs; Pets; Animals, Treatment of
Age range(s): Grades K-2
Major character(s): Kate, Child, Daughter; Mom, Mother, Spouse; Dad, Father, Spouse
Time period(s): 2000s (2001)
Locale(s): England

Summary: Kate awakens one summer morning with the idea to get a pup so her feet can have the company in bed that they've missed since the family cat died last winter. Mom and Dad agree to visit the animal shelter with Kate and they find a perfect pup. They also spot an older dog that tugs at their heartstrings, but they leave her behind. The first night at home with the puppy no one sleeps, but it may be memories of the older dog and not the pup's crying that bothers everyone. In the morning they return to the shelter to bring home one more dog and now everyone's ideas for a dog can be fulfilled. (32 pages)

Where it's reviewed:
Booklist, July 2001, page 2009
Bulletin of the Center for Children's Books, September 2001, page 16
Horn Book, September 2001, page 572
Riverbank Review, Winter 2001-2002, page 28
School Library Journal, July 2001, page 81

Awards the book has won:
ALA Notable Children's Books, 2002
Bulletin of the Center for Children's Books Blue Ribbon, 2001

Other books by the same author:
Max, 2000 (Publishers Weekly Best Book)
Benny: An Adventure Story, 1999 (School Library Journal Best Book)
Queenie, One of the Family, 1997

Other books you might like:
William Cole, *Have I Got Dogs!*, 1996
    A rhyming story describes different types of dogs.
Isabelle Harper, *Our New Puppy*, 1996
    The other family pets, including older dog Rosie, are slow to adjust to the new puppy that intrudes on their peaceful life.
Marc Simont, *The Stray Dog*, 2001
    After a sleepless night a family returns to the previous day's picnic spot to claim a stray dog as their own.

345

RHONDA GOWLER GREENE
JASON WOLFF, Illustrator

Jamboree Day
(New York: Orchard Books, 2001)

Subject(s): Animals; Stories in Rhyme
Age range(s): Grades K-2
Major character(s): Little Tree Frog, Frog
Time period(s): Indeterminate
Locale(s): Fictional Country

Summary: The jungle is rocking for Jamboree Day, a lively event that's held every May. Little Tree Frog with his megaphone shouts the news to all the animals. Hopping, flying, floating, bouncing, marching or leaping the animals travel to the jungle spot where the lively music is set to begin. Games, dancing, food and carnival rides entertain all ages until the day ends and as the stars appear the jungle animals depart, until next year. (32 pages)

Where it's reviewed:
Horn Book Guide, Spring 2002, page 44
Publishers Weekly, November 12, 2001, page 58

School Library Journal, January 2002, page 100

Other books by the same author:
Eek! Creak! Snicker, Sneak, 2002
The Stable Where Jesus Was Born, 1999
Barnyard Song, 1997 (School Library Journal Best Books)

Other books you might like:
Maryann Cocca-Leffler, *Jungle Halloween*, 2000
    A rhyming tale describes the jungle animal's preparations for and celebration of a festive Halloween.
Gail Jorgensen, *Crocodile Beat*, 1989
    Listening to the jungle sounds leads a crocodile to expect that dinner is coming but a lion foils those plans in this story in rhyme.
Judith Benet Richardson, *Come to My Party*, 1993
    Jungle animals feel reluctant to attend the birthday party for Rana the leopard.

346

STEPHANIE GREENE
MARTHA WESTON, Illustrator

Owen Foote, Super Spy
(New York: Clarion Books, 2001)

Subject(s): Spies; Honesty; Friendship
Age range(s): Grades 2-4
Major character(s): Owen Foote, Student—Elementary School, Friend; Joseph Hobbs, Student—Elementary School, Friend; Marty Mahoney, Principal
Time period(s): 2000s (2001)
Locale(s): United States

Summary: Spying on neighbors in his homemade camouflage hat made from his dad's boxer shorts becomes boring for Owen. Seeking more adventure, he plots with Joseph and two other students to spy on Mr. Mahoney's house. Watching the school principal work in his garden is not the excitement Owen expected from an ex-marine. When the other boys jostle Owen causing him to slip and roll down the embankment he finds Mr. Mahoney standing over him as he hears the sounds of retreating footsteps above him. Joseph does climb down the hill to support his friend and Mr. Mahoney gives them a week to think about their actions before returning to his house to discuss their behavior. (90 pages)

Where it's reviewed:
Booklist, January 1, 2002, page 857
Horn Book, November 2001, page 748
Publishers Weekly, November 19, 2001, page 70
School Library Journal, October 2001, page 118

Other books by the same author:
Owen Foote, Money Man, 2000
Owen Foote, Frontiersman, 1999 (School Library Journal Best Book)
Owen Foote, Soccer Star, 1998

Other books you might like:
Kate Banks, *Howie Bowles, Secret Agent*, 1999
    Howie adopts a false persona to gain acceptance at his new school but eventually realizes that no one knows the real Howie.

Betsy Duffey, *How to Be Cool in the Third Grade*, 1993
Third grade begins with one mishap after another, but eventually Robbie learns what it really means to be cool.

Johanna Hurwitz, *The Adventures of Ali Baba Bernstein*, 1985
Eight-year-old David Bernstein changes his name to something more exciting.

Gina Willner-Pardo, *Spider Storch's Teacher Torture*, 1997
When Spider's teacher announces her retirement he's sure it is his behavior that has driven her from the profession.

347

BARBARA GREENWOOD
HEATHER COLLINS, Illustrator

Gold Rush Fever: A Story of the Klondike, 1898

(Tonawanda, NY: Kids Can Press, 2001)

Subject(s): Gold Discoveries; Historical
Age range(s): Grades 5-8
Major character(s): Roy Olsen, Miner (gold); Tim Olsen, Miner (gold)
Time period(s): 1890s
Locale(s): Dawson City, Yukon Territory, Canada

Summary: Fifty years after convincing his brother Roy to take him and his inheritance to the Klondike, Tim reviews his memories of the famous gold rush of 1897. Telling his story, interspersed with diary entries and archival photographs, Tim relates the problems they confronted, from the ever-present gambling to cold and hunger, to the dance hall girls, other miners and the Mounted Police, in this look at a riotous time in American history. Roy finally realizes his dream of riches when he establishes himself as a shopkeeper while Tim becomes a reporter and circles the world for fifty years. (160 pages)

Where it's reviewed:
Booklist, December 15, 2001, page 726
Kirkus Reviews, September 1, 2001, page 1290
Quill & Quire, August 2001, page 31
Resource Links, December 2001, page 25
School Library Journal, October 2001, page 158

Other books by the same author:
A Pioneer Thanksgiving: A Story of Harvest Celebrations in 1841, 1999
A Pioneer Sampler: The Daily life of a Pioneer Family in 1840, 1998
The Last Safe House: A Story of the Underground Railroad, 1998

Other books you might like:
Will Hobbs, *Jason's Gold*, 1999
Jason tries to catch up with his brothers who've already left to hunt for gold in the Klondike.

Kathleen Karr, *Gold-Rush Phoebe*, 1998
Phoebe cuts her hair, dresses as a boy and, with her good friend Robbie, runs away for the gold fields of California.

Julie Lawson, *Destination Gold!*, 2001
The death of his father curtails his college plans, so Ned heads to the Klondike to find enough gold to support his mother and sister Sarah.

James Michener, *Journey*, 1989
Based on an episode from *Alaska*, this shorter book describes the effect that finding gold in the Klondike has on a group of British aristocrats.

348

KRISTIANA GREGORY

Five Smooth Stones: Hope's Diary

(New York: Scholastic Inc., 2001)

Series: My America
Subject(s): Historical; Diaries; American Colonies
Age range(s): Grades 3-5
Major character(s): Hope Penny Potter, 9-Year-Old, Daughter; Sarah Quinn, Widow(er), Quaker; Ethan Potter, Son, 13-Year-Old
Time period(s): 1770s (1776)
Locale(s): Philadelphia, Pennsylvania, American Colonies

Summary: The looming conflict between the colonists and the British reaches into Hope's happy life. First, her patriotic father leaves on a secret journey and then an accidental explosion fatally injures her neighbor as he guards gunpowder for General Washington. During the ensuing months, as tensions mount and hardships grow, Sarah becomes like another member of Hope's family, assisting with the birth of Hope's sister and evacuating with them to relatives in Valley Forge. Unfortunately, Ethan's impatience for news of their father sends him into the Tory camps in search of him and he is taken prisoner as a spy. While Hope, with her baby sister and mother find refuge outside the city, she knows not what will become of Ethan, her father, or the new nation struggling to free itself. Appended historical notes give background to the events of the time period. (106 pages)

Where it's reviewed:
Booklist, January 2001, page 960
Bulletin of the Center for Children's Books, April 2001, page 303
Horn Book Guide, Fall 2001, page 291

Other books by the same author:
Seeds of Hope: The Gold Rush Diary of Susanna Fairchild, California Territory, 1849, 2001 (Dear America)
The Stowaway: A Tale of California Pirates, 1995
The Legend of Jimmy Spoon, 1990
Jenny of the Tetons, 1989 (Golden Kite Award for Children's Fiction)

Other books you might like:
Lisa Banim, *A Spy in the King's Colony*, 1994
Emily and Maggie try to continue their routine activities despite the occupation of Boston by the British.

Elizabeth Massie, *Patsy's Discovery*, 1997
In 1776 Philadelphia, Patsy and a friend form the "Daughters of Liberty," a club dedicated to doing "good deeds."

Valerie Tripp, *Felicity Saves the Day: A Summer Story*, 1992
Felicity must choose between responsibility to her father and a desire to help his apprentice, Ben, run away to join George Washington's army.

349

KRISTIANA GREGORY

Seeds of Hope: The Gold Rush Diary of Susanna Fairchild, California Territory, 1849

(New York: Scholastic, 2001)

Series: Dear America
Subject(s): Frontier and Pioneer Life; Gold Discoveries; Diaries
Age range(s): Grades 5-8
Major character(s): Susanna Fairchild, 14-Year-Old; Clara Fairchild, 16-Year-Old; Dr. Fairchild, Doctor
Time period(s): 1840s (1849)
Locale(s): *California*, At Sea; Miner's Creek, California; San Francisco, California

Summary: What should have been a happy trip aboard the *California* for a family moving to Oregon turns to tragedy when Susanna's mother is swept overboard by a wave and the family's savings are lost when her father's jacket also lands in the ocean. Now in San Francisco Bay, with the crew having jumped ship, Susanna's father Dr. Fairchild decides to give up his plan to work as a doctor in Oregon and instead search for gold. Susanna and her sister Clara discuss his decision and choose to accompany him rather than to travel on to Oregon. Susanna uses her mother's journal and records their life in these camps as she wonders at the power of the word "gold," describes how gold is panned and tells of their daily life securing supplies and finding shelter in this continuing series. (184 pages)

Where it's reviewed:
Booklist, September 1, 2001, page 104
School Library Journal, July 2001, page 108
Voice of Youth Advocates, October 2001, page 276

Other books by the same author:
The Great Railroad Race: The Diary of Libby West, 1999 (Dear America)
Orphan Runaways, 1998
The Winter of Red Snow: The Diary of Abigail Jane Stewart, 1996 (Dear America)
Earthquake at Dawn, 1992

Other books you might like:
Karen Cushman, *The Ballad of Lucy Whipple*, 1996
    Thoroughly miserable that her mother has dragged the family to a small gold mining town in California, Lucy wants to return to Massachusetts.
Kathleen Karr, *Oregon, Sweet Oregon*, 1998
    Phoebe misses the adventure of trail life so when news of the California Gold Rush reaches her, she dresses as a boy and runs away to the gold fields.
Michael Morpurgo, *Twist of Gold*, 1992
    Sean and his sister Annie leave Ireland for American where they head west in search of their father who's in the gold camps.

350

ADELE GRIFFIN

Amandine

(New York: Hyperion, 2001)

Subject(s): Dishonesty; Emotional Problems; School Life
Age range(s): Grades 6-9
Major character(s): Delia Blaine, 9th Grader; Amandine Elroy-Bell, 9th Grader
Time period(s): 2000s
Locale(s): Alford, Massachusetts

Summary: New to James DeWolf High School, Delia is overweight, shy and lacking in self-confidence, which may explain why Delia is attracted to Amandine, an outrageous, look-at-me person, who is wickedly funny and quick to skewer. Amandine tells elaborate stories that skirt the truth, shares her drawings of ugly things and pulls Delia into a world that seeks weakness and then pounces on it. At first it's thrilling and exciting to be Amandine's friend, but gradually Delia realizes she's being manipulated and extricates herself from the friendship. When she does, Amandine retaliates and spreads vicious lies about Delia's father, lies that could destroy her family. Delia's weight hides an inner reserve of strength, and she needs that to survive as not everyone believes that Amandine is evil. (220 pages)

Where it's reviewed:
Booklist, September 15, 2001, page 226
Bulletin of the Center for Children's Books, October 2001, page 57
Horn Book, November 2001, page 748
Publishers Weekly, August 20, 2001, page 81
School Library Journal, November 2001, page 158

Awards the book has won:
ALA Quick Picks for Reluctant Young Adult Readers, 2002
ALA Best Books for Young Adults, 2002

Other books by the same author:
Witch Twins at Camp Bliss, 2002
Dive, 1999
The Other Shepards, 1998
Sons of Liberty, 1997
Split Just Right, 1997

Other books you might like:
Sue Ellen Bridgers, *Keeping Christina*, 1993
    Happy-go-lucky Annie befriends waif-like Christina, but rues the gesture when Christina becomes more and more controlling.
Carol Dines, *Best Friends Tell the Best Lies*, 1989
    Leah's friendship with Tamara is strained when she realizes that Tamara has been lying to her.
Anne Fine, *The Tulip Touch*, 1997
    Natalie's friend Tulip is exciting and stimulating, but has a streak of evil.
Cynthia Voigt, *Bad, Badder, Baddest*, 1997
    Mikey and Margalo aim to be the "bad girls" of their school, but they're angels compared to new student Gianette St. Etienne of New Orleans.

351

ADELE GRIFFIN

Witch Twins

(New York: Hyperion Books for Children, 2001)

Subject(s): Witches and Witchcraft; Twins; Remarriage
Age range(s): Grades 3-5
Major character(s): Luna Bundkin, Twin, 10-Year-Old; Claire Bundkin, Twin, 10-Year-Old; Arianna "Grandy" Bramblewine, Grandmother, Witch
Time period(s): 2000s (2001)
Locale(s): Philadelphia, Pennsylvania; Bramblewine, Pennsylvania

Summary: When Claire and Luna's divorced father announces his intention to remarry, his twin daughters fear that he may move to Texas. To stop the marriage Claire and Luna, only one-star witches, turn to Grandy, a five-star witch, for advice and a spell. Grandy refuses to meddle in destiny so Luna and Claire try to solve the problem without her help. The experience teaches the fledgling witches that human qualities of kindness and love can be more powerful than spells or can, at least, solve the problems caused by them. (154 pages)

Where it's reviewed:
Booklist, April 15, 2001, page 1552
Horn Book, September 2001, page 583
Kirkus Reviews, May 15, 2001, page 740
Publishers Weekly, July 2, 2001, page 76
School Library Journal, July 2001, page 82

Other books by the same author:
Split Just Right, 1997
Rainy Season, 1996

Other books you might like:
Catherine Dexter, *A Is for Apple, W Is for Witch*, 1996
    Ignoring her mother's warning, untrained Apple tries to cast a spell with unfortunate results.
Anne Mazer, *The Accidental Witch*, 1995
    When clumsy Bee tumbles into a circle of witches absorbing some of their power but none of their experience, the results are disastrous.
Jill Murphy, *The Worst Witch*, 1982
    As a first-year student, Mildred brings chaos to Miss Cackle's Academy for Witches.
P.J. Petersen, *I Hate Weddings*, 2000
    Dan's nervousness about attending his father's wedding and meeting his new family leads to unintended problems.

352

MARGOT GRIFFIN
P. JOHN BURDEN, Illustrator

Dancing for Danger: A Meggy Tale

(New York: Stoddart Kids, 2001)

Subject(s): Schools/Catholic Schools; Dancing; Courage
Age range(s): Grades 4-6
Major character(s): Meggy MacGillyCuddy, Dancer, Student; Dan MacGillyCuddy, Brother (of Meggy), Student; Master Cleary, Teacher

Time period(s): 18th century
Locale(s): County Kerry, Ireland

Summary: When the English occupied Ireland in the 1700s, they sought to subdue the Catholics and forbade them to have their own schools or to receive instruction in their religion. Schools were available, but the Irish Catholics chose not to attend the English ones; instead, they established their own secret "hedge schools." Meggy and her younger brother Dan attend one that is housed in an excavated cave until the soldiers come one day and destroy it. Two days later Master Cleary begins classes again in a clearing by the "stony books," but this time when the soldiers return they shoot Master Cleary as he's helping the children escape. Meggy staunches his wound and then, when a soldier comes too close to Cleary's hiding place, distracts him with her dancing, popping up in the meadow like a banshee and confusing him in this first novel. (93 pages)

Where it's reviewed:
Booklist, June 2001, page 1882
Resource Links, February 2001, page 12
School Library Journal, February 2002, page 134

Other books by the same author:
Secret of the Crystal Cave, 2002

Other books you might like:
Mauriel Phillips Joslyn, *Shenandoah Autumn: Courage under Fire*, 1998
    Though scared, Matilda and her mother smuggle wounded Will back to his regiment by claiming he's a deceased typhoid victim.
Gary Paulsen, *Nightjohn*, 1993
    Though Nightjohn suffers the loss of his toes as punishment, he continues to teach some of the slaves in a pit school he builds deep in the woods.
Gary D. Schmidt, *Anson's Way*, 1999
    Excited to be part of the Staffordshire Fecibles, Anson is conflicted when he's posted to Ireland and sees the oppression under which the Irish live.

353

PENI R. GRIFFIN

The Ghost Sitter

(New York: Dutton Children's Books, 2001)

Subject(s): Ghosts; Brothers and Sisters; Haunted Houses
Age range(s): Grades 4-6
Major character(s): Susie, 10-Year-Old, Spirit; Charlotte Verstuyft, Sister (older); Shannon Kohn, Neighbor, Friend (Charlotte's)
Time period(s): 2000s (2001)
Locale(s): Texas

Summary: For fifty years Susie, having promised her little sister that she would not go away, has been stuck waiting for her family to return to their home. Other families move in and out and the neighborhood rumor is that Susie haunts the house. Charlotte wants to think that Shannon is telling lies when she describes the house as haunted but events soon convince her that there is a ghost in the house. Charlotte and Shannon have to inform Susie that she is dead and arrange a meeting with her sister so she can be released from her promise and rest in peace. (131 pages)

Where it's reviewed:
Booklist, August 2001, page 2120
Horn Book, May 2001, page 323
Kirkus Reviews, May 1, 2001, page 659
School Library Journal, June 2001, page 149

Other books by the same author:
Margo's House, 1996
Vikki Vanishes, 1995
Switching Well, 1993

Other books you might like:
James M. Deem, *The Very Real Ghost Book of Christina Rose*, 1996
Christina and Danny's father moves them cross country to escape memories of their mother's death not realizing that he's bought a haunted house.
Cynthia DeFelice, *The Ghost of Fossil Glen*, 1998
Allie helps to uncover the mystery of Lucy's death many years earlier so her ghost can finally rest.
Hilary McKay, *The Amber Cat*, 1997
Two friends, recovering from the chicken pox, meet a ghost named Harriet who returns to visit them periodically.

⬛ **354**

ELISSA HADEN GUEST
CHRISTINE DAVENIER, Illustrator

Iris and Walter: True Friends

(San Diego: Gulliver Books/Harcourt, Inc., 2001)

Series: Iris and Walter. Book 2
Subject(s): Animals/Horses; Schools; Friendship
Age range(s): Grades 2-3
Major character(s): Iris, Friend, Student—Elementary School; Walter, Friend, Student—Elementary School; Rain, Horse; Miss Cherry, Teacher
Time period(s): 2000s (2001)
Locale(s): United States

Summary: In four brief chapters Iris and Walter offer each other moral and practical support. Iris wants to ride Rain, but she knows little about horses. Walter suggests ways in which Iris can teach Rain to trust her and finally Iris achieves her dream. The first day of school goes well for both students until Miss Cherry refers to Walter as "Walt." Walter doesn't like that but he doesn't have the courage to follow Iris's suggestion to just tell Miss Cherry. However, Iris does, through her support, give him an idea that solves the problem. Looks as if it'll be a good year. (44 pages)

Where it's reviewed:
Booklist, May 1, 2001, page 1678
Bulletin of the Center for Children's Books, September 2001, page 16
Horn Book Guide, Spring 2002, page 284
Publishers Weekly, June 25, 2001, page 74
School Library Journal, May 2001, page 122

Other books by the same author:
Iris and Walter and Baby Rose, 2002 (Iris and Walter, Book 3)

Iris and Walter, 2000 (Iris and Walter, Book 1)

Other books you might like:
James Howe, *Pinky and Rex and the Spelling Bee*, 1991
The support of a good friend can make life's most embarrassing moments a little easier to survive.
Tony Johnston, *Sparky & Eddie: The First Day of School*, 1997
A beginning chapter book introduces two friends entering school for the first time; the experience teaches them that some changes are acceptable.
Joan Robins, *Addie's Bad Day*, 1993
Good friend Max helps Addie overcome a problem so she can enjoy his birthday party.

⬛ **355**

JACQUELINE GUEST

Lightning Rider

(Custer, WA: Orca, 2001, c2000)

Subject(s): Mystery and Detective Stories; Motorcycles; Brothers and Sisters
Age range(s): Grades 7-10
Major character(s): January "Jan" Fournier, Indian (part white, part Indian), Motorcyclist; Grey Fournier, Indian (part white, part Indian), Motorcyclist; David McKenna, Police Officer; Sergeant Gellar, Police Officer; Josh Blakeman, 17-Year-Old, Cook
Time period(s): 2000s
Locale(s): Bragg Creek, Alberta, Canada

Summary: Jan can be found in one of three places, either at school, in the restaurant where she waitresses or on her motorcycle. More than anything she loves to ride the serpentine roads in the foothills of the Alberta Rockies where she lives. A Metis Indian, she and her older brother Grey are very close and often ride into the mountains together, but Jan's just been told he's in the intensive care unit of the Foothills Hospital. More startling news follows when Constable McKenna tells her that the bike her brother was riding was stolen. Though Jan feels certain her brother is innocent, Sergeant Gellar, a police officer with an aversion to Indians, is just as certain that Grey's guilty and is determined to make the stolen motorcycle charge stick. Knowing she won't receive any help from Gellar, who as much as warns her away from the case, she accepts the help offered by Josh and together they try to find the real culprit in a case that's as bewildering as some of those mountain roads. (162 pages)

Where it's reviewed:
Kliatt, November 2001, page 15
Resource Links, April 2001, page 23
Voice of Youth Advocates, October 2001, page 276

Other books by the same author:
Rink Rivals, 2002
Rookie Season, 2001
Triple Threat, 2000
Free Throw, 1999
Hat Trick, 1998

Other books you might like:

Terry Davis, *If Rock and Roll Were a Machine*, 1992
> Two very different people, English teacher Mr. Tanner and motorcycle shop owner Scott Shepard, help Bert find his worth and a '69 Harley-Davidson.

Lois Duncan, *I Know What You Did Last Summer*, 1973
> Four teens that take a vow of silence after they cause a hit-and-run accident are later tracked down, but not by the police.

Valerie Hobbs, *How Far Would You Have Gotten If I Hadn't Called You Back?*, 1995
> Feeling out of place in her new school where the kids like to party or drag race, Bron fits right in when she buys a 1946 Ford.

Luke Wallin, *Ceremony of the Panther*, 1987
> John, a sixteen-year-old Indian, is caught in the universal dilemma of blending family traditions with the expectations and prejudices of the outside world.

STEPHEN GULBIS, Author/Illustrator

Cowgirl Rosie and Her Five Baby Bison
(Boston: Little, Brown and Company, 2001)

Subject(s): Cowboys/Cowgirls; Animals/Buffalo; Lost and Found
Age range(s): Grades K-2
Major character(s): Rosie, Cowgirl, Rancher; "Snakey" Jake, Thief; Joe, Lawman (sheriff)
Time period(s): Indeterminate Past
Locale(s): West

Summary: As Cowgirl Rosie and her five baby bison walk to town, the babies vanish one by one. With Sheriff Joe's help, Cowgirl Rosie finds and confronts Snakey Jake. Unfortunately, the animals that emerge from the sack slung over Snakey Jake's shoulder are white not black as the missing bison should be. Cowgirl Rosie's effusive tears help to identify those flour-covered bison as her missing babies and Sheriff Joe apprehends Snakey Jake. Cowgirl's Rosie's reward for apprehending the thief will assure that she never loses her babies again while walking to town. The author's first book was originally published in Great Britain in 2000. (28 pages)

Where it's reviewed:
Booklist, May 15, 2001, page 1757
Children's Bookwatch, February 2001, page 4
Horn Book Guide, Fall 2001, page 257
Publishers Weekly, February 12, 2001, page 211
School Library Journal, May 2001, page 122

Other books you might like:

Nancy Antle, *Sam's Wild West Christmas*, 2000
> Sam and Rosie track thieves who have stolen Christmas gifts and captured a jolly man in a red suit.

Roy Gerrard, *Rosie and the Rustlers*, 1989
> A story in rhyme describes how Rosie catches the rustlers who have stolen her cattle.

Diane Stanley, *Saving Sweetness*, 1996
> A sheriff trying to catch an orphanage escapee is instead rescued by the runaway.

ROBIN JONES GUNN

I Promise
(Bloomington, MN: Bethany House, 2001)

Series: Christy and Todd: The College Years. Book 3
Subject(s): Weddings; Christian Life; College Life
Age range(s): Grades 6-10
Major character(s): Todd Spencer, Student—College; Christy Miller, Student—College
Time period(s): 2000s
Locale(s): Escondido, California

Summary: Christy and Todd are finally engaged, which opens up a whole new set of problems. Christy is extremely organized and wants not only to wait until they've graduated from college before getting married, but also to have all the details mapped out. On the other hand, Todd sees no reason to wait and thinks the sooner the better. And then Aunt Marti enters the fray with her version of how to organize a wedding. Whew! At times Christy and Todd wonder if it's going to work out or not in this last of a series. (285 pages)

Where it's reviewed:
Booklist, January 2002, page 841
Voice of Youth Advocates, December 2001, page 358

Other books by the same author:
As You Wish, 2000 (Christy and Todd: The College Years, Book 2)
Until Tomorrow, 2000 (Christy and Todd: The College Years, Book 1)

Other books you might like:

Carrie Bender, *Birch Hollow Schoolmarm*, 1999
> Dora dates Matthew until he leaves for the summer to work in California where misaddressed mail causes her lots of heartache.

Mary Christner Borntrager, *Rebecca*, 1989
> The romance that develops between a young Amish girl and a Mennonite man forces both of them to grow up.

Sarah Dessen, *That Summer*, 1996
> "That summer" was terrible when her sister married a boring man and her father divorced her mother, got a toupee and then a "trophy wife."

Betty Smith, *Joy in the Morning*, 1963
> Only their love for one another enables Annie and Carl to make their marriage work after their parents cut off their school funding.

ANNE GUTMAN
GEORG HALLENSLEBEN, Illustrator

Lisa's Airplane Trip
(New York: Alfred A. Knopf, 2001)

Series: Misadventures of Gaspard and Lisa
Subject(s): Air Travel; Airplanes; Travel
Age range(s): Preschool-Kindergarten
Major character(s): Lisa, Dog, Traveler
Time period(s): 1990s (1999)

Locale(s): In the Air

Summary: All alone on a very big plane Lisa flies across the ocean to meet her uncle in New York. When the lady next to her moves to a different seat Lisa stretches out for a nap until a tray of delicious food arrives. Then a movie starts but Lisa's too short to see it so she climbs on the back of the seat in front of her and accidentally spills her orange juice. A bath in the sink helps her clean the juice off before the plane lands. Originally published in France in 1999 (28 pages)

Where it's reviewed:

Booklist, February 1, 2001, page 1051
Christian Science Monitor, March 22, 2001, page 18
Horn Book, May 2001, page 311
Publishers Weekly, February 19, 2001, page 89
School Library Journal, September 2001, page 189

Other books by the same author:

Lisa in New York, 2002 (Misadventures of Gaspard and Lisa)
Gaspard and Lisa at the Museum, 2001 (Misadventures of Gaspard and Lisa)
Gaspard in the Hospital, 2001 (Misadventures of Gaspard and Lisa)
Gaspard on Vacation, 2001 (Misadventures of Gaspard and Lisa)

Other books you might like:

Jan Ormerod, *Miss Mouse Takes Off*, 2001
　　With her rag doll Miss Mouse in tow, a little girl experiences her first plane trip.
Anne F. Rockwell, *I Fly*, 1997
　　A boy's parents bid him good-bye and he boards the airplane to fly alone to his destination.
J. Otto Seibold, *Mr. Lunch Takes a Plane Ride*, 1993
　　Wacky illustrations complement the silly story of a dog's trip in the baggage compartment of a plane. Vivian Walsh, co-author.

359

DAN GUTMAN

The Edison Mystery

(New York: Simon & Schuster, 2001)

Series: Qwerty Stevens, Back in Time
Subject(s): Time Travel; Brothers and Sisters; Family Life
Age range(s): Grades 4-8
Major character(s): Robert Edward "Qwerty" Stevens, 13-Year-Old; Joey Dvorak, 13-Year-Old; Thomas Alva Edison, Historical Figure, Inventor; Barbara Stevens, 16-Year-Old, Sister (of Qwerty); Madison Stevens, Child, Sister (of Qwerty)
Time period(s): 2000s; 1870s (1879)
Locale(s): West Orange, New Jersey

Summary: Following an argument with his mother, Qwerty, so named after a mistake during a keyboarding lesson in third grade, relieves his anger the way he always does by going into their backyard and digging a hole. Their backyard has seen a lot of holes, but this time Qwerty actually finds a big wooden box with Thomas A. Edison's name on it. Qwerty's not surprised by his find, as he lives near Edison's former home, but he and his best friend Joey are astonished to find a time

machine inside the box along with a note from Edison saying "the world is not ready for this." Unsure whether or not to give the machine to a museum, Qwerty decides to test it and, after a quick trip to Spain, ends up in Edison's lab in 1879. His sister Barbara turns up next and both of them hear Edison admit he's not sure how to return them to the twenty first century. Their little sister Madison accidentally retrieves them and when they arrive home, Qwerty and Barbara discover how they've altered history. (201 pages)

Where it's reviewed:

Book Report, January 2002, page 60
Instructor, November 2001, page 17
School Library Journal, August 2001, page 182

Other books by the same author:

Shoeless Joe & Me, 2002 (Baseball Card Adventure)
Stuck in Time with Benjamin Franklin, 2002 (Qwerty Stevens, Back in Time)
Babe & Me, 2000 (Baseball Card Adventure)
Johnny Hangtime, 2000
The Million Dollar Shot, 1997
The Kid Who Ran for President, 1996

Other books you might like:

Scott Ciencin, *Dinoverse*, 1999
　　Bertram uses his science fair project to send himself and three other classmates back to prehistoric time where they blend right in as human-dinosaurs.
Sam Drexler, *Lost in Spillville*, 2000
　　Two runaway teens travel back in time after seeing an exhibit of the Bily brothers' carved clocks; now they must find the Bily brothers to return.
Annabel Johnson, *The Danger Quotient*, 1984
　　Living underground following a nuclear war, young genius Casey invents a time travel machine.
Jane Langton, *The Time Bike*, 2000
　　Eddy can't believe his uncle would send him an old-fashioned, klunky-looking bike to replace his stolen bike, until he looks at the dials!

360

DAN GUTMAN

The Million Dollar Kick

(New York: Hyperion, 2001)

Subject(s): Sports/Soccer; Contests
Age range(s): Grades 5-8
Major character(s): Whisper Nelson, 7th Grader; Jess Kirby, Computer Expert, 7th Grader; Ellie Gonzales, Soccer Player, 12th Grader
Time period(s): 2000s
Locale(s): Oklahoma City, Oklahoma

Summary: After kicking the ball into the wrong goal when she was a third grader, Whisper has never again played on a soccer team, or any other sports team. But now she's allowed her athletic little sister Briana to talk her into writing a slogan for their city's women's soccer team, the Oklahoma City Kick. Naturally Whisper's slogan wins, which might be great except the prize is to try to kick a twenty-yard penalty shot against the team's goalkeeper. If she succeeds, there's a one million dollar prize. To Whisper, this is the worst possible dilemma. But with the help of computer nerd Jess and soccer player Ellie, Whisper changes her mind about a lot of things and just does her best in this heart-warming story. (202 pages)

Where it's reviewed:
Booklist, November 15, 2001, page 571
Publishers Weekly, August 27, 2001, page 86
School Library Journal, December 2001, page 134

Other books by the same author:
Johnny Hangtime, 2000
Virtually Perfect, 1998
The Million Dollar Shot, 1997
The Kid Who Ran for President, 1996

Other books you might like:
Donna Jo Napoli, *Shelley Shock*, 2000
    None of the boys on the soccer team knows what to do when the new girl Shelley shows up for soccer practice.
Julie Anne Peters, *How Do You Spell G-E-E-K?*, 1996
    Though the friendship with Kim becomes strained, Ann works with new student Lurlene to prepare her for the National Spelling Bee.
Bill Wallace, *Never Say Quit*, 1993
    A team of misfits, coached by an alcoholic former principal, learns to work together as they develop into fine soccer players.

361

DAN GUTMAN

The Secret Life of Dr. Demented

(New York: Pocket Books/Archway, 2001)

Subject(s): Sports/Wrestling; Mothers and Sons
Age range(s): Grades 5-8
Major character(s): Wesley Brown, 14-Year-Old; Bonnie Brown, Single Parent, Mother (of Wesley); Landon "Dr. Demented" Wheeler, Wrestler (professional), Teacher (physical education)
Time period(s): 2000s
Locale(s): Humble, Texas

Summary: Undersized Wesley, often a target of teasing and bullying at school, is obsessed with professional wrestling, to the dismay of his mother. Bonnie doesn't want her son to know that his long-absent father was captain of his high school wrestling team and physically abusive, so she tries to convince Wesley of the dangers of violence. When Wesley discovers that their neighbor, who is also his PE teacher Landon Wheeler, is the famed pro wrestler Dr. Demented, he's sworn to secrecy. But what's he supposed to do when his mother begins dating Mr. Wheeler? (176 pages)

Where it's reviewed:
Kliatt, November 2001, page 15

Other books by the same author:
The Million Dollar Kick, 2001
Johnny Hangtime, 2000
Virtually Perfect, 1998
The Million Dollar Shot, 1997

Other books you might like:
Chad Henry, *Dogbreath Victorious*, 1999
    Tim and his alternate-rock band Dogbreath can't believe they're competing against his mother's band "The Angry Housewives."
Rich Wallace, *Wrestling Sturbridge*, 1996
    His senior year, Ben decides to go for the state title in the 135-pound wrestling class, even though it means wrestling against his best friend.
Sarah Weeks, *My Guy*, 2001
    Guy can't believe his mother plans to marry Jerry Zuckerman, father of Guy's enemy since kindergarten when Lana called him "Girlie Guy."

362

LILA GUZMAN
RICK GUZMAN, Co-Author

Lorenzo's Secret Mission

(Houston, TX: Pinata Books/Arte Publico Press, 2001)

Subject(s): Slavery; Identity; Revolutionary War
Age range(s): Grades 6-9
Major character(s): Lorenzo Bannister, 15-Year-Old; Bernardo de Galvez, Military Personnel (colonel), Historical Figure; Armand Bannister, Judge, Grandfather
Time period(s): 1770s (1776-1777)
Locale(s): New Orleans, Louisiana; Albemarle County, Virginia

Summary: To honor his dying father's wish, Lorenzo leaves San Antonio in search of his grandfather. In New Orleans, Lorenzo loses his haversack, becomes part of a melee and is thrown in jail before being released by Bernardo de Galvez, a former patient of his father's. Discovering that Lorenzo is trained as a medic, de Galvez arranges for him to travel aboard a flatboat up the Mississippi where his medical skills will supplement his intelligence gathering and distribution of supplies for the Americans. Lorenzo eventually reaches Virginia and finds his grandfather, Judge Bannister, whose sympathies lie with the British. Lorenzo also discovers secrets about his heritage in this book that illustrates the little-known involvement of the Spanish in the American Revolution. (153 pages)

Where it's reviewed:
School Library Journal, December 2001, page 134

Other books by the same author:
Green Slime and Jam, 2001

Other books you might like:
Kathy Balmes, *Thunder on the Sierra*, 2001
    With his father dead and vaqueros plotting to steal his beloved horse Fandango, Mateo leaves the ranch to seek his own adventure.
Joan Elizabeth Goodman, *Hope's Crossing*, 1998
    When Captain Wakeman joins General Washington, Loyalists storm his home, burn his house and kidnap his daughter Hope.
Gary Paulsen, *Sarny: A Life Remembered*, 1997
    Once freed, Sarny travels to New Orleans where she ac-

cepts a job with Miss Laura, an octoroon, and enjoys the creature comforts of her home.
Betsy Sterman, *Saratoga Secret*, 1998
   Though considered a child, Amith aids the American cause when he delivers a letter to the Continental Army warning of British Burgoyne's attack.

H

363

JESSIE HAAS
MARGOT APPLE, Illustrator

Runaway Radish
(New York: Greenwillow Books, 2001)

Subject(s): Animals/Horses; Humor; Pets
Age range(s): Grades 2-4
Major character(s): Radish, Pony, Runaway; Judy, Animal Lover, Equestrian; Nina, Animal Lover, Equestrian
Time period(s): Indeterminate Past
Locale(s): Vermont

Summary: Radish is a pony with a mind of his own and a desire to share his knowledge with novice equestrians. Judy is the first to benefit from Radish's teachings, but eventually she outgrows her pony and acquires a horse. Radish is not content to be retired so he is sold to Nina and returns to his role of tutor in the fine art of coping with a strong-willed, but gentle pony. Alas, Nina also grows up and again a horse takes Radish's place. This time Radish runs away to find his home with Judy. The perfect solution to Radish's dilemma occurs to Judy and, with Nina's approval, Radish becomes a pony at a summer camp where there are many novice riders just waiting for Radish's instruction. (56 pages)

Where it's reviewed:
Booklist, April 15, 2001, page 1552
Bulletin of the Center for Children's Books, July 2001, page 408
Horn Book Guide, Fall 2001, page 291
Horn Book, May 2001, page 324
School Library Journal, May 2001, page 122

Awards the book has won:
Horn Book Fanfare/Fiction, 2002
Bulletin of the Center for Children's Books Blue Ribbon, 2001

Other books by the same author:
Beware and Stogie, 1998
Be Well, Beware, 1996

A Blue for Beware, 1995

Other books you might like:
Jeanne Betancourt, *The Pony Pals Series*, 1994-
    The Pony Pals is a group of girls who enjoy riding and caring for their ponies.
Corinne Demas, *Perfect Pony*, 2000
    Jamie wonders if the advertisement she sees for a free pony could lead her to the perfect pony she seeks.
Dale Blackwell Gasque, *Pony Trouble*, 1998
    Two competitive cousins realize they need to work together or risk injuring a borrowed pony.
Marguerite Henry, *Brown Sunshine of Sawdust Valley*, 1996
    When the neglected mare Molly purchases at auction foals a mule, Molly learns how to care for and train Brown Sunshine too.

364

CHARLES HADDAD
STEVE PICA, Illustrator

Captain Tweakerbeak's Revenge: A Calliope Day Adventure
(New York: Delacorte Press, 2001)

Subject(s): Animals/Birds; Schools; Friendship
Age range(s): Grades 3-6
Major character(s): Calliope Day, 4th Grader, Sister (youngest); Noreen Catherwood, 4th Grader, Friend; Baby "Captain Tweakerbeak", Parrot
Time period(s): 1990s
Locale(s): South Orange, New York

Summary: Although the prim and proper Noreen seems to be the exact opposite of imaginative, impulsive Calliope, Calliope sees the potential for friendship and works to convince Noreen to agree to the idea. Success comes more easily than Calliope expects and now she's got to figure out what to do with a friend who commutes to school in a chauffeur-driven Mercedes and lives in a mansion. Developing an elaborate "show-and-tell" plot that will allow her to take Baby from Noreen is probably not the way most people would choose to develop a friendship, but Calliope is one of a kind. (185 pages)

Where it's reviewed:
Horn Book Guide, Fall 2001, page 306
Kirkus Reviews, May 1, 2001, page 660
School Library Journal, June 2001, page 116

Other books by the same author:
Meet Calliope Day, 1998

Other books you might like:
Beverly Cleary, *Ramona's World*, 1999
 Daisy, a new student, becomes fourth-grader Ramona's friend fulfilling one of her wishes for the school year.
Eth Clifford, *Harvey's Wacky Parrot Adventure*, 1990
 Begrudgingly Harvey accepts the help of his disliked cousin Nora in a search for hidden treasure.
Phyllis Reynolds Naylor, *The Girls' Revenge*, 1998
 Caroline's plan seems perfect to the actress wannabe and it does give her attention, but not the kind she expects.

365

MARGARET PETERSON HADDIX

Among the Impostors
(New York: Simon & Schuster, 2001)

Subject(s): Interpersonal Relations; Fear; Schools/Boarding Schools
Age range(s): Grades 5-7
Major character(s): Luke/Lee Garner/Grant, 12-Year-Old
Time period(s): Indeterminate Future
Locale(s): United States

Summary: As the third child in a society that allows only two children per family, Luke has been hidden in his home since birth. He now has a chance to assume the identity of a child killed in an unreported accident and attend school as Lee Grant. Taking the chance to come out of hiding, he enters Hendricks School where life turns upside down for him; instead of privacy, he's surrounded by classmates and instead of peace and tranquility he's hazed by his roommate. Escaping from the confusion of school life, Lee finds an open door and heads outside where he meets other third children, or "exnays," who gather in the woods and plot ways to escape. Lee worries about the Population Police who kill all third children and hopes that there are no traitors among the "exnays" in this sequel to *Among the Hidden*. (172 pages)

Where it's reviewed:
Booklist, April 15, 2001, page 1557
Bulletin of the Center for Children's Books, September 2001, page 17
Publishers Weekly, June 11, 2001, page 86
School Library Journal, July 2001, page 108
Voice of Youth Advocates, August 2001, page 213

Awards the book has won:
ALA Quick Picks for Reluctant Young Adult Readers, 2002

Other books by the same author:
Among the Betrayed, 2002
Turnabout, 2000
Among the Hidden, 1998

Running Out of Time, 1995

Other books you might like:
Arthur C. Clarke, *Childhood's End*, 1963
 The overlords land on the planet Earth and quickly assume control.
Louise Lawrence, *The Patchwork People*, 1994
 Stuck in different social classes, the only hope Hugh and Helen have for a life together is to become "patchwork people" and live in harmony with the land.
Deborah Moulton, *Children of Time*, 1989
 Ruled by computers, Earth is on the verge of war, but Lady Grey has a diabolical plan to adopt children and train them to assume control of Earth.

366

MARGARET PETERSON HADDIX
JANET HAMLIN, Illustrator

The Girl with 500 Middle Names
(New York: Simon & Schuster Books for Young Readers, 2001)

Subject(s): Schools; Parent and Child; Friendship
Age range(s): Grades 3-5
Major character(s): Janie Sams, 3rd Grader, Daughter Kimberly, 3rd Grader, Friend; Momma, Mother, Artisan (knitter)
Time period(s): 2000s (2001)
Locale(s): United States

Summary: With Janie's dad recovering from a work-related injury her family is financially strapped but Momma is so dissatisfied with the inadequacy of their inner city school that she's determined to move the family into a better school district. Momma supplements her secretarial wages by knitting sweaters with individual's names on consignment for a business in a nearby suburb. Compared to the attire of the wealthier students in her new school, Janie's wardrobe looks dated. When Janie takes to wearing Momma's rejected consigned sweaters to her new school Kimberly, who reaches out to Janie in friendship, thinks she's quite cool to have so many different middle names. (82 pages)

Where it's reviewed:
Bulletin of the Center for Children's Books, May 2001, page 338
Horn Book Guide, Fall 2001, page 291
Publishers Weekly, March 5, 2001, page 80
School Library Journal, June 2001, page 117

Other books by the same author:
Running Out of Time, 1995

Other books you might like:
Judith Caseley, *Jorah's Journal*, 1997
 In her journal, Jorah records her unhappy thoughts about her new home, school and difficulty making friends.
Judy Delton, *Kitty from the Start*, 1987
 Third grader Kitty adjusts to her family's move to a new neighborhood and her entry into a new school.
Bonnie Graves, *No Copycats Allowed!*, 1998
 The spelling of Gabrielle's long name gives her one more problem as she adjusts to a new school.

367
MARGARET PETERSON HADDIX

Takeoffs and Landings
(New York: Simon & Schuster, 2001)

Subject(s): Family Life; Travel; Mothers
Age range(s): Grades 6-9
Major character(s): Lori Lawson, 14-Year-Old; Charles Frederick "Chuck" Lawson, 15-Year-Old; Joan Lawson, Entertainer (motivational speaker)
Time period(s): 2000s
Locale(s): Pickford County, Ohio; Chicago, Illinois; Atlanta, Georgia

Summary: Lori and Chuck live with three younger siblings on their grandparents' farm while their mother supports the family by traveling around the country giving motivational speeches. Their father died eight years earlier in a tractor accident and ever since haven't seen much of their mother, but are now joining her for two weeks of speech making. Each is unsure of what lies ahead, but their mother's goal is to be reacquainted with her two oldest children. Lori is a popular teen who never wants to be different while Chuck is overweight, clumsy and very unsure of himself. The children think their mother is very self-assured, but on this trip she reveals more of herself and details of their father's accident. Though they don't become an instant family after only two weeks together, Lori does admit her anger at her mother's absence, Chuck becomes more self-confident and their mother becomes more like a mother to them. (201 pages)

Where it's reviewed:
Bulletin of the Center for Children's Books, October 2001, page 58
Kliatt, July 2001, page 9
Publishers Weekly, August 20, 2001, page 81
School Library Journal, August 2001, page 182
Voice of Youth Advocates, October 2001, page 276

Other books by the same author:
Among the Betrayed, 2002
Turnabout, 2000
Just Ella, 1999
Among the Hidden, 1998
Don't You Dare Read This, Mrs. Dunphrey, 1996

Other books you might like:
Diana Hendry, *Double Vision*, 1993
Neither popular, artistic or blessed with acting ability, Eliza doesn't like herself, a fact that changes as she begins to grow up.
Richard Peck, *Those Summer Girls I Never Met*, 1988
Drew and his sister Steph readjust their summer plans when their grandmother, whom they hardly know, invites them to join her on a senior citizen cruise.
Ruth Pennebaker, *Conditions of Love*, 1999
Sarah feels unloved and no longer special since her father died and she's left with her too-distant mother, the star of a television cooking show.

368
MICHAEL HAGUE, Author/Illustrator

Kate Culhane: A Ghost Story
(New York: SeaStar Books, 2001)

Subject(s): Ghosts; Folklore; Courage
Age range(s): Grades 4-6
Major character(s): Kate Culhane, Daughter (grieving), Young Woman
Time period(s): Indeterminate Past
Locale(s): Ireland

Summary: Kate lingers too long at her mother's grave and in the darkening shadows of the graveyard she accidentally steps on the fresh earth of a newly covered grave. Thus Kate is trapped and compelled to do the bidding of a voice that commands her to open the grave. The dead man that emerges from the coffin then requires Kate to carry him from house to house until he finds one free of holy water so he can dine. Though Kate is unable to resist his spell she is clever enough to outwit the dead man in the end, deny him what he seeks and gain what she desires. An introductory author's note gives the background for this mid-19th century Irish folktale. (34 pages)

Where it's reviewed:
Booklist, September 15, 2001, page 225
Bulletin of the Center for Children's Books, September 2001
Kirkus Reviews, June 15, 2001, page 863
Publishers Weekly, July 2, 2001, page 76
School Library Journal, September 2001, page 246

Awards the book has won:
IRA Children's Choices, 2002

Other books by the same author:
The Perfect Present, 1996 (IRA Children's Choices)
Teddy Bear, Teddy Bear, A Classic Action Rhyme, 1993
Michael Hague's World of Unicorns, 1986

Other books you might like:
Joan Aiken, *A Fit of Shivers: Tales for Late at Night*, 1992
Haunted houses, deceased daughters looking for revenge and vengeful ghosts comprise the short stories in this collection.
Janice Del Negro, *Lucy Dove*, 1998
Courage and determination to win a sack of gold enable Lucy Dove to complete a challenge to sew a pair of trousers in a haunted graveyard.
Robert D. San Souci, *Brave Margaret: An Irish Adventure*, 1999
In a retelling of a traditional tale, Margaret bravely faces adventure and danger to achieve her goal.
Jane Yolen, *Here There Be Ghosts*, 1998
A compilation of short stories and poems about ghosts gives the background for each story.

369

MARY DOWNING HAHN
DIANE DEGROAT, Illustrator

Anna on the Farm
(New York: Clarion Books, 2001)

Subject(s): Farm Life; Friendship; Orphans
Age range(s): Grades 3-5
Major character(s): Anna Sherwood, 9-Year-Old, Niece; Theodore Armiger, Orphan, Nephew; George Armiger, Uncle, Guardian (Theodore's); Aggie Armiger, Aunt, Spouse
Time period(s): 1910s (1914)
Locale(s): Baltimore, Maryland; Beltsville, Maryland

Summary: The prospect of escaping the hot city for a week with Uncle George and Aunt Aggie is exciting to Anna. When she arrives at the farm she's surprised and disappointed to meet Theodore who seems as unhappy to share Aunt Aggie and Uncle George as Anna is. The freedom from rigid social rules and dress on the farm allows Anna to wear overalls, swim in her drawers and braid her hair. Anna knows her mother would be horrified, but her boldness seems to help Theodore accept her. Still grieving the deaths of his parents Theodore needs a friend and before the week concludes he finds one in Anna. (152 pages)

Where it's reviewed:
Booklist, February 15, 2001, page 1136
Horn Book, May 2001, page 324
Kirkus Reviews, February 15, 2001, page 258
Publishers Weekly, April 9, 2001, page 76
School Library Journal, March 2001, page 209

Other books by the same author:
Anna All Year Round, 1999
Following My Own Footsteps, 1996
Stepping on the Cracks, 1991

Other books you might like:
Jane Buchanan, *Gratefully Yours*, 1997
    Orphan Hattie finds life on a farm an abrupt change for a city girl, but her adoptive farmer parents help her to also find love again.
Patricia MacLachlan, *Sarah, Plain and Tall*, 1985
    In a Newbery Medal winning title Sarah travels from Maine to the prairie farm of a widower and his two children in hopes she can ''make a difference.''
Laura Ingalls Wilder, *On the Banks of Plum Creek*, 1937
    A Newbery Honor Book in the Little House series describes the carefree life as well as the hardships of a farm family.

370

BRUCE HALE

Farewell, My Lunchbag
(San Diego: Harcourt, Inc., 2001)

Series: Chet Gecko Mystery. Case #3
Subject(s): Animals; Schools; Mystery and Detective Stories
Age range(s): Grades 3-6

Major character(s): Chet Gecko, Detective—Amateur, 4th Grader; Mrs. Bagoong, Reptile (iguana); Natalie Attired, Bird (mockingbird), Classmate (Chet's)
Time period(s): Indeterminate
Locale(s): Fictional Country (Emerson Hicky Elementary)

Summary: Food is near and dear to Chet Gecko's heart so when he learns from Mrs. Bagoong that a thief is depleting the supply in the school cafeteria he fears the lunchroom will close or Mrs. Bagoong will lose her job. With help from his partner, Natalie, Chet begins interviewing and searching for clues. Chet sets a trap for the thief but he's outsmarted, falls victim to his own love of food and becomes the suspect rather than the case solver. Now he faces slim pickings in the cafeteria and lifelong detention unless Natalie can help him nab the real crook. (107 pages)

Where it's reviewed:
Booklist, March 15, 2001, page 1398
Horn Book Guide, Fall 2001, page 306
Kirkus Reviews, March 1, 2001, page 332
Publishers Weekly, May 21, 2001, page 109
School Library Journal, April 2001, page 110

Other books by the same author:
The Hamster of the Baskervilles, 2002 (Chet Gecko Mystery, Case #5)
The Chameleon Wore Chartreuse, 2000 (Chet Gecko Mystery, Case #1)
The Mystery of Mr. Nice, 2000 (Chet Gecko Mystery, Case #2)

Other books you might like:
David A. Adler, *The Cam Jansen Series*, 1980-
    Using her photographic memory, Cam Jansen participates in the solving of a variety of mysteries.
Mary Pope Osborne, *Spider Kane and the Mystery at Jumbo Nightcrawler's*, 1993
    Spider Kane's case takes him to the seamy underworld of a supper club from which the good guys are being kidnapped.
Donald J. Sobol, *Encyclopedia Brown and the Case of the Slippery Salamander*, 1999
    Leroy ''Encyclopedia'' Brown is well known in his hometown of Idaville for solving cases that have even his police chief father stymied.

371

DENISE HAMILTON

The Jasmine Trade
(New York: Scribner, 2001)

Subject(s): Asian Americans; Suspense; Journalism
Age range(s): Grades 10-Adult
Major character(s): Marina Lu, 17-Year-Old, Crime Victim; Eve Diamond, Journalist; Mark Furukawa, Counselor
Time period(s): 2000s
Locale(s): Los Angeles, California

Summary: A car-jacking gone awry and Marina Lu dead at seventeen are typical stories that come across Eve Diamond's newspaper desk, but this one strikes her as a little different. What's a 17-year-old doing driving a luxury car, with a 2-

carat diamond on her hand and a wallet stuffed with bills to pay cash for the ten bridesmaids dresses she was ordering for her upcoming wedding? To get some leads on this story, she talks with Mark Furukawa, a counselor who works with all kinds of Asian American kids who are having difficulties, and he explains a little of the life these kids face. Eve is told about "parachute" kids who live here in the States, perhaps with an elderly relative or housekeeper, while their parents work back in Asia amassing more and more money. In essence, no one pays attention to where these teens go or what they do. When she begins to investigate the next layer, she finds a subculture of immigrant teens that survive by either being part of a gang or selling themselves sexually. The more Eve digs, the less people want her digging, as she confronts drug dealers and other criminals in a sobering first novel. (279 pages)

Where it's reviewed:
Booklist, May 15, 2001, page 1736
Globe & Mail, August 11, 2001, page D13
Kirkus Reviews, May 1, 2001, page 629
New York Times Book Review, August 5, 2001, page 17
Publishers Weekly, July 2, 2001, page 53

Other books you might like:
Ridley Pearson, *The First Victim*, 1999
    To investigate the shipping container found with both dead and live bodies of Chinese women, Melissa works in a sweatshop but then disappears.
S.J. Rozan, *A Bitter Feast*, 1998
    As a Chinese American, Lydia finds herself caught between both cultures as she investigates a missing person in New York's Chinatown.
Lisa See, *Flower Net*, 1997
    Police in China and America work to solve a case involving drowned bodies, one the American ambassador's son and the others, illegal Chinese immigrants.

372

JOYCE HANSEN

One True Friend

(New York: Clarion Books, 2001)

Subject(s): Friendship; Foster Homes; Letters
Age range(s): Grades 5-8
Major character(s): Amir Daniels, 14-Year-Old; Doris Williams, 12-Year-Old; Ronald Daniels, Child, Brother (of Amir)
Time period(s): 2000s
Locale(s): New York, New York (the Bronx); Syracuse, New York

Summary: Orphaned when his parents die of AIDS, then bounced from relatives to foster homes, Amir is determined to comply with his mother's wish that her children stay together. At present, he's been moved to a foster family who's been caring for his youngest brother Ronald, but Amir has other brothers and sisters to locate. Living in Syracuse, he writes letters to his good friend Doris from his Bronx neighborhood and they share their troubles, but are buoyed by the "one true friend" each enjoys. (160 pages)

Where it's reviewed:
Book Report, November 2001, page 62
Booklist, December 15, 2001, page 731
Bulletin of the Center for Children's Books, December 2001, page 141
School Library Journal, December 2001, page 134
Voice of Youth Advocates, October 2001, page 277

Other books by the same author:
The Heart Calls Home, 1999
I Thought My Soul Would Rise and Fly: The Diary of Patsy, a Freed Girl, 1997 (Dear America)
Out from This Place, 1988
Yellow Bird and Me, 1986

Other books you might like:
Alice Childress, *Rainbow Jordan*, 1981
    Many women help Rainbow recognize her self-worth as she is continually abandoned by her mother and placed in foster homes.
Christopher Paul Curtis, *Bud, Not Buddy*, 1999
    After being bounced from one foster home to another, Buddy finally runs away and is lucky enough to locate his grandfather.
Walter Dean Myers, *Motown and Didi*, 1984
    Among the drug use and despair of Harlem's inhabitants, Motown and Didi find one another, two teens who are determined to succeed.

373

JOAN HIATT HARLOW

Joshua's Song

(New York: Simon & Schuster/McElderry, 2001)

Subject(s): Change; Newspapers; Disasters
Age range(s): Grades 5-8
Major character(s): Joshua Harper, 13-Year-Old, Paperboy; Charlestown Charlie, Immigrant, Paperboy; Marc Muggeridge, Editor (newspaper)
Time period(s): 1910s (1919)
Locale(s): Boston, Massachusetts

Summary: Joshua and his mother are left with financial problems after the Influenza Epidemic of 1918 kills thousands of Americans, including his father. Though his mother was once one of Boston's elite, she's now forced to take in boarders, including a newspaper reporter Marc Muggeridge. Joshua gives up his private school and becomes one of Charlestown Charlie's newspaper boys, called a "newsie," but doesn't tell his mother as she'd think the job was beneath him. Bit by bit Joshua adjusts to the changes in his life, from his singing voice, which costs him a spot in the Boston Boys' Choir, to a new-found courage when he aids one of the victims of the Great Molasses Flood, in this historic tale. (176 pages)

Where it's reviewed:
Booklist, December 15, 2001, page 731
Publishers Weekly, October 29, 2001, page 64
School Library Journal, November 2001, page 158

Other books by the same author:
Star in the Storm, 2000

Other books you might like:

Robert Cormier, *Frenchtown Summer*, 1999
Eugene recounts events of his twelfth summer that helped him grow up, from delivering the newspaper to building a better relationship with his dad.

Carol Flynn Harris, *A Place for Joey*, 2001
Joey saves a policeman from the syrup of the molasses tank that explodes and realizes he will always stay in Boston and maybe become a policeman.

Gloria Skurzynski, *Good-Bye, Billy Radish*, 1992
Hank can't believe it when his friend Bazyli, nicknamed Billy Radish, dies during the influenza epidemic.

374

DAN HARPER
CARA MOSER, Illustrator
BARRY MOSER, Illustrator

Sit, Truman!

(San Diego: Harcourt, Inc., 2001)

Subject(s): Animals/Dogs; Pets; Behavior
Age range(s): Preschool-Grade 1
Major character(s): Truman, Dog; Oscar, Dog
Time period(s): 2000s (2001)
Locale(s): United States

Summary: Truman, a large, slobbery lovable dog, has a mind of his own. Little Oscar sits on command while Truman stands expectantly, waving one paw for attention. Truman thinks toilet bowls are a source of water and unattended lunches on the table must be waiting just for him. Oscar would like to share toys with Truman but sometimes Truman thinks Oscar is the toy. Walking two dogs of such disparate size is a challenging experience since Truman goes at his own pace and where he chooses. By the end of a long day Truman demonstrates just how nice he is by sleeping with Oscar on his very large dog bed. (32 pages)

Where it's reviewed:
Booklist, September 15, 2001, page 227
Horn Book Guide, Spring 2002, page 19
Publishers Weekly, August 20, 2001, page 79
School Library Journal, October 2001, page 119

Other books by the same author:
Telling Time with Big Mama Cat, 1998

Other books you might like:

Eric Copeland, *Milton, My Father's Dog*, 1994
When Fraser's parents go puppy shopping they come home with a one-year-old, rambunctious, enormous English sheep dog.

Alexandra Day, *Carl's Afternoon in the Park*, 1991
Carl, the family's pet rottweiler, looks after a puppy and a toddler while Mom visits with a friend.

Steven Kroll, *Oh, Tucker!*, 1998
A family's very large, exuberant dog seems to leave a trail of disaster behind him.

Cynthia Rylant, *The Henry and Mudge Series*, 1987-
The adventures of Henry and his lovable, slobbery dog Mudge entertain beginning readers.

375

JO HARPER

Delfino's Journey

(Lubbock, TX: Texas Tech University Press, 2001)

Subject(s): Illegal Immigrants; Indians of Mexico; Poverty
Age range(s): Grades 7-10
Major character(s): Delfino, 14-Year-Old, Indian (Aztec); Salvador, Cousin (of Delfino), Indian (Aztec); Bandit, Dog; Teresa, 18-Year-Old, Sister (of Delfino)
Time period(s): 2000s
Locale(s): Mexico; Texas

Summary: Worried about his pregnant married sister Teresa who needs good hospitalization for her delivery, Delfino and his cousin Salvador decide to enter the United States, find work and send money home. Almost drowning as they cross the Rio Grande, and deserted by the *coyote* they paid to help them across, the non-swimmers cling to the sinking boat and let the current carry them to the other side. Once on land their problems continue when they're picked up by the owner of a slave camp for laborers. Salvador has a special knack with animals and befriends Bandit, one of the camp's guard dogs, which makes it easier for the boys to escape. Making their way to Houston, Delfino and Salvador finally find jobs, help solve a murder and continue to rely on the Aztec teachings of their grandfather in this first novel. (184 pages)

Where it's reviewed:
Booklist, April 15, 2001, page 1545
Curriculum Review, April 2001, page 12

Other books you might like:

S. Beth Atkin, *Voices from the Fields: Children of Migrant Farmworkers Tell Their Stories*, 1993
Through interviews and poetry, teenage children of migrant workers share their dreams, family and friends. Nonfiction title.

Fran Leeper Buss, *Journey of the Sparrows*, 1991
Although life in America is difficult for illegal aliens, young Maria knows it's still better than the terror and killings that occur in El Salvador.

Francisco Jimenez, *The Circuit: Stories from the Life of a Migrant Child*, 1997
Stories based on the author's life as he moved from Mexico to California where he worked in the fields.

Gary Paulsen, *The Crossing*, 1987
Manny and Sergeant Lock's lives intertwine as each wants to escape, one from Mexico and one from the memories of Vietnam's horror.

376

KAREN HARPER

The Twylight Tower

(New York: Delacorte, 2001)

Series: Elizabeth I Mystery. Number 3
Subject(s): Mystery and Detective Stories; Historical
Age range(s): Grades 10-Adult

Major character(s): Elizabeth I, Royalty; Amy Robsart Dudley, Wife (of Lord Dudley), Nobleman; Robert Dudley, Nobleman

Time period(s): 16th century (1560)

Locale(s): England

Summary: Having ruled England for barely two years, Elizabeth I cannot afford gossip and scandal, for that gives her enemies opportunities to wrest the crown from her head. However, when her favorite lutenist falls to his death, her "Privy Plot Council," who has helped her in the past, decides the death was not accidental. Her servants begin their own investigation, which becomes more intense when Amy Robsart Dudley has a fall and dies. Normally this death would not create so much intrigue, but Amy is the frail wife of Robert Dudley, Elizabeth's childhood friend and the man she's flirted with all summer, in this third of a series. (289 pages)

Where it's reviewed:
Booklist, February 15, 2001, page 1119
Drood Review, January 2001, page 19
Globe & Mail, March 31, 2001, page D17
Library Journal, February 1, 2001, page 127
Publishers Weekly, February 26, 2001, page 62

Other books by the same author:
The Queen's Cure, 2002 (Elizabeth I Mystery, Number 4)
The Tidal Poole, 2000 (Elizabeth I Mystery, Number 2)
The Poyson Garden, 1999 (Elizabeth I Mystery, Number 1)

Other books you might like:
Fiona Buckley, *The Doublet Affair*, 1998
    Ursula agrees to spy for Queen Elizabeth I, but is kidnapped before she can determine if some friends are planning to overthrow the queen.
Ann Dukthas, *In the Time of the Poisoned Queen*, 1998
    Sickly Mary Tudor rules, Elizabeth I waits offstage, and the royalty receives strange letters, which lead to an investigation that reveals long-held secrets.
Kathy Lynn Emerson, *Face Down upon an Herbal*, 1998
    Susanna travels to Madderly Castle in Gloucester to work with Lady Madderly on her herbal manuscript, but murders require her attention instead.

GEORGE HARRAR

Parents Wanted

(Minneapolis, MN: Milkweed, 2001)

Subject(s): Adoption; Behavior

Age range(s): Grades 5-8

Major character(s): Andy Fleck, 12-Year-Old, Foster Child; Jeff Sizeracy, Foster Parent; Laurie Sizeracy, Foster Parent

Time period(s): 2000s

Locale(s): Massachusetts

Summary: With his father in jail, Andy's alcoholic mother decides she can no longer care for her attention deficit disorder son and gives him over to the state. After being kicked out of eight foster homes over the last two years, and attending countless adoption parties, Andy finally meets a childless couple that would like to adopt him, even when told all his behavior problems. At first Andy is willing to learn their rules, but he gradually reverts to his old behavior of dishonesty to get around problems, sassing Laurie and stealing money from Jeff. When he doesn't want to help with chores one weekend, he falsely accuses Jeff of child molestation and is returned to social services. Andy finally realizes that Laurie and Jeff really do love him, but now he may have ruined his chances of a permanent adoption and must try to convince authorities that he lied. (239 pages)

Where it's reviewed:
Booklist, December 15, 2001, page 723
Publishers Weekly, September 3, 2001, page 88
Riverbank Review, Winter 2001-2002, page 40
School Library Journal, November 2001, page 158
Voice of Youth Advocates, December 2001, page 60

Awards the book has won:
Milkweed Prize for Children's Literature, 2001

Other books by the same author:
First Tiger, 1999
Junk in Space, 1991

Other books you might like:
Jack Gantos, *Joey Pigza Swallowed the Key*, 1998
    When Joey's not on his medication, he sharpens his finger, cuts off the end of a classmate's nose and swallows his key.
Mary Quattlebaum, *Grover C. Graham and Me,* 2001
    Heading for his eighth foster home, Ben has learned to remain distant, but at the Torgles there's chaos, love and Grover, an abandoned fourteenth-month-old baby.
Hilma Wolitzer, *Toby Lived Here*, 1978
    Toby and her younger sister have different adjustment problems when they're sent to a foster home.

378

CAROL FLYNN HARRIS

A Place for Joey

(Honesdale, PA: Boyds Mill Press, 2001)

Subject(s): Emigration and Immigration; Historical

Age range(s): Grades 4-7

Major character(s): Giuseppe "Joey" Calabro, 12-Year-Old, Immigrant

Time period(s): 1920s

Locale(s): Boston, Massachusetts (north end of Boston)

Summary: Coming to America as a young boy, Joey doesn't know much about his homeland of Italy, just what he hears from his parents; he does, however, know that he loves living in the North End of Boston. Because Joey enjoys the sights, sounds and smells of the city, he doesn't share his parents' dream of buying a farm in the country and makes up his mind to drop out of school and find a job so that he can stay in the North End. One day he skips school and just happens to be on the waterfront when he hears an explosion and realizes a storage tank has exploded, destroying homes and buildings and spewing a flood of molasses into the street. His rescue of a policeman from the sticky syrup causes him to rethink his plans, move with his parents, but then return to the city when he's older, possibly to become a policeman, in this first novel. (90 pages)

Where it's reviewed:
Booklist, September 1, 2001, page 104
Publishers Weekly, March 26, 2001, page 93
School Library Journal, September 1, 2001, page 189
Voice of Youth Advocates, October 2001, page 277

Other books you might like:
Judie Angell, *One-Way to Ansonia*, 1985
    For immigrant Rose, the only way to achieve her dream of a home is to attend night school after working all day at the Griffin Cap Factory.
Robert Lehrman, *The Store That Mama Built*, 1992
    After moving to America, the Fried family has to adapt to their mother becoming a storeowner after the death of their father.
Marilyn Sachs, *Call Me Ruth*, 1982
    Russian immigrant Ruth and her mother can't agree on which culture to adopt, the old way or the new American way.
Gloria Skurzynski, *The Tempering*, 1983
    At the turn of the century, Karl must decide whether to stay in school or work in a steel mill.

379

ROBIE H. HARRIS
JAN ORMEROD, Illustrator

Goodbye Mousie
(New York: Margaret K. McElderry Books, 2001)

Subject(s): Death (of a Pet); Grief; Animals/Mice
Age range(s): Grades K-2
Major character(s): Mousie, Mouse; Daddy, Father; Mommy, Mother; Unnamed Character, Child, Son
Time period(s): 2000s (2001)
Locale(s): United States

Summary: When a little boy is unable to awaken his pet one morning he has difficulty accepting the truth of Daddy's observation that Mousie is dead. Daddy responds to his son's anger and tears with calm understanding and sincere expressions of sorrow. Mommy offers a shoebox to hold Mousie and her son gently fills it with items that he considers important to Mousie. Finally, they bury Mousie in the backyard and mark the spot with a carefully lettered sign proclaiming, ''Mousie is right here!'' (32 pages)

Where it's reviewed:
Booklist, September 1, 2001, page 114
Bulletin of the Center for Children's Books, October 2001, page 59
Kirkus Reviews, June 1, 2001, page 939
Publishers Weekly, July 30, 2001, page 83
School Library Journal, September 2001, page 190

Awards the book has won:
Publishers Weekly Best Children's Books, 2001

Other books by the same author:
Hi, New Baby!, 2000
Happy Birth Day!, 1996

Other books you might like:
Ezra Jack Keats, *Maggie and the Pirate*, 1979
    Maggie searches for her stolen pet cricket; death claims her pet, but Maggie finds a friend.
Holly Keller, *Goodbye, Max*, 1987
    Ben grieves for his dog, Max, expresses anger toward his parents and rejects the new puppy they offer.
Fred Rogers, *When a Pet Dies*, 1988
    The death of a pet arouses many conflicting emotions in a child.
Judith Viorst, *The Tenth Good Thing about Barney*, 1971
    When his cat dies, a young boy consoles himself by thinking of the ten best things her remembers about his pet.
Ruth Wallace-Brodeur, *Goodbye, Mitch*, 1995
    Michael's mom tries to prepare him for the inevitable death of his old cat.

380

TROON HARRISON

A Bushel of Light
(New York: Stoddart Publishing, 2001)

Subject(s): Twins; Orphans; Farm Life
Age range(s): Grades 5-8
Major character(s): Maggie Curnow, 14-Year-Old, Orphan; Thomasina Curnow, 14-Year-Old, Orphan; Matthew Howard, Farmer; Kathleen Howard, Wife (of Matthew); Lizzie Howard, Child
Time period(s): 1900s
Locale(s): St. Ives, England; Bridgenorth, Ontario, Canada

Summary: Maggie and her twin sister Thomasina, orphaned at the age of five, are separated when they're eight with Maggie sent to Canada to live with Matthew Howard's family where she immediately begins working on their farm. Now fourteen, it seems she's responsible for all the chores, from gardening to cooking, cleaning and even caring for the Howard's youngest daughter, Lizzie. Maggie is excited, though, because she's now old enough to be paid for her work and plans to use her wages to find her sister who she hears has been sent to Canada. Sadly she discovers that, though she can now earn a wage, she doesn't receive any money until she's twenty-one. Though the pull to find her twin is strong, the lack of money and her concern about abandoning Lizzie weigh heavily in Maggie's mind as she struggles to make a decision. (244 pages)

Where it's reviewed:
Resource Links, April 2001, page 24
School Library Journal, October 2001, page 158

Other books by the same author:
Goodbye to Atlantis, 2002

Other books you might like:
Lonnie Coleman, *Orphan Jim*, 1975
    Rather than let the schoolmarm put them in the Orphans' Home, Trudy and her brother Jim run away from home.
David DeVries, *Home at Last*, 1992
    New York-bred Billy has a hard time fitting in with the Anderson family after being sent to Nebraska by the Children's Aid Society.

Joan Lowery Nixon, *The Orphan Train Quartet*, 1987-1989
A series of books featuring the Kelly children who are sent West on the Orphan Train after their widowed mother realizes she cannot care for all of them.

Zilpha Keatley Snyder, *Gib Rides Home*, 1998
Gib jumps at the chance to leave the orphanage and work on Mr. Thornton's ranch, especially when he's able to care for the horses.

381

GERALD HAUSMAN
UTON HINDS, Co-Author

The Jacob Ladder
(New York: Scholastic/Orchard, 2001)

Subject(s): Poverty; Family Life; Fathers and Sons
Age range(s): Grades 5-8
Major character(s): Uton "Tall T" Hinds, 12-Year-Old; John "Brother John" Hinds, Father; Vera Watson, Neighbor, Witch (*obeah* lady)
Time period(s): 1960s
Locale(s): Oracabessa, Jamaica

Summary: Though Tall T loves his father, who's respected as a leader in their small town, he recognizes Brother John's weakness for rum and rolling the bone dice. When Tall T is twelve, the *obeah* woman living next door slips a voodoo potion into his father's soup and entices him to leave his family and move in with her. With three brothers and two sisters, it's up to Tall T to help his oldest brother support their family. Since he has no money for a school uniform anyway, he halts his education and toils at any odd job he can find. Luckily the local librarian, Miss Patterson, helps him continue his reading. His moment of self-worth comes when he's able to conquer his fear and climb up the steep cliff by means of fig vines, known locally as climbing Jacob's Ladder, a feat accomplished by only a few men, including his father. This fictionalized autobiography is based on the childhood of co-author Uton Hinds. (120 pages)

Where it's reviewed:
Book Report, September 2001, page 61
Booklist, May 1, 2001, page 1678
Kirkus Reviews, March 15, 2001, page 409
School Library Journal, April 2001, page 140
Voice of Youth Advocates, June 2001, page 122

Other books by the same author:
Tom Cringle: The Pirate and the Patriot, 2001
Tom Cringle: Battle on the High Seas, 2000
Coyote Bead, 1999
Night Flight, 1996

Other books you might like:
James R. Berry, *A Thief in the Village and Other Stories of Jamaica*, 1988
Nine stories that capture the quiet simplicity of Caribbean life on the island of Jamaica.

Hugh B. Cave, *Conquering Kilmarnie*, 1989
A story of the friendship of two young boys in Jamaica, one black and one white.

Phyllis Reynolds Naylor, *The Fear Place*, 1994
When his brother is lost, Doug doesn't hesitate to climb over a narrow ledge he calls his "fear place" to rescue him.

382

GERALD HAUSMAN
TAD HILLS, Illustrator

Tom Cringle: The Pirate and the Patriot
(New York: Simon & Schuster, 2001)

Series: Tom Cringle
Subject(s): Pirates; Slavery; Diaries
Age range(s): Grades 5-8
Major character(s): Tom Cringle, Sailor, 14-Year-Old; Sneezer, Dog (Newfoundland); Peter Mangrove, Sailor, Slave (former)
Time period(s): 1810s (1813)
Locale(s): *Kraaken*, At Sea

Summary: Promoted because of his bravery and heroic feats, Tom Cringle serves aboard the HMS *Kraaken* in the Caribbean, patrolling against slave runners and American ships. When the *Kraaken* captures a ship filled with stolen slaves, it falls to Tom to return them to their owner, an odious task to him. Accompanied by Sneezer and Tom's good friend and former slave Peter Mangrove, the men march their captives through the jungle of Jamaica to Cinnamon Hill plantation, but continually stave off attacks by the pirates who want to reclaim their goods in the second Tom Cringle adventure. (157 pages)

Where it's reviewed:
Booklist, September 15, 2001, page 222
Kirkus Reviews, July 1, 2001, page 939
School Library Journal, October 2001, page 160

Other books by the same author:
The Jacob Ladder, 2001
Tom Cringle: Battle on the High Seas, 2000 (Tom Cringle)
Doctor Moledinky's Castle: A Hometown Tale, 1995

Other books you might like:
Erik Christian Haugaard, *Under the Black Flag*, 1994
Sailing to England for boarding school, William is captured by Blackbeard, held for ransom and eventually becomes Blackbeard's cabin boy.

Iain Lawrence, *The Buccaneers*, 2001
Picking up a drifting sailor proves advantageous for John Spencer, aboard the schooner *Dragon*, when they're later attacked by pirates.

Geraldine McCaughrean, *The Pirate's Son*, 1998
In a rollicking escapade, orphans Nathaniel and his sister Maud accompany Tamo, son of a deceased pirate, to his home in Madagascar.

PETE HAUTMAN

Hole in the Sky

(New York: Simon & Schuster, 2001)

Subject(s): Quest; Diseases; Survival
Age range(s): Grades 7-10
Major character(s): Ceej Kane, Brother, Friend; Tim, Friend
Time period(s): 2020s (2028)
Locale(s): Grand Canyon

Summary: A deadly flu virus empties the earth and destroys civilization. In the post-apocalyptic world, Ceej and his friend Tim struggle to survive. When Ceej's sister goes missing, the two friends are determined to discover whether she has willingly joined the cultish marauders who deliberately try to infect others or if she has been kidnapped because she is a survivor. As they travel though Grand Canyon country, the boys meet a young Hopi girl who claims the spirit of her grandfather will guide them to the entrance to another, safer world. (179 pages)

Where it's reviewed:
Booklist, April 15, 2001, page 1554
Horn Book Magazine, May 2001, page 325
Publishers Weekly, May 14, 2001, page 83
School Library Journal, June 2001, page 149

Other books by the same author:
Stone Cold, 1998
Mr. Was, 1996

Other books you might like:
John Marsden, *The Dead of Night*, 1997
    Returning after a camping trip to a conquered land, Ellie and her friends struggle to survive.
Pat Murphy, *The City, Not Long After*, 1989
    Artists take over the city of San Francisco when a world wide plague decimates the world's population.
Jean Ure, *Plague*, 1991
    Returning home after a wilderness survival trip, several teens discover that everyone else has died of a plague.

384

GEOFFREY HAYES, Author/Illustrator

Patrick and the Big Bully

(New York: Hyperion Books for Children, 2001)

Series: Adventures of Patrick Brown. Number 1
Subject(s): Animals/Bears; Bullies; Imagination
Age range(s): Grades K-2
Major character(s): Patrick Brown, Bear, Bullied Child; Mama Bear, Bear, Mother; Big Bear, Bear, Bully
Time period(s): Indeterminate
Locale(s): Puttyville, Fictional Country

Summary: Patrick feels brave in his own yard imagining that he's a roaring dragon but he's a little concerned about Mama Bear's request that he walk to the corner store and buy cookies for lunch. With Mama Bear's encouragement he sets off and walks right into Big Bear who tries to take his money. Patrick manages to elude him and get the cookies but Big Bear follows him and tries to get the cookies. Then Patrick thinks of dragons, lets out his fiercest roar and hurries away from Big Bear again. (40 pages)

Where it's reviewed:
Horn Book Guide, Spring 2002, page 44
Publishers Weekly, October 1, 2001, page 61
School Library Journal, January 2002, page 101

Other books by the same author:
Patrick and His Grandpa, 1986
Patrick and Ted, 1984
Bear by Himself, 1976

Other books you might like:
Judith Caseley, *Bully*, 2001
    To stop Mack's bullying behavior Mickey tries to befriend him.
Ezra Jack Keats, *Goggles*, 1969
    In a Caldecott Honor Book two boys have to deal with neighborhood bullies who also want the motorcycle goggles they've found.
Gina Mayer, *Just a Bully*, 1999
    A bully at school causes problems for Little Critter and Little Sister.

385

JOE HAYES
JOSEPH DANIEL FIEDLER, Illustrator

Juan Verdades: The Man Who Couldn't Tell a Lie

(New York: Orchard Books, 2001)

Subject(s): Folklore; Honesty; Conduct of Life
Age range(s): Grades 2-5
Major character(s): Juan "Juan Verdades" Valdez, Foreman; don Ignacio, Rancher, Wealthy; don Arturo, Rancher, Gambler; Araceli, Daughter (don Arturo's)
Time period(s): Indeterminate Past
Locale(s): Southwest

Summary: The foreman on don Ignacio's ranch has such a reputation for honesty that he is known by all as Juan Verdades. While the simple fact of his truthfulness is accepted by all the ranchers don Arturo wagers his ranch that he can get Juan Verdades to tell don Ignacio a lie. Araceli plots with her father to achieve his goal and secretly to achieve one of her own. When don Arturo is certain that he's won the bet that he calls in all the other ranchers as witnesses, but Juan Verdades, in reporting his actions to don Ignacio, does so without lying. He uses a riddle to admit his guilt and don Arturo loses the bet. Don Ignacio will not accept the deed to don Arturo's ranch but asks that it be signed over to Juan Verdades. Now, Araceli is able to complete her secret plot and her family's ranch remains in the family when she weds Juan Verdades. (32 pages)

Where it's reviewed:
Booklist, December 1, 2001, page 646
Horn Book Guide, Spring 2002, page 118
Publishers Weekly, November 12, 2001, page 59
School Library Journal, December 2001, page 122

Other books by the same author:
Little Gold Star/Estrellita de Oro, 2000
A Spoon for Every Bite, 1996 (New Mexico's Land of Enchantment Children's Book Award)

Other books you might like:
Teresa Bateman, *The Ring of Truth*, 1997
Patrick's gift for blarney suffers when the king of the leprechauns gives him a ring that cannot be removed and requires him to always speak the truth.
Bill Cosby, *My Big Lie*, 1999
Little Bill's explanation as to why he is late for dinner is not truthful and he suffers the consequences.
Patricia C. McKissack, *The Honest-to-Goodness Truth*, 2000
Comments Libby makes while attempting to always be completely truthful offend her friends.

386

BETSY GOULD HEARNE

Wishes, Kisses, and Pigs
(New York: Simon & Schuster, 2001)

Subject(s): Wishes; Animals/Pigs; Magic
Age range(s): Grades 4-6
Major character(s): Louise Tolliver, 11-Year-Old; Willie Tolliver, Brother (of Louise); Clara Tolliver, Mother
Time period(s): 2000s
Locale(s): Tolliver's Hollow

Summary: Louise never intends for her brother to become a pig; matter of fact, she's not even sure that he is a pig, but she doesn't know what else to think for Willie hasn't been seen since the night he teases her about wishing on a star. One moment Willie is there, and the next he isn't, but the following day a white pig with blue eyes appears. Louise's mother Clara calls the sheriff who says he'll look for Willie, but about then Louise guesses the pig is really Willie and it's up to her to figure out how to get him back. And she'd better do it soon as some neighbors are making plans to fatten up the Tolliver's new pig while the sheriff's brother thinks the pig belongs to him. As Louise discovers, wishes and kisses make life magical. (133 pages)

Where it's reviewed:
Book, November 2001, page 75
Booklist, March 1, 2001, page 1278
Horn Book, May 2001, page 326
Publishers Weekly, March 26, 2001, page 93
School Library Journal, April 2001, page 140

Other books by the same author:
The Canine Connection: Stories about Dogs and Humans, 2003
Listening for Leroy, 1998

Other books you might like:
Ellen Conford, *Genie with the Light Blue Hair*, 1989
Jeannie receives an antique lamp complete with a blue Groucho Marx-like genie who's a little rusty in granting wishes.
Peni R. Griffin, *Switching Well*, 1993
When a fairy hears the wishes of Ada and Amber, she sends Ada forward in time and Amber back. Each quickly realizes she's traded one set of problems for another.
Jackie French Koller, *If I Had One Wish*, 1991
Alec wishes he'd never had a younger brother and, horror of horrors, his wish comes true. There's no sign of his little brother anywhere.
Joyce Sweeney, *The Dream Collector*, 1989
Becky's Christmas present to her family members of a self-help book to make wishes come true backfires when wishes come true in undesirable ways.

387

KEVIN HENKES, Author/Illustrator

Sheila Rae's Peppermint Stick
(New York: Greenwillow/HarperCollins Publishers, 2001)

Subject(s): Animals/Mice; Sisters; Sharing
Age range(s): Preschool-Kindergarten
Major character(s): Sheila Rae, Mouse, Sister (older); Louise, Mouse, Sister (younger)
Time period(s): Indeterminate
Locale(s): Fictional Country

Summary: Sheila Rae has a sweet, striped yummy looking peppermint stick and Louise wants one too. Sheila Rae expects her polite sister to correctly guess the number of stripes if she wants just one lick. Next Sheila Rae gives Louise the impossible task of reaching the stick while Sheila Rae stands on a stack of books and pillows piled on a stool. Of course, as Sheila Rae points out, there's the added problem that she does not have two sticks so can't give one away to Louise. Sheila Rae's plan collapses literally when the books, pillows and stool tip throwing Sheila Rae to the floor. Louise picks up half of the broken peppermint stick and both enjoy the sweet licks. (24 pages)

Where it's reviewed:
Booklist, August 2001, page 2180
Horn Book, September 2001, page 574
Kirkus Reviews, June 15, 2001, page 863
Publishers Weekly, September 10, 2001, page 95
School Library Journal, December 2001, page 104

Awards the book has won:
ALA Notable Children's Books, 2002
Parenting's Reading Magic Awards, 2001

Other books by the same author:
Wemberly Worried, 2000 (School Library Journal Best Books)
Oh!, 1999
Lilly's Purple Plastic Purse, 1996 (School Library Journal Best Books)
Owen, 1993 (Caldecott Honor Book)
Sheila Rae, the Brave, 1987

Other books you might like:
Russell Hoban, *A Birthday for Frances*, 1968
A Chompo bar makes such a delicious birthday gift for a sister that it's no surprise it's nibbled away on the walk home from the store.
Laura McGee Kvasnosky, *Zelda and Ivy*, 1998
Big sister Zelda tries to dominate the play activities with

her own ideas but little sister Ivy is learning how to fend for herself.

Rosemary Wells, *Max's Chocolate Chicken*, 1989

It looks as if older sister Ruby will find the most Easter eggs but Max makes off with the chocolate chicken prize anyway.

388

JOHN HERMAN

Labyrinth

(New York: Philomel, 2001)

Subject(s): Dreams and Nightmares; Fathers and Sons; Mythology

Age range(s): Grades 7-10

Major character(s): Gregory/Gregor Levi, 14-Year-Old; Virginia Powers, Girlfriend (of Jed), 16-Year-Old; Jed Turner, Student—High School, Motorcyclist; Minotaur, Mythical Creature

Time period(s): 2000s

Locale(s): United States

Summary: Life becomes difficult for Gregory after his father commits suicide and his mother begins a romance with someone from her past. Gregory hangs out with other misfits, including Jed and his girlfriend Virginia Powers, daughter of Gregory's father's boss and the man he thinks is responsible for the suicide. Gregory lives more and more dangerously, until he, Jed and Virginia decide to use the city's underground tunnels to burglarize homes and offices. At the same time, Gregory has weird dreams where he lives in a parallel world and is called Gregor. As Gregor, he's chosen as one of the ten Golden men who will be sent to their mother country to represent their nation, which is a nice way to say they'll be sacrificed to the Minotaur. Gregor's dream world and Gregory's real world gradually entwine and coalesce until he's not sure what's true and what isn't. (188 pages)

Where it's reviewed:
Bulletin of the Center for Children's Books, October 2001, page 59
Horn Book, July 2001, page 451
Publishers Weekly, June 4, 2001, page 81
School Library Journal, August 2001, page 183
Voice of Youth Advocates, June 2001, page 133

Other books by the same author:
Deep Waters, 1998

Other books you might like:
Ilene Cooper, *I'll See You in My Dreams*, 1997
Because so many of Karen's nightmares come true, she worries when her dreams about a friend's younger brother become dark and foreboding.

Priscilla Galloway, *Snake Dreamer*, 1998
Claiming to cure people who suffer from dreams of snakes, the two sisters are actually Gorgons searching for Medusa.

Brian Keaney, *No Need for Heroes*, 1989
Daughter of King Minos, Ariadne tells her version of the Minotaur myth, starting with the arrival of Daedalus and Icarus on her island.

Clemence McLaren, *Waiting for Odysseus*, 2000
As Odysseus returns home following the siege of Troy, his story is related through the eyes of four women in his life, beginning with his wife Penelope.

389

PATRICIA HERMES

The Starving Time: Elizabeth's Diary

(New York: Scholastic Inc., 2001)

Series: My America

Subject(s): American Colonies; American History; Diaries

Age range(s): Grades 3-5

Major character(s): Elizabeth "Lizzie" Barker, Settler, 9-Year-Old; Caleb Barker, Twin, 9-Year-Old; Pocahontas, Indian, Friend

Time period(s): 17th century (1609)

Locale(s): Jamestown, Virginia, American Colonies

Summary: Lizzie sends her first diary back to Caleb in England so he will know what to expect in this new land when the spring supply ship brings him to join the family. Though Lizzie's family has a house now the leadership of the settlement is fractured and the colonists fear the Indians. Food is scarce and with the winter also comes sickness that contributes to the loss of life. In an effort to help her family Lizzie sneaks out of the fort to a nearby Indian village seeking help from Pocohontas. Illness and fatigue keep Lizzie from fulfilling her mission but friendly Indians find her and lead the feverish child back to the fort then silently leave food at the fort's gate. Though the harsh winter takes her mother the spring brings a supply ship with Caleb aboard. A "Historical Note" completes the book. (107 pages)

Where it's reviewed:
Horn Book Guide, Fall 2001, page 291
School Library Journal, June 2001, page 118

Other books by the same author:
Our Strange New Land: Elizabeth's Diary, 2000 (My America)
On Winter's Wind, 1995
Nothing but Trouble, Trouble, Trouble, 1994

Other books you might like:
Jean Fritz, *The Double Life of Pocahontas*, 1983
The life of Pocahontas is intertwined with and influenced by the settlement of Jamestown.

Brendan January, *The Jamestown Colony*, 2001
A title in the nonfiction "We the People" series describes the first permanent English settlement in North America.

Gail Langer Karwoski, *Surviving Jamestown: The Adventures of Young Sam Collier*, 2001
Sam Collier, twelve-year-old page to John Smith, witnesses the hardship of life in the New World settlement at Jamestown.

PATRICIA HERMES

Westward to Home: Joshua's Diary
(New York: Scholastic Inc., 2001)

Series: My America
Subject(s): Frontier and Pioneer Life; American West; Diaries
Age range(s): Grades 3-5
Major character(s): Joshua Martin McCullough, 9-Year-Old, Pioneer
Time period(s): 1840s (1848)
Locale(s): St. Joseph, Missouri; Oregon

Summary: The excitement of embarking on a cross-country journey is evident in Joshua's diary entries, but as the trek gets underway his observations reflect the reality of the difficult journey. Dust chokes them as they walk, death through accident, illness or arrowshot takes lives of young and old, even one of Joshua's cousins. He and his family value the friendships made with fellow travelers while some others Joshua would prefer to leave by the side of the trail. Along the way Joshua knows fear and learns the meaning of courage. He works beside his family to assure their safe arrival in Oregon where they will make their new home. The book concludes with a "Historical Note." (108 pages)

Where it's reviewed:
Booklist, February 1, 2001, page 1053
Horn Book Guide, Fall 2001, page 292
Kirkus Reviews, December 1, 2000, page 1682

Other books by the same author:
The Starving Time: Elizabeth's Diary, 2001 (My America)
Calling Me Home, 1998
On Winter's Wind, 1995

Other books you might like:
Jane Kurtz, *I'm Sorry, Almira Ann*, 1999
   The tedium of Sarah's journey with her family on the Oregon Trail tests her patience and threatens her friendship with Almira Ann.
Marissa Moss, *Rachel's Journal: The Story of a Pioneer Girl*, 1998
   A fictionalized diary gives an account of daily life for a family traveling to California in 1850.
Elvira Woodruff, *Dear Levi: Letters from the Overland Trail*, 1994
   In letters to his younger brother, 12-year-old Austin Ives describes his journey from Pennsylvania to Oregon.

391
JOANNA HERSHON

Swimming
(New York: Ballantine, 2001)

Subject(s): Family Problems; Secrets; Brothers
Age range(s): Grades 10-Adult
Major character(s): Aaron Wheeler, Brother; Suzanne Hannon, Girlfriend (of Aaron's); Jack Wheeler, Brother; Lila Wheeler, Sister (of Aaron and Jack)
Time period(s): 1980s; 1990s
Locale(s): New Hampshire; New York, New York

Summary: Young Lila adores her two older brothers and is not aware of the jealousy and tension that lie between them. These expressions stay hidden until Aaron brings his girlfriend Suzanne to their home in the woods with its pond for swimming. Aaron's younger brother Jack captures Suzanne's interest and when Aaron finds them together, hits Jack hard enough to lead to tragedy. Aaron disappears, leaving Suzanne and Lila to face his parents. Ten years later Lila begins college, still wondering what really happened that night, but now determined to find out as she tracks down Suzanne in a haunting first novel of what was and what could have been. (356 pages)

Where it's reviewed:
Booklist, November 15, 2000, page 621
Kirkus Reviews, January 1, 2001, page 11
Library Journal, December 2000, page 188
Publishers Weekly, February 5, 2001, page 69

Other books you might like:
Jane Hamilton, *The Short History of a Prince*, 1998
   Now a 30-year-old man teaching school in a small town, Walter reviews his life and regrets some of the choices he made in his early adult years.
Sue Miller, *Family Pictures*, 1990
   The shortcomings and failings of a Chicago family are revealed in this look at forty years in the lives of the Eberhardts.
Michael C. White, *A Dream of Wolves: A Novel*, 2001
   Both obstetrician and medical examiner for Hubbard County, Doc fosters a child partly to atone for the guilt he feels over his own son's death.

392
KAREN HESSE

Witness
(New York: Scholastic, 2001)

Subject(s): Prejudice; Social Issues
Age range(s): Grades 6-9
Major character(s): Leanora Sutter, 12-Year-Old; Esther Hirsh, Child
Time period(s): 1920s
Locale(s): Vermont

Summary: Using free verse and distinctive voices, Hesse describes the reactions of eleven Vermonters when the Ku Klux Klan slithers into their town. The two girls most likely to be victims of Klan violence are Esther Hirsh, a young Jewish girl, and Leanora Sutter, a young black girl. Esther cannot understand why anyone would want to hurt her while Leanora is a little more aware of white hatred toward blacks, especially since she and her father are the only black people in town. The reader is also introduced to the town's newspaper editor, a couple who share opposite opinions of the Klan, a young Klan member who changes his mind after seeing Leanora's heroism, a preacher and others. Divided into five acts, this book begs to be read aloud as part of a reader's theater. (161 pages)

Where it's reviewed:
Bulletin of the Center for Children's Books, November 2001, page 103
Kliatt, September 2001, page 8
School Library Journal, August 20, 2001, page 80
School Library Journal, September 2001, page 225
Voice of Youth Advocates, October 2001, page 277

Awards the book has won:
School Library Journal Best Books, 2001
ALA Notable Children's Books, 2002

Other books by the same author:
Stowaway, 2000
A Light in the Storm: The Civil War Diary of Amelia Martin, 1999 (Dear America)
A Time of Angels, 1999
Out of the Dust, 1997
The Music of Dolphins, 1996

Other books you might like:
Mildred Barger Herschler, *The Darkest Corner*, 2000
One of Teddy's earliest recollections is the horror she felt at seeing her father with a group of sheeted men standing in front of the hanged body of her best friend's father.
Trudy Krisher, *Spite Fences*, 1994
The summer Maggie Pugh is thirteen remains embedded in her memory as the summer she realizes how racist her town is.
Carolyn Meyer, *White Lilacs*, 1993
The black community of Freedomtown opposes being moved to the sewer flats, but marches by the Ku Klux Klan stop their planned action.

393

AMY HEST
CLAIRE A. NIVOLA, Illustrator

The Friday Nights of Nana
(Cambridge, MA: Candlewick Press, 2001)

Subject(s): Grandmothers; Jews; Religious Traditions
Age range(s): Grades K-2
Major character(s): Jennie, Child, Sister (older); Nana, Grandmother, Cook
Time period(s): Indeterminate Past
Locale(s): United States

Summary: For Jennie Friday nights with Nana begin early in the day over tea and bread with jam. Jennie helps Nana by folding napkins, polishing candlesticks, making beds, cooking, and shopping for flowers. Finally it's time to don their Sabbath dresses and greet the other members of the family, including Jennie's parents and baby brother, as they arrive at Nana's home. Lighting the candles signals the time for Sabbath prayers and a shared meal to begin. (32 pages)

Where it's reviewed:
Booklist, October 1, 2001, page 334
Kirkus Reviews, July 1, 2001, page 939
Publishers Weekly, August 27, 2001, page 82
School Library Journal, October 2001, page 120
Smithsonian, November 2001, page 124

Awards the book has won:
Smithsonian's Notable Books for Children, 2001

Other books by the same author:
Mabel Dancing, 2000
When Jessie Came Across the Sea, 1997 (Notable Children's Trade Books in the Field of Social Studies)
Nana's Birthday Party, 1993 (Booklist Editors' Choice)

Other books you might like:
Joan C. Hawxhurst, *Bubbe and Gram: My Two Grandmothers*, 1993
Grandmothers of different faiths teach their grandchild about the customs of Judaism and Christianity.
Fran Manushkin, *Starlight and Candles: The Joys of the Sabbath*, 1995
Together, a family prepares for and celebrates the simple but never-ending joys of the Sabbath.
Roni Schotter, *Passover Magic*, 1995
Molly and Ben eagerly welcome the relatives arriving for the special Passover dinner.

394

AMY HEST
ANITA JERAM, Illustrator

Kiss Good Night
(Cambridge, MA: Candlewick Press, 2001)

Subject(s): Animals/Bears; Bedtime; Mothers and Sons
Age range(s): Preschool-Kindergarten
Major character(s): Sam, Bear, Son; Mrs. Bear, Bear, Mother
Time period(s): Indeterminate
Locale(s): Fictional Country

Summary: Mrs. Bear tucks Sam into bed on a stormy night. She reads Sam's favorite book, puts all his special friends under the covers with him and brings him warm milk. Still Sam waits as the wind howls and tossed branches hit the little house on Plum Street. Mrs. Bear reviews all the things she's done as part of the bedtime ritual, but can't seem to remember what Sam is waiting so patiently to receive. Finally, Mrs. Bear realizes it's a ''kiss good night'' Sam wants, again and again before he closes his eyes and allows sleep to overtake him. (32 pages)

Where it's reviewed:
Booklist, October 1, 2001, page 325
Kirkus Reviews, August 15, 2001, page 1213
Publishers Weekly, August 6, 2001, page 88
School Library Journal, November 2001, page 124

Other books by the same author:
Mabel Dancing, 2000
Off to School, Baby Duck!, 1999 (Booklist Editors' Choice)
In the Rain with Baby Duck, 1995 (Boston Globe-Horn Book Fanfare Award)

Other books you might like:
Kate Banks, *And If the Moon Could Talk*, 1998
Following a bedtime ritual with her parents, a child, wrapped in love, sleeps while the silent moon watches over all.
Mem Fox, *Sleepy Bears*, 1999
As winter nears Mother Bear calls her children inside for a bedtime rhyme before they sleep.

Russell Hoban, *Bedtime for Frances*, 1960
Frances is a master at avoiding sleep but her patient parents have a response for every problem.
Martin Waddell, *Can't You Sleep, Little Bear?*, 1988
Big Bear comforts Little Bear when a fear of the dark keeps him from dozing off.

395

JIM HEYNEN

The Boys' House: New and Selected Stories

(St. Paul, MN: Minnesota Historical Society Press, 2001)

Subject(s): Farm Life; Short Stories
Age range(s): Grades 7-12
Locale(s): Midwest

Summary: More than sixty short stories, culled from previous collections or written expressly for this book, reflect what it's like for some boys who live on a farm. Their grandfather offers them advice on milking cows that are kickers; leads them to find a robin's nest, but gets waylaid by memories of old farm equipment; and reminds them of how much harder his chores were than theirs. New discoveries await them every day from spotting the albino fox to locating sows buried under snowdrifts, catching the one-eyed pony or reviving a dying pigeon. And the characters they meet could fill another book, whether it be the lady who keeps geese in her house or their uncle Jack whose craziness is a matter of debate. Like the farm on which these stories take place, this collection is warm and redolent. (186 pages)

Where it's reviewed:
Booklist, July 2001, page 1980
Publishers Weekly, July 16, 2001, page 158

Awards the book has won:
Booklist Editors' Choice/Adult Books for Young Adults, 2001

Other books by the same author:
Fishing for Chickens: Short Stories about Rural Youth, 2001
Cosmos Coyote and William the Nice, 2000
Being Youngest, 1997
The One-Room Schoolhouse: Stories about the Boys, 1994

Other books you might like:
Alden R. Carter, *Growing Season*, 1984
The first year of farm life for a city family draws them all closer together.
Paula Fox, *The Western Wind*, 1993
Elizabeth resents being sent to her grandmother's for the summer, but that feeling fades as she hears the family stories her grandmother shares.
Gary Paulsen, *Alida's Song*, 1999
The boy is glad to leave his alcoholic parents and spend the summer working on the farm where his grandmother is the cook.

396

JIM HEYNEN, Editor

Fishing for Chickens: Short Stories about Rural Youth

(New York: Persea Books, 2001)

Subject(s): Short Stories; Rural Life; Farm Life
Age range(s): Grades 7-12
Locale(s): United States

Summary: The works of noted and lesser-known authors fill this anthology about the reality of farm life for young people. In Vicky Wicks's story "I Have the Serpent Brought" a young girl wants desperately to raise fox cubs as pets, but her father knows the danger they represent for his chickens and destroys them. A bird distracts Meg in Nancy Brown's "Burn Pile" and a fire that she's tending leaps out of control. The delicious smell of pineapple loses its appeal after the tediousness of factory work in "Pick Up Your Pine" by Kathleen Tyau. Balancing the frustration and hard work of farm life is a lighter piece called "Sugar Among the Chickens" by Lewis Nordan about a boy who baits his hook to catch a rooster when his mother won't let him walk to the town pond to fish. Other authors include Wallace Stegner, Alice Walker, Jim Heynen and Tomas Rivera. (177 pages)

Where it's reviewed:
Booklist, September 15, 2001, page 215
Kliatt, November 2001, page 23
Publishers Weekly, July 16, 2001, page 182
School Library Journal, October 2001, page 160
Voice of Youth Advocates, October 2001, page 274

Other books by the same author:
Standing Naked: New and Selected Poems, 2001
The Boys' House: New and Selected Stories, 2001
Cosmos Coyote and William the Nice, 2000
Being Youngest, 1997
The One-Room Schoolhouse: Stories about the Boys, 1994

Other books you might like:
Alden R. Carter, *Growing Season*, 1984
The first year of farm life for a city family draws them all closer together as each member pitches in to help the farm succeed.
Natalie Kinsey-Warnock, *As Long as There Are Mountains*, 1997
Iris's dream comes true when her uncle agrees to co-own the family farm with her which allows her to continue doing what she loves best—farming.
Gretchen Olson, *Joyride*, 1998
After a summer working on a berry farm rather than playing tennis, Jeff finds a new group of friends who prove to be warm and caring.
Gary Paulsen, *Harris and Me*, 1994
A summer of pig wrestling, outmaneuvering a testy barn cat and peeing on an electric fence make many memories for "Harris and me."

397

DAVID HILL

Time Out

(Chicago: Cricket Books, 2001)

Subject(s): Sports/Running; Family Problems; School Life
Age range(s): Grades 6-9
Major character(s): Kit, 16-Year-Old, Runner; Alrika, Runner (imaginary person)
Time period(s): 2000s
Locale(s): New Zealand

Summary: Frustrated at his parents' constant bickering, and feeling very much a loner at school, cross-country running is Kit's solace and salvation. While running one day, he's forced off the road by a large truck, leaps into a ditch and upon waking thinks he's in a parallel universe where he's happy and life with his aunt and uncle is warm and loving. Kit's surprised that he's now well liked at school and sees familiar faces of students and teachers. The only new face is Alrika, his running partner, who pushes and encourages him to do better as he finally awakens from this "other world" to discover he's in the hospital, but mentally happier and able to carry on with his life. (117 pages)

Where it's reviewed:
Book Report, January 2001, page 60
Bulletin of the Center for Children's Books, November 2001, page 104
School Library Journal, October 2001, page 160
Voice of Youth Advocates, February 2002, page 435

Other books by the same author:
Take It Easy, 1997
See Ya, Simon, 1994

Other books you might like:
Sis Deans, *Racing the Past*, 2001
    To avoid the school bully, Ricky walks home rather than ride the school bus.
John Herman, *Labyrinth*, 2001
    Gregory's home life is so troubled that he has weird dreams where he lives in a parallel world.
Kimberley Griffiths Little, *Enchanted Runner*, 1999
    Kendall visits his great-grandfather at the Acoma Pueblo and discovers his love of running comes from Armando who was an Acoma runner. 251-300 1

398

PAMELA SMITH HILL

The Last Grail Keeper

(New York: Holiday House, 2001)

Subject(s): Time Travel; Arthurian Legends; Magic
Age range(s): Grades 6-9
Major character(s): Felicity Jones, 16-Year-Old, Time Traveler; Vanessa Jones, Mother (of Felicity), Archaeologist; Morgan le Fey, Time Traveler, Sister (of King Arthur)
Time period(s): 2000s; Indeterminate Past
Locale(s): Glastonbury, England

Summary: Traveling with her mother to England for the summer, Felicity is bored staying in Glastonbury as her mother spends all her time working on a dig. The day Vanessa rushes home with the news that something big was found at the site is the first time Felicity faints and actually time travels. Gradually it's revealed that Felicity is one of the Grail Keepers, referred to in legends, and that the relic found at the site is probably the Holy Grail. Fellow time traveler Morgan le Fey helps her understand her role as protector of the Grail as she struggles with her special talents in this fantasy. (227 pages)

Where it's reviewed:
Booklist, November 15, 2001, page 565
Bulletin of the Center for Children's Books, February 2002, page 208
School Library Journal, December 2001, page 134

Other books by the same author:
A Voice from the Border, 1998
Ghost Horses, 1996

Other books you might like:
Ann Curry, *The Book of Brendan*, 1990
    Father Brendan and the characters from a magical book awaken King Arthur to help them save the monks of Holybury from the evil Myrddin.
Welwyn Wilton Katz, *The Third Magic*, 1989
    Replaying the Arthurian legend are Arddu from the world of Nwm, and Morgan from twentieth century Canada, who accidentally unite across time.
Katherine Paterson, *Parzival: The Quest of the Grail Knight*, 1998
    Unsophisticated Parzival wants to grow up and become a knight and, in his earnest, bumbling way, becomes the new Grail King.

399

LYNNE HINTON

The Things I Know Best

(New York: HarperSanFrancisco, 2001)

Subject(s): Psychic Powers; Family Life; Small Town Life
Age range(s): Grades 10-Adult
Major character(s): Tessa Lucille Ivy, Psychic, 18-Year-Old; Liddy Ivy, Psychic, 18-Year-Old; Mama Bertie Ivy, Psychic, Mother (of Tessa and Liddy); Grandma Pinot, Psychic, Grandmother (of Tessa and Liddy); Sterling Renfrow, Teenager, Boyfriend (of Tessa)
Time period(s): 2000s
Locale(s): Pleasant Cross, North Carolina

Summary: Though terrible with men and money, the women of the Ivy family are all strong and self-confident, probably because they have the sight, or what they refer to as the gift for "knowing." Their Grandma Pinot looks at the sky and forecasts the weather; their mother Mama Bertie knows when people will die, for which she receives a monthly allowance from the funeral director; Liddy reads palms and can tell you who you'll marry; while Tessa, the narrator and Liddy's twin, can interpret tea leaves and dreams. Now that the twins are older, Liddy's talking about moving to Atlanta while Tessa plans to remain in their small town. But then the Reverend

Renfrew and his biracial son Sterling come to town and Tessa's taken with Sterling, while Liddy meets the funeral director's nephew who's come to take over his uncle's business, in a delightful novel of a small Southern town. (159 pages)

Where it's reviewed:
Booklist, May 15, 2001, page 1731
Kirkus Reviews, May 1, 2001, page 608
Publishers Weekly, April 23, 2001, page 50

Other books by the same author:
Garden of Faith, 2002
Friendship Cake, 2000

Other books you might like:
Julie Cannon, *Truelove and Homegrown Tomatoes*, 2001
   Imo's life turns upside down when her husbands dies, but after a while she haunts the grocery store aisles looking for a husband.
Cathryn Clinton, *The Calling*, 2001
   Called to the Lord when she's only twelve, Esta Lea is amazed to discover she has the gift of healing, too.
Christine Lincoln, *Sap Rising*, 2001
   The townspeople of a rural Southern town have a world of memories, many of which are richly detailed in these interconnected stories.
Han Nolan, *Send Me Down a Miracle*, 1996
   Charity is astounded when artist Adrienne emerges from her home after several weeks of confinement and announces that she's visited with Jesus.

400

BRUCE HISCOCK, Author/Illustrator

Coyote and Badger: Desert Hunters of the Southwest

(Honesdale, PA: Boyds Mills Press, 2001)

Subject(s): Animals/Coyotes; Animals/Badgers; Deserts
Age range(s): Grades 1-4
Major character(s): Coyote, Coyote, Hunter; Badger, Badger, Hunter
Time period(s): 2000s
Locale(s): Chaco Canyon, New Mexico

Summary: The lack of vegetation following a spring drought makes hunting difficult for both Badger and Coyote because the small animals they usually hunt have no food. One night, when both are hungry, they come upon each other and begin hunting as a team. Badger has meat now to bring home to her pups and neither Coyote nor Badger go hungry. The drought continues through the summer forcing them to travel farther in search of food. One day Badger returns from a hunt to only one pup; an eagle has gotten the other one. Immediately Badger moves with her surviving pup and, once again, Coyote hunts alone. An "Author's Note" gives factual information about the animals and setting. (32 pages)

Where it's reviewed:
Booklist, April 15, 2001, page 1564
Horn Book Guide, Fall 2001, page 292
School Library Journal, August 2001, page 153

Other books by the same author:
When Will It Snow?, 1995
The Big Storm, 1993
The Big Tree, 1991

Other books you might like:
Tony Johnston, *Desert Song*, 2000
   The sun sets, the desert cools, and nocturnal animals such as coyotes come out to hunt.
Carolyn Lesser, *Storm on the Desert*, 1997
   The beauty and power of a desert storm are eloquently illustrated in an award-winning picture book.
Phyllis J. Perry, *Crafty Canines: Coyotes, Foxes, and Wolves*, 1999
   A nonfiction title describes characteristics, behavioral traits and habitats of some wild dog species including the coyote.

401

SID HITE

A Hole in the World

(New York: Scholastic, 2001)

Subject(s): Farm Life; Animals/Dogs; Coming-of-Age
Age range(s): Grades 6-9
Major character(s): Paul Shackleford, 15-Year-Old; Ada Vallencourt, Farmer; Hargrove Vallencourt, Farmer; Hennley Gray, Worker (hired hand); Einstein, Dog
Time period(s): 2000s
Locale(s): Fenton, Virginia

Summary: A lie, told to cover up for a friend, earns Paul a summer working on a farm for the Vallencourts, distant relatives of his parents. While Paul thinks he's being forced into servitude, his father sees it as an opportunity for Paul to lose his arrogance and gain some time for reflection. As Paul meets and works with the owners and their laborers, he finds enjoyment in the rhythm of farm work although he puzzles over this man Hennley Gray whom he is supposed to resemble. A valued hired hand, Hennley had terminal cancer and, rather than be dependent upon others, committed suicide. Part of his legacy is the memory of his integrity and just plain goodness while the other is his dog Einstein who becomes an integral part of Paul's summer. Hennley's ghost seems to be everywhere until a seance, followed by the death of Einstein, gives the ghost the peace he needs to be laid to rest in a strong coming of age tale. (204 pages)

Where it's reviewed:
Book Report, November 2001, page 62
Bulletin of the Center for Children's Books, November 2001, page 104
Publishers Weekly, November 11, 2001, page 60
School Library Journal, October 2001, page 162
Voice of Youth Advocates, October 2001, page 278

Awards the book has won:
Smithsonian's Notable Books for Children, 2001

Other books by the same author:
Cecil in Space, 1999
The Distance of Hope, 1998
Those Darn Dithers, 1996

An Even Break, 1995

Other books you might like:

Sue Ellen Bridgers, *Permanent Connections*, 1987
Bob is sent to stay at the family home in the Appalachian Mountains of North Carolina where taking care of relatives helps him find himself.

Alden R. Carter, *Up Country*, 1989
Carl Stagger is sent to live with farming relatives when his mother finally seeks help from an alcohol rehab center.

Gary Paulsen, *Alida's Song*, 1999
The boy is glad to escape his alcoholic parents and work on the farm where his grandmother is the cook.

402

HOLLY HOBBIE, Author/Illustrator

Toot & Puddle: I'll Be Home for Christmas

(Boston: Little, Brown and Company, 2001)

Subject(s): Christmas; Weather; Animals/Pigs
Age range(s): Grades K-2
Major character(s): Toot, Pig, Friend; Puddle, Pig, Friend; Tulip, Bird, Friend
Time period(s): 2000s (2000)
Locale(s): Woodcock Pocket; Edinburgh, Scotland

Summary: In a postcard from Scotland Toot promises to be home in time to decorate the Christmas tree, but Puddle begins to despair when an ice storm in Scotland delays all flights. When Toot finally reaches Boston, a snowstorm has brought land transportation to a standstill. Determined to fulfill his promise Toot begins walking through the cold snowy night until exhaustion forces him to stop. Then, he uses a memento from his trip to help him on his way to Tulip, Puddle and the tree that awaits its ornaments. (32 pages)

Where it's reviewed:
Booklist, September 15, 2001, page 235
Bulletin of the Center for Children's Books, November 2001, page 104
Publishers Weekly, September 24, 2001, page 52
School Library Journal, October 2001, page 66

Other books by the same author:
Toot & Puddle: Puddle's ABC, 2000
Toot & Puddle: You Are My Sunshine, 1999
Toot & Puddle: A Present for Toot, 1998
Toot & Puddle, 1997

Other books you might like:

Michael Bond, *Paddington Bear and the Christmas Surprise*, 1997
A visit from Santa assures Paddington that the jolly gentleman's marmalade is homemade.

Jonathan London, *Froggy's Best Christmas*, 2000
Max awakens Froggy from hibernation so the two friends can enjoy Christmas together for the first time.

James Stevenson, *Christmas at Mud Flat*, 2000
The animal residents of Mud Flat busily prepare for their communal holiday celebration.

403

VALERIE HOBBS

Tender

(New York: Frances Foster Books/Farrar Straus Giroux, 2001)

Subject(s): Fathers and Daughters; Diving
Age range(s): Grades 8-12
Major character(s): Olivia "Liv" Trager, 15-Year-Old; Mark Trager, Father (of Liv), Diver; Samantha "Sam", Girlfriend (of Mark's)
Time period(s): 2000s
Locale(s): Carpenteria, California

Summary: For Liv, the sorrow of losing her grandmother is bad enough, but to be forced to move to a small town along California's coast to live with the father who abandoned her after her mother died, is a major upheaval. Her father's long-term girlfriend Samantha makes it easy for Liv to like her, for she's more than willing to like Liv; her father Mark, however, is another story. A man of few words, he's an abalone diver who makes enough money for them to live, but not for extras. When Liv becomes her father's tender, the one who watches over his line when he's diving for abalone and his life hangs in her hands, they slowly begin a father-daughter relationship that should have started fifteen years ago. Just as the two of them begin to know and like one another, his girlfriend Sam is diagnosed with cancer. Liv realizes she's responding the same way her father did when her mother died—she wants to run away. With a grumpy father, a girlfriend whose head looks like a cue ball and a teen with attitude, it'll take a while for a real family to develop, but at least this family is headed in the right direction. (245 pages)

Where it's reviewed:
Booklist, August 2001, page 2107
Horn Book, September 2001, page 584
Publishers Weekly, August 27, 2001, page 86
School Library Journal, September 2001, page 225
Voice of Youth Advocates, October 2001, page 278

Other books by the same author:
Charlie's Run, 2000
Carolina Crow Girl, 1999
Get It While It's Hot, or Not, 1996
How Far Would You Have Gotten If I Hadn't Called You Back?, 1995

Other books you might like:

Pamela Brandt, *Becoming the Butlers*, 1990
After her mother leaves them, Rachel and her father struggle to come to terms with their new family makeup.

Monte Killingsworth, *Equinox*, 2001
Autumn is distraught when she thinks she'll have to choose between her mother, who seems so distant, and her father, who clearly loves her unconditionally.

Deborah Moulton, *Summer Girl*, 1992
Ten years after her parents divorce, Tommy is sent to live with her father. It's awkward at first, but they gradually build a relationship.

404

WILL HOBBS

Down the Yukon
(New York: HarperCollins, 2001)

Subject(s): Contests; Canoeing; Gold Discoveries
Age range(s): Grades 6-10
Major character(s): Jason Hawthorn, 16-Year-Old; Jamie Dunavant, Actress, 15-Year-Old; Burnt Paw, Dog; Cornelius Donner, Con Artist
Time period(s): 1890s
Locale(s): Dawson City, Yukon Territory, Canada; Nome, Alaska

Summary: Jason's string of bad luck in the Yukon continues as Dawson City burns, his brother Ethan loses their sawmill to the unscrupulous Cornelius Donner and attention is diverted from the Klondike area when gold is discovered in Nome. The return of his special friend Jamie on the first boat after the ice breakup renews his spirits, especially when she brings a poster announcing The Great Race. The Alaska Commercial Company is sponsoring a race from the riverbank at Dawson City to its warehouse in Nome with a $20,000 prize offered to the first two-person team to cross the finish line. Winning the race would enable Jason to buy back the sawmill, so he and Jamie sign up not realizing the adventure they will have. They, and the mutt Burnt Paw, join three hundred other participants heading to Nome by canoe, including the nefarious Cornelius Donner who will try anything to keep Jason from winning the race in this exciting sequel to *Jason's Gold*. (193 pages)

Where it's reviewed:
Book Report, September 2001, page 61
Booklist, April 1, 2001, page 1482
School Library Journal, May 2001, page 150
Voice of Youth Advocates, June 2001, page 122

Other books by the same author:
Wild Man Island, 2002
Jason's Gold, 1999
Ghost Canoe, 1997
Far North, 1996

Other books you might like:
Alden R. Carter, *Between a Rock and a Hard Place*, 1995
    A rite-of-passage canoe trip for two cousins almost turns to disaster when Randy loses his insulin and Mark must find help fast.
Kathleen Karr, *Gold-Rush Phoebe*, 1998
    Phoebe cuts her hair, dresses as a boy and, with her good friend Robbie, runs away for the gold fields of California.
James Michener, *Journey*, 1989
    Based on an episode from *Alaska*, this shorter book describes the effect that finding gold in the Klondike has on a group of British aristocrats.

405

MARY ANN HOBERMAN
MEILO SO, Illustrator

It's Simple, Said Simon
(New York: Alfred A. Knopf, 2001)

Subject(s): Animals/Tigers; Humor; Animals
Age range(s): Grades K-2
Major character(s): Simon, Child; Unnamed Character, Tiger
Time period(s): Indeterminate
Locale(s): Fictional Country

Summary: While walking Simon meets in turn a dog, a cat and a horse, responding to each one's challenge by demonstrating his ability to growl, stretch and jump. "It's simple," Simon says as he completes each task. Then Simon meets a tiger that has higher expectations for Simon when he growls, stretches and jumps but still Simon finds it simple to meet the challenge. Finally, Simon shows how simple it is to jump onto the tiger's back, but soon he realizes getting down will not be as easy because the hungry tiger has dinner plans. Simon makes plans to foil the tiger's intentions by simply swimming away so he'll be home in time for supper. (34 pages)

Where it's reviewed:
Bulletin of the Center for Children's Books, March 2001, page 262
Horn Book, March 2001, page 196
Publishers Weekly, March 19, 2001, page 99
Riverbank Review, Spring 2001, page 31
School Library Journal, March 2001, page 209

Other books by the same author:
You Read to Me, I'll Read to You: Very Short Stories to Read Together, 2001
The Two Sillies, 2000
One of Each, 1997 (School Library Journal Best Books)

Other books you might like:
Tim Egan, *Friday Night at Hodge's Cafe*, 1994
    Three tigers seem interested in dining on something that's not on the menu at Hodge's Cafe, but the restaurant's pet duck foils their plans.
Julius Lester, *Sam and the Tigers: A New Telling of Little Black Sambo*, 1996
    Sam struts off to school in his fine clothes that are claimed by a succession of tigers and later reclaimed (along with the butter) by Sam.
Maurice Sendak, *Where the Wild Things Are*, 1963
    Max gets away from the Land of the Wild Things in time to travel home before his supper cools.

406

MICHAEL HOEYE

The Sands of Time
(Portland, OR: Terfle Books, 2001)

Subject(s): Animals/Mice; Adventure and Adventurers
Age range(s): Grades 6-10

Major character(s): Hermux Tantamoq, Mouse, Detective—
Amateur; Mirrin Stenrill, Artist, Mouse; Birch Tentintrot-
ter, Chipmunk
Time period(s): Indeterminate
Locale(s): Pinchester, Fictional Country

Summary: In Pinchester, cats are off-limits as a topic of
discussion, a sensible rule when one considers that the town's
population consists almost entirely of small rodents. Some
residents question the very existence of cats. Marrin, an artist
friend of Hermux Tantamoq's, has painted the visions that
came to her during the three years she was blind with the
result being a large collection of paintings of cats. To the
horror of the populace, the local museum plans to mount an
exhibition of these works and there is much dissension and
talk of picketing and rioting. In the midst of this excitement,
an aged chipmunk appears who claims to have an old scroll
leading to an ancient tomb which contains the secrets of cats
and mice in this second adventure for Hermux. (300 pages)

Where it's reviewed:
Publishers Weekly, September 10, 2001, page 93

Other books by the same author:
Time Stops for No Mouse, 1999

Other books you might like:
Avi, *Ragwood: A Tale from Dimwood Forest*, 1999
Silverside, president of Felines Enraged about Rodents,
plans to eradicate the mice, but Ragwood leads the mice in
a pitched battle against the cats.
Brian Jacques, *Redwall Series*, 1987-
This charming series features the mice of Redwall who
defend their abbey against scurrilous animals and offer
refuge to their friends.
Robert C. O'Brien, *Mrs. Frisby and the Rats of NIMH*, 1971
Seeking help for her sick son from the rats living under the
rosebush, Mrs. Frisby is astounded to discover they've
escaped from the NIMH laboratory.

407

ALICE HOFFMAN

Aquamarine
(New York: Scholastic, 2001)

Subject(s): Friendship; Mermaids; Summer
Age range(s): Grades 6-9
Major character(s): Claire, 12-Year-Old; Hailey, 12-Year-
Old; Aquamarine, Mythical Creature (mermaid); Ray-
mond, Worker (snack bar)
Time period(s): 2000s
Locale(s): United States

Summary: This is a bittersweet summer for Claire and Hailey.
Best friends for years, they will part in the fall when Claire
moves to Florida with her grandparents. Their beach club the
Capri, where they hang out every day, is slated for demolition
and has become shabby and little used. One day they arrive
following a terrible storm and see a moody mermaid lying in
the pool, swept in by fierce waves. Aquamarine, as she's
called, wants to meet her true love, but the pool's chlorine
makes her sick. She agrees to return to the sea if Claire and
Hailey will fix her up with a date with Raymond, the cute

snack bar helper. The two friends assemble a delightful dinner
of tuna fish sandwiches, seaweed salad and sardines on toast,
dress Aquamarine in a special, hand-embroidered dress, place
her in a wheelchair and leave her to enjoy her evening with
Raymond. Though the two can't be together on land, Aquamarine leaves Raymond with a unique shell that he can use to
contact her in this first novel written for young people by a
noted adult author. (105 pages)

Where it's reviewed:
Booklist, March 1, 2001, page 1278
Bulletin of the Center for Children's Books, February 2001,
page 224
Kliatt, March 2001, page 10
Publishers Weekly, February 19, 2001, page 92
Voice of Youth Advocates, April 2001, page 52

Other books by the same author:
Indigo, 2002

Other books you might like:
Berlie Doherty, *Daughter of the Sea*, 1997
When the abandoned baby found in a fishing net is re-
claimed by a stranger, the tragic events that follow indicate
the stranger may be a seal.
Mollie Hunter, *The Mermaid Summer*, 1988
Eric laughs at the idea of mermaids, until mermaids wreck
his boat and leave him stranded for three years.
Donna Jo Napoli, *Sirena*, 1998
The mermaid Sirena meets the wounded sailor Philocetes
and the two fall in love, but Sirena's wish to become
mortal isn't granted.
Mary Pope Osborne, *Haunted Waters*, 1994
Lord Huldbrand marries the mysterious Undine but their
lives are changed forever by the lure of the sea in this
retelling of a nineteenth-century German fairy tale.
Susan Lynn Reynolds, *Strandia*, 1991
Telepathic Sand won't participate in an arranged marriage
for she'd rather be with the part-man, part-fish whom she
loves.

408

LOTTA HOJER, Author/Illustrator
DAN HOJER, Co-Author
ELISABETH KALLICK DYSSEGAARD, Translator

Heart of Mine: A Story of Adoption
(New York: R & S Books, 2001)

Subject(s): Adoption; Parent and Child; Babies
Age range(s): Grades K-2
Major character(s): Unnamed Character, Mother; Unnamed
Character, Father; Tu Thi, Baby, Adoptee
Time period(s): 2000s
Locale(s): Sweden; Asia

Summary: A phone call confirms the hopes of prospective
adoptive parents. On the other side of the world a little girl is
born who is to become their daughter. The mother and father
dream of Tu Thi and hang the picture they receive of her in
their apartment. Finally, they board a plane and fly to the
country where Tu Thi lives in a foster home. The love, which
began with the first phone call, grows stronger as the parents

prepare to return to their home with their daughter and begin their life together. Originally published in Sweden in 2000. (28 pages)

Where it's reviewed:
Booklist, August 2001, page 2130
Horn Book Guide, Fall 2001, page 258
School Library Journal, April 2001, page 110

Other books you might like:
Jamie Lee Curtis, *Tell Me Again about the Night I Was Born*, 1996
　A little girl knows the story of her adoption so well that she can fill in all the details of the story herself.
Karen Katz, *Over the Moon: An Adoption Tale*, 1997
　Receiving news of a baby's birth, a couple travels to another country to complete the process of adopting the child.
Rose Lewis, *I Love You Like Crazy Cakes*, 2000
　An American mother expresses her love for her adopted Chinese daughter.

409

JENNIFER L. HOLM

Boston Jane: An Adventure
(New York: HarperCollins, 2001)

Subject(s): Frontier and Pioneer Life; Indians of North America; Identity
Age range(s): Grades 6-9
Major character(s): Jane Peck, 16-Year-Old; William Baldt, Doctor (surgeon), Agent (Indian agent); Jehu Scudder, Sailor (first mate)
Time period(s): 1850s
Locale(s): Philadelphia, Pennsylvania; *Lady Luck*, At Sea; Washington (Washington Territory)

Summary: With no mother to rein in her exuberance, her busy doctor father lets tomboy Jane enjoy her childhood, which is unusual for a young girl living in Philadelphia in the nineteenth century. Jane, however, senses her lack of manners when nice-looking William arrives to be her father's apprentice and she immediately enrolls in Miss Heppelwhite's Young Ladies Academy where she learns etiquette, embroidery and how to deal with the help. William later travels to the Washington Territory and, when Jane is fifteen, writes and asks for her hand in marriage. Excited, she leaves on a treacherous, seasick-inducing journey to Shoalwater Bay where she discovers that William is off negotiating treaties with the Chinook Indians. Suddenly Miss Heppelwhite's training doesn't seem to be very helpful, as Jane was never taught how to deal with fleas, the proper way to sleep in a room full of drunken men, the best way to talk with the Chinook Indians or how to earn a living. Self-absorbed William finally reappears but by then Jane realizes that Jehu Scudder, a sailor she met on the journey, is probably a better match for anyone who plans to live in the wilderness. (273 pages)

Where it's reviewed:
Booklist, September 1, 2001, page 109
Horn Book, September 2001, page 584

Publishers Weekly, September 3, 2001, page 88
School Library Journal, August 2001, page 183
Voice of Youth Advocates, October 2001, page 278

Awards the book has won:
ALA Best Books for Young Adults, 2002

Other books by the same author:
Our Only Mae Amelia, 1999

Other books you might like:
Avi, *The True Confessions of Charlotte Doyle*, 1990
　Charlotte's adventures aboard the sailing ship *Seahawk* turn her from a proper young Victorian lady into a real sailor.
Brix McDonald, *Riding on the Wind*, 1998
　Though her stepmother tries to make her more ladylike, Carrie learned survival skills from her father and is happiest when she's astride a horse.
Philip Pullman, *The Ruby in the Smoke*, 1987
　Sally, an orphaned sixteen-year-old, outmaneuvers a host of villainous nineteenth-century figures to claim her inheritance and her independence.
Ann Turner, *Third Girl from the Left*, 1986
　Sary answers an ad for a mail-order bride and winds up in Montana married to a sixty-year-old rancher.
Joan Weir, *The Brideship*, 1999
　It's not until Sarah's aboard ship that the forty-eight orphans are told they're heading to the goldfields of British Columbia to be brides for the miners.

410

BARBARA WARE HOLMES

Following Fake Man
(New York: Knopf, 2001)

Subject(s): Mystery and Detective Stories; Fathers and Sons; Artists and Art
Age range(s): Grades 5-8
Major character(s): Homer Aldrich Winthrop, 12-Year-Old, Artist; Roger Sweeney, Friend (of Homer's); Catherine Winthrop, Linguist, Mother (of Homer); Madeleine, Housekeeper; Owen Castle, Artist
Time period(s): 2000s
Locale(s): Herring Cove, Maine

Summary: Homer knows nothing about his father other than the fact that he died when Homer was three; questions he asks his mother Catherine remain unanswered, and so Homer is left to wonder. His mother is very cold and distant so any mothering he receives is from the housekeeper, Madeleine, who does the best she knows how. The three travel to Maine and stay in his father's family home, which leaves Catherine in bed with a migraine and Homer free to explore and track down information about his father. His first activity, however, is befriending Roger, a local boy, who becomes Homer's best friend. Together the two follow the "fake man," a man who wears a disguise and travels to an island that houses an artist community. As the two boys discover, the "fake man" is really the noted artist Owen Castle who dons the disguise to paint in anonymity. Owen was also a friend of Homer's father and it's through him that Homer finally learns the truth about his dad and his death. Being told that he's just like his dad makes him feel great but also helps him understand his mother's reserve. The truth finally shakes his mother's grief, enables her to speak more openly with Homer and provides the two of them with a chance to become a family again. (228 pages)

Where it's reviewed:
Booklist, June 2001, page 1883
Bulletin of the Center for Children's Books, July 2001, page 409
Horn Book, July 2001, page 451
Publishers Weekly, May 21, 2001, page 108
School Library Journal, May 2001, page 150

Other books by the same author:
Letters to Julia, 1997

Other books you might like:
Mary Downing Hahn, *Following the Mystery Man*, 1988
  Madigan wishes she knew the father who abandoned her and is convinced the stranger renting a room from her grandmother is actually her father.
Hadley Irwin, *The Original Freddie Ackerman*, 1992
  With two new stepfamilies, Trevor decides to spend the summer in Maine with his great-aunts where he finally feels part of a family.
Wendelin Van Draanen, *Sammy Keyes and the Hotel Thief*, 1998
  Sammy tells the police about a thief she saw, but has difficulty making them believe her.

KIMBERLY WILLIS HOLT

Dancing in Cadillac Light
(New York: Putnam, 2001)

Subject(s): Grandfathers; Family Life; Small Town Life
Age range(s): Grades 6-8
Major character(s): Jaynell Lambert, 11-Year-Old; Racine Lambert, Sister; Grandpap, Grandfather
Time period(s): 1960s (1968)
Locale(s): Moon, Texas

Summary: It's the summer of 1968 and Jaynell is excited that her street has been blacktopped and men are going to walk on the moon. The same day they fix her street, her widowed Grandpap moves in with them rather than going to a nursing home. Jaynell loves having her grandfather in their home but becomes a little protective of him and covers up his odd quirks. She doesn't tell anyone about his visiting the cemetery and talking to the headstones, but there's no way she can hide his buying a 1962 emerald green Cadillac convertible. Suddenly Jaynell's days of "test-driving" all the cars at Clifton Bailey's Automobile and Salvage Parts are over and she's cruising around town with her grandfather while her sister Racine dances at night in the lights of the Cadillac's headlights. When Grandpap dies, the family discovers the Cadillac purchase was not the only oddity of his for he's also left the family home to the Pickens family, a group Jaynell's mother refers to as "white trash." Eventually Jaynell reveals some of the comments Grandpap made about the family home and her

family is more understanding of the legacy he left the Pickens. (167 pages)

Where it's reviewed:
Booklist, February 1, 2001, page 1053
Bulletin of the Center for Children's Books, March 2001, page 263
Horn Book, March 2001, page 207
Publishers Weekly, January 29, 2001, page 90
Voice of Youth Advocates, April 2001, page 42

Awards the book has won:
School Library Journal Best Books, 2001

Other books by the same author:
When Zachary Beaver Came to Town, 1999
Mister and Me, 1998
My Louisiana Sky, 1998

Other books you might like:
Joan Bauer, *Rules of the Road*, 1998
  Earning recognition for her salesmanship, teen Jenna is hired to drive elderly Mrs. Gladstone, of Gladstone Shoes, to her conference in Dallas.
Betty Levin, *Shadow-Catcher*, 2000
  Jonathan travels with his grandfather on his summer photography shoot when he photographs some underhanded shenanigans at a logging camp.
Chris Lynch, *Political Timber*, 1996
  Gordie's grandfather, the town's former mayor jailed for racketeering, intends to run Gordie for mayor and direct the campaign from his cell.
Barbara Park, *The Graduation of Jake Moon*, 2000
  Though his grandfather is diagnosed with Alzheimer's, Jake remembers that this man is still his beloved grandfather.

JOAN HOLUB
HIROE NAKATA, Illustrator

The Garden That We Grew
(New York: Viking, 2001)

Series: Viking Easy-to-Read. Level 2
Subject(s): Gardens and Gardening; Pumpkins; Stories in Rhyme
Age range(s): Grades K-2
Time period(s): 2000s (2001)
Locale(s): United States

Summary: A group of children plant and tend a garden. Carefully they water and weed the plot of earth. As the plants grow they notice the first buds of leaves and blossoms. Through sunny summer days the pumpkins grow and grow and grow. Finally the pumpkins are ready to harvest. Now the children are busy making pies, cookies and jack-o'-lanterns. (32 pages)

Where it's reviewed:
Booklist, July 2001, page 2023
Horn Book Guide, Spring 2002, page 67
Horn Book, July 2001, page 452
Kirkus Reviews, June 1, 2001, page 802
School Library Journal, August 2001, page 153

Other books by the same author:
Cinderdog and the Wicked Stepcat, 2001
Scat, Cats!, 2001 (Viking Easy-to-Read, Level 1)
The Pizza That We Made, 2001 (Viking Easy-to-Read, Level 2)
My First Book of Sign Language, 1996

Other books you might like:
Zoe Hall, *It's Pumpkin Time!*, 1994
Siblings describe the growth of the pumpkins in their specially planted jack-o'-lantern patch.
Teri Sloat, *Patty's Pumpkin Patch*, 1999
Patty plants her seeds and watches the pumpkins grow in this rhyming alphabet story.
Jeanne Titherington, *Pumpkin, Pumpkin*, 1986
Carefully Jamie plants a seed, tends the plant, carves the pumpkin and saves some seeds to plant in the spring.

KATHERINE HOLUBITSKY

Last Summer in Agatha
(Custer, WA: Orca Book Publishers, 2001)

Subject(s): Grief; Friendship; Brothers
Age range(s): Grades 6-9
Major character(s): Rachel Bennett, 16-Year-Old; Michael Bell, 11th Grader; Cory Sparks, 16-Year-Old; Taylor Sparshatt, 16-Year-Old
Time period(s): 2000s
Locale(s): Agatha, Alberta, Canada

Summary: Rather than spend the summer in a motel near her father's worksite, Rachel is happy to accept the invitation of her aunt and uncle to stay with them. Once she arrives, she quickly meets a group of friends, including an intriguing young man named Michael, and together they ride bikes, canoe, and enjoy the summer. Michael is still grieving over the death of his brother Nick and has a short fuse; in the past he's feuded with Cory and Taylor but their enmity has never gone beyond name calling. This year it escalates until a car is driven into a pond. Rachel feels caught in the middle, isn't sure how she feels about Michael and doesn't know how to stop this silly wrangling. (185 pages)

Where it's reviewed:
Kliatt, September 2001, page 8
Quill & Quire, May 2001, page 33
School Library Journal, December 2001, page 138
Voice of Youth Advocates, February 2002, page 435

Other books by the same author:
Alone at Ninety Foot, 1999

Other books you might like:
Charles Butler, *Timon's Tide*, 2000
Daniel has suffered guilt ever since his brother Timon's drug-related activities caught up with him and he was killed.
Robin Friedman, *How I Survived My Summer Vacation: And Lived to Tell the Story*, 2000
Determined to write the "great American novel" this summer, Jackie gets hung up on the second line.

Elizabeth Wennick, *Changing Jareth*, 2000
When Jareth and his friend cause an older man to have a heart attack and die, Jareth quits breaking into people's homes.
Carol Lynch Williams, *Carolina Autumn*, 2000
A year after losing her father and sister in a plane crash, Carolina's just beginning to show enthusiasm for the outside world.

414

ELIZABETH HONEY, Author/Illustrator

Fiddleback
(New York: Knopf, 2001)

Subject(s): Camps and Camping; Family Life; Diaries
Age range(s): Grades 5-7
Major character(s): Henni Octon, 12-Year-Old; Donna O'Sullivan, Counselor; Briquette, Dog (daschund)
Time period(s): 2000s
Locale(s): Warrangalla, Australia

Summary: A neighborhood camping trip turns into a high-spirited undertaking for Henni and her family as they "go bush" over the Christmas holidays. Henni faithfully records the travails of the five kids, six adults and the dog Briquette as they camp at a secluded spot along the Warrangalla River. The kids spend their nights sleeping in one huge tent and their days skinny-dipping in a pool, exploring their surroundings and playing games. Their idyllic times become serious when a lonely teenager arrives in search of his caseworker who's one of the campers. Discovery of a prized fiddleback tree, an ancient tree with beautiful markings that's used for making fiddles, leads to an encounter with greedy sawmill workers. But the most poignant moment comes when heavy rains trap them at their campsite and Donna goes into labor; only use of their cell phone helps the group delivery effort in this humorously told adventure from an Australian author. (204 pages)

Where it's reviewed:
Booklist, September 1, 2001, page 104
Bulletin of the Center for Children's Books, July 2001, page 409
Horn Book, September 2001, page 585
Publishers Weekly, June 18, 2001, page 82
School Library Journal, August 2001, page 184

Other books by the same author:
Don't Pat the Wombat, 2000
45 and 47 Stella Street and Everything That Happened, 1998
The Book of Little Books, 1996

Other books you might like:
Gary L. Blackwood, *Wild Timothy*, 1987
Separated from his father while on a camping trip, klutzy Timothy surprises everyone by surviving for three weeks before being discovered by hunters.
Peg Kehret, *Earthquake Terror*, 1996
A family camping trip turns to terror when an earthquake strikes and Jonathan and his younger sister Abby are surrounded by floodwaters.
Robin Klein, *Dresses of Red and Gold*, 1993
The Melling sisters and their cousin fill their summers with

rich activities in this simple story of family life in Australia after World War II.

Chris Lynch, *Babes in the Woods*, 1997
    Camping to become real men, the He-Men Women Haters Club is furious when they realize they're roughing it and the adults are living in a travel trailer.

415

DOROTHY HOOBLER
THOMAS HOOBLER, Co-Author

The 1940s: Secrets
(Brookfield, CT: The Millbrook Press, 2001)

Series: Century Kids
Subject(s): World War II
Age range(s): Grades 4-6
Major character(s): Esther Aldrich, 12-Year-Old; Gabriella Vivanti, 12-Year-Old; Ben Tamura, 13-Year-Old, Japanese American
Time period(s): 1940s
Locale(s): Chicago, Illinois; Los Alamos, New Mexico; Lake Chohobee Village, Maine

Summary: The Aldrich family feels the impact of World War II in different ways. Young Esther's parents are scientists who teach at the University of Chicago; suddenly they move and don't tell Esther, until they're on their way, that the family is going to Los Alamos to help with a secret project. Left behind in Chicago, Esther's best friend Gabriella wants to help with the war effort and starts a letter-writing campaign for the soldiers and sailors, but it's so successful she has to recruit volunteers, rent office space and put someone in charge. And Ben Tamura's family is lucky to move with some of Esther's relatives to their home in Maine and thus avoid being sent to the Japanese relocation camps in this fifth in a series. (175 pages)

Where it's reviewed:
Booklist, April 1, 2001, page 1483
School Library Journal, May 2001, page 154

Other books by the same author:
The 1970s: Arguments, 2002 (Century Kids)
The 1990s: Families, 2002 (Century Kids)
The 1980s: Earthsong, 2002 (Century Kids)
The 1950s: Music, 2001 (Century Kids)
The 1960s: Rebels, 2001 (Century Kids)
The 1920s: Luck, 2000 (Century Kids)
The 1930s: Directions, 2000 (Century Kids)

Other books you might like:
Barry Denenberg, *The Journal of Ben Uchida: Citizen 13559 Mirror Lake Internment Camp*, 1999
    After Pearl Harbor is bombed, Ben and his family are sent to an internment camp where Ben records his stay in a journal given to him by a friend.
LouAnn Bigge Gaeddert, *Friends and Enemies*, 2000
    Good friends discover their views about the war divide them, with Mennonite Jim believing in pacifism while Methodist William opts for patriotism.
Mary Pope Osborne, *My Secret War: The World War II Diary of Madeline Beck*, 2000

Just as Maddie adjusts to her new school, she and her mother learn her father's been wounded and they move to the West Coast to be near his hospital.

416

DOROTHY HOOBLER
THOMAS HOOBLER, Co-Author

The Demon in the Teahouse
(New York: Philomel Books, 2001)

Subject(s): Mystery and Detective Stories
Age range(s): Grades 6-9
Major character(s): Seikei Konoike, 14-Year-Old, Detective—Amateur; Judge Ooka, Judge; Umae, Entertainer (geisha)
Time period(s): 18th century
Locale(s): Edo, Japan

Summary: Now adopted by Judge Ooka and able to continue his samurai training, Seikei is sent to the Yoshiwara district of Edo, home of geishas and teahouses, to investigate several fires. Seikei finds a job as a messenger for the Teahouse of the Falling Cherry Blossoms where he acts as the judge's eyes and ears, and follows the path of the fires and three murders that lead to the famous geisha Umae. Accused of setting the fires, Seikei finds himself trapped on a rooftop with flames all around. Eventually distinguishing himself when he identifies the arsonist, he's learning his lessons in his quest to become a samurai warrior in this sequel to *The Ghost in the Tokaido Inn*. (182 pages)

Where it's reviewed:
Book Report, November 2001, page 63
Booklist, May 1, 2001, page 1612
Bulletin of the Center for Children's Books, June 2001, page 374
School Library Journal, June 2001, page 150
Voice of Youth Advocates, June 2001, page 122

Other books by the same author:
Real American Girls: Tell Their Own Stories, 1999
The Ghost in the Tokaido Inn, 1999
Sally Bradford: The Story of a Rebel Girl, 1997 (Her Story)
Promise Me the Moon, 1996

Other books you might like:
Eric Christian Haugaard, *The Boy and the Samurai*, 1991
    Saru, a street urchin, reminisces about how his life and the life of a samurai intertwined in sixteenth-century Japan.
Erik A. Kimmel, *Sword of the Samurai: Adventure Stories from Japan*, 1999
    Eleven stories relate the culture of these Japanese warriors who lived by strict rules and traditions.
Lucia St. Clair Robson, *The Tokaido Road: A Novel of Feudal Japan*, 1992
    This romance is filled with the customs and traditions of eighteenth-century Japan.

417

PATRICIA HOOPER
LYNN MUNSINGER, Illustrator

A Stormy Ride on Noah's Ark

(New York: G.P. Putnam's Sons, 2001)

Subject(s): Animals; Biblical Fiction; Stories in Rhyme
Age range(s): Grades K-3
Major character(s): Noah, Biblical Figure, Aged Person
Time period(s): Indeterminate Past
Locale(s): Earth

Summary: Animals of every type crowded in one large space on the ark creates some major sleeping problems. Lambs, rabbits, goats, mice and birds worry about sleeping when they are so near predators such as wolves, foxes, tigers and cats. As the storm intensifies and the ark tosses on the roiling water even the elephants, leopards and lions tremble with fear. Then the smallest animals step forward to offer comfort. Sparrow sings a song, mouse tells a tale, and spider weaves a web of sleep. By the time the animals awaken from their dreams the storm is finished. (32 pages)

Where it's reviewed:
Booklist, October 1, 2001, page 337
Horn Book Guide, Spring 2002, page 46
Horn Book, November 2001, page 736
School Library Journal, December 2001, page 104

Other books by the same author:
How the Sky's Housekeeper Wore Her Scarves, 1995
A Bundle of Beasts, 1987

Other books you might like:
Jonathan Allen, *Two by Two by Two*, 1995
  The Biblical story is reduced to a comic presentation of life aboard the ark as it floats over the flooded world.
Glen Rounds, *Washday on Noah's Ark*, 1985
  While the animals are concerned about sleeping, Mrs. Noah thinks about how to dry the clothes after 40 days of rain and improvises a clothesline.
Peter Spier, *Noah's Ark*, 1977
  The 1978 Caldecott Medal winner pictorially reenacts the story of the flood.

418

DEBORAH HOPKINSON
BETHANNE ANDERSEN, Illustrator

Bluebird Summer

(New York: Greenwillow Books, 2001)

Subject(s): Farm Life; Grandparents; Grief
Age range(s): Grades 2-4
Major character(s): Cody, Brother (younger), Child; Mags, Child, Sister (older); Gramps, Grandfather, Widow(er)
Time period(s): 2000s (2001)
Locale(s): United States

Summary: Mags and Cody visit Gramps as they do every summer, but this year is different because their grandmother is no longer alive to putter in her garden. Cody is the first to notice the absence of the bluebirds that formerly sang from the garden fence. Mags pulls weeds and plants flowers in the old garden in hopes of attracting the birds again. Cody has his own plans and soon he and Gramps are building bluebird houses to set up along the fence. The book concludes with factual information about bluebirds. (32 pages)

Where it's reviewed:
Booklist, April 15, 2001, page 1564
Horn Book Guide, Fall 2001, page 292
Kirkus Reviews, March 15, 2001, page 410
Publishers Weekly, April 23, 2001, page 78
School Library Journal, May 2001, page 123

Awards the book has won:
Notable Social Studies Trade Books for Young People, 2002

Other books by the same author:
A Band of Angels: A Story Inspired by the Jubilee Singers, 1999 (ALA Notable Book)
Maria's Comet, 1999
Birdie's Lighthouse, 1997 (Bulletin of the Center for Children's Books Blue Ribbon)
Sweet Clara and the Freedom Quilt, 1993 (IRA Children's Choice)

Other books you might like:
Lois Ehlert, *Planting a Rainbow*, 1988
  A mother and her child plant a family garden, carefully planning the placement of the flowers to create a rainbow of colors.
Mordicai Gerstein, *Daisy's Garden*, 1995
  Daisy is a gardener who cheerfully shares the work and the crop with bugs, birds and animals.
Elaine Moore, *Grandma's Garden*, 1993
  Together Grandma and Kim plant a garden, make a scarecrow and repair the damage of an early season thunderstorm.
Mary Beth Owens, *Counting Cranes*, 1993
  The life of the endangered whooping crane gracefully unfolds in an artistic portrayal that concludes with factual information about the birds.
James Preller, *Cardinal and Sunflower*, 1998
  Seeds strewn along a path provide immediate food for a pair of cardinals and begin a cycle of growth for new plants in the spring.

419

LAURIE MILLER HORNIK
DEBBIE TILLEY, Illustrator

The Secrets of Ms. Snickle's Class

(New York: Clarion Books, 2001)

Subject(s): Secrets; Schools; Magic
Age range(s): Grades 2-4
Major character(s): Ms. Snickle, Teacher; Lacey, Student—Elementary School
Time period(s): 2000s (2001)
Locale(s): Fictional Country (Murmer Street School)

Summary: As the new school year begins students in Ms. Snickle's class quickly learn that she is not like any other teacher they've ever had. She consigns the standardized tests to the recycle bin and gives homework that is supposed to stay at home (or it would be "schoolwork"). The only class rule she imposes is no telling secrets although she expects everyone to have one. Lacey has no secrets but she is busy learning the secrets of her classmates and her teacher. By learning and telling the secrets of her fellow students Lacey destroys the camaraderie in the room. When she informs the principal of Ms. Snickle's secret Lacey is expecting her to get in trouble but not to be fired. Alas, Lacey was mistaken and now she has to figure out how to get Ms. Snickle back before the author's first book concludes. (135 pages)

Where it's reviewed:
Bulletin of the Center for Children's Books, September 2001, page 18
Horn Book Guide, Fall 2001, page 307
Kirkus Reviews, April 1, 2001, page 498
Publishers Weekly, May 7, 2001, page 247
School Library Journal, August 2001, page 154

Other books you might like:
Louise Fitzhugh, *Harriet, the Spy*, 1964
Sneaking about her Manhattan neighborhood, Harriet records all she sees, good or bad about anybody and everything.
Mordecai Richler, *Jacob Two-Two's First Spy Case*, 1997
With help from his neighbor, Jacob investigates Mr. Greedyguts, his school's new headmaster, and the suspicious changes in the school lunches.
Barbara Robinson, *The Best School Year Ever*, 1994
The incorrigible Herdmans return to school making for a most unusual and challenging academic year.
Louis Sachar, *Wayside School Gets a Little Stranger*, 1995
The 30th floor of a school built sideways with classrooms atop one another rather than side-by-side is known for being a bit odd.

420

ANTHONY HOROWITZ

Stormbreaker

(New York: Philomel, 2001)

Series: Alex Rider Adventure
Subject(s): Spies; Terrorism; Orphans
Age range(s): Grades 6-9
Major character(s): Alex Rider, 14-Year-Old, Spy; Herod Sayle, Businessman
Time period(s): 2000s
Locale(s): London, England

Summary: Told that his uncle Ian died because he wasn't wearing his seat belt, Alex knows that's not true once he sees the bullet-raked windshield. It turns out that his uncle was not really a bank vice-president, but a secret agent working for British intelligence, a position that MI6 now asks Alex to assume. Once Alex agrees to help, he's sent to investigate Sayle Enterprises whose owner Herod Sayle has designed a supercomputer he plans to give every secondary school in England. Though it seems like a generous offer, the government is worried about some of the unfriendly countries with whom Sayle does business as well as whether or not there's a link between Sayle and the murder of Ian Rider. Alex makes use of all the hi-tech gadgets given to him by MI6 and,

pretending to be a computer nerd who wins a Sayle's Enterprises contest, investigates the company's factory where he finds clues left by his uncle. Mix a young James Bond with a young Indiana Jones and the result is Alex Rider. (192 pages)

Where it's reviewed:
Booklist, September 1, 2001, page 97
Bulletin of the Center for Children's Books, September 2001, page 18
Publishers Weekly, May 21, 2001, page 109
School Library Journal, June 2001, page 150
Voice of Youth Advocates, August 2001, page 202

Awards the book has won:
ALA Quick Picks for Reluctant Young Adult Readers, 2002

Other books by the same author:
Point Blank, 2002 (Alex Rider Adventure)
The Devil and His Boy, 2000
Death Walks Tonight, 1996
The Night of the Scorpion, 1984
The Devil's Door-Bell, 1983

Other books you might like:
Anthony Dana Arkin, *Captain Hawaii*, 1994
Exploding rafts, swarming spiders and a severed hand aren't what Arron expected to find when he and his parents came to Hawaii for a vacation.
Rob McGregor, *Indiana Jones and the Dance of the Giants*, 1991
Indiana and one of his students head off on a dangerous quest to locate a scroll that proves Merlin's existence.
Neal Shusterman, *The Eyes of Kid Midas*, 1992
The magical sunglasses Kevin finds on a sacred mountain answer his every wish, but his problems expand as each request is granted.

421

RUTH HOROWITZ
JOAN HOLUB, Illustrator

Breakout at the Bug Lab

(New York: Dial Books for Young Readers, 2001)

Series: Dial Easy-to-Read
Subject(s): Animals/Cockroaches; Animals/Insects; Brothers
Age range(s): Grades 1-3
Major character(s): Max, Cockroach; Leo, Brother (younger), Child; Unnamed Character, Brother, Narrator; Mom, Mother, Scientist
Time period(s): 2000s (2001)
Locale(s): United States

Summary: Max is more than another specimen in Mom's bug lab; Max is her pet. When he escapes from his cage on the day of a special presentation at the lab Leo and his brother hurry to find and recover the giant hissing cockroach before he can frighten the guests. An elderly stranger aids the recovery efforts. Later Leo and his brother learn that she is the famous person being honored that day at the lab. (48 pages)

Where it's reviewed:
Booklist, April 15, 2001, page 1568
Bulletin of the Center for Children's Books, July 2001, page 410

Horn Book, July 2001, page 453
Kirkus Reviews, April 15, 2001, page 586
School Library Journal, April 2001, page 112

Other books by the same author:
Crab Moon, 2000
Mommy's Lap, 1993
Bat Time, 1991

Other books you might like:
Janell Cannon, *Crickwing*, 2000
    Crickwing's talent for sculpture saves the cockroach and a colony of leaf-cutting ants from an invasion by army ants.
Karen Hartley, *Cockroach*, 1999
    A nonfiction title provides a factual introduction to cockroaches, their habitats and life cycle.
Kevin O'Malley, *Leo Cockroach . . . Toy Tester*, 1999
    Leo enjoys his secret, nightly ''job'' as a toy tester for a large company.

422

POLLY HORVATH

Everything on a Waffle

(New York: Farrar Straus Giroux, 2001)

Subject(s): Humor; Foster Homes; Parent and Child
Age range(s): Grades 5-8
Major character(s): Primrose Squarp, 11-Year-Old; Miss Perfidy, Aged Person; Jack Dion, Uncle; Miss Honeycutt, Counselor (school guidance counselor); Miss Bowzer, Restaurateur
Time period(s): 2000s
Locale(s): Coal Harbor, British Columbia, Canada

Summary: Primrose's mother sails out into a summer storm in search of her fisherman husband who is late returning home; when neither returns, the townspeople assume they've died and that Primrose is now an orphan. However, Primrose doesn't assume that, even though she is the only one convinced her parents are fine and will return home when they're rescued. Until that happens, however, she first stays with her neighbor Miss Perfidy who bills the Squarps' bank account for baby-sitting Primrose. With the account about to go dry, the town council is elated when Primrose's Uncle Jack comes into town and Primrose moves in with him, though that move proves dangerous when she accidentally loses a little toe and then the tip of her finger. Her guidance counselor Miss Honeycutt, who's perhaps more interested in Uncle Jack than in Primrose, is convinced she's in danger and sends her to stay with older, foster parents. Though Primrose's life seems jumbled, she always has the comfort of visiting Miss Bowzer, who owns the restaurant called The Girl on the Red Swing, where everything is served atop a waffle. In this delightfully funny book there's a recipe at the end of every chapter, including one for waffles! (150 pages)

Where it's reviewed:
Booklist, February 15, 2001, page 1137
Horn Book, March 2001, page 263
Publishers Weekly, April 9, 2001, page 75
School Library Journal, April 2001, page 144
Voice of Youth Advocates, June 2001, page 123

Awards the book has won:
Newbery Honor Book, 2002
Boston Globe-Horn Book Honor Book, 2001

Other books by the same author:
The Trolls, 1999
When the Circus Came to Town, 1996
The Happy Yellow Car, 1994

Other books you might like:
Betsy Byars, *The Not-Just-Anybody Family*, 1986
    Maggie and Vern have an amazing family—their mother's off with the rodeo, their brother's in the hospital and their grandfather's in the pokey.
Helen Cresswell, *The Bagthorpes Series*, 1978-
    The peculiar members of the Bagthorpe family confront one crisis after another.
Sid Hite, *Those Darn Dithers*, 1996
    Stilt walking, a dancing pig and an uncle who floats out to sea are just a few of the eccentric characters and adventures shared by the Dithers' family.
Gary Paulsen, *Harris and Me*, 1994
    A summer of pig wrestling, outmaneuvering a testy barn cat and peeing on an electric fence provides many memories for ''Harris and me.''

423

JAMES D. HOUSTON

Snow Mountain Passage

(New York: Knopf, 2001)

Subject(s): Wilderness Survival; Pioneers; Disasters
Age range(s): Grades 10-Adult
Major character(s): James Frazier ''Jim'' Reed, Leader (of expedition); Patty Read, Daughter (of Jim)
Time period(s): 1840s (1846-1847); 1920s
Locale(s): West; Sierra Nevada Mountains, California

Summary: In 1846 a group of wagons leaves Springfield, Illinois on a route to California just like hundreds of other wagons headed west, but this wagon train lives on in American history and imagination as the Donner Party. Narrated by Jim Reed, one of the leaders of the exploration, he reveals the dreams and visions shared by many of the pioneers as well as the harsh reality they find as they travel through storms, suffer from lack of food and argue with one another on the trail, just as they did at home with neighbors. One day Jim fights with one of the drovers and kills him in self-defense, but then is forced from the train, leaving his wife and children behind. He manages to cross the Sierra Nevada Mountains before the winter storms come, but then spends months trying to assemble a rescue team for his snowed-in family. Seventy-five years after this trek, his daughter Patty records her thoughts in ''Trail Notes'' where she is finally able to regard her father as a person and not the hero she always claimed him to be. (317 pages)

Where it's reviewed:
Book World, April 15, 2001, page 3
Booklist, April 1, 2001, page 1451
Kirkus Reviews, February 15, 2001, page 203
New York Times Book Review, April 8, 2001, page 29

Publishers Weekly, March 13, 2001, page 77

Other books by the same author:
The Last Paradise, 1998
In the Ring of Fire: A Pacific Basin Journey, 1997
Farewell to Manzanar, 1973

Other books you might like:
Sandra Dallas, *The Diary of Mattie Spenser*, 1997
　　Mattie keeps a diary as she marries and travels by Conestoga wagon to the Colorado Territories where she records her life on the prairie.
Cecelia Holland, *An Ordinary Woman*, 1999
　　Accompanying her husband, Nancy is part of an 1841 wagon train and is the first woman to enter California via the desert and the Sierra Nevadas.
Vilhelm Moberg, *Unto a Good Land*, 1954
　　Farmer Karl Nilsson, his wife and children leave Sweden for the United States and make their way to Minnesota by riverboat, foot and ox-drawn cart.
Nancy E. Turner, *These Is My Words: The Diary of Sarah Agnes Prine, 1881-1901*, 1998
　　Western pioneers Sarah and Jack live out a long and wonderful romance on the American frontier.

424

ARTHUR HOWARD, Author/Illustrator

Hoodwinked

(San Diego: Harcourt, Inc., 2001)

Subject(s): Pets; Witches and Witchcraft; Humor
Age range(s): Grades K-3
Major character(s): Mitzi, Child, Witch; Hoodwinked, Cat
Time period(s): Indeterminate
Locale(s): Fictional Country

Summary: As a lover of all things creepy, Mitzi seeks a suitably creepy pet at the pet store. She selects a slimy toad that is more interested in bugs than Mitzi so she exchanges it for two bats, but they also do not prove to be satisfactory pets. When a tiny kitten scratches at Mitzi's door on a rainy night she is repulsed by the kitten's adorable appearance, but lets it into the house anyway for one night. When the kitten proves to be just the right pet for Mitzi, she names him Hoodwinked and promises not to hold his looks against him. (32 pages)

Where it's reviewed:
Booklist, September 1, 2001, page 120
Bulletin of the Center for Children's Books, September 2001, page 19
Horn Book, January 2002, page 68
Publishers Weekly, September 24, 2001, page 42
School Library Journal, September 2001, page 190

Awards the book has won:
School Library Journal Best Books, 2001
IRA Children's Choices, 2002

Other books by the same author:
Cosmo Zooms, 1999 (IRA-CBC Children's Choices)
When I Was Five, 1996 (IRA-CBC Children's Choices)

Other books you might like:
Lauren Child, *I Want a Pet*, 1999
　　A little girl desperately wants a pet but has some difficulty choosing one that meets the requirements of her family.
Tres Seymour, *I Love My Buzzard*, 1994
　　A young boy who loves his buzzard as well as his squid, slugs and warthog reconsiders his priorities when his mom moves out to escape the menagerie.
James Stevenson, *Emma*, 1985
　　Not a typical witch, Emma even needs flying lessons.

425

ELIZABETH FITZGERALD HOWARD
PAT CUMMINGS, Illustrator

Lulu's Birthday

(New York: Greenwillow Books, 2001)

Subject(s): Birthdays; African Americans; Surprises
Age range(s): Grades K-2
Major character(s): Lulu, Aunt, Aged Person; Laurie, Niece, Child; J. Matthew, Nephew, Child
Time period(s): 2000s (2001)
Locale(s): United States

Summary: Lulu wants to celebrate her birthday by returning, with Laurie and J. Matthew, to one of the spots they enjoyed together during the children's summer visit with her. They consider holding her birthday celebration at the zoo, on the beach, in the movies, at a baseball game and during a ballet performance. J. Matthew and Laurie have something else planned for Lulu and she declares their surprise to be better than all the other ideas! (24 pages)

Where it's reviewed:
Booklist, January 2001, page 967
Horn Book Guide, Fall 2001, page 259
Kirkus Reviews, December 1, 2000, page 1682
Publishers Weekly, January 8, 2001, page 68
School Library Journal, February 2001, page 100

Other books by the same author:
What's in Aunt Mary's Room?, 1996
Aunt Flossie's Hats (and Crab Cakes Later), 1991
The Train to Lulu's, 1988

Other books you might like:
Cari Best, *Three Cheers for Catherine the Great!*, 1999
　　When Grandma insists on ''no presents'' for her birthday Sara creates a ''no present'' surprise for her special grandmother.
Amy Hest, *Jamaica Louise James*, 1996
　　Jamaica uses her birthday gift to create a surprise for Grammy's birthday.
Pat Mora, *A Birthday Basket for Tia*, 1992
　　Cecelia makes a special present for her family's celebration of Great Aunt Tia's 90th birthday.
Jeri Hanel Watts, *Keepers*, 1997
　　As a birthday gift for his grandmother, Kenyon compiles her oft-told family stories in a book.

426

GINGER HOWARD
LARRY DAY, Illustrator

William's House

(Brookfield, CT: The Millbrook Press, 2001)

Subject(s): Dwellings; Historical; American Colonies
Age range(s): Grades 1-3
Major character(s): William, Settler, Spouse; Elizabeth, Settler, Spouse
Time period(s): 17th century (1637-1638)
Locale(s): New England, American Colonies

Summary: After William and Elizabeth arrive in the New World with their two sons and the family dog, William builds a house in the style of his father's home in England. As the seasons evolve during their first year in this new land, William and Elizabeth notice the differences in climate and adjust the features of their home to make it more suitable to life in this country. By the time other relatives arrive a year later, William's house looks nothing like the one on which he modeled it yet it functions well in this environment as a home. (32 pages)

Where it's reviewed:
Booklist, March 15, 2001, page 1400
Bulletin of the Center for Children's Books, June 2001, page 375
Horn Book Guide, Fall 2001, page 259
Kirkus Reviews, February 1, 2001, page 184
School Library Journal, March 2001, page 212

Awards the book has won:
Notable Social Studies Trade Books for Young People, 2002

Other books by the same author:
A Basket of Bangles: How a Business Begins, 2002

Other books you might like:
Virginia Lee Burton, *The Little House*, 1942
The passage of time and family connections over generations is chronicled in the experiences of a house. Caldecott Medal Winner.
D.B. Johnson, *Henry Builds a Cabin*, 2002
Henry responds to his friends' helpful advice with the reasons why his cabin is not as small as it appears to them.
Emma Rogers, *Our House*, 1993
During its 200-year history many different families have lived in this house. Paul Rogers, co-author.
Anne Shelby, *Homeplace*, 1995
A grandmother traces the history of the family from the building of the family homestead by the great-great-great-great granpa to the present.

 427

JAMES HOWE, Editor

The Color of Absence: Twelve Stories about Loss and Hope

(New York: Atheneum/Simon & Schuster, 2001)

Subject(s): Short Stories; Grief

Age range(s): Grades 7-10
Time period(s): 2000s
Locale(s): United States

Summary: Though sad, loss and hope do not have to be dismal, as many of these pieces will illustrate. In ''Summer of Love'' by Annette Curtis Klause, the three-hundred-year-old vampire named Simon actually enters a church to rescue his cat Grimalkin and thereby gains a soul. A Labrador Retriever puppy bought to aid a mother's depression unfortunately sends her closer to suicide in C.B. Christiansen's story entitled ''Red Seven.'' And James Howe's ''Enchanted Night'' shows how the talents of a father can overwhelm a daughter's achievements. Jacqueline Woodson and Chris Lynch have an excerpt from a novel they're co-writing while other short story authors include Norma Fax Mazer, Michael J. Rosen, Virginia Euwer Wolff and Naomi Shihab Nye in this collection of twelve stories. (238 pages)

Where it's reviewed:
Booklist, July 2001, page 1999
Bulletin of the Center for Children's Books, December, 2001, page 142
Horn Book, September 2001, page 586
School Library Journal, September 2001, page 225
Voice of Youth Advocates, August 2001, page 199

Awards the book has won:
ALA Best Books for Young Adults, 2002

Other books by the same author:
The Misfits, 2001
The Watcher, 1997
The New Nick Kramer, or My Life as a Baby-Sitter, 1995
Dew Drop Dead, 1990

Other books you might like:
Donald R. Gallo, *No Easy Answers: Short Stories about Teenagers Making Tough Choices*, 1997
This strong collection of short stories features teens who face moral crises, such as peer pressure, computer blackmail or gangs.
David Gifaldi, *Rearranging and Other Stories*, 1998
Teenagers mature in many ways and the author captures the essence of coming of age in these stories.
M. Jerry Weiss, *From One Experience to Another*, 1997
Turning points in the lives of young adult authors become the basis for stories written for this exceptional collection.

428

JAMES HOWE

The Misfits

(New York: Simon & Schuster/Atheneum, 2001)

Subject(s): Elections; Teasing; School Life
Age range(s): Grades 5-8
Major character(s): Bobby Goodspeed, 7th Grader; Addie Carle, 7th Grader; Skeezie Tookis, 7th Grader; Joe Bunch, 7th Grader
Time period(s): 2000s
Locale(s): Paintbrush Falls, New York

Summary: The ''Gang of Five'' clings together as they are ''the misfits,'' those who will never be in the popular clique.

Though there are only four of them, fat Bobby, smart Addie, greaser Skeezie Tookis and effeminate Joe, they feel there's a kid out there somewhere who needs to belong and they save him a space. Tired of being called names, ranging from "fatso" to "beanpole" and "know it all" to "greaser" or "faggot," they decide to run for political office on the "No Name Party." Compiling a list of seventy names that they've each been called, they design campaign posters around these terms which show the offending word encircled with a slash through the word. Though they don't win the election, they do stir interest in their campaign and find the administration will help enforce their "No Name" contest. (274 pages)

Where it's reviewed:
Booklist, November 15, 2001, page 572
Horn Book, November 2001, page 750
Publishers Weekly, October 29, 2001, page 64
School Library Journal, November 2001, page 158
Voice of Youth Advocates, December 2001, page 359

Other books by the same author:
The Color of Absence: Twelve Stories about Loss and Hope, 2001
The Watcher, 1997
The New Nick Kramer, or My Life as a Baby-Sitter, 1995
Dew Drop Dead, 1990
The Celery Stalks at Midnight, 1983
Bunnicula, 1979

Other books you might like:
Elizabeth Cody Kimmel, *Visiting Miss Caples*, 2000
    When Jenna's friend Liv changes and assumes the role of queen, Jenna ignores her manipulations and finds a new friend.
Elizabeth Laird, *Secret Friends*, 1999
    Wanting to be part of the popular clique, Lucy teases Rafaella about her ears, but doesn't reveal that she and Rafaella are friends outside of school.
Richard Peck, *Princess Ashley*, 1987
    New student Chelsea is thrilled to be included in Ashley's "in" group, not realizing she's just being used.
Rob Thomas, *Slave Day*, 1997
    African American Keena Davenport writes a letter to the editor of the school newspaper urging students to boycott the demeaning ritual of "slave day."
Rachel Vail, *Wonder*, 1991
    Jessica's tumultuous seventh grade year finds her seesawing between being a social pariah and having her own clique.

JAMES HOWE
MELISSA SWEET, Illustrator

Pinky and Rex and the Just-Right Pet

(New York: Atheneum Books for Young Readers, 2001)

Series: Ready-to-Read. Level 3
Subject(s): Animals/Cats; Pets; Family Life
Age range(s): Grades 2-3
Major character(s): Pinky, 7-Year-Old, Brother (older); Amanda, Child, Sister; Patches, Cat
Time period(s): 2000s (2001)

Locale(s): United States

Summary: Pinky wants a dog, but his plans to convince his family of the value of his idea fail. Amanda's parents support her desire for a cat because a cat is less work. As luck would have it, someone is giving away free kittens at the grocery store and Pinky's family finds their pet. Amanda's a little possessive of Patches, but Pinky has the secret satisfaction of knowing that Patches visits him during the night, sleeps on his bed and plays with his feet under the covers. By the time Pinky's parents are willing to reward his responsible care of Patches by allowing him to get a dog, he's decided that cats make fine pets. (40 pages)

Where it's reviewed:
Booklist, March 1, 2001, page 1278
Horn Book Guide, Fall 2001, page 292
School Library Journal, May 2001, page 124

Other books by the same author:
Pinky and Rex and the Perfect Pumpkin, 1998 (Ready-to-Read, Level 3)
Pinky and Rex and the School Play, 1998 (Ready-to-Read, Level 3)
Pinky and Rex and the New Neighbors, 1997 (Ready-to-Read, Level 3)

Other books you might like:
Marion Dane Bauer, *Alison's Puppy*, 1997
    When Alison receives a kitten rather than the puppy she wants for her birthday she satisfies herself by naming the feline "Puppy."
Megan McDonald, *Beezy and Funnybone*, 2000
    Three humorous stories describe Beezy's relationship with her pet.
Maggie Stern, *George and Diggety*, 2000
    For George and his family having a pet like Diggety is sometimes challenging but always fun.

ETHAN HOWLAND

The Lobster War

(Chicago, IL: Front Street/Cricket Books, 2001)

Subject(s): Single Parent Families; Brothers; Fishing
Age range(s): Grades 7-10
Major character(s): Dain Harrington, 16-Year-Old, Fisherman (of lobsters); Edward "Eddie" Harrington, 19-Year-Old, Fisherman (of lobsters); Roger Gribbin, Fisherman (of lobsters)
Time period(s): 2000s
Locale(s): Maine

Summary: Living along the coast of Maine, it's natural that Dain wants to follow in the footsteps of his deceased father and be a lobsterman, though his mother pushes him in the direction of college. When Dain turns to his older brother Eddie for support, he realizes that they have grown apart as Eddie heads to his disreputable friend Roger's house to escape his mother's carping. With fall approaching Dain spends most of his time lobstering, though someone cuts his traps in the Narrows. Disappointed to learn his brother and Roger are the culprits, that knowledge doesn't stop Dain from heading out into a foggy storm to rescue them when Roger's boat goes aground. Dain finally sees that he has lots of options open to him and all of them can be explored, whether it be lobstering or attending college, in this first novel. (146 pages)

Where it's reviewed:
Book Report, September 2001, page 62
Booklist, April 15, 2001, page 1547
Kliatt, July 2001, page 10
School Library Journal, May 2001, page 154
Voice of Youth Advocates, June 2001, page 123

Other books you might like:
Cynthia DeFelice, *Death at Devil's Bridge*, 2000
    Ben's jeopardizes his job on a fishing charter when he carries sealed envelopes for "cool" Donny who may be involved in more than selling drugs.
Pete Fromm, *Blood Knot*, 1998
    This unusual collection of short stories focuses on fishing and the relationships that develop, or come close to ending, because of the sport.
Elizabeth Gilbert, *Stern Men*, 2000
    Ruth meets lobsterman Owney and decides the only way to marry him is to stop the fishing rights battle waged by lobstermen. Adult title.

431

SARAH HOYT

Ill Met by Moonlight
(New York, Ace Books, 2001)

Subject(s): Love; Fairies
Age range(s): Grades 9-Adult
Major character(s): William "Will" Shakespeare, Teacher; Anne "Nan" Shakespeare, Housewife; Quicksilver, Shape-changer (elf)
Time period(s): 16th century
Locale(s): Stratford-Upon-Avon, England

Summary: Young Will Shakespeare returns home from work exhausted and eager to see his wife Nan and their baby, only to find an empty house. Will is no ignorant county lout to fall prey to superstition; he quickly surmises that Nan has been called to her sister-in-law's aid as her child is born. Although exhausted form his walk home, the young schoolmaster resolves to retrieve his wife. His walk through the forest of Arden betrays him to his deepest fears. Where no light should be, a transparent castle glows, revealing Nan dancing with a supernaturally handsome king. The mysterious dark lady Quicksilver, one of the disinherited heirs to the fairy kingdom, approaches Will and offers a deal. Will's help in killing the treacherous fairy king can buy Nan's freedom. Nan, meanwhile, is plotting her own escape, while resisting the glamour of the elves. Can two mortals bargain for more than mere freedom when bartering with the good people? (274 pages)

Where it's reviewed:
Booklist, October 1, 2001, page 305
Library Journal, October 15, 2001, page 112
Magazine of Fantasy and Science Fiction, September 2001, page 96

Publishers Weekly, October 1, 2001, page 43

Other books you might like:
Emma Bull, *The War for the Oaks*, 1987
    A rock musician becomes a pawn in Faerie wars, but refuses to merely be used.
Pamela Dean, *Tam Lin*, 1991
    The queen of Fairy has taken a mortal man as tribute on a modern college campus. Can he be saved by a student?
Lisa Goldstein, *Strange Devices of the Sun and Moon*, 1993
    Elves and fairies stalk the streets of Elizabethan London.
Rebecca Lickiss, *Eccentric Circles*, 2001
    In addition to her great-grandmother's house, she also inherits the old lady's relationship with Fairie.

432

CHARLOTTE HUCK
ANITA LOBEL, Illustrator

The Black Bull of Norroway
(New York: Greenwillow Books, 2001)

Subject(s): Fairy Tales; Folklore; Love
Age range(s): Grades 2-5
Major character(s): Peggy Ann, Sister (youngest), Maiden; Black Bull of Norroway, Bull, Nobleman (enchanted)
Time period(s): Indeterminate Past
Locale(s): Norway

Summary: In family discussions of marriage Peggy Ann claims to only want a good, kind loving husband, even the Black Bull of Norroway. As her sisters set out to seek their future spouses, a wise woman sends the sisters on their way in the style they seek while Peggy Ann is sent riding on the Black Bull of Norroway. The bull is kind and gentle to Peggy Ann and because Peggy Ann treats the bull in the same way she learns that the Black Bull of Norroway is actually the Duke of Norroway under an evil spell. One more obstacle must be overcome before the Duke is completely free of the spell. As the spell breaks, Peggy Ann carelessly loses her beloved in the mist and toils for seven years to find and wed him. (40 pages)

Where it's reviewed:
Booklist, September 15, 2001, page 228
Bulletin of the Center for Children's Books, May 2001, page 339
Horn Book, May 2001, page 339
Riverbank Review, Fall 2001, page 47
School Library Journal, June 2001, page 137

Awards the book has won:
ALA Notable Children's Books, 2002
Notable Social Studies Trade Books for Young People, 2002

Other books by the same author:
Toads and Diamonds, 1996
Secret Places, 1993
Princess Furball, 1989

Other books you might like:
Lise Lunge-Larsen, *The Troll with No Heart in His Body: And Other Tales of Trolls from Norway*, 1999
    In each of these nine folktales trolls try to foil the hero or heroine's compassionate deeds.

Claire Martin, *Boots and the Glass Mountain*, 1992
    Boots, the youngest of three brothers, wins the hand of a
    princess in this retelling of a Norwegian folktale.
Ruth Sanderson, *Rose Red & Snow White*, 1997
    One of many retellings of the story explains the rewards
    for kindness freely offered by the sisters.
Katrin Tchana, *The Serpent Slayer*, 2000
    Eighteen folktales celebrate the strength and cleverness of
    heroines of diverse ages and cultures.
Jane Yolen, *Not One Damsel in Distress: World Folktales for
    Strong Girls*, 2000
    Thirteen folktales from twelve countries feature warriors,
    goddesses, pirates, princesses and ordinary courageous he-
    roes who just happen to be female.

433

TANYA HUFF

The Second Summoning

(New York: DAW Books, 2001)

Series: Keeper's Chronicles. Number 2
Subject(s): Love
Age range(s): Grades 9-Adult
Major character(s): Claire Hansen, Girlfriend, Sister; Dean
    McIsaac, Boyfriend; Austin, Cat; Diana Hansen, Sister;
    Samuel, Angel
Time period(s): 2000s
Locale(s): Canada

Summary: When *Summon the Keeper* ended, it was obvious to
everyone but Claire that she and Dean were a match made in
heaven. Claire just can't believe that a Keeper with her responsibilities for keeping evil under control can possibly be
meant for that kind of happiness. In spite of Austin's acid
comments, Claire sends Dean away for protection and now
Dean is insulted, Austin is sulking and Claire has to admit
she's miserable. By the time they get back together, the reunion is so glorious that the psychic energies bring Samuel, a
confused angel, into this dimension. Claire and interfering
little sister Diana are both determined to put matters right, but
it won't be as easy as just sending Samuel back where he
belongs. The powers of good and evil must be kept in balance,
and there's a demon on the loose who is having just as
difficult a time as Samuel! (416 pages)

Where it's reviewed:
Voice of Youth Advocates, December 2001, page 370

Other books by the same author:
Valor's Choice, 2000
The Quartered Sea, 1999
Summon the Keeper, 1998

Other books you might like:
Doranna Durgin, *A Feral Darkness*, 2001
    Druid isn't just a lost dog, he's a messenger from a god.
Gabriel King, *The Golden Cat*, 1999
    Evil is determined to eliminate the kitten who will become
    the long-prophesied Golden Cat.
Susan Fromberg Schaeffer, *The Autobiography of Foudini M.
    Cat*, 1997

Foudini gives you a cat's eye view of life from his beginnings as a foundling kitten to wise elderly tom.

434

DEAN HUGHES

Soldier Boys

(New York: Atheneum/Simon & Schuster, 2001)

Subject(s): World War II; Conduct of Life
Age range(s): Grades 7-10
Major character(s): Spencer Morgan, 17-Year-Old, Military
    Personnel; Dietrich "Dieter" Hedrick, 15-Year-Old, Mili-
    tary Personnel
Time period(s): 1930s; 1940s
Locale(s): Brigham City, Utah; Germany; Belgium

Summary: Two teens hurry into battle, victims of patriotism
and idealism. Spencer grows up on a farm in Utah and reaches
the age where he needs to prove himself, both to his family
and to a possible girlfriend, so he quits high school to train as
a paratrooper. In Germany, impressionable Dieter hears Hitler's warmongering and becomes a leader with Hitler youth,
moving from digging ditches along Germany's border to joining the army. Both boys experience the fear of war, the sight
of friends killed and eventually the questioning of why
they're involved in war. During the Battle of the Bulge their
paths cross when Spencer hears the cries of the wounded
Dieter and tries to rescue him in an act of great heroism. (162
pages)

Where it's reviewed:
Bulletin of the Center for Children's Books, March 2002,
    page 243
Horn Book, January 2002, page 77
Publishers Weekly, December 3, 2001, page 60
School Library Journal, November 2001, page 158
Voice of Youth Advocates, February 2002, page 435

Other books by the same author:
Grand Slam, 1999 (Scrappers, Number 9)
No Fear, 1999 (Scrappers, Number 8)
Team Picture, 1996
The Trophy, 1994
End of the Race, 1993

Other books you might like:
Grigory Baklanov, *Forever Nineteen*, 1989
    For Lt. Volodya Tretyakov, the war ends when an artillery
    shell explodes and he is "forever nineteen."
Michael Noonan, *McKenzie's Boots*, 1988
    Mature-looking though underage, Rod enlists in the Aus-
    tralian Army to fight in World War II where even the
    Japanese consider him a hero.
Erich Marie Remarque, *All Quiet on the Western Front*, 1929
    Of four German friends, only Paul survives the battles of
    World War I.

STEPHEN HUNECK, Author/Illustrator

Sally Goes to the Mountains

(New York: Harry N. Abrams, Inc., Publishers, 2001)

Subject(s): Animals/Dogs; Camps and Camping; Pets
Age range(s): Preschool-Kindergarten
Major character(s): Sally, Dog
Time period(s): 2000s (2001)
Locale(s): United States

Summary: Prior to their camping trip Sally's owners read a book about the various wild animals such as rabbits, beavers and moose living in the mountains. Sally settles down on her seat in the van to nap during the trip. Not until the van stops in the mountains does Sally realize that the all the animals she's been watching, chasing and sniffing have been in her dreams. Now she's ready to meet some real creatures. (32 pages)

Where it's reviewed:
Christian Science Monitor, June 14, 2001, page 18
Horn Book Guide, Fall 2001, page 260
New York Times Book Review, July 15, 2001, page 24
School Library Journal, July 2001, page 83
Smithsonian, November 2001, page 118

Awards the book has won:
Smithsonian's Notable Books for Children, 2001

Other books by the same author:
Sally Goes to the Farm, 2002
Sally Goes to the Beach, 2000
My Dog's Brain, 1997

Other books you might like:
Isabelle Harper, *My Dog Rosie*, 1994
    Rosie has an active day with Isabelle who feeds the pet, bathes him and takes him out for a game of catch before their nap.
Cynthia Rylant, *Tulip Sees America*, 1998
    A young man and his dog travel across America by car.
Jan Slepian, *Lost Moose*, 1995
    On an early morning walk, James spots a young moose separated from its mother on the wooded island where his family is vacationing.

AMY HUNTINGTON, Author/Illustrator

One Monday

(New York: Orchard Books, 2001)

Subject(s): Farm Life; Weather; Animals
Age range(s): Grades K-1
Major character(s): Annabelle, Child
Time period(s): 2000s
Locale(s): United States

Summary: Monday morning the sound of the barn's tin roof banging in the wind awakens Annabelle. Daily, the wind increases in strength, causing pigs' tails to straighten and hens' feathers to turn inside out. By Wednesday vegetables are being twisted out of the ground by the wind and on Friday frogs are riding the waves in the animals' water trough and the spots have been blown off the cow. Saturday the wind is so strong that Annabelle holds onto the fence to keep from being blown away. What a relief when the wind finally blows right out of town on Sunday but then on Monday, as the author's first book concludes, the rain begins. . . . (32 pages)

Where it's reviewed:
Booklist, February 1, 2002, page 946
Horn Book Guide, Spring 2002, page 46
Publishers Weekly, October 22, 2001, page 74
School Library Journal, December 2001, page 104

Other books you might like:
Mary Calhoun, *Jack and the Whoopee Wind*, 1987
    With friends in Whoopee, Wyoming Jack tries to tame a wind that is capable of blowing the feathers off a chicken.
Pat Hutchins, *The Wind Blew*, 1974
    A rhyming story describes the cumulative effect of a wind that blows away many objects.
G. Brian Karas, *The Windy Day*, 1998
    Most townspeople don't appreciate the havoc caused by a strong wind but one boy finds pleasure imagining all the places the wind has already traveled.
Phyllis Root, *One Windy Wednesday*, 1997
    One Wednesday on the farm the wind is so strong that the sound blows from one animal to another making the cows oink and the ducks moo.
Linda Arms White, *Comes a Wind*, 2000
    Two competitive brothers have to cooperate in order to rescue their mother after a strong wind carries her away and deposits her on the weather vane.

437

CAROL OTIS HURST
JAMES STEVENSON, Illustrator

Rocks in His Head

(New York: Greenwillow Books, 2001)

Subject(s): Collectors and Collecting; Hobbies; Museums
Age range(s): Grades 1-4
Major character(s): Unnamed Character, Father, Collector; Grace Johnson, Museum Curator
Time period(s): Indeterminate Past
Locale(s): Springfield, Massachusetts

Summary: A childhood interest in rocks starts a collection that continues to grow throughout a man's lifetime. For many years rocks remain a hobby as the man owns and operates a filling station until the Depression causes that business to fail. The rock collection moves to the attic of the family home and the man spends days when he cannot find work at a nearby museum. There he attracts the attention of Grace Johnson who notices how often he visits. She asks to see the man's collection and then gives him a job with the museum. Although he begins as a custodian he eventually becomes a curator. His life-long wish is fulfilled now that he can live his hobby all day long. (32 pages)

Where it's reviewed:
Booklist, June 2001, page 1890
Horn Book, July 2001, page 440

Publishers Weekly, April 30, 2001, page 78
Riverbank Review, Summer 2001, page 33
School Library Journal, June 2001, page 118

Awards the book has won:
Smithsonian's Notable Books for Children, 2001
Boston Globe-Horn Book Honor Book, 2001

Other books you might like:
Lynne Barasch, *Radio Rescue*, 2000
    Fascinated by wireless radio communication Robert learns Morse code and acquires his ham radio license.
Candace Fleming, *When Agnes Caws*, 1999
    Agnes, a gifted mimicker of birdcalls, travels the globe with her ornithologist mother in search of rare species.
Roma Gans, *Let's Go Rock Collecting*, 1997
    A nonfiction "Let's-Read-and-Find-Out" science series title for beginning rock collectors describes the characteristics of rocks and rock formations.

438

CAROL OTIS HURST

Through the Lock

(Boston: Lorraine/Houghton Mifflin, 2001)

Subject(s): Orphans; Canals; Historical
Age range(s): Grades 5-8
Major character(s): Walter Clark, 12-Year-Old; Etta Prentice, Orphan, 11-Year-Old; Jake Whittingham, Child
Time period(s): 19th century
Locale(s): Farmington Canal, Connecticut

Summary: Tired of her foster family who practically starve her and then make her pray over the leavings, Etta runs away and stumbles into a cabin alongside the new canal in Connecticut. Already holing up in the cabin is Walter who's fled his abusive, alcoholic father, but his father finds their cabin, drinks too much and dies. After returning his body to the family farm for burial, Walter and Etta next take in Jake, who helps at the general store and is unwilling to return to the Shaker settlement where his parents live. The three youngsters manage to convince the canal operators to let them work at one of the locks, which will provide them money and a bigger house. When the canal operators agree, as long as an adult resides with them, Walter has the opportunity to give his mother a place to live and Etta makes plans for her brother and sister to join them in this first novel based loosely on the life of the author's grandparents. (161 pages)

Where it's reviewed:
Book Report, November 2001, page 60
Bulletin of the Center for Children's Books, March 2001, page 264
Horn Book, March 2001, page 208
Publishers Weekly, April 30, 2001, page 79
Voice of Youth Advocates, April 2001, page 42

Other books by the same author:
In Plain Sight, 2002

Other books you might like:
Chester Aaron, *Lackawanna*, 1986
    During the Depression, Willy and other homeless children band together for survival.

Len Hilts, *Timmy O'Dowd and the Big Ditch: A Story of the Glory Days on the Old Erie Canal*, 1988
    Scrappy Tim is mortified when his citified, art-loving cousin Dennis arrives; only a canal emergency pulls them together.
William Mayne, *Gideon Ahoy!*, 1989
    Partially brain-damaged and deaf, Gideon's close-knit family buys a canal barge which will be operated by Gideon, his father and grandfather.
Carolyn Reeder, *Captain Kate*, 1999
    Kate enlists her stepbrother's help, while she captains their canal boat, to haul their cargo to market.

439

JOHANNA HURWITZ
PATIENCE BREWSTER, Illustrator

Lexi's Tale

(New York: SeaStar Books, 2001)

Series: Park Pals Adventure. Number 2
Subject(s): Animals/Squirrels; Animals/Guinea Pigs; Homeless People
Age range(s): Grades 2-5
Major character(s): Lexington "Lexi", Squirrel, Friend; Pee Wee, Guinea Pig, Friend; Stefan Klopot, Streetperson, Tourist (lost)
Time period(s): 2000s (2001)
Locale(s): New York, New York (Central Park)

Summary: Despite Lexi's efforts to teach his new friend PeeWee the ways of life in the park, he cannot dissuade PeeWee from befriending a homeless man who rescues him from a dog. PeeWee's familiar with humans and he senses that the man is friendly and kind although neither animal can understand the language he speaks. When Lexi finally agrees to help PeeWee his efforts lead to the man being taken away in a police car so Lexi follows, hiding in the same car in which the man is later driven to the relatives he was to meet when he arrived. PeeWee's ability to read enables him to learn Stefan's name when he finds a newspaper blowing through the park with an article about Stefan. Before the friendly stranger returns to Poland he visits the park one last time to leave a parting gift for PeeWee. (108 pages)

Where it's reviewed:
Booklist, December 15, 2001, page 731
Publishers Weekly, November 19, 2001, page 70
School Library Journal, October 2001, page 120

Other books by the same author:
PeeWee's Tale, 2000 (Park Pals Adventure, Number 1)
Llama in the Library, 1999
The Just Desserts Club, 1999
A Llama in the Family, 1994

Other books you might like:
Brooks Hansen, *Caesar's Antlers*, 1997
    Kindly Caesar uses his antlers to transport a sparrow with her nest of babies as she searches for her lost mate.
Wendy Orr, *Ark in the Park*, 2000
    Mr. and Mrs. Noah own a pet shop shaped like a ship in the park across the street from lonely Sophie's apartment.

Cynthia Rylant, *Gooseberry Park*, 1995

A dog, a bat and a hermit crab are stuck babysitting for young squirrels whose mother is lost after an ice storm destroys their tree home.

440

HAZEL HUTCHINS
SUSAN KATHLEEN HARTUNG, Illustrator

One Dark Night

(New York: Viking, 2001)

Subject(s): Animals/Cats; Weather; Grandparents
Age range(s): Grades K-2
Major character(s): Jonathan, Child, Animal Lover; Unnamed Character, Cat, Mother
Time period(s): 2000s (2001)
Locale(s): Canada

Summary: Distant thunder keeps Jonathan awake, looking out the window and guessing when the approaching storm will arrive. In the yard he sees a small animal and races downstairs to give a stray cat shelter. Jonathan is surprised when the cat scurries into house, drops a tiny kitten on the rug and runs out again. The storm is drawing near when the cat returns with another kitten and then leaves again. As the rain begins to pour Jonathan dashes outside to help the cat bring in the last kitten and then they all settle down to sleep on a dark, stormy night. (32 pages)

Where it's reviewed:
Booklist, May 15, 2001, page 1758
Bulletin of the Center for Children's Books, July 2001, page 410
Horn Book, July 2001, page 440
Kirkus Reviews, April 15, 2001, page 586
School Library Journal, June 2001, page 118

Awards the book has won:
IRA Children's Choices, 2002

Other books by the same author:
Two So Small, 2000
It's Raining, Yancy & Bear, 1998
Yancy & Bear, 1996

Other books you might like:
Aliki, *Tabby: A Story in Pictures*, 1995
A kitten's first year of life as a child's pet is chronicled in a photo-essay.
Debi Gliori, *Mr. Bear to the Rescue*, 2000
On a stormy night Mr. Bear responds to Mr. Rabbit-Bunn's plea for help after the destruction of a tree that housed his family.
Libba Moore Gray, *Is There Room on the Feather Bed?*, 1997
During a storm, the farm animals seek shelter in the teeny tiny house of the wee fat woman and her wee fat husband.
Holly Keller, *A Bed Full of Cats*, 1999
When Lee's lost cat comes home again she brings four kittens with her.

I

441

EVA IBBOTSON
KEVIN HAWKES, Illustrator

Dial-a-Ghost
(New York: Dutton, 2001)

Subject(s): Ghosts; Orphans
Age range(s): Grades 4-7
Major character(s): Oliver Smith, Orphan, Heir; Eric Wilkinson, Spirit; Adopta Wilkinson, Spirit; Fulton Snodde-Brittle, Uncle (of Oliver); Frieda Snodde-Brittle, Aunt (of Oliver)
Time period(s): 1940s
Locale(s): England

Summary: When the Wilkinson's country home takes a direct hit from a German bomb, the family is killed instantly, but their troubles are just beginning for now they're homeless ghosts. The only spot they find to haunt is a lingerie shop in London, which just isn't suitable for their children, son Eric and adopted daughter Adopta. Luckily there's the Dial-a-Ghost agency that promises to send them to a nice convent filled with mild-mannered nuns. The Dial-a-Ghost agency also deals directly with humans so when the despicable Fulton and Frieda Snodde-Brittle show up and request evil, dreadful ghosts, the agency sends them the Shriekers, two ghosts who hate children and wear rotting meat as jewelry. The Snodde-Brittles are guardians of Oliver Smith, their orphaned nephew who is heir to the family fortune, and they plan to scare him to death. By some strange stroke of luck, the folders are mixed up at the agency and the Shriekers are sent to the convent while the Wilkinsons are sent to Helton Hall where they are just what lonely Oliver needs in another delightful tale from this British author. (195 pages)

Where it's reviewed:
Bulletin of the Center for Children's Books, September 2001, page 20
Horn Book, September 2001, page 586
Publishers Weekly, July 9, 2001, page 68
School Library Journal, August 2001, page 184

Voice of Youth Advocates, December 2001, page 370

Awards the book has won:
Bulletin of the Center for Children's Books Blue Ribbon, 2001

Other books by the same author:
Journey to the River Sea, 2002
The Great Ghost Rescue, 2002
Island of the Aunts, 2000
Which Witch?, 1999
The Secret of Platform 13, 1998

Other books you might like:
Marianne Carus, *That's Ghosts for You!*, 2000
    If ghost stories are what you like to read, here's a collection of thirteen deliciously terrifying ones.
Dick King-Smith, *The Roundhill*, 2000
    A girl named Alice, who appears and disappears without making a sound, visits Evan in his special beech grove.
Lemony Snicket, *Unfortunate Events Series*, 1999-
    The Baudelaire children live up to the name of the series as their lives go from bad to worse after their parents are killed in a fire.
Stephanie S. Tolan, *Who's There?*, 1994
    Drew and Evan prove that the ghost of their grandfather's second wife was not the nice person everyone thinks she was.

442

MICK INKPEN, Author/Illustrator

Kipper's A to Z: An Alphabet Adventure
(San Diego: Red Wagon Books/Harcourt, Inc., 2001)

Subject(s): Animals/Dogs; Animals; Friendship
Age range(s): Preschool-Grade 1
Major character(s): Kipper, Dog, Friend; Arnold, Pig, Friend; Unnamed Character, Zebra
Time period(s): Indeterminate
Locale(s): Fictional Country

Summary: Arnold finds an ant and puts it in a small box to carry with him as he and Kipper meet up with other animals, some, like the caterpillar and the interesting insect small enough to go in Arnold's box but others, like the duck and the elephant that are definitely too large. An impatient zebra pops in and out of the adventure wondering when it will be his turn to be included in the story. Of course, the zebra has the special responsibility to proudly conclude Kipper and Arnold's alphabet adventure. First published in Great Britain in 2000. (58 pages)

Where it's reviewed:
Booklist, May 15, 2001, page 1758
Horn Book Guide, Fall 2001, page 233
Kirkus Reviews, February 1, 2001, page 184
Publishers Weekly, February 12, 2001, page 210
School Library Journal, June 2001, page 120

Awards the book has won:
Publishers Weekly Best Children's Books, 2001
ALA Notable Children's Books, 2002

Other books by the same author:
Kipper's Christmas Eve, 2000
The Great Pet Sale, 1999
Kipper's Snowy Day, 1996

Other books you might like:
Holly Hobbie, *Toot & Puddle: Puddle's ABC*, 2000
    Puddle teaches his friend Otto all the letters of the alphabet so Otto can write his name.
Maira Kalman, *What Pete Ate from A-Z*, 2001
    Pete is such a hungry dog he devours everything in sight from A to Z.
Mike Lester, *A Is for Salad*, 2000
    According to this humorous story "A Is for Salad" because the alligator is eating the salad and that's only the first letter of the alphabet.
Audrey Wood, *Alphabet Adventure*, 2001
    Before they can go to school the lower-case letters of the alphabet must rescue "i" and find his missing dot.

443

DAVID IVES

Monsieur Eek

(New York: HarperCollins, 2001)

Subject(s): Animals/Monkeys; Humor; Trials

Age range(s): Grades 5-7
Major character(s): Emmaline Perth, 13-Year-Old; Philip "Flurp the Town Fool" Flurp, 15-Year-Old; Lexter Shmink, Police Officer (bailiff); Monsieur Eek, Monkey
Time period(s): 17th century (1609)
Locale(s): MacOongafoondsen, Fictional Country

Summary: In the early 1600s, Emmaline and Flurp live in a small village with a population of twenty-one, a number that will reach twenty-two when a ship runs aground. Only Emmaline is brave enough to board and search the vessel where she finds a chimpanzee locked in a deserted cabin. The chimpanzee yells "Eek," the townspeople know he's a foreigner and since the French are foreigners, the animal must be a Frenchman, and they promptly name him Monsieur Eek. The less than honorable town bailiff Mr. Shmink decides that Monsieur Eek is a thief and threatens to hang him. Emmaline appoints herself as his lawyer and, with the help of Flurp, tries to save Monsieur Eek in this playwright's first novel for young people. (179 pages)

Where it's reviewed:
Book Report, January 2002, page 62
Booklist, June 2001, page 1883
Publishers Weekly, May 28, 2001, page 89
School Library Journal, June 2001, page 150
Voice of Youth Advocates, June 2001, page 133

Other books you might like:
Sid Hite, *Those Darn Dithers*, 1996
    Stilt walking, a dancing pig and an uncle who floats out to sea are just a few of the eccentric characters and adventures shared by the Dithers' family.
Polly Horvath, *Everything on a Waffle*, 2001
    When Primrose's parents are lost at sea, only she's convinced they're waiting for rescue, until they return, she's shuttled between foster homes.
Kate Klise, *Trial by Jury/Journal*, 2001
    Lily finds herself in the role of being the first-ever juvenile juror in the state of Missouri, as she duly records in her journal.
Lemony Snicket, *Unfortunate Events Series*, 1999-
    The Baudelaire children live up to the name of the series as their lives go from bad to worse after their parents are killed in a fire.

J

444

ELLEN JACKSON
MATT FAULKNER, Illustrator

Scatterbrain Sam

(Watertown, MA: Whispering Coyote/Charlesbridge, 2001)

Subject(s): Cooks and Cooking; Tall Tales; Folklore
Age range(s): Grades 3-5
Major character(s): Sam, Young Man, Hero; Maizie Mae, Young Woman, Pilot; Widder Woman, Sorceress
Time period(s): Indeterminate Past
Locale(s): United States

Summary: Sam grows tired of the local gossip about how scatterbrained he is and goes to Widder Woman for some kind of glue to stick his brains together. As it happens Widder Woman is cooking up a batch of glue stew but in order for it to work on Sam he needs to bring something that he loves to flavor the pot. Each time that Sam brings one of his pets he's too kind-hearted to throw the animal into the bubbling pot and Widder Woman gives him a riddle to solve instead. Maizie Mae helps the befuddled Sam with each riddle but still the pot needs something more. Finally Sam realizes he loves Maizie Mae but he doesn't want her in the pot either so he chooses to remain scatterbrained. Unfortunately, Maizie's sneeze tosses her into the pot and, thankfully Sam, without consulting his brains, reacts in just the right way to save her. Widder Woman says Sam glued his brains without her help and now he better marry Maizie Mae quickly. (32 pages)

Where it's reviewed:
Booklist, August 2001, page 2130
Horn Book Guide, Spring 2002, page 46
Kirkus Reviews, May 15, 2001, page 742
Publishers Weekly, June 25, 2001, page 71
School Library Journal, July 2001, page 83

Other books by the same author:
The Precious Gift: A Navaho Creation Myth, 1996
Brown Cow, Green Grass, Yellow Mellow Sun, 1995
The Impossible Riddle, 1995
Cinder Edna, 1994

Other books you might like:
Sid Fleischman, *McBroom's Wonderful One-Acre Farm: Three Tall Tales*, 1992
    A collection of humorous tall tales about Farmer Mc-Broom and his family was originally published in 1967.
Helen Ketteman, *Luck with Potatoes*, 1995
    Hard-luck farmer Clemmon Hardigree has a change of fortune when he grows a potato crop that comes complete with cows.
Sheila MacGill-Callahan, *To Capture the Wind*, 1997
    To free her betrothed from a pirate, Oonagh correctly answers four riddles.

445

JENNIFER RICHARD JACOBSON
ALISSA IMRE GEIS, Illustrator

Winnie Dancing on Her Own

(Boston: Houghton Mifflin Company, 2001)

Subject(s): Friendship; Ballet; Individuality
Age range(s): Grades 3-5
Major character(s): Winifred "Winnie" Fletcher, 8-Year-Old, Friend; Vanessa Wiley, 8-Year-Old, Friend; Zoe Johnson, 8-Year-Old, Friend
Time period(s): 2000s (2001)
Locale(s): United States

Summary: Ballet lessons threaten the three-year friendship of Winnie, Vanessa and Zoe. Winnie prefers the End-of-the-Alphabet Club's Tuesday afternoons at the library, but Vanessa and Zoe want to give dance a try. Awkward Winnie reluctantly joins her friends, but soon wants to quit the class. Although they're fearful that their different interests mean an end to their friendship, Vanessa, Winnie and Zoe find a way to maintain their individuality and stay friends. (105 pages)

Where it's reviewed:
Booklist, September 15, 2001, page 232
Bulletin of the Center for Children's Books, November 2001, page 105
Kirkus Reviews, August 1, 2001, page 1125

Publishers Weekly, August 6, 2001, page 90
School Library Journal, December 2001, page 104

Other books by the same author:
Moon Sandwich Mom, 1999
A Net of Stars, 1998

Other books you might like:
Beverly Cleary, *Ramona Quimby, Age 8*, 1981
    Spirited Ramona keeps her family guessing about her next
    adventure as she enters third grade in this Newbery Honor
    Book.
Michelle Edwards, *Pa Lia's First Day*, 1999
    Pa Lia's nervousness about entering a new school soon
    vanishes as she makes friends with Calliope and Howie.
David Elliott, *The Cool Crazy Crickets*, 2000
    Four friends start a club for the purpose of being friends for
    life.
Susan Wojciechowski, *Beany (Not Beanhead) and the Magic
    Crystal*, 1997
    Beany could use her magic crystal to solve her own prob-
    lems but instead she unselfishly gives it to an elderly
    neighbor.

446

BRIAN JACQUES
IAN SCHOENHERR, Illustrator

Castaways of the Flying Dutchman
(New York: Philomel Books, 2001)

Subject(s): Animals/Dogs; Heroes and Heroines; Angels
Age range(s): Grades 5-9
Major character(s): Nebuchadnezzar ''Neb/Ben'', Immortal;
    Denmark ''Den/Ned'', Dog (Labrador), Immortal; Cap-
    tain Vanderdecken, Sea Captain; Winifred Winn,
    Widow(er); Obadiah Smithers, Businessman (developer)
Time period(s): 17th century (1620s); 1890s (1896)
Locale(s): Copenhagen, Denmark; *Flying Dutchman*, At Sea;
    Chapelvale, England

Summary: A young boy, mute and abused by his stepbrothers,
is pushed by them into the sea where he luckily grabs a rope
and climbs aboard the ship the *Flying Dutchman*. Kept on to
help in the galley, along with the dog he lures on board, Neb
and Denmark begin a curious life aboard a ship captained by a
madman and sailed by a mutinous crew. Driven back as they
try to sail around Cape Horn, Captain Vanderdecken curses
the weather and the Lord; in turn, he and his ship are cursed by
an angel to forever sail the sea, as they become the ship of
legend. Neb and Den are tossed overboard and, because of
their innocent hearts, are saved from the curse. Instead they
are given immortality and speech, with the dog able to communicate telepathically with Neb, though they must always
do good throughout the world. Several hundred years later,
now referred to as Ben and Ned, they arrive in Chapelvale in
time to help Mrs. Winn find her missing deeds. They have
seven days to accomplish this to save the town from destruction by Mr. Smithers who wants to use the land to build a
quarry and cement factory. (327 pages)

Where it's reviewed:
Booklist, March 1, 2001, page 1271

Bulletin of the Center for Children's Books, March 2001,
    page 266
Horn Book, March 2001, page 208
Publishers Weekly, January 8, 2001, page 67
Voice of Youth Advocates, April 2001, page 53

Other books by the same author:
Tales from Redwall Series, 1987-

Other books you might like:
Joan Aiken, *Is Underground*, 1993
    Searching for her cousin Arun, Is finds him, along with
    other missing children, held captive in the underground
    mines and foundries of Holdernesse.
Gillian Chan, *The Carved Box*, 2001
    Newly arrived in Canada, Callum buys a large Newfound-
    land dog and the carved box that accompanies her.
Gerald Hausman, *Tom Cringle: Battle on the High Seas*, 2000
    After a storm hits his ship, Tom finds himself aboard a
    pirate ship.
Theodore Taylor, *Rogue Wave: And Other Red-Blooded Sea
    Stories*, 1996
    Eight stories of sea adventures will delight readers of all
    ages.

447

BRIAN JACQUES

Taggerung
(New York: Philomel Books, 2001)

Series: Tales from Redwall. Book 14
Subject(s): Animals; Adventure and Adventurers
Age range(s): Grades 6-10
Major character(s): Deyna/Tagg, Otter
Time period(s): Indeterminate Future
Locale(s): Mossflower Woods, Fictional Country

Summary: Redwall is still rejoicing in the birth of baby Deyna
when he disappears; as fans of the series will expect, this is
just the beginning of the adventures. A gang of roving ruffians
kidnaps the baby because they believe he is their prophesied
leader, the Taggerung who will bring them riches. Although
he is brought up by the gang far from the gentle atmosphere
and learning of Redwall, Tagg never becomes quite the villain
his foster family tries to create. Eventually Tagg finds his way
home where he's discovered to be the long-lost Deyna who
arrives just in time to save Redwall. (438 pages)

Where it's reviewed:
Booklist, August 2001, page 2120
Horn Book Magazine, November 2001, page 750
Kliatt, September 2001, page 10
Publishers Weekly, August 27, 2001, page 86
School Library Journal, October 2001, page 162

Other books by the same author:
Lord Brocktree, 2000 (Tales from Redwall, Book 13)
The Legend of Luke, 1999 (Tales from Redwall, Book 12)
Marlfox, 1998 (Tales from Redwall, Book 11)

Other books you might like:
Clare Bell, *Ratha's Creature*, 1983
    A race of intelligent, cat-like creatures finds its existence
    threatened by a similar species.

David Clement-Davies, *Fire Bringer*, 1999
    A long-prophesied child is born and leads his people, the deer, to freedom.
Tor Seidler, *The Wainscott Weasel*, 1993
    Determined to do the unexpected, a weasel embarks on a weird romance.

448

PAMELA JANE
VERA ROSENBERRY, Illustrator

Monster Mischief
(New York: Atheneum Books for Young Readers, 2001)

Subject(s): Halloween; Monsters; Stories in Rhyme
Age range(s): Grades K-2
Major character(s): Moe, Monster
Time period(s): Indeterminate
Locale(s): Fictional Country

Summary: Two monsters begin cooking stew in a garbage can and two other monsters arrive to add their live animal ingredients to the broth. Little Moe comes empty-handed but curious. Standing on a chair to get a better look in the pot Moe accidentally tips over the monster stew and frog, spider, lizard and bat quickly scurry from the room. Five unhappy, hungry monsters are relieved when a sixth monster comes to the door with a Halloween surprise, a bag of trick-or-treat candy. (32 pages)

Where it's reviewed:
Booklist, September 1, 2001, page 120
Bulletin of the Center for Children's Books, September 2001, page 20
Kirkus Reviews, August 1, 2001, page 1126
Publishers Weekly, September 24, 2001, page 42
School Library Journal, September 2001, page 190

Other books by the same author:
Monster Countdown, 2001
Halloween Hide-and-Seek, 1999
A-Boo-C: A Spooky Alphabet Story, 1998

Other books you might like:
Sean Diviny, *Halloween Motel*, 2000
    By the time a family realizes they're in the wrong motel on Halloween night the monsters are after them as they hastily leave this rhyming tale.
Judith Ross Enderle, *Six Creepy Sheep*, 1992
    Wearing their ghost costumes, six sheep set off for a night of Halloween fun. Stephanie G. Tessler, co-author.
Brian J. Heinz, *The Monster's Test*, 1996
    The fierce monsters become the frightened ones when they meet a group of trick-or-treaters.
Charlotte Huck, *A Creepy Countdown*, 1998
    Halloween symbols appear in a rhyming tale that uses the number one to ten and back again.

449

CAROLINE JANOVER
CHARLOTTE M. FREMAUX, Illustrator

How Many Days Until Tomorrow?
(Bethesda, MD: Woodbine House, 2000)

Subject(s): Grandfathers; Learning Disabilities; Brothers
Age range(s): Grades 4-7
Major character(s): Joshua "Josh" Grant, 12-Year-Old, Dyslexic; Simon Grant, Brother (of Joshua's), 13-Year-Old; Hobson Wilkes, Grandfather
Time period(s): 2000s
Locale(s): Seal Island, Maine

Summary: Josh is dismayed to learn that he and his older, know-it-all brother Simon, will spend a month in Maine visiting their grandparents. Being away from his friends is bothersome to Josh, especially after it becomes obvious that gruff Gramps prefers gifted Simon to dyslexic Josh. Thinking that he might have to run away, Josh gradually becomes enamored of island life, the wildlife he observes and the new friend he makes. When Gramps falls and dislocates his hip while repairing a dock, it's Josh who uses his wits, pulls Gramps out of the advancing tide and keeps him warm until the helicopter whisks him away to the hospital. By the end of Josh's stay, he and Gramps have found the good sides to one another in this sequel to *Josh: A Boy with Dyslexia*. (173 pages)

Where it's reviewed:
Booklist, January 2001, page 960
Children's Bookwatch, January 2001, page 3
School Library Journal, May 2001, page 154

Other books by the same author:
Zipper: The Kid with ADHD, 1997
The Worst Speller in Junior High, 1994
Josh: A Boy with Dyslexia, 1988

Other books you might like:
C.S. Adler, *Kiss the Clown*, 1986
    Joel covers up his problems of dyslexia by playing the role of class clown.
Norma Fox Mazer, *After the Rain*, 1987
    Rachel takes daily walks with her grumpy grandfather and is surprised to find they like one another, which makes his death harder to bear.
Zilpha Keatley Snyder, *The Runaways*, 1999
    Stuck in a desert town, Dani can't believe that she's been "adopted" by a kid whose dyslexia prevents him from reading, but not from being read to.

450

ROBIN JARVIS

The Crystal Prison
(New York: North-South/Sea Star, 2001)

Series: Deptford Mice Trilogy. Book 2
Subject(s): Supernatural; Animals/Mice; Animals/Rats
Age range(s): Grades 5-8

Major character(s): Audrey Brown, Mouse; Oswald Chitter, Mouse; Starwife, Squirrel; Madame Akkikuyu, Fortune Teller
Time period(s): 1980s
Locale(s): London, England (borough of Deptford); Fennywold, England

Summary: Having eradicated the evil Jupiter from his tyranny in the sewers, the mice return to their normal lives, though quite a few move to the country. Audrey is despondent because her good friend Oswald is near death and only the intervention of Starwife can save him, but Starwife enacts a fee for her services. Audrey must accompany, and remain with, the aging fortuneteller Madame Akkikuyu in the countryside of Fennywold. Madame Akkikuyu's healing touch and potions warm her to the hearts of the Fennywolders, but Audrey's city ways bring distrust and suspicion and when several murders occur, the town's mice are quick to accuse Audrey of being a witch. Thanks to several friends, Audrey is saved from a lynching, but realizes Jupiter is trying to work through Madame Akkikuyu's crystal globe to return to physical form. (240 pages)

Where it's reviewed:
Booklist, August 2001, page 2120
Kirkus Reviews, June 15, 2001, page 864
School Library Journal, November 2001, page 159
Voice of Youth Advocates, December 2001, page 370

Other books by the same author:
The Dark Portal, 2000 (Deptford Mice Trilogy, Book 1)
The Raven's Knot, 1996 (Tales from the Wyrd Museum)
The Woven Path, 1995 (Tales from the Wyrd Museum)

Other books you might like:
Avi, *The Dimwood Forest Tales*, 1995-
    The adventures of all the Dimwood Forest animals, from deer mice to porcupines, foxes and owls, are described in this series.
David Clement-Davies, *Fire Bringer*, 1999
    When evil leaders take over the herd, Rannoch's mother sends her young fawn, marked with the sign of a hero, far away from the malevolent deer.
Brian Jacques, *Redwall Series*, 1987-
    A charming series that features the mice of Redwall who defend their abbey against scurrilous animals and offer refuge to friends.

A.M. JENKINS

Damage
(New York: HarperCollins, 2001)

Subject(s): Depression; Sports/Football; Dating (Social Customs)
Age range(s): Grades 10-Adult
Major character(s): Austin Reid, 12th Grader, Football Player; Heather Mackenzie, 12th Grader; Curtis Hightower, 12th Grader, Football Player
Time period(s): 2000s
Locale(s): Parkersville, Texas

Summary: Austin's life should be wonderful for he's a senior and a football star, but the party-animal facade he shows friends hides his lack of energy for day-to-day activities. He dates Heather, considered one of the coolest girls in school, because of their shared loss of a father when young, Austin's to cancer and Heather's to suicide. Since Heather couldn't control her father's suicide, she tries to control everything else, even her sexual relationship with Austin, while Austin sinks deeper and deeper into depression. After Austin breaks up with Heather, he somehow finds the courage to tell his best friend Curtis that he's been thinking about committing suicide and for the first time feels he might be able to climb out of his abyss. (186 pages)

Where it's reviewed:
Booklist, September 15, 2001, page 227
Horn Book, September 2001, page 587
Publishers Weekly, November 12, 2001, page 60
School Library Journal, October 2001, page 162
Voice of Youth Advocates, October 2001, page 279

Awards the book has won:
Booklist Editors' Choice/Books for Youth, 2001
ALA Best Books for Young Adults, 2002

Other books by the same author:
Breaking Boxes, 1997

Other books you might like:
James W. Bennett, *I Can Hear the Mourning Dove*, 1990
    Shaken by her father's death, Grace attempts suicide, fails and is hospitalized.
Chris Crutcher, *Running Loose*, 1983
    When Louie's football coach asks him to take out an opposing player with an illegal hit, Louie refuses and quits the team.
Barbara Shoup, *Wish You Were Here*, 1994
    Jax tries to figure out who he is after his mother remarries, his father is critically injured, and Jax's inexperience with girls ruins some friendships.
Margaret Willey, *Saving Lenny*, 1990
    Foregoing college to live with Lenny, Jesse finally realizes his depression is destroying their relationship.

EMILY JENKINS
TOMEK BOGACKI, Illustrator

Five Creatures
(New York: Frances Foster Books/Farrar Straus Giroux, 2001)

Subject(s): Family Life; Animals/Cats; Pets
Age range(s): Grades 1-3
Major character(s): Unnamed Character, Child, Daughter; Unnamed Character, Father; Unnamed Character, Mother
Time period(s): 2000s (2001)
Locale(s): United States

Summary: A little girl describes the attributes and interests of the five creatures living in her home. The two cats share the interests of the human members of the family when they nap with the father or join the family sitting around the fire in the evening. Other interests, such as eating mice, belong to the cats alone. All five enjoy birds, but not for the same reason.

The humans can button and read while the cats cannot but all five creatures are capable of kissing others. (32 pages)

Where it's reviewed:
Booklist, March 15, 2001, page 1401
Bulletin of the Center for Children's Books, February 2001, page 226
Horn Book, March 2001, page 197
Publishers Weekly, March 26, 2001, page 91
School Library Journal, May 2001, page 124

Awards the book has won:
Boston Globe-Horn Book Honor Book, 2001
Bulletin of the Center for Children's Books Blue Ribbon, 2001

Other books you might like:
Lindsey Gardiner, *Here Come Poppy and Max*, 2000
    With her dog Max, Poppy plays an imaginative game, pretending to be different animals.
Anne Rockwell, *Long Ago Yesterday*, 1999
    Ten brief stories describe everyday family activities that are important to young children.
Caroline Uff, *Hello, Lulu*, 1999
    Meet Lulu's family, pets and friend in the first book about this outgoing character.

453

PATRICK JENNINGS

The Beastly Arms
(New York: Scholastic, 2001)

Subject(s): City and Town Life; Animals; Photography
Age range(s): Grades 5-8
Major character(s): Nicholas "Nickel" Dill, 11-Year-Old, Animal Lover; Miriam, Kangaroo Rat; Inez, 6th Grader; Julius Beasley/Beastley, Landlord, Animal Lover
Time period(s): 2000s
Locale(s): United States

Summary: Combining his love of nature and photography, Nickel often has his head in the clouds as he imagines their shapes as animals and photographs them. His good friend Inez is often with him, and she makes sure he doesn't walk into telephone poles or other obstacles when he's on a shoot. Miriam, his pet kangaroo rat, doesn't help much other than to keep him company. One day he and his mother search for a different apartment and find one that's affordable in the basement of the Beastly Arms, a strange building with an even more unusual landlord called Mr. Beastly. It doesn't take Nickel long to figure out something's amiss for he never sees other tenants and notices strange, animal-like odors and noises, all of which prompt him to explore the upper floors of the building. (314 pages)

Where it's reviewed:
Booklist, May 1, 2001, page 1678
Bulletin of the Center for Children's Books, October 2001, page 61
Horn Book, July 2001, page 454
Publishers Weekly, April 30, 2001, page 79
School Library Journal, April 2001, page 144

Other books by the same author:
Putnam and Pennyroyal, 1999
Faith and the Rocket Cat, 1998
Faith and the Electric Dogs, 1996

Other books you might like:
Winifred Elze, *Here, Kitty, Kitty*, 1996
    Reports of strange animals send Emma poking around an island where she discovers a time travel machine whose doors open to the Pleistocene Age.
Kate Gilmore, *The Exchange Student*, 1999
    A young alien with an obsessive fondness for animals comes to stay with an earth family.
Eva Ibbotson, *Island of the Aunts*, 2000
    When Aunts Etta, Coral and Myrtle need help caring for their creatures, they return to England and kidnap several children to be their assistants.

454

RICHARD W. JENNINGS

The Great Whale of Kansas
(Boston: Houghton Mifflin, 2001)

Subject(s): Fossils; Animals/Whales; Animals/Prehistoric
Age range(s): Grades 5-8
Major character(s): Unnamed Boy, 11-Year-Old, Narrator; Penny Whistle, Teacher (science); Tom White Cloud MacIntosh, Indian, Store Owner (bookstore)
Time period(s): 2000s
Locale(s): Melville, Kansas

Summary: Pretty much a loner, albeit a happy one, a young Kansas boy methodically digs a hole in his backyard for his fishpond, a birthday gift from his parents. As he digs and digs, he hears a metallic clank when the shovel hits something hard. Assuming it's a rock, he looks at it a little more carefully and realizes it's a bone. Further digging reveals five bones side by side and the young boy decides he needs a little more help with identification. His main sources of help are his science teacher, Miss Whistle, and her boyfriend Tom White Cloud, who realize he's found a fossil, but no one's sure what kind. When it looks as though he's unearthed a 25-foot mosasaur inside a whale, officials question the validity of his find. The State Museum of Natural History would like to own it and incorporate the fossil into a theme park and museum while his father would like to make a little money off his son's find. When Tom White Cloud looks into matters, he discovers the fossil is sited on Native American land and, based on an old treaty, the whale belongs to the Native Americans. A proper ceremony is performed, the whale is recovered and left in place, and the young boy proceeds with his plans to build his fishpond. (150 pages)

Where it's reviewed:
Booklist, June 2001, page 1884
Horn Book, September 2001, page 588
Kirkus Reviews, June 15, 2001, page 864
School Library Journal, August 2001, page 184
Voice of Youth Advocates, February 2002, page 435

Other books by the same author:
Orwell's Luck, 2000

Other books you might like:
Pam Conrad, *My Daniel*, 1989
> Julia and her brother discover dinosaur bones on their Nebraska ranch, an event saddened by the death of Daniel several days later.

Hope Norman Coulter, *Dry Bones*, 1990
> A puppy dragging a big bone fills Jonas's hometown with all kinds of speculation about the origin of the bone.

Kathryn Lasky, *The Bone Wars*, 1988
> In the 1870s, teens American Thad and Londoner Julian meet on a fossil dig in the Black Hills where their find astounds the paleontologists.

455

ANN-SOFIE JEPPSON
CATARINA KRUUSVAL, Illustrator
FRANCES CORRY, Translator

You're Growing Up, Pontus!
(New York: R & S Books, 2001)

Subject(s): Animals/Horses; Animals, Treatment of; Horsemanship
Age range(s): Grades 1-3
Major character(s): Pontus, Pony, Narrator; Patch, Cat; Unnamed Character, Child, Animal Lover
Time period(s): 1990s
Locale(s): Sweden

Summary: Pontus's owner, referred to by the pony as "the girl with the yellow mane" brings him to a stable from the pasture where he's been grazing leisurely all summer with friends. Pontus is concerned about being lonely but soon Patch appears, a friend from his earlier stay in the stable. During the winter months Pontus begins instruction on a lunge line and suffers a cold that requires treatment by the vet. Pontus is aware that his brother is winning competitions in something called show-jumping but Pontus is only interested in running in the woods so he hopes that's what the girl with the yellow mane means when she talks about dressage. Captioned drawings accompanying the story convey factual information about horses, their equipment and their care. Originally published in Sweden in 1997. (28 pages)

Where it's reviewed:
Horn Book Guide, Spring 2002, page 74
Kirkus Reviews, September 1, 2001, page 1292
School Library Journal, November 2001, page 124

Other books by the same author:
Here Comes Pontus, 2000

Other books you might like:
Jessie Haas, *Runaway Radish*, 2001
> Each time Radish's owner grows too big for her pony the animal is sold to another little girl who needs to learn all that Radish has to teach.

Dick King-Smith, *Sophie's Lucky*, 1996
> With aspirations of being a lady farmer, Sophie saves her money to buy a pony.

Barbara Ann Porte, *Harry's Pony*, 1997
> Zoning ordinances force Harry to donate the pony he wins in a contest to a riding facility for disabled children.

456

FRANCISCO JIMENEZ

Breaking Through
(Boston: Houghton Mifflin, 2001)

Subject(s): Mexican Americans; Migrant Labor
Age range(s): Grades 7-10
Major character(s): Francisco Jimenez, Mexican American, Teenager; Roberto Jimenez, Mexican American, Teenager
Time period(s): 1950s; 1960s
Locale(s): Santa Maria, California; Mexico

Summary: Though his father is in the United States with a green card, and his younger brothers were born in the United States, their mother, his older brother Roberto and Francisco are all illegal aliens. The Border Patrol picks up the boys from their classes and deports them, with the entire family leaving because they don't want to be separated. Once in Mexico, the three apply for and receive their visas, but only Roberto and Francisco return to Santa Maria. The plan is for the boys to earn enough money to bring back their family; meanwhile the family stays with an aunt while their father finds a healer for his back. In Santa Maria, Roberto and Francisco pick strawberries in the fields, then move up to waxing floors and cleaning windows. Frankie does well in school, though homework and working take up all his time, and is encouraged by his teachers to consider college in this sequel to *The Circuit*. (200 pages)

Where it's reviewed:
Book Report, May 2002, page 57
Booklist, September 1, 2001, page 109
Bulletin of the Center for Children's Books, January 2002, page 175
Riverbank Review, Fall 2001, page 38
School Library Journal, September 2001, page 225

Awards the book has won:
ALA Pura Belpre Honor Book, 2002
Smithsonian's Notable Books for Children, 2001

Other books by the same author:
The Circuit: Stories from the Life of a Migrant Child, 1999

Other books you might like:
Rudolfo A. Anaya, *Bless Me, Ultima*, 1976
> A story of growing up Chicano in the American Southwest during the 1940s.

Jerry McGinley, *Joaquin Strikes Back*, 1998
> Joaquin is not prepared for the racism he encounters when he moves from California to Michigan.

Gary Soto, *Jesse*, 1994
> Jesse knows the importance of an education to break his family's cycle of poverty, but he can't stay at home with his alcoholic stepfather.

457

ANGELA JOHNSON
BARRY MOSER, Illustrator

Those Building Men

(New York: Blue Sky Press/Scholastic, Inc., 2001)

Subject(s): Construction; Historical; American History
Age range(s): Grades 1-3
Time period(s): Indeterminate Past
Locale(s): United States

Summary: Men of many nationalities and races built this country. Working long days, digging canals, laying railroad tracks across the prairie or bridging a mountain gorge the men labored to make the nation great and strong. In the cities these men, these steel workers, these sky walkers created towering buildings as majestic as the western mountains. Men, strong and proud, built the nation from sea to shining sea. The book concludes with a note of tribute to all who labored whether man, woman or child. (32 pages)

Where it's reviewed:
Booklist, February 1, 2001, page 1055
Bulletin of the Center for Children's Books, February 2001, page 226
Horn Book Guide, Fall 2001, page 261
Kirkus Reviews, November 15, 2000, page 1615
School Library Journal, March 2001, page 236

Awards the book has won:
Notable Social Studies Trade Books for Young People, 2002

Other books by the same author:
Down the Winding Road, 2000
The Wedding, 1999
The Rolling Store, 1997

Other books you might like:
Elisa Bartone, *Peppe the Lamplighter*, 1993
  In a Caldecott Honor Book Peppe helps to support his immigrant family by lighting the city's street lamps.
Verla Kay, *Iron Horses*, 1999
  An illustrated story in rhyme describes the building of the transcontinental railroad.
Ian Wallace, *Boy of the Deeps*, 1999
  James works proudly beside his father deep underground in a coal mine.

458

PAUL BRETT JOHNSON, Author/Illustrator

Fearless Jack

(New York: Margaret K. McElderry Books, 2001)

Subject(s): Folklore; Appalachia; Problem Solving
Age range(s): Grades 2-5
Major character(s): Jack, Child, Son; Unnamed Character, Lawman (sheriff)
Time period(s): Indeterminate Past
Locale(s): Appalachians

Summary: Jack's mother hands him the last biscuit and sends him off to find work. Now Jack's not one for working but with a little luck and some quick thinking even his attempts to avoid a potential job end up making money. The sheriff is so impressed when Jack defeats the first wild varmint that he hires him to get rid of the second one. By the time Jack pockets the cash from the first two he's cunning enough to demand more money for the next task the sheriff has a mind for him to do. Jack's ready to mosey on home with his hard-earned money so he hopes the sheriff's rumor about giants isn't true. (32 pages)

Where it's reviewed:
Booklist, July 2001, page 2014
Bulletin of the Center for Children's Books, September 2001, page 21
Horn Book, September 2001, page 602
Publishers Weekly, May 28, 2001, page 87
School Library Journal, July 2001, page 95

Other books by the same author:
Bearhide and Crow, 2000
Mr. Persnickety and the Cat Lady, 2000
Old Dry Frye: A Deliciously Funny Tall Tale, 1999

Other books you might like:
Anthea Bell, *Jack in Luck*, 1992
  Jack's wages get spent on a series of trades as he buys a horse to exchange for a cow before deciding he doesn't need many possessions.
Tom Birdseye, *Look Out, Jack! The Giant Is Back!*, 2001
  A giant tracks Jack all the way to North Carolina to retrieve his slain brother's valuables.
Vivian French, *Lazy Jack*, 1995
  Jack's mother sends her sleepy son off to work but he can't seem to remember to bring his wages home to her.
M.C. Helldorfer, *Jack, Skinny Bones and the Golden Pancakes*, 1996
  Jack learns all of dishonest Granny's tricks and one day uses them to save himself and his pal Skinny Bones from Granny and the devil.

459

PAUL BRETT JOHNSON, Author/Illustrator

The Goose Who Went Off in a Huff

(New York: Orchard Books/Scholastic, Inc., 2001)

Subject(s): Animals/Geese; Animals/Elephants; Humor
Age range(s): Grades K-2
Major character(s): Magnolia, Goose; Miss Rosemary, Farmer, Aged Person; Gertrude, Cow; George, Pig
Time period(s): Indeterminate
Locale(s): United States

Summary: Miss Rosemary soon figures out that Magnolia's strange behavior reflects an unsatisfied maternal instinct. Magnolia doesn't take kindly to Miss Rosemary's assurance that in time she'll have a brood to care for so she vanishes. Miss Rosemary, Gertrude and George search the grounds of a traveling circus to no avail but finally notice Magnolia hiding in a shed on the farm. Neither promises of favorite foods nor orphan goose disguises donned by Gertrude and George convince Magnolia to rejoin her farm family. As the circus train departs, a strange noise in the bushes attracts everyone's attention. Miss Rosemary is not sure what to do with the lost baby elephant that missed the train, but Magnolia goes right into her mother routine and figuratively takes the large baby under her wing. (36 pages)

Where it's reviewed:
Booklist, May 15, 2001, page 1758
Horn Book Guide, Fall 2001, page 261
Kirkus Reviews, April 1, 2001, page 499
Publishers Weekly, April 23, 2001, page 76
School Library Journal, July 2001, page 83

Other books by the same author:
The Pig Who Ran a Red Light, 1999 (IRA/CBC Children's Choices)
A Perfect Pork Stew, 1998
The Cow Who Wouldn't Come Down, 1993 (School Library Journal Best Books)

Other books you might like:
Molly Bang, *Goose*, 1996
    A gosling feels out of place with her adoptive woodchuck family until she learns to fly—right back to the comfort of her woodchuck home.
Christel Desominaux, *Mrs. Hen's Big Surprise*, 2000
    Mrs. Hen hopes the egg she finds in her garden will give her lovely home the one thing it lacks, a baby chick to love.
Lynn Reiser, *The Surprise Family*, 1994
    Much to the surprise of a mother hen, the "chicks" she hatches from a clutch of abandoned eggs enjoy swimming—just like ducks.
Adele Sansone, *The Little Green Goose*, 1999
    An unusual egg from the woods gives Mr. Goose the opportunity to satisfy his desire to be a daddy.

460

RODNEY JOHNSON
JILL THOMPSON, Illustrator

The Secret of Dead Man's Mine
(Los Angeles: UglyTown Productions, 2001)

Series: Rinnah Two Feathers Mystery
Subject(s): Indians of North America; Mystery and Detective Stories; School Life
Age range(s): Grades 5-8
Major character(s): Rinnah Two Feathers, 13-Year-Old, Indian (Lakota Sioux); Tommy Red Hawk, Indian (Lakota Sioux); Meagen Paige, Student—Middle School
Time period(s): 2000s
Locale(s): Plainsville, South Dakota (Rosebud Sioux Reservation)

Summary: Several years ago Rinnah's dad died and now she and her mother, along with her grandparents, run the Circle Feather Lodge near the Sioux Reservation. Naturally curious, when Rinnah spies a stranger hanging around the old Jackson place, she decides to look into it. With her friends Tommy and Meagen they begin to put together the pieces of the puzzle and realize that someone is on the track of a lost gold mine. Ready to confront the thieves, the three friends instead find themselves held captive at gunpoint in an underground tunnel

while they hope the sheriff finds them before the gun fires. (248 pages)

Where it's reviewed:
School Library Journal, September 2001, page 226

Other books you might like:
C.S. Adler, *More than a Horse*, 1997
    Accompanying her mother to a job on a guest ranch, Leeann wants to ride but can't until she proves her worth to the ranch's head wrangler.
Dayle Campbell Gaetz, *Mystery from History*, 2001
    Katie and her friends discover that the sounds heard from the deserted mansion are not ghosts but art thieves, including the town's police chief.
Linda Shands, *Blind Fury*, 2001
    When a blizzard catches Wakara's father and brother by surprise up in the mountains, Wakara knows they're in danger and rides out to find them.

461

SUZANNE C. JOHNSON
DEBBIE TILLEY, Illustrator

Fribbity Ribbit!
(New York: Alfred A. Knopf, 2001)

Subject(s): Animals/Frogs and Toads; Humor; Family
Age range(s): Grades K-2
Major character(s): Unnamed Character, Child, Son
Time period(s): 2000s
Locale(s): United States

Summary: A young boy spots a frog in his backyard and attempts to catch it. The frog hops away and into the house where it leaps from one family member to another causing a commotion. The frog leaps into and out of the dog's bowl, hops across the computer keyboard, and even thumps up the stairs. Just when the family thinks they have it cornered it escapes once again back to the tranquility of the backyard. (36 pages)

Where it's reviewed:
Horn Book Guide, Spring 2002, page 21
Kirkus Reviews, June 1, 2001, page 802
Publishers Weekly, June 25, 2001, page 72
School Library Journal, August 2001, page 154

Other books you might like:
Wayne Campbell, *What a Catastrophe!*, 1986
    What happens when a boy brings a frog home for breakfast?
Robert Kalan, *Jump, Frog, Jump!*, 1981
    A frog tries to catch a fly while avoiding capture by anything higher on the food chain.
Mercer Mayer, *Frog on His Own*, 1973
    While walking with friends Frog decides to explore the park on his own.
Rick Walton, *Bullfrog Pops!*, 1999
    Seeking food, a hungry bullfrog climbs aboard a stagecoach heading for Ravenous Gulch.

462

JULIE JOHNSTON

In Spite of Killer Bees

(Plattsburgh, NY: Tundra Books, 2001)

Subject(s): Inheritance; Family Life; Sisters
Age range(s): Grades 7-10
Major character(s): Agatha Jane "Aggie" Quade, 14-Year-Old; Jeannie Quade, 17-Year-Old; Helen Quade, Waitress; Lily Quade, Aunt
Time period(s): 2000s
Locale(s): Port Desire, Canada

Summary: Ever since their father died and their mother abandoned them, Aggie and her two older sisters, Jeannie and Helen, have lived together but led separate lives. Now they receive word of their grandfather's death and an inheritance which could open new doors for them. Driving in a ramshackle car, they arrive in Port Desire only to find that the inheritance is the family home, with a tiny amount of money for utilities, but only if they can convince their Great Aunt Lily to leave her isolated island and live with them. The girls aren't sure living here is so great, especially after references to their thieving father are directed toward them, but lack of any other option keeps them in Port Desire. Aggie wants Helen and Jeannie to stay and try to be a family again, though she worries continually that they'll leave her. The girls gradually settle in, make friends, meet special guys, attend school and find jobs. As Christmas nears, the absence of a turkey doesn't stop them from inviting any and all of their friends and relatives to dinner in this warm tale of learning to become a family. (253 pages)

Where it's reviewed:
Booklist, January 2002, page 841
Bulletin of the Center for Children's Books, December 2001, page 143
Horn Book, January 2002, page 78
School Library Journal, December 2001, page 138
Voice of Youth Advocates, December 2001, page 360

Other books by the same author:
The Only Outcast, 1998
Adam and Eve and Pinch-Me, 1994
Hero of Lesser Causes, 1993

Other books you might like:
Louisa May Alcott, *Little Women*, 1868
    This classic story of family life stars the four March sisters—Jo, Meg, Beth and Amy.
Joan Bauer, *Hope Was Here*, 2000
    Hope is raised by her aunt Addie who leads a nomadic lifestyle cooking in various diners; wherever she works, Hope writes the message "Hope was here."
Sarah Dessen, *That Summer*, 1996
    As Haven thinks about this summer with its two weddings that she'd like to avoid, she remembers back to "that summer" when her life seemed better.
Jean Thesman, *When the Road Ends*, 1992
    Three foster children and a brain-damaged accident victim make a home and a family in a cabin located "when the road ends."

463

TONY JOHNSTON
TONY DITERLIZZI, Illustrator

Alien & Possum: Friends No Matter What

(New York: Simon & Schuster Books for Young Readers, 2001)

Series: Alien & Possum
Subject(s): Animals/Opossums; Aliens; Friendship
Age range(s): Grades 1-2
Major character(s): Possum, Opossum, Friend; Alien, Alien, Friend
Time period(s): Indeterminate
Locale(s): Fictional Country

Summary: Possum's quiet evening of stargazing becomes interesting when a spaceship crashes nearby and a strange creature wanders out. Initially fearful of Possum's strange sounds and dull gray color, the multi-colored Alien finally accepts Possum's offer of friendship. Possum teaches Alien that differences do not preclude a friendship and Alien carefully follows Possum's suggestions. Alien helps Possum tip over a trashcan so he can find some dinner and willingly reads Possum's bedtime story to him when his friend cannot stay awake to finish it. (48 pages)

Where it's reviewed:
Booklist, July 2001, page 2023
Kirkus Reviews, August 1, 2001, page 1126
Publishers Weekly, September 24, 2001, page 93
School Library Journal, September 2001, page 191
Tribune Books, August 26, 2001, page 4

Other books by the same author:
Alien & Possum: Hanging Out, 2002 (Alien & Possum)
Sparky & Eddie: Wild, Wild Rodeo!, 1998 (Hello, Reader!)
Sparky & Eddie: The First Day of School, 1997 (Hello, Reader!)

Other books you might like:
Laurie A. Jacobs, *So Much in Common*, 1994
    Although Philomena and Horace seem to have little in common, it is enough to build a friendship.
Arnold Lobel, *Frog and Toad Are Friends*, 1970
    In several brief stories Frog and Toad share some of the difficulties as well as the pleasures of friendship.
James Marshall, *George and Martha*, 1972
    The first book in a series about George and Martha uses several brief stories to describe the antics of two hippo buddies.
Cynthia Rylant, *Poppleton Forever*, 1998
    Poppleton's friend and neighbor Cherry Pie is both supportive and helpful with Poppleton's many little problems.

464

TONY JOHNSTON

Any Small Goodness: A Novel of the Barrio

(New York: Blue Sky/Scholastic, 2001)

Subject(s): Mexican Americans; Family Life
Age range(s): Grades 5-8

Major character(s): Arturo "Arthur" Rodriguez, Teenager, Mexican American
Time period(s): 2000s
Locale(s): Los Angeles, California

Summary: With his father's reminder to always make your own good if there's not enough, Arturo readjusts to life in a Los Angeles barrio after having spent his childhood in Mexico. His name becomes Anglicized, from Arturo to Arthur, which upsets his parents for each time he adopts another gringo way, they feel he's turning his back on his own culture. The closeness and kindness of people in the barrio is demonstrated everywhere from their elderly neighbor who sits all night in a tree to save a cat to the basketball pro who coaches at their school, but anonymously and for only a dollar, to the "book warrior" librarian. Even when the Rodriguez house is strafed in a drive-by shooting and Arturo's sister's favorite pink lunchbox is destroyed, a detective replaces it for her. Yes, Arturo is determined to see the goodness and begins his own gang to combat violence with kindness as the Green Needle Gang leaves Christmas trees and presents for families who would go without in a heart-warming first novel. (128 pages)

Where it's reviewed:
Bulletin of the Center for Children's Books, September 2001, page 21
Kirkus Reviews, June 15, 2001, page 865
Kliatt, July 2001, page 10
School Library Journal, September 2001, page 226
Voice of Youth Advocates, October 2001, page 279

Awards the book has won:
Smithsonian's Notable Books for Children, 2001

Other books you might like:
Rudolfo A. Anaya, *Bless Me, Ultima*, 1976
    A story of growing up Chicano in the American Southwest during the 1940s.
Danny Santiago, *Famous All over Town*, 1983
    The portrayal of life of a young Mexican American who lives in a California barrio.
Gary Soto, *Baseball in April: And Other Stories*, 1990
    Day to day life for young Hispanics living in California is realistically captured and related in this collection of eleven short stories.
Piri Thomas, *Stories from El Barrio*, 1980
    Eight sad and humorous stories and poems reflect Hispanic culture as experienced by children and teens.

465

TONY JOHNSTON
JOY ALLEN, Illustrator

My Best Friend Bear

(Flagstaff, AZ: Rising Moon, 2001)

Subject(s): Animals/Bears; Toys; Love
Age range(s): Grades K-1
Major character(s): Unnamed Character, Child, Narrator; Bear, Bear, Stuffed Animal; Mother, Mother
Time period(s): 2000s (2001)
Locale(s): United States

Summary: Bear is such a cherished old friend to a young girl that he's literally been loved until he's unrecognizable. When Bear is mistaken for a monkey, Mother knows it's time for some repairs. Using her daughter's picture as a guide, Mother fashions new ears, adds stuffing, replaces Bear's eyes and sews a new mouth. Then, because Bear is so brave, Mother sews on a heart. After Bear is washed and hung out to dry he's ready to resume life as a treasured companion in this tale originally published in Great Britain in 1989 as *My Friend Bear*. (32 pages)

Where it's reviewed:
Booklist, May 15, 2001, page 1758
Bulletin of the Center for Children's Books, May 2001, page 340
Horn Book Guide, Fall 2001, page 233
Publishers Weekly, February 26, 2001, page 84
School Library Journal, August 2001, page 154

Other books by the same author:
Clear Moon, Snow Soon, 2001
Desert Dog, 2001
Bigfoot Cinderrrrrella, 1999

Other books you might like:
Don Freeman, *Corduroy*, 1968
    A lonely, department store bear with a missing button eventually is purchased and given a loving home.
Kathryn Lasky, *Sophie and Rose*, 1998
    Sophie's mother helps to repair an old doll that is Sophie's companion and playmate.
Shulamith Levey Oppenheim, *I Love You, Bunny Rabbit*, 1995
    Micah's well-worn Bunny Rabbit is soiled with applesauce, chocolate milk and puddle mud, making it irreplaceable.

466

TONY JOHNSTON
FABRICIO VANDENBROECK, Illustrator

Uncle Rain Cloud

(Watertown, MA: Talewinds/Charlesbridge, 2001)

Subject(s): Aunts and Uncles; Language; Mexican Americans
Age range(s): Grades 1-3
Major character(s): Carlos, 3rd Grader, Nephew; Tomas, Uncle, Immigrant
Time period(s): 2000s (2001)
Locale(s): Los Angeles, California

Summary: Secretly, Carlos refers to his Uncle Tomas as "Uncle Rain Cloud" because the disgruntled man glowers when he must function in an English-speaking environment with Carlos interpreting for him. In the evenings when Tomas is free to speak Spanish with the family, he tells Carlos stories of Mexican gods with "tongue-twister" names. Finally, Carlos is able to tell his uncle how he feels about his attitude. Tio Tomas then admits that his hurt pride makes him fearful of speaking English. Carlos realizes that he and his uncle have something in common and together they devise a way to improve Tomas's English skills as Carlos continues to learn about the gods. A concluding pronunciation guide is provided for the god's names, but no glossary is given for the Spanish words included in the text. (32 pages)

Where it's reviewed:
Booklist, February 15, 2001, page 1134
Horn Book Guide, Fall 2001, page 261
School Library Journal, April 2001, page 113

Other books by the same author:
Day of the Dead, 1997
The Magic Maguey, 1996 (Smithsonian's Notable Books for Children)
The Iguana Brothers: A Tale of Two Lizards, 1995

Other books you might like:
Eve Bunting, *A Day's Work*, 1994
Although this immigrant grandfather cannot speak English, he knows the language of honesty and teaches its value to his grandson.
Jane Medina, *My Name is Jorge: On Both Sides of the River*, 1999
A collection of bilingual poems describes the varied experiences of a Mexican child attending an American school.
Pat Mora, *The Rainbow Tulip*, 1999
A young Mexican American student bridges two cultures as she learns English in school while using Spanish at home.

467

CARLA JOINSON

Diamond in the Dust

(New York: Dial Press, 2001)

Subject(s): Miners and Mining; Family Life; Coming-of-Age
Age range(s): Grades 6-10
Major character(s): Katy Ann Sollis, 16-Year-Old; Michael Stoner, Boyfriend (of Katy); Kenny Randall, Widower; Nate Sollis, Brother, Miner
Time period(s): 1900s (1905)
Locale(s): Buckeye City, Illinois

Summary: Born the oldest girl, Katy's now sixteen and, as her mother says, old enough to marry and leave their house as they can't afford to feed her. But Katy's always wanted more to life than being married to a coal miner with a half-dozen children running around her ankles; her dream is to move to St. Louis and become a type-writer or even a teacher. Her father's picks out mine foreman Kenny Randall, a widower with a bad temper, for her to marry, while Katy's sweet on Michael. But when her brother Nate is killed in the mines, Katy knows she has to leave, with or without Michael. (197 pages)

Where it's reviewed:
Book Report, September 2001, page 62
Children's Bookwatch, September 2001, page 3
Publishers Weekly, April 9, 2001, page 75
School Library Journal, June 2001, page 150
Voice of Youth Advocates, August 2001, page 202

Other books you might like:
Phyllis Reynolds Naylor, *Send No Blessings*, 1990
Beth doesn't want to spend her whole life in a double-wide

trailer in West Virginia, but is afraid she'll never achieve her dream of college.
Suzanne Newton, *Where Are You When I Need You?*, 1991
Missy's determination to attend college overcomes her family's disapproval and boyfriend Jim's reluctance to let her go.
N.A. Perez, *Breaker*, 1988
After Pat's father is killed in a mining accident, Pat begins working in the mines while his brother fights for improved labor conditions.

468

LYNNE JONELL
PETRA MATHERS, Illustrator

Mom Pie

(New York: G.P. Putnam's Sons, 2001)

Subject(s): Mothers; Mothers and Sons; Brothers
Age range(s): Grades K-2
Major character(s): Mommy, Mother, Cook; Robbie, Son, Brother (younger); Christopher, Son, Brother (older)
Time period(s): 2000s (2001)
Locale(s): United States

Summary: Mommy is so busy preparing a dinner for company that she has no time for Christopher and Robbie who feel lonely and upset when they are asked to leave the kitchen. Robbie declares that he does not like company even if Mommy is making three kinds of pie for dessert. Christopher suggests making a "Mom pie" and assures Robbie that it will not hurt Mommy at all. Robbie and Christopher gather symbols of Mommy that are soft, smooth, snuggly and fragrant. They top it off with a candle in Mommy's favorite color and present it to her just as the company arrives to take care of the last minute dinner details while Mommy enjoys her sons. (24 pages)

Where it's reviewed:
Booklist, March 15, 2001, page 1404
Horn Book, January 2001, page 83
Kirkus Reviews, December 1, 2000, page 1682
Publishers Weekly, January 1, 2001, page 92
School Library Journal, July 2001, page 84

Other books by the same author:
It's My Birthday, Too!, 1999 (Booklist Editors' Choice)
I Need a Snake, 1998 (School Library Journal Best Books)
Mommy Go Away!, 1997

Other books you might like:
Barbara Joosse, *I Love You the Purplest*, 1996
Competitive brothers vie for their mother's attention and affection but she loves and values each for their unique qualities.
Barbro Lindgren, *Benny's Had Enough!*, 1999
When Benny decides he's had enough of his mother's penchant for cleanliness he runs away to find another home, but not for long.
David Shannon, *No, David!*, 1998
In a Caldecott Honor Book, David's mom expresses her love for her son despite his behavior.

469

DIANA WYNNE JONES

Mixed Magics: Four Tales of Chrestomanci

(New York: Greenwillow Books, 2001)

Subject(s): Short Stories; Magic
Age range(s): Grades 6-10
Major character(s): Chrestomanci, Wizard

Summary: Chrestomanci, that powerful wizard with nine lives who is the subject of several of Jones' novels, is also the connecting link in these four stories. A terrifying child abuses the runaway warlock until he's rescued in the first story. In the second, a young warlock is almost tricked into evil by his own worst impulses, but saves himself in the end. A woman's dream cast goes on strike when she tries to push them into one more predictable dream to satisfy her audience, and a mysterious rebel wanders disruptively through Theare and time in the last. In each, Chrestomanci makes a brief appearance; tidying up, solving the mystery or saving the day and incidentally letting the reader know more about this intriguing character. (138 pages)

Where it's reviewed:
Booklist, April 15, 2001, page 1558
Horn Book Magazine, May 2001, page 327
Publishers Weekly, March 5, 2001, page 66
School Library Journal, July 2001, page 110
Times Educational Supplement, May 26, 2000, page 23

Other books by the same author:
Year of the Griffin, 2000
Deep Secret, 1999
Dark Lord of Derkholm, 1998

Other books you might like:
Ursula K. Le Guin, *Tales from Earthsea*, 2001
    Author LeGuin returns to the world of Earthsea and its people, including wizard Ged.
Patricia McKillip, *A Knot in the Grain and Other Stories*, 1994
    Fantasy and fairy tale stories with a magical twist.
David Skinner, *Thundershine: Tales of Metakids*, 1999
    Kids with powers beyond the ordinary are challenged by moral questions.

470

BARBARA JOOSSE
GISELLE POTTER, Illustrator

Ghost Wings

(San Francisco: Chronicle Books, 2001)

Subject(s): Grandmothers; Death; Love
Age range(s): Grades K-3
Major character(s): Grandmother, Grandmother, Aged Person; Unnamed Character, Child, Narrator
Time period(s): Indeterminate Past
Locale(s): Mexico

Summary: Grandmother is a young girl's friend, teacher and comforter. With Grandmother, the little girl visits the "Magic Circle" where the monarch butterflies gather at the conclusion of their annual migration. There, when a butterfly lands on her arm, she learns from Grandmother that the sensation from the gentle touch of a butterfly remains after the butterfly departs because they "carry the souls of the old ones." After Grandmother's death, as her family celebrates the Days of the Dead honoring the memories of deceased loved ones, a butterfly's touch restores the grieving girl's memories of Grandmother. (34 pages)

Where it's reviewed:
Booklist, April 15, 2001, page 1565
Bulletin of the Center for Children's Books, July 2001, page 411
Five Owls, Summer 2001, page 114
Publishers Weekly, April 2, 2001, page 64
School Library Journal, May 2001, page 125

Other books by the same author:
Nugget and Darling, 1997
I Love You the Purplest, 1996 (Golden Kite Award)
Mama, Do You Love Me?, 1991

Other books you might like:
George Ancona, *Pablo Remembers: The Fiesta of the Day of the Dead*, 1993
    Photographs illustrate the nonfiction title explaining the Mexican celebration honoring one's ancestors.
Gail Gibbons, *Monarch Butterfly*, 1989
    A nonfiction title depicts the life cycle of the monarch butterfly.
Virginia Kroll, *Butterfly Boy*, 1997
    Emilio learns about the habitat of the butterflies enjoyed by his invalid grandfather to assure they will be attracted to his yard annually.

471

BARBARA JOOSSE
BETSY LEWIN, Illustrator

A Houseful of Christmas

(New York: Henry Holt and Company, 2001)

Subject(s): Family; Grandmothers; Christmas
Age range(s): Grades K-2
Major character(s): Granny, Grandmother; Edgar, Dog; Fat Cat, Cat
Time period(s): 2000s
Locale(s): United States

Summary: Edgar shares Granny's enthusiasm for the Christmas holiday and the anticipation of a houseful of relatives. Fat Cat doesn't like the noisy crowd. When Granny finishes her preparations she waits with Edgar for the many family members to appear while Fat Cat hides glumly under a chair. During the Christmas celebrations the snow falls, the wind whooshes and by the time dinner is finished the weather conditions prevent the guests' departure. Granny doesn't mind and soon has the floor covered with blankets for everyone. It's hard to sleep on this crowded floor but Edgar offers comfort and becomes a soft pillow for three brothers. Even

Fat Cat finds one plump relative's chest to his liking as a comfortable bed. The clock ticks, the snow falls, the wind whirls and everyone sleeps. (32 pages)

Where it's reviewed:
Booklist, October 1, 2001, page 326
Publishers Weekly, September 24, 2001, page 52
School Library Journal, October 2001, page 66

Other books by the same author:
I Love You the Purplest, 1996
Snow Day!, 1995
Mama, Do You Love Me?, 1991

Other books you might like:
Louise Borden, *Just in Time for Christmas*, 1994
    As the relatives gather at Will's house to celebrate Christmas he's relieved to see his dog Luke reappear after five days.
Cynthia Rylant, *Henry and Mudge in the Family Trees*, 1997
    Henry's cousin Annie and her family host a family reunion where Henry and Mudge enjoy cake and tolerate sloppy kisses from relatives.
Cynthia Rylant, *The Relatives Came*, 1985
    A Caldecott Honor Book celebrates childhood memories of the joyful confusion of a houseful of relatives.

472

SHERRYL JORDAN

Secret Sacrament
(New York: HarperCollins, 2001)

Subject(s): Healing; Coming-of-Age
Age range(s): Grades 8-12
Major character(s): Gabriel, Healer
Time period(s): Indeterminate
Locale(s): Navora, Fictional Country

Summary: Gabriel is never able to meet his warrior father's expectations and, after accidentally witnessing the death of a slave woman, finds himself even more alienated. The woman gave him an amulet which brings the child strange visions of the life of the Shinali, a conquered people of the land who are held in contempt by Gabriel's father and most of Navorran society. After his father's death, Gabriel finds the courage to declare his intent to become a healer. Fortunately, Gabriel discovers a great deal of natural talent in his chosen field and he is chosen to study with special healers at the Citadel where he comes to the attention of the wily Empress of Navora. Trapped between unscrupulous politicians, Gabriel flees to the empty plains left to the Shinali where he discovers an unexpected destiny. (338 pages)

Where it's reviewed:
Booklist, February 15, 2001, page 1134
Bulletin of the Center for Children's Books, March 2001, page 266
Publishers Weekly, February 5, 2001, page 89
School Library Journal, February 2001, page 118
Voice of Youth Advocates, June 2001, page 133

Awards the book has won:
ALA Best Books for Young Adults, 2002

Other books by the same author:
The Raging Quiet, 1999
The Juniper Game, 1991
A Time of Darkness, 1990

Other books you might like:
Frank Herbert, *Dune*, 1965
    A boy from an alien world is embraced by a desert people as their savior.
Tamora Pierce, *Briar's Book*, 1999
    Briar's talent lies in healing and he enjoys exercising it until a plague without a cure strikes.
Elizabeth Anne Scarborough, *The Healer's War*, 1988
    A nurse finds her abilities much improved after an elderly Vietnamese man gives her an amulet.

473

MARIE-ODILE JUDES
MARTINE BOURRE, Illustrator
JOAN ROBINS, Translator

Max, the Stubborn Little Wolf
(New York: HarperCollins Publishers, 2001)

Subject(s): Animals/Wolves; Individuality; Fathers and Sons
Age range(s): Grades K-3
Major character(s): Max, Wolf, Son; Papa Wolf, Wolf, Father
Time period(s): Indeterminate
Locale(s): Fictional Country

Summary: Papa Wolf cannot interest Max in such proper wolf careers as chasing pigs. Max aspires to be a florist. Frustrated, Papa Wolf tries one plan after another to educate Max in what he considers to be more acceptable wolf behavior, but Max feels content with his aspirations. Although Papa Wolf's final idea does get Max to shift his goal from being a florist, his new occupational choice is not the one Papa Wolf sought. First published in France in 1996. (32 pages)

Where it's reviewed:
Booklist, February 1, 2001, page 1056
Bulletin of the Center for Children's Books, April 2001, page 305
Publishers Weekly, December 11, 2000, page 84
Riverbank Review, Fall 2001, page 31
School Library Journal, March 2001, page 212

Other books you might like:
Rebecca Bond, *Bravo, Maurice!*, 2000
    Maurice's relatives have ideas for his future career, but Maurice follows his own dreams.
Paul Fleischman, *Weslandia*, 1999
    To his conforming parents, Wesley's an embarrassment; to the school bullies, he's a target; by summer's end, the creative boy is a leader.
Bob Graham, *Max*, 2000
    Max's superhero parents and grandparents worry about his inability to fly because, without flight, he cannot uphold the family tradition.
Emily Arnold McCully, *The Amazing Felix*, 1993
    A concert pianist wants his son to show the same interest, but Felix seems to have a talent for magic tricks, not music.

Eileen Spinelli, *Boy, Can He Dance!*, 1993
   Tony's father expects him to become a chef and join the
   family business, but Tony's real gift is dancing.

K

KATHY KACER

Clara's War
(Toronto: Second Story Press, 2001)

Series: Holocaust Remembrance
Subject(s): Holocaust; Jews
Age range(s): Grades 4-7
Major character(s): Clara Berg, 13-Year-Old; Peter Berg, Brother (of Clara)
Time period(s): 1940s (1943)
Locale(s): Prague, Czechoslovakia; Terezin/Theresienstadt, Czechoslovakia

Summary: Clara, her younger brother Peter and her parents live in Prague when they are informed that, because they are Jewish, they are to relocate to the ghetto of Terezin, also called Theresienstadt, which they know is actually a concentration camp. Though the family goes in different directions during the day, and living conditions are harsh, the camp is not as uncomfortable as Auschwitz. Opportunities are available for schooling and the arts; when auditions are held for the opera *Brundibar*, Clara can hardly wait to try out. Soon the reasons for the new picket fence, the improved grounds and even the stage of the opera become apparent when the Red Cross comes to observe the camp and reports that the Jews are treated very well; perhaps the Red Cross didn't realize that of the 15,000 children who came through Terezin, only 132 would survive. (196 pages)

Where it's reviewed:
Kliatt, November 2001, page 16
School Library Journal, February 2002, page 134

Other books by the same author:
The Secret of Gabi's Dresser, 1999

Other books you might like:
Carol Matas, *Daniel's Story*, 1993
   Daniel's journal records his family's move from the ghetto to a concentration camp until only he and his father are left alive to march to Buchenwald.

Pamela Melnikoff, *Prisoner in Time: A Child of the Holocaust*, 2001
   During the Holocaust, Jan time travels to the sixteenth-century and meets Rabbi Loewe who made the famous golem, but this time it can't save Jan.
Gudrun Pausewang, *The Final Journey*, 1996
   Sheltered from Nazi terrorism, young Alice rides a cattle car to Auschwitz where she's happy to go to the showers and wash away the grime of the trip.
Barbara Rogasky, *The Golem*, 1996
   The story of the rabbi who creates a giant from clay, which miraculously comes to life and protects the Jews of sixteenth-century Prague.

MAIRA KALMAN, Author/Illustrator

What Pete Ate from A-Z
(New York: G.P. Putnam's Sons, 2001)

Subject(s): Animals/Dogs; Pets; Behavior
Age range(s): Grades 1-3
Major character(s): Pete, Dog; Poppy Wise, Sister (older), Narrator; Mookie Wise, Brother (younger)
Time period(s): 2000s (2001)
Locale(s): United States

Summary: Pete is one hungry canine. As Poppy tells the story, he eats everything from an accordion to yoyos and all with no apparent side effects. Poppy thinks Pete is a dreadful dog when he destroys her dear doll Dinky by ripping off her head. Before Mookie's Halloween costume is complete Pete gobbles the glue stick and then hurries on to Poppy's homework. In fact, Pete eats just about anything he encounters until he reaches his bowl of dog food (brand name Zug Zug) and devours zilch. (40 pages)

Where it's reviewed:
Booklist, September 1, 2001, page 115
Horn Book, January 2002, page 69
Kirkus Reviews, July 15, 2001, page 1028
Publishers Weekly, July 16, 2001, page 179

School Library Journal, September 2001, page 192

Awards the book has won:
Publishers Weekly Best Children's Books, 2001
School Library Journal Best Books, 2001

Other books by the same author:
Next Stop Grand Central, 1999 (Notable Social Studies Trade Books for Young People)
Swami on Rye (Max in India), 1995
Chicken Soup, Boots, 1993

Other books you might like:
Alyssa Satin Capucilli, *Mrs. McTats and Her Houseful of Cats*, 2001
   Twenty-four stray cats wander into Mrs. McTats home joining her cat Abner before Zoom, a puppy, appears at her door.
Nikki Grimes, *C Is for City*, 1995
   This illustrated story in rhyme introduces city life alphabetically.
Alastair Taylor, *Swollobog*, 2001
   Swollobog is a greedy dog with no concern about the alphabet; she only wants to eat, eat, and eat some more.

TERI KANEFIELD

Rivka's Way

(Chicago: Front Street/Cricket Books, 2001)

Subject(s): Jews; Marriage; Segregation
Age range(s): Grades 6-9
Major character(s): Rivka Liebermann, 15-Year-Old; Oskar Kara, Fiance(e), Student—Medical School; Mikulase "Mikul" Tomas, Orphan
Time period(s): 18th century (1778)
Locale(s): Prague, Czech Republic

Summary: Never having gone beyond the walls of her Jewish ghetto in Prague, Rivka wonders how she'll ever see what lies outside. Though her parents have arranged a marriage for her to the young medial student Oskar, Rivka would like a little taste of adventure before she settles down. Disguising herself as a boy, and taking off her yellow Jewish star, she ventures out and spends her first day of freedom digging potatoes. Subsequent forays follow and she meets a Gentile orphan named Mikul who works to pay off his parents' debts. When Rivka finds he's been arrested and put in jail for these debts, she wants to help but isn't sure what to do without giving away her identity. Luckily her fiance feels the same concern she does and settles Mikul's obligations so that he can join relatives in Germany in this first novel. (137 pages)

Where it's reviewed:
Booklist, April 1, 2001, page 1483
Kliatt, July 2001, page 10
Publishers Weekly, April 30, 2001, page 79
School Library Journal, March 2001, page 252
Voice of Youth Advocates, October 2001, page 279

Other books you might like:
Karen Hesse, *Letters from Rifka*, 1992
   Rifka's ringworm almost prevents her entry to America;

her immigration adventures are based on those of the author's great-aunt.
Pamela Melnikoff, *Plots and Players: The Lopez Conspiracy*, 1989
   When the Fernandez family lives in England during Elizabethan times, it has to practice its Jewish faith in secret.
Suzanne Fisher Staples, *Shabanu: Daughter of the Wind*, 1989
   Shabanu is told she will have to marry old, fat Rahim Sahib, which forces her to choose between family honor and her own identity.

G. BRIAN KARAS, Author/Illustrator

The Class Artist

(New York: Greenwillow Books, 2001)

Subject(s): Artists and Art; Schools; Individuality
Age range(s): Grades 1-3
Major character(s): Fred, Student—Elementary School, Brother (younger); Frances, Student—Elementary School, Classmate (Fred's); Martha, Sister (Fred's)
Time period(s): 2000s (2001)
Locale(s): United States

Summary: By the end of the first day of school the criticism Fred receives from Frances convinces him that he is not and never will be capable of drawing. After Martha shows Fred how to combine a circle and straight lines to make a pilgrim he begins to enjoy drawing. Then the teacher assigns an art project, giving the students one week to complete it. Fred has a great idea, but he's a little stuck on the execution. All his attempts fail to match his vision and on Friday Frances is quick to point out that Fred has not done his work. The understanding teacher suggests that Fred draw his feelings and from that opportunity, Fred finally completes the assignment though not in the way he'd originally planned. Even Frances is impressed. (32 pages)

Where it's reviewed:
Booklist, November 15, 2001, page 582
Bulletin of the Center for Children's Books, September 2001, page 22
Publishers Weekly, July 23, 2001, page 76
School Library Journal, September 2001, page 192
Smithsonian, November 2001, page 120

Awards the book has won:
Smithsonian's Notable Books for Children, 2001

Other books by the same author:
Bebe's Bad Dream, 2000
The Windy Day, 1998
Home on the Bayou: A Cowboy's Story, 1996 (Boston Globe-Horn Book Honor Book)

Other books you might like:
Peter Catalanotto, *Emily's Art*, 2001
   Emily's disappointed that her picture loses a school art contest because the judge does not like her choice of subject.
Valeri Gorbachev, *Peter's Picture*, 2000
   His neighbors' reaction to the picture he painted at school

diminishes Peter's feeling of pride in his artwork but his parents' response restores it.

Nancy Poydar, *Cool Ali*, 1996
Ali uses chalk and her artistic ability to create pictures on the sidewalk.

Sara Yamaka, *The Gift of Driscoll Lipscomb*, 1995
Annual gifts from an artist-neighbor teach Molly to see the colors in the world around her.

KATHLEEN KARR

Playing with Fire

(New York: Farrar Straus Giroux, 2001)

Subject(s): Psychic Powers; Occult; Mothers and Daughters
Age range(s): Grades 6-9
Major character(s): Greer Duquesne, 14-Year-Old, Psychic; Camille Duquesne, Psychic; Drake Morley, Con Artist; Amos Caldecott, Wealthy; Leo Rafferty, 16-Year-Old, Servant; Peg Rafferty, Servant, Sister (of Leo)
Time period(s): 1920s (1924)
Locale(s): Cliffside, New York (on Long Island)

Summary: Unsure about spending a summer in Mr. Caldecott's mansion on Long Island, Greer falls in love with the house as soon as she's shown her tower room that overlooks the ocean. In addition to her tower room, Greer is pleased to meet the teen servants of Peg and Leo and is happy when a romance develops between her and Leo. However, she's not so sure about what her "Uncle" Drake has cooked up for her mother. Greer's mother is Madame Camille, a spiritualist hired by Mr. Caldecott to conduct seances to contact his deceased wife, but Greer fears that Drake has a few crooked schemes in mind. As the seances are conducted, it turns out that Greer is being used as a medium and evil spirits are speaking through her, even providing clues to a past murder. Drake's evil side surfaces and he is institutionalized while Greer and her mother remain on the island and try to build a better relationship with one another. (185 pages)

Where it's reviewed:
Booklist, April 1, 2001, page 1483
Bulletin of the Center for Children's Books, May 2001, page 340
Kliatt, March 2001, page 10
Publishers Weekly, January 22, 2001, page 325
Voice of Youth Advocates, June 2001, page 133

Other books by the same author:
Bone Dry, 2002
Skullduggery, 2000
The Boxer, 2000
The Great Turkey Walk, 1998
Oh, Those Harper Girls! Or Young and Dangerous, 1992

Other books you might like:
Lois Duncan, *The Third Eye*, 1984
Unbidden visions of a small child in a terrifying situation compel a young woman to help police find a missing child.
Dorothy Gilman, *The Clairvoyant Countess*, 1975
Penniless, Madame Karitska advertises to do "Readings"

and when she meets Detective Pruden, has a chance to prove her clairvoyance.

Joan Lowery Nixon, *Spirit Seeker*, 1995
When her boyfriend is suspected of murdering his parents, Holly uses her psychic abilities to contact the spirit world.

479

GAIL LANGER KARWOSKI
PAUL CASALE, Illustrator

Surviving Jamestown: The Adventures of Young Sam Collier

(Atlanta, GA: Peachtree, 2001)

Subject(s): Discovery and Exploration
Age range(s): Grades 5-8
Major character(s): Sam Collier, 12-Year-Old, Apprentice; Nathaniel "Nate" Peacock, Apprentice; John Smith, Historical Figure, Explorer
Time period(s): 17th century (1606-1609)
Locale(s): Jamestown, Virginia; *Susan Constant*, At Sea

Summary: Sam can't believe his good fortune when he sails to the New World as an apprentice to John Smith; the second son of a farmer, he won't inherit his father's holdings, so Sam is ready for adventure. On board the *Susan Constant*, Sam and his friend Nate are in high spirits and ready to play anytime they're allowed on deck, though they quickly realize the hardships of a sea voyage. Once arrived in Jamestown, more reality hits them as the hard physical labor, sickness, Indian attacks and hunger threaten to overwhelm the colonists. When Smith receives severe injuries and must return to England, Sam is faced with the decision of returning with him or remaining in the New World. (198 pages)

Where it's reviewed:
Book Report, November 2001, page 63
Kliatt, July 2001, page 18
School Library Journal, August 2001, page 184
Voice of Youth Advocates, August 2001, page 202

Other books by the same author:
Seaman: The Dog Who Explored the West with Lewis & Clark, 1999

Other books you might like:
Sandra Forrester, *Wheel of the Moon*, 2000
Orphaned Pen is captured and sent to Jamestown where she is bought by a young couple to be their indentured servant.
Elizabeth Massie, *Winter of the Dead*, 2000
Orphaned and living as street thieves, Nathaniel and Richard jump at Captain Smith's offer to sail to the Jamestown Colony in exchange for labor.
Scott O'Dell, *The Serpent Never Sleeps: A Novel of Jamestown and Pocahontas*, 1987
Living in Jamestown, a young girl from England has the chance to meet Pocahontas.

VERLA KAY
DAN ANDREASEN, Illustrator

Tattered Sails

(New York: G.P. Putnam's Sons, 2001)

Subject(s): Voyages and Travels; American Colonies; Stories in Rhyme
Age range(s): Grades 1-3
Major character(s): Thomas, Child, Immigrant; Edward, Child, Immigrant; Mary Jane, Child, Immigrant
Time period(s): 17th century (1635)
Locale(s): London, England; Massachusetts, American Colonies

Summary: In search of a better life for Mary Jane, Thomas and Edward their parents leave the crowded, grimy streets of London behind and journey to the New World. The ship voyage is long, the living conditions deplorable, the storms terrifying but finally they arrive in the Massachusetts Bay Colony. Thomas and Edward play outdoors, Mary Jane cuddles a cornhusk doll and the family offers a prayer of thanks for their new life. (32 pages)

Where it's reviewed:
Booklist, October 15, 2001, page 401
Horn Book Guide, Spring 2002, page 47
Kirkus Reviews, August 1, 2001, page 1126
School Library Journal, September 2001, page 192

Awards the book has won:
Notable Social Studies Trade Books for Young People, 2002

Other books by the same author:
Covered Wagons, Bumpy Trails, 2000
Gold Fever, 1999
Iron Horses, 1999 (Notable Social Studies Trade Books for Young People)

Other books you might like:
Ginger Howard, *William's House*, 2001
    With his family William arrives in New England in 1637 and builds a replica of his father's English home, modifying it to suit seasonal differences.
Jean Van Leeuwen, *Across the Wide Dark Sea: The Mayflower Journey*, 1995
    With his family and many others Love Brewster bravely embarks on a journey to a new land in search of religious freedom.
Kate Waters, *On the Mayflower: Voyage of the Ship's Apprentice and a Passenger Girl*, 1996
    The first voyage of the Mayflower to America is seen through the shipboard experiences of two children.

481

JANICE KULYK KEEFER
JANET WILSON, Illustrator

Anna's Goat

(Custer, WA: Orca Book Publishers, 2001)

Subject(s): World War II; Refugees; Animals/Goats
Age range(s): Grades 2-4
Major character(s): Anna, Child, Refugee; Wanda, Sister (older), Refugee; Mama, Mother, Refugee
Time period(s): Indeterminate Past
Locale(s): Europe; Canada

Summary: Anna is born in a country far from her family's homeland. War forces Anna's parents and Wanda to seek refuge in another country where conditions are harsh. Anna is a small sickly baby and the local women help Mama care for her by loaning her a nanny goat. The goat provides companionship while Mama works in a factory all day and in the evenings Mama milks the goat to provide nourishment for the children. When the war ends, the family returns the nanny goat and begins a journey of many months to their home that they find destroyed by the war's bombs. Years later the grown up Anna moves to Canada where she sculpts animals, especially goats, in this fictionalized account of a refugee family's war experience. (32 pages)

Where it's reviewed:
Booklist, March 15, 2001, page 1404
Publishers Weekly, December 18, 2000, page 77
Quill & Quire, September 2000, page 60
Resource Links, December 2000, page 6
School Library Journal, May 2001, page 126

Other books you might like:
Eve Bunting, *Gleam and Glow*, 2001
    When a refugee family returns to their destroyed village they find that the pet fish they left in pond have multiplied giving them hope for renewal.
Page McBrier, *Beatrice's Goat*, 2001
    In her Ugandan village Beatrice's goat provides the means for her to receive an education and improve her family's life.
Robert Munsch, *From Far Away*, 1995
    Saoussan and her family move to Canada from war-torn Lebanon.

482

PEG KEHRET

The Hideout

(New York: Pocket/Minstrel, 2001)

Subject(s): Animals/Bears; Orphans; Poaching
Age range(s): Grades 4-7
Major character(s): Jeremy Holland, 13-Year-Old, Orphan; Ed, Wealthy, Uncle
Time period(s): 2000s
Locale(s): Seattle, Washington; Lindsburg

Summary: A random shooting at a Seattle mall leaves Jeremy's parents dead and Uncle Ed as his guardian. Upset at leaving Seattle to move to Chicago, Jeremy is aboard a train heading East when it derails leaving wounded and dead passengers scattered everywhere. Jeremy helps an older man whose legs are pinned, but when medical assistance arrives he wanders off into the woods to get away from the horror of the train wreck. Still grief-stricken over his parents' death, the carnage and noise is overwhelming as he seeks solitude. Stumbling over a well-stocked but deserted cabin, he decides that a week or so of quiet is exactly what he needs, so he moves in and thinks about the turns his life has recently taken. Hearing gunshots in the middle of the night, Jeremy has unwittingly landed in the midst of a bear poaching ring and is soon running for his life. (151 pages)

Where it's reviewed:
Booklist, May 1, 2001, page 1612
Horn Book, May 2001, page 341
School Library Journal, August 2001, page 185

Other books by the same author:
The Stranger Next Door, 2002
Saving Lilly, 2001
The Flood Disaster, 1999
The Secret Journey, 1999

Other books you might like:
Cynthia DeFelice, *Nowhere to Call Home*, 1999
   Orphaned during the Depression, Frances dresses like a boy and takes off to ride the rails rather than live with an aunt she doesn't know.
Gail Carson Levine, *Dave at Night*, 1999
   Each night Dave escapes from the Hebrew Home for Boys and enjoys the sights and sounds of Harlem during its Renaissance time.
Theodore Taylor, *The Weirdo*, 1991
   After being rescued by ''weirdo'' Chip, Sam works with him to save the swamp bears.

483

PEG KEHRET

Saving Lilly

(New York: Pocket/Minstrel, 2001)

Subject(s): Animals/Elephants; Animals, Treatment of; Circus
Age range(s): Grades 4-6
Major character(s): Erin Wrenn, 6th Grader; David Showers, 6th Grader; Lilly, Elephant
Time period(s): 2000s
Locale(s): Harborview

Summary: Challenged by their sixth grade teacher to read 300 books within the next six weeks, Erin and her best friend David join their classmates in reading at least eleven books each so their class can meet its goal and win a field trip. At the same time, their Talented and Gifted teacher assigns them a report on circus animals. As Erin and David work on their report, they become aware of the cruelty shown to circus animals, a cruelty borne out when they see the animals for the Glitter Tent Circus arrive in town. Ironically, by reading 300 books, their field trip is to the circus, a trip that Erin and David boycott. They're most concerned about the elephant Lilly, who is a victim of mistreatment, and when they hear the circus director plans to sell her to a hunting reserve, lead a campaign to buy Lilly. With car washes, bake sales, lawn mowing and baby-sitting, their class is determined to earn the $8,000 necessary to buy her and send her to an elephant sanctuary. Erin and David are amazed that two sixth graders achieve such a worthy cause. (148 pages)

Where it's reviewed:
Booklist, December 1, 2001, page 643
School Library Journal, November 2001, page 159

Other books by the same author:
Don't Tell Anyone, 2000
My Brother Made Me Do It, 2000
Searching for Candlestick Park, 1997

Other books you might like:
Eric Campbell, *Papa Tembo*, 1998
   One man's desire for revenge against the elephant Papa Tembo collides with the work of the Blake family, who watch and study Papa Tembo's herd.
Gillian Cross, *The Great American Elephant Chase*, 1993
   Runaway Tad finds himself in charge of an elephant and the daughter of the elephant's owner, both of whom he needs to transport safely to Nebraska.
Barbara Smucker, *Incredible Jumbo*, 1991
   Based on fact, this fictionalized account tells of Jumbo, the noted elephant with the P.T. Barnum Circus at the turn of the century.

484

HEATHER KELLERHALS-STEWART

Witch's Fang

(Vancouver, Canada: Polestar/Raincoast Books, 2001)

Subject(s): Mountaineering; Adventure and Adventurers
Age range(s): Grades 7-10
Major character(s): Todd Rushton, 17-Year-Old, Mountaineer; Jess Rushton, 17-Year-Old, Twin (of Todd); Howie, Mountaineer; Kurt Stone, Mountaineer; Leo, Mountaineer
Time period(s): 2000s
Locale(s): Witch's Fang, British Columbia, Canada

Summary: Though Todd hasn't climbed since his automobile accident, and no longer has much flexibility in the foot that was injured, he still loves mountain climbing and is dismayed to hear that his least-favorite person is planning to scale the previously unclimbed Witch's Fang. Todd talks his sister Jess and his friend Howie into making the ascent, allowing themselves two months to prepare for the arduous climb. They start their climb just as Kurt and his partner Leo depart, but Todd's group stops to rescue Leo from an avalanche. Kurt continues to the top, determined to reach the summit before Todd's group does, in a tense outdoor adventure. (168 pages)

Where it's reviewed:
School Library Journal, November 2001, page 159

Other books you might like:
Jon Krakauer, *Into Thin Air: A Personal Account of the Mt. Everest Disaster*, 1997
   A true story of the expedition where five people were killed while climbing the tallest mountain on earth. Nonfiction.
Robert Roper, *In Caverns of Blue Ice*, 1991
   Louise DeMaistre climbs in the Alps and the Himalayas, undeterred by the death of a brother in a climbing accident, in this work based on her life.
James R. Ullman, *Banner in the Sky*, 1954
   A young boy conquers the Citadel, the mountain which claimed his father's life.

DOUGLAS KELLEY

The Captain's Wife

(New York: Dutton, 2001)

Subject(s): Women; Sea Stories; Ships
Age range(s): Grades 9-Adult
Major character(s): Joshua Patten, Sea Captain; Mary Ann Patten, Sea Captain, 19-Year-Old; Keeler, Sailor (first mate)
Time period(s): 1850s
Locale(s): *Neptune's Car*, At Sea

Summary: Enjoying the first voyage she took with her sea captain husband, Mary Ann looks forward to their second trip when Joshua will try to set a record sailing his clipper ship *Neptune's Car* around the Cape of Good Horn and up to San Francisco in just one hundred days. The voyage should be thrilling but Keeler, the surly first mate hired just before they left, tries to start a mutiny and wounds Joshua in the process. With Keeler secure and in the brig, it falls to Mary Ann to assume her husband's role when he's ill, especially since she's the only other one who is able to navigate. Incredible is the only way to describe Mary as she cares for her husband, takes responsibility for the ship, stays on deck as much as humanly possible and conceals her pregnancy from the crew in this true story of a courageous young woman. (293 pages)

Where it's reviewed:
Booklist, July 2001, page 1981
Kirkus Reviews, July 1, 2001, page 891
Library Journal, August 2001, page 162
Publishers Weekly, July 30, 2001, page 61

Other books you might like:
Avi, *The True Confessions of Charlotte Doyle*, 1990
    Charlotte's adventures on the sailing ship *Seahawk* turn her from a proper Victorian lady to a real sailor.
Elizabeth Garrett, *The Sweet Trade*, 2001
    The exciting, illegal adventures of female pirates Anne Bonny and Mary Read in their life on the high seas.
Patrick O'Brian, *The Golden Ocean*, 1957
    In 1740 Commodore Anson sets out to travel around the globe; when he returns he has one ship and a tiny, but wealthy, crew.
Barbara Riefe, *Westward Hearts: The Amelia Dale Archer Story*, 1998
    Convinced she'll never get ahead in Philadelphia, Dr. Archer and her four grandchildren head to California which they hope will be kinder to women with careers.

STEVEN KELLOGG, Author/Illustrator

A Penguin Pup for Pinkerton

(New York: Dial Books for Young Readers, 2001)

Subject(s): Animals/Penguins; Animals/Dogs; Humor
Age range(s): Grades K-3
Major character(s): Pinkerton, Dog (Great Dane); Emily, Child, Student—Elementary School; Granny, Grandmother
Time period(s): 2000s (2001)
Locale(s): United States

Summary: As Pinkerton listens to Emily telling Granny about father emperor penguins hatching their eggs Pinkerton knows just what to do with the football he found that day. To Emily, Pinkerton's efforts to "hatch" the football are noteworthy enough to share with her class so Pinkerton comes to school with her for Show-and-Tell. An angry classmate recognizes his football and Pinkerton's vision of adoring penguin pups vanishes as the football is returned. Fortunately, while Emily and Pinkerton are at school Granny's been creating a solution that satisfies local football teams needing intact balls and Pinkerton's dreams. (32 pages)

Where it's reviewed:
Booklist, September 1, 2001, page 116
Horn Book, September 2001, page 574
Kirkus Reviews, July 15, 2001, page 1028
Publishers Weekly, October 29, 2001, page 65
School Library Journal, August 2001, page 155

Other books by the same author:
Prehistoric Pinkerton, 1987 (School Library Journal Best Book)
Tallyho, Pinkerton!, 1982 (Booklist Editors' Choice)
A Rose for Pinkerton, 1981 (Learning Best Book of the Year)
Pinkerton, Behave!, 1979 (Horn Book Fanfare)

Other books you might like:
Sheila W. Black, *Plenty of Penguins*, 1999
    This "Hello Reader!" science title gives factual information about several varieties of penguins.
Helen Lester, *Tacky and the Emperor*, 2000
    Unconventional Tacky's tendency to err creates a unique but enjoyable day for the visiting emperor penguin.
Jennifer Rae, *Dog Tales*, 1999
    Dogs play the leading roles in each of six fractured fairy tales.
Peggy Rathmann, *Officer Buckle and Gloria*, 1995
    Behind Officer Buckle's back, police dog Gloria acts out his safety tips, bringing new life to his dull assemblies. Caldecott Medal winner.
Alan Snow, *How Dogs Really Work!*, 1993
    A winner of the New York Times Best Illustrated Children's Book Award is a humorous instruction manual for dog owners.

MIJ KELLY
ALISON JAY, Illustrator

William and the Night Train

(New York: Farrar Straus Giroux, 2001)

Subject(s): Fantasy; Bedtime; Trains
Age range(s): Grades K-1
Major character(s): William, Child, Son
Time period(s): Indeterminate
Locale(s): Fictional Country

Summary: Passengers board the night train for the journey to tomorrow. William is in such a hurry to get to tomorrow that he's too excited to be quiet and sleep as the other passengers are doing. Frequently William asks when the train will reach tomorrow. His mother suggests a little trick, closing his eyes, so the train can depart the station. William tries the trick and sure enough, when he opens his eyes again, the train has reached its destination. Originally published in Great Britain in 2000. (32 pages)

Where it's reviewed:
Booklist, February 15, 2001, page 1135
Horn Book Guide, Fall 2001, page 234
Kirkus Reviews, February 1, 2001, page 185
Publishers Weekly, December 18, 2000, page 77
School Library Journal, March 2001, page 213

Other books you might like:
David McPhail, *The Train*, 1977
    Matthew boards his toy train for a fantastic bedtime journey.
Peggy Rathmann, *10 Minutes till Bedtime*, 1998
    The train in this bedtime tale offers hamster-guided tours of a child's frenetic bedtime routine.
Chris Van Allsburg, *The Polar Express*, 1985
    The Caldecott Medal winner relates the memory of a magical Christmas Eve train ride to the North Pole.

488

DEBORAH KENT

The Courage to Live
(New York: Pocket/Archway, 2001)

Series: Why Me?. Number 1
Subject(s): Diseases; School Life
Age range(s): Grades 7-10
Major character(s): Chloe Peterson, 15-Year-Old; Todd Bowers, Student—High School
Time period(s): 2000s
Locale(s): Illinois

Summary: Chloe is like every other teenager who tries to accomplish fifteen things at once and then stays constantly tired. Working at The Shelter, she meets Todd when he grabs a loose dog for her, a meeting that has potential to spice up her life. During this time Chloe suffers from terrible headaches and feels light-headed, but dismisses the symptoms as those of stress, especially when her father loses his job. Her doctor's suggestion of vitamins helps for a while, but gradually the symptoms return. Trying out for *The Sound of Music*, Chloe faints and is taken to the hospital where she undergoes a series of tests. Diagnosed with lupus, she worries about learning to live with this disease. (191 pages)

Where it's reviewed:
Booklist, May 1, 2001, page 1675
Kliatt, May 2001, page 21
Voice of Youth Advocates, April 2001, page 33

Other books by the same author:
Don't Cry for Yesterday, 2002 (Why Me?, Number 3)
Living with a Secret, 2001 (Why Me?, Number 2)

Other books you might like:
Jean Ferris, *Invincible Summer*, 1987
    Two teens meet and fall in love while undergoing treatment for leukemia, but only one survives.
Beth Goobie, *Before Wings*, 2001
    Barely surviving a brain aneurysm the previous year, Adrien's summer spent helping her aunt at Camp Lakeshore is so active that she quits expecting to die.
Lurlene McDaniel, *To Live Again*, 2001
    With her leukemia in remission for three years, Dawn's excited about her senior year until she's felled by a stroke that proves more debilitating than her cancer.

489

M.E. KERR (Pseudonym of Marijane Meaker)

Slap Your Sides
(New York: HarperCollins, 2001)

Subject(s): Pacifism; World War II; Quakers
Age range(s): Grades 7-10
Major character(s): Jubal Shoemaker, 15-Year-Old; Efram Elam "Bud" Shoemaker, Pacifist; Daria Daniel, 15-Year-Old
Time period(s): 1940s (1942-1945)
Locale(s): Sweet Creek, Pennsylvania

Summary: After Pearl Harbor, men everywhere are enlisting except for Quaker Bud Shoemaker who chooses conscientious objector status and works in a mental hospital instead. That decision leads to harassment for his family, messages about cowardice written on their department store windows and a decline in their business. It also causes his youngest brother Jubal to think about the difference between courage and cowardice, as Bud's work in the hospital proves dangerous and almost kills him. Jubal discovers the person writing on their store windows is Daria, a young girl whose twin brothers are fighting in the war and whose father has a popular radio show. Because he falls for her, he doesn't turn her in. Instead, forbidden by her father to see Jubal, the two meet secretly and spend Saturdays horseback riding together, until the day Jubal hears her scream in the barn. Rushing to protect her, Jubal accidentally kills a deranged young man and in that instant realizes how he's compromised all the beliefs by which he's been raised. Later he wonders if his action was worth it. (198 pages)

Where it's reviewed:
Bulletin of the Center for Children's Books, November 2001, page 106
Horn Book, November 2001, page 751
Publishers Weekly, October 20, 2001, page 65
School Library Journal, October 2001, page 162
Voice of Youth Advocates, October 2001, page 280

Awards the book has won:
Booklist Editors' Choice/Books for Youth, 2001

Other books by the same author:
What Became of Her?, 2000
Hello, I Lied, 1997
Linger, 1993
Night Kites, 1986

Other books you might like:

LouAnn Bigge Gaeddert, *Friends and Enemies*, 2000
William can't believe that his best friend Jim, who's a Mennonite, is so unpatriotic about World War II.

Nancy Price Graff, *A Long Way Home*, 2001
Riley learns about courage from Sam, a man scorned for being dishonorably discharged for refusing to carry a weapon during the Vietnam War.

Susan Hart Lindquist, *Summer Soldiers*, 1999
Because he doesn't believe in war, Mr. Morgan stays home on his farm, but exhibits courage when he gives his life to save some drowning horses.

490

BRAD KESSLER

Lick Creek

(New York: Scribner, 2001)

Subject(s): Miners and Mining; Mountain Life; Revenge
Age range(s): Grades 10-Adult
Major character(s): Ada Jenkins, Mother; Emily Jenkins, 18-Year-Old; Robert Daniels, Administrator (electric company); Joseph Gershon, Worker (lineman for electric company), Immigrant (Russian)
Time period(s): 1920s
Locale(s): Lick Creek, West Virginia

Summary: When Emily and her mother Ada hear the muffled boom, they know there's a problem in the coal mine, but they never think the explosion will take the lives of Emily's father, brother and first boyfriend. Struggling to get by, they accept a pittance from the electric company to install high tension wires on a right of way across their farm and Emily sells berries, mushrooms and goat cheese at the hotel where many of the electrical company's supervisors stay. One night Robert Daniels gets Emily drunk and rapes her, leaving Emily thirsting for vengeance which she carries out with small acts of sabotage. At the same time, a lineman is struck by lightning and carried to the Jenkins' home where Ada cares for him while Emily falls in love with him. But electricity is not yet done with Emily and Joseph for when they encounter Robert Daniels at the celebratory dinner, Emily's desire for vengeance resurges and changes their lives forever. (297 pages)

Where it's reviewed:
Booklist, January 2001, page 918
Kirkus Reviews, January 1, 2001, page 12
New York Times Book Review, April 1, 2001, page 19
Publishers Weekly, January 15, 2001, page 50
Voice of Youth Advocates, October 2001, page 280

Other books you might like:

David Baldacci, *Wish You Well*, 2000
Two New York city kids move to the mountain home of their great-grandmother where they adjust to the hardscrabble life of a coal town of 1940s Virginia.

Denise Giardina, *Storming Heaven*, 1988
10,000 coal miners march upon one town only to be met by U.S. military forces in a battle which leaves hundreds dead.

Lee Smith, *Fair and Tender Ladies*, 1988
For sixty-five years a young mountain girl writes a series of letters that describe life in the Appalachians.

491

CRISTINA KESSLER
JOELLEN MCALLISTER STAMMEN, Illustrator

Jubela

(New York: Simon & Schuster Books for Young Readers, 2001)

Subject(s): Animals/Rhinoceroses; Survival
Age range(s): Grades K-3
Major character(s): Jubela, Rhinoceros, Orphan; Unnamed Character, Rhinoceros
Time period(s): Indeterminate
Locale(s): Swaziland

Summary: A baby rhino doesn't understand the significance of the loud night noises or his mother's nudges encouraging him to run with her through the bush. Struggling to keep up, the young rhino can finally rest beside his mother after she crashes to the ground. In the hot light of morning, the mother does not stir and Jubela is afraid and hungry in this unfamiliar place. Finally the scent of danger forces Jubela to flee from his dead mother. He follows other animals until he recognizes a familiar scent and locates an old rhinoceros. She considers the baby for some time before accepting the responsibility of teaching him how to survive. A concluding note explains the true story on which the book is based. (32 pages)

Where it's reviewed:
Booklist, February 1, 2001, page 1056
Horn Book Guide, Fall 2001, page 262
Kirkus Reviews, December 15, 2000, page 1761
Publishers Weekly, January 15, 2001, page 75
School Library Journal, March 2001, page 213

Other books by the same author:
My Great-Grandmother's Gourd, 2000
Konte Chameleon Fine, Fine, Fine! A West African Folktale, 1997
One Night: A Story from the Desert, 1995 (Book Links Good Book)

Other books you might like:

Jeremy Grimsdell, *Kalinzu: A Story from Africa*, 1993
When Kalinzu, a buffalo calf, is separated from her mother, ox-peckers help her return to the security of the herd.

Bijou Le Tord, *Elephant Moon*, 1993
The way of life of elephants and other animals on the African plains is depicted.

Betsy Lewin, *Chubbo's Pool*, 1996
When Chubbo's water hole dries up the hippo regrets not being more generous with his animal neighbors who still have water.

492

HELEN KETTEMAN
MARY WHYTE, Illustrator

Mama's Way

(New York: Dial Books for Young Readers, 2001)

Subject(s): Clothes; Mothers and Daughters; Single Parent Families
Age range(s): Grades 1-4
Major character(s): Mama, Single Mother, Seamstress; Wynona Anderson, Daughter, 6th Grader; John Franklin Anderson, Brother (younger), Son
Time period(s): 2000s (2001)
Locale(s): United States

Summary: In a shop window Wynona spies a beautiful white dress, just perfect for her upcoming sixth grade graduation. The price, however, is beyond the family's budget so Wynona fears she will have to wear a classmate's hand-me-down. Recognizing her disappointment, Mama takes on some extra work and gives Wynona the money to buy the dress. Before they can go shopping John Franklin is injured while in Wynona's care and she sacrifices her graduation gift to help pay his emergency medical bill. Mama's way is to give up sleep in order to provide for her children so by graduation morning Wynona has a beautiful alteration of the secondhand dress to wear. (32 pages)

Where it's reviewed:
Booklist, February 15, 2001, page 1140
Bulletin of the Center for Children's Books, March 2001, page 267
Horn Book Guide, Fall 2001, page 262
Publishers Weekly, January 29, 2001, page 89
School Library Journal, March 2001, page 214

Other books by the same author:
Shoeshine Whittaker, 1999
I Remember Papa, 1998
Grandma's Cat, 1996
The Christmas Blizzard, 1995

Other books you might like:
Artie Ann Bates, *Ragsale*, 1995
    After a day of rummaging through the used items at ragsales sisters Eunice and Jessann share the excitement of opening their surprise bundles.
Marguerite De Angeli, *Thee, Hannah!*, 1940
    Hannah overcomes her envy of her friends' fashionable dresses when her plain Quaker attire attracts the attention of a runaway slave needing help.
Dolly Parton, *Coat of Many Colors*, 1994
    The knowledge that her colorful coat was lovingly made by her mother helps a young girl bear the teasing of schoolmates when she wears the garment.
Emily Rodda, *Something Special*, 1984
    While helping her mother sort clothes donated to the school fair, a daughter imagines the lives of the original owners.

493

CHIP KIDD

The Cheese Monkeys: A Novel in Two Semesters

(New York: Scribner, 2001)

Subject(s): College Life; Artists and Art; Humor
Age range(s): Grades 10-Adult
Major character(s): Unnamed character, Narrator, Student—College; Himillsy Dodd, Student—College; Winter Sorbeck, Professor
Time period(s): 1950s (1957-1958)
Locale(s): United States

Summary: A nameless college student, enrolled at his State University, decides to take the path of least resistance and become an art major. His first semester in Art 101 is spent trying to draw inanimate objects in pencil, all of which bore him. The best part of the class is meeting Himillsy, a fun-loving soul who is as bored and unstimulated by the class as nameless is. Their lives change when second semester rolls around and they sign up for Winter Sorbeck's class entitled Introduction to Commercial Art. As Winter explains, commercial art is to make people buy things whereas his class is really about graphic design which is to create and give ideas. Though the stereotype of the "know it all" professor, Sorbeck cajoles, intimidates, vilifies and humiliates his students to force them to think and be creative. He succeeds, but at a price, in this humorous first novel written by a book cover artist and set in an era before computers. (274 pages)

Where it's reviewed:
Booklist, September 1, 2001, page 51
Kirkus Reviews, August 1, 2001, page 1053
Library Journal, September 15, 2001, page 112
New York Times Book Review, October 21, 2001, page 34
Tribune Books, August 10, 2001, page 7

Other books you might like:
James Finney Boylan, *Getting In*, 1998
    A planned summer vacation to allow touring and interviewing at some of New England's preppiest colleges turns into a farcical road trip.
Tom Perrotta, *Joe College*, 2000
    Raised in a blue-collar home, Danny sometimes wonders what he's doing at Yale among all those wealthy students.
Ishmael Reed, *Japanese by Spring*, 1993
    Professor Chappie Puttbutt wishes to do well in academia, but never expects his Japanese tutor to buy his University in this satirical look at American colleges.

494

MONTE KILLINGSWORTH
JENNIFER DANZA, Illustrator

Equinox

(New York: Holt, 2001)

Subject(s): Islands; Mothers and Daughters; Fathers and Daughters
Age range(s): Grades 6-8

Major character(s): Autumn, 14-Year-Old; Harley, Father (of Autumn), Artisan (woodworker); Linda, Mother (of Autumn), Writer; Forrest, Artist
Time period(s): 2000s
Locale(s): Douglas Island, Washington (part of the San Juan Islands)

Summary: Life on tiny Douglas Island, in her family's log cabin that lacks electricity or an indoor shower, has been idyllic for Autumn and she's distressed to learn that her father Harley thinks they should move to the larger island where Autumn's mother works. Harley tells Autumn it's to make sure she enrolls in a better school, but it's also because he and his wife are ''drifting apart'' and perhaps the weekend-only visits are part of the problem. Autumn can't imagine living somewhere else and Forrest, an artist friend, gives her a journal to illustrate her favorite pieces of island living. When Autumn discovers that her mother and Jane, another islander, are in a long-term lesbian relationship, she understands the real reason her father wants to move, but is devastated by the knowledge. Distraught, she runs into the surf where the high equinox tide almost pulls her out to sea; luckily she is rescued by Forrest who helps Autumn adjust to life both on and off Douglas Island. (118 pages)

Where it's reviewed:
Booklist, August 2001, page 2107
Publishers Weekly, July 16, 2001, page 181
Riverbank Review, Winter 2001, page 35
School Library Journal, September 2001, page 226
Voice of Youth Advocates, October 2001, page 280

Other books by the same author:
Circle within a Circle, 1994
Eli's Song, 1991

Other books you might like:
Pamela Brandt, *Becoming the Butlers*, 1990
   After her mother leaves them, Rachel and her father struggle to come to terms with their new family makeup.
Carole Crowe, *Sharp Horns on the Moon*, 1998
   Living on a distant, isolated island, Ivy Marie is an unhappy teen who tires of being home-schooled and misses her deceased mother.
Tracy Mack, *Drawing Lessons*, 2000
   Rory's life turns upside down when she spots her beloved artist father, who guides her artistic talent, kissing his model.
Deborah Moulton, *Summer Girl*, 1992
   Ten years after her parents divorce, Tommy is sent to live with her father. It's awkward at first, but they gradually work out their relationship.

K.M. KIMBALL

The Star-Spangled Secret
(New York: Simon & Schuster/Aladdin, 2001)

Subject(s): War of 1812; Brothers and Sisters; Mystery and Detective Stories
Age range(s): Grades 4-7

Major character(s): Caroline Dorsey, 13-Year-Old; Charlie Dorsey, 14-Year-Old, Worker (aboard the *Liberty*); Sean Foley, Servant (indentured)
Time period(s): 1810s (1814)
Locale(s): Baltimore, Maryland; Elk Ridge, Maryland (family home); Philadelphia, Pennsylvania

Summary: At boarding school in Philadelphia, Caroline can't believe that her brother Charlie fell off his ship and drowned. Just a year older than Caroline, he's been serving aboard the privateer vessel *Liberty* and, according to Captain Moses, the crew has searched for but hasn't found his body. Something doesn't ring true for Caroline as Charlie's a wonderful swimmer, so she hurries home to Elk Ridge where she convinces the indentured servant Sean to drive her to Baltimore to investigate. Caroline asks questions of everyone, from the sailors around Baltimore harbor to President Madison, in her quest to discover what happened to her brother, and she turns up more secrets and spies than she ever imagined possible. Though Charlie is found alive, Sean has to make sure that Caroline and her mother are also safe after attempts are made on their lives. (234 pages)

Where it's reviewed:
Booklist, November 1, 2001, page 474
School Library Journal, November 2001, page 160

Other books by the same author:
The Secret of the Red Flame, 2002

Other books you might like:
Avi, *The True Confessions of Charlotte Doyle*, 1990
   A sea voyage under a tyrannical captain hones proper young lady Charlotte into a sailor who is able to fight for her life.
Harriette Gillem Robinet, *Washington City Is Burning*, 1996
   Virginia is one of Madison's slaves brought to the White House who stays to help other slaves escape, even though the British threaten the city.
Gloria Whelan, *Once on This Island*, 1995
   When their father leaves to fight in the War of 1812, a young girl and her brothers assume responsibility for their family's Michigan farm.

496

ERIC A. KIMMEL
KATYA KRENINA, Illustrator

A Cloak for the Moon
(New York: Holiday House, 2001)

Subject(s): Folklore; Jews; Quest
Age range(s): Grades 1-4
Major character(s): Haskel, Tailor, Traveler
Time period(s): Indeterminate Past
Locale(s): Tzafat, Fictional Country; China; Roof of the World, Fictional Country

Summary: Haskel believes the moon wants him to weave a cloth to keep her warm at night. The problem for Haskel is locating thread or a cloth that can adapt to the waxing and waning of the moon. His quest takes him on a long journey across the sea, through China to the Roof of the World where he finds the people grieving for the princess who cannot wed because she has no wedding dress. The dress that is traditionally passed on from queen to daughter is made of a cloth that shrinks and stretches to fit the wearer, but the hem is unraveling and no tailor can mend it. Haskel takes on the challenge, discovers how to weave the dress from moonbeams and takes as his reward one piece of thread. Using this scrap Haskel weaves a cloak for the moon. (32 pages)

Where it's reviewed:
Booklist, July 2001, page 2014
Bulletin of the Center for Children's Books, April 2001, page 304
Horn Book Guide, Fall 2001, page 262
Publishers Weekly, February 26, 2001, page 85
School Library Journal, May 2001, page 126

Awards the book has won:
Sydney Taylor Honor Book for Younger Readers, 2002

Other books by the same author:
Anansi and the Magic Stick, 2001
Why the Snake Crawls on Its Belly, 2001
Pumpkinhead, 2001

Other books you might like:
Marguerite W. Davol, *Batwings and the Curtain of Night*, 1997
  The Mother of All Things weaves a curtain to provide some respite from the bright sky; curious animals pierce it with their claws, creating stars.
Eric Hadley, *Legends of the Sun and Moon*, 1983
  Twelve traditional tales drawn from many cultures include legends related to both the sun and the moon.
Brian Wilcox, *Full Moon*, 2001
  In a dream fantasy a young boy uses his grandmother's birthday gift, a globe reminiscent of a full moon, to fly through the night sky.
Nancy Willard, *The Nightgown of the Sullen Moon*, 1983
  Finally, moon receives what she's long desired, an earthly nightgown.

497

ERIC A. KIMMEL
MICHAEL DOOLING, Illustrator

Robin Hook, Pirate Hunter!
(New York: Scholastic Press, 2001)

Subject(s): Pirates; Good and Evil; Conduct of Life
Age range(s): Grades 1-4
Major character(s): Robin Hook, Orphan, Hero; James Hook, Pirate, Sea Captain; Thatch, Pirate, Sea Captain
Time period(s): Indeterminate Past
Locale(s): *Sandpiper*, At Sea; *Avenger*, At Sea

Summary: Captain Hook retrieves a baby from the tentacles of a huge octopus and raises the child to be a pirate. Robin Hook is a different sort of lad and his kind heart does not take to pirate ways. When Robin releases three of Captain Hook's prisoners the pirate angrily dumps him on a deserted island. Robin wisely uses the time to learn the ways of animals and vows to rid the world of pirates. In time, pirates abandon other children on the island and together they build the *Sandpiper* and set off to bring pirates to justice. When Captain Thatch ransacks a nearby town and captures the residents, a parrot warns Robin Hook of their plight. In the *Sandpiper*, Robin and his crew force the *Avenger* onto a reef and rescue the prisoners. Robin's animal friends in the sea take care of the pirates. (32 pages)

Where it's reviewed:
Booklist, January 2001, page 967
Horn Book Guide, Fall 2001, page 262
Kirkus Reviews, December 15, 2001, page 1761
Publishers Weekly, February 19, 2001, page 90
School Library Journal, March 2001, page 214

Other books by the same author:
Gershon's Monster, 2000 (ALA Notable Children's Book)
Billy Lazroe and the King of the Sea, 1996
Onions and Garlic, 1996

Other books you might like:
Judy Cox, *Rabbit Pirates: A Tale of the Spinach Main*, 1999
  Retired pirates solve the problem of a customer at their restaurant whose primary interest is in eating the owners rather than ordering from the menu.
Pat Hutchins, *One-Eyed Jake*, 1994
  Bravely, the cook, the bo'sun and the cabin boy escape from evil Jake to lead the peaceful life of their dreams.
Emily Arnold McCully, *The Pirate Queen*, 1995
  The account of the life and adventures of a 16th-century pirate, Grania O'Malley, is based on both legend and history.
Colin McNaughton, *Captain Abdul's Pirate School*, 1994
  Maisie organizes a mutiny, overtakes wicked Captain Abdul and his crew and sails with the other students to the West Indies.

498

ERIC A. KIMMEL
JEFF SHELLY, Illustrator

Website of the Warped Wizard
(New York: Dutton, 2001)

Subject(s): Computer Games
Age range(s): Grades 4-6
Major character(s): Jessica Lyons, Computer Game Player; Matthew, Computer Game Player; Dennis, Mythical Creature (centaur)
Time period(s): 2000s
Locale(s): United States; Cyberspace

Summary: Tired of their old computer games, Jessica and Matt sign on to a new web site and enter the virtual-reality game Medieval Madness, and mad it is! When they order a centaur, a shorts-clad, surfer dude named Dennis shows up with a contract that stipulates how he can be used. On their virtual quest Jessica and Matt encounter an elf who's been downsized from his amusement park, Robin Hood's men now astride motorcycles and stealing from everyone, and Merlin, King Arthur and Guinevere. Returning home after they release King Arthur from an evil spell, Matt scrolls down to "Quit" but inadvertently hits "New Game." Uh-oh, here they go again. (118 pages)

Where it's reviewed:
Bulletin of the Center for Children's Books, March 2001, page 267
Publishers Weekly, January 22, 2001, page 324
School Library Journal, March 2001, page 252

Other books by the same author:
Website of the Cracked Cookies, 2001
One Good Tern Deserves Another, 1994

Other books you might like:
Mark Delaney, *The Vanishing Chip*, 1998
Four misfit teens unite to find a missing computer chip worth more than a million dollars.
Elisabeth Mace, *Under Siege*, 1990
Morris discovers that his Uncle Patrick has a computer reenactment of an entire miniature kingdom, complete with castle "under siege."
Vivian Vande Velde, *User Unfriendly*, 1991
A computer game played by Arvin and his friends becomes too lifelike and compromises their fantasy quest.

499

ERIC A. KIMMEL
JON GOODELL, Illustrator

ZigaZak!: A Magical Hanukkah Night

(New York: Doubleday Book for Young Readers, 2001)

Subject(s): Holidays, Jewish; Good and Evil; Magic
Age range(s): Grades 1-3
Major character(s): Unnamed Character, Demon, Shape-changer; Rabbi, Religious; Unnamed Character, Demon, Shape-changer
Time period(s): Indeterminate Past
Locale(s): Brisk, Europe

Summary: Such a Hanukkah! Dreidels sprout arms and legs, latkes fly through the air and menorah candles explode like fireworks. Alarmed, the townspeople rush to Rabbi's home as the two devils responsible for the mischief watch in amusement. Rabbi calmly grabs a flying latke and devours it, expresses delight at the sight of the dreidels and considers the exploding candles beautiful. The two frustrated devils appear in response to Rabbi's call, expecting punishment but instead Rabbi tricks them into using their power to produce Hanukkah gelt. The devils refuse Rabbi's offer to free them from darkness and attempt to frighten him by changing into various monsters. Undeterred, Rabbi withstands the onslaught and wisely uses one final request to rid the town of the demons. (32 pages)

Where it's reviewed:
Booklist, September 1, 2001, page 120
Bulletin of the Center for Children's Books, October 2001, page 62
Publishers Weekly, September 24, 2001, page 48
School Library Journal, October 2001, page 66

Other books by the same author:
Gershon's Monster, 2000 (ALA Notable Children's Book)
The Magic Dreidels: A Hanukkah Story, 1996
The Chanukkah Guest, 1990 (Sydney Taylor Award)

Hershel and the Hanukkah Goblins, 1989 (Caldecott Honor Book)

Other books you might like:
David A. Adler, *Chanukah in Chelm*, 1997
Mandel, a foolish synagogue caretaker, finds an indirect way to comply with Rabbi Nachman's request to locate a table for the menorah.
Naomi Howland, *Latkes, Latkes Good to Eat: A Chanukah Story*, 1999
Poor Sadie's kindness to an old woman is rewarded with a magic frying pan that produces latkes for Sadie and chaos for her greedy brothers.
Steve Sanfield, *The Feather Merchants and Other Tales of the Fools of Chelm*, 1991
Thirteen tales drawn from Jewish folklore offer humor and heritage.

500

PATRICE KINDL

Goose Chase

(Boston: Houghton Mifflin, 2001)

Subject(s): Fairy Tales; Love; Satire
Age range(s): Grades 6-10
Major character(s): Alexandria Aurora Fortunato, Orphan; Edmund, Royalty (prince); Claudio, Royalty (king)
Time period(s): Indeterminate
Locale(s): Gilboa, Fictional Country

Summary: Alexandria Aurora Fortunato may be an orphan goose girl made wealthy by a mysterious old woman and imprisoned in a tower by rivals for her hand, but she is no ordinary, passive fairy tale heroine! As she tells the story, spunky Alexandria doesn't intend to marry either of these rivals, instead she plans to escape and take her precious, magical geese with her. Escape she does, though it lands her in one danger after another, as Alexandria continually finds ways to foil the usual fate of princesses-in-towers. After many adventures, Prince Edmund's true heart is revealed, King Claudio's evil side is unmasked and the true identity of Alexandria and her geese is discovered in a denouement worthy of the most lurid melodrama. Alexandria's sassy tongue and pert attitude are the perfect medicine for anyone sick of one sweet heroine too many. (241 pages)

Where it's reviewed:
Booklist, September 15, 2001, page 225
Horn Book Magazine, July 2001, page 454
Publishers Weekly, March 19, 2001, page 99
School Library Journal, April 2001, page 144
Voice of Youth Advocates, June 2001, page 134

Awards the book has won:
Booklist Editors' Choice/Books for Youth, 2001

Other books by the same author:
The Woman in the Wall, 1997
Owl in Love, 1993

Other books you might like:
M.M. Kaye, *The Ordinary Princess*, 1984
An extraordinary princess, who sees herself as ordinary, decides to do what isn't expected of her.

Donna Jo Napoli, *The Magic Circle*, 1993
    In this unusual fairytale, the story of Hansel and Gretel is told by the witch, who sees herself as a victim.
Patricia C. Wrede, *Talking to Dragons*, 1985
    Not only is this princess too restless to stay at home in her father's castle, but she also decides to become housekeeper for a dragon!

501

MARCIA KING-GAMBLE

Change of Heart
(Washington, DC: BET/Arabesque, 2001)

Subject(s): Sports/Skiing; African Americans; Romance
Age range(s): Grades 10-Adult
Major character(s): Shayna DaCosta, Health Care Professional (physical therapist); Beaumont ''Beau'' Hill, Skier
Time period(s): 2000s
Locale(s): Denver, Colorado

Summary: Not many African Americans are found on the slopes skiing, and even fewer have the chance to be an Olympic champion, but Beau Hill is part of that small fraternity. A member of America's ski team, he has a brilliant career ahead of him until he takes a nasty fall and breaks his back. Angry and filled with self-pity, he's hospitalized and uninterested in anything, even getting better. Wheeled to therapy, he meets no-nonsense Shayna who doesn't reveal that her Olympic dreams were also halted. Goading, cajoling, or sweet-talking, Shayna is willing to try anything to get Beau to once again walk, and perhaps even ski. Many obstacles confront Beau before he returns to the world of skiing, especially when he learns that his fall may have been intentional, in this delightful romance. (282 pages)

Where it's reviewed:
Booklist, September 15, 2001, page 205

Other books by the same author:
Island Bliss, 2002
A Reason to Love, 2001
Island Magic, 2000
Under Your Spell, 1999
Eden's Dream, 1998

Other books you might like:
Rochelle Akers, *My Love's Keeper*, 2001
    Nicole enjoys her life and her job with an East Harlem family agency and tries to ignore her family's urgings to marry, until she meets her brother's friend Zachary.
Terry McMillan, *Waiting to Exhale*, 1992
    Four African American women in their thirties support one another as they wonder if they'll ever find the right man.
Janice Sims, *This Time Forever*, 2001
    African American police chief Kerry Everett investigates a brutal murder and not only catches the killer, but also the FBI agent sent to assist with the case.

502

DICK KING-SMITH
SUSIE JENKIN-PEARCE, Illustrator

Billy the Bird
(New York: Hyperion Books for Children, 2001)

Subject(s): Fantasy; Brothers and Sisters; Pets
Age range(s): Grades 2-4
Major character(s): Mary Bird, 8-Year-Old, Sister; Billy Bird, 4-Year-Old, Brother
Time period(s): 2000s
Locale(s): England

Summary: On a full moon night in early summer Mary discovers Billy soaring about his room. In the morning she confides in her pet guinea pig and cat seeking advice about this predicament. Sure that her parents will not believe her, Mary keeps Billy's ability a secret; an easy task because Billy is unaware of what he does during a full moon, the only time he's capable of flight. For almost a year Billy becomes lighter than air once a month until a lunar eclipse ends his magical powers. Only Mary and the pets remember with awe Billy's full-moon flights over the town. (67 pages)

Where it's reviewed:
Booklist, July 2001, page 2006
Horn Book Guide, Fall 2001, page 309
Publishers Weekly, April 23, 2001, page 78
School Librarian, Winter 2000, page 201
School Library Journal, June 2001, page 121

Other books by the same author:
Mysterious Miss Slade, 2000
Charlie Muffin's Miracle Mouse, 1999
A Mouse Called Wolf, 1997
Mr. Potter's Pet, 1996

Other books you might like:
Adele Geras, *The Fabulous Fantoras: Book One: Family Files*, 1998
    The first book of a fantasy series introduces the family members and the unique talents of each.
Marthe Jocelyn, *The Invisible Day*, 1997
    Finding a bag containing vanishing cream allows Billie to become invisible for a day; now she has to find the bag's owner and an antidote.
Ursula K. Le Guin, *Jane on Her Own: A Catwings Tale*, 1999
    Farm life bores Jane who puts her wings to good use and flies off to fine a home more suited to her.

DICK KING-SMITH
JILL BARTON, Illustrator

Lady Lollipop
(Cambridge, MA: Candlewick Press, 2001)

Subject(s): Prices and Princesses; Behavior; Animals/Pigs
Age range(s): Grades 2-4
Major character(s): Penelope, Royalty (princess), 8-Year-Old; Johnny Skinner, Animal Trainer, Orphan; Lollipop, Pig
Time period(s): Indeterminate Past

Locale(s): England

Summary: Spoiled Princess Penelope demands a pet for her eighth birthday present and not just any pet will do. Princess Penelope wants a pig. From the many pigs assembled on the palace grounds by royal command, Penelope selects the scrawniest, dirtiest pig of the lot and claims the pig's former owner as her personal pig keeper. So, Johnny Skinner and Lollipop move into a pig stall and Johnny begins teaching Penelope how to get Lollipop to obey her in the same way the pig obeys him. In the process, he also trains Penelope to be a kinder, gentler, more obedient human being, earns a cottage for himself as the under gardener to the queen and pleases the king so much that he promises to make the boy a duke. Lollipop, noble pig that she is, becomes Lady Lollipop. Originally published in Great Britain in 2000. (123 pages)

Where it's reviewed:
Booklist, April 15, 2001, page 1552
Bulletin of the Center for Children's Books, September 2001, page 22
Horn Book, May 2001, page 327
Publishers Weekly, June 4, 2001, page 80
School Library Journal, June 2001, page 121

Awards the book has won:
ALA Notable Children's Books, 2002

Other books by the same author:
Mysterious Miss Slade, 2000
The School Mouse, 1995 (School Library Journal Best Book)
Babe: The Gallant Pig, 1985 (Boston-Globe-Horn Book Honor Book)

Other books you might like:
Kathryn Cristaldi, *Princess Lulu Goes to Camp*, 1997
    Princess Lulu, a "royal pain," goes to camp to learn friendlier behavior.
George MacDonald, *The Lost Princess: A Double Story*, 1992
    Princess Rosamund receives help from a wise woman to help her change her spoiled behavior.
Ian Whybrow, *Little Wolf's Book of Badness*, 2000
    Little Wolf's problem is just the opposite from Penelope's; his parents think he's too good and send him away to Uncle Bigbad for lessons.

504

NATALIE KINSEY-WARNOCK
KATHLEEN KOLB, Illustrator

A Farm of Her Own

(New York: Dutton Children's Books, 2001)

Subject(s): Farm Life; Aunts and Uncles; Family
Age range(s): Grades K-3
Major character(s): Emma, Niece, Cousin; Ada, Aunt, Farmer; Will, Uncle, Farmer
Time period(s): Indeterminate Past
Locale(s): Sunnyside Farm, Vermont

Summary: Emma's first exposure to Sunnyside Farm is a summer visit but she falls in love with the farmer's life, the smell of hay, the farm animals and the swimming pond. Her cousins have no interest in the hard work of a farm, but Emma wants to be just like Aunt Ada. Uncle Will and Aunt Ada

work the farm until death stops them and the farm is sold. After Emma is grown she buys the farm to reclaim it for her family and to provide a summer retreat for her cousin's children. (32 pages)

Where it's reviewed:
Booklist, July 2001, page 2019
Bulletin of the Center for Children's Books, June 2001, page 376
Horn Book Guide, Fall 2001, page 262
School Library Journal, June 2001, page 122

Other books by the same author:
The Summer of Stanley, 1997 (Smithsonian's Notable Books for Children)
The Fiddler of the Northern Lights, 1996 (Smithsonian's Notable Books for Children)
The Bear That Heard Crying, 1993

Other books you might like:
Thomas Locker, *Family Farm*, 1988
    A family must work together and change with the times to maintain a successful farm.
Patricia MacLachlan, *All the Places to Love*, 1994
    Three generations live on a family farm that holds "all the places to love" that anyone could ever want.
Rosemary Wells, *Waiting for the Evening Star*, 1993
    Young Berty appreciates the simple pleasures of life in rural Vermont while his older brother is eager to see beyond the distant mountains.

505

SUSAN E. KIRBY

Hattie's Story

(New York: Aladdin/Simon & Schuster, 2001)

Series: American Quilts. Book 2
Subject(s): Quilts; Underground Railroad; Family Saga
Age range(s): Grades 4-6
Major character(s): Gram Jennie, Grandmother (of Lacey); Hattie Crosby, Child, Grandmother (great-great-great grandmother); Lacey Tandy, Child
Time period(s): 2000s; 1850s
Locale(s): Mount Hope Colony, Illinois; Funks Grove, Illinois

Summary: In the middle of the 19th century Illinois is a free state but slave catchers are allowed to pursue their trade within state boundaries. Hattie discovers her parents are part of the Underground Railroad and worries her best friend's father, the local constable, or the slave hunters will bother them. Because of her father's stance on slaves, Hattie's best friend isn't allowed to play with her anymore and her school day becomes very lonely. One runaway slave makes a special impression on Hattie when she tries to make sure her 13 children make it to freedom in Canada. Hattie is grandmother to Lacey's grandmother who tells the tale in this series based on the stories revealed by Gram Jennie's collection of family quilts. (186 pages)

Where it's reviewed:
School Library Journal, March 2001, page 252

Other books by the same author:
Daniel's Story, 2001 (American Quilts, Book 3)

Ida Lou's Story, 2001 (American Quilts, Book 4)
Ellen's Story, 2000 (American Quilts, Book 1)

Other books you might like:

Patricia Beatty, *Who Comes with Cannons?*, 1992
   Truth Hopkins and her Quaker family face problems during the Civil War but are able to help slaves escape.

Ann Rinaldi, *A Stitch in Time*, 1994
   When her siblings disperse in all directions, Hannah tries to bind them together by stitching a quilt pattern called Trust made of fabric from their trusted friends.

G. Clifton Wisler, *Caleb's Choice*, 1996
   Caleb must decide whether or not to help a runaway slave; his sense of justice prevails and he repays his debt to Ajax.

506

SUSAN E. KIRBY

Ida Lou's Story

(New York: Aladdin/Simon & Schuster, 2001)

Series: American Quilts. Book 4
Subject(s): Quilts; Family Saga; Circus
Age range(s): Grades 4-6
Major character(s): Gram Jennie, Grandmother (of Lacey); Lacey Tandy, Child; Florida Louisa ''Ida Lou'' Young, Teenager, Entertainer (trapeze artist); Sylvester ''Slick'' Baumgart, Teenager
Time period(s): 1910s
Locale(s): Bloomington, Illinois

Summary: Gram Jennie repairs another of her family's quilts, this time one made from the leftover scraps of circus costumes, and tells Lacey the story of her great-great aunt Ida Lou. Her father abandoned his family and Ida Lou, her brother and their mother struggle to make ends meet. Ida and new student Slick are both enthralled with the circus and work odd jobs to earn money for a ticket. Reading about the stars on the flying trapeze, Ida Lou yearns to perform, but an accidental fall down some stairs in her apartment building leaves her with broken legs and arm. Never one to quit, Ida Lou learns to walk again, rebuilds her strength and never gives up her desire to be a trapeze artist in this continuing series. (170 pages)

Where it's reviewed:
School Library Journal, December 2001, page 138

Other books by the same author:
Daniel's Story, 2001 (American Quilts, Book 3)
Hattie's Story, 2001 (American Quilts, Book 2)
Ellen's Story, 2000 (American Quilts, Book 1)

Other books you might like:

Marilyn Singer, *Circus Lunicus*, 2000
   A fairy lizard ensures that Solly gets to the Circus Lunicus, his first step in becoming one of its stars in this wonderfully wacky tale.

Barbara Smucker, *Incredible Jumbo*, 1991
   Based on fact, this fictionalized account tells of Jumbo, the noted elephant that starred in the P.T. Barnum Circus in the early 1900s.

Gloria Whelan, *Miranda's Last Stand*, 1999
   To earn enough money to renovate their inherited farm, Miranda and her mother join Buffalo Bill's Wild West Show.

507

DANIEL KIRK, Author/Illustrator

Bus Stop, Bus Go!

(New York: G.P. Putnam's Sons, 2001)

Subject(s): School Buses; Animals/Hamsters; Stories in Rhyme
Age range(s): Grades K-3
Major character(s): Joe, Driver (school bus); Tommy, Child, Student—Elementary School; Hammy, Hamster, Runaway
Time period(s): 2000s (2001)
Locale(s): United States

Summary: Joe and Tommy greet each other as Tommy climbs aboard the school bus carrying his pet's cage. The bus goes to the next stop as the curious riders question Tommy about Hammy. When Tommy notices that the cage is empty, the bus ride becomes a race to catch the hamster before Hammy reaches the front door and freedom. Tommy crawls along the bus floor past riders eating lunch, doing homework, and playing games. Some offer bits of food from their lunch boxes to tempt Hammy and finally he's caught as the bus stops at school and the children spill out. (32 pages)

Where it's reviewed:
Booklist, June 2001, page 1891
Bulletin of the Center for Children's Books, September 2001, page 23
Kirkus Reviews, May 15, 2001, page 742
Publishers Weekly, June 18, 2001, page 81
School Library Journal, September 2001, page 193

Other books by the same author:
Humpty Dumpty, 2000
Snow Family, 2000 (IRA Children's Choice)
Moondogs, 1999

Other books you might like:

Suzanne Bloom, *The Bus for Us*, 2001
   As each of a variety of vehicles nears the bus stop new student Tess asks her older brother, ''Is that the bus for us, Gus?''

Donald Crews, *School Bus*, 1984
   School buses deliver children to school and carry them safely home again in all kinds of weather.

Judy Hindley, *The Big Red Bus*, 1995
   When a wheel on the big red bus gets stuck in a pothole none of the traffic can get past.

508

DAVID KIRK, Author/Illustrator

Little Bird, Biddle Bird

(New York: Scholastic Press, 2001)

Series: Biddle Books
Subject(s): Animals/Birds; Stories in Rhyme; Food
Age range(s): Preschool-Kindergarten

Major character(s): Biddle Bird, Bird; Mommy, Bird, Mother
Time period(s): Indeterminate
Locale(s): Fictional Country

Summary: Mommy's not around and Biddle Bird is hungry so it's time to develop some independence. Little Biddle Bird considers caterpillar, slugs, peas, berries and bugs with wings wondering how to determine which is best to eat. Biddle Bird successfully wrestles a worm from the ground and feels quite full by the time Mommy returns to sing the praises of her little Biddle Bird. (32 pages)

Where it's reviewed:
Children's Bookwatch, June 2001, page 4
Horn Book Guide, Fall 2001, page 234
Publishers Weekly, March 12, 2001, page 93
School Library Journal, July 2001, page 84

Other books by the same author:
Little Pig, Biddle Pig, 2001 (Biddle Books)
Little Miss Spider, 1999
Miss Spider's ABC, 1998

Other books you might like:
Joyce Dunbar, *Baby Bird*, 1998
    A small blue bird, eager to fly, falls to the ground where it faces numerous dangers before it succeeds in flying back to safety.
P.D. Eastman, *Are You My Mother?*, 1960
    After falling from the nest, a lost baby bird searches for its mother.
Nancy Tafuri, *Will You Be My Friend?*, 2000
    Bunny tries to befriend Bird but Bird is too shy to respond at first.

509

ANNA KIRWAN

Victoria: May Blossom of Britannia, England, 1829

(New York: Scholastic, 2001)

Series: Royal Diaries
Subject(s): Princes and Princesses; Diaries
Age range(s): Grades 4-7
Major character(s): Victoire of Sax, Mother (of Victoria), Royalty (Duchess of Kent); John Conroy, Advisor (of finance); Alexandrina Victoria, Royalty (princess)
Time period(s): 1820s; 1830s (1829-1837)
Locale(s): London, England (Kensington Palace)

Summary: Well aware of the scrutiny under which she lives, Victoria still chafes at it and when she has the chance to steal a record book from the stable, does so to record all her private thoughts. Writing in secret, she describes her life as the niece of King George IV, with its accompanying intrigues of court life. From her mother and her mother's advisor Captain Conroy, she learns how to behave as a royal, dance in preparation for balls, and study for examinations in history, literature and religion. Though a child, she realizes the position to which she might one day succeed and, at the age of eighteen, becomes Queen of England in this continuing series. (219 pages)

Where it's reviewed:
Booklist, December 1, 2001, page 643
School Library Journal, January 2002, page 132
Voice of Youth Advocates, February 2002, page 436

Other books by the same author:
Juliet: Midsummer at Greenchapel, England, 1340, 1997 (Girlhood Journeys, Number 3)
Juliet: Rescue at Marlehead Manor, England, 1340, 1997 (Girlhood Journeys, Number 2)
Juliet: A Dream Takes Flight, England, 1339, 1996 (Girlhood Journeys, Number 1)

Other books you might like:
Kristiana Gregory, *Cleopatra VII: Daughter of the Nile*, 1999
    Diary entries for Cleopatra, ruler of Egypt, cover her years from twelve to fourteen as she prepares to become Egypt's ruler.
Kathryn Lasky, *Marie Antoinette: Princess of Versailles*, 2000
    Married to the Dauphin of France, Austrian Marie Antoinette gives up her childhood ways and struggles to adapt to marriage and life in France.
Carolyn Meyer, *Anastasia: The Last Grand Duchess, Russia, 1914*, 2000
    With the diary her grandmother gives her when she is twelve, Anastasia records her life as the youngest daughter of Tsar Nicholas II of Russia.
Carolyn Meyer, *Beware, Princess Elizabeth*, 2001
    Court life in sixteenth-century England is treacherous and constantly changing as Princess Elizabeth discovers when her half-sister Mary assumes the throne.

510

DAVID KLASS

You Don't Know Me

(New York: Farrar Straus Giroux, 2001)

Subject(s): Child Abuse; Self-Perception; Schools/High Schools
Age range(s): Grades 7-12
Major character(s): John, 14-Year-Old, Musician (tuba player); Violet Hayes, Musician (saxophone player); Arthur Flemingham Steenwilly, Teacher (orchestra); Stan, Teacher (orchestra)
Time period(s): 2000s
Locale(s): United States

Summary: John lives two lives, one during the day when he's "safe" at school and the other at night when Stan, his mother's live-in boyfriend, abuses him and makes him a partner in receiving stolen property. At school, which he refers to as anti-school because he doesn't think learning occurs there, he's often sarcastic and brushes off the interest and attempts to help from his teacher Mr. Steenwilly and another band member, Violet. At home he just tries to survive, especially since his mother works double shifts at a factory and is never there. He endures until he hears that his mother and "the man who is not my father" plan to marry and then he breaks down. Luckily Mr. Steenwilly intervenes when John returns home from a dance and Stan beats him severely, an act that opens John's mother eyes, and those of his community, to what's been happening to a young man who thinks no one knows him. (262 pages)

Where it's reviewed:
Booklist, March 1, 2001, page 1271
Horn Book, July 2001, page 455
Publishers Weekly, March 12, 2001, page 92
School Library Journal, March 2001, page 252
Voice of Youth Advocates, June 2001, page 123

Awards the book has won:
ALA Best Books for Young Adults, 2002

Other books by the same author:
Desperate Measures, 1998
Screen Test, 1997
Danger Zone, 1996
California Blue, 1994
A Different Season, 1988

Other books you might like:
Catherine Atkins, *When Jeff Comes Home*, 1999
　　Returned to his family after two and a half years of degradation at the hands of a kidnapper, Jeff finds it hard to adjust to normal life.
Glen Huser, *Touch of the Clown*, 1999
　　Though Cosmo's dying of cancer, he helps Barbara and her younger sister when they need a safe haven from their abusive father.
Rob Thomas, *Rats Saw God*, 1996
　　One English credit shy of graduation, Steve's guidance counselor suggests he write a 100-page essay about anything he knows.
Cynthia Voigt, *When She Hollers*, 1994
　　After years of sexual abuse by her stepfather, Tish comes to the breakfast table one morning with a knife and by day's end has a plan to stop him.

511

SHEILA SOLOMON KLASS

Little Women Next Door

(New York: Holiday House, 2000)

Subject(s): Family Life; Utopia/Dystopia; Friendship
Age range(s): Grades 4-8
Major character(s): Susan Wilson, 11-Year-Old; Louisa May Alcott, Historical Figure; Bronson Alcott, Historical Figure
Time period(s): 1840s (1843)
Locale(s): Massachusetts (near Harvard village)

Summary: Left motherless at the age of three weeks, Susan's intolerant father seems reminded only of his deceased wife when he interacts with Susan, which means there's little of a relationship between them. Lonely and hesitant to speak with strangers because of her stutter, Susan is initially shy when the Alcott family takes up residence on an adjoining farm, they call Fruitlands. Susan befriends the four girls, Anna, Louisa, Elizabeth and May, but becomes especially good friends with Louisa. Suddenly Susan's eyes are opened to the fun of having friends, being tutored by their brother, hearing the stories that Louisa writes and swinging on tree branches. Though the Alcotts experience their utopian venture for only

a year, it's enough time for Susan to realize the value education has for a girl, lose her stutter and learn to play a game of chess with her father. (188 pages)

Where it's reviewed:
Horn Book Guide, Spring 2001, page 75
Publishers Weekly, October 16, 2000, page 77
Riverbank Review, Spring 2001, page 42
School Library Journal, November 2000, page 157
Voice of Youth Advocates, April 2001, page 43

Other books by the same author:
The Uncivil War, 1998
A Shooting Star: A Novel about Annie Oakley, 1996
Rhino, 1993
The Bennington Stitch, 1985

Other books you might like:
Louisa May Alcott, *The Inheritance*, 1997
　　Reputed to have been written when the author was seventeen, this tale of a young orphan who becomes a wealthy woman turned up in family papers in the 1980s.
Louisa May Alcott, *Little Women*, 1868
　　This classic story of family life stars the four March sisters—Jo, Meg, Beth and Amy.
Jane Yolen, *The Gift of Sarah Barker*, 1981
　　Sister Sarah Barker and Brother Abel meet in a Shaker community but, once they fall in love, know they must leave the community if they hope to marry.

512

ELISA KLEVEN, Author/Illustrator

Sun Bread

(New York: Dutton Children's Books, 2001)

Subject(s): Food; Animals; Stories in Rhyme
Age range(s): Grades K-1
Major character(s): Unnamed Character, Dog, Baker
Time period(s): Indeterminate
Locale(s): Fictional Country

Summary: The dreary gray skies and cold wind of winter have the residents of a village wishing to see the sun again. The village baker tries to compensate by baking a huge, round, sunny loaf of bread. In the oven the dough seems to enlarge more than usual as the aroma attracts the residents to the bakery. The sight of the ''sun'' cheers everyone and samples of the warm bread fill the animals with thoughts of summer. The villagers' excited sounds awaken the sun and finally it breaks through the clouds to shine upon the village and add color and warmth to their world once again. (32 pages)

Where it's reviewed:
Booklist, May 1, 2001, page 1691
Horn Book Guide, Fall 2001, page 234
Kirkus Reviews, April 15, 2001, page 587
Publishers Weekly, May 21, 2001, page 106
School Library Journal, June 2001, page 122

Awards the book has won:
Parenting's Reading Magic Awards, 2001

Other books by the same author:
A Monster in the House, 1998

The Puddle Pail, 1997 (School Library Journal Best Book)
Hooray, a Pinata!, 1996 (Booklist Editors' Choice)

Other books you might like:
Betty G. Birney, *Pie's in the Oven*, 1996
  Grandma bakes an apple pie that attracts so many neighbors her grandson worries that there won't be any left for him.
Norah Dooley, *Everybody Bakes Bread*, 1996
  As Carrie visits the neighbors on a rainy day errand she is treated to a different kind of bread at each house in her multiethnic neighborhood.
Lynn Littlefield Hoopes, *The Unbeatable Bread*, 1996
  On a cold winter morning, Uncle John awakens with the desire to bake bread that is so unique it will wake the world and he succeeds.
Ferida Wolff, *Seven Loaves of Bread*, 1993
  The animals and neighbors depend on the bread Milly bakes and shares daily.

513

SUZY KLINE
FRANK REMKIEWICZ, Illustrator

Horrible Harry Goes to Sea
(New York: Viking, 2001)

Subject(s): Rivers; Boats and Boating; Schools
Age range(s): Grades 2-3
Major character(s): Miss Mackle, Teacher; Ida Burrell, 3rd Grader; Harry Spooger, 3rd Grader; Sidney LaFleur, 3rd Grader
Time period(s): 2000s (2001)
Locale(s): Connecticut

Summary: Inspired by Ida's report about an ancestor that sailed on the *Titanic* and survived, Miss Mackle's class researches other famous boats. In the process they discover a riverboat that sails the Connecticut River and plan a class trip on it. Even a trip on the river becomes exciting when Sidney can't be located and his hat is seen floating in the river. Harry's eager to rescue Sidney but the missing student is soon found in the snack area pretending to be a pirate, just like one of his ancestors, and wondering what's become of his hat. (58 pages)

Where it's reviewed:
Booklist, December 1, 2001, page 643
School Library Journal, November 2001, page 127

Other books by the same author:
Horrible Harry at Halloween, 2000
Horrible Harry Moves Up to Third Grade, 1998
Horrible Harry and the Purple People, 1997

Other books you might like:
Patricia Reilly Giff, *The Secret at the Polk Street School*, 1987
  One title in a series tells about the many adventures of students at Polk Street School.
Johanna Hurwitz, *Hurray for Ali Baba Bernstein*, 1989
  Expect the unexpected could be the motto for nine-year-old Ali Baba who rises above the turmoil.
Gina Willner-Pardo, *Spider Storch's Fumbled Field Trip*, 1998

Spider's teacher sends him back to the bus to wait for the class because of his misbehavior on a field trip.

514

KATE KLISE
M. SARAH KLISE, Illustrator

Trial by Jury/Journal
(New York: HarperCollins, 2001)

Subject(s): Diaries; Murder; Trials
Age range(s): Grades 5-8
Major character(s): Perry Keet, 6th Grader, Crime Victim; Lily Watson, 6th Grader, Juror; Anna Conda, Juror, Designer (of clothing); Fawn Papillon, Aged Person, Actress; Rhett Tyle, Wealthy, Businessman (zoo owner); Bob White, Crime Suspect
Time period(s): 2000s
Locale(s): Tyleville, Missouri

Summary: Because of a new state law, Lily is selected to be the first-ever juvenile juror in the state of Missouri. Thrilled though she is to have this honor, she's not happy that her teacher has turned it into an assignment and she's now required to keep a journal about the trial. Lily takes her task seriously, though, and collects newspaper accounts, interviews, notes to the jury and anything else she can find. The murder is premised on the disappearance, and presumed death, of young Perry Keet while volunteering at the zoo and Bob White is on trial for his murder. Zoo owner Rhett Tyle, and his girlfriend and jury member Anna Conda, are two regulars at the trial who seem to be hiding secrets. Lily's happy to make friends with Fawn Papillon, united by their joint writing projects as Fawn struggles to write her autobiography and Lily continues with her journal in this humorous take on a murder trial. (238 pages)

Where it's reviewed:
Booklist, September 1, 2001, page 106
Bulletin of the Center for Children's Books, April 2001, page 306
Horn Book, May 2001, page 328
Publishers Weekly, April 30, 2001, page 78
School Library Journal, June 2001, page 152

Other books by the same author:
Letters from Camp, 2000
Regarding the Fountain, 1999

Other books you might like:
Avi, *Nothing but the Truth*, 1991
  A student attempts to get out of homeroom by whistling through the National Anthem and the media blows the incident out of proportion.
Walter Dean Myers, *Darnell Rock Reporting*, 1994
  Though Darnell doesn't want to join the school newspaper, he's pleased when people pay attention to his words and respect his thoughts and ideas.
Todd Strasser, *Give a Boy a Gun*, 2000
  Interviews, coupled with facts about other shootings, tell the story of two boys who attend their school's dance and gun down students and teachers.

515

RON KOERTGE

The Brimstone Journals

(Cambridge, MA: Candlewick Press, 2001)

Subject(s): Violence; Schools/High Schools; Poetry
Age range(s): Grades 7-10
Major character(s): Boyd, 12th Grader
Time period(s): 2000s
Locale(s): United States

Summary: Through short poems fifteen students at Branston High School reveal problems experienced during their senior year in high school. The fifteen represent a wide range of students, from one struggling with anorexia to one who's being sexually abused, or from one who's very wealthy to one who's concerned about the environment. The students are linked together by Boyd, an angry young man, who believes that the only rule to follow is to break all the rules. Boyd has made a list of anyone and everyone who's ever made him mad, has built up an arsenal, and is ready to take action on Tuesday during first period. Luckily he reveals his plans to enough people that someone finally takes the initiative to call the police in this chilling look at high school today. (113 pages)

Where it's reviewed:
Booklist, April 15, 2001, page 1548
Bulletin of the Center for Children's Books, April 2001, page 307
Kliatt, March 2001, page 12
Publishers Weekly, February 12, 2001, page 213
Voice of Youth Advocates, August 2001, page 203

Awards the book has won:
ALA Best Books for Young Adults, 2002

Other books by the same author:
Confess-O-Rama, 1996
Tiger, Tiger, Burning Bright, 1994
The Harmony Arms, 1992
Mariposa Blues, 1991
The Boy in the Moon, 1990

Other books you might like:
Fran Arrick, *Where'd You Get the Gun, Billy?*, 1991
   Billy finds a Smith and Wesson .38 Chief Special and stuns his community when he shoots his girlfriend Lisa.
Walter Dean Myers, *Monster*, 1999
   Sixteen-year-old Steve narrates his trial from his jail cell, a trial to establish his role in the murder of a Harlem drug store owner.
Todd Strasser, *Give a Boy a Gun*, 2000
   Student interviews, coupled with facts about shootings, describe two unhappy boys who attend their school's dance and shoot students and teachers.
Virginia Walter, *Making Up Megaboy*, 1998
   One day Robbie Jones takes his father's gun, rides his bike to the liquor store and shoots Mr. Koh, though no one knows why.

516

MARC KORNBLATT

Understanding Buddy

(New York: Margaret K. McElderry/Simon & Schuster, 2001)

Subject(s): Sports/Soccer; Mutism; Grief
Age range(s): Grades 4-6
Major character(s): Sam Keeperman, 5th Grader; Buddy White, 5th Grader; Alex Kohler, 5th Grader
Time period(s): 2000s
Locale(s): Madison, Wisconsin

Summary: Sam is saddened to hear that his family's housekeeper died when her car hit a deer. Soon after, her son Buddy transfers to Sam's class, but only Sam knows that Buddy doesn't talk because he's grieving for his mother. When Buddy wears one of Sam's old shirts to school, Sam's best friend Alex and some other kids tease him about it, which sends Buddy deeper into his shell. Attempts are made to converse with Buddy, but it's only on the soccer field that Buddy begins to open up a little bit. With a mutual interest in soccer, Sam wants to be Buddy's friend though he knows to let the relationship develop at its own speed. (113 pages)

Where it's reviewed:
Book Report, November 2001, page 64
Booklist, February 1, 2001, page 1052
Bulletin of the Center for Children's Books, March 2001, page 268
Horn Book, March 2001, page 209
School Library Journal, April 2001, page 144

Other books by the same author:
Paul Revere and the Boston Tea Party, 1987 (Time Traveler, Number 5)
Flame of the Inquisition, 1986 (Time Machine, Number 15)
Mission to World War II, 1986 (Time Machine, Number 11)

Other books you might like:
Gerald Hausman, *Night Flight*, 1996
   Jeff and Max's friendship is strained when half-Jewish Jeff realizes Max's has a prejudiced attitude toward Jews.
Klaus Kordan, *Brothers Like Friends*, 1992
   Young Frank adores his older, half-brother Burkie and is devastated when a soccer injury proves fatal to him after World War II.
Cynthia Rylant, *Missing May*, 1992
   After Aunt May dies, Uncle Ob's hand-carved whirligigs stop and both he and Summer take time to grieve.

517

LYNNE KOSITSKY

A Question of Will

(Montreal: Roussan, 2000)

Series: Out of This World
Subject(s): Theater; Actors and Actresses; Historical
Age range(s): Grades 6-9
Major character(s): Perin ''Willow'' Willoughby, Time Traveler, Actor; John Pyke, Actor; William Shakespeare, His-

torical Figure, Writer (playwright); Edward de Vere, Historical Figure, Nobleman (Earl of Oxford)

Time period(s): 16th century

Locale(s): London, England

Summary: Part of a group studying in London, Perin is bored out of her mind listening to Mrs. Smithson lecture about William Shakespeare. Just as she thinks she'll keel over, the class is dismissed for their field trip and Perin finds herself once again trying to catch up with everyone else as they scurry to The Globe Theater. For a moment her vision blurs and when her focus returns she's clinging to a young man and all of London looks different. Luckily her smelly, dusty companion, named John Pyke, is heading toward the Theater where Will Shakespeare and his Chamberlain's Men perform. Not wanting to contradict everyone's assumption that she's a boy, Perin says her name is Willow and becomes Shakespeare's apprentice. Theories about Shakespeare's writing, his connection with Edward de Vere, who may have written some of the plays, and life in sixteenth century London fill the pages of this humorous work. (141 pages)

Where it's reviewed:
Kliatt, September 2001, page 24
Resource Links, October 2000, page 28
School Library Journal, November 2001, page 160
Voice of Youth Advocates, October 2001, page 291

Other books by the same author:
Rebecca's Flame, 1999
Candles, 1998 (Beloved Books)

Other books you might like:
Gary L. Blackwood, *The Shakespeare Stealer*, 1998
    Sent to copy Shakespeare's last play, Widge loses his duplicate and joins the cast to hunt for his illegal script of *The Tragedy of Hamlet*.
J.B. Cheaney, *The Playmaker*, 2000
    After his mother's death, Richard travels to London where he's lucky enough to find a job as an actor with Lord Chamberlain's Men.
Susan Cooper, *King of Shadows*, 1999
    In London to perform a Shakespearean play, Nat time travels to the 1590s where he has the part of Puck opposite Oberon as played by William Shakespeare.

518

AMY GOLDMAN KOSS

Stolen Words

(Middleton, WI: American Girl/Pleasant Company, 2001)

Series: AG Fiction

Subject(s): Vacations; Aunts and Uncles; Diaries

Age range(s): Grades 5-7

Major character(s): Robyn Gittleman, 11-Year-Old; Beth, Aunt

Time period(s): 2000s

Locale(s): Vienna, Austria

Summary: Robyn's family is on vacation, the first fun activity they've shared since their aunt Beth was killed in an automobile accident and Robyn's mother sank into depression. Robyn brings the journal Aunt Beth gave her and plans to

record the activities of their trip, but the first day they're in Vienna their luggage is stolen. Determined to fulfill Aunt Beth's wish for her to write daily, she begins another one and details not only their sightseeing but also everyone's attempt to come to terms with Aunt Beth's death. (145 pages)

Where it's reviewed:
Booklist, September 15, 2001, page 223
Kirkus Reviews, September 1, 2001, page 1293
Publishers Weekly, October 15, 2001, page 73
Voice of Youth Advocates, February 2002, page 436

Other books by the same author:
The Cheat, 2003
Strike Two, 2001
Smoke Screen, 2000
The Girls, 2000
The Ashwater Experiment, 1999

Other books you might like:
Sharon Creech, *Chasing Redbird*, 1997
    A project to clear a twenty-mile trail helps Zinn clear her mind about her aunt's death and other mysterious aspects of her family.
Iris Rosofsky, *My Aunt Ruth*, 1991
    Patty's glamorous Aunt Ruth, the soap opera actress, seems so lucky until she loses her legs to diabetes.
Carol Weston, *The Diary of Melanie Martin: Or How I Survived Matt the Brat, Michelangelo and the Leaning Tower of Pizza*, 2000
    Spending spring vacation in Italy is pretty exciting for Melanie, even though she has to put up with her six-year-old brother Matt.

519

AMY GOLDMAN KOSS

Stranger in Dadland

(New York: Dial Press, 2001)

Subject(s): Fathers and Sons; Interpersonal Relations; Divorce

Age range(s): Grades 4-7

Major character(s): John, 12-Year-Old; Beau Lubeck, 8th Grader; Cora, Girlfriend (of John's father); Iris, Niece (of Cora), 15-Year-Old; Matt, Father (of John)

Time period(s): 2000s

Locale(s): Los Angeles, California

Summary: Once again it's time for their annual week-long visit to their father in Los Angeles, but this summer Liz refuses to go because, as she explains, "There's just no room for me in Dadland." And she's right; Liz and John's father is either in a meeting or talking on the phone. John isn't ready to give up on his dad, so he flies from his home in Kansas and, sure enough, the first person he meets at the airport is the girlfriend of the summer, Cora. For the first three days he waits for his dad while he's in meetings, or he swims with Beau, a neighbor boy who knows more about his dad than John does, or they visit Cora and her niece Iris. The day comes when a beach trip is cancelled which allows John and his dad go rollerblading, but when his dad falls down and his knee swells up, they head to the hospital. Once Matt is incapacitated and can't go to work, he and John finally have a chance to get to know one another and "Dadland" becomes a happier place. (119 pages)

Where it's reviewed:
Booklist, March 1, 2001, page 1278
Horn Book, March 2001, page 210
Publishers Weekly, April 2, 2001, page 66
School Library Journal, March 2001, page 252
Voice of Youth Advocates, April 2001, page 43

Other books by the same author:
Stolen Words, 2001
Strike Two, 2001
Smoke Screen, 2000
The Girls, 2000
The Ashwater Experiment, 1999

Other books you might like:
Paula Danziger, *The Divorce Express*, 1982
Phoebe feels as though she's on the "divorce express" as she divides her time between her divorced parents.
Ron Koertge, *The Harmony Arms*, 1992
When Ron stays with his father at The Harmony Arms in Los Angeles, he meets so many eccentric people it makes his own father look normal.
Stella Pevsner, *Is Everyone Moonburned but Me?*, 2000
Hannah's parents are divorced and she toys with the idea of living with her father until she meets his girlfriend and her obnoxious son.

520

AMY GOLDMAN KOSS

Strike Two
(New York: Dial, 2001)

Subject(s): Sports/Softball; Cousins; Strikes and Lockouts
Age range(s): Grades 4-7
Major character(s): Gwendolyn "Gwen", Softball Player, Cousin; Jessica, Softball Player, Cousin
Time period(s): 2000s
Locale(s): United States

Summary: Cousins Gwen and Jess are almost like sisters, they're such good friends. Their fathers are twins who work for the *Press Gazette*, which sponsors the softball team the girls play on. All Gwen can think about is a summer filled with softball; even when her father announces he's on strike from the newspaper, she doesn't understand the ramifications of a strike. At first walking the picket line is fun, and seeing her dad every day is a rare treat, but she tires of his taking her to the pool or to the movies—these are activities she does with her friends. Then there are all the problems the strikes creates with her family for Jess's father is management and now works long hours and is never home. But worst of all for Gwen is the dissension on the softball team when strike problems show up at their field and her friendship with Jess is threatened. (134 pages)

Where it's reviewed:
Booklist, November 1, 2001, page 475
Bulletin of the Center for Children's Books, October 2001, page 63
Kliatt, September 2001, page 10

School Library Journal, September 2001, page 226
Voice of Youth Advocates, October 2001, page 280

Other books by the same author:
Stolen Words, 2001
Stranger in Dadland, 2001
Smoke Screen, 2000
The Girls, 2000
The Ashwater Experiment, 1999

Other books you might like:
James Lincoln Collier, *The Winchesters*, 1988
Though poor relations, when his uncle's employees at the factory go on strike, Chris is considered one of the "rich Winchesters."
Sue Macy, *Girls Got Game: Sports Stories & Poems*, 2001
Nine poems and an equal number of short stories describe some of the vast array of sports in which women are now able to participate.
Virginia Euwer Wolff, *Bat 6*, 1998
Two Oregon farm communities play softball against each other every summer, but this year racist feelings from World War II create trouble for both teams.

521

STEPHEN KRENSKY
S.D. SCHINDLER, Illustrator

How Santa Lost His Job
(New York: Simon & Schuster Books for Young Readers, 2001)

Subject(s): Elves; Santa Claus; Christmas
Age range(s): Grades K-3
Major character(s): Santa, Mythical Creature, Aged Person; Muckle, Mythical Creature (elf), Inventor; Clara, Postal Worker, Friend
Time period(s): Indeterminate
Locale(s): Fictional Country

Summary: The pre-Christmas Eve routine that Santa follows annually causes too much last-minute commotion in the opinion of efficient Muckle. Secretly, Muckle works on an idea to replace Santa. Despite Clara's attempts to explain to Muckle that Santa's job requires more than Muckle's invention, the *Deliverator* can do, the elves are so impressed with the machine's efficiency that they fire Santa. On Christmas Eve, loaded with toys, *Deliverator* takes off, only to fly in circles before crashing in the snow. Sheepishly the elves offer the job to Santa and the reindeer and no one tries to invent a replacement for him again. (32 pages)

Where it's reviewed:
Booklist, September 15, 2001, page 235
Bulletin of the Center for Children's Books, November 2001, page 106
Publishers Weekly, September 24, 2001, page 55
School Library Journal, October 2001, page 67

Other books by the same author:
How Santa Got His Job, 1998 (ALA Notable Children's Book)
We Just Moved!, 1998
My Teacher's Secret Life, 1996

Other books you might like:

Dean Morrissey, *The Christmas Ship*, 2000
    To help Father Christmas deliver gifts Joey and Sam the toymaker climb aboard a magical ship.

Tom Paxton, *The Story of Santa Claus*, 1995
    When an overworked woodcarver moves to the North Pole to receive help from elves with his toy production, he then must initiate a delivery system.

Tracey Campbell Pearson, *Where Does Joe Go?*, 1999
    The townspeople wonder where Joe, operator of a summer snack bar in town, goes each winter.

Elise Primavera, *Auntie Claus*, 1999
    By stowing away in Auntie Claus's luggage Sophie is able to learn the truth about Auntie Claus's annual winter business trip.

522

STEVEN KROLL

John Quincy Adams: Letters from a Southern Planter's Son
(New York: Winslow, 2001)

Series: Dear Mr. President
Subject(s): Indians of North America; Letters; Presidents
Age range(s): Grades 5-8
Major character(s): William Pratt, 12-Year-Old; John Quincy Adams, Political Figure (president), Historical Figure
Time period(s): 1820s (1825-1827)
Locale(s): Baldwin County, Georgia; Washington, District of Columbia; Quincy, Massachusetts

Summary: Upon the election of John Quincy Adams to the presidency, young William Pratt writes him a letter about the unfairness of the Treaty of Indian Springs, which took Indian land on the east of the Mississippi for white settlers and repaid the Indians with the same amount of land on the west side of the Mississippi. He wonders why the Indians can't just be left alone and states his views in his letter, views that spur Adams on to examine the treaty more closely. Their correspondence continues over several years as William describes his plantation life to Adams, with his feelings about slavery, a Christmas dinner, his school day and the planting season. In return, some of Adams's eccentricities emerge, such as his skinny-dipping in the Potomac River, along with his natural intelligence in this continuing series. (121 pages)

Where it's reviewed:
Booklist, January 2002, page 858
School Library Journal, December 2001, page 138

Other books by the same author:
Sweet America: An Immigrant's Story, 2000 (Jamestown's American Portraits)
When I Dream of Heaven: Angelina's Story, 2000 (Jamestown's American Portraits)

Other books you might like:

Jennifer Armstrong, *Theodore Roosevelt: Letters from a Young Coal Miner*, 2001
    A feeling of warmth and respect fills the letters between two unlikely correspondents, the coal miner Frank Kovacs and the president Teddy Roosevelt.

Jennifer Armstrong, *Thomas Jefferson: Letters from a Philadelphia Bookworm*, 2001
    Through a series of letters over five years, Amelia Hornsby of Philadelphia writes President Jefferson with her observations on the news of the day.

William Forrest, *Trail of Tears*, 1959
    When gold is found on Cherokee land in Georgia, the government forces the Indians out of their homes and marches them to Oklahoma.

Maureen Stock Sappey, *Letters from Vinnie*, 1999
    Vinnie is a great admirer of President Lincoln and wins a commission to sculpt a life-size statue of him to be placed in the Rotunda of the Capitol.

523

STEVEN KROLL
BARRY GOTT, Illustrator

Patches Lost and Found
(New York: Winslow Press, 2001)

Subject(s): Lost and Found; Animals/Guinea Pigs; Authorship
Age range(s): Grades K-3
Major character(s): Jenny, Child, Student—Elementary School; Patches, Guinea Pig; Mr. Griswold, Teacher
Time period(s): 2000s (2001)
Locale(s): United States

Summary: Jenny enjoys drawing pictures and playing with Patches, but writing is not as pleasurable as art. So, the day Mr. Griswold gives the class an assignment to write a story and Jenny arrives home to discover that Patches is lost, it is truly a sad day for her. She uses her artistic talent to make posters about Patches that she puts up all over the neighborhood. When she isn't searching the house or the yard, Jenny is drawing pictures of her fears about what has happened to Patches, but she is not completing her writing assignment because she has no ideas for a topic. Finally a neighbor discovers Patches in his yard and Jenny's mother helps her see that her pictures tell a wonderful story that only needs her words in order to complete Mr. Griswold's assignment. (32 pages)

Where it's reviewed:
Booklist, March 1, 2001, page 1277
Children's Bookwatch, August 2001, page 4
Horn Book Guide, Fall 2001, page 263
Kirkus Reviews, January 15, 2001, page 111
School Library Journal, May 2001, page 126

Awards the book has won:
Booklist Editors' Choice/Books for Youth, 2002

Other books by the same author:
Oh, Tucker!, 1998
The Pigrates Clean Up, 1993
The Magic Rocket, 1992

Other books you might like:
Jonathan Langley, *Missing!*, 2000
    When a school vacation changes Daisy's routine, her cat Lupin thinks something is wrong and Daisy thinks her cat is lost.

William Mayne, *Barnabas Walks*, 1986
When a guinea pig gets out of his cage in a classroom, a cat chases him.

Holly Meade, *John Willy and Freddy McGee*, 1998
Two bored guinea pigs escape through their open cage door and enjoy an afternoon of adventure running and hiding from the other pets.

JANE KURTZ

Jakarta Missing
(New York: HarperCollins, 2001)

Subject(s): Moving, Household; Family Life; Sisters
Age range(s): Grades 5-8
Major character(s): Dakar, 12-Year-Old; Jakarta, Sister (of Dakar), Basketball Player
Time period(s): 2000s
Locale(s): Nairobi, Kenya; Cottonwood, North Dakota

Summary: Having been brought up in various African countries while her do-gooder father helps occupants of third world countries, Dakar readjusts when her mother decides to return to her childhood home in North Dakota. Could there be greater distance between locales than Africa and North Dakota? Dakar has always been a fearful child, but with the presence of her older sister Jakarta, she's always managed to overcome those fears. Now Jakarta remains in Nairobi at her boarding school and Dakar's on her own. Before her dad whirls away on another rescue mission, this time to Guatemala, and her mother leaves to nurse a sick aunt, Jakarta luckily returns home after a bombing near her school so Dakar has the help she needs. Jakarta is unhappy at her change of scenery and throws herself into basketball, quickly becoming a star on her team. Though the family still seems to be at loose ends, unsure of where they want to live, Dakar knows she needs to put down roots and have a sense of family. (268 pages)

Where it's reviewed:
Bulletin of the Center for Children's Books, May 2001, page 341
Kliatt, March 2001, page 12
Publishers Weekly, April 2, 2001, page 65
School Library Journal, May 2001, page 154
Voice of Youth Advocates, June 2001, page 142

Other books by the same author:
Rain Romp, 2002
I'm Sorry, Almira Ann, 1999
The Storyteller's Beads, 1998

Other books you might like:
Joan Abelove, *Go and Come Back*, 1998
A visit by anthropologists to Alicia's Peruvian tribe teaches both groups about other cultures.

Hadley Irwin, *Sarah with an H*, 1996
Marti understands herself better after she witnesses the prejudice that fellow basketball player Jewish Sarah has to put up with during a game.

Barbara Kingsolver, *The Poisonwood Bible*, 1998
Determined to save the natives, missionary Nathan is unaware of the needs of both his family and the Congolese people in this adult title.

L

525

OFELIA DUMAS LACHTMAN

The Summer of El Pintor
(Houston: Arte Publico, 2001)

Subject(s): Moving, Household; Mystery and Detective Stories; Mexican Americans
Age range(s): Grades 7-10
Major character(s): Monica Ramos, 16-Year-Old; Antonia "Toni" Almayo, Teenager; Rob Almayo, Student—College; Francis "El Pintor" Mead, Artist, Grandfather
Time period(s): 2000s
Locale(s): Los Angeles, California

Summary: An embarrassing scandal forces Monica's naive father to resign from his high-level government job and spend all his savings on legal fees. The two return to Los Angeles to live in her deceased mother's childhood home in the barrio, where they are just grateful to have shelter. Though Monica misses her affluent lifestyle, she meets Toni and her older brother Rob and her neighbors are friendly and ready to help when her dad's out of town on business. She finds an old letter addressed to her mother from the painter El Pintor, a next-door neighbor, but the instructions warn not to open the letter and he is nowhere to be found. Rob and Monica finally locate him and discover that El Pintor is also Monica's grandfather. (235 pages)

Where it's reviewed:
Booklist, August 2001, page 2107
Publishers Weekly, June 4, 2001, page 81
School Library Journal, July 2001, page 110
Voice of Youth Advocates, December 2001, page 360

Other books by the same author:
Girl from Playa Blanca, 1999
Call Me Consuelo, 1997
Leticia's Secret, 1997

Other books you might like:
Diane Gonzales Bertrand, *Lessons of the Game*, 1999
  Concentrating on her first teaching job, Kaylene tries not to be distracted by Coach Garrison on whom she's had a crush for ten years.
Lori M. Carlson, *Barrio Streets, Carnival Dreams*, 1996
  Writers of Mexican, Cuban or Puerto Rican descent contribute writings descriptive of their cultural traditions.
Danny Santiago, *Famous All over Town*, 1983
  A realistic tale of a young Mexican American's life in a California barrio.

526

MERCEDES LACKEY

The Serpent's Shadow
(New York: DAW, 2001)

Subject(s): Magic; Romance
Age range(s): Grades 8-Adult
Major character(s): Maya Witherspoon, Doctor, Witch; Shavani, Witch, Aunt (of Maya); Peter Scott, Warlock
Time period(s): 1900s (1909)
Locale(s): London, England

Summary: The child of an Indian mother and an English father, Maya Witherspoon is accustomed to being a little different from her associates. When both her parents die in mysterious circumstances, Maya senses a magical danger in her native India that sends her across the world to England. Her mother had always told Maya that her magical talents lay in her father's native soil and that her teacher must perforce be from that land. Victorian England has plenty of other challenges for a young lady doctor who travels with two Indian servants and a menagerie that includes a monkey, a peacock, a falcon, a pair of mongooses and other exotic pets. In London, Maya must not only support her establishment, and ward off the danger coming from the aunt she has never known, but learn the magic she was born with from Peter Scott, an attractive but mysterious Englishman. (343 pages)

Where it's reviewed:
Booklist, February 15, 2001, page 1122
Kirkus Reviews, January 1, 2001, page 22
Library Journal, February 15, 2001, page 205

Locus, February 2001, page 27
Science Fiction Chronicle, February 2001, page 42

Awards the book has won:
Booklist Editors' Choice/Books for Young Adults, 2001

Other books by the same author:
Beyond World's End, 2001
Brightly Burning, 2000
The Black Swan, 1999

Other books you might like:
Glen Cook, *Water Sleeps*, 1999
   This tale of mercenaries and survival has its source in Indian mythology.
Barry Hughart, *Eight Skilled Gentlemen*, 1991
   A young man finds himself fleeing ancient Chinese demons while carrying a wise old man on his back; good thing his name is Number Ten Ox.
Philip Pullman, *The Ruby in the Smoke*, 1985
   Sally finds her father's Indian past comes to haunt her in Victorian London.

527
A. LAFAYE

Dad, in Spirit
(New York: Simon & Schuster Books for Young Readers, 2001)

Subject(s): Family; Fathers and Sons; Accidents
Age range(s): Grades 3-6
Major character(s): Ebon Jones, 9-Year-Old, Brother; Luke "Dad" Jones, Father, Researcher; Belinda Jane "B.J." Taggert, Friend (Ebon's), Neighbor
Time period(s): 2000s
Locale(s): Minneapolis, Minnesota

Summary: Ebon is sure that Dad, the consummate researcher, could explain what is happening. How can Dad, lying comatose in a hospital, appear in a spirit form to Ebon? Soon Ebon realizes that each time Dad's spirit leaves his body, alarm bells ring in his room as the hospitalized patient takes a turn for the worse. With help from B.J., Ebon tries to solve the mystery and figure out how to get Dad's spirit to stay in his body so he can recover and return permanently and completely to his family. (165 pages)

Where it's reviewed:
Booklist, July 2001, page 2006
Bulletin of the Center for Children's Books, July 2001, page 412
Kirkus Reviews, April 15, 2001, page 588
Publishers Weekly, June 4, 2001, page 81
School Library Journal, June 2001, page 152

Other books by the same author:
Nissa's Place, 1999
Strawberry Hill, 1999
The Year of the Sawdust Man, 1998

Other books you might like:
Peni R. Griffin, *Margo's House*, 1996
   Margo can't explain the astral projection happening to her but she knows the experience is an essential part of her unconscious father's recovery.

Ian McEwan, *The Daydreamer*, 1994
   Peter daydreams so much that he's not always sure when experiences are real and when they are imagined.
Emily Rodda, *The Timekeeper*, 1993
   Racing against time, Patrick travels to another dimension for help repairing a critical timepiece and then must save his siblings who follow him.

528
LESLIE LAFOY

Jackson's Way
(New York: Bantam, 2001)

Subject(s): American West; Romance
Age range(s): Grades 10-Adult
Major character(s): Jackson Stennett, Rancher; Billy Lindsay Weathers, Rancher; Lindsay MacPhaull, Businesswoman (manager)
Time period(s): 1830s
Locale(s): Texas; New York, New York

Summary: When Billy Weathers dies, Jackson inherits a ranch and a whole mess of trouble. A partner for seventeen years, Billy was also a father figure for Jackson whom he'd taken in when he was just a scared, angry teenager. Jackson knew the ranch had some debts, but Billy's legacies to others add to that debt, along with the news that Billy left behind three children. Told that he also inherits Billy's property in New York, Jackson travels there and meets his daughter Lindsay who's been managing the family business. They're forced to work together because the MacPhaull business is in trouble and requires shoring up, while Jackson needs the money to pay off the debts of the ranch. They have only sixty days to straighten out the finances, which might be possible; except that Jackson and Lindsay are trying to pretend they're not smitten over one another. (391 pages)

Where it's reviewed:
Booklist, September 15, 2001, page 208

Other books by the same author:
Come What May, 2002
Maddie's Justice, 2001
Daring the Devil, 1999

Other books you might like:
Lorraine Heath, *The Outlaw and the Lady*, 2001
   Angela Bainbridge can't believe the outlaw Lee Raven has kidnapped her, but does she really want to be rescued?
Meagan McKinney, *No Choice but Surrender*, 1998
   When Lady Morrow travels to her father's mansion, she finds American Avenel Slane has claimed it to settle a gambling debt.
Karen Robards, *Green Eyes*, 1990
   Anna is astounded that a jewel thief she met in England has followed her all the way to Ceylon.

529

PATRICIA LAKIN
STACEY SCHUETT, Illustrator

Fat Chance Thanksgiving
(Morton Grove, IL: Albert Whitman & Company, 2001)

Subject(s): Holidays; Neighbors and Neighborhoods; Apartments
Age range(s): Grades 1-3
Major character(s): Carla, Daughter, Student—Elementary School; Mama, Mother, Single Parent; Julio, Classmate, Neighbor
Time period(s): 2000s
Locale(s): New York, New York

Summary: For a year after a fire destroys their apartment building Carla reads her only surviving possession *A Pilgrim's Thanksgiving* nightly and imagines being a pilgrim girl at the feast table. A few weeks before Thanksgiving Mama and Carla move into another apartment and Carla begs Mama to have a Thanksgiving feast. ''Fat chance'' is Mama's reply considering the size of the apartment and their financial straits. Undeterred, Carla enlists the help of Julio and by Thanksgiving Day the residents of the building come together at a table set up in the building's lobby for a potluck feast. (32 pages)

Where it's reviewed:
Booklist, September 1, 2001, page 119
Bulletin of the Center for Children's Books, October 2001, page 64
Horn Book Guide, Spring 2002, page 48
Kirkus Reviews, August 15, 2001, page 1215
School Library Journal, October 2001, page 123

Other books by the same author:
Subway Sonata, 2001
The Little Mermaid, 1998
Dad and Me in the Morning, 1994
Don't Forget, 1994
The Palace of Stars, 1993

Other books you might like:
Joy Cowley, *Gracias, the Thanksgiving Turkey*, 1996
Thanksgiving dinner at Miguel's house is a roasted chicken rather than the turkey Miguel considers a pet.
Gail Gibbons, *Thanksgiving Day*, 1983
Simple text explains both the first Thanksgiving and the way we now celebrate the holiday.
Marion Hess Pomeranc, *The Can-Do Thanksgiving*, 1998
For Dee, Thanksgiving is especially meaningful this year when she helps a church feed the needy.
Sylvia Rosa-Casanova, *Mama Provi and the Pot of Rice*, 1997
Each neighbor in Mama Provi's apartment building offers an ethnic food for her to take to her sick granddaughter.

530

C. DREW LAMM
STACEY SCHUETT, Illustrator

Pirates
(New York: Hyperion Books for Children, 2001)

Subject(s): Pirates; Books and Reading; Brothers and Sisters
Age range(s): Grades 2-4
Major character(s): Ellery, Sister (older); Max, Brother (younger)
Time period(s): 2000s (2001)
Locale(s): United States

Summary: On a stormy night Ellery ignores Max's suggestions that she read books on some subject other than pirates. Despite Max's apparent fear, Ellery insists they read the books in the dark with only a flashlight and then she embellishes the tale so much that she begins to feel a little frightened too. When the flashlight dies, Ellery realizes that Max has vanished. Max isn't far; he's just making his point about choosing a different book. (34 pages)

Where it's reviewed:
Booklist, November 1, 2001, page 476
Kirkus Reviews, September 1, 2001, page 1294
Publishers Weekly, October 8, 2001, page 65
School Library Journal, November 2001, page 127

Other books by the same author:
The Prog Frince: A Mixed-Up Tale, 1999
Sea Lion Roars, 1997
Screech Owl at Midnight Hollow, 1996

Other books you might like:
Allan Ahlberg, *It Was a Dark and Stormy Night*, 1994
Kidnapped by a band of outlaws, Antonio skillfully crafts a tale that enables him to sneak away.
Rachel Isadora, *The Pirates of Bedford Street*, 1988
After Joey watches a pirate movie with his sisters he continues to imagine the action.
David McPhail, *Edward and the Pirates*, 1997
While Edward reads the stories come alive for him so vividly that he's kidnapped by the pirates in his book and must be saved by other literary heroes.

 531

LORNA LANDVIK

Welcome to the Great Mysterious
(New York: Ballantine, 2000)

Subject(s): Actors and Actresses; Down Syndrome; Romance
Age range(s): Grades 10-Adult
Major character(s): Geneva Jordan, Aunt, Singer (Broadway musicals); Rich, Nephew (of Geneva's), Mentally Challenged Person (Down syndrome); Conrad Torgerson, Handicapped (cerebral palsy); James O'Neal, Musician (pianist), Postal Worker
Time period(s): 2000s
Locale(s): New York, New York (Manhattan); Deep Lake, Minnesota

Summary: Though Geneva is used to playing a starring role on Broadway, her recent breakup with a boyfriend, along with her twin sister's request for help, send her to a small town in Minnesota where she will baby-sit her nephew. Rich has Down syndrome and his best friend Conrad has cerebral palsy, but Geneva handles her child-care activities with great determination and only a few mistakes. Small town life is a change of pace for Geneva and playing one day with Rich, they find an old box of toys that contains the scrapbook Geneva and her twin assembled years earlier. Called "The Great Mysterious," it contains questions about the meaning of life and responses from other family members, all of which start Geneva thinking about the life she's led. Meeting James, who himself led a career on stage, makes Geneva realize there are intriguing men who don't have the bad habit of falling for young actresses. This reevaluation of life offers Geneva choices she'd never before considered in a book filled with love. (324 pages)

Where it's reviewed:
Booklist, October 15, 2000, page 419
Kirkus Reviews, August 1, 2000, page 1062
Library Journal, August 2000, page 158
Publishers Weekly, July 31, 2000, page 67

Other books by the same author:
The Tall Pine Polka, 1999
Patty Jane's House of Curl, 1997
Your Oasis on Flame Lake, 1997

Other books you might like:
Sandra Dallas, *Alice's Tulips*, 2000
    Alice's cheerfulness is misinterpreted when her husband is away fighting in the Civil War, but luckily her mother-in-law defends her actions.
S.L. Rottman, *Head above Water*, 1999
    Skye feels her life overwhelming her when her boyfriend demands her time, time she should be spending with her Down syndrome brother Sunny.
Lee Smith, *Family Linen*, 1985
    A family funeral brings the relatives together and soon the family's dirty linen is aired in the light of a small Southern town.

GLENNA LANG, Author/Illustrator

Looking Out for Sarah
(Watertown, MA: Talewinds/Charlesbridge Publishing, 2001)

Subject(s): Animals/Dogs; Blindness; Work
Age range(s): Grades K-3
Major character(s): Sarah, Blind Person, Teacher; Perry, Dog
Time period(s): 2000s (2001)
Locale(s): Massachusetts

Summary: Perry enjoys his days of work with Sarah. A morning of errands takes Sarah and Perry to the grocery and the post office. As the only dog allowed in the grocery store Perry can savor the coolness of the floor and warm smells from the bakery. After returning home for water and a rest, Perry returns to work guiding Sarah and her guitar through the crowded train station so Sarah can travel to one of her schools for a music class. Later in the day Sarah and Perry go to the park for a game of catch, a time when Perry is free from the working harness. The first book also written by this children's book illustrator concludes with the factual basis for the story. (32 pages)

Where it's reviewed:
Booklist, November 1, 2001, page 483
Horn Book, September 2001, page 575
Kirkus Reviews, August 1, 2001, page 1127
Publishers Weekly, August 27, 2001, page 87
School Library Journal, September 2001, page 193

Other books you might like:
Caroline Arnold, *A Guide Dog Puppy Grows Up*, 1991
    A nonfiction title illustrated with photographs chronicles the raising of a puppy, its training as a guide dog and final placement with a blind person.
Eva Moore, *Buddy, the First Seeing Eye Dog*, 1996
    This "Hello Reader" title describes the early work experience of the first dog in America to be trained as a guide dog for the blind.
Nan Parsons Rossiter, *Rugby and Rosie*, 1997
    A family raises a puppy in preparation for its training as a guide dog for the blind.

MICHAEL LASER

6-321
(New York: Atheneum/Simon & Schuster, 2001)

Subject(s): School Life; Interpersonal Relations
Age range(s): Grades 5-7
Major character(s): Marc Chaikin, 6th Grader; Lily Wu, 6th Grader; John Fitzgerald Kennedy, Historical Figure, Government Official (president)
Time period(s): 1960s
Locale(s): New York, New York (Queens)

Summary: As Marc reviews his sixth grade year, he thinks about all that occurred in such a short amount of time. When he began the school year, his parents were together, he had never fallen in love and JFK was the president. Now it's all different. His high-ability class 6-321 is being bullied by the low-ability group in 6-309, his parents have separated and Marc and another boy in his class are competing for the attention of Lily Wu, who Marc thinks is the most perfect girl he's ever met. Worst of all, the kids in 6-309 have challenged 6-321 to a big fight, off school grounds. On the very day that President Kennedy is assassinated, Marc somehow finds the courage to tell his classmates how shameful it will be to fight on such a mournful day in this tale of reminiscences. (131 pages)

Where it's reviewed:
Booklist, January 2001, page 961
Bulletin of the Center for Children's Books, February 2001, page 228
Publishers Weekly, January 1, 2001, page 93
School Library Journal, May 2001, page 155
Voice of Youth Advocates, April 2001, page 43

Other books by the same author:
Children's Rules for Parents: Wit and Wisdom from Schoolchildren around the Country, 1987

Other books you might like:
Avi, *Don't You Know There's a War On?*, 2001
Howie reflects back on the year he had a crush on his teacher Miss Gossim and was certain their 5th grade principal was a spy for the Nazis.
Amy Gordon, *When JFK Was My Father*, 1999
Unhappy about the lack of interest shown in her by her dad, Georgia pretends that President Jack Kennedy is her father and writes him imaginary letters.
Nancy J. Hopper, *What Happened in Mr. Fisher's Room*, 1995
Lanie can't stand her teacher Mr. Fisher and plots to kill his fish, but when someone carries out her plan she is upset that she ever considered it.

534

KATHRYN LASKY
MARYLIN HAFNER, Illustrator

Starring Lucille
(New York: Alfred A. Knopf, 2001)

Subject(s): Ballet; Brothers and Sisters; Birthdays
Age range(s): Grades K-2
Major character(s): Lucille, Pig, Sister (younger); Franklin, Pig, Brother (older); Frances, Pig, Sister (older)
Time period(s): 2000s
Locale(s): Fictional Country

Summary: A tutu received as an early birthday gift inspires Lucille to plan a performance for her family at her birthday celebration. Despite jeering from Franklin and Frances, Lucille practices twirling, leaping, hopping and making curtsies in anticipation of her show. On the night of her big production, Franklin rides his bike into the living room wearing the tutu as a hat while Frances performs a tap dance. The parents intervene to reclaim the tutu from the jealous siblings and Lucille finally stars in a dance number that even Franklin and Frances admit is not bad for a four-year-old. (32 pages)

Where it's reviewed:
Booklist, October 1, 2001, page 326
Publishers Weekly, October 8, 2001, page 66
School Library Journal, January 2002, page 105

Other books by the same author:
Lucille's Snowsuit, 2000
The Emperor's Old Clothes, 1999
The Gates of the Wind, 1995

Other books you might like:
Ian Falconer, *Olivia*, 2000
Olivia, a pig with a mind of her own, tolerates her younger brother, tries on every outfit before making a decision, and dances during naptime.
Holly Hobbie, *Toot & Puddle: A Present for Toot*, 1998
Toot's birthday is coming and Puddle is trying to find the best gift for his friend.

Laura Joffe Numeroff, *If You Give a Pig a Pancake*, 1998
If an uninvited pig shows up for breakfast to share your pancakes, be prepared for a busy day.

535

DANIEL LAURENCE
CLAUDIO MUNOZ, Illustrator

Captain and Matey Set Sail
(New York: HarperCollins Publishers, 2001)

Series: I Can Read Book
Subject(s): Pirates; Humor; Individuality
Age range(s): Grades 1-3
Major character(s): Captain, Sea Captain, Pirate; Matey, Sailor, Pirate; Squawk, Parrot
Time period(s): Indeterminate Past
Locale(s): At Sea

Summary: Four brief stories capture the individuality of Captain and Matey. Thinking that their ship is incomplete without a parrot they steal one from a store and then can't agree on a name. The parrot, after a lot of squawking, finally gets their attention and they name the parrot Squawk because obviously that's its name. They also have different ideas as to proper pirate behavior including the song a pirate should sing while swabbing the decks. In the end they agree to disagree sometimes rather than risk their friendship in the author's first book. (64 pages)

Where it's reviewed:
Booklist, July 2001, page 2023
Bulletin of the Center for Children's Books, September 2001, page 24
Horn Book, January 2002, page 79
Kirkus Reviews, June 15, 2001, page 866
School Library Journal, November 2001, page 128

Other books you might like:
Ariane Dewey, *Lafitte, the Pirate*, 1985
Historical fiction in a beginning reader explores the exploits of a famous pirate.
William H. Hooks, *Lo-Jack and the Pirates*, 1991
A young boy kidnapped by pirates misunderstands their orders, follows them literally and inadvertently saves a ship by doing so.
Leonard Kessler, *The Pirate's Adventure on Spooky Island*, 1979
A bumbling pirate captain depends on his capable parrot to help him capture Bad Bart.

536

IAIN LAWRENCE

The Buccaneers
(New York: Delacorte, 2001)

Subject(s): Adventure and Adventurers; Sea Stories; Pirates
Age range(s): Grades 6-10
Major character(s): John Spencer, 17-Year-Old, Sailor; Stanley Butterfield, Sea Captain; Horn, Sailor; Bartholomew Grace, Pirate

Time period(s): 19th century
Locale(s): *Dragon*, At Sea

Summary: Sailing from London to Jamaica with a cargo of wool, John Spencer is aboard the schooner *Dragon*, recently acquired by his father, with his uncle at the helm and an inexperienced crew on board. Sailors are known for their superstitions and, when they pick up a man adrift at sea, there are conflicting opinions about whether Horn will bring them luck or be an albatross around their necks. When they meet the dreaded pirate, Captain Bartholomew Grace, Horn's knowledge of the pirate's trickery helps the crew outmaneuver him. Sharks, mosquitoes, a ghost ship of corpses and bouts of malaria are just a few of the disasters that John faces before he returns the *Dragon* to England, right back to the Tombstones in Cornwall where his adventures began in *The Wreckers*. (244 pages)

Where it's reviewed:
Booklist, May 15, 2001, page 1753
Bulletin of the Center for Children's Books, July 2001, page 413
Horn Book, July 2001, page 455
Publishers Weekly, July 30, 2001, page 86
School Library Journal, July 2001, page 110

Other books by the same author:
The Lightkeeper's Daughter, 2002
Lord of the Nutcracker Men, 2001
Ghost Boy, 2000
The Smugglers, 1999
The Wreckers, 1998

Other books you might like:
Sid Fleischman, *The Ghost in the Noonday Sun*, 1965
    Young Oliver is kidnapped by the pirate known as Captain Scratch and made to find the ghost of Gentleman Jack.
Gerald Hausman, *Tom Cringle: Battle on the High Seas*, 2000
    Off to sea aboard the *Bream*, Tom's eyesight makes him a perfect lookout for spotting pirate ships, though he never expects to sail aboard one.
Karen Hesse, *Stowaway*, 1999
    Running away from his abusive master, young butcher's apprentice Nicholas stows away on the *Endeavour* and has the adventure of his life.
Geraldine McCaughrean, *The Pirate's Son*, 1998
    Orphaned and penniless, Nathaniel and his sister Maud accompany Tamo, son of a deceased pirate, to his home in Madagascar in a rollicking escapade.

537

IAIN LAWRENCE

Lord of the Nutcracker Men

(New York: Delacorte, 2001)

Subject(s): World War I; Fathers and Sons; Toys
Age range(s): Grades 5-8
Major character(s): Johnny Briggs, Child; James Briggs, Father (of Johnny), Artisan (toy maker); Ivy Briggs, Aunt
Time period(s): 1910s
Locale(s): London, England; Cliffe, England; France

Summary: Johnny loves the set of thirty nutcracker soldiers his father carves for him and treasures them even more when his dad enlists to fight in World War I. While his dad fights overseas, Johnny lines up his soldiers and conducts imaginary battles. As the war progresses, London becomes too dangerous and Johnny is sent to live with Aunt Ivy. His father writes regularly, tells of the horrors of trench life, and encloses a hand-carved soldier with his missives; each of which reflects the incremental ravages of the war. Johnny continues to hold imaginary battles with his nutcrackers, as well as the "Tommys," "Pierres" and Huns sent by his father, but worries that he may be directing the outcome of actual battles in this quietly horrific book. (212 pages)

Where it's reviewed:
Booklist, November 1, 2001, page 474
Bulletin of the Center for Children's Books, October 2001, page 64
Publishers Weekly, October 8, 2001, page 65
School Library Journal, November 2001, page 160
Voice of Youth Advocates, December 2001, page 360

Awards the book has won:
School Library Journal Best Books, 2001
Publishers Weekly Best Children's Books, 2001

Other books by the same author:
The Lightkeeper's Daughter, 2002
The Buccaneers, 2001
Ghost Boy, 2000
The Smugglers, 1999
The Wreckers, 1998

Other books you might like:
Robert Cormier, *Tunes for Bears to Dance To*, 1992
    Henry would love to accept the money, but he can't destroy Mr. Levine's carving of his Holocaust-devastated town to earn it.
Michelle Magorian, *Good Night, Mr. Tom*, 1982
    Reclusive widower Tom Oakley and eight-year-old abused William Beech form a lasting friendship when William lives with Mr. Tom during World War II.
Cynthia Rylant, *I Had Seen Castles*, 1993
    An elderly man reflects on the ways his experiences in World War II have haunted him and changed his life.

538

JULIE LAWSON

Destination Gold!

(Custer, WA: Orca Book Publishers, 2001, c2000)

Subject(s): Gold Discoveries; Adventure and Adventurers
Age range(s): Grades 6-10
Major character(s): Edward "Ned" Turner, 16-Year-Old, Prospector; Sarah Turner, 12-Year-Old, Sister (of Ned); Montana Jim Daley, Con Artist, Gambler; Catherine, Runaway, 16-Year-Old; Frosty Jack Thurston, Prospector
Time period(s): 1890s
Locale(s): Victoria, British Columbia, Canada; Dawson, Yukon Territory, Canada

Summary: When the death of his father curtails his college plans, Ned decides the time is right to head to the Klondike, fine enough gold to support his mother and sister Sarah and return home. Extremely naive, he promptly loses his cash to the gambler Montana Joe, is taken in by Frosty Jack who helps him survive the winter and then heads for Dawson on earnings saved while working for Jack. Another victim of Montana Joe's is Catherine, sold to the gambler in a game, who manages to escape and heads to the Klondike thinking she'll leave her past behind and start over. At the same time, Ned's mother worries about not hearing from him so Sarah joins a neighboring family who's heading for the Klondike in hopes she can find Ned. Catherine, Sarah and Ned eventually all meet, but that no-good Montana Joe is not far behind in this work rich with historical detail. (210 pages)

Where it's reviewed:
Book Report, September 2001, page 63
Booklist, February 15, 2001, page 1128
Bulletin of the Center for Children's Books, April 2001, page 307
School Library Journal, July 2001, page 110
Voice of Youth Advocates, April 2001, page 44

Other books by the same author:
The Ghost of Avalanche Mountain, 2000
Goldstone, 1998
Turns on a Dime, 1998
Cougar Cove, 1996
Danger Game, 1996
White Jade Tiger, 1993

Other books you might like:
Will Hobbs, *Jason's Gold*, 1999
    Jason tries to catch up with his brothers who've already left to hunt for gold in the Klondike.
Kathleen Karr, *Oregon, Sweet Oregon*, 1998
    Phoebe misses the adventure of trail life so, when news of the California Gold Rush reaches her, she dresses as a boy and runs away to the gold fields.
Joann Mazzio, *Leaving Eldorado*, 1993
    Maude's left to live on her own in Eldorado, New Mexico, when the Yukon gold fever overwhelms her father.
Laurence Yep, *The Journal of Wong Ming-Chung: A Chinese Miner*, 2000
    Sent to America to help his uncles with gold mining, Wong's ability to read and write makes him the camp supervisor's choice to be his assistant.

539

URSULA K. LE GUIN

Tales from Earthsea
(New York: Harcourt, 2001)

Series: Earthsea
Subject(s): Short Stories; Fantasy; Magic
Age range(s): Grades 9-Adult

Summary: These stories are set both before and after the time of LeGuin's famous Earthsea novels. The first is set when sorcery is just beginning and is still a dangerous practice. One is a love story, one tells of Ged's time as archmage and one connects the time of the previous novels with the forthcoming *The Other Wind*. (296 pages)

Where it's reviewed:
Book World, June 24, 2001, page 13
Library Journal, May 15, 2001, page 166
New York Times Book Review, June 17, 2001, page 19
Publishers Weekly, March 5, 2001, page 66

Other books by the same author:
The Other Wind, 2001 (Earthsea)
Tehanu: The Last Book from Earthsea, 1990 (Earthsea)
The Farthest Shore, 1972 (Earthsea)
The Tombs of Atuan, 1971 (Earthsea)
A Wizard of Earthsea, 1968 (Earthsea)

Other books you might like:
Peter S. Beagle, *Giant Bones*, 1997
    Beagle revisits the world and people he created in *The Innkeeper's Song*, a world of danger, magic and bravery.
Charles De Lint, *Moonlight and Vines: A Newford Collection*, 1999
    Newford is very much like any city in our world, it's just that the people there are much more alert to the magic creeping through their streets.
Diana Wynne Jones, *Mixed Magics: Four Tales of Chrestomanci*, 2001
    Four stories that fill in some of the background of the mysterious Chrestomanci, who is featured in several of Jones' novels.

540

ANNETTE LEBOX
HARVEY CHAN, Illustrator

Wild Bog Tea
(Buffalo: Groundwood Book/Douglas & McIntyre, 2001)

Subject(s): Grandfathers; Seasons; Nature
Age range(s): Grades 1-3
Major character(s): Unnamed Character, Son (grandson), Narrator; Unnamed Character, Grandfather
Time period(s): Indeterminate Past
Locale(s): Blaney Bog, British Columbia, Canada

Summary: As a grandson grows from infant to adult his life is intertwined with his grandfather's through their exploration of a bog near the grandfather's home. The grandfather introduces the boy to the plants of the bog where they play hide and seek and dance with the cranes. As the plants and animals vary with the seasons, grandfather teaches the growing boy each one. From the bog they harvest wild cranberries and sprigs of Labrador tea to use in making wild bog tea when they return to the house. As an adult the grandson returns to walk alone to the bog, to dance alone with the cranes and to carry to his elderly grandfather the makings of wild bog tea and a report on the plants and animals visible during this hike. (32 pages)

Where it's reviewed:
Booklist, December 15, 2001, page 740
Globe & Mail, June 6, 2001, page D13
Horn Book Guide, Spring 2002, page 49
Quill & Quire, June 2001, page 51
School Library Journal, September 2001, page 193

Other books by the same author:
Miracle at Willowcreek, 1998
Miss Rafferty's Rainbow Socks, 1997
The Princess Who Danced with Cranes, 1997

Other books you might like:
Jim LaMarche, *The Raft*, 2000
Grandma, a self-proclaimed ''river rat'' teaches Nicky to appreciate the river and also to sketch the natural world he sees on it.
Thomas Locker, *Where the River Begins*, 1984
Grandfather's camping trip with two grandsons takes them upstream to locate the source of the river that flows past their home.
Jan B. Waboose, *Morning on the Lake*, 1998
In three brief stories a young boy and his Ojibwa grandfather share their love of nature during walks in the woods.

CHINLUN LEE, Author/Illustrator

The Very Kind Rich Lady and Her One Hundred Dogs

(Cambridge, MA: Candlewick Press, 2001)

Subject(s): Animals/Dogs; Pets; Animals, Treatment of
Age range(s): Grades K-1
Major character(s): Unnamed Character, Animal Lover, Wealthy
Time period(s): 2000s
Locale(s): Earth

Summary: A very kind, very rich woman names and provides a home to stray dogs. Her pets also receive lots of loving attention, healthy food, daily exercise and brushing. At the end of a busy day all one hundred dogs settle on and around the rich lady's bed for a good night's sleep. The author's first book is based on true story. (32 pages)

Where it's reviewed:
Booklist, May 15, 2001, page 1758
Horn Book Guide, Fall 2001, page 235
Kirkus Reviews, May 1, 2001, page 663
Publishers Weekly, May 28, 2001, page 86
School Library Journal, July 2001, page 84

Awards the book has won:
Parenting's Reading Magic Awards, 2001

Other books you might like:
Alyssa Satin Capucilli, *Mrs. McTats and Her Houseful of Cats*, 2001
After adopting the twenty-five stray cats that come to her door, Mrs. McTats welcomes a puppy that also seeks a home.
Charlotte Graeber, *Nobody's Dog*, 1998
With much deliberation and concern for her beautiful garden, Miss Pepper decides to adopt the stray dog in her neighborhood.
Marc Simont, *The Stray Dog*, 2001
For a week a family worries about the hungry dog at the park before returning to claim the mutt as their pet.

MILLY LEE
YANGSOOK CHOI, Illustrator

Earthquake

(New York: Frances Foster Books/Farrar Straus Giroux, 2001)

Subject(s): Earthquakes; Chinese Americans; Historical
Age range(s): Grades K-3
Major character(s): Unnamed Character, Daughter, Narrator; PoPo, Grandmother, Immigrant; MaMa, Mother, Immigrant
Time period(s): 1900s (1906)
Locale(s): San Francisco, California

Summary: A violent earthquake awakens a young girl and her family. Quickly dressing in many layers of clothes and packing as much as they can salvage from their apartment they hurry to the streets. The girl's father locates a cart in which they place their belongings and PoPo and MaMa who are unable to walk far because of their bound feet. By pushing and pulling the cart up and down the city's hilly streets with frequent stops to move debris out of the way the family makes it safely to Golden Gate Park where a tent city is being erected to house the city's residents. A concluding ''Author's Note'' gives the family history that inspired the story. (32 pages)

Where it's reviewed:
Bulletin of the Center for Children's Books, September 2001, page 25
Horn Book Guide, Spring 2002, page 50
Kirkus Reviews, June 1, 2001, page 803
Publishers Weekly, August 13, 2001, page 311
School Library Journal, September 2001, page 193

Awards the book has won:
Notable Social Studies Trade Books for Young People

Other books by the same author:
Nim and the War Effort, 1997 (ALA Notable Books for Children)

Other books you might like:
Judith Ross Enderle, *Francis, the Earthquake Dog*, 1996
Edward befriends a stray dog but then fears he's lost him when an earthquake destroys the city; Francis survives and is later found.
James House, *The San Francisco Earthquake*, 1989
A nonfiction title describes the 1906 earthquake and fire that destroy most of San Francisco.
Mary Pope Osborne, *Earthquake in the Early Morning*, 2001
In a ''Magic Tree House'' series title Jack and Annie travel through time back to 1906 San Francisco and experience the earthquake and fire.

543

KATHERINE LEINER
EDEL RODRIGUEZ, Illustrator

Mama Does the Mambo

(New York: Hyperion Books for Children, 2001)

Subject(s): Dancing; Grief; Mothers and Daughters
Age range(s): Grades 1-3

Major character(s): Mama, Mother, Widow(er); Sofia, Daughter; Eduardo, Gentleman
Time period(s): Indeterminate Past
Locale(s): Cuba

Summary: Sofia remembers her parents dancing at home and at Carnival. Everyone admired them but since her father's death, Mama does not dance. Many men try to become Mama's dancing partner, but Mama has no more interest in them than in dancing until Eduardo comes calling. Sofia likes Eduardo and she can see that Mama likes him too but Eduardo cannot dance. Carnival comes again and Sofia does not know what Mama will do when the music starts. During the rhumba Mama and Eduardo watch, when the band plays a chachacha they clap their hands and to the music of the merengue they sway. Then the conga player begins the beat for the mambo, Mama's favorite, and she takes the dance floor, beckoning to Sofia to be her partner. (36 pages)

Where it's reviewed:
Booklist, November 1, 2001, page 483
Bulletin of the Center for Children's Books, December 2001, page 145
Horn Book, January 2001, page 69
Publishers Weekly, September 24, 2001, page 93
School Library Journal, November 2001, page 128

Other books by the same author:
First Children: Growing Up in the White House, 1996
Halloween, 1993
Both My Parents Work, 1986

Other books you might like:
Susan Campbell Bartoletti, *Dancing with Dziadziu*, 1997
    Gabriella's elderly, widowed grandmother recalls youthful days dancing with her husband.
Libba Moore Gray, *My Mama Had a Dancing Heart*, 1995
    Remembering her mother's love for movement inspires a dancer's performance.
Leah Komaiko, *Aunt Elaine Does the Dance from Spain*, 1992
    Katy is amazed by the transformation in Aunt Elaine when she dons a Spanish costume and takes the stage at a dance show.
Eric Velasquez, *Grandma's Records*, 2001
    Memories of Grandma include summers listening to her collection of records, watching her dance and hearing stories of her Puerto Rican home.

MADELEINE L'ENGLE
CHRISTINE DAVENIER, Illustrator

The Other Dog

(New York: North-South/SeaStar Books, 2001)

Subject(s): Animals/Dogs; Babies; Sibling Rivalry
Age range(s): Grades 1-3
Major character(s): Touche L'Engle-Franklin, Dog (poodle); Jo, Daughter, Baby
Time period(s): Indeterminate Past
Locale(s): New York

Summary: It's difficult for Touche to comprehend why her family would want to acquire another dog, especially one as inadequate as Jo. It's true that Jo is quite capable of filling a lap, as is Touche, but this other dog has neither hair nor a tail and seems to be unaware that dogs never do their business in the house, white cloths or no. Finally, Touche comes to the conclusion that Jo is simply an inferior breed and decides to make the best of the situation for the family's sake. A concluding Author's Note introduces the poodle on which the story is based. (44 pages)

Where it's reviewed:
Bulletin of the Center for Children's Books, April 2001, page 308
Five Owls, Summer 2001, page 115
Publishers Weekly, February 12, 2001, page 212
Riverbank Review, Summer 2001, page 33
School Library Journal, May 2001, page 126

Awards the book has won:
Notable Social Studies Trade Books for Young People, 2002

Other books by the same author:
The Twenty-Four Days before Christmas: An Austin Family Story, 1984
The Anti-Muffins, 1980
A Wrinkle in Time, 1962 (Newbery Medal)

Other books you might like:
Gillian Johnson, *My Sister Gracie*, 2000
    The other dog added to Fabio's family actually is a dog, but still she's a disappointment to Fabio.
William Mayne, *Pandora*, 1996
    When her owners arrive home with a baby, Pandora, the cat, moves out temporarily.
Rosemary Wells, *McDuff and the Baby*, 1997
    McDuff's idyllic life with Fred and Lucy changes dramatically when they bring home a tiny, crying, time-consuming stranger.
Harriet Ziefert, *Pushkin Minds the Bundle*, 2000
    Pushkin is understandably jealous of the bundle named Pierre who receives so much attention and even claims Pushkin's favorite seat in the car.

HARRIET LERNER
SUSAN GOLDHOR, Co-Author
HELEN OXENBURY, Illustrator

Franny B. Kranny, There's a Bird in Your Hair!

(New York: HarperCollins Publishers, 2001)

Subject(s): Hair; Animals/Birds; Individuality
Age range(s): Grades K-2
Major character(s): Franny B. Kranny, Sister, Daughter; Bertha Kranny, Sister (younger), Daughter; Unnamed Character, Mother
Time period(s): 2000s (2001)
Locale(s): United States

Summary: The more her family complains about her hair the more Franny B. Kranny likes the long unruly mess. Franny doesn't mind that her hair snags her buttons or gets stuck in the refrigerator door. Franny loves everything about her hair except her mother's attempts to comb it or to convince her to have it more like Bertha's short, straight, uninteresting hair. When Franny's mother takes the girls to the hairdresser prior to a family reunion, Franny goes reluctantly but refuses to allow her hair to be cut. In an effort to please both Franny and her mother the hairdresser carefully piles the frizz on top of Franny's head and, as she leaves the shop, a bird nestles into it. Franny now feels special and refuses to dislodge the bird. Her hair is a definite conversation starter at the family reunion, but as soon as the day is over Franny cuts the topknot off and parks it in a tree for the bird. (36 pages)

Where it's reviewed:
Booklist, June 2001, page 1891
Bulletin of the Center for Children's Books, September 2001, page 25
Horn Book, July 2001, page 441
Publishers Weekly, May 21, 2001, page 107
School Library Journal, June 2001, page 122

Awards the book has won:
IRA Children's Choices, 2002

Other books by the same author:
What's So Terrible About Swallowing an Apple Seed?, 1996

Other books you might like:
Susan Garrison, *How Emily Blair Got Her Fabulous Hair*, 1995
    Emily enjoys styling her friend Pamela's curly locks while desperately seeking a remedy for her own straight hair.
Linda Breiner Milstein, *Amanda's Perfect Hair*, 1993
    Amanda does not think her curly, blond hair is as terrific as her friends do so she gives herself a haircut.
Donna Jo Napoli, *Albert*, 2001
    When cardinals build a nest in Albert's hand he rearranges his life style to accommodate the birds.
Tohby Riddle, *The Singing Hat*, 2001
    After napping under a tree Colin awakens to discover that a bird has made a nest in his hat.

546

DIANE LES BECQUETS

The Stones of Mourning Creek
(New York: Winslow Press, 2001)

Subject(s): Race Relations; Prejudice; Friendship
Age range(s): Grades 7-10
Major character(s): Francine "Francie" Grove, 14-Year-Old; Ruth "Ruthie" Taylor, 14-Year-Old; Harvey Mansfield, Con Artist
Time period(s): 1960s
Locale(s): Spring Gap, Alabama

Summary: Two months after her mother was murdered while saving a young black girl from being raped, Francie and her father are still grieving. African American Ruthie takes Francie home to her mother for treatment after a poisonous snake bites her; as the two girls become friendly, the white girls ostracize Francie. Her town of Little Spring Gap is at the mercy of Harvey Mansfield, an evil white man who's not only a buddy of the sheriff's but also controls the gambling and the

drinking in the town. When Francie and Ruthie hear that Harvey stages fights between young black men for gambling white men, one event leads to another and soon Ruthie is dead. This is a double loss for Francie since Ruthie is the girl her mother tried to save from being raped, in this first novel. (306 pages)

Where it's reviewed:
Publishers Weekly, December 3, 2001, page 61
School Library Journal, October 2001, page 163
Voice of Youth Advocates, February 2002, page 436

Awards the book has won:
ALA Best Books for Young Adults, 2002

Other books you might like:
John Armistead, *The $66 Summer*, 2000
    George and his black friend Bennett discover that Bennett's father didn't disappear but was murdered in the segregated south of the 1950s.
Mildred Barger Herschler, *The Darkest Corner*, 2000
    As a child, Teddy is horrified when she spots her father in the group of white-robed men who hang her best friend's father.
Nanci Kincaid, *Crossing Blood*, 1992
    Lucy grows up curious about the black family next door, but in these pre-integration days, kids of opposite races aren't supposed to socialize.
Trudy Krisher, *Spite Fences*, 1994
    The summer Maggie Pugh is thirteen remains embedded in her memory as the summer she realizes how racist her town is.
Mildred D. Taylor, *The Road to Memphis*, 1990
    The Logan family knows only too well the effects of racism and prejudice in the South of the 1940s.

547

HELEN LESTER
LYNN MUNSINGER, Illustrator

Score One for the Sloths
(Boston: Walter Lorraine/Houghton Mifflin Company, 2001)

Subject(s): Individuality; Schools; Humor
Age range(s): Grades K-3
Major character(s): Sparky, Sloth, Student
Time period(s): Indeterminate
Locale(s): Fictional Country (Sleepy Valley Sloth School)

Summary: Student sloths are as content as their teachers to sleep away the day except for their yawning lessons, berry lunch in the cafeteria, and recess. Their behavior is perfectly slothful and highly praised by their teacher and principal. New student Sparky upsets the balance with her perky energy and desire to read, play with blocks, and toot her horn. Sparky's feeling are hurt by the rejection of her friendly overtures but, as a sloth, she stands up for her classmates when a bureaucrat arrives to close the school for poor academic performance. Thanks to Sparky the official leaves the school so impressed that he allows the school to remain open. (32 pages)

Where it's reviewed:
Booklist, August 2001, page 2131

Horn Book, September 2001, page 576
Kirkus Reviews, June 1, 2001, page 803
Publishers Weekly, July 30, 2001, page 84
School Library Journal, October 2001, page 123

Other books by the same author:
Tacky and the Emperor, 2000
Hooway for Wodney Wat, 1999 (ALA Notable Children's Book)
Princess Penelope's Parrot, 1996

Other books you might like:
Maryann Cocca-Leffler, *Mr. Tanen's Ties*, 1999
    Students convince a fussy administrator that a blue-tie-only rule simply doesn't work at their school and save Mr. Tanen's unique tie collection.
Reeve Lindbergh, *The Awful Aardvarks Go to School*, 1997
    Four jolly aardvarks have too much energy. In only one day they forget every rule, anger the anteater and cause chaos in school.
Robert Munsch, *Get Out of Bed!*, 1998
    After sneaking in some late night television Amy is unable to wake up for school so her parents carry her there in her bed.

JULIUS LESTER
EMILIE CHOLLAT, Illustrator

Ackamarackus: Julius Lester's Sumptuously Silly Fantastically Funny Fables

(New York: Scholastic Press, 2001)

Subject(s): Fables; Animals; Humor
Age range(s): Grades 2-5
Time period(s): Indeterminate Past
Locale(s): Fictional Country

Summary: Six original fables offer lessons based on the problem solving strategies of animals. When a bee loses his buzz he unexpectedly finds true love with an open-minded, musically inclined bee. The many spouses of a lazy lion find a good use for his one talent. An ant with sore feet responds in anger to an anaconda and ends up with a huge ache in her stomach too. Each light-hearted fable concludes with two clearly stated morals proven by the story. (40 pages)

Where it's reviewed:
Booklist, February 1, 2001, page 1056
Bulletin of the Center for Children's Books, March 2001, page 268
Horn Book Guide, Fall 2001, page 293
Publishers Weekly, March 5, 2001, page 79
School Library Journal, March 2001, page 214

Awards the book has won:
Parenting's Reading Magic Awards, 2001

Other books by the same author:
What a Truly Cool World, 1999 (Bulletin of the Center for Children's Books Blue Ribbon)
Sam and the Tigers: A New Telling of Little Black Sambo, 1996 (School Library Journal Best Books)

The Last Tales of Uncle Remus, 1994

Other books you might like:
Robert Kraus, *Fables Aesop Never Wrote: But Robert Kraus Did*, 1994
    Fifteen original fables are written as spoofs of Aesop's traditional ones.
Arnold Lobel, *Fables*, 1980
    The illustrated collection of twenty original American fables won the Caldecott Medal.
Paul Rosenthal, *Yo, Aesop!: Get a Load of These Fables*, 1998
    Nine modern, humorous fables conclude, not with a moral, but with a "comment" by Aesop.

549

JULIUS LESTER

When Dad Killed Mom

(San Diego: Harcourt/Silver Whistle, 2001)

Subject(s): Murder; Brothers and Sisters; Family Problems
Age range(s): Grades 9-12
Major character(s): Jeremy Richards, 12-Year-Old; Jenna Richards, 14-Year-Old; Eric Richards, Doctor (psychologist), Professor; Rachel Richards, Crime Victim, Artist
Time period(s): 2000s
Locale(s): South Birchfield, New England

Summary: In school one day, Jenna and Jeremy receive the news that their father shot and killed their mother. Growing up, Jenny has always been her father Eric's favorite while Jeremy's artistic ways naturally paired him with his mother Rachel, so the siblings react in different ways to this news. Jeremy misses his mother terribly and moves into her studio to feel closer to her while his grandfather keeps an eye on him, via phone, from the main house. Jenna spends her time thinking about the relationships within the family, especially her tumultuous relationship with her mother. Jeremy finds his mother's diary, which reveals the lies their father has told them, and it helps them better understand the reasons behind the killing. When their father is on trial, angry Jeremy and Jenna erupt in the courtroom over the lying their father has done about his marriage and affairs with students. The two struggle to understand, but now need to concentrate on living their own lives in this powerful work. (183 pages)

Where it's reviewed:
Booklist, June 2001, page 1862
Bulletin of the Center for Children's Books, May 2001, page 342
Publishers Weekly, May 14, 2001, page 83
School Library Journal, May 2001, page 155
Voice of Youth Advocates, October 2001, page 280

Awards the book has won:
ALA Quick Picks for Reluctant Young Adult Readers, 2001

Other books by the same author:
Pharaoh's Daughter, 2000
Othello, 1995
Long Journey Home: Stories from Black History, 1972

Other books you might like:
Robert Hawks, *This Stranger, My Father*, 1988
    Patty can't believe that FBI agents surround her father

until she discovers he escaped from prison twenty years earlier.

Phyllis Reynolds Naylor, *Ice*, 1995
Chrissa doesn't understand why she hasn't seen her father in three years; by the time someone tells her he's in jail, she's able to handle the news.

Neal Shusterman, *What Daddy Did*, 1991
Preston knows his parents have agreed to separate, so he's unprepared for the police news that his father shot his mother and wounded himself.

550

GAIL CARSON LEVINE

The Two Princesses of Bamarre
(New York: HarperCollins, 2001)

Subject(s): Princes and Princesses; Magic; Self-Confidence
Age range(s): Grades 4-7
Major character(s): Meryl, Royalty (princess); Adeline "Addie", Royalty (princess); Rhys, Sorcerer; Vollys, Dragon
Time period(s): Indeterminate Past
Locale(s): Bamarre, Fictional Country

Summary: "The two princesses of Bamarre" are two sisters who love each other, but are total opposites. The eldest, Meryl, is bold and eager to find adventure, ready to emulate their country's hero whose good deeds are recorded in poetry. Addie, on the other hand, is timid and shy, afraid of spiders and happiest with her needlework. As luck would have it, Meryl comes down with the lethal "Gray Death" for which only dragons and fairies have the cure. Devastated at the thought of losing her sister, Addie finds a hidden strength and heads out in search of the cure. To help her, Rhys provides her with a magic cape and a tablecloth that prepares food on demand while her nursemaid presents a pair of seven league boots that belonged to Addie's mother. Along the way Addie meets all the creatures of Bamarre's kingdom, from fairies to ogres, specters and dragons, and is eventually taken prisoner by Vollys, the dragon who knows the cure to save Meryl. And Meryl is saved, although not in the way Addie imagined, while Addie finds her own happiness in a special, young sorcerer, as the good deeds of the two princesses are recorded in poetry. (241 pages)

Where it's reviewed:
Bulletin of the Center for Children's Books, October 2001, page 65
Kliatt, May 2001, page 12
Publishers Weekly, May 7, 2001, page 248
School Library Journal, May 2001, page 155
Voice of Youth Advocates, June 2001, page 134

Other books by the same author:
The Wish, 2000
Dave at Night, 1999
Princess Sonora and the Long Sleep, 1999
Ella Enchanted, 1997

Other books you might like:
Robin McKinley, *The Hero and the Crown*, 1984
Aerin proves her worth as daughter of the Damarian King when she slays the Black Dragon, with help from the Blue Sword.

Edith Pattou, *Hero's Song*, 1991
Reluctantly setting out to rescue his sister, Collun embarks on a journey that becomes an attempt to save their country.

Patricia C. Wrede, *Dealing with Dragons*, 1990
Princess Cimorene would rather be a dragon's captive princess than be forced to meet more boring suitors.

551

SONIA LEVITIN

Clem's Chances
(New York: Orchard/Scholastic, 2001)

Subject(s): Frontier and Pioneer Life; American West
Age range(s): Grades 5-8
Major character(s): Clem Fontayne, 14-Year-Old; Molly Warren, Girlfriend; Pierre Fontayne, Father
Time period(s): 1860s
Locale(s): Missouri; West; San Francisco, California

Summary: Clem's left alone on his Missouri farm with just a cow, a horse and some hens after his mother and baby sister die of the fever. Taken in by neighbors, he quickly discovers they just want his labor and his cow so he decides to head West to find his father Pierre who's searching for gold. With no money, Clem takes what jobs he can find along the trail; meets up with scalawags and good souls, a free-born slave and a Mormon family; is thrown from his horse; sees buffalo massacred and is smitten on cute Molly. Though he finally locates his father, he discovers that Pierre has made a life that doesn't include room for a son. After Clem accepts that, he knows he can rely on the resourcefulness that led him West in the first place to make his own life. (199 pages)

Where it's reviewed:
Book Report, November 2001, page 64
Booklist, September 15, 2001, page 223
Horn Book, November 2001, page 753
Publishers Weekly, October 29, 2001, page 64
School Library Journal, October 2001, page 165

Other books by the same author:
Dream Freedom, 2000
The Cure, 1999
The Singing Mountain, 1998
Yesterday's Child, 1997
Evil Encounter, 1996
Escape from Egypt, 1994

Other books you might like:
Sid Hite, *Stick and Whittle*, 2000
Melvin Fitchett meets Melvin Smyte on the Texas prairie and the two team up, call themselves Stick and Whittle, and search for Fitchett's love Evelyn.

Michael Morpurgo, *Twist of Gold*, 1993
Sean and his sister Annie leave Ireland for America where they head west to find their father.

Gary Paulsen, *Call Me Francis Tucket*, 1995
Captured by Pawnee Indians and then rescued by Mr. Grimes, Francis continues west across the prairie looking for his parents' wagon train.

Robert Lewis Taylor, *The Travels of Jaimie McPheeters*, 1958

Jaimie has many adventures as he and his alcoholic father travel west to the California gold fields.

ELIZABETH LEVY
MARK ELLIOT, Illustrator

Big Trouble in Little Twinsville
(New York: HarperCollins Publisher, 2001)

Subject(s): Twins; Sisters; Humor
Age range(s): Grades 3-5
Major character(s): Eve, 10-Year-Old, Sister (older); Amy, 4-Year-Old, Twin; May, 4-Year-Old, Twin
Time period(s): 2000s (2001)
Locale(s): Twin Falls

Summary: Four years ago Eve thought having a younger sibling was a great idea but she wasn't counting on twins. Amy and May have grown into messy, obnoxious almost five-year-olds who jump on Eve's bed, make a mess of her room and smear peanut butter on Eve's back thinking it's a tube of sunscreen lotion. Fortunately, Eve has two cousins her age who are much more sympathetic to her plight than her parents are. A week's vacation at the Twin Falls resort to attend a twins' festival sounds like a "twinmare" to Eve. Having her cousins come too should help, but when people see them together they are mistaken for triplets and the trouble begins. (89 pages)

Where it's reviewed:
Booklist, July 2001, page 2006
Bulletin of the Center for Children's Books, July 2001, page 414
Horn Book Guide, Fall 2001, page 310
School Library Journal, May 2001, page 128

Other books by the same author:
My Life as a Fifth Grade Comedian, 1997
Wolfman Sam, 1996
Cheater, Cheater, 1993

Other books you might like:
Judy Blume, *Superfudge*, 1980
    There may be only one of Fudge, but he's a little brother who causes plenty of trouble for Peter.
Judith Ross Enderle, *What's the Matter, Kelly Beans?*, 1996
    A family move forces Kelly to share a room with messy sister Erin
Jean Van Leeuwen, *Two Girls in Sister Dresses*, 1994
    As the older sister, Jennifer is alternately protective of Molly and jealous of the attention others give her.

553

ELIZABETH LEVY
BILL BASSO, Illustrator

Night of the Living Gerbil
(New York: HarperCollins Publishers, 2001)

Subject(s): Brothers; Pets; Death (of a Pet)

Age range(s): Grades 3-5
Major character(s): Robert Bamford, 7-Year-Old, Brother (younger); Sam Bamford, Brother (older), 9-Year-Old; Mabel, 7-Year-Old, Cousin
Time period(s): 2000s (2001)
Locale(s): New York, New York

Summary: A trip to the vet is not enough to save the life of Robert's pet gerbil. To soften the blow of his brother's loss Sam takes the pet's body to a new store in the neighborhood to have it stuffed as a surprise for Robert. He and Mabel decide to give the stuffed pet to Robert at a memorial service for the gerbil. When Sam sees the stuffed animal the first time, the pose looks so ferocious that he thinks it must have had an experience out of the movie *Night of the Living Dead* and been turned into a zombie. (84 pages)

Where it's reviewed:
Booklist, November 1, 2001, page 475
Kirkus Reviews, July 1, 2001, page 943
School Library Journal, November 2001, page 128

Other books by the same author:
Who Are You Calling a Wooly Mammoth?: Prehistoric America, 2001 (America's Horrible Histories)
Gorgonzola Zombies in the Park, 1993
Dracula Is a Pain in the Neck, 1983
Frankenstein Moved in on the Fourth Floor, 1979

Other books you might like:
David A. Adler, *The Many Troubles of Andy Russell*, 1998
    One of Andy's many troubles is figuring out how to locate and capture all his pet gerbils after they escape from their cage.
Suzy Kline, *Song Lee and the Hamster Hunt*, 1994
    During a visit to Song Lee's classroom, her pet hamster gets out of the cage.
Stephanie Spinner, *Bright Lights, Little Gerbil*, 1997
    In the fourth entry in the Weebie Zone series, Garth, who is able to talk to animals, loses his gerbil at a cat show in New York City.

554

WALDTRAUT LEWIN
ELIZABETH D. CRAWFORD, Translator

Freedom beyond the Sea
(New York: Delacorte, 2001)

Subject(s): Jews; Sea Stories; Voyages and Travels
Age range(s): Grades 7-10
Major character(s): Christopher Columbus, Historical Figure, Explorer; Esther/Pedro Marchadi/Fernandez, 16-Year-Old
Time period(s): 15th century (1492)
Locale(s): *Santa Maria*, At Sea

Summary: As Columbus sets out on his expedition to the New World, the young cabin boy Pedro signs up and, with his knowledge of reading and writing, becomes page to the admiral. But Pedro is really a girl, Esther Marchadi, who's fleeing from Spain after seeing her father burned at the stake for being a Jew. Grateful to be aboard the *Santa Maria*, Esther endures animosity from the crew for what they believe to be her favored position. She's approached by some who want her to spy for them while she fears for her life from a Jew who, fearing exposure, threatens to kill her. On top of all her other worries, she feel a strong romantic attachment to Columbus and finally has to reveal her true identity to him. Realizing the danger she's in, Columbus has her disembark in the Canary Islands in this work by a German author. (266 pages)

Where it's reviewed:
Booklist, September 15, 2001, page 223
Bulletin of the Center for Children's Books, December 2001, page 146
Horn Book, November 2001, page 753
School Library Journal, January 2002, page 137
Voice of Youth Advocates, December 2001, page 360

Other books you might like:
Jacqueline Dembar Greene, *One Foot Ashore*, 1994
   Portuguese Jews, Maria and her sister Isobel are kidnapped and sent to a Catholic monastery where monks try to eradicate the tenets of Judaism.
Gloria D. Miklowitz, *Secrets in the House of Delgado*, 2001
   Maria jealously tells a priest about her employers the Delgado family, which leads to Dr. Delgado's arrest and Maria's attempt to find them safe passage.
Ann Rinaldi, *Girl in Blue*, 2001
   Unwilling to marry the widower to whom she's been promised, Sarah leaves home disguised as a boy and joins the Union Army as Neddy Compton.

555

WENDY A. LEWIS

Graveyard Girl
(Alberta, Canada: Red Deer Press, 2000)

Subject(s): Short Stories; School Life
Age range(s): Grades 9-12
Time period(s): 1980s; 1990s
Locale(s): Lee, Ontario, Canada

Summary: In 1993 Ginger looks at her high school yearbook and thinks back to the time a group of her classmates reenacted the wedding of Prince Charles and Princess Diana. This "then and now" collection of stories tell of Ginger's old boyfriend who became a famous hockey player; the teen couple who disappointed their parents by marrying so young; classmates' battles with cancer and other diseases and the origin of Ginger's high school nickname, "the graveyard girl." This first novel by a Canadian author offers a remarkable array of characters who have their own unique stories to share. (189 pages)

Where it's reviewed:
Booklist, January 2001, page 940
Publishers Weekly, February 19, 2001, page 92
Resource Links, February 2001, page 30
School Library Journal, May 2001, page 156
Voice of Youth Advocates, June 2001, page 124

Other books you might like:
Peter Carver, *Close-ups*, 2000
   Written by Canadian authors of young adult fiction, this rich collection shows that the universal complexities of life are not only for teenagers.

Gillian Chan, *Golden Girl and Other Stories*, 1997
   The students at Elmwood High School have a wide range of interests, concerns and problems as evidenced by this collection of stories.
Tim Wynne-Jones, *Lord of the Fries and Other Stories*, 1999
   These seven short stories are deliciously witty and range from stopping a teacher's flirtation to the cause of a cook's crankiness.

556

REBECCA LICKISS

Eccentric Circles
(New York: Ace Books, 2001)

Subject(s): Magic; Fairies; Artists and Art
Age range(s): Grades 8-Adult
Major character(s): Piper Pied, Writer, Heiress; Aelvarim, Mythical Creature (elf)
Time period(s): 2000s
Locale(s): Colorado

Summary: Piper's family is notoriously odd, and the latest manifestation of their peculiarity is their apparent collusion to make Piper her great-grandmother's heir. Gran hasn't left all that much, just a tiny cottage that happens to have a yard that backs onto Fairie. Piper never suspects a thing until she comes down to breakfast and finds an incredibly handsome stranger sitting at the table. Aelvarim claims to be an elf, and he is very upset about Gran's death. Initially skeptical, Piper begins to wonder what is going on after a tour of Fairie and some close encounters with fairies, dwarves, wizards and magic. Aelvarim claims they have to find Gran's book, for without it Fairie will drift away and fall apart. As holes begin to appear in the fabric of reality, the search for the killer and the book becomes frantic. (218 pages)

Where it's reviewed:
Booklist, June 1, 2001, page 1856
Library Journal, November 1, 2001, page 120
Publishers Weekly, September 21, 2001, page 74

Other books you might like:
Marion Zimmer Bradley, *The Inheritor*, 1997
   The old house comes complete with witchcraft as part of the inheritance package.
Charles De Lint, *Moonlight and Vines: A Newford Collection*, 1999
   For another take on how stories might create reality, read "Saskia" from this collection by a master of the urban fairytale.
Rosemary Edghill, *The Sword of Maiden's Tears*, 1994
   The gorgeous young man who seems to be a mugging victim claims to be an elf trying to recover a stolen magical sword.

557

BRIAN LIES, Author/Illustrator

Hamlet and the Magnificent Sandcastle

(North Kingston, RI: Moon Mountain, 2001)

Subject(s): Sandcastles; Animals/Pigs; Friendship
Age range(s): Grades K-3
Major character(s): Hamlet, Pig, Friend; Quince, Porcupine, Friend
Time period(s): Indeterminate
Locale(s): Fictional Country

Summary: Quince does not think much of Hamlet's plan to build a huge sandcastle. The worrier recalls the calamities that have resulted from Hamlet's bright ideas and imagines a few new ones for this project. At a safe distance from the water Quince sets up his chair and umbrella so he can supervise Hamlet's work but the tired friend falls asleep. Water awakens him and he sees the castle surrounded by rapidly rising seawater. Quince struggles into Hamlet's massive structure as waves begin to destroy it. They make a boat out of Quince's umbrella and a sail from the beach chair to help them reach dry ground. After a wet trudge to the train station Hamlet treats Quince to a cup of hot chocolate as he thinks about his next great idea. (32 pages)

Where it's reviewed:
Booklist, January 1, 2002, page 866
Children's Bookwatch, March 2001, page 3
Publishers Weekly, June 4, 2001, page 80
School Library Journal, June 2001, page 124

Other books by the same author:
Hamlet and the Enormous Chinese Dragon Kite, 1994

Other books you might like:
Marsha Hayles, *Beach Play*, 1998
    A little girl's day by the sea includes playing in the surf and building a castle of sand.
Mick Inkpen, *Sandcastle*, 1999
    After completing his sandcastle Kipper searches the beach for the perfect adornment.
Brenda Shannon Yee, *Sand Castle*, 1999
    Many children join Jen as she quietly builds a sand castle; each one adds a different part until they complete an elaborate structure.

558

GRACE LIN, Author/Illustrator

Dim Sum for Everyone!

(New York: Alfred A. Knopf, 2001)

Subject(s): Cooks and Cooking; Food; Restaurants
Age range(s): Grades K-3
Major character(s): Ma-Ma, Mother; Ba-Ba, Father
Time period(s): 2000s
Locale(s): United States

Summary: A family with three daughters enjoys dining at a dim sum restaurant. From the carts rolling past their table Ma-Ma selects her favorite dish, sweet pork buns. Ba-Ba chooses fried shrimp while the girls take dishes of tofu, turnip cakes and egg tarts. Using chopsticks, the family shares all the dishes and at the conclusion of the meal the table is covered with many small, empty dishes. The history and culture of the dim sum tradition is appended. (28 pages)

Where it's reviewed:
Booklist, June 2001, page 1880
Horn Book Guide, Spring 2002, page 51
Kirkus Reviews, May 15, 2001, page 743
Publishers Weekly, July 16, 2001, page 183
School Library Journal, July 2001, page 84

Other books by the same author:
Ugly Vegetables, 1999 (Notable Social Studies Trade Books for Young People)

Other books you might like:
Sook Nyul Choi, *Halmoni and the Picnic*, 1993
    Yunmi's grandmother prepares traditional Korean food for a class picnic.
William Low, *Chinatown*, 1997
    Daily, a young boy walks with Grandma through the crowded streets of Chinatown.
Rosemary Wells, *Yoko*, 1998
    For International Food Day Yoko brings homemade sushi to share with her classmates.

559

CHRISTINE LINCOLN

Sap Rising

(New York: Pantheon, 2001)

Subject(s): Short Stories; African Americans; Small Town Life
Age range(s): Grades 10-Adult
Time period(s): 20th century
Locale(s): Grandville, South

Summary: In the rural Southern town of Grandville live a world of memories, many of which are richly detailed in these inter-connected stories that reflect the people and the area in which they live. The child abandoned by her mother; the father so beaten down by racism that he drinks too much; the city woman who appears and tells wonderful stories or the exuberant bride who's now a beaten down mother are some of the characters who flow back and forth, between and among the stories found in this collection. (164 pages)

Where it's reviewed:
Booklist, August 2001, page 2087
Library Journal, July 2001, page 128
People, September 17, 2001, page 57
Publishers Weekly, August 20, 2001, page 57
School Library Journal, December 2001, page 174

Other books you might like:
Dorisjean Austin, *Streetlights: Illuminating Tales of the Urban Black Experience*, 1996
    Forty-nine different authors each offer a story about living in the city, resulting in a varied mix of styles and experiences.
Alex Haley, *Mama Flora's Family*, 1998
    On Flora's eightieth birthday, she reflects on all she's seen,

from the Klan to civil rights and from segration to integration.

Dori Sanders, *Clover*, 1990
After losing her father, young Clover is raised in her black South Carolina community by her white Yankee stepmother.

Mildred D. Taylor, *Roll of Thunder, Hear My Cry*, 1976
During the Depression, Cassie and the rest of her family struggle to keep up their land payments in the South.

560

PIJA LINDENBAUM, Author/Illustrator
KJERSTI BOARD, Translator

Bridget and the Gray Wolves
(New York: R & S Books, 2001)

Subject(s): Schools/Preschool; Self-Confidence; Animals/Wolves
Age range(s): Grades K-2
Major character(s): Bridget, Preschooler
Time period(s): 2000s (2000)
Locale(s): Sweden

Summary: Fearful Bridget does not join in the carefree play of others at her day care center because jumping from the playhouse roof or petting a worm is simply too risky. On a walk through the woods Bridget loses her group. After waiting patiently for someone to return to get her, Bridget courageously begins walking back to day care. She seems a bit turned around because her walk takes her deeper into a spruce forest where she soon notices the yellow eyes of wolves peering at her from behind the trees. Calmly Bridget engages them in play as if they were her classmates but the wolves aren't very good with games. Bridget sings them a sad good night song and in the morning begins walking confidently back through the woods to day care. Originally published in Sweden in 2000. (32 pages)

Where it's reviewed:
Booklist, December 15, 2001, page 740
Bulletin of the Center for Children's Books, September 2001, page 25
Publishers Weekly, September 3, 2001, page 87
Riverbank Review, Fall 2001, page 29
School Library Journal, November 2001, page 128

Other books by the same author:
Boodil, My Dog, 1992 (New York Times Best Illustrated Children's Book)
Else-Marie and Her Seven Little Daddies, 1991

Other books you might like:
Marie-Louise Fitzpatrick, *Lizzy and Skunk*, 2000
Overly anxious Lizzy loses Skunk; conquering her fears enables her to find her special puppet.

Susan Meddaugh, *Hog-Eye*, 1995
While taking a short-cut to school through the woods a young pig is discovered by a wolf intent on making her into his next meal.

Clara Vulliamy, *Ellen and Penguin*, 1993
Until they meet a little girl with a toy monkey Ellen and her penguin are too shy to join the children playing at the park.

Ellen Stoll Walsh, *Pip's Magic*, 1994
In the process of searching for magic answers to his fear of the dark, Pip overcomes his problem on his own.

561

DEBORAH LISSON

Red Hugh: The Kidnap of Hugh O'Donnell
(Dublin, Ireland: The O'Brien Press, 2001, c1998)

Subject(s): Kidnapping; Historical
Age range(s): Grades 7-10
Major character(s): Hugh Roe "Red Hugh" O'Donnell, Teenager, Captive
Time period(s): 16th century (1580s)
Locale(s): Ballyshannon, Ireland; Dublin, Ireland

Summary: Elizabeth I sits upon the throne in England, fearful that Spain will invade and call upon Catholic Ireland to be its ally. Determined to subdue those barbarous Irish and convert them to Church of England, a trap is set to catch some of the nobility who will be kept as "hostages" in Dublin Castle. Using the ship *Matthew*, with its cargo of Spanish wine as enticement, Red Hugh and several of his friends come aboard for a sumptuous meal but are locked in their cabin instead. Captured and imprisoned in the castle, they try to escape but are caught and beaten. Finally on his fourth attempt, after four years of confinement, Red Hugh makes his escape but later loses his toes to the damage from frostbite in a true account from Ireland's history. (219 pages)

Where it's reviewed:
Booklist, December 1, 2001, page 638
Books for Keeps, May 2000, page 26
Kirkus Reviews, October 1, 2001, page 1427
School Library Journal, December 2001, page 138

Other books by the same author:
The Devil's Own, 1991

Other books you might like:
Kathryn Lasky, *Elizabeth I: Red Rose of the House of Tudor*, 1999
A series of fictionalized diary entries provides a look at Elizabeth's life during her early teen years as she strives for her father's attention.

Morgan Llywelyn, *Brian Boru: Emperor of the Irish*, 1995
The story of the courageous life of Brian Boru as he attempts to bring peace to Ireland.

Morgan Llywelyn, *Strongbow: The Story of Richard and Aoife*, 1996
Daughter of King Dermot, Aoife marries a Welsh mercenary who casts his lot with the Irish as they fight to reclaim her father's kingdom.

562

JEAN LITTLE
JENNIFER PLECAS, Illustrator

Emma's Yucky Brother
(New York: HarperCollins Publishers, 2001)

Subject(s): Brothers and Sisters; Adoption; Foster Children
Age range(s): Grades 1-2
Major character(s): Sally Gray, Friend (Emma's), Neighbor; Emma Frost, Daughter, Sister (older); Max, 4-Year-Old, Adoptee
Time period(s): 2000s (2001)
Locale(s): United States

Summary: As an experienced big sister Sally assures Emma that the brother her family is adopting will be a pest, just as her little brother is. Prior to leaving his foster home, Max visits Emma's family, plays with Sally's little brother and generally seems to prefer Sally to Emma, leaving Emma feeling a little jealous. Max also picks up a brotherly way of speaking and refers to Emma's homemade cookies as "yucky" and even uses the term to describe Emma. After Max's placement is final he runs away when Emma tells him to "get lost" while she and Sally play. After a frantic search of the neighborhood, Emma finds Max hiding in some bushes and their reunion provides the beginning of a true sibling bond. (64 pages)

Where it's reviewed:
Booklist, December 1, 2000, page 726
Bulletin of the Center for Children's Books, May 2001, page 343
Horn Book Guide, Fall 2001, page 285
Kirkus Reviews, January 15, 2001, page 112
School Library Journal, January 2001, page 103

Awards the book has won:
Parenting's Reading Magic Awards, 2001
ALA Notable Children's Books, 2002

Other books by the same author:
Emma's Magic Winter, 1998
Bats about Baseball, 1995
Revenge of the Small Small, 1992

Other books you might like:
Laurie Krasny Brown, *Rex and Lilly Playtime*, 1995
   In an easy reader, brother and sister dinosaurs enjoy three fun-filled play activities together.
James Howe, *Pinky and Rex and the New Baby*, 1993
   Content as the only child, Rex feels threatened by the arrival of an adopted baby brother and copes by becoming the perfect big sister.
Lois Lowry, *See You Around, Sam!*, 1996
   Life with a younger brother is full of surprises for Anastasia. The latest is Sam's decision to run away to Alaska.

563

BILL LITTLEFIELD

The Circus in the Woods
(Boston: Houghton Mifflin, 2001)

Subject(s): Vacations; Camps and Camping; Coming-of-Age
Age range(s): Grades 7-10
Major character(s): Molly, Student—College; Snow, Counselor, Aged Person; Nell, Nurse, Aged Person
Time period(s): 1990s
Locale(s): Vermont (near Burlington)

Summary: Now in college, Molly looks back on the summers her family used to spend in a cottage on a lake in Vermont, where they looked forward to the pancake breakfasts followed by day camp with Snow. One summer during her early teens, as she's trying to grow up and feeling very confused about life, Molly hears calliope music and pursues the sounds until she discovers a circus in the middle of the woods. She returns often to watch the acrobats, see the lions and meet with the fortuneteller Nell as she tries to understand her prophecies in a magical story about growing up. (199 pages)

Where it's reviewed:
Bulletin of the Center for Children's Books, December 2001, page 146
Publishers Weekly, November 5, 2001, page 69
School Library Journal, November 2001, page 160

Awards the book has won:
Smithsonian's Notable Books for Children, 2001

Other books by the same author:
Champions: Stories of Ten Remarkable Athletes, 1998

Other books you might like:
Ray Bradbury, *Something Wicked This Way Comes*, 1962
   When James and William discover the wonderful Pandemonium Shadow Show, they quickly wish they hadn't.
Sid Hite, *Those Darn Dithers*, 1996
   Stilt walking, a dancing pig and an uncle who floats out to sea are just a few of the adventures of the Dithers family.
Stephen King, *Needful Things: The Last Castle Rock Story*, 1991
   Cost for items at the new store "Needful Things" is cheap, just a token amount and completion of one deed chosen by the store's owner.

564

AMY LITTLESUGAR
FLOYD COOPER, Illustrator

Freedom School, Yes!
(New York: Philomel Books, 2001)

Subject(s): Schools; African Americans; Race Relations
Age range(s): Grades 2-4
Major character(s): Annie, Teacher, Volunteer; Jolie, Child, Student; Mama, Mother
Time period(s): 1960s (1964)
Locale(s): Chicken Creek, Mississippi

Summary: Mama is the only one in church willing to house the Freedom School teacher coming to town for the summer. The first night Annie is in their home a brick thrown through the window with a threatening note wrapped around it confirms Jolie's fears, but does not deter Mama from her commitment. The night after Annie speaks to the congregation, encouraging them to send their children to the school, arsonists burn the church. Freedom School is held under a tree while the church is rebuilt. Along with many others in her community, Jolie learns of the bravery of African Americans in our country's history and realizes she too can overcome her fears and achieve her goals. An Author's Note gives historical facts on which the story is based. (40 pages)

Where it's reviewed:
Booklist, February 15, 2001, page 1155
Bulletin of the Center for Children's Books, February 2001, page 229
Horn Book Guide, Fall 2001, page 293
Publishers Weekly, January 8, 2001, page 65
School Library Journal, January 2001, page 104

Awards the book has won:
IRA Teachers' Choices, 2002
Notable Social Studies Trade Books for Young People, 2002

Other books by the same author:
Tree of Hope, 1999
Shake Rag: From the Life of Elvis Presley, 1998
Josiah True and the Art Maker, 1995

Other books you might like:
Sandra Belton, *From Miss Ida's Front Porch*, 1993
    Stories told on Miss Ida's porch teach the children about past discriminations against black people and encourage pride in their heritage.
Robert Coles, *The Story of Ruby Bridges*, 1995
    Daily in 1960, six-year-old Ruby bravely faces angry mobs in order to exercise her right to attend an elementary school in the segregated South.
Elizabeth Fitzgerald Howard, *Virgie Goes to School with Us Boys*, 2000
    Strong-willed Virgie is sure she deserves the same chance for an education as her brothers and her parents agree.
Michael J. Rosen, *A School for Pompey Walker*, 1995
    With help from a white friend, Pompey Walker uses the system of slavery to get the income needed to achieve his goal of educating black children.

565

STAR LIVINGSTONE
MOLLY BANG, Illustrator

Harley

(New York: SeaStar Books/North-South, 2001)

Subject(s): Animals/Llamas; Animals/Sheep; Ranch Life
Age range(s): Grades 1-3
Major character(s): Harley, Llama; Unnamed Character, Shepherd
Time period(s): 2000s
Locale(s): Massachusetts

Summary: Although Harley fails his training to become a pack animal his independent, ornery nature is suited to the needs of a shepherd seeking a guard llama to protect her flock from coyotes. Harley enjoys the solitude and independence of his life in the mountain pasture and quickly becomes very protective of the sheep. Harley also looks forward to the daily visits of the shepherd and the treats she offers. The shepherd's experiment is successful. Harley enjoys the job and he does it well; no sheep are lost to coyotes now. The events in the author's first book are based on a real-life experience. (64 pages)

Where it's reviewed:
Booklist, April 1, 2001, page 1468
Bulletin of the Center for Children's Books, June 2001, page 379
Horn Book, July 2001, page 456
Riverbank Review, Summer 2001, page 39
School Library Journal, June 2001, page 125

Awards the book has won:
Horn Book Fanfare/Fiction, 2002
ALA Notable Children's Books, 2002

Other books you might like:
Susan Clymer, *Llama Pajamas*, 1996
    Sarah and her parents go on a camping vacation in Colorado using llamas as pack animals.
Johanna Hurwitz, *A Llama in the Family*, 1994
    Adjusting to his mother's purchase of a llama is challenging for Adam who expected the surprise to be a new bicycle.
Emilie U. Lepthien, *Llamas*, 1996
    This nonfiction title covers the historical significance of llamas as well as their contemporary uses.
Lynn M. Stone, *Llama Farms*, 1999
    The domestic production of llamas in United States as well as the characteristics of the animals is described in an illustrated nonfiction title.

566

LAURA LJUNGKVIST, Author/Illustrator

Toni's Topsy-Turvy Telephone Day

(New York: Harry N. Abrams, Inc., 2001)

Subject(s): Communication; Food; Humor
Age range(s): Grades K-3
Major character(s): Toni, Friend, Cousin; Ruth, Cousin; Kirk, Friend
Time period(s): 2000s
Locale(s): United States

Summary: Toni carefully plans the menu for a potluck dinner and then calls six friends to ask them to attend and bring one or two items. Unfortunately, Toni calls her friends at times when background noise makes it difficult for them to hear her. Thus, when Toni excitedly greets her arriving guests, she discovers that instead of food, everyone has arrived with a hungry person or animal. Ruth, who lives near an airport, comes with a pooch and a maid instead of punch and lemonade. A crying baby keeps Kirk from understanding Toni's request for hats and balloons so he shows up with cats and baboons. Even Toni's hurried call for a pizza delivery is misunderstood, but Toni and her guests enjoy the party anyway in the author's first book. (32 pages)

Where it's reviewed:
Booklist, June 2001, page 1892
Five Owls, Fall 2001, page 19
Horn Book Guide, Fall 2001, page 264
Publishers Weekly, May 21, 2001, page 106
School Library Journal, May 2001, page 128

Other books you might like:
Alma Flor Ada, *Dear Peter Rabbit*, 1994
  Goldilocks' written communication to her friends assures that everyone understands the party plans.
Jonathan Meres, *The Big Bad Rumor*, 2000
  Goose shouts the alarm about a big, bad, mad wolf on the way, but the other animals misunderstand the warning.
Nancy Elizabeth Wallace, *Tell-a-Bunny*, 2000
  Sunny's whispered phone communications with friends lead to a surprise birthday party for her brother that is not what Sunny plans.

567

WENDY LOGGIA

A Puppy of My Own
(New York: Bantam/Skylark, 2001)

Series: Woof!. Number 1
Subject(s): Animals/Dogs; Friendship; Pets
Age range(s): Grades 2-4
Major character(s): Emily Joy Conner, 3rd Grader, Friend; Kaia Hopkins, 3rd Grader, Friend; Lauren Parker, 3rd Grader, Friend
Time period(s): 2000s (2001)
Locale(s): United States

Summary: All Emily wants for her birthday is a yellow lab puppy. Sure that she's demonstrated her ability to be responsible Emily confidently tells Lauren and Kaia that she's getting a puppy but after she opens the gifts from her family she still has no puppy. Emily forces herself to be cheerful at her birthday sleepover but she stays mad at her parents for a few days. Then she feels guilty when an after school surprise trip with her brother and parents brings her to a breeder's home where a yellow lab puppy that wasn't quite old enough to come to her birthday party is waiting just for her. (105 pages)

Where it's reviewed:
Booklist, January 2001, page 961
Publishers Weekly, February 12, 2001, page 212
School Library Journal, September 2001, page 193

Other books by the same author:
Cute As a Button, 2001 (Woof!, Number 2)
No Dogs Ever, 2001 (Woof!, Number 4)
My New Best Friend, 2001 (Woof!, Number 3)

Other books you might like:
Helen Cresswell, *Meet Posy Bates*, 1992
  Posy tries to convince her mother that she should be allowed to have a pet.

Betsy Duffey, *Puppy Love*, 1992
  In a Pet Patrol series entry, Evie and Megan find it difficult to locate a good home for the runt of a litter of pups.
Dick King-Smith, *The Invisible Dog*, 1993
  Wishes come true for Janie when her conscientious care of an imaginary pet leads to her acquisition of a real one with the same characteristics.
Joan M. Lexau, *Trouble Will Find You*, 1994
  Diz tries to stay out of trouble for one day in order to prove to his parents that he can handle the responsibility of a pet dog.

568

JONATHAN LONDON
FRANK REMKIEWICZ, Illustrator

Froggy Eats Out
(New York: Viking, 2001)

Subject(s): Animals/Frogs and Toads; Restaurants; Behavior
Age range(s): Preschool-Grade 1
Major character(s): Froggy, Frog, Son; Froglina, Friend, Frog
Time period(s): 2000s
Locale(s): Fictional Country

Summary: Obviously Froggy is not accustomed to dining at a fancy restaurant with tablecloths and menus. As his parents try to celebrate their anniversary, Froggy tries to remember to be neat, quiet and keep his feet off the table. His menu knocks over the water glass and his singing while waiting impatiently for his meal is far from quiet. As he loudly slurps his spaghetti Froglina calls to him from another table. Embarrassed to be noticed by a girl, Froggy tries to hide under the table, pulling the tablecloth and dumping his spaghetti on his head. His parents recognize that it's a good time to leap frog to a fast food restaurant for something in eat. (32 pages)

Where it's reviewed:
Booklist, June 2001, page 1892
Children's Bookwatch, July 2001, page 6
Horn Book Guide, Fall 2001, page 264
Publishers Weekly, May 14, 2001, page 84
School Library Journal, August 2001, page 156

Awards the book has won:
IRA Children's Choices, 2002

Other books by the same author:
Froggy's Best Christmas, 2000
Froggy Plays Soccer, 1999 (IRA Children's Choice)
Froggy's Halloween, 1999

Other books you might like:
Phyllis Reynolds Naylor, *I Can't Take You Anywhere!*, 1997
  Amy Audrey is so prone to clumsiness that her parents prefer to stay at home rather than risk mishaps in public.
Patricia Polacco, *In Enzo's Splendid Gardens*, 1997
  While dining at an outdoor restaurant a boy drops a book and sets off an unexpected and rather messy chain of events.
Chris Raschka, *Table Manners*, 2001
  Chester gives Dudunya lessons in proper table manners prior to the final exam at a restaurant. Vladimir Radunsky, co-author.

569

JONATHAN LONDON
AARON LONDON, Co-Author
JILL KASTNER, Illustrator

White Water

(New York: Viking, 2001)

Subject(s): Sports/White Water Rafting; Rivers; Outdoor Life
Age range(s): Grades 1-3
Major character(s): Dad, Father; Unnamed Character, Son, Child
Time period(s): 2000s
Locale(s): Green River, Utah

Summary: Dad has some experience with white water rafting but the awe and excitement of a new adventure pervades his son's narration of their vacation trip down the Green River with a guided group. Three rafts loaded with gear and passengers row through the still stretches of water and plummet down rapids. Eagles soar overhead, wild horses gaze from high cliffs and the looming canyon walls reflect the light of the setting sun as the group relaxes at the conclusion of a day on the river. By journey's end it's obvious that the son shares Dad's love for the river and will return. (32 pages)

Where it's reviewed:
Booklist, June 2001, page 1892
Bulletin of the Center for Children's Books, May 2001, page 344
Horn Book Guide, Fall 2001, page 265
Publishers Weekly, June 11, 2001, page 85
School Library Journal, June 2001, page 125

Other books by the same author:
The Waterfall, 1999
At the Edge of the Forest, 1998
Old Salt, Young Salt, 1996
Honey Paw and Lightfoot, 1995

Other books you might like:
Meredith Hooper, *River Story*, 2000
    Beginning as a mountain stream fed by melting snow a river grows as it rushes to the sea.
Jim LaMarche, *The Raft*, 2000
    The discovery of a raft changes Nicky's unwelcome summer visit to Grandma's into one of exploration and independence.
Thomas Locker, *Where the River Begins*, 1984
    Grandfather's camping trip with two grandsons takes them upstream to locate the source of the river that flows past their home.

570

LENORE LOOK
YUMI HEO, Illustrator

Henry's First-Moon Birthday

(New York: Anne Schwartz Book/Atheneum Books for Young Readers, 2001)

Subject(s): Babies; Grandmothers; Chinese Americans
Age range(s): Grades K-3

Major character(s): Jenny, Sister (older), Child; GninGnin, Grandmother; Henry, Baby, Brother (younger)
Time period(s): 2000s (2001)
Locale(s): United States

Summary: Jenny, as the older sister "in charge of the house" since Henry's birth, is not sure that a crying baby deserves a celebration, but GninGnin knows the importance of the first-moon birthday tradition. GninGnin prepares the food, writes Henry's Chinese name with ink and a brush and decorates red cloth with characters expressing good luck. Jenny supervises, observes, spills ink on the kitchen floor and colors the lucky eggs red. When the relatives arrive they pay attention only to Henry who is sleeping peacefully so Jenny pinches him while no one is looking and then she goes to eat pigs' feet with her cousin. The visiting relatives may not notice, but Jenny's satisfied that GninGnin knows who is really in charge of this celebration. (32 pages)

Where it's reviewed:
Booklist, April 1, 2001, page 1470
Bulletin of the Center for Children's Books, March 2001, page 269
Publishers Weekly, April 9, 2001, page 73
Riverbank Review, Summer 2001, page 31
School Library Journal, June 2001, page 126

Awards the book has won:
ALA Notable Children's Books, 2002
Booklist Editors' Choice/Books for Youth, 2002

Other books by the same author:
Love as Strong as Ginger, 1999 (Booklist Editors' Choice)

Other books you might like:
Sook Nyul Choi, *The Best Older Sister*, 1997
    Sunhi feels jealous of her baby brother as preparations begin for a traditional Korean celebration of his first birthday.
Holly Keller, *Geraldine's Baby Brother*, 1994
    It takes some time for Geraldine to adjust to her noisy baby brother and all the attention he receives.
Carol Snyder, *One Up, One Down*, 1995
    With twins there is always one up when the other one is down keeping big sister Katie busy helping her parents.

571

CHRISTINE LOOMIS
ORA EITAN, Illustrator

Astro Bunnies

(New York: G.P. Putnam's Sons, 2001)

Subject(s): Animals/Rabbits; Space Travel; Stories in Rhyme
Age range(s): Preschool-Kindergarten
Time period(s): Indeterminate
Locale(s): Fictional Country

Summary: Bunnies in silver suits board a rocket and blast off for a tour of the Milky Way. They float past constellations, gather dust on the moon and greet bunnies from another planet. When their work in space is complete, the bunnies contentedly return to their home planet. (28 pages)

Where it's reviewed:
Booklist, February 15, 2001, page 1141
Bulletin of the Center for Children's Books, February 2001, page 229
Horn Book, January 2001, page 84
Riverbank Review, Spring 2001, page 30
School Library Journal, February 2001, page 102

Awards the book has won:
Bulletin of the Center for Children's Books Blue Ribbon, 2001

Other books by the same author:
Cowboy Bunnies, 1997
Rush Hour, 1996
The Hippo Hop, 1995

Other books you might like:
Frank Asch, *Mooncake*, 1978
　　Believing the moon is made of cake, Bear builds a rocket to fly there in order to taste it.
Nancy Coffelt, *Dogs in Space*, 1993
　　Dogs in astronaut gear travel through the solar system searching for playmates.
Daniel Pinkwater, *Guys from Outer Space*, 1989
　　A boy who travels to another planet with some space guys discovers talking rocks and other amazing things.
Michael Rosen, *Mission Ziffoid*, 1999
　　In this picture book a young boy visits the planet Ziffoid and meets the inhabitants.
Martha Weston, *Space Guys!*, 2000
　　In simple verse this easy reader describes a night visit from ''space guys'' to a young boy's home.
Dan Yaccarino, *Zoom! Zoom! Zoom! I'm Off to the Moon!*, 1997
　　Rhyming text and bright pictures describe a young boy's flight to the moon and return home.

572

PATTY LOVELL
DAVID CATROW, Illustrator

Stand Tall, Molly Lou Melon
(New York: G.P. Putnam's Sons, 2001)

Subject(s): Self-Acceptance; Grandmothers; Bullies
Age range(s): Grades K-3
Major character(s): Molly Lou Melon, Child, 1st Grader; Ronald Durkin, Bully, Student—Elementary School
Time period(s): Indeterminate
Locale(s): Fictional Country

Summary: In the author's first book a grandmother's advice enables Molly Lou to feel confident despite her short height, her loud voice, her clumsiness and her prominent teeth. When her family moves and Molly Lou enters a new school Ronald picks on a different characteristic of hers every day. Molly Lou's response to each of Ronald's remarks leaves other students impressed and Ronald feeling foolish. Finally, on the fifth day, Ronald makes a conciliatory offering by giving Molly Lou a stacking penny for her teeth. It looks as if Molly Lou's ability to accept her shortcomings is working in her favor again. (32 pages)

Where it's reviewed:
Bulletin of the Center for Children's Books, October 2001, page 66
Horn Book Guide, Spring 2002, page 51
Kirkus Reviews, June 15, 2001, page 867
Publishers Weekly, September 17, 2001, page 80
School Library Journal, October 2001, page 124

Other books you might like:
Judith Caseley, *Bully*, 2001
　　Mickey can't understand what's caused his friend Jack to become a bully, but some understanding and shared cookies help to restore the friendship.
Helen Lester, *Hooway for Wodney Wat*, 1999
　　Rodney Rat uses his speech impediment to get the best of a class bully during a game of Simon Says.
John Nickle, *The Ant Bully*, 1999
　　When Sid squirts Lucas the frustrated victim turns his squirt gun on some ants and suffers the consequences when he shrinks to ant size.

573

SUSAN LOWELL
RANDY CECIL, Illustrator

Dusty Locks and the Three Bears
(New York: Henry Holt and Company, 2001)

Subject(s): Folklore; Animals/Bears; Behavior
Age range(s): Grades K-3
Major character(s): Dusty Locks, Child, Runaway
Time period(s): Indeterminate Past
Locale(s): Fictional Country

Summary: Dusty Locks, a downright dirty little cowgirl, runs away from home to avoid a bath and seeks refuge in a cabin in the woods. Now, the cabin's residents, a bear family, are walking while their beans cool and before they return Dusty Locks has sampled all the beans and devoured one bowl. She's also tried out all three chairs and broken the smallest one and now she's sleeping in one of the beds. When the bears enter their cabin the smell tells them that no sandstorm made the mess they see. At first, the youngest bear suspects a skunk is in its bed but that's not the critter that leaps out the window. Dusty Locks runs home to her mother who's waiting to give her a bath and a hug. (32 pages)

Where it's reviewed:
Booklist, July 2001, page 2014
Bulletin of the Center for Children's Books, July 2001, page 414
Horn Book, July 2001, page 464
Publishers Weekly, May 21, 2001, page 107
School Library Journal, July 2001, page 96

Other books by the same author:
Cindy Ellen: A Wild West Cinderella, 2000
Little Red Cowboy Hat, 1997
The Bootmaker and the Elves, 1997 (IRA Children's Choice)
The Three Little Javelinas, 1992

Other books you might like:
Jan Brett, *Goldilocks and the Three Bears*, 1987
　　This illustrated retelling is true to the original tale of a

young girl who seeks shelter in a home, falls asleep and is found by three bears.

Lisa Campbell Ernst, *Goldilocks Returns*, 2000
To make up for her actions fifty years earlier, Goldi the locksmith returns to the bears' home and puts multiple locks on all the doors.

James Marshall, *Goldilocks and the Three Bears*, 1988
In a humorous version of the tale, three bears returning from a walk discover someone sleeping in Baby Bear's bed.

Heidi Petach, *Goldilocks and the Three Hares*, 1995
After Mama Hare burns the oatmeal the Hares go out to breakfast; Goldilocks drops by while they're gone.

Melodye Benson Rosales, *Leola and the Honeybears: An African-American Retelling of Goldilocks and the Three Bears*, 1999
Lost in the woods Leola wanders into the Honeybear's Inn for some food and a nap.

574

SALLIE LOWENSTEIN

Focus

(Kensington, MD: Lion Stone Books, 2001)

Subject(s): Science Fiction; Coming-of-Age
Age range(s): Grades 7-10
Major character(s): Andrew Haldran, 16-Year-Old
Time period(s): Indeterminate Future
Locale(s): Earth; Miners World, Planet—Imaginary

Summary: At a certain age, young people choose a profession and then are genetically augmented for compatibility with that profession by having all their unneeded traits stripped away. Unfortunately, Andrew likes everything and doesn't want to choose only one area of specialization. To prevent Andrew's augmentation, his father accepts a job on Miners World, an alien world where the minds of the indigenous inhabitants are "mined" by scientists to learn about their technology. Andrew and his family quickly realize Miners World is not as it appears and, after a while, even Andrew is ready to return to Earth and his augmentation. (284 pages)

Where it's reviewed:
Book Report, September 2001, page 63
Booklist, April 15, 2001, page 1554
School Library Journal, August 2001, page 185
Science Fiction Chronicle, April 2001, page 37
Voice of Youth Advocates, August 2001, page 214

Other books by the same author:
Evan's Voice, 1998
The Mt. Olympus Zoo, 1997

Other books you might like:
Charlotte Kerner, *Blueprint*, 2000
Siri resents being a clone of her talented concert pianist mother Iris.

Kathryn Lasky, *Star Split*, 1999
A genetically enhanced person, Darci is intrigued by the "original ones," those without the forty-eighth chromosome, until she meets a duplicate of herself.

Lois Lowry, *The Giver*, 1993
Set in a futuristic community that values sameness, Jonas is assigned his life-task but meeting the Giver helps him seek another world.

Robert Westall, *Futuretrack 5*, 1984
In a Britain of the future, people either live privileged lives in the Est class or lawless lives outside society's protection in the Unnem group.

575

NICOLE LUIKEN

Violent Eyes

(New York: Pocket/Pulse, 2001)

Subject(s): Genetic Engineering; Science Fiction
Age range(s): Grades 8-12
Major character(s): Angela Eastland, 17-Year-Old, Genetically Altered Being; Michael Vallant, 17-Year-Old, Genetically Altered Being
Time period(s): 1980s (1987); 2080s (2087)
Locale(s): Chinchaga, Canada

Summary: When Angel first meets Mike, the only thing they seem to have in common are their violet eyes. For some reason, Angel takes an instant dislike to him, but the dislike turns to like as Angel and Mike are thrown together in their classes and with their group of friends. As the two teens talk, they explore other commonalities, such as continual surveillance, living in the orphanage and frequent moves with their parents. They're different from their friends, yet Angel and Mike are similar, and they want to know why. Their search for the truth reveals they're part of a genetic engineering experiment called Renaissance and have been members of an historical immersion class supposedly living in 1987. When the two make their plans to escape the subterfuge and danger under which they lived, they know they'll enter the world of 2089, a world to which they're ready to adjust. (246 pages)

Where it's reviewed:
Booklist, June 2001, page 1865
Kliatt, May 2001, page 26
School Library Journal, January 22, 2001, page 325

Other books by the same author:
Silver Eyes, 2001

Other books you might like:
Marilyn Kaye, *Amy, Number Seven*, 1998
Amy is finally told that she was part of a government experiment that created thirteen clones; when the lab caught fire, only Amy was saved.

Charlotte Kerner, *Blueprint*, 2000
Siri resents being a clone of her talented concert pianist mother Iris.

Kathryn Lasky, *Star Split*, 1999
A genetically enhanced person, Darci is intrigued by the "original ones," those without the forty-eighth chromosome, until she meets a duplicate of herself.

Melinda Metz, *The Outsider*, 1998
Max doesn't want to let Liz know he's part of the 1947 spacecraft crash in Roswell, but when she's injured, he can't hide his special healing powers.

LOUISA LUNA

Brave New Girl

(New York: Pocket Books/MTV, 2001)

Subject(s): Coming-of-Age; Family Problems; Rape
Age range(s): Grades 10-Adult
Major character(s): Doreen Severna, 14-Year-Old; Tracey Severna, Sister (of Doreen's); Ted, 14-Year-Old; Matthew, Boyfriend (of Doreen's)
Time period(s): 2000s
Locale(s): Pasadena, California

Summary: Doreen feels like she doesn't have much in common with anyone in her family, from her type-A personality Dad to her carping mother to her too-cool sister. And then there's her brother Henry, exactly a decade older than her, who left home years ago. Her only friend is Ted who's just as much of an outsider as she is; Doreen figures they'll be buddies throughout high school as no one else will befriend them. Her sister Tracey dates twenty-one-year-old Matthew who considers himself irresistible and often flirts with Doreen. One night Matthew's flirting goes too far and he forces himself onto vulnerable Doreen in an act that has far-reaching implications. When the truth comes out during an ugly family scene, Doreen's father leaps to her defense in an edgy tale of adolescent alienation. (197 pages)

Where it's reviewed:
Booklist, April 15, 2001, page 1547
Kliatt, May 2001, page 21
Voice of Youth Advocates, February 2002, page 436

Other books by the same author:
Crooked, 2002

Other books you might like:
Stephen Chbosky, *The Perks of Being a Wallflower*, 1999
    In Charlie's freshman year he helps his pregnant older sister, adjusts to the suicide of a best friend and is hospitalized for depression.
Lou Kassem, *Odd One Out*, 1993
    At a sorority-fraternity initiation party, Alison's boyfriend Nic attempts to rape her to collect a one-hundred-dollar bet.
Walter Kirn, *Thumbsucker*, 1999
    With a family like Justin's, it's no wonder he can't control the urge to suck his thumb.
C.D. Payne, *Youth in Revolt: The Journals of Nick Twisp*, 1996
    Nick's diaries reveal his struggle to deal with his parents' divorce, figure out what high school's all about and examine his widening world.
J.D. Salinger, *The Catcher in the Rye*, 1951
    Trying to find himself, Holden Caulfield roams New York for three days, thinks back to his prep school days and mourns the loss of a younger brother.

577

MARY BETH LUNDGREN

Love, Sara

(New York: Holt, 2001)

Subject(s): Suicide; Diaries; Foster Homes
Age range(s): Grades 7-10
Major character(s): Sara Reichert, 11th Grader, Foster Child; Dulciana "Dulcie" Newton, 11th Grader, Adoptee; Jon Draper, 12th Grader, Football Player; Carol Reilly, Foster Parent
Time period(s): 2000s
Locale(s): Cleveland, Ohio

Summary: After being sexually abused by her father, and other men, and then bounced from one foster home to another, Sara's happy living with her current foster mother Carol, attending the same school two years in a row and having a best friend, Dulcie. Her story is told through her e-mail with Dulcie; journal entries she writes to Henri Toulouse-Lautrec, because she felt silly writing "Dear Diary;" and various short pieces of writing for her English Honors class. Dulcie starts dating wealthy Jon and Sara immediately worries that she'll lose her best friend, though she has a bigger problem when Dulcie's pregnant and Jon is kicked out of his home. The parents-to-be decide to commit suicide and Sara initially asks to be included in the pact as she and Carol have argued, but then she pulls back. Rushing to Jon's house, Sara sees them pull out of the garage and thinks the suicide has been prevented, but a few minutes later Jon tries to outrun a freight train and is hit crossing the tracks. Poor Sara doesn't know where to turn, except to Carol who finally convinces Sara that she is loved. (199 pages)

Where it's reviewed:
Bulletin of the Center for Children's Books, November 2001, page 107
Kliatt, September 2001, page 11
Publishers Weekly, November 12, 2001, page 60
School Library Journal, October 2001, page 165
Voice of Youth Advocates, December 2001, page 361

Other books you might like:
Eve Bunting, *Jumping the Nail*, 1991
    Dru's friend Elisa jumps off a ninety-foot cliff with her boyfriend; they survive the jump but peer pressure drives her to try it again.
Scott Johnson, *Overnight Sensation*, 1994
    When Kerry's new group of friends leads her away from her old, individualistic friend Madeline, she realizes she's made a mistake.
Julie Johnston, *Adam and Eve and Pinch-Me*, 1994
    Sara arrives at her latest foster home determined to stay detached but the eccentric, highly individual Huddleston's refuse to comply with Sarah's plan.

578

LISE LUNGE-LARSEN
MARY AZARIAN, Illustrator

The Race of the Birkebeiners
(Boston: Houghton Mifflin Company, 2001)

Subject(s): Kings, Queens, Rulers, etc.; Legends; Folklore
Age range(s): Grades 2-5
Major character(s): Inga, Mother, Widow; Hakon, Son, Royalty (prince); Torstein Skevla, Skier, Rescuer; Skervald Skrukka, Skier, Rescuer
Time period(s): 13th century (1206)
Locale(s): Norway

Summary: The enemies of a murdered king seek to destroy his heir, Prince Hakon. To save the baby, Birkebeiner warriors accompany Inga, Prince Hakon and their priest across treacherous mountains. When a winter storm threatens to strand them on the mountaintop with no shelter Skervald and Torstein take the baby and go on alone. Fortunately they stumble onto a snow-covered barn in which they find refuge from the storm before the group reassembles and continues on to a friendly town where Prince Hakon can be protected. The enemies of the royal family demand one more test of Inga to prove the legitimacy of Prince Hakon's claim to the throne. (32 pages)

Where it's reviewed:
Booklist, July 2001, page 2014
Bulletin of the Center for Children's Books, October 2001, page 67
Publishers Weekly, September 3, 2001, page 88
Riverbank Review, Fall 2001, page 54
School Library Journal, September 2001, page 217

Awards the book has won:
ALA Notable Children's Books, 2002

Other books by the same author:
The Legend of the Lady Slipper: An Ojibwe Tale, 1999
The Troll with No Heart in His Body: And Other Tales of Trolls from Norway, 1999 (ALA Notable Children's Book)

Other books you might like:
Carmen Agra Deedy, *The Yellow Star: The Legend of King Christian X of Denmark*, 2000
A legend from the recent past tells how a king protected the Jews of Denmark by donning a yellow star to protest the order of the occupying Nazis.
Virginia Haviland, *Favorite Fairy Tales Told in Norway*, 1961
This illustrated collection includes the familiar "Three Billy Goats Gruff," "Boots and the Troll" and other stories.
Gwyn Jones, *Scandinavian Legends and Folktales*, 1956
Twenty-four tales from the folklore of Scandinavian countries includes some from Norway.

579

HUGH LUPTON
SOPHIE FATUS, Illustrator

The Story Tree: Tales to Read Aloud
(New York: Barefoot Books, 2001)

Subject(s): Folklore; Animals; Multicultural
Age range(s): Grades 1-3
Time period(s): Indeterminate Past
Locale(s): Fictional Country

Summary: Seven stories from the oral storytelling tradition of seven cultures comprise this illustrated title. "The Magic Porridge Pot" from the Brothers Grimm tells of the gift of a magic pot in return for a little girl's kindness and the tasty problem that develops when someone other than the little girl uses the pot. Set in India, "Monkey See, Monkey Do" tells of the troubles a hat peddler has with monkeys when his cart tips over and spills its cargo. Based on an African American traditional tale, "The Sweetest Song" explains how a little girl who has wandered too far from home cleverly outwits a hungry wolf. Also included are "Little Lord Feather-Frock" based on a Russian tale, a Norwegian favorite "The Three Billy Goats Gruff," the English tale "The Little Red Hen" and "The Blue Coat." Concluding source notes explain the origins of the tales. (64 pages)

Where it's reviewed:
Booklist, October 1, 2001, page 321
Bulletin of the Center for Children's Books, November 2001, page 108
School Library Journal, November 2001, page 147
Smithsonian, November 2001, page 120

Awards the book has won:
Smithsonian's Notable Books for Children, 2001

Other books by the same author:
The Songs of Birds: Stories and Poems of Many Cultures, 2000
Freaky Tales: From Far and Wide, 1999
Tales of Wisdom and Wonder, 1998

Other books you might like:
Mary Ann Hoberman, *You Read to Me, I'll Read to You: Very Short Stories to Read Together*, 2001
Thirteen brief stories combine humor, rhyme and repetition to ensure an enjoyable bedtime read-aloud.
Celia B. Lottridge, *Ten Small Tales*, 1994
Familiar folktales are simply retold to make them accessible to younger readers.
Margaret Mayo, *Tortoise's Flying Lesson*, 1995
A collection of retold and adapted folktales tells of animals supporting, tricking and learning from one another.

580

CHRIS LYNCH

All the Old Haunts
(New York: HarperCollins, 2001)

Subject(s): Short Stories; Social Issues
Age range(s): Grades 9-12

Summary: "All the old haunts" appear in the lives of teens as they become aware of the realities of life and have to make personal decisions. In "Chlorine" a young teen reveals hatred of her grandfather, incapacitated by a stroke, but stops short of retaliating for all his abusive ways. A formerly alcoholic father becomes sober and devotes himself to soberness with the same skill he devoted to alcoholism, becoming a puritanical pain to everyone in "Foghorn." Cousins swim at a quarry one day and one jumps while the other doesn't; Nick returns from the dead to offer his cousin one last chance to jump. Horrible and horrific, these ten short stories will linger with readers. (185 pages)

Where it's reviewed:
Bulletin of the Center for Children's Books, October 2001, page 67
Horn Book, September 2001, page 588
Publishers Weekly, October 29, 2001, page 65
School Library Journal, November 2001, page 160
Voice of Youth Advocates, October 2001, page 281

Other books by the same author:
Freewill, 2001
Gold Dust, 2000
Extreme Elvin, 1999
Whitechurch, 1999
Political Timber, 1996

Other books you might like:
Roald Dahl, *Skin and Other Stories*, 2000
  Short stories, characterized by surprise endings, make up this collection written by a magical author.
Lois Duncan, *On the Edge: Stories on the Brink*, 2000
  Young adult authors contribute stories about people "on the edge," whether from sabotage, schizophrenia or fried fettuccine noodles.
Donald R. Gallo, *No Easy Answers: Short Stories about Teenagers Making Tough Choices*, 1997
  Teens star in these short stories as they face moral crises, such as peer pressure, computer blackmail or gang initiations.
Tim Wynne-Jones, *The Book of Changes: Stories*, 1995
  Seven stories narrated by teens tell of ordinary dilemmas in their lives, from school assignments to divorce.

581

CHRIS LYNCH

Freewill

(New York: HarperCollins, 2001)

Subject(s): Grief; Grandparents; Family Problems
Age range(s): Grades 9-12
Major character(s): Will, 17-Year-Old, Artisan; Angela, Athlete; Pops, Grandfather (of Will); Gran, Grandmother (of Will)
Time period(s): 1990s
Locale(s): United States

Summary: Told in the second person, Will's pain and grief after the death of his father and stepmother, who drowned in an automobile accident, is so strong it overrides everything else in his life. Living with his grandparents, he has managed to cut himself off from others his age, with the exception of Angela who is one of the few who can make him laugh. Longing to be a pilot, instead he's in a vocational high school where his skill as a woodworker is evident to his teacher Mr. Jacks, who is currently angry with him for not carving more gnomes and whirligigs. Instead Will seems called to make wooden sculptures, totem-like affairs that begin appearing at the sites of teen suicides. Uncertain of what's happening, Will feels he's become the "grim reaper" and is terrified. Eventually Will stumbles into necessary healing, though it's a jumbled affair of more totems, listening to his Pops about help, realizing he's lonely but not alone, and establishing his own memorial to his father in this thought-provoking work. (148 pages)

Where it's reviewed:
Booklist, May 15, 2001, page 1745
Bulletin of the Center for Children's Books, March 2001, page 270
Horn Book, July 2001, page 457
School Library Journal, March 2001, page 252
Voice of Youth Advocates, August 2001, page 203

Awards the book has won:
ALA Michael L. Printz Honor Book, 2002
ALA Best Books for Young Adults, 2002

Other books by the same author:
All the Old Haunts, 2001
Gold Dust, 2000
Extreme Elvin, 1999
Whitechurch, 1999
Political Timber, 1996

Other books you might like:
Chris Crutcher, *Ironman*, 1995
  Bo ends up in an Anger Management class because his domineering, sadistic father has turned him into a young man who resists any and all authority.
Paul Fleischman, *Whirligig*, 1998
  Brent's punishment for accidentally killing Lea Zamora is to set up whirligigs in the four corners of America.
A.M. Jenkins, *Damage*, 2001
  Written in the second-person, Austin's loss of his father leaves him with depression so deep it wraps around his soul.
Ben Mikaelsen, *Petey*, 1998
  Lonely teenager Trevor and cerebral palsy patient Petey form an unlikely bond with each growing and learning from the other.

582

MARY E. LYONS

Knockabeg: A Famine Tale

(Boston: Houghton Mifflin, 2001)

Subject(s): Famine Victims; Fairies
Age range(s): Grades 5-7
Major character(s): Eamon, Child
Time period(s): 1840s
Locale(s): Ireland

Summary: The Nuckelevee fairies destroyed the East Isle and now turn their sights to the West Isle, also known as Ireland. They put a curse on the potato vines so that the entire crop will be destroyed, which in turn will destroy the good fairies, known as the Trooping Ones, who live in Knockabeg. The Trooping Ones decide to battle the Nuckevelees, but realize they need a human to fight with them and to feed them. With young Eamon's help, the Trooping Ones manage to push back the bad Nuckelevee fairies in this work that highlights the grimness of the potato famine in Ireland. (118 pages)

Where it's reviewed:

Booklist, November 15, 2001, page 572
Publishers Weekly, July 23, 2001, page 78
School Library Journal, September 2001, page 226
Voice of Youth Advocates, October 2001, page 292

Other books by the same author:

Dear Ellen Bee: A Civil War Scrapbook of Two Union Spies, 2000

The Poison Place, 1997
Letters from a Slave Girl: The Story of Harriet Jacobs, 1992
Raw Head, Bloody Bones: African-American Tales of the Supernatural, 1991

Other books you might like:

Eileen Dunlop, *Tales of St. Patrick*, 1996
    The life of the saint identified with Ireland is fictionalized in this work, but is a compilation of fact and legend.
Patricia Reilly Giff, *Nory Ryan's Song*, 2000
    Nory is thrilled when tickets arrive so the family can travel to America, but her elderly neighbor Anna won't leave her home in Ireland.
Elizabeth Lutzeier, *The Coldest Winter*, 1991
    The coldest winter Ireland has ever known is also the year the potato crop fails and farmers and their families try to immigrate to America.

M

583

AMY MACDONALD
CAT BOWMAN SMITH, Illustrator

No More Nasty

(New York: Melanie Kroupa Books/Farrar Straus Giroux, 2001)

Subject(s): Teacher-Student Relationships; Schools; Humor
Age range(s): Grades 4-6
Major character(s): Simon Maxwell, 5th Grader, Nephew; Matilda "Aunt Mattie" Maxwell, Aunt (great aunt), Teacher (substitute)
Time period(s): 2000s (2001)
Locale(s): United States

Summary: While Simon is just as relieved as his classmates to learn that their mean, nasty teacher has chosen to retire with five weeks remaining in the school year he's absolutely dismayed to see that the substitute is his unconventional great aunt. Fortunately Aunt Mattie doesn't acknowledge the relationship and Simon remembers to call her Mrs. Maxwell as the other students do, but still he feels guilty about the subterfuge. Aunt Mattie treats the students, known as the worst fifth grade in the school, with respect and they respond to her expectations. In only a few weeks Aunt Mattie improves their vocabulary, teaches them about electricity by dismantling the annoying PA system and gives them a short-cut system of multiplication that enables them to achieve the winning score at the Math Bee for the first time. As their confidence improves Aunt Mattie expects them to tackle the goal of winning the Science Fair by working together to develop a presentation that's useful and original. (172 pages)

Where it's reviewed:
Booklist, September 1, 2001, page 106
Horn Book, November 2001, page 754
Kirkus Reviews, July 15, 2001, page 1029
Publishers Weekly, August 27, 2001, page 86
School Library Journal, September 2001, page 230

Other books by the same author:
No More Nice, 1996

Other books you might like:
David A. Adler, *School Trouble for Andy Russell*, 1999
    The substitute in Andy's classroom blames the creative underachiever for mishaps that are the work of another student.
Andrew Clements, *The Landry News*, 1999
    Fifth graders use their student-run newspaper to support their unconventional teacher when he is threatened with the loss of his job.
Jamie Gilson, *Thirteen Ways to Sink a Sub*, 1982
    A fourth grade class holds a contest to see who can be the first to make the substitute teacher cry.
Betty MacDonald, *Hello, Mrs. Piggle-Wiggle*, 1957
    Children's bad habits are no match for the creative cures of unorthodox Mrs. Piggle-Wiggle.
P.J. Petersen, *The Sub*, 1993
    The plan of two friends to switch places and fool a substitute teacher for a day backfires when she returns the next day also.

584

MARGARET READ MACDONALD
TIM COFFEY, Illustrator

Mabela the Clever

(Morton Grove, IL: Albert Whitman & Company, 2001)

Subject(s): Folklore; Folk Tales
Age range(s): Grades K-2
Major character(s): Mabela, Mouse, Heroine; Cat, Cat, Trickster
Time period(s): Indeterminate Past
Locale(s): Africa

Summary: Back in the time when mice were foolish and cats took advantage of that trait Cat visits the mouse village with a tempting offer. Eagerly the curious mice accept Cat's plan and go marching off, single file with Mabela, the smallest of the group at the lead. Foolishly the mice follow Cat's directions so they are not aware of what is happening as they loudly sing Cat's marching song. Mabela recalls her father's teachings to listen, look around, pay attention and move fast. When she follows her father's instructions, she quickly discovers she's the only mouse that's not in Cat's bag, but not for long. (32 pages)

Where it's reviewed:
Booklist, July 2001, page 2014
Bulletin of the Center for Children's Books, May 2001, page 345
Horn Book, September 2001, page 603
Publishers Weekly, May 14, 2001, page 81
School Library Journal, June 2001, page 139

Awards the book has won:
Charlotte Zolotow Award, Winner, 2001

Other books by the same author:
The Girl Who Wore Too Much: A Folktale from Thailand, 1998
Tuck-Me-In-Tales: Bedtime Stories from Around the World, 1996
The Old Woman Who Lived in a Vinegar Bottle, 1995

Other books you might like:
John Archambault, *A Beautiful Feast for a Big King Cat*, 1994
A young mouse taunts a large, hungry cat that stands between the mouse and the safety of home. Bill Martin, Jr., co-author.
Arnold Lobel, *Mouse Soup*, 1977
Mouse has a plan that he hopes will keep him out of Weasel's soup pot.
Gary Soto, *Chato's Kitchen*, 1995
Cool cat Chato's plans to dine on his dinner guests change abruptly when the mice arrive riding on the back of a dog.

585

SCARLETT MACDOUGAL

Have a Nice Life Series

(New York: Penguin Putnam/Alloy, 2001-)

Series: Have a Nice Life
Subject(s): Friendship; School Life; Future
Age range(s): Grades 9-12
Major character(s): Zola Mitchell, 12th Grader; Olivia Dawes, 12th Grader; Wilamina "Min" Weinstock, 12th Grader; Sally Wilder, 12th Grader; Clarence Terence, Angel
Time period(s): 2000s
Locale(s): Madison, Wisconsin

Summary: Intergalactic angel Clarence Terence, or fairy godmother as he likes to refer to himself, alights on Earth to show four young girls their karmic destinies so that he can attain his sixth incarnation. One look in his View-Master and he'll be able to show Zola, Olivia, Min and Sally what their futures will be and it's not a pretty sight. Each girl will have one chance to change her behavior, which in turn will alter her future. Unfortunately, tonight is their senior prom and these four girls are too busy with prom preparations like total waxing or learning to wear a backless bra, to pay any attention to Clarence; afterwards, none of the girls likes what she hears. As Clarence says, this new series is "kind of like *It's a Wonderful Life* meets *Terminator II*."

Where it's reviewed:
Kliatt, May 2001, page 24
Publishers Weekly, December 11, 2001, page 85
Voice of Youth Advocates, April 2001, page 32

Awards the book has won:
ALA Quick Picks for Reluctant Young Adult Readers, 2002

Other books by the same author:
Popover, 2001 (Have a Nice Life, Volume 3)
Score, 2001 (Have a Nice Life, Volume 4)
Play, 2000 (Have a Nice Life, Volume 2)
Start Here, 2000 (Have a Nice Life, Volume 1)

Other books you might like:
Ann Brashares, *The Sisterhood of the Traveling Pants*, 2001
Four friends, apart for the summer, decide that a pair of jeans, their rules for wearing and a schedule for mailing, will keep them united.
Thom Eberhardt, *Rat Boys: A Dating Experiment*, 2001
Marci and Summer lie about dates for the Spring Fling dance but, with the help of a magic ring, rats are transformed into their "hot" dates!
Louise Rennison, *Angus, Thongs and Full-Frontal Snogging: Confessions of Georgia Nicolson*, 2000
In her diary, Georgia records her interest in kissing, her appearance, and her opposition to most of what the adult world thinks is important.
Rosie Rushton, *Just Don't Make a Scene, Mum*, 1999
Five British teens find their lives connected through a radio show that lets them describe embarrassing moments in this first of a series.

586

PATRICIA MACLACHLAN

Caleb's Story

(New York: Joanna Cotler Books/HarperCollins Publishers, 2001)

Subject(s): Fathers and Sons; Forgiveness; Frontier and Pioneer Life
Age range(s): Grades 3-6
Major character(s): Caleb Witting, Son, Brother; Jacob "Papa" Witting, Father, Farmer; John "Grandfather" Witting, Father, Grandfather; Cassie Witting, 4-Year-Old, Daughter
Time period(s): 1910s (1918)
Locale(s): Kansas

Summary: Cassie is the first to see the stranger in the barn who turns out to be Papa's long lost father. Jacob is shocked and angry for he believes John Witting to be dead. Fascinated by this relative who seems to have appeared out of nowhere, Caleb records the family's interactions and tries to share his journal with Grandfather. When Caleb deduces that Grandfather is illiterate he quietly tutors him each evening. Very gradually, but long after Caleb and Cassie embrace Grandfather, Jacob overcomes his anger for what is past and becomes able to include his father in the family. (116 pages)

Where it's reviewed:
Booklist, September 1, 2001, page 107
Bulletin of the Center for Children's Books, October 2001, page 68

Horn Book, September 2001, page 590
Publishers Weekly, September 24, 2001, page 94
School Library Journal, September 2001, page 230

Other books by the same author:
Skylark, 1994
Sarah, Plain and Tall, 1985 (Newbery Medal)
Seven Kisses in a Row, 1983

Other books you might like:
Gerald Hausman, *The Jacob Ladder*, 2001
Tall T is now sure how he feels about his father's departure from the family but he knows he now has help out by working and getting an education.
Thomas L. Tedrow, *Good Neighbors*, 1992
During the harsh winter of 1905 a farm family and their neighbors work together to assure everyone's survival.
Laura Ingalls Wilder, *Farmer Boy*, 1953
The illustrated version of the previously published novel tells of Almanzo Wilder's boyhood on a farm in upstate New York.

587

PATRICIA MACLACHLAN
JANE DYER, Illustrator

The Sick Day
(New York: A Doubleday Book for Young Readers, 2001)

Subject(s): Illness; Fathers and Daughters; Family Life
Age range(s): Grades K-2
Major character(s): Emily, Daughter, Child; Father, Father, Writer; Mama, Mother
Time period(s): 2000s (2001)
Locale(s): United States

Summary: In an updated, newly illustrated version of a title originally published in 1979, Emily approaches Father in his writing room to list her aches and pains. She's alarmed to hear Father's opinion that she has a "bug" and is relieved by his explanation of the expression's meaning. Father tucks Emily into bed, brings her special blankets and animals and searches in vain for the thermometer. He humors her with music and stories and, the next day, Emily does the same for him while Mama stays home from work to clean up the mess. (32 pages)

Where it's reviewed:
Booklist, February 15, 2001, page 1141
Children's Bookwatch, May 2001, page 7
Horn Book Guide, Fall 2001, page 266
Publishers Weekly, May 28, 2001, page 90

Other books by the same author:
What You Know First, 1995
All the Places to Love, 1994 (Notable Children's Books in the Language Arts)
Mama One, Mama Two, 1982

Other books you might like:
Cathryn Falwell, *Dragon Tooth*, 1996
It's a loose tooth not an illness that makes Sara cranky, but still her patient Papa gives her an idea that helps Sara feel better and lose the tooth too!

Marilyn Hafner, *Mommies Don't Get Sick*, 1995
Daddy and Abby try to cope with the family household responsibilities while Mommy is sick in bed.
Vera Rosenberry, *When Vera Was Sick*, 1998
Father comforts Vera with flowers and a good night song when she is feeling sick and miserable with the chicken pox.

588

SUE MACY, Editor

Girls Got Game: Sports Stories & Poems
(New York: Holt, 2001)

Subject(s): Sports; Short Stories; Women
Age range(s): Grades 6-10

Summary: Nine poems and an equal number of short stories describe some of the vast array of sports in which women are now able to participate. From the editor Sue Macy comes "Batting after Sophie" in which the trials of batting second are frustrating to softball player Becky. Being the best pitcher around for stickball doesn't mean a thing when you're told that next season there'll be a baseball league, but girls aren't allowed to play, in "Beanie" by Jacqueline Woodson. From Nancy Boutilier come several poems including "The Rhythm of Strong" about being part of a rowing team. Lucy Jane Bledsoe, Virginia Euwer Wolff and Linnea Due are just a few of the other authors whose works appear in this collection. (152 pages)

Where it's reviewed:
Booklist, June 1, 2001, page 1858
Bulletin of the Center for Children's Books, June 2001, page 379
Horn Book, July 2001, page 458
School Library Journal, July 2001, page 123
Voice of Youth Advocates, August 2001, page 221

Other books by the same author:
Play Like a Girl: A Celebration of Women's Sports, 1999 (Nonfiction)
Whole New Ball Game: Story of the All-American Girls Professional Baseball League, 1999 (Nonfiction)
Winning Ways: A Photohistory of American Women in Sports, 1996 (Nonfiction)

Other books you might like:
David Klass, *A Different Season*, 1987
A female second baseman on the boys baseball team affects star pitcher Jim Roark's usually perfect throw.
Jeanne Schinto, *Show Me a Hero: Great Contemporary Stories about Sports*, 1995
Sports covers a multitude of emotions and reaches across a wide range of lifestyles and backgrounds in this collection of 21 stories.
Jerry Spinelli, *There's a Girl in My Hammerlock*, 1991
Maisie finds everyone against her when she joins the wrestling team, but she's determined to make it through the season.
Virginia Euwer Wolff, *Bat 6*, 1998
Two Oregon farm communities play softball against each

other every summer, but this year racist feelings from World War II create trouble for both teams.

589

MARIA ELENA MAGGI
GLORIA CALDERON, Illustrator
ELISA AMADO, Translator

The Great Canoe: A Karina Legend
(Toronto: Groundwood/Douglas & McIntyre, 2001)

Subject(s): Folklore; Indians of South America; Floods
Age range(s): Grades 1-4
Major character(s): Kaputano, Deity
Time period(s): Indeterminate Past
Locale(s): Venezuela

Summary: Kaputano, the Sky Dweller, warns the people that great rains will fall and cover the world. Most of the Karina people fail to heed Kaputano's words but the four couples that do build a large canoe. Into the finished canoe they gather two of each kind of animal and seed from every plant. Then the rains of which Kaputano warned begin and the land is soon flooded. When the rains stop and canoe comes to rest in a desolate place Kaputano helps to create a world in which the Karina people can live. An "Afterword" provides background for the legend originally published in Venezuela in 1998. (38 pages)

Where it's reviewed:
Booklist, November 15, 2001, page 577
Bulletin of the Center for Children's Books, December 2001, page 147
Horn Book, January 2002, page 88
Publishers Weekly, September 17, 2001, page 78
School Library Journal, October 2001, page 144

Awards the book has won:
Bulletin of the Center for Children's Books Blue Ribbon, 2001

Other books you might like:
Arthur Geisert, *After the Flood*, 1994
    After the water recedes, the ark is used for shelter and the work of repopulating the earth begins.
Pippa Goodhart, *Noah Makes a Boat*, 1997
    Noah's problem is that he has no experience in boat building but he's obedient and resourceful so he completes the task just as the rains begin.
Geraldine McCaughrean, *The Story of Noah and the Ark*, 1989
    Based on the Biblical story, Noah follows God's command to build an ark and load it with two of every animal.
Peter Spier, *Noah's Ark*, 1977
    A Caldecott Medal winner pictorially reenacts the well-known story of the flood.

590

BARBARA MAITLAND
NADINE BERNARD WESTCOTT, Illustrator

The Bookstore Burglar
(New York: Dutton Children's Books, 2001)

Series: Dutton Easy Reader
Subject(s): Animals/Cats; Stores, Retail; Burglary
Age range(s): Grades 1-3
Major character(s): Mr. Brown, Businessman, Store Owner; Cobweb, Cat; Unnamed Character, Criminal
Time period(s): 2000s (2001)
Locale(s): United States

Summary: In the sequel to *The Bookstore Ghost* Cobweb tries to alert Mr. Brown to the strange man in the bookshop who pockets the store's extra key. The store's "ghosts" understand Cobweb's cry for help and push books from the shelves onto the man but still Mr. Brown doesn't see the clues. Later, after he closes the shop for the night and leaves, the burglar returns, using the key to gain entrance. Cobweb and the store's "ghosts" (mice) succeed in frightening the burglar who runs away just as Mr. Brown comes downstairs to investigate the strange noises. (32 pages)

Where it's reviewed:
Booklist, November 1, 2001, page 486
Horn Book Guide, Spring 2002, page 68
School Library Journal, October 2001, page 124

Other books by the same author:
Moo in the Morning, 2000
My Bear and Me, 1999
The Bookstore Ghost, 1998 (Dutton Easy Reader)

Other books you might like:
David A. Adler, *Young Cam Jansen and the Missing Cookie*, 1996
    When Jason discovers his chocolate chip cookie missing from his lunch box Cam Jansen solves the mystery of its disappearance.
Erin Douglas, *Get That Pest!*, 2000
    On their third try Mom and Pop Nash capture the fox that's stealing eggs from the henhouse in this humorous "Green Light Reader."
Elizabeth Levy, *Parent's Night Fright*, 1998
    Charlene's leadership, Chip's invisibility and deaf Justin's lip-reading are used to solve the mystery of a missing short story.
Marjorie Weinman Sharmat, *The Nate the Great Series*, 1972-
    In a mystery series for beginning readers, Nate follows one clue after another in the style of Sherlock Holmes.

591

PETER MALONEY, Author/Illustrator
FELECIA ZEKAUSKAS, Illustrator

His Mother's Nose
(New York: Dial Books for Young Readers, 2001)

Subject(s): Family Life; Identity; Individuality
Age range(s): Grades K-3

Major character(s): Percival Puddicombe, Son, Child
Time period(s): Indeterminate Past
Locale(s): United States

Summary: Percival grows up feeling as if he's made of various parts of his relatives. He hears comments from other family members that he has his mother's nose, his brother's hair, or his father's eyes. Percival's aunt thinks he has her ear for music and his uncle's head for numbers. Trying to be simply Percival, he runs away and when he does, each family member loses the part of themselves that Percival shares. His mother awakens to find she has no nose; his sister can't talk because she has no mouth and his brother's bald. Percival makes his way to his grandparents' home where he looks at photo albums of his ancestors. Percival sees the family resemblance in all of them and realizes that he can be an individual and still share family traits. (40 pages)

Where it's reviewed:
Booklist, September 1, 2001, page 116
Horn Book Guide, Spring 2002, page 52
Kirkus Reviews, June 15, 2001, page 867
Publishers Weekly, August 6, 2001, page 88
School Library Journal, October 2001, page 124

Other books by the same author:
Belly Button Boy, 2000
The Magic Hockey Stick, 1999
Redbird at Rockefeller Center, 1997

Other books you might like:
Rebecca Bond, *Bravo, Maurice!*, 2000
    Maurice's relatives each see a resemblance between one of his features and one of their own.
Karla Kuskin, *I Am Me*, 2000
    A little girl surrounded by family members noting how her features remind them of one family member or another knows that she is actually ''me.''
Marilyn Singer, *The One and Only Me*, 2000
    To a young girl, having teeth like her uncle or a nose like grandma means nothing because she knows that she is completely unique.

592

CREINA MANSFIELD

Cherokee

(Dublin, Ireland: The O'Brien Press, 2001)

Subject(s): Grandfathers; Aunts and Uncles; Diaries
Age range(s): Grades 6-8
Major character(s): Gene Crawford, Orphan, 12-Year-Old; William ''Cherokee'' Crawford, Musician (saxophone player), Grandfather; Mrs. Walmsley, Social Worker; Joan Smythe, Aunt; Wesley Smythe, Cousin
Time period(s): 1990s
Locale(s): Clifftown, England (East Anglia)

Summary: Until he was twelve years old, Gene led a wonderful life traveling with his grandfather, the noted saxophone player Cherokee. However, his aunt Joan doesn't approve of this arrangement and when Gene arrives at Aunt Joan's for his annual summer visit, she manages to have Mrs. Walmsley from Social Services force him to stay. And keep a diary!

Gene solves that problem by keeping two diaries, one for Mrs. Walmsley and one for himself. Gradually he adjusts to Aunt Joan who cleans obsessively and cooks poorly. He even realizes that his wimpy cousin Wesley isn't all that bad, especially when Wesley figures out how to reunite Gene and Cherokee in this heart-warming story. (127 pages)

Where it's reviewed:
School Library Journal, November 2001, page 162

Other books by the same author:
My Nasty Neighbors, 1997

Other books you might like:
Christopher Paul Curtis, *Bud, Not Buddy*, 1999
    Tired of foster homes, Bud runs away to find his father, but instead locates his grandfather, the noted musician Herman E. Calloway.
Betty Levin, *Shadow-Catcher*, 2000
    Jonathan travels with his grandfather on his summer photography shoot when he photographs some underhanded shenanigans at a logging camp.
Chris Lynch, *Political Timber*, 1996
    Gordie's grandfather, the town's former mayor now jailed for racketeering, intends to run Gordie for mayor and direct the campaign from his cell.
Barbara Park, *The Graduation of Jake Moon*, 2000
    Though his grandfather is diagnosed with Alzheimer's, Jake remembers that this man is still his beloved grandfather.
Sue Townsend, *The Secret Diary of Adrian Mole, Aged 13 3/4*, 1982
    Adrian Mole, who often feels beleaguered and put upon, begins his diary the day he gets his first zit.

593

JULIET MARILLIER

Son of the Shadows

(New York: Tor, 2001)

Series: Sevenwaters Trilogy. Book 2
Subject(s): Love; Magic; Family
Age range(s): Grades 9-Adult
Major character(s): Liadan, Sister; Bran ''the Painted Man'', Warrior
Time period(s): Indeterminate Past
Locale(s): Ireland

Summary: Liadan is the daughter of Sorcha, heroine of *Daughter of the Forest*. As Sorcha sacrificed herself to save her seven brothers, who had been turned into swans, Liadan is the sacrifice that will continue to bind the factions of the family together. In the years since the brothers were saved, tensions have mounted with the English, despite Sorcha's marriage to one of them, and the leaders of Sevenwaters and their allies contemplate an all-out assault on their hereditary enemies. Peace has reigned most of Liadan's life, but it appears that war will dominate the rest of her days. Particularly aggravating are the assaults of the Painted Man, a mysterious attacker who appears from nowhere and disappears again. Liadan's quiet contemplation of her future is swept away when her kindness to a wounded man leads to a friendship with the hated and despised Painted Man. The tattoos that paint his skin cannot hide from Liadan that this is a tortured soul, not an instrument of evil, but Liadan's people would rather hear anything than the truth about Bran. (462 pages)

Where it's reviewed:
Booklist, May 15, 2001, page 1738
Library Journal, May 15, 2001, page 167
Publishers Weekly, April 16, 2001, page 49
Science Fiction Chronicle, May 2001, page 40

Other books by the same author:
Daughter of the Forest, 2000 (Sevenwaters Trilogy, Book 1)

Other books you might like:
Ann Chamberlin, *The Merlin of St. Gilles' Well*, 2000
    Joan of Arc is born as a follower of the old ways into a France full of magic.
Nancy McKenzie, *The High Queen*, 1995
    Guinevere's tragedy deepens as she falls more deeply in love with the wrong man.
Donna Jo Napoli, *Zel*, 1996
    In this retelling of Rapunzel, a young girl is held prisoner while her lover struggles through magical barriers to rescue her.

MICHELE MARINEAU
SUSAN OURIOU, Translator

Lean Mean Machines
(Calgary, Canada: Red Deer Press, 2001)

Series: Northern Lights Young Novels
Subject(s): School Life; Blackmail; Moving, Household
Age range(s): Grades 7-10
Major character(s): Laure Lupien, 10th Grader; Jeremy Martucci, 10th Grader; Christian Tougas, 11th Grader
Time period(s): 1990s
Locale(s): Montreal, Quebec, Canada

Summary: Attending a public high school, rather than her expensive private school, Laure hopes no one will find out that her lawyer father stole his client's money, bought and sold illegal drugs and then, when caught, committed suicide. But despicable Christian discovers her secret and uses the knowledge to try to blackmail Laure into an intimate relationship. Luckily Jeremy, whose locker is next to hers, extends a protective arm around her, throws the truth at Christian and forces Laure to confront her biggest fears. When Laure realize no lightning bolts come from the sky when talking about her father, she takes the first steps toward healing in this work translated from the French. (127 pages)

Where it's reviewed:
Quill & Quire, February 2001, page 39
Resource Links, October 2001, page 40
School Library Journal, November 2001, page 162
Voice of Youth Advocates, August 2001, page 204

Other books by the same author:
The Road to Chlifa, 1995

Other books you might like:
Laurie Halse Anderson, *Speak*, 1999
    Melinda is ostracized by classmates who think she dialed 911 to break up a party; when the truth comes out, she is vindicated.
A.C. LeMieux, *The TV Guidance Counselor*, 1993
    Upset about his parents' divorce, and forced to scale back financially, Michael uses his photography to shield himself from others.
Carol Sonenklar, *My Own Worst Enemy*, 1999
    When Eve's family faces financial problems and has to downsize, she lies to her new friends at school as she tries to be part of the snobbish clique.

595

JOHN MARSDEN

The Night Is for Hunting
(Boston: Houghton Mifflin, 2001)

Series: Tomorrow, When the War Began. Book 6
Subject(s): Survival; War
Age range(s): Grades 8-12
Major character(s): Ellie, Terrorist
Time period(s): 1990s
Locale(s): Australia

Summary: After rescuing four orphans in *Burning for Revenge*, Ellie finds the "ferals" are resistant to their attempts to help them which almost causes death or injury for the group. Reduced to five teenagers who have been fighting their country's takeover, Ellie's group is in "Hell," their term for an inaccessible ravine they discovered while on a camping trip. Hell has been their protection but recently signs indicate their safe spot may have been detected. Ellie is bothered by all the killing she's been forced to commit, though it's always been to save her friends or herself, in this sixth of a series. (246 pages)

Where it's reviewed:
Booklist, November 1, 2001, page 466
Kliatt, September 2001, page 11
School Library Journal, October 2001, page 165
Voice of Youth Advocates, December 2001, page 372

Other books by the same author:
Other Side of Dawn, 2002 (Tomorrow, When the War Began, Book 7)
Burning for Revenge, 2000 (Tomorrow, When the War Began, Book 5)
Darkness Be My Friend, 1999 (Tomorrow, When the War Began, Book 4)
A Killing Frost, 1998 (Tomorrow, When the War Began, Book 3)
The Dead of Night, 1997 (Tomorrow, When the War Began, Book 2)
Tomorrow, When the War Began, 1995 (Tomorrow, When the War Began, Book 1)

Other books you might like:
Harry Mazer, *A Boy at War: A Novel of Pearl Harbor*, 2001
    Adam's life turns upside down the Sunday he goes fishing

with friends in Pearl Harbor and sees his father's ship, and others, go up in flames.

Alice Mead, *Girl of Kosovo*, 2001
Zana is caught up in the war between Serbs and Albanians when family members are killed and her uncle threatens her best friend.

Gary Paulsen, *The White Fox Chronicles: Escape, Return, Breakout*, 2000
Cody is part of a resistance group of Americans fighting to regain control of their country from the Confederation of Consolidated Republics.

596

ANN M. MARTIN

Belle Teal

(New York: Scholastic Press, 2001)

Subject(s): Civil Rights Movement; Prejudice; Single Parent Families
Age range(s): Grades 4-7
Major character(s): Belle Teal Harper, 5th Grader, Friend; Clarice Baker, 5th Grader, Friend; Darryl Craig, 5th Grader (African American), Friend
Time period(s): 1960s (1962)
Locale(s): Coker Creek

Summary: The usual beginning of school excitement is compounded this year with the knowledge that three colored students will enter Coker Creek Elementary for the first time. For Belle Teal and Clarice the situation is interesting but not alarming for they have learned tolerance and acceptance of others in their families. Belle Teal is not prepared for the angry racist crowds outside the school as she arrives and when Darryl enters her classroom she's surprised by the reaction of some students. Clarice and Belle Teal soon learn that Darryl shares their interests in writing so they quickly begin to spend recess working together on a project. Not all of Belle Teal's ideas to include Darryl and help others see him as a person work effectively, but still Darryl values the simple acceptance and friendship that Belle Teal and Clarice offer. (214 pages)

Where it's reviewed:
Booklist, October 1, 2001, page 319
Horn Book, January 2002, page 81
Publishers Weekly, September 3, 2001, page 88
School Library Journal, September 2001, page 230
Voice of Youth Advocates, December 2001, page 361

Awards the book has won:
Notable Social Studies Trade Books for Young People, 2002

Other books by the same author:
The Doll People, 2000 (ALA Notable Children's Book, Laura Godwin, co-author)
Ten Kids, No Pets, 1988
Kristy's Great Idea, 1986
Stage Fright, 1984

Other books you might like:
Vaunda Micheaux Nelson, *Mayfield Crossing*, 1993
When the children of Mayfield Crossing are sent to larger Parkview Elementary they are treated as outsiders and judged by the color of their skin.

Mildred D. Taylor, *The Gold Cadillac*, 1987
An African-American family from Ohio, visiting relatives in the South, faces the racism that is a part of life in the South in the 1950s.

Ronder Thomas Young, *Learning by Heart*, 1993
In the 1960s Rachel becomes aware of racial prejudices and their impact on friendships in her small southern town.

597

RAFE MARTIN
DAVID SHANNON, Illustrator

The Shark God

(New York: Arthur A. Levine/Scholastic Press, 2001)

Subject(s): Animals/Sharks; Folklore; Legends
Age range(s): Grades K-3
Major character(s): Kauhuhu, Deity, Shape-changer; Unnamed Character, Child, Brother; Unnamed Character, Child, Sister
Time period(s): Indeterminate Past
Locale(s): Pacific Islands

Summary: When no one in their island community will help them free a shark, siblings do so by removing the tangled rope in which the shark is ensnared. On their way home the children violate the king's law by touching his drum and are condemned to death. Their parents plead for their children's lives, but the cruel king is unrelenting. Bravely, the parents seek Kauhuhu who listens to their tale and instructs them to prepare a canoe and wait at sea for their children. The parents comply, a great storm comes with huge waves that demolish the palace and the children ride out to sea on the palace gate to their grateful parents. Sources for the tale are included in the concluding "Author's Note."(32 pages)

Where it's reviewed:
Booklist, November 1, 2001, page 476
Horn Book, November 2001, page 761
Kirkus Reviews, September 1, 2001, page 1297
Publishers Weekly, November 5, 2001, page 67
School Library Journal, September 2001, page 218

Other books by the same author:
The Language of Birds, 2000
The Eagle's Gift, 1997
The Boy Who Lived with the Seals, 1993 (Booklist Editors' Choice)

Other books you might like:
Lee Wardlaw, *Punia and the King of Sharks: A Hawaiian Folktale*, 1997
The son of a fisherman, Punia tricks the King of Sharks in order to catch his lobsters.

Julie Stewart Williams, *Maui Goes Fishing*, 1991
The demigod Maui pulls the Hawaiian Islands out of the water with a giant fishing hook.

Laura E. Williams, *Torch Fishing with the Sun*, 1999
Makoa's grandfather catches the sun in his net every evening so the villagers can torch fish along the shore. After he dies the sun no longer sets.

RAFE MARTIN
KIMBERLY BULCKEN ROOT, Illustrator

The Storytelling Princess
(New York: G.P. Putnam's Sons, 2001)

Subject(s): Princes and Princesses; Storytelling; Marriage
Age range(s): Grades K-3
Major character(s): Unnamed Character, Royalty (prince); Unnamed Character, Royalty (princess), Storyteller
Time period(s): Indeterminate Past
Locale(s): Fictional Country

Summary: A prince who loves to read and a princess who seeks adventure are both told by their fathers that a marriage has been arranged for them. Each refuses the arrangement and counters the command. The prince will only marry someone who can tell him a tale for which he does not know the ending and the princess prefers to be washed into the sea by a storm. Both see their dreams fulfilled and inadvertently honor their parents' wishes. The princess, after surviving a storm-tossed sea, tells the prince the story of her adventure that brought her, in disguise, to his kingdom. (32 pages)

Where it's reviewed:
Booklist, July 2001, page 2014
Bulletin of the Center for Children's Books, July 2001, page 415
Kirkus Reviews, May 15, 2001, page 744
Publishers Weekly, June 25, 2001, page 72
School Library Journal, September 2001, page 199

Other books by the same author:
The Language of Birds, 2000
The Eagle's Gift, 1997
The Boy Who Lived with the Seals, 1993 (Booklist Editors' Choice)

Other books you might like:
J. Patrick Lewis, *Night of the Goat Children*, 1999
   Princess Birgitta, disguised as a hag, tells a convincing story to a group of outlaws and saves her town and her people.
Sheila MacGill-Callahan, *To Capture the Wind*, 1997
   To free her betrothed from a pirate, Oonagh must correctly answer four riddles.
Robert D. San Souci, *Brave Margaret: An Irish Adventure*, 1999
   In a retelling of a traditional tale, Margaret bravely faces adventure and danger to achieve her goal.
Marilyn Singer, *The Palace of the Ocean King*, 1995
   Mariana dives into the ocean that she fears in order to save her beloved Sylvain from the Ocean King.

CLAIRE MASUREL
KADY MACDONALD DENTON, Illustrator

Two Homes
(Cambridge, MA: Candlewick Press, 2001)

Subject(s): Divorce; Parent and Child; Dwellings
Age range(s): Preschool-Kindergarten
Major character(s): Alex, Child of Divorced Parents; Mommy, Mother, Divorced Person; Daddy, Father, Divorced Person
Time period(s): 2000s (2001)
Locale(s): United States

Summary: Alex has a Mommy and a Daddy and a home with each one. One home is in the city and one home is near the beach. Each home has a kitchen to cook in and a bedroom just for Alex. Friends come over to play at each home. Alex has two phone numbers, two toothbrushes and two parents who love their child very much. (32 pages)

Where it's reviewed:
Booklist, June 2001, page 1881
Horn Book Guide, Fall 2001, page 237
Kirkus Reviews, May 15, 2001, page 744
Riverbank Review, Winter 2001-2002, page 30
School Library Journal, August 2001, page 157

Awards the book has won:
Booklist Editors' Choice/Books for Youth, 2002

Other books by the same author:
Too Big, 1999
No, No, Titus!, 1997
Ten Dogs in the Window: A Countdown Book, 1997

Other books you might like:
Durga Bernhard, *To & Fro, Fast & Slow*, 2001
   A girl travels back and forth between mother and father, country home and city apartment always saying hello or good-bye to someone.
Judith Caseley, *Priscilla Twice*, 1995
   After her parents separate, Priscilla must adjust to life in two different households.
Sally Grindley, *A New Room for William*, 2000
   William is not happy to experience the changes forced by his parents' divorce but decorating his new room at Mom's house helps him adjust.
Judith Vigna, *I Live with Daddy*, 1997
   Following her parents' divorce Olivia lives with her father but writes a book about her mother's career in television.

600

CAROL MATAS

The War Within: A Novel of the Civil War
(New York: Simon & Schuster, 2001)

Subject(s): Civil War; Jews; Prejudice
Age range(s): Grades 5-8
Major character(s): Hannah Green, 13-Year-Old; Joanna Green, Sister; Jonathan Mazer, Military Personnel (Union Army)
Time period(s): 1860s
Locale(s): Holly Springs, Michigan; Memphis, Tennessee

Summary: Even though General Grant and his Union troops occupy their town, Hannah's family continues to operate their general store, her father and older brothers fight for the Confederacy and her sister even begins dating Union Captain Mazer. Then, because of concern over profiteering in cotton, General Order 11 appears which changes their lives. Though the Green family is Jewish, they've practiced their religion in secret, but now must acknowledge their faith as all Jews have been given twenty-four hours to leave any land that's under Grant's command. With their Southern way of life in total disarray, Hannah and the other members of her family head toward Memphis with nothing more than the clothes on their backs and a few personal items. Hannah reconsiders her life and her feelings, for she now hates the Union but also sees the parallels between being a slave and being a Jew in this fictional treatment of a little-known piece of the Civil War. (151 pages)

Where it's reviewed:
Booklist, April 1, 2001, page 1484
Bulletin of the Center for Children's Books, May 2001, page 346
Kirkus Reviews, April 15, 2001, page 589
School Library Journal, June 2001, page 152
Voice of Youth Advocates, June 2001, page 124

Other books by the same author:
Sparks Fly Upward, 2002
In My Enemy's House, 1999
Greater than Angels, 1998
The Garden, 1997
After the War, 1996

Other books you might like:
Pamela Smith Hill, *A Voice from the Border*, 1998
   When her father is killed in action and her home commandeered by a Union officer, Reeves comes to hate everything about the Yankees.
Gloria Houston, *Mountain Valor*, 1994
   After their farm is raided by Union soldiers, Valor dresses as a boy, rides into the Union camp, and rescues her family's belongings.
Ann Rinaldi, *In My Father's House*, 1993
   In a bizarre coincidence, the Civil War begins and ends on the McLean's land, with Lee surrendering to Grant in their parlor.

601

PETRA MATHERS, Author/Illustrator

Dodo Gets Married
(New York: Anne Schwartz Book/Atheneum Books for Young Readers, 2001)

Subject(s): Animals/Birds; Weddings; Courtship
Age range(s): Grades K-2
Major character(s): Dodo, Bird, Bride; Captain Vince, Bird, Amputee
Time period(s): Indeterminate
Locale(s): Fictional Country

Summary: Weekly Dodo rides past Captain Vince's house without gathering the courage to stop and meet him. Though Captain Vince notices her, he sits in the house mourning the loss of his leg in a helicopter accident and feeling useless. When Dodo finally stops to admire the windmill collection in the captain's yard, Vince watches warily from the window. A romance blossoms and soon wedding plans are being finalized. Alas, a bubble bath the night before the ceremony

somehow turns Dodo's plumage a brilliant and luminescent shade of green. While Dodo is horrified, Captain Vince still loves her and the wedding proceeds as planned. (32 pages)

Where it's reviewed:
Booklist, April 15, 2001, page 1566
Horn Book Guide, Fall 2001, page 266
Kirkus Reviews, April 1, 2001, page 502
Publishers Weekly, May 7, 2001, page 246
School Library Journal, May 2001, page 129

Other books by the same author:
A Cake for Herbie, 2000 (Horn Book Fanfare)
Lottie's New Friend, 1999
Lottie's New Beach Towel, 1998

Other books you might like:
Mary Jane Auch, *Hen Lake*, 1995
   Poulette, a determined hen ballerina, challenges a conceited barnyard peacock to talent contest.
Christine Davenier, *Leon and Albertine*, 1997
   Leon can't get Albertine to notice him until he does what comes naturally for pigs and his infectious joy touches even his beloved chicken.
Jef Kaminsky, *Poppy & Ella: 3 Stories about 2 Friends*, 2000
   Good friends Poppy and Ella do not always agree but they know just when and how to help each other.

602

GAY MATTHAEI
JEWEL GRUTMAN, Co-Author
ADAM CVIJANOVIC, Illustrator

The Sketchbook of Thomas Blue Eagle
(San Francisco: Chronicle Books, 2001)

Subject(s): Indians of North America; Entertainment
Age range(s): Grades 5-8
Major character(s): Thomas Blue Eagle, Indian (Lakota), 18-Year-Old; Echo, Indian (Lakota); Buffalo Bill Cody, Historical Figure (buffalo hunter), Entertainer; Annie Oakley, Historical Figure (sharpshooter)
Time period(s): 1880s
Locale(s): Pine Ridge Reservation, South Dakota; Europe

Summary: Returning to the Pine Ridge Reservation after school in Carlisle, Pennsylvania, Blue Eagle wants to marry Echo, but lacks the horses and cows needed as presents for her family. When Wild Bill Cody asks Blue Eagle to join his Wild West show, he accepts knowing he can save his money to marry Echo. After a tour of America, where Blue Eagle equals Annie Oakley in shooting and excels in riding, Cody's show crosses the Atlantic to tour Europe. What a trip! Blue Eagle meets European artists, sees the Pope, and is robbed. Returning home, Blue Eagle and Echo are reunited and his sketchbook, filled with drawings and memories of his travels, is returned. (62 pages)

Where it's reviewed:
Booklist, April 1, 2001, page 1468
Bulletin of the Center for Children's Books, May 2001, page 347
Christian Science Monitor, March 22, 2001, page 19
Publishers Weekly, March 19, 2001, page 102

Times Educational Supplement, June 22, 2001, page 522

Other books by the same author:
The Journal of Julia Singing Bear, 1996
The Ledgerbook of Thomas Blue Eagle, 1994

Other books you might like:
Judy Alter, *Cherokee Rose*, 1996
    Taught trick roping by her father, Tommy Jo signs up with Buffalo Bill's Wild West Show where she's known as Cherokee Rose.
Sherry Garland, *The Last Rainmaker*, 1997
    Running away from a cruel aunt, Caroline joins Shawnee Sam's Wild West Extravaganza where she meets her Native American grandfather, "the last rainmaker."
Sheila Solomon Klass, *A Shooting Star: A Novel about Annie Oakley*, 1996
    Phoebe Anne learns to shoot a rifle after her father dies and the family needs to be fed, a skill that comes in handy later in her life.
Gloria Whelan, *Miranda's Last Stand*, 1999
    To earn enough money to renovate their inherited farm, Miranda and her mother join Buffalo Bill's Wild West Show.

603

KEZI MATTHEWS

Scorpio's Child
(Chicago: Cricket Books, 2001)

Subject(s): Secrets; Family Problems; City and Town Life
Age range(s): Grades 6-9
Major character(s): Afton Dupree, 14-Year-Old; Deenie Mason, 15-Year-Old; Bailey, Uncle (of Afton), Convict
Time period(s): 1940s (1947)
Locale(s): Gillford, South Carolina

Summary: One day Afton's mother looks up and sees her brother Bailey on their doorstep, an uncle that Afton's never heard about? And why does her mother look so happy to see him? Secretive about Bailey, his mother lets the neighbors assume he's just been released from a prisoner of war camp. Afton's brother Francis was killed in World War II and her father is at sea in the Merchant Marine, so Afton is glad to see her mother happy, but Bailey is the strangest man she's ever met. Frustrated at her lack of information, Afton confides her curiosity and doubts about her uncle to her best friend Deenie, but all that does is make the townspeople suspicious of him when a local woman is found murdered. Afton finally learns the truth about Bailey, but not before Bailey flees from all the animosity directed toward him in this haunting look at the South after World War II. (152 pages)

Where it's reviewed:
Booklist, September 15, 2001, page 215
Bulletin of the Center for Children's Books, October 2001, page 68
Horn Book, January 2002, page 81
Publishers Weekly, November 5, 2001, page 70
School Library Journal, October 2001, page 166

Other books by the same author:
John Riley's Daughter, 2000

Other books you might like:
Patricia Reilly Giff, *Lily's Crossing*, 1997
    Lily's expected summer of bliss on the beach at Rockaway doesn't happen after her father is drafted in World War II.
Mary Downing Hahn, *Stepping on the Cracks*, 1991
    Margaret's dislike of bully Gordy changes when she helps him hide his pacifist brother, a World War II deserter.
Margaret Poynter, *A Time Too Swift*, 1990
    World War II changes Marjorie's life as she's forbidden to date a soldier, her brother's reported missing and some Japanese friends are interned.

604

JAMES MAYHEW, Author/Illustrator

Katie and the Sunflowers
(New York: Orchard Books, 2001)

Subject(s): Museums; Artists and Art; Fantasy
Age range(s): Grades K-3
Major character(s): Katie, Daughter (granddaughter); Grandma, Grandmother, Gardener
Time period(s): Indeterminate
Locale(s): Fictional Country

Summary: Rain interrupts Katie's work with Grandma in the garden giving them an opportunity to visit the art museum. While Grandma rests Katie is attracted to the warmth of Van Gogh's *Sunflowers*. The flowers look real enough to touch and for Katie they are. Unfortunately Katie knocks the vase over and the flowers spill prompting laughter from the girls in Gauguin's painting *Breton Girls Dancing*. Katie climbs inside the painting to get help, but the girl who agrees to do so brings her dog out of the painting too. The dog steals the sunflowers and runs away, causing more problems for Katie. Scrambling in and out of paintings and racing along museum corridors Katie manages to restore order before Grandma awakens. A concluding note gives information about Postimpressionism and the three artists featured in the title. (32 pages)

Where it's reviewed:
Booklist, June 2001, page 1894
Books for Keeps, March 2001, page 21
Kirkus Reviews, May 1, 2001, page 664
Publishers Weekly, June 4, 2001, page 82
School Library Journal, July 2001, page 85

Awards the book has won:
Notable Social Studies Trade Books for Young People, 2002

Other books by the same author:
Katie and the Impressionists, 1999
Katie and the Mona Lisa, 1999
Katie and the Dinosaurs, 1992

Other books you might like:
Bjorn Sortland, *Anna's Art Adventure*, 1999
    While on a trip to an art museum Anna finds herself inside several paintings.
Neil Waldman, *The Starry Night*, 1999
    Bernard finds Vincent van Gogh in Central Park and shows him around town.
Jacqueline Preiss Weitzmann, *You Can't Take a Balloon into the Metropolitan Museum*, 1998

While a young girl and her grandmother tour the museum a security guard chases the girl's balloon through the streets of New York.

605

HARRY MAZER

A Boy at War: A Novel of Pearl Harbor
(New York: Simon & Schuster, 2001)

Subject(s): World War II; Fathers and Sons
Age range(s): Grades 6-9
Major character(s): Adam Pelko, 14-Year-Old; Lieutenant Pelko, Military Personnel (Navy lieutenant); Davi Mori, 14-Year-Old
Time period(s): 1940s (1941)
Locale(s): Honolulu, Hawaii

Summary: Newly arrived in Hawaii, and conscious of his father's rank in the Navy, Adam tries to live up to all that is expected of him, but chafes at his father's order to not endanger his career by befriending any Japanese Americans. Not ready to give up his friendship with Davi, and a little defiant of his father, Adam goes fishing with Davi and another friend in Pearl Harbor on December 7. At first, the sounds of explosions don't seem real and Adam thinks it must be a practice exercise, but then the boys see bombs dropping and ships going up in smoke. Adam knows his father's been called back to the battleship *Arizona* and, when he sees it in flames, wonders if he'll ever again see his dad. In a few moments Adam has other worries as their fishing boat is bombed out from under them and the boys fight to survive in the maelstrom of smoke, oil slick, body parts and flames. Once Adam and his friends are safe on shore, someone thinks he's an enlisted sailor and Adam finds himself commandeered to fight the flames and rescue anyone he can in what he refers to as "a whole life lived in that one day." (104 pages)

Where it's reviewed:
Booklist, April 1, 2001, page 1481
Horn Book, May 2001, page 331
Publishers Weekly, May 7, 2001, page 247
School Library Journal, May 2001, page 156
Voice of Youth Advocates, June 2001, page 124

Other books by the same author:
The Wild Kid, 1998
The Dog in the Freezer: Three Novellas, 1997
Twelve Shots: Outstanding Short Stories about Guns, 1997
The Girl of His Dreams, 1987
Last Mission, 1979

Other books you might like:
Avi, *The Fighting Ground*, 1984
    In 1778 thirteen-year-old Jonathan goes to war and returns home the next day, but not before witnessing fear, horror, pain and death.
Graham Salisbury, *Under the Blood-Red Sun*, 1994
    After Pearl Harbor is bombed, American Tomi, born in Hawaii of Japanese parents, is viewed with suspicion because of his background.
Bill Wallace, *Aloha Summer*, 1997
    Initially excited by his father's new job in Hawaii, John is

dismayed at the racism he witnesses by other whites against Japanese, Hawaiian and Filipino workers.

606

NORMA FOX MAZER

Girlhearts
(New York: HarperCollins, 2001)

Subject(s): Grief; Orphans; Mothers and Daughters
Age range(s): Grades 6-9
Major character(s): Sarabeth Silver, Orphan, 13-Year-Old; Cynthia Ramos, Friend (of Sarabeth's mother); Leo, Boyfriend (of her mother); Pepper Black, Girlfriend (of Leo)
Time period(s): 2000s
Locale(s): Hinchville

Summary: Sarabeth, though poorer than her friends and living in a trailer with her widowed mother who cleans houses, is happy and well loved in this sequel to *Silver*. All that changes when her 29-year-old mother has a heart attack and dies. So lonely and alone, and so filled with grief that she's in a fog, Sarabeth doesn't know where to turn. Her mother's good friend Cynthia and her family take her in, but that means four people, including a baby, cramped into a small apartment; when Cynthia's husband makes his displeasure known, Sarabeth tries living with some of her friends, but that's not a workable solution. Next she considers locating her parents' parents, relatives who disowned her parents when her mother become pregnant as a teenager, but that visit doesn't turn up a possible home for her. As she's getting off the bus, an offer of a home comes from an unexpected source, the new girlfriend of her mother's ex-boyfriend Leo; strangely enough, this unrelated couple wants Sarabeth to live with them more than anyone else has. (210 pages)

Where it's reviewed:
Booklist, July 2001, page 2000
Bulletin of the Center for Children's Books, April 2001, page 310
Publishers Weekly, April 23, 2001, page 79
School Library Journal, May 2001, page 156
Voice of Youth Advocates, August 2001, page 204

Awards the book has won:
Smithsonian's Notable Books for Children, 2001

Other books by the same author:
Good Night, Maman, 1999
Crazy Fish, 1998
Missing Pieces, 1995
Out of Control, 1993
Silver, 1988

Other books you might like:
Carole Crowe, *Groover's Heart*, 2001
    Raised by her Aunt Viola with material goods, but no real love, Charlotte wants to meet her recovering alcoholic Uncle Charlie whose simple life appeals.
Cynthia DeFelice, *Nowhere to Call Home*, 1999
    Orphaned during the Depression, Frances dresses like a boy and takes off to ride the rails rather than live with an aunt she doesn't know.

Sid Fleischman, *Bo & Mzzz Mad*, 2001
    Orphaned, Bo's not sure whether to go to a foster home or contact his Martinka relatives who've had a long-standing feud with his side of the family.
Barbara Brooks Wallace, *Ghosts in the Gallery*, 2000
    Orphaned in China, Jenny travels to American to live with her grandfather Mr. Graymark, but he claims to know nothing about her.

607

SAM MCBRATNEY
KADY MACDONALD DENTON, Illustrator

In the Light of the Moon & Other Bedtime Stories

(New York: Kingfisher, 2001)

Subject(s): Bedtime; Toys; Short Stories
Age range(s): Grades K-2
Time period(s): Indeterminate
Locale(s): Fictional Country

Summary: A collection of eight original stories include "Brother Bear," reminiscent of a folktale and "Stop Daydreaming, Speedwell Bunting" about a reluctant tooth fairy. A child's special bear is lost in "Bargain Bear" and found again years later. Humor prevails in "Bentley—Go Gently" a story of a jealous pig and his attempts to be noticed. Young mice learn an important lesson about danger when they linger too late outside and something-in-the-sky that wants it's dinner swoops after them "In the Light of the Moon." (93 pages)

Where it's reviewed:
Booklist, February 1, 2002, page 942
Publishers Weekly, October 29, 2001, page 62
Quill & Quire, December 2001, page 27
School Library Journal, January 2002, page 106

Other books by the same author:
I'm Sorry, 2000
The Dark at the Top of the Stairs, 1996 (Booklist Editors' Choice)
Guess How Much I Love You, 1995 (Booklist Editors' Choice)

Other books you might like:
Mary Ann Hoberman, *You Read to Me, I'll Read to You: Very Short Stories to Read Together*, 2001
    A collection of brief stories and poems is designed for shared reading.
Richard Scarry, *Richard Scarry's Best Mother Goose Ever*, 1999
    This collection includes fifty nursery rhymes.
Margot Zemach, *Some from the Moon, Some from the Sun: Poems and Songs for Everyone*, 2001
    A compilation of traditional poems, songs and nursery rhymes is suitable for reading anytime.

608

PAGE MCBRIER
LORI LOHSTOETER, Illustrator

Beatrice's Goat

(New York: Anne Schwartz Book/Atheneum Books for Young Readers, 2001)

Subject(s): Animals/Goats; Education; Poverty
Age range(s): Grades K-3
Major character(s): Beatrice, 9-Year-Old, Daughter; Mugisa, Goat; Mama, Mother
Time period(s): 1990s
Locale(s): Kisinga, Uganda

Summary: Beatrice longs to go to school but she knows her poor family cannot afford the expense. When an international organization selects her family to receive a goat Beatrice works harder than ever to help Mama plant food and build an enclosure for the animal. When the goat arrives Beatrice names it Mugisa, meaning luck and within weeks the family discovers how lucky they are when Mugisa has twins. Once the kids are weaned Beatrice can sell the extra milk, saving the money for her family's needs. How happy she is when Mama announces that the first need to be met is Beatrice's need to go to school. (34 pages)

Where it's reviewed:
Booklist, February 15, 2001, page 1155
Bulletin of the Center for Children's Books, February 2001, page 230
Kirkus Reviews, November 15, 2000, page 1617
Publishers Weekly, January 22, 2001, page 323
School Library Journal, February 2001, page 103

Awards the book has won:
IRA Teachers' Choices, 2002

Other books by the same author:
Adventure in the Haunted House, 1986
Secret of the Old Garage, 1986
Oliver's Lucky Day, 1986

Other books you might like:
Laurie Halse Anderson, *Ndito Runs*, 1996
    Joyfully, Ndito runs across the Kenyan countryside to her schoolhouse.
Natalie Kinsey-Warnock, *The Summer of Stanley*, 1997
    For her ninth birthday Molly receives a goat rather than the bicycle she'd hope to get.
Catherine Stock, *Where Are You Going, Manyoni?*, 1993
    Manyoni saunters alone over the Zimbabwe plains until a friend joins her for the final trek to the village school.

609

BARBARA MCCLINTOCK, Author/Illustrator

Molly and the Magic Wishbone

(New York: Farrar Straus Giroux/Frances Foster Books, 2001)

Subject(s): Wishes; Brothers and Sisters; Magic
Age range(s): Grades K-3
Major character(s): Molly, Cat, Sister (older); Phylis, Cat, Sister (younger); Fairy Godmother, Cat

Time period(s): Indeterminate Past
Locale(s): Fictional Country

Summary: An old woman claiming to be Molly's Fairy Godmother tells her to save the bone from her fish dinner because the bone she receives will be a magic wishbone. Fairy Godmother forewarns Molly that the bone will grant only one wish. The bone appears as foretold and Molly's siblings have many suggestions for how she should use the wish. Each time a problem comes up Molly is able to solve it without wishing on the bone and everyone, but Phylis, forgets Molly has it. Phylis slips out of the house to find her own magic wishbone but she soon becomes lost in the crowded streets. Molly searches for her all day to no avail and finally decides how to use her magic wishbone. (32 pages)

Where it's reviewed:
Booklist, September 1, 2001, page 110
Children's Bookwatch, September 2001, page 5
Horn Book, January 2002, page 70
Publishers Weekly, November 5, 2001, page 66
School Library Journal, October 2001, page 124

Other books by the same author:
The Fantastic Drawings of Danielle, 1996 (Smithsonian's Notable Books for Children)
The Battle of Luke & Longnose, 1994
The Heartaches of a French Cat, 1989 (New York Times Best Illustrated Book)

Other books you might like:
Peter Collington, *Clever Cat*, 2000
   No fairy godmother intervenes to give Tibs the ability to participate in the human "rat race" but he's clever enough to return to the life of a cat.
Tim Egan, *Burnt Toast on Davenport Street*, 1997
   Belatedly, Arthur realizes that the fly offering to grant him three wishes must be magic.
J. Patrick Lewis, *At the Wish of the Fish: A Russian Folktale*, 1999
   A fool catches a talking fish, agrees to the fish's wish and becomes a wealthy man with more wits than he had at the beginning of the tale.

610

SHARON PIERCE MCCULLOUGH, Author/Illustrator

Bunbun at Bedtime

(New York: Barefoot Books, 2001)

Subject(s): Animals/Rabbits; Bedtime; Brothers and Sisters
Age range(s): Preschool
Major character(s): Bunbun, Rabbit, Brother; Bibi, Rabbit, Sister (younger); Benny, Rabbit, Brother (older)
Time period(s): Indeterminate
Locale(s): Fictional Country

Summary: Bibi's eating a snack and Benny cleans up toys, but Bunbun continues playing. Bunbun is not tired so he doesn't want to get ready for bed. His siblings brush their teeth and have a bath, but Bunbun plays until he hears an odd noise. The sound frightens Bunbun and he races to complete all the pre-bedtime routine and jump into bed in time for a good night kiss. (24 pages)

Where it's reviewed:
Booklist, October 1, 2001, page 326
Horn Book Guide, Spring 2002, page 23
Publishers Weekly, October 8, 2001, page 66
School Library Journal, November 2001, page 129

Other books by the same author:
Bunbun at the Fair, 2002
Bunbun, the Middle One, 2001

Other books you might like:
Russell Hoban, *Bedtime for Frances*, 1960
   Frances is a master at avoiding sleep, but her patient parents have a response for every problem.
Jonathan London, *Froggy Goes to Bed*, 2000
   Froggy feels exhausted from a busy day of play until he hears bedtime announced, then he begins searching for bath toys, pajamas and his toothbrush.
Caroline Uff, *Lulu's Busy Day*, 2000
   After a busy day of play Lulu cleans up her toys, has a bubble bath and settles into bed for a story and a good night's sleep.

611

EMILY ARNOLD MCCULLY, Author/Illustrator

Four Hungry Kittens

(New York: Dial Books for Young Readers, 2001)

Subject(s): Animals/Cats; Animals/Dogs; Farm Life
Age range(s): Grades K-1
Major character(s): Unnamed Character, Dog; Unnamed Character, Farmer; Unnamed Character, Cat, Mother
Time period(s): 2000s (2001)
Locale(s): United States

Summary: In a wordless picture book a mother cat hunts for food while her four kittens cavort in the barn. When the mother cat silently enters the feed room in search of mice just as the farmer exits the room, closing the door behind him, the mother cat is trapped. Her kittens become more and more hungry. Kindly, the watchful dog offers them his bone and scares away a hawk when the kittens wander into the open farmyard. The dog also attracts the farmer's attention to the closed feed room door so the mother can be freed to return to her kittens with their dinner. (32 pages)

Where it's reviewed:
Booklist, January 2001, page 968
Horn Book Guide, Fall 2001, page 265
Publishers Weekly, February 5, 2001, page 87
School Library Journal, March 2001, page 214
Tribune Books, April 15, 2001, page 4

Other books by the same author:
Monk Camps Out, 2000
Mouse Practice, 1999
Crossing the New Bridge, 1994

Other books you might like:
Margaret Wise Brown, *Big Red Barn*, 1995
   A day in the life of a barn introduces the many types of animals who live there.

Alexandra Day, *Good Dog, Carl*, 1997
   In a story without words, the illustrations portray Carl, the
   family dog, in his role as the babysitter.
Denise Fleming, *Mama Cat Has Three Kittens*, 1998
   One of Mama Cat's three kittens sleeps while the other two
   attend to her lessons on proper cat behavior.
Joan Sweeney, *Bijou, Bonbon & Beau: The Kittens Who
   Danced for Degas*, 1998
   Kittens born at a theater become favorites of the perform-
   ers and the audience when they appear, uninvited, onstage.

612

EMILY ARNOLD MCCULLY, Author/Illustrator

Grandmas Trick-or-Treat

(New York: HarperCollins Publishers, 2001)

Series: I Can Read Book
Subject(s): Halloween; Grandmothers; Bullies
Age range(s): Grades 1-2
Major character(s): Pip, Daughter (granddaughter), Child;
   Grandma Nan, Grandmother; Grandma Sal, Grandmother
Time period(s): 2000s (2001)
Locale(s): United States

Summary: Pip's grandmothers with their conflicting ideas
finally find common ground on Halloween. Grandma Nan
dislikes the holiday because she thinks it brings out the worst
in people. Grandma Sal, wearing a mummy costume, thinks
Pip and her friends need to be scarier. With her friends Pip
plans a trick on her grandmothers that turns out to be more
frightening for the trick-or-treaters than it is for the grandmothers. Oh well, at least they didn't lose their treats and they
have plenty to share. (48 pages)

Where it's reviewed:
Booklist, September 1, 2001, page 121
Bulletin of the Center for Children's Books, September 2001,
   page 27
Horn Book Guide, Spring 2002, page 68
Kirkus Reviews, August 2001, page 1129
School Library Journal, September 2001, page 184

Other books by the same author:
Grandmas at Bat, 1993 (I Can Read Book)
Grandmas at the Lake, 1990 (I Can Read Book)
The Grandma Mix-Up, 1988 (I Can Read Book)

Other books you might like:
Marion Dane Bauer, *Alison's Fierce and Ugly Halloween*,
   1997
   Alison's attempt to be scary on Halloween creates friction
   with her friend Cindy who has different ideas about the
   holiday.
Stephanie Calmenson, *Gator Halloween*, 1999
   A good deed sidetracks Amy and Allie so they miss entering the costume contest but they have a happy Halloween
   anyway.
Dav Pilkey, *Dragon's Halloween*, 1993
   In the fifth easy reader about Dragon, the kindly creature
   scares himself with his own pumpkin monster and then
   with sounds from his hungry stomach.

613

EMILY ARNOLD MCCULLY, Author/Illustrator

The Orphan Singer

(New York: Arthur A. Levine/Scholastic Press, 2001)

Subject(s): Singing; Talent; Poverty
Age range(s): Grades 1-3
Major character(s): Nina Dolci, Baby, Sister (younger); Anto-
   nio Dolci, Brother (older); Caterina, Orphan (presumed),
   Singer
Time period(s): 18th century
Locale(s): Venice, Italy

Summary: The Dolci family is blessed with musical talent but
lacks the financial resources to allow their children to receive
musical training. Antonio's parents sadly realize that he is
destined to be a basket maker all his life despite his beautiful
voice. When Nina is born and shows the same promise her
parents make the difficult decision to leave her, as an orphan,
at the *ospedalo* where she will be cared for and receive
musical instruction. The school names her Caterina and
indeed she is blessed with an outstanding voice but an independent, mischievous spirit. With Antonio, the parents visit
the conservatory whenever they can to get a glimpse of Nina
and she becomes so fond of them that she risks expulsion to
visit Antonio when he is ill. A concluding ''Author's Note''
explains the background for the story. (32 pages)

Where it's reviewed:
Booklist, November 15, 2001, page 582
Horn Book, September 2001, page 577
Publishers Weekly, October 22, 2001, page 76
School Library Journal, November 2001, page 129

Awards the book has won:
Notable Social Studies Trade Books for Young People, 2002

Other books by the same author:
Mirette & Bellini Cross Niagara Falls, 2000
Beautiful Warrior: The Legend of the Nun's Kung Fu, 1998
   (ALA Notable Book)
Little Kit or, the Industrious Flea Circus Girl, 1995
Mirette on the High Wire, 1992 (Caldecott Medal)

Other books you might like:
Candace Fleming, *Gabriella's Song*, 1997
   Inspired by the sounds of Venice, Gabriella hums a tune
   wherever she walks; a composer uses Gabriella's song to
   write a symphony.
Paolo Guarnieri, *A Boy Named Giotto*, 1999
   Cimabue recognizes artistic ability in a young shepherd
   and asks his parents to allow him to leave home and
   become his student in Florence.
Deborah Hopkinson, *A Band of Angels: A Story Inspired by
   the Jubilee Singers*, 1999
   In the 1870s a lack of money threatens the education of
   African American students at the Fisk School who form a
   small singing group to raise funds.

LURLENE MCDANIEL

To Live Again

(New York: Bantam, 2001)

Series: Dawn Rochelle Novel
Subject(s): Friendship; Illness
Age range(s): Grades 6-9
Major character(s): Dawn Rochelle, 12th Grader; Rhonda, 12th Grader; Jake Macka, Boyfriend (of Dawn's), 12th Grader
Time period(s): 2000s
Locale(s): United States

Summary: In remission for three years from her leukemia, Dawn's excited about her senior year until she's felled by a stroke that proves more debilitating than her cancer. Partial paralysis on her left side leaves her with a limp, speech that sounds slurred and mushy and a smile that's a little off-kilter. Embarrassed by her limp and her speech, Dawn experiences some depression until her naturally positive side takes over. With help from her best friend Rhonda, Jake who moves from friend to boyfriend and her continually supportive family, she prepares to overcome her latest medical problem. (151 pages)

Where it's reviewed:
Booklist, March 1, 2001, page 1272
Children's Bookwatch, June 2001, page 5
Kliatt, July 2001, page 20

Other books by the same author:
No Time to Cry, 1996 (Dawn Rochelle Novel)
I Want to Live, 1995 (Dawn Rochelle Novel)
Six Months to Live, 1995 (Dawn Rochelle Novel)
So Much to Live For, 1991 (Dawn Rochelle Novel)

Other books you might like:
Mary Lou Carney, *How Do You Hug an Angel?*, 1994
    All through the traumas of losing her mother and later regaining her hearing through surgery, Elise's guardian angel Herbie keeps her on track.
Priscilla Cummings, *A Face First*, 2001
    Having to wear a plastic mask on her face to reduce the scarring from her third degree burns, Kelley wonders if she'll ever again be able to face her classmates.
Jean Ferris, *Invincible Summer*, 1987
    Two teens meet and fall in love while undergoing treatment for leukemia, but only one survives.
Beth Goobie, *Before Wings*, 2001
    Barely surviving a brain aneurysm the previous year, Adrien's summer helping her aunt at Camp Lakeshore is so active that she quits expecting to die.

GERALD MCDERMOTT, Author/Illustrator

Jabuti the Tortoise: A Trickster Tale from the Amazon

(San Diego: Harcourt, Inc., 2001)

Subject(s): Indians of South America; Folklore; Animals/Turtles

Age range(s): Grades K-2
Major character(s): Jabuti, Turtle, Trickster; Vulture, Bird; King of Heaven, Bird, Deity
Time period(s): Indeterminate Past
Locale(s): Amazon, Brazil

Summary: Unlike the forest animals that have been tricked by Jabuti, the birds love the little tortoise for the sweet music he plays on his flute. Vulture, who cannot sing, is jealous of Jabuti and is only interested in having him for a meal. When the birds fly to a festival called by the King of Heaven, Jabuti wants to join in with his musical contribution, but he's unable to fly. Vulture seizes the opportunity to provide Jabuti's transportation as a way to finally put an end to the trickster. Though Vulture's plan is almost successful, the birds rescue Jabuti and are rewarded with colorful features while Vulture is condemned to a life of dullness by the angry King of Heaven. (32 pages)

Where it's reviewed:
Booklist, September 15, 2001, page 228
Kirkus Reviews, August 15, 2001, page 1217
Publishers Weekly, August 6, 2001, page 88
School Library Journal, September 2001, page 218

Awards the book has won:
IRA Children's Choices, 2002

Other books by the same author:
The Fox and the Stork, 1999
Musicians of the Sun, 1997 (Book Links Lasting Connections)
Raven: A Trickster Tale From the Pacific Northwest, 1993 (Caldecott Honor Book)
Arrow to the Sun, 1974 (Caldecott Medal)

Other books you might like:
Virginia Hamilton, *A Ring of Tricksters: Animal Tales from America, the West Indies, and Africa*, 1997
    Eleven read-aloud tales include tricksters from spiders to rabbits and the unwitting animals that bear the brunt of their cleverness.
Tololwa M. Mollel, *Ananse's Feast: An Ashanti Tale*, 1997
    Turtle Akye finds a way to give trickster Ananse a taste of his medicine.
Gayle Ross, *How Turtle's Back Was Cracked: A Traditional Cherokee Tale*, 1995
    Provoked wolves hurl boastful Turtle into the river to drown him, but he lands on a rock and survives with a cracked shell.

JANET MCDONALD

Spellbound

(New York: Farrar Straus Giroux, 2001)

Subject(s): Teen Parents; African Americans; Friendship
Age range(s): Grades 7-12
Major character(s): Raven Jefferson, 16-Year-Old, Single Mother; Dell Jefferson, Sister (of Raven); Aisha Ingram, Single Mother; Smokey Jefferson, Baby
Time period(s): 2000s
Locale(s): New York, New York (Brooklyn)

Summary: With her older sister Dell an outstanding role model for leaving the projects, Raven assumes she'll follow in her footsteps and attend college, but her plans are sidetracked when she becomes pregnant after a one-time encounter at a party. Now she's a high school dropout with a young son, Smokey, and spends time with her friend Aisha who's in a similar position. Dell hears of the Spell Success program, which offers a chance to win a college scholarship through a spelling bee contest, and Raven bones up on her spelling. Though she's always been a good student, she's not a good speller but with help from Aisha, along with a lot of teasing, she improves to the point that she wins the contest. For Raven, there's a chance for a better future, but for her friend Aisha, who's already on welfare, she'll probably remain in the projects in this first novel for young adults. (138 pages)

Where it's reviewed:
Booklist, November 1, 2001, page 476
Horn Book, January 2002, page 80
Publishers Weekly, November 19, 2001, page 68
School Library Journal, September 2001, page 230
Voice of Youth Advocates, October 2001, page 281

Awards the book has won:
ALA Best Books for Young Adults, 2002

Other books by the same author:
Project Girl, 1999 (adult title)

Other books you might like:
Connie Porter, *Imani All Mine*, 1999
    Tasha manages to juggle schoolwork, parenting classes and her son beloved Imani, until a drive-by shooting leaves her grief-stricken.
Rita Williams-Garcia, *Like Sisters on the Homefront*, 1995
    After becoming pregnant a second time, Gayle's mother marches her to the abortion clinic and then to Georgia to live with her parents.
Virginia Euwer Wolff, *Make Lemonade*, 1993
    LaVaughn and her single-parent mother make the most of life, though they're surrounded by poverty, gangs and tenements.
Jacqueline Woodson, *The Dear One*, 1991
    Feni resents the pregnant teenager from Harlem who comes to live with them in their upscale black community.

JOYCE MCDONALD

Shades of Simon Gray
(New York: Delacorte, 2001)

Subject(s): Space and Time; Cheating; Supernatural
Age range(s): Grades 7-10
Major character(s): Simon Gray, 11th Grader, Computer Expert; Devin McCafferty, 12th Grader; Jessup Wildemere, Spirit; Liz Shapiro, 11th Grader; Hannah Dobbler, Girlfriend (of Jessup), Criminal
Time period(s): 1990s; 1790s (1798)
Locale(s): Bellehaven, New Jersey

Summary: A plague of frogs strikes the town of Bellehaven the same night that Simon Gray crashes his car into the Liberty Tree, better known as the Hanging Tree to high school students. Though Simon lies comatose in a hospital bed, his spirit lingers near the tree where he meets the ghost of Jessup Wildemere, hanged two hundred years ago from the same tree. As they compare stories, each man finds he's committed a crime because of a woman. Simon steals teacher's tests from the school's computer system for Devin, a young girl who plays on his interest in her while Jessup is set up to kill the man who prevented Hannah from marrying him, her father. Thanks to Simon's friend Liz, who's researching the history around the Hanging Tree, he's pulled back from his comatose state in this eerie tale of injustice. (245 pages)

Where it's reviewed:
Booklist, January 2002, page 842
Bulletin of the Center for Children's Books, December 2001, page 148
Publishers Weekly, October 1, 2001, page 62
School Library Journal, November 2001, page 161
Voice of Youth Advocates, December 2001, page 372

Awards the book has won:
ALA Best Books for Young Adults, 2002

Other books by the same author:
Shadow People, 2000
Swallowing Stones, 1999
Comfort Creek, 1996
Mail-Order Kid, 1992

Other books you might like:
Norma Lehr, *Haunting at Black Water Cove*, 2000
    A request from the ghost Ruby Faye leads Kathy to investigate how Ruby was murdered in the early 1900s.
Phyllis Reynolds Naylor, *Jade Green: A Ghost Story*, 2000
    Judith's green-framed photo of her mother awakens the ghost of a former serving girl who luckily protects her from a murderous relative.
Carol Plum-Ucci, *The Body of Christopher Creed*, 2000
    Geeky Christopher Creed is missing and his classmates buzz with speculation as to whether he was murdered or kidnapped.
Kathryn Reiss, *Dreadful Sorry*, 1993
    Haunted by a fear of water and the song "Oh My Darling Clementine," Molly summers with her stepfamily in Maine who live in the house of her nightmares.

MEGAN MCDONALD
PETER REYNOLDS, Illustrator

Judy Moody Gets Famous
(Cambridge, MA: Candlewick Press, 2001)

Subject(s): Brothers and Sisters; Conduct of Life; Self-Esteem
Age range(s): Grades 2-4
Major character(s): Judy Moody, 3rd Grader, Sister (older); Stink Moody, Brother (younger); Frank Pearl, 3rd Grader, Friend (Judy's)
Time period(s): 2000s (2001)
Locale(s): Virginia

Summary: The sight of a classmate in a tiara won for being Queen Bee in a spelling contest is enough to put Judy in the mood to be famous. Her quest for fame runs into one stumbling block after another as her plans go awry. When Judy's attempt to set a world record for a human-centipede walk injures Frank she has time to think about someone else while waiting for Frank's broken finger to be set in the emergency room. Though Stink accuses her of stealing dolls from the hospital's play area, she soon shows him that she's really only trying to repair them. Secretly, Judy returns them to the hospital and soon a newspaper article appears about the "Phantom Doll Doctor." Finally, Judy is famous, anonymously, and that suits her mood just fine. (127 pages)

Where it's reviewed:
Horn Book, September 2001, page 589
Kirkus Reviews, June 15, 2001, page 867
Publishers Weekly, July 30, 2001, page 85
School Library Journal, October 2001, page 124

Awards the book has won:
ALA Notable Children's Books, 2002
IRA Children's Choices, 2002

Other books by the same author:
Judy Moody, 2000 (Publishers Weekly Best Books)
Shadows in the Glasshouse, 2000 (History Mysteries, Number 7)
The Bridge to Nowhere, 1993

Other books you might like:
Kate Banks, *Howie Bowles and Uncle Sam*, 2000
    When Howie erroneously receives a tax bill for someone else with the same name he fears becoming very well known as a prisoner.
Diane DeGroat, *Annie Pitts, Burger Kid*, 2000
    Annie, aspiring actress, feels confident that she'll win the Burger Barn poster contest and fulfill her desire for fame.
Betsy Duffey, *Spotlight on Cody*, 1998
    Nothing goes right for Cody as he tries to find some "talent" to perform for the school's talent show.
Stephanie Greene, *Owen Foote, Money Man*, 2000
    Owen seeks cash not fame to use in ordering supplies such as fake vomit from a catalog, but his ideas yield more problems than income.

619

MEGAN MCDONALD
PAUL BRETT JOHNSON, Illustrator

Reptiles Are My Life
(New York: Orchard Books, 2001)

Subject(s): Animals/Reptiles; Animals/Insects; Friendship
Age range(s): Grades K-2
Major character(s): Amanda Frankenstein, Animal Lover (insects), Classmate, Student—Elementary School; Maggie, Animal Lover (reptiles), Friend (Amanda's), Student—Elementary School; Emily Elligator, Student—Elementary School (new), Animal Lover (reptiles)
Time period(s): 1990s
Locale(s): United States

Summary: Maggie and Amanda's interest in different species forms the basis of a friendship that is threatened by the arrival of a new student. Emily is also a lover of reptiles, a fact that attracts Maggie and soon has the two girls playing together to

the exclusion of Amanda. When the class bully complains that Emily and Maggie are sticking out their tongues at him Amanda comes to their defense by explaining to the teacher that they're pretending to be snakes and snakes smell with their tongues. Maggie and Emily are grateful to Amanda and realize that three can be friends even though Amanda's more interested in insects than reptiles. (32 pages)

Where it's reviewed:
Horn Book Guide, Spring 2002, page 51
Kirkus Reviews, July 1, 2001, page 943
School Library Journal, August 2001, page 156

Other books by the same author:
The Night Iguana Left Home, 1999
Insects Are My Life, 1995
Is This a House for Hermit Crab?, 1990

Other books you might like:
Judith Caseley, *Mr. Green Peas*, 1995
    Norman, a child with no pets, is excited to become the temporary caretaker of an iguana.
Lynne Jonell, *I Need a Snake*, 1998
    Robbie's sure he needs a pet snake; Mommy's confident Robbie will wait until he's grown and living in his own home before he has a snake.
Faith McNulty, *A Snake in the House*, 1994
    A snake that a young boy brings home escapes and hides in the house for days before finally finding a way to freedom.

620

MEGAN MCDONALD
PAUL BACHEM, Illustrator
LASZLO KUBINYA, Illustrator

Shadows in the Glasshouse
(Middleton, WI: Pleasant Co./American Girl, 2000)

Series: History Mysteries
Subject(s): Mystery and Detective Stories; Orphans; Kidnapping
Age range(s): Grades 4-7
Major character(s): Meredith "Merry" Shipman, 12-Year-Old, Orphan; Angelo, Apprentice (glassblower); Margaret Shipman Leak, Sister (of Merry)
Time period(s): 17th century (1621)
Locale(s): Jamestown, Virginia; *Flying Hart*, At Sea

Summary: Tempted by a hot meat pie, Merry finds herself kidnapped and put aboard ship headed for a life as an indentured servant in Jamestown, far away from her beloved sister Margaret in London. Arriving in the New World, Merry is sold for eighty pounds of tobacco, which binds her to the master of the glasshouse where she assists with menial chores. Staying with the Webbes, who begrudge even the straw pallet they give her for sleeping, Merry realizes they want to steal Angelo's secret formula for making *cristallo*, a clear glass from Italy. The two try to stop the Webbes from their plans, but find themselves in trouble instead. By book's end, all is resolved and Merry and her sister are reunited in this book of a continuing series. (131 pages)

Where it's reviewed:
School Library Journal, February 2001, page 118

Other books you might like:

Sandra Forrester, *Wheel of the Moon*, 2000
Living with a group of fellow orphans, Pen's group is caught, tossed on board ship and sent to Jamestown to be indentured servants.

Elizabeth Massie, *1609: Winter of the Dead: A Novel about the Founding of Jamestown*, 2000
Two orphans sail to the New World in exchange for labor aboard ship, confident that previous survival by living on their wits can be done again.

Ann Rinaldi, *The Journal of Jasper Jonathan Pierce: A Pilgrim Boy*, 2000
Jasper is happy to have the chance to sail aboard the *Mayflower* for the new world until he realizes his brother has been left behind.

CHRISTINE MCDONNELL
MARTHA DOTY, Illustrator

Ballet Bug

(New York: Viking, 2001)

Subject(s): Ballet; Sports/Hockey; Friendship
Age range(s): Grades 3-6
Major character(s): Bea Nash, Hockey Player, Dancer; Rebecca, Friend, Dancer; Margaret, Dancer, Friend
Time period(s): 2000s (2001)
Locale(s): United States

Summary: Until viewing a ballet video at Rebecca's birthday sleepover Bea had never been interested in dance, but now she's been bitten by the "ballet bug." Bea enrolls in classes, working to keep up with ballet and ice hockey practices. In the locker room she meets Margaret who's enrolled in a more advanced class and offers Bea suggestions to help her improve. With Margaret's encouragement Bea auditions successfully for a part in *The Nutcracker*; Rebecca and Margaret also have roles. Jealous twins from Bea's class try to sabotage Margaret's performance but are caught in the act and the show concludes with just enough vacation left for Bea to teach Margaret how to ice skate. (96 pages)

Where it's reviewed:
Bulletin of the Center for Children's Books, October 2001, page 69
Kirkus Reviews, July 15, 2001, page 1030
School Library Journal, September 2001, page 193

Other books by the same author:
It's a Deal, Dogboy, 1998
Just for the Summer, 1987
Toad Food & Measle Soup, 1982

Other books you might like:

Patricia Reilly Giff, *Rosie's Nutcracker Dreams*, 1996
Rosie dreams of dancing the lead role in this year's production of *The Nutcracker*.

Sally Warner, *Ellie & the Bunheads*, 1997
Ellie confides in her diary as she tries to sort out her feelings and decide whether to continue with ballet training.

Rita Williams-Garcia, *Blue Tights*, 1988
Joyce's attempts at classical ballet are defeated by her physical development, but she finds her niche in an African dance troupe.

Laurence Yep, *Ribbons*, 1996
Robin must give up dance lessons when her grandmother moves into her family's home.

622

JAMIE MCEWAN
SANDRA BOYNTON, Illustrator

The Heart of Cool

(New York: Simon & Schuster Books for Young Readers, 2001)

Series: Ready-to-Read. Level 3
Subject(s): Schools; Self-Acceptance; Sports/Skateboarding
Age range(s): Grades 2-3
Major character(s): Bobby North, Bear (polar bear), Student—Elementary School; Harry Haller, Moose, Student—Elementary School; Siggy Sidewinder, Student—Elementary School, Bully
Time period(s): Indeterminate
Locale(s): Fictional Country

Summary: Bobby not only wants to fit in at his new school, he wants to be as cool as Harry. To achieve his goal Bobby watches Harry's behavior, acquires a used skateboard and learns to use it, and practices in front of the mirror at home acting just like Harry. Any time Bobby makes the slightest mistake, Siggy taunts him. Bobby stays focused on his goal and achieves what Harry calls "the heart of cool," a state of being in which coolness no longer matters. Siggy doesn't get it, but Harry understands. (48 pages)

Where it's reviewed:
Bulletin of the Center for Children's Books, April 2001, page 310
Horn Book Guide, Fall 2001, page 286
Kirkus Reviews, April 15, 2001, page 590
School Library Journal, August 2001, page 156

Other books by the same author:
The Story of Grump and Pout, 1991

Other books you might like:

Kate Banks, *Howie Bowles, Secret Agent*, 1999
On his third move in one year Howie becomes Secret Agent Bean Burger rather than expend the energy adjusting to a new group of classmates.

Betsy Duffey, *Hey, New Kid!*, 1996
To impress classmates in his new school Cody makes up a new identity rather than tell people the truthful, boring story of his life.

Andrea Davis Pinkney, *Solo Girl*, 1997
Learning to jump double dutch helps Cass feel accepted by other girls in her new neighborhood.

623

LYN ROSSITER MCFARLAND
JIM MCFARLAND, Illustrator

Widget

(New York: Farrar Straus Giroux, 2001)

Subject(s): Animals/Dogs; Animals/Cats; Humor
Age range(s): Preschool
Major character(s): Widget, Dog; Mrs. Diggs, Animal Lover,
Aged Person
Time period(s): Indeterminate Past
Locale(s): United States

Summary: On a cold, wet night Widget, a hungry stray,
searches for a home. When he peeks his head inside a little
door of a house he spots six cats, six beds, and six bowls of
food. Mrs. Diggs intercepts Widget as he hurries toward the
food and explains that "the girls" don't like dogs so Widget
cannot stay. Widget really wants a home so he begins to
meow. Then he imitates the cats' hissing and spitting behavior. By the time Widget finishes using the litter box and
playing with the cats' toys they are so confused that they
allow him to remain. Widget makes a great playmate for the
cats and, one day, his ability to bark like a dog comes in handy
too. (32 pages)

Where it's reviewed:
Booklist, November 1, 2001, page 477
Kirkus Reviews, August 1, 2001, page 1129
Publishers Weekly, September 24, 2001, page 92
School Library Journal, August 2001, page 156

Awards the book has won:
Booklist Editors' Choice/Books for Youth, 2002
Book Links' Lasting Connections, 2002

Other books by the same author:
The Pirate's Parrot, 2000

Other books you might like:
Ruth Brown, *Copycat*, 1994
Buddy, the family cat, tries to imitate the behaviors of the
other family pets and hurts himself when he gnaws the
dog's bone.
Lydia Monks, *The Cat Barked?*, 1999
A cat considers the far better life that a dog appears to have
but decides she still prefers being a feline; the dog however
might switch places.
Rosemary Wells, *McDuff Moves In*, 1997
McDuff, a West Highland terrier, falls out of a
dogcatcher's truck and runs off in search of a home.

624

COLLEEN O'SHAUGHNESSY MCKENNA
STEPHANIE ROTH, Illustrator

Third Grade Stinks!

(New York: Holiday House, 2001)

Subject(s): Schools; Behavior; Problem Solving
Age range(s): Grades 2-4
Major character(s): Gordie Barr, 3rd Grader, Friend; Lamont
Hayes, 3rd Grader, Friend; Lucy Diaz, 3rd Grader

Time period(s): 2000s (2001)
Locale(s): United States

Summary: Gordie has plans for third grade carefully detailed
in his planner and they do not include sharing a locker with
Lucy Diaz. How could his teacher do this to him? Gordie
wants to share a locker with Lamont so together the boys
come up with a plan that they hope will force Lucy to abandon
Gordie as a locker mate. Not only is Lucy unfazed by the
stinky items, including Limburger cheese, the boys put in the
locker but she also likes the cheese so much that she considers
it a "gift." When Lamont and Gordie discover that Lucy
shares their interest in baseball it begins to look as if Gordie
may have to revise some of his plans for the year. (99 pages)

Where it's reviewed:
Booklist, December 15, 2001, page 731
Bulletin of the Center for Children's Books, November 2001,
page 109
School Library Journal, November 2001, page 129

Other books by the same author:
Camp Murphy, 1993
Good Grief, Third Grade, 1993
Eeenie, Meanie, Murphy, No, 1990

Other books you might like:
Mary Jane Auch, *I Was a Third Grade Science Project*, 1998
Josh agrees to help Brian with his plans for a science
project and ends up being the one hypnotized into thinking
he's a cat.
Paula Danziger, *Amber Brown Is Not a Crayon*, 1994
Third grade is a confusing and sad time for Amber because
her best friend is moving.
Betsy Duffey, *How to Be Cool in the Third Grade*, 1993
Being assigned "Book Buddy" to the meanest kid in class
is not part of Robbie's plan to be cool, but learning to be
more understanding of others is.

625

PATRICIA C. MCKISSACK
JERRY PINKNEY, Illustrator

Goin' Someplace Special

(New York: Anne Schwartz Book/Atheneum Books for Young Readers,
2001)

Subject(s): Segregation; African Americans; Civil Rights
Age range(s): Grades 2-4
Major character(s): 'Tricia Ann, Child; Mama Frances,
Grandmother; Blooming Mary, Aged Person, Gardener
Time period(s): 1950s
Locale(s): Nashville, Tennessee

Summary: Reluctantly, Mama Frances allows 'Tricia Ann to
make her first solo journey to "Someplace Special" in town.
'Tricia Ann is confident that she's ready to ride the bus and
walk the streets of her segregated city without her grandmother beside her. When the colored section of the bus becomes full, 'Tricia Ann gives her seat to an older woman,
glares at the empty seats in the white section and expresses
annoyance at the unfairness of the Jim Crow system. 'Tricia
Ann stops to rest in a park but notices that the benches are for
"Whites Only." When 'Tricia Ann tires of the journey

through bigotry she seeks solace in a familiar church's garden. Though she wishes for Mama Frances to comfort her, it is Blooming Mary who gives her courage to continue her trip to "Someplace Special," the public library where all are welcome. A concluding Author's Note explains the childhood memories on which the story is based. (34 pages)

Where it's reviewed:
Booklist, August 2001, page 2117
Bulletin of the Center for Children's Books, September 2001, page 28
Horn Book, November 2001, page 736
Publishers Weekly, August 6, 2001, page 89
School Library Journal, September 2001, page 199

Awards the book has won:
ALA Notable Children's Books, 2002
Coretta Scott King Illustrator Award, 2002

Other books by the same author:
The Honest-to-Goodness Truth, 2000 (School Library Journal Best Books)
Ma Dear's Aprons, 1997 (Book Links Lasting Connections)
Mirandy and Brother Wind, 1988 (Caldecott Honor Book)

Other books you might like:
Evelyn Coleman, *White Socks Only*, 1996
    In 1950s Mississippi a young black child wearing white socks naively drinks from the "whites only" water fountain with unexpected consequences.
William Miller, *Night Golf*, 1999
    The only time James can play on the town's "whites only" golf course is secretly at night after the facility closes.
William Miller, *Richard Wright and the Library Card*, 1997
    In the segregated South it is illegal for 17-year-old Richard to check out a library book, but he still finds a way to satisfy his desire to read.
Margaree King Mitchell, *Granddaddy's Gift*, 1997
    Despite threats and humiliation in the segregated 1960s, Granddaddy stands up for his constitutional right to vote.

626

KIM MCLARIN

Meeting of the Waters
(New York: Morrow, 2001)

Subject(s): Interracial Dating; Newspapers
Age range(s): Grades 10-Adult
Major character(s): Porter Stockman, Journalist; Lenora "Lee" Page, Journalist
Time period(s): 1990s
Locale(s): Los Angeles, California; Philadelphia, Pennsylvania

Summary: Covering the aftermath of the trial of the four white policeman in the Rodney King beating case, Porter is foolishly on the streets of LA watching the riot and interviewing bystanders when the crowd turns on him. Coming unexpectedly to his rescue is another reporter, a black woman named Lenora, who manages to get him to safety and then leaves. For Porter, it's love at first sight but he despairs of ever seeing her again until the day she arrives in his newsroom at the *Philadelphia Record* having left her job at the *Baltimore Sun*.

Porter wants to date Lee but she's suspicious of his intentions and puts him off as long as she can. When she finally accepts a date, the two begin a relationship that is hard for both of them as the race card continually intercedes until all they have to rely on is their love for one another. (338 pages)

Where it's reviewed:
Booklist, August 2001, page 2087
Kirkus Reviews, August 15, 2001, page 1155
Library Journal, October 15, 2001, page 108
Redbook, December 2001, page G-1

Other books by the same author:
Taming It Down, 1998

Other books you might like:
Leslie Esdaile, *Rivers of the Soul*, 2001
    Returning to Philly after her divorce, Toni finds even her homegirls don't want a single woman around their husbands.
Terry McMillan, *Disappearing Acts*, 1989
    Construction worker Franklin and music teacher Zora begin a relationship that suffers from racism that Franklin has encountered throughout life.
Jacqueline Woodson, *If You Come Softly*, 1998
    Black Miah and white Ellie meet and fall in love at their prep school. Just as they're ready to tell their parents, Miah is shot to death.

627

SEAN MCMULLEN

Eyes of the Calculor
(New York: Tor, 2001)

Series: Greatwinter Trilogy. Number 3
Subject(s): Cultural Conflict; Artificial Intelligence
Age range(s): Grades 11-Adult
Major character(s): Highliber Franzas Dramren, Librarian; Saireme Airlord Samodel, Military Personnel; Martyne Caderine, Religious; Rangen Derris, Student
Time period(s): 40th century
Locale(s): Australica, Fictional Country; Earth

Summary: In this final volume of the Greatwinter trilogy, the precariously balanced political situation is pushed into chaos when the orbiting Mirrorsun destroys all electrical engines and the world's most advanced civilizations are returned to primitive conditions. Some, like the Library of Libris, are able to immediately put plans in motion to restore the recently replaced technologies. Highliber Dramren is decisively ruthless in conscripting the best and the brightest to work the manual relays that will keep the Library computing. Rangen Derris, one of the Library's most promising students, is equally determined not to be trapped. In North American, meanwhile, less technological disruption allows the Airlords to press their campaign to fly to Australica; led by Samodel, a daring long-term project is launched. Some people refuse to be deflected from personal business, however. Brother Martyne, a member of a cloistered order of martial arts monks, overcomes all barriers and returns to the layman's world when he learns of his sister's rape and murder;

avenging her death may lead to more than just Martyne's peace. (529 pages)

Where it's reviewed:
Booklist, September 15, 2000, page 201
Kirkus Reviews, August 15, 2001, page 1175

Other books by the same author:
The Miocene Arrow, 2000
Soul in the Great Machine, 1999
The Centurion's Empire, 1999

Other books you might like:
William Gibson, *Idoru*, 1996
    In a dystopian future, an artificial intelligence plots to make herself real.
Garth Nix, *Lirael: Daughter of the Clayr*, 2001
    Lirael's time in the Library of the Clayr suggests a very different kind of power.
Walter Jon Williams, *Metropolitan*, 1995
    The battle for control is waged in fire and information.

628

COLIN MCNAUGHTON, Author/Illustrator

Oomph!

(San Diego: Harcourt, Inc., 2001)

Series: Preston Pig Story
Subject(s): Animals/Pigs; Animals/Wolves; Beaches
Age range(s): Grades K-1
Major character(s): Preston Pig, Pig, Son; Maxine "Max", Pig, Friend; Mr. Wolf, Wolf
Time period(s): Indeterminate
Locale(s): Fictional Country

Summary: Preston's family takes off for a week's vacation at the beach oblivious to the fact that lying atop the inflatable raft tied to the car's roof is Mr. Wolf, packed and ready for the holiday. All week, Mr. Wolf lurks in the background as Preston, smitten with new friend Maxine, enjoys a variety of beach activities with her and doesn't notice the danger. Mr. Wolf tries to catch them as they surf, but he wipes out. The day they dig a big hole on the beach Mr. Wolf falls into it and when they explore tidal pools Mr. Wolf slips on the seaweed. As Preston and his family depart Max notices the wolf on the roof rack, but Preston is sure she's joking. (28 pages)

Where it's reviewed:
Booklist, March 15, 2001, page 1405
Horn Book Guide, Fall 2001, page 266
Kirkus Reviews, March 15, 2001, page 416
Magpies, March 2001, page 27
School Library Journal, July 2001, page 85

Other books by the same author:
Yum!: A Preston Pig Story, 1999 (IRA Children's Choices)
Preston's Goal, 1998 (Preston Pig Story)
Oops!, 1997 (Preston Pig Story)

Other books you might like:
Amy Axelrod, *Pigs on a Blanket*, 1996
    Mr. and Mrs. Pig plan an impromptu trip to the beach with their family.

Gael Crisp, *The Tale of Gilbert Alexander Pig*, 2000
    Gilbert Alexander wants to be left alone to practice his music but a wolf follows him wherever he goes; finally they agree to work together.
Steven Kellogg, *The Three Little Pigs*, 1997
    The pigs in this humorous retelling face a tough-looking hungry wolf trying to order piglet from their waffle wagon.

629

MARGARET MEACHAM

Quiet! You're Invisible

(New York: Holiday House, 2001)

Subject(s): Time Travel; Bullies; School Life
Age range(s): Grades 3-5
Major character(s): Hoby Hobson, Bullied Child, 5th Grader; Harold "Hammerhead" Jones, Bully, Neighbor; Zircus "Zirc" Orflandu, Time Traveler
Time period(s): 2000s (2001)
Locale(s): United States

Summary: Hoby has enough problems just being a neighbor to the local bully but then he discovers Zirc who has accidentally transported himself to this millennium in his father's new space cruiser. Hoby's life becomes more complicated as he tries to help Zirc return to his own time before his absence is discovered. In the brief time Zirc has been in this time zone he's also run afoul of Hammerhead but he can avoid the bully by becoming invisible if his dematerializer is working. Unfortunately, Hammerhead gets his hands on the battery to Zirc's space cruiser and until Zirc can recharge it, he's stuck here. Before Hammerhead will return the battery he demands that Hoby steal an answer sheet to a math test. Both Zirc and Hoby are reluctant to comply with the demand but they try, unsuccessfully, to do it. Out of fear and desperation, Zirc sets a trap for Hammerhead that doesn't work as planned, but Hoby finds the courage to tackle the bully and retrieve the battery so Zirc can escape. (114 pages)

Where it's reviewed:
Booklist, January 1, 2002, page 858
School Library Journal, November 2001, page 129

Other books by the same author:
Boy on the Beach, 1992
The Secret of Heron Creek, 1991

Other books you might like:
Betsy Duffey, *Alien for Rent*, 1999
    Quite unintentionally J.P. and Lexie direct the powers of a small fuzzy alien against the school bully with unexpected results.
Dyan Sheldon, *My Brother Is a Superhero*, 1996
    Adam and his friend try to handle a problem with three bullies but they are grateful when Adam's older brother intervenes.
Laurence Yep, *Cockroach Cooties*, 2000
    For Bobby and his brother Teddy, bugs become the secret weapon against Arnie, a bully with a long memory who's out to get them.

630

ALICE MEAD

Girl of Kosovo

(New York: Farrar Straus Giroux, 2001)

Subject(s): Prejudice; Friendship; War
Age range(s): Grades 6-10
Major character(s): Zana Dugolli, 11-Year-Old; Lena Goran, Friend (of Zana)
Time period(s): 1990s
Locale(s): Gllogovc, Yugoslavia (Republic of Kosovo); Belgrade, Yugoslavia (Republic of Serbia)

Summary: In Kosovo, Zana tries to live by her father's admonition to not let her heart be filled with hate, though that's difficult at times when you're caught in a war between two ethnic groups. As Albanians, Zana and her family try to escape a Serbian attack but her father and brothers are killed and her foot is severely injured. Hospitalized for several months as her wound becomes infected, Zana worries about her family, her once-friend, Serbian Lena, who's not allowed to play with her anymore and whether peace will ever return to her country. Returning home to her tiny village, her uncle and brother want to retaliate against the Serbs, including Lena's family, but Zana stands beside her friend to avert their plan in this heartbreaking story of war. (113 pages)

Where it's reviewed:
Booklist, March 15, 2001, page 1401
Bulletin of the Center for Children's Books, June 2001, page 390
Publishers Weekly, March 19, 2001, page 100
School Library Journal, March 2001, page 254
Voice of Youth Advocates, June 2001, page 125

Other books by the same author:
Junebug in Trouble, 2002
Soldier Mom, 1999
Junebug and the Reverend, 1998
Adem's Cross, 1996
Junebug, 1995

Other books you might like:
Daniella Carmi, *Samir and Yonatan*, 2000
    Palestinian Samir becomes friends with all the children at the Jewish hospital, but especially Yonatan who teaches him how to use the computer.
Gaye Hicyilmaz, *Smiling for Strangers*, 2000
    Leaving behind her mortally wounded grandfather, who urges her to flee, Nina ''smiles for strangers'' as she makes her way to safety in England.
Anna Levine, *Running on Eggs*, 1999
    Two young girls, one Arab and one Jewish, become friends because of their love for running.

631

HOLLY MEADE, Author/Illustrator

A Place to Sleep

(New York: Marshall Cavendish, 2001)

Subject(s): Animals; Sleep; Bedtime

Age range(s): Preschool-Grade 1
Time period(s): Indeterminate
Locale(s): Earth

Summary: Where do animals sleep? Seals sleep on beaches, bears in tree branches while cats stretch out on the couch. Elephants sleep standing up and hippos snooze in oozy mud. Rabbit heads to a burrow, fish keep their eyes open but sleepy children curl up in bed to dream. (32 pages)

Where it's reviewed:
Booklist, September 1, 2001, page 117
Bulletin of the Center for Children's Books, December 2001, page 148
Publishers Weekly, October 1, 2001, page 60
Riverbank Review, Winter 2001-2002, page 32
School Library Journal, September 2001, page 199

Other books by the same author:
The Rabbit's Bride, 2001
John Willy and Freddy McGee, 1998

Other books you might like:
Kathi Appelt, *Bayou Lullaby*, 1995
    A rhyming lullaby about the animals of the bayou soothes a little girl at bedtime.
Margaret Wise Brown, *Little Donkey Close Your Eyes*, 1995
    Animals throughout the world are putting their kittens, lambs, fawns and children to sleep.
Mirra Ginsburg, *Asleep, Asleep*, 1992
    Animals are quietly bid good night until only a sleepy child and the wind are awake.

632

PAMELA MELNIKOFF

Prisoner in Time: A Child of the Holocaust

(Philadelphia, PA: Jewish Publication Society, 2001)

Subject(s): Holocaust; Jews; Time Travel
Age range(s): Grades 6-9
Major character(s): Jan Weiss, 12-Year-Old; Judah Loewe ben Bezalel, Religious (rabbi); Golem, Mythical Creature
Time period(s): 1940s; 16th century
Locale(s): Prague, Czechoslovakia

Summary: When the Nazis invade Prague, Jan's family life changes forever. Initially the Weiss's contend with food rationing, isolation from non-Jews and the closing of their businesses, but then Jan's physician father is rounded up and sent off to the front to care for wounded German soldiers. Finally all Jews are deported to Terezin, also called Theresienstadt after the Empress Maria Theresa. Jan's mother, grandfather, and sisters prepare to leave but he will remain behind, hidden in the attic of some friends. After a year of confinement he walks outside for an hour, which is long enough for his presence to be reported to the Gestapo, putting his friends in jeopardy and forcing him to leave. Heading to the Jewish cemetery, he finds an amulet that enables him to time travel back to the sixteenth century when Rabbi Loewe made a giant golem which scared all those who were prejudiced against the Jews. If only Jan could stay back then he wouldn't be sent to Terezin where only 150 of 150,000 children survived. (142 pages)

Where it's reviewed:
Booklist, October 1, 2001, page 312
School Library Journal, December 2001, page 138

Other books by the same author:
Plots and Players: The Lopez Conspiracy, 1989

Other books you might like:
Sonia Levitin, *The Golem and the Dragon Girl*, 1993
When Jonathan moves into Laurel's old house, he worries there's a golem living there so Laurel returns to lure away her great-grandfather's spirit.
Malka Penn, *Ghosts and Golems: Haunting Tales of the Supernatural*, 2001
Original short stories by ten different authors offer a look at Jewish culture while also adding a dollop of suspense.
Barbara Rogasky, *The Golem*, 1996
The story of the rabbi who creates a giant from clay, which miraculously comes to life and protects the Jews of sixteenth-century Prague.
Jane Yolen, *The Devil's Arithmetic*, 1988
Hannah opens the symbolic door to Elijah during Passover Seder, only to find herself part of a Jewish family headed for a concentration camp.

633

MELINDA METZ

Gifted Touch

(New York: HarperCollins/Avon, 2001)

Series: Fingerprints. Number 1
Subject(s): Psychic Powers; School Life
Age range(s): Grades 7-10
Major character(s): Rachel ''Rae'' Voight, Psychic, 11th Grader; Anthony Fascinelli, 17-Year-Old; Jesse Bevan, 13-Year-Old
Time period(s): 2000s
Locale(s): United States

Summary: In her junior year of high school, Rae suddenly has random thoughts going through her head, thoughts she labels ''not-her-thoughts.'' Scared when ''let me pass the physics test'' or ''Rae thinks she's so cool'' run through her head, she has a breakdown in the school cafeteria and is hospitalized. Group therapy introduces her to people who don't shun her, like the students at her school, but one day someone from group tries to kill her with a bomb. By now Rae has figured out that when she touches an object, she picks up the thoughts of the last users, and realizes that someone has set up Anthony. With the help of Jesse from group, the two track down the real bomber and Anthony is released from jail. As Rae later confides to Anthony, she also found evidence of a payoff to the bomber from someone who has targeted her to die in this first of a series. (216 pages)

Where it's reviewed:
Publishers Weekly, April 9, 2001, page 76
School Library Journal, August 2001, page 186
Voice of Youth Advocates, April 2001, page 33

Awards the book has won:
ALA Quick Picks for Reluctant Young Adult Readers, 2002

Other books by the same author:
Payback, 2002 (Fingerprints, Number 7)
Betrayed, 2001 (Fingerprints, Number 5)
Fingerprints, 2001 (Fingerprints, Number 3)
Secrets, 2001 (Fingerprints, Number 4)
Revelations, 2001 (Fingerprints, Number 6)
Trust Me, 2001 (Fingerprints, Number 2)

Other books you might like:
Claudio Apone, *My Grandfather, Jack the Ripper*, 2000
Using his psychic ability, Andy describes the contents of a mysterious room to determine its connection to the legendary Jack the Ripper.
Jenny Carroll, *When Lightning Strikes*, 2001
After being struck by lightning, Jessica gains the ability to sense the location of missing children.
David Lubar, *Hidden Talents*, 1999
At the alternative school, Martin helps his roommates use their special abilities, like telekinesis and precognition, to stop bullies from sabotage.

634

CAROLYN MEYER

Beware, Princess Elizabeth

(San Diego: Harcourt, 2001)

Series: Young Royal Book
Subject(s): Princes and Princesses; Sisters; Historical
Age range(s): Grades 6-9
Major character(s): Elizabeth, Royalty (princess), Historical Figure; Mary Tudor, Royalty (queen), Historical Figure; Edward VI, Royalty (king), Historical Figure
Time period(s): 16th century (1547-1558)
Locale(s): Hatfield, England; London, England

Summary: The intrigue of court life in sixteenth-century England is complicated, treacherous and constantly changing. Into this world is born Elizabeth I, daughter of Henry VIII and Anne Boleyn, who was later beheaded. Elizabeth and her older sister Mary vie with one another, partly because Elizabeth's mother replaced Mary's mother and partly because each eyes the throne. This book begins when Elizabeth's beloved father dies and her life becomes dependent upon the good will of whoever's seated on the throne ruling England. The love Elizabeth feels for her younger brother Edward, her feelings of dislike toward her staunchly Catholic half-sister Mary, her adaptability to changing rules at court and her interactions with various other court officials are well-captured in this fictionalized tale of her life before she becomes the queen. (214 pages)

Where it's reviewed:
Book Report, November 2001, page 64
Booklist, March 1, 2001, page 1278
School Library Journal, May 2001, page 156
Voice of Youth Advocates, June 2001, page 125

Other books by the same author:
Anastasia: The Last Grand Duchess, Russia, 1914, 2000 (Royal Diaries)

Isabel: Jewel of Castilla, 2000 (Royal Diaries)
Mary, Bloody Mary, 1999

Other books you might like:

E.L. Konigsburg, *A Proud Taste for Scarlet and Miniver*, 1973
     Eleanor of Aquitaine narrates the events of her life from her home in Heaven.
Kathryn Lasky, *Elizabeth I: Red Rose of the House of Tudor*, 1999
     A series of fictionalized diary entries provides a look at Elizabeth's life during her early teen years as she strives for her father's attention. Royal Diaries.
Jane Yolen, *Queen's Own Fool: A Novel of Mary Queen of Scots*, 2000
     After Nicola performs for Queen Mary, she is invited to be Mary's personal ''fool,'' a job she accepts for she believes she will always be able to tell Queen Mary the truth.

SUSAN MEYERS
MARLA FRAZEE, Illustrator

Everywhere Babies

(San Diego: Harcourt, Inc., 2001)

Subject(s): Babies; Parent and Child; Stories in Rhyme
Age range(s): Preschool-Kindergarten
Time period(s): 2000s
Locale(s): United States

Summary: Despite differences in appearance babies share a myriad of common experiences. Every day they are dressed, kissed, rocked and fed. Noisy babies squeal, giggle and cry. Babies are carried in backpacks and pushed in strollers. They play with toys, books and stuffed animals while growing day by day. Babies are born and babies are loved. (32 pages)

Where it's reviewed:
Booklist, March 1, 2001, page 1288
Horn Book, May 2001, page 312
Kirkus Reviews, March 1, 2001, page 334
Riverbank Review, Summer 2001, page 30
School Library Journal, May 2001, page 129

Awards the book has won:
Horn Book Fanfare/Picture Book, 2002
School Library Journal Best Books, 2001

Other books by the same author:
Insect Zoo, 1991
Pearson, a Harbor Seal Pup, 1981
The Truth about Gorillas, 1980

Other books you might like:
Kathy Henderson, *The Baby Dances*, 1999
     As the seasons change, a baby grows under the watchful eyes of a loving family.
Amy Schwartz, *Some Babies*, 2000
     At bedtime Baby wants Mommy to describe the play antics and dress of all the babies at the park.
Charles R. Smith Jr., *Brown Sugar Babies*, 2000
     Babies in a photographic essay come in all shades of brown—some peanut butter creamy, some cinnamon spice and some sweet as honey.

CHARLOTTE MIDDLETON, Author/Illustrator

Tabitha's Terrifically Tough Tooth

(New York: Phyllis Fogelman Books, 2001)

Subject(s): Growing Up; Problem Solving; Fairies
Age range(s): Grades K-2
Major character(s): Tabitha, Child, Daughter
Time period(s): 2000s (2000)
Locale(s): England

Summary: When Tabitha learns that the tooth fairy leaves money in exchange for teeth she's determined that her wobbly tooth will be out before bedtime. Unfortunately, her strategies for tooth removal are creative but ineffective. Unexpectedly, Tabitha sneezes and her terrifically tough tooth flies across the room. Content to have her problem resolved Tabitha leaves a note for the tooth fairy and drifts off to sleep as the author's first book, originally published in Great Britain in 2000, concludes. (32 pages)

Where it's reviewed:
Booklist, April 15, 2001, page 1566
Horn Book Guide, Fall 2001, page 267
Kirkus Reviews, May 1, 2001, page 664
Publishers Weekly, April 30, 2001, page 77
School Library Journal, June 2001, page 126

Other books you might like:
Cathryn Falwell, *Dragon Tooth*, 1996
     Although her loose tooth is painful, Sara is not sure she wants her father to yank it out.
Robert Munsch, *Andrew's Loose Tooth*, 1998
     A painful, loose tooth defies various unique attempts at extraction.
Martin Silverman, *My Tooth Is Loose!*, 1991
     Georgie's friends offer unappealing advice when they learn that Georgie has a loose tooth.

CHINA MIEVILLE

Perdido Street Station

(New York: Del Rey, 2001)

Subject(s): Utopia/Dystopia; Love; Magic
Age range(s): Grades 10-Adult
Major character(s): Isaac Dan der Grimnebulin, Scientist; Lin, Alien, Artist; Derkhan Blueday, Journalist; Yagharek, Alien, Criminal
Time period(s): Indeterminate
Locale(s): New Crobuzon, Fictional City

Summary: In the weird crumbling metropolis of New Crobuzon, corrupt politicians, gang bosses, scientists with magical abilities and strange alien races compete for survival. Isaac is a neer-do-well scientific genius whose refusal to accept any kind of discipline has put him on the fringes of the scientific community. For one thing, he carries on a relationship with Lin, one of the khephri bug-women. He also tries to find a way to help Yagharek, one of the winged, flying Garuda, whose wings have been amputated by his own people for crimes he refuses to name. Isaac is inspired by the challenge of restoring Yagharek's flying ability and decides not to worry about the moral questions. As part of his research, he collects anything with wings and is not particular about how he obtains them; one creature that comes into his hands is a bizarre caterpillar of unknown species. While Lin is hired by a gang lord to sculpt his portrait, Isaac finally begins to see a solution to Yagharek's problem. Unfortunately, his friend Derkham has stumbled onto some ugly political truths, which will enrage Lin's employer, endanger Isaac and imperil all of New Crobuzon. As dangerous secrets are revealed, the caterpillar emerges from its cocoon and the real threat becomes apparent. (710 pages)

Where it's reviewed:
Book World, June 24, 2001, page 13
Booklist, February 15, 2001, page 1122
Library Journal, February 15, 2001, page 204
New Scientist, April 7, 2001, page 49
Publishers Weekly, January 8, 2001, page 52

Other books by the same author:
King Rat, 1999

Other books you might like:
Melvin Burgess, *Bloodtide*, 2001
  An alternate, but equally bleak vision of a metropolitan future featuring gang warfare.
Mary Gentle, *Rats and Gargoyles*, 1990
  The city's architecture plays an important role in this swords and sorcery tale.
Sean McMullen, *Eyes of the Calculor*, 2001
  If civilization does not collapse to the inner city, then the dystopian future might pit man, minus his machines, against the intelligent mammals of the sea.

638

BEN MIKAELSEN

Touching Spirit Bear
(New York: HarperCollins, 2001)

Subject(s): Animals/Bears; Anger; Indians of North America
Age range(s): Grades 7-10
Major character(s): Cole Matthews, 15-Year-Old, Criminal; Peter Driscal, 9th Grader, Crime Victim; Garvey, Parole Officer; Edwin, Indian (Tlingit)
Time period(s): 2000s
Locale(s): Minneapolis, Minnesota; Drake, Alaska (island off the coast of Alaska)

Summary: Mean, arrogant and vicious, Cole is always in trouble for fighting and not controlling his violent temper, actions he's learned from his alcoholic, abusive father. His latest episode, when he beat classmate Peter so badly the boy is permanently damaged, requires a different type of punishment, one from which his wealthy father's lawyers can't extricate him. His parole officer Grundy suggests ''Circle Justice,'' a Native American alternative sentencing, whereby Cole will be sent to live alone on a remote Alaskan island with supplies, shelter, and the time needed to rethink his life and his actions. Cole agrees to this figuring he'll just swim off the island and escape, but before he can try to leave he meets an

adversary he can't defeat, the Spirit Bear. Left badly wounded after the attack, Cole is rescued by his parole officer and Edwin, a Tlingit elder. After hospitalization, Cole knows he needs to not only return to the island to complete his sentence but also help his victim, Peter, begin to heal, though he's not sure the courts will agree. (241 pages)

Where it's reviewed:
Book Report, September 2001, page 64
Booklist, January 2001, page 940
Bulletin of the Center for Children's Books, May 2001, page 347
School Library Journal, February 2001, page 122
Voice of Youth Advocates, June 2001, page 126

Awards the book has won:
ALA Best Books for Young Adults, 2002

Other books by the same author:
Red Midnight, 2002
Peter, 1998
Countdown, 1996
Stranded, 1995
Sparrow Hawk Red, 1993

Other books you might like:
Alden R. Carter, *Up Country*, 1989
  Carl Stagger is sent to live with farming relatives when his mother finally seeks help from an alcohol rehab center.
Chris Crutcher, *The Crazy Horse Electric Game*, 1987
  Hit by a pitch, Willie's sense of balance is impaired and, unable to accept his disability, runs away from home.
Gary Paulsen, *Hatchet*, 1987
  Enroute to visit his father, Brian's plane crashes in the Canadian Northwoods; as the sole survivor, he relies on his hatchet to stay alive.
Deb Vanasse, *A Distant Enemy*, 1997
  Part Eskimo and part white, Joseph is an angry young man who tries to live in the traditions of his Eskimo culture but goes about everything the wrong way.

639

GLORIA D. MIKLOWITZ

Secrets in the House of Delgado
(Grand Rapids, MI: Eerdmans, 2001)

Subject(s): Jews; Prejudice; Inquisition
Age range(s): Grades 7-10
Major character(s): Maria Sanchez, Orphan, Servant; Angelica Delgado, 11-Year-Old; Juan Pablo Delgado, Brother (of Angelica); Francisco Sanchez, Uncle (of Maria), Sea Captain
Time period(s): 15th century
Locale(s): Caceres, Spain; Palos, Spain

Summary: When Columbus is exploring new worlds, his sponsors Ferdinand and Isabella rule a country racked by the Spanish Inquisition where any non-Catholic is ferreted out, questioned, tortured and perhaps even burned at the stake. An orphaned Catholic girl, Maria, approaches her priest about finding work and he sends her to the Delgado family where she will be the maid to their daughter Angelica. Because the Delgado family are Conversos, people originally Jewish but who generations earlier converted to Catholicism, Maria has been told to report to the priest anything that indicates the family also practices Judaism. At first she is very happy with this family that welcomes her and treats her more as a companion to their daughter than a maid; Maria even has a crush on their oldest son and thinks he's interested in her. When Juan Pablo's engagement to another Converso is announced, Maria's jealousy unloosens her tongue and her innocuous comments to the priest are heard differently than she intends. When Dr. Delgado is arrested and questioned, Maria realizes the impact of her words and scrambles to find her uncle to secure the family safe passage out of Spain. (182 pages)

Where it's reviewed:
Book Report, January 2002, page 63
Bulletin of the Center for Children's Books, November 2001, page 111
Kliatt, September 2001, page 12
School Library Journal, October 2001, page 166
Voice of Youth Advocates, December 2001, page 361

Other books by the same author:
Camouflage, 1998
Masada: The Last Fortress, 1998
Past Forgiving, 1995
The Killing Boy, 1993
Desperate Pursuit, 1992

Other books you might like:
Jacqueline Dembar Greene, *One Foot Ashore*, 1994
    Portuguese Jews, Maria and her sister Isobel are kidnapped and sent to a Catholic monastery where monks try to eradicate the tenets of Judaism.
Waldtraut Lewin, *Freedom beyond the Sea*, 2001
    Elizabeth, the daughter of a Jewish rabbi, flees the Inquisition disguised as a ship's cabin boy and sails with Columbus aboard the *Santa Maria*.
Pamela Melnikoff, *Plots and Players: The Lopez Conspiracy*, 1989
    Living in England during the reign of Elizabeth I, the Lopez family is forced to practice Judaism in secret.

640

WILLIAM MILLER
CHARLOTTE RILEY-WEBB, Illustrator

Rent Party Jazz

(New York: Lee & Low Books Inc., 2001)

Subject(s): Music and Musicians; Depression (Economic); African Americans
Age range(s): Grades 2-5
Major character(s): Sonny Comeaux, Son, Student; Mama, Single Mother, Unemployed; Smilin' Jack, Musician
Time period(s): 1930s
Locale(s): New Orleans, Louisiana

Summary: Sonny works in the morning before school delivering coal to help his Mama pay the rent but when Mama loses her job he knows he doesn't make enough to cover all the expenses. Mama's job search is unproductive but Sonny has better luck solving their financial problems when he stops to listen to Smilin' Jack on his way home from school. Smilin'

Jack tells Sonny about rent parties and offers to play at one for Sonny's family. Sonny spreads the word, the neighbors come and by the end of an evening of great music and good fun Sonny and Mama have a bucket full of coins that will more than pay the rent. An "Afterword" gives the background information about "rent parties" and the role they played in the development of jazz. (32 pages)

Where it's reviewed:
Booklist, November 15, 2001, page 582
Horn Book Guide, Spring 2002, page 52
Publishers Weekly, October 15, 2001, page 71
Riverbank Review, Winter 2001-2002, page 32
School Library Journal, November 2001, page 130

Awards the book has won:
Notable Social Studies Trade Books for Young People, 2002

Other books by the same author:
The Piano, 2000
Night Golf, 1999
Richard Wright and the Library Card, 1997 (Smithsonian's Notable Books for Children)

Other books you might like:
Debbi Chocolate, *The Piano Man*, 1998
    An old man's daughter buys the piano he once played for silent movies and presents it to her father as a gift.
Linda England, *The Old Cotton Blues*, 1998
    Dexter learns to make the music that he feels within him come to life on a used harmonica as he plays the "Old Cotton Blues."
Libba Moore Gray, *Little Lil and Swing-Singing Sax*, 1996
    When her uncle pawns his sax to buy medicine for her sick mother, Little Lil knows she must get it back so her mother can hear the healing music.
Alan Schroeder, *Satchmo's Blues*, 1996
    A fictionalized biography of Louis Armstrong's childhood in New Orleans depicts the influence of the city sounds on his desire to play the cornet.

641

CLAUDIA MILLS
CATHERINE STOCK, Illustrator

Gus and Grandpa at Basketball

(New York: Farrar Straus Giroux, 2001)

Subject(s): Sports/Basketball; Grandfathers; Competition
Age range(s): Grades 1-3
Major character(s): Gus, Basketball Player, Son; Grandpa, Grandfather; Daddy, Father
Time period(s): 2000s (2001)
Locale(s): Colorado

Summary: Gus's first experience with team sports is a bit overwhelming. He enjoys practicing with his teammates and shooting hoops alone at Grandpa's house, but the noisy games are no fun. Gus's parents attend his games and Daddy yells advice to Gus that confuses and stresses him. Grandpa sensitively stays home until Gus asks him to come to the last game of the season. Then Grandpa turns off his hearing aid so the noise of the crowd doesn't bother him and gestures to Gus to do the same in his mind. When Gus returns to the court, pretending he cannot hear the crowd's noises, he performs much better and actually shoots the winning goal. (48 pages)

Where it's reviewed:
Booklist, November 15, 2001, page 574
Horn Book, November 2001, page 754
Kirkus Reviews, June 15, 2001, page 868
School Library Journal, September 2001, page 200

Awards the book has won:
ALA Notable Children's Books, 2002

Other books by the same author:
Gus and Grandpa and Show-and-Tell, 2000
Gus and Grandpa and the Two-Wheeled Bike, 1999
Gus and Grandpa Ride the Train, 1998

Other books you might like:
Robert Burleigh, *Hoops*, 1997
    An illustrated prose poem expresses the intensity of the game, the drive of the players and the joy of basketball.
John Coy, *Strong to the Hoop*, 1999
    James joins his older brother's pick-up game when a player is injured and uses determination and skill to guard a bigger opponent.
Bill Martin Jr., *Swish!*, 1997
    On the final play of a basketball game, teamwork scores the winning goal for the Cardinals.

642

LAUREN MILLS, Author/Illustrator
DENNIS NOLAN, Illustrator

The Dog Prince
(Boston: Little, Brown and Company, 2001)

Subject(s): Behavior; Magic; Princes and Princesses
Age range(s): Grades 1-4
Major character(s): Nana, Mythical Creature (fairy), Aged Person; Eliza, Maiden; Prince, Dog, Royalty
Time period(s): Indeterminate Past
Locale(s): Fictional Country

Summary: Nana transforms a disagreeable, spoiled prince into a drooling bloodhound that is shooed away from the castle when he tries to return home. Lonely, thirsty and hungry he finds a home with Eliza, a goat herder he treated rudely when he was a human prince. From Eliza, Prince the dog learns manners, loyalty and love. When a chimera slithers into the farm to devour Eliza's goats Prince fights the beast and would be killed if not for Eliza distracting the chimera with a broom swat. Still Prince seems mortally wounded and Eliza weeps for her pet, professing her love, thus breaking Nana's spell. In true fairy tale form they all live happily ever after though Eliza has to get another dog. (32 pages)

Where it's reviewed:
Booklist, November 15, 2001, page 583
Horn Book Guide, Spring 2002, page 76
Publishers Weekly, October 8, 2001, page 64
School Library Journal, December 2001, page 106

Other books by the same author:
Fairy Wings, 1995 (Golden Kite Award, Illustration)
Tatterhood and the Hobgoblins, 1993

The Rag Coat, 1991

Other books you might like:
Laura Krauss Melmed, *Prince Nautilus*, 1994
    Kindly Fiona is rewarded when her unselfish actions free a Prince from an evil spell.
Jennifer Rae, *Dog Tales*, 1999
    Dogs play the leading roles in each of six fractured fairy tales.
Laurence Yep, *The Dragon Prince: A Chinese Beauty and the Beast Tale*, 1997
    To save her father's life a poor farmer's daughter agrees to marry a dragon.

643

FRANCES MINTERS
JANIE BYNUM, Illustrator

Too Big, Too Small, Just Right
(San Diego: Harcourt, Inc., 2001)

Subject(s): Language; Animals/Rabbits; Stories in Rhyme
Age range(s): Preschool-Kindergarten
Major character(s): Unnamed Character, Rabbit, Friend; Unnamed Character, Rabbit, Friend; Unnamed Character, Mouse
Time period(s): Indeterminate
Locale(s): Fictional Country

Summary: While playing, two rabbit friends discover that some toys are too big or too small, too high or too low, but together they find a way to enjoy them that is just right. A little mouse tags along and participates in the solutions such as when it provides the small amount of weight needed to balance the seesaw. One rabbit roller skates too fast and the other skates too slowly, but by helping each other they can skate together at just the right pace. Too many balloons lift one rabbit off the ground while too few isn't much fun. However, when each friend has a balloon they're happy. (32 pages)

Where it's reviewed:
Booklist, May 1, 2001, page 1692
Children's Bookwatch, April 2001, page 4
Horn Book Guide, Fall 2001, page 238
Publishers Weekly, February 12, 2001, page 210
School Library Journal, April 2001, page 118

Other books by the same author:
Chicken for a Day, 2000 (Step into Reading)
Sleepless Beauty, 1996
Cinder-Elly, 1994

Other books you might like:
Stella Blackstone, *Baby High, Baby Low*, 1997
    Pairs of babies demonstrate opposite traits; if one is happy, the other's sad and if one's hot the other baby is cold.
Nina Crews, *A High, Low, Near, Far, Loud, Quiet Story*, 1999
    Photographs of the daily routine of a city-dwelling brother and sister contrast concepts such as high and low; near and far; large and small.
Mick Inkpen, *Kipper's Book of Opposites*, 1995
    The antics of a playful dog depict a variety of conceptual terms expressing opposites.

644

KATHRYN MITCHELL

Proud and Angry Dust

(Boulder, CO: University Press of Colorado, 2001)

Subject(s): African Americans; Murder; Oil
Age range(s): Grades 10-Adult
Major character(s): Barnett Lindsay, Uncle, Teenager; Theodore Roosevelt Bullmoose O'Malley, Teenager; Elliott Singer, Lawyer; Betsy Singer, Teenager
Time period(s): 1920s
Locale(s): Knox Plains, Texas

Summary: Moose is a young boy of mixed African American and Irish blood whose small town in Texas changes overnight when oil is discovered in the black folks' section of town, a section to which they've been relegated by the whites. Until now Moose and his uncle Barnett, who's Moose's age, have concentrated on pranks, school and running their general store, with help from Moose's mom. But suddenly swindlers, girls of the night and the white population want to extricate some of that money for their own wallets. Moose is bothered because of several murders but meeting the black lawyer Elliott Singer enables him to see that justice will be done. Moose takes advantage of the oil discovery, and its accompanying wealth, to pursue his goal of becoming a research chemist, and during a summer program at Tuskegee he meets Elliott's sister Betsy and falls in love. (233 pages)

Where it's reviewed:
Booklist, June 2001, page 1848
Kirkus Reviews, May 1, 2001, page 614

Other books you might like:
David Anthony Durham, *Gabriel's Story*, 2001
    African American Gabriel finds himself dragged to the Kansas plains by his mother who is remarrying; miserable, he runs away on an adventure that makes him glad to return home.
Carolyn Meyer, *White Lilacs*, 1993
    The black community of Freedomtown opposes being moved to the sewer flats, but violence and marches by the Ku Klux Klan stop their action.
Clay Reynolds, *Monuments*, 2000
    Hugh's quiet summer disappears when his town decides to demolish an ugly old building.

645

LOUISE MOERI

The Devil in Ol' Rosie

(New York: Atheneum/Simon & Schuster, 2001)

Subject(s): Ranch Life; Fathers and Sons; Animals/Horses
Age range(s): Grades 5-8
Major character(s): Rosie, Horse; John "Wart" Nolan, 12-Year-Old
Time period(s): 1900s (1907)
Locale(s): Oregon

Summary: Once again Ol' Rosie takes advantage of an unlatched gate, only this time she's followed into the cattle pasture by the family's other horses. Normally Wart's pa would round them up, but Wart's mother is in labor and needs her husband so young Wart is sent out on a lame horse. Knowing his family will starve if the horses aren't found, Wart understands the responsibility he's been given, but it's a lot to ask of a twelve-year-old. His twenty-four hour trek is a test of his mettle as his horse is injured, Wart's hand is cut, his eye abraded, a cougar stalks the young colt and a blizzard engulfs them. By Wart's return, with a string of horses behind him, he has earned his father's respect and the discarding of his nickname. (202 pages)

Where it's reviewed:
Booklist, February 15, 2001, page 1137
Bulletin of the Center for Children's Books, March 2001, page 272
Horn Book, January 2001, page 94
Publishers Weekly, January 8, 2001, page 67
School Library Journal, March 2001, page 254

Other books by the same author:
The Forty-Third War, 1989
Downwind, 1984
First the Egg, 1982
Save Queen of Sheba, 1981

Other books you might like:
Gretel Ehrlich, *A Blizzard Year: Timmy's Almanac of the Seasons*, 1999
    A terrible blizzard destroys most of their cattle and Timmy worries that her parents will lose their ranch.
Phyllis Reynolds Naylor, *The Fear Place*, 1994
    When his brother is lost, Doug doesn't hesitate to climb over a narrow ledge he calls his "fear place" to rescue him.
Linda Shands, *Blind Fury*, 2001
    Wakara's father and brother are caught up in the mountains by a blizzard, but Wakara knows they're in danger and rides out to find them.
Laura E. Williams, *The Ghost Stallion*, 1999
    Though secretly envying the stallion his freedom, Mary Elizabeth knows he has to be caught as he's stealing the mares of the ranchers.
G. Clifton Wisler, *Mustang Flats*, 1997
    Thrilled his dad's home from the Civil War, Alby resents his father blaming him for damage to the farm caused by a cyclone.

646

SUSIE MORGENSTERN
SERGE BLOCH, Illustrator
GILL ROSNER, Translator

A Book of Coupons

(New York: Viking, 2001)

Subject(s): Teachers; Schools; Gifts
Age range(s): Grades 4-6
Major character(s): Hubert Noel, Teacher; Charles, 5th Grader; Incarnation Perez, Principal
Time period(s): 1990s (1999)
Locale(s): France (Marie Curie School)

Summary: All summer Charles and his classmates look forward to meeting their new teacher so they are quite surprised to enter the classroom and find Monsieur Noel, a person who looks much too old to be described as a new teacher. Monsieur Noel's approach to teaching is new and different from anything they've experienced at Marie Curie School. The students quickly learn to appreciate the "gifts" the teacher passes out, beginning with the "Book of Coupons" but also including texts, field trips and tests. Incarnation Perez is horrified by Monsieur Noel's unconventional teaching and seizes an opportunity to force him to retire. His gift from his students on the final day of school is a giant coupon for a happy retirement. The book was originally published in France as *Joker* in 1999. (62 pages)

Where it's reviewed:
Booklist, April 1, 2001, page 1471
Horn Book, May 2001, page 332
Kirkus Reviews, April 15, 2001, page 591
Riverbank Review, Winter 2001-2002, page 34
School Library Journal, May 2001, page 129

Awards the book has won:
Mildred L. Batchelder Honor Book, 2002
ALA Notable Children's Books, 2002

Other books by the same author:
Secret Letters from 0 to 10, 1998 (Booklist Editor's Choice)

Other books you might like:
Andrew Clements, *The Landry News*, 1999
    Mr. Larson's teaching style is unconventional, but effective as his students' demonstrate in order to save his job.
Kirkpatrick Hill, *The Year of Miss Agnes*, 2000
    Miss Agnes has unorthodox, but effective teaching methods that win the appreciation of her students.
Gregory Maguire, *Four Stupid Cupids*, 2000
    Miss Earth's students attempt to do a little matchmaking for their beloved teacher prior to Valentine's Day.

647

SUSIE MORGENSTERN
GILL ROSSNER, Translator

Three Days Off
(New York: Viking, 2001)

Subject(s): Conduct of Life; Schools/High Schools; Teachers
Age range(s): Grades 7-10
Major character(s): William Lesmarais, 15-Year-Old; Miss March, Teacher
Time period(s): 2000s
Locale(s): Valenciennes, France

Summary: It's all William can do to force himself out of bed in the morning to go to school, and when he sits in class he's on automatic pilot with everything tuned out. That's the way it's been for ten years and he doesn't see it changing. One day his earnest young teacher Miss March tries to break through his zombie state and demands to know what he's dreaming. Unfortunately William tells her, and is then suspended for three days. As he wanders around, several events occur that nudge him out of his state of ennui. He spends time with an American tourist who's left everything behind and is searching for a better life, but knows it can't be found. William spends another day helping two blue-collar workers who remind him of the importance of school. Then on the third day, he travels to Lille and meets a college student with whom he thinks he'll make headway, but finds out she has a boyfriend. By book's end he's grown a little wiser, tells his mother of his suspension and writes an account of his adventures, along with an apology to Miss March. (89 pages)

Where it's reviewed:
Booklist, December 15, 2001, page 724
Horn Book, November 2001, page 755
Kirkus Reviews, October 1, 2001, page 1429
Publishers Weekly, October 29, 2001, page 65
School Library Journal, December 2001, page 139

Other books by the same author:
Princesses Are People, Too: Two Modern Fairy Tales, 2002
A Book of Coupons, 2001
Secret Letters from 0 to 10, 1998

Other books you might like:
Stephen Chbosky, *The Perks of Being a Wallflower*, 1999
    In Charlie's freshman year he helps his pregnant older sister, adjusts to the suicide of a best friend and is hospitalized for depression.
J.D. Salinger, *The Catcher in the Rye*, 1951
    Trying to find himself, Holden Caulfield roams New York City for three days, thinks over his prep school days and mourns the loss of his younger brother.
Rob Thomas, *Rats Saw God*, 1996
    One English credit shy of graduation, Steve's guidance counselor suggests he write a 100-page essay about anything he knows.

648

JACLYN MORIARTY

Feeling Sorry for Celia
(New York: St. Martin's, 2001)

Subject(s): Letters; School Life; Friendship
Age range(s): Grades 8-12
Major character(s): Elizabeth Clarry, 15-Year-Old; Celia Buckley, Runaway; Christina Kratovac, Student—High School
Time period(s): 2000s
Locale(s): Sydney, Australia

Summary: Through a series of letters, fridge notes from her mother and messages from such made-up organizations as "The Association of Teenagers" or the "Take a Deep Breath and Calm Down Society," Elizabeth tells about the year her friend Celia ran away to join the circus. Of course, more events occurr that year, beginning with the pen pal letter writing assignment from Elizabeth's teacher where she meets her total opposite in Christina, a student at a nearby school; trains for half-marathon runs because she likes how it feels when you stop running; and meets and loses a special boy. Elizabeth constantly worries about Celia who constantly runs away, but after rescuing her from the circus and losing her boyfriend to Celia, Elizabeth begins to pay attention to her own special talents in a very funny first novel. (276 pages)

Where it's reviewed:
Book Report, May 2001, page 60
Booklist, November 15, 2001, page 621
Kliatt, March 2001, page 12
School Library Journal, May 2001, page 156
Voice of Youth Advocates, April 2001, page 44

Awards the book has won:
ALA Best Books for Young Adults, 2002

Other books you might like:
Catherine Clark, *Truth or Dairy*, 2000
    When her boyfriend dumps her, Courtney throws herself into student government, working and giving up boys!
Louise Rennison, *Angus, Thongs and Full-Frontal Snogging: Confessions of Georgia Nicolson*, 2000
    In her diary, Georgia records her interest in kissing, her appearance and her opposition to most of what the adult world thinks is important.
Rosie Rushton, *Just Don't Make a Scene, Mum*, 1999
    In this first of a series, five British teens find their lives connected through a radio show that lets them describe embarrassing moments.

649

GERALD MORRIS

Parsifal's Page
(Boston: Houghton Mifflin, 2001)

Subject(s): Knights and Knighthood; Arthurian Legends; Middle Ages
Age range(s): Grades 6-9
Major character(s): Piers/Pierre, Page; Parsifal, Knight; Ither, Knight
Time period(s): Indeterminate Past
Locale(s): England

Summary: Growing up feasting on the stories of his mother's experiences as a French lady-in-waiting, Piers wishes to be a page or a squire, anything but an apprentice to his father, the blacksmith. He gets his wish when a knight appears at the smithy, though his time with Sir Ither is short when Parsifal defeats Ither. Piers, who now calls himself Pierre, attaches to Parsifal to help him locate the Holy Grail and thus join the Knights of the Round Table. Though Pierre tries to assist, he often doesn't know as much as Parsifal does and the two end up in a humorous romp in this retelling of the Arthurian legend. (232 pages)

Where it's reviewed:
Booklist, April 15, 2001, page 1558
Bulletin of the Center for Children's Books, April 2001, page 310
Horn Book, May 2001, page 333
School Library Journal, April 2001, page 146
Voice of Youth Advocates, June 2001, page 134

Other books by the same author:
The Savage Damsel and the Dwarf, 2000
The Squire, the Knight, & His Lady, 1999
The Squire's Tale, 1998

Other books you might like:
Anne E. Crompton, *Gawain and Lady Green*, 1997
    Sir Gawain looks at the court of King Arthur and its unique code of chivalry and honor.
Joan Elizabeth Goodman, *The Winter Hare*, 1996
    Will's dream to become a knight comes true when he helps Empress Matilda escape and is permitted to use the winter hare on his shield.
Katherine Paterson, *Parzival: The Quest of the Grail Knight*, 1998
    Once Parzival decides he wants to become a knight; the earnest but bumbling young man mounts a sway-backed nag and searches for King Arthur's court.

650

DEAN MORRISSEY, Author/Illustrator
STEPHEN KRENSKY, Co-Author

The Moon Robber
(New York: HarperCollins Publishers, 2001)

Series: Magic Door. Book 1
Subject(s): Fantasy; Time Travel; Stealing
Age range(s): Grades 2-5
Major character(s): Michael, 10-Year-Old; Sarah, 10-Year-Old; Joey, 6-Year-Old; Mogg, Mythical Creature (giant)
Time period(s): Indeterminate; Indeterminate Past
Locale(s): Old Bridgeport, Fictional Country; Great Kettles, Fictional Country

Summary: Rumbling in the magic shop causes an unused door to open permitting Joey, Sarah and Michael to enter the Great Kettle, a land on the other side of time. In this strange land the children feel the ground tremble again and they soon learn that it's not an earthquake but Mogg walking which causes the shaking. As they explore this new place they enter the moon and accidentally dislodge it from its moorings disturbing the man in the moon. More alarming is Mogg who grabs the moon and carries it to his home. By nightfall Joey, Sarah and Michael realize that Mogg is afraid of the dark and they must find a solution to his problem before they return home if the moon is to be free to rise each night. (64 pages)

Where it's reviewed:
Booklist, April 15, 2001, page 1559
Horn Book Guide, Fall 2001, page 293
Publishers Weekly, June 11, 2001, page 86
School Library Journal, September 2001, page 200

Other books by the same author:
The Winter King, 2002 (Magic Door, Book 2)
The Great Kettles: A Tale of Time, 1997
Ship of Dreams, 1994 (New York Times Best Illustrated Book)

Other books you might like:
Hazel Hutchins, *The Prince of Tarn*, 1997
    A fictional character comes to life and expects Fred to return him to his homeland.
Mary Pope Osborne, *Pirates Past Noon*, 1994
    In the fourth book in the Magic Tree House series Jack and Annie travel back in time and place to a deserted island with buried treasure.

Jon Scieszka, *The Not-So-Jolly Roger*, 1991
The Time Warp trio travels back in time to the days of pirates and hidden treasure.

651

DONNA MORRISSEY

Kit's Law

(New York: Mariner/Houghton Mifflin, 2001)

Subject(s): Coming-of-Age; Mothers and Daughters; Mentally Handicapped
Age range(s): Grades 11-Adult
Major character(s): Kit Pitman, Teenager; Josie Pitman, Mother (of Kit), Mentally Challenged Person; Lizzy Pitman, Grandmother; Sidney "Sid" Ropson, Teenager; Dr. Hodgins, Doctor
Time period(s): 1950s
Locale(s): Fox's Cove, Newfoundland, Canada (Haire's Hollow)

Summary: In this raw, untamed novel, reflective of her surroundings along Newfoundland's coast, Kit lives in a decrepit gully shack with her beloved grandmother Lizzy and mentally challenged mother Josie, the town tramp. Lizzy keeps their odd little family together, and protects Kit from the sneers of the townspeople, but when she dies the townspeople want to place Kit in an orphanage and Josie in an asylum. Kit fights ferociously against this, aided by the kindly Dr. Hodgins, who's one of the few who knows the identity of her father. Other distractions enter Kit's life when the minister sends his son Sid to spy on them, but the plan backfires when Sid and Kit fall in love with one another. There's also a murderer loose, a crazed drunkard named Shine with whom her mother is often seen. Kit's life tips upside down when the secrets about her father are revealed, but her companionship with her mother and her own inner resources, plus some good friends, will see her through this latest calamity in an engaging first novel. (385 pages)

Where it's reviewed:
Booklist, April 1, 2001, page 1452
Kirkus Reviews, March 1, 2001, page 284
Publishers Weekly, April 9, 2001, page 49
Tribune Books, July 1, 2001, page 6

Awards the book has won:
ALA Alex Award, 2002

Other books you might like:
Thomas Hardy, *Far from the Madding Crowd*, 1874
With three suitors, Bathsheba first marries the wastrel, then the farmer who goes insane and finally settles down with solid Gabriel.
Harper Lee, *To Kill a Mockingbird*, 1970
The lives of Scout and her younger brother change when their father defends a black man accused of raping a white woman in 1930s Alabama.
Annie Proulx, *Shipping News*, 1993
A former newspaper man returns to his family's ancestral town in Newfoundland accompanied by his aging aunt and young daughters.

Marilynne Robinson, *Housekeeping*, 1980
Eccentricity abounds in Ruth's home as she's raised by her aging grandmother and two elderly aunts.

652

BARRY MOSER, Author/Illustrator

The Three Little Pigs

(Boston: Little, Brown and Company, 2001)

Subject(s): Folklore; Animals/Pigs; Animals/Wolves
Age range(s): Grades K-3
Major character(s): Big Mama Pig, Mother, Pig; Unnamed Character, Pig, Brother; Unnamed Character, Wolf
Time period(s): Indeterminate Past
Locale(s): Fictional Country

Summary: In a humorously illustrated retelling of the traditional tale Big Mama Pig sends her three little pigs out into the world with the admonition that they beware of the wolf. The first pig in his straw house soon falls victim to the huffing and puffing wolf, as does the second pig in the house of sticks. The brick house (made with "Wolfe Pruf" cement) of the third pig proves to more than the wolf can huff and puff down. The wolf turns to subterfuge, but the third pig stays one step ahead of him and gleefully lets the wolf know just how he's been outwitted. Finally, in frustration, the wolf climbs down the pig's chimney, becoming the victim of the pig's final plan. (32 pages)

Where it's reviewed:
Booklist, June 2001, page 1886
Bulletin of the Center for Children's Books, March 2001, page 272
Horn Book, May 2001, page 340
Publishers Weekly, March 12, 2001, page 90
School Library Journal, May 2001, page 145

Other books by the same author:
Good and Perfect Gifts: An Illustrated Retelling of O. Henry's The Gift of the Magi, 1997
Tucker Pfeffercorn: An Old Story Retold, 1994

Other books you might like:
Gavin Bishop, *The Three Little Pigs*, 1989
In this retelling of the three little pigs in search of their fortunes the hip wolf, with sunglasses and Walkman, still meets the stew pot in the end.
Steven Kellogg, *The Three Little Pigs*, 1997
The pigs in this humorous retelling face a tough-looking hungry wolf trying to order piglet from their waffle wagon.
James Marshall, *The Three Little Pigs*, 1989
The inimitable illustrator retells the classic story with humor and originality.
Jon Scieszka, *The True Story of the 3 Little Pigs*, 1989
This version of the classic tale takes a different look at just what happened with those three little pigs.

RICHARD MOSHER

Zazoo: A Novel

(New York: Clarion Books, 2001)

Subject(s): Grandfathers; Orphans; Secrets
Age range(s): Grades 6-10
Major character(s): Zazoo, Orphan, 13-Year-Old; Marius, 16-Year-Old; Grand-Pierre, Grandfather, Resistance Fighter (during World War II); Felix Klein, Pharmacist
Time period(s): 1980s
Locale(s): France

Summary: For the last eleven years, Zazoo has been happily living with her adoptive grandfather, Grand-Pierre, in his lockkeeper's house beside a canal. Originally from Vietnam, Zazoo was orphaned when she was a baby and left Vietnam when she was two. When the stranger Marius bicycles to their village and asks her about a pharmacist named Klein, she realizes that not only doesn't she know much about her Vietnamese family, she knows nothing about Grand-Pierre except that he was a hero during the French Resistance. Thanks to Marius, secrets emerge from the "awful time" of World War II, including old loves and not speaking to the pharmacist, and old hurts are finally healed in this beautifully told story. (248 pages)

Where it's reviewed:
Booklist, December 15, 2001, page 724
Kliatt, September 2001, page 12
Publishers Weekly, December 3, 2001, page 61
School Library Journal, November 2001, page 162
Voice of Youth Advocates, October 2001, page 282

Awards the book has won:
ALA Best Books for Young Adults, 2002
School Library Journal Best Books, 2001

Other books by the same author:
The Taxi Navigator, 1998

Other books you might like:
Kimberly Willis Holt, *Dancing in Cadillac Light,* 2001
    Jaynelle's grandfather moves in with her family and she's appointed to "keep an eye" on him, but covers up his quirks rather than reporting them.
Christa Laird, *But Can the Phoenix Sing?: A Compelling Story of Unrelenting Courage in Nazi-Occupied Poland,* 1995
    Rich better understands his stepfather Misha's strictness when he reads an autobiographical letter written by Misha describing his life as a partisan fighter in Warsaw.
Eugenie Melnyk, *My Darling Elia,* 1999
    Separated during the Holocaust, Elia comes close to being reunited with his wife Anna, whom he hasn't seen in forty years, when he finds a locket he made for her at a flea market.
Barbara Park, *The Graduation of Jake Moon,* 2000
    Though his grandfather is diagnosed with Alzheimer's, Jake remembers that this man is still his beloved grandfather.

MARISSA MOSS, Author/Illustrator

Oh Boy, Amelia!

(Middleton, WI: Pleasant Company Publications, 2001)

Subject(s): Gender Roles; Schools; Sisters
Age range(s): Grades 3-5
Major character(s): Amelia, Sister (younger), Student; Cleo, Sister (older), Student; Oliver, 13-Year-Old, Boyfriend
Time period(s): 2000s (2001)
Locale(s): Oopa, Oregon

Summary: Amelia absolutely has to figure out why Cleo is beginning to act more like a normal human being. The answer is Oliver. Cleo's got a crush on a boy and wants to impress him so she's changed her behavior. Amelia is not totally pleased with the changes she sees but they do make her wonder about gender roles. Is it really necessary for girls to pretend they need help from boys? If Amelia's bad at sewing in her Life Skills class, but good with the woodworking project is she any less a girl? Before the book concludes Amelia finds some answers and Cleo finds some balance. (40 pages)

Where it's reviewed:
Booklist, January 1, 2002, page 859
Horn Book Guide, Spring 2002, page 76
Publishers Weekly, July 16, 2001, page 183
School Library Journal, October 2001, page 126

Awards the book has won:
IRA Children's Choices, 2002

Other books by the same author:
Madam Amelia Tells All, 2001
Amelia Works It Out, 2000
Amelia's Family Ties, 2000
The All-New Amelia, 1999

Other books you might like:
Carol Gorman, *The Miraculous Makeover of Lizard Flanagan,* 1994
    Tomboy Lizard enters middle school observing the changes in her friends and wondering about her own transition from athletic kid to middle school girl.
Phyllis Reynolds Naylor, *All but Alice,* 1992
    Alice quickly tires of being popular, especially if it means she's supposed to be mean to her good friend Patrick.
Louis Sachar, *Marvin Redpost: Is He a Girl?,* 1993
    A friend's assertion that kissing your own elbow will make one a girl has Marvin wondering just what such a change would mean.

MARISSA MOSS, Author/Illustrator

Rose's Journal: The Story of a Girl in the Great Depression

(San Diego: Silver Whistle/Harcourt, Inc., 2001)

Series: Young American Voices
Subject(s): Depression (Economic); Farm Life; Family Life

Age range(s): Grades 3-5
Major character(s): Rose Samuels, Sister, 11-Year-Old; Floyd Samuels, Brother, 14-Year-Old; Father, Farmer
Time period(s): 1930s (1935)
Locale(s): Keota, Kansas

Summary: Three years of drought and dust storms are changing everything that Rose knows. Father is unhappy and irritable all the time. Floyd, who wants to be an artist not a farmer, runs away to Chicago and New York. Lots of people leave the area but Father will not abandon the farm that's been in his family for three generations. Still, Rose doesn't know how they can survive but she has a farmer's hope that tomorrow will be better and events prove that adage to be true. Just as Floyd finds his true calling in the city Rose realizes that farming is in her blood and she will be the one to succeed Father some day. A concluding "Author's Note" gives additional facts about the time period. (54 pages)

Where it's reviewed:
Horn Book Guide, Spring 2002, page 82
School Library Journal, December 2001, page 108

Awards the book has won:
Notable Social Studies Trade Books for Young People, 2002

Other books by the same author:
Hannah's Journal: The Story of an Immigrant Girl, 2000 (Young American Voices)
Emma's Journal: The Story of a Colonial Girl, 1999 (Young American Voices)
Rachel's Journal: The Story of a Pioneer Girl, 1998 (Young American Voices)

Other books you might like:
C. Coco De Young, *A Letter to Mrs. Roosevelt*, 1999
    Margo uses a class assignment in letter writing to request that Eleanor Roosevelt help save her family's home.
Patricia MacLachlan, *Skylark*, 1994
    Drought causes crop failure and forces many families to leave their prairie homes.
Margot Theis Raven, *Angels in the Dust*, 1997
    A picture book for older readers poignantly depicts harsh living conditions in the Oklahoma panhandle during the Dust Bowl of the 1930s
Jerry Stanley, *Children of the Dust Bowl: The True Story of the School at Weedpatch Camp*, 1992
    An award-winning nonfiction title shows that living conditions didn't improve for families of farmers forced to become migrant workers.

656

JIM MURPHY

My Face to the Wind: The Diary of Sarah Jane Price, a Prairie Teacher, Broken Bow, Nebraska, 1881

(New York: Scholastic, 2001)

Series: Dear America
Subject(s): Teachers; City and Town Life; Diaries
Age range(s): Grades 5-8

Major character(s): Sarah Jane Price, 14-Year-Old, Teacher; Miss Kizer, Landlord (boardinghouse owner)
Time period(s): 1880s (1881-1882)
Locale(s): Broken Bow, Nebraska

Summary: After her father dies from a bout of diphtheria that sweeps through their little town, Sarah struggles to pay the rent at Miss Kizer's boarding house. When the town feels that Sarah should be sent to an orphanage, which is just a polite way of saying workhouse, Sarah decides to bump her age up a few years and asks to replace her father as the town's schoolteacher. Though some people are opposed, and there's a dearth of textbooks or other materials, Sarah makes do in an abandoned sod house until the roof is blown off during a storm. After managing to escort each child safely home, the townspeople regard her quite differently and decide to build a proper school. Sarah records the good and bad times of teaching, her unruly students and the grief she feels over losing her father in her diary in this continuing series. (175 pages)

Where it's reviewed:
Booklist, December 1, 2001, page 644
Kirkus Reviews, October 15, 2001, page 1489
Kliatt, November 2001, page 9
School Library Journal, December 2001, page 139
Voice of Youth Advocates, February 2002, page 437

Other books by the same author:
A Young Patriot: The American Revolution as Experienced by One Boy, 1998
The Journal of James Edmond Pease: A Civil War Union Soldier, 1998 (My Name Is America)
West to a Land of Plenty: The Diary of Teresa Angelino Viscardi, 1998 (Dear America)

Other books you might like:
Bess Aldrich, *A Lantern in Her Hand*, 1924
    Abbie gives up her singing career to raise her children in a sod house on the Nebraska prairie.
Avi, *The Secret School*, 2001
    When Ida hears that her one-room school will close because her teacher resigned, Ida swears her classmates to secrecy and becomes their teacher.
Linda Lael Miller, *Rachel*, 1999
    Accepting a friend's request to teach in Sweetwater, Montana, Rachel is unhappy with the town's chicken-coop sized schoolhouse.

657

PATTI BELING MURPHY, Author/Illustrator

Elinor and Violet: The Story of Two Naughty Chickens

(Boston: Little, Brown and Company, 2001)

Subject(s): Behavior; Animals/Chickens; Humor
Age range(s): Grades K-2
Major character(s): Violet Poulet, Chicken, Friend (Elinor's); Elinor, Chicken, Sister; Lucy, Aunt (Elinor's), Chicken
Time period(s): Indeterminate
Locale(s): Fictional Country

Summary: When very naughty Violet visits her grandmother for a week she befriends Elinor who previously has been only a little bit naughty. Now the duo are into mischief all the time and Elinor often finds herself in the time-out corner. Violet's shenanigans peak when Aunt Lucy visits with the promise of taking everyone out to tea. Unfortunately, one of Violet's naughty ideas is to pretend Aunt Lucy's purse is pirate treasure and hide it so no one can go anywhere until it is found. Seeing Aunt Lucy's disappointment, Elinor finds the hidden "treasure" so everyone can enjoy tea with Aunt Lucy. Whether Elinor learns a lesson or not remains to be seen next year when Violet promises to visit her grandmother for the entire summer rather than one week. (32 pages)

Where it's reviewed:
Booklist, May 15, 2001, page 1759
Horn Book, March 2001, page 199
Kirkus Reviews, January 15, 2001, page 114
Publishers Weekly, March 12, 2001, page 89
School Library Journal, June 2001, page 126

Other books you might like:
Babette Cole, *Bad habits!*, 1999
   Lucretzia's schoolmates happily copy her obnoxious antics until they find themselves on the receiving end of some bad behavior.
Jack Gantos, *Not So Rotten Ralph*, 1994
   Sarah's pet is a cat with deplorable behavior, but she loves Ralph anyway.
James Marshall, *Wings: A Tale of Two Chickens*, 1986
   Adventurous Winnie accepts a ride in a fox's hot air balloon forcing her sensible friend Harriet to plan a rescue mission.

658

RITA MURPHY

Black Angels
(New York: Delacorte, 2001)

Subject(s): African Americans; Racially Mixed People; Civil Rights Movement
Age range(s): Grades 5-8
Major character(s): Celli Jenkins, 11-Year-Old; Ellery Jenkins, 14-Year-Old; Sophie Carter, Cook; Pearl Jenkins, Grandmother
Time period(s): 1960s (1961)
Locale(s): Mystic, Georgia

Summary: Since school let out, Celli's seen the black angels and, with the beginning of the town's troubles, sees them more often. Celli lives with her older brother Ellery; their mother, who spends the month of July with her older sister; and Sophie, their cook who stays with them during July. Sophie's pretty outspoken and when the Freedom Riders come to their southern town, Sophie helps lead the protests which eventually lands her in jail. The Freedom Riders bring Celli's other grandmother to town, the mother of her long-departed father, and Celli's astounded to see that Grandmother Pearl is black. Unaware of her biracial heritage, Celli better understands not only why the angels she sees are black but also why she needs to spring Sophie from jail in this story of the early days of the Civil Rights Movement. (163 pages)

Where it's reviewed:
Bulletin of the Center for Children's Books, March 2001, page 272
Horn Book, March 2001, page 272
Kirkus Reviews, March 1, 2001, page 336
Publishers Weekly, February 5, 2001, page 89
School Library Journal, July 2001, page 111

Other books by the same author:
Night Flying, 2000

Other books you might like:
Christopher Paul Curtis, *The Watsons Go to Birmingham—1963*, 1995
   Heading south to visit Grandmother, the Watson family's high spirits falter when a church in Birmingham blows up and four children are killed.
Trudy Krisher, *Spite Fences*, 1994
   The summer Maggie Pugh is thirteen remains embedded in her memory as the summer she realizes how racist her town is.
Harriette Gillem Robinet, *Walking to the Bus-Rider Blues*, 2000
   During the Montgomery bus boycott, Alfa, Zinnia and Big Mama walk everywhere and see some wrongs righted as they adjust to the "bus-rider blues."

659

SHIRLEY ROUSSEAU MURPHY

Cat Spitting Mad
(New York: HarperCollins, 2001)

Subject(s): Animals/Cats; Mystery and Detective Stories
Age range(s): Grades 9-Adult
Major character(s): Max Harper, Police Officer (chief of police); Joe Grey, Cat, Detective—Amateur; Dulcie, Cat, Detective—Amateur; Kit, Cat (kitten)
Time period(s): 2000s
Locale(s): Molena Point, California

Summary: Those cats that talk and read are back again with a heinous crime to solve involving their friend Max Harper. Now Joe Grey will be the first to admit that he loves to tease the police chief Max by leaving an anonymous crime solver hint on his voice mails, but he also has great admiration for the man. It's natural, then, that Joe Grey is concerned when it appears that Max is being framed for the murder of two women and kidnapping of a teen who were horseback riding along a mountain trail. As the search proceeds for the missing teen, there's also a cougar and a serial killer loose in those hills and Joe Grey, Dulcie and Kit have their paws full. (228 pages)

Where it's reviewed:
Booklist, December 1, 2000, page 697
Drood Review of Mystery, November 2000, page 18
Library Journal, January 2001, page 162
Publishers Weekly, December 11, 2000, page 67
School Library Journal, May 2001, page 176

Other books by the same author:
Cat Laughing Last, 2001
Cat to the Dogs, 2000

Cat in the Dark, 1999
Cat Raise the Dead, 1997
Cat on the Edge, 1996

Other books you might like:

Garrison Allen, *Movie Cat*, 1999
 Amateur sleuths Penelope Warren, owner of Mycroft and Company mystery bookstore, and Mycroft the twenty-five-pound Abyssinian cat, find another dead body.

Lillian Jackson Braun, *The Cat Who Said Cheese*, 1996
 A food event goes awry and Qwilleran and his two Siamese cats investigate the explosion that killed a housewife.

Anne McCaffrey, *No One Noticed the Cat*, 1996
 A magical cat protects a young king while he comes of age.

660

T.M. MURPHY

The Secrets of Code Z

(Exeter, NH: J.N. Townsend Publishing, 2001)

Series: Belltown Mystery. Case 5
Subject(s): Mystery and Detective Stories
Age range(s): Grades 5-8
Major character(s): Orville Jacques, Detective—Amateur, 16-Year-Old; Vanessa Hyde, Girlfriend
Time period(s): 2000s
Locale(s): Belltown, Massachusetts (town on Cape Cod)

Summary: Orville's having a wonderful time at the Winter Carnival with his special date Vanessa until a fortuneteller says he's "surrounded by death" in a portent that too quickly comes true. Finding a body in the ocean sends him off on another mystery to solve, this time one involving the CIA, a Russian scientist from the Chernobyl disaster, a rookie newspaper reporter and a few too many murders in Orville's fifth adventure. (134 pages)

Where it's reviewed:
Booklist, May 15, 2001, page 1753
Kliatt, November 2001, page 17
School Library Journal, July 2001, page 111

Other books by the same author:
The Secrets of the Twisted Cross, 2002 (Belltown Mystery, Case 6)
The Secrets of Pilgrim Pond, 1997 (Belltown Mystery, Case 4)
The Secrets of Belltown, 1996 (Belltown Mystery, Case 1)
The Secrets of Cain's Castle, 1996 (Belltown Mystery, Case 3)
The Secrets of Cranberry Beach, 1996 (Belltown Mystery, Case 2)

Other books you might like:
Michael Dahl, *The Horizontal Man*, 1999
 Finn spots a gold Mayan relic of his parents' in a neighbor's apartment, investigates and is kidnapped.

Mark Delaney, *Of Heroes and Villains*, 1999
 Invited to attend a comic book convention, the Misfits dodge bullets and fires to recover the new Hyperman movie.

Susan Murray, *Mayhem on Maui*, 1999
 On a trip to Hawaii, K.C. and her brother tangle with the Japanese mafia.

Gloria Skurzynski, *Deadly Waters*, 1999
 The theft of a camera belonging to three young people sets off an investigation into the deaths of manatees.

Eric Wilson, *Code Red at the Mall*, 2000
 Liz and Tom help their father as he investigates a series of bombs left at an opulent mall that features a hotel, theme areas, an indoor aquarium and lots of stores.

661

MARGARET MUSGROVE
JULIA CAIRNS, Illustrator

The Spider Weaver: A Legend of Kente Cloth

(New York: The Blue Sky Press/Scholastic, Inc., 2001)

Subject(s): Folklore; Animals/Spiders; Cultures and Customs
Age range(s): Grades 1-4
Major character(s): Nana Koragu, Artisan (weaver); Nana Ameyaw, Artisan (weaver)
Time period(s): Indeterminate Past
Locale(s): Bonwire, Ghana

Summary: Although they are experienced weavers, Nana Koragu and Nana Ameyaw find inspiration for a new weaving style in a unique spider's web. Their attempt to carry the fragile web home to copy fails, but they return to the location early the next morning and watch the spider all day as she creates a new web. When Koragu and Ameyaw return to their village they adapt their looms so they can use the spider's patterns. In time they begin to dye their traditional black and white threads so their products are of many colors and become known as kente cloth. An "Afterword" gives the history of kente cloth and the origins of the story. (34 pages)

Where it's reviewed:
Booklist, February 15, 2001, page 1156
Bulletin of the Center for Children's Books, March 2001, page 273
Horn Book Guide, Fall 2001, page 345
Publishers Weekly, February 12, 2001, page 211
School Library Journal, February 2001, page 113

Other books by the same author:
Ashanti to Zulu, 1976 (Caldecott Medal)

Other books you might like:
Debbi Chocolate, *Kente Colors*, 1997
 Rhyming text and vivid illustrations explain the history, making and use of kente cloth.

Angela Shelf Medearis, *Seven Spools of Thread*, 2000
 This award-winning title offers another tale to explain the origin of kente cloth.

Jeanette Winter, *My Baby*, 2001
 Her native land in Mali inspires Nakunte as she paints designs on the traditional cloth that she creates for her baby.

662

ANNA MYERS

Stolen by the Sea
(New York: Walker, 2001)

Subject(s): Hurricanes; Jealousy; Orphans
Age range(s): Grades 5-8
Major character(s): Maggie McKenna, 12-Year-Old; Felipe Ortega, Orphan
Time period(s): 1900s
Locale(s): Galveston, Texas

Summary: Maggie realizes she shouldn't be jealous, but she can't help it. She knows her father prefers boys to girls, which means if her pregnant mother gives birth to a son, her dad won't care as much for her. She knows this is true because he'd rather spend time with Felipe, the Mexican boy from the orphanage, than take long walks along the beach with Maggie, as he used to do. One day that summer her father takes her mother to Houston to see the doctor, leaving Maggie in Galveston with the servants and a storm brewing. The storm proves worse than anyone imagined and Felipe remains with Maggie as rising water traps them both on the top floor of the McKenna home. As the two struggle to save themselves, and others around them, Maggie realizes the insignificance of her jealousy and concentrates on what's really important. (121 pages)

Where it's reviewed:
Book Report, January 2002, page 63
Kirkus Reviews, October 1, 2001, page 1429
School Library Journal, November 2001, page 162

Other books by the same author:
When the Bough Breaks, 2000
Captain's Command, 1999
Ethan between Us, 1998
The Keeping Room, 1997
Fire in the Hills, 1996

Other books you might like:
John Dowd, *Rare and Endangered: A Caribbean Island Eco-Adventure*, 2000
    Jim and Julie are held captive by poachers as a hurricane approaches.
Sherry Garland, *The Silent Storm*, 1993
    Left mute after the hurricane that killed her parents, Alyssa faces another storm three years later, but this time must speak to help her grandfather.
Theresa Nelson, *Devil Storm*, 1987
    Left in charge of his mother and sisters when his father heads to Galveston on business, Walter has no idea that a huge hurricane is brewing.
Robert Newton Peck, *Arly's Run*, 1991
    Running away from the work farm, Arly flees to Moore Haven to the family that will take him in, but arrives just after a hurricane devastates the town.

663

CHRISTOPHER MYERS, Author/Illustrator

Fly!
(New York: Jump at the Sun/Hyperion Books for Children, 2001)

Subject(s): Animals/Birds; Animals, Treatment of; Friendship
Age range(s): Grades 1-4
Major character(s): Jawanza, Child; Roderick Jackson Montgomery, Aged Person, Animal Lover
Time period(s): 2000s
Locale(s): United States

Summary: From his top-floor apartment Jawanza watches children playing in the streets where he is forbidden to go. He's intrigued by the pigeons swarming in the sky near the apartment rooftop and imagines the letters and numbers they form in flight. When Jawanza yells out his window to the pigeons the answer to his questions comes from an elderly man leaning over the edge of the roof. Jawanza hurries up the stairs to the roof where he finds a flock of birds and meets Roderick Jackson Montgomery the Three from whom he learns important lessons about birds and friendship. (32 pages)

Where it's reviewed:
Publishers Weekly, December 3, 2001, page 58
School Library Journal, December 2001, page 108

Other books by the same author:
Wings, 2000 (ALA Notable Children's Book)
Black Cat, 1999 (Coretta Scott King Honor Book for Illustration)

Other books you might like:
Robert J. Blake, *Fledgling*, 2000
    From high atop a building in Brooklyn Fledging fearfully begins her first flight.
Jane Kurtz, *Only a Pigeon*, 1997
    An Ethiopian boy raises homing pigeons behind his home in Addis Ababa.
Cynthia Rylant, *The Bird House*, 1998
    Birds gathering at the home of an elderly woman attract the attention of a young homeless girl who enjoys watching them.
Nick Williams, *How Birds Fly*, 1997
    A nonfiction title explains how the shape of bird's bodies makes flight possible.

664

WALTER DEAN MYERS

The Journal of Biddy Owens: The Negro Leagues, Birmingham, Alabama, 1948
(New York: Scholastic, 2001)

Series: My Name Is America
Subject(s): Sports/Baseball; African Americans; Segregation
Age range(s): Grades 5-8
Major character(s): Biddy Owens, 17-Year-Old, Manager (Sports) (equipment); Jackie Robinson, Historical Figure, Baseball Player
Time period(s): 1940s (1948)

Locale(s): Birmingham, Alabama; Midwest; South

Summary: It's the opening of baseball season and Biddy revels in the excitement. As the equipment manager for the Birmingham Black Barons, he also occasionally plays right field. He'd love to play more, but at only 135 pounds he's a little light and, deep down, knows he'll probably never be a good enough ball player. So for now, Biddy's content to travel with the team where he records all that occurs both in Birmingham and on the road. In 1948 America, though Jackie Robinson is now playing pro ball, Biddy still encounters problems with the Ku Klux Klan, is forced to sit in the balcony of movie theatres, and lives with the Jim Crow laws. Though he'll always be a baseball fan, he realizes the importance of an education and begins planning for college and a journalism career in this continuing series. (139 pages)

Where it's reviewed:
BookPage, May 2001, page 26
Bulletin of the Center for Children's Books, July 2001, page 416
Kirkus Reviews, March 15, 2001, page 418
School Library Journal, April 2001, page 146
Voice of Youth Advocates, August 2001, page 204

Other books by the same author:
Handbook for Boys, 2002
The Journal of Joshua Loper: A Black Cowboy, 1999 (My Name Is America)
The Journal of Scott Pendleton Collins: A World War II Soldier, 1999 (My Name Is America)
Slam!, 1996
The Righteous Revenge of Artemis Bonner, 1992

Other books you might like:
Evelyn Coleman, *Circle of Fire*, 2001
  Black Mendy and her white friend Jeffrey team up to halt the Ku Klux Klan from bombing Highlander Folk School where Mrs. Roosevelt is to speak.
Patricia C. McKissack, *Black Diamond: The Story of the Negro Baseball League*, 1994
  A history of the time before 1947 when blacks were not allowed to play major league baseball.
Robert Newton Peck, *Extra Innings*, 2001
  Tate heals with the help of the stories told by his adopted Aunt Vidalia who traveled with the all-black baseball team Ethiopia's Clowns.
Mildred D. Taylor, *The Gold Cadillac*, 1987
  A loving Ohio family is not prepared for the prejudice they experience while in Mississippi.

N

665

AN NA

A Step from Heaven

(Asheville, NC: Front Street Books, 2001)

Subject(s): Korean Americans; Family Life; Emigration and Immigration
Age range(s): Grades 8-12
Major character(s): Young Ju Park, Immigrant; Joon Ho Park, Immigrant
Time period(s): 1980s; 1990s
Locale(s): Republic of Korea; United States

Summary: Flying through the sky to America, Young Ju thinks they are moving to Heaven, but upon landing in America, her uncle informs her that America is "a step from heaven." As the Park family discovers, it's several steps from heaven as their inflexible father has difficulty making a success of any of his businesses and her mother holds down two menial jobs. Young Ju and her brother Joon Ho are the ones who learn English and act as translators for their confused parents, yet the siblings are often just as confused as the parents as they adapt to a new culture. Their father's increased bitterness leads to alcoholism and abusiveness toward his family, especially Young Ju's mother. Remembering that in America she has choices, Young Ju steps outside her cultural norm and calls 911 when her father is beating her mother. Embarrassed and feeling ineffective, her father returns to Korea leaving Young Ju, Joon Ho and her mother behind in this first novel. (156 pages)

Where it's reviewed:
Booklist, June 2001, page 1881
Bulletin of the Center for Children's Books, July 2001, page 416
Publishers Weekly, April 2, 2001, page 65
School Library Journal, May 2001, page 156
Voice of Youth Advocates, June 2001, page 126

Awards the book has won:
School Library Journal Best Books, 2001
ALA Michael L. Printz Award, 2002

Other books you might like:
Haemi Balgassi, *Tae's Sonata*, 1997
    Tae struggles with being "the Asian girl" in her classroom, but being paired with sensitive Josh for a report helps her discard her ethnic worries.
Sook Nyul Choi, *Gathering of Pearls*, 1994
    A freshman in college in New York, Korean Sookan must adjust to cultural differences, homesickness and the loss of her dear mother.
Amy Tan, *The Joy Luck Club*, 1989
    Four women who fled from China in the 1940s meet weekly to play Mah-Jongg, tell stories and keep alive their culture and their memories.

666

BEVERLEY NAIDOO

The Other Side of Truth

(New York: HarperCollins, 2001)

Subject(s): Refugees; Brothers and Sisters
Age range(s): Grades 7-10
Major character(s): Sade Solaja, 12-Year-Old; Femi Solaja, Child; Folarin Solaja, Father (of Femi and Sade), Journalist (*Speak*); Dele Solaja, Professor, Uncle
Time period(s): 2000s
Locale(s): Lagos, Nigeria; London, England

Summary: Sade's father is a journalist who is a marked man for writing of the abuses by the Nigerian government; unfortunately when an attempt is made on his life, assassins mistakenly shoot his wife. Sade and her younger brother Femi are whisked out of Nigeria and sent by plane to London where Uncle Dele is to meet them. By the time they reach London, their escort has disappeared and Uncle Dele, unbeknownst to the youngsters, has gone into hiding. Picked up by the police, Sade and Femi become part of the foster system and, though their family is kind to them, are bullied by their schoolmates who make fun of their background. Sade is miserable at school and unsure of where her father might be. When he suddenly appears in London, he is arrested and jailed for entering illegally. Realizing the need for help, Sade alerts the television news to their plight, knowing it's the only way her father will be released in this look at the repercussive fallout from telling the truth. (252 pages)

Where it's reviewed:
Booklist, September 1, 2001, page 110
Horn Book, November 2001, page 756
Publishers Weekly, September 17, 2001, page 81
School Library Journal, September 2001, page 231
Voice of Youth Advocates, October 2001, page 282

Awards the book has won:
Carnegie Medal, 2002
ALA Best Books for Young Adults, 2002

Other books by the same author:
No Turning Back: A Novel of South Africa, 1997
Chain of Fire, 1990
Journey to Jo'Burg: A South African Story, 1986

Other books you might like:
Chinua Achebe, *Girls at War, and Other Stories*, 1973
Stories that recount the problems that occur when Nigerian customs clash with modern Africa.
Simi Bedford, *Yoruba Girl Dancing*, 1992
Simi makes major adjustments when she leaves her Nigerian grandparents' servant-filled house for boarding school in England.
Jonathan Scott Fuqua, *The Reappearance of Sam Webber*, 1999
When Sam's father disappears, he and his mother move to a poorer section of Baltimore where Sam attends a new school and lives in perpetual fear of the bullies.

LENSEY NAMIOKA
AKI SOGABE, Illustrator

The Hungriest Boy in the World
(New York: Holiday House, 2001)

Subject(s): Food; Problem Solving; Humor
Age range(s): Grades K-3
Major character(s): Jiro, Child, Son; Hunger Monster, Monster, Shape-changer
Time period(s): Indeterminate Past
Locale(s): Japan

Summary: Because Jiro has a bad habit of putting anything from pebbles to seaweed in his mouth it's only natural that he does the same with the purple blob he finds on the beach and so it happens that Jiro swallows the Hunger Monster. Now Jiro must satisfy the Hunger Monster's constant cries for more food and, if food is not available, Jiro will devour fishing nets, his quilt, or the seating cushions in order to feed the Hunger Monster. Once his family realizes what is causing Jiro's insatiable appetite they devise a plan to trick the Hunger Monster into leaving Jiro's body and his appetite returns to normal. (32 pages)

Where it's reviewed:
Booklist, April 1, 2001, page 1479
Horn Book, May 2001, 313
Kirkus Reviews, February 15, 2001, page 263

The New Advocate, Winter 2002, page 75
School Library Journal, April 2001, page 119

Other books by the same author:
The Laziest Boy in the World, 1998
The Loyal Cat, 1995

Other books you might like:
Henrik Drescher, *The Boy Who Ate Around*, 1994
Mo eats around his unappetizing dinner until he's consumed the world and is left with his plate, heartburn and the inevitable burp.
Betsy Everitt, *TV Dinner*, 1994
Daisy Lee's distinctive food habits give new meaning the term TV dinner.
Simms Taback, *There Was an Old Lady Who Swallowed a Fly*, 1997
Inventive illustrations in a Caldecott Honor Book depict the sequence of items an old lady swallows trying to calm the tickling of a fly inside her.

668

DONNA JO NAPOLI
JIM LAMARCHE, Illustrator

Albert
(San Diego: Silver Whistle/Harcourt, Inc., 2001)

Subject(s): Animals/Birds; Animals, Treatment of; Conduct of Life
Age range(s): Grades 1-4
Major character(s): Albert, Recluse, Animal Lover
Time period(s): 2000s
Locale(s): United States

Summary: In the young adult novelist's first picture book, solitary Albert follows a daily ritual to determine whether or not to leave his apartment for a walk. Albert's personal barometer is a hand stretched through the grillwork of his open window to test the weather. Invariably, Albert decides that the weather is not suitable for venturing out, so he stays inside. His outlook begins to change the day his outstretched hand is used by a pair of cardinals to build a nest. Too kind to simply pull his hand in and destroy the nest, Albert stays at the window, arm outstretched, fascinated by the birds' activity. For weeks Albert stands. As the eggs incubate, Albert's beard grows. The male cardinal brings food to his mate and to Albert. By the time the four baby birds learn to fly, Albert has learned that the sights and sounds of the world outside his window hold the promise of adventure and, like the fledglings, he's ready to explore the world, in any weather. (32 pages)

Where it's reviewed:
Booklist, March 1, 2001, page 1288
Bulletin of the Center for Children's Books, April 2001, page 312
Horn Book Guide, Fall 2001, page 268
Publishers Weekly, March 5, 2001, page 78
School Library Journal, May 2001, page 130

Awards the book has won:
School Library Journal Best Books, 2001

Other books you might like:

Melissa Milich, *Miz Fannie Mae's Fine New Easter Hat*, 1997
Mama's new Easter hat becomes the sight of a ''miracle'' when the decorative eggs begin hatching during the church service.

Tracey Campbell Pearson, *The Purple Hat*, 1997
When Annie's favorite lost hat is found with a full bird's nest in the crown she realizes the birds need it more than she does for now.

Toby Riddle, *The Singing Hat*, 2001
Awakening from a nap in the park Colin discovers that a bird has built a nest in his hair and he modifies his life to accommodate nature's needs.

669

DONNA JO NAPOLI
RICHARD TCHEN, Co-Author
AMY WALROD, Illustrator

How Hungry Are You?
(New York: Atheneum Books for Young Readers, 2001)

Subject(s): Food; Mathematics; Sharing
Age range(s): Grades K-3
Major character(s): Unnamed Character, Rabbit, Friend; Unnamed Character, Frog, Friend; Unnamed Character, Fox
Time period(s): Indeterminate
Locale(s): Fictional Country

Summary: A hungry frog plans a picnic with a rabbit who's making twelve sandwiches to share between the two of them. Then they meet other animals that also want to attend the picnic. The frog is willing to include any that agree to bring food. As the numbers of participants grow the variety of foods in the picnic increases while the number of each item available decreases. As twelve animals arrive at the picnic site to divide up twelve of each food item a hungry fox, with no food to share, appears. The frog doesn't want to include the fox, but other animals agree to divide everything in half so each of the first twelve animals gets something and then the fox will share what is not eaten with the animals that are still hungry. (32 pages)

Where it's reviewed:
Booklist, September 15, 2001, page 233
Horn Book Guide, Spring 2002, page 53
Kirkus Reviews, July 15, 2001, page 1032
Publishers Weekly, August 20, 2001, page 80
School Library Journal, October 2001, page 126

Other books by the same author:
Albert, 2001 (School Library Journal Best Books)

Other books you might like:
Elinor J. Pinczes, *One Hundred Hungry Ants*, 1993
Marching to a picnic one hundred ants stop so often to divide themselves into different groups that they arrive too late to find any food to divide.

Joanne Rocklin, *One Hungry Cat*, 1997
Tom bakes snacks to share with friends but he samples some while working and now faces a division problem and hungry friends.

Harriet Ziefert, *Rabbit and Hare Divide an Apple*, 1998
While Rabbit and Hare argue about who will eat which portion of a mushroom a sly skunk makes off with the whole thing.

670

DONNA JO NAPOLI

Three Days
(New York: Dutton, 2001)

Subject(s): Kidnapping; Fathers and Daughters
Age range(s): Grades 5-9
Major character(s): Jackie Holt, Kidnap Victim; Claudia, Mother (of deceased child)
Time period(s): 2000s
Locale(s): Italy

Summary: Joining her father on his three-week business trip to Italy, Jackie feels so much younger than usual as she holds her father's hand and lets him be in charge, until the night they're returning to their hotel after dinner and her father has a heart attack while driving. Pulled over to the side of the road, Jackie screams for help for what seems forever until two men stop and pick her up. Thinking they're taking her to the police, Jackie isn't worried until they take her to their farmhouse where she meets kindly Claudia. No one speaks English but after several days she figures out that she's being kept captive, evidently to replace Claudia's daughter who died recently. Jackie is beside herself with worry about her father's body and her mother's whereabouts, until she convinces Claudia to help her escape. On the train heading to town, Jackie sees a newspaper article about her father's accident and her mother's arrival in Italy and immediately feels better. (151 pages)

Where it's reviewed:
Booklist, October 1, 2001, page 312
Bulletin of the Center for Children's Books, November 2001, page 112
Horn Book, September 2001, page 590
School Library Journal, August 2001, page 186
Voice of Youth Advocates, August 2001, page 204

Awards the book has won:
School Library Journal Best Books, 2001

Other books by the same author:
Daughter of Venice, 2002
Beast, 2000
Shelley Shock, 2000
Crazy Jack, 1999
Spinners, 1999

Other books you might like:
James Duffy, *Missing*, 1988
Kate Prescott is missing but her runaway history keeps everyone from worrying until the police realize she got into a stranger's car.

Norma Fox Mazer, *The Solid Gold Kid*, 1977
A rich boy is kidnapped and held for ransom, but the kidnappers take four other teens, too.

Willo Davis Roberts, *Hostage*, 2000
Sent home from school for medication, Kaci interrupts

thieves who panic and throw her into the back of their stolen car.

ALAN NAYES

Gargoyles

(New York: Tor/Forge, 2001)

Subject(s): Genetic Engineering; Medical Thriller
Age range(s): Grades 10-Adult
Major character(s): Amoreena Daniels, Student—Graduate (medical school), Mother (surrogate); Geneva Daniels, Cancer Patient
Time period(s): 2000s
Locale(s): California; Guatemala

Summary: When Amoreena's cancer-stricken mother Geneva reveals that she used medical insurance money to pay for her daughter's medical school fees, Amoreena doesn't know how to obtain the new $30,000 treatment that would help her mother. The Women's Clinic offers her a chance to earn $50,000 if she'll agree to become a surrogate mother. Seeing this as a chance to solve her problems, Amoreena quickly agrees. After artificial insemination, she realizes the movement she feels in her womb shouldn't be occurring this early in a pregnancy; then a medical intern warns her that the Women's Clinic is not as upright as it appears. Finally she receives hints that the clinic may be an organ factory where women are impregnated with genetic material from baboons and pigs to produce a creature from which organs can be harvested. Taken to Guatemala to give birth, Amoreena isn't sure how to escape the nightmare in this first novel. (380 pages)

Where it's reviewed:
Booklist, August 2001, page 2089
Kirkus Reviews, July 15, 2001, page 969
Publishers Weekly, September 3, 2001, page 65

Other books you might like:
Robin Cook, *Mutation*, 1989
　Using genetic engineering, infertility expert Dr. Frank implants a ''perfect'' child in his wife but realizes an evil monster has been born.
Linda Grant, *Lethal Genes*, 1996
　Biotechnology is a potentially profitable area and the idea that people can become thinner leads to greedy behavior.
Ira Levin, *Rosemary's Baby*, 1967
　After their baby is born, Guy and Rosemary Woodhouse lead a nightmare existence.

PHYLLIS REYNOLDS NAYLOR

Alice Alone

(New York: Simon & Schuster, 2001)

Series: Alice
Subject(s): Interpersonal Relations; Schools/High Schools; Single Parent Families
Age range(s): Grades 6-9

Major character(s): Alice Kathleen McKinley, 9th Grader; Patrick Long, 9th Grader; Penny, 9th Grader
Time period(s): 2000s
Locale(s): Silver Spring, Maryland

Summary: Alice and her friends have finally arrived!! High school is both more and less than they thought it would be. The work is interesting, they're split into different classes and coursework leads the friends in still other directions. Alice is excited to be part of the newspaper staff, but it requires so much of her time that she doesn't see Patrick as often. This leaves him free to spend time with new student Penny who has set her sights on him. Soon Alice and Patrick end their two-year romance, Patrick and Penny become the new couple and Alice is left feeling very lonely. Advice flows from everyone, including her family and her best friends, but Alice stands on her own and gains self-confidence as she encounters each rock in the road in this continuing saga. (229 pages)

Where it's reviewed:
Booklist, May 15, 2001, page 1745
Bulletin of the Center for Children's Books, May 2001, page 348
Horn Book, July 2001, page 459
School Library Journal, June 2001, page 152
Voice of Youth Advocates, August 2001, page 205

Other books by the same author:
Simply Alice, 2002
Starting with Alice, 2002
The Grooming of Alice, 2000
Alice on the Outside, 1999
Achingly Alice, 1998

Other books you might like:
Nora Raleigh Baskin, *What Every Girl (Except Me) Knows*, 2001
　Gabby's journal records everything she thinks she should know to be a grown-up woman, important stuff that she would ask her mother, if only she had one.
Ann Brashares, *The Sisterhood of the Traveling Pants*, 2001
　Four friends, apart for the summer, decide that a pair of jeans, their rules for wearing and a schedule for mailing, will keep them united over the summer.
Catherine Clark, *Truth or Dairy*, 2000
　Courtney looks forward to the beginning of her senior year, but finds she's going to be on her own when her boyfriend Dave breaks up with her.

PHYLLIS REYNOLDS NAYLOR

The Boys Return

(New York: Delacorte Press, 2001)

Subject(s): Brothers; Sisters; Humor
Age range(s): Grades 3-6
Major character(s): Caroline Malloy, 4th Grader, Sister (youngest); Wally Hatford, 4th Grader, Brother (middle child); Tony Benson, 6th Grader, Brother
Time period(s): 1990s
Locale(s): Buckman, West Virginia

Summary: Wally and his brothers are excited to learn that the five Benson brothers will be spending spring vacation in Buckman. The Malloy sisters, whose family is renting the Benson's house for a year, wonder what tricks the Benson and Hatford boys are plotting against the three girls. The girls are right to be suspicious because Tony arrives with a carefully developed idea to convince the Malloy girls that Caroline's room is haunted by the ghost of a former occupant. The trick frightens Caroline but her suspicious older sister researches local history at the library and finds factual evidence that Tony's story cannot be true. The Malloy's retaliatory plan almost succeeds in convincing Tony that the ''ghost'' is really after him. What really seems to be after one or all of them or at least some tasty garbage is a cougar that Caroline sees entering the Malloy garage. Quickly she closes the door trapping the cougar and, unfortunately, Wally inside. (132 pages)

Where it's reviewed:
Booklist, December 15, 2001, page 732
Horn Book Guide, Spring 2002, page 90
Publishers Weekly, November 19, 2001, page 70
School Library Journal, October 2001, page 167

Other books by the same author:
A Spy Among the Girls, 2000
A Traitor Among the Boys, 1999
The Girls' Revenge, 1998
Boys Against Girls, 1994
The Boys Start the War, 1993
The Girls Get Even, 1993

Other books you might like:
Alane Ferguson, *The Practical Joke War*, 1991
   Tricks the Dillon children play on each other escalate to such a point that they call it quits and use the shared experience as a basis for friendship.
Ann M. Martin, *Karen's Big Joke*, 1992
   On April Fool's Day Karen plans her best joke yet to use on her family.
Dyan Sheldon, *My Brother Is a Visitor from Another Planet*, 1993
   Adam's older brother Keith takes advantage of his trusting nature and convinces Adam that he's an alien needing assistance to reach his spaceship.

674

SHIRLEY NEITZEL
NANCY WINSLOW PARKER, Illustrator

I'm Not Feeling Well Today
(New York: Greenwillow Books/HarperCollins Publishers, 2001)

Subject(s): Illness; Stories in Rhyme; Parent and Child
Age range(s): Grades K-2
Major character(s): Unnamed Character, Child
Time period(s): 2000s (2001)
Locale(s): United States

Summary: A child awakens to report feeling ill and lists items needed for the day beginning with tissues and continuing through an extra blanket, another pillow, and the family cat for comfort. Then, for entertainment, the child wants finger puppets, jigsaw puzzles, and the television for cartoons. The list of requirements grows longer until the mother begins doubting the severity of the child's illness especially when the child's been observed doing flips in bed. Miraculously, upon hearing that a snowfall during the night has closed the schools, the child happily reports feeling well enough to take advantage of the snowfall. (32 pages)

Where it's reviewed:
Booklist, April 15, 2001, page 1566
Horn Book, May 2001, page 314
Kirkus Reviews, March 15, 2001, page 418
School Library Journal, July 2001, page 86

Other books by the same author:
I'm Taking a Trip on My Train, 1999
The House I'll Build for the Wrens, 1997
We're Making Breakfast for Mother, 1997

Other books you might like:
Moira Fain, *Snow Day*, 1996
   Snow closes school for the day and Maggie enjoys sledding instead of doing her homework.
Barbara M. Joosse, *Snow Day!*, 1995
   Snow forces cancellation of school, giving Robby and his family a day to play outside.
Peter O'Donnell, *Carnegie's Excuse*, 1993
   Carnegie offers an interesting excuse for his tardiness and failure to complete his homework
Jean Van Leeuwen, *Oliver and Amanda and the Big Snow*, 1995
   Oliver and his younger sister enjoy sledding, tossing snowballs and making a snow pig.

675

LESLEA NEWMAN
ERIKA OLLER, Illustrator

Cats, Cats, Cats!
(New York: Simon & Schuster Books for Young Readers, 2001)

Subject(s): Animals/Cats; Stories in Rhyme; Humor
Age range(s): Grades K-2
Major character(s): Mrs. Brown, Aged Person, Animal Lover
Time period(s): Indeterminate
Locale(s): Fictional Country

Summary: Mrs. Brown is a lover of cats. She has sixty for pets and each one is adored. Cats sleep on the couch, the chairs and the banister while Mrs. Brown cleans. When she drinks her coffee cats sleep on the kitchen counter and if she's eating lunch they are draped over the table and floor, snoring away. In the evening after she's groomed, cuddled and fed each cat, Mrs. Brown retires to bed and the sleepy cats come alive. They sew, they read, they cook, they knit and they party all night. In the morning, as Mrs. Brown awakes to greet the day, the cats return to snoozing. (28 pages)

Where it's reviewed:
Booklist, February 15, 2001, page 1141
Bulletin of the Center for Children's Books, March 2001, page 274
Kirkus Reviews, January 1, 2001, page 55
Publishers Weekly, January 15, 2001, page 75
School Library Journal, March 2001, page 215

Other books by the same author:
Matzo Ball Moon, 1998
Too Far Away to Touch, 1995
Saturday Is Payday, 1993

Other books you might like:
Alyssa Satin Capucilli, *Mrs. McTats and Her Houseful of Cats*, 2001
    Mrs. McTats lives contentedly with one cat but each time a stray appears she welcomes it to her household also.
Adele Geras, *Sleep Tight, Ginger Kitten*, 2001
    A young boy's pet wanders inside and out before finding the perfect spot for a nap.
Joan Holub, *Scat, Cats!*, 2001
    A rhyming easy reader describes a house that is overrun by mischievous cats.

676

JENNY NIMMO
DEBBIE BOON, Illustrator

Something Wonderful

(San Diego: Harcourt, Inc., 2001)

Subject(s): Animals/Chickens; Individuality; Self-Confidence
Age range(s): Grades K-2
Major character(s): Little Hen, Chicken; Arthur, Rooster; Mrs. Field, Spouse, Farmer
Time period(s): Indeterminate Past
Locale(s): Fictional Country

Summary: Little Hen is the only chicken in the hen house without a trophy or a ribbon to show how special she is. When Little Hen declares her intention to do ''something wonderful'' too the others, with the exception of Arthur, laugh at her. On a hot day the other chickens wander into the cooler woods and lay eggs in a nest there but then they return to the hen house, abandoning the eggs. Mrs. Fields is concerned later to discover that there are no eggs and no Little Hen. Only Arthur cares and worries about Little Hen while she's gone. Mrs. Fields jumps for joy many days later when Little Hen struts into the barnyard leading five chicks and Arthur gives her a special prize. (28 pages)

Where it's reviewed:
Booklist, September 15, 2001, page 233
Horn Book Guide, Spring 2002, page 25
Kirkus Reviews, July 1, 2001, page 944
Publishers Weekly, June 18, 2001, page 80
School Library Journal, September 2001, page 202

Other books by the same author:
Esmerelda and the Children Next Door, 2000
The Starlight Cloak, 1993
The Witches and the Singing Mice, 1993

Other books you might like:
Antonia Barber, *Gemma and the Baby Chick*, 1993
    Gemma warms a rejected egg until it hatches and then returns the baby chick to its sleeping mother.
Lynn Reiser, *The Surprise Family*, 1994
    A mother hen loves the ''chicks'' she's hatched from a clutch of abandoned eggs even though they enjoy swimming just like the ducks that they are.

Mary Wormell, *Hilda Hen's Search*, 1994
    Hilda Hen, definitely a special chicken, confidently searches until she finds a perfectly original spot for her nest.

677

GARTH NIX

Lirael: Daughter of the Clayr

(New York: HarperCollins, 2001)

Subject(s): Quest; Coming-of-Age
Age range(s): Grades 8-12
Major character(s): Lirael, Librarian; Sameth, Royalty (prince)
Time period(s): Indeterminate
Locale(s): Old Kingdom, Fictional Country

Summary: Lirael refuses to accept the fact that she will never have the Sight, which is common to her people. The Clayr are a community of clairvoyant women and Lirael is an orphan without gifts among the people with whom she longs to belong. To hide her shame, Lirael takes a job as a sub-librarian, which gives her access to the books and creatures of magic hidden in the Library. Prince Sameth feels equally alienated, in his case because everyone expects him to become the next Abhorsen, the figure that commands the Dead. Lirael meets the weird Disreputable Dog and together they flee across the Old Kingdom, adding Sameth and the mysterious Mogget, a talking cat that is probably more than he seems, to their entourage. The foursome know they are to perform some important task, but are unsure what that task is in this sequel to *Sabriel*. (496 pages)

Where it's reviewed:
Booklist, April 15, 2001, page 1557
Horn Book Magazine, July 2001, page 459
Publishers Weekly, March 19, 2001, page 101
School Library Journal, May 2001, page 157
Voice of Youth Advocates, August 2001, page 215

Awards the book has won:
ALA Best Books for Young Adults, 2002

Other books by the same author:
Above the Veil, 2001
Aenir, 2001
Sabriel, 1995

Other books you might like:
Mary Brown, *The Unlikely Ones*, 1986
    An enchanted girl and a group of unusual animals flee a wicked witch.
Peter Dickinson, *The Ropemaker*, 2001
    A foursome sets off into an unknown land in search of the wizard who can renew their valley's magical protections.
Meredith Ann Pierce, *Treasure at the Heart of the Tanglewood*, 2001
    Hannah escapes the thrall of the wizard and sets off on a quest to discover who she is and where she comes from.

JOAN LOWERY NIXON

Maria's Story: 1773

(New York: Delacorte Press, 2001)

Series: Young Americans: Colonial Williamsburg. Number 5
Subject(s): Historical; Newspapers; Gender Roles
Age range(s): Grades 3-6
Major character(s): Maria Rind, 9-Year-Old, Daughter; Clementina Rind, Mother, Widow(er); William Rind, Brother (older), Apprentice
Time period(s): 1770s (1773)
Locale(s): Williamsburg, Virginia, American Colonies

Summary: Maria and her family have little time to grieve her father's untimely death. Clementina is determined to continue publishing his newspaper and expects Maria to take on the duties of the household and care for her three younger brothers. Seeing lazy William chosen to help with the printing business while she labors in the expected place of a girl frustrates Maria who decides to teach herself to read and write so she can join the family business. Greater troubles await a family whose father dies leaving debts but Maria's practical spirit helps Clementina find a way to overcome the troubles. The book concludes with factual information about the time period. (167 pages)

Where it's reviewed:
Booklist, January 1, 2002, page 859
Horn Book Guide, Spring 2002, page 90
School Library Journal, December 2001, page 141

Other books by the same author:
Will's Story: 1771, 2001 (Young Americans: Colonial Williamsburg, Number 4)
Ann's Story: 1747, 2000 (Young Americans: Colonial Williamsburg, Number 1)
Caesar's Story: 1759, 2000 (Young Americans: Colonial Williamsburg, Number 2)
Aggie's Home, 1998 (Orphan Train Children, Number 3)

Other books you might like:
Valerie Tripp, *Felicity Saves the Day: A Summer Story*, 1992
Felicity is torn between responsibility to her father and a desire to help his apprentice who wants to run away and join Washington's army.
Jean Van Leeuwen, *Hannah of Fairfield*, 1999
Eight-year-old Hannah learns household tasks such as knitting and spinning while her brothers help in the fields or in the father's clock shop.
Kate Waters, *Mary Geddy's Day*, 1999
A photo essay reenacts one day in the life of a ten-year-old resident of Williamsburg in 1776.

JOAN LOWERY NIXON

Playing for Keeps

(New York: Delacorte, 2001)

Subject(s): Mystery and Detective Stories; Refugees; Cruise Ships

Age range(s): Grades 6-10
Major character(s): Rose Ann Marstead, 16-Year-Old; Gloria "Glory" Marstead, Grandmother; Enrique "Ricky" Urbino, Refugee, Baseball Player
Time period(s): 2000s
Locale(s): Caribbean (aboard a cruise ship)

Summary: Smuggled out of Cuba to Haiti and then on board a cruise ship, Ricky hopes to be granted asylum in America where he can join his uncle who's a professional baseball player. But tragedy strikes when the man who helped smuggle him out of Cuba is found dead and Ricky's a suspect, once authorities find him. Also on this cruise ship is Rose, roommate of her grandmother Glory who's playing bridge onboard the ship, who immediately noticed good-looking Ricky. Once the two officially meet, and Ricky explains his problem to her, Rose leaps right in to prove Ricky's innocence in another YA mystery from a top-notch author. (197 pages)

Where it's reviewed:
Book Report, January 2002, page 64
Booklist, May 1, 2001, page 1612
Bulletin of the Center for Children's Books, July 2001, page 417
School Library Journal, July 2001, page 112
Voice of Youth Advocates, August 2001, page 205

Other books by the same author:
Trap, 2002
Nobody's There, 2000
Who Are You?, 1999
Murdered, My Sweet, 1997
Search for the Shadow Man, 1996

Other books you might like:
Anilu Bernardo, *Jumping Off to Freedom*, 1996
Fleeing from Cuba, David and his father share a raft with two dangerous strangers, which makes their journey a death-defying trip of survival.
John Dowd, *Hogsty Reef: A Caribbean Island Eco-Adventure*, 1999
Helping on a scientific study in the Caribbean, Jim meets and agrees to help hide Marcel, a Haitian refugee.
Richard Peck, *Those Summer Girls I Never Met*, 1988
Drew and his sister Steph's summer plans change drastically when his grandmother takes them on a senior citizen cruise.

680

JOSEPHINE NOBISSO
GLO COALSON, Illustrator

The Moon's Lullaby

(New York: Orchard Books, 2001)

Subject(s): Sleep; Bedtime; Parent and Child
Age range(s): Grades K-2
Time period(s): 2000s
Locale(s): Earth

Summary: Somewhere in the world as the day ends a baby yawns and begins a sequence of yawns that travel around the world. The baby's mother yawns and then the dog. The moon sees the dog yawning and, hard as she tries, she catches hold of that yawn and it goes with her to families in countries around the globe until it comes to a tiny baby cuddled by its mother under a desert awning and the cycle begins again. (32 pages)

Where it's reviewed:
Booklist, January 1, 2002, page 867
Horn Book Guide, Spring 2002, page 53
School Library Journal, December 2001, page 108

Other books by the same author:
For the Sake of a Cake, 1993
Grandma's Scrapbook, 1991
Grandpa Loved, 1991 (Parent's Magazine Best Children's Book of the Year)

Other books you might like:
Kate Banks, *And If the Moon Could Talk*, 1998
Following a bedtime ritual with her parents a child, wrapped in love, sleeps while the silent moon watches over all.
Margaret Wise Brown, *Goodnight Moon*, 1947
In a classic of bedtime stories, a little rabbit's evening ritual is to say goodnight to everything in sight, including the moon, shining outside.
Megan McDonald, *My House Has Stars*, 1996
All over the world youngsters from many different homes can see the stars shining overhead and enjoy the shared experience.

681

HAN NOLAN

Born Blue

(San Diego: Harcourt, 2001)

Subject(s): Mothers and Daughters; Singing; Drugs
Age range(s): Grades 9-12
Major character(s): Mama Linda, Addict (heroin); Harmon W. James, Foster Child; Janie "Leshaya" English, Abandoned Child, Singer
Time period(s): 2000s
Locale(s): Mobile, Alabama; Birmingham, Alabama; Atlanta, Georgia

Summary: Abandoned by her heroin-addicted mother to foster homes, Janie finds nothing but abusive white people until she meets her foster brother Harmon, a sweet African American boy. He introduces her to some of the great "ladies" who sing jazz or the blues, like Aretha Franklin or Billie Holiday, and Janie finds something she cares about—music. She attends church with Harmon and his black social worker and there she hears more music, but also has a chance to sing and realizes the power of her own voice. One day she realizes that black people have always been nice to her, while white people haven't, so she'd like to be black. She changes her name to Leshaya, mimics Harmon's speech, while adding some of her own made-up dialect, and wants to be the next great blues singer. Mama Linda returns for her, only this time sells her to her dealer, which starts Leshaya down the same path as Mama Linda: drugs, sex and finally pregnancy. Leshaya seems to self-destruct better than anything and whenever she meets someone nice, she "burns her bridges" before giving the relationship a chance to go anywhere. She hurts Harmon and

is disloyal to a friend; the only good thing she does is allow her brown-skinned child to be adopted. Reunited with her mother helps her see where she'll end up, though it may not be enough to stop her self-destructive behavior, as she cares for her mother before she dies of AIDS in another powerful book from a noted young adult author. (277 pages)

Where it's reviewed:
Booklist, September 15, 2001, page 217
Horn Book, January 2002, page 82
Kliatt, November 2001, page 9
School Library Journal, November 2001, page 162
Voice of Youth Advocates, October 2001, page 282

Awards the book has won:
School Library Journal Best Books, 2001
ALA Best Books for Young Adults, 2002

Other books by the same author:
A Face in Every Window, 1999
Dancing on the Edge, 1997
Send Me Down a Miracle, 1996
If I Should Die Before I Wake, 1994

Other books you might like:
Melvin Burgess, *Smack*, 1998
A horrifying account of two young teen runaways who are quickly dragged down into heroin addiction.
Janet Fitch, *White Oleander*, 1999
The only child of a single mother, Astrid is devastated when her mother murders her boyfriend.
Linda Glovach, *Beauty Queen*, 1998
A stint at topless dancing to earn enough money to flee her abusive home leads Samantha into a heroin addiction from which there's no escape.
Graham McNamee, *Hate You*, 1999
A talented songwriter, Alice can't sing the songs she writes because of the damage done to her vocal cords when her father choked her.

682

ROBERT NORDAN

The Secret Road

(New York: Holiday House, 2001)

Subject(s): Underground Railroad; Slavery; Quakers
Age range(s): Grades 4-7
Major character(s): Laura Milford, Teenager; Charity Buchanan, Aunt, Quaker; Jesse Buchanan, Uncle, Farmer; Rosetta, Slave
Time period(s): 2000s
Locale(s): South

Summary: Young Laura spends the summer on the farm of her Quaker aunt and uncle, far from the refinement of her family's plantation. She's glad to give up the formal teas, women's chatter and ritualistic manners for the freedom of playing with no restrictions. This year Laura realizes Aunt Charity and Uncle Jesse are part of the Underground Railroad and are hiding Rosette under their meat house. Concerned about light-skinned Rosette, and eager to help, Laura suggests the two travel as sisters to reach Rosette's husband in Philadelphia. Dogged by a slave catcher, at one point Laura and Rosette even seek safety in a traveling side show exhibition and are spirited to safety by the carnival owner. Laura takes Rosette as far as she can, before handing her off to the next set of escorts, but wonders if she made it to safety. That winter a letter arrives from Rosette that sets her mind at ease. (202 pages)

Where it's reviewed:

Booklist, September 15, 2001, page 217
Kirkus Reviews, October 1, 2001, page 1429
School Library Journal, October 2001, page 167
Voice of Youth Advocates, December 2001, page 362

Other books by the same author:

Dead and Breakfast, 2001 (adult title)
Death Beneath the Christmas Tree, 1993 (adult title)

Other books you might like:

Jennifer Armstrong, *Steal Away*, 1992
Yankee Susannah and her personal slave run away to-gether to freedom and a friendship that lasts through the years.

Lois Walfrid Johnson, *Escape into the Night*, 1995
Libby's quiet life changes when she meets the cabin boy on her father's ship and together they assist runaway slaves to reach the Underground Railroad.

Norma Johnston, *Over Jordan*, 1999
Masquerading as a bossy Southern belle, Roxana travels by riverboat to Cincinnati to assist with the escape of her servant Joss and Joss's boyfriend.

Mary E. Lyons, *Letters from a Slave Girl: The Story of Harriet Jacobs*, 1992
After seven years spent hiding in her grandmother's small storeroom, Harriet eventually escapes along the Underground Railroad.

Carolyn Reeder, *Across the Lines*, 1997
Edward and Simon have been more than master and slave, but when Union soldiers overtake Edward's plantation, Simon seizes the chance to escape.

O

683

BARBARA O'CONNOR

Moonpie and Ivy

(New York: Farrar Straus Giroux, 2001)

Subject(s): Mothers and Daughters; Aunts and Uncles; Country Life
Age range(s): Grades 5-8
Major character(s): Moonpie, 11-Year-Old; Pearl Patterson, 12-Year-Old; Ruby Patterson, Single Mother; Ivy Patterson, Aunt
Time period(s): 2000s
Locale(s): Derwood, Georgia

Summary: When her mother Ruby dumps her with another stranger, Pearl's not at all surprised, though this time the stranger is her mother's estranged sister Ivy. Welcomed by Aunt Ivy, Pearl hesitates to respond too much for she knows her mother will eventually return for her. She's also welcomed by the strange looking next-door neighbor Moonpie, whose home situation isn't much better than Pearl's except that he's loved by his sickly, beer-guzzling grandmother. When Moonpie's grandmother dies and Ivy and her new husband take in Moonpie as a foster child, Pearl feels even more alone and unwanted. Ivy reminds her that she hasn't let herself become attached to Pearl because she knows Ruby will come back and snatch her away. Sure enough, Ruby returns and soon she and Pearl head for Arizona, but this time Pearl's armed not only with the knowledge of what a normal family could be like but also with Aunt Ivy's phone number. (152 pages)

Where it's reviewed:
Booklist, May 1, 2001, page 1682
Bulletin of the Center for Children's Books, May 2001, page 333
Kliatt, March 2001, page 13
School Library Journal, May 2001, page 157
Voice of Youth Advocates, June 2001, page 126

Other books by the same author:
Me and Rupert Goody, 1999

Beethoven in Paradise, 1997

Other books you might like:
Patricia Calvert, *Yesterday's Daughter*, 1986
　　When her mother shows up to reclaim her, Leenie retreats to the swampland she loves.
Kimberly Willis Holt, *My Louisiana Sky*, 1998
　　Bright Tiger loves her parents but doesn't realize they're mentally handicapped until she's older and her grandmother dies.
Patricia MacLachlan, *Journey*, 1991
　　Abandoned by his mother, Journey's sorrow is eased when his grandfather helps him replace destroyed family photos.
Richard Peck, *Strays Like Us*, 1998
　　Molly and Will, next door neighbors living with relatives, have each been "dropped off" by troubled parents and call themselves "strays."
Ruth White, *Belle Prater's Boy*, 1996
　　Cousins Gypsy and Woodrow learn to grieve together, Woodrow for his mother and Gypsy for her father who committed suicide.

684

SUSAN HEYBOER O'KEEFE
ROBIN SPOWART, Illustrator

Love Me, Love You

(Honesdale, PA: Boyds Mills Press, 2001)

Subject(s): Love; Animals/Rabbits; Stories in Rhyme
Age range(s): Preschool
Major character(s): Unnamed Character, Rabbit, Mother; Unnamed Character, Rabbit, Child
Time period(s): Indeterminate
Locale(s): Fictional Country

Summary: As a mother rabbit interacts with her young offspring, they share expressions of love based on their activities. The young rabbit is clear that the mother's love will remain constant despite mischief such as putting oatmeal in its fur and not in its mouth. The rabbit child feels confident that the loving mother rabbit will accept choices in clothing and play activities. The young rabbit loves the mother rabbit so much that it even offers to share its delicious thumb with the mother rabbit. (32 pages)

Where it's reviewed:
Booklist, April 15, 2001, page 1566
Horn Book Guide, Fall 2001, page 239
Publishers Weekly, February 5, 2001, page 87
School Library Journal, April 2001, page 119

Other books by the same author:
Angel Prayers: Prayers for All Children, 1999
Good Night, God Bless, 1999
One Hungry Monster: A Counting Book in Rhyme, 1989

Other books you might like:
Kathi Appelt, *Oh My Baby, Little One*, 2000
    Love is the invisible bond that links Mama Bird and Baby Bird when they are apart.
Margaret Wise Brown, *The Runaway Bunny*, 1942
    Mother bunny loves her baby too much to let him run away so she finds him each time he escapes.
Sam McBratney, *Guess How Much I Love You*, 1995
    Little Nutbrown Hare enjoys playing a game with his father in which each professes the magnitude of his love for the other.

685

ISAAC OLALEYE
CHRIS DEMAREST, Illustrator

Bikes for Rent!

(New York: Orchard Books, 2001)

Subject(s): Bicycles and Bicycling; Work; Problem Solving
Age range(s): Grades K-3
Major character(s): Lateef, Child, Worker; Babatunde, Businessman
Time period(s): Indeterminate Past
Locale(s): Erin, Nigeria

Summary: Lateef eyes the bikes at Babatunde's rental stand knowing that his parents cannot afford the rental fees. Lateef's desire to ride with the other boys is strong and his willingness to work to achieve his goal enables him to save enough money to rent a small bike and learn to ride. Gradually he's able to handle a larger bike and join the village boys riding down the hill and doing stunts. Babatunde reluctantly rents his only new bicycle to Lateef. Unfortunately, Lateef, trying to impress the others, crashes and damages the bike. To repay Babatunde for the repairs, Lateef works at his stand learning enough about bicycle repair to build one of his own from spare parts. (32 pages)

Where it's reviewed:
Booklist, August 2001, page 2132
Bulletin of the Center for Children's Books, June 2001, page 381
Kirkus Reviews, April 15, 2001, page 591
Publishers Weekly, April 30, 2001, page 77
School Library Journal, July 2001, page 86

Other books by the same author:
In the Rainfield: Who Is the Greatest?, 2000 (Notable Social Studies Trade Books for Young People)

Lake of the Big Snake: An African Rain Forest Adventure, 1998
The Distant Talking Drum: Poems from Nigeria, 1995 (ALA Notable Book)

Other books you might like:
Luis Garay, *Pedrito's Day*, 1997
    Pedrito saves his shoeshine money to buy a bicycle but when he loses his aunt's money he must repay her from his savings.
Tololwa M. Mollel, *My Rows and Piles of Coins*, 1999
    Saruni secretly saves the few coins he earns in hopes of buying a bicycle to help transport his mother's goods to market.
Audrey Wood, *The Red Racer*, 1996
    Nona thinks that if she can get rid of her old bike somehow the shiny new red one in the store window will become hers.

686

MATTHEW OLSHAN

Finn: A Novel

(Baltimore, MD: Bancroft Press, 2001)

Subject(s): Runaways; Illegal Immigrants; Grandparents
Age range(s): Grades 8-12
Major character(s): Chloe/Finn Wilder, Teenager; Silvia Morales, Immigrant, Servant
Time period(s): 2000s
Locale(s): United States

Summary: After a chaotic childhood with her unstable mother, Chloe moves in with her grandparents who live in a quiet, peaceful middle-class neighborhood. The biggest excitement occurs when her grandparents discover their maid Silvia's pregnant and kick her out of the house. Chaos returns when Chloe's crazy mother and new husband kidnap Chloe and force her to rob her grandparents' home. Faking her own death, Chloe meets up with Silvia and the two take off for California and the baby's father. Their roller coaster journey takes them through suburbs and projects, railroad yards and a night in the park where Chloe sees more of street life than she wants. A friend of Chloe's comes forward to help just as Silvia goes into labor in this wild first novel. (180 pages)

Where it's reviewed:
Booklist, April 1, 2001, page 1471
Kliatt, March 2001, page 13
School Library Journal, April 2001, page 146
Voice of Youth Advocates, April 2001, page 45

Other books you might like:
Fran Leeper Buss, *Journey of the Sparrows*, 1991
    Although life in America is difficult for illegal aliens, young Maria knows it's still better than the terror and killings of El Salvador.
Liza Fosburgh, *Cruise Control*, 1988
    Tired of his dysfunctional family life, Gussie takes Jimbo and runaway Flame on a trip south where they stay with an aunt and uncle who have a nice, stable home.
Willo Davis Roberts, *Hostage*, 2000
    Kaci interrupts thieves who kidnap her, and her older, nosy

neighbor, but this unlikely pair manages to escape from their captors.

Mark Twain, *The Adventures of Huckleberry Finn*, 1885
The classic adventure of the slave Jim and young Huck, two runaways who flee Huck's abusive father and float down the Mississippi River.

687

SOREN OLSSON
ANDERS JACOBSSON, Co-Author
KEVIN READ, Translator

In Ned's Head
(New York: Atheneum/Simon & Schuster, 2001)

Subject(s): Diaries; Humor; School Life
Age range(s): Grades 4-6
Major character(s): Ned Floyd, 11-Year-Old; Nadia Nelson, Girlfriend (of Ned), 6th Grader; Nicholas ''Nugget'', Bully, 6th Grader
Time period(s): 2000s
Locale(s): Sweden

Summary: Though admitting that boys don't usually keep diaries, Ned remains anonymous as he renames himself Treb and records all his daily thoughts, adventures and mishaps in a blue diary decorated with a skull and crossbones. He treads lightly around Nugget, the class bully, as he tries to one-up him with exaggerated deeds; starts a rock band that's loud, but not necessarily good; is ecstatic when he discovers that Nadia really does like him and wishes fervently that his father would get a better car. A popular series in Sweden, Ned's humorous adventures will appeal to preteens anywhere. (133 pages)

Where it's reviewed:
Booklist, April 1, 2001, page 1471
Bulletin of the Center for Children's Books, March 2001, page 264
Publishers Weekly, February 26, 2001, page 87
Riverbank Review, Summer 2001, page 40
School Library Journal, June 2001, page 153

Other books you might like:
Judith Clarke, *The Heroic Life of Al Capsella*, 1990
Al longs to be normal but finds it impossible when he's been named Almeric by Mr. And Mrs. Capsella, as he refers to his eccentric parents.
Sue Townsend, *The Secret Diary of Adrian Mole, Aged 13 3/4*, 1982
Adrian Mole, who often feels beleaguered and put upon, begins his diary the day he gets his first zit.
Paul Zindel, *The Amazing and Death-Defying Diary of Eugene Dingman*, 1987
Eugene spends the summer working at a resort in the Catskills where he lusts after the waitress Della, who ignores him for the vile short order cook.

688

JAN ORMEROD, Author/Illustrator

Miss Mouse Takes Off
(New York: HarperCollins Publishers, 2001)

Subject(s): Dolls and Dollhouses; Air Travel; Airplanes
Age range(s): Preschool-Kindergarten
Major character(s): Miss Mouse, Doll, Stuffed Animal; Unnamed Character, Child, Daughter; Unnamed Character, Mother, Passenger
Time period(s): 2000s (2001)
Locale(s): In the Air

Summary: Miss Mouse narrates her experience as the traveling companion to a young girl and her mother who journey from a cold, wintry city to the child's grandmother's warm locale. Several times Miss Mouse almost joins the baggage or becomes lost, but each time conscientious workers retrieve her. On the plane Miss Mouse becomes a playmate linking the little girl and the boy in the seat in front of her until Miss Mouse flips into a lunch tray and completes her journey with a green ear. After lunch, watching the movie helps everyone have a nap before landing. (32 pages)

Where it's reviewed:
Booklist, June 2001, page 1894
Bulletin of the Center for Children's Books, July 2001, page 418
Horn Book, September 2001, page 578
Publishers Weekly, June 25, 2001, page 72
School Library Journal, July 2001, page 86

Awards the book has won:
Parenting's Reading Magic Awards, 2001

Other books by the same author:
Miss Mouse's Day, 2001
Who's Whose, 1998
Miss MacDonald Has a Class, 1996

Other books you might like:
Barbro Lindgren, *Sam's Teddy Bear*, 1982
Sam's faithful doggie helps recover his lost teddy bear.
Shulamith Levey Oppenheim, *I Love You, Bunny Rabbit*, 1995
Micah's well-worn Bunny Rabbit is soiled with applesauce, chocolate milk and puddle mud, making it irreplaceable.
Adrian Reynolds, *Pete and Polo's Big School Adventure*, 2000
The first day of school is not quite the same as a plane ride but it still seems a little scary to Polo, a toy bear carried by Pete to school.

689

JAN ORMEROD, Author/Illustrator

Miss Mouse's Day
(New York: HarperCollins Publishers, 2001)

Subject(s): Animals/Mice; Toys; Playing
Age range(s): Preschool-Grade 1

Major character(s): Miss Mouse, Mouse, Stuffed Animal; Unnamed Character, Child, Friend
Time period(s): 2000s
Locale(s): England

Summary: Miss Mouse's day begins and ends with a cuddle from her friend. Between cuddles Miss Mouse and her pal stay busy with art projects, playing outside and building houses in the sandbox. When her friend slips in the mud while carrying Miss Mouse the poor animal is forgotten for hours while her friend is taken inside for a bath. After dark, a flashlight beam locates her in the mud. After a quick wash and a spin in the dryer, Miss Mouse joins her friend for a story, a kiss and a good night cuddle. (32 pages)

Where it's reviewed:
Booklist, March 15, 2001, page 1401
Horn Book, March 2001, page 200
Kirkus Reviews, December 1, 2000, page 1686
Publishers Weekly, January 1, 2001, page 91
School Library Journal, March 2001, page 218

Other books by the same author:
Miss Mouse Takes Off, 2001 (Parenting's Reading Magic Award)
Who's Whose, 1998
When We Went to the Zoo, 1991

Other books you might like:
Kim Lewis, *My Friend Harry*, 1995
    James and Harry, a toy elephant, go everywhere together until James enters school.
Barbro Lindgren, *Sam's Teddy Bear*, 1982
    Sam's dog helps recover his special teddy bear.
Shulamith Levey Oppenheim, *I Love You, Bunny Rabbit*, 1995
    Micah's well-worn Bunny Rabbit is soiled with applesauce, chocolate milk and puddle mud, making it irreplaceable.
Caroline Uff, *Lulu's Busy Day*, 2000
    Lulu's active day concludes with a bubble bath, brushing her teddy bear's teeth and hearing a story before snuggling into bed with her bear.
Martin Waddell, *Small Bear Lost*, 1996
    When Small Bear is left on a train he manages to find his way home to the little girl who lost him.

690

WENDY ORR
KERRY MILLARD, Illustrator

Nim's Island

(New York: Alfred A. Knopf, 2001)

Subject(s): Islands; Survival; Animals
Age range(s): Grades 3-5
Major character(s): Nim Rusoe, Daughter; Alex Rover, Writer, Rescuer; Jack Rusoe, Father, Scientist
Time period(s): 1990s (1999)
Locale(s): Fictional Country

Summary: Jack's three-day plankton collection trip becomes much longer when the rudder on the boat breaks in a storm. Nim has to push the memories of her mother's loss at sea from her mind and continue with the many chores on their island home. Though Nim feels a little lonely and concerned she has an iguana, a sea lion and a turtle for company in addition to e-mails from Alex who is doing research for a book and messages from Jack delivered by a frigate bird. Before Jack can return the island's volcano erupts and Nim injures her knee in a fall. Alex comes to rescue her but an unexpected, severe storm leaves her in the sea needing to be rescued by Nim and her friends. The storm makes Jack's return more difficult too but one of Nim's research experiments floats his way enabling him to reach the island. Originally published in Australia in 1999. (125 pages)

Where it's reviewed:
Kirkus Reviews, December 15, 2000, page 1764
Los Angeles Times Book Review, March 25, 2001, page 6
Publishers Weekly, February 19, 2001, page 91
School Librarian, Winter 2000, page 202
School Library Journal, February 2001, page 104

Other books by the same author:
Ark in the Park, 2000
A Light in Space, 1994
Pegasus & Ooloo-Moo-loo, 1993

Other books you might like:
Eva Ibbotson, *Island of the Aunts*, 2000
    Aging sisters resort to kidnapping children in order to care for the marine animals at their secluded island home.
Astrid Lindgren, *Pippi Longstocking*, 1950
    With only a monkey and horse for companions parentless Pippi lives an intriguing life.
Johann D. Wyss, *The Swiss Family Robinson*, 1949
    A family shipwrecked on an island finds a way to survive in a classic story.

691

MARY POPE OSBORNE
SAL MURDOCCA, Illustrator

Christmas in Camelot

(New York: Stepping Stone/Random House, 2001)

Series: Magic Tree House
Subject(s): Time Travel; Magic; Arthurian Legends
Age range(s): Grades 2-5
Major character(s): Annie, Sister, Time Traveler; Jack, Brother, Time Traveler; Morgan, Sorceress, Friend
Time period(s): 2000s (2001); Indeterminate Past
Locale(s): Frog Creek, Pennsylvania; Camelot, Fictional Country; Otherworld, Fictional Country

Summary: As Jack and Annie walk home from school to begin their Christmas vacation Annie notices that the magic tree house has returned to the woods. Morgan is not inside, but they do find an invitation to celebrate Christmas in Camelot. The Camelot to which the Magic Tree House transports them is an unhappy one. Morgan explains that magic has been banned for the king blames it for the loss of his three best knights. A magician more powerful than Morgan appears in the guise of a knight seeking help with a quest to save Camelot and Annie eagerly accepts the task. Jack writes down the riddle they are to follow and Annie takes the red cloak offered by the mysterious knight. By using the magical gifts and the deciphered riddle Jack and Annie travel to Otherworld, locate and free the three knights and acquire the magical water that will restore joy to Camelot. (115 pages)

Where it's reviewed:
Booklist, December 15, 2001, page 732
Horn Book Guide, Spring 2002, page 76
Publishers Weekly, September 24, 2001, page 56
School Library Journal, October 2001, page 68

Other books by the same author:
Stage Fright on a Summer Night, 2002 (Magic Tree House, Number 25)
Twister on Tuesday, 2001 (Magic Tree House, Number 23)
Dingoes at Dinnertime, 2000 (Magic Tree House, Number 20)
Pirates Past Noon, 1994 (Magic Tree House, Number 4)

Other books you might like:
Edward Eager, *Knight's Castle*, 1956
    Four children magically travel to an earlier time when Ivanhoe and Robin Hood were living.
K.H. McMullan, *Sir Lancelot, Where Are You?*, 1999
    Three knights-in-training seek to save Sir Lancelot from Morgan's sorcery.
Jon Scieszka, *Knights of the Kitchen Table*, 1991
    Joe's birthday present is a book that holds the power to transport him and his two friends to other times and places.
Nancy Springer, *I Am Morgan LeFay*, 2001
    Young Morgan begins to understand her magical powers and connection to the fairies.
Elizabeth Winthrop, *The Castle in the Attic*, 1985
    A toy castle received as a gift leads William to unexpected magical adventures.

692

ADAM OSTERWEIL
CRAIG SMITH, Illustrator

The Comic Book Kid
(Asheville, NC: Front Street, 2001)

Subject(s): Time Travel; Cartoons and Comics; Fathers and Sons
Age range(s): Grades 4-6

Major character(s): Brian, 12-Year-Old, Collector; Paul, 12-Year-Old, Collector
Time period(s): Multiple Time Periods (from 75 million BC to the future)
Locale(s): Springs, New York (on Long Island)

Summary: Brian and Paul have one claim to fame in their middle school—between them they have over 5,000 action adventure comic books, carefully preserved in plastic covers. Their care at preservation stems from the time Brian accidentally spilled fruit punch over his dad's 1939 issue of the very first Superman comic book, an act for which Brian has never forgiven himself. One day the boys receive a special comic book with blank pages and a metal ring. Reading the directions, they kiddingly tell the ring 75 million BC and find themselves swimming in the Atlantic Ocean with prehistoric sea creatures. Frantically yelling ''Home,'' they return to Brian's laundry room. Thus begin their adventures with time travel, adventures which mysteriously fill the blank panels of their Timequest comic book as they anger prehistoric cave dwellers, try to find another 1939 Superman comic book, and meet aliens from the future, while also trying to complete their homework. (151 pages)

Where it's reviewed:
Booklist, May 15, 2001, page 1753
School Library Journal, August 2001, page 186

Other books you might like:
Mark Delaney, *Of Heroes and Villains*, 1999
    Invited to attend a comic book convention, the Misfits dodge bullets and fires to recover the new Hyperman movie.
Mel Gilden, *Harry Newberry and the Raiders of the Red Drink*, 1989
    Harry thinks his mother is the heroine of his favorite comic book, until she's kidnapped by the evil Bonnie Android who's looking for a lost recipe.
Norma Howe, *The Adventures of Blue Avenger*, 1999
    After drawing his cartoon superhero for several years, David decides to become the Blue Avenger and dresses the part as he charges forth to do good deeds.
Robert Silverberg, *Project Pendulum*, 1987
    Twins Eric and Sean become human ends of a time pendulum with one twin swinging forward in time while the other swings backward.

P

693

MARGIE PALATINI
GLIN DIBLEY, Illustrator

Tub-boo-boo
(New York: Simon & Schuster Books for Young Readers, 2001)

Subject(s): Problem Solving; Humor; Parent and Child
Age range(s): Grades K-3
Major character(s): Lucy Hathaway, Sister, Narrator; Henry Hathaway, Brother; Mother, Mother
Time period(s): 2000s
Locale(s): United States

Summary: At the conclusion of Henry's bubble bath he tries to stop a drip from the faucet by using his toe and becomes stuck. Mother puts her fingers into the spigot to dislodge Henry's toe and becomes entrapped also. Next Henry's dad gets his tie mixed up with the fingers but somehow Mother grabs the cell phone from his shirt pocket and calls for help. The police officer that responds adds to the problem and he calls a plumber who disconnects the faucet from the wall but does nothing for the fingers and toes. Lucy comes to the rescue by dumping ice cream into the unplugged end of the faucet thus chilling the jammed appendages and one by one they all come free. (34 pages)

Where it's reviewed:
Booklist, September 1, 2001, page 117
Bulletin of the Center for Children's Books, October 2001, page 70
Kirkus Reviews, July 1, 2001, page 945
Publishers Weekly, August 20, 2001, page 79
School Library Journal, October 2001, page 128

Other books by the same author:
Bedhead, 2000
Ding Dong Ding Dong, 1999
Piggie Pie!, 1995 (ALA Notable Book)

Other books you might like:
Tedd Arnold, *No More Water in the Tub!*, 1995
    William's bath water overflows and carries William, still in the tub, out the door and down the apartment stairs.
Cynthia DeFelice, *Casey in the Bath*, 1996
    To make baths more appealing to Casey his mother buys soap from a traveling salesman; only Casey knows the magical power it has.
Chad Stuart, *The Ballymara Flood*, 1996
    Stuck faucets turn a simple bath into a flood that quickly covers the town in a humorous rhyming story.

694

MARGIE PALATINI
RICHARD EGIELSKI, Illustrator

The Web Files
(New York: Hyperion Books for Children, 2001)

Subject(s): Literature; Humor; Mystery and Detective Stories
Age range(s): Grades 2-4
Major character(s): Dirty Rat, Rat, Thief; Ducktective Web, Duck, Detective—Police; Bill, Duck, Detective—Police
Time period(s): Indeterminate Past
Locale(s): Fictional Country

Summary: Ducktective Web and his partner Bill pursue a case involving a hen's purloined purple peppers, tasty tomatoes taken from some horses and leafy lettuce lifted from a sheep. Recognizing the thief to be a salad eater, Web and Bill head for the hideout of Dirty Rat, known for nefarious deeds and scrounging through garbage. Dirty Rat denies the accusations but Ducktective Web spots the tell tale signs of salad on the chin of the suspect and books him on three charges of "vegetable vagrancy, offensive bad breath and not using a napkin." It's an open and shut case; Dirty Rat gets six months of farm labor. (32 pages)

Where it's reviewed:
Booklist, May 1, 2001, page 1690
Bulletin of the Center for Children's Books, February 2001, page 232

Horn Book, May 2001, page 314
Publishers Weekly, May 14, 2001, page 81
School Library Journal, November 2001, page 132

Awards the book has won:
ALA Notable Children's Books, 2002

Other books by the same author:
Bedhead, 2000
Ding Dong Ding Dong, 1999
Piggie Pie!, 1995 (ALA Notable Children's Book)

Other books you might like:
Doug Cushman, *Inspector Hopper*, 2000
Confidently, Inspector Hopper, Private Bug, tackles the problems of other insects in his community.
Bruce Whatley, *Detective Donut and the Wild Goose Chase*, 1997
Fortunately for dimwit Detective Donut his partner Mouse is clever enough to retrieve the Maltese Dodo from the nefarious Goose.
David Wisniewski, *Tough Cookie*, 1999
When Tough Cookie gets the news that his former partner's been badly hurt by Fingers he decides to put an end to Fingers once and for all.

695

BARBARA PARK
DENISE BRUNKUS, Illustrator

Junie B. Jones Is a Graduation Girl
(New York: Random House, 2001)

Series: Junie B. Jones. Number 17
Subject(s): Schools; Behavior; Individuality
Age range(s): Grades 1-3
Major character(s): Junie B. Jones, 6-Year-Old; Mrs., Teacher
Time period(s): 2000s
Locale(s): United States

Summary: Junie B. Jones, a one-of-a-kind, act-before-thinking kind of a girl is graduating from kindergarten. The excitement of having a box containing a white cap and gown for the ceremony coupled with the admonition not to wear it before the big night requires more self-control than Junie B. can muster. So, when one of her stuffed animals spills his grape juice on her bookcase she grabs the closest thing she can to mop it up and that, unfortunately, is her white graduation gown. Junie B. sees her error and tries to rectify it but when she can't get the grape juice stains out she enhances them with purple marker. The truth comes out on graduation night when Junie B. sadly puts on her gown and the other students in Room 9, in a show of solidarity, decorate their own gowns with colored markers while Mrs. is in the hall trying to console Junie B. As Mrs. says in her graduation remarks, this is the most colorful class she's ever had. (69 pages)

Where it's reviewed:
Horn Book Guide, Spring 2002, page 76
Instructor, August 2001, page 20

Other books by the same author:
Junie B., First Grader (at Last!), 2001 (Junie B. Jones, Number 18)

Junie B. Jones Has a Peep in Her Pocket, 2000 (Junie B. Jones, Number 15)
Junie B. Jones Is (Almost) a Flower Girl, 1999 (Junie B. Jones, Number 13)

Other books you might like:
Beverly Cleary, *The Ramona Series*, 1952-1999
Irrepressible Ramona and her family endure school problems and sibling squabbles with love and a sense of humor.
Johanna Hurwitz, *Starting School*, 1998
Even separate classrooms can't keep twins Marcus and Marius from causing problems for their teachers.
Lois Lowry, *Zooman Sam*, 1999
Sam's family pulls together to make a costume the night before career day in his preschool classroom.
Bonnie Pryor, *Jumping Jenny*, 1992
During Jenny's kindergarten year she stays busy adjusting to many changes.

696

LINDA SUE PARK

A Single Shard
(New York: Clarion Books, 2001)

Subject(s): Artists and Art; Apprentices
Age range(s): Grades 5-8
Major character(s): Tree-Ear, Orphan, Apprentice; Crane-Man, Handicapped; Min, Artisan (potter)
Time period(s): 12th century
Locale(s): Ch'ul'po, Republic of Korea

Summary: Raised by Crane-Man, so called because of his withered leg, the orphan Tree-Ear is entranced with the exquisite celadon pottery made by the artisans in their village. Though he longs to become a potter, apprenticeships are kept within the family and Tree-Ear continues his daily routine of finding enough food for the two men to eat. One day he accidentally breaks a piece of pottery made by the celebrated potter Min and must work for Min to repay his debt. Tree-Ear wisely turns this servitude into an apprenticeship and is finally entrusted with delivering two pots to the royal court at Songdo. Beset by robbers along the way who shatter the celadon vases, Tree-Ear doesn't give up on his mission and arrives in Songdo with but "a single shard" in this award-winning work. (152 pages)

Where it's reviewed:
Booklist, April 1, 2001, page 1483
Bulletin of the Center for Children's Books, March 2001, page 275
New York Times Book Review, February 10, 2002, page 21
Publishers Weekly, March 5, 2001, page 80
School Library Journal, May 2001, page 158

Awards the book has won:
Newbery Medal, 2002
ALA Best Books for Young Adults, 2002

Other books by the same author:
When My Name Was Keoko, 2002
The Kite Fighters, 2000
Seesaw Girl, 1999

Other books you might like:

Michael Cadnum, *The Book of the Lion*, 2000
    In twelfth-century England a young apprentice finds himself assigned as a squire to the crusader Sir Nigel.

Alden R. Carter, *Crescent Moon*, 1999
    Jeremy helps his Uncle Mac carve an Indian statue to replace one destroyed because it was considered offensive.

Jean Ferris, *Across the Grain*, 1990
    From the old woodcarver Sam, Will learns patience and the importance of making life easier by going with the grain.

Mary Stolz, *Pangur Ban*, 1988
    In Ireland in the ninth century, a young boy enters a monastery where he learns to illuminate manuscripts.

ELIZABETH PARTRIDGE
AKI SOGABE, Illustrator

Oranges on Golden Mountain

(New York: Dutton Children's Books, 2001)

Subject(s): Emigration and Immigration; Chinese Americans; Fishing
Age range(s): Grades 1-4
Major character(s): Jo Lee, Child, Son; Fourth Uncle, Uncle, Immigrant; Unnamed Character, Mother, Widow
Time period(s): Indeterminate Past
Locale(s): China; California

Summary: Two years of drought force Jo Lee's mother to send him to Golden Mountain to earn a living fishing with Fourth Uncle. She gives Jo Lee branches from the family's orange trees to plant in his new home. After long days of fishing Jo Lee tends the tiny orange trees as a small reminder of his homeland. Finally, they grow enough to produce a few blossoms and Jo Lee pays the letter writer to send a message to his mother and sister with the promise of oranges when they are able to join him on Golden Mountain. An ''Afterword'' gives factual information on the migration of Chinese to America in the mid to late 1800s. (40 pages)

Where it's reviewed:
Booklist, January 2001, page 970
Bulletin of the Center for Children's Books, February 2001, page 233
Publishers Weekly, December 11, 2000, page 84
Riverbank Review, Spring 2001, page 38
School Library Journal, March 2001, page 218

Other books by the same author:
Annie and Bo and the Big Surprise, 2002
Pig's Eggs, 2000
Clara and the Hoodoo Man, 1999

Other books you might like:

Eleanor Coerr, *Chang's Paper Pony*, 1988
    In 1850s San Francisco, Chang longs for a pony that he knows his immigrant parents cannot afford.

Mary Watson, *The Butterfly Seeds*, 1995
    When Jake immigrates to America he brings ''butterfly'' seeds from Grandpa to plant in memory of his homeland.

Yin, *Coolies*, 2001
    Two brothers leave their Chinese homeland to join other immigrants working to build the transcontinental railroad.

CLARE PASTORE

Fiona McGilray's Story: A Voyage from Ireland in 1849

(New York: Penguin, 2001)

Series: Journey to America
Subject(s): Irish Potato Famine; Emigration and Immigration; Brothers and Sisters
Age range(s): Grades 5-8
Major character(s): Fiona Marie McGilray, 12-Year-Old, Immigrant; Patrick McGilray, 16-Year-Old, Immigrant; Mrs. Broder, Wealthy; Liam Hanley, Cousin
Time period(s): 1840s
Locale(s): County Wexford, Ireland; Boston, Massachusetts

Summary: At first Fiona's family isn't bothered by the plague that destroys Ireland's potatoes for their father has a good job raising flax, but when the English owner shuts down the farm, her father is left jobless. Fiona's older sister dies of typhus and their father is caught stealing grain from the warehouses and sent to jail, though Fiona and Patrick were also with him the night he was caught. Deciding it's best if the two children leave Ireland, Fiona and Patrick sail to Boston where they hope to find their cousins. After landing, they discover difficulty of finding work and are surprised to be called dirty Irish. Just as Fiona's feeling discouraged, she meets Mrs. Broder who hires her to help in her garden and provides the clue they need to find their cousins the Hanleys. When Liam hears of their plight, he provides Fiona and Patrick with a place to live and arranges passage for the rest of their family in this first of a series. (184 pages)

Where it's reviewed:
Booklist, March 15, 2001, page 1399
Voice of Youth Advocates, August 2001, page 206

Other books by the same author:
Aniela Kaminski's Story: A Voyage from Poland During World War II, 2001 (Journey to America)
Chantrea Conway's Story: A Voyage from Cambodia in 1975, 2001 (Journey to America)

Other books you might like:

Marita Conlon-McKenna, *Wildflower Girl*, 1992
    After losing her parents in Ireland's Great Famine, Peggy comes to America where she's lucky enough to find a position in a wealthy home.

Betty Cummings, *Now Ameriky*, 1979
    The potato famine forces Bridget to travel to America where she knows she'll be poor, but at least able to find food.

Elizabeth Lutzeier, *The Coldest Winter*, 1991
    Evicted from their home when their crops fail in the coldest winter ever in Ireland, the only hope for the Kennedy family is to sail to America.

Michael Morpurgo, *Twist of Gold*, 1992
    Sean and his sister Annie leave Ireland for American

where they head west in search of their father who's in the gold camps.

ALEXS D. PATE

West of Rehoboth

(New York: Morrow, 2001)

Subject(s): African Americans; Mystery and Detective Stories
Age range(s): Grades 10-Adult
Major character(s): Edward Massey, 12-Year-Old; Edna Hull, Aunt, Store Owner; Rufus Brown, Uncle
Time period(s): 1960s
Locale(s): Philadelphia, Pennsylvania; West Rehoboth, Delaware

Summary: It's summer again and for Edward, his mother and his sister, that means leaving their home in a rough neighborhood of North Philadelphia and traveling to West Rehoboth where they'll stay with Aunt Edna. His mother waitresses and picks up money to supplement the family income, his sister Sarah plays in the sand and Edward, well, this summer Edward decides to emulate his favorite detective, Hercule Poirot. Told to call this man who lives in a shack behind Aunt Edna's home Uncle Rufus, Edward has wondered about him for five years, wondered why he drinks so much and where he goes when he disappears for days at a time. This is the summer he decides to investigate, learns more than he wants to about Jim Crow and puts his life in danger. (241 pages)

Where it's reviewed:
Booklist, September 1, 2001, page 54
Kirkus Reviews, September 1, 2001, page 1239
Publishers Weekly, August 27, 2001, page 54

Other books by the same author:
Amistad, 1997
Finding Makeba, 1996
Losing Absalom, 1994

Other books you might like:
O.H. Bennett, *The Colored Garden*, 2000
   Grandmother Ruth teaches Sarge about his heritage through her vegetable garden that's part of an old slave cemetery.
J. California Cooper, *Family*, 1991
   Clora, a slave who commits suicide to stop her master's unwanted attention, remains a ghost and watches over her family for one hundred years.
Jonathan Scott Fuqua, *The Reappearance of Sam Webber*, 1999
   When Sam lives in perpetual fear of the bullies at his new school, only his friendship with the black janitor helps him survive.
Ntozake Shange, *Betsy Brown: A Novel*, 1985
   Three generations of a well-to-do black family living in St. Louis are represented in this work that takes place in 1957 when the schools are desegregated.

700

KATHERINE PATERSON
EMILY ARNOLD MCCULLY, Illustrator

The Field of the Dogs

(New York: HarperCollins Publishers, 2001)

Subject(s): Animals/Dogs; Stepfathers; Bullies
Age range(s): Grades 4-6
Major character(s): Josh, Son, Stepson; Manch, Dog; Wes Rockett, Bully, Neighbor
Time period(s): 2000s
Locale(s): Vermont

Summary: Not much is going right for Josh since his mom remarried and has a baby needing her attention. He has no friends in his new home and local kids, especially Wes, seem to resent him as a "flatlander" from Virginia. Looking for his dog one afternoon leads Josh to a field in which Manch is playing with other dogs. Josh is surprised to discover that he can understand the dogs and he hears their concern about a rival dog gang threatening them. After one of Manch's friends is hurt by a snowplow while fighting with the other dogs' leader, Josh attempts to help the situation by stealing a gun from his stepfather's locked cabinet and shooting the leader of the pack. Josh knows little about guns so his plan fails and the other dogs are ready to attack him when Manch leaps into the fray. Frightened that Manch will be killed Josh hurries to Wes's house and asks for help. His willingness to reach out saves Manch and could signal the end of Josh's loneliness in his new home. (90 pages)

Where it's reviewed:
Booklist, September 15, 2001, page 223
Bulletin of the Center for Children's Books, February 2001, page 233
Kirkus Reviews, December 1, 2000, page 1686
Publishers Weekly, January 1, 2001, page 93
School Library Journal, February 2001, page 122

Other books by the same author:
Preacher's Boy, 1999 (Booklist Editors' Choice)
Jip: His Story, 1996 (ALA Notable Book)
Flip-Flop Girl, 1994 (School Library Journal Best Books)

Other books you might like:
Avi, *The Good Dog*, 2001
   McKinley, "head dog" in his town, plots to rescue a dog being abused by its owner.
Susan Hart Lundquist, *Wander*, 1998
   James and Sary find a stray dog that provides needed love and comfort following their mother's death.
Phyllis Reynolds Naylor, *Shiloh*, 1991
   In a Newbery Medal winner Marty tries to hide a beagle from the dog's abusive owner.

KATHERINE PATERSON
JANE CLARK BROWN, Illustrator

Marvin One Too Many

(New York: HarperCollins Publishers, 2001)

Series: I Can Read Book
Subject(s): Books and Reading; Schools; Fathers and Sons
Age range(s): Grades 1-3
Major character(s): Marvin Gates, 1st Grader, Brother (younger); Ms. Brown, Teacher; May Gates, Sister (older)
Time period(s): 2000s (2001)
Locale(s): United States

Summary: With May's help, Marvin locates his classroom on the first day of school and hurries in only a little late but still Ms. Brown says he's "one too many" because she has no desk for him. When it comes to reading, Marvin also feels as if he is "one too many" because he just can't seem to master it. Ms. Brown sends a note home to Marvin's parents but Marvin thinks they're too busy with the dairy farm to read to him so he discards the note. When a big snow storm hits, Marvin is happy not go to school but he also feels responsible for the storm and the problems the loss of power make for his beloved cows and his parents. Finally, he admits to his parents about his inability to read and learns that his father was also the last in his class to start reading. (48 pages)

Where it's reviewed:
Booklist, July 2001, page 2023
Kirkus Reviews, July 1, 2001, page 945
Publishers Weekly, October 8, 2001, page 67
School Library Journal, September 2001, page 202

Awards the book has won:
Parenting's Reading Magic Awards, 2001

Other books by the same author:
Celia and the Sweet, Sweet Water, 1998
Marvin's Best Christmas Present Ever, 1997 (School Library Journal Best Books)
The Smallest Cow in the World, 1991

Other books you might like:
Marc Brown, *Arthur's Reading Race*, 1996
    Arthur challenges his younger sister to prove her claim that she can read in this beginning reader.
Patricia Reilly Giff, *Today was a Terrible Day*, 1980
    For Ronald Morgan this school day brings one problem after another.
Dr. Seuss, *I Can Read with My Eyes Shut!*, 1978
    The Cat in the Hat shows Young Cat how much fun reading can be in a rhyming book for beginning readers.

EDITH PATTOU
TRICIA TUSA, Illustrator

Mrs. Spitzer's Garden

(San Diego: Harcourt, Inc., 2001)

Subject(s): Teachers; Gardens and Gardening; Schools
Age range(s): Grades K-2

Major character(s): Mrs. Spitzer, Teacher; Mr. Merrick, Principal
Time period(s): Indeterminate Past
Locale(s): United States (Tremont Elementary School)

Summary: At Tremont Elementary School Mr. Merrick delivers seeds representing a new group of students to Mrs. Spitzer's classroom. Throughout the school year Mrs. Spitzer plants, waters, tends and weeds the garden encouraging optimal growth in each little plant. The class record player provides music for the growing plants whether they are tall and slender, low and bushy, brightly colored or not. When the year concludes Mrs. Spitzer's job is temporarily over but she knows the plants will continue growing in someone else's care and, at the end of summer, Mr. Merrick will once again bring her a supply of seeds. (32 pages)

Where it's reviewed:
Horn Book Guide, Spring 2002, page 54
Kirkus Reviews, March 15, 2001, page 419
Publishers Weekly, March 26, 2001, page 92
School Library Journal, April 2001, page 120
Southern Living, August 2001, page 48

Other books you might like:
Julie Dannenberg, *First Day Jitters*, 2000
    Sarah Jane Hartwell, a first year teacher, has multiple excuses for staying in bed on the first day of school.
Robert Munsch, *We Share Everything!*, 1999
    This kindergarten teacher's first day reminders about sharing are taken literally by two of her students.
Nancy Poydar, *First Day, Hooray!*, 1999
    Students, teachers, bus drivers and other school employees prepare for the beginning of a new school year.

MARY E. PEARSON

Scribbler of Dreams

(San Diego: Harcourt, 2001)

Subject(s): Love; Honesty; Feuds
Age range(s): Grades 7-10
Major character(s): Kaitlin "Kait" Malone, 12th Grader; Bram Crutchfield, Artist, 12th Grader
Time period(s): 2000s
Locale(s): Twin Oaks, California

Summary: Brought up to hate the Crutchfields, Kaitlin feels anger even more now that her father's in jail for killing Robert Crutchfield in what he claims is an accident. With her family facing financial difficulties, Kait and her sister forego their private Christian school and attend the public high school enrolled under their mother's maiden name. Scribbling in her journal helps Kait as she struggles to fit in, though seeing a good-looking guy named Bram also helps. The two finally meet, but Kait's confused as Bram's not only one of the despicable Crutchfields, but also the son of the man her father killed. Reading a journal written years ago by Maggie Crutchfield, Kait learns of the incident that started the feud, the anger of one sister against the other pregnant, unmarried one, and realizes that neither side has been guiltless in this 100-year-old war. Though she must finally tell Bram who she is, each of them is able to put the past behind them in this tearjerker romance. (223 pages)

Where it's reviewed:
Booklist, April 15, 2001, page 1553
Bulletin of the Center for Children's Books, May 2001, page 350
Publishers Weekly, April 9, 2001, page 75
School Library Journal, May 2001, page 158
Voice of Youth Advocates, June 2001, page 126

Other books by the same author:
David v. God, 2000

Other books you might like:
Sid Fleischman, *Bo & Mzzz Mad*, 2001
    When Bo's left an orphan, he's unsure whether or not to contact his Martinka relatives who've always feuded with his Gamage side of the family.
Dakota Lane, *Johnny Voodoo*, 1996
    Deirdre has difficulty adjusting to life in Louisiana until she falls in love with Johnny, but calling him Johnny Voodoo at a party drives him away.
Hilary McKay, *Exiles in Love*, 1998
    Big Grandma warns them that "the family failing is falling in love," and usually with unsuitable men. The Conroy girls are proving Big Grandma's correct.
Ann Rinaldi, *The Coffin Quilt: The Feud between the Hatfields and the McCoys*, 1999
    The Hatfields and the McCoys have inflicted pain and injury on one another for so long they don't even remember how the feud started.

704

RICHARD PECK

Fair Weather

(New York: Dial, 2001)

Subject(s): Family Life; Humor; Fairs
Age range(s): Grades 5-8
Major character(s): Rosie Beckett, 13-Year-Old; Lottie Beckett, 17-Year-Old; Buster Beckett, Child; Grandad Fuller, Grandfather; Euterpe Fuller Fleischacker, Widow, Aunt
Time period(s): 1890s (1893)
Locale(s): Bulldog Crossing, Illinois; Chicago, Illinois

Summary: Rosie can't believe their good fortune. Aunt Euterpe has sent four train tickets so she, Buster and Lottie, along with their mother, can attend the World's Fair in Chicago. Never having left her family's farm, Rosie can hardly wait, especially when her mother decides she can't go and has Granddad mail back her ticket, for this means the siblings will be on their own. Rosie, Buster and Lottie board the train when, to their amazement, it makes an unauthorized stop and crotchety, unpredictable Granddad hops on. When the four, plus Granddad's dog, invade Aunt Euterpe's home, everything turns upside down and the lazy maid and cook leave after the first day. Never mind, there are lots of things to eat and see at the fair as they marvel at the electric light, ride the wheel invented by George Ferris and ogle the Midway sights. And poor Aunt Euterpe, who's tried for years to be accepted

in Chicago society, is mortified when her relatives embarrass her in front of the grand dame of that society. The Beckett family's trip to the big city is a life-changing adventure for everyone. (139 pages)

Where it's reviewed:
Bulletin of the Center for Children's Books, October 2001, page 70
Horn Book, November 2001, page 757
Publishers Weekly, July 23, 2001, page 77
School Library Journal, September 2001, page 231
Voice of Youth Advocates, October 2001, page 282

Awards the book has won:
ALA Best Books for Young Adults, 2002
Smithsonian's Notable Books for Children, 2001

Other books by the same author:
A Year Down Yonder, 2000
A Long Way from Chicago, 1998
Strays Like Us, 1998
The Last Safe Place on Earth, 1995
Those Summer Girls I Never Met, 1988

Other books you might like:
Jane Cutler, *The Song of the Molimo*, 1998
    Harry attends the St. Louis World's Fair and has the time of his life, even meeting and befriending the Pygmy Ota Benga.
Sherry Garland, *The Last Rainmaker*, 1997
    Running away from a cruel aunt, Caroline joins Shawnee Sam's Wild West Extravaganza where she meets her Native American grandfather, "the last rainmaker."
Sid Hite, *Dither Farm*, 1992
    Dither Farm is fairly quiet until Aunt Emma arrives and then the family is struck with a kidnapping, a flying carpet and several romances.
Mary Stolz, *Bartholomew Fair*, 1990
    Everyone who attends Bartholomew Fair that day in 1597 returns home changed, including Elizabeth I.

705

ROBERT NEWTON PECK

Extra Innings

(New York: HarperCollins, 2001)

Subject(s): Sports/Baseball; Family Life; African Americans
Age range(s): Grades 6-9
Major character(s): Tate Bannock Stonemason, 16-Year-Old; Abbott Bristol Stonemason, Grandfather (great-grandfather of Tate); Vidalia "Viddy" Abbott, Aunt (great-aunt of Tate), Adoptee
Time period(s): 2000s; 1930s
Locale(s): Florida; South

Summary: A horrendous plane explosion kills the Stonemason family members except for Tate, whose now shattered leg squelches his dream of pitching in the major leagues. Tate moves to his great-grandfather's Florida mansion where he tries to heal both his leg and his spirits. Surprisingly, it's his Aunt Vidalia, adopted by Great-Granddad Stonemason when she was just a young girl, who provides the healing touch through stories of her childhood. A young African-American, she was abandoned on the team bus of all-black baseball team Ethiopia's Clowns, who traveled throughout the South during the Depression days playing exhibition games. Vidalia became the daughter and the mother to these ball players until the team disbanded, at which point she was adopted by Abbott Stonemason and raised in his white family. Now in her seventies, her tales of life with this baseball team make Tate aware of his inclination to write and when she dies, he knows a book will be a lasting tribute to her. (176 pages)

Where it's reviewed:
Booklist, February 2001, page 1046
Bulletin of the Center for Children's Books, March 2001, page 275
Publishers Weekly, January 15, 2001, page 76
School Library Journal, March 2001, page 255
Voice of Youth Advocates, August 2001, page 206

Other books by the same author:
Horse Thief, 2002
The Cowboy Ghost, 1999
Nine Man Tree, 1998
Arly's Run, 1991
A Day No Pigs Would Die, 1973

Other books you might like:
Richard Peck, *A Long Way from Chicago*, 1998
    Joey and his sister Mary Alice hear many warm and funny stories and learn unusual lessons during the summers they spend with their grandmother.
Joseph Romain, *The Mystery of the Wagner Whacker*, 1998
    Ghosts from the past repair a special baseball bat machine, much to the delight of Matt and the well-being of his uncle.
K. Smith, *Skeeter*, 1989
    A chance meeting leads to friendship for two white boys and an old black man named Skeeter.

706

MALKA PENN, Editor
THEODOR BLACK, Illustrator

Ghosts and Golems: Haunting Tales of the Supernatural

(Philadelphia, PA: The Jewish Publication Society, 2001)

Subject(s): Short Stories; Jews; Supernatural
Age range(s): Grades 5-8

Summary: Original short stories by ten different authors offer a look at Jewish culture while also adding a dollop of suspense. Malka Penn's "The Shadow of the Golem" tells of Joey's experience in the Old-New Synagogue in Prague when he hears first-hand about the Golem. "The Ghost of Leah Levy" encourages Aliza to join her so that the two Jewish girls won't ever be lonely again in a haunting tale by Rivka Widerman. Angry that he's vacationing in Jerusalem rather than celebrating his bar mitzvah at home, Dan wanders into a secret tunnel and meets ghosts from the past in "Jerusalem Tunnel" by Hanna Bandes Geshelin. Seven other short stories add to Jewish lore. (128 pages)

Where it's reviewed:
Booklist, November 15, 2001, page 570
School Library Journal, February 2002, page 135

Other books by the same author:
The Hanukkah Ghosts, 1995

Other books you might like:
Sandy Asher, *With All My Heart, with All My Mind: Thirteen Stories about Growing Up Jewish*, 1999
    Stories that examine the issue of growing up Jewish, especially when trying to reconcile centuries of tradition with the modern world.
Pamela Melnikoff, *Prisoner in Time: A Child of the Holocaust*, 2001
    During the Holocaust, Jan time travels to the sixteenth century and meets Rabbi Loewe who made the golem, but this time it can't save Jan.
Barbara Rogasky, *The Golem*, 1996
    The story of the rabbi who creates a giant from clay, which miraculously comes to life and protects the Jews of sixteenth-century Prague.

707

SUSAN PERABO

The Broken Places

(New York: Simon & Schuster, 2001)

Subject(s): Fathers and Sons; Fires; Fear
Age range(s): Grades 10-Adult
Major character(s): Sonny Tucker, Fire Fighter; Paul Tucker, 12-Year-Old; Ian Finch, Teenager
Time period(s): 2000s
Locale(s): Casey, Pennsylvania

Summary: Life is idyllic for young Paul as he grows up in his small town where his deceased grandfather was fire chief and his father is a firefighter. One day an explosion levels a house and Ian Finch, a rebellious, swastika-tattooed teenager is trapped inside. Paul's father Sonny attempts to rescue him but a second wall falls, burying both of them under the rubble. Paul and his mother both think the worst so are relieved when, hours later, Sonny emerges carrying Ian. Though Ian's foot was cut off to save him, the media and the townspeople hail Sonny as a hero, which turns the Tucker family upside down. Sonny seems drawn to the teen he rescued, which is puzzling to Paul, but when the truth of the rescue comes out there's even more for Paul to accept in this first novel. (254 pages)

Where it's reviewed:
Booklist, August 2001, page 2090
BookPage, August 2001, page 27
Entertainment Weekly, August 17, 2001, page 67
Publishers Weekly, August 6, 2001, page 63
School Library Journal, October 2001, page 196

Other books by the same author:
Who Was I Supposed to Be: Short Stories, 1999

Other books you might like:
Nevada Barr, *Firestorm*, 1996
    Ranger Anna Pigeon volunteers as a medic at a spike camp of firefighters in northern California and almost dies when trapped in a firestorm.
Leif Enger, *Peace Like a River*, 2000
    Young Rube describes exactly what happens the year his

older brother shoots two intruders, is jailed and escapes in a humorous, touching story.

Luanne Rice, *Home Fires*, 1995
Having lost her daughter in a tragic fire, Anne builds a new life with a firefighter badly scarred by an earlier blaze.

Alan Watt, *Diamond Dogs*, 2000
When Neil accidentally kills a freshman, his father protects him and the two are locked in a silent bond.

708

THOMAS PERRY

Death Benefits

(New York: Random, 2001)

Subject(s): Mystery and Detective Stories
Age range(s): Grades 10-Adult
Major character(s): John Walker, Analyst (insurance company); Max Stillman, Insurance Investigator; Ellen Snyder, Insurance Agent; Mary Catherine ''Serena'' Casey, Computer Expert
Time period(s): 2000s
Locale(s): San Francisco, California; Miami Beach, Florida; New Hampshire

Summary: McLaren Life and Casualty Insurance Company has just given away twelve million to the wrong person, a fact not realized until the real beneficiary shows up a few days later to claim his death benefit. The company calls in security consultant Max Stillman who invites John Walker, one-time boyfriend of the agent who authorized the payout, to accompany him out of town. It seems agent Ellen Snyder is missing and has left a convoluted paper trail, which Max thinks, will be easier to follow if John accompanies him. The two hopscotch around the country from the Midwest to Florida and finally up to New Hampshire, accompanied by a computer guru who wants to be called Serena. Finding the murdered body of Ellen is just the beginning of a huge insurance scam. (383 pages)

Where it's reviewed:
Booklist, October 15, 2000, page 424
New York Times Book Review, January 28, 2001, page 16
People, February 5, 2001, page 43
Publishers Weekly, November 6, 2000, page 69
Voice of Youth Advocates, October 2001, page 282

Other books by the same author:
Pursuit, 2001
Blood Money, 2000
Shadow Woman, 1999
Face-Changers, 1998
Dance for the Dead, 1996

Other books you might like:
Robert Crais, *Hostage*, 2001
Several years ago Police Chief Talley made the wrong call in a hostage situation and now is scared he'll make another incorrect decision.

Jeffery Deaver, *The Empty Chair*, 2000
Poisoning of the environment by a local North Carolina company, the kidnapping of two women and a misunderstood teenager give Lincoln Rhyme his latest case.

Dick Francis, *Odds Against*, 1966
After crippling his hand in a racing accident, Sid Hailey turns to investigating and uses his horse racing knowledge to his advantage.

709

K.M. PEYTON

Blind Beauty

(New York: Dutton/Penguin Putnam, 2001, c1999)

Subject(s): Animals/Horses; Horse Racing; Family Problems
Age range(s): Grades 6-10
Major character(s): Tessa Blackthorn, Teenager; Maurice Morrison-Pleydell, Businessman (real estate developer), Stepfather
Time period(s): 1990s
Locale(s): England

Summary: It's no wonder Tessa's been kicked out of three boarding schools with a father who abandoned her and an insecure mother who remarried a cruel, money-grubber. Now that's she's between schools, her stepfather sends her to work at his Sparrows Wyck farm. Unhappy to be assigned an ungainly horse called Buffoon, Tessa's attitude changes when she finds out he's the offspring of Shiner, a blind horse she loved as a child, and works to bring him along for racing. When Maurice rigs the Grand National so that his horse wins and Shiner comes in seventh, Tessa is so angry she stabs him and spends several years in a detention center. Returning to the stable after she's been released, she once again tries to turn Buffoon into a champion in another exciting horse story. (360 pages)

Where it's reviewed:
Book Report, September 2001, page 65
Bulletin of the Center for Children's Books, February 2001, page 234
Publishers Weekly, January 29, 2001, page 90
School Library Journal, March 2001, page 255
Voice of Youth Advocates, April 2001, page 46

Other books by the same author:
Snowfall, 1998
Going Home, 1982
Midsummer Night's Dream, 1978
Prove Yourself a Hero, 1978

Other books you might like:
Enid Bagnold, *National Velvet*, 1935
Velvet Brown wins a horse in a lottery and later rides him in the Grand National Steeplechase.

Mary Casanova, *Stealing Thunder*, 1999
When Libby thinks Mr. Porter is harming her favorite horse Thunder, she steals the horse but then discovers Porter's plans to collect insurance money.

Steven Farley, *The Black Stallion's Steeplechaser*, 1997
One of the progeny of Black Stallion, a temperamental horse named Black Storm, is on track to be a champion until he throws his owner.

Deborah Savage, *Under a Different Sky*, 1997
When wealthy Lara sees Ben riding Galaxy, she helps him

realize his dream of being an Olympic rider, while he helps her recover after her suicide attempt.

RODMAN PHILBRICK

The Journal of Douglas Allen Deeds, The Donner Party Expedition, 1846
(New York: Scholastic, 2001)

Series: My Name Is America
Subject(s): Wilderness Survival; Diaries; Disasters
Age range(s): Grades 5-8
Major character(s): Douglas Allen Deeds, Orphan, 15-Year-Old
Time period(s): 1840s (1846-1847)
Locale(s): West; Sierra Nevada Mountains, California

Summary: When both his parents die, young Douglas leaves Missouri with a family who has a son his age and thus becomes part of the Donner Party Expedition. With his new journal in hand, he records their trek across the prairie, the inexperience of the trip's leaders and their eventual conflict. He also reports on the wagon train's reliance on a poorly written set of travel directions, which causes them to be in the Sierra Nevada Mountains where they're trapped by the first snows of winter. Douglas doesn't take part in the cannibalism that saved so many others, though is aware of it, in this continuing series. (158 pages)

Where it's reviewed:
Booklist, January 2002, page 859
Kliatt, November 2001, page 10
School Library Journal, December 2001, page 142

Other books by the same author:
REM World, 2000
The Last Book in the Universe, 2000
Max the Mighty, 1998
The Fire Pony, 1996
The Haunting, 1995

Other books you might like:
Connie Brummel Crook, *The Hungry Year*, 2001
    During their first harsh winter in Canada, only the help of the Mohawk Indians keeps Kate and her siblings from starving.
James D. Houston, *Snow Mountain Passage*, 2001
    Team leader Jim Reed tells of his conflicts with the Donners, his eventual dismissal from the train and subsequent rescue of the stranded group.
George R. Stewart, *Ordeal by Hunger: The Story of the Donner Party*, 1960
    This overview of the tragedy endured by inexperienced pioneers was compiled from diaries of survivors and other contemporary accounts.

711

MEREDITH ANN PIERCE

Treasure at the Heart of the Tanglewood
(New York: Viking, 2001)

Subject(s): Magic; Coming-of-Age; Quest
Age range(s): Grades 7-10
Major character(s): Hannah, Healer
Time period(s): Indeterminate
Locale(s): Fictional Country

Summary: Brown Hannah lives on the edge of the woods, has no memory of her previous life and ministers to the local villagers as a healer. Once a month, she pulls out the flowers that grow in her hair and brews a tonic for the wizard who lives in the wood. This is a painful and debilitating process, although the wizard makes light of it. Periodically, knights appear and announce that they have come to fight the golden boar who lives in the wood. Even though Hannah has never seen the boar, terrible sounds come from the wood and none of the knights ever returns. At last, a knight comes who engages more than Hannah's passing sympathy. She wants to save him from whatever fate awaits him and follows him into the wood. What she finds there convinces her that the wizard is not to be trusted and starts her on a journey of revelation across the world. (241 pages)

Where it's reviewed:
Booklist, April 15, 2001, page 1557
Bulletin of the Center for Children's Books, July 2001, page 419
Horn Book Magazine, July 2001, page 460
Publishers Weekly, May 7, 2001, page 248
School Library Journal, June 2001, page 153

Awards the book has won:
Booklist Editors' Choice/Books for Youth, 2001

Other books by the same author:
Dark Moon, 1992
The Pearl of the Soul of the World, 1990
A Gathering of Gargoyles, 1984

Other books you might like:
Mary Brown, *The Unlikely Ones*, 1986
    A girl with no memory, accompanied by a strange assortment of beasts, set out to free themselves from enslavement by a wicked witch.
Geraldine McCaughrean, *The Stones are Hatching*, 2000
    Phelim's drab upbringing offered him no room for imaginative stories, so he's unsure how to fill his role as Jack'o'Green.
Sheri S. Tepper, *Singer from the Sea*, 1999
    The blood of innocents provides some powerful old men with nearly endless lives.

TAMORA PIERCE

Squire
(New York: Random House, 2001)

Series: Protector of the Small. Book 3

Subject(s): Coming-of-Age; Adventure and Adventurers
Age range(s): Grades 6-10
Major character(s): Kelandry, Teenager, Animal Lover; Lord Raoul, Warrior
Time period(s): Indeterminate
Locale(s): Tortall, Fictional Country

Summary: Kel's endurance in the page program is rewarded when she becomes Lord Raoul's squire. Initially disappointed not to become squire to the legendary Lady Alanna, Lord Raoul, commander of the King's Own, quickly shows Kel enough action to distract her from any regrets. Her adventures involve centaurs, floods and baby griffins, and her faithful horse, dog and sparrows continue to play their parts. Kel even finds time to become interested in boys, as something other than sparring partners, and begins a friendship with Alanna. Looming in the background, however, is the Ordeal, the night she must spend alone in the magical chamber to prove herself a knight. When Joren, the bully with whom Kel has battled throughout her education, fails, Kel begins to have real fears about the weaknesses the Ordeal is meant to expose. (416 pages)

Where it's reviewed:
Booklist, September 1, 2001, page 97
Bulletin of the Center for Children's Books, June 2001, page 382
Horn Book Magazine, July 2001, page 460
School Library Journal, August 2001, page 186
Voice of Youth Advocates, August 2001, page 215

Awards the book has won:
ALA Best Books for Young Adults, 2002

Other books by the same author:
Street Magic, 2001
Page, 2000 (Protector of the Small, Book 2)
First Test, 1999 (Protector of the Small, Book 1)

Other books you might like:
Robin McKinley, *The Blue Sword*, 1982
  Harry can't see any reason why being a princess should keep her from defending her people against dangers like dragons, so she sets out to do just that.
Sherwood Smith, *Wren to the Rescue*, 1990
  When her royal friends are in trouble, Wren literally flies to their aid.
Jane Yolen, *Sister Light, Sister Dark*, 1988
  A sisterhood of warrior women finds it useful to have a shadow sister to watch their backs; unfortunately, bright sunlight undoes the magic.

713

DAV PILKEY, Author/Illustrator

Captain Underpants and the Wrath of the Wicked Wedgie Woman

(New York: Blue Sky Press/Scholastic, Inc., 2001)

Series: Captain Underpants. 5th Epic Novel
Subject(s): Cartoons and Comics; Humor; Teacher-Student Relationships
Age range(s): Grades 2-5

Major character(s): George Beard, Friend, Student—Elementary School; Harold Hutchins, Friend, Student—Elementary School; Mr. Krupp, Principal; Ms. Ribble, Teacher (retiring)
Time period(s): 2000s
Locale(s): Piqua, Ohio (Jerome Horwitz Elementary School)

Summary: George and Harold's cartoon celebrating the retirement of Ms. Ribble earns them a trip to the principal's office and there they begin their usual pranks. George and Harold's plans backfire and they inadvertently transform crabby Ms. Ribble into Wicked Wedgie Woman who is determined to defeat Captain Underpants. Wicked Wedgie Woman ties up George and Harold and builds robots in their image that she programs to defeat Captain Underpants. Meanwhile one of Wicked Wedgie Woman's plans goes awry and the real George and Harold escape to locate Captain Underpants before Wicked Wedgie Woman can complete her plan for total world domination. (176 pages)

Where it's reviewed:
Booklist, January 1, 2002, page 859
Horn Book Guide, Spring 2002, page 90
Kirkus Reviews, July 15, 2001, page 1032
Publishers Weekly, October 8, 2001, page 66
School Library Journal, October 2001, page 129

Other books by the same author:
Captain Underpants and the Perilous Plot of Professor Poopypants, 2000 (Captain Underpants, 4th Epic Novel)
Captain Underpants and the Attack of the Talking Toilets, 1999 (Captain Underpants, 2nd Epic Novel)
Captain Underpants and the Invasion of the Incredibly Naughty Cafeteria Ladies from Outer Space, 1999 (Captain Underpants, 3rd Epic Novel)

Other books you might like:
Stan Berenstain, *The Berenstain Bear Scouts and the Run-Amuck Robot*, 1997
  Professor Actual Factual has no control over his latest invention, a supercharged robot destroying Bear Country, if the scouts can't stop it.
Marilyn Sadler, *Bobo Crazy*, 2001
  In the first series entry for "Zenon, Girl of the 21st Century," a popular robotic pet turns on its owners making Zenon glad she has an "uncool" Bobo.
Stephanie Spinner, *Be First in the Universe*, 2000
  Alien Jack seeks the DNA from a set of twins with nasty dispositions to use in an experiment on the planet Gemini.

714

ISABEL PIN, Author/Illustrator
ROSEMARY LANNING, Translator

The Seed

(New York: North-South Books, 2001)

Subject(s): Animals/Insects; Greed; Allegories
Age range(s): Grades 2-5
Time period(s): Indeterminate
Locale(s): Fictional Country

Summary: Two tribes of insects covet the object that lands on the boundary between their territories. The Scarabs study the orb scientifically while the Chafers use scholarly records to determine the nature of the unknown thing. Both reach the same conclusion: it is a cherry seed. The tribes, knowing the potential for a tree and its fruit, make plans to gain control of the seed. While their energies go into preparing for the war that they think will inevitably come, the seed becomes wedged in the ground, sprouts and grows into a tree that spreads its branches across the territories of both tribes thus averting conflict. (32 pages)

Where it's reviewed:
Booklist, May 15, 2001, page 1760
Horn Book Guide, Fall 2001, page 270
The New Advocate, Winter 2002, page 76
Publishers Weekly, February 26, 2001, page 84
School Library Journal, July 2001, page 86

Other books you might like:
Geraldine McCaughrean, *The Cherry Tree*, 1991
   War destroys their village and kills their father but hope survives in a cherry tree seedling nurtured by two siblings.
Dav Pilkey, *World War Won*, 1987
   Two kings and their subjects race to build the tallest stack of weapons; the wind soon shows what is strongest.
Dr. Seuss, *The Butter Battle Book*, 1984
   The stupidity of war is obvious as Zooks and Yooks take sides against each other because of the different way in which each group butters bread.
Priscilla Turner, *The War Between the Vowels and the Consonants*, 1996
   Vowels and consonants stop fighting when they realize what they can accomplish by cooperating.

715

ANDREA DAVIS PINKNEY
BRIAN PINKNEY, Illustrator

Mim's Christmas Jam
(San Diego: Gulliver Books/Harcourt, Inc., 2001)

Subject(s): African Americans; Christmas; Family Life
Age range(s): Grades K-3
Major character(s): Saraleen, Sister, Daughter; Royce, Brother, Son; Mim, Mother; Pap, Father, Construction Worker
Time period(s): 1910s (1915)
Locale(s): Wildroot, Pennsylvania; New York, New York

Summary: Christmas won't be the same this year with Pap in New York helping to build the new subway. Mim assures Saraleen and Royce that she'll still make her famous jam and they'll decorate a jar to send to Pap. When the jam arrives on Christmas Eve Pap offers a taste to the two mean foremen on his site who have refused to give the work crew time off for the holiday. The jam is so delicious the foremen relent and shut down the site for Christmas thus giving Pap the opportunity to make it back to Wildroot with some co-workers. (32 pages)

Where it's reviewed:
Booklist, September 15, 2001, page 236
Bulletin of the Center for Children's Books, November 2001, page 113

Horn Book Guide, Spring 2002, page 54
Publishers Weekly, September 24, 2001, page 50
School Library Journal, October 2001, page 68

Other books by the same author:
Duke Ellington: The Piano Prince and His Orchestra, 1998 (Caldecott Honor Book)
Pretty Brown Face, 1997
Bill Pickett: Rodeo Ridin' Cowboy, 1996

Other books you might like:
Marie Bradby, *The Longest Wait*, 1998
   As a blizzard rages Thomas wonders if his father, a rural letter carrier, will make it home safely.
Candice F. Ransom, *One Christmas Dawn*, 1996
   During the winter of 1917 a young mountain girl's father leaves his family to find work in the city and they wonder if he'll be home for Christmas.
Irene Smalls, *Irene Jennie and the Christmas Masquerade: The Johnkankus*, 1996
   Irene Jennie's parents have been rented out to a nearby plantation so she sadly awaits Christmas Day and hopes for their return.

716

DANIEL PINKWATER
ANDY RASH, Illustrator

Fat Camp Commandos
(New York: Scholastic Press, 2001)

Subject(s): Self-Acceptance; Camps and Camping; Humor
Age range(s): Grades 3-5
Major character(s): Ralph Nebula, Camper (runaway), Brother; Sylvia Nebula, Sister (Ralph's), Camper (runaway); Mavis Goldfarb, Camper (runaway), Witch
Time period(s): 2000s (2001)
Locale(s): Mountainburg, New York (Camp Noo Yoo); Pokooksie, New York

Summary: Resentful that their parents send them to Camp Noo Yoo, Sylvia and Ralph eagerly agree to the plan Mavis presents to sneak away from camp and ride the bus back to Pokooksie where they can hide out for the remainder of the summer at her house. Fortunately, her parents are fossil hunting in Africa and the gardener doesn't mind having them around. Initially, the three overweight children spend their time harassing thin people, asserting their right to be fat and generally getting revenge on people who refuse to accept them as happy, fat people. A brush with the law gets them involved in a theater production using only overweight members of the community and they discover a positive way to accept their size and communicate their worth to others. (89 pages)

Where it's reviewed:
Booklist, April 15, 2001, page 1553
Bulletin of the Center for Children's Books, June 2001, page 382
Horn Book, May 2001, page 334
Publishers Weekly, May 21, 2001, page 108
School Library Journal, May 2001, page 158

Awards the book has won:
IRA Children's Choices, 2002

Other books by the same author:
The Werewolf Club Meets Dorkula, 2001 (Werewolf Club, Number 3)
The Magic Pretzel, 2000 (Werewolf Club, Number 1)
Mush, a Dog from Space, 1995

Other books you might like:
Kate Klise, *Letters from Camp*, 1999
    Siblings communicate suspicions about the summer camp's operators in their letters home.
Marissa Moss, *Amelia Takes Command*, 1998
    Confidence gained at Space Camp helps Amelia confront her problems with the school bully.
Julie Anne Peters, *Revenge of the Snob Squad*, 1998
    Sixth grade outcasts band together to take on their tormentor.
Todd Strasser, *Help! I'm Trapped in the First Day of Summer Camp*, 1997
    Jake is bored by continually reliving the events of the first day of camp.

DANIEL PINKWATER
JILL PINKWATER, Illustrator

Irving and Muktuk: Two Bad Bears

(Boston: Houghton Mifflin Company, 2001)

Subject(s): Animals/Bears; Food; Problem Solving
Age range(s): Grades K-3
Major character(s): Irving, Bear; Muktuk, Bear; Officer Bunny, Rabbit, Lawman
Time period(s): 1990s
Locale(s): Yellowtooth, Arctic; Bayonne, New Jersey

Summary: Annually the town of Yellowtooth hosts a Blueberry Muffin Festival that attracts both residents and hungry polar bears with a passion for muffins. Officer Bunny spots Irving and Muktuk each year despite the disguises they don and has them transported by helicopter to a remote spot above the Arctic Circle. By the next year's festival, Irving and Muktuk have managed to return dressed in a different disguise that fools everyone except vigilant Officer Bunny. Finally, Officer Bunny posts a bears-for-sale ad on the Internet and a zoo in New Jersey calls to offer Irving and Muktuk a home in the "muffin capital of the world," as the city is known. It's possible that the bears will not return for next year's festival. (32 pages)

Where it's reviewed:
Booklist, September 15, 2001, page 233
Bulletin of the Center for Children's Books, November 2001, page 113
Publishers Weekly, September 3, 2001, page 89
School Library Journal, September 2001, page 202
Smithsonian, November 2001, page 120

Awards the book has won:
Smithsonian's Notable Books for Children, 2001

Other books by the same author:
Ice Cream Larry, 1999 (IRA Children's Choices)

Rainy Morning, 1999
At the Hotel Larry, 1997

Other books you might like:
Joann Adinolfi, *The Egyptian Polar Bear*, 1994
    Stranded on an iceberg floating south, Nanook ends up in the Mediterranean Sea and becomes the pet of a 10-year-old king.
Don Freeman, *Bearymore*, 1976
    Rather than plan his new circus act, Bearymore settles down for his winter's hibernation.
Janet Stevens, *Tops and Bottoms*, 1995
    Bear is the brunt of the joke in this Caldecott Honor book about how clever gardener Hare shares his crop.

718

DANIEL PINKWATER
JILL PINKWATER, Illustrator

The Werewolf Club Meets Dorkula

(New York: Atheneum Books for Young Readers, 2001)

Series: Werewolf Club. Number 3
Subject(s): Werewolves; Clubs; Humor
Age range(s): Grades 3-5
Major character(s): Billy Furball, Werewolf, Student—Elementary School; Henry Count Dorkula, Bat, Student—Elementary School; Lucy Fang, Student—Elementary School, Werewolf
Time period(s): 2000s
Locale(s): United States (Watson Elementary School)

Summary: Lucy is the first member of the Werewolf Club to suspect that something is odd about new club member Henry. Obviously he's not a werewolf, but anyone can join the club. However, is he a vampire, as he claims? Billy calls him master and does his bidding, but Henry shows no interest in biting people. Lucy wonders if the shortage of fruit in all the local stores could be connected to the mystery of Henry. When Lucy confronts Henry she learns that he's a "fruitpire" because he changes into a fruit bat rather than a vampire bat and it's his great great great great uncle who is consuming all the fruits and vegetables in town. The club members help Henry "steak" his uncle and so stop his fruit thievery and Billy admits to a willingness to be a slave to anyone offering food. (65 pages)

Where it's reviewed:
Booklist, September 15, 2001, page 223
Horn Book Guide, Spring 2002, page 77

Other books by the same author:
The Werewolf Club Meets Oliver Twit, 2002 (Werewolf Club, Number 5)
The Werewolf Club Meets the Hound of the Basketballs, 2001 (Werewolf Club, Number 4)
The Werewolf Club: The Lunchroom of Doom, 2000 (Werewolf Club, Number 2)

Other books you might like:
Dan Greenburg, *Don't Count on Dracula*, 2000
    The prize Zack wins in a contest is to meet horror film star Mella Bugosi whose odd habits make Zack wonder if the actor actually is a vampire.

James Howe, *Bunnicula: A Rabbit Tale of Mystery*, 1979
Harold, the family dog, suspects that the new family pet Bunnicula is a vampire rabbit that drains the juice from vegetables.

Eric Sanvoisin, *The Ink Drinker*, 1998
The unusual vampire in this story survives by slurping the print from the pages of books.

719

PATRICIA POLACCO, Author/Illustrator

Mr. Lincoln's Way
(New York: Philomel Books, 2001)

Subject(s): Prejudice; Schools; Bullies
Age range(s): Grades 1-4
Major character(s): Mr. Lincoln, Principal; Eugene Esterhause, Bully, Student—Elementary School
Time period(s): 2000s
Locale(s): Haslett, Michigan

Summary: With the exception of Eugene, everyone thinks Mr. Lincoln is a "cool" principal. Eugene doesn't seem to like anyone, especially anyone who looks different from him and he's known to tease and bully students of other races. When Mr. Lincoln observes that Eugene has an interest in and knowledge of birds he enlists Eugene's help in preparing the school's atrium so that it will attract more birds. Mr. Lincoln uses the variety of birds that come to the atrium as a metaphor for the many races of students in the school that he expects Eugene to treat with same kindness that he shows for the birds. (40 pages)

Where it's reviewed:
Booklist, September 1, 2001, page 117
Horn Book Guide, Spring 2002, page 55
Kirkus Reviews, July 15, 2001, page 1033
Publishers Weekly, July 9, 2001, page 67
School Library Journal, August 2001, page 158

Awards the book has won:
IRA Teachers' Choices, 2002

Other books by the same author:
The Butterfly, 2000 (Notable Social Studies Trade Books for Young People)
Welcome Comfort, 1999 (Smithsonian's Notable Books for Children)
Thank You, Mr. Falker, 1998 (Notable Social Studies Trade Books for Young People)

Other books you might like:
Maryann Cocca-Leffler, *Mr. Tanen's Ties*, 1999
Mr. Apple, administrator, considers it inappropriate for a principal to wear ties as expressive as Mr. Tanen's but the students think otherwise.

Sharon Creech, *A Fine, Fine School*, 2001
Mr. Keene is so proud of his fine school that the principal thinks more, more, more of the same will make the school even better.

Cynthia Rylant, *The Bird House*, 1998
A house where birds gather attracts a homeless girl who tries to avoid discovery; the birds alert the old woman in the home and she takes in the girl.

720

BARBARA ANN PORTE
ROSEMARY FEIT COVEY, Illustrator

Beauty and the Serpent: Thirteen Tales of Unnatural Animals
(New York: Simon & Schuster, 2001)

Subject(s): Short Stories; Animals; Supernatural
Age range(s): Grades 6-10
Major character(s): Lavinia Drumm, Librarian, Storyteller
Time period(s): 2000s
Locale(s): United States (Ernestine Wilde Alternative High School)

Summary: Whenever the students at the Ernestine Wilde Alternative High School misbehave, their teachers send them to the library and, if they're lucky the librarian Ms. Drumm tells them a story. But her stories aren't warm, feel-good stories, instead they're about animals, that may or may not be human, and the unusual things they do. Whether it be Aunty Squirrel with her two-diamond ring and mismatched eyes, or a puppy from hell, or a snake tattoo that almost kills its wearer, these tales feature animals that act in unexpected, and very unnatural, ways. (117 pages)

Where it's reviewed:
School Library Journal, November 2001, page 183
Voice of Youth Advocates, February 2002, page 450

Other books by the same author:
Hearsay: Strange Tales from the Middle Kingdom, 1998
Black Elephants with a Brown Ear (in Alabama), 1996
Something Terrible Happened, 1994
I Only Made Up the Roses, 1987

Other books you might like:
Lois Duncan, *Night Terrors: Stories of Shadow and Substance*, 1996
Madness, witchcraft, horror, suspense and mystery reside in these tales that magnify the terror hiding in the darkness of night.

Judith Gorog, *Three Dreams and a Nightmare: And Other Tales of the Dark*, 1988
Building on the theme of dreams, these fourteen tales range from remakes of well-known campfire tales to some that are downright chilling.

Malka Penn, *Ghosts and Golems: Haunting Tales of the Supernatural*, 2001
Original short stories by ten different authors offer a look at Jewish culture while also adding a dollop of suspense.

R.L. Stine, *The Haunting Hour: Chills in the Dead of the Night*, 2001
Voodoo cookies, graveyard romps and ghostly requests add touches of terror to these ten short stories.

721

RANDY POWELL

Run If You Dare
(New York: Farrar Straus Giroux, 2001)

Subject(s): Fathers and Sons; Identity; Family Life

Age range(s): Grades 7-10
Major character(s): Gardner Dickinson, 10th Grader; Aidan Skeepbo, 10th Grader; Cam Dickinson, Father, Unemployed; Annie Harris, 10th Grader
Time period(s): 2000s
Locale(s): Seattle, Washington

Summary: Gardner's father loses his job and isn't looking too hard for another, instead he's playing golf and even contemplates the Senior Tour. At first Gardner is so absorbed in his own interests that he's oblivious to his mother's return to work and his sister's classes at the community college. Gradually he realizes that his idolized father has a decided lack of ambition. To compensate for his being "just like his dad," Gardner begins a physical fitness program, joins the track team at school and chops and sells firewood. For sanity he relies on hanging out with his childhood friend Skeepbo and Annie, a girl who's just moved back to town. When his father mentions his desire to leave and search for a new kind of life, Gardner knows he and the rest of his family will survive whatever decision his dad makes in this coming of age story. (185 pages)

Where it's reviewed:
Horn Book, May 2001, page 335
Kliatt, March 2001, page 14
Publishers Weekly, February 12, 2001, page 213
School Library Journal, March 2001, page 256
Voice of Youth Advocates, June 2001, page 127

Other books by the same author:
Three Clams and an Oyster, 2002
Tribute to Another Dead Rock Star, 1999
The Whistling Toilets, 1996
My Underrated Year, 1988

Other books you might like:
Cynthia D. Grant, *Mary Wolf*, 1995
    When Mary's father loses his job, he takes his family on a long vacation in an RV while Mary wants only the security of home.
Joyce McDonald, *Comfort Creek*, 1996
    Her father's employer closes the phosphate mine, her mother leaves to join a band and Quinn's father moves the rest of his family to some swampland.
Heather Quarles, *A Door Near Here*, 1998
    Katherine's alcoholic, divorced mother is fired and takes to her room, which leaves Katherine wondering how she's supposed to care for her siblings.

DAVID POYER

Fire on the Waters
(New York: Simon & Schuster, 2001)

Subject(s): Civil War; Sea Stories
Age range(s): Grades 10-Adult
Major character(s): Micah Eaker, Father (of Eli), Wealthy; Elisha "Eli" Eaker, Military Personnel (Naval officer); Parker Bucyrus Tresevant, Military Personnel (captain); Kar Claiborne, Military Personnel (lieutenant); Araminta Van Velsor, Cousin, Fiance(e)

Time period(s): 1860s (1861)
Locale(s): New York, New York; USS *Owanee*, At Sea

Summary: North and South are at odds with each other, which leaves the nation in a state of flux and forces young men to declare their loyalties as they enlist for either the Union or Confederate side. Eli decides to join the Union navy, partly to provoke his domineering father and partly to postpone the forthcoming marriage to his cousin Araminta. Volunteering without pay aboard the USS *Owanee*, the ship is sent to defend Fort Sumter, the last Union stronghold in the south. Unsure of his nautical abilities, Eli is at least sure of his loyalties, unlike his two top-ranked officers who are both from Virginia. Captain Tresevant has already decided to resign and give up his command, though he hasn't yet informed his crew, a decision that will affect his second in command, fellow Virginian Lt. Clairborne, in this first of a trilogy. (443 pages)

Where it's reviewed:
Booklist, July 2001, page 1983
Kirkus Reviews, April 15, 2001, page 533
Library Journal, May 15, 2001, page 165
Publishers Weekly, June 18, 2001, page 56

Other books by the same author:
Black Storm, 2002
China Sea, 2000
Thunder on the Mountain, 1998
Tomahawk, 1998
As the Wolf Loves Winter, 1996

Other books you might like:
Bernard Cornwell, *Rebel*, 1993
    Northern Nathaniel Starbuck happens to be in the South when struck by "rebel fever" and joins the Southern side, more for adventure than the cause.
C.S. Forester, *Mr. Midshipman Hornblower*, 1950
    First in the series, this work describes the early days of Hornblower's sailing career from being a novice to his commission as a lieutenant.
James Reasoner, *Manassas*, 1999
    Will Brannon gives up his sheriff position and joins the Confederate army in this first of an eight-volume series.
Kenneth Lewis Roberts, *The Lively Lady*, 1931
    Captain Nason, of *The Lively Lady*, fights sea battles during the War of 1812 and winds up captive in an English prison.

TERRY PRATCHETT

Amazing Maurice and His Educated Rodents: A Novel of Discworld
(New York: HarperCollins, 2001)

Subject(s): Crime and Criminals; Animals/Cats; Animals/Rats
Age range(s): Grades 8-12
Major character(s): Maurice, Cat; Dangerous Beans, Rat; Peaches, Rat; Keith, Orphan, Musician; Malicia Grim, Daughter
Time period(s): Indeterminate
Locale(s): Bad Blintz, Fictional City

Summary: When rats start foraging in the dump of the University of Wizards, it only leads to trouble as they wind up with an unlikely leader in the talking cat Maurice. A born con artist, Maurice sees the somewhat naive rats, that have christened themselves with names they chose before understand what they were reading, as the perfect partners in crime. He ropes in Keith, a talented but somewhat vague young musician, and the entire menagerie tours from town to town pulling the Pied Piper scam. Unfortunately for Maurice, the rats are getting smarter and, led by Dangerous Beans and Peaches, the whole group develops a conscience. The rats are ready to abandon the game, but Maurice convinces them to do one more job. Too bad he chooses the town of Bad Blintz, where things go wrong when Malicia Grim figures out the scam. This is the first *Discworld* novel aimed at the YA audience. (241 pages)

Where it's reviewed:
Booklist, January 1, 2002, page 842
Bulletin of the Center for Children's Books, February 2002, page 217
Publishers Weekly, November 5, 2001, page 70
School Library Journal, December 2001, page 142
Voice of Youth Advocates, February 2002, page 450

Awards the book has won:
ALA Best Books for Young Adults, 2002

Other books by the same author:
The Fifth Elephant: A Novel of Discworld, 2000
The Truth: A Novel of Discworld, 2000
Carpe Jugulum: A Novel of Discworld, 1998

Other books you might like:
Tanya Huff, *Summon the Keeper*, 1998
   Austin the cat calls on all his powers of sarcasm to keep his human in line when summoned to close the door into hell.
Patrice Kindl, *Goose Chase*, 2001
   A tart-tongued goose girl is determined to save her beloved geese no matter how many kings or princes want to marry her.
Henry Wilson, *The Coachman Rat*, 1989
   What happens to a rat that has been transformed into a coachman by a magic spell?

724

MIRJAM PRESSLER
BRIAN MURDOCK, Translator

Shylock's Daughter

(New York: Penguin Putnam/Phyllis Fogelman Books, 2001)

Subject(s): Jews; Fathers and Daughters; Prejudice
Age range(s): Grades 9-12
Major character(s): Jessica, 16-Year-Old; Shylock, Banker (moneylender); Lorenzo, Nobleman; Dalilah, Foster Child; Hannah Meshullam, Friend (of Jessica)
Time period(s): 16th century (1560s)
Locale(s): Venice, Italy

Summary: For teenager Jessica, life in the Jewish ghetto is drab and gloomy, especially compared to the sparkle and excitement of life in Venice itself. Leaving the ghetto to visit her friend Hannah, a Shepardic Jew who enjoys a freer life-style than Jessica, she meets the nobleman Lorenzo and is instantly infatuated. Her father is the Jewish moneylender Shylock, featured in Shakespeare's *The Merchant of Venice*, and the contrast between her life and Lorenzo's is almost insurmountable. The thought that Jessica might leave behind her father, her foster sister Dalilah, her home and her religion, as well as steal from her father, is unimaginable. However the desire for freedom from the ghetto, a richer standard of living, and the love of Lorenzo exert a powerful tug and she leaves. By book's end, Jessica wonders if she's really free now that she's out of the ghetto, Dalilah realizes she'll always be alone and senses the freedom of that and Shylock disappears after the disastrous loan he made in this author's attempt to explain Shakespeare's famous play. (266 pages)

Where it's reviewed:
Booklist, April 1, 2001, page 1484
Bulletin of the Center for Children's Books, July 2001, page 420
Publishers Weekly, June 25, 2001, page 74
School Library Journal, June 2001, page 154
Voice of Youth Advocates, October 2001, page 283

Other books by the same author:
Halinka, 1998

Other books you might like:
Teri Kanefield, *Rivka's Way*, 2001
   Rivka is curious about what lies beyond the walls of her Jewish ghetto in Prague, so she dresses as a boy, removes her yellow Jewish star and goes exploring.
Julius Lester, *Othello*, 1995
   This retelling of Shakespeare's classic play of lies and jealousy follows the same plot but changes some of the characters.
Gloria D. Miklowitz, *Secrets in the House of Delgado*, 2001
   Maria tells a priest about her employers the Delgado family, which leads to Dr. Delgado's arrest and Maria's attempt to find them safe passage from Spain.

725

MARJORIE PRICEMAN, Author/Illustrator

It's Me, Marva!: A Story about Color & Optical Illusions

(New York: Alfred A. Knopf, 2001)

Subject(s): Inventors and Inventions; Science; Humor
Age range(s): Grades 2-5
Major character(s): Marva, Inventor
Time period(s): 2000s
Locale(s): United States

Summary: Ketchup from Marva's latest invention splatters her with so much red goo that she considers becoming a redhead. Her at-home attempt to dye her hair results in an orange head of hair when the red dye combines with Marva's yellow hair. A trip to a professional who first removes the existing color yields pink hair. After staring at the polka dot wallpaper while waiting for her hair to dry Marva glances in the mirror and thinks the afterimages of the dots are measles spots on her face. Marva has no better luck with her laundry when she combines blue jeans with a yellow scarf and a red shirt and pulls a green scarf and purple shirt out of the machine. Marva's day is one of visual tricks and discoveries that are explained in concluding notes about the science behind color and optical illusions. (34 pages)

Where it's reviewed:
Booklist, August 2001, page 2132
Horn Book Guide, Fall 2001, page 270
Horn Book, June 2001, page 443
Publishers Weekly, June 4, 2001, page 80
School Library Journal, July 2001, page 86

Other books by the same author:
Froggie Went A-Courting, 2000
Emeline at the Circus, 1999 (Bulletin of the Center for Children's Books Blue Ribbon)
How to Make an Apple Pie and See the World, 1994 (ALA Notable Book)
Friend or Frog, 1989

Other books you might like:
Eric Carle, *Hello, Red Fox*, 1998
Multi-colored guests at Little Frog's birthday party show off their complimentary colors.
Leo Lionni, *Little Blue and Little Yellow: A Story for Pippo and Other Children*, 1959
Best friends Little Blue and Little Yellow hug and become green.
Cynthia Rylant, *Mr. Putter & Tabby Paint the Porch*, 2000
Pets create a multi-colored mess as Mr. Putter attempts to paint his porch.
Ellen Stoll Walsh, *Mouse Paint*, 1989
Three white mice fall in and out of jars of primary colored paint, confusing a cat as they change colors.
Hans Wilhelm, *I Love Colors!*, 2000
In a beginning reader, a small white dog experiments with three jars of paint in primary colors until his coat of fur is rainbow colored.

726

JAMES PROIMOS, Author/Illustrator

The Many Adventures of Johnny Mutton
(San Diego: Harcourt, Inc., 2001)

Subject(s): Animals/Sheep; Schools; Individuality
Age range(s): Grades 2-4
Major character(s): Johnny Mutton, Sheep, Student—Elementary School; Momma Mutton, Mother
Time period(s): Indeterminate
Locale(s): Fictional Country

Summary: Abandoned on Momma Mutton's doorstop, Johnny is adopted by the nearsighted woman and raised as a unique little boy. Momma Mutton encourages Johnny's self-expression so his individuality quickly distinguishes him from most of his conforming classmates. While others bring the teacher apples, Johnny gives him a bag of marshmallows. When the rest of the class dons witch and pirate costumes for Halloween, Johnny comes as a runny nose and forges a friendship with a classmate dressed as a box of tissues. Although Momma Mutton tries to develop Johnny's ball handling skills, Johnny opts for water ballet rather than basketball and

he's quite successful just as Momma Mutton encourages him to be. (42 pages)

Where it's reviewed:
Booklist, June 2001, page 1872
Bulletin of the Center for Children's Books, July 2001, page 420
Horn Book, September 2001, page 591
Publishers Weekly, April 30, 2001, page 78
School Library Journal, May 2001, page 131

Other books by the same author:
The Loudness of Sam, 1999 (IRA/CBC Children's Choice)

Other books you might like:
Stan Berenstain, *The Goofy, Goony Guy*, 2001
Sister Bear is unsure what to make of the new student in her class because of his unusual behavior.
Mem Fox, *The Straight Line Wonder*, 1996
Ignoring the warnings of his friends a straight line seeks to express his individuality by curving and bending into different shapes.
Christopher Myers, *Wings*, 2000
The support of just one person gives Ikarus the confidence to accept his wings and put them to good use.
Dav Pilkey, *Ricky Ricotta's Giant Robot: An Adventure Novel*, 2000
Ricky's friendship with Robot helps solve a bully problem for the kind student.

727

ALICE PROVENSEN, Author/Illustrator

The Master Swordsman & The Magic Doorway: Two Legends from Ancient China
(New York: Simon & Schuster Books for Young Readers, 2001)

Subject(s): Talent; Short Stories; Fantasy
Age range(s): Grades 2-5
Time period(s): Indeterminate Past
Locale(s): China

Summary: In the first of two original stories a young resident of a poor village beset by bandits seeks a master swordsman to teach him how to defend his village. The master's instruction consists of assigning laborious chores and hurling talking objects at the youth until he becomes strong and agile. The master then awards him a sword with instructions to use it only to chop cabbage. The second story describes an artist's relationship with the emperor who commissions a large wall mural. The artist's work is so stunning that the emperor plans to kill the artist as soon as the mural is completed rather than have him paint for anyone else. It takes years to complete the mural and, when it is finally declared finished, the artist reveals that he has painted his way to freedom. (40 pages)

Where it's reviewed:
Booklist, September 15, 2001, page 223
Horn Book, January 2002, page 71
Publishers Weekly, October 29, 2001, page 63
School Library Journal, November 2001, page 133
Smithsonian, November 2001, page 120

Awards the book has won:
Parenting's Reading Magic Awards, 2001
Smithsonian's Notable Books for Children, 2001

Other books by the same author:
An Owl and Three Pussycats, 1994
The Glorious Flight: Across the Channel with Louis Bleriot, 1983 (Caldecott Medal)
The Year at Maple Hill Farm, 1978

Other books you might like:
Stefan Czernecki, *The Cricket's Cage: A Chinese Folktale*, 1997
    A lucky cricket helps a lowly carpenter design a model of a tower that is acceptable to the emperor thus saving the carpenter's life.
Marguerite W. Davol, *The Paper Dragon*, 1997
    Armed with his paints, scrolls and wits, artist Mi Fei faces a dragon that threatens his beloved village.
Demi, *The Greatest Treasure*, 1998
    For Li, a poor farmer, the sound of his children singing is a greater treasure than the bag of coins given to him by a wealthy neighbor.

728

PHILIP PULLMAN
IAN BECK, Illustrator

Puss in Boots: The Adventures of That Most Enterprising Feline
(New York: Alfred A. Knopf, 2001)

Subject(s): Fairy Tales; Folklore; Animals/Cats
Age range(s): Grades 1-4
Major character(s): Jacques, Brother (youngest); Puss, Cat; Ogre, Monster, Shape-changer
Time period(s): Indeterminate Past
Locale(s): Fictional Country

Summary: After his father's death Jacques inherits Puss, a schemer with imaginative plans for a better life for Jacques. With Puss's ideas and Jacques's courage the duo are soon rescuing a kidnapped princess from Ogre before he can fulfill his plans to marry her. With help from the princess they trick Ogre into answering questions that solve perplexing problems near his castle thus improving life for others. Then Puss has the last laugh and a satisfying snack when he encourages the Ogre to demonstrate his shape-changing ability. This retelling of Perrault's classic was originally published in England in 2000. (26 pages)

Where it's reviewed:
Booklist, July 2001, page 2015
Bulletin of the Center for Children's Books, September 2001, page 32
Kirkus Reviews, July 15, 2001, page 1033
Publishers Weekly, June 25, 2001, page 72
School Library Journal, August 2001, page 172

Other books by the same author:
I Was a Rat!, 2000 (School Library Journal Best Books)
The Firework-Maker's Daughter, 1999 (Booklist Editor's Choice)
Count Karlstein, 1998

Other books you might like:
Paul Galdone, *Puss in Boots*, 1976
    A poor man's cat outwits an evil giant enabling the poor master to gain both fortune and the hand of a princess.
Charles Perrault, *Puss in Boots*, 1990
    In this translation of the French fairy tale illustrated by Marcellino a cat uses only a sack and a pair of boots to acquire wealth for its master.
Anne Rockwell, *Puss in Boots and Other Stories*, 1988
    The illustrated collection of twelve stories includes a re-telling of Puss in Boots.

729

SIMON PUTTOCK
ALISON JAY, Illustrator

A Ladder to the Stars
(New York: Henry Holt and Company, 2001)

Subject(s): Wishes; Old Age; Birthdays
Age range(s): Grades 1-4
Major character(s): Unnamed Character, 7-Year-Old; Unnamed Character, Aged Person
Time period(s): Indeterminate Past
Locale(s): Fictional Country

Summary: On her seventh birthday a little girl's wish on a star expresses her desire to climb into the sky and dance across it with the star. A little star hears the wish and consults with the moon, the sun, wind, clouds and the weather to send a special seed to earth that will grow tall enough to allow the wish to come true. One hundred years later when the tree's branches are tickling the sun as it passes the star goes to tell the little girl that her wish is fulfilled. Now celebrating her 107th birthday, the grown-up girl can't remember her wish and only with encouragement from the star does she climb the tree. Her wish made so long ago comes true and the old woman dances with the star for eternity. (32 pages)

Where it's reviewed:
Books for Keeps, May 2001, page 6
Horn Book Guide, Spring 2002, page 56
Magpies, July 2001, page 30
Publishers Weekly, October 8, 2001, page 64
School Library Journal, January 2002, page 108

Other books by the same author:
Squeaky Clean, 2002
A Story for Hippo: A Book About Loss, 2001
Here I Am! Said Smedley, 2001

Other books you might like:
Helen V. Griffith, *Dream Meadow*, 1994
    An elderly woman and her devoted dog who wish only to run freely through the meadow finally achieve their dream.
Shelley Jackson, *The Old Woman and the Wave*, 1998
    After many years of living fearfully beneath a curling wave an old woman learns to appreciate the gifts of friendship offered by the wave.
Minna Jung, *William's Ninth Life*, 1993
    For his ninth life William is offered many choices but he wishes to remain as the pet of his elderly companion Elizabeth.

Q

730

ROBERT QUACKENBUSH, Author/Illustrator

Batbaby Finds a Home

(New York: Random House, 2001)

Series: Step into Reading. Step 2
Subject(s): Animals/Bats; Nature; Environmental Problems
Age range(s): Grades 1-3
Major character(s): Batbaby, Bat, Son; Squirrel, Squirrel, Friend; Woodpecker, Woodpecker, Friend
Time period(s): 2000s
Locale(s): United States

Summary: At daybreak, just as Batbaby and his parents are settling into sleep in the eaves of their old barn home a bulldozer levels the structure and they hurriedly fly away in search of a new roosting spot. They find many places that look perfect at first but in which flaws soon become obvious. The church steeple is too loud when the bells ring, a house's cellar also contains a hungry cat, and a nearby house attic already has an occupant. Other places are equally problematic and Batbaby's family doesn't know where to turn. Batbaby seeks help from Squirrel and Woodpecker who show him a bat house on the side of a newly built home. Finally, they've found the perfect roosting spot! Factual information about bats appears in a concluding section entitled ''The Truth about Bats.'' (48 pages)

Where it's reviewed:
School Library Journal, February 2002, page 110

Other books by the same author:
Batbaby, 1997
Henry's Important Date, 1993
Evil Under the Sea: A Miss Mallard Mystery, 1992

Other books you might like:
Annie Cannon, *The Bat in the Boot*, 1996
  Two children find a baby bat in their father's boot, feed and care for it all day and wait for the mother bat to return for it after dark

Ann Earle, *Zipping, Zapping, Zooming Bats*, 1995
  A nonfiction title in the ''Let's-Read-and-Find-Out Science'' series describes the benefits of bats the environment.
Gail Gibbons, *Bats*, 1999
  Characteristics of different types of bats and suggestions for protecting them are included in this nonfiction title.
Ruth Horowitz, *Bat Time*, 1991
  As night falls, Leila and her father watch bats feeding on insects in their yard.

731

MARY QUATTLEBAUM

Grover C. Graham and Me

(New York: Delacorte, 2001)

Subject(s): Parent and Child; Foster Homes; Babies
Age range(s): Grades 4-7
Major character(s): Ben Watson, 11-Year-Old, Foster Child; Grover C. Graham, Baby, Foster Child; Tracey Graham, Mother (of Grover); Eileen Torgle, Foster Parent; Mr. Torgle ''Mr. T'', Foster Parent
Time period(s): 1990s
Locale(s): Greenfield, Virginia

Summary: Heading for his eighth foster home, Ben has learned to tune out everything and remain distant so that he won't become attached. But at the Torgles, there's always chaos and love as well as Grover, another abandoned child but one who's only fourteen-months-old. A bond develops between the two boys and soon Ben's reading Dr. Spock's manual to himself and *Hop on Pop* to Grover. All goes well until Grover's mother Tracey, a young girl who was overwhelmed by motherhood, begins making sporadic visits to see her son. Grover and Tracey become competitive over Grover as each view for Grover's attention. When Tracey leaves Grover alone one day, Ben instinctively runs away with him without thinking of how he'll feed or care for Grover. Caught, Ben reacts the only way he knows and arranges to leave the Torgles and go to a juvenile home, but gradually common sense takes over as he swallows his pride and asks the Torgles if he can remain with them. (179 pages)

Where it's reviewed:
Horn Book, January 2002, page 83
School Library Journal, October 2001, page 167

Other books you might like:
Patricia Calvert, *When Morning Comes*, 1989
Runaway Cat finally finds a home with foster mother Annie Bowen, a middle-aged, frumpy bee farmer whose heart is made of honey.
Julie Johnston, *Adam and Eve and Pinch-Me*, 1994
Though she's determined to remain detached from her new foster family, Sara's no match for the eccentric Huddleston family.
Hilma Wolitzer, *Toby Lived Here*, 1978
Toby and her younger sister have different adjustment problems when they're sent to a foster home.

732

MARY QUATTLEBAUM
TIM LADWIG, Illustrator

The Shine Man: A Christmas Story

(Grand Rapids, MI: Eerdmans Books for Young Readers, 2001)

Subject(s): Conduct of Life; Christmas; Depression (Economic)
Age range(s): Grades 1-4
Major character(s): Larry, Streetperson, Worker (shoeshine man); Boy, Child, Streetperson
Time period(s): 1930s (1932)
Locale(s): United States

Summary: Larry hops off a train in a large city and sets up his shoeshine stand hoping to make a little money before Christmas. Alas, times are hard and no one has a nickel to spare for a shoeshine. The only shoes that stop are old ones on the feet of Boy, a child lacking a hat or gloves to keep him warm. Boy is attracted to a ''spoolie'' doll that Larry's making, but instead of giving away his Christmas angel Larry gives Boy his hat. Each time Boy stops Larry gives away another item of clothing to make the child more comfortable and finally on Christmas Eve he gives Boy the ''spoolie'' and a shoeshine as a gift. A far greater gift awaits Larry, one given from one Shine Man to another. (32 pages)

Where it's reviewed:
Booklist, September 1, 2001, page 121
Horn Book Guide, Spring 2002, page 56
Publishers Weekly, September 24, 2001, page 53
School Library Journal, October 2001, page 68

Other books by the same author:
Aunt CeeCee, Aunt Belle, and Mama's Surprise, 1999
Underground Train, 1997
A Year on My Street, 1996

Other books you might like:
Sharon Chmielarz, *Down at Angel's*, 1994
Two sisters befriend an elderly, reclusive carpenter, give him a special homemade Christmas gift and receive one of his beautiful tables in return.
Katherine Paterson, *Angels and Other Strangers*, 1979
A collection of original short stories reflects on some of the mysteries of the Christmas season.
Susan Wojciechowski, *The Christmas Miracle of Jonathan Toomey*, 1995
A gifted woodcarver learns to listen carefully to the suggestions of a young boy as he strives to complete a nativity set.

R

733

ELSA OKON RAEL
MARYANN KOVALSKI, Illustrator

Rivka's First Thanksgiving

(New York: Margaret K. McElderry Books, 2001)

Subject(s): Holidays; Jews; Emigration and Immigration
Age range(s): Grades 1-3
Major character(s): Rivka Rabin, 9-Year-Old, Immigrant; Bubbeh, Grandmother, Immigrant; Yoshe Preminger, Religious (rabbi), Aged Person
Time period(s): 1910s
Locale(s): New York, New York (Lower East Side)

Summary: Based on her teacher's description of Thanksgiving, Rivka thinks the American holiday is perfect for an immigrant family such as hers. Bubbeh is doubtful that it is appropriate for Jews and seeks the counsel of Rabbi Preminger. Being unfamiliar with the holiday, Rabbi Preminger interviews Rivka and, after consideration, decides that Thanksgiving is not for Jews. Rivka writes a letter to Rabbi Preminger explaining the similarities, as she sees them, between the pilgrims search for religious freedom in this new land and the reasons that Jewish immigrants have come to America. Rivka's reasoning when she compares Thanksgiving with the Jewish seder convinces the rabbi that perhaps this American tradition is also suitable for Jewish immigrants in America and Rivka celebrates her first Thanksgiving. (32 pages)

Where it's reviewed:
Booklist, September 15, 2001, page 236
Bulletin of the Center for Children's Books, November 2001, page 113
Publishers Weekly, September 24, 2001, page 46
School Library Journal, November 2001, page 133

Awards the book has won:
Sydney Taylor Book Award for Younger Readers, 2002
Notable Social Studies Trade Books for Young People, 2002

Other books by the same author:
When Zaydeh Dances on Eldridge Street, 1997
What Zeesie Saw on Delancey Street, 1996 (ALA Notable Children's Book)
Marushka's Egg, 1993

Other books you might like:
Barbara Cohen, *Molly's Pilgrim*, 1990
    Molly, a Russian Jewish immigrant, celebrates Thanksgiving for the first time.
Gail Gibbons, *Thanksgiving Day*, 1983
    Simple text explains both the first Thanksgiving and the way we now celebrate the holiday.
Marion Hess Pomeranc, *The Can-Do Thanksgiving*, 1998
    Thanksgiving is especially meaningful for Dee this year when she helps a church feed the needy.
Michael J. Rosen, *A Thanksgiving Wish*, 1999
    Recreating the Thanksgiving dinner that recently deceased Bubbe traditionally cooked blows all the fuses and makes the meal a neighborhood effort.

734

GLORIA RAND
TED RAND, Illustrator

Sailing Home: A Story of a Childhood at Sea

(New York: North-South Books, 2001)

Subject(s): Historical; Sea Stories; Family
Age range(s): Grades 2-5
Major character(s): Matilda Madsen, Sister (oldest), Narrator; Albert Madsen, Brother, Son; Mads Albert Madsen, Father, Sea Captain
Time period(s): 1890s; 1900s (1896-1910)
Locale(s): *John Ena*, At Sea

Summary: Matilda, the oldest of four children relates the tale of her family's life at sea in a fictionalized account of the Madsen family. Captain Madsen plies the seas hauling cargo in the *John Ena*, a four-masted bark. Matilda tells of the family's many and unique pets gathered from their travels around the world and of the animals her mother keeps in order to supplement their diet with eggs and fresh meat. A governess lives aboard to teach the three older children their lessons, an activity that Albert avoids by hiding on the ship until Captain Madsen finds him. The development of the faster but less spacious steamship ends the family's opportunity to travel together. (32 pages)

Where it's reviewed:
Booklist, November 1, 2001, page 479
Bulletin of the Center for Children's Books, October 2001, page 71
Publishers Weekly, September 10, 2001, page 93
School Library Journal, October 2001, page 129
Smithsonian, November 2001, page 124

Awards the book has won:
Smithsonian's Notable Books for Children, 2001
Notable Social Studies Trade Books for Young People, 2002

Other books by the same author:
A Home for Spooky, 1998
Baby in a Basket, 1997
Aloha, Salty!, 1996

Other books you might like:
Richard Berleth, *Mary Patten's Voyage*, 1994
    When the ship's captain falls ill, his pregnant wife takes command and brings the clipper ship safely to port.
Loretta Krupinski, *Bluewater Journal: The Voyage of the Sea Tiger*, 1995
    Benjamin Slocum records the daily events of the voyage on his father's clipper ship from Boston to the Sandwich Islands.
Kathryn Lasky, *Born in the Breezes: The Seafaring Life of Joshua Slocum*, 2001
    In the late 19th century Joshua Slocum, sea captain, and his wife raise their children aboard his sailing vessels.

735

MARIE RAPHAEL

Streets of Gold

(New York: Persea Books, 2001)

Subject(s): Emigration and Immigration; Historical
Age range(s): Grades 7-10
Major character(s): Marisia Bolinski, 15-Year-Old; Stefan Bolinski, Brother; Sofia Cybulski, 16-Year-Old
Time period(s): 1900s (1901)
Locale(s): Poland; New York, New York

Summary: The Russian soldiers club Marisia's brother Stefan and take him away to join the army, but several months later he runs away and returns home. Hiding Stefan in the hay during the day isn't a way to live, either, so the family secretly leaves their home and travels to America to start a new life. On board ship, Marisia befriends Sofia, which is to prove fortuitous when the Bolinski parents return to Germany after denied admittance to Ellis Island when their youngest daughter is found to have tuberculosis. Marisia finds life in America is harder than she thought, but she works for Sofia's family and at least has a place to live, nurses Stefan when he's

injured on the job, and is determined to continue her drawing in this first novel. (215 pages)

Where it's reviewed:
Kliatt, July 2001, page 21
Voice of Youth Advocates, October 2001, page 283

Other books you might like:
Judie Angell, *One-Way to Ansonia*, 1985
    For 1890s immigrant Rose Olshansky, the only way to achieve her dream is to attend night school after working all day in a factory.
Susan Campbell Bartoletti, *A Coal Miner's Bride: The Diary of Anetka Kaminska*, 2000
    When Anetka and her brother Josef travel to America from Poland, so does Private Nasevich who saved her from the attentions of a Russian sergeant.
Karen Hesse, *Letters from Rifka*, 1992
    Rifka's ringworm prevents her admission to America.
Joan Lowery Nixon, *Land of Hope*, 1992
    Rebekah and her family flee the Russian pograms for America, but once in New York City find the streets are not "paved with gold."

736

CHRIS RASCHKA, Author/Illustrator

Little Tree

(New York: Hyperion Books for Children, 2001)

Subject(s): Trees; Christmas; Poetry
Age range(s): Grades K-3
Time period(s): Indeterminate
Locale(s): Fictional Country

Summary: The poem "little tree" by e. e. cummings provides both the introduction and the inspiration for the story of a little tree fulfilling its dream of being a Christmas tree. After traveling by truck and train to a big city the little tree waits in a Christmas tree lot until a family chooses it. A cab ride and lift in an elevator bring the little tree to the family's apartment where lights and ornaments wait to be placed on the tree's branches making the little tree's wish complete. (24 pages)

Where it's reviewed:
Bulletin of the Center for Children's Books, November 2001, page 114
Horn Book Guide, Spring 2002, page 173
Publishers Weekly, September 24, 2001, page 49
School Library Journal, October 2001, page 63

Other books by the same author:
Table Manners, 2001 (Vladimir Radunsky, co-author)
Waffle, 2001
Ring! Yo?, 2000
Like Likes Like, 1999

Other books you might like:
Michael Cutting, *The Little Crooked Christmas Tree*, 1990
    Because a tree shelters a dove it grows crookedly and cannot be chosen to be a Christmas tree although it has the true spirit of the season.
Satomi Ichikawa, *What the Little Fir Tree Wore to the Christmas Party*, 2001
    Initially disappointed not to go to the "party" that's been

the topic of conversation on the tree farm a fir tree is satisfied by snow-covered branches.

Dav Pilkey, *Dragon's Merry Christmas*, 1991
  Dragon finds a tree that is absolutely perfect for his Christmas tree, so perfect in fact that he refuses to chop it down.

CHRIS RASCHKA, Author/Illustrator
VLADIMIR RADUNSKY, Illustrator

Table Manners
(Cambridge, MA: Candlewick Press, 2001)

Subject(s): Human Behavior; Cultures and Customs; Humor
Age range(s): Grades 1-4
Major character(s): Chester, Friend; Dudunya, Friend
Time period(s): Indeterminate
Locale(s): Fictional Country

Summary: Chester thinks Dudunya eats like a pig and begins instruction in proper table manners including the use of utensils and napkins. Dudunya needs to know the rationale for plates, glasses, napkins and utensils and Chester is only too happy to offer illustrated explanations. Chester also expounds on the virtue of chewing one's food, the consequences for not doing so and the accidents that can occur if one speaks with one's mouth full. At the final exam, a meal in a restaurant, Dudunya figures out that the way to conclude the meal successfully is to not eat. (26 pages)

Where it's reviewed:
Booklist, January 1, 2002, page 867
Bulletin of the Center for Children's Books, December 2001, page 150
Horn Book Guide, Spring 2002, page 56
Publishers Weekly, October 29, 2001, page 62
School Library Journal, November 2001, page 134

Other books you might like:
Caralyn Buehner, *It's a Spoon Not a Shovel*, 1995
  Animal characters in a variety of situations provide a humorous introduction to proper social behavior.
Cheryl Chapman, *Pass the Fritters, Critters*, 1993
  Animals learn the magic of the word "please" in a rhyming story about table manners.
Seslye Joslin, *What Do You Do, Dear?*, 1958
  An illustrated nonfiction title gives etiquette advice in a companion title to *What Do You Say, Dear?*.
Harriet Ziefert, *Someday We'll Have Very Good Manners*, 2001
  Siblings are aware of the behavior expected of them when they grow up but the illustrations show the reality of their present behavior.

SILVER RAVENWOLF

Witches' Key to Terror
(St. Paul, MN: Llewellyn Publications, 2001)

Series: Witches' Chillers

Subject(s): Witches and Witchcraft; Mystery and Detective Stories
Age range(s): Grades 9-12
Major character(s): Bethany Salem, 10th Grader, Witch; Cricket Bindart, 16-Year-Old, Twin; Tad Bindart, 16-Year-Old, Twin
Time period(s): 2000s
Locale(s): Cedar Crest, New York

Summary: Cricket's tired of covering for her brother Tad who's supposed to work in the orchard with her, but evidently is sneaking out to date some of the local girls. Their strict father won't be happy if he finds out Cricket is falling behind in her studies because she's pulling double duty. Being homeschooled, Cricket and Tad don't have a wide circle of friends, so when they find dead rabbits left in their mailbox, accompanied by threatening notes, Cricket turns to a group she's read about in the newspaper—the Cedar Crest witches. Contacting Bethany about a missing migrant worker, the dead rabbits and a poisoned apple, Cricket watches as the coven casts spells and uses its psychic ability to determine what's going on at Bindart Orchard. (264 pages)

Where it's reviewed:
School Library Journal, October 2001, page 168

Other books by the same author:
Beneath a Mountain Moon, 2002
Witches' Night of Fear, 2001 (Witches' Chillers)
Murder at Witches Bluff: A Novel of Suspense and Magic, 2000
Witches' Night Out, 2000 (Witches' Chillers)

Other books you might like:
Isobel Bird, *Circle of Three Series*, 2001-
  Kate, Cooper and Annie become interested in witchcraft and progress from casting a simple love spell on a boy at their school to learning more about Wiccan history and ceremonies.
Lynne Ewing, *Into the Cold Fire*, 2000
  The Daughters of the Moon is formed when four friends discover they have unusual powers, which range from invisibility to time travel to premonitions.
Jean Thesman, *The Other Ones*, 1999
  Bridget finally acknowledges her powers when she helps a friend shape shift to falcon form so she can escape from her human body.

CELIA REES

Witch Child
(Cambridge, MA: Candlewick Press, 2001)

Subject(s): Witches and Witchcraft; Diaries; Puritans
Age range(s): Grades 6-10
Major character(s): Mary Newbury, Witch; Jaybird, Indian
Time period(s): 17th century
Locale(s): Beulah, Massachusetts

Summary: When her grandmother is accused of being a witch, Mary watches as her only family member she knows is tortured and then executed. A benevolent stranger whisks Mary away and sends her to America, masquerading as a Puritan, where she accompanies the group to the wilderness settlement of Beulah and tries to live by their rules. Frequenting the forested area to find herbs needed for healing, Mary meets and befriends Jaybird, grandson of an Indian shaman. Their friendship, coupled with her healing talents, makes the community suspicious that she is a witch, an emissary of the devil. When a formal accusation is made, Mary's diary ends abruptly as she heads to the wilderness with boy's clothing, food, a blanket and moccasins in this book that has a sequel in the works. (261 pages)

Where it's reviewed:
Booklist, October 15, 2001, page 389
Bulletin of the Center for Children's Books, July 2001, page 421
Publishers Weekly, June 25, 2001, page 73
School Library Journal, August 2001, page 188
Voice of Youth Advocates, October 2001, page 284

Awards the book has won:
ALA Best Books for Young Adults, 2002

Other books by the same author:
Sorceress, 2002
The Truth Out There, 2000
Blood Sinister, 1999

Other books you might like:
Gilbert B. Cross, *A Witch Across Time*, 1990
When Hannah visits her elderly aunt's New England home, she is used as a medium by a young girl hanged for witchcraft three hundred years earlier.
Kathryn Lasky, *Beyond the Burning Time*, 1995
Young Mary struggles to rescue her mother from hanging as a witch, all part of the hysteria surrounding the Salem witch trials.
Ann Rinaldi, *A Break with Charity: A Story about the Salem Witch Trials*, 1992
Susannah English relates her horror when she realizes the outcome of the "game" of witchcraft played by some girls in her village.
Elizabeth Spears, *The Witch of Blackbird Pond*, 1958
Orphaned in Barbados, Kit finds she is ill-equipped to fit into the Puritan society of New England where she now lives with her relatives.

740

KATHRYN REISS

Riddle of the Prairie Bride
(Middleton, WI: Pleasant Company/American Girl, 2001)

Series: History Mysteries
Subject(s): Frontier and Pioneer Life; Mail Order Brides; Mystery and Detective Stories
Age range(s): Grades 5-7
Major character(s): Caroline/Lucy Fairchild/Dotson, Mail Order Bride; Ida Kate Deming, 12-Year-Old; Henry Clay Deming, Father, Farmer; Henry Fairchild, Baby
Time period(s): 1870s (1878)
Locale(s): Hays City, Kansas

Summary: Ida Kate can hardly wait for the arrival of the train bearing her father's mail-order bride and her young son,

partly for some relief from the chores Ida Kate has inherited since her mother died two years ago. Caroline and her son Hanky settle in but something's not right about this woman. Her hair's the wrong color, she's short rather than tall and she's not allergic to the cat. After a little snooping, Ida Kate's afraid this woman is an imposter, perhaps even a murderess, in this tale set on the Kansas prairie. (162 pages)

Where it's reviewed:
Booklist, April 1, 2001, page 1484
School Library Journal, May 2001, page 158

Other books by the same author:
Paint by Magic: A Time Travel Mystery, 2002
The Strange Case of Baby H, 2002 (History Mysteries)
Paperquake, 1998
Pale Phoenix, 1994
Time Windows, 1991

Other books you might like:
Frances Arrington, *Bluestem*, 2000
Depressed from living on the prairie and losing babies in two successive winters, Polly and Jessie's mother walks out of their home one day and never returns.
Patricia MacLachlan, *Sarah, Plain and Tall*, 1986
Caleb and Anna are entranced by the mail-order bride from Maine who travels West to be a new mother for them.
Ann Turner, *Third Girl from the Left*, 1986
Young, adventuresome Sary answers an ad for a mail-order bride and winds up in Montana married to a sixty-year-old rancher.

741

J.J. RENEAUX
JAMES RANSOME, Illustrator

How Animals Saved the People: Animal Tales from the South
(New York: HarperCollins Publishers, 2001)

Subject(s): Folklore; Folk Tales; Animals
Age range(s): Grades 4-7
Time period(s): Indeterminate Past
Locale(s): South

Summary: Eight tales from the oral traditions of six different cultures settled in the South are retold by the late author. Native American stories include "How Bear People Lost Fire" and the title story "How Animals Saved the People." From Appalachia comes "The Golly Whumper" while a mixture of European settlers in the Deep South told variations of the monster tale "The Poopampareno." African American traditions give us the pourquoi tale "How Miz Gator Lost Her Pea-Green Suit" and the haunted house tale "Waiting for BooZoo." Derived from the Cajun tradition is the retelling entitled "Buzzard and Hawk" while "Bouki and Lapin Divide the Crops" has Creole roots. A glossary, source notes and bibliography conclude the collection. (64 pages)

Where it's reviewed:
Booklist, February 15, 2001, page 1136
Bulletin of the Center for Children's Books, March 2001, page 276
Horn Book, March 2001, page 220

Publishers Weekly, December 18, 2000, page 77
School Library Journal, January 2001, page 122

Awards the book has won:
IRA Children's Choices, 2002
Notable Social Studies Trade Books for Young People, 2002

Other books by the same author:
Why Alligator Hates Dog: A Cajun Folktale, 1995
Haunted Bayou and Other Cajun Ghost Stories, 1994
Cajun Folktales, 1992

Other books you might like:
Virginia Hamilton, *A Ring of Tricksters: Animal Tales from America, the West Indies, and Africa*, 1997
Eleven tales grouped by geographic area of origin and united by the trickster theme include the familiar Anasi and the less well-known Cunnie Rabbit.
Neil Philip, *Stockings of Buttermilk: American Folktales*, 1999
Sixteen tales from the European tradition are retold as they evolved after reaching America's shores.
Robert D. San Souci, *Cut from the Same Cloth: American Women of Myth, Legend and Tall Tale*, 1993
The illustrated collection of twenty tales is drawn from folk tales, ballads and popular stories.

742

LOUISE RENNISON

On the Bright Side, I'm Now the Girlfriend of a Sex God: Further Confessions of Georgia Nicolson

(New York: HarperCollins, 2001)

Subject(s): Dating (Social Customs); Humor; Diaries
Age range(s): Grades 7-10
Major character(s): Georgia Nicolson, 14-Year-Old; Angus, Cat; Robbie "Sex God", 17-Year-Old; Libby Nicolson, Sister (of Georgia), Child
Time period(s): 2000s
Locale(s): England

Summary: Georgia's back and this time her diary entries reveal her fear of moving to New Zealand, or "Kiwi-a-gogo land" as she calls it, where her father is now working. This transfer couldn't come at a worse time for Georgia's finally hooked Robbie, better known as the Sex God, "SG" for short. This on top of her other trials, such as pimples, a sister who likes to suck on Georgia's nose, the increasing size of that nose, and her still crazy, half Scottish wildcat Angus. But then tragedy strikes when SG decides Georgia's too young for him and suggests another mate for her. Georgia takes that information and uses it to lure SG back to her in this non-stop craziness of a sequel to *Angus, Thongs, and Full-Frontal Snogging*. (243 pages)

Where it's reviewed:
Book Report, November 2001, page 65
Booklist, May 15, 2001, page 1751
Publishers Weekly, February 26, 2001, page 87
School Library Journal, May 2001, page 159
Voice of Youth Advocates, June 2001, page 128

Awards the book has won:
ALA Quick Picks for Reluctant Young Adult Readers, 2002

Other books by the same author:
Knocked Out by My Nunga-Nungas: Further, Further Confessions of Georgia Nicolson, 2002
Angus, Thongs and Full-Frontal Snogging: Confessions of Georgia Nicolson, 2000

Other books you might like:
Thom Eberhardt, *Rat Boys: A Dating Experiment*, 2001
Marci and Summer lie about dates for the Spring Fling dance, but with the help of a magic ring, rats are transformed into "hot" dates!
Scarlett Macdougal, *Have a Nice Life Series*, 2001-
Four girls, shown their not-too-pretty karmic destinies by an intergalactic angel, have a chance to change their behavior.
Rosie Rushton, *Just Don't Make a Scene, Mum*, 1999
In this first of a series, five British teens find their lives connected through a radio show that lets them describe embarrassing moments.
Ellen Wittlinger, *Razzle*, 2001
Kenyon almost gives up tall and independent Razzle for a self-centered sexpot who throws him aside when he can't help her with a modeling career.

743

MARILYN REYNOLDS

Love Rules

(Buena Park, CA: Morning Glory Press, 2001)

Series: True-to-Life Series from Hamilton High
Subject(s): Prejudice; Sports/Football; Homosexuality/Lesbianism
Age range(s): Grades 9-12
Major character(s): Lynn Wright, 17-Year-Old, 12th Grader; Katherine "Kit" Dandridge, 12th Grader; Conan, 12th Grader, Football Player
Time period(s): 2000s
Locale(s): Hamilton Heights, California

Summary: Lynn's senior year becomes extremely complicated when she's caught up in the prejudices and biases felt by her best friend and her boyfriend. Lynn and Kit have been friends since they were eleven and Lynn will stand by her no matter what, even when Kit comes out of the closet and reveals her lesbianism. Lynn loves her friend but finds it difficult to see Kit suffer the verbal and physical abuse heaped on her. Some of the most homophobic members of their school are the guys on the football team and Lynn has just started dating one of them, Conan who's African American. When she receives criticism from some students for dating him, she better understands the prejudice both Conan and Kit face every day. Then Kit is attacked and injured by some members of the football team but the principal looks the other way because of the upcoming playoffs; only a lawsuit forces disciplinary action in this chilling look at the high schools of today. (270 pages)

Where it's reviewed:
Book, September 2001, page 91
Booklist, August 2001, page 2107

Kliatt, July 2001, page 12
School Library Journal, September 2001, page 232
Voice of Youth Advocates, October 2001, page 284

Other books by the same author:
If You Loved Me, 1999 (True-to-Life Series from Hamilton High)
Baby Help, 1997 (True-to-Life Series from Hamilton High)
But What About Me?, 1996 (True-to-Life Series from Hamilton High)
Telling, 1996 (True-to-Life Series from Hamilton High)

Other books you might like:
Chris Crutcher, *Whale Talk*, 2001
The special privileges accorded to athletes, especially those on the football and basketball team, are what has kept talented TJ from playing sports at his high school.
Sharon M. Draper, *Romiette and Julio*, 1999
African American Romiette and Hispanic Julio date and anticipate problems from their parents, but are unprepared for the response of a local gang.
Nancy Garden, *Lark in the Morning*, 1991
Gillian's concerned when the family's tool shed is burglarized as it contains her diary with thoughts about her lesbianism.
Alex Sanchez, *Rainbow Boys*, 2001
Jason, Kyle and Nelson face their senior year, and life-changing decisions, as they deal with their sexual identity.
Laura Torres, *November Ever After*, 1999
At first Amy is disturbed that her best friend Sara has a lesbian relationship with Anita, but eventually realizes that Sara will always be her best friend.
Ellen Wittlinger, *Hard Love*, 1999
John thinks he's found the love for which he's been searching when he meets Marisol, only to discover she's in love with another girl.

744

DAVID RICE

Crazy Loco
(New York: Dial, 2001)

Subject(s): Short Stories; Mexican Americans
Age range(s): Grades 7-12
Locale(s): Texas

Summary: Based on stories from the author's life, this collection of nine shares daily events of Mexican American families living in the Rio Grande Valley in South Texas. When the "California Cousins" come to visit, their Texas cousins are ready with booby-trapped outhouses. Though Harry complains about his grandfather when the family lives together, it's "Papa Lalo" who buys him a tuxedo to wear to the *quinceanera* parties. Pedro is taught to be an altar boy by Father Bob's two current altar boys who more closely resemble bodyguards in "Last Mass." Other stories describe the "Crazy Loco" dog that liked to sit behind the wheel or the chance a young girl receives for an education in "She Flies" in a spirited collection. (135 pages)

Where it's reviewed:
Booklist, May 15, 2001, page 1747

Bulletin of the Center for Children's Books, September 2001, page 32
Horn Book, September 2001, page 592
School Library Journal, June 2001, page 154
Voice of Youth Advocates, June 2001, page 128

Awards the book has won:
ALA Best Books for Young Adults, 2002

Other books you might like:
Rudolfo A. Anaya, *My Land Sings: Stories from the Rio Grande*, 1999
Original stories are combined with folkloric retellings that continue the tradition of Mexican and Native American folklore.
Lori M. Carlson, *Where Angels Glide at Dawn: New Stories from Latin America*, 1990
The flavor of Latin American culture is captured in this unique collection of stories that have been translated into English.
Victor Martinez, *Parrot in the Oven: Mi Vida*, 1996
Mexican American teen Manny and his family fight to stay together and make a success of their lives in America.
Carolyn Meyer, *Rio Grande Stories*, 1994
Seventh graders at Rio Grande Junior High School write their own stories to assemble into a book for a school fundraiser.

745

JAMES RICE, Author/Illustrator

Victor Lopez at the Alamo
(Gretna, LA: Pelican Publishing Co., 2001)

Subject(s): War; Coming-of-Age
Age range(s): Grades 5-8
Major character(s): Victor Lopez, 14-Year-Old; General Santa Anna, Historical Figure, Military Personnel; John Daugherty, Rancher
Time period(s): 1830s
Locale(s): Mexico; Texas

Summary: Helping his mother and uncle beside their little house in Mexico, Victor can't believe all the soldiers he sees walk past, but his interest is misinterpreted by two soldiers who are conscripting all boys of suitable age. Though his mother tells the soldier that Victor is fourteen and too young to fight, she is finally convinced otherwise, with the aid of a few coins, and Victor becomes part of the Mexican army. Generalissimo Santa Anna plans to take his army north to Texas to take care of the rebellious Tejanos and Victor, unhappily, marches along to battles at the Alamo and at Goliad. Luckily, at the battle of San Jacinto, a friendly Texan named John not only saves him but also offers him a job on his cattle ranch, which Victor happily accepts. (125 pages)

Where it's reviewed:
School Library Journal, December 2001, page 142

Other books you might like:
Avi, *The Fighting Ground*, 1984
In 1778 13-year-old Jonathan goes to war, returning home the next day but not before witnessing fear, horror, pain and death.

Sherry Garland, *In the Shadow of the Alamo*, 2001
Conscripted into the Mexican Army, Lorenzo marches with Santa Anna to the Alamo where he learns that some privates are more heroic than generals.

D. Anne Love, *I Remember the Alamo*, 1999
Jessie is upset when she finds out her family plans to move from Kentucky to Mexican Texas to help fight for Texas's independence.

G. Clifton Wisler, *All for Texas: A Story of Texas Liberation*, 2000
Drawn to Texas because of the promise of land in exchange for helping fight the Mexicans, Jeff and his mother prove to be hardy settlers.

746

GEORGE C. RICHARDSON
DIANNA BURNS, Illustrator

Drummer
(San Jose, CA: Writer's Showcase, 2001)

Subject(s): Civil War; African Americans
Age range(s): Grades 6-9
Major character(s): Johnny Jackson, Slave, Runaway; Jacob Smith, 13-Year-Old, Military Personnel (drummer boy); Major Harrell, Military Personnel
Time period(s): 1860s
Locale(s): Frederick, Maryland; Philadelphia, Pennsylvania; Baltimore, Maryland

Summary: When a chance to escape arises, young slave Johnny takes it and flees from his Confederate officer master to a Union camp five miles north. Major Harrell allows him to stay and Jacob, the white drummer boy, is excited to have a companion who wants to learn how to drum. Johnny wants to join the Union army, but Major Harrell's unit already has a drummer boy, but when told of an all-colored unit forming near Philadelphia, he's eager to join them. Finding this unit could be a problem as there are bounty hunters and Confederate soldiers eager to grab Johnny and return him to his master to collect the reward. With help from friends of Major Harrell, Johnny manages to elude a bounty hunter and make his way to the First Pennsylvania Colored infantry, Company A. (82 pages)

Where it's reviewed:
School Library Journal, December 2001, page 143

Other books you might like:
Sandra Forrester, *Sound the Jubilee*, 1995
Slaves Maddie and her parents escape when the Union Army is nearby, but Maddie discovers that some Yankee soldier are as racist as Confederate ones.

Mary Downing Hahn, *Promises to the Dead*, 2000
Jesse promises a dying, runaway slave that he'll accompany her light-skinned son to Baltimore, though a slave catcher tracks their every move.

G. Clifton Wisler, *Red Cap*, 1991
Young Union drummer Ransom J. Powell, who lies about his age to join the army, is one of the few to survive the rigors of Andersonville Prison.

747

TOHBY RIDDLE, Author/Illustrator

The Singing Hat
(New York: Farrar Straus Giroux, 2001)

Subject(s): Animals/Birds; Fathers and Daughters; Animals, Treatment of
Age range(s): Grades K-3
Major character(s): Colin Jenkins, Businessman, Single Father; Unnamed Character, Daughter
Time period(s): 2000s (2000)
Locale(s): Australia

Summary: A simple nap under a tree complicates Colin's life in ways he never anticipated. While Colin sleeps a bird builds a nest on his head. He's reluctant to dislodge it and his daughter wants him to keep it but others are not as understanding. Colin loses friends, a job and his home because of the bird's nest. He returns to the tree thinking he can place the nest, now with two birds, there but the branches are taken. Just as a stranger remarks about the rarity of the birds they take flight and soar away. Free to remove the nest, Colin places it near a window where, from time to time, odd objects appear. First published in Australia in 2000. (32 pages)

Where it's reviewed:
Booklist, February 15, 2001, page 1141
Horn Book Guide, Fall 2001, page 271
Kirkus Reviews, February 1, 2001, page 187
Publishers Weekly, February 19, 2001, page 89
School Library Journal, July 2001, page 87

Other books by the same author:
The Great Escape from City Zoo, 1999
A Most Unusual Dog, 1994
Careful With That Ball, Eugene!, 1991

Other books you might like:
Harriet Lerner, *Franny B. Kranny, There's a Bird in Your Hair!*, 2001
For a brief time Franny loves the attention of having a bird's nest in her frizzy hair but soon she cuts off her topknot/nest to put in a tree.

Donna Jo Napoli, *Albert*, 2001
Reclusive Albert becomes more outgoing in order to accommodate the needs of a pair of birds that build a nest on his hand.

Katherine Paterson, *Marvin's Best Christmas Present Ever*, 1997
When birds nest in the Christmas wreath Marvin makes for his family it's left hanging until the eggs hatch.

748

ANN RINALDI

The Education of Mary: A Little Miss of Color
(New York: Jump at the Sun/Hyperion, 2000)

Subject(s): Race Relations; Prejudice; Schools/Boarding Schools
Age range(s): Grades 6-8

Major character(s): Mary Harris, 13-Year-Old; Sarah Harris, 18-Year-Old; Prudence Crandall, Quaker
Time period(s): 19th century (1832)
Locale(s): Canterbury, Connecticut
Summary: Mary differs from her older sister Sarah, for she is content to receive secret schooling from Miss Crandall in return for duties as a servant, whereas Sarah wants to be the first black student enrolled at Miss Crandall's school. Miss Crandall, who's a Quaker, runs the Canterbury Female Seminary in Connecticut, a school for young white girls from wealthy families. When challenged about her policy of enrolling only white girls, especially since Quakers espouses equality, Miss Crandall closes down and reopens the school to black girls. Sarah and several other students are swept up in the abolitionist movement, but Miss Crandall claims she is interested only in education. Mary views some of this discourse a little suspiciously, but is happy to make her mark as part of the Underground Railroad in this work based on historical fact. (254 pages)

Where it's reviewed:
Book Report, March 2001, page 62
Bulletin of the Center for Children's Books, January 2001, page 194
School Library Journal, January 2001, page 134
Voice of Youth Advocates, February 2001, page 426

Other books by the same author:
Millicent's Gift, 2002
Numbering All the Bones, 2002
Girl in Blue, 2001
The Staircase, 2000 (Great Episodes)
Amelia's War, 1999

Other books you might like:
Mary E. Lyons, *Letters from a Slave Girl: The Story of Harriet Jacobs*, 1992
   After seven years spent hiding in her grandmother's small storeroom, Harriet eventually escapes along the Underground Railroad.
Robert Nordan, *The Secret Road*, 2001
   Spending the summer with her Quaker aunt and uncle, Laura helps a slave escape to freedom via the Underground Railroad.
Gary Paulsen, *Nightjohn*, 1993
   Nightjohn risks his life to teach his fellow slaves to read.

ANN RINALDI

Girl in Blue
(New York: Scholastic, 2001)

Subject(s): Civil War; Spies; Identity, Concealed
Age range(s): Grades 7-10
Major character(s): Sarah Louisa/Neddy Wheelock/Compton, Military Personnel, Spy; Allan Pinkerton, Historical Figure; Lieutenant Sheldon, Military Personnel; Rose Greenhow, Spy
Time period(s): 1860s
Locale(s): Casey's Mill, Michigan; Washington, District of Columbia

Summary: Tired of her father's abuse and unwilling to marry the widower to whom she's been promised, Sarah leaves home disguised as a boy and joins the Union Army as Neddy Compton. At first she helps at the hospital in Washington, but later the Second Michigan is sent to fight at the Battle of Bull Run in Manassas. Sarah kills a man before her identity is accidentally revealed and she's forced to leave the army. Introduced to Allan Pinkerton, she's offered a job. Sarah becomes a spy in the home of Rose Greenhow, a Confederate sympathizer, and figures out Rose's method of sending messages in her intricate tapestries. She also loses her heart to Lt. Sheldon, one of Rose Greenhow's guards, though Sarah's unsure of his loyalties to the Union. In this piece of historical fiction by a prolific author, Rinaldi's character Sarah is based on the life of Sarah Emma Edmonds. (310 pages)

Where it's reviewed:
Booklist, April 1, 2001, page 1484
Bulletin of the Center for Children's Books, June 2001, page 384
Publishers Weekly, March 19, 2001, page 100
School Library Journal, March 2001, page 256
Voice of Youth Advocates, April 2001, page 46

Other books by the same author:
Millicent's Gift, 2002
The Journal of Jasper Jonathan Pierce: A Pilgrim Boy, 2000 (My Name Is America)
The Staircase, 2000
Amelia's War, 1999
The Coffin Quilt: The Feud between the Hatfields and the McCoys, 1999

Other books you might like:
Kathleen Ernst, *The Night Riders of Harper's Ferry*, 1997
   The Union soldiers think Mahalia's twin brother is a member of the Confederate Army; they don't realize it's Mahalia in disguise.
Mary E. Lyons, *Dear Ellen Bee: A Civil War Scrapbook of Two Union Spies*, 2000
   Miss Bet arranges for Liza, the daughter of her freed slaves, to work for Jefferson Davis where she can spy and send Miss Bet the information.
Carroll Thomas, *Matty's War*, 1999
   Matty attends Hartford Female Seminary with her cousin Neely, but it's just a cover until she can leave to enlist in the Union Army.
Florida Ann Town, *With a Silent Companion*, 2000
   With no men left to support Margaret and her mother, she disguises herself as a man to seek entry into medical school.

KAREN RIVERS

Waiting to Dive
(Custer, WA: Orca Book Publishers, 2001)

Subject(s): Stepfamilies; Friendship; Diving
Age range(s): Grades 4-6
Major character(s): Carly, 10-Year-Old, Friend; Montana, Friend, Diver; Samantha, Friend, Diver
Time period(s): 2000s (2000)

Locale(s): Victoria, British Columbia, Canada

Summary: Carly and her best friend Montana meet Samantha in the diving class they're taking during summer vacation. Carly invites Montana and Samantha on a weekend visit to the family's remote cabin when her stepsiblings are with their mother. A fun-filled day of exploring tidal pools, building sandcastles and diving from a rock after the tide comes in ends tragically when Montana dives too deeply and breaks her back. Carly's depression over Montana's injury affects her confidence with her diving lessons. Gradually, both girls recover. (105 pages)

Where it's reviewed:
Booklist, March 1, 2001, page 1281
Bulletin of the Center for Children's Books, April 2001, page 313
Resource Links, February 2001, page 18
School Library Journal, May 2001, page 159

Other books you might like:
David A. Adler, *Andy and Tamika*, 1999
    While Tamika's parents recover from an automobile accident she lives with her friend Andy's family.
Sally Warner, *Sort of Forever*, 1998
    Nana's diagnosis of leukemia makes Cady wonder how long the best friends will be together.
Gina Willner-Pardo, *Jumping into Nothing*, 1999
    Sophie's fear of the high dive at the community pool threatens her friendship with Annaliese.

BETHANY ROBERTS
DOUG CUSHMAN, Illustrator

Thanksgiving Mice!
(New York: Clarion Books, 2001)

Subject(s): Animals/Mice; Holidays; Stories in Rhyme
Age range(s): Preschool-Grade 1
Time period(s): Indeterminate
Locale(s): Fictional Country

Summary: A group of mice put on a play representing the story of the original pilgrims. From the long sea voyage to the harsh living conditions of the first winter in this new land the mice imaginatively portray the historical events. The play concludes with the first feast giving thanks for a bountiful harvest as the appreciative audience joins the performers in dining on the props. (32 pages)

Where it's reviewed:
Booklist, September 1, 2001, page 121
Horn Book Guide, Spring 2002, page 26
School Library Journal, September 2001, page 204

Other books by the same author:
Christmas Mice!, 2000
Valentine Mice!, 1998
Halloween Mice!, 1995

Other books you might like:
Alice Dalgleish, *The Thanksgiving Story*, 1954
    The struggle for survival in their new home is shown

through the experience of one Pilgrim family in this Caldecott Honor Book.
Steven Kroll, *Oh, What a Thanksgiving!*, 1988
    While waiting to celebrate his family's meal David imagines what it must have been like to be at the first Thanksgiving.
Abby Levine, *This Is The Turkey*, 2000
    In a rhyming story a boy describes the Thanksgiving meal that he shares with his extended family.

752
KATHERINE ROBERTS

Spellfall
(New York: Scholastic, 2001)

Subject(s): Magic; Coming-of-Age
Age range(s): Grades 6-10
Major character(s): Natalie, 12-Year-Old; Hawk, Wizard
Time period(s): 2000s
Locale(s): Millenium Green, England

Summary: Natalie has never known her mother, and her father refuses to talk about her. Although she misses a mother's love, Natalie never suspects that ignorance about her mother could be dangerous. On a perfectly ordinary trip to the grocery store, Natalie picks up what she thinks is a piece of trash, only to find herself enmeshed in a mysterious world of spells and magic. The unscrupulous wizard Hawk knows that Natalie is capable of great power and is determined to stop at nothing until Natalie is under his control. (247 pages)

Where it's reviewed:
Booklist, November 15, 2001, page 574
Children's Bookwatch, September 2001, page 2
Kirkus Reviews, September 1, 2001, page 1300
Publishers Weekly, October 1, 2001, page 62
School Library Journal, October 2001, page 168

Other books by the same author:
Crystal Mask, 2002
Song Quest, 1999

Other books you might like:
Diane Duane, *So You Want to Be A Wizard*, 1983
    Nita and Kit are astonished to discover that they have magical powers and the ability to travel between dimensions.
J.K. Rowling, *Harry Potter and the Sorcerer's Stone*, 1998
    An orphan boy discovers that he comes from a talented wizard family, in spite of his "muggle" relatives.
Jan Seigel, *Prospero's Children*, 2000
    A motherless brother and sister discover that they have the blood of Atlantis in their veins.

WILLO DAVIS ROBERTS

Buddy Is a Stupid Name for a Girl
(New York: Atheneum/Simon & Schuster, 2001)

Subject(s): Mystery and Detective Stories; Aunts and Uncles; Grandfathers

Age range(s): Grades 4-7
Major character(s): Amy Kate ''Buddy'' Adams, 6th Grader; Bart Adams, 17-Year-Old; Addie Ostrom, Aunt, Writer; Cassie Miller, Aunt; Max Miller, Cousin
Time period(s): 2000s
Locale(s): Washington; Haysville, Montana

Summary: With their dad finally hired as a long-distance trucker, Bart and Buddy are relieved to know the rent can now be paid, but their good fortune is short-lived when the landlord evicts them anyway. After one night spent sleeping in their car, Bart decides to search for their dad and puts Buddy on a bus to Montana to stay with their maternal aunts. Not having been close to her aunts Cassie and Addie, Buddy's apprehensive about this decision and cries all the way to Haysville. Once there she learns that both aunts disliked her mother because they think she stole the profits from the sale of the family store. Luckily Aunt Cassie's stepson Max teams up with Buddy and the two find the missing money up in the attic, where it's been since the last time Buddy's mother was home. By book's end, Buddy asks everyone to please call her by her real name, Amy Kate, as ''Buddy is a stupid name for a girl.'' (218 pages)

Where it's reviewed:
Bulletin of the Center for Children's Books, February 2001, page 234
Publishers Weekly, February 5, 2001, page 89

Other books by the same author:
Undercurrents, 2002
Hostage, 2000
The Kidnappers: A Mystery, 1998
Caught!, 1994
What Could Go Wrong?, 1989

Other books you might like:
Barbara Hall, *Dixie Storms*, 1990
    Fourteen-year-old Dutch is the glue binding together her motherless Virginia farm family.
Kezi Matthews, *John Riley's Daughter*, 2000
    Dropped off at her maternal grandmother's house five years ago by her folksinger father, Memphis argues with her aunt, which makes her even more sad.
Louise Moeri, *The Devil in Ol' Rosie*, 2001
    After surviving a blizzard and a stalking cougar, Wart comes home with his family's horses and asks his father to call him by his given name, John.

754

BARBARA ROBERTSON

Rosemary Meets Rosemarie

(New York: Winslow Press, 2001)

Series: The Hourglass Adventures. Number 1
Subject(s): Grandmothers; Magic; Time Travel
Age range(s): Grades 4-6
Major character(s): Rosemary Rita Hampton, 10-Year-Old, Time Traveler; Rosemary Regina ''Mimi'' Ryan, Grandmother
Time period(s): 2000s (2001); 1870s (1870)
Locale(s): Greenville, South Carolina; Berlin, Germany

Summary: In celebration of her tenth birthday Rosemary Rita receives ten packages from Grandma Mimi. The contents of the first nine boxes are so exciting and mysterious that Rosemary Rita ignores Grandma Mimi's written instructions and opens the tenth box, revealing an old hourglass. Innocently turning the hourglass over while holding a postcard written to her great-great-great grandmother transports Rosemary Rita back in time to 1870s Berlin where she meets the relative as a 10-year-old. While the trip is an interesting way to learn family history and be introduced to customs of the time, Rosemary Rita does wonder how she'll find her way home again. The answer arrives in a package to her relative. (123 pages)

Where it's reviewed:
Bookpage, July 2001, page 30
Publishers Weekly, May 28, 2001, page 89
School Library Journal, October 2001, page 168

Other books by the same author:
Rosemary and the Island Treasure: Back to 1947, 2001 (Hourglass Adventures, Number 4)
Rosemary in Paris: Back to 1889, 2001 (Hourglass Adventures, Number 2)
Rosemary at Sea: Back to 1919, 2001 (Hourglass Adventures, Number 3)

Other books you might like:
Yvonne MacGrory, *The Secret of the Ruby Ring*, 1994
    On the eve of her eleventh birthday Lucy receives a magical family ring and uses one of the wishes it grants to journey to the past to Langley Castle.
Mary Pope Osborne, *Earthquake in the Early Morning*, 2001
    In the twenty-forth Magic Tree House adventure Jack and Annie find themselves in 1906 San Francisco on the morning of the great earthquake.
Elvira Woodruff, *The Orphan of Ellis Island: A Time-Travel Adventure*, 1997
    An unexpected trip back in time to Italy helps Dominic understand his unknown family history and the reasons for his ancestors' immigration to America.
Jane Yolen, *The Pictish Child*, 1999
    Molly receives a talisman from one of her grandmother's friends that sets in motion a series of magical events.

755

HARRIETTE GILLEM ROBINET

Missing from Haymarket Square

(New York: Jean Karl/Simon & Schuster, 2001)

Subject(s): Labor Conditions; Historical; Riots
Age range(s): Grades 5-7
Major character(s): Dinah Bell, 12-Year-Old, Seamstress; Olive Schaeffer, 12-Year-Old, Seamstress; Ben Schaeffer, 16-Year-Old, Worker (factory); Napoleon, Dog; Noah Bell, Father (of Dinah), Activist (labor)
Time period(s): 1880s (1886)
Locale(s): Chicago, Illinois

Summary: In the latter part of the nineteenth century immigrants fill Chicago's tenements, immigrants from Europe as well as emigrants from the south following the end of slavery.

Dinah and her family share a one-room tenement apartment with an Austrian and a Polish. Because money is very tight, Dinah and her Austrian friends Olive and Ben "humbug" several nights a week and steal money from the pockets of the rich in order to buy food. Dinah's father Noah is active in the labor movement and the entire family plans to be part of the march in support of an eight-hour working day. Pinkerton detectives snatch her dad to prevent his marching in Haymarket Square but Dinah is determined to use her street smarts, and her dog Napoleon's keen nose, to find him in this sobering look at the life of the poor. (143 pages)

Where it's reviewed:
Booklist, October 1, 2001, page 318
Bulletin of the Center for Children's Books, October 2001, page 71
Publishers Weekly, June 18, 2001, page 81
School Library Journal, July 2001, page 112
Voice of Youth Advocates, October 2001, page 284

Other books by the same author:
Walking to the Bus-Rider Blues, 2000
Forty Acres and Maybe a Mule, 1998
Washington City Is Burning, 1996
If You Please, President Lincoln, 1995
Mississippi Chariot, 1994

Other books you might like:
Elizabeth Massie, *Not with Our Blood*, 2000
    After the Civil War, Patrick's family moves north to work in the factories and have a better life, but factory conditions are terrible.
Jay Parini, *The Patch Boys*, 1988
    Sammy diCantini grows up quickly one summer when his older brother is injured trying to organize a union in a Pennsylvania mining town.
Katherine Paterson, *Lyddie*, 1991
    Lyddie hates being an inn servant and leaves to work in a factory where her interest in unions causes her to be fired for "moral turpitude."
Gloria Skurzynski, *Rockbuster*, 2001
    Orphaned young, Tommy toils in the mines but resists being involved in the labor movement, choosing instead to become a lawyer and help all people.

C. KELLY ROBINSON

Between Brothers

(New York: Villard/Strivers Row, 2001)

Subject(s): African Americans; College Life; Drugs
Age range(s): Grades 10-Adult
Major character(s): Nico Lane, Drug Dealer; Terence "Bootstrapper" Davidson, Student—College; Larry "Smooth Operator" Whitaker, Student—College; Brandon "Choirboy" Bailey, Student—College; Oscar Jarvis "O.J." Peters, Student—College, Religious (minister)
Time period(s): 2000s
Locale(s): Washington, District of Columbia

Summary: The Ellis Community Center, which has just lost government funding from the city, is an after-school refuge for kids who heed the message to stay off the streets and avoid drugs, which bothers the main drug dealer Nico Lane. Upset that kids are telling his dealers they're stupid to sell, Nico approaches the director and tries to buy her off, but she kicks him out of her office. Angry, he vows to find another way to close down Ellis. Meanwhile at Highland University, four brothers try to raise funds to help Ellis but find themselves vulnerable because of the campaign. Terrence is forced to choose between Ellis and helping his brother; O.J.'s second career as a minister is threatened; Larry's bid for student association president is damaged and Brandon's hopes for med school are on the line. Once the four realize what's happening, they become even more determined in their commitment to Ellis and one another, which surprises the drug dealer. (373 pages)

Where it's reviewed:
Booklist, September 15, 2001, page 196
Kirkus Reviews, August 15, 2001, page 1158

Other books by the same author:
Not All Dogs, 1999

Other books you might like:
Tajuana Butler, *Sorority Sisters*, 1998
    A first novel starring five African American college students, all from different background, who pledge the same sorority and become friends.
R.M. Johnson, *The Harris Men*, 1999
    After abandoning his family twenty years earlier, Julius has been diagnosed with terminal cancer and wants to become reacquainted with his sons before he dies.
Omar Tyree, *Just Say No!*, 2001
    Two buddies from North Carolina find success after college with John Williams as a star singer and Darin Harmon as his manager, until John can't say no to drugs.

757

ANNE ROCKWELL
PAUL MEISEL, Illustrator

Morgan Plays Soccer

(New York: HarperCollins Publishers, 2001)

Subject(s): Sports/Soccer; Animals/Bears; Animals
Age range(s): Grades K-2
Major character(s): Morgan Brownbear, Bear, Neighbor; Nina Jane Monkey, Monkey, Soccer Player
Time period(s): Indeterminate
Locale(s): Fictional Country

Summary: Morgan dons the new shirt he receives from his aunt and goes out to play at his new house. Nina Jane assumes from the shirt that Morgan must play soccer. Poor Morgan knows so little about soccer that he doesn't even know his aunt sent him a soccer jersey. Nina Jane convinces Morgan to join her team and helps him improve his skills, but still Morgan can't seem to remember not to catch the ball. The coach solves that problem by making Morgan the goalie, a position he plays quite well. (36 pages)

Where it's reviewed:
Booklist, August 2001, page 2132
Kirkus Reviews, June 15, 2001, page 87

Publishers Weekly, July 16, 2001, page 179
School Library Journal, August 2001, page 158

Other books by the same author:
Valentine's Day, 2001
Career Day, 2000
Our Earth, 1998

Other books you might like:
Anthony Browne, *Willy the Wizard*, 1996
    Willy the chimpanzee gains the confidence to play on a team of gorillas when he's given a special pair of soccer boots.
Jonathan London, *Froggy Plays Soccer*, 1999
    Despite the instructions shouted by his dad from the sidelines Froggy makes an unintentional error in his first championship soccer game.
Colin McNaughton, *Preston's Goal*, 1998
    As usual, Preston is oblivious to the consequences of his actions as he kicks his soccer ball along the street.

758

ANNE ROCKWELL, Author/Illustrator

Welcome to Kindergarten
(New York: Walker & Company, 2001)

Subject(s): Schools; Mothers and Sons; School Life
Age range(s): Preschool-Kindergarten
Major character(s): Tim, Child, Son; Mrs. Jardin, Teacher; Unnamed Character, Mother
Time period(s): 2000s (2001)
Locale(s): United States

Summary: Tim receives an invitation from Mrs. Jardin to visit the kindergarten classroom as a preview for his school experience. The departing students and the room look very big to Tim but his mother assures him that the space is only big enough for learning. Tim explores the classroom's science center, art space, math corner, and reading center anticipating his future days as a student. The room also has a writing table, a weatherboard and a clock to tell when it is time for recess. At the snack table Tim and another potential student eat cookies made in the cooking center. By the time Tim's visit concludes the kindergarten room looks to be just right. (32 pages)

Where it's reviewed:
Booklist, June 2001, page 1895
Horn Book Guide, Fall 2001, page 271
Publishers Weekly, March 12, 2001, page 93
School Library Journal, May 2001, page 133

Other books by the same author:
Valentine's Day, 2001
Career Day, 2000
The Boy Who Wouldn't Obey: A Mayan Legend, 2000
Bumblebee, Bumblebee, Do You Know Me?: A Garden Guessing Game, 1999
Pumpkin Day, Pumpkin Night, 1999

Other books you might like:
Nancy Carlson, *Look Out Kindergarten, Here I Come!*, 1999
    Henry's enthusiasm for school wanes as he approaches the building.

Amy Schwartz, *Annabelle Swift, Kindergartner*, 1988
    Advice from her experienced big sister helps Annabelle have a successful first day of kindergarten.
Mary Serfozo, *Benjamin Bigfoot*, 1993
    Benjamin's reservations about beginning kindergarten vanish after a visit to the teacher.
Joseph Slate, *Miss Bindergarten Gets Ready for Kindergarten*, 1996
    Even teachers prepare for the opening of a school year.

759

EMILY RODDA

Rowan and the Travelers
(New York: Greenwillow Books, 2001)

Subject(s): Fantasy; Heroes and Heroines; Courage
Age range(s): Grades 3-6
Major character(s): Rowan, Son, Hero; Zeel, Adoptee, Daughter; Ogden, Storyteller, Father (Zeel's)
Time period(s): Indeterminate Past
Locale(s): Rin, Fictional Country; Pit of Unrin, Fictional Country

Summary: In the sequel to *Rowan of Rin* a visit from the Travelers makes the people of Rin suspicious of the nomadic group's motives. As the people of Rin begin to fall asleep by some unknown force, Rowan thinks the answers to saving his family and his village lie with the Travelers. After Rowan confers with Ogden, he is selected to accompany Zeel into the evil Pit of Unrin to locate a long lost city that could offer a solution. The truth Rowan discovers enables him, with help from Zeel, Ogden and other Travelers, to save Rin and gives Ogden a tale worthy to be told around campfires for years to come. Originally published in Australia in 1994. (170 pages)

Where it's reviewed:
Booklist, November 15, 2001, page 574
Bulletin of the Center for Children's Books, October 2001, page 72
Publishers Weekly, November 19, 2001, page 70
School Library Journal, January 2002, page 140

Other books by the same author:
Rowan and the Keeper of the Crystal, 2002
Rowan of Rin, 2001
The Forest of Silence, 2001

Other books you might like:
Ursula K. Le Guin, *A Wizard of Earthsea*, 1991
    A young wizard combats the evil that he unwittingly released as an apprentice.
Tamora Pierce, *Sandry's Book*, 1997
    This entry in the Circle of Magic series features Sandry, a young magician in training at the Winding Circle Temple.
J.K. Rowling, *Harry Potter and the Sorcerer's Stone*, 1997
    In order to save Hogwart's from the evil sorcerer that killed his parents Harry and his friends must find the hidden sorcerer's stone.

EMILY RODDA

Rowan of Rin
(New York: Greenwillow Books, 2001)

Series: Rowan of Rin. #1
Subject(s): Fantasy; Heroes and Heroines; Courage
Age range(s): Grades 3-6
Major character(s): Rowan, Child, Animal Lover; Strong Jonn, Adventurer; Sheba, Witch, Aged Person
Time period(s): Indeterminate
Locale(s): Rin, Fictional Country

Summary: Inexplicably the stream that provides water to the village stops flowing into the pond from which the bukshah drink. The life of the villagers is dependent on these beasts that cannot drink well water. Saving the village requires a quest to the top of a nearby mountain atop which lives a dragon. The villagers seek help from Sheba who gives them a riddle and a map that is only visible when held by timid Rowan, the village bukshah herder. Seven villagers begin the quest, but as Sheba prophesizes each finds his or her courage defeated by the mountain and they turn back to Rin. Finally, Strong Jonn and Rowan continue, but it is up to Rowan to complete the quest, defeat the dragon and restore the flow of life-giving water. Originally published in Australia in 1993. (151 pages)

Where it's reviewed:
Booklist, May 1, 2001, page 1682
Bulletin of the Center for Children's Books, June 2001, page 385
Horn Book, July 2001, page 461
School Library Journal, June 2001, page 154
Science Fiction Chronicle, August 2001, page 36

Other books by the same author:
Rowan and the Travelers, 2001 (Rowan of Rin, #2)
Dread Mountain, 2000 (Deltora Quest, #5)
The Timekeeper, 1992
The Best-Kept Secret, 1988

Other books you might like:
Lloyd Alexander, *The Iron Ring*, 1997
    After losing his kingdom to Jaya in a dice game, Tamar is honor bound to comply with the command to journey to Jaya's palace and face his fate.
Gail Carson Levine, *Ella Enchanted*, 1997
    In a Newbery Honor Book, Ella is cursed with obedience and must go on a quest seeking freedom from the curse in order to save those she cares about.
J.R.R. Tolkien, *The Hobbit*, 1938
    In the first book of a fantasy trilogy, a Hobbit finds himself on a journey that grows increasingly treacherous.
Cynthia Voigt, *Jackaroo*, 1985
    To help the People through hard times an innkeeper's daughter goes on a quest to learn the truth behind the legend of the hero Jackaroo.

COLBY RODOWSKY

Clay
(New York: Farrar Straus Giroux, 2001)

Subject(s): Kidnapping; Mental Illness; Brothers and Sisters
Age range(s): Grades 5-8
Major character(s): Elsie/Linda Clay "L.C." McPhee/McGee, 11-Year-Old; Tommy/Timmy McPhee/McGee, Autistic, Child; Violet Hassie, Store Owner (sub shop)
Time period(s): 2000s
Locale(s): Baltimore, Maryland; Richmond, Virginia

Summary: For the last four years Elsie and her autistic brother Tommy have been dragged from one garden apartment to another, forbidden to talk to strangers, not allowed to tell anyone their real name and kept away from school by their mentally ill mother. Elsie's parents are divorced, because of differing opinions about Tommy's mental condition, and their father had been given custody until their mother kidnapped them. Now Tommy's sick and, afraid of discovery, their mother won't take him to the doctor. Elsie feels she has to do something so gives sub shop owner Vi a note asking for help and listing their apartment number, but is momentarily frozen when the FBI knocks on her door. Though Elsie and Tommy are reunited with their father, returning home is harder than she imagined it would be. (166 pages)

Where it's reviewed:
Booklist, May 1, 2001, page 1683
Bulletin of the Center for Children's Books, March 2001, page 277
Publishers Weekly, January 8, 2001, page 67
School Library Journal, April 2001, page 148
Voice of Youth Advocates, June 2001, page 128

Other books by the same author:
Spindrift, 2000
The Turnabout Shop, 1998
Remembering Mog, 1996
Sydney, Invincible, 1995
Hannah in Between, 1994
Lucy Peale, 1992

Other books you might like:
Amy Ehrlich, *Where It Stops, Nobody Knows*, 1988
    Nina is surprised when her mother is arrested for kidnapping her, but joining her birth family proves most traumatic of all.
Norma Fox Mazer, *Taking Terri Mueller*, 1983
    Terri's father kidnaps her to prevent her from seeing her mother.
Susan Beth Pfeffer, *Twice Taken*, 1994
    While watching a television show, Brooks recognizes her father's picture and realizes he took her from her mother's custody eleven years ago.
Laura Roybal, *Billy*, 1994
    Taken by his natural father, six years later Billy's real identity is discovered and he's returned to his legal guardians in Iowa.
Cherylyn Stacey, *How Do You Spell Abducted?*, 1996
    On a court-ordered two week vacation with their father,

Debbie realizes he means to kidnap them when they cross over into Canada.

LISA WALLER ROGERS

Get Along, Little Dogies: The Chisholm Trail Diary of Hallie Lou Wells: South Texas, 1878

(Lubbock, TX: Texas Tech University Press, 2001)

Series: Lone Star Journals. Book 1
Subject(s): Cattle Drives; American West; Diaries
Age range(s): Grades 5-8
Major character(s): Harriet Lucretia ''Hallie Lou'' Wells, 14-Year-Old; Paloma Maria ''Dovey Mae'', Servant, 15-Year-Old
Time period(s): 1870s (1878)
Locale(s): Victoria, Texas; Dodge City, Kansas

Summary: The cattle are rounded up and her father's ready to start the drive, once again leaving Hallie Lou behind. Furious that only boys and men ever drive the cattle, she pleads her case to accompany them, especially when she hears of her mother's pregnancy and her father's decision to stay home with her. Successful in her plea, Hallie Lou and her maid ride in a buggy alongside the men and she records the events in Hallie Lou's diary, everything from cute cowboys to sunburned skin, shooting of buffalo and the dust, thirst and dreadful food typical of a cattle drive. Hallie Lou is a spunky young lady and her diary entries reflect her sense of daring and adventure. (174 pages)

Where it's reviewed:
Curriculum Review, September 2001, page 13
School Library Journal, July 2001, page 112

Other books by the same author:
The Great Storm: The Hurricane Diary of J.T. King, Galveston, Texas 1900, 2002 (Lone Star Journals, Book 2)
The Texas Sampler: Historic Recollections, 1998

Other books you might like:
Brian Burks, *Wrango*, 1999
   A fictionalized story of George McJunkin who survives a rattler's bite, nabs a thief and cares for horses on a cattle drive along the Chisholm Trail.
Ric Lynden Hardman, *Sunshine Rider: The First Vegetarian Western*, 1998
   Wylie signs up as an assistant cook on a cattle drive where he's put in charge of Roselle, a pet that's part buffalo and part longhorn.
Louise Moeri, *The Devil in Ol' Rosie*, 2001
   After surviving a blizzard and a stalking cougar, Wart comes home with his family's horses and asks his father to call him by his given name, John.
Walter Dean Myers, *The Journal of Joshua Loper: A Black Cowboy*, 1999
   Joshua's skill with a gun and his ability to sing keep his spirits up on a grueling, dust-laden cattle drive that turns a boy into a man.

STEPHEN ROOS

The Gypsies Never Came

(New York: Simon & Schuster, 2001)

Subject(s): Physically Handicapped; Schools; Self-Acceptance
Age range(s): Grades 5-8
Major character(s): Augie Knapp, 6th Grader; Lydie Rose Meisenheimer, 6th Grader, Teenager
Time period(s): 2000s
Locale(s): Warsaw Junction, Pennsylvania

Summary: Augie keeps his deformed left hand covered with a flesh-colored glove and endures the jibes and comments of some of his classmates. Convinced that this stub of a hand is why his father divorced his mother, he hates his deformity. Working in a dry cleaner after school, he collects the ephemera he finds in people's pockets, from notes to receipts, reports cards and even family photos, as these items make him feel part of a family he keeps them safely locked away in an old suitcase. While not perfect, Augie feels he's made a secure life for himself, until Lydie Rose drives into town and signs herself up for sixth grade in Augie's classroom. For some reason, she takes a shine to Augie and tries to do too much for him. She steals his suitcase, writes his genetics paper for him and wants to see his hand, all the while telling him that he's special, as he'll find out when the gypsies come for him. (117 pages)

Where it's reviewed:
Booklist, March 1, 2001, page 1281
Bulletin of the Center for Children's Books, May 2001, page 351
Horn Book, May 2001, page 336
Publishers Weekly, February 12, 2001, page 213
School Library Journal, February 2001, page 122

Other books by the same author:
Recycling George, 2002
Who's Been Sleeping in My Grave?, 1999
Thirteenth Summer, 1992
You'll Miss Me When I'm Gone, 1988
Confessions of a Wayward Preppie, 1986

Other books you might like:
Tim Bowler, *Midget*, 1995
   Midget is a young handicapped man whose birth causes the death of his mother and the everlasting hatred of his older brother.
Iain Lawrence, *Ghost Boy*, 2000
   Grieving and no longer feeling part of his family, ''ghost boy,'' so named for his albinism, runs away from home with the Hunter and Green's Traveling Circus.
John Marsden, *So Much to Tell You*, 1987
   Through her journal Marina reveals the sad story of her facial disfigurement, caused when her father threw acid and it accidentally landed on her.
Terry Trueman, *Stuck in Neutral*, 2000
   Only Shawn appreciates his perfect recall and great sense of humor because his cerebral palsy is so profound he lacks the muscle control to speak.

764

KAREN ROOSA
MAGGIE SMITH, Illustrator

Beach Day
(New York: Clarion Books, 2001)

Subject(s): Beaches; Stories in Rhyme; Playing
Age range(s): Preschool-Grade 1
Time period(s): 2000s
Locale(s): United States

Summary: A day at the beach begins with parents, children, grandma and the dog carrying the day's supplies across the dunes to the sandy shore. To the roaring and crashing sounds of the waves they set up their umbrella and spread the blanket. With other families they splash in the waves, dig in the sand, play catch and eat a big picnic lunch. As the sun sets, the author's first book concludes with families packing their towels, umbrellas and toys to begin the homeward journey after a happy beach day. (32 pages)

Where it's reviewed:
Booklist, May 1, 2001, page 1694
Horn Book Guide, Fall 2001, page 240
Kirkus Reviews, March 1, 2001, page 337
Publishers Weekly, April 23, 2001, page 76
School Library Journal, April 2001, page 121

Other books you might like:
Aliki, *Those Summers*, 1996
    Children frolic in the waves, enjoying a carefree family vacation at the seashore.
Douglas Florian, *A Beach Day*, 1990
    A family shares a relaxing day at the beach looking for sea shells.
Troon Harrison, *The Long Weekend*, 1994
    For his birthday Michael chooses to spend three days playing at the beach with his mom.
Stephen Huneck, *Sally Goes to the Beach*, 2000
    Sally, a black lab, loves a day at the beach with her family.

 765

PHYLLIS ROOT
JILL BARTON, Illustrator

Rattletrap Car
(Cambridge, MA: Candlewick Press, 2001)

Subject(s): Automobiles; Family; Problem Solving
Age range(s): Grades K-2
Major character(s): Poppa, Father, Driver; Junie, Daughter, Sister (older); Jakie, Son, Brother
Time period(s): Indeterminate Past
Locale(s): United States

Summary: It's so hot on the farm that Poppa and his children want to find relief at the lake. Poppa's not sure the old car is up to the trip, but with encouragement from Junie, Jakie and even the baby, he agrees to load up the supplies for their venture. As soon they leave home the first disaster befalls the old car and Junie uses her beach ball as a spare tire. Next the floor falls off and Jakie, with help from the chocolate marsh-mallow fudge delight, sticks his surfboard on as a replacement. Even the baby has an idea to help the car get to its destination. The rattletrap car finally reaches the cool lake thanks to the family's persistence, ingenuity, and a few children's toys. (32 pages)

Where it's reviewed:
Booklist, April 1, 2001, page 1479
Horn Book Guide, Fall 2001, page 272
Kirkus Reviews, April 1, 2001, page 504
Publishers Weekly, April 30, 2001, page 77
School Library Journal, June 2001, page 128

Awards the book has won:
Booklist Editors' Choice/Books for Youth, 2002

Other books by the same author:
Soggy Saturday, 2001
Kiss the Cow!, 2000
Grandmother Winter, 1999

Other books you might like:
Faye Gibbons, *Mama and Me and the Model T*, 1999
    When Mr. Long arrives home with the family's first car Mama takes everyone for an exciting ride about the farm.
Margaret Mahy, *The Rattlebang Picnic*, 1994
    Grandma's inedible pizza saves her family when their old car loses a wheel as they flee their picnic site just ahead of lava from an exploding volcano.
Lynn Plourde, *Pigs in the Mud in the Middle of the Rud*, 1997
    A Maine farm family is loaded in the Model T with no way to go until Granny convinces the pig to get out of the road.

766

MELODYE BENSON ROSALES, Author/Illustrator

Minnie Saves the Day
(Boston: Little, Brown and Company, 2001)

Series: Adventures of Minnie. Book 1
Subject(s): Dolls and Dollhouses; Toys; African Americans
Age range(s): Grades 3-5
Major character(s): Hester Merriweather, Sister (younger), Daughter; Annie Merriweather, Sister (older), Daughter; Minnie, Doll; Papa, Father, Railroad Worker (porter)
Time period(s): 1930s (1933)
Locale(s): Chicago, Illinois (Bronzeville)

Summary: When Papa returns from a trip down south he brings Hester a doll specially made for her by her grandma. Each scrap of family clothes her grandmother used for the rag doll represents a piece of family history. Hester "introduces" Minnie to all her other toys but after Hester falls asleep Minnie discovers that she and the other dolls become real and capable of conversation and movement. The next day Hester wants to help her mother by baking a cake but she falls asleep so Minnie tackles the job with some unexpected help from one of Annie's older toys. The book concludes with a photo-essay of Chicago's African American history and a pound cake recipe. (84 pages)

Where it's reviewed:
Booklist, April 15, 2001, page 1553
Bulletin of the Center for Children's Books, June 2001, page 385

Horn Book Guide, Fall 2001, page 294
Publishers Weekly, March 26, 2001, page 93
School Library Journal, July 2001, page 88

Other books by the same author:
'Twas the Night B'fore Christmas: An African-American Version, 1996

Other books you might like:
Rumer Godden, *The Doll's House*, 1976
　Two little girls enjoy adventures with their Victorian dollhouse and the family of dolls that live in it.
Jan Karon, *Jeremy: The Tale of an Honest Bunny*, 2000
　A handmade bunny comes to life when named and decides to make his own way to his new owner in America rather than be shipped in a box.
Ann M. Martin, *The Doll People*, 2000
　When Kate's away or asleep her dollhouse family comes to life.
Yona Zeldis McDonough, *The Dollhouse Magic*, 2000
　During dreary days of the 1930s Depression two sisters enjoy playing with an elderly neighbor's dollhouse.

767

MICHAEL J. ROSEN
MELISSA IWAI, Illustrator

Chanukah Lights Everywhere
(San Diego: Gulliver Books/Harcourt, Inc., 2001)

Subject(s): Holidays, Jewish; Family; Cultures and Customs
Age range(s): Preschool-Kindergarten
Major character(s): Unnamed Character, 5-Year-Old, Brother (older); Mom, Mother
Time period(s): 2000s
Locale(s): United States

Summary: A young boy relates the nightly events as his family celebrates Chanukah. Relatives come in to enjoy Mom's latkes or to play dreidel with the boy and his sister. Sometimes the boy's family goes visiting others, even friends of different faiths. Everywhere the boy sees lights reminding him of the Jewish celebration of the Festival of Lights. Factual information about Chanukah concludes the book. (26 pages)

Where it's reviewed:
Booklist, September 1, 2001, page 122
Bulletin of the Center for Children's Books, November 2001, page 114
Children's Bookwatch, September 2001, page 6
Publishers Weekly, September 24, 2001, page 48
School Library Journal, October 2001, page 68

Other books by the same author:
Our Eight Nights of Hanukkah, 2000
A Thanksgiving Wish, 1999 (Notable Social Studies Trade Books for Young People)
Bonesy and Isabel, 1995

Other books you might like:
David A. Adler, *One Yellow Daffodil: A Hanukkah Story*, 1995
　The kindness of a neighborhood family helps lonely Morris Kaplan celebrate his faith once again.

Amy Ehrlich, *The Story of Hanukkah*, 1989
　The historical beginnings of the traditions of Hanukkah are simply presented in this picture book.
Marissa Moss, *The Ugly Menorah*, 1996
　After learning the history of Grandma's ugly menorah Rachel understands why it is so important to her recently widowed grandmother.

768

LIZ ROSENBERG
JOANNA YARDLEY, Illustrator

Eli's Night Light
(New York: Orchard Books/Scholastic, Inc., 2001)

Subject(s): Bedtime; Sleep; Problem Solving
Age range(s): Grades K-1
Major character(s): Eli, Child, Son
Time period(s): 2000s (2001)
Locale(s): United States

Summary: The evening that Eli's night light burns out after his parents are asleep, he searches his dark room for an alternative to use. Eli notices the glowing numerals on his clock, the splash of a passing car's headlights on his wall, and the hall light streaming through the crack of his partially opened door. The light that Eli finally chooses for a substitute is one he knows will not burn out anytime soon and then he sleeps. (32 pages)

Where it's reviewed:
Booklist, June 2001, page 1895
Horn Book Guide, Fall 2001, page 272
Kirkus Reviews, April 1, 2001, page 505
Publishers Weekly, May 14, 2001, page 80
School Library Journal, August 2001, page 160

Other books by the same author:
The Silence in the Mountains, 1999
Eli and Uncle Dawn, 1997
Moonbathing, 1996 (Smithsonian's Notable Books for Children)

Other books you might like:
Kate Banks, *And If the Moon Could Talk*, 1998
　A brilliant moon shines into a child's bedroom illuminating all that it would tell—if only the moon could talk.
Betsy James, *Flashlight*, 1997
　Grandpa gives his visiting granddaughter a flashlight to help her overcome her fear of sleeping in his strange dark living room.
Jan Ormerod, *Moonlight*, 1982
　Illustrations alone portray a young girl's moonlit bedtime ritual in this wordless picture book.

769

SUSAN L. ROTH, Author/Illustrator

Grandpa Blows His Penny Whistle Until the Angels Sing
(New York: Barefoot Books, 2001)

Subject(s): Family Relations; Faith; Grandfathers

Age range(s): Grades 1-4
Major character(s): Little Boy James, 7-Year-Old, Brother (younger); Grandpa, Grandfather; Honey, Sister (older), Narrator
Time period(s): Indeterminate Past
Locale(s): United States

Summary: Despite Honey's warnings Little Boy James refuses to dress for church. Instead he runs out to ride the horse, walk barefoot along the fence and climb a ladder to the barn roof. Grandpa comes out to hold the ladder and to coax Little Boy James down, but Little Boy James accidentally falls from the roof and lands flat on his back in the garden. When the doctor comes they carry Little Boy James into the house and pray for the once active child who now lies completely still and quiet. Grandpa leaves the house intent on having a conversation with God. With Honey he walks to the church seeking a miracle. As the preacher drones on, Grandpa begins to play his penny whistle and the sad tune calls the angels into the church. When a crowd of singing angels forms Grandpa leads them back to the house where they crowd into the room with Little Boy James. In a few minutes Little Boy James sits up and proclaims that when Grandpa plays his penny whistle he can hear the angels singing. (40 pages)

Where it's reviewed:
Booklist, April 1, 2001, page 1479
Horn Book Guide, Fall 2001, page 272
Kirkus Reviews, April 1, 2001, page 505
Publishers Weekly, May 28, 2001, page 85
School Library Journal, May 2001, page 133

Other books by the same author:
Brave Martha and the Dragon, 1996
The Biggest Frog in Australia, 1996
Another Christmas, 1992

Other books you might like:
Valiska Gregory, *Looking for Angels*, 1996
    Grandpa, who sees with the eyes of a poet, teaches Sarah to look carefully at the world around her and she will see angels.
Helen V. Griffith, *Georgia Music*, 1986
    The music on a Georgia farm includes nature's sounds and those coming from a loving grandfather's mouth organ.
Natalie Kinsey-Warnock, *The Bear That Heard Crying*, 1993
    A toddler lost in the woods near her family's colonial homestead is miraculously found alive after being cared for by a bear for several days.

770

SUSAN L. ROTH, Author/Illustrator

Happy Birthday Mr. Kang

(Washington, D.C.: National Geographic Society, 2001)

Subject(s): Birthdays; Chinese Americans; Wishes
Age range(s): Grades 2-5
Major character(s): Mr. Kang, Aged Person, Grandfather; Birdie, Bird; Sam, Son (grandson), 7-Year-Old
Time period(s): 2000s
Locale(s): New York, New York

Summary: At Mr. Kang's 70th birthday celebration, memories of his homeland and his grandfather's hua mei bird lead him to wish to own such a bird. Each of Mr. Kang's three wishes comes true and Mr. Kang begins a new ritual of visiting the park every Sunday with Birdie where they socialize with the other Chinese Americans and their birds. Sam is impressed that Birdie came all the way from China by plane, but he's also concerned that Birdie should be free, not kept in a cage. Although he's been in America for 43 years, at times Mr. Kang feels "caged" here so he heeds Sam's words and, on the Sunday that Sam walks with him to the park, Mr. Kang sets Birdie free. When Sam and his grandfather return to the apartment, Birdie is waiting on the railing. (32 pages)

Where it's reviewed:
Booklist, January 2001, page 971
Bulletin of the Center for Children's Books, April 2001, page 314
Kirkus Reviews, January 15, 2001, page 114
Publishers Weekly, November 27, 2000, page 76
School Library Journal, February 2001, page 105

Other books by the same author:
Grandpa Blows His Penny Whistle Until the Angels Sing, 2001
Cinnamon's Day Out: A Gerbil Adventure, 1998
The Biggest Frog in Australia, 1996

Other books you might like:
Sherry Garland, *The Lotus Seed*, 1993
    An immigrant to America uses a lotus seed to connect to her birthplace and share her heritage with her children and grandchildren.
Allen Say, *Grandfather's Journey*, 1993
    A grandson completes his grandfather's journey between homeland and adopted land, memory and desire in this Caldecott Medal winner.
Amy Tan, *The Moon Lady*, 1992
    Now living in the United States, a grandmother reminisces about her childhood in China.

771

NICOLE RUBEL, Author/Illustrator

A Cowboy Named Ernestine

(New York: Dial Books for Young Readers, 2001)

Subject(s): American West; Mail Order Brides; Cowboys/Cowgirls
Age range(s): Grades K-3
Major character(s): Ernestine O'Reilly, Mail Order Bride, Cowboy; Texas Teeth, Cowboy
Time period(s): Indeterminate Past
Locale(s): Lizard Lick, Texas

Summary: The sight of the grizzly, dirty groom awaiting Ernestine as she steps off the stagecoach is enough to make her wish she could afford to return to Ireland. Since she can't, she uses her wits to disguise herself as a cowboy and sneak away from her predicament before the preacher shows up. With more gumption than experience, Ernestine survives with the help of Texas Teeth who finds her lost in the desert. She joins his cattle drive, learns to ride and throw a lasso and manages to disguise her sex until she's secretly entered in a bull-riding contest at a rodeo and loses her hat. With the truth of her identity now obvious, she and Texas Teeth are soon wed. (32 pages)

Where it's reviewed:
Booklist, April 1, 2001, page 1480
Horn Book Guide, Fall 2001, page 272
Kirkus Reviews, December 15, 2000, page 1765
Publishers Weekly, January 22, 2001, page 323
School Library Journal, March 2001, page 219

Other books by the same author:
Conga Crocodile, 1993
The Ghost Family Meets Its Match, 1992
Goldie's Nap, 1991
Goldie, 1989
It Came From the Swamp, 1988

Other books you might like:
Robert Kinerk, *Slim and Miss Prim*, 1998
    Cattle-rustling kidnappers are no match for the non-stop lecturing from Miss Prim about their behavior; soon she and Slim are free and heading for the altar.
Susan Lowell, *Cindy Ellen: A Wild West Cinderella*, 2000
    Cindy Ellen wows Joe Prince at the rodeo, but at midnight departs leaving only a spur in the dust and Joe, determined to find and marry her.
Steve Sanfield, *The Great Turtle Drive*, 1996
    Considering the high cost of turtle soup, a cowboy thinks he's found a way to strike it rich.
Diane Stanley, *Raising Sweetness*, 1999
    Prompted by a letter from Sweetness, Lucy Locket returns to Possum Trot to marry the Sheriff, Sweetness' adoptive father, and resume her teaching job.

772

KAREN GRAY RUELLE, Author/Illustrator

Spookier Than a Ghost
(New York: Holiday House, 2001)

Series: Holiday House Reader. Level 2
Subject(s): Halloween; Brothers and Sisters; Family Life
Age range(s): Grades 1-2
Major character(s): Harry, Brother (older), Cat; Emily, Sister, Cat
Time period(s): Indeterminate
Locale(s): Fictional Country

Summary: On October first Harry and Emily begin planning their costumes for Halloween. Emily wants hers to be a surprise so she won't even give Harry a clue about what she's making. She does give him a hand though with his dinosaur costume by making the head for him. Harry returns the favor by praising her costume when it doesn't turn out as Emily hopes. He also explains her costume plan at each house and, for having an original idea, Emily gets extra treats that she kindly shares with Harry when they return home from a night of trick or treating. (32 pages)

Where it's reviewed:
Booklist, September 15, 2001, page 236
Horn Book Guide, Spring 2002, page 69

School Library Journal, September 2001, page 204

Other books by the same author:
Snow Valentines, 2000 (Holiday House Reader, Level 2)
The Monster in Harry's Backyard, 1999 (Holiday House Reader, Level 2)
The Thanksgiving Beast, 1999 (Holiday House Reader, Level 2)

Other books you might like:
Marion Dane Bauer, *Alison's Fierce and Ugly Halloween*, 1997
    Alison's attempt to be scary on Halloween creates friction with her friend Cindy.
Robin Michal Koontz, *Chicago and the Cat: The Halloween Party*, 1994
    On Halloween night nothing seems to go the way Chicago and the cat plan.
Dav Pilkey, *Dragon's Halloween*, 1993
    Kindly Dragon first scares himself with the pumpkin monster he makes and then with the sounds from his hungry stomach.

773

PATRICIA H. RUSHFORD

Stranded
(Bloomington, MN: Bethany House, 2001)

Series: Jennie McGrady Mystery. Number 14
Subject(s): Mystery and Detective Stories; Drugs; Cults
Age range(s): Grades 7-10
Major character(s): Jennie McGrady, Detective—Amateur, Teenager; Helen Bradley, Grandmother, Pilot; Eric, Religious (member of Desert Colony), Teenager; Donovan, Religious (member of Desert Colony), Con Artist
Time period(s): 2000s
Locale(s): Oregon

Summary: Jennie accompanies her grandmother as they fly to eastern Oregon where they'll meet up with family members for a ski vacation. While her grandmother Helen takes the aerial photographs she needs for a secret government assignment, Jennie has the chance to put her flying lessons to use. A storm engulfs the Piper Cherokee and Jennie is glad to have her grandmother assume the controls, but the plane ices up, stalls and crashes on landing. Helen is unconscious and Jennie leaves her to find help at the religious settlement they've flown over. She meets Eric, one of the Desert Colony members, and he takes her to the settlement for shelter. Some men from the settlement ride out to search, but refuse to take Jennie along; when they return they claim they've found neither a plane nor her grandmother. Jennie speaks to Donovan, the leader, and though he assures her his group is doing all they can to find the missing plane and its pilot, Jennie's convinced there's something amiss with this Desert Colony. Why else would her grandmother have been taking pictures? And where is her grandmother? (171 pages)

Where it's reviewed:
Voice of Youth Advocates, October 2001, page 284

Other books by the same author:
Grave Matters, 2002 (Jennie McGrady Mystery, Number 15)

Abandoned, 1999 (Jennie McGrady Mystery, Number 12)
In Too Deep, 1996 (Jennie McGrady Mystery, Number 8)
Silent Witness, 1993 (Jennie McGrady Mystery, Number 2)

Other books you might like:
Linda Crew, *Brides of Eden*, 2001
Joshua mesmerizes the women of Corvallis, Oregon and they join his church eager to become the "Second Mary" with Joshua ready to father the child.
Marilyn Levy, *No Way Home*, 1990
Billy's mother is part of a fanatical religious cult, which won't let him leave when his three-week visit has ended.
T.M. Murphy, *The Secrets of Code Z*, 2001
Amateur detective Orville contends with the CIA, a Russian scientist, a rookie newspaper reporter and a few too many murders in this fifth adventure.
Joan Lowery Nixon, *Murdered, My Sweet*, 1997
A murder takes place and everyone assumes Jenny's mystery writer mother can solve the crime, but her mother can write a good mystery, not solve one.
Frank Peretti, *Hangman's Curse*, 2001
Part of a secret government project, Elisha and Elijah infiltrate a high school where the bullies suffer from a strange form of madness.

774

MARISABINA RUSSO, Author/Illustrator

Come Back, Hannah!

(New York: Greenwillow Books/HarperCollins Publishers, 2001)

Subject(s): Babies; Mothers and Daughters; Parent and Child
Age range(s): Preschool
Major character(s): Hannah, Baby, Daughter; Mama, Mother
Time period(s): 2000s (2001)
Locale(s): United States

Summary: Hannah is no longer content to sit on the floor near Mama. Hannah is crawling and Mama chases after her because she doesn't "come back" on her own. Blocks, balls, and books hold Hannah's interest for a little while but then she crawls away looking for another activity. Mama calls to Hannah to come back, but Hannah keeps crawling. Mama gathers Hannah into her lap and reads a book with her before tucking Hannah into her crib for a nap. (32 pages)

Where it's reviewed:
Booklist, August 2001, page 2133
Horn Book Guide, Fall 2001, page 240
Kirkus Reviews, March 1, 2001, page 338
School Library Journal, July 2001, page 88

Awards the book has won:
Charlotte Zolotow Award, Highly Commended, 2002

Other books by the same author:
Under the Table, 1997
Alex Is My Friend, 1992
The Line-Up Book, 1986 (IRA Children's Picture Book Award)

Other books you might like:
Adele Aron Greenspun, *Bunny and Me*, 2000
Baby and Bunny imitate each other's behavior but when

Bunny hops away Baby's left feeling sad until Bunny reappears.
Kathy Henderson, *The Baby Dances*, 1999
Gradually, during a baby's first year of life she learns to smile, roll over, crawl and take her first steps.
Peter McCarty, *Baby Steps*, 2000
Month by month baby Suki grows and changes until she takes her first steps.

775

MARGRIET RUURS
ANDREW KISS, Illustrator

When We Go Camping

(Plattsburgh, NY: Tundra Books, 2001)

Subject(s): Camps and Camping; Animals; Nature
Age range(s): Grades K-2
Major character(s): Unnamed Character, Child, Sister; Unnamed Character, Child, Brother
Time period(s): 2000s (2001)
Locale(s): British Columbia, Canada

Summary: A family camping trip is a time to explore nature, fish, and canoe on the lake. Hiking through the woods allows siblings to view elk from afar while a pause for a closer look along the trail gives time to observe butterflies and robins seeking worms. Berries are ripe for the picking and the trout are delicious cooked over an open fire. As the day ends the family gathers to roast marshmallows and tell tales around the campfire. A concluding legend identifies the animal tracks on each page and gives information about each animal. (32 pages)

Where it's reviewed:
Booklist, December 15, 2001, page 741
Children's Bookwatch, July 2001, page 6
Horn Book Guide, Spring 2002, page 272
Resource Links, June 2001, page 5
School Library Journal, July 2001, page 88

Other books by the same author:
Emma's Cold Day, 2002
A Pacific Alphabet, 2001
Emma and the Coyote, 1999
Emma's Eggs, 1997
A Mountain Alphabet, 1996

Other books you might like:
Marion Dane Bauer, *When I Go Camping with Grandma*, 1995
A child and her grandmother share a loving relationship on a camping trip.
Lindsay Barrett George, *Around the Pond: Who's Been Here?*, 1996
As three children walk along a lake path in search of blueberries they notice signs of animal life and successfully identify eight animals.
Cynthia Rylant, *Henry and Mudge and the Starry Night*, 1998
A family camping trip includes hiking, singing around the campfire and quiet times with Henry's dog Mudge.

Ashley Wolff, *Stella and Roy Go Camping*, 1999
> On a camping trip Stella uses her book of animal tracks to identify the prints Roy sees as they hike.

776

PAM MUNOZ RYAN
JOE CEPEDA, Illustrator

Mice and Beans

(New York: Scholastic Press, 2001)

Subject(s): Birthdays; Animals/Mice; Cultures and Customs
Age range(s): Grades K-2
Major character(s): Rosa Maria, Grandmother, Cook; Little Catalina, 7-Year-Old
Time period(s): 2000s
Locale(s): United States

Summary: For a week, Rosa Maria, whose big heart can accommodate anything except a mouse, plans and prepares for Little Catalina's seventh birthday party. Each night as she completes the day's plans she sets a mousetrap before retiring, but by the following evening the mousetrap has vanished. Rosa Maria believes she's being forgetful, but unbeknownst to her, as soon as the lights are out mice scurry about to gather items for their own celebration. The helpful creatures also complete one very important task that Rosa Maria has forgotten and she finally realizes not only that her tiny home has mice, but also how beneficial they can be. A concluding glossary and pronunciation guide identifies the Spanish words used in the text. (32 pages)

Where it's reviewed:
Booklist, September 15, 2001, page 233
Bulletin of the Center for Children's Books, October 2001, page 73
Kirkus Reviews, August 1, 2001, page 1131
Publishers Weekly, September 17, 2001, page 79
School Library Journal, October 2001, page 130

Awards the book has won:
ALA Notable Children's Books, 2002

Other books by the same author:
Amelia and Eleanor Go for a Ride, 1999 (ALA Notable Children's Book)
Armadillos Sleep in Dugouts: And Other Places Animals Live, 1997
California Here We Come!, 1997

Other books you might like:
Becky Chavarria-Chairez, *Magda's Tortillas: Las Tortillas de Magda*, 2000
> In honor of her seventh birthday Magda is allowed to help Abuela make the tortillas for the family celebration.
Benjamin Alire Saenz, *Grandma Fina and Her Wonderful Umbrellas*, 1999
> Grandma Fina receives so many umbrellas for her birthday that she's able to share with all her friends.
Vivian Sathre, *Three Kind Mice*, 1997
> Three mice bake a cake as a birthday surprise for a cat
Gary Soto, *Chato and the Party Animals*, 2000
> Chato plans a big celebration for his friend Novio Boy, a former pound kitty who has never had a birthday party.

777

SARA RYAN

Empress of the World

(New York: Viking, 2001)

Subject(s): Homosexuality/Lesbianism; Friendship; School Life
Age range(s): Grades 9-12
Major character(s): Nicola "Nic" Lancaster, Student, Musician (viola); Battle Hall Davies, Student, 16-Year-Old; Isaac, Student; Katrina, Student, Computer Expert
Time period(s): 2000s
Locale(s): United States

Summary: Attending the Siegel Institute Summer Program for Gifted Students is a great opportunity for bright kids, who often don't fit in at their own schools, to excel in exciting, demanding coursework; take Nicola, she's interested in archaeology, but also plays the viola and is interested in the theater. The best aspect of the Institute, however, is the opportunity to make friends with like-minded, talented teens. On the first day, Nic meets Battle, Katrina and Isaac with whom she stays friends the entire eight-weeks, though not without a little flare up now and again. What amazes Nic is that she and Battle fall for one another in a relationship that moves easily from friendship, to romance, to kissing and then sneaking out at night to be with one another in this first novel. (213 pages)

Where it's reviewed:
Booklist, July 2001, page 2000
Horn Book, September 2001, page 594
Publishers Weekly, July 23, 2001, page 78
School Library Journal, July 2001, page 113
Voice of Youth Advocates, August 2001, page 206

Awards the book has won:
ALA Best Books for Young Adults, 2002

Other books you might like:
Francesca Lia Block, *Weetzie Bat*, 1989
> Offbeat Weetzie and Dirk each find their true love, though not with one another, in this witty, bizarre, modern-day fairy tale.
Nancy Garden, *Annie on My Mind*, 1982
> Lisa and Annie fall in love but are afraid to tell anyone of their relationship.
Laura Torres, *November Ever After*, 1999
> At first Amy is disturbed that her best friend Sara has a relationship with Anita, but eventually realizes that Sara can still be her best friend.

778

CYNTHIA RYLANT
G. BRIAN KARAS, Illustrator

The Case of the Puzzling Possum

(New York: Greenwillow Books, 2001)

Series: High-Rise Private Eyes. Case #3
Subject(s): Animals; Mystery and Detective Stories; Problem Solving
Age range(s): Grades 2-4

Major character(s): Bunny Brown, Rabbit, Detective—Private; Jack Jones, Raccoon, Detective—Private; Mr. Riley, Store Owner, Dog; Freddy, Opossum, Musician
Time period(s): 2000s (2001)
Locale(s): Fictional Country

Summary: A call to Bunny from Mr. Riley sends the two detectives hurrying to Mr. Riley's store to investigate a case of a vanishing and reappearing trombone. At the moment it's not in the window, but Bunny searches for clues anyway. The mud and hay that she finds suggest some link between the trombone's disappearance and the flier posted in Mr. Riley's shop about a hayride. Bunny and Jack attend the hayride and spot the trombone in the brass band accompanying the ride. By following the musician as he returns the trombone, they learn why the possum takes the instrument and suggest a way for him to pay for it so he no longer needs to "borrow" it from the store. (48 pages)

Where it's reviewed:
Booklist, December 1, 2000, page 708
Horn Book, March 2001, page 212
Kirkus Reviews, February 15, 2001, page 264
Publishers Weekly, January 8, 2001, page 69
School Library Journal, April 2001, page 121

Other books by the same author:
The Case of the Climbing Cat, 2000 (High Rise Private Eyes, Case #2)
The Case of the Missing Monkeys, 2000 (High Rise Private Eyes, Case #1)
Mr. Putter & Tabby Toot the Horn, 1998

Other books you might like:
Eth Clifford, *Flatfoot Fox and the Case of the Bashful Beaver,* 1995
   Detective Flatfoot Fox gives his assistant, Secretary Bird, an opportunity to solve the mystery of Bashful Beaver's stolen button bag.
Howard Goldsmith, *The Twiddle Twins Music Box Mystery,* 1997
   Timothy and Tabitha discover the identity of the thief who takes a family's music box.
Elizabeth Levy, *Parent's Night Fright,* 1998
   In the sixth title in the Invisible Inc. series, a group of amateur sleuths track a prize-winning story that appears to be as invisible as Chip.

779

CYNTHIA RYLANT
G. BRIAN KARAS, Illustrator

The Case of the Troublesome Turtle
(New York: Greenwillow Books, 2001)

Series: High-Rise Private Eyes. Case Number 4
Subject(s): Animals; Sports/Football; Mystery and Detective Stories
Age range(s): Grades 2-3
Major character(s): Bunny Brown, Rabbit, Detective—Private; Jack Jones, Raccoon, Detective—Private; Mr. Paris, Store Owner, Hippopotamus
Time period(s): 2000s (2001)

Locale(s): United States

Summary: Mr. Paris seeks the help of Bunny and Jack because, every Friday, balloons are being stolen from a display at the entrance to his toy store. Bunny notes the clues while Jack attempts to determine if the store stocks a toy in which he's interested. Bunny redirects Jack's attention to their task; deductive reasoning puts them on the track of the thief. On-site investigation confirms the detectives' suspicions and a cleverly worded note to the culprit solves the problem for everyone. (48 pages)

Where it's reviewed:
Booklist, May 15, 2001, page 1753
Horn Book Guide, Fall 2001, page 286
Horn Book, May 2001, page 337
School Library Journal, July 2001, page 88

Other books by the same author:
The Case of the Puzzling Possum, 2001 (High-Rise Private Eyes, Case Number 3)
The Case of the Climbing Cat, 2000 (High-Rise Private Eyes, Case Number 2)
The Case of the Missing Monkeys, 2000 (High-Rise Private Eyes, Case Number 1)

Other books you might like:
David A. Adler, *The Cam Jansen Series,* 1980-
   When confronted with a mystery needing a solution, Cam relies on her photographic memory.
Eth Clifford, *Flatfoot Fox and the Case of the Bashful Beaver,* 1995
   Detective Flatfoot Fox gives his assistant, Secretary Bird, an opportunity to solve the mystery of Bashful Beaver's stolen button bag.
Elizabeth Levy, *The Snack Attack Mystery,* 1996
   The third entry in the Invisible, Inc. series investigates a classroom's vanishing snacks.
Marjorie Weinman Sharmat, *Nate the Great and the Missing Key,* 1981
   Annie turns to Nate for help when her friend hides Annie's key in a safe place and gives her a poem full of clues to its location.

780

CYNTHIA RYLANT
MARK TEAGUE, Illustrator

The Great Gracie Chase: Stop That Dog!
(New York: The Blue Sky Press/Scholastic, Inc., 2001)

Subject(s): Animals/Dogs; Pets; Runaways
Age range(s): Preschool-Grade 1
Major character(s): Gracie, Dog, Runaway
Time period(s): Indeterminate Past
Locale(s): United States

Summary: Gracie leads a simple, contented life as the smaller of two family dogs living in quiet harmony with the family cat and goldfish. The arrival of house painters disrupts Gracie's routine. Her barking to complain about the noisy painters in her house only causes them to put her outside. Gracie is so offended by this action that she slips out the gate and takes herself for a walk. Immediately she's missed, but she never looks back and the great Gracie chase begins. The more people who come running after Gracie the faster she runs until she reaches the security of her now quiet home. (32 pages)

Where it's reviewed:
Booklist, February 15, 2001, page 1142
Bulletin of the Center for Children's Books, March 2001, page 278
Horn Book Guide, Fall 2001, page 272
Kirkus Reviews, February 1, 2001, page 188
School Library Journal, April 2001, page 121

Awards the book has won:
IRA Children's Choices, 2002

Other books by the same author:
Bunny Bungalow, 1999
The Cookie-Store Cat, 1999
The Bookshop Dog, 1996

Other books you might like:
Arthur Howard, *Cosmo Zooms*, 1999
   Cosmo fails to notice that his chosen nap spot has wheels; soon he's zooming down the hill on a skateboard and gaining the admiration of other dogs.
Gillian Johnson, *My Sister Gracie*, 2000
   Gracie, the dog Fabio's family gets from the pound to be his companion is completely opposite his hopes and expectations.
Steven Kroll, *Oh, Tucker!*, 1998
   Tucker's family loves their large, exuberant and clumsy dog despite the inadvertent messes he creates in the house.
Nancy Van Laan, *Little Baby Bobby*, 1997
   When Bobby's baby buggy begins rolling down the hill everyone joins the chase to rescue the errant stroller.

781

CYNTHIA RYLANT
TIM BOWERS, Illustrator

Little Whistle
(San Diego: Harcourt, Inc., 2001)

Subject(s): Animals/Guinea Pigs; Toys; Pets
Age range(s): Preschool-Grade 1
Major character(s): Little Whistle, Guinea Pig
Time period(s): 2000s
Locale(s): Toytown

Summary: Little Whistle lives in a toy store where he sleeps by day and visits his friends at night, when the toys come alive. When he's chilly, he dons a coat loaned by a sailor and sometimes a bear's hat. If Little Whistle visits friends in a distant part of the store he rides the train. Little Whistle enjoys a variety of acquaintances because every day some toys are sold while other new items arrive to replace them. Toytown is the perfect home for contented Little Whistle. (32 pages)

Where it's reviewed:
Booklist, February 15, 2001, page 1142
Bulletin of the Center for Children's Books, May 2001, page 351
Horn Book Guide, Fall 2001, page 240
Publishers Weekly, April 2, 2001, page 63
School Library Journal, May 2001, page 134

Other books by the same author:
Little Whistle's Dinner Party, 2001
Bunny Bungalow, 1999
The Cookie-Store Cat, 1999

Other books you might like:
Don Freeman, *Corduroy*, 1968
   A lonely department-store bear with a missing button eventually is purchased and given a loving home.
Holly Meade, *John Willy and Freddy McGee*, 1998
   Life in a cage is boring to two guinea pigs that seize the first opportunity to get out, explore the house and have a little fun.
Kevin O'Malley, *Leo Cockroach . . . Toy Tester*, 1999
   Leo enjoys his nightly work as the self-appointed toy tester for Waddatoy Toys.
Margaret Shannon, *Gullible's Troubles*, 1998
   Gullible Guineapig's teasing relatives try to take advantage of him but he gets the last laugh.

782

CYNTHIA RYLANT
TIM BOWERS, Illustrator

Little Whistle's Dinner Party
(San Diego: Harcourt, Inc., 2001)

Subject(s): Animals/Guinea Pigs; Toys; Stores, Retail
Age range(s): Grades K-1
Major character(s): Little Whistle, Guinea Pig, Friend
Time period(s): Indeterminate
Locale(s): Fictional Country

Summary: Little Whistle invites all his toy store friends to a party at midnight. Into a shopping cart he places a stove, a teakettle and dishes from the toy store shelves. Special food items he's saved for the occasion are placed into the oven. The dishes Little Whistle uses to set a "table" on the counter near his cage. His friends arrive while Little Whistle is searching for dessert, but soon everyone gathers around the table for an enjoyable meal in the company of good friends. (32 pages)

Where it's reviewed:
Booklist, October 1, 2001, page 326
Children's Bookwatch, September 2001, page 6
Horn Book Guide, Spring 2002, page 58
Kirkus Reviews, September 1, 2001, page 1300
School Library Journal, October 2001, page 130

Other books by the same author:
Little Whistle, 2001
Bunny Bungalow, 1999
The Cookie-Store Cat, 1999

Other books you might like:
Jane Hissey, *Old Bear*, 1997
   Old Bear is stuck in the attic and some stuffed animal friends work to free him.
Rosemary Wells, *Bunny Party*, 2001
   Max and Ruby can't agree on which toys are invited to the party they're planning for Grandma's birthday.
Dare Wright, *The Lonely Doll*, 1957
   Edith is a lonely doll until two stuffed bears move into her house.

783

CYNTHIA RYLANT
ARTHUR HOWARD, Illustrator

Mr. Putter & Tabby Feed the Fish

(San Diego: Harcourt, Inc., 2001)

Series: Mr. Putter & Tabby
Subject(s): Animals/Cats; Problem Solving; Pets
Age range(s): Grades 2-3
Major character(s): Mr. Putter, Aged Person; Tabby, Cat; Zeke, Dog
Time period(s): 2000s (2001)
Locale(s): United States

Summary: Mr. Putter's childhood love of goldfish leads him to purchase three from the local shop and set them up in a bowl at home. He expects that watching the fish will provide good exercise for Tabby's tail, but Tabby becomes so transfixed by the fish swimming in the bowl that she twitches and bats and cannot pull herself away even to sleep or eat. Mr. Putter covers the fish bowl with a pillowcase, but Tabby scoots under it so he tries putting a pail over the bowl. While the pail solves the Tabby problem, it doesn't allow Mr. Putter to observe the goldfish so he gives them to his neighbor. The fish do not excite her pet, Zeke, but they do lull him to sleep. (44 pages)

Where it's reviewed:
Booklist, May 1, 2001, page 1684
Horn Book Guide, Fall 2001, page 286
Kirkus Reviews, January 15, 2001, page 115
School Library Journal, May 2001, page 134
Tribune Books, March 25, 2001, page 5

Other books by the same author:
Mr. Putter & Tabby Paint the Porch, 2000 (Mr. Putter & Tabby)
Mr. Putter & Tabby Take the Train, 1998 (Mr. Putter & Tabby)
Mr. Putter & Tabby Toot the Horn, 1998 (Mr. Putter & Tabby)

Other books you might like:
Nancy Coffelt, *Tom's Fish*, 1994
    Tom is fascinated by his birthday present, a goldfish that swims upside down.
Claudia Mills, *Gus and Grandpa*, 1997
    The first book in a series introduces Gus and the warm, loving relationship he has with Grandpa.
Maggie Stern, *George and Diggety*, 2000
    George administers a doggie IQ test to his pet and realizes he should enjoy Diggety for his other admirable traits.

784

CYNTHIA RYLANT
MARK TEAGUE, Illustrator

Poppleton in Winter

(New York: Blue Sky Press/Scholastic Inc, 2001)

Series: Poppleton. Book 8
Subject(s): Animals/Pigs; Winter; Friendship

Age range(s): Grades 1-3
Major character(s): Poppleton, Pig, Friend; Cherry Sue, Llama, Friend; Patrick, Bird, Friend
Time period(s): Indeterminate
Locale(s): Fictional Country

Summary: Poppleton lovingly measures the icicles that form on his house each winter. Or he did until Patrick accidentally flew into one, starting a domino effect that drops the icicles into the snowy yard. Together Patrick and Poppleton use the icicles to make a lovely picket fence. In the second story, Poppleton busies himself making a bust of Cherry Sue but he has difficulty remembering the details of her features. After he knocks on her door for the third time, Cherry Sue comes to his house to model. No one has time for a sleigh ride with Poppleton in the final story so he's feeling a little glum. Then his three busy friends show up at Poppleton's house and he learns why they were too busy. They were making the food for his surprise birthday party. The day concludes with a sleigh ride too! (48 pages)

Where it's reviewed:
Bulletin of the Center for Children's Books, December 2001, page 152
Horn Book Guide, Spring 2002, page 62
Kirkus Reviews, September 1, 2001, page 152
School Library Journal, October 2001, page 130

Other books by the same author:
Poppleton Has Fun, 2000 (Poppleton, Book 7)
Poppleton in Fall, 1999 (Poppleton, Book 6)
Poppleton in Spring, 1999 (Poppleton, Book 5)

Other books you might like:
Stephen Krensky, *Lionel in the Winter*, 1994
    In four brief easy-to-read stories Lionel makes the most of the winter weather that others in his family dislike.
Arnold Lobel, *Frog and Toad All Year*, 1976
    Through all the seasons of the year Frog and Toad's friendship endures.
Jean Van Leeuwen, *Oliver and Amanda and the Big Snow*, 1995
    Siblings Oliver and Amanda enjoy the day romping in the snow with their parents.

785

CYNTHIA RYLANT
WENDY ANDERSON HALPERIN, Illustrator

Summer Party

(New York: Simon & Schuster Books for Young Readers, 2001)

Series: Cobble Street Cousins. Book 5
Subject(s): Cousins; Aunts and Uncles; Surprises
Age range(s): Grades 2-4
Major character(s): Tess, 9-Year-Old, Cousin, Niece; Rosie, 9-Year-Old, Sister (Lily's), Cousin (Tess's); Lily, 9-Year-Old, Sister (Rosie's), Cousin (Tess's)
Time period(s): 1990s
Locale(s): United States

Summary: Rosie, Lily and Tess are feeling sad and happy all at the same time. Their parents are returning from their world tour and, although they're excited to see them, they are feeling blue because their year of living together in their aunt's attic is coming to an end. While planning a surprise to welcome their parents, the three cousins also make plans to have a reunion every summer. The first one will come sooner than they expect because a surprise announcement at the party gives them news of their aunt's wedding later in the summer. (54 pages)

Where it's reviewed:
Booklist, June 2001, page 1884
Horn Book Guide, Spring 2002, page 78
School Library Journal, May 2001, page 134

Other books by the same author:
Some Good News, 1999 (Cobble Street Cousins, Book 4)

Special Gifts, 1999 (Cobble Street Cousins, Book 3)
A Little Shopping, 1998 (Cobble Street Cousins, Book 2)

Other books you might like:
Beverly Cleary, *The Ramona Series*, 1952-1999
Irrepressible Ramona and her family endure school problems and sibling squabbles with love and a sense of humor.
Maud Hart Lovelace, *Betsy-Tacy and Tib*, 1941
The warmth of small town neighbors and the shared activities of close friends make this work a timeless classic.
Marilyn Sachs, *JoJo & Winnie: Sister Stories*, 1999
Although Winnie is often an annoying little sister, JoJo reaches out to comfort her when Winnie's excluded from a neighborhood birthday party.

S

786

MARILYN SADLER
ROGER BOLLEN, Illustrator

Bobo Crazy
(New York: Random House, 2001)

Series: Zenon, Girl of the 21st Century. #1
Subject(s): Robots; Pets; Space Colonies
Age range(s): Grades 2-4
Major character(s): Zenon "Zee" Kar, 5th Grader, Friend; Nebula "Neb", 5th Grader, Friend; Bobo Dog, Robot
Time period(s): 2040s (2049)
Locale(s): Space Station 9, Space Station

Summary: Zee would prefer to be like Neb and all the other kids on the Space Station and own the latest brand of robotic pet, but her father buys a cheaper, and to Zee inferior, model. The Bobo Dog has no mouth and cannot do Zee's homework for her as the other robotic pet can. Zee is so annoyed and embarrassed to have the Bobo Dog following her that she treats it unkindly and it vanishes. The popular robotic pet becomes vicious toward its owners and the teacher fails Neb and their classmates who used their robots to do the homework. Suddenly, Bobo Dog looks more appealing and Zee wishes she could find her stellar pet robot. A concluding glossary defines the space slang used in the book. (88 pages)

Where it's reviewed:
Booklist, April 1, 2001, page 1473
Horn Book Guide, Fall 2001, page 295
Kirkus Reviews, December 1, 2000, page 1688
Publishers Weekly, January 22, 2001, page 324
School Library Journal, February 2001, page 105

Other books by the same author:
Zenon Kar, Spaceball Star, 2001 (Zenon, Girl of the 21st Century, #2)
The Parakeet Girl, 1997
Zenon, Girl of the 21st Century, 1996
P.J. Funnybunny Camps Out, 1993

Other books you might like:
Stan Berenstain, *The Berenstain Bear Scouts and the Run-Amuck Robot*, 1997
Professor Actual Factual has no control over his latest invention, a supercharged robot destroying Bear Country if the scouts can't stop it.
Margaret Mahy, *Raging Robots and Unruly Uncles*, 1993
Twin brothers reconsider their opinion of their children after two out-of-control robots visit them.
Dav Pilkey, *Ricky Ricotta's Giant Robot: An Adventure Novel*, 2000
Dr. Stinky creates a destructive Robot but forgets to program his invention to be nasty and mean so the giant Robot becomes the friend Ricky seeks.

787

RENE SALDANA JR.

The Jumping Tree
(New York: Delacorte, 2001)

Subject(s): Mexican Americans; Fathers and Sons; Family Life
Age range(s): Grades 6-9
Major character(s): Rey Castaneda, Teenager
Time period(s): 2000s
Locale(s): Nuevo Penitas, Texas; Mexico

Summary: Though young Rey lives in Texas, he and his family often cross the border into Mexico to visit family, which makes him part of his close-knit Mexican family as well as his American community. Rey wants to emulate his elders, like his dad who can say no to drinking, but he also has a "macho" streak when he's with his peers. A rite of passage in his neighborhood is to jump from one mesquite tree to another, but when Rey jumps, his shorter legs cause him to fall and break his wrist in this first novel. (181 pages)

Where it's reviewed:
Book Report, November 2001, page 66
Booklist, May 15, 2001, page 1747

Bulletin of the Center for Children's Books, September 2001, page 34
Kirkus Reviews, May 1, 2001, page 665
School Library Journal, June 2001, page 154

Other books you might like:

Molly Bang, *Tiger's Fall*, 2001
Never one to pass up a dare, Lupe climbs the old fig tree but skipping back down loses her balance, falls and is paralyzed.

Victor Martinez, *Parrot in the Oven: Mi Vida*, 1996
Mexican American teen Manny and his family fight to stay together and make a success of their lives in America.

Jerry McGinley, *Joaquin Strikes Back*, 1998
Moving from California to Michigan, Mexican American Joaquin is unprepared for the racism he confronts at his new school.

David Rice, *Crazy Loco*, 2001
The importance of family is featured in this collection of short stories about Mexican Americans living in a small south Texas town.

Gary Soto, *Baseball in April: And Other Stories*, 1990
Day-to-day life for young Hispanics is related in these eleven short stories.

788

GRAHAM SALISBURY

Lord of the Deep

(New York: Delacorte, 2001)

Subject(s): Fishing; Stepfathers
Age range(s): Grades 6-8
Major character(s): Mikey Donovan, 13-Year-Old; Bill Monks, Stepfather (of Mikey), Sea Captain; Cal, Fisherman; Ernie, Fisherman; Alison ''Ali'', 15-Year-Old, Daughter (of Cal)
Time period(s): 2000s
Locale(s): Maui, Hawaii; *Crystal-C*, At Sea (off Kona Coast of Hawaii)

Summary: As the youngest deckhand in the fleet, Mikey's thrilled and honored that his stepfather Bill asked for his help aboard his fishing boat the *Crystal-C*. Their charter trips have been great until Cal and Ernie come aboard, two sportsmen who make a mockery of that term, accompanied by Cal's daughter Alison. Mikey and Alison befriend one another and when Mikey has to go under the boat to cut free a tangled line, he's glad of her presence. Cal and Ernie want to catch a blue marlin and, having already lost one, are delighted when another strikes. Bill's help reeling in the marlin negates its championship size, but that doesn't bother the two brothers who offer him a sizable fee to modify the record. To Mikey's dismay, Bill accepts the bribe. Mikey has difficulty understanding that his stepfather took the money to maintain his charter fishing business, which provides for their family, including his blind half-brother. (182 pages)

Where it's reviewed:
Booklist, August 2001, page 2108
Horn Book, September 2001, page 595
Publishers Weekly, July 30, 2001, page 86
School Library Journal, August 2001, page 188

Voice of Youth Advocates, August 2001, page 206

Awards the book has won:
School Library Journal Best Books, 2001
ALA Best Books for Young Adults, 2002

Other books by the same author:
Island Boyz, 2002
Jungle Dogs, 1998
Shark Bait, 1997
Under the Blood-Red Sun, 1994
Blue Skin of the Sea, 1992

Other books you might like:

Marion Dane Bauer, *Face to Face*, 1991
A white water rafting trip to reunite Michael with his father is disastrous, but shows Michael the worth of his solid stepfather.

Cynthia DeFelice, *Death at Devil's Bridge*, 2000
Ben jeopardizes his summer job on a charter fishing boat when he lets himself enjoy the attention of a friendship with drug dealer Donny.

James DeVita, *Blue*, 2001
Bored and dreaming of the blue marlin fish that leap out of the water, Morgan awakens to find he's turning into one.

Ernest Hemingway, *The Old Man and the Sea*, 1952
Though Santiago loses his fish to sharks, knowing he caught one will restore his standing with the villagers who think he has bad luck.

789

KAREN SALMANSOHN

One Puppy, Three Tales

(Berkeley, CA: Tricycle Press, 2001)

Series: Alexandra Rambles On!. Book 1
Subject(s): Mothers and Daughters; Fathers and Daughters; Interpersonal Relations
Age range(s): Grades 4-6
Major character(s): Alexandra, 12-Year-Old
Time period(s): 2000s
Locale(s): United States

Summary: This riotous book, illustrated in hot colors of lime, pink, purple and blue, with sidebar commentaries and whimsical, doodling illustrations, features Alexandra who has lots to say about her life and her family. She's embarrassed by her cabaret singing mother who wears zebra stripes, isn't sure which school clique is right for her and doesn't understand why her father's always too busy to talk to her. (64 pages)

Where it's reviewed:
Kirkus Reviews, March 1, 2001, page 338
Publishers Weekly, March 12, 2001, page 91
School Library Journal, June 2001, page 156

Other books by the same author:
Wherever I Go, There I Am, 2002 (Alexandra Rambles On, Book 3)
Oh, and Another Thing, 2001 (Alexandra Rambles On, Book 2)

Other books you might like:

Amy Goldman Koss, *Smoke Screen*, 2000
> To interest a cute guy, Mitzi tells a lie about her mother's health but the lie is discovered when her mother receives a mound of get-well cards.

Dona Schenker, *The Secret Circle*, 1998
> Though Jamie would love to belong to a group of friends, the task "The Secret Circle" requires for membership is more than she's willing to do.

Susan Shreve, *Goodbye, Amanda the Good*, 2000
> One day Amanda rebels against being an obedient, intelligent student and dyes her hair black to match her black clothes and thinks of joining "The Club."

Rachel Vail, *Wonder*, 1991
> Jessica's tumultuous seventh grade year finds her seesawing between being a social pariah and having her own clique.

790

BARNEY SALTZBERG, Author/Illustrator

The Problem with Pumpkins: A Hip & Hop Story

(San Diego: Gulliver/Harcourt, Inc., 2001)

Subject(s): Halloween; Problem Solving; Friendship
Age range(s): Grades K-2
Major character(s): Hip, Hippopotamus, Friend; Hop, Rabbit, Friend
Time period(s): Indeterminate
Locale(s): Fictional Country

Summary: The only problem Hip and Hop are having with pumpkins is Hop's insistence that only one of them can wear a pumpkin costume for Halloween and Hop is the one. Poor Hip! She really wants to be a pumpkin too. She tries a pirate costume but it doesn't suit her. Hop offers suggestions for other costume ideas but Hip decides if she can't be a pumpkin she'll just go home. Hop, faced with the prospect of trick-or-treating alone, has a change of heart and makes Hip a pumpkin costume so the friends can go out happily together. (40 pages)

Where it's reviewed:
Booklist, September 15, 2001, page 236
Horn Book Guide, Spring 2002, page 58
Kirkus Reviews, July 15, 2001, page 1034
Publishers Weekly, September 24, 2001, page 43
School Library Journal, September 2001, page 205

Other books by the same author:
The Soccer Mom from Outer Space, 2000
The Flying Garbanzos, 1998
This Is a Great Place for a Hot Dog Stand, 1995

Other books you might like:

Holly Hobbie, *Toot & Puddle: You Are My Sunshine*, 1999
> The sun shines but Toot mopes so Puddle and Tulip try to cheer their friend.

Jef Kaminsky, *Poppy & Ella: 3 Stories about 2 Friends*, 2000
> Poppy and Ela are great friends who agree about everything and even when they disagree they are still friends.

Arnold Lobel, *Frog and Toad All Year*, 1976
> Through all the seasons of the year Frog and Toad's friendship endures.

James Marshall, *George and Martha*, 1972
> The first book in a series about George and Martha uses several brief humorous stories to describe the antics of two hippo buddies.

791

ALEX SANCHEZ

Rainbow Boys

(New York: Simon & Schuster, 2001)

Subject(s): Homosexuality/Lesbianism; Interpersonal Relations; Schools/High Schools
Age range(s): Grades 9-12
Major character(s): Jason Carillo, Basketball Player, 12th Grader; Kyle Meeks, 12th Grader, Homosexual; Nelson "Nelly" Glassman, 12th Grader, Homosexual
Time period(s): 2000s
Locale(s): United States

Summary: In this first novel, three seniors face a year during which each will make life-changing decisions as well as become closer friends. Jason is the basketball star with the girlfriend whose dreams increasingly include men; Kyle is gay but unable to come out to anyone but himself; and Kyle's friend Nelson is a "flaming gay" who isn't practicing at the moment. Because of Nelson's mother's activism in PFLAG, the Parents, Families and Friends of Lesbians and Gays, Nelson decides to establish a Gay-Straight Alliance at his school and is helped by Kyle. When Jason attends a meeting of Rainbow Youth to try to understand his conflicting actions and dreams, he's as surprised to see Kyle and Nelson there as they are to see him. And that's when life becomes even more complicated for Nelson really likes Kyle while Kyle has had a crush on Jason for a long time. Jason has been oblivious to Kyle's emotions until he attends this meeting and the three begin to open up to one another in this realistic look at the romantic difficulties facing young gay teens. Don't be surprised that the conflicts sound the same as those in heterosexual relationships for the participants are all teenagers facing love, often for the first time. (245 pages)

Where it's reviewed:
Bulletin of the Center for Children's Books, November 2001, page 91
Kliatt, September 2001, page 12
Publishers Weekly, November 26, 2001, page 62
School Library Journal, October 2001, page 169
Voice of Youth Advocates, December 2001, page 362

Awards the book has won:
ALA Best Books for Young Adults, 2002

Other books you might like:

Michael Cart, *My Father's Scar*, 1996
> After Evan is beaten up for announcing that he's gay, Andy worries that he did nothing to help.

Jean Ferris, *Eight Seconds*, 2000
> Attending rodeo camp and riding a bull is thrilling, but

then so are his feelings for fellow cowboy Kit, which leaves John mulling over some truths about himself.

M.E. Kerr, *Hello, I Lied*, 1997

Though Lang finds himself attracted to Huguette, he realizes only Eric makes him truly happy, which confirms his homosexuality.

William Taylor, *The Blue Lawn*, 1999

Good-looking David is interested in tough guy Theo which forces them to consider their feelings for one another.

Ellen Wittlinger, *Hard Love*, 1999

John thinks he's found the love for which he's been searching when he meets Marisol, only to discover she's in love with another girl.

792

RUTH SANDERSON, Author/Illustrator

The Golden Mare, the Firebird, and the Magic Ring

(Boston: Little, Brown and Company, 2001)

Subject(s): Folklore; Magic; Folk Tales
Age range(s): Grades 1-4
Major character(s): Alexi, Hunter; Golden Mare, Horse; Yelena the Fair, Maiden
Time period(s): Indeterminate Past
Locale(s): Russia

Summary: Elements from several Russian folktales contribute to this original story of Alexi, seeker of adventure and fortune. Hearing hoofbeats approaching in a dark forest Alexi prepares his bow to fell a deer but instead a mare appears. Golden Mare asks that her life be spared and Alexi willingly does so. The Golden Mare becomes Alexi's steed assuring his success as one of the tsar's huntsman but also angering the tsar because the mare refuses to allow anyone but Alexi to ride her. The frustrated tsar sends Alexi on a series of seemingly impossible quests but Alexi achieves each one with the aid of the magical Golden Mare. One quest brings Yelena the Fair to the tsar who seeks to marry her but Yelena has a magic ring that spares her from marriage to the old man and enables Alexi to achieve the fortune he seeks. (32 pages)

Where it's reviewed:
Booklist, April 1, 2001, page 1463
Horn Book Guide, Fall 2001, page 346
Kirkus Reviews, March 15, 2001, page 421
Publishers Weekly, April 9, 2001, page 74
School Library Journal, April 2001, page 135

Other books by the same author:
The Crystal Mountain, 1999 (Notable Social Studies Trade Books for Young People)
Rose Red & Snow White, 1997
Papa Gatto: An Italian Fairy Tale, 1995

Other books you might like:
Mary Casanova, *The Hunter: A Chinese Folktale*, 2000
Hai Li Bu's kindness to a snake earns him a reward enabling him to be a successful hunter but it also carries a warning that could mean his death.

Brad Kessler, *The Firebird*, 1996

An archer, assisted by a magical horse, completes the Tsar's demands and gains the hand of the princess.

Elizabeth Winthrop, *The Little Humpbacked Horse: A Russian Tale*,

With the support of his faithful horse, a peasant succeeds in becoming Tsar of Russia.

793

BARBARA SANTUCCI
ANDREA SHINE, Illustrator

Loon Summer

(Grand Rapids, MI: Eerdmans Books for Young Readers, 2001)

Subject(s): Divorce; Fathers and Daughters; Animals/Birds
Age range(s): Grades 1-4
Major character(s): Rainie, Child of Divorced Parents; Dad, Father
Time period(s): 2000s (2001)
Locale(s): United States

Summary: The sad call of loons awakens Rainie and reminds her that, for the first time, only she and Dad are at the cottage. Rainie can't understand why her parents cannot stay together for life as the loons do. Dad assures Rainie that the two of them will continue to visit the lake cottage every summer. Each familiar experience feels different to Rainie and is a painful reminder that her parents do not live together. During the summer Rainie and Dad build new memories as they enjoy fishing and berry picking in a slightly different way than they did when there were three at the lake cottage. As Rainie and Dad pack the car at the end of summer, the loons fly away to conclude the author's first book. (32 pages)

Where it's reviewed:
Children's Bookwatch, June 2001, page 3
Publishers Weekly, May 28, 2001, page 88
Riverbank Review, Winter 2001, page 30
School Library Journal, August 2001, page 160

Other books you might like:
Roni Schotter, *Missing Rabbit*, 2002
Kara uses her stuffed rabbit to help her adjust to the constant moving between her mother's and father's houses after her parent's divorce.

Andrea Spalding, *Me and Mr. Mah*, 1999
His parents' divorce forces a young boy to leave his farm home on the prairie and move to a city far from his father.

Judith Vigna, *Mommy and Me by Ourselves Again*, 1987
A little girl feels lonely following her parent's divorce until relatives arrive for a birthday celebration.

Elizabeth Winthrop, *As the Crow Flies*, 1998
Annually, Michael's father visits him for one week and they stay together in a hotel; the rest of the year phone calls connect them.

JOHN SAUL

The Manhattan Hunt Club

(New York: Ballantine, 2001)

Subject(s): Suspense; Homeless People; Murder
Age range(s): Grades 10-Adult
Major character(s): Jeff Converse, Student—College
Time period(s): 2000s
Locale(s): New York, New York (Manhattan)

Summary: Bright architecture student Jeff Converse hustles to help a badly beaten woman, but then is falsely accused of committing the crime. Sentenced to prison, the van taking him to Rikers Island is hit and catches on fire, but not before Jeff is pulled to what he thinks is safety. Taken to a subway stop, he is sent into the subterranean world of tunnels that crisscross, loop and dead end under the streets of New York. There he meets gangs of homeless who control this underground world as well as an odd group of predators, the business and civic leaders of New York, who have turned these tunnels into their own private hunt club. Jeff is now the hunted and his only hope of salvation lies in returning to the aboveground world, an act not too easy to achieve, in another tale of terror from a popular author. (313 pages)

Where it's reviewed:
Booklist, May 1, 2001, page 1595
Kirkus Reviews, June 1, 2001, page 768
Library Journal, August 2001, page 166
People Weekly, August 20, 2001, page 41
Publishers Weekly, May 21, 2001, page 78

Other books by the same author:
Nightshade, 2000
The Right Hand of Evil, 1999
The Presence, 1997
Black Lightning, 1995
Sleepwalk, 1990

Other books you might like:
Jeffery Deaver, *The Coffin Dancer*, 1998
    Quadriplegic Lincoln Rhyme and his assistant Amelia Sachs track down the "Coffin Dancer," a man who eliminates witnesses any way he can.
Iris Johansen, *The Killing Game*, 1999
    Forensic sculptor Eve Duncan escapes to a tropical island, but is called home when bodies are found in Georgia, one of whom could be her missing daughter.
James Patterson, *Pop! Goes the Weasel*, 1999
    When "Jane Does" are being murdered in Washington, D.C., Alex is told to not waste time on the investigation, but ignores his boss as he's sure a serial killer is at work.

795

APRIL PULLEY SAYRE
JOELLEN MCALLISTER STAMMEN, Illustrator

Crocodile Listens

(New York: Greenwillow Books/HarperCollins Publishers, 2001)

Subject(s): Animals/Crocodiles; Animals

Age range(s): Grades K-3
Major character(s): Crocodile, Crocodile, Mother
Time period(s): Indeterminate
Locale(s): Nile River, Africa

Summary: Ignoring the sounds of passing giraffes, warthogs and frogs, Crocodile lies quietly beside the river, listening. Then she stands and deep beneath the sand, her babies hear the sounds of her feet. The hatchlings need help and when Crocodile hears their cries she begins to dig. Soon the sand covering the eggs is pushed aside and the young crocodiles emerge from their eggs. To protect her young from a hungry mongoose, Crocodile scoops them into her mouth and carries them to the river. In the Nile they learn to swim, hunt and survive, riding on Crocodile's back whenever they need to rest. A concluding note gives additional information about the Nile crocodile. (24 pages)

Where it's reviewed:
Bulletin of the Center for Children's Books, October 2001, page 74
Horn Book Guide, Spring 2002, page 58
Kirkus Reviews, August 15, 2001, page 1221
School Library Journal, October 2001, page 130

Other books by the same author:
Shadows, 2002
Dig Wait Listen: A Desert Toad's Tale, 2001 (Booklist Editors' Choice)
It's My City!: A Singing Map, 2001
Turtle, Turtle, Watch Out!, 2000

Other books you might like:
Roy Gerrard, *Croco'nile*, 1994
    When Hamut and Nekatu are kidnapped on the Nile their crocodile friend comes to their rescue just in time.
Jonathan London, *Crocodile: Disappearing Dragon*, 2001
    Life in a mangrove swamp holds many challenges for a crocodile and her newly hatched offspring.
Karen Wallace, *Imagine You Are a Crocodile*, 1997
    This picture book introduces crocodiles and their habitat by asking the reader to imagine being one of the animals.

APRIL PULLEY SAYRE
BARBARA BASH, Illustrator

Dig Wait Listen: A Desert Toad's Tale

(New York: Greenwillow Books, 2001)

Subject(s): Animals/Frogs and Toads; Deserts; Nature
Age range(s): Grades K-2
Major character(s): Unnamed Character, Toad
Time period(s): 2000s
Locale(s): Southwest

Summary: Beneath the ground a spadefoot toad patiently waits. As protection from the dry desert climate she's burrowed into the sand where she listens for the sound of rain. She hears the soft sounds of a scorpion, the tapping sounds of a woodpecker on a nearby cactus and the loud crunching of the park ranger's boots. Finally, the sound of distant thunder precedes the drumming of the heavy rain on the ground and the toad knows it is time to dig out of the burrow. She joins other toads in a rapidly growing puddle where the female toads lay eggs that are fertilized by the males. The eggs hatch and develop before the puddle dries up and the toads return to safety beneath the desert floor. (32 pages)

Where it's reviewed:
Booklist, June 2001, page 1881
Bulletin of the Center for Children's Books, May 2001, page 352
Horn Book, July 2001, page 476
Kirkus Reviews, April 1, 2001, page 505
School Library Journal, June 2001, page 129

Awards the book has won:
Booklist Editors' Choice/Books for Youth, 2002

Other books by the same author:
Turtle, Turtle, Watch Out!, 2000
Home at Last: A Song of Migration, 1998
Coral Reef, 1996

Other books you might like:
Richard E. Albert, *Alejandro's Gift*, 1994
    To attract and thank the desert creatures that befriend him, lonely Alejandro digs a waterhole that becomes an oasis.
Vivian French, *Growing Frogs*, 2000
    With Mom's help a little girl collects frog spawn from a pond and watches the frogs' development in her home aquarium.
Barbara Ann Porte, *Tale of a Tadpole*, 1997
    The tadpole that Francine carefully raises surprises her by developing into a toad rather than the frog she expected.
Jane Yolen, *Welcome to the Sea of Sand*, 1996
    An illustrated poetic exploration of the desert environment concludes with factual information.

797

SIMON SCARROW

Under the Eagle: A Tale of Military Adventure and Reckless Heroism with the Roman Legions
(New York: Thomas Dunne/St. Martin's, 2001)

Subject(s): Historical; Roman Empire; Gold
Age range(s): Grades 10-Adult
Major character(s): Lucius Cornelius Macro, Military Personnel (centurion); Quintus Licinius Cato, Military Personnel (second-in-command to Macro)
Time period(s): 1st century
Locale(s): Germany; England

Summary: A slave who can read and write and an officer who is illiterate and fears discovery; luckily these two serve together and help one another. Centurion Macro is part of the Roman army's Second Legion currently fighting in Germany, but fears if his illiteracy is discovered, he'll be demoted back to a common soldier. His second in command is Cato, a former imperial slave, who's been forced to join the army and is held in contempt by the other soldiers for his previously easy life. However, Cato proves his mettle and earns his officer rank in the eyes of the other legionnaires. The Second Legion receives orders to Britain, considered the most barba-

rous country of all, and Cato takes advantage of their change to teach Macro to read and write. There's more to their expedition than many realize for one-hundred years earlier a trunk of gold was left buried in a bog. The politics of Rome remain tangled as someone plots to use the found gold as a means to ascend the throne in this adventurous first novel. (246 pages)

Where it's reviewed:
Booklist, August 2001, page 2091
Kirkus Reviews, July 1, 2001, page 896

Other books you might like:
Gillian Bradshaw, *Imperial Purple*, 1988
    Asked to weave a purple cloak too large for the current ruler, Demetrias knows there's a conspiracy afoot against Emperor Theodosius II.
Lindsey Davis, *Silver Pigs*, 1989
    Falco, a hard-boiled detective in a toga, investigates a plot to overthrow the Empire by sending ingots of silver to Rome.
Robert Graves, *I, Claudius*, 1934
    Lame Claudius survives many plots, conspiracies and intrigues to eventually become emperor.

798

ROSALYN SCHANZER, Author/Illustrator

Davy Crockett Saves the World
(New York: HarperCollins Publishers, 2001)

Subject(s): Tall Tales; Folklore; Legends
Age range(s): Grades K-3
Major character(s): Davy Crockett, Hero, Frontiersman
Time period(s): Indeterminate Past
Locale(s): United States

Summary: Halley's Comet threatens to destroy earth and Davy Crockett is called on to stop it. Davy climbs a high mountain where the comet sees him and roars down to devour him. Davy's angered by the sight of the comet and leaps on it as the comet whirls around frantically trying to shake Davy off. Failing that, the comet dives into the ocean to drown Davy but instead its fire is put out and its ice melts. Davy now grabs the bit of the tail still visible, spins Halley's Comet around and flings it far into space thus setting it on a different orbital path so the planet will not be threatened in the future. (32 pages)

Where it's reviewed:
Booklist, November 15, 2001, page 573
Kirkus Reviews, June 15, 2001, page 872
Publishers Weekly, July 23, 2001, page 77
School Library Journal, August 2001, page 160

Awards the book has won:
Booklist Editors' Choice/Books for Youth, 2002
IRA Children's Choices, 2002

Other books by the same author:
Gold Fever!: Tales from the California Gold Rush, 1999
How We Crossed the West: The Adventures of Lewis & Clark, 1997
My First Jewish Word Book, 1992

Other books you might like:

Ariane Dewey, *The Narrow Escapes of Davy Crockett*, 1993
   Stories based on The Crockett Almanacs include these tall
   tales about America's folk hero.
Steven Kellogg, *Sally Ann Thunder Ann Whirlwind Crockett:
A Tall Tale*, 1995
   According to this tall tale, Sally Ann rescues and marries
   Davy Crockett.
Audrey Wood, *The Bunyans*, 1996
   The story of larger-than-life Paul Bunyan humorously pre-
   sents the legendary folk hero as a family man.

 799

JULIAN SCHEER
RONALD HIMLER, Illustrator

A Thanksgiving Turkey
(New York: Holiday House, 2001)

Subject(s): Grandfathers; Animals/Turkeys; Farm Life
Age range(s): Grades 2-5
Major character(s): Granddad, Grandfather, Farmer; Un-
   named Character, 13-Year-Old, Narrator
Time period(s): Indeterminate Past
Locale(s): Virginia

Summary: Thirteen is not an age to give up one's friends and
move to a small farm in Virginia, but there's no other way
around it when this teen's mother says it's time to give
Granddad a hand with the farm. Rural life turns out not to be
too bad. The grandson learns to do farm chores and identify
the tracks of wild animals in the nearby woods. Granddad
enjoys the challenge of hunting wild turkey and teaches his
grandson how to use the turkey call and judge the age of the
turkey by the length of its "beard." After months of fruitless
hunting for one old tom Granddad finally sees the majestic old
bird but hasn't the heart to see it dead and the family eats
store-bought turkey for Thanksgiving dinner. (32 pages)

Where it's reviewed:

Booklist, September 1, 2001, page 122
Bulletin of the Center for Children's Books, October 2001,
   page 75
Kirkus Reviews, July 15, 2001, page 1034
Publishers Weekly, September 24, 2001, page 46
School Library Journal, September 2001, page 205

Other books by the same author:

By the Light of the Captured Moon, 2001
Upside Down Day, 1968
Rain Makes Applesauce, 1964 (Caldecott Honor Book)

Other books you might like:

Eve Bunting, *A Turkey for Thanksgiving*, 1991
   Mr. and Mrs. Moose change to a vegetarian menu after
   their live turkey causes them to have second thoughts
   about the Thanksgiving meal.
Denys Cazet, *Minnie and Moo and the Thanksgiving Tree*,
2000
   To avoid being part of Thanksgiving dinner, various farm
   animals join the turkeys hiding from the farmer's wife in
   Minnie and Moo's tree.

Joy Cowley, *Gracias, the Thanksgiving Turkey*, 1996
   Miguel convinces his family to eat chicken on Thanksgiving rather than his pet turkey, Gracias.

800

GARY D. SCHMIDT

Straw into Gold
(New York: Clarion Books, 2001)

Subject(s): Fairy Tales; Greed
Age range(s): Grades 6-9
Major character(s): Tousle, Foster Child; Innes, Blind Person,
   Revolutionary; Da, Father (of Tousle); Beryn, Nobleman
   (lord)
Time period(s): Indeterminate Past
Locale(s): Wolverham, England; St. Eynsham Abbey, En-
   gland

Summary: What would have happened if the Queen hadn't
been able to guess Rumplestiltskin's name and her son had
been taken away from her? In this adaptation, a young lad
named Tousle and his funny, little father Da travel to Wol-
versham where they witness the parade of one hundred rebels
condemned to execution unless someone pleads for their
lives. That someone is Tousle, supported by the Queen, who
is given a chance to save the rebels if he can answer the
King's question "What fills a hand fuller than a skein of
gold?" Allowed seven days to find the answer, Tousle is
given the blind rebel Innes as his guide, and the two set off to
find the Queen at St. Evynsham Abbey, for they are certain
she knows the answer. Following behind them are the men of
Lord Beryn, who want them dead, and the King's Grip, who
thinks Tousle may lead him to the funny, little man who can
spin straw into gold in another twist on the famous fairy tale.
(172 pages)

Where it's reviewed:

Book Report, November 2001, page 66
Booklist, August 2001, page 2108
Bulletin of the Center for Children's Books, September 2001,
   page 35
School Library Journal, August 2001, page 188
Voice of Youth Advocates, February 2002, page 451

Awards the book has won:

Bulletin of the Center for Children's Books Blue Ribbon,
   2001

Other books by the same author:

Mara's Stories: Glimmers in the Darkness, 2002
Anson's Way, 1999
The Sin Eater, 1996

Other books you might like:

Emma Donoghue, *Kissing the Witch: Old Tales in New Skins*,
1997
   Thirteen familiar fairy tales are retold from a feminist
   slant.
Donna Jo Napoli, *Spinners*, 1999
   In this replay of the fairy tale, Rumplestiltskin loses again
   but never realizes this time he's lost to his daughter.

Vivian Vande Velde, *The Rumpelstiltskin Problem*, 2000
  Six tales that each offer a different alternative to the
  original fairytale *Rumpelstiltskin*.

801

JAN NEUBERT SCHULTZ

Horse Sense

(Minneapolis, MN: Carolrhoda Books, 2001)

Subject(s): Animals/Horses; Farm Life; Robbers and Outlaws
Age range(s): Grades 4-7
Major character(s): Will Sasse, 14-Year-Old; Henry Sasse, Father, Farmer; Jesse James, Outlaw, Historical Figure; Frank James, Outlaw, Historical Figure; Star, Horse (mare)
Time period(s): 1870s (1876)
Locale(s): Northfield, Minnesota

Summary: Growing up on a farm, Will and his father disagree about horse raising; his father wants big, strong horses that can pull a plow while Will wants to breed horses that can be ridden. One day at a horse auction Will talks to a stranger named Jesse about his wish to breed his mare Star. Jesse, his brother Frank and two other cowboys even come by the farm for dinner one night where Jesse not only asks a lot of questions about the town but also lets his stallion loose in the pasture with Star. Later Will realizes Jesse is part of the infamous James-Younger gang that robs a bank in Northfield. When he discovers that his mare is gone, and a stallion has been left in her place, Will knows Jesse stole Star and joins the posse to search for the gang and his horse. Will's offered a chance to ride with Jesse, but knows he'd rather stay on the good side of the law in a work based on the author's family history. (177 pages)

Where it's reviewed:
Booklist, August 2001, page 2121
Bookpage, August 2001, page 31
Publishers Weekly, July 23, 2001, page 77
School Library Journal, October 2001, page 170

Other books by the same author:
Firestorm, 2002

Other books you might like:
Warwick Downing, *Kid Curry's Last Ride*, 1989
  A boring summer at his grandmother's turns into an adventure when Alex meets bank robber Kid Curry and they make a "bank withdrawal."
Sid Fleischman, *Bandit's Moon*, 1998
  When orphan Annyrose is captured by Joaquin Murieta and his outlaws, she's horrified at his misdeeds but tries to teach him to read.
Willo Davis Roberts, *Jo and the Bandit*, 1992
  Jo is used as bait to catch stagecoach robbers.

802

AMY SCHWARTZ, Author/Illustrator

The Boys Team

(New York: Richard Jackson Book/Atheneum Books for Young Readers, 2001)

Subject(s): School Life; Playing; Friendship
Age range(s): Preschool-Grade 1
Major character(s): Oscar, Kindergartner, Friend; Eddie, Kindergartner, Friend; Jacob, Kindergartner, Friend
Time period(s): 2000s (2001)
Locale(s): United States

Summary: Jacob explains how he, Oscar and Eddie comprise the Boys Team, bigger than the preschoolers they once were and reveling in their status as kindergarteners. This threesome is inseparable. They build with blocks, eat lunch together and spread out their mats side by side at rest time but certainly not to sleep. After school the boys take karate and swimming classes together and for Halloween they trick or treat as the same scary character. Sometimes, if it fits their schedule, they allow a girl to join them, but never on a Friday, a day reserved for the Boys Team. (40 pages)

Where it's reviewed:
Booklist, November 1, 2001, page 485
Horn Book, January 2002, page 72
Publishers Weekly, November 5, 2001, page 66
Riverbank Review, Winter 2001-2002, page 26
School Library Journal, January 2002, page 110

Other books by the same author:
Some Babies, 2000
How to Catch an Elephant, 1999
Annabelle Swift, Kindergartner, 1988

Other books you might like:
John Burningham, *The Friend*, 1975
  A young boy enjoys playing with his good friend Arthur.
James Howe, *Horace and Morris but Mostly Dolores*, 1999
  Three adventure-loving pals fearlessly engage in activities that they probably shouldn't be doing, but feel compelled to try.
Tony Johnston, *Sparky & Eddie: The First Day of School*, 1997
  Inseparable friends learn to adapt to change when they enter school and are assigned to different classrooms.
Charlotte Zolotow, *My Friend John*, 2000
  A little boy and his best friend John share all the important things in life in this newly illustrated reissue of a 1968 title.

803

VIRGINIA FRANCES SCHWARTZ

If I Just Had Two Wings

(Niagara Falls, NY: Stoddart Kids, 2001)

Subject(s): Underground Railroad; Slavery
Age range(s): Grades 6-9
Major character(s): Phoebe, Slave, 13-Year-Old; Liney, Slave, 19-Year-Old
Time period(s): 19th century

Locale(s): Alabama

Summary: The only sibling who hasn't been sold off to other masters, Phoebe works in the fields picking cotton and dreams of freedom, but is thankful to still be with her parents. Hearing that she is to be sold, she joins the slave Liney and her two children as the foursome heads North based on rumors they've heard about the Underground Railroad. Using their limited information, Phoebe and Liney hope to find enough sympathetic people to help them reach Canada. (221 pages)

Where it's reviewed:
Booklist, December 1, 2001, page 630
Kliatt, January 2002, page 8
School Library Journal, December 2001, page 143
Voice of Youth Advocates, December 2001, page 33

Other books by the same author:
Send One Angel Down, 2000

Other books you might like:
Elisa Carbone, *Stealing Freedom*, 1998
   Without her family to support her, Ann Maria's life as a slave is horrible until a stranger helps her escape on the Underground Railroad to Canada.
Gloria Houston, *Bright Freedom's Song: A Story of the Underground Railroad*, 1998
   Bright Freedom's father was an indentured servant, which explains his commitment to using the Underground Railroad to save slaves.
Kathryn Lasky, *True North: A Novel of the Underground Railroad*, 1996
   Reaching Canada together, runaway slave Afrika and Lucy later exchange hundreds of letters, but five decades pass before they are reunited.

804

JON SCIESZKA
LANE SMITH, Illustrator

Baloney (Henry P)
(New York: Viking, 2001)

Subject(s): Aliens; School Life; Humor
Age range(s): Grades 2-4
Major character(s): Henry P. Baloney, Alien, Student; Miss Bugscuffle, Teacher, Alien
Time period(s): Indeterminate
Locale(s): Fictional Country

Summary: Facing Miss Bugscuffle and the potential for ''Permanent Lifelong Detention,'' Henry P. Baloney mentally scrambles for a believable excuse or at least one that will satisfy his teacher. Henry has a lot of experience concocting excuses for tardiness but the one he tells Miss Bugscuffle about his misplaced ''zimulis'' is truly a masterpiece. The simple act of attempting to attend school prepared with ''zimulis'' (pencil) in hand leads Henry on a potentially dangerous adventure from which he's lucky to have arrived alive though a little late. Unfortunately, Henry's unable to begin work because he's misplaced his ''zimulis'' again. A concluding ''decoder'' defines the ''alien'' words used in the text and gives their actual origin. (32 pages)

Where it's reviewed:
Booklist, May 15, 2001, page 1751
Bulletin of the Center for Children's Books, May 2001, page 352
Horn Book, May 2001, page 316
Publishers Weekly, April 30, 2001, page 76
School Library Journal, May 2001, page 134

Awards the book has won:
Parenting's Reading Magic Awards, 2001
IRA Children's Choices, 2002

Other books by the same author:
Squids Will Be Squids: Fresh Morals, Beastly Fables, 1998
Math Curse, 1995 (ALA Notable Books for Children)
The Stinky Cheese Man and Other Fairly Stupid Tales, 1992 (ALA Notable Books for Children)
The True Story of the 3 Little Pigs, 1989 (ALA Notable Books for Children)

Other books you might like:
Susan Meddaugh, *Hog-Eye*, 1995
   This little pig has a far-fetched excuse for being absent from school when she was only trying to avoid tardiness.
Mark Teague, *The Secret Shortcut*, 1996
   Rather than risk being late for school again, Floyd and Wendell use a shortcut that leads them into a jungle filled with obstacles.
Patricia Rae Wolff, *The Toll-Bridge Troll*, 1995
   Daily, Trigg must outsmart a troll demanding a toll in order to cross the bridge and arrive at school on time.

805

JON SCIESZKA
ADAM MCCAULEY, Illustrator

Sam Samurai
(New York, Viking, 2001)

Series: Time Warp Trio
Subject(s): Time Travel; Poetry; Humor
Age range(s): Grades 3-6
Major character(s): Joe, Friend, Time Traveler; Sam, Friend, Time Traveler; Fred, Friend, Time Traveler
Time period(s): 2000s (2001); 17th century (1600s)
Locale(s): New York, New York (Brooklyn); Japan

Summary: As usual, Sam, Fred and Joe have no intention of going anywhere but, while working on a homework assignment to write haiku, they inadvertently trigger the magic in Joe's blue book and end up in old Japan. Knowing just enough about samurai to fear for their lives the trio finds their circumstances complicated by a malfunctioning ''auto-translator'' component of their book. Realizing that they cannot get home until they locate the book they set off with a friendly samurai for the shogun's castle to find it. Along the way they offend a war leader and are fortunate to be rescued by their great granddaughters who just happen to be time traveling too. The girls have taken the time to study the book more carefully than Joe, Fred and Sam so they are able to use the knowledge effectively to locate the book and use it as part of their audience before the shogun as the six travelers make their escape in the green mist. (88 pages)

Where it's reviewed:
Booklist, November 1, 2001, page 475
Horn Book Guide, Spring 2002, page 92
School Library Journal, November 2001, page 136

Other books by the same author:
See You Later, Gladiator, 2000 (Time Warp Trio)
It's All Greek to Me, 1999 (Time Warp Trio)
Summer Reading Is Killing Me!, 1998 (Time Warp Trio)

Other books you might like:
Emma Bradford, *Kat and the Emperor's Gift*, 1998
   Kat's time machine carries her to the court of Kublai Khan in thirteenth-century China.
Edward Eager, *Seven-Day Magic*, 1962
   Susan checks out a library book that unexpectedly brings magic into her life.
Eric A. Kimmel, *Sword of the Samurai: Adventure Stories from Japan*, 1999
   Eleven stories telling of the service, courage and honor of the samurai concludes with a glossary of terms and source notes for the stories.

806

MELISSA SCOTT
LISA A. BARNETT, Co-Author

Point of Dreams
(New York: Tor, 2001)

Subject(s): Magic; Mystery; Romance
Age range(s): Grades 11-Adult
Major character(s): Nicholas Rathe, Police Officer; Philip Eslingen, Actor
Time period(s): Indeterminate
Locale(s): Astreiant, Fictional City

Summary: In this sequel to *Point of Hopes*, Pointsman Nicholas Rathe returns with an even more delicate case. The city-state of Astreiant has gone wild over a new play, and a threat to its premiere is perceived as a threat to the ruling family. The play cannot premier without the customary banquets, but someone with a grudge and the magical ability to influence action and perceptions, is creating mischief through the fad of flower forcing and arranging. Since no one knows the identity of the mischief-maker, or which arrangements are magical, Rathe is charged with discovering the danger before it is too late. He enlists the help of his love, Philip Eslingen, recently hired by the theatre as an instructor in arms and fencing. Eslingen is able to spy on the outrageous doings of the cast and crew from behind the scenes, as the city's rich and powerful jockey for sexual partners, recognition and political position. As the backstabbing becomes literal, Rathe fears for Eslingen's safety. (352 pages)

Where it's reviewed:
Booklist, February 15, 2001, page 1122
Kirkus Reviews, December 15, 2000, page 1727
Library Journal, February 15, 2001, page 204
Publishers Weekly, January 8, 2001, page 52

Other books by the same author:
Point of Hopes, 1995

Other books you might like:
Kate Ross, *The Devil in Music*, 1997
   An English dandy attempts to unravel an Italian mystery involving a dead Count, a lady's glove and a missing tenor.
Martha Wells, *The Death of the Necromancer*, 1998
   A noble thief and his gang must solve the puzzle of criminal necromancer before it causes their deaths.
Elizabeth Wiley, *The Well-Favored Man*, 1993
   A young mage suddenly finds he has inherited his family's problems with dragons, monsters and disaffected relatives.

807

RICHARD SCRIMGER
GILLIAN JOHNSON, Illustrator

Bun Bun's Birthday
(Plattsburgh, NY: Tundra Books, 2001)

Subject(s): Family Life; Birthdays; Jealousy
Age range(s): Grades K-2
Major character(s): Winifred, Child, Sister (older); Eugene, Child, Brother; Brenda "Bun Bun", Sister (youngest), 1-Year-Old
Time period(s): 2000s (2001)
Locale(s): Canada

Summary: It's just not fair, in Winifred's opinion, that Bun Bun should be having a birthday. Winifred's accustomed to being the family member with the birthday that follows Eugene's celebration, but all the decorations and the cake today are for Bun Bun. When Winifred learns that she, too, had a first birthday party, although she doesn't remember it, she decides to enjoy this celebration as if it is her own and tell Bun Bun all about it when she's older. (24 pages)

Where it's reviewed:
Bulletin of the Center for Children's Books, April 2001, page 314
Horn Book Guide, Fall 2001, page 274
Quill & Quire, March 2001, page 57
Resource Links, April 2001, page 6
School Library Journal, June 2001, page 129

Other books by the same author:
Princess Bun Bun, 2002

Other books you might like:
Russell Hoban, *A Birthday for Frances*, 1968
   Frances is so distracted by the attention her little sister is receiving that she absentmindedly eats the Chompo bar intended as her birthday present.
Lynne Jonell, *It's My Birthday, Too!*, 1999
   Robbie may be the younger brother but he still thinks he should be invited to Christopher's birthday party.
Lenore Look, *Henry's First-Moon Birthday*, 2001
   Jen-Jen organizes the festivities for baby brother Henry's one-month birthday celebration in accordance with Chinese tradition.

RICHARD SCRIMGER

A Nose for Adventure

(Toronto, Canada: Tundra Books, 2001)

Subject(s): Aliens; Humor; Physically Handicapped
Age range(s): Grades 5-8
Major character(s): Alan Dingwall, 13-Year-Old; Frieda Miller, 14-Year-Old, Handicapped; Sally, Dog; Norbert, Alien
Time period(s): 2000s
Locale(s): New York, New York

Summary: Flying to New York to see his dad, Alan is alternately made fun of or beaten at arm wrestling by his seatmate, Frieda, who's returning from a trip to the doctor. Arriving at the airport, it's no surprise that Alan's father isn't there to greet him, but it is a surprise when Frieda and her wheelchair are almost kidnapped. Sensing danger, Alan wheels her away and as the two are in line to catch a cab, he's reunited with Norbert, the alien from Jupiter who used to live in Alan's nose. They also meet Sally, the dog in whose nose Norbert had been living. Thank heavens! Norbert is there just in time to help Alan and Frieda elude the smugglers who used Frieda's wheelchair to hide an Egyptian artifact in a madcap adventure. (176 pages)

Where it's reviewed:
Booklist, February 15, 2001, page 1138
Quill & Quire, December 2000, page 32
Resource Links, February 2001, page 19
School Library Journal, April 2001, page 149
Voice of Youth Advocates, April 2001, page 56

Other books by the same author:
The Nose from Jupiter, 1998
The Way to Schenectady, 1998
Still Life with Children: Tales of Family Life, 1997

Other books you might like:
Terry Farish, *Why I'm Already Blue*, 1989
    Though her next-door neighbor Gus is in a wheelchair, his upbeat outlook on life helps Lucy survive her parent's divorce and her unmarried sister's pregnancy.
Gail Gauthier, *Club Earth*, 1999
    Will and Robby are delighted with their alien guests, especially Sal, short for saliva, who plans to turn their home into an intergalactic tourist spot.
Willo Davis Roberts, *What Could Go Wrong?*, 1989
    Gracie knows that any flight can go awry when her cousin Charlie is along and sure enough, soon they're chased around the airport by criminals.
William Sleator, *The Night the Heads Came*, 1996
    The alien invasion seems silly at first, but it slowly becomes clear that we are losing.

809

MARCUS SEDGWICK

Witch Hill

(New York: Delacorte, 2001)

Subject(s): Witches and Witchcraft; Ghosts; Fires

Age range(s): Grades 6-10
Major character(s): James "Jamie" Fraser, 12-Year-Old; Jane, Aunt (of Jamie)
Time period(s): 2000s
Locale(s): Crownhill, England

Summary: A fire destroys Jamie's home and he's left traumatized by the thought that he didn't rescue his baby sister. Sent to live with Aunt Jane while he tries to recover, he finds he's gone from one nightmare to another for his presence in Crownhill stirs up past terror, a terror begun when Crownhill was called Cronehill, the site of witch burnings. Now Jamie has riled up the ghosts of the girl falsely accused of being a witch, along with the real witch, as he finds himself in the midst of another house fire in this suspenseful tale. (147 pages)

Where it's reviewed:
Booklist, October 1, 2001, page 320
Books for Keeps, July 2001, page 25
Bulletin of the Center for Children's Books, October 2001, page 75
School Librarian, Summer 2001, page 103
School Library Journal, September 2001, page 232

Other books by the same author:
Floodland, 2001

Other books you might like:
E.L. Konigsburg, *Silent to the Bone*, 2000
    Falsely accused of hurting his sister, mute Branwell is not able to defend himself until his best friend devises a way to break through his silence.
Ann Rinaldi, *A Break with Charity: A Story about the Salem Witch Trials*, 1992
    Susannah English relates her horror when she realizes the outcome of the "game" of witchcraft played by some girls in her village.
Vivian Vande Velde, *Magic Can Be Murder*, 2000
    Nola and her mother practice their witchcraft in secret to keep from being executed.
Tim Wynne-Jones, *Stephen Fair*, 1998
    Stephen has strange dreams of a fire and a baby crying, dreams that are finally explained when he understands a family secret.

810

TOR SEIDLER
BRETT HELQUIST, Illustrator

The Revenge of Randal Reese-Rat

(New York: Farrar Straus Giroux, 2001)

Subject(s): Animals/Rats; City and Town Life; Weddings
Age range(s): Grades 4-6
Major character(s): Montague "Monty" Mad-Rat, Rat, Bridegroom; Isabel Moberly-Rat, Rat, Bride; Randal Reese-Rat, Rat; Maggie Mad-Rat, Rat, Cousin (of Montague)
Time period(s): 2000s
Locale(s): Africa; New York, New York

Summary: Montague wins the rat of his dreams, the beautiful Isabel. As the two prepare for their wedding nuptials, they await the arrival of relatives, including Cousin Maggie from

Africa. The night of the wedding, a terrible fire destroys Montague and Isabel's home and is thought to be the work of Isabel's rejected suitor, Randal. With an all-out rat-hunt under way for Randal, he prepares to exact revenge from those who would accuse him of such a heinous crime, but his plans fall by the wayside when he meets the beautiful Maggie. When Maggie has to sail home to Africa, Randal finds a way to accompany her in this sequel to *A Rat's Tale*. (233 pages)

Where it's reviewed:

Booklist, November 1, 2001, page 479
Kirkus Reviews, August 15, 2001, page 1221
New York Times Book Review, November 18, 2001, page 52
Publishers Weekly, July 30, 2001, page 85
School Library Journal, October 2001, page 170

Other books by the same author:

Brothers Below Zero, 2002
Terpin, 2002, 198
The Tar Pit, 2001, c19
A Rat's Tale, 1999, c19

Other books you might like:

Avi, *Ragwood: A Tale from Dimwood Forest*, 1999
    Ragwood helps the mice of Amperville in a successful battle against the cats of F.E.A.R., Felines Enraged About Rodents.
Brian Jacques, *Redwall Series*, 1987-
    This charming series features the mice of Redwall who defend their abbey against scurrilous animals and offer refuge to friends.
Robert C. O'Brien, *Mrs. Frisby and the Rats of NIMH*, 1971
    Seeking help for her sick son from the rats living under the rosebush, Mrs. Frisby is amazed to discover they've escaped from the NIMH laboratory.

811

BARBARA SEULING
PAUL BREWER, Illustrator

Robert and the Great Pepperoni

(Chicago: Cricket Books, 2001)

Subject(s): Pets; Animals/Dogs; Schools
Age range(s): Grades 2-3
Major character(s): Robert Dorfman, 2nd Grader, Brother (younger); Buster, Rabbit
Time period(s): 2000s (2001)
Locale(s): United States

Summary: All Robert really wants is a dog but his parents won't let him have one so he begins a pet sitting service. While Robert gets lots of business it all seems to end up with him acquiring pets that people can no longer keep. Instead of a dog, Robert now has a tarantula, two birds and a rabbit. Surprise! Make that seven rabbits. Buster turns out to be a girl. When Robert has the opportunity to provide a foster home to an unwanted dog his parents are not as willing to accept another pet but they do relent. Robert has a big job to make Pepperoni adoptable by teaching him commands and training him not to use the house for his bathroom. Robert proves to be a good teacher and Pepperoni finds a new home

with the perfect family that welcomes Robert's visits. (118 pages)

Where it's reviewed:

Horn Book, January 2002, page 83
School Library Journal, October 2001, page 131

Other books by the same author:

Oh No, It's Robert, 1999
Winter Lullaby, 1998
Elephants Can't Jump and Other Freaky Facts about Animals, 1985

Other books you might like:

Betsy Duffey, *Puppy Love*, 1992
    In a Pet Patrol series entry, Evie and Megan find it difficult to locate a good home for the runt of a litter of pups.
Karen Hesse, *Sable*, 1994
    In order to keep the stray dog that wanders into the yard of her mountain home, Tate must demonstrate the ability to care for it responsibly.
Barbara Moe, *Dog Days for Dudley*, 1994
    Dudley is overjoyed when his parents finally agree to allow him to have a pet dog.
Colby Rodowsky, *Not My Dog*, 1999
    Adopting great-aunt Margaret's dog does not satisfy Ellie's desire for a puppy.

812

BARBARA SEULING
GREG NEWBOLD, Illustrator

Spring Song

(San Diego: Gulliver Books/Harcourt, Inc., 2001)

Subject(s): Spring; Animals; Stories in Rhyme
Age range(s): Grades K-1
Time period(s): Indeterminate
Locale(s): Earth

Summary: Spring comes to the mountains melting the snow and awakening the black bear hungry for fish. Spring warms the prairie farmlands and the moles begin digging new tunnels. Spring breezes in the forest call striped skunks out of their dens. Wetland reeds grow tall in spring as bullfrogs croak all night. Eagles soar as buds appear on trees looking for a spot to build their nest. Rabbits dine on clover, butterflies emerge from cocoons and children fly kites. Spring is here. (32 pages)

Where it's reviewed:

Booklist, April 14, 2001, page 1566
Children's Bookwatch, April 2001, page 4
Kirkus Reviews, February 15, 2001, page 265
Publishers Weekly, February 26, 2001, page 84
School Library Journal, May 2001, page 135

Other books by the same author:

Winter Lullaby, 1998
The Triplets, 1980
The Teeny Tiny Woman: An Old English Ghost Tale, 1976

Other books you might like:

Nancy White Carlstrom, *Raven and River*, 1997
An Alaskan river and the animals living nearby gradually awaken from winter's chill and welcome spring.

Jean Craighead George, *Look to the North: A Wolf Pup Diary*, 1997
Signs of seasonal change that appear in the lower forty-eight states are related to the growth of wolf cubs in Alaska.

Reeve Lindbergh, *North Country Spring*, 1997
Bear cubs tumble, frogs peep and geese fly as the natural world awakens to spring's call.

813

DARREN SHAN

Cirque du Freak: A Living Nightmare

(Boston: Little, Brown, 2001)

Series: Saga of Darren Shan. Book 1
Subject(s): Vampires; Horror; Animals/Spiders
Age range(s): Grades 7-10
Major character(s): Darren Shan, 12-Year-Old; Madame Octa, Spider (tarantula); Mr. Crepsley, Vampire; Steve Leopard, 12-Year-Old
Time period(s): 2000s
Locale(s): England

Summary: A group of friends read of the freak show "Cirque du Freak" coming to town, but are able to buy only two tickets. Darren and his friend Steve head to an old theater to see these advertised oddities of nature, including Mr. Crepsley and his poisonous spider Madame Octa. Reminded of a pet tarantula he had as a child, Darren is entranced with the spider and decides to steal her. Lingering behind, Darren overhears a conversation between Steve and Mr. Crepsley and learns that Mr. Crepsley is a vampire, but even that doesn't stop his desire to have Madame Octa. Successfully stealing the spider, he learns to control her through a mixture of flute music and his thoughts but then she bites Steve. Forced to locate Mr. Crepsley and ask for an antidote, Darren promises to become the vampire's servant. (266 pages)

Where it's reviewed:
Booklist, April 15, 2001, page 1559
Bulletin of the Center for Children's Books, June 2001, page 386
Publishers Weekly, February 19, 2001, page 92
School Library Journal, May 2001, page 159
Voice of Youth Advocates, April 2001, page 56

Other books by the same author:
Cirque du Freak: Tunnels of Blood, 2002 (Saga of Darren Shan, Book 3)
Cirque du Freak: The Vampire's Assistant, 2001 (Saga of Darren Shan, Book 2)

Other books you might like:
M.T. Anderson, *Thirsty*, 1997
As Chris approaches adolescence, he is dismayed to realize that he has an increasing thirst for blood, a sure sign he'll become a vampire.

Amelia Atwater-Rhodes, *Demon in My View*, 2000
Jessica doesn't realize it, but she's about to be caught between vampires who want to claim her as one of theirs and good witches who will try to save her.

M.C. Sumner, *The Coach*, 1994
There's no way Chris can tell the police that the reason there are so many dead people is because they were all vampires.

814

DARREN SHAN

Cirque du Freak: The Vampire's Assistant

(Boston: Little, Brown, 2001)

Series: The Saga of Darren Shan. Book 2
Subject(s): Vampires; Horror
Age range(s): Grades 7-10
Major character(s): Darren Shan, 12-Year-Old; Mr. Crepsley, Vampire; Evra Von, Entertainer (snake boy); Sam Grest, Friend
Time period(s): 2000s
Locale(s): England

Summary: In this second of the *Cirque du Freak* series, Darren is now a half-vampire and has been studying with Mr. Crepsley for several months, though he can't yet bring himself to drink human blood. Returning to the freak show, Darren is assigned to room with Evra and assist with his chores, including feeding the Little People and the Wolf Man. The two become friends and extend their friendship to Sam, a local boy who hangs around the freak show. To supply food for the performers, Darren occasionally kills a sheep from one of the surrounding farms, but the farmers are becoming suspicious about their losses. One outsider sets off a tragic string of events when he loosens the lock on the WolfMan's cage, which in turn gives Darren a chance to carry on the memory of his friend by finally drinking human blood. (241 pages)

Where it's reviewed:
Booklist, September 15, 2001, page 224
Publishers Weekly, August 27, 2001, page 86
School Library Journal, August 2001, page 188
Voice of Youth Advocates, October 2001, page 294

Other books by the same author:
Cirque du Freak: Tunnels of Blood, 2002 (The Saga of Darren Shan, Book 3)
Cirque du Freak: A Living Nightmare, 2001 (The Saga of Darren Shan, Book 1)

Other books you might like:
Richie Tankersley Cusick, *Vampire*, 1991
Spending the summer with her Uncle Jake, Darcy looks a little warily at him as teenage girls are found with lipstick bite marks on their necks.

Anne Rice, *Interview with the Vampire*, 1976
The life of a two-hundred-year-old vampire is recounted, detail by gory detail.

R.L. Stine, *Goodnight Kiss*, 1992
Matt and his girlfriend April become unwitting victims when two vampires set up a competition to see who can be first to turn someone into an "Eternal One."

M.C. Sumner, *The Coach*, 1994
Chris Delaney isn't about to tell the police that the reason there are so many dead people is because they were all vampires and had to be killed.

LINDA SHANDS

Blind Fury
(Grand Rapids, MI: Revell/Baker Book House Co., 2001)

Series: Wakara of Eagle Lodge. Book 2
Subject(s): Brothers and Sisters; Ranch Life; Single Parent Families
Age range(s): Grades 6-8
Major character(s): Wakara Windsong "Kara" Sheridan, 15-Year-Old, Indian (part Indian and part Irish); Tia Louise Sanchez, Student—High School; Greg Sheridan, Brother (of Kara); Anne Lightfoot, Indian (Nez Perce), House-keeper
Time period(s): 2000s
Locale(s): Oregon

Summary: Though Wakara still misses her mom, who was killed last year in an automobile accident, she, her brothers and father readjust to life on their ranch. Helping the family is their new housekeeper, Anne Lightfoot, from the Nez Perce reservation. A regular visitor to their ranch is Wakara's good friend Tia who hunts on the Internet for information about Wakara's Indian heritage, running over with every new fact she finds. New disaster hits the family when a blizzard catches her father and brother Greg in the mountains, far from the ranch. Sensing they're in danger, Wakara rides out to find and bring them home. (172 pages)

Where it's reviewed:
Booklist, May 1, 2001, page 1684

Other books by the same author:
White Water, 2001 (Wakara of Eagle Lodge, Book 3)
Wild Fire, 2001 (Wakara of Eagle Lodge, Book 1)

Other books you might like:
Gretel Ehrlich, *A Blizzard Year: Timmy's Almanac of the Seasons*, 1999
A terrible blizzard destroys most of their cattle and Timmy worries that her parents will lose their ranch.
Will Hobbs, *Bearstone*, 1990
Cloyd finds his Indian heritage as he battles for survival in the Colorado mountains.
Louise Moeri, *The Devil in Ol' Rosie*, 2001
When Ol' Rosie escapes, leading the rest of the family's horses with her, Wart is sent to round them up on a trip that includes a stalking cougar and an advancing blizzard.
Gary Paulsen, *The Haymeadow*, 1992
Because one of the ranch hands is sick, John spends the summer by himself up in the haymeadow with six thousand sheep, two horses and four dogs.

MARJORIE WEINMAN SHARMAT
MITCHELL SHARMAT, Co-Author
MARTHA WESTON, Illustrator

Nate the Great and the Big Sniff
(New York: Delacorte Press, 2001)

Subject(s): Department Stores; Animals/Dogs; Mystery and Detective Stories
Age range(s): Grades 2-3
Major character(s): Nate the Great, Detective—Amateur, Friend; Sludge, Dog; Annie, Friend
Time period(s): 2000s (2001)
Locale(s): United States

Summary: Nate the Great works his biggest case with no help from his sidekick Sludge because locating Sludge is the case. Sludge vanishes while Nate is shopping in a large department store. Annie gives Nate the Great the first clue; Sludge went into the store. Nate searches for Sludge by following directions given by clerks who have seen a dog. When Nate finally sees a wagging tail under a bed it belongs to Annie's dog not his. Now Nate puts on his thinking cap and realizes Sludge knows that the first thing Nate does when he's on a case is eat pancakes. Once Nate heads for the store's restaurant he has no problem locating his sidekick. (48 pages)

Where it's reviewed:
Booklist, November 2001, page 487
Horn Book Guide, Spring 2002, page 69
Kirkus Reviews, July 15, 2001, page 1035
School Library Journal, October 2001, page 131

Other books by the same author:
Nate the Great: San Francisco Detective, 2000
Nate the Great and the Monster Mess, 1999
Nate the Great and Me, 1998

Other books you might like:
David A. Adler, *My Dog and the Green Sock Mystery*, 1986
Items are vanishing at Andy's house and it's his friend Jenny's dog that solves the mystery of the disappearances.
Patricia Reilly Giff, *Mary Moon Is Missing*, 1998
Amateur detective Minnie tries to locate a missing homing pigeon.
Cynthia Rylant, *The Case of the Missing Monkeys*, 2000
While Detectives Bunny and Jack eat breakfast the diner owner reports a stolen glass monkey and asks them to take the case.

817

AARON SHEPARD, Adaptor
DAVID WISNIEWSKI, Illustrator

Master Man: A Tall Tale of Nigeria
(New York: HarperCollins Publishers, 2001)

Subject(s): Tall Tales; Folklore; Cartoons and Comics
Age range(s): Grades 1-4
Major character(s): Shadusa, Spouse; Shettu, Spouse; Master Man, Mythical Creature (giant)
Time period(s): Indeterminate Past

Locale(s): Nigeria

Summary: Boasting of his strength, Shadusa suggests his wife call him "Master Man," an idea Shettu thinks is unwise. When Shadusa learns of another calling himself "Master Man" he seeks to meet him. However, after finding Master Man's home and seeing the piles of elephant bones, Shadusa regrets coming. Before he can leave, Master Man returns home with another elephant to eat; Shadusa hides until he thinks its safe to run away. With the angry giant in pursuit, Shadusa races on past farmers and porters until he runs into another stranger sitting beside a huge pile of elephant bones. This enormous stranger also claims to be "Master Man." As the two giant men fight over the name, their struggle lifts them into the air where they can sometimes be heard to this day whenever the clouds rumble with the sound that some call thunder. A concluding author's note gives the background for the tale. (32 pages)

Where it's reviewed:
Bulletin of the Center for Children's Books, February 2001, page 236
Horn Book, January 2001, page 102
Publishers Weekly, January 1, 2001, page 92
Riverbank Review, Summer 2001, page 32
School Library Journal, February 2001, page 115

Other books by the same author:
The Crystal Heart: A Vietnamese Legend, 1998
The Maiden of Northland: A Hero Tale of Finland, 1996
The Legend of Lightning Larry, 1993

Other books you might like:
Lloyd Alexander, *How the Cat Swallowed Thunder*, 2000
    When Mother Holly's cat foolishly swallows some of the evidence of her mischievous behavior she begins to purr.
Beatrice Orcutt Harrell, *How Thunder and Lightning Came to Be: A Choctaw Legend*, 1995
    Choctow legend explains thunder as an early warning system for storms devised inadvertently by two clumsy birds trying to please the Great Sun Father.
Junko Morimoto, *The Two Bullies*, 1999
    Two self-proclaiming strongmen are secretly relieved that circumstances prevent a direct confrontation between them.

818

SHARON SHINN

Summers at Castle Auburn

(New York: Ace Books, 2001)

Subject(s): Coming-of-Age; Magic; Romance
Age range(s): Grades 8-Adult
Major character(s): Coriel "Corie", Sister; Elisandra, Royalty; Bryan, Royalty (prince)
Time period(s): Indeterminate
Locale(s): Fictional Country

Summary: As a child, Corie is enchanted by her summers at Castle Auburn where she is companion to her adored half-sister Elisandra and lives in the lap of luxury. But Corie's summers are balanced by the rest of the year, which she spends with her Grandmother, a notable herbalist and healer. As she grows up, Corie begins to see that not everything is perfect at Castle Auburn. For one thing, she begins to worry about the ailora, the magical captives of the rulers, that are able to soothe empathically. Corie also begins to realize that Prince Bryan, the idol of her childhood, may not be the husband her sister deserves; in fact, Corie begins to wonder if she saw anything clearly during her childhood summers at Castle Auburn. (355 pages)

Where it's reviewed:
Booklist, April 15,2001, page 1544
Kliatt, July 2001, page 27
Publishers Weekly, April 2, 2001, page 44
Science Fiction Chronicle, July 2001, page 44
Voice of Youth Advocates, August 2001, page 216

Awards the book has won:
ALA Best Books for Young Adults, 2002

Other books by the same author:
Heart of Gold, 2000
Wrapt in Crystal, 1999
The Alleluia Files, 1998

Other books you might like:
Patricia Briggs, *The Hob's Bargain*, 2001
    Aren is determined to do whatever it takes to win the aid of the magical hob, even live with him.
Lois McMaster Bujold, *The Curse of Chalion*, 2001
    Saving the heirs to Chalion may require more than just a willingness to die for them, a little luck might be needed, too.
Teresa Edgerton, *The Queen's Necklace*, 2001
    When Wil pursues the goblin plot to take over the kingdoms, he is surprised to find his best ally is his wife.

819

SUSAN SHREVE

Blister

(New York: Arthur A. Levine Books/Scholastic Press, 2001)

Subject(s): Family Problems; Moving, Household; Schools
Age range(s): Grades 4-6
Major character(s): Alyssa "Blister" Reed, 10-Year-Old, Daughter; Daisy G., Grandmother, Dancer; Jack Reed, Father, Businessman
Time period(s): 2000s
Locale(s): Meadowville, Connecticut; North Haven, Connecticut

Summary: Alyssa thinks it's the stillbirth of her baby sister that causes her perfect world to crumble so that she becomes nothing but a blister irritating her parents' failing marriage. Daisy G. assures Alyssa that life is not perfect, her parents' problems are not new and that she, like her grandmother, must be elastic and bounce back from adversity. Blister's mother falls into a deep depression following the baby's death as her marriage disintegrates. Blister's angry when Jack Reed moves his family into a city apartment, forcing her to enter a new school. Then, he moves out on his family without acknowledging the affair he's having. Blister discovers the evidence during a visit to Jack's apartment and takes some of the woman's belongings thus bringing the family's secrets out into the open and forcing her parents to look beyond their own needs and consider their responsibility to their daughter. By following Daisy G.'s advice to be "elastic" Blister proves herself to be resilient enough to survive the loss of perfection in her life. (153 pages)

Where it's reviewed:
Booklist, September 15, 2001, page 224
Bulletin of the Center for Children's Books, November 2001, page 115
Publishers Weekly, August 27, 2001, page 85
School Library Journal, November 2001, page 162

Awards the book has won:
ALA Notable Children's Books, 2002

Other books by the same author:
Ghost Cats, 1999
Jonah the Whale, 1998
The Formerly Great Alexander Family, 1995
Amy Dunn Quits School, 1993

Other books you might like:
Lynne Reid Banks, *Alice-by-Accident*, 2000
  Alice, illegitimate child of her single mum, enjoys a relationship with her paternal grandmother although she's never met her father.
Patricia Hermes, *Someone to Count On*, 1993
  Sam, daughter of unconventional Elizabeth, experiences a period of stability while living temporarily with someone she can count on, her grandfather.
Susan Patron, *Maybe Yes, Maybe No, Maybe Maybe*, 1993
  In an award-winning title, middle child PK begrudgingly adjusts to a move to a new apartment with her mother and two sisters.
Cynthia Voigt, *Dicey's Song*, 1981
  After being abandoned by their mother, Dicey and her younger siblings make a long journey on foot to their eccentric grandmother's home.
Deborah Wiles, *Love, Ruby Lavender*, 2001
  Ruby's eccentric grandmother helps her cope with the accidental death of her grandfather.

820

JAN SIEGEL

The Dragon Charmer
(New York: Del Rey, 2000)

Subject(s): Magic; Friendship
Age range(s): Grades 10-Adult
Major character(s): Fernanda "Fern" Capel, Witch, Sister; Gaynor Mobberley, Friend; Will Capel, Brother (of Fern); Ragginbone, Sorcerer; Morgus, Witch
Time period(s): 2000s
Locale(s): Yarrowdale, England (Yorkshire)

Summary: In this sequel to *Prospero's Children*, Fern has decided to turn her back on her magical abilities. Plunging into a normal life, she becomes a public relations consultant and is engaged to an older man who seems eminently safe. Fern agrees to a home wedding in spite of her misgivings about Yarrowdale and, with her best friend Gaynor, the two leave London for Yorkshire. There things go wrong from the

start as Gaynor is the target of uncanny experiences and Fern is in denial. Will, on the other hand, isn't surprised that something goes wrong with his sister and tries to reassure Gaynor and explain about their past. Meanwhile, Will seeks reassurance from Ragginbone, the sorcerer who aided them in their first trouble. Will's and Ragginbone's worst fears come to pass when Fern and Gaynor go for a night out on the eve of Fern's wedding. Fern's spirit is stolen from her body and Gaynor wanders in a terrifying spirit world before finding her way back for help. But no one can reach Fern, who is the prisoner of Morgus, an ancient witch with a vendetta. (364 pages)

Where it's reviewed:
Booklist, June 1, 2001, page 1856
Kirkus Reviews, May 15, 2001, page 715
Publishers Weekly, June 11, 2001, page 67
Science Fiction Chronicle, July 2001, page 42

Other books by the same author:
Witch Queen, 2002
Prospero's Children, 1999

Other books you might like:
Peter S. Beagle, *Tamsin*, 1999
  What kind of mysterious danger can terrify a girl who has been dead for hundreds of years?
Charles de Lint, *The Dreaming Place*, 1990
  When Nina is threatened by a magical danger from a place beyond space and time, her cousin Ash tries to rescue her.
Margaret Mahy, *The Changeover*, 1984
  Laura must use her suppressed powers as a witch if she wants to save her little brother's life.

821

JUDY SIERRA
WILL HILLENBRAND, Illustrator

Preschool to the Rescue
(San Diego: Gulliver Books/Harcourt, Inc., 2001)

Subject(s): Weather; Problem Solving; Stories in Rhyme
Age range(s): Preschool-Grade 1
Time period(s): Indeterminate
Locale(s): Fictional Country

Summary: In the schoolhouse yard there is a deep, creepy mud puddle that devours all traffic on a rainy day. First a pizza van becomes stuck then the police car and even the tow truck that comes to pull the other vehicles out. A backhoe and fire engine meet the same fate. As the rain abates and the clouds thin the preschoolers race outside to the rescue (or is it recess) and soon the toys are out of the mud. To prevent a recurrence, the playful students next consume the mud puddle by making mud pies, cakes, pizza and cookies. (32 pages)

Where it's reviewed:
Booklist, April 15, 2001, page 1566
Bulletin of the Center for Children's Books, April 2001, page 314
Horn Book, May 2001, page 317
Publishers Weekly, March 19, 2001, page 98
School Library Journal, May 2001, page 135

Other books by the same author:
The Beautiful Butterfly: A Folktale from Spain, 2000
The Gift of the Crocodile: A Cinderella Story, 2000
There's a Zoo in Room 22, 2000
Counting Crocodiles, 1997

Other books you might like:
Jonathan London, *Puddles,* 1997
   A brother and sister delight in the puddles and mud that
   await after a storm.
Lynn Plourde, *Pigs in the Mud in the Middle of the Rud,* 1997
   A large mud puddle blocks the road when it becomes full
   of pigs and other farm animals attracted by the commotion.
Jack Prelutsky, *Rainy, Rainy Saturday,* 1980
   Fourteen poems celebrate the fun to be had on a rainy day,
   even if you're stuck inside.
Mary Lyn Ray, *Mud,* 1996
   Between winter and spring, conditions are perfect for mak-
   ing and enjoying terrific mud.

822

DIANE SILVEY

Raven's Flight

(Vancouver: Raincoast Books, 2001)

Subject(s): Sisters; Drugs; Homeless People
Age range(s): Grades 7-10
Major character(s): Raven, 15-Year-Old; Marcie, Sister, Ad-
   dict; Rita, Cousin
Time period(s): 2000s
Locale(s): Egmont, British Columbia, Canada; Vancouver,
   British Columbia, Canada

Summary: Raven's older sister Marcie leaves their home in
British Columbia to accompany their cousin Rita to Vancouver where she plans to find a good job as well as have her own
apartment, car, clothes and maybe even a boyfriend. After a
few weeks, Rita calls to say that Marcie's missing; Raven's
the only one in the family who can leave so she uses her
college tuition savings for the bus ticket to Vancouver. Rita
doesn't meet Raven at the bus station, which means a creepy
walk to the apartment for Raven, who's wondering what she's
gotten into. Sleeping on Marcie's mattress, Raven finds the
diary that she usually keeps and gets her first clues that
something's very wrong in Marcie's life. The next day, armed
with Marcie's photo, she searches the streets named in the
diary, though most people either don't know Marcie or don't
want to admit it. Finally two homeless people report on a
kidnapping ring that captures children and smuggles them
across the Pacific where they're auctioned off to work in
sweatshops. Though terrified, Raven's determined to find her
sister who by now has become addicted to drugs in a chilling
work. (120 pages)

Where it's reviewed:
School Library Journal, December 2001, page 146

Other books by the same author:
Spirit Quest, 2001

Other books you might like:
Melvin Burgess, *Smack,* 1998
   A horrifying account of two young teen runaways who are
   quickly dragged down into heroin addiction.
Linda Glovach, *Beauty Queen,* 1998
   A stint at topless dancing to earn enough money to flee her
   abusive home leads Samantha into a heroin addiction from
   which there's no escape.
Han Nolan, *Born Blue,* 2001
   Abandoned by her heroin-addicted mother, Janie grows up
   to share the same, self-destructive behavior.

823

MARC SIMONT, Author/Illustrator

The Stray Dog

(New York: HarperCollins Publishers, 2001)

Subject(s): Animals/Dogs; Family Life; Pets
Age range(s): Grades K-3
Major character(s): Unnamed Character, Child, Sister (older);
   Unnamed Character, Child, Brother (younger); Willy, Dog
Time period(s): 2000s (2001)
Locale(s): United States

Summary: A playful dog joins a family as they enjoy a picnic.
The children name the dog Willy, feed it hot dogs and play
with it until the parents insist that it is time to head home.
Believing that the dog has a home, they leave Willy behind,
but thoughts of him fill their minds during the week. On
Saturday they return to the same picnic spot. When Willy
races past with a dog warden in pursuit of the stray, the
children quickly intervene to cleverly claim Willy as their
own. This time, when the picnic concludes, Willy joins his
new family for the trip home. The award-winning illustrator's
story is based on a friend's true tale. (32 pages)

Where it's reviewed:
Bulletin of the Center for Children's Books, March 2001,
   page 279
Horn Book, January 2001, page 86
Publishers Weekly, December 4, 2000, page 72
Riverbank Review, Spring 2001, page 34
School Library Journal, February 2001, page 106

Awards the book has won:
Caldecott Honor Book, 2002
Boston Globe-Horn Book Honor Book, 2001

Other books you might like:
Robert J. Blake, *Dog,* 1994
   An elderly man initially rebuffs a dog's attempts to make a
   home with him.
Gloria Rand, *A Home for Spooky,* 1998
   Annie secretly feeds an abandoned dog until the dog's
   health deteriorates and he needs medical treatment to save
   his life.
Tres Seymour, *Pole Dog,* 1993
   An abandoned dog sits forlornly near a telephone pole
   until rescued by a sympathetic family.

824

MARCIA SIMPSON

Sound Tracks

(Scottsdale, AZ: Poisoned Pen, 2001)

Subject(s): Animals/Whales; Mystery and Detective Stories
Age range(s): Grades 10-Adult
Major character(s): Liza Romero, Librarian, Sea Captain; Henry Sizemore, Crime Victim
Time period(s): 2000s
Locale(s): Wrangell, Alaska

Summary: With her policeman husband dead after a drug bust gone wrong, Liza leaves the lower forty-eight and moves to Alaska where she buys an old fishing boat and runs a delivery service for both ordered goods and library books. Returning home after one trip something strikes her boat and nearly turns it over. Liza assumes she's hit rocks, but instead a whale has hit the *Salmon Eye*. Later she sees other whales beaching themselves and realizes something's amiss for whales are known for their navigational abilities. Henry Sizemore, the wildlife protection agent, starts investigating and even orders hydrophones to see if underground noises are diverting the whales. When he turns up drowned, followed by several other murders, Liza begins her own investigation in this top-notch mystery. (244 pages)

Where it's reviewed:
Booklist, June 2001, page 1853
Publishers Weekly, April 30, 2001, page 60

Other books by the same author:
Crow in Stolen Colors, 2000

Other books you might like:
Nevada Barr, *Endangered Species*, 1997
    Sabotage, a plane crash and loggerhead turtles combine as Anna Pigeon searches for the murderer of two men.
Sue Henry, *Murder on the Yukon Quest*, 1999
    Running her dogs on the thousand-mile Yukon Quest is a new race for both Jessie and her dogs, but so is the ransom money she's carrying.
Christopher Lane, *A Shroud of Midnight Sun: An Inupiat Eskimo Mystery*, 2000
    Ray Attla, a vacationing Inupiat police officer, doesn't plan on the bicycle crash that sends him into berry bushes that conceal a corpse.
Dana Stabenow, *Hunter's Moon*, 1999
    Kate guides wealthy German hunters into the Alaska woods where some successfully bag a moose while others meet gruesome deaths.

825

MARILYN SINGER
MARIE-LOUISE GAY, Illustrator

Didi and Daddy on the Promenade

(New York: Clarion Books, 2001)

Subject(s): Fathers and Daughters; City and Town Life; Parent and Child
Age range(s): Preschool-Kindergarten
Major character(s): Didi, Child, Daughter; Daddy, Father
Time period(s): 2000s (2000)
Locale(s): New York, New York (Brooklyn Heights Promenade)

Summary: Sunday morning. Excited Didi. Sleepy Daddy. Hurry, hurry, let's walk on the Promenade. Away Didi races as Daddy calls for her to go slow, but each time Didi says no; she can't slow down because she needs to jump and dance and see and hear everything. When Didi meets a friend walking with her father they stop for a while at the playground until rain begins to fall. Daddy wants to head home, but Didi wants to finish the walk. The rain becomes a thunderstorm and now it's Didi's turn to say slow to Daddy and hear a negative response as he grabs Didi's hand and the two run home, wet but happy from their walk on the Promenade. (32 pages)

Where it's reviewed:
Booklist, April 1, 2001, page 1480
Bulletin of the Center for Children's Books, April 2001, page 315
Horn Book Guide, Fall 2001, page 275
Publishers Weekly, February 12, 2001, page 210
School Library Journal, May 2001, page 135

Other books by the same author:
Monster Museum, 2001
Solomon Sneezes: A-Choo, 1999
In the Palace of the Ocean King, 1995
Chester, the Out-of-Work Dog, 1992

Other books you might like:
Thierry Courtin, *Daddy and Me*, 1997
    One Daddy plus one child equals lots of fun on Daddy's day off.
Caroline Uff, *Lulu's Busy Day*, 2000
    Preschooler Lulu's busy day includes going to the park until rain forces her to return home.
John Wallace, *Little Bean's Friend*, 1997
    Daddy sends Little Bean out to play in the yard with her dog Bouncer and she meets the little boy who lives next door.

826

PETER SIS, Author/Illustrator

Ballerina!

(New York: Greenwillow Books, 2001)

Subject(s): Dancing; Ballet; Imagination
Age range(s): Preschool-Kindergarten
Major character(s): Terry, Dancer, Child
Time period(s): 2000s
Locale(s): United States

Summary: Terry combines her imagination with her love of dance and colored costumes to transform a simple mirror in her room into a succession of scenes from famous ballets. In a red leotard Terry is one character and in blue she's dancing another ballet. With her white feather boa she dips low to perform *Swan Lake* and in a violet cape she dances *Cinderella*. The best performance is the one that uses seven different colored scarves for then she can imagine all the roles. (26 pages)

Where it's reviewed:
Booklist, April 1, 2001, page 1480
Bulletin of the Center for Children's Books, May 2001, page 353
Publishers Weekly, March 26, 2001, page 92
Riverbank Review, Fall 2001, page 28
School Library Journal, April 2001, page 122

Other books by the same author:
Dinosaur!, 2000
Ship Ahoy!, 1999
Trucks Trucks Trucks, 1999 (Horn Book Fanfare)

Other books you might like:
Lucy Dickens, *Dancing Class*, 1992
    Five young aspiring dancers have the opportunity to perform as birds during class.
Kay Gallwey, *Dancing Daisy*, 1994
    After seeing her first ballet, Daisy is determined to become a ballerina.
Patricia Lee Gauch, *Tanya and Emily and the Dance for Two*, 1994
    Tanya's free-spirited, unconventional dance technique inspires creativity in Emily, a proper ballerina.
Rachel Isadora, *Lili at Ballet*, 1993
    Four times a week Lili attends ballet classes hoping to achieve her dream of being a ballerina.

827

GLORIA SKURZYNSKI

Rockbuster

(New York: Atheneum/Simon & Schuster, 2001)

Subject(s): Labor and Labor Classes; Miners and Mining; Prejudice
Age range(s): Grades 6-10
Major character(s): Tommy Quinlan, 18-Year-Old, Miner (coal); Jim McInerny, Miner (coal); Bill Haywood, Historical Figure, Leader (union boss); Eugenie Farnham, Girlfriend (of Tommy); Joe Hill, Historical Figure, Musician (labor leader)
Time period(s): 1910s
Locale(s): Castle Gate, Utah; Chicago, Illinois

Summary: When Tommy is just ten-years-old he accompanies his Uncle Jim to Idaho to deliver funds to a union boss accused of murder, Big Bill Haywood. When Tommy accidentally reveals that Uncle Jim is a union man, Pinkerton detectives intervene, hustle Jim off the train and murder him. With both Tommy's father and uncle dead, Tommy supports his mother by working in the mines as a trapper, one who opens the trap door for the miners. This gives him time to learn to play Uncle Jim's guitar and soon he finds himself playing for dances, where he meets Eugenie, the mine owner's daughter. Falling in love with one another, they keep their relationship secret for each knows their parents wouldn't approve. With Tommy's union background, and his musical ability, he's asked to serve as a troubadour for the union movement. When he travels to Chicago to play for Joe Hill's funeral he's discouraged by all the lies he hears from some of the other union people, including Big Bill Haywood. That's when he resolves to return home and go to law school so he

can work for justice for all people, not just poor people. (253 pages)

Where it's reviewed:
Kirkus Reviews, October 15, 2001, page 1493
Kliatt, November 2001, page 10
Publishers Weekly, November 19, 2001, page 68
School Library Journal, December 2001, page 146
Voice of Youth Advocates, December 2001, page 364

Other books by the same author:
The Clones, 2002
Spider's Voice, 1999
Virtual War, 1997
Good-Bye, Billy Radish, 1992

Other books you might like:
Mary Casanova, *Riot*, 1996
    Bryan is relieved when his father admits he was wrong to set fire to the homes of non-union workers who replaced him at the paper mill.
Jay Parini, *The Patch Boys*, 1988
    Sammy diCantini grows up quickly one summer when his older brother is injured trying to organize a union in a Pennsylvania mining town.
Katherine Paterson, *Lyddie*, 1991
    Lyddie hates being an inn servant and leaves to work in a factory, but her interest in unions causes her to be fired for "moral turpitude."
N.A. Perez, *Breaker*, 1988
    After Pat's father is killed in a mining accident, Pat begins working in the mines while his brother fights for improved labor conditions.
Ann Turnbull, *No Friend of Mine*, 1995
    Two young English boys befriend one another, though one is the son of the mine owner and the other is the son of a miner.

828

JOSEPH SLATE
ASHLEY WOLFF, Illustrator

Miss Bindergarten Takes a Field Trip with Kindergarten

(New York: Dutton Children's Books, 2001)

Subject(s): School Life; Teachers; Animals
Age range(s): Grades K-1
Major character(s): Miss Bindergarten, Teacher, Dog
Time period(s): Indeterminate
Locale(s): Fictional Country

Summary: Miss Bindergarten takes her alphabetical class on a walking field trip through the community. The students view sights at the bakery, fire station, post office and library and make comments in the order in which their names appear in the alphabet. A community park provides a resting spot for the tired group to enjoy snacks and review the different shapes they've seen at each place. (32 pages)

Where it's reviewed:
Booklist, October 1, 2001, page 326
Horn Book Guide, Spring 2002, page 28
Publishers Weekly, July 2, 2001, page 78

School Library Journal, September 2001, page 206

Awards the book has won:
IRA Children's Choices, 2002

Other books by the same author:
Miss Bindergarten Stays Home from Kindergarten, 2000
Miss Bindergarten Celebrates the 100th Day of Kindergarten, 1998
Miss Bindergarten Gets Ready for Kindergarten, 1996

Other books you might like:
Paulette Bourgeois, *Franklin's Class Trip*, 1999
Franklin's anticipation of a class trip ends when Beaver tells him the museum houses real dinosaurs.
Anna Grossnickle Hines, *What Joe Saw*, 1994
Joe's classmates focus on the destination as the group walks to the duck pond but Joe observes everything along the way too.
Grace Maccarone, *The Class Trip*, 1999
In a rhyming "Hello Reader" story Sam loses his group during a class trip to the zoo.

829

WILLIAM SLEATOR

Marco's Millions
(New York: Dutton, 2001)

Subject(s): Space and Time; Psychic Powers; Aliens
Age range(s): Grades 6-9
Major character(s): Marco, 12-Year-Old, Brother (of Lilly); Lilly, 11-Year-Old, Sister (of Marco)
Time period(s): 1970s; 1980s
Locale(s): United States

Summary: When his sister Lilly asks Marco to accompany her to the basement, he has no idea what Lilly has found in the old root cellar. Explaining that she can see lights coming from one wall, Marco investigates and passes through the wall into a tunnel that leads to another world. Inhabited by purple, insect-like creatures that are trying to placate their god, they seek help telepathically from Lilly who refuses to travel through the tunnel. For Marco, who as a child rode buses and trains wherever they would go, entering the tunnel is exhilarating and he returns again and again. He finds a "naked singularity" that not only controls time but is also pocked with worm holes that allow him to travel to millions of other worlds in this prequel to *The Boxes*. (161 pages)

Where it's reviewed:
Bulletin of the Center for Children's Books, July 2001, page 423
Horn Book, May 2001, page 337
Publishers Weekly, May 21, 2001, page 108
School Library Journal, June 2001, page 156
Voice of Youth Advocates, June 2001, page 135

Other books by the same author:
Boltzmon!, 1999
Rewind, 1999
The Boxes, 1998
The Beasties, 1997
The Night the Heads Came, 1996

Other books you might like:
Vivien Alcock, *The Red-Eared Ghosts*, 1997
Because of the resemblance of Mary to her grandmother, aliens lure her into a parallel universe; to escape, she must use all her cleverness.
Kate Gilmore, *The Exchange Student*, 1999
A young alien with an obsessive fondness for animals comes to stay with an earth family.
Lesley Howarth, *Maphead*, 1994
Maphead leaves his parallel universe to travel to Earth to find his human mother, but first must learn to speak English.
Diana Wynne Jones, *The Lives of Christopher Chant*, 1988
As he dreams, Christopher travels to distant and fascinating worlds.

830

CHARLES R. SMITH JR., Author/Illustrator

Loki & Alex: The Adventures of a Dog & His Best Friend
(New York: Dutton Children's Books, 2001)

Subject(s): Animals/Dogs; Pets; Humor
Age range(s): Grades K-3
Major character(s): Alex, Child; Loki, Dog
Time period(s): 2000s (2001)
Locale(s): United States

Summary: Photographs capture a trip to the park from the perspective of both a boy and his dog. Alex is confident that he knows all about Loki, his pet and best friend, but captions beneath each photo suggest that neither completely appreciates the other's view of the relationship. Loki thinks Alex's expression shows how happy he is to see his dog scrounging in the garbage to find treats. Alex thinks he's being kind to give Loki a turn on the slide when Loki is actually terrified. Both agree that a hug after a trip to the park is the best treat of all. (32 pages)

Where it's reviewed:
Booklist, June 2001, page 1896
Bulletin of the Center for Children's Books, July 2001, page 423
Horn Book Guide, Fall 2001, page 275
Kirkus Reviews, June 1, 2001, page 805
School Library Journal, July 2001, page 88

Awards the book has won:
Parenting's Reading Magic Awards, 2001

Other books by the same author:
Brown Sugar Babies, 2000
Tall Tales: Six Amazing Basketball Dreams, 2000

Other books you might like:
Janice Boland, *A Dog Named Sam*, 1996
Sam's enthusiasm for fetching, water play and nighttime activity create problems for his family.
Cynthia Rylant, *The Henry and Mudge Series*, 1987-
The adventures of Henry and his lovable, slobbery dog Mudge entertain beginning readers.
Alan Snow, *How Dogs Really Work!*, 1993
A winner of the New York Times Best Illustrated Chil-

dren's Book Award is a humorous instruction manual for dog owners.

Andrea Zimmerman, *My Dog Toby*, 2000

A little girl is confident that her beloved pet is smart enough to learn just one trick and she tries many strategies to show that she's correct.

831

CYNTHIA LEITICH SMITH

Rain Is Not My Indian Name
(New York: HarperCollins, 2001)

Subject(s): Indians of North America; Grief; Photography
Age range(s): Grades 6-9
Major character(s): Cassidy Rain Berghoff, 14-Year-Old; Georgia Wilhelm, Aunt; Natalie Michelle Lewis, Editor (newspaper), Fiance(e) (of Fynn); Fynnegan ''Fynn'' Berghoff, Brother (of Rain)
Time period(s): 2000s
Locale(s): Hannesburg, Kansas

Summary: After losing her mother six years earlier, Rain enjoys life again and on her birthday realizes her friend Galen could become a romantic interest. The next morning she hears he's been killed in a traffic accident and Rain returns to her grief shell. Refusing to see anyone, she avoids his funeral, gives up her beloved photography and stays in her room. Six months later her brother Fynn's fiancee Natalie urges Rain to attend the Native American youth camp operated by her Aunt Georgia, but Rain resists, agreeing only to photograph the camp for the local newspaper. When there's talk of cutting funding to the camp, Rain realizes she would like to learn more about her Ojibway, Creek and Cherokee heritage, mixed though it is with Scots-Irish and German. (135 pages)

Where it's reviewed:
Book Report, September 2001, page 66
Bulletin of the Center for Children's Books, September 2001, page 35
Publishers Weekly, July 9, 2001, page 68
School Library Journal, June 2001, page 156
Voice of Youth Advocates, June 2001, page 128

Other books by the same author:
Indian Shoes, 2002

Other books you might like:
Rebecca Busselle, *A Frog's-Eye View*, 1990
When Neela's plan for romance doesn't pan out, she gladly accepts her Great-Aunt Amelia's offer of photography lessons.
Julie Reece Deaver, *Say Goodnight, Gracie*, 1988
Morgan's life comes to an abrupt halt when her best friend Jimmy is killed in an automobile accident.
Jennifer Owings Dewey, *Navajo Summer*, 1998
Not wishing to spend the summer with either parent while they're divorcing, Jamie stays with a Navajo family she's met and enjoys the pace of their lives.
Jacqueline Guest, *Lightning Rider*, 2001
Jan defends her jailed brother Grey against a policeman who dislike Indians and has charged Grey with motorcycle theft.

832

LINDA SMITH
KATHRYN BROWN, Illustrator

When Moon Fell Down
(New York: HarperCollins Publishers, 2001)

Subject(s): Animals/Cows; Stories in Rhyme; Fantasy
Age range(s): Grades K-3
Major character(s): Moon, Celestial Body; Cow, Cow
Time period(s): Indeterminate Past
Locale(s): Earth

Summary: When Moon falls down into a field he is ecstatic to experience first hand all the things he's viewed from afar. Curious Cow approaches and Moon offers her a ride over the town. Together they stroll the streets of the town as Moon gazes into the windows of the shops that previously he's only known by their rooftops. With the dawn, Cow and Moon return to the farm to be scolded by the irate farmer for leaving the places where they belong and so ends their memorable night. (32 pages)

Where it's reviewed:
Booklist, April 1, 2001, page 1472
Horn Book Guide, Fall 2001, page 275
Kirkus Reviews, April 15, 2001, page 593
Publishers Weekly, May 14, 2001, page 81
School Library Journal, July 2001, page 88

Awards the book has won:
Booklist Editors' Choice/Books for Youth, 2002

Other books you might like:
Mary-Claire Helldorfer, *Moon Trouble*, 1994
When the moon falls in the river the local folk know to call Paul Bunyan to solve the problem.
Rodney Rigby, *The Night the Moon Fell Asleep*, 1993
Overtired by too many late nights, the moon falls asleep and crashes to the ground, requiring a community effort to restore her to the night sky.
Susan Whitcher, *Moonfall*, 1993
Sylvie finds the fallen moon in a neighbor's lilac bush and tries to restore its luster.

833

MAGGIE SMITH, Author/Illustrator

Desser the Best Ever Cat
(New York: Alfred A. Knopf, 2001)

Subject(s): Animals/Cats; Death; Pets
Age range(s): Grades K-2
Major character(s): Desser, Cat; Dad, Father; Unnamed Character, Daughter, Narrator
Time period(s): Indeterminate Past
Locale(s): United States

Summary: Desser's been the best cat ever since he wandered into Dad's life long before his marriage and the birth of his children. In those days, the cat was called Dexter, but Dad's first child's pronunciation soon changed that. Desser is a source of comfort during chicken pox and a playmate just about any time. Desser grows older and eventually the family must face the fact that Desser is near death. Despite her parents' comfort, the little girl is sad to lose her best ever cat. The family buries Desser under his favorite tree with all the toys and treats he could ever need because Desser's the best. (40 pages)

Where it's reviewed:
Booklist, February 15, 2001, page 1142
Horn Book Guide, Fall 2001, page 275
Kirkus Reviews, February 15, 2001, page 265
Publishers Weekly, March 26, 2001, page 93
School Library Journal, July 2001, page 89

Awards the book has won:
Publishers Weekly Best Children's Books, 2001

Other books by the same author:
Dear Daisy, Get Well Soon, 2000
Counting Our Way to Maine, 1995
My Grandma's Chair, 1992

Other books you might like:
Robie H. Harris, *Goodbye Mousie*, 2001
    A little boy wakes up to find his pet mouse lifeless and his parents sensitively help him accept Mousie's death and grieve for his loss.
Ann M. Martin, *Leo the Magnificat*, 1996
    A fluffy black and white cat wanders into a churchyard and make himself at home for the rest of his long life.
Judith Viorst, *The Tenth Good Thing about Barney*, 1971
    When his cat dies, a young boy consoles himself by thinking of the ten best things he remembers about his pet.
Ruth Wallace-Brodeur, *Goodbye, Mitch*, 1995
    Michael's mom tries to prepare him for the inevitable death of his old cat.

834

ROLAND SMITH

Zach's Lie

(New York: Hyperion, 2001)

Subject(s): Drugs; Identity, Concealed
Age range(s): Grades 5-9
Major character(s): Jack/Zachary Colin Osborne/Granger, 13-Year-Old; Sam Sebesta, Maintenance Worker (school janitor); Catalin Cristobal, 7th Grader; Alonzo Aznar, Drug Dealer
Time period(s): 2000s
Locale(s): Elko, Nevada

Summary: Jack's dad is arrested for drug trafficking and agrees to cooperate with the government, an act that sends thugs to terrorize his family. Agreeing to become part of the Witness Protection Program, Jack becomes Zach and he, his mother and sister are moved to a small town in Nevada where Jack has difficulty adjusting to his new name and his new life. For a sense of well being he maintains his old journal, which contains identifying information about his family; is helped at school by Sam, the school custodian; and meets a special girl, Catalin. Catalin's grandfather is a Basque sheepherder with a sheep camp in the mountains, a camp that offers safety to Zach when his journal is stolen and given to the drug lord Aznar. With help from Sam, the drug lord is subdued but his

family's identity has been compromised and they must move again in this suspenseful story. (211 pages)

Where it's reviewed:
Book Report, May 2001, page 61
Booklist, May 15, 2001, page 1754
Publishers Weekly, June 25, 2001, page 73
School Library Journal, June 2001, page 156
Voice of Youth Advocates, June 2001, page 128

Awards the book has won:
ALA Quick Picks for Reluctant Young Adult Readers, 2002

Other books by the same author:
The Captain's Dog: My Journey with the Lewis and Clark Tribe, 1999
The Last Lobo, 1999
Sasquatch, 1998
Jaguar, 1997
Thunder Cave, 1995

Other books you might like:
Barbara Abercrombie, *Run for Your Life*, 1984
    Mystery writer Sarah Flynn finds her entire family is in jeopardy when a deranged killer begins following the plot of her latest book.
Robert Cormier, *In the Middle of the Night*, 1995
    Because of an incident years ago, Denny's family moves often, changing houses, phone numbers and schools.
Lois Duncan, *Don't Look Behind You*, 1989
    Though April's family is part of a Witness Security Program, April inadvertently reveals their whereabouts and places her family in danger.
James Stevenson, *The Unprotected Witness*, 1997
    Pete, his grandmother and his best friend Rootie travel to the Ozarks for the funeral of his father, killed while part of the Witness Protection Program.

835

WILL SMITH
KADIR NELSON, Illustrator

Just the Two of Us

(New York: Scholastic Press, 2001)

Subject(s): Fathers and Sons; Love; Growing Up
Age range(s): Grades K-2
Major character(s): Daddy, Single Father; Unnamed Character, Son
Time period(s): 2000s
Locale(s): United States

Summary: A father recalls the joy of his son's birth, the wonder of a tiny life, the challenge of the responsibility of raising him to be a good man. Daddy knows the importance of his influence in his son's life and he strives to balance love, discipline and knowledge as he watches his son grow all the while knowing that the day will come when the son will want to be independent and Daddy must trust that he's fulfilled his role. (32 pages)

Where it's reviewed:
Booklist, July 2001, page 2021
Children's Bookwatch, April 2001, page 4
Kirkus Reviews, April 15, 2001, page 593

Publishers Weekly, April 30, 2001, page 76
School Library Journal, June 2001, page 129

Awards the book has won:
Notable Social Studies Trade Books for Young People, 2002

Other books you might like:
Margaret Park Bridges, *If I Were Your Father*, 1999
    While sharing activities with his father a little boy imagines himself in the role.
Mercer Mayer, *Just Me and My Dad*, 1977
    The illustrations depict what actually happens during a father and son camping adventure.
Charlotte Zolotow, *A Father Like That*, 1971
    To his mom a young boy offers a description of the ideal father.

836

GORDON SNELL, Editor

Thicker Than Water: Coming-of-Age Stories by Irish and Irish American Writers

(New York: Delacorte, 2001)

Subject(s): Short Stories; Coming-of-Age; Irish Americans
Age range(s): Grades 9-12
Time period(s): 2000s
Locale(s): Ireland; United States

Summary: Twelve Irish or Irish American authors contribute stories, unique for their scenes of Irish life, yet reflective of the feelings of teens everywhere. Consider Chris Lynch's "Off Ya Go, So" about a young couple discussing the need for an abortion, but knowing they'll have to travel to England as abortions are outlawed in Ireland. Emma Donoghue's story, "Thicker than Water," features two sisters who unnecessarily embarrass one another at their mother's second wedding. Marita Conlon-Mckenna chillingly portrays the conflict between Catholic and Protestant in "Good Girl." Works by Maeve Binchey, Peter Cunningham, June Considine and Jenny Roche are included as well as other authors perhaps not as well known to American audiences. (237 pages)

Where it's reviewed:
Book Report, September 2001, page 69
Booklist, January 2001, page 941
Horn Book, March 2001, page 213
Publishers Weekly, February 26, 2001, page 88
School Library Journal, May 2001, page 160

Other books by the same author:
Phantom Horseman, 1997
Curse of Werewolf Castle, 1996
Dangerous Treasure, 1996
Mystery of Monk Island, 1996

Other books you might like:
Robin Klein, *Tearaways: Stories to Make You Think Twice*, 1991
    Suspenseful stories by an Australian author about people who seem trustworthy, but who actually have many flaws.
John Loughery, *First Sightings: Stories of American Youth*, 1993

Arranged chronologically by the age of the protagonist, these twenty stories illustrate the coming of age phenomena in America.
Anne Mazer, *A Walk in My World: International Short Stories about Youth*, 1998
    Young people worldwide share similar experiences as shown in these sixteen stories by international authors.
Budge Wilson, *The Dandelion Garden*, 1995
    Self-discovery is the theme of this collection of short stories by a Canadian author.

837

ZILPHA KEATLEY SNYDER

Spyhole Secrets

(New York: Delacorte, 2001)

Subject(s): Grief; Moving, Household; Family Problems
Age range(s): Grades 4-7
Major character(s): Hallie Meredith, 6th Grader; Zachary Crestman, Child
Time period(s): 2000s
Locale(s): Irvington

Summary: Moving to a small apartment with her mother, Hallie's still angry about her father's accidental death, which forced her mother to sell their house, give away their pets and send Hallie to a new school. One afternoon Hallie returns to her new apartment, subdivided from an old mansion, and decides to explore the attic that tenants use for storage. Hallie hopes to find a secret hiding place, some spot to call her own, and is drawn to the boarded-up tower window through which a ray of blue light shines. Finding a hole through which she can peek, she peers into the living room of the high-rise apartment built right next to the converted mansion. The first occupant she spots is a sullen teenage girl with blonde hair and Hallie imagines all kinds of stories about her. Weeks of observation convince her that a troubled family lives there, with a daughter who carries around a gun and parents who argue continually, all of which make her own problems shrink in size and importance. Eventually meeting the son at the library, Hallie discovers that her imagination has run unchecked but it has helped her begin to heal. (186 pages)

Where it's reviewed:
Book Report, November 2001, page 66
Booklist, May 1, 2001, page 1612
Bulletin of the Center for Children's Books, October 2001, page 77
Publishers Weekly, July 2, 2001, page 76
School Library Journal, June 2001, page 156 .

Other books by the same author:
Gib and the Gray Ghost, 2000
The Runaways, 1999
Fool's Gold, 1993
Libby on Wednesday, 1990
And Condors Danced, 1987

Other books you might like:
Audrey Couloumbis, *Getting Near to Baby*, 1999
    Sitting on the roof to be "near to Baby" is Willa Jo's

favorite spot since her baby sister died after drinking contaminated water.

Adrienne Ross, *In the Quiet*, 2000

Sammy and her good friend Bones dig holes hoping to find some object that will help Sammy reconnect with her deceased mother's spirit.

Laura Torres, *November Ever After*, 1999

After Amy's mother dies, her minister father throws himself into work while Amy quits attending church.

838

KEVIN SOMERS
DIANA CAIN BLUTHENTHAL, Illustrator

Meaner than Meanest
(New York: Hyperion Books for Children, 2001)

Subject(s): Witches and Witchcraft; Magic; Behavior
Age range(s): Grades K-3
Major character(s): Hisss, Cat; Unnamed Character, Witch, Aged Person; Daisy, Child
Time period(s): Indeterminate
Locale(s): Fictional Country

Summary: A mean old hag tries to create a monster that is meaner than the meanest thing she knows, Hisss. Consulting her recipes the hag cooks a vile mixture of spiders, snails, snakes and scorpions in her pot. She gathers the pot's foam into a cocoon that she tends carefully by talking to it and reading it horror stories. At the moment the cocoon prepares to open the hag notices that she's forgotten a critical ingredient but it's too late. The creature that steps out of the cocoon is not a mean monster but an overly sweet little girl. Every attempt the hag makes to frighten Daisy is met with unfailing sweetness to which Hisss responds thus making the hag even more annoyed. Daisy has to coax the hag out of bed on Halloween night so the trick or treating can begin. The hag is really in for a surprise now as the author's first book concludes. (32 pages)

Where it's reviewed:
Bulletin of the Center for Children's Books, November 2001, page 116
Kirkus Reviews, August 15, 2001, page 1222
Publishers Weekly, September 24, 2001, page 42
School Library Journal, November 2001, page 136

Other books you might like:
Addie Adam, *Hilda and the Mad Scientist*, 1995
Helpful Hilda's do-good housekeeping plans unintentionally foil Dr. Weinerstein's monster-making experiments.
Pat Hutchins, *Three-Star Billy*, 1994
A monster who doesn't want to be in school learns that his temper tantrum earns him three stars from the teacher.
Anne Wilsdorf, *Philomene*, 1992
Captured by a disagreeable witch, Philomene takes her by surprise when she befriends the witch's monster and they create their own spell.

839

SONYA SONES

What My Mother Doesn't Know
(New York: Simon & Schuster, 2001)

Subject(s): Dating (Social Customs); Love; School Life
Age range(s): Grades 7-10
Major character(s): Sophie, 15-Year-Old; Robin Murphy, Boyfriend
Time period(s): 2000s
Locale(s): Boston, Massachusetts

Summary: Sophie's in love, first with Dylan who practically clings to her side, but then that infatuation fades. Then there's Chaz who she meets over the Internet, but luckily discovers he's a pervert before she actually meets him in person. While looking for the next "Mr. Right," she finds him! In the Museum of Fine Arts, she meets the perfect boyfriend, Robin Murphy, the one she's liked from afar who's in her art class. He makes her laugh, they can talk to one another, and his kisses cause her to melt; now all she has to do is convince her friends that he's really not a jerk in this book written in free verse. (259 pages)

Where it's reviewed:
Booklist, November 15, 2001, page 573
Kliatt, September 2001, page 13
Publishers Weekly, October 15, 2001, page 72
School Library Journal, October 2001, page 171
Voice of Youth Advocates, October 2001, page 284

Awards the book has won:
Booklist Editors' Choice/Books for Youth, 2001
ALA Best Books for Young Adults, 2002

Other books by the same author:
Stop Pretending: What Happened When My Big Sister Went Crazy, 1999

Other books you might like:
Robert Cormier, *Frenchtown Summer*, 1999
In free verse Eugene thinks over all that occurred during the summer he was twelve and how those events contributed to his growing up.
Mame Farrell, *And Sometimes Why*, 2001
Athletic Chris and artistic Jack have been friends since first grade; now that they're older, they realize they'll have to work at remaining friends.
Phyllis Reynolds Naylor, *The Alice Series*, 1985-
Motherless Alice and her friends Pamela, Elizabeth and Patrick survive all the traumas of junior high, peer pressure and dating, but now await high school.

840

JESSICA SPANYOL, Author/Illustrator

Carlo Likes Reading
(Cambridge, MA: Candlewick Press, 2001)

Subject(s): Animals/Giraffes; Books and Reading; Literacy
Age range(s): Preschool-Kindergarten
Major character(s): Carlo, Giraffe
Time period(s): Indeterminate

Locale(s): Fictional Country

Summary: Everywhere Carlo goes he sees words and words are just what a reader like Carlo enjoys. He can read his bedroom, his breakfast or the bathroom because everything is labeled. Sometimes Carlo's mom reads to him and sometimes Carlo reads to the cat or a friend or even the ducks at the park in the author's first book. (26 pages)

Where it's reviewed:
Booklist, November 1, 2001, page 485
Kirkus Reviews, August 1, 2001, page 132
Publishers Weekly, September 3, 2001, page 86
School Library Journal, October 2001, page 132
Smithsonian, November 2001, page 120

Awards the book has won:
Smithsonian's Notable Books for Children, 2001

Other books you might like:

Deborah Bruss, *Book! Book! Book!*, 2001
Even the bored farm animals enjoy reading a story now and then.

Robert Burleigh, *I Love Going Through This Book*, 2001
An eager reader describes the pleasure of getting lost in a book.

P.K. Hallinan, *Just Open a Book*, 1995
A rhyming story tells how simple it is to have an adventure—open a book.

Rosemary Wells, *Read to Your Bunny*, 1998
The importance of reading daily is emphasized in brief text and cozy pictures of mother and father bunnies reading to their youngsters.

841

BRITNEY SPEARS
LYNNE SPEARS, Co-Author

A Mother's Gift
(New York: Delacorte, 2001)

Subject(s): Singing; Schools; Mothers and Daughters
Age range(s): Grades 5-9
Major character(s): Holly Faye Lovell, 14-Year-Old, Singer; Wanda Jo Lovell, Seamstress; Tyler Norwood, Mechanic, Boyfriend (of Holly's)
Time period(s): 2000s
Locale(s): Biscay, Mississippi; Hattiesburg, Mississippi

Summary: Young Holly Faye lives with her mother Wanda Jo in a small Southern town, poor but happy in their world. Holly Faye sings in the church choir and school musicals, but really wants to be a glamorous singer when she grows up. Her boyfriend manages to get her an audition at the noted Haverty School of Music where she is offered a full scholarship. Knowing her mother can't afford the tuition, she accepts, but upon arriving finds how out of place she looks compared to the wealthy students. Being the youngest person ever selected to sing at the Haverty Talent Hour, and finding the truth about her own birth, give Holly Faye much-needed confidence in this work by a popular singing star and her mother. (227 pages)

Where it's reviewed:
Entertainment Weekly, April 27, 2001, page 13

Girls' Life, April 2001, page 12
Knight-Ridder/Tribune News Service, June 27, 2001, page K2921
Publishers Weekly, April 23, 2001, page 78

Awards the book has won:
ALA Quick Picks for Reluctant Young Adult Readers, 2002

Other books by the same author:
Britney Spears' Heart to Heart, 2000 (nonfiction)
Britney Spears: Oops! . . . I Did It Again, 2000 (nonfiction)

Other books you might like:

Gillian Cross, *Chartbreaker*, 1987
Becoming the lead singer for the rock band "Kelp" is the last thing Janis Mary Finch thinks will happen when she runs away from home.

Vy Higginsen, *Mama, I Want to Sing*, 1992
Against her mother's wishes, Doris takes first prize at the Apollo Theater's Amateur Night and moves on to a successful musical career.

Phyllis Reynolds Naylor, *Send No Blessings*, 1990
Beth doesn't want to spend her whole life in a doublewide trailer in West Virginia, but is afraid she'll never achieve her dream of college.

Katherine Paterson, *Come Sing, Jimmy Jo*, 1985
Though Jimmy Jo joins his blues family as a famous singer, he'd rather be doing something else.

Rhea Beth Ross, *Hillbilly Choir*, 1991
Laurie's singing ability provides her with a chance to leave her small town, though it's hard to leave her grandmother and her friends.

842

EILEEN SPINELLI
CHRISTY HALE, Illustrator

A Safe Place Called Home
(New York: Marshall Cavendish, 2001)

Subject(s): Fear; Stories in Rhyme; Parent and Child
Age range(s): Grades K-2
Major character(s): Unnamed Character, Child, Son
Time period(s): 2000s
Locale(s): United States

Summary: The walk home from school can seem frightening to a young boy who encounters a barking dog, older kids running, storm clouds and lightening. Sirens wail, bullies glare, bumblebees appear and the boy goes faster and faster in his desire to reach home. The leaves whirl menacingly in the wind and the scared little boy smiles to finally be in the safety of his parents' arms at home. (32 pages)

Where it's reviewed:
Booklist, October 1, 2001, page 330
Bulletin of the Center for Children's Books, September 2001, page 36
Horn Book Guide, Spring 2002, page 59
School Library Journal, February 2002, page 112

Other books by the same author:
Kittycat Lullaby, 2001
Night Shift Daddy, 2000
Six Hogs on a Scooter, 2000

Other books you might like:
Valiska Gregory, *Kate's Giants*, 1995
　Kate imagines scary things behind the attic door; her parents help her find the courage to confront her fears.
Kevin Henkes, *Sheila Rae, the Brave*, 1987
　Brave Sheila Rae and her timid sister Louise become lost and it is Louise who courageously finds the way home.
Martin Waddell, *Let's Go Home, Little Bear*, 1993
　The sound of the "Drippers" and "Plodders" in the woods frighten Little Bear so much that Big Bear carries him home.

843

EILEEN SPINELLI
JANE DYER, Illustrator

Sophie's Masterpiece: A Spider's Tale
(New York: Simon & Schuster Books for Young Readers, 2001)

Subject(s): Animals/Spiders; Boarding Houses; Talent
Age range(s): Grades K-3
Major character(s): Sophie, Spider, Artist; Unnamed Character, Young Woman, Mother
Time period(s): Indeterminate Past
Locale(s): United States (Beekman's Boardinghouse)

Summary: Sophie's artistry is noted and appreciated by her family long before she ventures out to make a home for herself at Beekman's Boardinghouse. Unfortunately, the landlady and the tenants do not appreciate Sophie's attempts to add some beauty to the dingy interior. Finally Sophie finds a haven in a knitting basket in a third floor room. Her journey has been exhausting and Sophie rests more than she spins. The young woman resident of the room does not chase Sophie away, but simply knits until she's made booties and a baby sweater. With no money to buy new yarn, the woman cannot knit a blanket for her baby. Sophie goes to work on her masterpiece, a blanket for the newborn, into which she weaves moonlight, snowflakes, quiet songs, bits of pine scent and her heart. (32 pages)

Where it's reviewed:
Booklist, April 15, 2001, page 1551
Bulletin of the Center for Children's Books, July 2001, page 424
Horn Book, July 2001, page 444
Publishers Weekly, May 14, 2001, page 81
School Library Journal, May 2001, page 135

Awards the book has won:
Booklist Editors' Choice/Books for Youth, 2002

Other books by the same author:
A Safe Place Called Home, 2001
Kittycat Lullaby, 2001
Night Shift Daddy, 2000
Six Hogs on a Scooter, 2000
When Mama Comes Home, 1998
Where Is the Night Train Going?: Bedtime Poems, 1996

Other books you might like:
Eric Carle, *The Very Busy Spider*, 1984
　A busy little spider ignores the distracting farm animals and focuses on completing her web.

Melissa Kajpust, *A Dozen Silk Diapers*, 1993
　A spider and her children make a gift for the baby who is born in their manger home.
Margaret Musgrove, *The Spider Weaver: A Legend of Kente Cloth*, 2001
　A spider's intricate web inspires two weavers to try new patterns.
Jeanette Winter, *My Baby*, 2001
　During her pregnancy, a mother lovingly designs and creates a painted cloth for her baby.

844

STEPHANIE SPINNER
TERRY BISSON, Co-Author

Expiration Date: Never
(New York: Delacorte Press, 2001)

Subject(s): Twins; Aliens; Science Fiction
Age range(s): Grades 3-5
Major character(s): Tessa Gibson, Twin, Sister; Tod Gibson, Twin, Brother; Gemini Jack, Alien, Twin; Nigel Throbber, Musician
Time period(s): 2000s (2001)
Locale(s): United States

Summary: Tod and Tessa feel excited and a bit perplexed to discover that Gemini Jack is back in his virtual shop at the mall. Apparently the solution they devised for his planet's problems in *Be First in the Universe* was not successful. Tod and Tessa have to admit that what Jack did to "help" them on Earth is becoming a little annoying too. Jack agrees to give Tod and Tessa the DNA necessary to undo his earlier experiment and they offer to think of a solution to his planet's problem. Unfortunately having Nigel Throbber practicing drum solos all night in the barn keeps them from sleeping or thinking. As it turns out, Nigel and his drums are just the solution that Gemini Jack needs for his planet. (115 pages)

Where it's reviewed:
Booklist, August 2001, page 2122
Bulletin of the Center for Children's Books, July 2001, page 424
Horn Book Guide, Fall 2001, page 316
Kirkus Reviews, April 1, 2001, page 506
School Library Journal, July 2001, page 89

Other books by the same author:
Be First in the Universe, 2000
Gerbilitis, 1996 (Ellen Weiss, co-author)
The Mummy's Tomb, 1985

Other books you might like:
Eve Bunting, *Wanna Buy an Alien?*, 2000
　By following the directions on his odd birthday gift Ben actually brings a space ship to Earth, but he's not sure it has friendly intentions.
Gery Greer, *Jason and the Escape from Bat Planet*, 1993
　In a series entry, Jason and his alien friend Coop rescue an absent-minded professor imprisoned in outer space. Bob Ruddick, co-author.

Daniel Pinkwater, *Ned Feldman, Space Pirate*, 1994
  Ned discovers Captain Lugo, an alien pirate, under the kitchen sink and accompanies him on a trip through space.

845

MICHAEL SPOONER

Daniel's Walk

(New York: Holt, 2002)

Subject(s): Frontier and Pioneer Life; Robbers and Outlaws; American West
Age range(s): Grades 6-9
Major character(s): Daniel LeBlanc, 14-Year-Old; Thompson Haggard, Thief; James Clyman, Historical Figure, Wagonmaster; Johnny, Slave (freed); Rosalie McCulloch, Orphan, 14-Year-Old
Time period(s): 1840s
Locale(s): Caldwell, Missouri; West; Rocky Mountains

Summary: For some reason, Daniel hears a "voice" warning him that his father needs help and Daniel knows he must find and lend him a hand. Unfortunately, his father's trapping animals in the Rocky Mountains and Daniel doesn't know how to find one person in that vast wilderness, but he's determined and decides to follow the wagon trails. On his third night out, he spots a scar-faced man called Haggard stealing horses from a wagon train and takes a shot at him; though Haggard escapes, Daniel is certain the man will one day find and hurt him. When James Clyman invites him to join his wagon train, Daniel is quick to accept his offer for the safety it provides and the friends he meets, including the freed slave Johnny and the young orphan Rosalie. Haggard later kidnaps Daniel and Rosalie and takes them to Daniel's father, a well-known outlaw who hates the white man for destroying the Native Americans. The trek has been arduous for Daniel as he's been shot at, stabbed, starved and nearly sold to the Indians; when his reunion with his father doesn't go as expected, Daniel is glad to return to Missouri. (212 pages)

Where it's reviewed:
Booklist, December 15, 2001, page 724
Bulletin of the Center for Children's Books, November 2001, page 116
Kliatt, September 2001, page 13
School Library Journal, October 2001, page 172
Voice of Youth Advocates, December 2001, page 364

Other books you might like:
Patricia Calvert, *Bigger*, 1994
  As Tyler journeys to find his father and bring him back after the Civil War, he is accompanied by the abused dog Bigger.
Kristiana Gregory, *Jimmy Spoon and the Pony Express*, 1994
  Riding fifty miles over harsh terrain is an exhausting but exhilarating job for Jimmy as he rides for the Pony Express.
Sonia Levitin, *Clem's Chances*, 2001
  Clem finally finds his father, who headed West in search of gold, but realizes Pierre doesn't have room in his life for a son.
Gary Paulsen, *Call Me Francis Tucket*, 1995
  Captured by Pawnee Indians and then rescued by Mr.

Grimes, Francis continues west across the prairie looking for his parents' wagon train.

846

NANCY SPRINGER

I Am Morgan Le Fay

(New York: Philomel, 2001)

Series: Tale from Camelot
Subject(s): Magic; Family
Age range(s): Grades 8-12
Major character(s): Morgan, Sorceress; Thomas, Warrior
Time period(s): Indeterminate Future
Locale(s): England

Summary: Young Morgan's life is twisted from the moment she witnesses the Uther Pendragon's magically aided rape of her mother Igraine. With her father dead and her mother a captive of Uther, Morgan is strangely alone and her emerging powers will soon mark her even more clearly. Although Igraine is besotted with the baby boy she bears Uther, Morgan remains ambivalent about him and grows into her powers in isolation, with only her childhood nurse and sister for company. Her experiences are in the strange, magical world of the fey, and when she falls in love with her childhood friend Thomas she is unprepared for love's demands. Her pain only deepens when she tries to reach out to her mother and her brother, now King Arthur. (227 pages)

Where it's reviewed:
Booklist, February 1, 2001, page 304
Bulletin of the Center for Children's Books, April 2001, page 315
Horn Book Magazine, November-December 2001, page 781
Publishers Weekly, December 4, 2000, page 74
School Library Journal, March 2001, page 256

Other books by the same author:
I Am Mordred: A Tale from Camelot, 1998
Fair Peril, 1996
Looking for Jamie Bridger, 1995

Other books you might like:
Marion Zimmer Bradley, *The Mists of Avalon*, 1982
  Morgaine tells the story of Arthur's reign and the slow triumph of Christianity over the older pagan ways.
Sarah L. Thomson, *The Dragon's Son*, 2001
  The first of these four short stories retells Morgan's version of the Arthurian legend.
Elizabeth Wein, *The Winter Prince*, 1993
  Two brothers, one weak and one strong, are caught in a battle for the throne of Britain.

847

NANCY SPRINGER

Rowan Hood: Outlaw Girl of Sherwood Forest

(New York: Philomel, 2001)

Subject(s): Fathers and Daughters; Adventure and Adventurers; Identity, Concealed

Age range(s): Grades 4-8
Major character(s): Rosemary/Rowan ''Ro'', 13-Year-Old; Ettarde ''Etty'', Royalty (princess); Lionel, Musician; Tykell, Dog (wolf-dog); Robin Hood, Father, Outlaw
Time period(s): 12th century
Locale(s): Sherwood Forest, England

Summary: When her mother, a noted healer, is killed by the local lord's men, who also burn her house, Rosemary has no choice but to search for her father, the infamous Robin Hood, who has never been told of her existence. Cutting her hair, dressing as a boy and calling herself Rowan, she heads to Sherwood Forest. Along the way she gathers several companions including the wolf-dog Tykell, a ''gentle giant'' musician Lionel and the runaway princess Etty. Finding Robin Hood, Rowan explains their relationship but declines his invitation to stay at his camp with his men. Instead she sets up her own band where her first task is to rescue Robin from the Sheriff of Nottingham in this alternate tale. (170 pages)

Where it's reviewed:
Booklist, April 15, 2001, page 1561
Bulletin of the Center for Children's Books, September 2001, page 36
Kliatt, May 2001, page 14
School Library Journal, July 2001, page 114
Voice of Youth Advocates, June 2001, page 136

Other books by the same author:
Outlaw Minstrel of Sherwood Forest: A Tale of Rowan Hood, 2002
I am Mordred: A Tale from Camelot, 1998
The Boy on a Black Horse, 1994
The Red Wizard, 1990
Not on a White Horse, 1988

Other books you might like:
Michael Cadnum, *In a Dark Wood*, 1998
    At last the ''evil'' Sheriff of Nottingham has a chance to tell his side of the story, from the problems with his unfaithful wife to his fear of being a coward.
Robin McKinley, *The Outlaws of Sherwood*, 1988
    A realistic reworking of the story of Robin Hood with Robin as a more ordinary man.
Theresa Tomlinson, *The Forestwife*, 1995
    In a retelling of the legend of Robin Hood, Mary runs away from an arranged marriage, finds shelter with the Forestwife and learns to be an herbalist.
Jane Yolen, *Sherwood: Original Stories from the World of Robin Hood*, 2000
    Eight stories explore the life around Sherwood Forest, though not necessarily from the original Robin Hood's perspective.

848

JOHN STADLER, Author/Illustrator

What's So Scary?

(New York: Orchard Books, 2001)

Subject(s): Animals; Books and Reading; Artists and Art
Age range(s): Grades 1-3

Major character(s): Unnamed Character, Dog; Unnamed Character, Artist (illustrator)
Time period(s): Indeterminate
Locale(s): Fictional Country

Summary: A dog suspects the illustrator of drawing his character into the wrong book. The dog knows the title of the planned book is *Dog's Big Birthday Sleepover* not *What's So Scary?* As the animal guests arrive for the dog's birthday party everyone has to scurry out of the way of the unseen, clumsy illustrator who has knocked over the paint. They race from page to page of the book trying to escape the paint and searching for the book's end. When the illustrator slips in the paint and drops the brush the dog picks it up and paints a solution to the problem. (32 pages)

Where it's reviewed:
Children's Bookwatch, May 2001, page 7
Horn Book Guide, Fall 2001, page 276
Kirkus Reviews, May 1, 2001, page 667
School Library Journal, August 2001, page 162

Other books by the same author:
The Cats of Mrs. Calamari, 1997
Ready, Set, Go!, 1996
The Adventures of Snail at School, 1993

Other books you might like:
Tanya Linch, *My Duck*, 2000
    Imaginative Tanya creates two characters with independent ideas that keep appearing in her class artwork despite the teacher's complaints
Ellen Stoll Walsh, *Jack's Tale*, 1997
    Reluctantly, Jack agrees to an author's request to walk through a story he's writing from beginning to end.
Bruce Whatley, *Wait! No Paint!*, 2001
    The illustrator changes the outcome of a familiar story when he spills his juice and runs out of red paint.
David Wiesner, *The Three Pigs*, 2001
    Characters set the direction for this retelling as they wander in and out of the pages of different stories with varying illustrative styles.

849

DIANE STANLEY
HOLLY BERRY, Illustrator

Joining the Boston Tea Party

(New York: Joanna Cotler/HarperCollins Publishers, 2001)

Series: Time-Traveling Twins
Subject(s): Historical; Time Travel; Twins
Age range(s): Grades 2-4
Major character(s): Grandma, Grandmother, Time Traveler; Liz, Twin, Time Traveler; Lenny, Twin, Time Traveler
Time period(s): 1770s (1773)
Locale(s): Boston, Massachusetts, American Colonies

Summary: Liz and Lenny know that a summer visit to Grandma's house will be a time for many activities, including time travel with the help of Grandma's magic hat. Lenny chooses a picture of an ancestor to visit and they all depart for Boston to explore the political and social events surrounding the Boston Tea Party. Their relatives give them period clothes to wear so they won't be conspicuous and their history lesson begins. A concluding "Author's Note" adds historical background for the story.

Where it's reviewed:
Booklist, September 15, 2001, page 224
Horn Book, November 2001, page 769
Kirkus Reviews, August 1, 2001, page 1132
Publishers Weekly, August 6, 2001, page 91
School Library Journal, August 2001, page 162

Awards the book has won:
IRA Children's Choices, 2002

Other books by the same author:
Roughing It on the Oregon Trail, 2000 (Time-Traveling Twins)
Raising Sweetness, 1999
Rumpelstiltskin's Daughter, 1997

Other books you might like:
Louise Borden, *Sleds on Boston Common: A Story from the American Revolution*, 2000
   One of the inconveniences of life in occupied Boston, not being able to sled on the best hill, is resolved in a picture book for older readers.
Katherine Kirkpatrick, *Redcoats and Petticoats*, 1999
   The role of the Strong family of Long Island in conveying secret messages to the American forces is described in this illustrated historical fiction.
Karen B. Winnick, *Sybil's Night Ride*, 2000
   The teenaged daughter of an American Colonel rides all night to alert her father and his troops of a British attack on a nearby town.

850

DIANE STANLEY

The Mysterious Matter of I.M. Fine
(New York: HarperCollins, 2001)

Subject(s): Magic; Books and Reading; Mystery and Detective Stories
Age range(s): Grades 4-6
Major character(s): Franny, 6th Grader; Scott "Beamer" Connolly, 6th Grader; Ida Mae "I.M." Fine, Writer
Time period(s): 2000s
Locale(s): Baltimore, Maryland; Wimberly, Pennsylvania

Summary: Starting the year at yet another new school, Franny keeps to herself until the day Beamer sits across the lunch table from her and the two become friends. They both notice that many of the students in their lunchroom are playing with Jelly Worms and recall that popular author I.M. Fine has written a book called *The Worm Turns*. Several weeks later a virus goes around the school and students are bedridden with piercing headaches, which might be linked to Fine's next book. But when *Sinister Serpent Surprise* is released and students across the country begin slithering like snakes, it's obvious to Franny and Beamer that something in Fine's books causes these reactions. The two friends track down the author and discover she is Ida Mae Fine who uses her writings to retaliate for her father's death many years earlier. (201 pages)

Where it's reviewed:
Booklist, July 2001, page 2007
School Library Journal, August 2001, page 189

Other books by the same author:
A Time Apart, 1999

Other books you might like:
Otto Coontz, *The Night Walkers*, 1982
   The children of Covendale are plagued by a disease that keeps them away from sun and light but free to roam the streets at night.
Kathryn Lasky, *Memoirs of a Book Bat*, 1994
   Harper's father discovers religion and becomes a banned books organizer, driving his family from town to town while Harper reads what her father bans.
R.L. Stine, *The Fear Street Series*, 1989-
   Still popular, this horror series written for young adults has led to several spinoffs, including *Goosebumps* and *The Nightmare Room*.

851

SANDRA STEEN
SUSAN STEEN, Co-Author
G. BRIAN KARAS, Illustrator

Car Wash
(New York: G.P. Putnam's Sons, 2001)

Subject(s): Imagination; Brothers and Sisters; Fathers
Age range(s): Preschool-Grade 1
Major character(s): Unnamed Character, Father, Driver; Unnamed Character, Child, Twin; Unnamed Character, Child, Twin
Time period(s): 2000s (2001)
Locale(s): United States

Summary: Lunch out with their dad is delayed when the family's car drives through a big mud puddle. Now the real adventure begins as the twin siblings imagine that their car is a submarine and the components of the car wash are undersea objects. The sea foams with soap bubbles and the enormous red arms of an octopus noisily scrub the car's roof. Finally, the car and its occupants safely emerge from the deeps to continue their journey to a drive-through restaurant. Oops! Now the inside of the car needs cleaning. (32 pages)

Where it's reviewed:
Booklist, January 2001, page 971
Bulletin of the Center for Children's Books, January 2001, page 198
Five Owls, January 2001, page 66
Kirkus Reviews, November 15, 2000, page 1620
School Library Journal, January 2001, page 108

Awards the book has won:
Bulletin of the Center for Children's Books Blue Ribbon, 2001
ALA Notable Children's Books, 2002

Other books by the same author:
Historic St. Augustine, 1997 (Places in American History)
Independence Hall, 1994 (Places in American History)
Colonial Williamsburg, 1993 (Places in American History)

Other books you might like:

Joan Anderson, *Sally's Submarine*, 1995
    Sally uses a cardboard submarine and her vivid imagination to enjoy a day under the sea.
Byron Barton, *My Car*, 2001
    Sam takes good care of his car. He drives it safely to his job where he climbs aboard a bus for a day's work.
Grace Maccarone, *Cars! Cars! Cars!*, 1995
    An illustrated rhyming story describes many types of cars.
Margaret Mahy, *The Rattlebang Picnic*, 1994
    Rapidly approaching lava brings a family's picnic to an abrupt end but Grandma's inedible pizza replaces a lost wheel, allowing the family to flee.

852

WILLIAM STEIG
TERYL EUVREMER, Illustrator

Toby, What Are You?

(New York: Joanna Cotler Books/HarperCollins Publishers, 2001)

Subject(s): Parent and Child; Imagination; Playing
Age range(s): Preschool-Grade 1
Major character(s): Toby, Son, Animal
Time period(s): Indeterminate
Locale(s): Fictional Country

Summary: Toby's game begins when his father, returning home from work, finds him stretched on the stoop in front of the door pretending to be a doormat. The game continues all evening with one parent or another trying to guess what Toby is enacting. Sometimes the parents do not guess correctly, but Toby tells them what he is. Finally it's time for Toby's dad to pretend to be the horse that's carrying cowboy Toby to bed. (32 pages)

Where it's reviewed:

Booklist, May 1, 2001, page 1693
Horn Book Guide, Fall 2001, page 242
Kirkus Reviews, April 1, 2001, page 507
Publishers Weekly, May 14, 2001, page 84
School Library Journal, May 2001, page 135

Other books by the same author:

Wizzil, 2000
Pete's a Pizza, 1998 (Booklist Editors' Choice)
Toby, Where Are You?, 1997 (Child Magazine Best Book of the Year)

Other books you might like:

Kady MacDonald Denton, *Would They Love a Lion?*, 1995
    Using a reversible bathrobe for a costume, Anna "becomes" many different animals, each of them loved by her family.
Lisa McCourt, *I Love You, Stinky Face*, 1997
    No matter what horrid creature her child imagines becoming, Mama's sure that her love will never end.
Janice May Udry, *Is Susan Here?*, 1993
    Imaginative Susan "disappears" one day, but stays nearby disguised as various animals before surprising her parents by returning at bedtime.

853

TED STENHOUSE

Across the Steel River

(Tonawanda, NY: Kids Can Press, 2001)

Subject(s): Racism; Indians of North America; Friendship
Age range(s): Grades 5-8
Major character(s): Will Samson, 6th Grader; Arthur, Indian (Blackfoot)
Time period(s): 1950s (1952)
Locale(s): Grayson, Canada

Summary: In this first novel, white Will and Indian Arthur are walking along the railroad tracks one day when they come across Yellowfly, an Indian decorated during World War II, who's lying there beaten almost to death. Though the local mounted police say he was hit by a train, Will and Arthur know that's not true and decide to find the people responsible. But in the Canada of the 1950s, there's a great deal of prejudice against the Native American and even Will has to look inside himself and reconsider his own attitudes in this tale of friendship. (222 pages)

Where it's reviewed:

Booklist, January 2002, page 845
Quill & Quire, August 2001, page 31
Resource Links, October 2001, page 42
School Library Journal, October 2001, page 172
Voice of Youth Advocates, February 2002, page 440

Other books you might like:

Will Hobbs, *Bearstone*, 1990
    Cloyd discovers his Indian heritage as he battles for survival in the Colorado Mountains.
Jerrie Oughton, *Music from a Place Called Half Moon*, 1995
    When her father suggests that the Vine Street Baptist Church admit everyone in town, including the Indian children, Edie Jo's family is shunned.
Marsha Qualey, *Revolutions of the Heart*, 1993
    Cory becomes interested in Native American Mac and immediately becomes the recipient of outrage, lewd notes and disdain from her community.

854

MAGGIE STERN
BLANCHE SIMS, Illustrator

Singing Diggety

(New York: Orchard Books/Scholastic, Inc., 2001)

Series: Orchard Chapters
Subject(s): Animals/Dogs; Talent; Humor
Age range(s): Grades 2-3
Major character(s): George, Child, Brother; Diggety, Dog; Dad, Father
Time period(s): 2000s (2001)
Locale(s): United States

Summary: Three brief stories continue the antics of George and his lovable, but not completely cooperative pet. George forgets his whistle when he takes Diggety to Obedience School and Diggety will not follow commands. Substituting the harmonica he finds in his pocket, George does elicit a response from Diggety, but not the one he expects. While attending a costume party for dogs Diggety does not wait his turn to play the games and must sit out the contests, but George wins a prize for his dalmatian costume. In order to bring Diggety to school for show and tell, George must also bring a parent. Fortunately Dad comes along wearing his dog tie and following George's commands because Diggety takes a nap, ignoring his assignment. (48 pages)

Where it's reviewed:
Bulletin of the Center for Children's Books, October 2001, page 78
Horn Book, September 2001, page 595
School Library Journal, August 2001, page 163

Other books by the same author:
George and Diggety, 2000 (Orchard Chapters)
George, 1999 (Orchard Chapters)
Acorn Magic, 1998

Other books you might like:
Megan McDonald, *Beezy and Funnybone*, 2000
    In one of three brief stories Beezy's attempt to teach Funnybone to "fetch" is more successful than she intends.
Claudia Mills, *Gus and Grandpa and Show-and-Tell*, 2000
    Grandpa helps Gus solve his problem selecting something for show-and-tell.
Cynthia Rylant, *The Henry and Mudge Series*, 1987-
    The satisfying friendship between a boy and his dog is portrayed in many books about Henry and his lovable, slobbery dog Mudge.

 855

JANET STEVENS, Author/Illustrator
SUSAN STEVENS CRUMMEL, Co-Author

And the Dish Ran Away with the Spoon
(San Diego: Harcourt, Inc., 2001)

Subject(s): Literature; Humor; Stories in Rhyme
Age range(s): Grades 1-3
Major character(s): Cat, Cat, Musician; Dog, Dog; Cow, Cow
Time period(s): Indeterminate Past
Locale(s): Fictional Country

Summary: Cat awakens very tired Cow and Dog to alert them to the fact that, while the dish and the spoon ran away, as their rhyme's conclusion requires, they have not yet returned to the story. Cow and Dog would prefer changing the ending of the rhyme so they can continue to sleep but Cat insists that they search for the characters missing from their nursery rhyme. While they do not locate them in the first few locations they search, Dog does spot a piece of chipped china on the floor as the threesome cleverly escape from a hungry wolf. When they finally find the missing pair, dish is broken into so many pieces that only the repair shop that fixes Humpty Dumpty can put her back together again in time for the characters to take their places in preparation for their story to be read once again. (48 pages)

Where it's reviewed:
Booklist, April 1, 2001, page 1472
Horn Book, July 2001, page 444

Publishers Weekly, April 9, 2001, page 74
Riverbank Review, Fall 2001, page 28
School Library Journal, May 2001, page 135

Awards the book has won:
ALA Notable Children's Books, 2002

Other books by the same author:
Cook-a-Doodle-Doo!, 1999
Shoe Town, 1999
My Big Dog, 1999

Other books you might like:
Gennifer Choldenko, *Moonstruck: The True Story of the Cow Who Jumped over the Moon*, 1997
    The cow's jumping coach explains the challenge and the training required for a cow to jump over the moon.
Lisa Campbell Ernst, *Goldilocks Returns*, 2000
    To ease the guilt of her misdeeds fifty years earlier, Goldi, a locksmith, returns (uninvited) to the three bears' home to protect it from intruders.
David T. Greenberg, *Whatever Happened to Humpty Dumpty?: And Other Surprising Sequels to Mother Goose Rhymes*, 1999
    Retellings of traditional nursery rhymes conclude with new, humorous endings suggesting what really happened to the characters.
Joanne Oppenheim, *Eency Weency Spider*, 1991
    In an expanded tale of the spider washed down the waterspout, Eency Weency meets other nursery rhyme characters.
Rachel Vail, *Over the Moon*, 1998
    Director Hi Diddle Diddle tries to make the cow follow the nursery rhyme script and jump over (not under or through) the moon.

856

IAN STEWART

Flatterland: Like Flatland, Only More So
(Cambridge, MA: Perseus Publishing, 2001)

Subject(s): Mathematics; Physics; Fantasy
Age range(s): Grades 9-12
Major character(s): Victoria "Vikki" Line, Teenager, Mythical Creature; Space Hopper, Mythical Creature
Time period(s): 21st century
Locale(s): Mathiverse, Fictional Country (dimensional universe which includes all space, times, and dimension)

Summary: Vikki Line inhabits Flatland, the two dimensional reality first described in Edwin Abbott's *Flatland*. All Flatland's females are lines and all the males are polygons and no one and nothing has more than two dimensions. Flatland gets along just fine that way, thank you, until teenager Vikki discovers the manuscript of her heretic great-great-grandfather A. Line. In it, Albert Line describes his adventures when an incredible Stranger, who calls himself a sphere, takes the two-dimensional Line to visit the two-dimensional world, and sets off speculations about the possibility of even more dimensions. Vikki's father is horrified that this skeleton in the family closet has been discovered and confiscates the book, but it's too late as Vikki has scanned it onto her computer.

Eventually she discovers the way to summon a two-dimensional being and embarks on her own comprehensive voyage of discovery guided by a weird orange creature that calls itself Space Hopper. (304 pages)

Where it's reviewed:
Analog, October 2001, page 132
Booklist, May 15, 2001, page 1739
Publishers Weekly, April 2, 2001, page 43
School Library Journal, November 2001, page 194
Wall Street Journal, May 18, 2001, page W13

Other books by the same author:
Wheelers, 2000
Figments of Reality: The Culture of the Curious Mind, 1997
Another Fine Math You've Got Me Into, 1992

Other books you might like:
George Alec Effinger, *Schrodinger's Kitten*, 1988
A young Arab woman commits a murder motivated by physics.
Jostein Gaarder, *Sophie's World: A Novel About the History of Philosophy*, 1994
Mysterious letters draw Sophie into a survey of philosophy.
Wendy Isdell, *A Gebra Named Al: A Novel*, 1993
Julie's difficulties with her math homework land her in the Land of Mathematics, where she is lucky to meet Al who helps her return home.
William Sleator, *The Boy Who Reversed Himself*, 1986
A foolhardy mathematical experiment lands two teens in a dangerous environment with rules they only dimly understand.

857

SARAH STEWART
DAVID SMALL, Illustrator

The Journey
(New York: Farrar Straus Giroux, 2001)

Subject(s): Amish; City and Town Life; Diaries
Age range(s): Grades 2-4
Major character(s): Hannah, Child, Vacationer; Mother, Mother, Vacationer; Clara, Aunt
Time period(s): 2000s (2001)
Locale(s): United States; Chicago, Illinois

Summary: Aunt Clara's kindness gives Hannah an amazing birthday treat, a trip to Chicago with Mother and her friend. Through daily entries in her diary Hannah describes the wonder of her first trip away from her family's farm while the illustrations portray the parallels between her experiences in the big city and her simple Amish life. By week's end, Hannah reflects on the wonder of all she's experienced on the trip and just how much she misses her family, even her brothers. (36 pages)

Where it's reviewed:
Bulletin of the Center for Children's Books, April 2001, page 316
Horn Book, March 2001, page 202
Publishers Weekly, January 8, 2001, page 66
Riverbank Review, Spring 2001, page 31

School Library Journal, March 2001, page 220

Awards the book has won:
Publishers Weekly Best Children's Books, 2001
Smithsonian's Notable Books for Children, 2001

Other books by the same author:
The Gardener, 1997 (Caldecott Honor Book)
The Library, 1995
The Money Tree, 1991

Other books you might like:
Merle Good, *Reuben and the Quilt*, 1999
When a quilt is stolen from their yard an Amish family puts the matching pillowcases out with a note for the thief and the quilt returns.
Barbara Mitchell, *Down Buttermilk Lane*, 1993
Mam, Dat and their children, an Old Order Amish family in Pennsylvania, travel to town by horse and buggy for needed supplies.
Patricia Polacco, *Just Plain Fancy*, 1990
The peacock that hatches from the unusual egg Naomi finds causes her to worry that such a beautiful bird may violate her simple Amish lifestyle.

858

JOHN WARREN STEWIG
JOHANNA WESTERMAN, Illustrator

Mother Holly
(New York: Cheshire Studio/North-South Books, 2001)

Subject(s): Fairy Tales; Folk Tales; Conduct of Life
Age range(s): Grades 1-4
Major character(s): Rose, Stepsister, Stepdaughter; Blanche, Stepsister, Daughter; Mother Holly, Aged Person
Time period(s): Indeterminate Past
Locale(s): Fictional Country

Summary: Without complaining, Rose obeys her demanding stepmother's every request, including her command that she jump into the well to retrieve a dropped spindle. Rose finds herself in an enchanted land where her sweet nature enables her to live and be rewarded by Mother Holly for her kind service. When she's allowed to return to her home, the jealous stepmother sends Blanche down the well to receive the same good fortune. True to her selfish nature, Blanche does not behave kindly toward others and her lack of experience with housework prevents her from serving Mother Holly as Rose did. By her laziness Blanche causes many problems. Finally, she demands to leave and Mother Holly happily sends her on her way with rewards befitting her disagreeable nature. (32 pages)

Where it's reviewed:
Booklist, July 2001, page 2015
Bulletin of the Center for Children's Books, October 2001, page 78
Kirkus Reviews, July 1, 2001, page 947
Publishers Weekly, November 15, 2001, page 71
School Library Journal, September 2001, page 215

Other books by the same author:
Moon's Choice, 1993
Stone Soup, 1991

The Fisherman and His Wife, 1988

Other books you might like:
Amy Ehrlich, *The Random House Book of Fairy Tales*, 1985
    Nineteen familiar fairy tales are included in the illustrated volume.
Peter Hansard, *Jig, Fig, and Mrs. Pig*, 1995
    Jig's kindness to a disguised wizard is rewarded with a gift of gold and diamonds; when bully Fig tries to get the same he receives toads and snakes.
Charlotte Huck, *Toads and Diamonds*, 1996
    A kind stepdaughter receives a reward of diamonds and flowers each time she speaks; her bitter stepsister gets toads and snakes instead.

859

R.L. STINE

The Haunting Hour: Chills in the Dead of the Night
(New York: HarperCollins, 2001)

Subject(s): Short Stories; Horror
Age range(s): Grades 5-8

Summary: A master of horror unleashes ten more short stories that will simultaneously amuse and horrify. A trunk containing the ghost of a young girl accompanies a teenager on a family cruise in "Take Me With You." Trying to give a friend a little of his own medicine, three boys entomb him inside a snowman, but the trick backfires in "Revenge of the Snowman." And "The Bad Baby-Sitter" teaches her charges to made voodoo mud cookies, but the family dog causes some unexpected results. Mummies, graveyard romps and ghostly requests add more touches of terror. (153 pages)

Where it's reviewed:
Publishers Weekly, September 24, 2001, page 94
Voice of Youth Advocates, February 2002, page 451

Other books by the same author:
When Good Ghouls Go Bad, 2001
Ghost in the Mirror, 2000
Liar Liar, 2000 (Nightmare Room, Number 4)
Attack of the Mutant, 1999
Weekend at Poison Lake, 1999

Other books you might like:
Joan Aiken, *A Fit of Shivers: Tales for Late at Night*, 1992
    Scary stories guaranteed to give the reader "a fit of shivers."
Bruce Coville, *Odder than Ever*, 1999
    Stories that are scary or sad, fantastic or funny, can be found in this companion to *Oddly Enough*.
Collin McDonald, *The Chilling Hour: Tales of the Real and Unreal*, 1992
    Eight terrifying tales will keep readers up late shivering in fright as they explore tension-filled stories.

860

CATHERINE STOCK, Author/Illustrator

Gugu's House
(New York: Clarion Books, 2001)

Subject(s): Grandmothers; Artists and Art; Drought
Age range(s): Grades 1-3
Major character(s): Gugu, Grandmother, Artist; Kukamba, Child
Time period(s): 2000s (2001)
Locale(s): Zimbabwe

Summary: A long bus ride brings Kukamba from her city home to Gugu's colorful one perched like an oasis in the midst of the dry, brown countryside. Using mud and dung, Gugu sculpts animal statues and teaches Kukamba how to make smaller versions of them. Then they gather materials such as ash, clay, cattle dung and charcoal to make the decorative paints for their creations. When the rains finally come Kukamba joins the villagers in celebrating the life-giving moisture. Only after the sun returns does Kukamba see the destruction caused by the heavy rains that washed away their colorful artwork and turned their animals to lumps of mud. Patiently, Gugu takes Kukamba into the hills to see the gift brought by the rains in the colors of flowers, trees, and birds. A concluding "Author's Note" gives background for the story and a glossary of terms used. (32 pages)

Where it's reviewed:
Booklist, February 15, 2001, page 1154
Horn Book Guide, Fall 2001, page 277
School Library Journal, April 2001, page 122

Awards the book has won:
Charlotte Zolotow Award, Highly Commended, 2002

Other books by the same author:
Island Summer, 1999
Where Are You Going, Manyoni?, 1993
Easter Surprise, 1991
Armien's Fishing Trip, 1990

Other books you might like:
Verna Aardema, *Bringing the Rain to Kapiti Plain: A Nandi Tale*, 1981
    A rhyming retelling of an African folktale explains how Ki-pat brings the rain to the dry Kapiti Plain and its wildlife.
Maya Angelou, *My Painted House, My Friendly Chicken, and Me*, 1994
    A picture book highlights the customs of the Ndebele people of South Africa, including their decoratively painted homes.
Ifeoma Onyefulu, *Grandfather's Work*, 1998
    A native healer in Nigeria, Grandfather explains the natural sources he uses for his work.
Diane Stewart, *The Dove*, 1993
    The sight of a dove inspires Lindi and her grandmother after a flood destroys their crops in Natal, South Africa.

JULIAN STOCKWIN

Kydd

(New York: Scribner, 2001)

Subject(s): Sea Stories
Age range(s): Grades 10-Adult
Major character(s): Thomas Paine Kidd, Military Personnel (seaman); Nicholas Renzi, Military Personnel (seaman), Wealthy
Time period(s): 1790s (1793)
Locale(s): *Duke William*, At Sea

Summary: With the Revolutionary War in America finally over, Britain now turns its attention to France, with whom it's fought many wars and battles. Needing seamen to man its ships for this military foray, the British government impresses young men into service, regardless of their nautical experience. Tom Kydd normally works as a wig-maker, but finds himself aboard the *Duke William* where he learns to be a seaman through trial and error. He's terrified of being washed overboard, sees a friend killed when he's caught in the sails, listens as some sailors talk of mutiny and becomes acquainted with Nicholas Renzi, a fellow seaman. Though not his chosen career, Tom is loyal to Britain and feels proud of his nautical ability in this first of a new series. (254 pages)

Where it's reviewed:
Booklist, April 1, 2001, page 1454
Books, Spring 2001, page 26
Kirkus Reviews, April 15, 2001, page 535
Publishers Weekly, June 4, 2001, page 59

Other books by the same author:
Artemis, 2002

Other books you might like:
C.S. Forester, *Mr. Midshipman Hornblower*, 1950
    First in the series, this work describes the early days of Hornblower's sailing career from being a novice to his commission as a lieutenant.
Wilder Perkins, *Hoare and the Matter of Treason*, 2001
    Commander Bartholomew Hoare of the Royal Navy commands a ship whose purpose is to act as a floating spy center in this last of a trilogy.
David Poyer, *Fire on the Waters*, 2001
    Loyal to the Union cause, inexperienced seaman Eli decides to join the navy and volunteers to work without pay in this first of a Civil War trilogy.

862

BRAD STRICKLAND

The Tower at the End of the World

(New York: Dial, 2001)

Subject(s): Magic; Supernatural; Wizards
Age range(s): Grades 5-8
Major character(s): Lewis Barnavelt, Orphan, 13-Year-Old; Jonathan Barnavelt, Uncle, Sorcerer; Florence Zimmerman, Witch; Rose Rita Pottinger, Student—Junior High School; Ishmael Izard, Wizard

Time period(s): 1950s
Locale(s): New Zebedee, Michigan; Porcupine Bay, Michigan (on Lake Superior)

Summary: On vacation on an island in Lake Superior, Lewis and his uncle Jonathan, along with their friends Rose Rita and Mrs. Zimmerman, help Rose Rita's grandfather who is house sitting. Lewis and Rose Rita are a little perplexed about their island as it doesn't appear on any map and they begin to wonder if there's a little magic afoot. Soon they discover that the evil Ishmael Izard is determined to destroy the world and the only way to stop the destruction is to find the doomsday clock, in this sequel to John Bellair's first book *The House with a Clock in Its Walls*. (146 pages)

Where it's reviewed:
Booklist, September 1, 2001, page 111
Kirkus Reviews, August 1, 2001, page 1133
School Library Journal, September 2001, page 234
Voice of Youth Advocates, October 2001, page 294

Other books by the same author:
The Beast under the Wizard's Bridge, 2000
The Wrath of the Grinning Ghost, 1999
The Bell, the Book, and the Spellbinder, 1997
The Hand of the Necromancer, 1996

Other books you might like:
Joseph Bruchac, *Skeleton Man*, 2001
    After her parents disappear and a unknown great-uncle shows up, Molly wonders why he looks like the Skeleton Man of her father's Mohawk Indian tales.
Norma Lehr, *Haunting at Black Water Cove*, 2000
    While cabin sitting at Blue Lakes, the spirit of Ruby Faye contacts Kathy and asks for help in determining how she died.
Robert Norman, *Albion's Dream: A Novel of Terror*, 1992
    Playing the board game Albion's Dream propels Edward into a struggle between good and evil.

863

KEN STUCKEY

Conflict in California

(Grand Rapids, MI: Baker Books, 2001)

Series: Orly Mann Racing Team
Subject(s): Sports/Auto Racing; Emotional Problems
Age range(s): Grades 7-10
Major character(s): Paola Pellegrini, Mechanic; Loren Janine, Race Car Driver; Orly Mann, Race Car Driver; Hildy Hornbrook, Lawyer
Time period(s): 2000s
Locale(s): California; Charlotte, North Carolina

Summary: Because it's an off weekend for the racers in the Winston Cup Series of NASCAR racing, some of Orly Mann's pit crew fly to California to see family and relax. Paola and some of his friends hop in his car and head to the National Hot Rod Association's drag race where their paths cross that of Loren, a top-notch drag racer who's become addicted to drugs to overcome her fear of crashing while racing. Meanwhile Orly and his team are dismayed to learn they might lose their major sponsor, Speed King Oil, which also sponsors Loren's drag racing car. This incident reintroduces Hildy Hornbrook, daughter of the owner of Speed King Oil, to Orly's life, which dredges up painful memories for him in a continuing series by a former racing car driver. (208 pages)

Where it's reviewed:
School Library Journal, November 2001, page 164

Other books by the same author:
Doubt at Daytona, 1999
Slowdown at Sears Point, 1999

Other books you might like:
Millys N. Altman, *Racing in Her Blood*, 1980
    More than anything, Jane wants to be a racecar driver and eventually teams up with her twin brother to achieve her dream.
Frank Bonham, *Speedway Contender*, 1964
    Colton is much more interested in cars than he is in attending schools, even building himself a car for racing.
Herb Karl, *The Toom County Mud Race*, 1992
    For English class, Jackie Lee records the adventures he and his friends have as he races his '69 Chevy pick-up through mud and slime.

T

864

NANCY TAFURI, Author/Illustrator

Silly Little Goose!
(New York: Scholastic Press, 2001)

Subject(s): Animals/Geese; Farm Life; Animals
Age range(s): Preschool
Major character(s): Goose, Goose
Time period(s): 2000s
Locale(s): United States

Summary: Goose is on a mission to create a nest but the other animals think her choices are silly. First she selects a nice, warm place on some hay but that's the pigs' bed so she moves on to a nice, soft place but it is the kittens' home so she continues her search. Each spot on the farm already belongs to another animal that refuses to relinquish it to Goose. Finally Goose finds the farmer's hat, blown off in the wind. The hat is just what Goose is seeking and the farmer doesn't try to take it from her. Finally, Goose builds her nest, lays her eggs and waits for her eight goslings to hatch. (32 pages)

Where it's reviewed:
Booklist, February 1, 2001, page 1058
Horn Book Guide, Fall 2001, page 242
Kirkus Reviews, March 1, 2001, page 339
Publishers Weekly, March 12, 2001, page 88
School Library Journal, April 2001, page 123

Awards the book has won:
Parenting's Reading Magic Awards, 2001

Other books by the same author:
Will You Be My Friend?, 2000
Snowy Flowy Blowy: A Twelve Months Rhyme, 1999
Have You Seen My Duckling?, 1984 (Caldecott Honor Book)

Other books you might like:
Joan L. Nodset, *Who Took the Farmer's Hat?*, 1963
  A farmer searches for his lost hat not realizing it's been carried away by the wind and put to good use.

Tracey Campbell Pearson, *The Purple Hat*, 1997
  The bird that finds Annie's beloved, lost purple hat uses it for a nest.
Mary Wormell, *Hilda Hen's Search*, 1994
  Hilda Hen confidently searches until she finds a perfectly original spot for her nest.

865

NANCY TAFURI, Author/Illustrator

Where Did Bunny Go?
(New York: Scholastic Press, 2001)

Subject(s): Animals/Rabbits; Animals/Birds; Friendship
Age range(s): Preschool-Kindergarten
Major character(s): Bunny, Rabbit, Friend; Bird, Bird, Friend; Squirrel, Squirrel, Friend; Chipmunk, Chipmunk, Friend
Time period(s): Indeterminate
Locale(s): United States

Summary: Best friends Bunny and Bird awaken to see new snow covering the ground. Eagerly they join with Squirrel and Chipmunk to play "Follow the Leader" and "Hide and Seek." Bird finds Squirrel and Chipmunk but she can't find Bunny's hiding spot. Chipmunk and Squirrel help Bird search for Bunny but still he can't be found. When Bunny overhears Chipmunk saying that Bunny ran away, he leaps from the hollow log in which he's hiding and assures Bird of their friendship. (32 pages)

Where it's reviewed:
Booklist, December 1, 2001, page 651
Horn Book Guide, Spring 2002, page 29
School Library Journal, December 2001, page 112

Other books by the same author:
Silly Little Goose!, 2001
Will You Be My Friend?, 2000
Snowy Flowy Blowy: A Twelve Months Rhyme, 1999
I Love You, Little One, 1998

Other books you might like:
Kim Lewis, *Friends*, 1997
    Sam becomes angry with his visiting friend Alice, but not for long.
Todd Starr Palmer, *Rhino and Mouse*, 1994
    Despite their obvious differences, Rhino and Mouse enjoy a close friendship.
Nancy Willard, *A Starlit Somersault Downhill*, 1993
    A rabbit somersaults down snow-covered banks while its friend bear hibernates in a nearby den.

866

JANET TASHJIAN

The Gospel According to Larry
(New York: Holt, 2001)

Subject(s): Identity; Coming-of-Age; Humor
Age range(s): Grades 8-12
Major character(s): Joshua/Larry "Josh" Swensen, 17-Year-Old, 12th Grader; Beth, 12th Grader
Time period(s): 2000s
Locale(s): Boston, Massachusetts

Summary: Written as a report, with hilarious footnotes, this tells the story of an idealistic young man. Ever since he was young, Josh has wanted to make the world better, improve it, keep people moving forward, just as Darwin's theories explained about evolution. Tired of consumerism and celebrities, of the adoration of Beth, the girl he loves, for yet another less than bright jock, and of people glued to television sets, he sets up a web site called www.thegospelaccordingtolarry.com, where he anonymously sets forth his ideas. His "sermons" become widely-read, his web site receives thousands of hits, discussion groups for his ideas spread across the country, and suddenly Josh is caught up in all he preaches against. When his identity is finally disclosed, he follows the example of Tom Sawyer and fakes his own death, resolved to first fix himself before he again tries to fix the world. (227 pages)

Where it's reviewed:
Booklist, November 1, 2001, page 471
Horn Book, January 2002, page 84
Publishers Weekly, December 3, 2001, page 61
School Library Journal, October 2001, page 172
Voice of Youth Advocates, December 2001, page 364

Awards the book has won:
ALA Best Books for Young Adults, 2002
Booklist Editors' Choice/Books for Youth, 2001

Other books by the same author:
Multiple Choice, 1999
Tru Confessions, 1997

Other books you might like:
Stephen Chbosky, *The Perks of Being a Wallflower*, 1999
    In Charlie's freshman year he helps his pregnant older sister, adjusts to the suicide of a best friend, and is hospitalized for depression.
Michael Morpurgo, *The War of Jenkins' Ear*, 1995
    At boarding school Toby meets Simon Christopher, who claims to be the reincarnated Jesus Christ.

Rob Thomas, *Rats Saw God*, 1996
    One English credit shy of graduation, Steve's guidance counselor suggests he write a 100-page essay about anything he knows.

867

ELEANORA E. TATE

The Minstrel's Melody
(Middleton, WI: Pleasant Company/American Girl, 2001)

Series: History Mysteries
Subject(s): African Americans; Music and Musicians; Race Relations
Age range(s): Grades 4-7
Major character(s): Orphelia Bruce, 12-Year-Old, Musician (pianist); Madame Meritta, Entertainer
Time period(s): 1900s (1904)
Locale(s): Calico Creek, Missouri; St. Louis, Missouri

Summary: With an exquisite voice and her piano-playing ability, Orphelia is ready for the talent show hosted by Madame Meritta and doesn't even mind that she has to include her off-key singing sister. But when Orphelia misbehaves, her mother cancels the sister act, though she allows them to attend the talent show. Frustrated, Orphelia runs away that night and joins Madame Meritta and her Marvelous Traveling Troubadours as they travel around the state, preparing for their performance at the St. Louis World's Fair. Though Orphelia struggles with the racism she encounters, she also discovers some family secrets in this continuing series. (163 pages)

Where it's reviewed:
Booklist, April 1, 2001, page 1488
School Library Journal, August 2001, page 189

Other books by the same author:
A Blessing in Disguise, 1995
Front Porch Stories at the One-Room School, 1992
The Secret of Gumbo Grove, 1987

Other books you might like:
Marthe Jocelyn, *Earthly Astonishments*, 2000
    Sold to a school for her sewing abilities, Josephine runs away to join a freak show where the fact she's a dwarf makes her feel part of their family.
Patricia C. McKissack, *Color Me Dark: The Diary of Nellie Lee Love, the Great Migration North*, 2000
    The Love family moves north to Chicago for better jobs, but encounters racism as established black families look down upon families from the south.
Alison Smith, *Billy Boone*, 1989
    When Billy decides she wants to play the trumpet, only her grandmother supports the idea of girls playing this instrument.
Erika Tamar, *The Midnight Train Home*, 2000
    Entrusted to the Children's Aid Society, Deirdre is unhappy with her new family and joins a vaudeville troupe whose members easily become her family.

868

CLIFTON L. TAULBERT
E.B. LEWIS, Illustrator

Little Cliff's First Day of School

(New York: Dial Books for Young Readers, 2001)

Subject(s): Schools; Fear; Grandmothers
Age range(s): Grades K-2
Major character(s): Cliff, 1st Grader; Mama Pearl, Grandmother (great-grandmother), Spouse; Poppa Joe, Grandfather (great-grandfather), Spouse
Time period(s): 1950s
Locale(s): South

Summary: Mama Pearl and Poppa Joe are bursting with pride just thinking about Little Cliff heading off to his first day of school. Little Cliff looks forward to the day as if it might be his last. He says good-bye to his toys and his favorite climbing tree as daily he becomes more fearful. The morning of the first day of school Little Cliff only wants to stay home with his great grandparents. He tries to hide under the house but Mama Pearl will see him in school and she walks him there herself. When they arrive at the schoolyard and Cliff spots his friends playing, Little Cliff realizes that there just might be some fun to this learning after all and he races off to join them before the bell rings. (32 pages)

Where it's reviewed:
Booklist, May 15, 2001, page 1760
Horn Book, July 2001, page 446
Kirkus Reviews, May 1, 2001, page 668
Publishers Weekly, July 2, 2001, page 78
School Library Journal, June 2001, page 131

Other books by the same author:
Little Cliff and the Cold Place, 2002
Little Cliff and the Porch People, 1999 (Notable Social Studies Trade Books for Young People)

Other books you might like:
Nancy Bo Flood, *I'll Go to School, If . . .* , 1997
   A frightened little boy offers conditions under which he'll go to school for the first time; his practical mom suggests more realistic alternatives.
Elizabeth Fitzgerald Howard, *Virgie Goes to School with Us Boys*, 2000
   Virgie's brothers may be reluctant to return to school, especially with a girl, but Virgie looks forward to this opportunity to receive an education.
Vera Rosenberry, *Vera's First Day of School*, 1999
   Vera's eager for the first day of school until she sees the crowded schoolyard; then she has second thoughts about entering the building.

869

ALASTAIR TAYLOR, Author/Illustrator

Swollobog

(Boston: Houghton Mifflin Company, 2001)

Subject(s): Animals/Dogs; Behavior; Humor
Age range(s): Grades 1-3

Major character(s): Meg, Child, Daughter; Swollobog, Dog
Time period(s): 2000s
Locale(s): England

Summary: In the author's first children's book, Meg clearly understands that Swollobog's eating problem is one of greed. It matters not to Swollobog how often or how recently she's eaten, if even the thought of food wanders into the mind of someone nearby, Swollobog is waiting and begging to share. It's not only food that Swollobog devours. She's also been known to down the bowl in which it's served. While attending a fair with her family, Swollobog gulps down a helium balloon and soars away over the sea. It takes some ingenuity as well as the assistance of a champion kite flyer, a fisherman, and thoughts of cheese to retrieve Swollobog, but finally she makes it back to shore, hungry for something more substantial such as Meg's bike. (32 pages)

Where it's reviewed:
Booklist, March 15, 2001, page 1405
Bulletin of the Center for Children's Books, April 2001, page 316
Kirkus Reviews, March 1, 2001, page 339
Publishers Weekly, March 12, 2001, page 89
School Library Journal, May 2001, page 135

Awards the book has won:
Bulletin of the Center for Children's Books Blue Ribbon, 2001

Other books you might like:
Robert Bender, *A Most Unusual Lunch*, 1994
   As various animals eat their way up the food chain, each takes on characteristics of the animal just eaten until the last animal belches.
Betsy Everitt, *TV Dinner*, 1994
   Daisy Lee's distinctive food habits give new meaning to the term TV dinner.
Bill Grossman, *My Sister Ate One Hare*, 1996
   One hare is only the beginning of the items consumed by a little sister in this rhyming tale.
Maira Kalman, *What Pete Ate from A-Z*, 2001
   Pete eats everything in sight, including things a dog shouldn't devour and he does it all in alphabetical order.

870

KIM TAYLOR

Cissy Funk

(New York: HarperCollins, 2001)

Subject(s): Mothers and Daughters; Depression; Family Problems
Age range(s): Grades 6-9
Major character(s): Narcissus Louise "Cissy" Funk, 13-Year-Old; Jonas Funk, Brother (of Cissy); Vera Funk, Aunt; Maxine, Lesbian
Time period(s): 1930s (1935)
Locale(s): Ransom, Colorado; Denver, Colorado

Summary: Cissy doesn't understand why, since her baby sister died, her mother beats her but doesn't touch her brother. She's left to fend for herself as Jonas dreams of escape, staying only to provide a little protection for Cissy, and her father's moved away to work in Denver; Cissy retreats to the movie theater whenever life gets too rough at home. Luckily her aunt Vera shows up for a visit and, at the sight of Cissy's bruises, whisks her away to Denver, but that's only a temporary solution as Vera is penniless and in love with Maxine. Returned to Rose on the farm, Cissy waits for the first blow to come from her mother but receives a larger one when Aunt Vera reveals that she's really Cissy's mother in this first novel. (211 pages)

Where it's reviewed:
Booklist, August 2001, page 2109
Bulletin of the Center for Children's Books, May 2001, page 354
Publishers Weekly, May 28, 2001, page 89
School Library Journal, May 2001, page 160
Voice of Youth Advocates, August 2001, page 207

Other books you might like:
Alane Ferguson, *Secrets*, 1997
    T.J. reels with the news that he's adopted, but after running away to live with his birth mother, realizes that his dad's home is the perfect spot for him.
Elizabeth Van Steenwyk, *Maggie in the Morning*, 2001
    Though unsettling, by summer's end Maggie has learned who she really is and the news isn't so bad.
Sally Warner, *How to Be a Real Person (in Just One Day)*, 2001
    Kara thinks if she lies and follows her made-up rules, no one will know how unhinged her mother has become.

MARILYN TAYLOR

Faraway Home
(Dublin, Ireland: O'Brien Press, 2000)

Subject(s): Holocaust; Brothers and Sisters
Age range(s): Grades 5-8
Major character(s): Karl Muller, Teenager; Rosa Muller, Child; Judy Simons, Teenager; Nathaniel "Peewee" Crawford, Teenager
Time period(s): 1930s; 1940s (1938-1941)
Locale(s): Vienna, Austria; Millisle, Northern Ireland

Summary: As Karl watches the Nazis march through Vienna after successfully annexing Austria, he worries about what will happen to his Jewish family. When the family business is destroyed and his father and uncle imprisoned, Karl and his sister Rosa are put on a *Kindertransport* that takes them to Millisle Farm in Ireland. There they join other Jewish refugees in what seems to be a haven of safety. Karl makes friends with several local children, including Judy who is Jewish and Peewee who is Catholic. When Belfast is bombed, the terror of the war returns to Karl and he fears that his parents will never be able to escape from Austria. (221 pages)

Where it's reviewed:
Book Report, January 2001, page 62
Booklist, March 1, 2001, page 1283
Books for Keeps, July 2000, page 26
Kliatt, November 2000, page 17

Other books by the same author:
Call Yourself a Friend, 1998

Could This Be Love, I Wondered, 1998
Could I Love a Stranger?, 1998

Other books you might like:
Ellen Howard, *A Different Kind of Courage*, 1996
    Bertrand and Zina meet on a refugee train in Europe, where they're part of a group that makes it to safety in America.
Kit Pearson, *Looking at the Moon*, 1992
    Norah was evacuated to Canada from England three years ago and worries that she'll forget what her parents look like.
Irene N. Watts, *Remember Me: A Search for Refuge in Wartime Britain*, 2000
    Part of *Kindertransport*, Marianne is sent to London but stays with a family in Wales where she finds it best not to mention that she's a German Jew.

MILDRED D. TAYLOR

The Land
(New York: Penguin Putnam/Fogelman, 2001)

Subject(s): Racially Mixed People; Prejudice; African Americans
Age range(s): Grades 7-10
Major character(s): Paul-Edward Logan, Landowner; Mitchell Thomas, Friend
Time period(s): 19th century (after Reconstruction)
Locale(s): Georgia; Mississippi

Summary: With a mother who's a slave and her white master as his father, Paul-Edward walks that fine line of being half white and living in the South after the Civil War. Though taught to read and write by his father, and friendly with his half-brothers, Paul-Edward knows he'll always be considered colored by the white folks and thought uppity by the black folks. His no-win situation worsens as he becomes older and he and his best friend Mitchell eventually run away, leaving Georgia for Mississippi where Paul-Edward finds work training horses, then clearing lumber and eventually making furniture. Though proficient in all his trades, it's not enough for him to secure a loan to buy some land, which is his overriding dream. A contract with a white man is ripped in two after several years of work, leaving him still landless; it takes complicated financial arrangements before he owns his acreage and it costs him the life of his friend Mitchell. This prequel enriches *Roll of Thunder, Hear My Cry* in its look at life during Reconstruction for former slaves. (375 pages)

Where it's reviewed:
Booklist, August 2001, page 2108
Bulletin of the Center for Children's Books, October 2001, page 78
Horn Book, September 2001, page 596
School Library Journal, August 2001, page 190
Voice of Youth Advocates, October 2001, page 285

Awards the book has won:
ALA Coretta Scott King Award, 2002
ALA Best Books for Young Adults, 2002

Other books by the same author:
The Well, 1995
The Road to Memphis, 1989
The Gold Cadillac, 1987
Let the Circle Be Unbroken, 1981
Roll of Thunder, Hear My Cry, 1976

Other books you might like:
Walter Dean Myers, *The Glory Field,* 1994
   The saga of the Lewis family, who went from slaves to freemen, is firmly rooted in the family plot of land.
Gary Paulsen, *Sarny: A Life Remembered,* 1997
   Once freed, Sarny travels to New Orleans where she accepts a job with Miss Laura, an octoroon, and enjoys the creature comforts of her home.
Harriette Gillem Robinet, *Forty Acres and Maybe a Mule,* 1998
   When the government's offer of forty acres and a mule is rescinded, Pascal and Gideon rely on found treasure to buy land on Georgia's Sea Islands.

873

THEODORE TAYLOR

A Sailor Returns

(New York: Blue Sky/Scholastic, 2001)

Subject(s): Grandfathers; Physically Handicapped; Sea Stories
Age range(s): Grades 4-6
Major character(s): Evander "Evan" Bryant, 11-Year-Old; Buddy Jensen, 11-Year-Old; Thomas "Chips" Pentreath, Grandfather, Sailor; Mike Hodge, Bully
Time period(s): 1910s (1914)
Locale(s): Portsmouth, Virginia

Summary: With a club foot that keeps him from playing sports, and makes him a prime target of bullies, and a father who's always too busy to take him fishing, Evan finds life pretty dull during the summer. But a letter arrives from his mother's father, who was thought to have drowned thirty years ago, saying he would like to come for a visit. Wow, Evan can't believe he has a grandfather and can hardly wait for him to arrive; the moment he does, the two bond. Evan and his good friend Buddy are taught to fish, learn how to make a boat and Evan even learns how to retaliate against Mike, the bully who always picks on him. Grandpa Tom has secrets in his past from the rough life he led as a ship's carpenter, and he's paid his time for a murder committed in self-defense, he just has to work up his nerve to tell his daughter. Before he can, a nearby neighbor is murdered and during questioning by the police, Grandpa Tom explains his past and realizes that his family still loves and supports him in this touching, simple tale. (159 pages)

Where it's reviewed:
Booklist, May 1, 2001, page 1684
Bulletin of the Center for Children's Books, March 2001, page 280
Publishers Weekly, May 21, 2001, page 108
Voice of Youth Advocates, April 2001, page 150
Voice of Youth Advocates, June 2001, page 128

Other books by the same author:
The Boy Who Could Fly without a Motor, 2002
The Trouble with Tuck, 2000
Rogue Wave: And Other Red-Blooded Sea Stories, 1996
Sweet Friday Island, 1994
Timothy of the Cay, 1993
The Cay, 1969

Other books you might like:
Natalie Kinsey-Warnock, *In the Language of Loons,* 1998
   After a rough school year at home, Arlis spends a wonderful summer with his grandfather as he learns about nature.
Norma Fox Mazer, *After the Rain,* 1987
   Rachel takes daily walks with her grumpy grandfather and is surprised to find they like one another, which makes his death harder to bear.
Richard Peck, *A Long Way from Chicago,* 1998
   Joey and his sister Mary Alice hear many warm, funny stories and learn unusual lessons during the summers they spend with their grandmother.

874

SAMUEL TENENBAUM, Author/Illustrator
RICHARD UNGAR, Illustrator

Rachel Captures the Moon

(Plattsburgh, New York: Tundra Books, 2001)

Subject(s): Folklore; Jews; Humor
Age range(s): Grades 2-5
Major character(s): Simon, Father, Carpenter; Rachel, Child, Daughter
Time period(s): Indeterminate Past
Locale(s): Chelm, Fictional Country

Summary: The moon fascinates the people of Chelm and they would like to capture it and keep it near. The first villager with a plan is Simon who builds a ladder that reaches into the sky, but not far enough to catch the moon. Each night a different villager with a different skill tries but the weaver, the cook, the fisherman, and the musician each fail to entice the moon out of the sky and into the streets of Chelm. Finally Rachel proposes a solution and it works! This adaptation is the author/illustrator's first picture book. (32 pages)

Where it's reviewed:
Horn Book Guide, Spring 2002, page 122
Publishers Weekly, November 15, 2001, page 68
School Library Journal, December 2001, page 129

Other books you might like:
Jonathan Emmett, *Bringing Down the Moon,* 2001
   Mole wants the moon but his attempts to bring it down fail until he sees the moon's reflection in a puddle and thinks he's finally succeeded.
Rodney Rigby, *The Night the Moon Fell Asleep,* 1993
   Overtired, the moon falls asleep and crashes to the ground, requiring a community effort to restore her to the night sky.
James Thurber, *Many Moons,* 1943
   A Caldecott Medal winner tells of a Princess whose wish for the moon is finally fulfilled by the Court Jester.

SHERI S. TEPPER

The Fresco
(New York: HarperCollins/Eos, 2000)

Subject(s): Artists and Art; Aliens; Women
Age range(s): Grades 11-Adult
Major character(s): Benita Alvarez-Shipton, Diplomat
Time period(s): Indeterminate Future
Locale(s): Earth; Pistach, Fictional Country

Summary: Life is a rather dreary business for Benita until the day she is chosen by the Pistach as their sole go-between with the powers of Earth. In a reverse on take-us-to-your-leader, the Pistach send Benita to the leaders of Earth to offer their friendship and advanced technology, if only mankind will abandon certain practices. Naturally, these practices are held near and dear by some, so the Pistach somewhat high-handedly make their points. Aliens approach the offended parties with a much less benign agenda and the race for the hearts and minds of Earthlings is on. As the Pistach solve world problems like environmental destruction, drug abuse and mistreatment of women, they themselves begin to suffer a crisis of faith involving the famous fresco at the center of their philosophical beliefs. The delegation from Earth, including Benita, may have an opportunity to return the kindness of the Pistach. (406 pages)

Where it's reviewed:
Analog Science Fiction and Fact, February 2001, page 130
Booklist, November 15, 2000, page 625
Kirkus Reviews, September 15, 2000, page 1321
Library Journal, October 15, 2000, page 107
Publishers Weekly, October 16, 2000, page 53

Other books by the same author:
The Family Tree, 1997
Gibbon's Decline and Fall, 1996
Shadow's End: A Novel, 1994

Other books you might like:
Iain Banks, *Look to Windward*, 2001
   The premiere of a symphony by an exiled composer becomes a focus for an assassin and an artificial intelligence who are both haunted by tragic memories.
Terry Bisson, *The Pickup Artist*, 2001
   Hank's troubles all begin with his uncontrollable longing to hear a banned recording.
Elizabeth Moon, *Remnant Population*, 1996
   An elderly woman inadvertently makes herself man's representative to an alien species when she secretly stays behind as a planet is evacuated.
Katie Waitman, *The Merro Tree*, 1997
   Mikk is willing to risk everything to perform the only art that is able to encompass all of his talents, and he'll have to, because it's been banned across the known universe.

JEAN THESMAN

In the House of the Queen's Beasts
(New York: Viking, 2001)

Subject(s): Friendship; Family Problems; Self-Perception
Age range(s): Grades 6-9
Major character(s): Emily Shepherd, 14-Year-Old; Rowan Tucker, 14-Year-Old
Time period(s): 2000s
Locale(s): Seattle, Washington

Summary: Emily is so happy to move to a new home, away from her old neighborhood with the kids who teased her about a facial scar. Thanks to plastic surgery, Emily is ready to begin a new life, though she still feels a little shy. One of the best features of Emily's new home is the wonderful tree house in the backyard, but she finds it's occupied by Rowan, the girl who lives in the house behind theirs. Each is a little reticent, but the girls become friends as together they decorate the tree house, including the addition of Rowan's beautiful carved animals, called the "queen's beasts." Part of a loving family, Emily doesn't understand Mr. Tucker's abusive actions and it opens her eyes to her good fortune. For Rowan, hearing about Emily's warm, supportive family gives hope that hers might, one day, improve—and it does. (166 pages)

Where it's reviewed:
Booklist, February 15, 2001, page 1128
Horn Book, March 2001, page 214
Publishers Weekly, March 26, 2001, page 94
School Library Journal, March 2001, page 256
Voice of Youth Advocates, April 2001, page 47

Other books by the same author:
Between, 2002
Calling the Swan, 2000
The Other Ones, 1999
The Tree of Bells, 1999
The Ornament Tree, 1996
The Rain Catchers, 1991

Other books you might like:
Jean Ferris, *Across the Grain*, 1990
   Will's guardian sister drags him to a new home in the desert where Will's friendship with an aging woodcarver helps him stand up to her.
Katherine Martin, *Night Riding*, 1989
   Prin's not sure what to do when she realizes her friend Mary Faith's father is a child abuser.
June Rae Wood, *About Face*, 1999
   Two girls with dissimilar backgrounds, Glory who worries about her birthmark and Marvalene who travels with the carnival, become unlikely friends.

877

JEAN THESMAN

A Sea So Far
(New York: Viking, 2001)

Subject(s): Earthquakes; Social Classes; Orphans

Age range(s): Grades 7-10
Major character(s): Kate Keely, Orphan, 15-Year-Old; Jolie Logan, 17-Year-Old, Invalid
Time period(s): 1900s (1906-1907)
Locale(s): San Francisco, California; Dublin, Ireland

Summary: In 1906, San Franciscans are hit by a terrible earthquake, which leaves much of their city destroyed or in flames. Two young girls whose lives will intertwine are affected by that earthquake, Kate the young orphan who must seek work after she and her aunt lose their home and Jolie, a scarlet fever survivor who loses her mother. Almost a year after the quake, Kate is hired as a companion to Jolie and worries that she's made a mistake in accepting the assignment. Jolie is depressed and still mourns her mother while Kate is always upbeat and ready to laugh. Gradually the two girls grow to understand and accept one another and when asked, Kate agrees to accompany Jolie to Ireland to visit the estate her aunt plans to leave her. Kate has another reason for accepting as Ireland was the home of her mother and it's always been her wish to visit there. Matter of fact, Kate's half thinking of leaving Jolie once she's delivered her to her aunt, but once in Ireland prefers to remain with Jolie in an old-fashioned story of friendship. (195 pages)

Where it's reviewed:
Booklist, October 15, 2001, page 392
Kliatt, July 2001, page 14
Publishers Weekly, November 12, 2001, page 59
School Library Journal, October 2001, page 173
Voice of Youth Advocates, October 2001, page 285

Other books by the same author:
Between, 2002
Calling the Swan, 2000
The Other Ones, 1999
The Tree of Bells, 1999
The Ornament Tree, 1996

Other books you might like:
Paige Dixon, *May I Cross Your Golden River?*, 1975
  Though he's only eighteen, Jordan accepts his fatal muscular-vascular disease knowing his family will help him live as normally as possible.
Kristiana Gregory, *Earthquake at Dawn*, 1992
  Photographer Edith happens to be in San Francisco when the 1906 earthquake strikes and, in defiance of the mayor's orders, photographs the destruction.
Thelma Hatch Wyss, *A Stranger Here*, 1993
  Her summer spent taking care of Aunt May, who's "dying" of a rheumatic heart, turns out to be intriguing.

878

CARROLL THOMAS (Pseudonym of Carole Shmurak and Thomas Ratliff)
LARRY HOWARD, Illustrator

Blue Creek Farm: A Matty Trescott Novel

(Hanover, NH: Smith and Kraus, 2001)

Subject(s): Farm Life; Historical
Age range(s): Grades 6-9
Major character(s): Matilda "Matty" Trescott, 12-Year-Old

Time period(s): 1860s
Locale(s): Blue Creek Farm, Kansas

Summary: Matty unknowingly prepares herself for war in this prequel to *Matty's War*, which describes her life as a motherless girl growing up on a farm in Kansas. Though she misses her mother, Matty has learned to assume the household responsibilities and farm chores as her family adjusts to drought conditions. It's difficult, though, to ignore the presence of Bill Quantrill and his Raiders and every household lives in fear of a raid by these guerrillas on their homes and farms. (186 pages)

Where it's reviewed:
Booklist, April 1, 2001, page 1488
Voice of Youth Advocates, June 2001, page 129

Other books by the same author:
Ring Out Wild Bells, 2001
Matty's War, 1999

Other books you might like:
Craig Crist-Evans, *Moon over Tennessee*, 1999
  A young teenaged boy and his father join the Civil War, not to fight slavery but because of their great love for their farmland.
Jennifer Johnson Garrity, *The Bushwhackers: A Civil War Adventure*, 1999
  Innocent victims of the hatred of war, Jacob and his sister Eliza flee from their burning home after bushwhackers shoot their father, a Union sympathizer.
Hadley Irwin, *Jim Dandy*, 1994
  Between losing his mother and living with his stepfather's strictness, Caleb's life on the frontier is harsh but raising the young foal Dandy brings him joy.

879

FRANCES THOMAS
ROSS COLLINS, Illustrator

One Day, Daddy

(New York: Hyperion Books for Children, 2001)

Subject(s): Monsters; Parent and Child; Imagination
Age range(s): Preschool-Grade 1
Major character(s): Little Monster, Son; Father Monster, Father
Time period(s): Indeterminate
Locale(s): Fictional Country

Summary: Little Monster has great plans for his future. He explains to Father Monster that he's interested in space exploration. He'll begin with a trip to the moon but he'll continue on to Mars and perhaps Jupiter and Saturn too. Father Monster promises to wave while Little Monster is on the moon but Little Monster knows he'll be too far away to see. He may hitch a ride on a comet's tail or discover a new star but he plans to definitely come back home when his explorations conclude. (28 pages)

Where it's reviewed:
Bulletin of the Center for Children's Books, October 2001, page 79
Horn Book Guide, Spring 2002, page 29
Publishers Weekly, June 18, 2001, page 80

School Library Journal, September 2001, page 207

Other books by the same author:
What If?, 1999 (Bulletin of the Center for Children's Books Blue Ribbon)
The Bear and Mr. Bear, 1995
The Prince and the Cave, 1992

Other books you might like:
Christine Loomis, *Astro Bunnies*, 2001
Bunnies on rockets explore space and return home in time for bed in a rhyming tale.
Lisa McCourt, *I Miss You, Stinky Face*, 1999
Stinky Face imagines implausible problems that could prevent his traveling mother's return but she assures him she'll overcome them all.
Ann Tompert, *Little Fox Goes to the End of the World*, 1984
Little Fox imagines a dangerous journey to the end of the world with a safe return to her home where her mother will be waiting.

880

KATE THOMPSON

The Beguilers

(New York: Dutton, 2001)

Subject(s): Coming-of-Age; Magic; Quest
Age range(s): Grades 6-10
Major character(s): Rilka, Teenager; Marik, Teenager
Time period(s): Indeterminate
Locale(s): Planet—Imaginary

Summary: Rilka is a misfit in her tradition-ridden village. She is allergic to the chuffies, the empathic creatures who absorb negative feelings and are everyone else's best crutch. She's miserable at the choices available for her future, so she refuses to state a Great Intention, the public goal that will earn her adulthood. But one night, she follows a beguiler, the mysterious beings said to lure people to their deaths, and is inspired to catch one and solve their mystery. The villagers ostracize her, but Rilka sets off in search of the beguilers anyway. Her journey leads to many discoveries, including the truth about beguilers, but Rilka would never survive their danger without the help of Marik, a blind porter who helps her realize she can't do everything alone. (183 pages)

Where it's reviewed:
Horn Book Magazine, January 2002, page 85
Kliatt, September 2001, page 14
Publishers Weekly, October 29, 2001, page 65
School Library Journal, October 2001, page 173
Times Educational Supplement, June 8, 2001, page 20

Other books by the same author:
Midnight's Choice, 1999
Wild Blood, 1999
Switchers, 1998

Other books you might like:
Aiden Beaverson, *The Hidden Arrow of Maether*, 2000
A mysterious sign sends a girl off on a religious quest in search of her heritage.

Lois Lowry, *The Giver*, 1993
Coming of age in a seemingly perfect society should be joyful, shouldn't it?
Sharon Shinn, *Summers at Castle Auburn*, 2001
As she gets older, Corie becomes uncomfortable with the way her people use the beautiful captive ailora.

881

LAUREN THOMPSON
LINDA S. WINGERTER, Illustrator

One Riddle, One Answer

(New York: Scholastic Press, 2001)

Subject(s): Problem Solving; Mathematics; Fairy Tales
Age range(s): Grades 3-5
Major character(s): Aziza, Daughter (of Sultan); Ahmed, Farmer
Time period(s): Indeterminate Past
Locale(s): Persia

Summary: A sultan desiring to find a husband for his daughter accepts Aziza's solution. She devises a riddle and her father agrees to allow her to marry the man who can correctly answer it. Aziza travels to many cities and towns where men attempt to answer the riddle but none do so successfully. Just as Aziza is ready to turn home defeated, Ahmed, a farmer who shares Aziza's love of numbers, appears and wins her hand by answering the riddle correctly. The solution is explained at the conclusion of the book. (32 pages)

Where it's reviewed:
Booklist, February 1, 2001, page 1058
Bulletin of the Center for Children's Books, April 2001, page 317
Horn Book Guide, Fall 2001, page 296
Publishers Weekly, February 19, 2001, page 91
School Library Journal, April 2001, page 123

Awards the book has won:
IRA Teachers' Choices, 2002

Other books by the same author:
Mouse's First Valentine, 2002
Love One Another: The Last Days of Jesus, 2000
Mouse's First Halloween, 2000
Mouse's First Christmas, 1999

Other books you might like:
Demi, *One Grain of Rice*, 1997
Rani seeks payment from the raja of only one grain of rice, to be doubled daily for thirty days, thus ending the villagers' hunger during a drought.
Ellen Jackson, *The Impossible Riddle*, 1996
A Czar uses a riddle to foil his daughter's would-be suitors rather than have her marry.
Greg Tang, *The Grapes of Math: Mind Stretching Math Riddles*, 2001
Rhyming clues to riddles and computer art add to this introduction to innovative problem solving strategies.

882

SARAH L. THOMSON

The Dragon's Son

(New York: Scholastic/Orchard, 2001)

Subject(s): Arthurian Legends; Love; Short Stories
Age range(s): Grades 8-12
Major character(s): Nimue, Wife, Mother; Morgan, Sister; Luned, Servant; Medraud, Son
Time period(s): Indeterminate Past
Locale(s): England

Summary: In these four stories the Arthurian legends are explored from some untraditional perspectives. In the first, Nimue's love and trust the bard leads to the death of her son when he's sacrificed for the good of the kingdom. Morgan similarly finds her trust in her brother betrayed from her point of view. Luned saves her queen through her quick thinking and manipulations, but loses her own beloved. Medraud plays out the hatred his mother Morgan has taught him and brings vengeance to his father in the final tale. (181 pages)

Where it's reviewed:
Booklist, May 1, 2001, page 1675
Bulletin of the Center for Children's Books, July 2001, page 425
Kliatt, May 2001, page 15
School Library Journal, July 2001, page 114
Voice of Youth Advocates, June 2001, page 136

Other books you might like:
Anne McCaffrey, *Black Horses for the King*, 1996
   Galwyn tells his version of Arthur's tale.
Gerald Morris, *The Squire, His Knight & His Lady*, 1999
   The squire to one of the knights of the Round Table hopes that someday he can be a bit more important.
Nancy Springer, *I Am Morgan Le Fay*, 2001
   Morgan explains her bitterness towards her family in this retelling of Arthur's story.

883

CATE TIERNAN

Book of Shadows

(New York: Penguin/Puffin, 2001)

Series: Sweep. Book 1
Subject(s): Witches and Witchcraft; Schools/High Schools
Age range(s): Grades 8-12
Major character(s): Cal Blaire, 12th Grader, Witch; Bree Warren, 11th Grader; Morgan Rowlands, 11th Grader, Witch
Time period(s): 2000s
Locale(s): Widow's Vale, New York

Summary: Morgan and her best friend Bree, thrilled to finally be upper classmen at Widow's Vale High School, stop in their tracks on the first day of school when they spot good-looking new student, Cal Blaire. Cal is a relaxed, self-confident guy who, after a few weeks of school, invites some of the juniors and seniors to join him one evening for food and fun at a field outside of town. About twenty teens gather there, though the number dwindles after Cal explains that he's a Wiccan and

asks them to join him in celebrating the harvest by forming a circle. To Morgan's amazement, she exhibits Wiccan traits. When the coven celebrates Samhain, Morgan makes "magick," clear signs that she's a blood witch in this first of a series. (187 pages)

Where it's reviewed:
Booklist, February 15, 2001, page 1129
Los Angeles Times Book Review, June 10, 2001, page 16
Publishers Weekly, December 18, 2000, page 79
Science Fiction Chronicle, June 2001, page 40
Voice of Youth Advocates, April 2001, page 32

Awards the book has won:
ALA Quick Picks for Reluctant Young Adult Readers, 2002

Other books by the same author:
Awakening, 2001 (Sweep, Book 5)
The Coven, 2001 (Sweep, Book 2)
The Bloodwitch, 2001 (Sweep, Book 3)
Dark Magick, 2001 (Sweep, Book 4)
Spellbound, 2001 (Sweep, Book 6)

Other books you might like:
Isobel Bird, *Circle of Three Series*, 2001-
   Kate, Cooper and Annie become interested in witchcraft and progress from casting a simple love spell to learning more about Wiccan history and rites.
Lynne Ewing, *Into the Cold Fire*, 2000
   The Daughters of the Moon is formed when four friends discover they have unusual powers, from invisibility to time travel to premonitions.
Silver RavenWolf, *Witches' Night Out*, 2000
   Bethany's Thursday night group has previously gathered for innocuous charms, but tonight they call up the Hounds of the Wild Hunt to locate a killer.

884

REBECCA TINGLE

The Edge on the Sword

(New York: Putnam, 2001)

Subject(s): Kings, Queens, Rulers, etc.; Vikings; Coming-of-Age
Age range(s): Grades 7-10
Major character(s): Aethelflaed "Flaed", Royalty, Historical Figure; Ethelred of Mercia, Historical Figure, Nobleman; Red, Bodyguard; Alfred, Royalty (king), Historical Figure
Time period(s): 9th century
Locale(s): West Saxony, England

Summary: At the age of fifteen, Flaed is told of her betrothal to Ethelred of Mercia, a man she doesn't know, but one who is a friend and ally of her father, King Alfred. Having just received instruction in reading and writing, Flaed understands the importance of this alliance, but squirms at the restriction of the bodyguard Red, sent by her future husband. The day she eludes Red is the day she heads straight into disaster and must be saved by him. That incident also marks the beginning of her training in defensive techniques including the use of weapons, such as the sword, shield and dagger; horsemanship; and battle strategy. As she travels to her wedding, she calls upon Red's training when Danish raiders attack her train in this remarkable first novel. (277 pages)

Where it's reviewed:
Booklist, April 15, 2001, page 1551
Bulletin of the Center for Children's Books, October 2001, page 79
Publishers Weekly, July 2, 2001, page 77
School Library Journal, July 2001, page 114
Voice of Youth Advocates, August 2001, page 207

Awards the book has won:
ALA Best Books for Young Adults, 2002

Other books you might like:
Michael Cadnum, *Raven of the Waves*, 2001
Vikings overrun his village but Wiglaf, a young boy with a withered arm, is saved; he in turn helps save the wounded men who just killed his family.
Frances Mary Hendry, *Quest for a Maid*, 1990
Marie, the "Maid of Norway," survives a shipwreck and an ambush while on her way to join Prince Edward on Scotland's throne.
Eloise McGraw, *The Striped Ships*, 1991
Young Jilly tells the story of the Norman invasion of Saxon England through her work on the famed Bayeux Tapestry.
Joan Wolf, *The Edge of Light*, 1990
During the ninth century Alfred the Great unifies the Saxons and prevents the Danes from invading England. Adult title.

885

BETSY TOBIN

Bone House

(New York: Scribner, 2001)

Subject(s): Prostitution; Country Life; Servants
Age range(s): Grades 10-Adult
Major character(s): Unnamed Girl, Narrator, Servant (chambermaid); Dora, Prostitute, Crime Victim; Johann "Long Boy", Son (of Dora); Edward, Landowner (lives in Great House), Handicapped
Time period(s): 17th century
Locale(s): England

Summary: In the latter part of the Elizabethan era, when "bone house" refers to the body, Dora has been an accepted, indeed loved, prostitute and member of a small English town. Though she offers her favors to all the men, the women seek her out as a confidante and friend; when she's found dead at the bottom of a ravine, the townspeople are dismayed. This dismay turns to worry when it's revealed that she was pregnant and foretold her own death. A young chambermaid, daughter of the town midwife, quietly begins her own investigation while she works at the manor, home of crippled, deformed Edward. When a painter arrives to begin a portrait of Edward's mother, Edward also asks for a likeness of Dora. This necessitates the exhumation of her body, but when the grave is opened, Dora's body is missing. The disposition of the body and the identity of the murderer are worrisome events to ponder in this engrossing first novel. (219 pages)

Where it's reviewed:
Booklist, January 2001, page 925
Library Journal, January 2001, page 158
New York Times Book Review, February 25, 2001, page 30
Publishers Weekly, December 4, 2000, page 50
School Library Journal, June 2001, page 184

Awards the book has won:
School Library Journal Best Books, 2001

Other books you might like:
Geraldine Brooks, *Year of Wonders*, 2001
Grief, vengeance, and profit-making overtake village life when a small seventeenth-century English village walls itself in when struck by the plague.
Tracy Chevalier, *Girl with a Pearl Earring*, 2000
To help her family, Griet works as a servant in the home of the painter Vermeer, but she and his wife have a misunderstanding and Griet leaves.
Robert Nye, *Mrs. Shakespeare*, 2000
Anne Hathaway compares Shakespeare's quiet home in Stratford to the wild life available to him in London.

886

STEPHANIE S. TOLAN

Flight of the Raven

(New York: HarperCollins, 2001)

Subject(s): Militia Movements; Terrorism; African Americans
Age range(s): Grades 7-10
Major character(s): Elijah Raymond, Child, Psychic; Amber Landis, 12-Year-Old; Charles Landis, Terrorist
Time period(s): Indeterminate Future
Locale(s): Adirondack Mountains, New York

Summary: The Ark was a facility for young people with special psychic talents and many of them were especially opposed to violence. When it is disbanded, Elijah runs away into the Adirondack Mountains where, ironically, he is found by members of the Free Mountain Militia who are intent on using terrorism to change the American government. He meets Amber, the daughter of its leader Charles, who dismisses the "necessary losses" as a means of achieving their goal. With Elijah's ability to communicate telepathically, a talent he also detects in Amber, and his skill with computers, he is made a vital member of the militia, though their violence is in opposition to his beliefs. He and Amber discuss the group's violent tactics, but when her father decides to unleash a potent strain of smallpox, Elijah knows he must direct his telepathy to prevent this act of terrorism in a sequel to *Welcome to the Ark*. (294 pages)

Where it's reviewed:
Booklist, October 15, 2001, page 396
Kirkus Reviews, October 1, 2001, page 1435
School Library Journal, October 2001, page 173
Voice of Youth Advocates, October 2001, page 295

Other books by the same author:
Surviving the Applewhites, 2002
Ordinary Miracles, 1999
The Face in the Mirror, 1998
Welcome to the Ark, 1996

Who's There?, 1994

Other books you might like:

David Lubar, *Hidden Talents*, 1999
At the alternative school, Martin helps his roommates use their special abilities of telekinesis and precognition to stop bullies from sabotage.

John Marsden, *A Killing Frost*, 1998
Ellie and her friends continue their guerrilla activities against the foreign army, which invaded Australia.

Gary Paulsen, *The White Fox Chronicles: Escape, Return, Breakout*, 2000
Cody is part of a resistance group of Americans fighting to regain control of their country from the Confederation of Consolidated Republics.

887

MICHELE TORREY
BARBARA JOHANSEN NEWMAN, Illustrator

The Case of the Gasping Garbage
(New York: Dutton Children's Books, 2001)

Series: Doyle and Fossey, Science Detectives. Book 1
Subject(s): Science; Mystery and Detective Stories; Scientific Experiments
Age range(s): Grades 3-5
Major character(s): Drake Doyle, 5th Grader, Detective—Amateur; Nell Fossey, 5th Grader, Scientist (amateur)
Time period(s): 2000s (2001)
Locale(s): Mossy Lake

Summary: A series of problems require the services of science detectives Drake and Nell. An alarmed classmate calls Drake to report a monster in her garbage can. Astute detective work and the scientific method help Nell and Drake test their hypothesis and solve the mystery. Nell calls on Drake to help save the town's population of leopard frogs and Nell's mom gives her a clue that solves the dilemma of a truck stuck under a bridge. Together they respond to a classmate with an anonymous love letter; their scientific experiment identifies the author. The methods for conducting each experiment are included at the conclusion of the book. (71 pages)

Where it's reviewed:
Booklist, August 2001, page 2122
Bulletin of the Center for Children's Books, June 2001, page 388
School Library Journal, August 2001, page 164

Other books by the same author:
The Case of the Mossy Lake Monster, 2002 (Doyle and Fossey, Science Detectives, Book 2)
Bottle of Eight and Pieces of Rum, 1998

Other books you might like:
Bruce Hale, *The Chameleon Wore Chartreuse*, 2000
Fourth-grader Chet's reputation as an effective private eye is well known to other students who contact him to solve tough cases.

Barbara Joosse, *Alien Brain Fryout*, 2000
In Book four of the Wild Willie Mystery series the amateur sleuths decide they must keep their town free from aliens.

Donald J. Sobol, *Encyclopedia Brown, Boy Detective*, 1979
Confident and affordable, Encyclopedia Brown opens a detective agency in this first book in a popular series.

Gertrude Chandler Warner, *The Boxcar Children Mystery Series*, 1953-
Four children are involved in a variety of mysteries in this timeless series.

888

RODERICK TOWNLEY

The Great Good Thing
(New York: Atheneum/Simon & Schuster, 2001)

Subject(s): Books and Reading; Dreams and Nightmares; Princes and Princesses
Age range(s): Grades 4-7
Major character(s): Sylvie, Royalty (princess); Claire, Grandmother; Lily, Daughter (granddaughter)
Time period(s): Indeterminate
Locale(s): United States

Summary: Waiting among the pages of a fairytale is Princess Sylvie, bored beyond belief because no Reader has opened her book in quite a while. But then in one day, there are two Readers, one an unappealing boy who drips jelly almost on Sylvie's toes and one a caring girl who cleans off the jelly and begins to read their story. Something strikes Sylvie and she breaks a rule of fairytale characters when she looks right into Claire's eyes and the two establish a bond. This bond helps Sylvie, who refuses to marry Prince Riggeloff before she accomplishes one "great good thing." Making use of the bond, Sylvie and members of her court enter Claire's subconscious where Sylvie has adventures far beyond her usual reserved court life. That unappealing boy manages to burn the book, but by then Sylvie is able to permanently implant herself and many of the book's characters in Claire's mind, tucked away in a little corner where they're not thought of very often. As Claire lies dying, Sylvie accomplishes her "great good thing" by prompting Claire's granddaughter Lily into remembering and writing down the story, thereby breathing life into Sylvie and her court in a delightful, multilayered tale. (216 pages)

Where it's reviewed:
Booklist, March 15, 2001, page 1398
Kliatt, May 2001, page 14
Publishers Weekly, May 21, 2001, page 108
School Library Journal, July 2001, page 114
Voice of Youth Advocates, April 2001, page 57

Other books by the same author:
Night Errands: How Poets Use Dreams, 2000

Other books you might like:
Lewis Carroll, *Alice's Adventures in Wonderland*, 1865
When Alice falls down a rabbit's hole, she enters a fantasy world populated with strange, funny, cruel and unusual characters.

Michael Ende, *The Neverending Story*, 1984
An overweight boy enters the book he's reading to save the land of Fantastica from devastation.

William Goldman, *The Princess Bride*, 1973
This humorous adventure stars a perfect hero and a beautiful heroine, complete with princes and daring friends.

Donn Kushner, *A Book Dragon*, 1988
A dragon has guarded the illuminated manuscript *Book of Hours* for five hundred years, but now shrinks to insect size to stay in the bookstore.

889

DON TREMBATH

Frog Face and the Three Boys
(Custer, WA: Orca, 2001)

Series: Black Belt
Subject(s): Sports/Karate; School Life; Humor
Age range(s): Grades 4-7
Major character(s): Jeffrey "Stewie" Stewart, 7th Grader; Charles "Charlie" Cairns, 7th Grader; Sidney Martin, 7th Grader; "Frog Face" Duncan, Principal
Time period(s): 2000s
Locale(s): Emville, Alberta, Canada

Summary: When three boys end up in the principal's office for three very different offenses, Mr. Duncan, also known as Frog Face, realizes that detention isn't going to make these boys behave any better so he tries something different. He enrolls the three of them in his son's karate classes where their usual coping skills don't work. Charlie the liar can no longer lie his way out of sessions; shy Jeffrey has to defend himself and fighting Sidney now finds himself on the receiving end, usually knocked over by a girl! The three boys not only change and grow as they take their karate classes, but also have a lot of fun in this first of a series. (157 pages)

Where it's reviewed:
Booklist, March 1, 2001, page 1283
Quill & Quire, December 2000, page 32
Resource Links, December 2000, page 13
School Library Journal, September 2001, page 234

Other books by the same author:
The Popsicle Journal, 2002 (Harper Winslow Series)
The Missing Finger, 2001
Lefty Carmichael Has a Fit, 2000
A Beautiful Place on Yonge Street, 1998
A Fly Named Alfred, 1997

Other books you might like:
Jack Gantos, *Joey Pigza Swallowed the Key*, 1998
Unless he takes his medication, Joey is an out of control kid who sticks his finger in the pencil sharpener, swallows his house key or careens off desks.

Gail Gauthier, *A Year with Butch and Spike*, 1998
After a year sandwiched between the two troublemakers Spike and Butch, ideal student Jasper realizes there's more to life than being perfect.

Chris Lynch, *Johnny Chesthair*, 1997
Two boys start a club that has only one rule—no girls! Their worst moment comes when they confront archenemy Monica and her cookie-selling Girl Scouts.

890

MICHAEL O. TUNNELL

Brothers in Valor: A Story of Resistance
(New York: Holiday House, 2001)

Subject(s): Holocaust; World War II; Resistance Movements
Age range(s): Grades 6-10
Major character(s): Rudi Ollenik, Resistance Fighter; Helmuth Hubener, Resistance Fighter; Karl Schneider, Resistance Fighter
Time period(s): 1930s; 1940s (1937-1942)
Locale(s): Hamburg, Germany

Summary: Rudi, Helmuth and Karl are just young boys when Hitler comes to power but they notice the disappearance of their Jewish friends, witness the horror of *Kristallnacht* and realize their country needs to be free of vermin like Hitler. All members of a small congregation of the Mormon Church, they're frustrated that the church isn't standing up to Hitler and decide to do something. After secretly listening to the BBC broadcasts over a short wave radio, they prepare handbills detailing the truth about Hitler and the war and distribute the flyers until someone reports their actions to the Nazis. Arrested, they are questioned, tortured and Helmuth is executed by beheading while Rudi and Karl are sent to jail in this work, based on historical fact, about three brave teenagers. (260 pages)

Where it's reviewed:
Booklist, May 1, 2001, page 1676
Bulletin of the Center for Children's Books, September 2001, page 37
Publishers Weekly, May 28, 2001, page 89
School Library Journal, June 2001, page 158
Voice of Youth Advocates, August 2001, page 208

Other books by the same author:
School Spirits, 1997
The Children of Topaz: The Story of a Japanese American Internment Camp: Based on a Classroom Diary, 1996

Other books you might like:
Sebastian Faulk, *Charlotte Gray*, 1999
When Charlotte's RAF pilot is lost over France, she travels there to search for him, joins the Resistance and is caught up in the war effort.

Lois Lowry, *Number the Stars*, 1989
Annemarie fears for her Jewish friend's life when the Germans occupy her Copenhagen neighborhood.

Bjarne B. Reuter, *The Boys of St. Petri*, 1994
Sons of a local minister, Lars and Gunnar lead their Danish classmates in acts of resistance against the Nazis.

891

SANDY TURNER, Author/Illustrator

Silent Night
(New York: Atheneum Books for Young Readers, 2001)

Subject(s): Animals/Dogs; Santa Claus; Christmas
Age range(s): Grades 2-4
Major character(s): Unnamed Character, Dog

Time period(s): Indeterminate
Locale(s): Fictional Country

Summary: The family pet tries to alert everyone to an intruder in the night by barking, yapping and woofing. Everyone, with the exception of the dog, in this story is silent, but the night resonates with the sounds of the dog trying to tell the family about the fat, red guy who just came down the chimney. No one seems to catch on to the dog's warning but the next morning they find a scrap of red fabric on the floor near the fireplace. The exhausted dog simply sleeps as the author's first book concludes. (32 pages)

Where it's reviewed:
Booklist, October 1, 2001, page 330
Bulletin of the Center for Children's Books, November 2001, page 118
Horn Book, November 2001, page 739
Publishers Weekly, September 24, 2001, page 49
School Library Journal, October 2001, page 70

Other books by the same author:
Grow Up, 2002

Other books you might like:
Nancy Antle, *Sam's Wild West Christmas*, 2000
  Sam tracks two thieves who have stolen gifts and tied up a fellow in a red suit that they found on the cabin roof.
David McPhail, *Santa's Book of Names*, 1993
  Poor reader Edward helps Santa with his list of name and receives a fitting gift in return.
Chris Van Allsburg, *The Polar Express*, 1985
  The Caldecott Medal winner relates a child's memory of a magical Christmas Eve ride to the North Pole.

CATHLEEN TWOMEY

Charlotte's Choice

(Honesdale, PA: Boyds Mills Press, 2001)

Subject(s): Orphans; Abuse; Friendship

Age range(s): Grades 6-9
Major character(s): Charlotte Ann Matthews, 13-Year-Old; Jesse Irwin, 14-Year-Old, Abuse Victim; Aaron Phelps, Store Owner
Time period(s): 1900s (1905)
Locale(s): Turner's Crossing, Missouri

Summary: When the orphan train pulls out of Turner's Crossing, Jesse is one of those who remains in town, first staying with a spinster and then moving to the home of Mr. Phelps, a shopkeeper. She and Charlotte become fast friends and Jesse enjoys the warmth she finds in the Matthews home, while Charlotte admires Jesse's spunk and independence. Jesse finally confides to Charlotte that Mr. Phelps abuses her, though she makes Charlotte promise to never tell. When Jesse kills Mr. Phelps and is arrested for his murder, Charlotte doesn't know what to do. Should she break her promise to Jesse and tell, which would certainly free her, or should she be silent and preserve Jesse's pride? Whatever decision Charlotte makes will be painful, both for her and for Jesse. (184 pages)

Where it's reviewed:
Booklist, January 2002, page 845
School Library Journal, December 2001, page 147
Voice of Youth Advocates, February 2002, page 440

Other books you might like:
Katherine Martin, *Night Riding*, 1989
  The night Mary Faith's father tries to accost Prin while she's riding her horse is when she realizes her friend is being abused.
Joan Lowery Nixon, *The Orphan Train Quartet*, 1987-1989
  A series of books featuring the Kelly children who are sent West on the Orphan Train after their widowed mother realizes she can't care for them.
Susan Beth Pfeffer, *Justice for Emily*, 1997
  After three girls taunt and push her friend Gracie into the street to her death, Emily returns to make sure the three are punished.

U

893

MYRON UHLBERG
SONJA LAMUT, Illustrator

Lemuel the Fool
(Atlanta: Peachtree Publishers, 2001)

Subject(s): Folk Tales; Voyages and Travels; Humor
Age range(s): Grades K-3
Major character(s): Lemuel, Fisherman, Spouse; Essie, Spouse, Housewife; Sol, Son, Child
Time period(s): Indeterminate Past
Locale(s): Fictional Country

Summary: Though only a simple fisherman, Lemuel dreams of an enchanted village across the sea. Essie considers Lemuel a fool to sail away from his home and family, but Lemuel is determined to find this village of his dreams. As he travels, Lemuel loses consciousness when stormy seas rock the boat and he hits his head. When he comes to, the storm is past and the boat is sailing toward a harbor that looks very much like his own village. Lemuel is astonished that this enchanted village has a woman named Essie with a boy named Sol who claim to be his wife and son. Feeling bewildered Lemuel sneaks back to his boat to sail home but falls asleep as the vessel sails of its own accord. This time when Lemuel enters the harbor he recognizes the village as his own and hurries home to Essie and Sol who await the silly fool. (32 pages)

Where it's reviewed:
Booklist, April 15, 2001, page 1567
Horn Book Guide, Fall 2001, page 278
Kirkus Reviews, February 15, 2001, page 266
Publishers Weekly, February 5, 2001, page 88
School Library Journal, August 2001, page 164

Other books by the same author:
Mad Dog McGraw, 2000 (IRA Children's Choice)
Flying over Brooklyn, 1999

Other books you might like:
Steven Kellogg, *The Three Sillies*, 1999
    A gentleman locates three people sillier than those in the family of the woman he wishes to wed in order to win her hand.
Eric A. Kimmel, *The Adventures of Hershel of Ostropol*, 1995
    Ten stories relate the misfortunes of a wandering beggar who approaches barriers on the road of life with wit, determination and inventiveness.
Arthur Ransome, *The Fool of the World and the Flying Shop*, 1968
    The peasant in this Caldecott Medal winning folktale is no fool as his attention to good advice enables him to marry the princess.
Steve Sanfield, *The Feather Merchants and Other Tales of the Fools of Chelm*, 1991
    Thirteen tales drawn from Jewish folklore offer humor and heritage.

894

JEAN URE
CHRIS FISHER, Illustrator
PETER BAILEY, Illustrator

Skinny Melon and Me
(New York: Holt, 2001)

Subject(s): Diaries; Divorce; Stepfathers
Age range(s): Grades 5-7
Major character(s): Cherry Louise Waterton, 11-Year-Old; Melanie "Skinny Melon" Skinner, 11-Year-Old; Roland Butter, Artist (children's book illustrator)
Time period(s): 2000s
Locale(s): London, England

Summary: Responding to a teacher's advice that keeping a diary helps "clean out the cupboard" of her mind, Cherry begins filling the pages in hers. Her entries range from school lunches, her best friend Melanie's grief and her own lack of a pet. But the one person about whom Cherry can write volumes is the awful Roland Butter, now married to her mother. A children's illustrator, he continually slips messages written in rebus under her door to try to win over her affections, and she consigns them all to the trashcan. A trip to visit her dad and his new wife helps her see the worth of her stepfather, especially when her dad makes it obvious there's not room in his life for his new family and Cherry too. When Roland finds the perfect pet for her, Cherry finally admits him into her life. (202 pages)

Where it's reviewed:
Booklist, January 2001, page 961
Bulletin of the Center for Children's Books, March 2001, page 280
Publishers Weekly, November 27, 2000, page 77
School Library Journal, January 2001, page 134
Voice of Youth Advocates, April 2001, page 47

Other books by the same author:
The Children Next Door, 1996
Plague, 1991
The Other Side of the Fence, 1988

Other books you might like:
Mary Jane Auch, *Mom Is Dating Weird Wayne*, 1988
Jenna is horrified that her mother is dating that weird weatherman who always dresses in costume on his television program.
Morse Hamilton, *The Garden of Eden Motel*, 1999
Del enjoys getting to know his new stepfather, a seed company inspector, on his summer trip west with him.
Susan Beth Pfeffer, *Devil's Den*, 1998
Joey takes his time trying to decide whether or not to be adopted by his stepfather Ben.
Cheryl Ware, *Catty-Cornered*, 1998
Venola keeps a journal of the time she stays with her grandmother and goes to bed at 7:30 p.m., lives with thirteen cats and watches only religious programs on TV.

895

ANDREA U'REN, Author/Illustrator

Pugdog
(New York: Farrar Straus Giroux, 2001)

Subject(s): Animals/Dogs; Pets; Gender Roles
Age range(s): Grades 1-2
Major character(s): Pugdog, Dog; Mike, Animal Lover
Time period(s): 2000s (2001)
Locale(s): United States

Summary: In the author's first book, a trip to the vet brings Pugdog's idyllic ''dog's life'' to an abrupt halt. When unobservant pet owner Mike learns from the vet that Pugdog is a she not a he, Mike stops treating her to bones, romps in the park, and belly scratches because such behaviors are not ''ladylike.'' Even worse, Mike takes Pugdog to a doggy salon where she is bathed and dressed in an uncomfortable frock. Pugdog grows so miserable that she runs away to enjoy the park on her own terms once again. When Mike finds his pet happily digging holes in her torn, dirty frock, he realizes that dog behavior cannot be stereotyped and promises to let her return to doggy ways. (32 pages)

Where it's reviewed:
Booklist, March 1, 2001, page 1258
Horn Book, March 2001, page 203
Kirkus Reviews, February 15, 2001, page 266

Publishers Weekly, January 29, 2001, page 88
School Library Journal, June 2001, page 131

Other books you might like:
James Howe, *Pinky and Rex and the Just-Right Pet*, 2001
A new pet kitten for the family endears itself to Pinky who really wanted a dog.
Chinlun Lee, *The Very Kind Rich Lady and Her One Hundred Dogs*, 2001
No matter her pets' gender, the dogs all receive the same love and care from the kind rich lady.
Rick Walton, *That's My Dog!*, 2001
The owner of a large, red, smelly, dirty dog proudly describes his mischievous pet.

896

VERONICA URIBE
GLORIA CALDERON, Illustrator
ELISA AMADO, Translator

Buzz Buzz Buzz
(Toronto: Groundwood Books, 2001)

Subject(s): Fantasy; Sleep; Brothers and Sisters
Age range(s): Grades K-1
Major character(s): Juliana, Child, Sister; Andres, Child, Brother (younger)
Time period(s): Indeterminate
Locale(s): Fictional Country

Summary: Juliana and Andres are tucked in bed but unable to sleep because of the buzzing of a mosquito. Together they run outside and into the jungle beseeching the animals to help them get rid of the mosquito. Finally an owl agrees to help the children return home. When they do, the mosquito follows and a frog sitting on the windowsill slurps it right down. Finally, Juliana and Andres can sleep. Originally published in Venezuela in 1999. (28 pages)

Where it's reviewed:
Booklist, July 2001, page 2022
Kirkus Reviews, June 1, 2001, page 806
The New Advocate, Winter 2002, page 76
Publishers Weekly, May 28, 2001, page 86
School Library Journal, August 2001, page 164

Other books by the same author:
Classic Children's Tales, 1998

Other books you might like:
Verna Aardema, *Why Mosquitoes Buzz in People's Ears: A West African Tale*, 1975
A Caldecott Medal winning folktale offers the mosquito's perspective on why the pesky insects buzz in people's ears.
Gary Bilezikian, *While I Slept*, 1990
Noisy night sounds do not keep this little boy awake.
Fran Manushkin, *Peeping and Sleeping*, 1994
The distant and continuous sound of peeping keeps Barry from sleeping so he and his father go to investigate the source.
Teri Sloat, *The Thing that Bothered Farmer Brown*, 1995
An annoying mosquito keeps tired Farmer Brown from enjoying his night's sleep.

V

897

ALAIN VAES, Author/Illustrator

The Princess and the Pea
(Boston: Little, Brown and Company, 2001)

Subject(s): Fairy Tales; Humor; Princes and Princesses
Age range(s): Grades K-3
Major character(s): Ralph, Royalty (prince), Bachelor; Frieda, Royalty (queen), Mother; Opaline "Opal" von Highbredde, Royalty (princess), Mechanic
Time period(s): Indeterminate
Locale(s): Upper Crestalia, Fictional Country; Lower Crestalia, Fictional Country

Summary: Prince Ralph's desire to marry does not please Queen Frieda who fears he may want one of her precious gems for an engagement ring. To assure that nothing comes between her and her jewel collection, Queen Frieda devises increasingly impossible tests for the princesses seeking to win her son's approval. Despondent, Prince Ralph drives through Upper Crestalia until he reaches the border of little known Lower Crestalia where his car breaks down. His rescuer is a mechanic and tow truck driver who also happens to be the crown princess of Lower Crestalia. Prince Ralph hurries home with Princess Opal determined to make her his bride and, by a fortunate turn of events, he does. (32 pages)

Where it's reviewed:
Booklist, July 2001, page 2015
Bulletin of the Center for Children's Books, October 2001, page 80
Kirkus Reviews, July 1, 2001, page 948
Publishers Weekly, July 23, 2001, page 77
School Library Journal, September 2001, page 207

Other books by the same author:
Reynard the Fox, 1994
The Porcelain Pepper Pot, 1985
The Wild Hamster, 1985

Other books you might like:
Hans Christian Andersen, *The Princess and the Pea*, 1978
    Paul Galdone's illustrated retelling of the classic fairy tale explains how a princess verifies her royalty.
Sucie Stevenson, *The Princess and the Pea*, 1992
    A pea felt through twenty mattresses and twenty feather beds keeps a princess from sleeping but assures her marriage to the prince.
Harriet Ziefert, *The Princess and the Pea*, 1996
    This version of Andersen's fairy tale is retold as an easy reader.

898

EDO VAN BELKOM, Editor

Be Afraid!: Tales of Horror
(Plattsburgh, NH: Tundra Books, 2000)

Subject(s): Short Stories; Horror
Age range(s): Grades 8-12

Summary: Fifteen horrifying tales make up this collection of short stories written for teens and about teens. In Tim Wynne Jones's "The iBook" a young thief makes a serious mistake when he steals a laptop from an author, reads the story written there and has the audacity to sign his name, a name easily deleted. A high school freshman wonders what her senior stepbrother is up to when he seems to have their parents under his control; determined not to let that happen to her, she finds herself unable to resist his request to drive her car in Edmund Plante's story "In the Middle of the Night." And Ellen has a hard time telling her best friend Margaret, who's now a ghost, that she's dating Margaret's former boyfriend in Scott Nicholson's work "In the Heart of November." Other authors include Monica Hughes, Ed Gorman, Nancy Etchemendy and Joe R. Lansdale, to name a few, in this truly scary anthology of stories that prove everyday life often contains the greatest horrors. (178 pages)

Where it's reviewed:
Booklist, February 1, 2001, page 1046
Quill & Quire, September 2000, page 62

Resource Links, October 2000, page 31
School Library Journal, March 2001, page 258
Science Fiction Chronicle, October 2000, page 61

Other books by the same author:
Death Drives a Semi: Horror Stories, 2001
Martyrs, 2001

Other books you might like:
Mark Baker, *My Favorite Horror Story*, 2000
Writers of horror fiction share their favorite story in this collection of tried and true favorites that also includes a history of horror.
Paul Jennings, *Undone!: More Mad Endings*, 1995
A superb collection of tales featuring unusual characters such as a boy wearing a cape of live bats or a girl who brings her aunt's toe to school.
Arielle North Olson, *Ask the Bones: Scary Stories from around the World*, 1999
Fourteen different countries, ranging from Uzbekistan to the United States and Iceland to Iraq, are represented in this collection of twenty-two ghostly folktales.

899

WENDELIN VAN DRAANEN

Flipped

(New York: Knopf, 2001)

Subject(s): Romance; Family Life; Schools/Middle Schools
Age range(s): Grades 5-8
Major character(s): Julianna ''Juli'' Baker, 8th Grader; Bryce Loski, 8th Grader; Chet Duncan, Grandfather (of Bryce)
Time period(s): 2000s
Locale(s): United States

Summary: When Juli's a second grader, Bryce moves into her neighborhood and, after seeing his beautiful eyes, she instantly flips. Bryce, on the other hand, can't put enough distance between them as he ducks her pushy ways. Now eighth graders, their feelings have ''flipped.'' Juli raises chickens, the remnant of a science fair project, and gives away their eggs to her neighbors, including Bryce's family. Now she hears that not only have they thrown away the eggs, but that Bryce also makes unkind comments about her family's messy yard, causing Juli to reevaluate her feelings about loving him. From Bryce's new perspective, Juli is a unique individual and he can't believe he's avoided her all those years. It takes the help of Bryce's grandfather Chet, sitting in a sycamore tree and really looking at the world, and a conversation with her mother to realize she needs to take a second look at Bryce. (212 pages)

Where it's reviewed:
Book Report, March 2002, page 52
Booklist, December 15, 2001, page 732
Publishers Weekly, September 10, 2001, page 93
School Library Journal, November 2001, page 165
Voice of Youth Advocates, December 2001, page 365

Awards the book has won:
School Library Journal Best Books, 2001

Other books by the same author:
Sammy Keyes and the Search for Snake Eyes, 2002

Sammy Keyes and the Hollywood Mummy, 2001
Sammy Keyes and the Curse of Moustache Mary, 2000
Sammy Keyes and the Runaway Elf, 1999

Other books you might like:
Jennifer L. Holm, *Boston Jane: An Adventure*, 2001
Neither Miss Heppelwhite's training, nor William's nice looks, matter to Jane when she puts them in perspective of her new life in the Washington Territory.
Gayle Pearson, *Don't Call It Paradise*, 1999
Visiting a friend, Maddie can't believe how cute her older brother is, though Bean tries to warn her that Buddy is still mean as a snake.
Jerry Spinelli, *Jason and Marceline*, 1986
As Jason begins ninth grade, he tries to understand girls, especially Marceline.

900

WENDELIN VAN DRAANEN

Sammy Keyes and the Hollywood Mummy

(New York: Knopf, 2001)

Subject(s): Mothers and Daughters; Mystery and Detective Stories; Actors and Actresses
Age range(s): Grades 6-9
Major character(s): Samantha ''Sammy'' Keyes, Detective—Amateur, 13-Year-Old; Marissa McKenze, 13-Year-Old; Lana/Dominique Keyes/Windsor, Actress, Mother (of Sammy); Max Mueller, Agent
Time period(s): 2000s
Locale(s): Santa Martina, California; Hollywood, California

Summary: Sammy lives with her grandmother after her mother moves to Hollywood to become a star, but Sammy decides it's time she pay a call on her mother. She and her friend Marissa catch a bus to Hollywood where she finds her mother is one of a dozen roommates sharing a Spanish villa run by the agent Max Mueller. Sammy is disgusted to learn that her mother now calls herself Dominique Windsor, claims to be ten years younger than she really is and has a new, dyed hairdo. Of course Dominique now isn't old enough to be Sammy's mother, so she palms Sammy off as her niece. None of this makes Sammy feel very welcome, but when her mother's competitor for a coveted role is found dead, Sammy stays on to investigate. (256 pages)

Where it's reviewed:
Booklist, March 1, 2001, page 1272
Horn Book, May 2001, page 338
New York Times Book Review, August 12, 2001, page 24
School Library Journal, February 2001, page 122

Other books by the same author:
Sammy Keyes and the Search for Snake Eyes, 2002
Flipped, 2001
Sammy Keyes and the Runaway Elf, 1999
Sammy Keyes and the Sisters of Mercy, 1999
Sammy Keyes and the Hotel Thief, 1998

Other books you might like:
Joachim Friedrich, *4 1/2 Friends and the Secret Cave*, 2001
Collin and Steffi set up a detective agency but admit her

twin brother when he reports finding a cave with a treasure map dated from the 1950s.

Dorothy Hoobler, *The Demon in the Teahouse*, 2001
Adopted by Judge Ooka, Seikei helps with his investigations and is sent to a teahouse when suspicious fires are set and three people murdered.

Anthony Horowitz, *Stormbreaker*, 2001
After his uncle dies, Alex helps British intelligence and, armed with lots of hi-tech gadgets, investigates the computer giant Sayle Enterprises.

901

NANCY VAN LAAN
VICTORIA CHESS, Illustrator

Teeny Tiny Tingly Tales
(New York: Anne Schwartz/Atheneum Books for Young Readers, 2001)

Subject(s): Horror; Short Stories; Stories in Rhyme
Age range(s): Grades K-3
Time period(s): Indeterminate
Locale(s): Fictional Country

Summary: Three brief rhyming stories grow progressively more alarming. "Old Doctor Wango Tango" has a collection of motley animals that he treats indifferently and doesn't feed so when he rides the horse to a hilltop with the other animals by his side they all blow away in the wind. "It" comes down the stairs in bits and pieces, reassembles itself and goes for a stroll. In the final story, a little old lady finds a hairy toe in the pea patch and promptly buries it. Later, she hear a moaning sound seeking the return of the hairy toe so she digs it up and hurls it away in the direction of the sound. (32 pages)

Where it's reviewed:
Booklist, October 15, 2001, page 402
Bulletin of the Center for Children's Books, September 2001, page 38
Horn Book, September 2001, page 578
Publishers Weekly, August 13, 2001, page 311
School Library Journal, January 2002, page 112

Other books by the same author:
When Winter Comes, 2000 (Charlotte Zolotow Highly Commended Book)
So Say the Little Monkeys, 1998 (School Library Journal Best Book)
Little Baby Bobby, 1997

Other books you might like:
Joanna Cole, *Bony-Legs*, 1983
A young girl's compassion toward mistreated animals gives her the magic she needs to escape from Baba Yaga.

Cynthia DeFelice, *Cold Feet*, 2000
A bagpiper with newly found boots is surprised by a knock at the door from a corpse seeking the return of his feet.

Diane Goode, *Diane Goode's Book of Scary Stories and Songs*, 1994
The not-too-terrifying collection of scary stories also includes poems and songs.

Kay Winters, *The Teeny Tiny Ghost*, 1997
The teeny, tiny, timid ghost has difficulty doing his haunting homework because he scares himself so easily.

902

JEAN VAN LEEUWEN
BRAD SNEED, Illustrator

Sorry
(New York: Phyllis Fogelman Books, 2001)

Subject(s): Brothers; Family Relations; Behavior
Age range(s): Grades 1-4
Major character(s): Ebenezer, Brother, Farmer; Obadiah, Brother, Farmer (dairy)
Time period(s): Indeterminate Past
Locale(s): New England

Summary: Ebenezer and Obadiah live and farm together; Obadiah milks the cow and Ebenezer plows the fields and plants the corn. One winter morning Obadiah comments that the oatmeal is lumpy; Ebenezer takes offense and dumps the bowl on Obadiah's head. Thus begins a feud that lasts for generations because neither brother is willing to be the first to say "sorry." When the spring thaw makes it possible, Obadiah saws the house in half and hauls his part over to the next hilltop where he begins a dairy farm. Ebenezer plants corn and builds walls with the stones from the field to keep out the cows. Neither marriages nor the arrival of children and grandchildren soften the brothers' hearts enough for them to apologize. The disagreement continues long after any descendants can recall the original reason for it. It finally ends when two cousins meet unexpectedly at Ebenezer's wall under one of Obadiah's apple trees and apologize. (32 pages)

Where it's reviewed:
Booklist, June 2001, page 1896
Bulletin of the Center for Children's Books, September 2001, page 38
Kirkus Reviews, April 15, 2001, page 594
Publishers Weekly, May 21, 2001, page 107
School Library Journal, May 2001, page 138

Other books by the same author:
Oliver and Albert, Friends Forever, 2000
Across the Wide Dark Sea: The Mayflower Journey, 1995
Going West, 1992

Other books you might like:
Clyde Robert Bulla, *The Stubborn Old Woman*, 1980
A stubborn old woman refuses to leave her home that is falling into the river until she meets a stubborn young girl who's equally adamant about going.

Sam McBratney, *I'm Sorry*, 2000
An argument could be end of a good friendship but the two children realize what they'd lose if they did not apologize.

Tres Seymour, *Jake Johnson: The Story of a Mule*, 1999
Mrs. Puckett tries lighting a fire under Farmer Puckett's stubborn mule in hopes that will make him move; she's partially successful.

William Steig, *Spinky Sulks*, 1998
Spinky pouts for days before telling his family what's bothering him.

Janice May Udry, *Let's Be Enemies*, 1988
After their disagreement James and John decide to be enemies rather than friends; a decision that enables them to rebuild their relationship.

903

JULIA VAN NUTT
ROBERT VAN NUTT, Illustrator

Skyrockets and Snickerdoodles: A Cobtown Story from the Diaries of Lucky Hart

(New York: Doubleday Book for Young Readers, 2001)

Subject(s): Diaries; Holidays; City and Town Life
Age range(s): Grades 2-4
Major character(s): Lucky Hart, 10-Year-Old; Buckeye, Goat
Time period(s): 1840s (1845)
Locale(s): Cobtown

Summary: As Lucky records in her diary Cobtown begins its Fourth of July celebration as the town of Carbuncle because no one in town can locate the original town marker to prove the town's name. The townsfolk are not happy about this name change so when Buckeye races off with the umpire's straw hat and climbs to the top of the train station thus dislodging the ivy on the side. They are thrilled to find the stone marker under the vine. The baseball team goes on to defeat their opponent, the picnic offers food galore and the fireworks are spectacular. It's a Fourth of July to remember! (34 pages)

Where it's reviewed:
Booklist, September 1, 2001, page 111
Horn Book Guide, Fall 2001, page 296
Kirkus Reviews, May 1, 2001, page 669
Publishers Weekly, July 2, 2001, page 78
School Library Journal, July 2001, page 90

Other books by the same author:
Pignapped!: A Cobtown Story from the Diaries of Lucky Hart, 2000
Pumpkins from the Sky?: A Cobtown Story from the Diaries of Lucky Hart, 1999
The Mystery of Mineral Gorge: A Cobtown Story from the Diaries of Lucky Hart, 1999

Other books you might like:
Jane Resh Thomas, *Celebration!*, 1997
  On the Fourth of July relatives gather at Maggie's house for swimming, games, a picnic and sparklers.
Jean Van Leeuwen, *A Fourth of July on the Plains*, 1997
  A wagon train heading to Oregon stops for a day so everyone can celebrate Independence Day.
Wendy Watson, *Hooray for the Fourth of July*, 1992
  A small town's observance of America's birthday includes a parade, picnic and fireworks.

904

ELIZABETH VAN STEENWYK

Maggie in the Morning

(Grand Rapids, MI: Eerdman's, 2001)

Subject(s): Family Life; Identity; Secrets
Age range(s): Grades 4-6
Major character(s): Maggie Calhoun, 11-Year-Old; Cooper Calhoun, Child; Ida Mae George, Friend (of Maggie); Bess, Aunt; Dick, Uncle
Time period(s): 1940s (1941)
Locale(s): Oquawka, Illinois

Summary: It's summer and Maggie and her little brother Cooper are visiting their aunt and uncle while their pregnant mother is home on bed rest and their father prepares to move the family to his new job in California. This summer, Maggie becomes aware of little oddities, memories of a woman who used to visit her, hints from her grandmother of a need to talk, and family photographs that disappear. A new friend, Ida Mae, tells her point-blank that she's not Maggie Calhoun, which is an unsettling thought. By summer's end, Maggie has learned a little bit more about who she really is, and the news isn't so bad. (128 pages)

Where it's reviewed:
Booklist, January 2002, page 860
School Library Journal, December 2001, page 148

Other books by the same author:
A Traitor Among Us, 1998
Three Dog Winter, 1987
Ride to Win, 1979
Rivals on Ice, 1978

Other books you might like:
Alane Ferguson, *Secrets*, 1997
  T.J. reels with the news that he's adopted, but after running away to live with his birth mother, realizes that his dad's home is the perfect spot for him.
Adele Griffin, *Split Just Right*, 1997
  When Danny finds the father she's never known, she also discovers a deeper appreciation for her artistic single mom.
Richard Peck, *A Long Way from Chicago*, 1998
  Joey and his sister Mary Alice hear many warm and funny stories, and learn unusual lessons, during the summers they spend with their grandmother.

905

SUSANNA VANCE

Sights

(New York: Delacorte, 2001)

Subject(s): Mothers and Daughters; Self-Perception; Schools/High Schools
Age range(s): Grades 7-10
Major character(s): Baby Girl, 9th Grader, Psychic; Selda, Student—High School; Dempster, Student—High School
Time period(s): 1950s
Locale(s): Cot

Summary: Baby Girl claims she was in her mother's womb for more than eleven months and during that time she received the Sight; it's true she has the sight, it's just that sometimes her interpretation of events is a little strange. She knows her father doesn't like her, probably because she's not petite like her mother, and has tried several times to kill her. When her mother catches her father in the act, she and Baby Girl leave and drive across nine states until they reach Cot, named for its apricot product. Adored by her mother, and the classmates she left behind, Baby Girl is surprised to start school and find herself an outcast, partly because she's so large. She links up with two other outcasts, Selda and Dempster, discovers her love of music and forms a band with her two outcast friends. It takes a while for Baby Girl to sort out high school, her band friends and herself, but sort them out she does until she's back to liking herself in this first novel for young adults. (215 pages)

Where it's reviewed:
Booklist, February 15, 2001, page 1129
Horn Book, March 2001, page 214
Publishers Weekly, March 19, 2001, page 100
School Library Journal, July 2001, page 115
Voice of Youth Advocates, August 2001, page 208

Awards the book has won:
ALA Best Books for Young Adults, 2002

Other books you might like:
Cathryn Clinton, *The Calling*, 2001
  Called to the Lord when she's only twelve, Esta Lea is amazed to discover she has the gift of healing, too.
Gail Carson Levine, *The Wish*, 2000
  Wilma is granted one wish by an elderly woman and sees herself become popular, but what will happen when the school year ends?
David Lubar, *Hidden Talents*, 1999
  At the alternative school, Martin helps his roommates use their special abilities of telekinesis and precognition to stop bullies from sabotage.
Jerry Spinelli, *Stargirl*, 2000
  Stargirl rocks Mica High School when she arrives, but her naivete doesn't prepare her for the fickle roller coaster of popularity that lurks for nonconformists.

906

VIVIAN VANDE VELDE

Alison, Who Went Away

(Boston: Houghton Mifflin, 2001)

Subject(s): Sisters; Missing Persons; Family Problems
Age range(s): Grades 6-9
Major character(s): Susan/Sybil Casselman, 9th Grader; Connie Miraglia, 9th Grader; Alison Casselman, Crime Victim
Time period(s): 2000s
Locale(s): Port Champlain, New York

Summary: Interested in finding dates for an upcoming dance, a difficult proposition when one attends an all-girls school, Sybil's best friend Connie arranges for them to try out for roles in a play at a nearby all-boys school. Sybil's overprotective mother eventually grants permission and the two girls expand their pool of eligible males. Yet Sybil can never shrug off the knowledge that her rebellious sister Alison hasn't been seen in three years, not since she was arrested on a solicitation charge. The family thinks a local serial killer probably murdered her, but he dies not revealing all his victims. Therapy eventually helps the family understand that they will likely never know what happened to Alison and that they need to stop shouldering the blame as Alison was a troubled young lady. (211 pages)

Where it's reviewed:
Booklist, April 1, 2001, page 1458

Bulletin of the Center for Children's Books, April 2001, page 318
Publishers Weekly, February 5, 2001, page 89
School Library Journal, April 2001, page 151
Voice of Youth Advocates, June 2001, page 130

Other books by the same author:
Being Dead: Stories, 2001
Magic Can Be Murder, 2000
The Rumpelstiltskin Problem, 2000
There's a Dead Person Following My Sister Around, 1999
A Coming Evil, 1998

Other books you might like:
Michael Cadnum, *Zero at the Bone*, 1996
  Everyone in Cray's family is left feeling ''zero at the bone'' when his older sister Anita never returns home from work.
Robert Cormier, *Tenderness*, 1997
  When a girl he cares for accidentally drowns, a serial killer knows the police will claim he murdered her.
Meredith Daneman, *Francie and the Boys*, 1989
  When Francie's chosen to star in a play put on by a London boys' school, she's not prepared for the jealousies that arise.
Colby Rodowsky, *Remembering Mog*, 1996
  As Annie prepares to graduate, ''remembering Mog'' isn't hard to do since her older sister was shot to death in a robbery the night before her graduation.
Jean Thesman, *Calling the Swan*, 2000
  Skylar talks to her sister Alexandra all the time, even though Alexandra was kidnapped three years ago and hasn't been seen since.

907

VIVIAN VANDE VELDE

Being Dead

(San Diego: Harcourt, 2001)

Subject(s): Short Stories; Horror; Supernatural
Age range(s): Grades 7-10

Summary: The dead don't always stay dead as this collection of short stories will prove. In ''The Ghost'' several college students rent a house in which a murder took place, but leave when their belongings are unpacked, to the disappointment of a trickster ghost. The victim of a hit-and-run accident returns to remind the unaware teenage driver who hit her of what she's done. ''October Chill'' features a volunteer museum docent with a brain tumor who meets a young man from Colonial times. Four more tales will delight, shock and scare young readers. (203 pages)

Where it's reviewed:
Booklist, September 1, 2001, page 97
Bulletin of the Center for Children's Books, September 2001, page 39
Horn Book, November 2001, page 758
School Library Journal, September 2001, page 234
Voice of Youth Advocates, December 2001, page 374

Awards the book has won:
ALA Best Books for Young Adults, 2002

Other books by the same author:
Heir Apparent, 2002
Curses Inc. and Other Stories, 1997
Tales from the Brothers Grimm and the Sister Weird, 1995

Other books you might like:
Roald Dahl, *Skin and Other Stories*, 2000
   Short stories, characterized by surprise endings, make up this collection written by a magical author.
Anne Mazer, *A Sliver of Glass and Other Uncommon Tales*, 1996
   Each of these short page turners concludes with an extra twist.
Thomas McKean, *Into the Candlelight Room and Other Strange Tales*, 1999
   Five short stories, written in the form of letters, a diary entry and a college admissions essay, reveal the quirky, macabre side of people.
Michael Stearns, *A Nightmare's Dozen: Stories from the Dark*, 1996
   Fourteen psychologically horrifying tales, from such authors as Jane Yolen, Bruce Coville, Sherwood Smith and others, make up this work.

908

ANAIS VAUGELADE, Author/Illustrator
MARIE-CHRISTINE ROUFFIAC, Translator
TOM STREISSGUTH, Translator

The War

(Minneapolis, MN: Carolrhoda Books, Inc., 2001)

Subject(s): War; Princes and Princesses; Fables
Age range(s): Grades 3-5
Major character(s): Fabien, Royalty (prince); Julius, Royalty (prince)
Time period(s): Indeterminate Past
Locale(s): Fictional Country

Summary: Two armies fight daily for so many years that no one remembers how or why the war between the Blue and the Red began. With the size of the armies dwindling Prince Julius, of the Reds, challenges Prince Fabien, of the Blues, to a duel to settle the war once and for all. Prince Fabien doesn't think much of war and doesn't really like to ride a horse so he appears on the battlefield astride a sheep. The bleating sheep startles Prince Julius's horse so that it rears and the Prince falls off, strikes his head and dies. The Red king is angry with Prince Fabien for cheating and Fabien's father is angry because he did nothing. Banished from his home, Prince Fabien fashions a plan that tricks the Red and Blue kings into cooperating to assure their survival while he goes off to live peacefully in the Yellow kingdom. Originally published in France in 1998. (32 pages)

Where it's reviewed:
Booklist, March 15, 2001, page 1399
Bulletin of the Center for Children's Books, April 2001, page 318
Horn Book, March 2001, page 204
Publishers Weekly, February 5, 2001, page 87
School Library Journal, April 2001, page 124

Awards the book has won:
IRA Children's Choices, 2002
Notable Social Studies Trade Books for Young People, 2002

Other books you might like:
Isabel Pin, *The Seed*, 2001
   As two insect tribes prepare to battle for ownership of a cherry seed wedged on the boundary between their lands, a tree grows providing fruit for all.
Dr. Seuss, *The Butter Battle Book*, 1984
   The stupidity of war is obvious as Zooks and Yooks take sides against each other because of the different way in which each group butters bread.
Priscilla Turner, *The War Between the Vowels and the Consonants*, 1996
   The Vowels and Consonants stop fighting when they realize what they can accomplish by cooperating.
Jean Van Leeuwen, *Sorry*, 2001
   A feud between two brothers continues through many generations until no one can remember how it began or why it continues.

909

MARCIA VAUGHAN
ANN SCHWENINGER, Illustrator

We're Going on a Ghost Hunt

(San Diego: Silver Whistle/Harcourt, Inc., 2001)

Subject(s): Halloween; Ghosts; Stories in Rhyme
Age range(s): Grades K-2
Major character(s): Unnamed Character, Child, Sister; Unnamed Character, Child, Brother
Time period(s): 2000s (2001)
Locale(s): United States

Summary: Accompanied by a little dog, two trick-or-treaters search for a ghost. They go past a haunted house and over a muddy swamp, feeling no fear, none at all. Bravely they scurry past bats, run past skeleton bones and crawl slowly through a cave. When they come face to face with a big, white, swirly ghost-like creature they hurriedly retrace their steps and scamper into the house where their mother is waiting to read them a story. (32 pages)

Where it's reviewed:
Booklist, September 15, 2001, page 237
Horn Book Guide, Spring 2002, page 30
Publishers Weekly, September 24, 2001, page 42
School Library Journal, September 2001, page 207

Other books by the same author:
Snap!, 1996
The Dancing Dragon, 1996
Whistling Dixie, 1995 (ALA Notable Book)

Other books you might like:
Nancy White Carlstrom, *What a Scare, Jessie Bear*, 1999
   Participating in Halloween is fun, but also a little scary for Jessie Bear.
Sam McBratney, *The Dark at the Top of the Stairs*, 1996
   Three young mice climb the stairs to see what lurks in the dark at the top.

Michael Rosen, *We're Going on a Bear Hunt*, 1989
Bravely a group sets off in search of a bear until, arriving at their goal, they hurriedly retreat.

910

ERIC VELASQUEZ, Author/Illustrator

Grandma's Records
(New York: Walker & Company, 2001)

Subject(s): Grandmothers; Music and Musicians; Puerto Rican Americans
Age range(s): Grades 1-3
Major character(s): Grandma, Grandmother; Daisy, Dog; Unnamed Character, Child
Time period(s): Indeterminate Past
Locale(s): New York, New York (Spanish Harlem)

Summary: With Daisy and a suitcase full of summer clothes a young boy with two working parents goes to live with Grandma every summer as soon as school ends. Grandma's collection of records keeps their days filled with music; the album covers inspire the boy's art. When Grandma's nephew and his band from Puerto Rico come to New York to perform they visit Grandma and give her two tickets for their concert. Hearing the music performed live is an exciting new experience that inspires the boy and Grandma to create music shows right in Grandma's apartment. The first book also written by this children's book illustrator is based on childhood memories. (32 pages)

Where it's reviewed:
Booklist, May 15, 2001, page 1761
Horn Book Guide, Fall 2001, page 279
Kirkus Reviews, April 15, 2001, page 594
Publishers Weekly, May 7, 2001, page 246
School Library Journal, September 2001, page 207

Other books you might like:
Mark Karlins, *Music over Manhattan*, 1998
With instructions from Uncle Louie, Bernie learns to play the trumpet so well that the music floats over Manhattan.
Eileen Kurtis-Kleinman, *When Aunt Lena Did the Rhumba*, 1997
Weekly, when Aunt Lena arrives home from the matinee, she shows Sophie the highlights of the musical she's just seen.
Vera B. Williams, *Music, Music for Everyone*, 1984
While Grandma is ill and confined to bed Rosa and her friends make music to cheer her.

911

TJIBBE VELDKAMP
PHILIP HOPMAN, Illustrator

The School Trip
(Asheville, NC: Front Street Books, Inc., 2001)

Subject(s): Schools; Problem Solving; Individuality
Age range(s): Grades 1-3
Major character(s): Davy, Student—Elementary School, Son
Time period(s): Indeterminate

Locale(s): Europe

Summary: Reports of bullies, homework and strict teachers have Davy a bit apprehensive about his first day of school. The day goes well though after all because Davy builds his own school with scraps that he finds. The next day Davy adds wheels to his structure so he can "go far" in school as his mother suggests. Davy's school rolls down the hill and goes farther than he planned by crashing into the actual school he's supposed to be attending. At recess the other students are so interested in Davy's mobile school that they quietly attach the wheels to their school and roll it away. Originally published in the Netherlands in 2000. (32 pages)

Where it's reviewed:
Booklist, August 2001, page 2133
Horn Book Guide, Fall 2001, page 279
School Library Journal, July 2001, page 90

Other books by the same author:
22 Orphans, 1998 (Silver Brush Award)

Other books you might like:
Marsha Wilson Chall, *Bonaparte*, 2000
Jean Claude runs away from his new boarding school to find his pet Bonaparte not knowing that the dog searches for him at the Paris school.
Nancy Bo Flood, *I'll Go to School If . . .* , 1997
A frightened little boy offers conditions under which he will go to school for the first time, but his practical mom suggests alternatives.
Vera Rosenberry, *Vera's First Day of School*, 1999
Vera's initial eagerness to enter school fades at the sight of it and she returns home to hide under the bed; her mother walks back to class with her.

ROSS VENOKUR

The Autobiography of Meatball Finkelstein
(New York: Delacorte, 2001)

Subject(s): Humor; Weight Control; Magic
Age range(s): Grades 4-8
Major character(s): Meatball Finkelstein, 13-Year-Old; Precious Finkelstein, 15-Year-Old, Sister (of Meatball); Rufus Delaney, Bully
Time period(s): 2000s
Locale(s): United States

Summary: When Meatball was born, he weighed 27 pounds and 4 ounces. His two-year-old sister Precious took one look at him and said her first word, "Meatball." Meatball has been a big boy ever since and, coupling his first name with the fact that he's a vegetarian, makes him the perfect target for Rufus, the school bully. One day in the cafeteria, to defy Rufus, Meatball swallows a meatball, which unleashes a freak tornado. Realizing that one taste of meat has given him secret powers to change into other creatures or objects, Meatball has to be careful not to be exploited by his principal in this madcap comedy. (154 pages)

Where it's reviewed:
Bulletin of the Center for Children's Books, September 2001, page 39

School Library Journal, August 2001, page 190

Other books by the same author:
The Cookie Company, 2000
The Amazing Frecktacle, 1998

Other books you might like:
Steven Cousins, *Frankenbug*, 2001
Fed up with Jeb's teasing about his insects, Adam creates "Frankenbug," brings it to life with fireflies and uses "Frankie" to scare Jeb.
Betsy Gould Hearne, *Wishes, Kisses, and Pigs*, 2001
Wishing on a star, Louise's brother somehow turns into a white pig with blue eyes.
Laurence Yep, *Cockroach Cooties*, 2000
When Bobby finds out the bully who bothers his brother is scared of roaches, he borrows a large one from an entomologist.

913

JUDITH VIORST
ROBIN PREISS GLASSER, Illustrator

Super-Completely and Totally the Messiest
(New York: Atheneum Books for Young Readers, 2001)

Subject(s): Cleanliness; Sisters; Individuality
Age range(s): Grades 1-4
Major character(s): Olivia, Sister (older), Narrator; Sophie, Sister (younger); Jake, Brother
Time period(s): 2000s (2001)
Locale(s): United States

Summary: Olivia cannot understand it. Despite the stunning example of neatness she, the big sister, offers, Sophie is absolutely the clumsiest, messiest person in the world. She's even worse than Jake who's only somewhat sloppy. The creative clutter of Sophie's room completely hides her at times especially if she opens her closet door. Sophie's not just messy at home, she's messy everywhere. Sophie can destroy a wrapped birthday gift (and her pretty dress) while walking to the party or demolish seven sandcastles simply walking on the beach with her bucket and towel. And her hair . . . well, you get the picture. For all that, Olivia does conclude Sophie has some admirable qualities and she is trying to improve. (32 pages)

Where it's reviewed:
Booklist, February 2, 2001, page 1058
Bulletin of the Center for Children's Books, June 2001, page 389
Publishers Weekly, January 22, 2001, page 323
School Library Journal, March 2001, page 224
Teacher Librarian, June 2001, page 44

Other books by the same author:
Alexander, Who's Not (Do You Hear Me? I Mean It!) Going to Move, 1995
The Good-Bye Book, 1988
Alexander, Who Used to Be Rich Last Sunday, 1978

Other books you might like:
Mem Fox, *Harriet, You'll Drive Me Wild!*, 2000
Quite unintentionally, or so she says, Harriet is at the center of an escalating series of messes that frustrate her patient mother.
Phyllis Reynolds Naylor, *I Can't Take You Anywhere!*, 1997
Clumsy Amy Audrey seems to inadvertently create disaster wherever she goes.
Elise Petersen, *Tracy's Mess*, 1995
Tracy appears to be fastidious but wait until you see what's behind her bedroom door!

914

FRANS VISCHER, Author/Illustrator

Jimmy Dabble
(New York: Dutton Children's Books, 2001)

Subject(s): Parent and Child; Fantasy; Farm Life
Age range(s): Grades 3-5
Major character(s): Jimmy Dabble, Son, Animal Lover; Maggie Dabble, Mother, Housewife; Hank Dabble, Father, Farmer; Oma, Grandmother, Traveler
Time period(s): Indeterminate
Locale(s): Fictional Country

Summary: Just before Jimmy's ninth birthday Oma arrives for an extended visit. Frugal Mr. and Mrs. Dabble have not informed Oma that she has a grandson and she's excited to greet the shy boy. Once Jimmy recovers from the shock of this outgoing, exuberant person who is so very different from his drab, serious parents he learns there is more to life than work. Oma introduces Jimmy to fantasy literature, encourages his exploration of the nearby woods, and seems quite understanding of his ability to converse with the farm animals. The changes in Jimmy cause his parents to become even stricter and their actions inadvertently lead to problems that cause greater financial hardship. When it appears they may lose the farm, Jimmy puts his newly discovered imagination and his gift with animals to good use and raises enough money to save the day in the author's first book. (151 pages)

Where it's reviewed:
Horn Book Guide, Spring 2002, page 79
Kirkus Reviews, June 1, 2001, page 807
Publishers Weekly, July 9, 2001, page 68
School Library Journal, August 2001, page 164

Other books you might like:
Roald Dahl, *Charlie and the Chocolate Factory*, 1963
Charlie's dreary, impoverished life changes dramatically when he wins the opportunity to tour Willa Wonka's factory.
Susie Morgenstern, *Secret Letters from 0 to 10*, 1998
Ernest's sheltered, monotonous life with Grandmother opens to new possibilities when outgoing Victoria joins his class and becomes his friend.
E.B. White, *Charlotte's Web*, 1952
The runt pig that Fern rescues becomes Charlotte's best friend in the barnyard; Charlotte uses her talents to save Wilbur's life.

W

915

BERNARD WABER, Author/Illustrator

Fast Food! Gulp! Gulp!

(Boston: Walter Lorraine Books/Houghton Mifflin Company, 2001)

Subject(s): Food; Restaurants; Stories in Rhyme
Age range(s): Grades K-2
Major character(s): Colonel Mane, Lion, Restaurateur; Cook, Pig, Cook
Time period(s): Indeterminate
Locale(s): Fast Food Town, Fictional Country

Summary: Colonel Mane encourages speed in his chain of fast food restaurants. He wants the food prepared rapidly and eaten quickly. The kitchen crew includes a cook, a chopper, a wrapper, a server, and someone to take phone orders. Colonel Mane's system works efficiently until Cook becomes fed up with the pace and walks out to start her own restaurant, a quiet, slow-paced vegetarian establishment. (32 pages)

Where it's reviewed:
Publishers Weekly, October 15, 2001, page 70
School Library Journal, September 2001, page 208
Smithsonian, November 2001, page 120

Awards the book has won:
Smithsonian's Notable Books for Children, 2001

Other books by the same author:
The Mouse that Snored, 2000
Lyle at Christmas, 1998
A Lion Named Shirley Williamson, 1996

Other books you might like:
Jim Aylesworth, *The Burger and the Hot Dog*, 2001
Twenty-three humorous poems describe the behavior of food items after the restaurant closes for the night.
Stephanie Calmenson, *Dinner at the Panda Palace*, 1991
A story in rhyme describes a restaurant so crowded that Mr. Panda finds innovative ways of seating his many patrons.
Maggie S. Davis, *The Rinky-Dink Cafe*, 1988
Hungry Pig takes a restaurant's advertisement "Dinners Made to Order" to heart and stomach and keeps the cook hopping.
Toby Speed, *Brave Potatoes*, 2000
Potatoes bravely foil Chef Hackemup's plans to add vegetables to the pot of chowder brewing on the stove.

916

MARTIN WADDELL
DAVID PARKINS, Illustrator

Webster J. Duck

(Cambridge, MA: Candlewick Press, 2001)

Subject(s): Animals/Ducks; Animals; Mothers and Sons
Age range(s): Preschool-Grade 1
Major character(s): Webster J. Duck, Duck, Son; Mother Duck, Duck, Mother
Time period(s): Indeterminate
Locale(s): Fictional Country

Summary: The moment Webster J. Duck emerges from his egg he begins looking for his mother. When he questions the dog he knows from the barking response that cannot be his mother. The same logic applies to the sheep and the cow. Poor motherless Webster sits and cries as the three animals call loudly in their own voices in hopes of attracting his mother's attention. They succeed only in frightening the little duck whose quiet quacking finally elicits a loud quacking response and Mother Duck appears. (28 pages)

Where it's reviewed:
Booklist, November 15, 2001, page 584
Horn Book Guide, Spring 2002, page 30
Kirkus Reviews, August 1, 2001, page 1134
Publishers Weekly, June 18, 2001, page 80
School Library Journal, July 2001, page 90

Other books by the same author:
Good Job, Little Bear, 1999 (IRA Children's Choice)
Who Do You Love?, 1999
Yum, Yum, Yummy!, 1998

Other books you might like:

Frank Asch, *Baby Duck's New Friend*, 2001
Baby Duck befriends a rubber duck and follows it so far from home that he wonders how he'll find his mama.

P.D. Eastman, *Are You My Mother?*, 1960
A lost baby bird questions many different animals while searching for its mother.

Keiko Kasza, *A Mother for Choco*, 1992
A bear adopts a young bird that is searching for its mother.

LEA WAIT

Stopping to Home

(New York: Simon & Schuster/Margaret McElderry Books, 2001)

Subject(s): Orphans; Brothers and Sisters; Widows/Widowers
Age range(s): Grades 4-6
Major character(s): Abigail "Abbie" Chambers, 11-Year-Old; Seth Chambers, Brother (of Abbie), Child; Lydia Chase, Widow(er)
Time period(s): 1800s (1806)
Locale(s): Wiscasset, Maine

Summary: With her mother dead of smallpox and her seldom-seen father at sea somewhere, Abbie is determined to keep her young brother Seth out of the orphanage. Going to work for Mrs. Chase, Abbie exchanges housemaid duties for room and board and feels content until Captain Chase also dies of smallpox and Mrs. Chase's financial situation changes. When Abbie realizes Mrs. Chase is pregnant, she resolves to help her begin a millinery business so they can remain together as a family in this first novel. (152 pages)

Where it's reviewed:

Booklist, November 15, 2001, page 567
Bulletin of the Center for Children's Books, December 2001, page 154
Horn Book, January 2001, page 85
Publishers Weekly, November 5, 2001, page 69
School Library Journal, October 2001, page 174

Other books by the same author:

Shadows at the Fair: An Antique Print Mystery, 2002

Other books you might like:

Kristiana Gregory, *Orphan Runaways*, 1998
Miserable in the orphanage, Danny and Judd run away in search of their gold miner uncle.

Jim Murphy, *My Face to the Wind: The Diary of Sarah Jane Price, a Prairie Teacher, Broken Bow, Nebraska, 1881*, 2001
After her father dies, Sarah is left alone at Miss Kizer's boarding house until she decides to ask to replace him as the town's schoolteacher.

Zilpha Keatley Snyder, *Gib Rides Home*, 1998
For young Gib, a chance to leave the orphanage and work on Mr. Thornton's ranch is the next best thing to being adopted.

PAMELA WALKER

Pray Hard

(New York: Scholastic, 2001)

Subject(s): Spirituality; Grief; Fathers
Age range(s): Grades 5-8
Major character(s): Amelia Forrest, 12-Year-Old; J.E. "Brother Mustard Seed" Abernathy, Convict
Time period(s): 2000s
Locale(s): Kentucky

Summary: In the year following her father's plane crash while he was on a missionary run, Amelia's certain her popper toy, which she hid in the plane, caused the accident. Amelia's father was a crop duster pilot who also visited prisons as part of his Baptist missionary responsibility. At the moment there's a strange man on Amelia's doorstep claiming to be Brother Mustard Seed, saved by her father Jed while serving time in prison, who has had a vision of her father. Oh, Amelia can hardly wait for her mother to return from the beauty parlor, but when her mother returns, she welcomes Brother Mustard Seed and invites him to stay so they can both cry away their sadness. Though Amelia doesn't want to admit it, it's thanks to Brother Mustard Seed that she and her mother learn to cope with their grief. Best of all is the knowledge that her green popper toy wasn't even in the plane when it crashed in this offbeat first novel. (172 pages)

Where it's reviewed:

Book Report, May 2001, page 62
Booklist, March 1, 2001, page 1283
Publishers Weekly, April 9, 2001, page 75
School Library Journal, July 2001, page 115
Voice of Youth Advocates, August 2001, page 208

Other books you might like:

Cathryn Clinton, *The Calling*, 2001
Called to the Lord when she's only twelve, Esta Lea is amazed to discover she has the gift of healing, too.

Han Nolan, *Send Me Down a Miracle*, 1996
Astonishment floods Charity when artist Adrienne emerges from her home after several weeks of confinement and announces that she's visited with Jesus.

Gary Paulsen, *The Tent*, 1995
Corey feels guilty as he watches his father con people out of their money in his new character of traveling preacher.

919

BARBARA BROOKS WALLACE

Secret in St. Something

(New York: Atheneum/Simon & Schuster)

Subject(s): Brothers; Poverty; Homeless People
Age range(s): Grades 5-8
Major character(s): Robin, 11-Year-Old, Streetperson; Danny, Baby; Hawker Doak, Stepfather
Time period(s): 1890s
Locale(s): New York, New York

Summary: With his mother and father both dead, Robin and his younger brother Danny are at the mercy of their cruel stepfather who beats and abuses Robin at the slightest provocation. Hawker now threatens Robin with factory work and plans to send Danny to a "baby farm," which propels Robin into action. That night he grabs his little brother and runs away, planning to leave Danny on the steps of a church where some rich family will find and adopt him. Stumbling into the basement of the church "St. Something" to stay for the night, Robin tumbles into the lair of a group of street boys who were all brought up in large families and display a great deal of knowledge about tending babies. With the help of these well meaning but poor lads, Robin manages to earn enough money to survive in this tale that has a storybook ending. (149 pages)

Where it's reviewed:
Booklist, May 15, 2001, page 1754
Bulletin of the Center for Children's Books, October 2001, page 80
Horn Book, September 2001, page 597
Kirkus Reviews, May 15, 2001, page 747
School Library Journal, July 2001, page 116

Other books by the same author:
Peppermints in the Palace, 2002
Ghosts in the Gallery, 2000
Cousins in the Castle, 1996
Sparrows in the Scullery, 1996
The Twin in the Tavern, 1993

Other books you might like:
Chester Aaron, *Lackawanna*, 1986
   During the Depression, six youngsters band together as a family, scrounging and panhandling to support themselves.
Isabelle Holland, *Paperboy*, 1999
   Caught stealing a paper, once Kevin proves he can read the news he's hired on as a messenger by the newspaper's publisher and begins his journalism career.
Brooks McNamara, *The Merry Muldoons and the Brighteyes Affair*, 1992
   Forced to burgle a home, the Muldoons vaudeville team winds up with the diamonds and runs away from New York City to escape the criminal Brighteyes.

920

ALICE WALSH
GEOFF BUTLER, Illustrator

Heroes of Isle Aux Morts
(Plattsburgh, NY: Tundra Books, 2001)

Subject(s): Animals/Dogs; Shipwrecks; Historical
Age range(s): Grades 2-5
Major character(s): Anne Harvey, Daughter, Rescuer; Hairy Man, Dog (Newfoundland), Rescuer
Time period(s): 1830s (1832)
Locale(s): Isle aux Morts, Newfoundland, Canada

Summary: On a stormy morning Anne sees the flares from a ship run aground in the rough seas. Quickly she wakens her father and brother and they launch the dory, struggling through the waves toward the foundering ship. When they are as close as they can safely get they send Hairy Man swimming to the ship with a rope. Hairy Man returns to the dory with another rope that they row to shore and tie to a pole. A breeches buoy is set up and all the passengers and crew are safely removed from the ship. (32 pages)

Where it's reviewed:
Booklist, June 2001, page 1897
Bulletin of the Center for Children's Books, April 2001, page 320
Horn Book Guide, Fall 2001, page 297
Quill & Quire, March 2001, page 58
School Library Journal, October 2001, page 133

Other books by the same author:
Uncle Farley's Teeth, 1998

Other books you might like:
Odds Bodkin, *Ghost of the Southern Belle: A Sea Tale*, 1999
   After the *Southern Belle* sinks without a trace during a nor'easter she returns to haunt other schooners that she races to their doom.
Betsy Byars, *My Dog, My Hero*, 2000
   Eight stories describing the heroic efforts of dogs include one about a Newfoundland that jumps into an icy river to save another dog.
Wolfram Hanel, *Rescue at Sea!*, 1999
   The crew of a foundering fishing boat make it safely to shore but their dog is still aboard and Paul decides to save it.

921

ELLEN STOLL WALSH, Author/Illustrator

Dot & Jabber and the Great Acorn Mystery
(San Diego: Harcourt, Inc., 2001)

Subject(s): Animals/Mice; Trees; Nature
Age range(s): Grades K-2
Major character(s): Dot, Mouse, Detective; Jabber, Mouse, Detective
Time period(s): Indeterminate
Locale(s): Fictional Country

Summary: Dot and Jabber consider themselves detectives and the mystery Dot decides to solve is how an oak tree came to be growing where it is. There is no mature oak tree in sight yet somehow an acorn made its way to this spot and a tree is now growing. First Dot and Jabber locate the big oak tree and then they hypothesize how the acorn could travel so far. Jabber wants to eat the acorns under the big tree but Dot says they're clues to be inspected for wings or feet. When a squirrel comes and steals a clue the intrepid detectives follow and discover that the squirrel buries the acorn. Mystery solved! Jabber returns to eat the leftover clues while Dot searches for the next mystery. (40 pages)

Where it's reviewed:
Booklist, October 1, 2001, page 330
Horn Book Guide, Spring 2002, page 30
Kirkus Reviews, June 15, 2001, page 873
Publishers Weekly, September 3, 2001, page 87
School Library Journal, September 2001, page 208

Other books by the same author:
Mouse Magic, 2000
Samantha, 1996
Pip's Magic, 1994

Other books you might like:
Jim Arnosky, *Crinkleroot's Guide to Knowing the Trees*, 1991
> A nonfiction title describes how to identify trees and how animals use trees for shelter and food.
Eve Bunting, *Someday a Tree*, 1993
> Alice is grateful that she saved acorns from the ancient oak tree that's been killed by illegally dumped chemicals.
Gerda Muller, *Around the Oak*, 1994
> When Ben and Caroline visit their uncle, a forest ranger, their adventures provide opportunities for learning more about the forest.

922

JO WALTON

The King's Name
(New York: Tor, 2001)

Subject(s): Arthurian Legends; Politics
Age range(s): Grades 11-Adult
Major character(s): Sulien ap Gwien, Military Personnel; Urdo, Royalty (king)
Time period(s): Indeterminate Past
Locale(s): Tir Tanagiri, Fictional Country

Summary: Sulien inherits her family's property so, as custom dictates, she withdraws from Urdo's court to manage it. Urdo has established a peace which holds across the land, but the deeds of the past are slowly surfacing to threaten it. Becoming aware of this when her own sister attempts to poison her, Sulien finds a web of treachery stretching across the entire country and encompassing many of her former comrades. Letters are intercepted and lost, meanings are twisted, and once-soothed old wounds become active grievances. Sulien rushes to the site of a projected invasion where an old friend lands an army to march against Urdo's peace. Though in time to avert disaster, she's not in time to prevent the demise of peace in this sequel to *The King's Peace*. (304 pages)

Where it's reviewed:
Booklist, October 15, 2001, page 388
Publishers Weekly, November 12, 2001, page 46

Other books by the same author:
The King's Peace, 2000

Other books you might like:
Marion Zimmer Bradley, *The Mists of Avalon*, 1982
> The sorceress Morgan, Arthur's sister, tells the story of his rise and fall from her perspective.
Mary Gentle, *The Books of Ash Series*, 1999-2000
> In this alternate history world Ash is a fierce Joan of Arc, who leads her men against the English, the Germans, and a magical darkness.
Jack Whyte, *The Singing Sword*, 1999
> Whyte's Arthurian saga shares the strong Roman influence that is such a part of *The King's Name*.

923

JO WALTON

The King's Peace
(New York: Tor, 2000)

Subject(s): Arthurian Legends; War
Age range(s): Grades 11-Adult
Major character(s): Sulien ap Gwien, Military Personnel; Urdo, Royalty (king)
Time period(s): Indeterminate Past
Locale(s): Tir Tanagiri, Fictional Country

Summary: Sulien is raised as a warrior and preserver of the civilization of the past. As she reaches womanhood, an attack on her family's holdings leads to her brother's death and Sulien's rape. In a fury, Sulien goes for help and winds up in another battle that allows her to prove herself and join Urdo's troops. Urdo is the Arthur of this world, battling the disintegration of civilization, fighting for peace and justice, yet doomed by fate. Sulien joins her fate to his and becomes indispensable to his military victories. (416 pages)

Where it's reviewed:
Booklist, October 1, 2000, page 327
Kirkus Reviews, September 1, 2000, page 1241
Library Journal, October 15, 2000, page 108
Magazine of Fantasy and Science Fiction, January 2001, page 29
Publishers Weekly, October 2, 2000, page 65

Other books by the same author:
The King's Name, 2001

Other books you might like:
Catherine Christian, *The Pendragon*, 1978
> The remnants of Roman culture in Britain band together to drive out the Saxon invaders.
Stephen R. Lawhead, *The Pendragon Cycle*, 1987-1997
> A retelling of the Arthurian myth with Arthur and Merlin as the principle characters.
Jack Whyte, *The Skystone*, 1996
> In post-Roman Britain, a sword is forged from the mysterious metal of a stone that has fallen from the sky.

924

HELEN WARD
WAYNE ANDERSON, Illustrator

The Tin Forest
(New York: Dutton Children's Books, 2001)

Subject(s): Ecology; Fantasy; Recycling (Waste)
Age range(s): Grades 1-3
Major character(s): Unnamed Character, Aged Person
Time period(s): Indeterminate
Locale(s): Fictional Country

Summary: An old man living in a barren wasteland littered with scraps of metal and assorted discards tries to clear away and organize the junk near his home but his efforts seem futile. He dreams nightly of a beautiful forest filled with animals, birds and flowers but nothing changes until he has the idea to fashion his dream out of scrap metal. The tin forest grows and in it he perches tin birds, frogs, lizards and cats. After the forest is complete the wind blows a real bird into it for a brief stay. The bird returns with a mate and each carries seeds in their beaks. The old man tends the seeds, plants grow, flowers bloom and soon the man's dream comes true as the drab tin forest is overtaken by real, colorful vegetation and wildlife. (36 pages)

Where it's reviewed:
Booklist, September 15, 2001, page 233
Bulletin of the Center for Children's Books, September 2001, page 38
Kirkus Reviews, August 1, 2001, page 1134
Publishers Weekly, August 27, 2001, page 84
School Library Journal, October 2001, page 133

Other books by the same author:
The King of the Birds, 1997
The Golden Pear, 1991
The Moonrat and the White Turtle, 1990

Other books you might like:
Lady Borton, *Junk Pile!*, 1997
    Creative Jamie uses discards from her father's junkyard to fashion "flower" arrangements in her yard.
Holly Keller, *Grandfather's Dream*, 1994
    Grandfather's dream is to see the wetlands restored to their prewar condition so the Sarus cranes can return to their habitat.
Dr. Seuss, *The Lorax*, 1971
    The Lorax sadly recounts the environmental changes that come with "progress."
Andrea Zimmerman, *Trashy Town*, 1999
    Mr. Gilly goes through his day as a trash collector.

SALLY WARNER

Bad Girl Blues
(New York: HarperCollins, 2001)

Subject(s): Friendship; School Life; Animals, Treatment of
Age range(s): Grades 5-8
Major character(s): Mary McQuinn "Quinney" Todd, 6th Grader, 12-Year-Old; Marguerite Harper, 6th Grader; Brynn "Brynnie", 6th Grader
Time period(s): 2000s
Locale(s): Lake Geneva, New York

Summary: Best friends since they were little, Quinney realizes she is growing apart from Marguerite and Brynnie, all of whom are finding different interests and different friends. Quinney's thrilled that a shelter for stray animals is opening and can hardly wait to volunteer, though neither Brynnie nor Marguerite would enjoy that. Marguerite is the one who's trying to grow up the fastest and even though the school year's only a week old, she's already cut school to go riding with some drunk high school kids and has been in an accident. Marguerite's attitude after the accident makes Quinney realize how difficult it is to be a friend with her, but then Quinney's mother invites her to move in with them. Yikes! What should Quinney do in this sequel to *Totally Confidential*. (212 pages)

Where it's reviewed:
Booklist, July 2001, page 2007
Kirkus Reviews, May 1, 2001, page 669
Publishers Weekly, June 25, 2001, page 74
School Library Journal, July 2001, page 116
Voice of Youth Advocates, October 2001, page 285

Other books by the same author:
Finding Hattie, 2001
Sister Split, 2001
Totally Confidential, 2000
Sort of Forever, 1998
Some Friend, 1996

Other books you might like:
Paula Danziger, *Snail Mail No More*, 2000
    When Tara moves away, she and Elizabeth correspond by e-mail and find it's easy to stay in touch, though not necessarily easy to stay friends.
Amy Goldman Koss, *The Girls*, 2000
    A group of five friends reduces itself to four as leader Candace decides Maya is out of the clique.
Laura Peyton Roberts, *Get a Life*, 1998
    In this inspirational series, eight students at Clearwater Crossing High School form a small club that specializes in community service.
Rachel Vail, *The Friendship Ring Series*, 1991-1998
    Friends learn that growing up can be tough, even when it's just choosing ballet or a social life, wanting a best friend or learning to be yourself.

SALLY WARNER

Finding Hattie
(New York: HarperCollins, 2001)

Subject(s): Cousins; Orphans; Schools/Boarding Schools
Age range(s): Grades 6-9
Major character(s): Harriet "Hattie" Knowlton, Orphan; Sophia "Sophie" Hubbard, Cousin (of Hattie); Charles "Charley" Hubbard, Uncle (of Hattie); Margaret Hubbard, Aunt (of Hattie); Minnie Bonsteel, Student; Fannie Macintosh, Student
Time period(s): 1880s
Locale(s): New York, New York; Tarrytown, New York

Summary: After everyone in her immediate family dies, Hattie moves in with her wealthy Aunt Margaret, Uncle Charley and Cousin Sophie. Not raised with the same degree of riches, Hattie's often intimidated by the formality that wealth seems to demand in the Hubbard's home. When school begins in the fall, she follows Sophie to Miss Bulkley's Seminary for Young Ladies where her cousin and her "Quartette" of friends make an effort to include Hattie in their activities. Though Hattie does feel like the "poor relative," the Quartette never speaks of her financial situation, and it's only Minnie who loves to jab at Hattie whenever she can. When Fannie arrives at school, bringing her Western ways with her, Hattie is relieved that there's another outcast and doesn't reach out to befriend Fannie right away for fear of offending the Quartette. Hattie finally learns that she needs to follow her own inclinations when dealing with people in this work based on the author's great-grandmother. (227 pages)

Where it's reviewed:
Booklist, February 1, 2001, page 1054
Bulletin of the Center for Children's Books, June 2001, page 390
Horn Book, May 2001, page 338
Publishers Weekly, January 1, 2001, page 93
Voice of Youth Advocates, August 2001, page 209

Other books by the same author:
This Isn't about the Money, 2002
Sister Split, 2001 (American Girl Fiction)
Totally Confidential, 2000
Sort of Forever, 1998
Ellie & the Bunheads, 1997

Other books you might like:
Michelle Magorian, *Back Home*, 1984
    Returning to England after evacuation to American during World War II, Rusty has a hard time adjusting to boarding school life.
Ann Rinaldi, *The Staircase*, 2000
    Lizzy's not prepared for the cruel treatment she receives when she attends the boarding school run by the Sisters of Loretto in Santa Fe.
Erika Tamar, *The Midnight Train Home*, 2000
    Entrusted to the Children's Aid Society, Deirdre dislikes her new family and joins a vaudeville troupe whose members easily become like her own kin.

927

SALLY WARNER

How to Be a Real Person (in Just One Day)
(New York: Knopf/Borzoi, 2001)

Subject(s): Mothers and Daughters; Mental Illness; Family Problems
Age range(s): Grades 5-8
Major character(s): Kara Biggs, 6th Grader; Stephanie Miller, 6th Grader, Friend (of Kara); Mr. Benito, Teacher
Time period(s): 2000s
Locale(s): Pasadena, California

Summary: When her mother takes her medication, she can be a lot of fun, but since Kara's dad moved a few hours away to take a new job, her mother's stayed in her bedroom and Kara's barely holding everything together. Not wanting to let anyone know about her mother's demented state, for fear they'll hospitalize her, Kara lies to her friend Stephanie, her father and even her teacher Mr. Benito, but it's getting harder for Kara to maintain the facade and keep up her schoolwork. She makes lists for herself, such as "How to Survive Listening to Your Maybe-Crazy Mother" or "How to Blend In" just to endure each day while she hopes her mother will improve. *The Island of the Blue Dolphin* becomes not only her favorite book, but also her refuge as she compares her plight to that of the book's heroine. Luckily on this pivotal Thursday, her father calls the house when Kara's not home, talks to

her mother and realizes the situation; Kara's last list is "How to Glue Your Life Back Together." (123 pages)

Where it's reviewed:
Booklist, February 15, 2001, page 1139
Bulletin of the Center for Children's Books, March 2001, page 280
Publishers Weekly, January 1, 2001, page 93
School Library Journal, February 2001, page 123
Voice of Youth Advocates, August 2001, page 209

Other books by the same author:
Bad Girl Blues, 2001
Finding Hattie, 2001
Sister Split, 2001
Totally Confidential, 2000
Sort of Forever, 1998

Other books you might like:
A.E. Cannon, *Amazing Gracie*, 1991
    Gracie hopes her mother's remarriage will help her overcome depression for even Gracie doesn't know how to prevent another suicide attempt.
Terry Spencer Hesser, *Kissing Doorknobs*, 1998
    It's hard to help Tara when her behavior becomes so obsessive than it takes her thirty minutes to complete her doorknob ritual to leave her house.
Louise Plummer, *A Dance for Three*, 2000
    The roles switch for Hannah and her agoraphobic mother when Hannah discovers she's pregnant and her boyfriend abandons her.
Amy Bronwen Zemser, *Beyond the Mango Tree*, 1998
    Sarina's obsessive, overprotective mother often ties her to the mango tree to keep her from leaving the yard.

928

SALLY WARNER

Sister Split
(Middleton, WI: Pleasant Company/American Girl, 2001)

Subject(s): Sisters; Divorce
Age range(s): Grades 4-6
Major character(s): Ivy Miller, 11-Year-Old; Lacey Miller, 15-Year-Old
Time period(s): 2000s
Locale(s): United States

Summary: Ivy knows her parents haven't been happy recently, especially after her father agrees to a new job, so separation isn't unexpected, but she is shocked when her sister Lacey informs her that she's always hated her. Lacey moves in with her father and Ivy remains with her mother, but escalates the problem when she divorces Lacey; after all, if parents can do it, why can't sisters? Eventually their parents decide to just leave the two girls locked in a room until they come out hugging, a solution Ivy is glad to try. (141 pages)

Where it's reviewed:
Booklist, January 2002, page 860

Other books by the same author:
Bad Girl Blues, 2001
Finding Hattie, 2001
How to Be a Real Person (in Just One Day), 2001

Totally Confidential, 2000
Sort of Forever, 1998

Other books you might like:

Barbara Dana, *Necessary Parties*, 1987
    When his parents file for divorce, Chris Mills hires an unconventional lawyer who tries to block their action.
Anne Fine, *Alias Madame Doubtfire*, 1988
    The Hilliards are divorced, but Daniel Hilliard wears a turban and heavy makeup to secure the job as housekeeper to his children.
Mary E. Ryan, *My Sister Is Driving Me Crazy*, 1991
    Mattie decides that eighth grade will be the year she breaks free of her twin—no more identical haircuts or clothes!

SUNNY WARNER, Author/Illustrator

The Moon Quilt
(Boston: Walter Lorraine Books/Houghton Mifflin Company, 2001)

Subject(s): Quilts; Animals/Cats; Old Age
Age range(s): Grades 1-4
Major character(s): Unnamed Character, Aged Person, Artisan (quilter); Unnamed Character, Cat
Time period(s): Indeterminate Past
Locale(s): United States

Summary: On a June day an old woman dozes, dreaming of the husband who was lost at sea many years ago. At night, when she sews, she incorporates the images of her dream and the fabric of her long life into the quilt she's making. By day she plants seeds for pumpkins and flowers and tends the plants as they grow. By night as the moon wanes and grows she adds her life experiences and summer activities to the quilt. When the pumpkins ripen she makes pies for the neighborhood children and invites them to carve jack o' lanterns prior to trick or treating. After adding the children to the quilt she adds her cat and an image of herself. Now, on a full moon November night, the quilt is complete as is the full life of an old woman and her cat. (32 pages)

Where it's reviewed:
Booklist, April 15, 2001, page 1567
Horn Book Guide, Fall 2001, page 280
Kirkus Reviews, February 15, 2001, page 266
Publishers Weekly, March 12, 2001, page 91
School Library Journal, April 2001, page 124

Other books by the same author:
Madison Finds a Line, 1999
The Magic Sewing Machine, 1997

Other books you might like:
Mindy Dwyer, *Quilt of Dreams*, 2000
    After her grandmother's death, Kate completes the quilt her grandmother was working on and finds a wealth of family memories in the process.
Helen V. Griffith, *Dream Meadow*, 1994
    An elderly woman and her aged dog spend their days dreaming of youth as life slowly slips away from each of them.
Patricia Polacco, *The Keeping Quilt*, 1988
    A special quilt connects four generations of one family.

930

WENDY WAX
TODD DONEY, Illustrator

Empire Dreams
(New York: Silver Moon Press, 2000)

Series: Adventures in America
Subject(s): Depression (Economic); Jews; Indians of North America
Age range(s): Grades 4-6
Major character(s): Junie Mae Singer, 11-Year-Old; Daniel A. Hill, Indian (Mohawk)
Time period(s): 1930s
Locale(s): New York, New York (Manhattan); New York, New York (Brooklyn)

Summary: The construction of the Empire State Building is fascinating to Julie and she not only maintains a scrapbook but also slips away as often as she can to watch it being built. One day Julie discovers that her father is out of work, though not telling anyone, and she travels into Manhattan to find employment at her uncle's shirt collar factory doing piecework. While sitting in the park one afternoon working on a collar, she meets Daniel, a young Mohawk Indian, whose brother is one of the "Skywalkers" building the skyscraper. Daniel's brother falls off the Empire State Building, but plans to return to work after an anticipated year-long recovery and her father finally talks to his family about cutbacks in his architectural business in this continuing series. (91 pages)

Where it's reviewed:
Curriculum Review, November 2000, page 14
Horn Book Guide, Spring 2001, page 69
School Library Journal, March 2001, page 258

Other books you might like:
Patricia Beatty, *Sarah and Me and the Lady from the Sea*, 1989
    Marcella and her family adjust to a simpler life in their summer home on the Washington coast after their father suffers a business loss.
Barbara Corcoran, *The Sky Is Falling*, 1988
    Annah's middle-class world comes crashing down during the Depression when her father loses his banking job.
Carol Flynn Harris, *A Place for Joey*, 2001
    Joey enjoys the sights, sounds and smells of the city of Boston so he decides to drop out of school and find a job so that he can stay.

931

BETH NIXON WEAVER

Rooster
(New York: Winslow Press, 2001)

Subject(s): Drugs; Mentally Handicapped; Family Problems
Age range(s): Grades 7-10
Major character(s): Rooster Rosada, 13-Year-Old, Mentally Challenged Person; Kady Palmer, 15-Year-Old; Jon Hamilton, 12th Grader, Wealthy; Tony Rosada, 17-Year-Old
Time period(s): 1960s (1969)

Locale(s): Florida

Summary: The lure of the life of rich folks, which is in such contrast to her struggling migrant parents' orange grove, proves irresistible to Kady when she becomes infatuated with wealthy Jon. Escaping from her home whenever she can, Kady meets Jon, and his equally wealthy but arrogant friends, in their spot in the woods as they smoke pot or eat brownies enhanced with a dash of marijuana. One afternoon Rooster, a brain-damaged teenager who idolizes Kady, follows her and helps himself to the brownies. Unaware of what Rooster's done, Kady is horrified when he thinks he can fly and falls from a tree, seriously injuring himself. That act awakens Kady to the shallowness of her new "friends," the worth of her down-to-earth, loving parents and the potential of Rooster's brother Tony to be a much better match for her in this first novel. (301 pages)

Where it's reviewed:
Booklist, July 2001, page 2000
Horn Book, July 2001, page 461
Publishers Weekly, July 2, 2001, page 77
School Library Journal, June 2001, page 158
Voice of Youth Advocates, February 2002, page 441

Awards the book has won:
ALA Best Books for Young Adults, 2002

Other books you might like:
Edward Bloor, *Tangerine,* 1997
Legally blind Paul and his family move to Tangerine, Florida, where Paul plays soccer and slowly faces the truth about his brother's role in his blindness.
Gretchen Olson, *Joyride,* 1998
Jeff's country club friends seem shallow after he spends a summer picking berries with Hispanic migrant workers.
Mirjam Pressler, *Shylock's Daughter,* 2001
The desire to escape her Jewish ghetto is so strong that Jessica leaves behind her religion and her father, though she takes his savings.

932

WILL WEAVER

Memory Boy

(New York: HarperCollins, 2001)

Subject(s): Family Life; Wilderness Survival; Futuristic Fiction

Age range(s): Grades 7-10

Major character(s): Miles Arthur Newell, 16-Year-Old

Time period(s): 2000s (2006-2008)

Locale(s): Minneapolis, Minnesota; Birch Bay, Minnesota

Summary: Two years earlier volcanoes in the Cascade Mountain Range exploded, hurling lava, debris and ash up into the air. Tired of enduring the falling ash, exorbitant prices, looting and general chaos that followed, Miles's family decides to leave the urban area of Minneapolis. The Newells recycle their boat and their bicycles to construct a "land boat" and head north to live in their lakefront cabin, but upon arriving discover the sheriff is allowing two other families to live there. Unsure of where to go next, Miles remembers an oral history project and the kindly old man he interviewed who

used to have a cabin in these woods. Recalling the other woodland lore he was told, Miles and his family put the instructions to use as they hunt, fish and gather plants in order to survive in this tale of the future. (152 pages)

Where it's reviewed:
Book Report, November 2001, page 67
Booklist, February 1, 2001, page 1046
Publishers Weekly, January 22, 2001, page 325
School Library Journal, June 2001, page 158
Voice of Youth Advocates, August 2001, page 218

Other books by the same author:
Hard Ball, 1998
Farm Team, 1995
Striking Out, 1993

Other books you might like:
Gary L. Blackwood, *The Dying Sun,* 1989
James and his family homestead in frigid, sparsely populated Missouri as the United States is in the grip of a new Ice Age.
Caroline Macdonald, *The Lake at the End of the World,* 1989
In 2025, Diana and her parents fear they are the only inhabitants left on Earth, until Diana discovers an unusual underground cult.
Johann D. Wyss, *The Swiss Family Robinson,* 1814
A much-loved classic about a family that uses all its ingenuity to survive after being shipwrecked on an island.

933

SARAH WEEKS

My Guy

(New York: Laura Geringer/HarperCollins, 2001)

Subject(s): Parent and Child; Remarriage; Humor

Age range(s): Grades 4-7

Major character(s): Guy Strang, 13-Year-Old; Lana Zuckerman, 13-Year-Old; Buzz Adams, 13-Year-Old; Jerry Zuckerman, Musician (piccolo player), Clown; Lorraine Strang, Mother (of Guy), Single Parent

Time period(s): 2000s

Locale(s): Cedar Springs, New Jersey

Summary: Guy can't believe his mother plans to marry Jerry Zuckerman, father of Lana, Guy's enemy since kindergarten when she called him "Girlie Guy" because of the pink mittens he wore. Luckily, Lana's just as upset as Guy is, and the two declare a truce while they plan their battle strategy to halt this marriage. Lana, Guy and his best friend Buzz design a dreadful dinner party for the two lovebirds which has its desired effect, though Guy's now left with a despondent mother which might be worse than having Lana as a stepsister. It's all pretty wild and crazy as the two parents eventually get back together and Guy and Lana learn to tolerate one another. (186 pages)

Where it's reviewed:
Booklist, August 2001, page 2123
Bulletin of the Center for Children's Books, June 2001, page 390
Horn Book, July 2001, page 462
Publishers Weekly, May 21, 2001, page 109

School Library Journal, May 2001, page 160

Other books by the same author:
Guy Wire, 2002
Guy Time, 2000
Regular Guy, 1999

Other books you might like:
Mary Jane Auch, Mom Is Dating Weird Wayne, 1988
    Jenna is horrified that her mother is dating that weird weatherman who always dresses in costume on his television program.
Anne Fine, My War with Goggle-Eyes, 1989
    Kitty brings out all her artillery in an attempt to get rid of Gerald Faulkner, the man her mother is dating.
Morris Gleitzman, Puppy Fat, 1996
    Keith changes his goal from reuniting his separated parents to improving their appearances so each will be able to attract a new partner.
Francess Lantz, Stepsister from the Planet Weird, 1997
    Megan and Ariel hate one another, but when their parents plan to marry, the two have no choice but to work together to keep their parents apart.

934

NICHOLAS WEINSTOCK

As Long as She Needs Me

(New York: Cliff Street/HarperCollins, 2001)

Subject(s): Publishing; Weddings; Journalism
Age range(s): Grades 10-Adult
Major character(s): Oscar Campbell, Assistant (publisher); Lauren LaRose, Journalist (wedding columnist); Dawn Davis, Publisher
Time period(s): 2000s
Locale(s): New York, New York

Summary: For ten years Oscar has been personal assistant to Dawn, president and publisher of Dawn Books and local harridan. He has learned to endure her tantrums and her outrageous demands, but her latest is almost beyond his abilities. Dawn plans to marry soon and wants Oscar to plan a secret wedding for about five-hundred people, an event for which he has no experience. Luckily he flies to his college roommate's wedding and there meets Lauren LaRose, a wedding columnist who's jaded by all the theme events that are now the fad. The two strike a deal with Oscar agreeing to do all her editing if she'll help him plan the wedding. Oscar has two goals, to date Lauren and prevent Dawn from marrying a womanizer in this humorous first novel. (245 pages)

Where it's reviewed:
Booklist, March 1, 2001, page 1229
Kirkus Reviews, February 1, 2001, page 142
Publishers Weekly, March 19, 2001, page 73
School Library Journal, December 2001, page 175
US Weekly, April 23, 2001, page 69

Other books you might like:
Melissa Bank, The Girls' Guide to Hunting and Fishing, 1999
    Going by the romance rules Jane does everything wrong; maybe she should follow her mother's advice and just be herself.

Jane Green, Mr. Maybe, 2001
    Confusing wealth for Mr. Right, Libby dates a rich bachelor who proves boring and bumbling.
Dorothy West, The Wedding, 1995
    When light-skinned Shelby marries a white man, her white grandmother relates the history of their racially mixed family.

935

ROSEMARY WELLS, Author/Illustrator

Bunny Party

(New York: Viking, 2001)

Subject(s): Animals/Rabbits; Brothers and Sisters; Birthdays
Age range(s): Preschool-Kindergarten
Major character(s): Max, Rabbit, Brother (younger); Ruby, Rabbit, Sister (older); Grandma, Rabbit, Grandmother
Time period(s): Indeterminate
Locale(s): Fictional Country

Summary: Ruby wants Max to help her make name cards for the guests attending Grandma's birthday party. Max doesn't like the guests that Ruby invited and he wants to make room for his stuffed animals and toys. Each time Ruby leaves the table to work on party preparations Max disguises one of his guests and seats it at the table. Grandma arrives before Ruby can evict the party crashers and Max foils Ruby's plans once again. (28 pages)

Where it's reviewed:
Booklist, August 2001, page 2133
Horn Book, September 2001, page 579
Kirkus Reviews, August 15, 2001, page 1222
Publishers Weekly, October 15, 2001, page 73
School Library Journal, August 2001, page 166

Other books by the same author:
Max Cleans Up, 2000
Bunny Cakes, 1997
Bunny Money, 1997

Other books you might like:
Russell Hoban, A Birthday for Frances, 1968
    A Chompo bar makes such a delicious birthday gift for a sister that it's no surprise it's nibbled away on the walk home from the store.
Pat Hutchins, It's MY Birthday!, 1999
    Little monster Billy has difficulty sharing the gifts he receives at his birthday party.
Nancy Elizabeth Wallace, Tell-a-Bunny, 2000
    A phone call to plan a surprise party begins a series of distorted messages changing the party plans in a way that surprises the hostess.

936

ROSEMARY WELLS, Author/Illustrator

Felix Feels Better

(Cambridge, MA: Candlewick Press, 2001)

Subject(s): Illness; Fear; Animals/Guinea Pigs
Age range(s): Preschool-Kindergarten

Major character(s): Felix, Guinea Pig, Son; Mama, Guinea Pig, Mother; Dr. Duck, Duck, Doctor
Time period(s): Indeterminate Past
Locale(s): Fictional Country

Summary: Oh my, poor Felix awakens the morning after he's eaten too many sweets and stayed up after his bedtime to feel so poorly that he cannot eat Mama's delicious pancakes. Even her lovingly prepared chamomile tea and sugared prunes do not help Felix perk up. Fresh air is Mama's next healthy recommendation but when Felix does not make his motorcycle noises while playing she knows she has a sick child who needs to see the doctor. Felix's fear of visiting Dr. Duck's office vanishes when Mama is allowed to remain with him. Two spoonfuls of Dr. Duck's ''Happy Tummy'' medicine, a long nap and Felix is ready to make plans for an exciting day. (32 pages)

Where it's reviewed:
Booklist, May 1, 2001, page 1693
Bulletin of the Center for Children's Books, June 2001, page 391
Kirkus Reviews, March 15, 2001, page 423
Publishers Weekly, June 4, 2001, page 79
School Library Journal, May 2001, page 138

Awards the book has won:
Bulletin of the Center for Children's Books Blue Ribbon, 2001
Parenting's Reading Magic Awards, 2001

Other books by the same author:
Max Cleans Up, 2000
Read to Your Bunny, 1998
Yoko, 1998 (Booklist Editors' Choice)
Bunny Cakes, 1997

Other books you might like:
H.M. Ehrlich, *Dr. Duck*, 2000
　　When dedicated Dr. Duck falls ill his patients arrive to care for him until he's able to return to work.
Claire Masurel, *Too Big*, 1999
　　Charlie's large toy dinosaur is just the right size to comfort him on a trip to the doctor's office.
Vera Rosenberry, *When Vera Was Sick*, 1998
　　Vera is miserable when she's sick, but as soon as she's better she's eager to play outside.

937

ROSEMARY WELLS, Author/Illustrator
JODY WHEELER, Illustrator

Mama, Don't Go!

(New York: Hyperion Books for Children, 2001)

Series: Yoko and Friends—School Days. Number 1
Subject(s): Schools; Fear; Animals/Cats
Age range(s): Grades K-2
Major character(s): Yoko, Cat, Kindergartner; Mrs. Jenkins, Teacher, Dog; Timothy, Raccoon, Kindergartner
Time period(s): Indeterminate
Locale(s): Fictional Country

Summary: On the first day of school, many things about Yoko's classroom appeal to her, but when her mother tries to leave, she begins to cry. Each day Yoko is able to allow her mother to leave for a few minutes with her promise that she'll be right back but still she cannot stay in class all day without her. Timothy explains to Yoko that parents always come back, but Yoko is still not sure. Mrs. Jenkins devises a plan that Yoko accepts and finally she is able to give her mother the freedom of a day out of the classroom. (32 pages)

Where it's reviewed:
Horn Book Guide, Spring 2002, page 69
Publishers Weekly, October 8, 2001, page 67
School Library Journal, January 2002, page 112

Other books by the same author:
Be My Valentine, 2001 (Yoko and Friends School Days, Number 5)
The School Play, 2001 (Yoko and Friends School Days, Number 2)
The Halloween Parade, 2001 (Yoko and Friends School Days, Number 3)

Other books you might like:
Kevin Henkes, *Wemberly Worried*, 2000
　　Wemberly's worries about beginning school vanish when she enters the classroom and the teacher introduces her to Jewel who is also clutching a doll.
Jutta Langreutter, *Little Bear Goes to Kindergarten*, 1997
　　Although Little Bear enjoys everything about his first day in kindergarten he still doesn't want his mother to leave.
Jonathan London, *Froggy Goes to School*, 1996
　　Froggy's feeling nervous about his first day of school, but he survives and enjoys the day.
Margaret Wild, *Tom Goes to Kindergarten*, 2000
　　Tom's parents have so much fun on Tom's first day of school that they want to stay with him again, but he no longer needs their support.

938

ROSEMARY WELLS
SUSAN JEFFERS, Illustrator

McDuff Goes to School

(New York: Hyperion Books for Children, 2001)

Subject(s): Animals/Dogs; Neighbors and Neighborhoods; Pets
Age range(s): Grades K-2
Major character(s): McDuff, Dog; Marie-Antoinette, Dog; Celeste de Gaulle, Neighbor
Time period(s): Indeterminate Past
Locale(s): Barkedelphia

Summary: When McDuff's owners welcome the new neighbors and their obedient Marie-Antoinette they realize that McDuff needs to go to school. Celeste decides to enroll Marie-Antoinette in the same class and she practices daily with her pet as the teacher suggests. Poor McDuff! His owners are too busy so he watches Marie-Antoinette and Celeste and soon he's following along with Celeste's French commands from his side of the picket fence. On graduation day McDuff is disqualified for failing to heed his owner's directions while Marie-Antoinette wins the prize for best student. Then McDuff surprises everyone by responding to

Celeste's commands in French. A concluding glossary helps non-Francophiles understand directions as well as McDuff and Marie-Antoinette. (32 pages)

Where it's reviewed:
Booklist, October 1, 2001, page 330
Horn Book, January 2002, page 73
Kirkus Reviews, August 15, 2001, page 1222
Publishers Weekly, September 3, 2001, page 89
School Library Journal, December 2001, page 114

Other books by the same author:
McDuff's New Friend, 1998
McDuff Moves In, 1997
McDuff and the Baby, 1997 (Publishers Weekly's Best Children's Book)

Other books you might like:
Jane Goodall, *Dr. White*, 1999
   The health inspector thinks dogs have no place in hospitals yet the medical staff knows the healing benefit of Dr. White's visits with ill children.
Steven Kroll, *Oh, Tucker!*, 1998
   Despite the chaos Tucker creates in their home a dog's owners find it difficult to scold him.
Jean Davies Okimoto, *A Place for Grace*, 1993
   Too small to realize her ambition to become a guide dog for the blind, Grace is trained to be a companion for a deaf person.
Alan Snow, *How Dogs Really Work!*, 1993
   A winner of the New York Times Best Illustrated Children's Book Award is a humorous instruction manual for dog owners.

939

ROSEMARY WELLS, Author/Illustrator

Yoko's Paper Cranes
(New York: Hyperion Books for Children, 2001)

Subject(s): Grandmothers; Birthdays; Gifts
Age range(s): Grades K-2
Major character(s): Yoko, Child, Daughter (granddaughter); Obaasan, Grandmother, Cat; Ojiisan, Grandfather, Cat
Time period(s): Indeterminate Past
Locale(s): Japan; California

Summary: Yoko's memories of her younger days in Japan include feeding the cranes in Obaasan's garden and learning from Ojiisan the skill of folding origami cranes. Now Yoko lives in America and she's looking for an idea for Obaasan's winter birthday gift. Remembering how important the cranes are to Obaasan and knowing they migrate for the winter, Yoko uses skills she learned from Ojiisan to make three cranes in different colors. The cranes fly in an airplane package all the way to her grandparents' home where they are hung in the window. (36 pages)

Where it's reviewed:
Booklist, September 15, 2001, page 233
Bulletin of the Center for Children's Books, December 2001, page 155
Kirkus Reviews, August 15, 2001, page 1223
Publishers Weekly, August 20, 2001, page 79

School Library Journal, November 2001, page 138

Other books by the same author:
Mama Don't Go, 2001 (Yoko and Friends School Days, Number 1)
Emily's First 100 Days of School, 2000 (Bulletin of the Center for Children's Books Blue Ribbon)
Yoko, 1998 (Booklist Editors' Choice)
Bunny Money, 1997

Other books you might like:
Amy Hest, *Nana's Birthday Party*, 1993
   Cousins Maggie and Brette work together to create a special birthday gift for Nana.
Irmgard Kneissler, *Origami: A Children's Book*, 1992
   A nonfiction book describes the process for folding a variety of origami shapes.
Virginia Kroll, *Pink Paper Swans*, 1994
   Janetta becomes the "fingers" for her arthritic neighbor Mrs. Tsujimoto and learns to fold origami.
Laura Krauss Melmed, *Little Oh*, 1997
   One of the origami shapes folded by a potter comes to life.

940

BRIGITTE WENINGER
EVE THARLET, Illustrator
ROSEMARY LANNING, Translator

Happy Easter, Davy!
(New York: North-South Books, 2001)

Subject(s): Animals/Rabbits; Family; Holidays
Age range(s): Grades K-2
Major character(s): Dan, Rabbit, Brother (older); Davy, Rabbit, Brother; Father Rabbit, Rabbit, Father
Time period(s): Indeterminate
Locale(s): Fictional Country

Summary: Dan excitedly tells his family the news of an Easter Bunny living in their woods that will bring them gifts. Father Rabbit has never met an Easter Bunny so the family goes off in search of the neighbor to ask why they've not received gifts in the past. Alas, they cannot find the Easter Bunny and, with the exception of Davy, return home. Rather than see his siblings disappointed, Davy works all day to decorate "eggs" and make gifts to hide at dawn on Easter morning. (32 pages)

Where it's reviewed:
Booklist, April 1, 2001, page 1480
Horn Book Guide, Fall 2001, page 280
Publishers Weekly, February 19, 2001, page 93

Other books by the same author:
Merry Christmas, Davy!, 1998
Will You Mind the Baby, Davy?, 1997
Where Have You Gone, Davy?, 1996

Other books you might like:
Helen Rossendale, *Bunny's Easter Eggs*, 2001
   Bunny's late for the parade because he can't remember where he put the eggs!
Gerlinda Wiencirz, *Teddy's Easter Secret*, 2001
   By following a rabbit with a basket a teddy bear learns an Easter secret.

Hans Wilhelm, *More Bunny Trouble*, 1989
Ralph interrupts his Easter egg decorating with the other bunnies to locate his baby sister.

NANCY WERLIN

Black Mirror

(New York: Dial, 2001)

Subject(s): Murder; Schools/Boarding Schools; Self-Acceptance
Age range(s): Grades 8-12
Major character(s): Frances Leventhal, 16-Year-Old; Daniel Leventhal, Brother, Crime Victim; Saskia Sweeney, 16-Year-Old, Girlfriend (of Daniel); Andy Jankowski, Maintenance Worker, Mentally Challenged Person; Yvette Wiles, Teacher (art)
Time period(s): 2000s
Locale(s): Lattimore, Massachusetts

Summary: Unhappy with her short, round appearance and her half Japanese, half Jewish ethnic identity, Frances chooses to be a loner who immerses herself in art. Not surprisingly, her art teacher and a handicapped handyman on campus are the only ones she considers friends. Both she and her brother Daniel are scholarship students at Pettingill School where Daniel is very involved in Unity Service, which also happens to be their financial sponsor. But then Daniel commits suicide through a heroin overdose and Frances is stunned for she didn't know her brother had a drug problem. To try to understand his death, Frances joins Unity Service but is met with hostility, even from Daniel's girlfriend Saskia. Now Frances wonders if Daniel's death really was suicide, if there's a drug group on campus and whether or not she's a target because of her curiosity in another thriller from a top-notch mystery writer. (249 pages)

Where it's reviewed:
Bulletin of the Center for Children's Books, October 2001, page 81
Kliatt, September 2001, page 14
Publishers Weekly, November 12, 2001, page 60
School Library Journal, September 2001, page 234
Voice of Youth Advocates, October 2001, page 286

Awards the book has won:
ALA Best Books for Young Adults, 2002

Other books by the same author:
Locked Inside, 2000
The Killer's Cousin, 1998
Are You Alone on Purpose?, 1994

Other books you might like:
W. Edward Blain, *Passion Play*, 1990
A Virginia boarding school harbors a killer who strikes again and again, terrorizing students, faculty and parents.
Chris Crutcher, *Whale Talk*, 2001
T.J. stands out in his white community partly for his ability to stand on his own and partly because he's an adopted, biracial teen.
Stephen Dobyns, *Boy in the Water*, 1999
Noted psychologist Jim Hawthorne assumes the headmaster job at a school for "troubled" students and finds himself with a murderous cook.
Sharon E. Heisel, *Eyes of a Stranger*, 1996
As Merissa investigates the empty, whirling carousel she is caught by a serial killer who has eliminated four other girls.
M.E. Kerr, *Fell Back*, 1989
As John Fell investigates the death of fellow student Paul Lasher, he follows a path that leads to a larger-than-life drug scam.

VALERIE WILSON WESLEY

Willimena and the Cookie Money

(New York: Jump at the Sun/Hyperion Books for Children, 2001)

Subject(s): Sisters; Money; Problem Solving
Age range(s): Grades 2-4
Major character(s): Willimena "Willie" Thomas, 7-Year-Old, Sister (younger); Tina Thomas, Sister (older), 9-Year-Old; Amber Washington, 7-Year-Old, Friend
Time period(s): 2000s (2001)
Locale(s): United States

Summary: Amber and Willie can rattle off a list of problems with their older sisters. Willie can also recall times when Tina's been helpful like helping her practice her cookie sales routine. Willie was so successful she sold more cookies than anyone in the troop. The only problem is Willie used some of the money to buy lunches for two hungry kids on her street and now it's time to turn in the money. Willie doesn't know what to do. Tina offers to help again with an idea for a money making project. Their efforts are not completely successful as fundraisers but Willie does learn from the experience that the only way out is to tell the truth. This is the first children's book for an author of adult novels. (124 pages)

Where it's reviewed:
Horn Book Guide, Fall 2001, page 297
Kirkus Reviews, June 1, 2001, page 807
Publishers Weekly, June 18, 2001, page 81
School Library Journal, August 2001, page 166

Other books you might like:
Ann Cameron, *Gloria's Way*, 2000
Gloria faces the trials and tribulations of childhood with support from friends and family.
Beverly Cleary, *Ramona Quimby, Age 8*, 1981
Spirited Ramona keeps her family guessing about her next adventure as she enters third grade in this Newbery Honor Book.
Stephanie Greene, *Owen Foote, Money Man*, 2000
When Owen thinks he's in trouble with the IRS he desperately tries a series of unsuccessful moneymaking schemes.
Marilyn Singer, *Josie to the Rescue*, 1999
Josie's desire to help her family is admirable but it's soon obvious that her value to the family is not in her money-making ability.

943

BRUCE WHATLEY, Author/Illustrator

Wait! No Paint!
(New York: HarperCollins Publishers, 2001)

Subject(s): Animals/Pigs; Animals/Wolves; Artists and Art
Age range(s): Grades K-3
Major character(s): Unnamed Character, Artist (illustrator); Unnamed Character, Wolf
Time period(s): Indeterminate
Locale(s): Fictional Country

Summary: Feeling somewhat cramped in their house with seventy-three other pigs, three little pigs set off to build homes of their own. Before the wolf can blow down first pig's straw house a glass of orange juice spills on it and the soggy house collapses. Another interruption from the unseen illustrator keeps the wolf from blowing down the second house and by the time the three pigs are gathered in the brick house the illustrator runs out of red paint and the pigs lose their pink coloration. Even worse, they cannot build a hot fire to foil the wolf that's climbing down the chimney to gobble them up. The pigs demand to be removed from the story and the illustrator complies by drawing them into another fairy tale. (32 pages)

Where it's reviewed:
Booklist, August 2001, page 2133
Horn Book, September 2001, page 580
New York Times Book Review, May 20, 2001, page 20
Publishers Weekly, June 11, 2001, page 85
School Library Journal, July 2001, page 91

Awards the book has won:
IRA Children's Choices, 2002

Other books by the same author:
Captain Pajamas: Defender of the Universe, 1999 (Rosie Smith, co-author)
My First Nursery Rhymes, 1999
The Teddy Bear's Picnic, 1996

Other books you might like:
Lauren Child, *Beware of the Storybook Wolves*, 2001
    After two hungry wolves emerge from a storybook Herb frantically shakes a fairy godmother out of another book to help him with the problem.
Barry Moser, *The Three Little Pigs*, 2001
    The traditional tale is retold with adherence to the familiar text while the illustrations add humor.
David Wiesner, *The Three Pigs*, 2001
    Three pigs take control of events in the story by simply walking (or flying) off the page and into another tale where they seek refuge from the wolf.

944

NADIA WHEATLEY
MATT OUTLEY, Illustrator

Luke's Way of Looking
(La Jolla, CA: Kane/Miller Book Publishers, 2001)

Subject(s): Artists and Art; Teacher-Student Relationships; Imagination
Age range(s): Grades 1-4
Major character(s): Luke, Student, Child; Mr. Barraclough, Teacher
Time period(s): 1990s (1999)
Locale(s): Australia

Summary: Luke is definitely the odd one out in his classroom of conformists who all see the world in the same way, Mr. Barraclough's way. Friday Art class is especially difficult for Luke because Mr. Barraclough expects realism in the student's art and Luke's paintings express his own imaginative way of seeing the world. Luke's way infuriates Mr. Barraclough. One Friday morning, rather than go to school, Luke wanders into a large building that happens to be an art museum. When Luke sees the imaginative, surrealistic, contemporary and abstract paintings and sculptures he finally feels that he belongs. Luke ventures back to school in time for Friday afternoon's art class and even Mr. Barraclough is left speechless by his rendering of a watermelon. (36 pages)

Where it's reviewed:
Horn Book Guide, Spring 2002, page 62
Kirkus Reviews, September 1, 2001, page 1302
Publishers Weekly, November 5, 2001, page 68

Other books by the same author:
My Place, 1989

Other books you might like:
Anthony Browne, *Willy the Dreamer*, 1998
    As Willy sits, dozing, in an armchair the images of his dreams appear on each page in the style of various artists and illustrators.
Peter Catalanotto, *Emily's Art*, 2001
    Emily is disappointed to lose a school art contest because she's chosen to submit a drawing of her dog and the judge is afraid of dogs.
Michael Garland, *Dinner at Magritte's*, 1995
    Pierre's home is so quiet and boring that he visits his artist neighbors where things are not exactly as they seem to the eye.
Barbara McClintock, *The Fantastic Drawings of Danielle*, 1996
    Papa does not approve of Danielle's fanciful drawings but they do lead to a paid position as an assistant to Madame Beton.

945

GERARD WHELAN

The Guns of Easter
(Dublin, Ireland: O'Brien Press, 2000)

Subject(s): Revolutions; Family Life

Age range(s): Grades 6-10
Major character(s): Jimmy Conway, 12-Year-Old
Time period(s): 1910s (1916)
Locale(s): Dublin, Ireland

Summary: Jimmy has been the "man of the family" for his mother and two sisters while his father is away from home fighting for the British during World War I. Rebels in Ireland are trying to gain freedom for their country from England and turn the city upside down when they seize a Dublin post office and begin shooting. For Jimmy's family, this is a big problem as they rely on their father's paycheck but won't receive it if the post office is closed. It's now up to Jimmy to find food for the family, even though it means his going out in the midst of the fighting and then trying to return home before the curfew begins. In his travels, he sees good and bad on each side and finds his loyalties divided between the Irish rebels and the British soldiers. (167 pages)

Where it's reviewed:
Booklist, March 1, 2001, page 1272

Awards the book has won:
Bisto Book of the Year/Eilis Dillon Award, 1997

Other books by the same author:
A Winter of Spies, 2002
Out of Nowhere, 2001
The Dream Invader, 1997

Other books you might like:
Aubrey Flegg, *Katie's War*, 2000
   Katie's older brother is ready to join with other Irish rebels who oppose the treaty with England, but Katie's afraid this will harm their father.
Margot Griffin, *Dancing for Danger: A Meggy Tale*, 2001
   When British soldiers trap their "hedge school" teacher, Irish Meggy distracts them when she dances like a banshee.
Gary D. Schmidt, *Anson's Way*, 1999
   Excited to be part of the Staffordshire Fecibles, Anson is conflicted when he's posted to Ireland and sees the oppression under which the Irish live.

946

GLORIA WHELAN

Angel on the Square
(New York: HarperCollins, 2001)

Subject(s): Revolutions; Mothers and Daughters; Historical
Age range(s): Grades 6-10
Major character(s): Ekaterina "Katya" Ivanona Baranova, Teenager; Irina Ivanova Baranova, Mother (of Katya), Noblewoman (countess); Nicholas Alexandrovitch Romanov II, Ruler (tsar), Historical Figure; Alexandra Romanov, Wife (of Tsar Nikolai II), Historical Figure; Anastasia Nicholaievna, Royalty (Grand Duchess), Historical Figure; Mikhail Sergeyevich "Misha" Gnedich, 16-Year-Old, Revolutionary
Time period(s): 1910s (1913-1918)
Locale(s): St. Petersburg, Russia; Russia (Alexander Palace)

Summary: Her mother Irina is asked to be lady-in-waiting to the Empress, and Katya is thrilled for it means they'll live in Alexander Palace and she'll be a companion to the Grand Duchess Anastasia. Having grown up in a wealthy family, Katya is accustomed to the perks that come to the rich and is only vaguely aware of the discontent felt by the common people. Trying to open her eyes to the domestic problems is Misha, the orphaned son of friends of theirs, who has joined the student revolutionaries. When the Tsar is forced to abdicate, Katya and her mother leave for their summer home, which they find in shambles. Katya finally looks around and notices the wounded soldiers, working children and poor conditions under which most Russians live and realizes that the Tsar was not as kindly a man as she thought in this tale of pomp and poverty. (293 pages)

Where it's reviewed:
Booklist, September 15, 2001, page 215
Publishers Weekly, July 16, 2001, page 182
Riverside Review, Fall 2001, page 36
School Library Journal, October 2001, page 175
Voice of Youth Advocates, October 2001, page 286

Other books by the same author:
The Wanigan: A Life on the River, 2002
Homeless Bird, 2000
Miranda's Last Stand, 1999
Friends, 1997

Other books you might like:
Felice Holman, *The Wild Children*, 1983
   After the Bolshevik Revolution, Eric and other homeless children beg and rob to survive.
Carolyn Meyer, *Anastasia: The Last Grand Duchess, Russia, 1914*, 2000
   With the diary her grandmother gave her when she was twelve, Anastasia records her life as the youngest daughter of Tsar Nicholas II of Russia.
Joanne Rocklin, *Strudel Stories*, 1999
   In tribute to their grandfather, Lori and her sister make strudel, his favorite dish, and recount the flight of their family from Odessa, Russia.

947

CAROLYN WHITE
LAURA DRONZEK, Illustrator

The Adventure of Louey and Frank
(New York: Greenwillow Books, 2001)

Subject(s): Animals/Bears; Animals/Rabbits; Friendship
Age range(s): Grades K-3
Major character(s): Louey, Rabbit, Friend; Frank, Bear, Friend
Time period(s): Indeterminate
Locale(s): At Sea; Fictional Country

Summary: Seeking adventure Louey and Frank craft a boat from old shoes with a sock for a sail. Frank packs marshmallows and Louey brings pickle sandwiches for the voyage. When they come upon a large blue shape, the friends disagree as to whether they've landed on a rock or a whale for their picnic. Louey feels confident they're building the fire on a rock with a geyser; Frank has different ideas. The heat from the fire causes the rock/whale to roll and dump the friends into the sea. The boat sinks, a storm comes up and Louey and Frank find refuge on a brown prickly log/fish floating in the sea. After reaching dry land, Louey and Frank agree that they've had an adventure. (24 pages)

Where it's reviewed:
Booklist, January 2001, page 975
Bulletin of the Center for Children's Books, March 2001, page 282
Horn Book Guide, Fall 2001, page 243
Publishers Weekly, January 8, 2001, page 66
School Library Journal, March 2001, page 224

Other books by the same author:
Whuppity Stoorie: A Scottish Folktale, 1997
The Tree House Children: An African Folktale, 1994

Other books you might like:
Helen Lester, *Tacky in Trouble*, 1998
Tacky has an unexpected trip when the wind catches his flowered shirt and he sails away to a rocky island.
Brian Lies, *Hamlet and the Magnificent Sandcastle*, 2001
Quince fashions a boat from his beach chair and umbrella to rescue Hamlet when the tide comes in and destroys Hamlet's sandcastle.
H.A. Rey, *Whiteblack the Penguin Sees the World*, 2000
After Whiteblack's boat collides with an iceberg his travels become all the more adventurous as he gathers material for his radio show.

948

ELLEN EMERSON WHITE

Kaiulani: The People's Princess, Hawaii, 1889

(New York: Scholastic, 2001)

Series: Royal Diaries
Subject(s): Diaries; Princes and Princesses
Age range(s): Grades 5-8
Major character(s): Victoria Kawekiu Lunalilo Kala Cleghorn, Royalty (princess), Historical Figure; Liliuokalani, Royalty (queen)
Time period(s): 1880s; 1890s (1899-1893)
Locale(s): Waikiki, Hawaii; England; Washington, District of Columbia

Summary: Heir to the throne through her aunt Queen Liliuokalani, Princess Kaiulani writes in her diary of her daily life at home in Hawaii, her friendship with the author Robert Louis Stevenson and her fear at being sent to school in England. Even the encouragement from her Scottish father about his good memories of England doesn't help her mindset. Leaving Hawaii when she's thirteen, Kaiulani travels to the United States by boat, then across the US by train and finally reaches England after another ocean voyage. Though away from home, she hears of and worries about the political activities in Hawaii as the United States wishes to take control of her island. Kaiulani also worries about her slowly failing health, especially after the overthrow of Queen Liliuokalani. She returns to the United States to explain why her people and the islands need to remain independent, but

dies at the young age of twenty-three, never succeeding to the throne that was removed from her family. (238 pages)

Where it's reviewed:
Booklist, April 1, 2001, page 1488
Kliatt, May 2001, page 14
School Library Journal, June 2001, page
Voice of Youth Advocates, October 2001, page 286

Other books by the same author:
The Journal of Patrick Seamus Flaherty: United States Marine Corps, 2002 (My Name Is America)
Where Have All the Flowers Gone?: The Diary of Molly Mackenzie Flaherty, 2002 (Dear America)
Voyage on the Great Titanic: The Diary of Margaret Ann Brady, 1998 (Dear America)

Other books you might like:
Kristiana Gregory, *Cleopatra VII: Daughter of the Nile*, 1999
Diary entries for Cleopatra, ruler of Egypt, cover her years from twelve to fourteen as she prepares to become Egypt's ruler.
Anna Kirwan, *Victoria: May Blossom of Britannia, England, 1829*, 2001
The thoughts of the future Queen Victoria reside in a record book she steals from the stable and tell of her preparation to become queen.
Kathryn Lasky, *Marie Antoinette: Princess of Versailles*, 2000
Married to the Dauphin of France, Austrian Marie Antoinette gives up her childhood ways and struggles to adapt to marriage and life in France.
Carolyn Meyer, *Anastasia: The Last Grand Duchess, Russia, 1914*, 2000
With the diary her grandmother gives her when she is twelve, Anastasia records her life as the youngest daughter of Tsar Nicholas II of Russia.

949

IAN WHYBROW
ADRIAN REYNOLDS, Illustrator

Sammy and the Robots

(New York: Orchard Books, 2001)

Subject(s): Robots; Grandmothers; Problem Solving
Age range(s): Grades K-1
Major character(s): Sammy, Child, Son (grandson); Gran, Grandmother; Mom, Mother (Sammy's)
Time period(s): 2000s
Locale(s): England

Summary: When Sammy shows his broken robot to Gran she sends it to the robot hospital and then offers to help Sammy make a new robot, but before she can her cough worsens and she is taken to the hospital. Sammy makes a new robot with a little help from Mom and he finishes in time to bring the robot to the hospital when they go to visit Gran. Sammy is too young to go into Gran's room but he sneaks in anyway so the robot can blast away Gran's cough. Then he hurries home to make five more robots just for Gran and soon she's feeling well enough to come home on the very day that the robot hospital returns Sammy's original, repaired robot. Originally published in Great Britain in 2000. (28 pages)

Where it's reviewed:
Children's Book and Play Review, May 2001, page 21
Children's Bookwatch, June 2001, page 3
Horn Book Guide, Fall 2001, page 243
School Library Journal, July 2001, page 91

Other books by the same author:
Sammy and the Dinosaurs, 1999 (Smithsonian's Notable Books for Children)
A Baby for Grace, 1998
Harry and the Snow King, 1998

Other books you might like:
Rebecca Nevers Fellows, *A Lei for Tutu*, 1998
    When Tutu's hospitalization curtails plans to make a lei, Nahoa sneaks flowers into her grandmother's room to the benefit of her health.
Laura Joffe Numeroff, *What Grandmas Do Best, What Grandpas Do Best*, 2000
    Grandmas and Grandpas each have unique ways to share their love with their grandchildren.
Dan Yaccarino, *If I Had a Robot*, 1996
    Phil imagines the many advantages of a family robot that he could send to piano lessons in his place or to whom he could feed his vegetables.

950

DAVID WIESNER, Author/Illustrator

The Three Pigs
(New York: Clarion Books, 2001)

Subject(s): Animals/Pigs; Literature; Fairy Tales
Age range(s): Grades 1-4
Major character(s): Unnamed Character, Pig; Unnamed Character, Wolf; Unnamed Character, Cat; Unnamed Character, Dragon
Time period(s): Indeterminate Past
Locale(s): Fictional Country

Summary: Three little pigs set out to build their homes of straw, sticks and bricks as the story book wolf follows along to destroy their homes and gobble them up. This time, the wolf's huffing and puffing blows the first pig right off the pages of the story and gives the precocious porker an idea to save the others. The story line continues with the befuddled wolf wondering what's going on while the three pigs knock the pages of the storybook down, construct a paper airplane from one page and soar away. After they crash they wander into the pages of other books, save a dragon from a knight and befriend a fiddling cat. Then they rebuild their story just as the wolf arrives to blow down the brick house. Here the story literally falls apart and the three pigs with their new friends rewrite the ending and live happily ever . . . you get the idea. (40 pages)

Where it's reviewed:
Booklist, May 15, 2001, page 1761
Bulletin of the Center for Children's Books, May 2001, page 355
Horn Book, May 2001, page 341

Publishers Weekly, February 26, 2001, page 86
School Library Journal, April 2001, page 126

Awards the book has won:
Caldecott Medal, 2002
School Library Journal Best Books, 2001

Other books by the same author:
Sector 7, 1999 (ALA Notable Children's Books)
June 29, 1999, 1992
Tuesday, 1991 (Caldecott Medal)

Other books you might like:
Lauren Child, *Beware of the Storybook Wolves*, 2001
    When the wolves in Herb's storybook come alive one night he calls on the help of characters from another book.
Jon Scieszka, *The True Story of the 3 Little Pigs*, 1989
    Misunderstood A. Wolf presents his side of the story about just what happened between him and those three pigs.
Janet Stevens, *And the Dish Ran Away with the Spoon*, 2001
    Cat, Dog and Cow search for the missing Dish and Spoon before it's time for their nursery rhyme to be read again.
Eugene Trivizas, *The Three Little Wolves and the Big Bad Pig*, 1993
    A familiar tale takes a new turn when the big, bad pig tries to outmaneuver the three little wolves and ends up surprising himself.

951

MARGARET WILD
RON BROOKS, Illustrator

Fox
(La Jolla, CA: Kane/Miller Book Publishers, 2001)

Subject(s): Friendship; Animals; Conduct of Life
Age range(s): Grades 2-4
Major character(s): Magpie, Bird, Friend; Dog, Dog, Friend; Fox, Fox
Time period(s): Indeterminate
Locale(s): Fictional Country

Summary: Dog rescues Magpie from a forest fire and shelters her in his cave while she heals. Depressed and angry to realize that she'll never fly again because of her burned wing, Magpie is slow to accept the wisdom of Dog's counsel based on his experience as a dog that is blind in one eye. Wisely, Dog encourages Magpie to climb on his back and he runs with her so she can once again experience the sensation of flight. The two friends are content until Fox appears. Lonely and bitter, he manipulates the initially suspicious Magpie into leaving Dog and carries her swiftly out to the desert where he abandons her. Betrayed but determined Magpie slowly begins hopping home to Dog's cave. Originally published in Australia in 2000. (32 pages)

Where it's reviewed:
Booklist, November 15, 2001, page 585
Children's Bookwatch, August 2001, page 4
Horn Book Guide, Spring 2002, page 63
Publishers Weekly, October 8, 2001, page 65
School Library Journal, December 2001, page 114

Awards the book has won:
Children's Book Council of Australia Award, Best Picture Book, 2001

Other books by the same author:
The Pocket Dogs, 2001
Big Cat Dreaming, 1997
Old Pig, 1996

Other books you might like:
Pat Pflieger, *The Fog's Net*, 1994
    The fog betrays Devora and takes her brother despite receiving a newly woven net; fortunately Devora cleverly wove a way to save him into the net.
Rafik Schami, *Albert & Lila*, 1999
    Despite being farm outcasts, Albert and Lila spot a predatory fox and willingly develop a plan to save the other animals from it.
Ursel Scheffler, *The Return of Rinaldo, the Sly Fox*, 1993
    Rinaldo may be able to outwit Detective Bruno, but can he deceive his beautiful dinner companion?

952

MARGARET WILD
ANN JAMES, Illustrator

Midnight Babies
(New York: Clarion Books, 2001)

Subject(s): Babies; Behavior; Fantasy
Age range(s): Preschool
Major character(s): Baby Brenda, Baby, Sister (younger); Baby Mario, Baby
Time period(s): Indeterminate
Locale(s): Midnight Cafe, Fictional Country

Summary: With her family sleeping, Baby Brenda quietly sneaks out of bed and down the stairs. After raiding the refrigerator for goodies to pack in her backpack she sneaks out the cat door and meets her baby friends for a trip to the Midnight Cafe. Upon arrival they discover Baby Mario and his friends scowling to see them arrive. The unfriendly faces vanish when Baby Mario notices the wagon full of a wibbly-wobbly, jiggly-joggly treat. Now all the babies smile, dance and eat the night away before crawling or toddling back to their homes. Baby Brenda is not at all hungry for breakfast! (32 pages)

Where it's reviewed:
Booklist, February 15, 2001, page 1135
Horn Book Guide, Fall 2001, page 243
Kirkus Reviews, February 1, 2001, page 191
Publishers Weekly, February 5, 2001, page 87
School Library Journal, April 2001, page 126

Awards the book has won:
Booklist Editors' Choice/Books for Youth, 2002

Other books by the same author:
Tom Goes to Kindergarten, 2000
Big Cat Dreaming, 1997
Our Granny, 1994 (Booklist Editors' Choice)

Other books you might like:
Remy Charlip, *Sleepytime Rhyme*, 1999
    In this lyrical bedtime story the baby actually sleeps, safe in a mother's arms.
Nina Laden, *The Night I Followed the Dog*, 1994
    Dogs, too, have a secret nightlife while their families sleep.
Susan Meyers, *Everywhere Babies*, 2001
    Babies of all shapes, sizes and colors are everywhere, playing, eating, sleeping and most of all, being loved.

953

MARGARET WILD
KERRY ARGENT, Illustrator

Nighty Night
(Atlanta: Peachtree, 2001)

Subject(s): Animals; Bedtime
Age range(s): Preschool-Grade 1
Time period(s): Indeterminate
Locale(s): Fictional Country

Summary: Young animals on the farm have tricks planned for their parents. As each parent bids goodnight to the young of its species the reply is the sound made by a different species. It takes a while to get the ducks, chicks, pigs, and lambs back in their proper beds so the "Nighty Night" refrain can begin again. This time the offspring have other excuses, such as needing water and wanting more kisses, for not going to sleep. Finally they're all settled and the weary parents gather for a cup of tea. First published in Australia in 2000. (36 pages)

Where it's reviewed:
Booklist, September 1, 2001, page 118
Bulletin of the Center for Children's Books, September 2001, page 40
Kirkus Reviews, September 1, 2001, page 1303
Publishers Weekly, July 9, 2001, page 66
School Library Journal, September 2001, page 208

Other books by the same author:
Tom Goes to Kindergarten, 2000
Big Cat Dreaming, 1997
Old Pig, 1996

Other books you might like:
Margaret Wise Brown, *Little Donkey Close Your Eyes*, 1998
    Animals throughout the world are bid good night in this gentle poem.
Mem Fox, *Time for Bed*, 1993
    All over the world mothers are putting their kittens, lambs, fawns and children to sleep.
Carole Lexa Schaefer, *Down in the Woods at Sleepytime*, 2000
    Various animal mothers encourage their babies to settle down for "sleepytime" but each species claims to have an important activity to complete.
Jane Yolen, *How Do Dinosaurs Say Good Night?*, 2000
    A succession of human parents show a range of emotions as they try to coax their dinosaurs into bed in this award-winning picture book.

MARGARET WILD
STEPHEN MICHAEL KING, Illustrator

The Pocket Dogs
(New York: Scholastic Press, 2001)

Subject(s): Animals/Dogs; Clothes; Lost and Found
Age range(s): Grades K-2
Major character(s): Mr. Pockets, Animal Lover; Biff, Dog; Buff, Dog
Time period(s): 2000s
Locale(s): Australia

Summary: Biff and Buff are just the right size to ride in the large pockets of Mr. Pockets coat. Daily, Mr. Pockets settles Biff in the right pocket and Buff in the left pocket before beginning a leisurely stroll to the shops. All goes well until Biff's foot pokes through a small hole in the right pocket. The hole grows larger but Mr. Pockets takes no notice of the problem. Biff, however, dreams of falling out and becoming lost. Buff sympathizes, but neither dog is able to communicate the concern effectively to Mr. Pockets. Alas, Biff's fears come true and he falls out of the pocket in the grocery store where he is surrounded by legs, none of them belonging to Mr. Pockets. This tale of a lost, and fortunately found, pet was originally published in Australia in 2000. (32 pages)

Where it's reviewed:
Booklist, February 1, 2001, page 1051
Bulletin of the Center for Children's Books, March 2001, page 283
Horn Book Guide, Fall 2001, page 281
Publishers Weekly, April 2, 2001, page 63
School Library Journal, June 2001, page 132

Other books by the same author:
Midnight Babies, 2001 (Booklist Editors' Choice, Books for Youth)
Tom Goes to Kindergarten, 2000
Big Cat Dreaming, 1997
Our Granny, 1994

Other books you might like:
Ian Beck, *Home before Dark*, 1997
A teddy bear, dropped in the park by its owner, attempts to find his way home while it is still daylight.
Ann Braybrooks, *Plenty of Pockets*, 2000
In order to find items in his cluttered home, Henry sews pockets on his overalls to store everything from pets to pots so nothing is lost.
Emmy Payne, *Katy No-Pocket*, 1973
A mother kangaroo without a pocket has a real problem until a sympathetic carpenter gives her his work apron.

DEBORAH WILES
JEROME LAGARRIGUE, Illustrator

Freedom Summer
(New York: Anne Schwartz Book/Atheneum Books for Young Readers, 2001)

Subject(s): African Americans; Race Relations; Friendship
Age range(s): Grades 2-5
Major character(s): John Henry Waddell, Child, Friend (Joe's); Annie Mae Waddell, Cook, Housekeeper; Joe, Child, Friend (John Henry's)
Time period(s): 1960s (1964)
Locale(s): South

Summary: Every morning Annie Mae arrives by bus for her day's work at Joe's house. In summer John Henry rides the bus with her so he and Joe can play all day. They dam the creek to make a swimming hole and walk to the general store where Joe goes in to buy ice pops for both since John Henry's not allowed in the store. The enactment of the Civil Rights Act opens previously segregated public facilities to all and Joe makes plans with John Henry to be the first ones in the public pool. When they arrive the boys are dismayed to see the county trucks filling the pool with asphalt. As they slowly walk home they stop for an ice pop and enter the store together for the first time. An introductory author's note gives background for the story. (32 pages)

Where it's reviewed:
Booklist, February 15, 2001, page 1158
Bulletin of the Center for Children's Books, February 2001, page 239
Horn Book, May 2001, page 317
Publishers Weekly, December 4, 2000, page 72
School Library Journal, February 2001, page 107

Awards the book has won:
IRA Teachers' Choices, 2002

Other books you might like:
Evelyn Coleman, *White Socks Only*, 1996
In 1950s Mississippi a young black child stands in her white socks to drink from a "whites only" water fountain with unexpected consequences.
Robert Coles, *The Story of Ruby Bridges*, 1995
Courageously six-year-old Ruby, the first black child to attend a formerly all-white school, faces angry white protesters.
William Miller, *Night Golf*, 1999
The only time James can play on the town's "whites only" golf course is at night after the course closes.
Jacqueline Woodson, *The Other Side*, 2001
Two girls, one white and one black, refuse to let a fence or local prejudice keep them from playing together.

956

DEBORAH WILES

Love, Ruby Lavender
(San Diego: Gulliver Books/Harcourt, Inc., 2001)

Subject(s): Grandparents; Self-Reliance; Death
Age range(s): Grades 4-6
Major character(s): Ruby Lavender, 9-Year-Old, Child of Divorced Parents; Eula "Miss Eula" Dapplevine, Grandmother, Widow(er); Dove Ishee, 9-Year-Old, Friend
Time period(s): Indeterminate Past
Locale(s): Halleluia, Mississippi

Summary: What will Ruby do all summer without Miss Eula, the grandma with whom she liberates aged laying hens before they can become someone's stew and the confidant for whom she leaves correspondence in their secret "mailbox" in a tree? Ruby is losing her status as Miss Eula's only grandchild and, worse, she's losing Miss Eula temporarily when her grandmother goes to Hawaii to visit her son, his wife, and newborn daughter. Miss Eula also wants to get away from memories of the accidental death of her husband the previous summer. Ruby tries to do that too but the daughter of the accident's other victim never lets Ruby forget who was driving the car that summer night. Dove's arrival in town to visit her uncle, the newly arrived teacher, and her willingness to befriend both Ruby and her archenemy provides some focus to Ruby's activity during Miss Eula's absence. As an amateur anthropologist and a curious newcomer, Dove also uncovers the information needed to open a way to heal the relationship between two grieving members of the small community. The author's first novel is based on memories of growing up in a small Southern town. (188 pages)

Where it's reviewed:
Booklist, May 1, 2001, page 1684
Bulletin of the Center for Children's Books, September 2001, page 41
Horn Book Guide, Fall 2001, page 318
School Library Journal, April 2001, page 152
Southern Living, August 2001, page 48

Awards the book has won:
ALA Notable Children's Books, 2002

Other books you might like:
Sharon Creech, *Chasing Redbird*, 1997
    Grieving for Aunt Jessie and worried by Uncle Nate's increasingly bizarre behavior, Zinny looks for solace and finds answers to family mysteries.
Cynthia Rylant, *Missing May*, 1992
    A Newbery Award winner looks at the impact of May's death on her husband of many years and his orphaned niece.
B.J. Stone, *Ola's Wake*, 2000
    Through stories overheard at Ola's wake, Josie learns about the great grandmother she never knew and her single mother's childhood.

957

MELISSA WILEY
DAN ANDREASEN, Illustrator

On Tide Mill Lane
(New York: HarperCollins, 2001)

Series: Charlotte Years
Subject(s): Family Life; War of 1812
Age range(s): Grades 4-6
Major character(s): Charlotte Tucker, Child
Time period(s): 1810s
Locale(s): Roxbury, Massachusetts

Summary: This series, an extension of Laura Ingalls Wilder's *Little House* books, features Charlotte Tucker, the grandmother of Laura. Living in Massachusetts in the early 1800s, Charlotte stays busy with household chores, watching her baby sister, making candles, picking bayberries or learning to sew a sampler. The War of 1812 forms the background for her life as she worries about the young men from her community who have gone off to fight. The war finally ends and the family successfully weathers a hurricane in this second book about Charlotte. (258 pages)

Where it's reviewed:
Booklist, February 15, 2001, page 1139

Other books by the same author:
Down to the Bonny Glen, 2001 (Martha Years)
The Far Side of the Loch, 2000 (Martha Years)
Little House by Boston Bay, 1999 (Charlotte Years)
Little House in the Highlands, 1999 (Martha Years)

Other books you might like:
Roger Lea MacBride, *Bachelor Girl*, 1999
    This last in the series *The Rose Years* features Rose Wilder Lane, youngest daughter of Laura Ingalls Wilder, and was written by a friend of Rose's.
Gloria Whelan, *Once on This Island*, 1995
    When their father leaves to fight in the War of 1812, a young girl and her brothers assume responsibility for their family's Michigan farm.
Laura Ingalls Wilder, *The Little House on the Prairie Series*, 1932-1941
    Offering a slice of daily life in the unsettled West, this series contains the well-known stories of the Ingalls family.

958

DOUG WILHELM

Raising the Shades
(New York, Farrar Straus Giroux, 2001)

Subject(s): Alcoholism; Fathers and Sons
Age range(s): Grades 6-8
Major character(s): Casey Butterfield, 7th Grader, Child of an Alcoholic; Oscar Terry, 7th Grader; Julie Butterfield, Aunt
Time period(s): 2000s
Locale(s): New Hampshire

Summary: Ever since his parents divorced and his mother moved out taking his over-achieving older sister, Casey's become more and more of a loner with no time to hang out with his friend Oscar. He races home after school to wash the breakfast dishes, pick up the beer bottles from the night before and, sometimes, mop up his dad's vomit. Then Casey stays close to the kitchen while his father starts dinner in case the food burns while his dad's wandered into the garage to smoke a little pot. Casey's Aunt Julia calls with an offer of help, but it will require Casey's assistance as it involves an interventionist. Unsure of what to do, as he doesn't want to lose what little relationship he and his dad have, Casey decides to take matters in his own hands after being embarrassed by his father in front of his friends. (181 pages)

Where it's reviewed:
Booklist, July 2001, page 2000
Bulletin of the Center for Children's Books, May 2001, page 355
Kliatt, March 2001, page 15
School Library Journal, May 2001, page 160
Voice of Youth Advocates, June 2001, page 130

Other books by the same author:
Gold Medal Secret, 1996 (Choose Your Own Adventure, Number 173)
Underground Railroad, 1996 (Choose Your Own Adventure, Number 175)
Shadow of the Swastika, 1995 (Choose Your Own Adventure, Number 163)
Gunfire at Gettysburg, 1994 (Choose Your Own Adventure, Number 151)

Other books you might like:
Bruce Brooks, *Vanishing*, 1999
    Rather than live with her alcoholic mother and stepfather, or her father who lives with his cold mother, Alice quits eating and stays in the hospital.
Paula Fox, *The Moonlight Man*, 1986
    Spending a month with the father she has always seen as a romantic figure opens Catherine's eyes to the realization he's an alcoholic.
S.L. Rottman, *Hero*, 1997
    Angry over his father's abandonment and his abusive mother's alcoholism, meeting crusty Mr. Hassler enriches Sean's life.

959

KATE WILHELM

Desperate Measures
(New York: St. Martin's Minotaur, 2001)

Subject(s): Mystery and Detective Stories; Trials; Fathers and Daughters
Age range(s): Grades 10-Adult
Major character(s): Barbara Holloway, Lawyer; Frank Holloway, Lawyer; Gus Marchand, Farmer, Crime Victim; Graham Minick, Doctor (psychiatrist); Alexander "Alex" Feldman, Handicapped, Artist
Time period(s): 2000s
Locale(s): Opal Creek, Oregon

Summary: When a murder occurs, it's often convenient if there's a scapegoat, and in this small town in Oregon, such a person exists: Alex Feldman who was born with a horrible facial deformity. Surgery could only correct so much and then he was sent home to indifferent parents; after a suicide attempt, psychiatrist Graham Minick offered to raise him and Alex has lived with him ever since. Now a successful cartoonist, he maintains his anonymity, until the body of Gus Marchand is found. A religious bigot, Marchand has spread evil lies about Alex and the community instantly considers him a suspect. Lawyer Barbara Holloway believes Alex is innocent and sets out to prove her case, even though her father is the lawyer for another potential suspect, in this continuing series. (387 pages)

Where it's reviewed:
Booklist, May 1, 2001, page 1643
Kirkus Reviews, May 15, 2001, page 712
Publishers Weekly, June 25, 2001, page 50
School Library Journal, October 2001, page 196

Other books by the same author:
Skeletons, 2002
No Defense, 2000
The Deepest Water, 2000
Defense for the Devil, 1999
The Good Children, 1998

Other books you might like:
Marjorie Kellogg, *Tell Me That You Love Me, Junie Moon*, 1968
    Recovering from facial scarring, Junie Moon befriends a paraplegic and a terminally ill patient and the three decide to set up house together.
John Marsden, *So Much to Tell You*, 1987
    Through her journal, Marina reveals the sad story of her facial disfigurement caused when her father unintentionally threw acid on her.
Christine Sparks, *The Elephant Man*, 1995
    Born deformed, John Merrick has been forced into a workhouse or made part of a freak show.

960

MARGARET WILLEY
HEATHER SOLOMON, Illustrator

Clever Beatrice
(New York: Atheneum Books for Young Readers, 2001)

Subject(s): Folklore; Tall Tales; Giants
Age range(s): Grades K-3
Major character(s): Beatrice, Child, Daughter; Mister Giant, Giant
Time period(s): Indeterminate Past
Locale(s): Michigan

Summary: The morning that Beatrice and her mother eat the last of their porridge, the clever girl decides to make her way into the north woods to "get some money." Beatrice's mother knows that the only way to make a living in the north woods is be a lumberjack or gamble with the rich giant. Beatrice, being a slight child, chooses the giant. After walking far into the north woods, Beatrice boldly awakens Mister Giant and proposes a bet. Sure of his strength and confident that he will win, Mister Giant accepts. When Beatrice outwits him he pays her the promised gold and proposes another wager in an attempt to get his money back. Beatrice accepts Mister Giant's bets each time and finally goes home with his entire sack of gold while Mister Giant considers himself fortunate to have avoided the problems that would have developed had clever Beatrice won his proposed contests. (32 pages)

Where it's reviewed:
Bulletin of the Center for Children's Books, October 2001, page 82
Horn Book, November 2001, page 763
Publishers Weekly, July 30, 2001, page 84
Riverbank Review, Fall 2001, page 47
School Library Journal, October 2001, page 147

Awards the book has won:
Bulletin of the Center for Children's Books Blue Ribbon, 2001
Horn Book Fanfare/Folklore, 2002

Other books by the same author:
Thanksgiving with Me, 1998

Other books you might like:
Mary Pope Osborne, *Kate and the Beanstalk*, 2000
    Kate makes three trips up the beanstalk and into a giant's castle to retrieve stolen items and return them to a slain knight's family.
Audrey Wood, *Rude Giants*, 1993
    Persuasive Beatrix convinces two rude giants to clean up their act and become good neighbors.
Jane Yolen, *Not One Damsel in Distress: World Folktales for Strong Girls*, 2000
    Thirteen folktales relate the bravery of women known through the traditional literature of many countries.

961

ANNIE MORRIS WILLIAMS
LINSEY DOOLITTLE, Illustrator

Gwyneth's Secret Grandpa
(Conway, MA: Field Stone Publishers, 2001)

Series: Family History Adventures for Young Readers. Book 1
Subject(s): World War II; Family Problems; Grandfathers
Age range(s): Grades 4-6
Major character(s): Gwyneth Bryn "Gwynnie" Thompson, 12-Year-Old; David "Davie" Thompson, Military Personnel (Marines); Elizabeth "Beth" Hopkins, Fiance(e); Martin Griffith, Grandfather (of Gwynnie); Annie McIntosh, Aunt (of Gwynnie)
Time period(s): 1940s (1942)
Locale(s): Youngstown, Ohio; Warren, Ohio

Summary: Gwynnie is surprised when her brother Davie lets her accompany him the day he drives to Warren to find their grandfather, a man she didn't even know existed. Having no luck that day, they return home and Davie leaves to take part in World War II. On a trip with Davie's fiancee Beth, they at least find the correct house, but no one answers when they knock on the door. Because gas is rationed, a return trip by car isn't possible, so Gwynnie takes the bus to Warren instead.

This time her trip's successful, she meets her grandfather Martin and her aunt Annie and learns about her mother's side of the family in a work brimming with details of life on the Homefront. (167 pages)

Where it's reviewed:
School Library Journal, October 2001, page 175

Other books you might like:
Betsy Byars, *Coast to Coast*, 1992
    Faced with going into a retirement home, Pop and his granddaughter Birch sneak off for one last cross-country flight in his Piper J-3 Cub.
Julie Reece Deaver, *First Wedding, Once Removed*, 1990
    Pokie's beloved brother leaves for college where he meets Nell and, to Pokie's dismay and initial jealousy, marries her within the year.
Maureen Pople, *The Other Side of the Family*, 1988
    Sent from England to Australia during WWII, Kate stays with her father's mother and discovers how wrong the stories are about Grandmother Tucker.

962

LAURA E. WILLIAMS

Up a Creek
(New York: Holt, 2001)

Subject(s): Mothers and Daughters; Single Parent Families; Conservation
Age range(s): Grades 5-8
Major character(s): Starshine Bott, 13-Year-Old, 8th Grader; Jenna Charbonet, 13-Year-Old, 8th Grader; Lucy "Memaw" Bott, Grandmother (of Starshine); Miracle Bott, Activist, Mother (of Starshine)
Time period(s): 2000s
Locale(s): Louisiana

Summary: Outrageous first name! Outrageous mother! Starshine is tired of the teasing she receives from other middle school kids about her first name, but she's even more tired of the causes for which her mother fights. Miracle takes on the town council for their plan to cut down the old oak trees in the town square; when her protest march is ignored, Miracle climbs one of the trees and refuses to come down. No matter how much Starshine pleads with her, Miracle claims the trees have no one to speak for them and she won't leave. Eventually Starshine asks questions about her unknown father and for the first time Miracle considers leaving her tree, but when she starts down she slips, falls and is hospitalized. With Miracle out of the tree, men and machines move in and begin chopping away. Hearing the noise Starshine climbs one tree, her friend Jenna another, and soon other classmates are up in the trees, which halts the cutting, at least for a little while. (135 pages)

Where it's reviewed:
Booklist, January 2001, page 941
Bulletin of the Center for Children's Books, February 2001, page 240
Publishers Weekly, December 11, 2000, page 85
School Library Journal, January 2001, page 135
Voice of Youth Advocates, April 2001, page 47

Other books by the same author:
The Mystery of the Missing Tiger, 2002
The Executioner's Daughter, 2000
The Ghost Stallion, 1999
The Spider's Web, 1999
Behind the Bedroom Wall, 1996

Other books you might like:
Cynthia DeFelice, *Lostman's River*, 1994
   Tyler is upset when the man he guides into the swamp's secret rookery doesn't take photographs as promised, but instead kills the birds for their feathers.
Monte Killingsworth, *Eli's Song*, 1991
   Upset that an old-growth forest is to be cut, young Eli "tree sits" until a lawyer agrees to take his case to court.
Theodore Taylor, *The Weirdo*, 1991
   After being rescued by "weirdo" Chip, whose scars have made him reclusive, Sam works with him to save the bears in the swamp.
Marion Woodson, *The Amazon Influence*, 1994
   Nick would like to become friends with Allison, but the possibility is doubtful since her father is boss of a logging company and his mother is a crusading environmentalist.

963

LORI AURELIA WILLIAMS

Shayla's Double Brown Baby Blues

(New York: Simon & Schuster, 2001)

Subject(s): Family Life; African Americans; Alcoholism
Age range(s): Grades 7-10
Major character(s): Shayla Dubois, 13-Year-Old; Kambia Elaine Major, 13-Year-Old, Writer, Abuse Victim; Anderson Fox, Father (of Shayla); Lemm Turley, Alcoholic, 13-Year-Old; Gift Marie Fox, Baby (half-sister of Shayla)
Time period(s): 2000s
Locale(s): Houston, Texas

Summary: Shayla can't believe that her new half-sister Gift is born on her birthday and their mutual father, whom Shayla hardly ever sees, has turned into a "doting daddy." Unhappy about sharing her day with a half-sister, her grandmother chides Shayla to remember that Gift's birth is only a "little rain" in her life. If that's true, then her friends Kambia and Lemm have hurricanes in their lives. Thanks to Shayla, last year Kambia received the help she needed after her foster family forced her into prostitution, but now some cruel person sends her ugly reminders of that time. Lemm is new in Shayla's life, an honor roll student who's an alcoholic, and she reaches out to help him in the same way in this sequel to *When Kambia Elaine Flew in from Neptune*. (300 pages)

Where it's reviewed:
Booklist, July 2001, page 2000
Horn Book, September 2001, page 598
Kliatt, July 2001, page 15
Publishers Weekly, August 13, 2001, page 313
Voice of Youth Advocates, October 2001, page 286

Other books by the same author:
When Kambia Elaine Flew in from Neptune, 2000

Other books you might like:
Jan Cheripko, *Imitate the Tiger*, 1996
   Severely beaten while on a drinking binge, Chris is finally in a rehabilitation center where he's forced to reexamine his life and learn to let go of his past.
Nikki Grimes, *Jazmin's Notebook*, 1998
   After being shuttled between foster homes, Jazmin finally has a permanent home with her older sister and records this newfound happiness in her journal.
Glen Huser, *Touch of the Clown*, 1999
   Barbara and her younger sister are beaten by her alcoholic father before a friend intervenes to place both girls in a good foster home.
Hadley Irwin, *Can't Hear You Listening*, 1990
   Tracy doesn't know where to turn for help when her good friend Stanley denies having a problem with either alcohol or drugs.

964

MARK LONDON WILLIAMS

Ancient Fire

(Berkeley, CA: Tricycle Press, 2001)

Series: Danger Boy. Book 1
Subject(s): Time Travel; Science Fiction
Age range(s): Grades 5-8
Major character(s): Eli Sandusky, 12-Year-Old, Time Traveler; Clyne, Dinosaur; Thea, 13-Year-Old; Sandusky Sands, Scientist, Father (of Eli)
Time period(s): 2010s (2019); 5th century B.C. (419)
Locale(s): Sonoma, California (Valley of the Moon); Alexandria, Egypt

Summary: Eli's scientist dad works with time spheres and their practical application on traveling backwards through time, however his experiments aren't always successful as evidenced by the disappearance of Eli's mom. Eli accidentally sticks his hand into the middle of an experiment and suddenly lands in Clyne's spaceship, knocking it off course so that the two land in Alexandria in the middle of a riot. Clyne and Eli bump into Thea, the only daughter of Hypatia, the last librarian in Alexandria, who's accused of being a witch and is the cause of the riot. This topsy-turvy, time travel adventure winds through the alleys of ancient Alexandria in the first of what looks to be an exciting series. (167 pages)

Where it's reviewed:
Publishers Weekly, March 26, 2001, page 94
School Library Journal, April 2001, page 152

Other books by the same author:
Dino Sword, 2001 (Danger Boy, Number 2)

Other books you might like:
Scott Ciencin, *Dinoverse*, 1999
   Bertram uses his science fair project to send him and three others back to prehistoric times where they blend right in as human-dinosaurs.
Anthony Horowitz, *Stormbreaker*, 2001
   After his uncle's death, Alex agrees to take his place helping British intelligence and investigates the computer giant Sayle Enterprises.

Richard Peck, *Lost in Cyberspace*, 1995
Josh's computer geek friend Aaron manages to transport the two boys back to 1923 in a crazy, madcap adventure.

965

VERA B. WILLIAMS, Author/Illustrator

Amber Was Brave, Essie Was Smart
(New York: Greenwillow Books, 2001)

Subject(s): Sisters; Family Problems; Working Mothers
Age range(s): Grades 2-4
Major character(s): Amber, Sister (younger), Child; Essie, Child, Sister (older); Wilson, Bear, Stuffed Animal
Time period(s): Indeterminate Past
Locale(s): United States

Summary: Sisters Amber and Essie depend on each other for company, solace and nurture as their mother works long hours during their father's imprisonment. When they feel especially sad or lonely they form a "best sandwich" with Wilson in the middle and draw warmth from their closeness. The poverty inherent in this difficult life situation is evident in the food (or lack thereof) available for snacks and meals. Brave Amber can convince the grocer to let them have milk on credit. Smart Essie figures out problems and teaches Amber to write in cursive. Without warning, their mother disrupts the sisters' routine by staying home from work on a Friday and shopping for groceries. Saturday morning, the doorbell rings announcing their father's return. (72 pages)

Where it's reviewed:
Booklist, September 15, 2001, page 227
Bulletin of the Center for Children's Books, September 2001, page 3
Horn Book, September 2001, page 608
Riverbank Review, Fall 2001, page 36
School Library Journal, September 2001, page 209

Awards the book has won:
Publishers Weekly Best Children's Books, 2001
School Library Journal Best Books, 2001

Other books by the same author:
Scooter, 1993 (ALA Notable Book)

Other books you might like:
Lisa Westberg Peters, *The Hayloft*, 1995
Two sisters living on a farm share a memorable summer.
Marilyn Sachs, *JoJo & Winnie: Sister Stories*, 1999
For JoJo and Winnie, having a sister means sharing when neither wants to share.
Maria Testa, *Nine Candles*, 1996
When Raymond visits his incarcerated mother on his seventh birthday she promises to be home with him when his cake had nine candles.
Jean Van Leeuwen, *Two Girls in Sister Dresses*, 1994
As the older sister, Jennifer is alternately protective of Molly and jealous of the attention others give her.

966

RITA WILLIAMS-GARCIA

Every Time a Rainbow Dies
(New York: HarperCollins, 2001)

Subject(s): Rape; Animals/Birds
Age range(s): Grades 9-12
Major character(s): Thulani, 16-Year-Old; Ysa, Crime Victim, Student—College (clothing designer)
Time period(s): 2000s
Locale(s): New York, New York (Brooklyn)

Summary: While tending to his pigeons atop his brother's home in Brooklyn, Thulani sees a young girl attacked in the alley below. Though he's too late to stop the rape, he scares away her attackers and helps the girl to her home. Frightened and upset, she slams the door in Thulani's face, an act he understands and one that doesn't stop his consuming interest in her, even returning to the scene of the rape. There he finds her peacock-colored skirt, which he takes home and affixes to his wall as a reminder. Thulani gently pursues the girl, named Ysa, and gradually the two share their life stories and future plans. For Thulani, it's the first time since his mother died that he's had an interest in anything other than his birds and Ysa's career plans spark him to think of his own goals. Though it's inevitable they'll drift apart, Thulani at least knows he'll return to Jamaica where his father still lives and where his mother is buried. (166 pages)

Where it's reviewed:
Booklist, December 15, 2000, page 809
Horn Book, March 2001, page 216
School Library Journal, February 2001, page 123
School Library Journal, January 8, 2001, page 68
Voice of Youth Advocates, June 2001, page 130

Awards the book has won:
Booklist Editors' Choice/Books for Youth, 2001
ALA Best Books for Young Adults, 2002

Other books by the same author:
Like Sisters on the Homefront, 1995
Fast Talk on a Slow Track, 1991
Blue Tights, 1988

Other books you might like:
Robert Cormier, *We All Fall Down*, 1991
An act of vandalism turns into tragedy with far-reaching effects for Jane, her injured sister and the boys involved.
Marilyn Reynolds, *But What About Me?*, 1996
Erica finally realizes that she needs to break up with her boyfriend Danny after the night he's so drunk he can't prevent her being raped.
Frances Temple, *Tonight, by Sea*, 1995
Paulie can't imagine leaving Haiti, but when her best friend is killed, she knows it's time to flee and tell the world their story.

CONNIE WILLIS

Passage

(New York: Bantam, 2001)

Subject(s): Death; Love; Near-Death Experience
Age range(s): Grades 10-Adult
Major character(s): Joanna Lander, Scientist; Richard Wright, Scientist
Time period(s): 2000s
Locale(s): Denver, Colorado (Mercy General Hospital)

Summary: Mercy General Hospital seems designed to frustrate Joanna's research in near-death experiences. The maze-like layout means it's almost impossible to get from one place to another, the hospital administration insists she wear a beeper that constantly interrupts her at critical moments, and a smarmy, feel-good author writing books on NDEs has been given the run of Mercy General because the trustees love him. Things seem to be looking up when Dr. Richard Wright arrives, a neurologist who's discovered a drug that seems to mimic NDEs physiologically. He needs Joanna to interview his subjects and help him determine if they really are experiencing near-death. Joanna's superior interview skills quickly reduce Richard's viable pool of test subjects to almost nil, but they also confirm that these people seem to be having an NDE. Desperate for volunteers, Joanna agrees to become a subject herself, and her eerie experience quickly refocuses their research. Is it really possible that the tunnel, the light, and the figures in white are aboard the sinking *Titanic*? (594 pages)

Where it's reviewed:
Booklist, March 15, 2001, page 1361
Library Journal, April 15, 2001, page 135
Locus, March 2001, page 21
Publishers Weekly, March 15, 2001, page 67
School Library Journal, April 15, 2001, page 135

Awards the book has won:
School Library Journal Best Books, 2001

Other books by the same author:
To Say Nothing of the Dog, or How We Found the Bishop's Bird Stump at Last, 1997
Bellwether, 1996
Promised Land, 1996

Other books you might like:
Kage Baker, *In the Garden of Iden*, 1997
 Scientifically trained cyborgs travel through time but are not immune to the most dangerous human ill—love.
Peter S. Beagle, *A Dance for Emilia*, 2000
 In this gentle haunting, love finds a way to reach back to life from beyond death.
Rachel Pollack, *Godmother Night*, 1996
 The incarnation of Death makes a strange and frightening spectacle as she comes for the doomed with her motorcycle gang.

BUDGE WILSON
SUSAN TOOKE, Illustrator

A Fiddle for Angus

(Plattsburgh, New York: Tundra Books, 2001)

Subject(s): Music and Musicians; Family; Talent
Age range(s): Grades 1-3
Major character(s): Angus, Son, Brother (younger); Big Murdoch MacDougall, Musician, Teacher; Molly, Sister, Singer
Time period(s): 2000s (2001)
Locale(s): Cape Breton, Nova Scotia, Canada

Summary: Everyone in Angus's family plays a musical instrument except Molly who sings and Angus who hums along with the tune. Although his family thinks his humming is an important part of their musical medley, Angus is sad not to be able to do something more. When his parents agree that he's old enough to get an instrument Angus curbs his excitement enough to consider carefully a variety of possibilities before deciding that a fiddle is the musical instrument that's right for him. Initially, the squawks that come from the fiddle as Angus pulls the bow across the strings are so discouraging that he wonders where the music is hiding. Lessons from Big Murdoch MacDougal and lots of practice enable Angus to draw the music out of the fiddle and become a full participant with his musical family. (32 pages)

Where it's reviewed:
Booklist, October 15, 2001, page 402
Horn Book Guide, Spring 2002, page 63
School Library Journal, October 2001, page 134

Other books by the same author:
The Fear of Angelina Domino, 2000
Duff the Giant Killer, 1997
The Long Wait, 1997

Other books you might like:
David F. Birchman, *A Green Horn Blowing*, 1997
 A migrant worker introduces a young boy to the joy of music and leaves his trumpet behind for the boy when he leaves the farm.
Marianna Dengler, *Fiddlin' Sam*, 1999
 After a nomadic life fiddling in the Ozarks, Fiddlin' Sam finds a boy with a gift for music to whom he can pass his talent and his fiddle.
Harriett Diller, *Big Band Sound*, 1996
 When her makeshift drum set goes out with the trash Arlis searches for other discards and creates more drums.
George Ella Lyon, *Five Live Bongos*, 1994
 Five lively children create the "Found Sound Band" with everyday household items and discards.
Lloyd Moss, *Zin! Zin! Zin! A Violin*, 1995
 Playful rhymes and zany illustrations introduce the instruments of the orchestra.

969

DAWN WILSON

Saint Jude

(Greensboro, NC: Tudor Publishers, 2001)

Subject(s): Mental Illness
Age range(s): Grades 9-12
Major character(s): Taylor Jay Drysdale, 18-Year-Old, Mentally Ill Person
Time period(s): 2000s
Locale(s): Asheville, North Carolina

Summary: Diagnosed with bipolar disorder, Taylor is medicated with lithium but when that doesn't help, is taken to St. Jude's Academy. Living in a group home is stressful for Taylor as there are rules, restrictions and no guarantee of when she can go home. One group member commits suicide, the director resigns and the group home begins to dissolve when no new members are admitted. Taylor proves a lot to herself during her stay, from surviving being dumped by her boyfriend to now attending college and playing her beloved guitar as she tries to make it on her own. (171 pages)

Where it's reviewed:
Booklist, November 1, 2001, page 471
School Library Journal, November 2001, page 166

Other books you might like:
Lisa Rowe Fraustino, *Ash: A Novel*, 1995
    Again and again Ash and his family try to save his older, schizophrenic brother from suicide attempts.
Patricia McCormick, *Cut*, 2000
    Callie won't talk, either during group sessions or with the therapist, until another patient is admitted who has the same self-cutting problem as Callie.
Shelley Stoehr, *Crosses*, 1991
    Nancy and Katie deal with their problems by cutting themselves with glass, their fingernails or any sharp object.
Ruth White, *Memories of Summer*, 2000
    After they move to Michigan, Lyric realizes that her sister Summer's tics and phobias are worsening as her mental condition deteriorates.

970

JACQUELINE WILSON
NICK SHARRATT, Illustrator

Bad Girls

(New York: Delacorte Press, 2001)

Subject(s): Bullies; Friendship; Schools
Age range(s): Grades 4-6
Major character(s): Mandy White, 10-Year-Old, Bullied Child; Tanya, Foster Child, 14-Year-Old
Time period(s): 1990s (1996)
Locale(s): England

Summary: Bullied by three girls in her class Mandy, the only child of older parents, dashes into the street and is struck by a bus. Her concerned mother attempts to get the school to stop the problem but it worsens. When Tanya moves into the foster home across the street she takes a liking to Mandy who reminds her of a younger sister from whom she's separated. Mandy, while excited to have Tanya as a friend and grateful for the protection she offers against the bullies, also is concerned about Tanya's habit of shoplifting. Rather than see the friendship end Mandy agrees not to complain about it and Tanya agrees not to steal anything for Mandy. Eventually, during a shopping trip with Mandy, Tanya is caught and arrested. Through their brief friendship Mandy learns self-confidence and as the new school year begins she has a new friend and a teacher who tackles the bullying issue in a positive way. Originally published in Great Britain in 1996. (165 pages)

Where it's reviewed:
Booklist, January 1, 2001, page 962
Bulletin of the Center for Children's Books, March 2001, page 283
Kirkus Reviews, December 15, 2000, page 1767
Publishers Weekly, January 8, 2001, page 68
School Library Journal, March 2001, page 258

Awards the book has won:
IRA Children's Choices, 2002

Other books by the same author:
The Story of Tracy Beaker, 2001
Double Act, 1998 (Smarties Prize)
Elsa, Star of the Shelter!, 1996

Other books you might like:
C. Anne Scott, *Lizard Meets Ivana the Terrible*, 1999
    When Lizzie moves in with her grandmother and enters a new school she worries about making friends.
Dyan Sheldon, *My Brother Is a Superhero*, 1996
    When three bullies harass Adam and his friend they try to handle the problem but are grateful when Adam's older brother intervenes.
Susan Shreve, *Joshua T. Bates Takes Charge*, 1993
    Joshua finally finds the courage to stand up to the school bully and stop his abusive treatment of others.

971

JACQUELINE WILSON
NICK SHARRATT, Illustrator

The Story of Tracy Beaker

(New York: Delacorte Press, 2001)

Subject(s): Foster Homes; Foster Children; Mothers and Daughters
Age range(s): Grades 4-6
Major character(s): Tracy Beaker, 10-Year-Old, Foster Child; Cam Lawson, Writer; Peter Ingham, Orphan, Friend
Time period(s): 1990s (1991)
Locale(s): England

Summary: As Tracy points out in her personal book that she's writing about her life it is certainly not her fault that she's living in another children's home and that her former foster home placements did not work out. Any day now Tracy believes her mother will return to get her so those other situations don't really matter and because she'll be leaving soon she doesn't need to make any friends in this home. Peter has never been in this situation before and he'd really like

Tracy to be his friend so she reluctantly agrees because beneath the tough exterior of this child, who never cries but sometimes has ''hay fever,'' lies a sensitive soul. Befriended by Cam, who's trying to do an article about foster care, Tracy has hopes that the single woman will become her foster mom. At least Cam accepts her as she is so Tracy has one positive relationship in a title originally published in England in 1991. (136 pages)

Where it's reviewed:
Booklist, June 2001, page 1884
Bulletin of the Center for Children's Books, April 2001, page 321
Horn Book, September 2001, page 598
Kirkus Reviews, June 15, 2001, page 873
School Library Journal, July 2001, page 116

Other books by the same author:
Bad Girls, 2001
The Lottie Project, 1999
The Suitcase Kid, 1997

Other books you might like:
Betsy Byars, *The Pinballs*, 1977
    Three foster children cope with loneliness by learning to care about others and themselves.
Adrian Fogelin, *Anna Casey's Place in the World*, 2001
    For now, Anna's ''place'' is a foster home in Florida and adjusting to it is difficult.
Katherine Paterson, *The Great Gilly Hopkins*, 1978
    Eleven-year-old Gilly longs to live with her mother and rejects those who reach out to her in friendship.

972

JACQUELINE WILSON
NICK SHARRATT, Illustrator

Vicky Angel
(New York: Delacorte, 2001)

Subject(s): Death; Grief; Guilt
Age range(s): Grades 5-8
Major character(s): Jade Marshall, 9th Grader; Vicky Waters, 9th Grader; Mrs. Wainwright, Counselor (grief)
Time period(s): 2000s
Locale(s): England

Summary: Friends since nursery school, Jade is Vicky's shadow, and lives in her shadow, until the day she tries to speak up for herself about her intent to attend a drama club meeting. Vicky counters with their need to join the Fun Run Club, which Jade hates, at which point they have a tiff and Vicky walks away into the path of an oncoming car. Though grief-stricken without her best friend, Jade is heartened when Vicky returns as an angel and pops in and out of her life. Sometimes Vicky amuses her, but at other times taunts her and keeps Jade away from her classmates, acting as though she doesn't want Jade to have other friends. This continues until Jade sees the grief counselor, Mrs. Wainwright, who helps her see how restrictive and one-sided her friendship was with Vicky, which in turn gives Jade the strength to let her go. (171 pages)

Where it's reviewed:
Booklist, November 15, 2001, page 575
Bulletin of the Center for Children's Books, October 2001, page 83
Publishers Weekly, August 13, 2001, page 313
School Library Journal, October 2001, page 175
Voice of Youth Advocates, December 2001, page 375

Awards the book has won:
Bulletin of the Center for Children's Books Blue Ribbon, 2001

Other books by the same author:
Girls in Love, 2002
Girls under Pressure, 2002
The Story of Tracy Beaker, 2001
The Lottie Project, 1999
Double Act, 1998

Other books you might like:
Julie Reece Deaver, *Say Goodnight, Gracie*, 1988
    Morgan's life comes to an abrupt halt when her dear friend Jimmy is killed in an automobile accident.
Louise Hawes, *Rosey in the Present Tense*, 1999
    Though killed in an automobile accident, Rosey returns to her boyfriend Franklin.
Peter Pohl, *I Miss You, I Miss You!*, 1999
    When Cilla is hit and killed by a car, her twin Tina is not sure she can survive.
Robert Westall, *The Promise*, 1990
    Valerie dies during World War II, a bomb obliterates her grave, and her ghost remembers Bob's promise to find her if she's ever lost.

973

NANCY HOPE WILSON

Mountain Pose
(New York: Farrar Straus Giroux, 2001)

Subject(s): Grandmothers; Diaries; Inheritance
Age range(s): Grades 5-7
Major character(s): Eleanor ''Ellie'' Dunklee, 12-Year-Old; Aurelia Sprague, Grandmother; Lyman Sprague, Uncle
Time period(s): 2000s
Locale(s): Hampton, Massachusetts; Hart Farm, Vermont

Summary: When Ellie is only five, her mother dies; seven years later, her mother's mother, the hateful Aurelia, dies and leaves Ellie as sole heir to Hart Farm. Ellie can't believe it, especially because Aurelia left her son, Ellie's Uncle Lyman, only an empty wooden chest. Aurelia had only one other request for Ellie, and that was to read the family diaries, which her father asks her not to do as anything Aurelia did was usually tinged with bitterness and hate. Ellie loves her professor father, but she is also curious about this woman who raised her mother, so she reads the diaries, even solving the code in which some of them are written. As she learns about the six generations of women, the family history of abuse becomes evident, even through Aurelia's time, which at least explains some of her behavior. Sharing her discovery with her father and Uncle Lyman helps them begin a healing process in this quiet, reflective work. (233 pages)

Where it's reviewed:
Booklist, August 2001, page 2123
Bulletin of the Center for Children's Books, June 2001, page 391
Publishers Weekly, April 2, 2001, page 66
School Library Journal, April 2001, page 152
Voice of Youth Advocates, June 2001, page 130

Other books by the same author:
Flapjack Waltzes, 1998
Becoming Felix, 1996
The Reason for Janey, 1994
Bringing Nettie Back, 1992

Other books you might like:
Irene Bennett Brown, *Answer Me, Answer Me*, 1985
    After Gram's death, Bryn discovers a large bank account that allows her to search for her unknown parents.
Kevin Henkes, *The Birthday Room*, 1999
    Ben gives up his studio to turn it into a guest bedroom so that his estranged uncle will come visit Ben's family.
Jan O'Donnell Klaveness, *Keeper of the Light*, 1990
    Ian thinks his grandmother doesn't care about him, but after her death finds he's inherited everything.

974

KEN WILSON-MAX, Author/Illustrator

Max's Starry Night
(New York: Jump at the Sun/Hyperion Books for Children, 2001)

Subject(s): Fear; Friendship; Problem Solving
Age range(s): Preschool-Kindergarten
Major character(s): Max, Child; Little Pink, Pig, Toy; Big Blue, Elephant, Toy
Time period(s): Indeterminate
Locale(s): Fictional Country

Summary: Max and Little Pink hurry outside before bedtime to make a wish on a star, but Big Blue refuses to join them. With encouragement, fearful Big Blue finally comes out to wish that he could not be afraid of the dark. Little Pink teases Big Blue for being afraid but Max tries to help him and reminds Little Pink of the things that he finds frightening. Finally Max devises a way for Big Blue to feel comfortable while they all wish on a star in the comfort of Max's room. (28 pages)

Where it's reviewed:
Booklist, January, 2001, page 975
Horn Book Guide, Fall 2001, page 243
Publishers Weekly, January 22, 2001, page 323
School Library Journal, March 2001, page 224

Other books by the same author:
Big Silver Space Shuttle, 2000
Max Loves Sunflowers, 1999
Max's Money, 1999
Max, 1998
Wake Up; Sleep Tight, 1998

Other books you might like:
Russell Hoban, *Bedtime for Frances*, 1960
    Frances imagines so many scary things in her room that she is unable to sleep.

Ellen Stoll Walsh, *Pip's Magic*, 1994
    Unexpectedly, while searching for answers to his fear of the dark, Pip overcomes his problem.
Mary Wormell, *Hilda Hen's Scary Night*, 1996
    To reach the safety of the hen house, Hilda Hen must cross the dark and forbidding yard.

975

JEANETTE WINTER, Author/Illustrator

My Baby
(New York: Frances Foster Books/Farrar Straus Giroux, 2001)

Subject(s): Artists and Art; Babies
Age range(s): Grades K-3
Major character(s): Nakunte, Artist, Mother
Time period(s): Indeterminate Past
Locale(s): Mali

Summary: As a child Nakunte observes her mother painting bogolan cloth and gradually learns to create her own designs with mud and a painting stick. After her marriage, Nakunte begins working on a special cloth for the baby that will be born in the spring. She carefully selects the best mud and the leaves to color it before planning her designs. Then, Nakunte allows the cultural and natural elements in her environment to inspire the designs she carefully paints in black on the white cloth in which she will wrap her baby. (32 pages)

Where it's reviewed:
Booklist, February 15, 2001, page 1158
Five Owls, Fall 2001, page 20
Publishers Weekly, January 1, 2001, page 91
Riverbank Review, Spring 2001, page 33
School Library Journal, April 2001, page 126

Other books by the same author:
Rock-a-Bye Baby, 1999
My Name Is Georgia: A Portrait, 1998
Josefina, 1996 (Bulletin of the Center for Children's Books Blue Ribbon)

Other books you might like:
Debbi Chocolate, *On the Day I Was Born*, 1995
    Relatives celebrate a newborn's birth with gifts of a kente cloth and a kofia.
Niki Daly, *Jamela's Dress*, 1999
    Jamela is so attracted to her mother's new dress fabric that she uses it to fashion an outfit for herself and parades about her village.
Margaret Musgrove, *The Spider Weaver: A Legend of Kente Cloth*, 2001
    In Ghana, a spider's intricate web inspires two weavers to try new patterns as they create cloth on their looms.

976

ELIZABETH WINTHROP
BETSY LEWIN, Illustrator

Dumpy La Rue
(New York: Henry Holt and Company, 2001)

Subject(s): Dancing; Animals/Pigs; Stories in Rhyme

Age range(s): Grades K-2
Major character(s): Dumpy La Rue, Pig, Dancer
Time period(s): Indeterminate
Locale(s): Fictional Country

Summary: Dumpy's got rhythm and he wants to dance despite the objections of his family that pigs simply don't do that sort of thing. Dumpy does and soon he's got most of the animals swinging and swaying to their individual inner beats. At first Dumpy's family tries to ignore him but even they are taken in by the joyful exuberance of the animals and soon the entire barnyard is dancing in Dumpy's ballet. (36 pages)

Where it's reviewed:
Booklist, March 15, 2001, page 1406
Bulletin of the Center for Children's Books, July 2001, page 426
Children's Bookwatch, June 2001, page 4
Horn Book Guide, Fall 2001, page 281
School Library Journal, May 2001, page 139

Other books by the same author:
Promises, 2000
As the Crow Flies, 1998
A Little Humpbacked Horse: A Russian Tale, 1997
Bear and Roly-Poly, 1996
Asleep in a Heap, 1993

Other books you might like:
Janie Bynum, *Otis*, 2000
    A clean pig that dislikes mud is a pig searching for a friend and fastidious Otis finds one when he meets Little Frog, another mud hater.
Ellen Stoll Walsh, *Hop Jump*, 1993
    Other frogs may hop, but an independently minded blue frog learns to dance instead.
Piotr Wilkon, *Rosie the Cool Cat*, 1991
    Unlike the others in her family, Rosie expresses her individuality by becoming a rock star.

977

ELIZABETH WINTHROP

Franklin Delano Roosevelt: Letters from a Mill Town Girl

(New York: Winslow, 2001)

Series: Dear Mr. President
Subject(s): Letters; Presidents; Depression (Economic)
Age range(s): Grades 5-8
Major character(s): Emma Bartoletti, 12-Year-Old; Franklin Delano Roosevelt, Political Figure (president)
Time period(s): 1930s (1933-1936)
Locale(s): North Adams, Massachusetts; Washington, District of Columbia

Summary: As her father's working hours are reduced and the family's finances dwindle, Emma's aunt suggests she write the president to find out why their lives are changing. Emma, daughter of Italian immigrants, does just that and thus begins a three-year correspondence between the two. When Emma questions some of Roosevelt's actions, he responds and recommends she listen to his weekly radio addresses. She describes her home life, the cutbacks her family makes to survive, and how their mill town is changing while the president describes ways he's helping the entire country. Part of a continuing series, this book explains everyday life during the time of the Depression. (153 pages)

Where it's reviewed:
Booklist, February 1, 2002, page 942
School Library Journal, December 2001, page 148

Other books by the same author:
The Battle for the Castle, 1993
The Castle in the Attic, 1985

Other books you might like:
Jennifer Armstrong, *Theodore Roosevelt: Letters from a Young Coal Miner*, 2001
    A feeling of warmth and respect fills the letters between two unlikely correspondents, the coal miner Frank Kovacs and the president Teddy Roosevelt.
Cynthia DeFelice, *Nowhere to Call Home*, 1999
    During the Depression, Francie's left an orphan when her father commits suicide rather than face bankruptcy after losing his factories.
Steven Kroll, *John Quincy Adams: Letters from a Southern Planter's Son*, 2001
    Letters between William Pratt and President Adams discuss plantation life, slavery, Pratt's school day and life in the White House.

978

ELLEN WITTLINGER

Razzle

(New York: Simon & Schuster, 2001)

Subject(s): Family Life; Photography; Friendship
Age range(s): Grades 8-12
Major character(s): Kenyon "Ken" Baker, 15-Year-Old, Photographer; Razzle Penney, Teenager; Harley, 16-Year-Old
Time period(s): 2000s
Locale(s): Truro, Massachusetts

Summary: Moving from Boston wasn't his idea, thinks Kenyon as he settles in for a summer of working on the vacation cottages his parents bought as their retirement income. In exchange for his handyman work, Ken lives in one of the cottages and uses it as a darkroom for his photography. He meets a wonderful subject for portraits when he bumps into Razzle who runs the recycling center at the town dump. Tall, thin, and buzz-cut, this independent teenager lives with her grandmother and brother, away from her alcoholic, promiscuous mother. Ken and Razzle enjoy their times together as Ken takes a series of photos he plans to exhibit, but their light-heartedness is destroyed when Harley, the town sexpot who dreams of being a model, befriends Ken. Warned about the many boyfriends Harley has tossed aside, poor Ken is swept off his feet for no "babe" has ever expressed interest in him before, even though his foolhardiness could mean the end of Razzle's friendship. (247 pages)

Where it's reviewed:
Booklist, November 1, 2001, page 477
Horn Book, November 2001, page 758
Kliatt, September 2001, page 14

School Library Journal, September 2001, page 235
Voice of Youth Advocates, October 2001, page 287

Awards the book has won:
ALA Best Books for Young Adults, 2002

Other books by the same author:
The Long Night of Leo and Bree, 2002
Gracie's Girl, 2000
What's in a Name?, 2000
Hard Love, 1999
Noticing Paradise, 1995

Other books you might like:
Rebecca Busselle, *A Frog's-Eye View*, 1990
   When Neela's strategy for romance doesn't pan out, she gladly accepts her Great-Aunt Amelia's offer of photography lessons.
Ann Herrick, *The Perfect Guy*, 1989
   Rebecca's attempt to make her new stepbrother fall for her backfires and she almost loses out on the best guy of all.
M.E. Kerr, *Night Kites*, 1989
   Erick's folks are so busy caring for his AIDS-stricken brother, they don't know he spends his afternoons in Nicki Marr's room.
Norma Klein, *Just Friends*, 1990
   Isabel and Stuart have been close friends for years, but it's not until Stuart starts dating her best friend that Isabel recognizes his worth.

979

GRETCHEN WOELFLE
NICOLA BAYLEY, Illustrator

Katje, the Windmill Cat
(Cambridge, MA: Candlewick Press, 2001)

Subject(s): Animals/Cats; Floods; Babies
Age range(s): Grades K-3
Major character(s): Katje, Cat; Anneke, Baby; Nico, Father, Spouse; Lena, Mother, Spouse
Time period(s): 15th century (1421)
Locale(s): Netherlands

Summary: Katje's idyllic life as Nico's pet ends when he marries. Rather than face scolding from Lena, Katje retreats to Nico's mill where she keeps the mice under control. At night when the adults sleep, Katje sneaks into the house and gently rocks Anneke's cradle by leaping from side to side. On a stormy day Lena brings food to Nico at the mill and Katje hurries to the house to visit Anneke. A dam breaks rapidly flooding the village and the cradle, with Anneke and Katje, floats away in the swirling water. Nico and Lena in a rowboat pursue the bobbing cradle that Katje keeps balanced by leaping from side to side as the sea rocks it until Nico and Lena rescue them. A concluding note gives the historical background for the story. (28 pages)

Where it's reviewed:
Booklist, February 1, 2002, page 940
Horn Book Guide, Spring 2002, page 63
Kirkus Reviews, August 15, 2001, page 1223
Publishers Weekly, September 10, 2001, page 92
School Library Journal, November 2001, page 139

Other books by the same author:
The Wind at Work: An Activity Guide to Windmills, 1997

Other books you might like:
Norma Green, *The Hole in the Dike*, 1974
   In this adaptation a courageous little boy saves his country when he notices a hole in the dike and takes action.
Thomas Locker, *The Boy Who Held Back the Sea*, 1987
   A picture book adaptation from *Hans Brinker, or, The Silver Skates* retells the story of the boy who saves the town by blocking a leak in the dike.
George Ella Lyon, *One Lucky Girl*, 2000
   A tornado picks up Becky's crib and carries it away, depositing it in a field where her family finds her, still sleeping.
Gloria Rand, *Baby in a Basket*, 1997
   Trappers find a baby, securely bundled in a basket, hours after a sleigh tips over during an Alaskan snowstorm and the basket falls out.

980

VIRGINIA EUWER WOLFF

True Believer
(New York: Atheneum/Simon & Schuster, 2001)

Subject(s): Single Parent Families; Conduct of Life; Poverty
Age range(s): Grades 7-12
Major character(s): Verna LaVaughn, 15-Year-Old, 10th Grader; Jody, Homosexual
Time period(s): 2000s
Locale(s): United States

Summary: Living with her mother in a small, inner-city apartment, LaVaughn faces daily violence and poverty, but tries to keep her focus on college. She moves up to an advanced biology class and after school Grammar Build-Up lessons, moving beyond her friends academically. LaVaughn also sets herself apart from some childhood friends when she chooses not to join a "Cross Your Legs for Jesus" group, especially when her friend Jody moves back into the neighborhood. Jody is one fine-looking young man and LaVaughn is interested in him, even asking him to join her at a school dance. Surprising him with cookies one day, she enters his apartment to see him kissing another boy and her world momentarily falls apart. The resilience she showed in *Make Lemonade* returns and LaVaughn has all the support she needs to forgive Jody and accept him as her friend. (264 pages)

Where it's reviewed:
Booklist, February 1, 2001, page 1051
Bulletin of the Center for Children's Books, May 2001, page 329
Horn Book, January 2001, page 98
Publishers Weekly, December 18, 2000, page 79
School Library Journal, January 2001, page 136

Awards the book has won:
ALA Michael L. Printz Honor Book, 2002
ALA Best Books for Young Adults, 2002

Other books by the same author:
Bat 6, 1998
Make Lemonade, 1993

The Mozart Season, 1991
Probably Still Nick Swanson, 1988

Other books you might like:

Joyce Annette Barnes, *Promise Me the Moon*, 1997
Though Annie is rejected for a magnet school, a trip to visit relatives, an inheritance and eventual acceptance to McAllen High reinforce her self-esteem.

Evelyn Coleman, *Born in Sin*, 2001
Keisha can't believe her misguided principal enrolls her in a summer program for ''at risk'' students after she'd been tentatively accepted at Avery University.

Ellen Wittlinger, *Hard Love*, 1999
John thinks he's found the love for which he's been searching when he meets Marisol, only to discover she's in love with another girl.

981

DIANE WOLKSTEIN
STEVE JOHNSON, Illustrator
LOU FANCHER, Illustrator

The Day Ocean Came to Visit

(San Diego: Gulliver Books/Harcourt, Inc., 2001)

Subject(s): Folklore; Floods
Age range(s): Grades K-3
Major character(s): Sun, Celestial Body, Spouse; Moon, Celestial Body, Spouse; Ocean, Friend
Time period(s): Indeterminate Past
Locale(s): Nigeria

Summary: In this retelling of a Nigerian folktale Sun and Moon live happily in a bamboo hut constructed by Sun. By day Sun enjoys riding about on the back of a giraffe and visiting friends while Moon prefers to stay at home working in her garden. One day, after riding far, Sun meets Ocean and is fascinated by her tales. Ocean desires to meet Moon but Moon refuses to leave her garden and travel to Ocean. Sun enlarges their home and invites Ocean to come to them. Although she initially demurs, Ocean does agree to travel to Sun and Moon's home. Of course, by entering, Ocean floods them out. Sun and Moon leap from the roof into the sky where they live to this day with their children, the stars. (32 pages)

Where it's reviewed:
Booklist, July 2001, page 2015
Horn Book Guide, Spring 2002, page 123
Kirkus Reviews, July 1, 2001, page 949
Publishers Weekly, August 13, 2001, page 311
School Library Journal, August 2001, page 174

Other books by the same author:
White Wave: A Chinese Tale, 1996
Little Mouse's Painting, 1992
The Banza: A Haitian Story, 1981
The Red Lion: A Tale of Ancient Persia, 1977

Other books you might like:
Ashley Bryan, *Beat the Story-Drum, Pum-Pum*, 1987
An illustrated collection retells five Nigerian folktales.

Elphinstone Dayrell, *Why the Sun and the Moon Live in the Sky: An African Folktale*, 1968
When sun and moon lived on earth their house was too

small for a visit from their friend water so they moved to the sky. Caldecott Honor Book.

Mary-Joan Gerson, *Why the Sky Is Far Away: A Nigerian Folktale*, 1992
Considering itself misused by the peasants, the sky responds by moving farther away.

982

AUDREY WOOD
BRUCE WOOD, Illustrator

Alphabet Adventure

(New York: Blue Sky Press/Scholastic, Inc., 2001)

Subject(s): Letters; Lost and Found; Writing
Age range(s): Preschool-Grade 1
Major character(s): Charley, Child, Student
Time period(s): Indeterminate
Locale(s): United States

Summary: The lower case letters from Charley's alphabet set eagerly march to school to help some lucky child learn their ABCs. When the lower case ''i'' trips and falls off a bridge the other letters link together to rescue her. Unfortunately her dot is lost. Frantically the letters search for the dot or a substitute but nothing seems to work. Finally, the dot comes out of hiding to rejoin her letter and the 26 letters hurry to school just in time to spell their first word, ''Charley.'' (36 pages)

Where it's reviewed:
Booklist, September 1, 2001, page 118
Horn Book Guide, Spring 2002, page 32
Kirkus Reviews, July 1, 2001, page 949
Publishers Weekly, July 2, 2001, page 75
School Library Journal, September 2001, page 209

Other books by the same author:
Jubal's Wish, 2000
Sweet Dream Pie, 1998
The Flying Dragon Room, 1996

Other books you might like:
Mirko Gabler, *The Alphabet Soup*, 1992
Zack is just what witch twins need to complete their alphabet soup.

Holly Hobbie, *Toot & Puddle: Puddle's ABC*, 2000
Otto wants to write his name so his friend Puddle teaches him the letters of the alphabet.

Bob Reese, *ABC*, 1992
In a rhyming story a teacher shows students how letters go together to make words.

983

JACQUELINE WOODSON
E.B. LEWIS, Illustrator

The Other Side

(New York: G.P. Putnam's Sons, 2001)

Subject(s): Race Relations; Friendship; Summer
Age range(s): Grades 1-4

Major character(s): Annie Paul, Child, Neighbor; Clover, Child, Narrator; Mama, Mother
Time period(s): Indeterminate Past
Locale(s): United States

Summary: The summer Clover notices a girl sitting atop the fence that runs through her town, dividing white folks from black ones, the fence seems bigger than usual to Clover. Mama's told Clover not to go to the other side of the fence, but every day she sees that girl sitting there, alone. When it rains the girl is there in her raincoat, dancing in the puddles or sitting on the fence. Finally, Clover courageously approaches the fence and joins Annie. Both girls agree that, though they've been told not to go to the other side, no one's told them not to sit atop the dividing line. Eventually, Clover's friends include Annie in their game of jump rope and Annie and Clover are joined by a group of girls sitting on the fence who watch the world and ponder how long the fence will remain. (32 pages)

Where it's reviewed:
Booklist, February 15, 2001, page 1154
Bulletin of the Center for Children's Books, February 2001, page 211
Publishers Weekly, December 4, 2000, page 73
Riverbank Review, Spring 2001, page 33
School Library Journal, January 2001, page 112

Awards the book has won:
ALA Notable Children's Books, 2002
School Library Journal Best Books, 2001

Other books by the same author:
Sweet, Sweet Memory, 2000
We Had a Picnic This Sunday Past, 1997
Martin Luther King, Jr., and His Birthday, 1990

Other books you might like:
Margaret Carlson, *The Canning Season*, 1999
    One hot summer in the 1950s two girls of different races find their friendship challenged by society's expectations.
K. Scott Conover, *Can I Play Too?*, 1998
    New to the neighborhood, a young boy in orthopedic braces must convince the other children to let him join in their games.
William Miller, *Night Golf*, 1999
    The only time James can play on the town's "whites only" golf course is at night after the course is closed.

984

JACQUELINE WOODSON
FLOYD COOPER, Illustrator

Sweet, Sweet Memory

(New York: Jump at the Sun/Hyperion Books for Children, 2000)

Subject(s): Death; Grief; Grandparents
Age range(s): Grades 1-4
Major character(s): Grandma, Grandmother; Grandpa, Grandfather; Sarah, Daughter (grandaughter)
Time period(s): Indeterminate Past
Locale(s): United States

Summary: The relatives gather to remember Grandpa and Sarah doesn't want to share a story, but one of her uncles says

exactly what she's thinking. It seems Grandpa gave the same advice to so many that anyone who knew him can recall that "everyone and everything goes on and on," just like Grandpa said. Before he died, Grandpa planted his garden and Sarah and Grandma enjoy its harvest of sweet, sweet memories through the summer and into the fall. (32 pages)

Where it's reviewed:
Black Issues Book Review, July 2001, page 74
Booklist, February 15, 2001, page 1158
Bulletin of the Center for Children's Books, May 2001, page 357
Horn Book Guide, Fall 2001, page 282
School Library Journal, April 2001, page 126

Other books by the same author:
Our Gracie Aunt, 2002
The Other Side, 2001
We Had a Picnic This Sunday Past, 1997

Other books you might like:
Trish Cooke, *The Grandad Tree*, 2000
    Grandad's apple tree lives on after his death reminding Vin and Leigh of happy times when Grandad played his fiddle in the tree's shade.
Mem Fox, *Sophie*, 1994
    Because Granpa has always been part of Sophie's life his death leaves a sense of emptiness that, in time, is filled.
Marisabina Russo, *Grandpa Abe*, 1996
    Grandpa Abe dies leaving nine-year-old Sarah with memories and the ability to perform his magic thumb trick.
Jane Yolen, *Grandad Bill's Song*, 1994
    With support from family and friends, a young boy begins to accept his feelings following his grandfather's death.

985

MARY WORMELL, Author/Illustrator

Bernard the Angry Rooster

(New York: Farrar Straus Giroux, 2001)

Subject(s): Animals/Roosters; Farm Life; Behavior
Age range(s): Preschool-Kindergarten
Major character(s): Bernard, Rooster; Lucy, Child
Time period(s): 2000s
Locale(s): Scotland

Summary: Bernard shocks the barnyard animals one day when the previously happy, proud rooster reacts angrily to anyone and everything in his path. He chases Lucy when she brings the food, leaps at the sleeping cat and pecks the tail of the dog. Bernard has no answer to those questioning his cross mood but, when he jumps onto the back of the pony and is bucked high onto the stable roof, the answer emerges. From the rooftop Bernard is able to climb a tree and now he is higher than the new rooster-shaped weather vane just installed atop the farmhouse. With help from his friends Bernard will continue to be the "top" rooster. (32 pages)

Where it's reviewed:
Booklist, May 1, 2001, page 1694
Bulletin of the Center for Children's Books, April 2001, page 322
Horn Book Guide, Fall 2001, page 244

Publishers Weekly, February 19, 2001, page 89
School Library Journal, July 2001, page 91

Other books by the same author:
Why Not?, 2000
Hilda Hen's Scary Night, 1996
Hilda Hen's Happy Birthday, 1995

Other books you might like:
Bill Martin Jr., *Chicken Chuck*, 2000
　　A rooster's inflated sense of self-importance shatters when he spots a circus poster with a horse that has not one, but two blue feathers on his head.
Bill Peet, *Cock-a-Doodle Dudley*, 1990
　　Cocky Dudley thinks that he controls the daily rising of the sun.
Janet Stevens, *Cook-a-Doodle-Doo!*, 1999
　　Bored with a steady diet of chicken feed, Big Brown Rooster takes charge in the kitchen and makes strawberry shortcake, with help from his friends.

986

CATHERINE WRIGHT
HOWARD FINE, Illustrator

Steamboat Annie and the Thousand-Pound Catfish

(New York: Philomel Books, 2001)

Subject(s): Fishing; Tall Tales; Singing
Age range(s): Grades 1-4
Major character(s): Steamboat Annie, Fisherman, Political Figure (mayor); Ernie, Fish
Time period(s): Indeterminate Past
Locale(s): Pleasant, Indiana; Ohio River

Summary: To save her town from the ravages of Ernie, a grumpy catfish that has already eaten boats, a dock and the church in his attempts to end the cheerful singing of the citizens, Steamboat Annie decides to fish for the rascal. She hooks him on the second try and then battles the mammoth fish up and down the river for a year and a half before she finally hauls him in and then flings the catfish all the way to California where he lands in an old gold mine. The town rebuilds and returns to singing without fear of Ernie in the author's first book for children. (32 pages)

Where it's reviewed:
Booklist, July 2001, page 2015
Bulletin of the Center for Children's Books, September 2001, page 41
Publishers Weekly, October 29, 2001, page 63
School Library Journal, October 2001, page 134

Other books you might like:
Anne Isaacs, *Swamp Angel*, 1994
　　An original tall tale and Caldecott Honor Book describes the achievements of Angelica and how she earns her nickname.
Patricia C. McKissack, *A Million Fish . . . More or Less*, 1992
　　None of Hugh Thomas' fish are as big as Ernie, but he sure does catch a lot of them.
Alexis O'Neill, *Loud Emily*, 1998
　　Emily's voice is so loud it can be heard over the sounds of

a storm at sea thus attracting whales that help to save the ship.
Kenneth Oppel, *Peg and the Whale*, 2000
　　When Peg tries to catch a whale she ends up being swallowed by one but manages to live comfortably in the whale's belly.

987

DON WULFFSON

Soldier X

(New York: Viking/Penguin, 2001)

Subject(s): World War II; Identity, Concealed
Age range(s): Grades 8-12
Major character(s): Erik Brandt, 16-Year-Old, Military Personnel; Tamara, Nurse (aide)
Time period(s): 1940s
Locale(s): Tarnapol, Russia

Summary: On his sixteenth birthday and with only three weeks of training, Erik is aboard a train with other teens from Hitler Youth, who are sent to the Russian front in a last effort stand. Erik assumes his knowledge of the Russian language will keep him away from the enemy lines and busy with interpreting, but that proves wrong when he's shoved into a ditch and faces a heavy Russian attack. Wounded, Erik takes a desperate chance and switches uniforms with a dead Russian soldier, is taken to a Russian hospital and feigns amnesia. His command of the Russian language, learned from his mother and her parents, aids his charade and he is called Soldier X. Recovering from his wounds, he remains at the hospital as an orderly and falls in love with the nurse's aide Tamara, the only one who sees through his disguise. When the hospital is attacked, Erik and Tamara help the patients to safety and then the two flee, running away from Germans and Russians as they try to escape from the horror of war. (226 pages)

Where it's reviewed:
Booklist, May 1, 2001, page 1676
Horn Book, July 2001, page 463
Publishers Weekly, January 20, 2001, page 90
School Library Journal, March 2001, page 258
Voice of Youth Advocates, April 2001, page 48

Awards the book has won:
Bulletin of the Center for Children's Books Blue Ribbon, 2001
Christopher Awards/Young Adult, 2002

Other books by the same author:
Still More Scary Stories for Stormy Nights, 1997 (Jim Charbonneau, co-author)
Aliens: Extraterrestrial Tales of Terror, 1996
Mega Scary Stories for Sleep-Overs, 1996

Other books you might like:
Grigory Baklanov, *Forever Nineteen*, 1989
　　For Lt. Volodya Tretyakov, the war ends when an artillery shell explodes and he is "forever nineteen."
Robert Cormier, *Heroes*, 1998
　　After being wounded in World War II, Francis finds there are many different types of heroes.

Dean Hughes, *Soldier Boys*, 2001
Two teens hurry into battle, one from Utah and one from Germany, never imagining they'll face one another in the Battle of the Bulge.

Walter Dean Myers, *The Journal of Scott Pendleton Collins: A World War II Soldier*, 1999
Proud that his grandfather fought in the Civil War and his father in World War I, Scott has his turn in the D-Day Invasion.

988

SHARON DENNIS WYETH

Freedom's Wings: Corey's Diary
(New York: Scholastic, Inc., 2001)

Series: My America
Subject(s): Underground Railroad; Slavery; African Americans
Age range(s): Grades 3-6
Major character(s): Corey Birdsong, 9-Year-Old, Slave (fugitive); Daddy, Slave, Blacksmith; Mama, Mother, Slave
Time period(s): 1850s (1857-1858)
Locale(s): Kentucky; Ohio

Summary: Corey's fortunate that his father is literate and teaches him to read and write though they both know the danger if the master discovers their secret. When Corey overhears talk that Daddy will be sold for a good price because of his skills, he tells his parents and Daddy runs away to find freedom. Months later a white man comes to the plantation, ostensibly to buy a horse and asks Corey to teach him about local birds. From him, Mama and Corey learn that Daddy is alive and heading to Ohio. With the help of many people opposed to slavery, Corey and Mama make their journey on the Underground Railroad to Daddy and freedom. (101 pages)

Where it's reviewed:
Horn Book Guide, Fall 2001, page 297
School Library Journal, June 2001, page 160

Awards the book has won:
Notable Social Studies Trade Books for Young People, 2002

Other books by the same author:
Tomboy Trouble, 1998
Ginger Brown: The Nobody Boy, 1997
The Winning Stroke, 1996

Other books you might like:
Patricia C. McKissack, *A Picture of Freedom: The Diary of Clotee, a Slave Girl*, 1997
Clotee, a literate twelve-year-old house slave considers running away in this "Dear America" series entry set in 1859.

Joan Lowery Nixon, *Caesar's Story: 1759*, 2000
Caesar is chosen to be a personal servant and must leave his family to live in the "Big House" and attend to his master's every need.

Connie Porter, *Meet Addy: An American Girl*, 1993
When the master sells her father and brother, Addy and her mother escape from their North Carolina plantation to freedom in the North.

Marcia Vaughan, *The Secret to Freedom*, 2001
Great Aunt Lucy tells a story of the Underground Railroad helping a runaway slave.

989

SHARON DENNIS WYETH

A Piece of Heaven
(New York: Knopf, 2001)

Subject(s): Family Problems; Emotional Problems; African Americans
Age range(s): Grades 6-9
Major character(s): Mahalia "Haley" Moon, 13-Year-Old; Otis Moon, 15-Year-Old (juvenile delinquent); D'Angola Jackson, Musician (pianist), Teacher
Time period(s): 2000s
Locale(s): New York, New York

Summary: At the moment, the only stability in Haley's life is her job cleaning up Jackson's back yard before his adult daughter comes to visit. At home, on her birthday, she watches as her depressed mother breaks down and checks herself into the hospital. At first Haley and her brother Otis do all right living on their own, but then Otis is arrested for selling stolen goods and is sent to a juvenile detention center which leaves Haley by herself. She'd be content to stay in their one-room apartment, but Social Services places her in a group home. Though her family life is in turmoil, Haley returns every afternoon to Jackson's backyard where little by little she brings order out of chaos and leaves each day feeling rewarded for her efforts. Best of all is the friendship she and Jackson have, one without a loving daughter and the other without a father. (200 pages)

Where it's reviewed:
Book Report, September 2001, page 67
Booklist, February 15, 2001, page 1129
Bulletin of the Center for Children's Books, March 2001, page 284
Publishers Weekly, December 4, 2000, page 73
School Library Journal, February 2001, page 123

Other books by the same author:
Flying Free: Corey's Underground Railroad Diary, 2002
Once on This River, 1998
Be Mine, 1997
In Deep Water, 1996

Other books you might like:
Paul Fleischman, *Seedfolks*, 1997
Telling their stories in alternating chapters, thirteen people describe how the lima beans planted in a vacant city lot conjure up memories and images from their past.

Patricia Baird Greene, *The Sabbath Garden*, 1993
African American teen Opie and her Jewish neighbor Solomon Leshko form an unlikely friendship as they build a "Sabbath Garden" for their community.

Angela Johnson, *Songs of Faith*, 1998
Doreen and her younger brother Bobo react in different ways to their parents' divorce, though each needs time to heal.

990

TIM WYNNE-JONES

The Boy in the Burning House
(New York: Farrar Straus Giroux, 2001)

Subject(s): Murder; Mystery and Detective Stories; Farm Life
Age range(s): Grades 7-10
Major character(s): Jim Hawkins, 14-Year-Old; Ruth Rose, 16-Year-Old; Eldon Fisher, Religious; Hub Hawkins, Farmer, Crime Victim
Time period(s): 2000s
Locale(s): Ontario, Canada

Summary: Two years ago Jim's dad, Hub Hawkins, disappeared and everyone assumes he committed suicide, though Jim's not so sure anymore. Ruth Rose, stepdaughter of the preacher, stalks up to Jim and says some crazy things, even alleging that her stepfather, Eldon Fisher, killed Jim's father. She adds the tidbit that Eldon is being blackmailed by someone who knows about a killing that happened thirty years ago, back when good friends Eldon and Hub were young men. Because Ruth is crazy and needs to be on medication, Jim's not sure whether to believe or discount her accusation, but decides it won't hurt to look into the story of the young man who died in a burning house. Once he does, he finds that Ruth Rose's accusation is true. Unfortunately the pastor decides to eliminate everyone who knows the truth, beginning with Jim and Ruth. (214 pages)

Where it's reviewed:
Booklist, September 1, 2001, page 97
Horn Book, November 2001, page 759
Publishers Weekly, September 24, 2001, page 94
School Library Journal, October 2001, page 176
Voice of Youth Advocates, October 2001, page 287

Other books by the same author:
Boys' Own: An Anthology of Canadian Fiction for Young Readers, 2001
Lord of the Fries and Other Stories, 1999
Stephen Fair, 1998
The Maestro, 1996
Some of the Kinder Planets, 1995

Other books you might like:
Lynn Hall, *Murder in a Pig's Eye*, 1990
  Bodie searches all over Henry Silver's farm, including the manure pile, to find the body of Henry's wife who he's sure has been murdered.
Karen Harper, *Down to the Bone*, 2000
  When two men enter Rachel's life a year after her husband Sam died in a freak barn accident, she begins to wonder if Sam's death was really murder?
Alice Hoffman, *The River King*, 2000
  His fellow students at posh Haddan School dislike Gus so when they drown him, everyone agrees to cover up the crime.
Nancy Werlin, *The Killer's Cousin*, 1998
  Though his cousin Lily taunts and harasses him, David doesn't give up on her and eventually saves her from a suicide attempt.

Y

991

DAN YACCARINO
ADAM MCCAULEY, Illustrator

The Lima Bean Monster
(New York: Walker & Company, 2001)

Subject(s): Food; Monsters; Fantasy
Age range(s): Grades K-3
Major character(s): Sammy, Son, Child; Chester, Child, Friend; Lima Bean Monster, Monster
Time period(s): Indeterminate
Locale(s): Fictional Country

Summary: Never, ever in his life has Sammy eaten a lima bean yet his mother continues to serve them in a variety of ways in hopes he'll try just one. Finally, Sammy finds a new way to hide the beans and he's able to sneak away from the table, pretending the beans have been devoured. Actually, Sammy buries the beans in a vacant lot on his street. When Chester learns of the strategy he adds his despised vegetables to the hole. Soon every kid on the street is throwing vegetables (and a few unwanted, inedible items) into the hole. The plan seems to be working until lightning hits the vegetable dump and Lima Bean Monster, a creature hungry for "human beans," emerges from the hole. The only way to defeat Lima Bean Monster is . . . gulp! (32 pages)

Where it's reviewed:
Booklist, September 1, 2001, page 118
Horn Book Guide, Spring 2002, page 64
Kirkus Reviews, July 1, 2001, page 949
Publishers Weekly, July 30, 2001, page 84
School Library Journal, September 2001, page 209

Awards the book has won:
IRA Children's Choices, 2002

Other books by the same author:
Deep in the Jungle, 2000
First Day on a Strange New Planet, 2000
An Octopus Followed Me Home, 1997
If I Had a Robot, 1996

Other books you might like:
Henrik Drescher, *The Boy Who Ate Around*, 1994
When Mo faces a meal he doesn't enjoy he simply eats around it.
Mary Ann Hoberman, *The Seven Silly Eaters*, 1997
The Peters family has seven children with definite food preferences and a tired mother trying to please each one.
David Shannon, *A Bad Case of Stripes*, 1998
When Camilla refuses to eat lima beans she breaks out in stripes, spots, and assorted colors.

992

DAN YACCARINO, Author/Illustrator

New Pet
(New York: Hyperion, 2001)

Series: Blast Off Boy and Blorp. 2nd
Subject(s): Pets; Space Travel; Aliens
Age range(s): Grades 1-3
Major character(s): Blast Off Boy, Human, Student—Exchange; Blorp, Alien, Student—Exchange; Blinky, Hippopotamus
Time period(s): Indeterminate Future
Locale(s): United States; Planet—Imaginary

Summary: Blast Off Boy misses having a pet but the enormous, slobbery schloppo his alien host family gives him as a surprise is a bit more of a pet than the little dog he left behind. Blorp on the other hand happily adopts a baby hippo that follows him home from school. The teacher notes that a baby hippopotamus has escaped from the zoo and suggests that Blorp return Blinky to his mother. So, Blorp learns to be content with the companionship of Blast Off Boy's small dog and Blast Off Boy learns to acceptance the odd behavior of schloppo because that's the best they can do while on the exchange program. (34 pages)

Where it's reviewed:
Booklist, December 1, 2001, page 645
Horn Book Guide, Spring 2002, page 80
Kirkus Reviews, September 1, 2001, page 1304

Publishers Weekly, September 3, 2001, page 89
School Library Journal, December 2001, page 116

Other books by the same author:
First Day on a Strange New Planet, 2000 (Blast Off Boy and Blorp)
An Octopus Followed Me Home, 1997
If I Had a Robot, 1996 (IRA Children's Choice)

Other books you might like:
Nancy Coffelt, *Dogs in Space*, 1993
Dogs in astronaut gear travel through the solar system searching for playmates.
Daniel Kirk, *Moondogs*, 1999
Will builds a rocket to fly to the moon and get a moondog for a pet but he decides to keep the dog that stows away on the rocket instead.
Jake Wolf, *Daddy, Could I Have an Elephant?*, 1995
His father objects to an elephant as a pet so Tony suggests getting a python or a flamingo instead.

993

BRENDA SHANNON YEE
DEBBIE TILLEY, Illustrator

Hide & Seek
(New York: Orchard Books, 2001)

Subject(s): Animals/Mice; Games; Stories in Rhyme
Age range(s): Preschool-Kindergarten
Major character(s): Unnamed Character, Mouse, Narrator; Unnamed Character, Aged Person
Time period(s): 2000s (2001)
Locale(s): United States

Summary: One little mouse tries to tip toe across the kitchen without being observed by the woman in the room. The mouse almost makes it to the door when the woman notices it. The mouse scurries into the dark laundry room and leaps into a crate. When the mouse peeks out to see if the coast is clear it finds itself eyeball to eyeball with the woman and both are frightened. The mouse thinks the game was such fun it hopes to play again. (32 pages)

Where it's reviewed:
Booklist, May 15, 2001, page 1761
Children's Bookwatch, May 2001, page 7
Horn Book Guide, Fall 2001, page 244
Kirkus Reviews, April 1, 2001, page 510
School Library Journal, July 2001, page 92

Other books by the same author:
Sand Castle, 1999

Other books you might like:
Henrietta, *A Mouse in the House: A Real-Life Game of Hide and Seek*, 2001
A mouse hides in the birthday preparations on each page of a photographic essay.
Linnea Riley, *Mouse Mess*, 1997
The nighttime forays of this mouse leave a mess in the kitchen for the family to find in the morning.
Judy Waite, *Mouse, Look Out!*, 1998
Seeking shelter, a hungry mouse explores an abandoned

house, unaware that a cat stalks it while the cat doesn't notice the dog following.
Wong Herbert Yee, *Eek! There's a Mouse in the House*, 1992
In a rhyming tale a little girl tries to catch a mouse in the house by sending in larger and larger animals.

994

LAURENCE YEP

Angelfish
(New York: Penguin Putnam, 2001)

Subject(s): Ballet; Chinese Americans; Animals/Fish
Age range(s): Grades 5-8
Major character(s): Robin Lee, Dancer (ballerina); Mr. Cao, Dancer (ballerina), Aged Person
Time period(s): 2000s
Locale(s): San Francisco, California

Summary: Tired of Thomas teasing her about gaining weight and being hard to lift during ballet rehearsal, Robin swings her book bag at him but, to her horror, it flies out of her hand and crashes through a plate glass window of a pet fish store. Mr. Cao comes running out, fussing away, and Robin offers to work for three months, without pay, after her daily ballet rehearsal. Somewhat mollified he agrees but, as Robin quickly discovers, he's a very crabby old man who makes constant cracks about her being a "bunhead" as if he hates ballerinas; he also seems angry that she's only half-Chinese. Eventually Robin discovers that Mr. Cao was an accomplished ballet dancer in China but during the Cultural Revolution was disgraced and his toes on one foot were cut off. Anger and bitterness have overtaken his life, but once Robin figures out the reasons for his crabbiness, she introduces him to her ballet teacher and enlists his help in costume and set design. Once Mr. Cao learns to stand up for himself and not give in to his family, he makes a better life for himself in this continuation of Yep's books featuring Robin. (216 pages)

Where it's reviewed:
Booklist, May 15, 2001, page 1754
Children's Bookwatch, September 2001, page 2
Kliatt, May 2001, page 16
Publishers Weekly, June 25, 2001, page 74
School Library Journal, June 2001, page 160

Other books by the same author:
The Cook's Family, 1998
Ribbons, 1996

Other books you might like:
Lorri Hewitt, *Dancer*, 1999
When Stephanie loses out on the lead in *Sleeping Beauty*, she wonders if, being African American, she's chosen the wrong career.
Sally Warner, *Ellie & the Bunheads*, 1997
Ellie reaches the age where she must decide for herself whether or not she wishes to continue her ballet training.
Dori Jones Yang, *The Secret Voice of Gina Zhang*, 2000
Newly arrived in America, Chinese Jinna wants her classmates to know she's smart, but can't get the words out of her mouth.

LAURENCE YEP

Lady of Ch'iao Kuo: Warrior of the South, Southern China, A.D. 531

(New York: Scholastic, 2001)

Series: Royal Diaries
Subject(s): Diaries; Princes and Princesses; War
Age range(s): Grades 5-8
Major character(s): Redbird, Royalty (princess); Master Chen, Teacher
Time period(s): 6th century (530s)
Locale(s): Kingfisher Hill, China; Kao-liang, China

Summary: As members of the Hsien tribe, Princess Redbird and her family try to learn the ways of the Chinese as they want to live in peace with them. To help, Redbird is sent to school in the Chinese colony where she not only learns their customs and their language, but also how to read, thanks to Master Chen. One day the Dog Head tribe attacks both the Hsien and the Chinese and Princess Redbird comes home from school to use her logic and help her people create alliances to defeat their attackers. When her father is killed, Princess Redbird's job becomes harder, but her instinct for tact and diplomacy helps achieve peace. (300 pages)

Where it's reviewed:
Booklist, November 15, 2001, page 575
School Library Journal, December 2001, page 149

Other books by the same author:
Dream Soul, 2000
The Journal of Wong Ming-Chung: A Chinese Miner, 2000 (My Name Is America)
The Amah, 1999
The Cook's Family, 1998
Ribbons, 1996

Other books you might like:
Lloyd Alexander, *The Remarkable Journey of Prince Jen*, 1991
    On a quest to locate the Heavenly Kingdom, sheltered Prince Jen loses his gifts and his bodyguards, but meets the people of his realm.
Katherine Paterson, *Rebels of the Heavenly Kingdom*, 1988
    Wang Lee is kidnapped by bandits and then rescued by girl warrior Mei Lin in this story of China's Taiping Rebellion.
Barbara Ann Porte, *Hearsay: Strange Tales from the Middle Kingdom*, 1998
    This collection of fifteen stories is a combination of legend, Chinese lore and the author's imagination.

996

YIN

CHRIS SOENTPIET, Illustrator

Coolies

(New York: Philomel Books, 2001)

Subject(s): Chinese Americans; Brothers; Railroads
Age range(s): Grades 1-4

Major character(s): Shek, Brother (older), Immigrant; Wong, Brother (younger), Immigrant; PawPaw, Grandmother, Storyteller
Time period(s): 2000s; 1860s (1864-1869)
Locale(s): Canton, China; West; San Francisco, California

Summary: Yin's first book relates the history of the Chinese railroad laborers through a story PawPaw tells her grandson to explain the tradition of honoring the family's ancestors. At a time of extreme poverty in Canton, Shek and Wong leave their mother and siblings to travel to America for work. The construction of the railroad is difficult and dangerous but allows the brothers to send money home to their family for food. With the completion of the railroad Shek and Wong settle in San Francisco and save enough money to bring the rest of the family to this land of opportunity. (40 pages)

Where it's reviewed:
Booklist, February 1, 2001, page 1059
Horn Book, May 2001, page 204
Publishers Weekly, December 11, 2000, page 85
Riverbank Review, Spring 2001, page 38
School Library Journal, March 2001, page 230

Awards the book has won:
ALA Notable Children's Books, 2002

Other books you might like:
Darice Bailer, *The Last Rail*, 1996
    A picture book for older readers describes the building of the transcontinental railroad through the eyes of a young observer.
Verla Kay, *Iron Horses*, 1999
    Succinct rhyming text describes the creation of the nation's first transcontinental railroad.
Elizabeth Partridge, *Oranges on Golden Mountain*, 2001
    Jo Lee's mother sends him to America with a bundle of cuttings from her orange trees to plant and remind him of home.

997

JANE YOLEN
ROBERT J. HARRIS, Co-Author

Odysseus in the Serpent Maze

(New York: HarperCollins, 2001)

Series: Young Heroes. Number 1
Subject(s): Mythology; Heroes and Heroines; Adventure and Adventurers
Age range(s): Grades 5-8
Major character(s): Odysseus, 13-Year-Old, Royalty (prince of Ithaca); Mentor, Friend (of Odysseus); Helen, Royalty (princess of Sparta); Penelope, Teenager
Time period(s): Indeterminate Past
Locale(s): Greece

Summary: Meet teenaged Odysseus, and his sidekick Mentor, as the two begin their many adventures, starting with the purloined spear from his grandfather that Odysseus is using to hunt the Boar of Parnassus. Oh, but that's a minor adventure compared to their return to Ithaca when their ship encounters a storm and the two boys are rescued by pirates who've already kidnapped sensible Penelope (future wife of Odysseus) and her self-absorbed cousin Helen (soon to be of Troy). Odysseus manages an escape for all of them, but there's still the Labyrinth, inhabited by the multi-headed serpent Ladon, waiting for them in this humorous take on Greek mythology and the first in a new series. (248 pages)

Where it's reviewed:
Booklist, April 15, 2001, page 1561
Bulletin of the Center for Children's Books, May 2001, page 357
Instructor, September 2001, page 30
Publishers Weekly, February 19, 2001, page 91
School Library Journal, July 2001, page 116

Other books by the same author:
Atalanta and the Arcadian Beast, 2003 (Young Heroes, Number 2)
Girl in a Cage, 2002
Queen's Own Fool: A Novel of Mary Queen of Scots, 2000

Other books you might like:
Brian Keaney, *No Need for Heroes*, 1989
    Daughter of King Minos, Ariadne tells her version of the Minotaur myth, beginning with the arrival of Daedalus and Icarus on her island.
Clemence McLaren, *Inside the Walls of Troy: A Novel of the Women Who Lived the Trojan War*, 1996
    The legendary beauty Helen of Troy, along with Cassandra, relate events of the Trojan War as seen through their eyes.
Clemence McLaren, *Waiting for Odysseus*, 2000
    As Odysseus returns home following the siege of Troy, his story is related through the eyes of four women in his life, beginning with his wife Penelope.

998

ARTHUR YORINKS
DAVID SMALL, Illustrator

Company's Going

(New York: Hyperion Books for Children, 2001)

Subject(s): Aliens; Humor; Space Travel
Age range(s): Grades 1-3
Major character(s): Moe, Spouse, Space Explorer; Shirley, Spouse, Space Explorer
Time period(s): Indeterminate
Locale(s): Bellmore; Planet—Imaginary (Nextoo)

Summary: The two aliens that visited Moe and Shirley in *Company's Coming* are so impressed with the hospitality that they invite Moe and Shirley to travel to Nextoo to cater their sister's wedding. Shirley is honored, Moe is apprehensive and the space ship's flight is bumpy because the vehicle is overloaded with Shirley's luggage. Upon landing, Moe and Shirley are mistaken for invading Martians by one of the aliens and blasted by his ray gun. It looks as if the caterers are goners but Shirley recovers at the mention of food and awakens Moe. The morning after the wedding reception the spaceship delivers Moe and Shirley to Bellmore and then returns to Nextoo, leaving the hosts sad to see their company gone. (32 pages)

Where it's reviewed:
Booklist, January 1, 2002, page 868
Horn Book, January 2002, page 74
Publishers Weekly, November 15, 2001, page 68
School Library Journal, February 2002, page 116

Other books by the same author:
Company's Coming, 2000 (reissue of 1988 edition)
Tomatoes from Mars, 1999 (IRA Children's Choice)
The Miami Giant, 1995

Other books you might like:
Neal Layton, *Smile If You're Human*, 1999
    An alien family comes to Earth to photograph a human but they land in a zoo and have difficulty determining which creature is a human.
David McPhail, *Tinker and Tom and the Star Baby*, 1998
    Tinker repairs a spaceship that lands in his yard while the alien Star Baby eats the cat's food and levitates kitchen objects.
Daniel Pinkwater, *Guys from Outer Space*, 1989
    A boy who travels to another planet with some space guys discovers talking rocks and other amazing things.
Michael Rosen, *Mission Ziffoid*, 1999
    A young boy gives a humorous description of his brother's visit to the planet Ziffoid.

999

ED YOUNG, Author/Illustrator

Monkey King

(New York: HarperCollins Publishers, 2001)

Subject(s): Folklore; Magic; Animals/Monkeys
Age range(s): Grades 2-5
Major character(s): Monkey, Monkey, Trickster
Time period(s): Multiple Time Periods
Locale(s): China

Summary: Based on a portion of a Chinese epic, *Journey to the West*, the concluding "Author's Note" sets this tale in the T'ang dynasty. Simply being declared king of the monkeys is not enough adventure for Monkey so he studies for hundreds of years with a master and learns magic tricks such as changing shape and disappearing. At times Monkey uses his magic for good but many times he's simply mischievous. Depending on how he chooses to use his magical talents Monkey is sometimes rewarded while other times the magic gets him into trouble. (38 pages)

Where it's reviewed:
Booklist, February 1, 2001, page 1058
Bulletin of the Center for Children's Books, April 2001, page 322
Kirkus Reviews, January 1, 2001, page 76
Publishers Weekly, January 15, 2001, page 74
School Library Journal, February 2001, page 108

Awards the book has won:
Notable Social Studies Trade Books for Young People, 2002

Other books by the same author:
The Lost Horse: A Chinese Folktale, 1998
Mouse Match: A Chinese Folktale, 1997 (Booklist Editors' Choice)

Donkey Trouble, 1995

Other books you might like:

Verna Aardema, *Princess Gorilla and a New Kind of Water*, 1988

An African folktale explains that monkeys live in trees as punishment for being dishonest with a king and his daughter.

Linda Fang, *The Ch'i-lin Purse: A Collection of Ancient Chinese Stories*, 1995

The collection includes illustrated retellings of nine folktales from China.

Laurence Yep, *City of Dragons*, 1995

With a caravan of kind giants, a young outcast journeys beneath the sea to the City of Dragons.

Z

1000

JANE BRESKIN ZALBEN, Author/Illustrator

Don't Go!
(New York: Clarion Books, 2001)

Subject(s): Schools; Fear; Animals/Elephants
Age range(s): Grades K-1
Major character(s): Daniel, Elephant, Preschooler; Mr. Berry, Teacher, Dog
Time period(s): Indeterminate
Locale(s): Fictional Country

Summary: On his first day in school Daniel doesn't want his mother to leave him. Once he's able to join the group and listen to the story Mr. Berry is reading he begins to feel more comfortable. Daniel makes friends and has fun with the classroom activities. Still, by the end of the day he's very happy to see his mother again and to show her his picture of the first day of school. A concluding editor's note gives tips for a successful school beginning and the recipe for Daniel's cookies is included. (32 pages)

Where it's reviewed:
Booklist, August 2001, page 2134
Horn Book Guide, Spring 2002, page 32
Kirkus Reviews, July 1, 2001, page 950
Publishers Weekly, June 18, 2001, page 80
School Library Journal, September 2001, page 209

Other books by the same author:
The Magic Menorah: A Modern Chanukah Tale, 2001
Pearl's Marigolds for Grandpa, 1997
Pearl Plants a Tree, 1995

Other books you might like:
Paulette Bourgeois, *Franklin Goes to School*, 1995
    Friends help Franklin conquer his nervousness about entering school for the first time.
Kevin Henkes, *Wemberly Worried*, 2000
    Wemberly worries about everything, especially beginning school.

Amy Hest, *Off to School, Baby Duck!*, 1999
    With Grandpa Duck's support Baby Duck overcomes her fears, enters school for the first time and makes a friend before the day is over.

1001

HARRIET ZIEFERT
EMILIE BOON, Illustrator

No Kiss for Grandpa
(New York: Orchard Books, 2001)

Subject(s): Animals/Cats; Grandfathers; Playing
Age range(s): Preschool-Kindergarten
Major character(s): Louie, Cat, Son; Grandpa, Cat, Grandfather
Time period(s): Indeterminate
Locale(s): Fictional Country

Summary: Louie's in a "NO!" phase, rejecting any suggestions from Grandpa as they play and refusing to give him a kiss. Patiently Grandpa follows Louie's ideas for playing on the beach by making a cake NOT a sand castle and pretending to march in a band rather than play ball. After Louie and Grandpa go home again they read books together until it's Grandpa's turn to say, "No," because he has to leave. Now, Louie's ready to offer him ONE kiss. (24 pages)

Where it's reviewed:
Horn Book Guide, Fall 2001, page 244
Kirkus Reviews, May 15, 2001, page 748

Other books by the same author:
Someday We'll Have Very Good Manners, 2001
Pushkin Minds the Bundle, 2000
Talk, Baby!, 1999

Other books you might like:
Eve Bunting, *Can You Do This, Old Badger?*, 2000
    Old Badger may no longer be fast or agile but during their day together Little Badger comes to appreciate the value of what he can share.

Anita Jeram, *Contrary Mary*, 1995
> Mary is having an uncooperative day and everything she does is contrary.

Anne Rockwell, *No! No! No!*, 1995
> A little boy has a difficult day when everything seems to go wrong; by bedtime he feels hopeful that tomorrow will be better.

1002

HARRIET ZIEFERT
DONALD SAAF, Illustrator

What Do Ducks Dream?
(New York: G.P. Putnam's Sons, 2001)

Subject(s): Animals; Sleep; Stories in Rhyme
Age range(s): Preschool-Grade 1
Major character(s): Sigmund, Farmer
Time period(s): Indeterminate Past
Locale(s): Fictional Country

Summary: Under the night sky Sigmund doses in a chair as the animals sleep while dreaming of fantastic adventures. Horses dream of galloping across the sea, cows see themselves in sailboats on fields of hay and ducks fly by on bikes. At night wild animals do not sleep. Wide-awake, they prowl and make plans for their next meal of chickens, eggs or mice. Sigmund's children and their pets dream dreams that they hope will come true in the morning. (32 pages)

Where it's reviewed:
Five Owls, Fall 2001, page 21
Kirkus Reviews, April 1, 2001, page 510
Publishers Weekly, June 4, 2001, page 80
Riverbank Review, Summer 2001, page 34
School Library Journal, June 2001, page 132

Other books by the same author:
Murphy Meets the Treadmill, 2001
Someday We'll Have Very Good Manners, 2001
Ode to Humpty Dumpty, 2001

Other books you might like:
Nancy Kapp Chapman, *Doggie Dreams*, 2000
> Silly, colorful illustrations enliven a rhyming text about bones, phones, planes and other dreams of dogs.

Naomi Shihab Nye, *Benito's Dream Bottle*, 1995
> Benito believes that the source of dreams is a bottle within each person that must periodically be refilled.

Chris Van Allsburg, *Ben's Dreams*, 1998
> While studying for a geography test Ben falls asleep and dreams he's traveling past the monuments of the world.

1003

PAUL ZINDEL

The Gadget
(New York: HarperCollins, 2001)

Subject(s): Spies; World War II; Nuclear Weapons
Age range(s): Grades 6-10
Major character(s): Stephen Orr, 13-Year-Old; Alexei Nagavatsk, Spy

Time period(s): 1940s (1944-1945)
Locale(s): London, England; Los Alamos, New Mexico

Summary: Sent from battle-scarred London after he witnesses the death of his favorite cousin, Stephen now lives with his scientist father in Los Alamos, a secret military base in New Mexico. Though Stephen was originally concerned about getting along with his distant father, not he wonders if he'll ever see him since he's working on some secret project called "the gadget." Stephen and his friend Alexei, whose father also works on the base, are determined to find out about the gadget. They witness the detonation of the atomic bomb in the desert but are seen and returned by soldiers to Los Alamos. Upset about the bomb and his father's role in its manufacture, Stephen runs away to Alexei's father's ranch but discovers too late that both Nagavatsks are Russian spies who will kill rather than release him. (184 pages)

Where it's reviewed:
Booklist, January 2001, page 941
Kliatt, March 2001, page 15
Publishers Weekly, January 8, 2001, page 68
School Library Journal, February 2001, page 123
Voice of Youth Advocates, August 2001, page 210

Other books by the same author:
Night of the Bat, 2001
Rats, 1999
Raptor, 1998
Reef of Death, 1998
The Doom Stone, 1995

Other books you might like:
Avi, *Don't You Know There's a War On?*, 2001
> Howie reflects back on the year he had a crush on his teacher Miss Gossim and was certain their fifth grade principal was a spy for the Nazis.

Barry Denenberg, *One Eye Laughing, the Other Weeping: The Diary of Julie Weiss*, 2000
> Julie's father has the foresight to make her learn English; when the Nazis invade Austria, he sends her to an aunt in America.

Dorothy Hoobler, *The 1940s: Secrets*, 2001
> During World War II her parents move Esther with them to Los Alamos where they work on a secret government project.

Michelle Magorian, *Good Night, Mr. Tom*, 1982
> Reclusive widower Tom Oakley and eight-year-old abused William Beech form a lasting friendship when William lives with Mr. Tom during World War II.

1004

PAUL ZINDEL

Night of the Bat
(New York: Hyperion, 2001)

Subject(s): Animals/Bats; Monsters
Age range(s): Grades 6-9
Major character(s): Jake Lefkowitz, 15-Year-Old; Dr. Lefkowitz, Scientist
Time period(s): 2000s
Locale(s): Amazon River, Brazil

Summary: Jake flies to the Amazon to join his father in a research project on bats where he also hopes to test his echolocation machine, called Gizmo, that locates bats even through the thick canopy of trees. Once Jake arrives he immediately heads up the ladders into the canopy where he finds the remains of two members missing from Dr. Lefkowitz's team. A mutated giant bat continues to catch members of the research team as his snack and Dr. Lefkowitz wants to catch the bat alive. When this doesn't work out and more lives are in danger, it falls to Jake to provide assistance in another tale of horror from a popular author. (129 pages)

Where it's reviewed:
Booklist, June 2001, page 1865
Bulletin of the Center for Children's Books, July 2001, page 427
Publishers Weekly, July 30, 2001, page 86
School Library Journal, September 2001, page 235
Voice of Youth Advocates, June 2001, page 136

Awards the book has won:
ALA Quick Picks for Reluctant Young Adult Readers, 2002

Other books by the same author:
Rats, 1999
Raptor, 1998
Reef of Death, 1998
The Doom Stone, 1995
Loch: A Novel, 1994

Other books you might like:
Barbara Block, *In Plain Sight*, 1996
    Pet storeowner Robin has her hands full when a friend is murdered, a high school student is missing and the bat population explodes.
Kenneth Oppel, *Sunwing*, 2000
    The young bat Shade searches for his father but is lured into a man-made cage to be used as a weapon against humans.
John Peel, *Talons*, 1993
    Teen Kari helps a scientist excavate a stone covered with runic writings, but has horrid dreams of a winged creature ready to attack.

1005

LINDA ZINNEN

The Truth about Rats, Rules, & Seventh Grade

(New York: HarperCollins, 2001)

Subject(s): Mothers and Daughters; Animals/Dogs; School Life
Age range(s): Grades 4-7
Major character(s): Larch Ann Waysorta, 7th Grader; Charles Randall Prouty, Maintenance Worker; Elaine Mae Waysorta, Mother (of Larch), Single Parent
Time period(s): 2000s
Locale(s): Pottsville, Ohio

Summary: Larch is now a seventh grader and realizes that life if easier if one lives by the Rules, especially the Rule that she never talk about her father with her mother Elaine. Larch is also tired of living in their moldering, rat-occupied trailer with a mother who smokes and sleeps too much. One day, to complete a class assignment on local history, Larch interviews the custodian Mr. Prouty and is furious when she learns that her mother was driving the car the day her father was killed in the automobile accident. But, because Larch knows the Rules, she has difficulty talking to her mother about her new knowledge. The rat situation at least improves when Mr. Prouty gives Larch a stray dog that's eliminated many of the rats in the school basement in this first novel that finds Larch rethinking the Rules. (153 pages)

Where it's reviewed:
Booklist, April 1, 2001, page 1472
Bulletin of the Center for Children's Books, June 2001, page 393
Publishers Weekly, January 15, 2001, page 76
School Library Journal, February 2001, page 123

Other books you might like:
Priscilla Cummings, *A Face First*, 2001
    Kelley's car accident leaves her wearing a plastic facial mask to reduce the scarring from her third degree burns, an accident caused by her mother's driving.
Barbara Ware Holmes, *Following Fake Man*, 2001
    Homer's mother won't discuss his deceased father, but when Homer meets his father's best friend, it's the breakthrough he and his mother need.
Susan Shreve, *Goodbye, Amanda the Good*, 2000
    Tired of living by the rules, Amanda rebels when she becomes a seventh grader, dyes her hair black and wears only black clothes.

1006

PAM ZOLLMAN

Don't Bug Me!

(New York: Holiday House, 2001)

Subject(s): Animals/Insects; Brothers and Sisters; Teasing
Age range(s): Grades 4-6
Major character(s): Megan Hollander, 6th Grader; Charlie Bettencourt, 6th Grader; Alexander Hollander, Child, Brother (of Megan); Belinda, 6th Grader
Time period(s): 2000s
Locale(s): United States

Summary: All the students in Megan's sixth-grade-only school have the same science assignment: collect twenty-five insects. Megan's been working on her project and has many insects mounted and labeled on a piece of corkboard in her room, but there's a problem. Her little brother Alexander loves bugs and he take all her "dead" bugs, buries them and conducts funeral services over their mass grave. Megan is beside herself and now, every time an insect is spotted at her house, Alexander wants to claim it as his pet. Life isn't much better at school with her classmate Charlie teasing her about needing more bugs. Desperate to complete her assignment, she and her friend Belinda sneak into the school kitchen, which they think will be the mother lode of insects, but end up in detention in this humorous first novel. (134 pages)

Where it's reviewed:
Booklist, July 2001, page 2007

Kirkus Reviews, June 1, 2001, page 808
Publishers Weekly, June 11, 2001, page 86
School Library Journal, October 2001, page 176

Other books you might like:
Steven Cousins, *Frankenbug*, 2001
Fed up with Jeb's teasing about his interest in insects, Adam creates the monster "Frankenbug," brings it to life with fireflies and scares Jeb.
Jean Craighead George, *The Fire Bug Connection: An Ecological Mystery*, 1993
Maggie and a graduate student try to figure out why her firebugs die before they transform from their larval state.
Laurence Yep, *Cockroach Cooties*, 2000
When Bobby finds out the bully who's bothering his brother is scared of roaches, he borrows a large one from an entomologist.

1007

N.F. ZUCKER

Benno's Bear

(New York: Dutton, 2001)

Subject(s): Animals/Bears; Fathers and Sons; Crime and Criminals
Age range(s): Grades 5-7
Major character(s): Benno, 11-Year-Old; Bear, Bear; Officer Pikche, Police Officer; Katorna "Kat" Pikche, Baker
Time period(s): Indeterminate Past
Locale(s): Europe (somewhere in Central Europe)

Summary: Benno, Bear and his father have a wonderful arrangement, his father plays the concertina, Bear dances and Benno picks the pockets of the bystanders, until they're all caught. Now his father's in jail for seven months, Bear is in the zoo and Benno is taken in by Officer Pikche and his wife Kat. Benno can't believe his good fortune to be in a home where he's warm and there's so much food he doesn't need to save any, while at school he discovers his love of reading. Accused of stealing the teacher's purse, he runs away to Bear, releases her from the zoo and the two head to the forest where Benno thinks they can live. Benno quickly realizes this plan won't work so he leaves Bear in the woods and returns to the city where his father, newly released from jail, is ready to begin their pickpocketing scheme. Having seen another way of life, Benno doesn't wish to return to stealing and, when offered a chance to work for Mrs. Pikche in her bakery, leaps at the chance to support his father in this first novel for young people. (244 pages)

Where it's reviewed:
Bulletin of the Center for Children's Books, December 2001, page 156
Horn Book, November 2001, page 759
Kirkus Reviews, October 1, 2001, page 1435
School Library Journal, October 2001, page 176
Voice of Youth Advocates, April 2002, page 48

Awards the book has won:
Smithsonian's Notable Books for Children, 2001

Other books you might like:
Kate DiCamillo, *The Tiger Rising*, 2001
Taking pity on a caged tiger he's been hired to feed, Rob releases him, but that results in unexpected tragedy.
Harriet Graham, *A Boy and His Bear*, 1996
When Dickon sees a bear cub being abused in the London Bear Garden, he frees the cub and flees to France to escape the Bear Catcher.
Ben Mikaelsen, *Rescue Josh McGuire*, 1991
Rather than turn in an orphaned bear cub to the Fish and Game Department, Josh flees into the mountains with the cub just as an early snowstorm approaches.

1008

MARKUS ZUSAK

Fighting Ruben Wolfe

(New York: Arthur A. Levine/ Scholastic, 2001)

Subject(s): Sports/Boxing; Brothers
Age range(s): Grades 7-10
Major character(s): Ruben Wolfe, Boxer, Brother; Cameron "Cam" Wolfe, Boxer, Brother
Time period(s): 2000s
Locale(s): Australia

Summary: With their proud, injured father unwilling to go on the dole and their mother working two jobs, Cameron and his older brother Ruben accept Perry Cole's offer to fight for his organized boxing racket. The matches are illegal but the $50 from a win really helps, as do the tips if you lose but do so with a "big heart." Ruben is a natural fighter, always willing to scrap, while narrator Cam excels at getting up after being hit. Eventually the two brothers have to face their fears and fight each other in this Australian author's first novel. (219 pages)

Where it's reviewed:
Booklist, February 15, 2001, page 1129
Bulletin of the Center for Children's Books, March 2001, page 284
Horn Book, March 2001, page 217
Publishers Weekly, February 26, 2001, page 87
School Library Journal, March 2001, page 258

Awards the book has won:
ALA Best Books for Young Adults, 2002

Other books you might like:
Michael Cadnum, *Redhanded*, 2000
To obtain money to compete in the Golden Gloves West Coast tournament, Steve reluctantly agrees to Chad's scheme of robbery.
Robert Lipsyte, *The Contender*, 1967
Alfred learns that in boxing, as in life, it's more important to be a contender than a winner.
Chris Lynch, *Shadow Boxer*, 1993
Monty proves to be a good boxer until he views the brutal video of his father's last fight and reconsiders the sport.
Peter Weston Wood, *To Swallow a Toad*, 1987
A miserable home life has made Pete Watt hungry for boxing's Golden Gloves title.

Series Index

This index alphabetically lists series to which books featured in the entries belong. Beneath each series name, book titles are listed alphabetically, with author names, age-level code(s) and entry numbers also included. The age-level codes are as follows: *p* Preschool, *b* Beginning Reader, *e* Elementary School (Grades 2-5), *m* Middle School (Grades 5-8), *h* High School (Grades 9-12), and *a* Adult.

Young Americans: Colonial Williamsburg
Maria's Story: 1773 - Joan Lowery Nixon   e,
    m   678

Young Heroes
Odysseus in the Serpent Maze - Jane Yolen   m   997

Young Royal Book
Beware, Princess Elizabeth - Carolyn Meyer
    m   634

Young Wizards
The Wizard's Dilemma - Diane Duane   m, h   251

Zenon, Girl of the 21st Century
Bobo Crazy - Marilyn Sadler   e   786

Award Index

This index lists major awards given to books featured in the entries. Books are listed alphabetically beneath the name of the award, with author name, age-level code(s) and entry numbers also included. The age-level codes are as follows: *p* Preschool, *b* Beginning Reader, *e* Elementary School (Grades 2-5), *m* Middle School (Grades 5-8), *h* High School (Grades 9-12), and *a* Adult.

ALA Alex Award

Gabriel's Story - David Anthony Durham   *h, a* 255

Kit's Law - Donna Morrissey   *h, a* 651

Peace Like a River - Leif Enger   *h, a* 278

Year of Wonders - Geraldine Brooks   *h, a* 101

ALA Best Books for Young Adults

All That Remains - Bruce Brooks   *m, h* 100

Amandine - Adele Griffin   *m* 350

Amazing Maurice and His Educated Rodents: A Novel of Discworld - Terry Pratchett   *h* 723

Being Dead - Vivian Vande Velde   *m, h* 907

Black Mirror - Nancy Werlin   *h* 941

Born Blue - Han Nolan   *h* 681

Boston Jane: An Adventure - Jennifer L. Holm   *m* 409

Breathing Underwater - Alex Flinn   *h* 295

The Brimstone Journals - Ron Koertge   *m, h* 515

The Color of Absence: Twelve Stories about Loss and Hope - James Howe   *m, h* 427

Crazy Loco - David Rice   *m, h* 744

Damage - A.M. Jenkins   *h* 451

The Edge on the Sword - Rebecca Tingle   *m, h* 884

Empress of the World - Sara Ryan   *h* 777

Every Time a Rainbow Dies - Rita Williams-Garcia   *h* 966

Fair Weather - Richard Peck   *m* 704

Feeling Sorry for Celia - Jaclyn Moriarty   *h* 648

Fighting Ruben Wolfe - Markus Zusak   *m, h* 1008

Freewill - Chris Lynch   *h* 581

The Gospel According to Larry - Janet Tashjian   *h* 866

The Land - Mildred D. Taylor   *m, h* 872

Lirael: Daughter of the Clayr - Garth Nix   *h* 677

Lord of the Deep - Graham Salisbury   *m* 788

Love and Sex: Ten Stories of Truth - Michael Cart   *h* 143

Of Sound Mind - Jean Ferris   *m, h* 286

On the Fringe - Donald R. Gallo   *m, h* 308

The Other Side of Truth - Beverley Naidoo   *m, h* 666

The Rag and Bone Shop - Robert Cormier   *m, h* 183

Rainbow Boys - Alex Sanchez   *h* 791

Razzle - Ellen Wittlinger   *h* 978

Rooster - Beth Nixon Weaver   *m, h* 931

Secret Sacrament - Sherryl Jordan   *h* 472

Seek - Paul Fleischman   *m, h* 290

Shades of Simon Gray - Joyce McDonald   *m, h* 617

Shadow of the Hegemon - Orson Scott Card   *h, a* 139

Sights - Susanna Vance   *m, h* 905

A Single Shard - Linda Sue Park   *m* 696

The Sisterhood of the Traveling Pants - Ann Brashares   *m, h* 99

Spellbound - Janet McDonald   *m, h* 616

Squire - Tamora Pierce   *m, h* 712

The Stones of Mourning Creek - Diane Les Becquets   *m, h* 546

Summers at Castle Auburn - Sharon Shinn   *h, a* 818

Touching Spirit Bear - Ben Mikaelsen   *m, h* 638

Troy - Adele Geras   *h, a* 327

True Believer - Virginia Euwer Wolff   *m, h* 980

Whale Talk - Chris Crutcher   *h* 199

What My Mother Doesn't Know - Sonya Sones   *m, h* 839

Witch Child - Celia Rees   *m, h* 739

You Don't Know Me - David Klass   *m, h* 510

Zazoo: A Novel - Richard Mosher   *m, h* 653

ALA Coretta Scott King Award

The Land - Mildred D. Taylor   *m, h* 872

ALA Michael L. Printz Award

A Step from Heaven - An Na   *h* 665

ALA Michael L. Printz Honor Book

Freewill - Chris Lynch   *h* 581

The Ropemaker - Peter Dickinson   *m, h* 232

True Believer - Virginia Euwer Wolff   *m, h* 980

ALA Notable Children's Books

And the Dish Ran Away with the Spoon - Janet Stevens   *p* 855

The Black Bull of Norroway - Charlotte Huck   *p, e* 432

Blister - Susan Shreve   *e, m* 819

A Book of Coupons - Susie Morgenstern   *e, m* 646

Car Wash - Sandra Steen   *p* 851

Coolies - Yin   *p, e* 996

Emma's Yucky Brother - Jean Little   *b* 562

The Gawgon and the Boy - Lloyd Alexander   *m* 11

Goin' Someplace Special - Patricia C. McKissack   *p, e* 625

Gus and Grandpa at Basketball - Claudia Mills   *b* 641

Harley - Star Livingstone   *b* 565

Henry's First-Moon Birthday - Lenore Look   *p* 570

The Hero of Ticonderoga - Gail Gauthier   *m* 320

The Hickory Chair - Lisa Rowe Fraustino   *p* 300

Judy Moody Gets Famous - Megan McDonald   *e* 618

Kipper's A to Z: An Alphabet Adventure - Mick Inkpen   *p* 442

Lady Lollipop - Dick King-Smith   *e* 503

Let's Get a Pup! Said Kate - Bob Graham   *p* 344

Love, Ruby Lavender - Deborah Wiles   *e, m* 956

Love That Dog - Sharon Creech   *e, m* 192

Mice and Beans - Pam Munoz Ryan   *p* 776

Olivia Saves the Circus - Ian Falconer   *p* 282

The Other Side - Jacqueline Woodson   *p, e* 983

The Race of the Birkebeiners - Lise Lunge-Larsen   *p, e* 578

The Ropemaker - Peter Dickinson   *m, h* 232

Sheila Rae's Peppermint Stick - Kevin Henkes   *p* 387

Skeleton Man - Joseph Bruchac   *m* 110

Storm Warriors - Elisa Carbone   *m* 138

The Web Files - Margie Palatini   *p, e* 694

Witness - Karen Hesse   *m* 392

ALA Pura Belpre Honor Book

Breaking Through - Francisco Jimenez   *m, h* 456

ALA Quick Picks for Reluctant Young Adult Readers

Amandine - Adele Griffin   *m* 350

Among the Impostors - Margaret Peterson Haddix   *m* 365

The Black Book (Diary of a Teenage Stud) Series - Jonah Black   *h* 79

Book of Shadows - Cate Tiernan   *h* 883

Breathing Underwater - Alex Flinn   *h* 295

Darkness Before Dawn - Sharon M. Draper   *h* 249

Gifted Touch - Melinda Metz   *h* 633

Have a Nice Life Series - Scarlett Macdougal   *h* 585

Love and Sex: Ten Stories of Truth - Michael Cart   *h* 143

A Mother's Gift - Britney Spears   *m* 841

Night of the Bat - Paul Zindel   *m* 1004

On the Bright Side, I'm Now the Girlfriend of a Sex God: Further Confessions of Georgia Nicolson - Louise Rennison   *m, h* 742

Princess in the Spotlight - Meg Cabot   *m, h* 131

Rat Boys: A Dating Experiment - Thom Eberhardt   *m* 258

Shattered Mirror - Amelia Atwater-Rhodes   *h* 30

So Mote It Be - Isobel Bird   *m, h* 73

Stormbreaker - Anthony Horowitz   *m* 420

When Dad Killed Mom - Julius Lester   *h* 549

Zach's Lie - Roland Smith   *m* 834

Barnes & Noble's Discover Great New Writers Award for Fiction

Peace Like a River - Leif Enger   *h, a* 278

Time Index

This index chronologically lists the time settings in which the featured books take place. Main headings refer to a century; where no specific time is given, the headings MULTIPLE TIME PERIODS, INDETERMINATE PAST, INDETERMINATE FUTURE, AND INDETERMINATE are used. The 18th through 21st centuries are broken down into decades when possible. (Note: 1800s, for example, refers to the first decade of the 19th century.) Featured titles are listed alphabetically beneath time headings, with author names, age-level code(s) and entry numbers also included. The age-level codes are as follows: *p* Preschool, *b* Beginning Reader, *e* Elementary School (Grades 2-5), *m* Middle School (Grades 5-8), *h* High School (Grades 9-12), and *a* Adult.

Time Index

Geographic Index

This index provides access to all featured books by geographic settings—such as countries, continents, oceans, and planets. States and provinces are indicated for the United States and Canada. Also interfiled are headings for fictional place names (Spaceships, Imaginary Planets, etc.). Sections are further broken down by city or the specific name of the imaginary locale. Book titles are listed alphabetically under headings, with author names, age-level code(s) and entry numbers also included. The age-level codes are as follows: *p* Preschool, *b* Beginning Reader, *e* Elementary School (Grades 2-5), *m* Middle School (Grades 5-8), *h* High School (Grades 9-12), and *a* Adult.

AFGHANISTAN

Kabul

The Breadwinner - Deborah Ellis   *m* 274

AFRICA

Bintou's Braids - Sylviane A. Diouf   *p* 235
Dark Inheritance - W. Michael Gear   *a* 322
Mabela the Clever - Margaret Read MacDonald
    p 584
Mansa Musa: The Lion of Mali - Khephra Burns   *e*,
    m 127
The Revenge of Randal Reese-Rat - Tor Seidler
    e 810

Nile River

Crocodile Listens - April Pulley Sayre   *p* 795

AMERICAN COLONIES

MASSACHUSETTS

Tattered Sails - Verla Kay   *p* 480

Boston

Joining the Boston Tea Party - Diane Stanley   *p*,
    e 849

NEW ENGLAND

William's House - Ginger Howard   *p, e* 426

PENNSYLVANIA

Philadelphia

Five Smooth Stones: Hope's Diary - Kristiana Gregory
    e 348

VIRGINIA

Jamestown

The Starving Time: Elizabeth's Diary - Patricia
Hermes   *e* 389

Williamsburg

Maria's Story: 1773 - Joan Lowery Nixon   *e*,
    m 678

ARCTIC

Nutik, the Wolf Pup - Jean Craighead George
    p 325

Kangit

Nutik & Amaroq Play Ball - Jean Craighead George
    p 324

Yellowtooth

Irving and Muktuk: Two Bad Bears - Daniel Pinkwater
    p 717

ASIA

Heart of Mine: A Story of Adoption - Lotta Hojer
    p 408
Song of the Axe - John R. Dann   *a* 209

AT SEA

The Adventure of Louey and Frank - Carolyn White
    p 947
Captain and Matey Set Sail - Daniel Laurence
    b 535
The Merbaby - Teresa Bateman   *p, e* 61

Avenger
Robin Hook, Pirate Hunter! - Eric A. Kimmel   *p*,
    e 497

California
*Seeds of Hope: The Gold Rush Diary of Susanna
    Fairchild, California Territory, 1849* - Kristiana
    Gregory   *m* 349

Crystal-C
Lord of the Deep - Graham Salisbury   *m* 788

Dragon
The Buccaneers - Iain Lawrence   *m, h* 536

Duke William
Kydd - Julian Stockwin   *a* 861

Flying Dutchman
Castaways of the Flying Dutchman - Brian Jacques
    m 446

Flying Hart
Shadows in the Glasshouse - Megan McDonald   *e*,
    m 620

John Ena
Sailing Home: A Story of a Childhood at Sea - Gloria
    Rand   *p, e* 734

Kraaken
Tom Cringle: The Pirate and the Patriot - Gerald
    Hausman   *m* 382

Lady Luck
Boston Jane: An Adventure - Jennifer L. Holm
    m 409

Neptune's Car
The Captain's Wife - Douglas Kelley   *a* 485

Pretty Anne
The Sweet Trade - Elizabeth Garrett   *a* 318

Sandpiper
Robin Hook, Pirate Hunter! - Eric A. Kimmel   *p*,
    e 497

Santa Maria
Freedom beyond the Sea - Waldtraut Lewin   *m*,
    h 554

Susan Constant
*Surviving Jamestown: The Adventures of Young Sam
    Collier* - Gail Langer Karwoski   *m* 479

USS Owanee
Fire on the Waters - David Poyer   *a* 722

AUSTRALIA

Fighting Ruben Wolfe - Markus Zusak   *m, h* 1008
Luke's Way of Looking - Nadia Wheatley   *p, e* 944
The Night Is for Hunting - John Marsden   *h* 595
The Pocket Dogs - Margaret Wild   *p* 954
The Singing Hat - Tohby Riddle   *p* 747

Sydney
Feeling Sorry for Celia - Jaclyn Moriarty   *h* 648

Warrangalla
Fiddleback - Elizabeth Honey   *m* 414

AUSTRIA

Vienna
Faraway Home - Marilyn Taylor   *m* 871
Stolen Words - Amy Goldman Koss   *m* 518

Geographic Index

Subject Index

This index lists subjects which are covered in the featured titles. These can include such things as family life, animals, personal and social problems, historical events, ethnic groups, and story types, e.g. Mystery and Detective Stories. Beneath each subject heading, titles are arranged alphabetically with author names, age-level code(s) and entry numbers also included. The age-level codes are as follows: *p* Preschool, *b* Beginning Reader, *e* Elementary School (Grades 2-5), *m* Middle School (Grades 5-8), *h* High School (Grades 9-12), and *a* Adult.

Buzz Buzz Buzz - Veronica Uribe   p 896
The Eye of the Stone - Tom Birdseye   e, m 75
A Fish Named Spot - Jennifer P. Goldfinger   p 337
Flatterland: Like Flatland, Only More So - Ian Stewart   h 856
Issola - Steven Brust   h, a 112
Jimmy Dabble - Frans Vischer   e 914
Katie and the Sunflowers - James Mayhew   p 604
Larky Mavis - Brock Cole   p, e 170
The Lima Bean Monster - Dan Yaccarino   p 991
The Master Swordsman & The Magic Doorway: Two Legends from Ancient China - Alice Provensen   p, e 727
Midnight Babies - Margaret Wild   p 952
The Moon Robber - Dean Morrissey   e 650
Rowan and the Travelers - Emily Rodda   e 759
Rowan of Rin - Emily Rodda   e, m 760
Sir Apropos of Nothing - Peter David   h, a 214
The Snail House - Allan Ahlberg   p 10
The Spy Wore Shades - Martha Freeman   e, m 301
Tales from Earthsea - Ursula K. Le Guin   h, a 539
Ted - Tony DiTerlizzi   p 237
The Tin Forest - Helen Ward   p 924
Tree Girl - T.A. Barron   e, m 55
When Moon Fell Down - Linda Smith   p 832
William and the Night Train - Mij Kelly   p 487

Farm Life

Anna on the Farm - Mary Downing Hahn   e 369
Bernard the Angry Rooster - Mary Wormell   p 985
Blue Creek Farm: A Matty Trescott Novel - Carroll Thomas   m 878
Bluebird Summer - Deborah Hopkinson   p, e 418
The Boy in the Burning House - Tim Wynne-Jones   m, h 990
The Boys' House: New and Selected Stories - Jim Heynen   m, h 395
A Bushel of Light - Troon Harrison   m 380
A Farm of Her Own - Natalie Kinsey-Warnock   p 504
Fishing for Chickens: Short Stories about Rural Youth - Jim Heynen   m, h 396
Four Hungry Kittens - Emily Arnold McCully   p 611
Grandpa's Overalls - Tony Crunk   p 198
Hank's Story - Jane Buchanan   e 113
A Hole in the World - Sid Hite   m 401
Horse Sense - Jan Neubert Schultz   e, m 801
Jimmy Dabble - Frans Vischer   e 914
Nursery Crimes - Arthur Geisert   p, e 323
Oliver's Milk Shake - Vivian French   p 302
One Monday - Amy Huntington   p 436
Piper - Natale Ghent   m 328
Prairie School - Avi   b, e 37
Rose's Journal: The Story of a Girl in the Great Depression - Marissa Moss   e 655
Silly Little Goose! - Nancy Tafuri   p 864
A Thanksgiving Turkey - Julian Scheer   p, e 799
There's a Cow in the Cabbage Patch - Stella Blackstone   p 81

Fathers

Car Wash - Sandra Steen   p 851
My Dad - Anthony Browne   p 107
Pray Hard - Pamela Walker   m 918

Fathers and Daughters

Desperate Measures - Kate Wilhelm   a 959
Didi and Daddy on the Promenade - Marilyn Singer   p 825
Equinox - Monte Killingsworth   m 494
Loon Summer - Barbara Santucci   p 793
One Puppy, Three Tales - Karen Salmansohn   e 789
Open Season - C.J. Box   a 97

Rowan Hood: Outlaw Girl of Sherwood Forest - Nancy Springer   e, m 847
Shylock's Daughter - Mirjam Pressler   h 724
The Sick Day - Patricia MacLachlan   p 587
The Singing Hat - Tohby Riddle   p 747
Tender - Valerie Hobbs   h 403
Three Days - Donna Jo Napoli   m 670

Fathers and Sons

Benno's Bear - N.F. Zucker   m 1007
A Boy at War: A Novel of Pearl Harbor - Harry Mazer   m 605
Breathing Underwater - Alex Flinn   h 295
The Broken Places - Susan Perabo   a 707
Caleb's Story - Patricia MacLachlan   e, m 586
The Comic Book Kid - Adam Osterweil   e 692
Dad, in Spirit - A. LaFaye   e, m 527
Danger in Disguise - Mary Alice Downie   m 245
The Devil in Ol' Rosie - Louise Moeri   m 645
Following Fake Man - Barbara Ware Holmes   m 410
Ghost Soldier - Elaine Marie Alphin   m 13
I Lost My Dad - Taro Gomi   p 339
The Jacob Ladder - Gerald Hausman   m 381
The Jumping Tree - Rene Saldana Jr.   m 787
Just the Two of Us - Will Smith   p 835
Labyrinth - John Herman   m, h 388
Lord of the Nutcracker Men - Iain Lawrence   m 537
Marvin One Too Many - Katherine Paterson   b 701
Max, the Stubborn Little Wolf - Marie-Odile Judes   p 473
My Brother, the Robot - Bonnie Becker   e 65
Peace Like a River - Leif Enger   h, a 278
Plunking Reggie Jackson - James W. Bennett   h 69
Racing the Past - Sis Deans   m 220
Raising the Shades - Doug Wilhelm   m 958
Run If You Dare - Randy Powell   m, h 721
Seek - Paul Fleischman   m, h 290
Storm Warriors - Elisa Carbone   m 138
Stranger in Dadland - Amy Goldman Koss   e, m 519
Ted - Tony DiTerlizzi   p 237
Uncle Daddy - Ralph Fletcher   e, m 293

Fear

Among the Impostors - Margaret Peterson Haddix   m 365
The Broken Places - Susan Perabo   a 707
Don't Go! - Jane Breskin Zalben   p 1000
Felix Feels Better - Rosemary Wells   p 936
Little Cliff's First Day of School - Clifton L. Taulbert   p 868
Mama, Don't Go! - Rosemary Wells   b 937
Max's Starry Night - Ken Wilson-Max   p 974
A Safe Place Called Home - Eileen Spinelli   p 842
Scared Stiff - Katie Davis   p 217

Feuds

Scribbler of Dreams - Mary E. Pearson   m, h 703

Fires

The Broken Places - Susan Perabo   a 707
Dot the Fire Dog - Lisa Desimini   p 227
The Ghost and Mrs. Hobbs - Cynthia DeFelice   e, m 221
Witch Hill - Marcus Sedgwick   m, h 809

Fishing

The Biggest Fish in the Lake - Margaret Carney   p, e 140
The Lobster War - Ethan Howland   m, h 430
Lord of the Deep - Graham Salisbury   m 788

Oranges on Golden Mountain - Elizabeth Partridge   p, e 697
Steamboat Annie and the Thousand-Pound Catfish - Catherine Wright   p, e 986

Floods

The Day Ocean Came to Visit - Diane Wolkstein   p 981
The Great Canoe: A Karina Legend - Maria Elena Maggi   p, e 589
In Sunlight, in a Beautiful Garden - Kathleen Cambor   a 135
Katje, the Windmill Cat - Gretchen Woelfle   p 979

Folk Tales

Children of the Dragon: Selected Tales from Vietnam - Sherry Garland   e, m 315
The Golden Mare, the Firebird, and the Magic Ring - Ruth Sanderson   p, e 792
How Animals Saved the People: Animal Tales from the South - J.J. Reneaux   e, m 741
Hungry! Hungry! Hungry! - Malachy Doyle   p 246
Lemuel the Fool - Myron Uhlberg   p 893
Mabela the Clever - Margaret Read MacDonald   p 584
Mother Holly - John Warren Stewig   p, e 858
Skeleton Man - Joseph Bruchac   m 110
The Tale of Tricky Fox: A New England Trickster Tale - Jim Aylesworth   p 39

Folklore

The Black Bull of Norroway - Charlotte Huck   p, e 432
Clever Beatrice - Margaret Willey   p 960
A Cloak for the Moon - Eric A. Kimmel   p, e 496
Davy Crockett Saves the World - Rosalyn Schanzer   p 798
The Day Ocean Came to Visit - Diane Wolkstein   p 981
Dusty Locks and the Three Bears - Susan Lowell   p 573
The Famous Adventures of Jack - Berlie Doherty   e 239
Fearless Jack - Paul Brett Johnson   p, e 458
The Golden Mare, the Firebird, and the Magic Ring - Ruth Sanderson   p, e 792
The Great Canoe: A Karina Legend - Maria Elena Maggi   p, e 589
How Animals Saved the People: Animal Tales from the South - J.J. Reneaux   e, m 741
How Chipmunk Got His Stripes: A Tale of Bragging and Teasing - Joseph Bruchac   p 108
Is My Friend at Home?: Pueblo Fireside Tales - John Bierhorst   e 72
Jabuti the Tortoise: A Trickster Tale from the Amazon - Gerald McDermott   p 615
Juan Verdades: The Man Who Couldn't Tell a Lie - Joe Hayes   p, e 385
Kate Culhane: A Ghost Story - Michael Hague   e, m 368
Mabela the Clever - Margaret Read MacDonald   p 584
Master Man: A Tall Tale of Nigeria - Aaron Shepard   p, e 817
Monkey King - Ed Young   p, e 999
Petite Rouge: A Cajun Red Riding Hood - Mike Artell   p, e 22
Puss in Boots: The Adventures of That Most Enterprising Feline - Philip Pullman   p, e 728
The Race of the Birkebeiners - Lise Lunge-Larsen   p, e 578
Rachel Captures the Moon - Samuel Tenenbaum   p, e 874
Scatterbrain Sam - Ellen Jackson   p, e 444
The Shark God - Rafe Martin   p 597

Subject Index

Pets

Agapanthus Hum and Major Bark - Joy Cowley
   b   189

Billy the Bird - Dick King-Smith   *e*   502

Bobo Crazy - Marilyn Sadler   *e*   786

The Cats of Cuckoo Square: Two Stories - Adele
   Geras   *e*   326

Desser the Best Ever Cat - Maggie Smith   *p*   833

A Fish Named Spot - Jennifer P. Goldfinger   *p*   337

Five Creatures - Emily Jenkins   *p*   452

The Good Dog - Avi   *e, m*   36

The Great Gracie Chase: Stop That Dog! - Cynthia
   Rylant   *p*   780

Hoodwinked - Arthur Howard   *p*   424

Let's Get a Pup! Said Kate - Bob Graham   *p*   344

Little Whistle - Cynthia Rylant   *p*   781

*Loki & Alex: The Adventures of a Dog & His Best
   Friend* - Charles R. Smith Jr.   *p*   830

McDuff Goes to School - Rosemary Wells   *p*   938

Mr. Putter & Tabby Feed the Fish - Cynthia Rylant
   b   783

Mrs. McTats and Her Houseful of Cats - Alyssa Satin
   Capucilli   *p*   137

New Pet - Dan Yaccarino   *e*   992

Night of the Living Gerbil - Elizabeth Levy   *e*   553

One Day at Wood Green Animal Shelter - Patricia
   Casey   *p*   146

Pinky and Rex and the Just-Right Pet - James Howe
   b, e   429

Pugdog - Andrea U'Ren   *p*   895

A Puppy of My Own - Wendy Loggia   *e*   567

Robert and the Great Pepperoni - Barbara Seuling
   e   811

Rufferella - Vanessa Gill-Brown   *p*   331

Runaway Radish - Jessie Haas   *e*   363

Sally Goes to the Mountains - Stephen Huneck
   p   435

Sit, Truman! - Dan Harper   *p*   374

Stella's Dancing Days - Sandy Asher   *p*   25

The Stray Dog - Marc Simont   *p*   823

Tiger Trouble! - Diane Goode   *p*   341

The Very Kind Rich Lady and Her One Hundred Dogs
   - Chinlun Lee   *p*   541

What Pete Ate from A-Z - Maira Kalman   *p*   475

What's Cooking, Jamela? - Niki Daly   *p*   206

Photography

The Beastly Arms - Patrick Jennings   *m*   453

Rain Is Not My Indian Name - Cynthia Leitich Smith
   m   831

Razzle - Ellen Wittlinger   *h*   978

Physically Handicapped

The Gypsies Never Came - Stephen Roos   *m*   763

A Nose for Adventure - Richard Scrimger   *m*   808

Prairie School - Avi   *b, e*   37

A Sailor Returns - Theodore Taylor   *e*   873

Tiger's Fall - Molly Bang   *e*   48

Physics

Flatterland: Like Flatland, Only More So - Ian Stewart
   h   856

Pilgrims and Pilgrimages

We Gather Together . . . Now Please Get Lost! - Diane
   DeGroat   *p*   222

Pioneers

Snow Mountain Passage - James D. Houston
   a   423

Pirates

The Buccaneers - Iain Lawrence   *m, h*   536

Captain and Matey Set Sail - Daniel Laurence
   b   535

Corsair - Chris Bunch   *h, a*   116

Little Badger, Terror of the Seven Seas - Eve Bunting
   p   120

Pirates - C. Drew Lamm   *p, e*   530

Robin Hook, Pirate Hunter! - Eric A. Kimmel   *p,
   e*   497

The Sweet Trade - Elizabeth Garrett   *a*   318

Tom Cringle: The Pirate and the Patriot - Gerald
   Hausman   *m*   382

Plague

Year of Wonders - Geraldine Brooks   *h, a*   101

Playing

Beach Day - Karen Roosa   *p*   764

The Boys Team - Amy Schwartz   *p*   802

Flip and Flop - Dawn Apperley   *p*   17

Miss Mouse's Day - Jan Ormerod   *p*   689

Naughty! - Caroline Castle   *p*   148

No Kiss for Grandpa - Harriet Ziefert   *p*   1001

Nutik & Amaroq Play Ball - Jean Craighead George
   p   324

Toby, What Are You? - William Steig   *p*   852

When Poppy and Max Grow Up - Lindsey Gardiner
   p   312

Poaching

The Hideout - Peg Kehret   *e, m*   482

Poetry

The Brimstone Journals - Ron Koertge   *m, h*   515

Little Tree - Chris Raschka   *p*   736

Love That Dog - Sharon Creech   *e, m*   192

Sam Samurai - Jon Scieszka   *e, m*   805

Political Thriller

Shadow of the Hegemon - Orson Scott Card   *h,
   a*   139

Politics

Deep Doo-Doo and the Mysterious E-Mail - Michael
   Delaney   *e*   224

Defender - C.J. Cherryh   *h, a*   155

The King's Name - Jo Walton   *h, a*   922

Poverty

Beatrice's Goat - Page McBrier   *p*   608

Delfino's Journey - Jo Harper   *m, h*   375

The Jacob Ladder - Gerald Hausman   *m*   381

The Orphan Singer - Emily Arnold McCully
   p   613

Out of the Night That Covers Me: A Novel - Pat
   Cunningham Devoto   *a*   229

Secret in St. Something - Barbara Brooks Wallace
   m   919

True Believer - Virginia Euwer Wolff   *m, h*   980

Pregnancy

Plunking Reggie Jackson - James W. Bennett   *h*   69

Prejudice

Belle Teal - Ann M. Martin   *e, m*   596

Circle of Fire - Evelyn Coleman   *m*   172

The Education of Mary: A Little Miss of Color - Ann
   Rinaldi   *m*   748

Girl of Kosovo - Alice Mead   *m, h*   630

Half a Heart - Rosellen Brown   *a*   105

The Land - Mildred D. Taylor   *m, h*   872

Love Rules - Marilyn Reynolds   *h*   743

Mr. Lincoln's Way - Patricia Polacco   *p, e*   719

Rockbuster - Gloria Skurzynski   *m, h*   827

Secrets in the House of Delgado - Gloria D. Miklowitz
   m, h   639

Shylock's Daughter - Mirjam Pressler   *h*   724

The Stones of Mourning Creek - Diane Les Becquets
   m, h   546

Walk Across the Sea - Susan Fletcher   *m*   294

The War Within: A Novel of the Civil War - Carol
   Matas   *m*   600

Witness - Karen Hesse   *m*   392

Presidents

*Franklin Delano Roosevelt: Letters from a Mill Town
   Girl* - Elizabeth Winthrop   *m*   977

*John Quincy Adams: Letters from a Southern Planter's
   Son* - Steven Kroll   *m*   522

*Thomas Jefferson: Letters from a Philadelphia
   Bookworm* - Jennifer Armstrong   *m*   19

Princes and Princesses

Beware, Princess Elizabeth - Carolyn Meyer
   m   634

The Dog Prince - Lauren Mills   *p, e*   642

The Great Good Thing - Roderick Townley   *e,
   m*   888

Kaiulani: The People's Princess, Hawaii, 1889 - Ellen
   Emerson White   *m*   948

Lady Lollipop - Dick King-Smith   *e*   503

*Lady of Ch'iao Kuo: Warrior of the South, Southern
   China, A.D. 531* - Laurence Yep   *m*   995

The Princess and the Pea - Alain Vaes   *p*   897

Princess in the Spotlight - Meg Cabot   *m, h*   131

The Storytelling Princess - Rafe Martin   *p*   598

The Two Princesses of Bamarre - Gail Carson Levine
   m   550

Victoria: May Blossom of Britannia, England, 1829 -
   Anna Kirwan   *e, m*   509

The War - Anais Vaugelade   *p, e*   908

Problem Solving

Bikes for Rent! - Isaac Olaleye   *p*   685

The Case of the Puzzling Possum - Cynthia Rylant
   b, e   778

Eli's Night Light - Liz Rosenberg   *p*   768

Fearless Jack - Paul Brett Johnson   *p, e*   458

The Hungriest Boy in the World - Lensey Namioka
   p   667

Hungry! Hungry! Hungry! - Malachy Doyle   *p*   246

Irving and Muktuk: Two Bad Bears - Daniel Pinkwater
   p   717

Look Out, Jack! The Giant Is Back! - Tom Birdseye
   p, e   76

Max's Starry Night - Ken Wilson-Max   *p*   974

Mr. Putter & Tabby Feed the Fish - Cynthia Rylant
   b   783

One Riddle, One Answer - Lauren Thompson   *p,
   e*   881

Preschool to the Rescue - Judy Sierra   *p*   821

The Problem with Pumpkins: A Hip & Hop Story -
   Barney Saltzberg   *p*   790

Rattletrap Car - Phyllis Root   *p*   765

Sammy and the Robots - Ian Whybrow   *p*   949

The Scarecrow's Hat - Ken Brown   *p*   102

Scared Stiff - Katie Davis   *p*   217

The School Trip - Tjibbe Veldkamp   *p*   911

Tabitha's Terrifically Tough Tooth - Charlotte
   Middleton   *p*   636

Third Grade Stinks! - Colleen O'Shaughnessy McKenna   *e*   624
Tub-boo-boo - Margie Palatini   *p*   693
Willimena and the Cookie Money - Valerie Wilson Wesley   *e*   942

Prohibition Era

Moonshiner's Gold - John R. Erickson   *m*   279

Prostitution

Bone House - Betsy Tobin   *h, a*   885

Psychic Powers

Gifted Touch - Melinda Metz   *m, h*   633
Just Imagine - Pat Lowery Collins   *m*   177
Marco's Millions - William Sleator   *m*   829
My Grandfather, Jack the Ripper - Claudio Apone   *m*   16
Playing with Fire - Kathleen Karr   *m*   478
The Seeing Stone - Kevin Crossley-Holland   *m, h*   196
The Things I Know Best - Lynne Hinton   *a*   399
When Lightning Strikes - Jenny Carroll   *m, h*   142

Publishing

As Long as She Needs Me - Nicholas Weinstock   *a*   934

Puerto Rican Americans

Grandma's Records - Eric Velasquez   *p, e*   910

Pumpkins

The Garden That We Grew - Joan Holub   *b*   412

Puritans

Witch Child - Celia Rees   *m, h*   739

Quakers

The Secret Road - Robert Nordan   *e, m*   682
Slap Your Sides - M.E. Kerr   *m, h*   489

Quest

The Beguilers - Kate Thompson   *m, h*   880
A Cloak for the Moon - Eric A. Kimmel   *p, e*   496
Hole in the Sky - Pete Hautman   *m, h*   383
Lirael: Daughter of the Clayr - Garth Nix   *h*   677
The Ropemaker - Peter Dickinson   *m, h*   232
Treasure at the Heart of the Tanglewood - Meredith Ann Pierce   *m, h*   711

Quilts

Hattie's Story - Susan E. Kirby   *e*   505
Ida Lou's Story - Susan E. Kirby   *e*   506
The Moon Quilt - Sunny Warner   *p, e*   929

Quinceanera

Quinceanera Means Sweet 15 - Veronica Chambers   *m*   152

Race Relations

The Education of Mary: A Little Miss of Color - Ann Rinaldi   *m*   748
Freedom School, Yes! - Amy Littlesugar   *p, e*   564
Freedom Summer - Deborah Wiles   *p, e*   955

The Minstrel's Melody - Eleanora E. Tate   *e, m*   867
The Other Side - Jacqueline Woodson   *p, e*   983
The Stones of Mourning Creek - Diane Les Becquets   *m, h*   546

Racially Mixed People

Black Angels - Rita Murphy   *m*   658
Half a Heart - Rosellen Brown   *a*   105
The Land - Mildred D. Taylor   *m, h*   872
Valley of the Moon: The Diary of Maria Rosalia De Milagros, Sonoma Valley, Alta California, 1846 - Sherry Garland   *m*   317
Whale Talk - Chris Crutcher   *h*   199

Racism

Across the Steel River - Ted Stenhouse   *m*   853
A Day for Vincent Chin and Me - Jacqueline Turner Banks   *e*   50

Radio

Seek - Paul Fleischman   *m, h*   290

Railroads

Casey Jones - Allan Drummond   *p*   250
Coolies - Yin   *p, e*   996
The Holy Road - Michael Blake   *a*   83
Two Little Trains - Margaret Wise Brown   *p*   104

Ranch Life

Blind Fury - Linda Shands   *m*   815
The Devil in Ol' Rosie - Louise Moeri   *m*   645
Harley - Star Livingstone   *b*   565

Rape

Brave New Girl - Louisa Luna   *h*   576
Darkness Before Dawn - Sharon M. Draper   *h*   249
Every Time a Rainbow Dies - Rita Williams-Garcia   *h*   966

Recycling (Waste)

The Tin Forest - Helen Ward   *p*   924

Refugees

Anna's Goat - Janice Kulyk Keefer   *p, e*   481
The Other Side of Truth - Beverley Naidoo   *m, h*   666
Playing for Keeps - Joan Lowery Nixon   *m, h*   679

Reincarnation

A Dance for Emilia - Peter S. Beagle   *h, a*   63

Relatives

Aunt Claire's Yellow Beehive Hair - Deborah Blumenthal   *p*   88
The Hickory Chair - Lisa Rowe Fraustino   *p*   300

Religion

The Calling - Cathryn Clinton   *m, h*   169
Heresy - Anselm Audley   *h, a*   33
Priestess of Avalon - Marion Zimmer Bradley   *h, a*   98

Religious Traditions

The Friday Nights of Nana - Amy Hest   *p*   393

Remarriage

Ghost Soldier - Elaine Marie Alphin   *m*   13
My Guy - Sarah Weeks   *e, m*   933
Witch Twins - Adele Griffin   *e*   351

Resistance Movements

Brothers in Valor: A Story of Resistance - Michael O. Tunnell   *m, h*   890
Under a War-Torn Sky - L.M. Elliott   *m, h*   273

Responsibility

My Car - Byron Barton   *p*   57

Restaurants

Dim Sum for Everyone! - Grace Lin   *p*   558
Fast Food! Gulp! Gulp! - Bernard Waber   *p*   915
Froggy Eats Out - Jonathan London   *p*   568

Revenge

Lick Creek - Brad Kessler   *a*   490

Revolutionary War

Lorenzo's Secret Mission - Lila Guzman   *m*   362
Through the Wormhole - Robert J. Favole   *m*   284

Revolutions

Angel on the Square - Gloria Whelan   *m, h*   946
The Guns of Easter - Gerard Whelan   *m, h*   945

Riots

Missing from Haymarket Square - Harriette Gillem Robinet   *m*   755

Rivers

Horrible Harry Goes to Sea - Suzy Kline   *e*   513
White Water - Jonathan London   *p, e*   569

Robbers and Outlaws

Daniel's Walk - Michael Spooner   *m*   845
Horse Sense - Jan Neubert Schultz   *e, m*   801
The Man Who Wore All His Clothes - Allan Ahlberg   *e*   9
Nursery Crimes - Arthur Geisert   *p, e*   323

Robots

Bobo Crazy - Marilyn Sadler   *e*   786
My Brother, the Robot - Bonnie Becker   *e*   65
Sammy and the Robots - Ian Whybrow   *p*   949

Roman Empire

Under the Eagle: A Tale of Military Adventure and Reckless Heroism with the Roman Legions - Simon Scarrow   *a*   797

Romance

Change of Heart - Marcia King-Gamble   *a*   501
The Curse of Chalion - Lois McMaster Bujold   *h, a*   115
Echo - Francesca Lia Block   *h*   84

Small Town Life

Dancing in Cadillac Light - Kimberly Willis Holt
   m   411
Four Corners - Diane Freund   *a*   304
Sap Rising - Christine Lincoln   *a*   559
The Things I Know Best - Lynne Hinton   *a*   399

Social Classes

Falling Angels - Tracy Chevalier   *a*   156
In Sunlight, in a Beautiful Garden - Kathleen Cambor
   a   135
A Sea So Far - Jean Thesman   *m, h*   877

Social Conditions

Coram Boy - Jamila Gavin   *m, h*   321

Social Issues

All the Old Haunts - Chris Lynch   *h*   580
A Day for Vincent Chin and Me - Jacqueline Turner
   Banks   *e*   50
Witness - Karen Hesse   *m*   392

Space and Time

Anne Frank and Me - Cherie Bennett   *m*   68
Marco's Millions - William Sleator   *m*   829
Shades of Simon Gray - Joyce McDonald   *m,*
   h   617

Space Colonies

Bobo Crazy - Marilyn Sadler   *e*   786

Space Travel

Astro Bunnies - Christine Loomis   *p*   571
Company's Going - Arthur Yorinks   *p, e*   998
New Pet - Dan Yaccarino   *e*   992

Spies

The Gadget - Paul Zindel   *m, h*   1003
Girl in Blue - Ann Rinaldi   *m, h*   749
Owen Foote, Super Spy - Stephanie Greene   *e*   346
Stormbreaker - Anthony Horowitz   *m*   420

Spirituality

Pray Hard - Pamela Walker   *m*   918

Sports

All That Remains - Bruce Brooks   *m, h*   100
Girls Got Game: Sports Stories & Poems - Sue Macy
   m, h   588

Sports/Auto Racing

Conflict in California - Ken Stuckey   *m, h*   863

Sports/Baseball

All the Way Home - Patricia Reilly Giff   *e*   330
Extra Innings - Robert Newton Peck   *m*   705
The Journal of Biddy Owens: The Negro Leagues,
   Birmingham, Alabama, 1948 - Walter Dean Myers
   m   664
Plunking Reggie Jackson - James W. Bennett   *h*   69
Tartabull's Throw - Henry Garfield   *h*   313
Till Tomorrow - John Donahue   *m*   240

Sports/Basketball

Finding Forrester - James W. Ellison   *a, h*   276
Gus and Grandpa at Basketball - Claudia Mills
   b   641

Sports/Boxing

Fighting Ruben Wolfe - Markus Zusak   *m, h*   1008

Sports/Football

The Case of the Troublesome Turtle - Cynthia Rylant
   b, e   779
Damage - A.M. Jenkins   *h*   451
Love Rules - Marilyn Reynolds   *h*   743

Sports/Hockey

Ballet Bug - Christine McDonnell   *e, m*   621
Finnie Walsh - Steven Galloway   *a*   309

Sports/Karate

Frog Face and the Three Boys - Don Trembath   *e,*
   m   889

Sports/Running

Racing the Past - Sis Deans   *m*   220
Time Out - David Hill   *m, h*   397

Sports/Skateboarding

The Heart of Cool - Jamie McEwan   *b, e*   622

Sports/Skiing

Change of Heart - Marcia King-Gamble   *a*   501

Sports/Soccer

The Million Dollar Kick - Dan Gutman   *m*   360
Morgan Plays Soccer - Anne Rockwell   *p*   757
Understanding Buddy - Marc Kornblatt   *e*   516

Sports/Softball

Strike Two - Amy Goldman Koss   *e, m*   520

Sports/Swimming

Born in Sin - Evelyn Coleman   *h*   171
Whale Talk - Chris Crutcher   *h*   199

Sports/White Water Rafting

White Water - Jonathan London   *p, e*   569

Sports/Wrestling

The Secret Life of Dr. Demented - Dan Gutman
   m   361

Spring

Robin's Home - Jeannine Atkins   *p*   29
Splish, Splash, Spring - Jan Carr   *p*   141
Spring Song - Barbara Seuling   *p*   812

Stealing

The Moon Robber - Dean Morrissey   *e*   650

Stepfamilies

Waiting to Dive - Karen Rivers   *e, m*   750

Stepfathers

The Field of the Dogs - Katherine Paterson   *e,*
   m   700
Lord of the Deep - Graham Salisbury   *m*   788
Skinny Melon and Me - Jean Ure   *m*   894

Stores, Retail

The Bookstore Burglar - Barbara Maitland   *b*   590
Little Whistle's Dinner Party - Cynthia Rylant
   p   782
Math Man - Teri Daniels   *p*   208

Stories in Rhyme

Altoona Up North - Janie Bynum   *p*   130
And the Dish Ran Away with the Spoon - Janet
   Stevens   *p*   855
Astro Bunnies - Christine Loomis   *p*   571
Beach Day - Karen Roosa   *p*   764
Bear in Sunshine - Stella Blackstone   *p*   80
Bus Stop, Bus Go! - Daniel Kirk   *p*   507
Casey Jones - Allan Drummond   *p*   250
Castles, Caves, and Honeycombs - Linda Ashman
   p   26
Cats, Cats, Cats! - Leslea Newman   *p*   675
Dancing Class - H.M. Ehrlich   *p*   265
Dumpy La Rue - Elizabeth Winthrop   *p*   976
Everywhere Babies - Susan Meyers   *p*   635
Farm Flu - Teresa Bateman   *p*   59
Fast Food! Gulp! Gulp! - Bernard Waber   *p*   915
The Garden That We Grew - Joan Holub   *b*   412
Hide & Seek - Brenda Shannon Yee   *p*   993
Hushabye - John Burningham   *p*   126
I Love Going Through This Book - Robert Burleigh
   p   124
I Love You Because You're You - Liza Baker   *p*   44
I'm Not Feeling Well Today - Shirley Neitzel
   p   674
Jamboree Day - Rhonda Gowler Greene   *p*   345
Last Night at the Zoo - Michael Garland   *p*   314
Little Bird, Biddle Bird - David Kirk   *p*   508
Little Green - Keith Baker   *p*   43
Love Me, Love You - Susan Heyboer O'Keefe
   p   684
The Magical, Mystical, Marvelous Coat - Catherine
   Ann Cullen   *p*   200
Maxwell's Magic Mix-Up - Linda Ashman   *p*   27
Monster Mischief - Pamela Jane   *p*   448
More Parts - Tedd Arnold   *p, e*   20
Mrs. McTats and Her Houseful of Cats - Alyssa Satin
   Capucilli   *p*   137
One of the Problems of Everett Anderson - Lucille
   Clifton   *p*   168
Petite Rouge: A Cajun Red Riding Hood - Mike Artell
   p, e   22
A Plump and Perky Turkey - Teresa Bateman   *p*   62
Polar Bolero: A Bedtime Dance - Debi Gliori
   p   334
Preschool to the Rescue - Judy Sierra   *p*   821
Pumpkin Eye - Denise Fleming   *p*   292
Room on the Broom - Julia Donaldson   *p*   241
A Safe Place Called Home - Eileen Spinelli   *p*   842
Splish, Splash, Spring - Jan Carr   *p*   141
Spring Song - Barbara Seuling   *p*   812
A Stormy Ride on Noah's Ark - Patricia Hooper
   p   417
Sun Bread - Elisa Kleven   *p*   512
Tattered Sails - Verla Kay   *p*   480
Teeny Tiny Tingly Tales - Nancy Van Laan   *p*   901
Thanksgiving Mice! - Bethany Roberts   *p*   751
There's a Cow in the Cabbage Patch - Stella
   Blackstone   *p*   81

World War I

Lord of the Nutcracker Men - Iain Lawrence
    m   537

World War II

The 1940s: Secrets - Dorothy Hoobler   e   415
Anna's Goat - Janice Kulyk Keefer   p, e   481
A Boy at War: A Novel of Pearl Harbor - Harry
    Mazer   m   605

Brothers in Valor: A Story of Resistance - Michael O.
    Tunnell   m, h   890
Don't You Know There's a War On? - Avi   m   35
The Gadget - Paul Zindel   m, h   1003
Gwyneth's Secret Grandpa - Annie Morris Williams
    e   961
Slap Your Sides - M.E. Kerr   m, h   489
Soldier Boys - Dean Hughes   m, h   434
Soldier X - Don Wulffson   h   987
Under a War-Torn Sky - L.M. Elliott   m, h   273

Writing

Alphabet Adventure - Audrey Wood   p   982

Zoos

Last Night at the Zoo - Michael Garland   p   314
Notes from a Liar and Her Dog - Gennifer Choldenko
    m   162

Character Name Index

This index alphabetically lists the major characters in each featured title. Each character name is followed by a description of the character. Citations also provide titles of the books featuring the character, listed alphabetically if there is more than one title, with author names, age-level code(s) and entry numbers also included. The age-level codes are as follows: *p* Preschool, *b* Beginning Reader, *e* Elementary School (Grades 2-5), *m* Middle School (Grades 5-8), *h* High School (Grades 9-12), and *a* Adult.

A

Abbott, Vidalia "Viddy" (Aunt; Adoptee)
Extra Innings - Robert Newton Peck   *m* 705

Abernathy, J.E. "Brother Mustard Seed" (Convict)
Pray Hard - Pamela Walker   *m* 918

Abner (Cat)
Mrs. McTats and Her Houseful of Cats - Alyssa Satin Capucilli   *p* 137

Achilles (Genius)
Shadow of the Hegemon - Orson Scott Card   *h, a* 139

Ada (Aunt; Farmer)
A Farm of Her Own - Natalie Kinsey-Warnock   *p* 504

Adams, Amy Kate "Buddy" (6th Grader)
Buddy Is a Stupid Name for a Girl - Willo Davis Roberts   *e, m* 753

Adams, Bart (17-Year-Old)
Buddy Is a Stupid Name for a Girl - Willo Davis Roberts   *e, m* 753

Adams, Buzz (13-Year-Old)
My Guy - Sarah Weeks   *e, m* 933

Adams, John Quincy (Political Figure; Historical Figure)
John Quincy Adams: Letters from a Southern Planter's Son - Steven Kroll   *m* 522

Adeline "Addie" (Royalty)
The Two Princesses of Bamarre - Gail Carson Levine   *m* 550

Adolpho (Witch)
The Pillars of the World - Anne Bishop   *h, a* 77

Adrian, Jason (11-Year-Old; Wizard)
The Magickers - Emily Drake   *m* 248

Aelvarim (Mythical Creature)
Eccentric Circles - Rebecca Lickiss   *h, a* 556

Aethelflaed "Flaed" (Royalty; Historical Figure)
The Edge on the Sword - Rebecca Tingle   *m, h* 884

Agon "Axe Man" (Prehistoric Human)
Song of the Axe - John R. Dann   *a* 209

Ahmed (Farmer)
One Riddle, One Answer - Lauren Thompson   *p, e* 881

Ahvren, Viv (Military Personnel; 18-Year-Old)
A Matter of Profit - Hilari Bell   *h, a* 67

al-Aya, Tariq (Rescuer; Traveler)
Mansa Musa: The Lion of Mali - Khephra Burns   *e, m* 127

Albert (Recluse; Animal Lover)
Albert - Donna Jo Napoli   *p, e* 668

Alcott, Bronson (Father; Historical Figure)
Becoming Little Women: Louisa May at Fruitlands - Jeannine Atkins   *e, m* 28

Alcott, Bronson (Historical Figure)
Little Women Next Door - Sheila Solomon Klass   *e, m* 511

Alcott, Louisa May (Historical Figure; 11-Year-Old)
Becoming Little Women: Louisa May at Fruitlands - Jeannine Atkins   *e, m* 28

Alcott, Louisa May (Historical Figure)
Little Women Next Door - Sheila Solomon Klass   *e, m* 511

Aldrich, Esther (12-Year-Old)
The 1940s: Secrets - Dorothy Hoobler   *e* 415

Alex (Friend; Student—Elementary School)
Daniel's Mystery Egg - Alma Flor Ada   *b* 1

Alex (Child)
Loki & Alex: The Adventures of a Dog & His Best Friend - Charles R. Smith Jr.   *p* 830

Alex (Nephew; Magician)
Maxwell's Magic Mix-Up - Linda Ashman   *p* 27

Alex (Child of Divorced Parents)
Two Homes - Claire Masurel   *p* 599

Alexandra (12-Year-Old)
One Puppy, Three Tales - Karen Salmansohn   *e* 789

Alexandrina Victoria (Royalty)
Victoria: May Blossom of Britannia, England, 1829 - Anna Kirwan   *e, m* 509

Alexi (Hunter)
The Golden Mare, the Firebird, and the Magic Ring - Ruth Sanderson   *p, e* 792

Alfred (Royalty; Historical Figure)
The Edge on the Sword - Rebecca Tingle   *m, h* 884

Alice (Friend; Babysitter)
Emily and Alice Baby-Sit Burton - Joyce Champion   *b, e* 153

Alien (Alien; Friend)
Alien & Possum: Friends No Matter What - Tony Johnston   *b* 463

Alison "Ali" (15-Year-Old; Daughter)
Lord of the Deep - Graham Salisbury   *m* 788

Allen, Ethan (Historical Figure)
The Hero of Ticonderoga - Gail Gauthier   *m* 320

Almayo, Antonia "Toni" (Teenager)
The Summer of El Pintor - Ofelia Dumas Lachtman   *m, h* 525

Almayo, Rob (Student—College)
The Summer of El Pintor - Ofelia Dumas Lachtman   *m, h* 525

Alnor (Grandfather)
The Ropemaker - Peter Dickinson   *m, h* 232

Alrika (Runner)
Time Out - David Hill   *m, h* 397

Alvarez-Shipton, Benita (Diplomat)
The Fresco - Sheri S. Tepper   *h, a* 875

Amanda (Child; Sister)
Pinky and Rex and the Just-Right Pet - James Howe   *b, e* 429

Amaroq (Child; Eskimo)
Nutik & Amaroq Play Ball - Jean Craighead George   *p* 324

Amaroq (Eskimo; Brother)
Nutik, the Wolf Pup - Jean Craighead George   *p* 325

Amber (Sister; Child)
Amber Was Brave, Essie Was Smart - Vera B. Williams   *e* 965

Ambriel (Amnesiac)
Stained Glass - Michael Bedard   *m, h* 66

Amelia (Sister; Student)
Oh Boy, Amelia! - Marissa Moss   *e* 654

Ameyaw, Nana (Artisan)
The Spider Weaver: A Legend of Kente Cloth - Margaret Musgrove   *p, e* 661

Amy (4-Year-Old; Twin)
Big Trouble in Little Twinsville - Elizabeth Levy   *e* 552

Anderson, Elizabeth "Lizzie" (9-Year-Old; Child of Divorced Parents)
By Lizzie - Mary Eccles   *e* 259

Anderson, Ellie (Sister; 2-Year-Old)
By Lizzie - Mary Eccles   *e* 259

Anderson, Everett (Student—Elementary School; Son)
One of the Problems of Everett Anderson - Lucille Clifton   *p* 168

Anderson, John Franklin (Brother; Son)
Mama's Way - Helen Ketteman   *p, e* 492

Anderson, Norman (Brother; 12-Year-Old)
By Lizzie - Mary Eccles   *e* 259

Anderson, Tamika (Friend; 4th Grader)
Andy Russell, NOT Wanted by the Police - David A. Adler   *e* 5

Anderson, Wynona (Daughter; 6th Grader)
Mama's Way - Helen Ketteman   *p, e* 492

Andreas, Nicholas "Nick" (16-Year-Old; Wealthy)
Breathing Underwater - Alex Flinn   *h* 295

Andres (Child; Brother)
Buzz Buzz Buzz - Veronica Uribe   *p* 896

Andy (10-Year-Old; Brother)
A Castle on Viola Street - DyAnne DiSalvo   *p* 236

Angela (Athlete)
Freewill - Chris Lynch   *h* 581

Angelica (Cousin)
Tiger's Fall - Molly Bang   *e* 48

Angelo (Apprentice)
Shadows in the Glasshouse - Megan McDonald   *e, m* 620

Angus (Son; Brother)
A Fiddle for Angus - Budge Wilson   *p, e* 968

Angus (Cat)
On the Bright Side, I'm Now the Girlfriend of a Sex God: Further Confessions of Georgia Nicolson - Louise Rennison   *m, h* 742

Anna (Child; Refugee)
Anna's Goat - Janice Kulyk Keefer   *p, e* 481

Annabel (Sister; Bride)
The Reluctant Flower Girl - Lynne Barasch   *p* 53

Annabelle (Child)
One Monday - Amy Huntington   *p* 436

Anneke (Baby)
Katje, the Windmill Cat - Gretchen Woelfle   *p* 979

Annie (Child; Niece)
Aunt Claire's Yellow Beehive Hair - Deborah Blumenthal   *p* 88

Annie (Sister; Time Traveler)
Christmas in Camelot - Mary Pope Osborne   *e* 691

Annie (Teacher; Volunteer)
Freedom School, Yes! - Amy Littlesugar   *p, e* 564

Annie (Cousin)
The Gawgon and the Boy - Lloyd Alexander   *m* 11

Annie (Friend)
Nate the Great and the Big Sniff - Marjorie Weinman Sharmat   *b* 816

Antonella (Child)
Antonella and Her Santa Claus - Barbara Augustin   *p* 34

ap Gwien, Sulien (Military Personnel)
The King's Name - Jo Walton   *h, a* 922
The King's Peace - Jo Walton   *h, a* 923

April (Sister; Child)
The Reluctant Flower Girl - Lynne Barasch   *p* 53

Apropos (Bastard Son; Handicapped)
Sir Apropos of Nothing - Peter David   *h, a* 214

Aquamarine (Mythical Creature)
Aquamarine - Alice Hoffman   *m* 407

Araceli (Daughter)
Juan Verdades: The Man Who Couldn't Tell a Lie - Joe Hayes   *p, e* 385

Ari (Witch)
The Pillars of the World - Anne Bishop   *h, a* 77

Arkanian, Petra (Genius)
Shadow of the Hegemon - Orson Scott Card   *h, a* 139

Armiger, Aggie (Aunt; Spouse)
Anna on the Farm - Mary Downing Hahn   *e* 369

Armiger, George (Uncle; Guardian)
Anna on the Farm - Mary Downing Hahn   *e* 369

Armiger, Theodore (Orphan; Nephew)
Anna on the Farm - Mary Downing Hahn   *e* 369

Armstrong, Diane "Dee" (Student—College)
Compass in the Blood - William E. Coles Jr.   *m, h* 173

Armstrong, Jake (Musician; Detective—Amateur)
The Protestor's Song - Mark Delaney   *m* 223

Arnold (Pig; Friend)
Kipper's A to Z: An Alphabet Adventure - Mick Inkpen   *p* 442

Arthur (Indian)
Across the Steel River - Ted Stenhouse   *m* 853

Arthur (Rooster)
Something Wonderful - Jenny Nimmo   *p* 676

Arthur "Art" (17-Year-Old)
Love Trilogy - Kate Cann   *h* 136

Ash, Paula (10th Grader)
Death on Sacred Ground - Harriet K. Feder   *m, h* 285

Ashbrook, Alexander (Musician)
Coram Boy - Jamila Gavin   *m, h* 321

Attired, Natalie (Bird; Classmate)
Farewell, My Lunchbag - Bruce Hale   *e, m* 370

Auntie (Baboon; Aunt)
Altoona Up North - Janie Bynum   *p* 130

Austin (Cat)
The Second Summoning - Tanya Huff   *h, a* 433

Autumn (14-Year-Old)
Equinox - Monte Killingsworth   *m* 494

Aziza (Daughter)
One Riddle, One Answer - Lauren Thompson   *p, e* 881

Aznar, Alonzo (Drug Dealer)
Zach's Lie - Roland Smith   *m* 834

B

Ba-Ba (Father)
Dim Sum for Everyone! - Grace Lin   *p* 558

Babatunde (Businessman)
Bikes for Rent! - Isaac Olaleye   *p* 685

Baboona, Altoona (Baboon; Niece)
Altoona Up North - Janie Bynum   *p* 130

Baby Bert (Son; Baby)
The Adventures of Bert - Allan Ahlberg   *p* 8

Baby Brenda (Baby; Sister)
Midnight Babies - Margaret Wild   *p* 952

Baby "Captain Tweakerbeak" (Parrot)
Captain Tweakerbeak's Revenge: A Calliope Day Adventure - Charles Haddad   *e, m* 364

Baby Duck (Duck; Baby)
Baby Duck's New Friend - Frank Asch   *p* 24

Baby Girl (9th Grader; Psychic)
Sights - Susanna Vance   *m, h* 905

Baby Mario (Baby)
Midnight Babies - Margaret Wild   *p* 952

Badger (Badger; Hunter)
Coyote and Badger: Desert Hunters of the Southwest - Bruce Hiscock   *p, e* 400

Bailey (Uncle; Convict)
Scorpio's Child - Kezi Matthews   *m* 603

Bailey, Brandon "Choirboy" (Student—College)
Between Brothers - C. Kelly Robinson   *a* 756

Bailey, Sistine (6th Grader)
The Tiger Rising - Kate DiCamillo   *m* 231

Baker, Clarice (5th Grader; Friend)
Belle Teal - Ann M. Martin   *e, m* 596

Baker, Julianna "Juli" (8th Grader)
Flipped - Wendelin Van Draanen   *m* 899

Baker, Kenyon "Ken" (15-Year-Old; Photographer)
Razzle - Ellen Wittlinger   *h* 978

Baldt, William (Doctor; Agent)
Boston Jane: An Adventure - Jennifer L. Holm   *m* 409

Baloney, Henry P. (Alien; Student)
Baloney (Henry P) - Jon Scieszka   *p, e* 804

Bamford, Robert (7-Year-Old; Brother)
Night of the Living Gerbil - Elizabeth Levy   *e* 553

Bamford, Sam (Brother; 9-Year-Old)
Night of the Living Gerbil - Elizabeth Levy   *e* 553

Bandit (Dog)
Delfino's Journey - Jo Harper   *m, h* 375

Banks, John (Historical Figure; Military Personnel)
Through the Wormhole - Robert J. Favole   *m* 284

Banks, Michael (9th Grader; Equestrian)
Through the Wormhole - Robert J. Favole   *m* 284

Bannerjee, Ravi (Royalty; Patient)
The Year of My Indian Prince - Ella Thorp Ellis   *m, h* 275

Bannister, Armand (Judge; Grandfather)
Lorenzo's Secret Mission - Lila Guzman   *m* 362

Bannister, Lorenzo (15-Year-Old)
Lorenzo's Secret Mission - Lila Guzman   *m* 362

Baranova, Ekaterina "Katya" Ivanona (Teenager)
Angel on the Square - Gloria Whelan   *m, h* 946

Baranova, Irina Ivanova (Mother; Noblewoman)
Angel on the Square - Gloria Whelan   *m, h* 946

Barker, Caleb (Twin; 9-Year-Old)
The Starving Time: Elizabeth's Diary - Patricia Hermes   *e* 389

Barker, Elizabeth "Lizzie" (Settler; 9-Year-Old)
The Starving Time: Elizabeth's Diary - Patricia Hermes   *e* 389

Barker, Moffat "Moffie" (Dog; Twin)
Meet the Barkers: Morgan and Moffat Go to School - Tomie DePaola   *p* 225

Barker, Morgan "Morgie" (Dog; Twin)
Meet the Barkers: Morgan and Moffat Go to School - Tomie DePaola   *p* 225

Barnavelt, Jonathan (Uncle; Sorcerer)
The Tower at the End of the World - Brad Strickland   *m* 862

Barnavelt, Lewis (Orphan; 13-Year-Old)
The Tower at the End of the World - Brad Strickland   *m* 862

Barr, Gordie (3rd Grader; Friend)
Third Grade Stinks! - Colleen O'Shaughnessy McKenna   *e* 624

Bartlett, Alicia (Child; Victim)
The Rag and Bone Shop - Robert Cormier   *m, h* 183

Bartoletti, Emma (12-Year-Old)
Franklin Delano Roosevelt: Letters from a Mill Town Girl - Elizabeth Winthrop   *m* 977

Bat (Bat; Mother)
Bat Loves the Night - Nicola Davies   p   216

Batbaby (Bat; Son)
Batbaby Finds a Home - Robert Quackenbush
b   730

Baumgart, Sylvester "Slick" (Teenager)
Ida Lou's Story - Susan E. Kirby   e   506

Beaker, Tracy (10-Year-Old; Foster Child)
The Story of Tracy Beaker - Jacqueline Wilson   e,
m   971

Bean (Genius)
Shadow of the Hegemon - Orson Scott Card   h,
a   139

Bean, Clarice (Child; Niece)
Clarice Bean: Guess Who's Babysitting? - Lauren
Child   p, e   159

Beans (Dog)
A Fine, Fine School - Sharon Creech   p   191

Bear (Bear)
Bear in Sunshine - Stella Blackstone   p   80
Benno's Bear - N.F. Zucker   m   1007
*How Chipmunk Got His Stripes: A Tale of Bragging
and Teasing* - Joseph Bruchac   p   108

Bear (Bear; Stuffed Animal)
My Best Friend Bear - Tony Johnston   p   465

Beard, George (Friend; Student—Elementary
School)
*Captain Underpants and the Wrath of the Wicked
Wedgie Woman* - Dav Pilkey   e   713

Beasley/Beastley, Julius (Landlord; Animal Lover)
The Beastly Arms - Patrick Jennings   m   453

Beatrice (9-Year-Old; Daughter)
Beatrice's Goat - Page McBrier   p   608

Beatrice (Child; Daughter)
Clever Beatrice - Margaret Willey   p   960

Beckett, Buster (Child)
Fair Weather - Richard Peck   m   704

Beckett, Lottie (17-Year-Old)
Fair Weather - Richard Peck   m   704

Beckett, Rosie (13-Year-Old)
Fair Weather - Richard Peck   m   704

Beezer, Ebenezer (Aged Person)
A Plump and Perky Turkey - Teresa Bateman   p   62

Belinda (6th Grader)
Don't Bug Me! - Pam Zollman   e   1006

Belinda (Centipede; Mother)
*Harry the Poisonous Centipede's Big Adventure:
Another Story to Make You Squirm* - Lynne Reid
Banks   e   52

Bell, Dinah (12-Year-Old; Seamstress)
Missing from Haymarket Square - Harriette Gillem
Robinet   m   755

Bell, Michael (11th Grader)
Last Summer in Agatha - Katherine Holubitsky
m   413

Bell, Noah (Father; Activist)
Missing from Haymarket Square - Harriette Gillem
Robinet   m   755

Bennett, Rachel (16-Year-Old)
Last Summer in Agatha - Katherine Holubitsky
m   413

Benno (11-Year-Old)
Benno's Bear - N.F. Zucker   m   1007

Benny (Rabbit; Brother)
Bunbun at Bedtime - Sharon Pierce McCullough
p   610

Benson, Tony (6th Grader; Brother)
The Boys Return - Phyllis Reynolds Naylor   e,
m   673

Berg, Clara (13-Year-Old)
Clara's War - Kathy Kacer   e, m   474

Berg, Peter (Brother)
Clara's War - Kathy Kacer   e, m   474

Berghoff, Cassidy Rain (14-Year-Old)
Rain Is Not My Indian Name - Cynthia Leitich Smith
m   831

Berghoff, Fynnegan "Fynn" (Brother)
Rain Is Not My Indian Name - Cynthia Leitich Smith
m   831

Berkeley, George (Maintenance Worker)
Stained Glass - Michael Bedard   m, h   66

Bernard (Elephant; Preschooler)
Bernard Goes to School - Joan Elizabeth Goodman
p   342

Bernard (Rooster)
Bernard the Angry Rooster - Mary Wormell   p   985

Bert (Father; Spouse)
The Adventures of Bert - Allan Ahlberg   p   8

Bert (Farmer; Spouse)
The Great Pig Search - Eileen Christelow   p   163

Beryn (Nobleman)
Straw into Gold - Gary D. Schmidt   m   800

Bess (Aunt)
Maggie in the Morning - Elizabeth Van Steenwyk
e   904

Beth (12th Grader)
The Gospel According to Larry - Janet Tashjian
h   866

Beth (Aunt)
Stolen Words - Amy Goldman Koss   m   518

Beto (Child; Son)
Beto and the Bone Dance - Gina Freschet   p   303

Betriz (Noblewoman)
The Curse of Chalion - Lois McMaster Bujold   h,
a   115

Bettencourt, Charlie (6th Grader)
Don't Bug Me! - Pam Zollman   e   1006

Bevan, Jesse (13-Year-Old)
Gifted Touch - Melinda Metz   m, h   633

Bibi (Rabbit; Sister)
Bunbun at Bedtime - Sharon Pierce McCullough
p   610

Bibliogoth (Scholar; Alien)
A Matter of Profit - Hilari Bell   h, a   67

Biddle Bird (Bird)
Little Bird, Biddle Bird - David Kirk   p   508

Bidson, Ida (14-Year-Old; Teacher)
The Secret School - Avi   e, m   38

Bidson, Noah (9-Year-Old; Nephew)
Prairie School - Avi   b, e   37

Biff (Dog)
The Pocket Dogs - Margaret Wild   p   954

Big Bear (Bear; Bully)
Patrick and the Big Bully - Geoffrey Hayes   p   384

Big Blue (Elephant; Toy)
Max's Starry Night - Ken Wilson-Max   p   974

Big Hippo (Hippopotamus; Mother)
Naughty! - Caroline Castle   p   148

Big Mama Pig (Mother; Pig)
The Three Little Pigs - Barry Moser   p   652

Big Wolf (Wolf)
Beware of the Storybook Wolves - Lauren Child   p,
e   158

Big Zeb (Zebra; Mother)
Naughty! - Caroline Castle   p   148

Biggs, Kara (6th Grader)
How to Be a Real Person (in Just One Day) - Sally
Warner   m   927

Bill (Duck; Detective—Police)
The Web Files - Margie Palatini   p, e   694

Bindart, Cricket (16-Year-Old; Twin)
Witches' Key to Terror - Silver RavenWolf   h   738

Bindart, Tad (16-Year-Old; Twin)
Witches' Key to Terror - Silver RavenWolf   h   738

Bintou (Daughter; Sister)
Bintou's Braids - Sylviane A. Diouf   p   235

Bird (Bird; Friend)
Where Did Bunny Go? - Nancy Tafuri   p   865

Bird, Billy (4-Year-Old; Brother)
Billy the Bird - Dick King-Smith   e   502

Bird, Mary (8-Year-Old; Sister)
Billy the Bird - Dick King-Smith   e   502

Birdie (Bird)
Happy Birthday Mr. Kang - Susan L. Roth   p,
e   770

Birdsong, Corey (9-Year-Old; Slave)
Freedom's Wings: Corey's Diary - Sharon Dennis
Wyeth   e, m   988

Bishop, John (Political Figure; Crime Victim)
Green Grow the Victims - Jeanne M. Dams   a   207

Black, Caroline (Suffragette)
Falling Angels - Tracy Chevalier   a   156

Black, Jonah (17-Year-Old)
The Black Book (Diary of a Teenage Stud) Series -
Jonah Black   h   79

Black, Pepper (Girlfriend)
Girlhearts - Norma Fox Mazer   m   606

Black Bull of Norroway (Bull; Nobleman)
The Black Bull of Norroway - Charlotte Huck   p,
e   432

Blackheart, Lilliana "Lili" (Healer; Wizard)
The Queen's Necklace - Teresa Edgerton   h, a   260

Blackheart, Wilrowan "Wil" (Nobleman; Spouse)
The Queen's Necklace - Teresa Edgerton   h, a   260

Blackthorn, Tessa (Teenager)
Blind Beauty - K.M. Peyton   m, h   709

Blaine, Delia (9th Grader)
Amandine - Adele Griffin   m   350

Blaire, Cal (12th Grader; Witch)
Book of Shadows - Cate Tiernan   h   883

Blake, Dorothea (Widow; Wealthy)
The Maiden of Mayfair - Lawana Blackwell   a   82

Blakeman, Josh (17-Year-Old; Cook)
Lightning Rider - Jacqueline Guest   m, h   355

Blanche (Stepsister; Daughter)
Mother Holly - John Warren Stewig   p, e   858

Blast Off Boy (Human; Student—Exchange)
New Pet - Dan Yaccarino   e   992

Blinky (Hippopotamus)
New Pet - Dan Yaccarino   e   992

Bloom, Cleo (Girlfriend; Designer)
What Every Girl (Except Me) Knows - Nora Raleigh
Baskin   m   58

Blooming Mary (Aged Person; Gardener)
Goin' Someplace Special - Patricia C. McKissack   p,
e   625

Blorp (Alien; Student—Exchange)
New Pet - Dan Yaccarino   e   992

Blossom (Cat)
The Cats of Cuckoo Square: Two Stories - Adele Geras   e   326

Blue Eagle, Thomas (Indian; 18-Year-Old)
The Sketchbook of Thomas Blue Eagle - Gay Matthaei   m   602

Blue Kangaroo (Kangaroo; Stuffed Animal)
Where Are You, Blue Kangaroo? - Emma Chichester Clark   p   157

Blueday, Derkhan (Journalist)
Perdido Street Station - China Mieville   h, a   637

Bobo Dog (Robot)
Bobo Crazy - Marilyn Sadler   e   786

Bolinski, Marisia (15-Year-Old)
Streets of Gold - Marie Raphael   m, h   735

Bolinski, Stefan (Brother)
Streets of Gold - Marie Raphael   m, h   735

Bonifacio, Lorenzo (15-Year-Old; Military Personnel)
In the Shadow of the Alamo - Sherry Garland   m   316

Bonny, Anne (Pirate)
The Sweet Trade - Elizabeth Garrett   a   318

Bonsteel, Minnie (Student)
Finding Hattie - Sally Warner   m   926

Boomer, Kinsasha Rosa Parks "Kinchy" (Friend; Anthropologist)
The Transmogrification of Roscoe Wizzle - David Elliott   e   272

Borgia, Lucifer di S'Embowelli (Brother)
Pure Dead Magic - Debi Gliori   e, m   335

Bott, Lucy "Memaw" (Grandmother)
Up a Creek - Laura E. Williams   m   962

Bott, Miracle (Activist; Mother)
Up a Creek - Laura E. Williams   m   962

Bott, Starshine (13-Year-Old; 8th Grader)
Up a Creek - Laura E. Williams   m   962

Bowers, Todd (Student—High School)
The Courage to Live - Deborah Kent   m, h   488

Bowzer (Restaurateur)
Everything on a Waffle - Polly Horvath   m   422

Boy (Child; Streetperson)
The Shine Man: A Christmas Story - Mary Quattlebaum   p, e   732

Boyd (12th Grader)
The Brimstone Journals - Ron Koertge   m, h   515

Braddock, Peter (Detective—Amateur)
The Protestor's Song - Mark Delaney   m   223

Bradley, Helen (Grandmother; Pilot)
Stranded - Patricia H. Rushford   m, h   773

Bramblewine, Arianna "Grandy" (Grandmother; Witch)
Witch Twins - Adele Griffin   e   351

Bran "the Painted Man" (Warrior)
Son of the Shadows - Juliet Marillier   h, a   593

Branden, Michael (Professor)
Clouds without Rain - P.L. Gaus   a   319

Brandt, Erik (16-Year-Old; Military Personnel)
Soldier X - Don Wulffson   h   987

Brenda "Bun Bun" (Sister; 1-Year-Old)
Bun Bun's Birthday - Richard Scrimger   p   807

Brennan, Kelley Anne (12-Year-Old; Patient)
A Face First - Priscilla Cummings   m   201

Brennan, Leah (Sister; Student—College)
A Face First - Priscilla Cummings   m   201

Brian (12-Year-Old; Collector)
The Comic Book Kid - Adam Osterweil   e   692

Bridget (Preschooler)
Bridget and the Gray Wolves - Pija Lindenbaum   p   560

Briggs, Ivy (Aunt)
Lord of the Nutcracker Men - Iain Lawrence   m   537

Briggs, James (Father; Artisan)
Lord of the Nutcracker Men - Iain Lawrence   m   537

Briggs, Johnny (Child)
Lord of the Nutcracker Men - Iain Lawrence   m   537

Briquette (Dog)
Fiddleback - Elizabeth Honey   m   414

Bromfield, Harriet "Harry" (Journalist)
Compass in the Blood - William E. Coles Jr.   m, h   173

Brother Fox (Fox)
The Tale of Tricky Fox: A New England Trickster Tale - Jim Aylesworth   p   39

Brown, Amber (7-Year-Old; Friend)
It's Justin Time, Amber Brown - Paula Danziger   e   210

Brown, Amber (2nd Grader; Friend)
What a Trip, Amber Brown - Paula Danziger   e   211

Brown, Audrey (Mouse)
The Crystal Prison - Robin Jarvis   m   450

Brown, Bonnie (Single Parent; Mother)
The Secret Life of Dr. Demented - Dan Gutman   m   361

Brown, Bunny (Rabbit; Detective—Private)
The Case of the Puzzling Possum - Cynthia Rylant   b, e   778
The Case of the Troublesome Turtle - Cynthia Rylant   b, e   779

Brown, Patrick (Bear; Bullied Child)
Patrick and the Big Bully - Geoffrey Hayes   p   384

Brown, Rufus (Uncle)
West of Rehoboth - Alexs D. Pate   a   699

Brown, Wesley (14-Year-Old)
The Secret Life of Dr. Demented - Dan Gutman   m   361

Brown Squirrel (Squirrel)
How Chipmunk Got His Stripes: A Tale of Bragging and Teasing - Joseph Bruchac   p   108

Brownbear, Morgan (Bear; Neighbor)
Morgan Plays Soccer - Anne Rockwell   p   757

Bruce, Orphelia (12-Year-Old; Musician)
The Minstrel's Melody - Eleanora E. Tate   e, m   867

Bryan (Royalty)
Summers at Castle Auburn - Sharon Shinn   h, a   818

Bryant, Evander "Evan" (11-Year-Old)
A Sailor Returns - Theodore Taylor   e   873

Brynn "Brynnie" (6th Grader)
Bad Girl Blues - Sally Warner   m   925

Bubbeh (Grandmother; Immigrant)
Rivka's First Thanksgiving - Elsa Okon Rael   p, e   733

Buchanan, Charity (Aunt; Quaker)
The Secret Road - Robert Nordan   e, m   682

Buchanan, Jesse (Uncle; Farmer)
The Secret Road - Robert Nordan   e, m   682

Buckeye (Goat)
Skyrockets and Snickerdoodles: A Cobtown Story from the Diaries of Lucky Hart - Julia Van Nutt   e   903

Buckley, Celia (Runaway)
Feeling Sorry for Celia - Jaclyn Moriarty   h   648

Buckner, Josh (3rd Grader; Friend)
I Was a Third Grade Spy - Mary Jane Auch   e   32

Buff (Dog)
The Pocket Dogs - Margaret Wild   p   954

Bunbun (Rabbit; Brother)
Bunbun at Bedtime - Sharon Pierce McCullough   p   610

Bunch, Joe (7th Grader)
The Misfits - James Howe   m   428

Bundkin, Claire (Twin; 10-Year-Old)
Witch Twins - Adele Griffin   e   351

Bundkin, Luna (Twin; 10-Year-Old)
Witch Twins - Adele Griffin   e   351

Bunny (Rabbit; Friend)
Where Did Bunny Go? - Nancy Tafuri   p   865

Burke, Coley (12th Grader; Baseball Player)
Plunking Reggie Jackson - James W. Bennett   h   69

Burns, Nicole "Nicole Bernhardt" (10th Grader)
Anne Frank and Me - Cherie Bennett   m   68

Burnt Paw (Dog)
Down the Yukon - Will Hobbs   m, h   404

Burrell, Ida (3rd Grader)
Horrible Harry Goes to Sea - Suzy Kline   e   513

Burton (Dog)
Emily and Alice Baby-Sit Burton - Joyce Champion   b, e   153

Buster (Rabbit)
Robert and the Great Pepperoni - Barbara Seuling   e   811

Butler (Servant)
Artemis Fowl - Eoin Colfer   m   174

Butter, Roland (Artist)
Skinny Melon and Me - Jean Ure   m   894

Butterfield, Casey (7th Grader; Child of an Alcoholic)
Raising the Shades - Doug Wilhelm   m   958

Butterfield, Julie (Aunt)
Raising the Shades - Doug Wilhelm   m   958

Butterfield, Stanley (Sea Captain)
The Buccaneers - Iain Lawrence   m, h   536

C

Caderine, Martyne (Religious)
Eyes of the Calculor - Sean McMullen   h, a   627

Cairns, Charles "Charlie" (7th Grader)
Frog Face and the Three Boys - Don Trembath   e, m   889

Cal (Fisherman)
Lord of the Deep - Graham Salisbury   m   788

Calabro, Giuseppe "Joey" (12-Year-Old; Immigrant)
A Place for Joey - Carol Flynn Harris   e, m   378

Caldecott, Amos (Wealthy)
Playing with Fire - Kathleen Karr   m   478

Caleb (Cowboy; Brother)
Gabriel's Story - David Anthony Durham   h, a   255

Calhoun, Cooper (Child)
Maggie in the Morning - Elizabeth Van Steenwyk   e   904

Calhoun, Maggie (11-Year-Old)
Maggie in the Morning - Elizabeth Van Steenwyk   e   904

Callahan, Nita (Wizard; Daughter)
The Wizard's Dilemma - Diane Duane   m, h   251

Cameron, Bren (Diplomat)
Defender - C.J. Cherryh   h, a   155

Campbell, Oscar (Assistant)
As Long as She Needs Me - Nicholas Weinstock
   a   934

Capel, Fernanda "Fern" (Witch; Sister)
The Dragon Charmer - Jan Siegel   h, a   820

Capel, Will (Brother)
The Dragon Charmer - Jan Siegel   h, a   820

Captain (Sea Captain; Pirate)
Captain and Matey Set Sail - Daniel Laurence
   b   535

Captain (Dog)
Private Captain: A Novel of Gettysburg - Marty Crisp
   m   194

Captain Vanderdecken (Sea Captain)
Castaways of the Flying Dutchman - Brian Jacques
   m   446

Captain Vince (Bird; Amputee)
Dodo Gets Married - Petra Mathers   p   601

Carey, Chipper (12-Year-Old; Orphan)
Chipper - James Lincoln Collier   m   176

Carillo, Jason (Basketball Player; 12th Grader)
Rainbow Boys - Alex Sanchez   h   791

Carla (Daughter; Student—Elementary School)
Fat Chance Thanksgiving - Patricia Lakin   p,
   e   529

Carle, Addie (7th Grader)
The Misfits - James Howe   m   428

Carlo (Giraffe)
Carlo Likes Reading - Jessica Spanyol   p   840

Carlos (3rd Grader; Nephew)
Uncle Rain Cloud - Tony Johnston   p   466

Carly (10-Year-Old; Friend)
Waiting to Dive - Karen Rivers   e, m   750

Carnegie, Andrew (Historical Figure; Industrialist)
In Sunlight, in a Beautiful Garden - Kathleen Cambor
   a   135

Carolinus (Wizard)
The Dragon and the Fair Maid of Kent - Gordon
   Dickson   h, a   233

Carr, January (Orphan)
Heaven Eyes - David Almond   m   12

Carroll, Arthur "Artie" (Victim)
Prowlers - Christopher Golden   h   336

Carter, Mercy "Munnonock" (11-Year-Old)
The Ransom of Mercy Carter - Caroline B. Cooney
   m   181

Carter, Raylene (Con Artist; Computer Expert)
The Onion Girl - Charles De Lint   h, a   219

Carter, Sophie (Cook)
Black Angels - Rita Murphy   m   658

Casey, Anna (12-Year-Old; Foster Child)
Anna Casey's Place in the World - Adrian Fogelin
   m   296

Casey, Danny (Student—Middle School)
Above and Beyond - Susan Bonners   m   91

Casey, Mary Catherine "Serena" (Computer Expert)
Death Benefits - Thomas Perry   a   708

Casselman, Alison (Crime Victim)
Alison, Who Went Away - Vivian Vande Velde
   m   906

Casselman, Susan/Sybil (9th Grader)
Alison, Who Went Away - Vivian Vande Velde
   m   906

Castaneda, Rey (Teenager)
The Jumping Tree - Rene Saldana Jr.   m   787

Castle, Owen (Artist)
Following Fake Man - Barbara Ware Holmes
   m   410

Cat (Cat; Musician)
And the Dish Ran Away with the Spoon - Janet
   Stevens   p   855

Cat (Cat; Trickster)
Mabela the Clever - Margaret Read MacDonald
   p   584

Caterina (Orphan; Singer)
The Orphan Singer - Emily Arnold McCully
   p   613

Cathan (Nobleman; Wizard)
Heresy - Anselm Audley   h, a   33

Catherine (Runaway; 16-Year-Old)
Destination Gold! - Julie Lawson   m, h   538

Catherwood, Noreen (4th Grader; Friend)
*Captain Tweakerbeak's Revenge: A Calliope Day
   Adventure* - Charles Haddad   e, m   364

Catisha (Insect)
Clara Caterpillar - Pamela Duncan Edwards
   p   263

Catlett, Lucy (13-Year-Old)
My Grandfather, Jack the Ripper - Claudio Apone
   m   16

Cato, Quintus Licinius (Military Personnel)
*Under the Eagle: A Tale of Military Adventure and
   Reckless Heroism with the Roman Legions* - Simon
   Scarrow   a   797

Catty (Witch)
Into the Cold Fire - Lynne Ewing   m, h   281

Cavanaugh, Patrick (Fire Fighter)
Green Grow the Victims - Jeanne M. Dams   a   207

Cazaril (Warrior)
The Curse of Chalion - Lois McMaster Bujold   h,
   a   115

Chaikin, Marc (6th Grader)
6-321 - Michael Laser   m   533

Chambers, Abigail "Abbie" (11-Year-Old)
Stopping to Home - Lea Wait   e   917

Chambers, Margaret (Teacher)
Esther's Pillow - Marlin Fitzwater   a   288

Chambers, Seth (Brother; Child)
Stopping to Home - Lea Wait   e   917

Chamblee, Richeson Francis (Military Personnel;
   Spirit)
Ghost Soldier - Elaine Marie Alphin   m   13

Charbonet, Jenna (13-Year-Old; 8th Grader)
Up a Creek - Laura E. Williams   m   962

Charles (5th Grader)
A Book of Coupons - Susie Morgenstern   e, m   646

Charlestown Charlie (Immigrant; Paperboy)
Joshua's Song - Joan Hiatt Harlow   m   373

Charley (Child; Student)
Alphabet Adventure - Audrey Wood   p   982

Charlie (Child; Brother)
I Am NOT Sleepy and I Will NOT Go to Bed - Lauren
   Child   p   160

Chase, Lydia (Widow(er))
Stopping to Home - Lea Wait   e   917

Cherry Sue (Llama; Friend)
Poppleton in Winter - Cynthia Rylant   b   784

Chester (Child; Friend)
The Lima Bean Monster - Dan Yaccarino   p   991

Chester (Friend)
Table Manners - Chris Raschka   p, e   737

Chicken (Chicken)
The Scarecrow's Hat - Ken Brown   p   102

Chief Carlson (Police Officer)
Mystery from History - Dayle Campbell Gaetz   e,
   m   307

Chief McCallister (Police Officer)
Frankenbug - Steven Cousins   e, m   185

Chin, Vincent (Historical Figure; Crime Victim)
A Day for Vincent Chin and Me - Jacqueline Turner
   Banks   e   50

Chip (6th Grader)
My Brother, the Robot - Bonnie Becker   e   65

Chipmunk (Chipmunk; Friend)
Where Did Bunny Go? - Nancy Tafuri   p   865

Chitter, Oswald (Mouse)
The Crystal Prison - Robin Jarvis   m   450

Chrestomanci (Wizard)
Mixed Magics: Four Tales of Chrestomanci - Diana
   Wynne Jones   m, h   469

Christmas (Chicken)
What's Cooking, Jamela? - Niki Daly   p   206

Christopher (Son; Brother)
Mom Pie - Lynne Jonell   p   468

Circus Girl (Entertainer; Friend)
Circus Girl - Tomek Bogacki   p   90

Claiborne, Kar (Military Personnel)
Fire on the Waters - David Poyer   a   722

Claire (12-Year-Old)
Aquamarine - Alice Hoffman   m   407

Claire (Grandmother)
The Great Good Thing - Roderick Townley   e,
   m   888

Clara (Insect; Friend)
Clara Caterpillar - Pamela Duncan Edwards
   p   263

Clara (Postal Worker; Friend)
How Santa Lost His Job - Stephen Krensky   p   521

Clara (Aunt)
The Journey - Sarah Stewart   p, e   857

Clarence (Pig; Traveler)
Clarence and the Great Surprise - Jean Ekman Adams
   p   3

Clark, Walter (12-Year-Old)
Through the Lock - Carol Otis Hurst   m   438

Clarry, Elizabeth (15-Year-Old)
Feeling Sorry for Celia - Jaclyn Moriarty   h   648

Claude (Aged Person; Farmer)
All the Way Home - Patricia Reilly Giff   e   330

Claude (Alligator)
Petite Rouge: A Cajun Red Riding Hood - Mike Artell
   p, e   22

Claudia (Mother)
Three Days - Donna Jo Napoli   m   670

Claudio (Royalty)
Goose Chase - Patrice Kindl   m, h   500

Claus, Peter (Son; Child)
Peter Claus and the Naughty List - Lawrence David
   p   213

Cleghorn, Victoria Kawekiu Lunalilo Kala (Royalty;
   Historical Figure)
Kaiulani: The People's Princess, Hawaii, 1889 - Ellen
   Emerson White   m   948

Cleo (Sister; Student)
Oh Boy, Amelia! - Marissa Moss   e   654

Cleveland, Vanessa (Witch)
Into the Cold Fire - Lynne Ewing   m, h   281

Cliff (1st Grader)
Little Cliff's First Day of School - Clifton L. Taulbert
p 868

Clover (Child; Narrator)
The Other Side - Jacqueline Woodson   p, e 983

Clyman, James (Historical Figure; Wagonmaster)
Daniel's Walk - Michael Spooner   m 845

Clyne (Dinosaur)
Ancient Fire - Mark London Williams   m 964

Cobweb (Cat)
The Bookstore Burglar - Barbara Maitland   b 590

Cody (Brother; Child)
Bluebird Summer - Deborah Hopkinson   p, e 418

Cody, Buffalo Bill (Historical Figure; Entertainer)
The Sketchbook of Thomas Blue Eagle - Gay Matthaei
m 602

Coleman, Duane "Denny" (5th Grader)
Don't You Know There's a War On? - Avi   m 35

Coleman, Kitty (Mother; Suffragette)
Falling Angels - Tracy Chevalier   a 156

Coleman, Maude (Child)
Falling Angels - Tracy Chevalier   a 156

Colette "Coll" (16-Year-Old)
Love Trilogy - Kate Cann   h 136

Collier, Sam (12-Year-Old; Apprentice)
*Surviving Jamestown: The Adventures of Young Sam
Collier* - Gail Langer Karwoski   m 479

Collin (Detective—Amateur)
4 1/2 Friends and the Secret Cave - Joachim Friedrich
e 305
41/2 Friends and the Disappearing Bio Teacher -
Joachim Friedrich   e 306

Colonel Mane (Lion; Restaurateur)
Fast Food! Gulp! Gulp! - Bernard Waber   p 915

Columbus, Christopher (Historical Figure; Explorer)
Freedom beyond the Sea - Waldtraut Lewin   m,
h 554

Comeaux, Sonny (Son; Student)
Rent Party Jazz - William Miller   p, e 640

Conan (12th Grader; Football Player)
Love Rules - Marilyn Reynolds   h 743

Conda, Anna (Juror; Designer)
Trial by Jury/Journal - Kate Klise   m 514

Connaire (Royalty)
The Destruction of the Inn - Randy Lee Eickhoff   h,
a 266

Conner, Emily Joy (3rd Grader; Friend)
A Puppy of My Own - Wendy Loggia   e 567

Connolly, Scott "Beamer" (6th Grader)
The Mysterious Matter of I.M. Fine - Diane Stanley
e 850

Conor (Gang Member)
Bloodtide - Melvin Burgess   h, a 123

Conroy, John (Advisor)
Victoria: May Blossom of Britannia, England, 1829 -
Anna Kirwan   e, m 509

Converse, Jeff (Student—College)
The Manhattan Hunt Club - John Saul   a 794

Conway, Jimmy (12-Year-Old)
The Guns of Easter - Gerard Whelan   m, h 945

Cook (Pig; Cook)
Fast Food! Gulp! Gulp! - Bernard Waber   p 915

Cooper, Jackson (13-Year-Old)
The Eye of the Stone - Tom Birdseye   e, m 75

Coppercorn, Jilly (Artist; Sister)
The Onion Girl - Charles De Lint   h, a 219

Cora (Girlfriend)
Stranger in Dadland - Amy Goldman Koss   e,
m 519

Coram, Thomas (Historical Figure)
Coram Boy - Jamila Gavin   m, h 321

Coriel "Corie" (Sister)
Summers at Castle Auburn - Sharon Shinn   h,
a 818

Cornelius (Insect; Friend)
Clara Caterpillar - Pamela Duncan Edwards
p 263

Coughlin, Chris (Swimmer; Mentally Challenged
Person)
Whale Talk - Chris Crutcher   h 199

Cousin Smith (Landowner; Neighbor)
A Bus of Our Own - Freddi Williams Evans   p,
e 280

Cow (Cow)
And the Dish Ran Away with the Spoon - Janet
Stevens   p 855
When Moon Fell Down - Linda Smith   p 832

Coyote (Coyote; Hunter)
Coyote and Badger: Desert Hunters of the Southwest -
Bruce Hiscock   p, e 400

Crackers (Cat)
Crackers - Becky Bloom   p 85

Craig, Darryl (5th Grader; Friend)
Belle Teal - Ann M. Martin   e, m 596

Crandall, Annie (10th Grader)
So Mote It Be - Isobel Bird   m, h 73

Crandall, Prudence (Quaker)
The Education of Mary: A Little Miss of Color - Ann
Rinaldi   m 748

Crane-Man (Handicapped)
A Single Shard - Linda Sue Park   m 696

Crawford, Gene (Orphan; 12-Year-Old)
Cherokee - Creina Mansfield   m 592

Crawford, Nathaniel "Peewee" (Teenager)
Faraway Home - Marilyn Taylor   m 871

Crawford, William "Cherokee" (Musician;
Grandfather)
Cherokee - Creina Mansfield   m 592

Creffield, Franz Edmund (Religious)
Brides of Eden - Linda Crew   m, h 193

Crepsley (Vampire)
Cirque du Freak: The Vampire's Assistant - Darren
Shan   m, h 814

Crestman, Zachary (Child)
Spyhole Secrets - Zilpha Keatley Snyder   e, m 837

Cricklestein, Adam (6th Grader; Animal Lover)
Frankenbug - Steven Cousins   e, m 185

Cringle, Tom (Sailor; 14-Year-Old)
Tom Cringle: The Pirate and the Patriot - Gerald
Hausman   m 382

Crispers, Howard Bellington "Howie" (5th Grader)
Don't You Know There's a War On? - Avi   m 35

Cristobal, Catalin (7th Grader)
Zach's Lie - Roland Smith   m 834

Crockett, Davy (Hero; Frontiersman)
Davy Crockett Saves the World - Rosalyn Schanzer
p 798

Crocodile (Crocodile; Mother)
Crocodile Listens - April Pulley Sayre   p 795

Crosby, Hattie (Child; Grandmother)
Hattie's Story - Susan E. Kirby   e 505

Crutchfield, Bram (Artist; 12th Grader)
Scribbler of Dreams - Mary E. Pearson   m, h 703

Culhane, Kate (Daughter; Young Woman)
Kate Culhane: A Ghost Story - Michael Hague   e,
m 368

Curnow, Maggie (14-Year-Old; Orphan)
A Bushel of Light - Troon Harrison   m 380

Curnow, Thomasina (14-Year-Old; Orphan)
A Bushel of Light - Troon Harrison   m 380

Cybulski, Sofia (16-Year-Old)
Streets of Gold - Marie Raphael   m, h 735

D

Da (Father)
Straw into Gold - Gary D. Schmidt   m 800

Dabble, Hank (Father; Farmer)
Jimmy Dabble - Frans Vischer   e 914

Dabble, Jimmy (Son; Animal Lover)
Jimmy Dabble - Frans Vischer   e 914

Dabble, Maggie (Mother; Housewife)
Jimmy Dabble - Frans Vischer   e 914

DaCosta, Shayna (Health Care Professional)
Change of Heart - Marcia King-Gamble   a 501

Dad (Father)
Desser the Best Ever Cat - Maggie Smith   p 833
I Lost My Dad - Taro Gomi   p 339

Dad (Father; Spouse)
Let's Get a Pup! Said Kate - Bob Graham   p 344

Dad (Father)
Loon Summer - Barbara Santucci   p 793
More Parts - Tedd Arnold   p, e 20
Singing Diggety - Maggie Stern   b, e 854
White Water - Jonathan London   p, e 569

Daddy (Father)
Didi and Daddy on the Promenade - Marilyn Singer
p 825

Daddy (Slave; Blacksmith)
Freedom's Wings: Corey's Diary - Sharon Dennis
Wyeth   e, m 988

Daddy (Father)
Goodbye Mousie - Robie H. Harris   p 379
Gus and Grandpa at Basketball - Claudia Mills
b 641

Daddy (Single Father)
Just the Two of Us - Will Smith   p 835

Daddy (Father; Divorced Person)
Two Homes - Claire Masurel   p 599

Daisy (Dog)
Grandma's Records - Eric Velasquez   p, e 910

Daisy (Child)
Meaner than Meanest - Kevin Somers   p 838

Daisy G. (Grandmother; Dancer)
Blister - Susan Shreve   e, m 819

Dakar (12-Year-Old)
Jakarta Missing - Jane Kurtz   m 524

Daley, Montana Jim (Con Artist; Gambler)
Destination Gold! - Julie Lawson   m, h 538

Dalilah (Foster Child)
Shylock's Daughter - Mirjam Pressler   h 724

Dan (Rabbit; Brother)
Happy Easter, Davy! - Brigitte Weninger   p 940

Dandridge, Katherine "Kit" (12th Grader)
Love Rules - Marilyn Reynolds   h 743

Dangerous Beans (Rat)
*Amazing Maurice and His Educated Rodents: A Novel
of Discworld* - Terry Pratchett   h 723

don Arturo (Rancher; Gambler)
Juan Verdades: The Man Who Couldn't Tell a Lie - Joe Hayes   *p, e*   385

don Ignacio (Rancher; Wealthy)
Juan Verdades: The Man Who Couldn't Tell a Lie - Joe Hayes   *p, e*   385

Donner, Cornelius (Con Artist)
Down the Yukon - Will Hobbs   *m, h*   404

Donohue, Hank (12-Year-Old; Orphan)
Hank's Story - Jane Buchanan   *e*   113

Donohue, Peter "Pete" (Orphan; Runaway)
Hank's Story - Jane Buchanan   *e*   113

Donovan (Religious; Con Artist)
Stranded - Patricia H. Rushford   *m, h*   773

Donovan, Mikey (13-Year-Old)
Lord of the Deep - Graham Salisbury   *m*   788

Dora (Prostitute; Crime Victim)
Bone House - Betsy Tobin   *h, a*   885

Dora (Aunt; Paraplegic)
Prairie School - Avi   *b, e*   37

Dorfman, Robert (2nd Grader; Brother)
Robert and the Great Pepperoni - Barbara Seuling   *e*   811

Dorkula, Henry Count (Bat; Student—Elementary School)
The Werewolf Club Meets Dorkula - Daniel Pinkwater   *e*   718

Dorrant, Jason (12-Year-Old)
The Rag and Bone Shop - Robert Cormier   *m, h*   183

Dorsey, Caroline (13-Year-Old)
The Star-Spangled Secret - K.M. Kimball   *e, m*   495

Dorsey, Charlie (14-Year-Old; Worker)
The Star-Spangled Secret - K.M. Kimball   *e, m*   495

Dot (Mouse; Detective)
Dot & Jabber and the Great Acorn Mystery - Ellen Stoll Walsh   *p*   921

Dot (Dog)
Dot the Fire Dog - Lisa Desimini   *p*   227

Dougherty, Lorraine "Rainey" (Child)
Four Corners - Diane Freund   *a*   304

Dove (Horse)
One Unhappy Horse - C.S. Adler   *m*   4

Doyle, Drake (5th Grader; Detective—Amateur)
The Case of the Gasping Garbage - Michele Torrey   *e*   887

Doyle, Naomi (Cook)
The Maiden of Mayfair - Lawana Blackwell   *a*   82

Doyle, William (Student—College; Nephew)
The Maiden of Mayfair - Lawana Blackwell   *a*   82

Drake, Jake (3rd Grader; Narrator)
Jake Drake, Know-It-All - Andrew Clements   *e*   166

Dramren, Franzas (Librarian)
Eyes of the Calculor - Sean McMullen   *h, a*   627

Draper, Jon (12th Grader; Football Player)
Love, Sara - Mary Beth Lundgren   *m, h*   577

Driscal, Peter (9th Grader; Crime Victim)
Touching Spirit Bear - Ben Mikaelsen   *m, h*   638

Drumm, Lavinia (Librarian; Storyteller)
Beauty and the Serpent: Thirteen Tales of Unnatural Animals - Barbara Ann Porte   *m, h*   720

Drysdale, Taylor Jay (18-Year-Old; Mentally Ill Person)
Saint Jude - Dawn Wilson   *h*   969

Dubois, Shayla (13-Year-Old)
Shayla's Double Brown Baby Blues - Lori Aurelia Williams   *m, h*   963

Duck, Mother (Duck; Mother)
Webster J. Duck - Martin Waddell   *p*   916

Duck, Webster J. (Duck; Son)
Webster J. Duck - Martin Waddell   *p*   916

Ducktective Web (Duck; Detective—Police)
The Web Files - Margie Palatini   *p, e*   694

Dudley, Amy Robsart (Wife; Nobleman)
The Twylight Tower - Karen Harper   *a*   376

Dudley, Robert (Nobleman)
The Twylight Tower - Karen Harper   *a*   376

Dudunya (Friend)
Table Manners - Chris Raschka   *p, e*   737

Dugolli, Zana (11-Year-Old)
Girl of Kosovo - Alice Mead   *m, h*   630

Dulcie (Cat; Detective—Amateur)
Cat Spitting Mad - Shirley Rousseau Murphy   *a*   659

Dunavant, Jamie (Actress; 15-Year-Old)
Down the Yukon - Will Hobbs   *m, h*   404

Dunbar/Dances with Wolves, John (Warrior; Military Personnel)
The Holy Road - Michael Blake   *a*   83

Duncan, Chet (Grandfather)
Flipped - Wendelin Van Draanen   *m*   899

Duncan, "Frog Face" (Principal)
Frog Face and the Three Boys - Don Trembath   *e, m*   889

Dunklee, Eleanor "Ellie" (12-Year-Old)
Mountain Pose - Nancy Hope Wilson   *m*   973

Dunnegan, Vern (Game Warden)
Open Season - C.J. Box   *a*   97

Dupree, Afton (14-Year-Old)
Scorpio's Child - Kezi Matthews   *m*   603

Duquesne, Camille (Psychic)
Playing with Fire - Kathleen Karr   *m*   478

Duquesne, Greer (14-Year-Old; Psychic)
Playing with Fire - Kathleen Karr   *m*   478

Durkin, Ronald (Bully; Student—Elementary School)
Stand Tall, Molly Lou Melon - Patty Lovell   *p*   572

Dusty Locks (Child; Runaway)
Dusty Locks and the Three Bears - Susan Lowell   *p*   573

Dutton, Brett (13-Year-Old)
Dark Inheritance - W. Michael Gear   *a*   322

Dutton, Jim (Anthropologist)
Dark Inheritance - W. Michael Gear   *a*   322

Dvorak, Joey (13-Year-Old)
The Edison Mystery - Dan Gutman   *e, m*   359

Dwyer, Jack (19-Year-Old; Saloon Keeper/Owner)
Prowlers - Christopher Golden   *h*   336

E

Eaker, Elisha "Eli" (Military Personnel)
Fire on the Waters - David Poyer   *a*   722

Eaker, Micah (Father; Wealthy)
Fire on the Waters - David Poyer   *a*   722

Eamon (Child)
Knockabeg: A Famine Tale - Mary E. Lyons   *m*   582

Eastland, Angela (17-Year-Old; Genetically Altered Being)
Violent Eyes - Nicole Luiken   *h*   575

Ebenezer (Brother; Farmer)
Sorry - Jean Van Leeuwen   *p, e*   902

Echo (Narrator)
Echo - Francesca Lia Block   *h*   84

Echo (Indian)
The Sketchbook of Thomas Blue Eagle - Gay Matthaei   *m*   602

Eckert, Angela "Angie" (Spouse)
The Dragon and the Fair Maid of Kent - Gordon Dickson   *h, a*   233

Eckert, James "Jim" (Spouse; Warrior)
The Dragon and the Fair Maid of Kent - Gordon Dickson   *h, a*   233

Ed (Wealthy; Uncle)
The Hideout - Peg Kehret   *e, m*   482

Eddie (Kindergartner; Friend)
The Boys Team - Amy Schwartz   *p*   802

Edgar (Dog)
Clarence and the Great Surprise - Jean Ekman Adams   *p*   3
A Houseful of Christmas - Barbara Joosse   *p*   471

Edison, Thomas Alva (Historical Figure; Inventor)
The Edison Mystery - Dan Gutman   *e, m*   359

Edmund (Royalty)
Goose Chase - Patrice Kindl   *m, h*   500

Eduardo (Gentleman)
Mama Does the Mambo - Katherine Leiner   *p, e*   543

Edward (Landowner; Handicapped)
Bone House - Betsy Tobin   *h, a*   885

Edward (Child; Immigrant)
Tattered Sails - Verla Kay   *p*   480

Edward VI (Royalty; Historical Figure)
Beware, Princess Elizabeth - Carolyn Meyer   *m*   634

Edward "Ed" (Uncle)
Groover's Heart - Carole Crowe   *e*   197

Edwin (Indian)
Touching Spirit Bear - Ben Mikaelsen   *m, h*   638

Eena "Spear Woman" (Prehistoric Human)
Song of the Axe - John R. Dann   *a*   209

Eilan/Julia Helena (Mother; Religious)
Priestess of Avalon - Marion Zimmer Bradley   *h, a*   98

Einstein (Dog)
A Hole in the World - Sid Hite   *m*   401

Eli (Child; Son)
Eli's Night Light - Liz Rosenberg   *p*   768

Elinor (Chicken; Sister)
Elinor and Violet: The Story of Two Naughty Chickens - Patti Beling Murphy   *p*   657

Elisandra (Royalty)
Summers at Castle Auburn - Sharon Shinn   *h, a*   818

Eliza (Maiden)
The Dog Prince - Lauren Mills   *p, e*   642

Elizabeth (Royalty; Historical Figure)
Beware, Princess Elizabeth - Carolyn Meyer   *m*   634

Elizabeth (Settler; Spouse)
William's House - Ginger Howard   *p, e*   426

Elizabeth I (Royalty)
The Twylight Tower - Karen Harper   *a*   376

Ellery (Sister)
Pirates - C. Drew Lamm   *p, e*   530

Fossey, Nell (5th Grader; Scientist)
The Case of the Gasping Garbage - Michele Torrey
   e 887

Fournier, Grey (Indian; Motorcyclist)
Lightning Rider - Jacqueline Guest m, h 355

Fournier, January "Jan" (Indian; Motorcyclist)
Lightning Rider - Jacqueline Guest m, h 355

Fourth Uncle (Uncle; Immigrant)
Oranges on Golden Mountain - Elizabeth Partridge
   p, e 697

Fowl, Artemis (12-Year-Old)
Artemis Fowl - Eoin Colfer m 174

Fox (Fox)
Fox - Margaret Wild p, e 951

Fox, Anderson (Father)
Shayla's Double Brown Baby Blues - Lori Aurelia
Williams m, h 963

Fox, Gift Marie (Baby)
Shayla's Double Brown Baby Blues - Lori Aurelia
Williams m, h 963

Frances (Student—Elementary School; Classmate)
The Class Artist - G. Brian Karas p 477

Frances (Pig; Sister)
Starring Lucille - Kathryn Lasky p 534

Frank (Bear; Friend)
The Adventure of Louey and Frank - Carolyn White
   p 947

Frank, Anne (Historical Figure)
Anne Frank and Me - Cherie Bennett m 68

Frankenbug "Frankie" (Insect)
Frankenbug - Steven Cousins e, m 185

Frankenstein, Amanda (Animal Lover; Classmate;
Student—Elementary School)
Reptiles Are My Life - Megan McDonald p 619

Franklin (Pig; Brother)
Starring Lucille - Kathryn Lasky p 534

Franny (6th Grader)
The Mysterious Matter of I.M. Fine - Diane Stanley
   e 850

Fraser, James "Jamie" (12-Year-Old)
Witch Hill - Marcus Sedgwick m, h 809

Fred (Student—Elementary School; Brother)
The Class Artist - G. Brian Karas p 477

Fred (Friend; Time Traveler)
Sam Samurai - Jon Scieszka e, m 805

Freddy (Opossum; Musician)
The Case of the Puzzling Possum - Cynthia Rylant
   b, e 778

Frieda (Royalty; Mother)
The Princess and the Pea - Alain Vaes p 897

Frith, Anna (Servant; Widow(er))
Year of Wonders - Geraldine Brooks h, a 101

Froggy (Frog; Son)
Froggy Eats Out - Jonathan London p 568

Froglina (Friend; Frog)
Froggy Eats Out - Jonathan London p 568

Frost, Emma (Daughter; Sister)
Emma's Yucky Brother - Jean Little b 562

Fumiko (Servant)
The Yokota Officers Club - Sarah Bird h, a 74

Funk, Jonas (Brother)
Cissy Funk - Kim Taylor m 870

Funk, Narcissus Louise "Cissy" (13-Year-Old)
Cissy Funk - Kim Taylor m 870

Funk, Vera (Aunt)
Cissy Funk - Kim Taylor m 870

Furball, Billy (Werewolf; Student—Elementary
School)
The Werewolf Club Meets Dorkula - Daniel Pinkwater
   e 718

Furukawa, Mark (Counselor)
The Jasmine Trade - Denise Hamilton a 371

G

Gabriel (Healer)
Secret Sacrament - Sherryl Jordan h 472

Gallegar, Benjamin "Ben" (7th Grader)
Dangling - Lillian Eige e, m 267

Gamage, Bo (Orphan; 12-Year-Old)
Bo & Mzzz Mad - Sid Fleischman m 291

Gardiner, Meshak (Mentally Challenged Person)
Coram Boy - Jamila Gavin m, h 321

Gardiner, Otis (Con Artist)
Coram Boy - Jamila Gavin m, h 321

Garner/Grant, Luke/Lee (12-Year-Old)
Among the Impostors - Margaret Peterson Haddix
   m 365

Garth "Math Man" (Worker)
Math Man - Teri Daniels p 208

Garvey (Parole Officer)
Touching Spirit Bear - Ben Mikaelsen m, h 638

Gaskitt, Gloria (9-Year-Old; Twin)
The Man Who Wore All His Clothes - Allan Ahlberg
   e 9

Gaskitt, Gus (9-Year-Old; Twin)
The Man Who Wore All His Clothes - Allan Ahlberg
   e 9

Gates, Marvin (1st Grader; Brother)
Marvin One Too Many - Katherine Paterson b 701

Gates, May (Sister)
Marvin One Too Many - Katherine Paterson b 701

Gates, Russell "Rusty" (11-Year-Old; Detective—
Amateur)
Mystery from History - Dayle Campbell Gaetz e,
m 307

Gecko, Chet (Detective—Amateur; 4th Grader)
Farewell, My Lunchbag - Bruce Hale e, m 370

Gemini Jack (Alien; Twin)
Expiration Date: Never - Stephanie Spinner e 844

General Santa Anna (Military Personnel; Historical
Figure)
In the Shadow of the Alamo - Sherry Garland
   m 316

General Santa Anna (Historical Figure; Military
Personnel)
Victor Lopez at the Alamo - James Rice m 745

Gentle One (Child; Sister)
Stella's Dancing Days - Sandy Asher p 25

George (Pig)
The Goose Who Went Off in a Huff - Paul Brett
Johnson p 459

George (Friend; Centipede)
*Harry the Poisonous Centipede's Big Adventure:
Another Story to Make You Squirm* - Lynne Reid
Banks e 52

George (Child; Brother)
Singing Diggety - Maggie Stern b, e 854

George, Ida Mae (Friend)
Maggie in the Morning - Elizabeth Van Steenwyk
   e 904

Germondo, Howard "Germ" (Friend; Student—
Middle School)
Fur-Ever Yours, Booker Jones - Betsy Duffey e,
m 252

Gershon, Joseph (Worker; Immigrant)
Lick Creek - Brad Kessler a 490

Gertrude (Cow)
The Goose Who Went Off in a Huff - Paul Brett
Johnson p 459

Gibson, Tessa (Twin; Sister)
Expiration Date: Never - Stephanie Spinner e 844

Gibson, Tod (Twin; Brother)
Expiration Date: Never - Stephanie Spinner e 844

Gilbert (Student—Elementary School)
We Gather Together . . . Now Please Get Lost! - Diane
DeGroat p 222

Gillespie, Aimee Anne (7th Grader; Dancer)
Only the Lonely - Laura Dower e 244

Gino (Child; Friend)
Antonella and Her Santa Claus - Barbara Augustin
   p 34

Girl (Child; Daughter)
The Christmas Promise - Susan Campbell Bartoletti
   p, e 56

Gittleman, Robyn (11-Year-Old)
Stolen Words - Amy Goldman Koss m 518

Gladd, Will (Handicapped)
Just Ask Iris - Lucy Frank m 299

Glassman, Nelson "Nelly" (12th Grader;
Homosexual)
Rainbow Boys - Alex Sanchez h 791

Gnedich, Mikhail Sergeyevich "Misha" (16-Year-
Old; Revolutionary)
Angel on the Square - Gloria Whelan m, h 946

GninGnin (Grandmother)
Henry's First-Moon Birthday - Lenore Look
   p 570

Gogo (Grandmother)
What's Cooking, Jamela? - Niki Daly p 206

Golden Mare (Horse)
The Golden Mare, the Firebird, and the Magic Ring -
Ruth Sanderson p, e 792

Goldfarb, Mavis (Camper; Witch)
Fat Camp Commandos - Daniel Pinkwater e 716

Golem (Mythical Creature)
Prisoner in Time: A Child of the Holocaust - Pamela
Melnikoff m 632

Gonzales, Ellie (Soccer Player; 12th Grader)
The Million Dollar Kick - Dan Gutman m 360

Goodspeed, Bobby (7th Grader)
The Misfits - James Howe m 428

Goose (Goose)
Silly Little Goose! - Nancy Tafuri p 864

Goran, Lena (Friend)
Girl of Kosovo - Alice Mead m, h 630

Gordon, Matt (Brother)
Racing the Past - Sis Deans m 220

Gordon, Ricky (11-Year-Old)
Racing the Past - Sis Deans m 220

Gorgeous (Dog)
41/2 Friends and the Disappearing Bio Teacher -
Joachim Friedrich e 306

Gossim, Rolanda (Teacher)
Don't You Know There's a War On? - Avi m 35

Grace (Friend)
The Summer of Riley - Eve Bunting e 122

Grace, Bartholomew (Pirate)
The Buccaneers - Iain Lawrence m, h 536

Gracie (Dog; Runaway)
The Great Gracie Chase: Stop That Dog! - Cynthia Rylant   p   780

Graham, Cassel (Child; Cousin)
Piper - Natale Ghent   m   328

Graham, Cindy (Aunt)
Piper - Natale Ghent   m   328

Graham, Emily (Lawyer)
On the Street Where You Live - Mary Higgins Clark   a   165

Graham, Grover C. (Baby; Foster Child)
Grover C. Graham and Me - Mary Quattlebaum   e, m   731

Graham, Norman (Uncle; Teacher)
Piper - Natale Ghent   m   328

Graham, Tracey (Mother)
Grover C. Graham and Me - Mary Quattlebaum   e, m   731

Gram Jennie (Grandmother)
Hattie's Story - Susan E. Kirby   e   505
Ida Lou's Story - Susan E. Kirby   e   506

Gramlich, Eb (Foster Child)
Anna Casey's Place in the World - Adrian Fogelin   m   296

Grampa (Aged Person)
Heaven Eyes - David Almond   m   12

Gramps (Grandfather; Widow(er))
Bluebird Summer - Deborah Hopkinson   p, e   418

Gramps (Grandfather)
Butterfly Buddies - Judy Cox   e   190

Gran (Grandmother)
Freewill - Chris Lynch   h   581

Gran (Grandmother; Aged Person)
The Hickory Chair - Lisa Rowe Fraustino   p   300

Gran (Grandmother)
Sammy and the Robots - Ian Whybrow   p   949

Grand-mere (Grandmother; Duck)
Petite Rouge: A Cajun Red Riding Hood - Mike Artell   p, e   22

Grand-Pierre (Grandfather; Resistance Fighter)
Zazoo: A Novel - Richard Mosher   m, h   653

Grandad Fuller (Grandfather)
Fair Weather - Richard Peck   m   704

Granddad (Grandfather; Farmer)
A Thanksgiving Turkey - Julian Scheer   p, e   799

Grandma (Rabbit; Grandmother)
Bunny Party - Rosemary Wells   p   935

Grandma (Grandmother)
Grandma's Records - Eric Velasquez   p, e   910

Grandma (Spouse; Dog)
Grandpa's Overalls - Tony Crunk   p   198

Grandma (Grandmother; Time Traveler)
Joining the Boston Tea Party - Diane Stanley   p, e   849

Grandma (Grandmother; Gardener)
Katie and the Sunflowers - James Mayhew   p   604

Grandma (Grandmother; Aged Person)
See You Soon Moon - Donna Conrad   p   179

Grandma (Grandmother; Storyteller)
The Snail House - Allan Ahlberg   p   10

Grandma (Grandmother)
Sweet, Sweet Memory - Jacqueline Woodson   p, e   984

Grandma Marilyn (Grandmother; Aged Person)
Aunt Claire's Yellow Beehive Hair - Deborah Blumenthal   p   88

Grandma Nan (Grandmother)
Grandmas Trick-or-Treat - Emily Arnold McCully   b   612

Grandma Pinot (Psychic; Grandmother)
The Things I Know Best - Lynne Hinton   a   399

Grandma Sal (Grandmother)
Grandmas Trick-or-Treat - Emily Arnold McCully   b   612

Grandma Soukeye (Grandmother; Aged Person)
Bintou's Braids - Sylviane A. Diouf   p   235

Grandmere (Grandmother)
Princess in the Spotlight - Meg Cabot   m, h   131

Grandmother (Grandmother; Aged Person)
Ghost Wings - Barbara Joosse   p   470

Grandpa (Grandfather; Fisherman)
The Biggest Fish in the Lake - Margaret Carney   p, e   140

Grandpa (Grandfather)
Grandpa Blows His Penny Whistle Until the Angels Sing - Susan L. Roth   p, e   769

Grandpa (Farmer; Dog)
Grandpa's Overalls - Tony Crunk   p   198

Grandpa (Grandfather)
Gus and Grandpa at Basketball - Claudia Mills   b   641

Grandpa (Cat; Grandfather)
No Kiss for Grandpa - Harriet Ziefert   p   1001

Grandpa (Grandfather)
Sweet, Sweet Memory - Jacqueline Woodson   p, e   984

Grandpap (Grandfather)
Dancing in Cadillac Light - Kimberly Willis Holt   m   411

Granny (Grandmother)
A Houseful of Christmas - Barbara Joosse   p   471

Granny (Grandmother; Aged Person)
One More Wednesday - Malika Doray   p   242

Granny (Grandmother)
A Penguin Pup for Pinkerton - Steven Kellogg   p   486

Grant (Student—College; Boyfriend)
Wurst Case Scenario - Catherine Clark   h   164

Grant, Joshua "Josh" (12-Year-Old; Dyslexic)
How Many Days Until Tomorrow? - Caroline Janover   e, m   449

Grant, Simon (Brother; 13-Year-Old)
How Many Days Until Tomorrow? - Caroline Janover   e, m   449

Granville, Ann Elizabeth "Annie" (12-Year-Old)
The Gramma War - Kristin Butcher   m   129

Granville, Claire (Sister)
The Gramma War - Kristin Butcher   m   129

Granville, Fiona "Gramma" (Grandmother)
The Gramma War - Kristin Butcher   m   129

Gray, Hennley (Worker)
A Hole in the World - Sid Hite   m   401

Gray, Sally (Friend; Neighbor)
Emma's Yucky Brother - Jean Little   b   562

Gray, Simon (11th Grader; Computer Expert)
Shades of Simon Gray - Joyce McDonald   m, h   617

Great-Aunt Ray (Aunt; Aged Person)
Aunt Claire's Yellow Beehive Hair - Deborah Blumenthal   p   88

Green, Hannah (13-Year-Old)
The War Within: A Novel of the Civil War - Carol Matas   m   600

Green, Joanna (Sister)
The War Within: A Novel of the Civil War - Carol Matas   m   600

Green, Sarah (Witch)
Shattered Mirror - Amelia Atwater-Rhodes   h   30

Greenhow, Rose (Spy)
Girl in Blue - Ann Rinaldi   m, h   749

Greg (Student—Elementary School; Abuse Victim)
One of the Problems of Everett Anderson - Lucille Clifton   p   168

Grest, Sam (Friend)
Cirque du Freak: The Vampire's Assistant - Darren Shan   m, h   814

Gribbin, Roger (Fisherman)
The Lobster War - Ethan Howland   m, h   430

Griffin, Kate (Widow; Single Mother)
A Long Way Home - Nancy Price Graff   m   343

Griffin, Riley (7th Grader)
A Long Way Home - Nancy Price Graff   m   343

Griffith, Martin (Grandfather)
Gwyneth's Secret Grandpa - Annie Morris Williams   e   961

Griffiths, Bonehead (Bully)
Genius Games - Narinder Dhami   e   230

Grim, Malicia (Daughter)
Amazing Maurice and His Educated Rodents: A Novel of Discworld - Terry Pratchett   h   723

Grove, Francine "Francie" (14-Year-Old)
The Stones of Mourning Creek - Diane Les Becquets   m, h   546

Gugu (Grandmother; Artist)
Gugu's House - Catherine Stock   p   860

Guidry, Leonard "Lenny" (Father)
Seek - Paul Fleischman   m, h   290

Gullane, Mouse (Orphan)
Heaven Eyes - David Almond   m   12

Gus (Student—Elementary School; Child)
The Bus for Us - Suzanne Bloom   p   86

Gus (Basketball Player; Son)
Gus and Grandpa at Basketball - Claudia Mills   b   641

Guzman, Juanita (7-Year-Old; Sister; Child of Divorced Parents)
How Tia Lola Came to Visit/Stay - Julia Alvarez   e, m   15

Guzman, Miguel (Brother; Nephew; Child of Divorced Parents)
How Tia Lola Came to Visit/Stay - Julia Alvarez   e, m   15

Gwendolyn "Gwen" (Softball Player; Cousin)
Strike Two - Amy Goldman Koss   e, m   520

H

Haggard, Thompson (Thief)
Daniel's Walk - Michael Spooner   m   845

Haig-Ereildoun, Angus (Government Official; Writer)
Do Try to Speak as We Do: The Diary of an American Au Pair - Marjorie Leet Ford   a   297

Haig-Ereildoun, Claire (Deaf Person; Child)
Do Try to Speak as We Do: The Diary of an American Au Pair - Marjorie Leet Ford   a   297

Haig-Ereildoun, Prudence "Pru" (11-Year-Old)
Do Try to Speak as We Do: The Diary of an American Au Pair - Marjorie Leet Ford   a   297

Haig-Ereildoun, Trevor (Child)
Do Try to Speak as We Do: The Diary of an American Au Pair - Marjorie Leet Ford   *a*   297

Hailey (12-Year-Old)
Aquamarine - Alice Hoffman   *m*   407

Hairy Man (Dog; Rescuer)
Heroes of Isle Aux Morts - Alice Walsh   *p, e*   920

Hakon (Son; Royalty)
The Race of the Birkebeiners - Lise Lunge-Larsen   *p, e*   578

Haldran, Andrew (16-Year-Old)
Focus - Sallie Lowenstein   *m, h*   574

Haller, Harry (Moose; Student—Elementary School)
The Heart of Cool - Jamie McEwan   *b, e*   622

Halston, William (11-Year-Old)
The Summer of Riley - Eve Bunting   *e*   122

Hambrick, Nicole (Teenager)
Ghost Soldier - Elaine Marie Alphin   *m*   13

Hambrick, Paige (Professor)
Ghost Soldier - Elaine Marie Alphin   *m*   13

Hamilton, Jon (12th Grader; Wealthy)
Rooster - Beth Nixon Weaver   *m, h*   931

Hamlet (Pig; Friend)
Hamlet and the Magnificent Sandcastle - Brian Lies   *p*   557

Hammond, Kate (9th Grader; Swimmer)
Through the Wormhole - Robert J. Favole   *m*   284

Hammy (Hamster; Runaway)
Bus Stop, Bus Go! - Daniel Kirk   *p*   507

Hampton, Rosemary Rita (10-Year-Old; Time Traveler)
Rosemary Meets Rosemarie - Barbara Robertson   *e, m*   754

Hangerman, Kyle (Friend)
The Foreigner - Meg Castaldo   *a*   147

Hanley, Liam (Cousin)
Fiona McGilray's Story: A Voyage from Ireland in 1849 - Clare Pastore   *m*   698

Hannah (Baby; Daughter)
Come Back, Hannah! - Marisabina Russo   *p*   774

Hannah (8-Year-Old; Niece)
Hannah's Bookmobile Christmas - Sally Derby   *p, e*   226

Hannah (Child; Vacationer)
The Journey - Sarah Stewart   *p, e*   857

Hannah (Sister; Child)
The Snail House - Allan Ahlberg   *p*   10

Hannah (Healer)
Treasure at the Heart of the Tanglewood - Meredith Ann Pierce   *m, h*   711

Hannon, Suzanne (Girlfriend)
Swimming - Joanna Hershon   *a*   391

Hansen, Bobby (Child)
4 1/2 Friends and the Secret Cave - Joachim Friedrich   *e*   305

Hansen, Claire (Girlfriend; Sister)
The Second Summoning - Tanya Huff   *h, a*   433

Hansen, Diana (Sister)
The Second Summoning - Tanya Huff   *h, a*   433

Hardaway, Jonathan (Coach)
Darkness Before Dawn - Sharon M. Draper   *h*   249

Harley (Father; Artisan)
Equinox - Monte Killingsworth   *m*   494

Harley (Llama)
Harley - Star Livingstone   *b*   565

Harley (16-Year-Old)
Razzle - Ellen Wittlinger   *h*   978

Harold (Bridegroom; Young Man)
The Reluctant Flower Girl - Lynne Barasch   *p*   53

Harper, Belle Teal (5th Grader; Friend)
Belle Teal - Ann M. Martin   *e, m*   596

Harper, Joshua (13-Year-Old; Paperboy)
Joshua's Song - Joan Hiatt Harlow   *m*   373

Harper, Marguerite (6th Grader)
Bad Girl Blues - Sally Warner   *m*   925

Harper, Max (Police Officer)
Cat Spitting Mad - Shirley Rousseau Murphy   *a*   659

Harrington, Dain (16-Year-Old; Fisherman)
The Lobster War - Ethan Howland   *m, h*   430

Harrington, Edward "Eddie" (19-Year-Old; Fisherman)
The Lobster War - Ethan Howland   *m, h*   430

Harris, Annie (10th Grader)
Run If You Dare - Randy Powell   *m, h*   721

Harris, Mary (13-Year-Old)
The Education of Mary: A Little Miss of Color - Ann Rinaldi   *m*   748

Harris, Sarah (18-Year-Old)
The Education of Mary: A Little Miss of Color - Ann Rinaldi   *m*   748

Harry (Centipede; Son)
Harry the Poisonous Centipede's Big Adventure: Another Story to Make You Squirm - Lynne Reid Banks   *e*   52

Harry (Brother; Cat)
Spookier Than a Ghost - Karen Gray Ruelle   *b*   772

Hart, Lucky (10-Year-Old)
Skyrockets and Snickerdoodles: A Cobtown Story from the Diaries of Lucky Hart - Julia Van Nutt   *e*   903

Hartman, Aviva "Vivi" (10th Grader)
Death on Sacred Ground - Harriet K. Feder   *m, h*   285

Harvey, Anne (Daughter; Rescuer)
Heroes of Isle Aux Morts - Alice Walsh   *p, e*   920

Haskel (Tailor; Traveler)
A Cloak for the Moon - Eric A. Kimmel   *p, e*   496

Hassie, Violet (Store Owner)
Clay - Colby Rodowsky   *m*   761

Hatford, Wally (4th Grader; Brother)
The Boys Return - Phyllis Reynolds Naylor   *e, m*   673

Hathaway, Henry (Brother)
Tub-boo-boo - Margie Palatini   *p*   693

Hathaway, Lucy (Sister; Narrator)
Tub-boo-boo - Margie Palatini   *p*   693

Hawk (Wizard)
Spellfall - Katherine Roberts   *m, h*   752

Hawkins, Hub (Farmer; Crime Victim)
The Boy in the Burning House - Tim Wynne-Jones   *m, h*   990

Hawkins, Jim (14-Year-Old)
The Boy in the Burning House - Tim Wynne-Jones   *m, h*   990

Hawthorn, Jason (16-Year-Old)
Down the Yukon - Will Hobbs   *m, h*   404

Hayes, Lamont (3rd Grader; Friend)
Third Grade Stinks! - Colleen O'Shaughnessy McKenna   *e*   624

Hayes, Violet (Musician)
You Don't Know Me - David Klass   *m, h*   510

Haywood, Bill (Historical Figure; Leader)
Rockbuster - Gloria Skurzynski   *m, h*   827

Heart's Delight (Orphan)
Larky Mavis - Brock Cole   *p, e*   170

Heaven Eyes (Orphan)
Heaven Eyes - David Almond   *m*   12

Hector (7th Grader)
Trino's Time - Diane Gonzales Bertrand   *m*   70

Hedrick, Dietrich "Dieter" (15-Year-Old; Military Personnel)
Soldier Boys - Dean Hughes   *m, h*   434

Helen (Royalty)
Odysseus in the Serpent Maze - Jane Yolen   *m*   997

Henrietta "Henry" (Librarian)
The Pickup Artist - Terry Bisson   *h, a*   78

Henry (Baby; Brother)
Henry's First-Moon Birthday - Lenore Look   *p*   570

Herb (Child; Son)
Beware of the Storybook Wolves - Lauren Child   *p, e*   158

Hightower, Curtis (12th Grader; Football Player)
Damage - A.M. Jenkins   *h*   451

Hill, Beaumont "Beau" (Skier)
Change of Heart - Marcia King-Gamble   *a*   501

Hill, Daniel A. (Indian)
Empire Dreams - Wendy Wax   *e*   930

Hill, Joe (Historical Figure; Musician)
Rockbuster - Gloria Skurzynski   *m, h*   827

Hill, Raspberry (13-Year-Old)
Money Hungry - Sharon G. Flake   *m*   289

Hinds, John "Brother John" (Father)
The Jacob Ladder - Gerald Hausman   *m*   381

Hinds, Uton "Tall T" (12-Year-Old)
The Jacob Ladder - Gerald Hausman   *m*   381

Hip (Friend; Bear)
Flip and Flop - Dawn Apperley   *p*   17

Hip (Hippopotamus; Friend)
The Problem with Pumpkins: A Hip & Hop Story - Barney Saltzberg   *p*   790

Hirsh, Esther (Child)
Witness - Karen Hesse   *m*   392

Hisss (Cat)
Meaner than Meanest - Kevin Somers   *p*   838

Hobbs, Joseph (Student—Elementary School; Friend)
Owen Foote, Super Spy - Stephanie Greene   *e*   346

Hobson, Hoby (Bullied Child; 5th Grader)
Quiet! You're Invisible - Margaret Meacham   *e*   629

Hodge, Mike (Bully)
A Sailor Returns - Theodore Taylor   *e*   873

Hoff, Posie (Girlfriend)
The Black Book (Diary of a Teenage Stud) Series - Jonah Black   *h*   79

Hogg, Marshall (Cowboy; Criminal)
Gabriel's Story - David Anthony Durham   *h, a*   255

Holland, Jeremy (13-Year-Old; Orphan)
The Hideout - Peg Kehret   *e, m*   482

Hollander, Alexander (Child; Brother)
Don't Bug Me! - Pam Zollman   *e*   1006

Hollander, Megan (6th Grader)
Don't Bug Me! - Pam Zollman   *e*   1006

Holloway, Barbara (Lawyer)
Desperate Measures - Kate Wilhelm   *a*   959

Holloway, Frank (Lawyer)
Desperate Measures - Kate Wilhelm   *a*   959

Jansen, Cam (Detective—Amateur; Friend)
Cam Jansen and the School Play Mystery - David A. Adler   *e*   6

Jawanza (Child)
Fly! - Christopher Myers   *p, e*   663

Jaybird (Indian)
Witch Child - Celia Rees   *m, h*   739

Jeff (Student—Elementary School; Brother)
A Bus of Our Own - Freddi Williams Evans   *p, e*   280

Jefferson, Dell (Sister)
Spellbound - Janet McDonald   *m, h*   616

Jefferson, Raven (16-Year-Old; Single Mother)
Spellbound - Janet McDonald   *m, h*   616

Jefferson, Smokey (Baby)
Spellbound - Janet McDonald   *m, h*   616

Jefferson, Thomas (Historical Figure; Government Official)
Thomas Jefferson: Letters from a Philadelphia Bookworm - Jennifer Armstrong   *m*   19

Jen (Aunt; Mother)
Oliver's Milk Shake - Vivian French   *p*   302

Jenkins, Ada (Mother)
Lick Creek - Brad Kessler   *a*   490

Jenkins, Celli (11-Year-Old)
Black Angels - Rita Murphy   *m*   658

Jenkins, Colin (Businessman; Single Father)
The Singing Hat - Tohby Riddle   *p*   747

Jenkins, Ellery (14-Year-Old)
Black Angels - Rita Murphy   *m*   658

Jenkins, Emily (18-Year-Old)
Lick Creek - Brad Kessler   *a*   490

Jenkins, Judge (6th Grader)
A Day for Vincent Chin and Me - Jacqueline Turner Banks   *e*   50

Jenkins, Jury (6th Grader)
A Day for Vincent Chin and Me - Jacqueline Turner Banks   *e*   50

Jenkins, Pearl (Grandmother)
Black Angels - Rita Murphy   *m*   658

Jennie (Child; Sister)
The Friday Nights of Nana - Amy Hest   *p*   393

Jenny (Sister; Child)
Henry's First-Moon Birthday - Lenore Look   *p*   570

Jenny (Child; Student—Elementary School)
Patches Lost and Found - Steven Kroll   *p*   523

Jensen, Buddy (11-Year-Old)
A Sailor Returns - Theodore Taylor   *e*   873

Jessica (16-Year-Old)
Shylock's Daughter - Mirjam Pressler   *h*   724

Jessica (Student—Elementary School; Sister)
Stop, Drop, and Roll - Margery Cuyler   *p*   202

Jessica (Softball Player; Cousin)
Strike Two - Amy Goldman Koss   *e, m*   520

Jessie (Child; Friend)
Kate Can't Wait - Marilyn Eisenstein   *p*   269

Jewels, Bentley (Aged Person; Uncle)
The Calling - Cathryn Clinton   *m, h*   169

Jewels, Peter Earl (Uncle; Con Artist)
The Calling - Cathryn Clinton   *m, h*   169

Jill (Young Woman)
The Famous Adventures of Jack - Berlie Doherty   *e*   239

Jimena (Witch)
Into the Cold Fire - Lynne Ewing   *m, h*   281

Jimenez, Francisco (Mexican American; Teenager)
Breaking Through - Francisco Jimenez   *m, h*   456

Jimenez, Roberto (Mexican American; Teenager)
Breaking Through - Francisco Jimenez   *m, h*   456

Jin Woo (Baby; Adoptee)
Jin Woo - Eve Bunting   *p*   119

Jiro (Child; Son)
The Hungriest Boy in the World - Lensey Namioka   *p*   667

Jo (Daughter; Baby)
The Other Dog - Madeleine L'Engle   *p*   544

Jo-Jo (5-Year-Old; Sister)
The Days of Summer - Eve Bunting   *p*   117

Jo Lee (Child; Son)
Oranges on Golden Mountain - Elizabeth Partridge   *p, e*   697

Joan (Cousin; 13-Year-Old)
Four Corners - Diane Freund   *a*   304

Jody (Homosexual)
True Believer - Virginia Euwer Wolff   *m, h*   980

Joe (Driver)
Bus Stop, Bus Go! - Daniel Kirk   *p*   507

Joe (Lawman)
Cowgirl Rosie and Her Five Baby Bison - Stephen Gulbis   *p*   356

Joe (Child; Friend)
Freedom Summer - Deborah Wiles   *p, e*   955

Joe (Friend; Time Traveler)
Sam Samurai - Jon Scieszka   *e, m*   805

Joe Grey (Cat; Detective—Amateur)
Cat Spitting Mad - Shirley Rousseau Murphy   *a*   659

Joey (6-Year-Old)
The Moon Robber - Dean Morrissey   *e*   650

Joey (Student—Elementary School; Friend)
The Name Jar - Yangsook Choi   *p*   161

Johann "Long Boy" (Son)
Bone House - Betsy Tobin   *h, a*   885

Johannsen, Mary Jo (Student—College; Roommate)
Wurst Case Scenario - Catherine Clark   *h*   164

Johansson, Hilda (Servant; Detective—Amateur)
Green Grow the Victims - Jeanne M. Dams   *a*   207

John (12-Year-Old)
Stranger in Dadland - Amy Goldman Koss   *e, m*   519

John (14-Year-Old; Musician)
You Don't Know Me - David Klass   *m, h*   510

Johnny (Slave)
Daniel's Walk - Michael Spooner   *m*   845

Johns, Solomon (Farmer; Stepfather)
Gabriel's Story - David Anthony Durham   *h, a*   255

Johnson, Grace (Museum Curator)
Rocks in His Head - Carol Otis Hurst   *p, e*   437

Johnson, Zoe (8-Year-Old; Friend)
Winnie Dancing on Her Own - Jennifer Richard Jacobson   *e*   445

Jolie (Child; Student)
Freedom School, Yes! - Amy Littlesugar   *p, e*   564

Jonathan (Child; Animal Lover)
One Dark Night - Hazel Hutchins   *p*   440

Jones, Ebon (9-Year-Old; Brother)
Dad, in Spirit - A. LaFaye   *e, m*   527

Jones, Felicity (16-Year-Old; Time Traveler)
The Last Grail Keeper - Pamela Smith Hill   *m*   398

Jones, Harold "Hammerhead" (Bully; Neighbor)
Quiet! You're Invisible - Margaret Meacham   *e*   629

Jones, Jack (Raccoon; Detective—Private)
The Case of the Puzzling Possum - Cynthia Rylant   *b, e*   778
The Case of the Troublesome Turtle - Cynthia Rylant   *b, e*   779

Jones, John Luther "Casey" (Engineer; Railroad Worker)
Casey Jones - Allan Drummond   *p*   250

Jones, John Paul (Father)
Whale Talk - Chris Crutcher   *h*   199

Jones, Junie B. (6-Year-Old)
Junie B. Jones Is a Graduation Girl - Barbara Park   *e*   695

Jones, Libba (Sister; Student—Middle School)
Fur-Ever Yours, Booker Jones - Betsy Duffey   *e, m*   252

Jones, Luke "Dad" (Father; Researcher)
Dad, in Spirit - A. LaFaye   *e, m*   527

Jones, The Tao "T.J." (12th Grader; Swimmer)
Whale Talk - Chris Crutcher   *h*   199

Jones, Vanessa (Mother; Archaeologist)
The Last Grail Keeper - Pamela Smith Hill   *m*   398

Jones, Walter "Booker" (Writer; Friend)
Fur-Ever Yours, Booker Jones - Betsy Duffey   *e, m*   252

Jordan, Geneva (Aunt; Singer)
Welcome to the Great Mysterious - Lorna Landvik   *a*   531

Jordan, Jack (8th Grader)
And Sometimes Why - Mame Farrell   *m*   283

Joseph (Cyborg)
The Graveyard Game - Kage Baker   *h, a*   42

Josh (Son; Stepson)
The Field of the Dogs - Katherine Paterson   *e, m*   700

Josh (Fisherman; Brother)
The Merbaby - Teresa Bateman   *p, e*   61

Jubela (Rhinoceros; Orphan)
Jubela - Cristina Kessler   *p*   491

Judge Ooka (Judge)
The Demon in the Teahouse - Dorothy Hoobler   *m*   416

Judy (Animal Lover; Equestrian)
Runaway Radish - Jessie Haas   *e*   363

Juliana (Child; Sister)
Buzz Buzz Buzz - Veronica Uribe   *p*   896

Julie (Sister; Eskimo)
Nutik, the Wolf Pup - Jean Craighead George   *p*   325

Julio (Classmate; Neighbor)
Fat Chance Thanksgiving - Patricia Lakin   *p, e*   529

Julius (Royalty)
The War - Anais Vaugelade   *p, e*   908

Junie (Daughter; Sister)
Rattletrap Car - Phyllis Root   *p*   765

K

Ka (Prehistoric Human)
Song of the Axe - John R. Dann   *a*   209

Kagan, Sam (Writer)
A Dance for Emilia - Peter S. Beagle   *h, a*   63

Lee, Robin (Dancer)
Angelfish - Laurence Yep   m   994

Lefkowitz, Jake (15-Year-Old)
Night of the Bat - Paul Zindel   m   1004

Lemon, Silas (Grandfather)
The Memory Prisoner - Thomas Bloor   m   87

Lemuel (Fisherman; Spouse)
Lemuel the Fool - Myron Uhlberg   p   893

Lena (Mother; Spouse)
Katje, the Windmill Cat - Gretchen Woelfle   p   979

L'Engle-Franklin, Touche (Dog)
The Other Dog - Madeleine L'Engle   p   544

Lenny (Twin; Time Traveler)
Joining the Boston Tea Party - Diane Stanley   p,
    e   849

Leo (Brother; Child)
Breakout at the Bug Lab - Ruth Horowitz   b   421

Leo (Child; Friend)
The Cool Crazy Crickets to the Rescue! - David Elliott
    e   271

Leo (Boyfriend)
Girlhearts - Norma Fox Mazer   m   606

Leo (Mountaineer)
Witch's Fang - Heather Kellerhals-Stewart   m,
    h   484

Leopard, Steve (12-Year-Old)
Cirque du Freak: A Living Nightmare - Darren Shan
    m, h   813

Leslie (Nurse)
A Face First - Priscilla Cummings   m   201

Lesmarais, William (15-Year-Old)
Three Days Off - Susie Morgenstern   m, h   647

Leventhal, Daniel (Brother; Crime Victim)
Black Mirror - Nancy Werlin   h   941

Leventhal, Frances (16-Year-Old)
Black Mirror - Nancy Werlin   h   941

Levi, Gregory/Gregor (14-Year-Old)
Labyrinth - John Herman   m, h   388

Lewis (Cyborg)
The Graveyard Game - Kage Baker   h, a   42

Lewis, Arful (Dog)
I Was a Third Grade Spy - Mary Jane Auch   e   32

Lewis, Brian (3rd Grader; Friend)
I Was a Third Grade Spy - Mary Jane Auch   e   32

Lewis, Eddie (3rd Grader)
The Day Eddie Met the Author - Louise Borden
    e   93

Lewis, Natalie Michelle (Editor; Fiance(e))
Rain Is Not My Indian Name - Cynthia Leitich Smith
    m   831

Lexington "Lexi" (Squirrel; Friend)
Lexi's Tale - Johanna Hurwitz   e   439

Liadan (Sister)
Son of the Shadows - Juliet Marillier   h, a   593

Lidsmod (17-Year-Old)
Raven of the Waves - Michael Cadnum   h   132

Liebermann, Rivka (15-Year-Old)
Rivka's Way - Teri Kanefield   m   476

Lieutenant Pelko (Military Personnel)
A Boy at War: A Novel of Pearl Harbor - Harry
    Mazer   m   605

Lieutenant Sheldon (Military Personnel)
Girl in Blue - Ann Rinaldi   m, h   749

Lightfoot, Anne (Indian; Housekeeper)
Blind Fury - Linda Shands   m   815

Liliuokalani (Royalty)
Kaiulani: The People's Princess, Hawaii, 1889 - Ellen
    Emerson White   m   948

Lilly (11-Year-Old; Sister)
Marco's Millions - William Sleator   m   829

Lilly (Elephant)
Saving Lilly - Peg Kehret   e   483

Lily (Daughter)
The Great Good Thing - Roderick Townley   e,
    m   888

Lily (Child; Daughter)
Home before Dark - Ian Beck   p   64

Lily (Cousin; Daughter)
Oliver's Milk Shake - Vivian French   p   302

Lily (9-Year-Old; Sister; Cousin)
Summer Party - Cynthia Rylant   e   785

Lily (Tiger)
Tiger Trouble! - Diane Goode   p   341

Lily (Child)
Where Are You, Blue Kangaroo? - Emma Chichester
    Clark   p   157

Lima Bean Monster (Monster)
The Lima Bean Monster - Dan Yaccarino   p   991

Lin (Alien; Artist)
Perdido Street Station - China Mieville   h, a   637

Linda (Mother; Writer)
Equinox - Monte Killingsworth   m   494

Lindsay, Barnett (Uncle; Teenager)
Proud and Angry Dust - Kathryn Mitchell   a   644

Line, Victoria "Vikki" (Teenager; Mythical
Creature)
Flatterland: Like Flatland, Only More So - Ian Stewart
    h   856

Liney (Slave; 19-Year-Old)
If I Just Had Two Wings - Virginia Frances Schwartz
    m   803

Lionel (Musician)
Rowan Hood: Outlaw Girl of Sherwood Forest -
    Nancy Springer   e, m   847

Lirael (Librarian)
Lirael: Daughter of the Clayr - Garth Nix   h   677

Lisa (Dog; Traveler)
Lisa's Airplane Trip - Anne Gutman   p   358

Lisano (7th Grader)
Trino's Time - Diane Gonzales Bertrand   m   70

Little Badger (Badger; Pirate)
Little Badger, Terror of the Seven Seas - Eve Bunting
    p   120

Little Boy James (7-Year-Old; Brother)
*Grandpa Blows His Penny Whistle Until the Angels
    Sing* - Susan L. Roth   p, e   769

Little Catalina (7-Year-Old)
Mice and Beans - Pam Munoz Ryan   p   776

Little Green (Bird)
Little Green - Keith Baker   p   43

Little Hen (Chicken)
Something Wonderful - Jenny Nimmo   p   676

Little Hippo (Hippopotamus; Friend)
Naughty! - Caroline Castle   p   148

Little Louis (Son; Rabbit)
I Am the King! - Nathalie Dieterle   p   234

Little Monster (Son)
One Day, Daddy - Frances Thomas   p   879

Little Pink (Pig; Toy)
Max's Starry Night - Ken Wilson-Max   p   974

Little Red Hen (Chicken; Mother)
With Love, Little Red Hen - Alma Flor Ada   p   2

Little Red Riding Hood (Child; Friend)
With Love, Little Red Hen - Alma Flor Ada   p   2

Little Tree Frog (Frog)
Jamboree Day - Rhonda Gowler Greene   p   345

Little Whistle (Guinea Pig)
Little Whistle - Cynthia Rylant   p   781

Little Whistle (Guinea Pig; Friend)
Little Whistle's Dinner Party - Cynthia Rylant
    p   782

Little Wolf (Wolf)
Beware of the Storybook Wolves - Lauren Child   p,
    e   158

Little Zeb (Zebra; Baby)
Naughty! - Caroline Castle   p   148

Liz (Twin; Time Traveler)
Joining the Boston Tea Party - Diane Stanley   p,
    e   849

Lockwood, Anna Sophia "Annie" (Time Traveler)
For All Time - Caroline B. Cooney   m, h   180

Loewe ben Bezalel, Judah (Religious)
Prisoner in Time: A Child of the Holocaust - Pamela
    Melnikoff   m   632

Logan, Jolie (17-Year-Old; Invalid)
A Sea So Far - Jean Thesman   m, h   877

Logan, Paul-Edward (Landowner)
The Land - Mildred D. Taylor   m, h   872

Loki (Dog)
*Loki & Alex: The Adventures of a Dog & His Best
    Friend* - Charles R. Smith Jr.   p   830

Lola (Sister; Child)
I Am NOT Sleepy and I Will NOT Go to Bed - Lauren
    Child   p   160

Lollipop (Pig)
Lady Lollipop - Dick King-Smith   e   503

Lomister, Gilbert (Principal)
Don't You Know There's a War On? - Avi   m   35

Long, Patrick (9th Grader)
Alice Alone - Phyllis Reynolds Naylor   m   672

Lopez, Victor (14-Year-Old)
Victor Lopez at the Alamo - James Rice   m   745

Lord Raoul (Warrior)
Squire - Tamora Pierce   m, h   712

Lorenzo (Nobleman)
Shylock's Daughter - Mirjam Pressler   h   724

Loretta (Nurse)
All the Way Home - Patricia Reilly Giff   e   330

Loretta (Aunt; Traveler)
A Fish Named Spot - Jennifer P. Goldfinger   p   337

Loski, Bryce (8th Grader)
Flipped - Wendelin Van Draanen   m   899

Louey (Rabbit; Friend)
The Adventure of Louey and Frank - Carolyn White
    p   947

Louie (Cat; Son)
No Kiss for Grandpa - Harriet Ziefert   p   1001

Louis (Child; Blind Person)
The Hickory Chair - Lisa Rowe Fraustino   p   300

Louise (7-Year-Old; Sister)
Maxwell's Magic Mix-Up - Linda Ashman   p   27

Louise (Mouse; Sister)
Sheila Rae's Peppermint Stick - Kevin Henkes
    p   387

Lovell, Holly Faye (14-Year-Old; Singer)
A Mother's Gift - Britney Spears   m   841

Lovell, Wanda Jo (Seamstress)
A Mother's Gift - Britney Spears   m   841

Lowell, Carmen Lucille (15-Year-Old)
The Sisterhood of the Traveling Pants - Ann Brashares m, h 99

Lu, Marina (17-Year-Old; Crime Victim)
The Jasmine Trade - Denise Hamilton a 371

Lubeck, Beau (8th Grader)
Stranger in Dadland - Amy Goldman Koss e, m 519

Lucas (Religious)
The Crusader - Michael Alexander Eisner a 270

Luchesi, Nancie (Patient)
The Year of My Indian Prince - Ella Thorp Ellis m, h 275

Lucian (Fairy)
The Pillars of the World - Anne Bishop h, a 77

Lucille (Pig; Sister)
Starring Lucille - Kathryn Lasky p 534

Lucy (Child)
Bernard the Angry Rooster - Mary Wormell p 985

Lucy (Aunt; Chicken)
Elinor and Violet: The Story of Two Naughty Chickens - Patti Beling Murphy p 657

Lucy (Mouse; Sister)
Estelle and Lucy - Anna Alter p 14

Luke (Student; Child)
Luke's Way of Looking - Nadia Wheatley p, e 944

Lulu (Aunt; Aged Person)
Lulu's Birthday - Elizabeth Fitzgerald Howard p 425

Lulu (Daughter; Child)
My Grandmother Is a Singing Yaya - Karen Scourby D'Arc p 212

Luned (Servant)
The Dragon's Son - Sarah L. Thomson h, a 882

Lupe (11-Year-Old; Handicapped)
Tiger's Fall - Molly Bang e 48

Lupien, Laure (10th Grader)
Lean Mean Machines - Michele Marineau m, h 594

Lupin (Wolf)
The Good Dog - Avi e, m 36

Lynch, Eliza (Mother; Widow(er))
Gabriel's Story - David Anthony Durham h, a 255

Lynch, Gabriel (15-Year-Old; Runaway)
Gabriel's Story - David Anthony Durham h, a 255

Lyons, Jessica (Computer Game Player)
Website of the Warped Wizard - Eric A. Kimmel e 498

M

Ma-Ma (Mother)
Dim Sum for Everyone! - Grace Lin p 558

Mabel (7-Year-Old; Cousin)
Night of the Living Gerbil - Elizabeth Levy e 553

Mabela (Mouse; Heroine)
Mabela the Clever - Margaret Read MacDonald p 584

Mable Jean (Student—Elementary School; Sister)
A Bus of Our Own - Freddi Williams Evans p, e 280

MacBean, Rory (Uncle; Farmer)
The Carved Box - Gillian Chan m 154

MacDougall, Big Murdoch (Musician; Teacher)
A Fiddle for Angus - Budge Wilson p, e 968

MacGillyCuddy, Dan (Brother; Student)
Dancing for Danger: A Meggy Tale - Margot Griffin e 352

MacGillyCuddy, Meggy (Dancer; Student)
Dancing for Danger: A Meggy Tale - Margot Griffin e 352

Macintosh, Fannie (Student)
Finding Hattie - Sally Warner m 926

MacIntosh, Tom White Cloud (Indian; Store Owner)
The Great Whale of Kansas - Richard W. Jennings m 454

Macka, Jake (Boyfriend; 12th Grader)
To Live Again - Lurlene McDaniel m 614

Mackenzie, Heather (12th Grader)
Damage - A.M. Jenkins h 451

MacKinley, Jeffrey "Jeff" (Student—High School)
A Group of One - Rachna Gilmore m, h 332

MacPhaull, Lindsay (Businesswoman)
Jackson's Way - Leslie LaFoy h, a 528

MacPherson, Antonia Jane "Ant" (12-Year-Old; 6th Grader)
Notes from a Liar and Her Dog - Gennifer Choldenko m 162

Macpherson, Duncan (Father; Accountant)
Danger in Disguise - Mary Alice Downie m 245

MacPherson, Elizabeth (Sister)
Notes from a Liar and Her Dog - Gennifer Choldenko m 162

Macpherson, Jamie (14-Year-Old)
Danger in Disguise - Mary Alice Downie m 245

MacPherson, Katherine (Sister)
Notes from a Liar and Her Dog - Gennifer Choldenko m 162

Macro, Lucius Cornelius (Military Personnel)
Under the Eagle: A Tale of Military Adventure and Reckless Heroism with the Roman Legions - Simon Scarrow a 797

Mad-Rat, Maggie (Rat; Cousin)
The Revenge of Randal Reese-Rat - Tor Seidler e 810

Mad-Rat, Montague "Monty" (Rat; Bridegroom)
The Revenge of Randal Reese-Rat - Tor Seidler e 810

Madame Akkikuyu (Fortune Teller)
The Crystal Prison - Robin Jarvis m 450

Madame Meritta (Entertainer)
The Minstrel's Melody - Eleanora E. Tate e, m 867

Madame Octa (Spider)
Cirque du Freak: A Living Nightmare - Darren Shan m, h 813

Madeleine (Housekeeper)
Following Fake Man - Barbara Ware Holmes m 410

Madison, Bree (10th Grader)
Plunking Reggie Jackson - James W. Bennett h 69

Madsen, Albert (Brother; Son)
Sailing Home: A Story of a Childhood at Sea - Gloria Rand p, e 734

Madsen, Mads Albert (Father; Sea Captain)
Sailing Home: A Story of a Childhood at Sea - Gloria Rand p, e 734

Madsen, Matilda (Sister; Narrator)
Sailing Home: A Story of a Childhood at Sea - Gloria Rand p, e 734

Maggie (Animal Lover; Friend; Student—Elementary School)
Reptiles Are My Life - Megan McDonald p 619

Magnolia (Goose)
The Goose Who Went Off in a Huff - Paul Brett Johnson p 459

Magpie (Bird; Friend)
Fox - Margaret Wild p, e 951

Mags (Child; Sister)
Bluebird Summer - Deborah Hopkinson p, e 418

Maguire, Jack "Blackjack" (Uncle; Convict)
Above and Beyond - Susan Bonners m 91

Mahoney, Marty (Principal)
Owen Foote, Super Spy - Stephanie Greene e 346

Maizie Mae (Young Woman; Pilot)
Scatterbrain Sam - Ellen Jackson p, e 444

Major, Kambia Elaine (13-Year-Old; Writer; Abuse Victim)
Shayla's Double Brown Baby Blues - Lori Aurelia Williams m, h 963

Major Bark (Dog)
Agapanthus Hum and Major Bark - Joy Cowley b 189

Major Harrell (Military Personnel)
Drummer - George C. Richardson m 746

Major Quilan (Military Personnel; Alien)
Look to Windward - Iain Banks h, a 49

Malloy, Caroline (4th Grader; Sister)
The Boys Return - Phyllis Reynolds Naylor e, m 673

Malloy, Daniel (Political Figure)
Green Grow the Victims - Jeanne M. Dams a 207

Malone, Kaitlin "Kait" (12th Grader)
Scribbler of Dreams - Mary E. Pearson m, h 703

Mama (Mother; Refugee)
Anna's Goat - Janice Kulyk Keefer p, e 481

Mama (Mother)
Beatrice's Goat - Page McBrier p 608
Come Back, Hannah! - Marisabina Russo p 774

MaMa (Mother; Immigrant)
Earthquake - Milly Lee p 542

Mama (Mother)
Elsie Times Eight - Natalie Babbitt p 41

Mama (Mother; Single Parent)
Fat Chance Thanksgiving - Patricia Lakin p, e 529

Mama (Guinea Pig; Mother)
Felix Feels Better - Rosemary Wells p 936

Mama (Mother)
Freedom School, Yes! - Amy Littlesugar p, e 564

Mama (Mother; Slave)
Freedom's Wings: Corey's Diary - Sharon Dennis Wyeth e, m 988

Mama (Mother; Refugee)
Gleam and Glow - Eve Bunting p, e 118

Mama (Mother; Widow(er))
Mama Does the Mambo - Katherine Leiner p, e 543

Mama (Single Mother; Seamstress)
Mama's Way - Helen Ketteman p, e 492

Mama (Mother)
One More Wednesday - Malika Doray p 242
One of the Problems of Everett Anderson - Lucille Clifton p 168
The Other Side - Jacqueline Woodson p, e 983

Mama (Single Mother; Unemployed)
Rent Party Jazz - William Miller p, e 640

Mama (Bird; Mother)
Robin's Home - Jeannine Atkins   p 29

Mama (Mother)
The Sick Day - Patricia MacLachlan   p 587
What's Cooking, Jamela? - Niki Daly   p 206

Mama Bear (Bear; Mother)
Patrick and the Big Bully - Geoffrey Hayes   p 384

Mama Duck (Duck; Mother)
Baby Duck's New Friend - Frank Asch   p 24

Mama Frances (Grandmother)
Goin' Someplace Special - Patricia C. McKissack   p,
e 625

Mama Linda (Addict)
Born Blue - Han Nolan   h 681

Mama Pearl (Grandmother; Spouse)
Little Cliff's First Day of School - Clifton L. Taulbert
p 868

Manch (Dog)
The Field of the Dogs - Katherine Paterson   e,
m 700

Mangrove, Peter (Sailor; Slave)
Tom Cringle: The Pirate and the Patriot - Gerald
Hausman   m 382

Mann, Orly (Race Car Driver)
Conflict in California - Ken Stuckey   m, h 863

Manning, Mariel (Adoptee)
All the Way Home - Patricia Reilly Giff   e 330

Manning, Skye (Student—High School)
The Sky's the Limit - Mitzi Dale   m 205

Mansfield, Harvey (Con Artist)
The Stones of Mourning Creek - Diane Les Becquets
m, h 546

Marazol, Marisol (14-Year-Old)
Quinceanera Means Sweet 15 - Veronica Chambers
m 152

Marchadi/Fernandez, Esther/Pedro (16-Year-Old)
Freedom beyond the Sea - Waldtraut Lewin   m,
h 554

Marchand, Gus (Farmer; Crime Victim)
Desperate Measures - Kate Wilhelm   a 959

Marchand, Paul (15-Year-Old; Handyman)
Before Wings - Beth Goobie   m, h 340

Marcie (Sister; Addict)
Raven's Flight - Diane Silvey   m, h 822

Marco (12-Year-Old; Brother)
Marco's Millions - William Sleator   m 829

Marcus (Child; Friend)
The Cool Crazy Crickets to the Rescue! - David Elliott
e 271

Margaret (Dancer; Friend)
Ballet Bug - Christine McDonnell   e, m 621

Marie-Antoinette (Dog)
McDuff Goes to School - Rosemary Wells   p 938

Marik (Teenager)
The Beguilers - Kate Thompson   m, h 880

Marina (5-Year-Old; Sister)
Gleam and Glow - Eve Bunting   p, e 118

Marius (16-Year-Old)
Zazoo: A Novel - Richard Mosher   m, h 653

Marley (Dog)
A Mile from Ellington Station - Tim Egan   p 264

Marnie (Student—Elementary School)
Math Man - Teri Daniels   p 208

Marpessa (Sister; Artisan)
Troy - Adele Geras   h, a 327

Marshall, Jade (9th Grader)
Vicky Angel - Jacqueline Wilson   m 972

Marshall, Rich (Father)
Whale Talk - Chris Crutcher   h 199

Marstead, Gloria "Glory" (Grandmother)
Playing for Keeps - Joan Lowery Nixon   m, h 679

Marstead, Rose Ann (16-Year-Old)
Playing for Keeps - Joan Lowery Nixon   m, h 679

Martha (Sister)
The Class Artist - G. Brian Karas   p 477

Martin, Jennifer (14-Year-Old; Beauty Queen)
Rat Boys: A Dating Experiment - Thom Eberhardt
m 258

Martin, Jennifer Atwood (Child)
Above and Beyond - Susan Bonners   m 91

Martin, Sidney (7th Grader)
Frog Face and the Three Boys - Don Trembath   e,
m 889

Martinka, Charlie "Paw Paw" (Aged Person; Actor)
Bo & Mzzz Mad - Sid Fleischman   m 291

Martinka, Juna (Aunt; Artist)
Bo & Mzzz Mad - Sid Fleischman   m 291

Martinka, Madeleine "Mzzz Mad" (13-Year-Old)
Bo & Mzzz Mad - Sid Fleischman   m 291

Martucci, Jeremy (10th Grader)
Lean Mean Machines - Michele Marineau   m,
h 594

Martyn (Student—Boarding School)
The Hole - Guy Burt   a 128

Marva (Inventor)
*It's Me, Marva!: A Story about Color & Optical
Illusions* - Marjorie Priceman   p, e 725

Marva (Pig; Businesswoman)
Nursery Crimes - Arthur Geisert   p, e 323

Marvel, Marty Q. (Magician)
The Frog Principal - Stephanie Calmenson   p 134

Mary (Aunt; Librarian)
Hannah's Bookmobile Christmas - Sally Derby   p,
e 226

Mary Jane (Child; Immigrant)
Tattered Sails - Verla Kay   p 480

Masera, Iban "Gil" (Animal Trainer)
A Feral Darkness - Doranna Durgin   h, a 254

Mason, Deenie (15-Year-Old)
Scorpio's Child - Kezi Matthews   m 603

Massey, Edward (12-Year-Old)
West of Rehoboth - Alexs D. Pate   a 699

Massimo (Student—Graduate)
My Grandfather, Jack the Ripper - Claudio Apone
m 16

Master Chen (Teacher)
*Lady of Ch'iao Kuo: Warrior of the South, Southern
China, A.D. 531* - Laurence Yep   m 995

Master Cleary (Teacher)
Dancing for Danger: A Meggy Tale - Margot Griffin
e 352

Master Man (Mythical Creature)
Master Man: A Tall Tale of Nigeria - Aaron Shepard
p, e 817

Master Melwyn (Aged Person; Fisherman)
Tree Girl - T.A. Barron   e, m 55

Mastriani, Douglas "Dougie" (Mentally Ill Person)
When Lightning Strikes - Jenny Carroll   m, h 142

Mastriani, Jessica Antonia (Psychic; 16-Year-Old)
When Lightning Strikes - Jenny Carroll   m, h 142

Mateo (Orphan; 13-Year-Old)
Thunder on the Sierra - Kathy Balmes   e, m 47

Matey (Sailor; Pirate)
Captain and Matey Set Sail - Daniel Laurence
b 535

Matt (Father)
Stranger in Dadland - Amy Goldman Koss   e,
m 519

Matthew (Boyfriend)
Brave New Girl - Louisa Luna   h 576

Matthew (Computer Game Player)
Website of the Warped Wizard - Eric A. Kimmel
e 498

Matthews, Charlotte Ann (13-Year-Old)
Charlotte's Choice - Cathleen Twomey   m 892

Matthews, Cole (15-Year-Old; Criminal)
Touching Spirit Bear - Ben Mikaelsen   m, h 638

Maurice (Cat)
*Amazing Maurice and His Educated Rodents: A Novel
of Discworld* - Terry Pratchett   h 723

Max (Cockroach)
Breakout at the Bug Lab - Ruth Horowitz   b 421

Max (Rabbit; Brother)
Bunny Party - Rosemary Wells   p 935

Max (4-Year-Old; Adoptee)
Emma's Yucky Brother - Jean Little   b 562

Max (Wolf; Son)
Max, the Stubborn Little Wolf - Marie-Odile Judes
p 473

Max (Child)
Max's Starry Night - Ken Wilson-Max   p 974

Max (Father; Spouse)
A Mountain of Blintzes - Barbara Diamond Goldin
p 338

Max (Brother)
Pirates - C. Drew Lamm   p, e 530

Max (Dog)
When Poppy and Max Grow Up - Lindsey Gardiner
p 312

Maxine (Lesbian)
Cissy Funk - Kim Taylor   m 870

Maxine "Max" (Pig; Friend)
Oomph! - Colin McNaughton   p 628

Maxwell (Magician; Uncle)
Maxwell's Magic Mix-Up - Linda Ashman   p 27

Maxwell, Matilda "Aunt Mattie" (Aunt; Teacher)
No More Nasty - Amy MacDonald   e, m 583

Maxwell, Ring (7th Grader)
Dangling - Lillian Eige   e, m 267

Maxwell, Simon (5th Grader; Nephew)
No More Nasty - Amy MacDonald   e, m 583

May (4-Year-Old; Twin)
Big Trouble in Little Twinsville - Elizabeth Levy
e 552

Mazer, Jonathan (Military Personnel)
The War Within: A Novel of the Civil War - Carol
Matas   m 600

McCafferty, Devin (12th Grader)
Shades of Simon Gray - Joyce McDonald   m,
h 617

McCallister, Jeb (Bully; 6th Grader)
Frankenbug - Steven Cousins   e, m 185

McCarthy, Bugsie (Bully; 6th Grader)
Racing the Past - Sis Deans   m 220

McCourt, Caitlin Alyssa (Abuse Victim; Girlfriend)
Breathing Underwater - Alex Flinn   h 295

McCulloch, Rosalie (Orphan; 14-Year-Old)
Daniel's Walk - Michael Spooner   m 845

Miss Mouse (Doll; Stuffed Animal)
Miss Mouse Takes Off - Jan Ormerod   *p*   688

Miss Mouse (Mouse; Stuffed Animal)
Miss Mouse's Day - Jan Ormerod   *p*   689

Miss Perfidy (Aged Person)
Everything on a Waffle - Polly Horvath   *m*   422

Miss Rosemary (Farmer; Aged Person)
The Goose Who Went Off in a Huff - Paul Brett Johnson   *p*   459

Miss Stretchberry (Teacher)
Love That Dog - Sharon Creech   *e, m*   192

Miss Wing (Teacher)
Butterfly Buddies - Judy Cox   *e*   190

Mister Giant (Giant)
Clever Beatrice - Margaret Willey   *p*   960

Mitchell, Sam (Carpenter)
A Long Way Home - Nancy Price Graff   *m*   343

Mitchell, Zola (12th Grader)
Have a Nice Life Series - Scarlett Macdougal   *h*   585

Mitzi (Child; Witch)
Hoodwinked - Arthur Howard   *p*   424

Mobberley, Gaynor (Friend)
The Dragon Charmer - Jan Siegel   *h, a*   820

Moberly-Rat, Isabel (Rat; Bride)
The Revenge of Randal Reese-Rat - Tor Seidler   *e*   810

Moe (Spouse; Space Explorer)
Company's Going - Arthur Yorinks   *p, e*   998

Moe (Monster)
Monster Mischief - Pamela Jane   *p*   448

Moe (Son; Brother)
A Mountain of Blintzes - Barbara Diamond Goldin   *p*   338

Moffett, Christy "Chris" (8th Grader)
And Sometimes Why - Mame Farrell   *m*   283

Mogg (Mythical Creature)
The Moon Robber - Dean Morrissey   *e*   650

Molly (Student—College)
The Circus in the Woods - Bill Littlefield   *m, h*   563

Molly (Sister; Singer)
A Fiddle for Angus - Budge Wilson   *p, e*   968

Molly (Cat; Sister)
Molly and the Magic Wishbone - Barbara McClintock   *p*   609

Molly (Student—Middle School)
Skeleton Man - Joseph Bruchac   *m*   110

Mom (Mother)
Breakout at the Bug Lab - Ruth Horowitz   *b*   421

Mom (Single Mother; Journalist)
By Lizzie - Mary Eccles   *e*   259

Mom (Mother)
Chanukah Lights Everywhere - Michael J. Rosen   *p*   767

Mom (Mother; Sister)
Clarice Bean: Guess Who's Babysitting? - Lauren Child   *p, e*   159

Mom (Mother; Daughter)
The Days of Summer - Eve Bunting   *p*   117

Mom (Mother)
Home before Dark - Ian Beck   *p*   64

Mom (Mother; Spouse)
Let's Get a Pup! Said Kate - Bob Graham   *p*   344

Mom (Mother)
More Parts - Tedd Arnold   *p, e*   20
Sammy and the Robots - Ian Whybrow   *p*   949

Momma (Mother; Artisan)
The Girl with 500 Middle Names - Margaret Peterson Haddix   *e*   366

Momma (Mother; Elephant)
Squeak's Good Idea - Max Eilenberg   *p*   268

Momma Chang (Mother; Cook)
The Runaway Rice Cake - Ying Chang Compestine   *p*   178

Mommy (Mother)
Goodbye Mousie - Robie H. Harris   *p*   379

Mommy (Bird; Mother)
Little Bird, Biddle Bird - David Kirk   *p*   508

Mommy (Mother; Cook)
Mom Pie - Lynne Jonell   *p*   468

Mommy (Mother; Divorced Person)
Two Homes - Claire Masurel   *p*   599

Mompellion, Michael (Religious)
Year of Wonders - Geraldine Brooks   *h, a*   101

Monkey (Monkey; Trickster)
Monkey King - Ed Young   *p, e*   999

Monkey, Nina Jane (Monkey; Soccer Player)
Morgan Plays Soccer - Anne Rockwell   *p*   757

Monks, Bill (Stepfather; Sea Captain)
Lord of the Deep - Graham Salisbury   *m*   788

Monsieur Eek (Monkey)
Monsieur Eek - David Ives   *m*   443

Montana (Friend; Diver)
Waiting to Dive - Karen Rivers   *e, m*   750

Montgomery, Keisha (12th Grader)
Darkness Before Dawn - Sharon M. Draper   *h*   249

Montgomery, Roderick Jackson (Aged Person; Animal Lover)
Fly! - Christopher Myers   *p, e*   663

Moo (Cow)
Minnie and Moo Meet Frankenswine - Denys Cazet   *b*   150

Moody, Judy (3rd Grader; Sister)
Judy Moody Gets Famous - Megan McDonald   *e*   618

Moody, Stink (Brother)
Judy Moody Gets Famous - Megan McDonald   *e*   618

Moon (Celestial Body; Spouse)
The Day Ocean Came to Visit - Diane Wolkstein   *p*   981

Moon (Celestial Body)
When Moon Fell Down - Linda Smith   *p*   832

Moon, Charlie (Police Officer; Indian)
Grandmother Spider - James D. Doss   *a*   243

Moon, Mahalia "Haley" (13-Year-Old)
A Piece of Heaven - Sharon Dennis Wyeth   *m*   989

Moon, Otis (15-Year-Old)
A Piece of Heaven - Sharon Dennis Wyeth   *m*   989

Moonpie (11-Year-Old)
Moonpie and Ivy - Barbara O'Connor   *m*   683

Morag (Fairy)
The Pillars of the World - Anne Bishop   *h, a*   77

Morales, Silvia (Immigrant; Servant)
Finn: A Novel - Matthew Olshan   *h*   686

Morgan (Sorceress; Friend)
Christmas in Camelot - Mary Pope Osborne   *e*   691

Morgan (Sister)
The Dragon's Son - Sarah L. Thomson   *h, a*   882

Morgan (Sorceress)
I Am Morgan Le Fay - Nancy Springer   *h*   846

Morgan, Kate (10th Grader)
So Mote It Be - Isobel Bird   *m, h*   73

Morgan, Spencer (17-Year-Old; Military Personnel)
Soldier Boys - Dean Hughes   *m, h*   434

Morgus (Witch)
The Dragon Charmer - Jan Siegel   *h, a*   820

Mori, Davi (14-Year-Old)
A Boy at War: A Novel of Pearl Harbor - Harry Mazer   *m*   605

Morley, Drake (Con Artist)
Playing with Fire - Kathleen Karr   *m*   478

Morrison-Pleydell, Maurice (Businessman; Stepfather)
Blind Beauty - K.M. Peyton   *m, h*   709

Moscovitz, Lilly (9th Grader)
Princess in the Spotlight - Meg Cabot   *m, h*   131

Moses, Bobby (Entertainer)
The Yokota Officers Club - Sarah Bird   *h, a*   74

Mother (Cat; Mother)
Estelle and Lucy - Anna Alter   *p*   14

Mother (Mother; Vacationer)
The Journey - Sarah Stewart   *p, e*   857

Mother (Mother)
My Best Friend Bear - Tony Johnston   *p*   465
Tub-boo-boo - Margie Palatini   *p*   693

Mother Claus (Mother; Spouse)
Peter Claus and the Naughty List - Lawrence David   *p*   213

Mother Greenwood (Aged Person; Storyteller)
The Famous Adventures of Jack - Berlie Doherty   *e*   239

Mother Holly (Aged Person)
Mother Holly - John Warren Stewig   *p, e*   858

Mousie (Mouse)
Goodbye Mousie - Robie H. Harris   *p*   379

Mr. Barraclough (Teacher)
Luke's Way of Looking - Nadia Wheatley   *p, e*   944

Mr. Benito (Teacher)
How to Be a Real Person (in Just One Day) - Sally Warner   *m*   927

Mr. Berry (Teacher; Dog)
Don't Go! - Jane Breskin Zalben   *p*   1000

Mr. Brockhurst (Teacher)
The Gramma War - Kristin Butcher   *m*   129

Mr. Brown (Businessman; Store Owner)
The Bookstore Burglar - Barbara Maitland   *b*   590

Mr. Bundy (Principal; Frog)
The Frog Principal - Stephanie Calmenson   *p*   134

Mr. Cao (Dancer; Aged Person)
Angelfish - Laurence Yep   *m*   994

Mr. Crepsley (Vampire)
Cirque du Freak: A Living Nightmare - Darren Shan   *m, h*   813

Mr. Gaskitt (Father)
The Man Who Wore All His Clothes - Allan Ahlberg   *e*   9

Mr. Gianini (Teacher)
Princess in the Spotlight - Meg Cabot   *m, h*   131

Mr. Giant (Giant)
Look Out, Jack! The Giant Is Back! - Tom Birdseye   *p, e*   76

Mr. Griswold (Teacher)
Patches Lost and Found - Steven Kroll   *p*   523

Mr. Jackson (Worker)
Falling Angels - Tracy Chevalier   *a*   156

Mr. Kang (Aged Person; Grandfather)
Happy Birthday Mr. Kang - Susan L. Roth   *p, e*   770

Mr. Keene (Principal)
A Fine, Fine School - Sharon Creech   *p*   191

Mr. Kim (Store Owner)
The Name Jar - Yangsook Choi   *p*   161

Mr. Krupp (Principal)
Captain Underpants and the Wrath of the Wicked Wedgie Woman - Dav Pilkey   *e*   713

Mr. Lexeter (Librarian)
The Memory Prisoner - Thomas Bloor   *m*   87

Mr. Lincoln (Principal)
Mr. Lincoln's Way - Patricia Polacco   *p, e*   719

Mr. Martin (Teacher)
Stop, Drop, and Roll - Margery Cuyler   *p*   202

Mr. Merrick (Principal)
Mrs. Spitzer's Garden - Edith Pattou   *p*   702

Mr. Mud (Landlord)
Tiger Trouble! - Diane Goode   *p*   341

Mr. Olson (Farmer; Alcoholic)
Hank's Story - Jane Buchanan   *e*   113

Mr. Paris (Store Owner; Hippopotamus)
The Case of the Troublesome Turtle - Cynthia Rylant   *b, e*   779

Mr. Pockets (Animal Lover)
The Pocket Dogs - Margaret Wild   *p*   954

Mr. Popovich (Manager (Stage))
Milo's Hat Trick - Jon Agee   *p*   7

Mr. Putter (Aged Person)
Mr. Putter & Tabby Feed the Fish - Cynthia Rylant   *b*   783

Mr. Riley (Store Owner; Dog)
The Case of the Puzzling Possum - Cynthia Rylant   *b, e*   778

Mr. Santangelo (Teacher)
The Hero of Ticonderoga - Gail Gauthier   *m*   320

Mr. Simet (Teacher; Coach)
Whale Talk - Chris Crutcher   *h*   199

Mr. Torgle "Mr. T" (Foster Parent)
Grover C. Graham and Me - Mary Quattlebaum   *e, m*   731

Mr. Trent (Detective—Police)
The Rag and Bone Shop - Robert Cormier   *m, h*   183

Mr. Wolf (Wolf)
Oomph! - Colin McNaughton   *p*   628

Mrs. (Teacher)
Junie B. Jones Is a Graduation Girl - Barbara Park   *e*   695

Mrs. Bagoong (Reptile)
Farewell, My Lunchbag - Bruce Hale   *e, m*   370

Mrs. Bear (Bear; Mother)
Kiss Good Night - Amy Hest   *p*   394

Mrs. Bert (Mother; Spouse)
The Adventures of Bert - Allan Ahlberg   *p*   8

Mrs. Broder (Wealthy)
Fiona McGilray's Story: A Voyage from Ireland in 1849 - Clare Pastore   *m*   698

Mrs. Brown (Aged Person; Animal Lover)
Cats, Cats, Cats! - Leslea Newman   *p*   675

Mrs. Byrd (Bird; Teacher)
We Gather Together . . . Now Please Get Lost! - Diane DeGroat   *p*   222

Mrs. Diggs (Animal Lover; Aged Person)
Widget - Lyn Rossiter McFarland   *p*   623

Mrs. Field (Spouse; Farmer)
Something Wonderful - Jenny Nimmo   *p*   676

Mrs. Gaskitt (Taxi Driver; Mother)
The Man Who Wore All His Clothes - Allan Ahlberg   *e*   9

Mrs. Gourd (Teacher)
Math Man - Teri Daniels   *p*   208

Mrs. Haig-Ereildoun (Mother)
Do Try to Speak as We Do: The Diary of an American Au Pair - Marjorie Leet Ford   *a*   297

Mrs. Hobbs (Widow(er))
The Ghost and Mrs. Hobbs - Cynthia DeFelice   *e, m*   221

Mrs. Jardin (Teacher)
Welcome to Kindergarten - Anne Rockwell   *p*   758

Mrs. Jenkins (Teacher; Dog)
Mama, Don't Go! - Rosemary Wells   *b*   937

Mrs. Maxwell (Teacher)
Shrinking Violet - Cari Best   *p, e*   71

Mrs. McTats (Animal Lover)
Mrs. McTats and Her Houseful of Cats - Alyssa Satin Capucilli   *p*   137

Mrs. Morrow (Teacher)
The Day Eddie Met the Author - Louise Borden   *e*   93

Mrs. Spitzer (Teacher)
Mrs. Spitzer's Garden - Edith Pattou   *p*   702

Mrs. Wainwright (Counselor)
Vicky Angel - Jacqueline Wilson   *m*   972

Mrs. Walmsley (Social Worker)
Cherokee - Creina Mansfield   *m*   592

Ms. Benson (Teacher)
Cam Jansen and the School Play Mystery - David A. Adler   *e*   6

Ms. Brown (Teacher)
Marvin One Too Many - Katherine Paterson   *b*   701

Ms. Clayton (Teacher)
The School Story - Andrew Clements   *e, m*   167

Ms. Fair (Teacher)
Emily's Art - Peter Catalanotto   *p*   149

Ms. Ribble (Teacher)
Captain Underpants and the Wrath of the Wicked Wedgie Woman - Dav Pilkey   *e*   713

Ms. Shepherd (Dog; Teacher)
Meet the Barkers: Morgan and Moffat Go to School - Tomie DePaola   *p*   225

Ms. Snickle (Teacher)
The Secrets of Ms. Snickle's Class - Laurie Miller Hornik   *e*   419

Ms. Turner (Librarian; Rabbit)
D.W.'s Library Card - Marc Brown   *p*   103

Ms. Witherspoon "Cat Lady" (Aged Person; Animal Lover)
Just Ask Iris - Lucy Frank   *m*   299

Muckle (Mythical Creature; Inventor)
How Santa Lost His Job - Stephen Krensky   *p*   521

Mueller, Max (Agent)
Sammy Keyes and the Hollywood Mummy - Wendelin Van Draanen   *m*   900

Muggeridge, Marc (Editor)
Joshua's Song - Joan Hiatt Harlow   *m*   373

Mugisa (Goat)
Beatrice's Goat - Page McBrier   *p*   608

Muktuk (Bear)
Irving and Muktuk: Two Bad Bears - Daniel Pinkwater   *p*   717

Muller, Karl (Teenager)
Faraway Home - Marilyn Taylor   *m*   871

Muller, Rosa (Child)
Faraway Home - Marilyn Taylor   *m*   871

Mulligan, Pinch (Gang Member)
Chipper - James Lincoln Collier   *m*   176

Murdoch, Callum (15-Year-Old; Orphan)
The Carved Box - Gillian Chan   *m*   154

Murieta, Joaquin (Historical Figure; Thief)
Thunder on the Sierra - Kathy Balmes   *e, m*   47

Murphy, Molly (Immigrant; Detective—Amateur)
Murphy's Law - Rhys Bowen   *a*   96

Murphy, Robin (Boyfriend)
What My Mother Doesn't Know - Sonya Sones   *m, h*   839

Musa, Abubakari (Brother; Royalty)
Mansa Musa: The Lion of Mali - Khephra Burns   *e, m*   127

Musa, Kankan (Kidnap Victim; Royalty)
Mansa Musa: The Lion of Mali - Khephra Burns   *e, m*   127

Mutton, Johnny (Sheep; Student—Elementary School)
The Many Adventures of Johnny Mutton - James Proimos   *e*   726

Mutton, Momma (Mother)
The Many Adventures of Johnny Mutton - James Proimos   *e*   726

N

Nagavatsk, Alexei (Spy)
The Gadget - Paul Zindel   *m, h*   1003

Nakunte (Artist; Mother)
My Baby - Jeanette Winter   *p*   975

Nana (Mythical Creature; Aged Person)
The Dog Prince - Lauren Mills   *p, e*   642

Nana (Grandmother; Cook)
The Friday Nights of Nana - Amy Hest   *p*   393

Napoleon (Dog)
Missing from Haymarket Square - Harriette Gillem Robinet   *m*   755

Nash, Bea (Hockey Player; Dancer)
Ballet Bug - Christine McDonnell   *e, m*   621

Natalie (12-Year-Old)
Spellfall - Katherine Roberts   *m, h*   752

Nate the Great (Detective—Amateur; Friend)
Nate the Great and the Big Sniff - Marjorie Weinman Sharmat   *b*   816

Nebuchadnezzar "Neb/Ben" (Immortal)
Castaways of the Flying Dutchman - Brian Jacques   *m*   446

Nebula, Ralph (Camper; Brother)
Fat Camp Commandos - Daniel Pinkwater   *e*   716

Nebula, Sylvia (Sister; Camper)
Fat Camp Commandos - Daniel Pinkwater   *e*   716

Nebula "Neb" (5th Grader; Friend)
Bobo Crazy - Marilyn Sadler   *e*   786

Nell (Nurse; Aged Person)
The Circus in the Woods - Bill Littlefield   *m, h*   563

Nelson, Hannah (Mother; Editor)
The School Story - Andrew Clements   *e, m*   167

Nelson, Nadia (Girlfriend; 6th Grader)
In Ned's Head - Soren Olsson   *e*   687

Nelson, Whisper (7th Grader)
The Million Dollar Kick - Dan Gutman   *m*   360

Nelson/Day, Natalie/Cassandra (Writer; 12-Year-Old)
The School Story - Andrew Clements   *e, m*   167

Nergal (Friend; 1st Grader)
Horus's Horrible Day - Shana Corey   e 182

Newbury, Mary (Witch)
Witch Child - Celia Rees   m, h 739

Newell, Miles Arthur (16-Year-Old)
Memory Boy - Will Weaver   m, h 932

Newton, Dulciana "Dulcie" (11th Grader; Adoptee)
Love, Sara - Mary Beth Lundgren   m, h 577

Nicholaievna, Anastasia (Royalty; Historical Figure)
Angel on the Square - Gloria Whelan   m, h 946

Nicholas "Nugget" (Bully; 6th Grader)
In Ned's Head - Soren Olsson   e 687

Nichols, Allie (11-Year-Old; Friend)
The Ghost and Mrs. Hobbs - Cynthia DeFelice   e, m 221

Nichols, Michael (4-Year-Old; Brother)
The Ghost and Mrs. Hobbs - Cynthia DeFelice   e, m 221

Nickowsky, Pete (6th Grader; Writer)
Deep Doo-Doo and the Mysterious E-Mail - Michael Delaney   e 224

Nico (Father; Spouse)
Katje, the Windmill Cat - Gretchen Woelfle   p 979

Nicolson, Georgia (14-Year-Old)
On the Bright Side, I'm Now the Girlfriend of a Sex God: Further Confessions of Georgia Nicolson - Louise Rennison   m, h 742

Nicolson, Libby (Sister; Child)
On the Bright Side, I'm Now the Girlfriend of a Sex God: Further Confessions of Georgia Nicolson - Louise Rennison   m, h 742

Nikolas (Vampire; Twin)
Shattered Mirror - Amelia Atwater-Rhodes   h 30

Nimue (Wife; Mother)
The Dragon's Son - Sarah L. Thomson   h, a 882

Nina (Animal Lover; Equestrian)
Runaway Radish - Jessie Haas   e 363

Noah (Slave; Fugitive)
Stealing South: A Story of the Underground Railroad - Katherine Ayres   m, h 40

Noah (Biblical Figure; Aged Person)
A Stormy Ride on Noah's Ark - Patricia Hooper   p 417

Noel, Hubert (Teacher)
A Book of Coupons - Susie Morgenstern   e, m 646

Nolan, John "Wart" (12-Year-Old)
The Devil in Ol' Rosie - Louise Moeri   m 645

Nora (Sister; 4th Grader)
The Days of Summer - Eve Bunting   p 117

Norbert (Detective—Amateur)
4 1/2 Friends and the Secret Cave - Joachim Friedrich   e 305
41/2 Friends and the Disappearing Bio Teacher - Joachim Friedrich   e 306

Norbert (Alien)
A Nose for Adventure - Richard Scrimger   m 808

North, Bobby (Bear; Student—Elementary School)
The Heart of Cool - Jamie McEwan   b, e 622

Norwood, Tyler (Mechanic; Boyfriend)
A Mother's Gift - Britney Spears   m 841

Nuadha's Silver Druid "Druid" (Dog; Mythical Creature)
A Feral Darkness - Doranna Durgin   h, a 254

Nutik (Wolf)
Nutik & Amaroq Play Ball - Jean Craighead George   p 324
Nutik, the Wolf Pup - Jean Craighead George   p 325

Nutria, Walter (Student)
Beatnik Rutabagas from Beyond the Stars - Quentin Dodd   m, h 238

Nygerski, Cyrus (Baseball Player)
Tartabull's Throw - Henry Garfield   h 313

O

Oakley, Annie (Historical Figure)
The Sketchbook of Thomas Blue Eagle - Gay Matthaei   m 602

Obaasan (Grandmother; Cat)
Yoko's Paper Cranes - Rosemary Wells   p 939

Obadiah (Brother; Farmer)
Sorry - Jean Van Leeuwen   p, e 902

O'Brien, Sophie (Girlfriend)
The Black Book (Diary of a Teenage Stud) Series - Jonah Black   h 79

O'Brien, Terrence "O.B." (12-Year-Old)
Till Tomorrow - John Donahue   m 240

O'Carr, Alex (Twin; Child)
The Hungry Year - Connie Brummel Crook   m 195

O'Carr, Kate (12-Year-Old)
The Hungry Year - Connie Brummel Crook   m 195

O'Carr, Ryan (Twin; Child)
The Hungry Year - Connie Brummel Crook   m 195

Ocean (Friend)
The Day Ocean Came to Visit - Diane Wolkstein   p 981

O'Connor, Kathleen (Mother)
Murphy's Law - Rhys Bowen   a 96

Octon, Henni (12-Year-Old)
Fiddleback - Elizabeth Honey   m 414

O'Dell, Sean (Mythical Creature)
Harp O' Gold - Teresa Bateman   p, e 60

O'Donnell, Hugh Roe "Red Hugh" (Teenager; Captive)
Red Hugh: The Kidnap of Hugh O'Donnell - Deborah Lisson   m, h 561

Odysseus (13-Year-Old; Royalty)
Odysseus in the Serpent Maze - Jane Yolen   m 997

Officer Bunny (Rabbit; Lawman)
Irving and Muktuk: Two Bad Bears - Daniel Pinkwater   p 717

Officer Pikche (Police Officer)
Benno's Bear - N.F. Zucker   m 1007

O'Flannery, Megan (Scientist)
The Phoenix Code - Catherine Asaro   h, a 23

Ogden (Storyteller; Father)
Rowan and the Travelers - Emily Rodda   e 759

Ogre (Monster; Shape-changer)
Puss in Boots: The Adventures of That Most Enterprising Feline - Philip Pullman   p, e 728

Ojiisan (Grandfather; Cat)
Yoko's Paper Cranes - Rosemary Wells   p 939

Old Badger (Badger)
Little Badger, Terror of the Seven Seas - Eve Bunting   p 120

Olga (Pig)
Minnie and Moo Meet Frankenswine - Denys Cazet   b 150

Olivares, Trino (13-Year-Old)
Trino's Time - Diane Gonzales Bertrand   m 70

Oliver (13-Year-Old; Boyfriend)
Oh Boy, Amelia! - Marissa Moss   e 654

Oliver (Child; Nephew)
Oliver's Milk Shake - Vivian French   p 302

Olivia (Pig; Sister)
Olivia Saves the Circus - Ian Falconer   p 282

Olivia (Sister; Narrator)
Super-Completely and Totally the Messiest - Judith Viorst   p, e 913

Ollenik, Rudi (Resistance Fighter)
Brothers in Valor: A Story of Resistance - Michael O. Tunnell   m, h 890

Olsen, Christian (Drug Dealer)
The Foreigner - Meg Castaldo   a 147

Olsen, Roy (Miner)
Gold Rush Fever: A Story of the Klondike, 1898 - Barbara Greenwood   m 347

Olsen, Tim (Miner)
Gold Rush Fever: A Story of the Klondike, 1898 - Barbara Greenwood   m 347

Olson, Jo (Spouse)
Hank's Story - Jane Buchanan   e 113

Oma (Grandmother; Traveler)
Jimmy Dabble - Frans Vischer   e 914

O'Malley (Crime Victim)
Murphy's Law - Rhys Bowen   a 96

O'Malley, Theodore Roosevelt Bullmoose (Teenager)
Proud and Angry Dust - Kathryn Mitchell   a 644

Omar Ben Ali (Orphan)
Benny and Omar - Eoin Colfer   m 175

O'Neal, James (Musician; Postal Worker)
Welcome to the Great Mysterious - Lorna Landvik   a 531

Opal (Student—Elementary School; Friend)
Shrinking Violet - Cari Best   p, e 71

Ordway, Bennet (6th Grader; Inventor)
Deep Doo-Doo and the Mysterious E-Mail - Michael Delaney   e 224

O'Reilly, Ernestine (Mail Order Bride; Cowboy)
A Cowboy Named Ernestine - Nicole Rubel   p 771

Orflandu, Zircus "Zirc" (Time Traveler)
Quiet! You're Invisible - Margaret Meacham   e 629

Orlando, Alexandra Rockangela "Alex" (Saleswoman; Niece)
The Foreigner - Meg Castaldo   a 147

Orlando, Anthony Carmine (Uncle)
The Foreigner - Meg Castaldo   a 147

Orr, Stephen (13-Year-Old)
The Gadget - Paul Zindel   m, h 1003

Ortega, Felipe (Orphan)
Stolen by the Sea - Anna Myers   m 662

Osborne/Granger, Jack/Zachary Colin (13-Year-Old)
Zach's Lie - Roland Smith   m 834

Oscar (Kindergartner; Friend)
The Boys Team - Amy Schwartz   p 802

Oscar (Dog)
Sit, Truman! - Dan Harper   p 374

Osi (Cat)
The Spy Wore Shades - Martha Freeman   e, m 301

Ostrom, Addie (Aunt; Writer)
Buddy Is a Stupid Name for a Girl - Willo Davis Roberts   e, m 753

O'Sullivan, Donna (Counselor)
Fiddleback - Elizabeth Honey   m 414

Tentintrotter, Birch (Chipmunk)
The Sands of Time - Michael Hoeye   *m, h*   406

Terence, Clarence (Angel)
Have a Nice Life Series - Scarlett Macdougal
   h   585

Teresa (18-Year-Old; Sister)
Delfino's Journey - Jo Harper   *m, h*   375

Terry (Dancer; Child)
Ballerina! - Peter Sis   *p*   826

Terry, Oscar (7th Grader)
Raising the Shades - Doug Wilhelm   *m*   958

Tess (Child; Student—Elementary School)
The Bus for Us - Suzanne Bloom   *p*   86

Tess (9-Year-Old; Cousin; Niece)
Summer Party - Cynthia Rylant   *e*   785

Tessa (Prehistoric Human)
The Eye of the Stone - Tom Birdseye   *e, m*   75

Texas Teeth (Cowboy)
A Cowboy Named Ernestine - Nicole Rubel   *p*   771

Thatch (Pirate; Sea Captain)
Robin Hook, Pirate Hunter! - Eric A. Kimmel   *p,*
   e   497

Thea (13-Year-Old)
Ancient Fire - Mark London Williams   *m*   964

Thomas (Warrior)
I Am Morgan Le Fay - Nancy Springer   *h*   846

Thomas (Child; Immigrant)
Tattered Sails - Verla Kay   *p*   480

Thomas, Mitchell (Friend)
The Land - Mildred D. Taylor   *m, h*   872

Thomas, Tina (Sister; 9-Year-Old)
Willimena and the Cookie Money - Valerie Wilson
   Wesley   *e*   942

Thomas, Willimena "Willie" (7-Year-Old; Sister)
Willimena and the Cookie Money - Valerie Wilson
   Wesley   *e*   942

Thompson, David "Davie" (Military Personnel)
Gwyneth's Secret Grandpa - Annie Morris Williams
   e   961

Thompson, Gwyneth Bryn "Gwynnie" (12-Year-
   Old)
Gwyneth's Secret Grandpa - Annie Morris Williams
   e   961

Thompson, Mendy Anna (12-Year-Old)
Circle of Fire - Evelyn Coleman   *m*   172

Thorp, April (16-Year-Old; Patient)
The Year of My Indian Prince - Ella Thorp Ellis   *m,*
   h   275

Throbber, Nigel (Musician)
Expiration Date: Never - Stephanie Spinner   *e*   844

Thulani (16-Year-Old)
Every Time a Rainbow Dies - Rita Williams-Garcia
   h   966

Thurston, Frosty Jack (Prospector)
Destination Gold! - Julie Lawson   *m, h*   538

Thyme Penelope (Student—College)
Wurst Case Scenario - Catherine Clark   *h*   164

Tia Lola (Aunt)
How Tia Lola Came to Visit/Stay - Julia Alvarez   *e,*
   m   15

Tibby (15-Year-Old; Clerk)
The Sisterhood of the Traveling Pants - Ann Brashares
   m, h   99

Tiernan, Brick (Runaway)
All the Way Home - Patricia Reilly Giff   *e*   330

Tiger (Animal)
The Tiger Rising - Kate DiCamillo   *m*   231

Tilja (Daughter)
The Ropemaker - Peter Dickinson   *m, h*   232

Tillie (Student—Elementary School; Sister)
A Fine, Fine School - Sharon Creech   *p*   191

Tim (Child; Student—Elementary School)
Circus Girl - Tomek Bogacki   *p*   90

Tim (Friend)
Hole in the Sky - Pete Hautman   *m, h*   383

Tim (Child; Son)
Welcome to Kindergarten - Anne Rockwell   *p*   758

Timothy (Raccoon; Kindergartner)
Mama, Don't Go! - Rosemary Wells   *b*   937

Toby (Son; Animal)
Toby, What Are You? - William Steig   *p*   852

Todd, Mary McQuinn "Quinney" (6th Grader; 12-
   Year-Old)
Bad Girl Blues - Sally Warner   *m*   925

Tolliver, Clara (Mother)
Wishes, Kisses, and Pigs - Betsy Gould Hearne
   e   386

Tolliver, Louise (11-Year-Old)
Wishes, Kisses, and Pigs - Betsy Gould Hearne
   e   386

Tolliver, Willie (Brother)
Wishes, Kisses, and Pigs - Betsy Gould Hearne
   e   386

Tom (Minstrel)
Harp O' Gold - Teresa Bateman   *p, e*   60

Tom (6-Year-Old; Brother)
Stop, Drop, and Roll - Margery Cuyler   *p*   202

Tomas (Uncle; Immigrant)
Uncle Rain Cloud - Tony Johnston   *p*   466

Tomas, Mikulase "Mikul" (Orphan)
Rivka's Way - Teri Kanefield   *m*   476

Tommy (Child; Student—Elementary School)
Bus Stop, Bus Go! - Daniel Kirk   *p*   507

Tommy (6th Grader)
A Day for Vincent Chin and Me - Jacqueline Turner
   Banks   *e*   50

Toni (Friend; Cousin)
Toni's Topsy-Turvy Telephone Day - Laura Ljungkvist
   p   566

Tookis, Skeezie (7th Grader)
The Misfits - James Howe   *m*   428

Toot (Pig; Friend)
Toot & Puddle: I'll Be Home for Christmas - Holly
   Hobbie   *p*   402

Torgerson, Conrad (Handicapped)
Welcome to the Great Mysterious - Lorna Landvik
   a   531

Torgle, Eileen (Foster Parent)
Grover C. Graham and Me - Mary Quattlebaum   *e,*
   m   731

Tougas, Christian (11th Grader)
Lean Mean Machines - Michele Marineau   *m,*
   h   594

Tousle (Foster Child)
Straw into Gold - Gary D. Schmidt   *m*   800

Townley, Willard (Art Dealer; Con Artist)
A Lovely Illusion - Tessa Barclay   *a*   54

Trager, Mark (Father; Diver)
Tender - Valerie Hobbs   *h*   403

Trager, Olivia "Liv" (15-Year-Old)
Tender - Valerie Hobbs   *h*   403

Tree-Ear (Orphan; Apprentice)
A Single Shard - Linda Sue Park   *m*   696

Trescott, Matilda "Matty" (12-Year-Old)
Blue Creek Farm: A Matty Trescott Novel - Carroll
   Thomas   *m*   878

Tresevant, Parker Bucyrus (Military Personnel)
Fire on the Waters - David Poyer   *a*   722

Triblue's Spitfire "Piper" (Dog)
Piper - Natale Ghent   *m*   328

'Tricia Ann (Child)
Goin' Someplace Special - Patricia C. McKissack   *p,*
   e   625

Tricky Fox (Fox; Trickster)
The Tale of Tricky Fox: A New England Trickster Tale
   - Jim Aylesworth   *p*   39

Trowbridge, Doris "Weird Doris" (Antiques
   Dealer)
Rat Boys: A Dating Experiment - Thom Eberhardt
   m   258

Truman (Dog)
Sit, Truman! - Dan Harper   *p*   374

Tu Thi (Baby; Adoptee)
Heart of Mine: A Story of Adoption - Lotta Hojer
   p   408

Tucker, Charlotte (Child)
On Tide Mill Lane - Melissa Wiley   *e*   957

Tucker, Paul (12-Year-Old)
The Broken Places - Susan Perabo   *a*   707

Tucker, Rowan (14-Year-Old)
In the House of the Queen's Beasts - Jean Thesman
   m   876

Tucker, Sonny (Fire Fighter)
The Broken Places - Susan Perabo   *a*   707

Tudor, Mary (Royalty; Historical Figure)
Beware, Princess Elizabeth - Carolyn Meyer
   m   634

Tulip (Bird; Friend)
Toot & Puddle: I'll Be Home for Christmas - Holly
   Hobbie   *p*   402

Tumble (Elephant)
Squeak's Good Idea - Max Eilenberg   *p*   268

Turley, Lemm (Alcoholic; 13-Year-Old)
Shayla's Double Brown Baby Blues - Lori Aurelia
   Williams   *m, h*   963

Turner, Edward "Ned" (16-Year-Old; Prospector)
Destination Gold! - Julie Lawson   *m, h*   538

Turner, Jed (Student—High School; Motorcyclist)
Labyrinth - John Herman   *m, h*   388

Turner, Sarah (12-Year-Old; Sister)
Destination Gold! - Julie Lawson   *m, h*   538

Tuway (Assistant)
Out of the Night That Covers Me: A Novel - Pat
   Cunningham Devoto   *a*   229

Two Feathers, Rinnah (13-Year-Old; Indian)
The Secret of Dead Man's Mine - Rodney Johnson
   m   460

Tykell (Dog)
Rowan Hood: Outlaw Girl of Sherwood Forest -
   Nancy Springer   *e, m*   847

Tyle, Rhett (Wealthy; Businessman)
Trial by Jury/Journal - Kate Klise   *m*   514

U

Umae (Entertainer)
The Demon in the Teahouse - Dorothy Hoobler
   m   416

Wolfe, Ruben (Boxer; Brother)
Fighting Ruben Wolfe - Markus Zusak   *m, h*   1008

Wong (Brother; Immigrant)
Coolies - Yin   *p, e*   996

Wood, Adrien (15-Year-Old; Counselor)
Before Wings - Beth Goobie   *m, h*   340

Wood, Erin (Aunt; Administrator)
Before Wings - Beth Goobie   *m, h*   340

Woodpecker (Woodpecker; Friend)
Batbaby Finds a Home - Robert Quackenbush
    b   730

Woodward, Paul (Hockey Player)
Finnie Walsh - Steven Galloway   *a*   309

Woodward, Robert (Father; Amputee)
Finnie Walsh - Steven Galloway   *a*   309

Wrenn, Erin (6th Grader)
Saving Lilly - Peg Kehret   *e*   483

Wright, Jan (12-Year-Old)
One Unhappy Horse - C.S. Adler   *m*   4

Wright, Keisha (14-Year-Old; Swimmer)
Born in Sin - Evelyn Coleman   *h*   171

Wright, Lynn (17-Year-Old; 12th Grader)
Love Rules - Marilyn Reynolds   *h*   743

Wright, Richard (Scientist)
Passage - Connie Willis   *h, a*   967

Wu, Lily (6th Grader)
6-321 - Michael Laser   *m*   533

X

Xanthe (Sister; Nurse)
Troy - Adele Geras   *h, a*   327

Y

Yagharek (Alien; Criminal)
Perdido Street Station - China Mieville   *h, a*   637

Yann (Witch)
The Merlin of the Oak Woods - Ann Chamberlin   *h, a*   151

Yaya (Grandmother; Singer)
My Grandmother Is a Singing Yaya - Karen Scourby D'Arc   *p*   212

Yelena the Fair (Maiden)
The Golden Mare, the Firebird, and the Magic Ring - Ruth Sanderson   *p, e*   792

Ygnacio (Religious)
Valley of the Moon: The Diary of Maria Rosalia De Milagros, Sonoma Valley, Alta California, 1846 - Sherry Garland   *m*   317

Yoko (Cat; Kindergartner)
Mama, Don't Go! - Rosemary Wells   *b*   937

Yoko (Child; Daughter)
Yoko's Paper Cranes - Rosemary Wells   *p*   939

Young, Florida Louisa "Ida Lou" (Teenager; Entertainer)
Ida Lou's Story - Susan E. Kirby   *e*   506

Ysa (Crime Victim; Student—College)
Every Time a Rainbow Dies - Rita Williams-Garcia   *h*   966

Z

Zalinski, Dov (13-Year-Old)
Brother Enemy - Robert Elmer   *m*   277

Zalinski, Natan (Brother; Resistance Fighter)
Brother Enemy - Robert Elmer   *m*   277

Zazoo (Orphan; 13-Year-Old)
Zazoo: A Novel - Richard Mosher   *m, h*   653

Zeel (Adoptee; Daughter)
Rowan and the Travelers - Emily Rodda   *e*   759

Zeke (Dog)
Mr. Putter & Tabby Feed the Fish - Cynthia Rylant   *b*   783

Ziller, Mahrai (Musician; Alien)
Look to Windward - Iain Banks   *h, a*   49

Zimmerman, Florence (Witch)
The Tower at the End of the World - Brad Strickland   *m*   862

Zoey (3rd Grader; Classmate)
Butterfly Buddies - Judy Cox   *e*   190

Zoom (Dog)
Mrs. McTats and Her Houseful of Cats - Alyssa Satin Capucilli   *p*   137

Zuckerman, Jerry (Musician; Clown)
My Guy - Sarah Weeks   *e, m*   933

Zuckerman, Lana (13-Year-Old)
My Guy - Sarah Weeks   *e, m*   933

Zwake, Finnegan (13-Year-Old; Detective—Amateur)
The Viking Claw - Michael Dahl   *m*   204

Character Name Index

Character Description Index

This index alphabetically lists descriptions of the major characters in featured titles. The descriptions may be occupations (doctor, lawyer, etc.) or may describe persona (amnesiac, runaway, teenager, etc.). For each description, character names are listed alphabetically. Book titles, author names, age-level code(s) and entry numbers are also included. The age-level codes are as follows: *p* Preschool, *b* Beginning Reader, *e* Elementary School (Grades 2-5), *m* Middle School (Grades 5-8), *h* High School (Grades 9-12), and *a* Adult.

1-YEAR-OLD

Brenda "Bun Bun"
Bun Bun's Birthday - Richard Scrimger   *p*   807

2-YEAR-OLD

Anderson, Ellie
By Lizzie - Mary Eccles   *e*   259

Flop
Flip and Flop - Dawn Apperley   *p*   17

3-YEAR-OLD

Daniels, Danny
What a Trip, Amber Brown - Paula Danziger   *e*   211

4-YEAR-OLD

Amy
Big Trouble in Little Twinsville - Elizabeth Levy   *e*   552

Bird, Billy
Billy the Bird - Dick King-Smith   *e*   502

Max
Emma's Yucky Brother - Jean Little   *b*   562

May
Big Trouble in Little Twinsville - Elizabeth Levy   *e*   552

Nichols, Michael
The Ghost and Mrs. Hobbs - Cynthia DeFelice   *e*, *m*   221

Witting, Cassie
Caleb's Story - Patricia MacLachlan   *e*, *m*   586

5-YEAR-OLD

Flip
Flip and Flop - Dawn Apperley   *p*   17

Jo-Jo
The Days of Summer - Eve Bunting   *p*   117

Marina
Gleam and Glow - Eve Bunting   *p*, *e*   118

Unnamed Character
Chanukah Lights Everywhere - Michael J. Rosen   *p*   767

6-YEAR-OLD

Joey
The Moon Robber - Dean Morrissey   *e*   650

Jones, Junie B.
Junie B. Jones Is a Graduation Girl - Barbara Park   *e*   695

Tom
Stop, Drop, and Roll - Margery Cuyler   *p*   202

7-YEAR-OLD

Bamford, Robert
Night of the Living Gerbil - Elizabeth Levy   *e*   553

Brown, Amber
It's Justin Time, Amber Brown - Paula Danziger   *e*   210

Daniels, Justin
It's Justin Time, Amber Brown - Paula Danziger   *e*   210

Guzman, Juanita
How Tia Lola Came to Visit/Stay - Julia Alvarez   *e*, *m*   15

Little Boy James
Grandpa Blows His Penny Whistle Until the Angels Sing - Susan L. Roth   *p*, *e*   769

Little Catalina
Mice and Beans - Pam Munoz Ryan   *p*   776

Louise
Maxwell's Magic Mix-Up - Linda Ashman   *p*   27

Mabel
Night of the Living Gerbil - Elizabeth Levy   *e*   553

Pinky
Pinky and Rex and the Just-Right Pet - James Howe   *b*, *e*   429

Sam
Happy Birthday Mr. Kang - Susan L. Roth   *p*, *e*   770

Thomas, Willimena "Willie"
Willimena and the Cookie Money - Valerie Wilson Wesley   *e*   942

Unnamed Character
A Ladder to the Stars - Simon Puttock   *p*, *e*   729

Washington, Amber
Willimena and the Cookie Money - Valerie Wilson Wesley   *e*   942

8-YEAR-OLD

Bird, Mary
Billy the Bird - Dick King-Smith   *e*   502

Fletcher, Winifred "Winnie"
Winnie Dancing on Her Own - Jennifer Richard Jacobson   *e*   445

Hannah
Hannah's Bookmobile Christmas - Sally Derby   *p*, *e*   226

Johnson, Zoe
Winnie Dancing on Her Own - Jennifer Richard Jacobson   *e*   445

Penelope
Lady Lollipop - Dick King-Smith   *e*   503

Viktor
Gleam and Glow - Eve Bunting   *p*, *e*   118

Wiley, Vanessa
Winnie Dancing on Her Own - Jennifer Richard Jacobson   *e*   445

9-YEAR-OLD

Anderson, Elizabeth "Lizzie"
By Lizzie - Mary Eccles   *e*   259

Bamford, Sam
Night of the Living Gerbil - Elizabeth Levy   *e*   553

Barker, Caleb
The Starving Time: Elizabeth's Diary - Patricia Hermes   *e*   389

Barker, Elizabeth "Lizzie"
The Starving Time: Elizabeth's Diary - Patricia Hermes   *e*   389

Beatrice
Beatrice's Goat - Page McBrier   *p*   608

Bidson, Noah
Prairie School - Avi   *b*, *e*   37

Birdsong, Corey
Freedom's Wings: Corey's Diary - Sharon Dennis Wyeth   *e*, *m*   988

Gaskitt, Gloria
The Man Who Wore All His Clothes - Allan Ahlberg   *e*   9

Gaskitt, Gus
The Man Who Wore All His Clothes - Allan Ahlberg   *e*   9

Ishee, Dove
Love, Ruby Lavender - Deborah Wiles *e, m* 956

Jones, Ebon
Dad, in Spirit - A. LaFaye *e, m* 527

Lavender, Ruby
Love, Ruby Lavender - Deborah Wiles *e, m* 956

Lily
Summer Party - Cynthia Rylant *e* 785

McCullough, Joshua Martin
Westward to Home: Joshua's Diary - Patricia Hermes *e* 390

Potter, Hope Penny
Five Smooth Stones: Hope's Diary - Kristiana Gregory *e* 348

Rabin, Rivka
Rivka's First Thanksgiving - Elsa Okon Rael *p, e* 733

Rind, Maria
Maria's Story: 1773 - Joan Lowery Nixon *e, m* 678

Rosie
Summer Party - Cynthia Rylant *e* 785

Rowanna "Anna"
Tree Girl - T.A. Barron *e, m* 55

Sherwood, Anna
Anna on the Farm - Mary Downing Hahn *e* 369

Tess
Summer Party - Cynthia Rylant *e* 785

Thomas, Tina
Willimena and the Cookie Money - Valerie Wilson Wesley *e* 942

White, Rivers
Uncle Daddy - Ralph Fletcher *e, m* 293

10-YEAR-OLD

Andy
A Castle on Viola Street - DyAnne DiSalvo *p* 236

Beaker, Tracy
The Story of Tracy Beaker - Jacqueline Wilson *e, m* 971

Bundkin, Claire
Witch Twins - Adele Griffin *e* 351

Bundkin, Luna
Witch Twins - Adele Griffin *e* 351

Carly
Waiting to Dive - Karen Rivers *e, m* 750

Danny
Riding the Tiger - Eve Bunting *e* 121

Eve
Big Trouble in Little Twinsville - Elizabeth Levy *e* 552

Hampton, Rosemary Rita
Rosemary Meets Rosemarie - Barbara Robertson *e, m* 754

Hart, Lucky
Skyrockets and Snickerdoodles: A Cobtown Story from the Diaries of Lucky Hart - Julia Van Nutt *e* 903

Michael
The Moon Robber - Dean Morrissey *e* 650

Reed, Alyssa "Blister"
Blister - Susan Shreve *e, m* 819

Sarah
The Moon Robber - Dean Morrissey *e* 650

Susie
The Ghost Sitter - Peni R. Griffin *e, m* 353

White, Mandy
Bad Girls - Jacqueline Wilson *e, m* 970

Wizzle, Roscoe
The Transmogrification of Roscoe Wizzle - David Elliott *e* 272

11-YEAR-OLD

Adrian, Jason
The Magickers - Emily Drake *m* 248

Alcott, Louisa May
Becoming Little Women: Louisa May at Fruitlands - Jeannine Atkins *e, m* 28

Benno
Benno's Bear - N.F. Zucker *m* 1007

Bryant, Evander "Evan"
A Sailor Returns - Theodore Taylor *e* 873

Calhoun, Maggie
Maggie in the Morning - Elizabeth Van Steenwyk *e* 904

Carter, Mercy "Munnonock"
The Ransom of Mercy Carter - Caroline B. Cooney *m* 181

Chambers, Abigail "Abbie"
Stopping to Home - Lea Wait *e* 917

David
The Gawgon and the Boy - Lloyd Alexander *m* 11

Dearborn, Charlotte
Groover's Heart - Carole Crowe *e* 197

Delgado, Angelica
Secrets in the House of Delgado - Gloria D. Miklowitz *m, h* 639

Dill, Nicholas "Nickel"
The Beastly Arms - Patrick Jennings *m* 453

Dugolli, Zana
Girl of Kosovo - Alice Mead *m, h* 630

Floyd, Ned
In Ned's Head - Soren Olsson *e* 687

Gates, Russell "Rusty"
Mystery from History - Dayle Campbell Gaetz *e, m* 307

Gittleman, Robyn
Stolen Words - Amy Goldman Koss *m* 518

Gordon, Ricky
Racing the Past - Sis Deans *m* 220

Haig-Ereildoun, Prudence "Pru"
Do Try to Speak as We Do: The Diary of an American Au Pair - Marjorie Leet Ford *a* 297

Halston, William
The Summer of Riley - Eve Bunting *e* 122

Jenkins, Celli
Black Angels - Rita Murphy *m* 658

Jensen, Buddy
A Sailor Returns - Theodore Taylor *e* 873

Lambert, Jaynell
Dancing in Cadillac Light - Kimberly Willis Holt *m* 411

Lilly
Marco's Millions - William Sleator *m* 829

Lupe
Tiger's Fall - Molly Bang *e* 48

McPhee/McGee, Elsie/Linda Clay "L.C."
Clay - Colby Rodowsky *m* 761

Miller, Ivy
Sister Split - Sally Warner *e* 928

Minners, Dougie
The Spy Wore Shades - Martha Freeman *e, m* 301

Moonpie
Moonpie and Ivy - Barbara O'Connor *m* 683

Nichols, Allie
The Ghost and Mrs. Hobbs - Cynthia DeFelice *e, m* 221

Parvana
The Breadwinner - Deborah Ellis *m* 274

Philips, Wesley
Piper - Natale Ghent *m* 328

Prentice, Etta
Through the Lock - Carol Otis Hurst *m* 438

Robin
Secret in St. Something - Barbara Brooks Wallace *m* 919

Samuels, Rose
Rose's Journal: The Story of a Girl in the Great Depression - Marissa Moss *e* 655

Seldomridge, Danny
Private Captain: A Novel of Gettysburg - Marty Crisp *m* 194

Singer, Junie Mae
Empire Dreams - Wendy Wax *e* 930

Skinner, Melanie "Skinny Melon"
Skinny Melon and Me - Jean Ure *m* 894

Squarp, Primrose
Everything on a Waffle - Polly Horvath *m* 422

Tolliver, Louise
Wishes, Kisses, and Pigs - Betsy Gould Hearne *e* 386

Unnamed Boy
The Great Whale of Kansas - Richard W. Jennings *m* 454

Waterton, Cherry Louise
Skinny Melon and Me - Jean Ure *m* 894

Watson, Ben
Grover C. Graham and Me - Mary Quattlebaum *e, m* 731

Wilson, Susan
Little Women Next Door - Sheila Solomon Klass *e, m* 511

12-YEAR-OLD

Aldrich, Esther
The 1940s: Secrets - Dorothy Hoobler *e* 415

Alexandra
One Puppy, Three Tales - Karen Salmansohn *e* 789

Anderson, Norman
By Lizzie - Mary Eccles *e* 259

Bartoletti, Emma
Franklin Delano Roosevelt: Letters from a Mill Town Girl - Elizabeth Winthrop *m* 977

Bell, Dinah
Missing from Haymarket Square - Harriette Gillem Robinet *m* 755

Brennan, Kelley Anne
A Face First - Priscilla Cummings *m* 201

Brian
The Comic Book Kid - Adam Osterweil *e* 692

Bruce, Orphelia
The Minstrel's Melody - Eleanora E. Tate *e, m* 867

Calabro, Giuseppe "Joey"
A Place for Joey - Carol Flynn Harris *e, m* 378

Carey, Chipper
Chipper - James Lincoln Collier *m* 176

13-YEAR-OLD

Mori, Davi
A Boy at War: A Novel of Pearl Harbor - Harry Mazer   *m*   605

Nicolson, Georgia
On the Bright Side, I'm Now the Girlfriend of a Sex God: Further Confessions of Georgia Nicolson - Louise Rennison   *m, h*   742

Pati
Panther - Martin Booth   *e*   92

Pelko, Adam
A Boy at War: A Novel of Pearl Harbor - Harry Mazer   *m*   605

Price, Sarah Jane
My Face to the Wind: The Diary of Sarah Jane Price, a Prairie Teacher, Broken Bow, Nebraska, 1881 - Jim Murphy   *m*   656

Quade, Agatha Jane "Aggie"
In Spite of Killer Bees - Julie Johnston   *m, h*   462

Renaldo, Amelia "Mia"
Princess in the Spotlight - Meg Cabot   *m, h*   131

Richards, Jenna
When Dad Killed Mom - Julius Lester   *h*   549

Rider, Alex
Stormbreaker - Anthony Horowitz   *m*   420

Rosario, Magdalena
Quinceanera Means Sweet 15 - Veronica Chambers   *m*   152

Samuels, Floyd
Rose's Journal: The Story of a Girl in the Great Depression - Marissa Moss   *e*   655

Sasse, Will
Horse Sense - Jan Neubert Schultz   *e, m*   801

Severna, Doreen
Brave New Girl - Louisa Luna   *h*   576

Shepherd, Emily
In the House of the Queen's Beasts - Jean Thesman   *m*   876

Simon "Si"
Panther - Martin Booth   *e*   92

Taylor, Ruth "Ruthie"
The Stones of Mourning Creek - Diane Les Becquets   *m, h*   546

Ted
Brave New Girl - Louisa Luna   *h*   576

Tucker, Rowan
In the House of the Queen's Beasts - Jean Thesman   *m*   876

Weingarten, Summer
Rat Boys: A Dating Experiment - Thom Eberhardt   *m*   258

Wells, Harriet Lucretia "Hallie Lou"
Get Along, Little Dogies: The Chisholm Trail Diary of Hallie Lou Wells: South Texas, 1878 - Lisa Waller Rogers   *m*   762

Whitehall, Jeffrey
Circle of Fire - Evelyn Coleman   *m*   172

Wright, Keisha
Born in Sin - Evelyn Coleman   *h*   171

15-YEAR-OLD

Alison "Ali"
Lord of the Deep - Graham Salisbury   *m*   788

Baker, Kenyon "Ken"
Razzle - Ellen Wittlinger   *h*   978

Bannister, Lorenzo
Lorenzo's Secret Mission - Lila Guzman   *m*   362

Bolinski, Marisia
Streets of Gold - Marie Raphael   *m, h*   735

Bonifacio, Lorenzo
In the Shadow of the Alamo - Sherry Garland   *m*   316

Clarry, Elizabeth
Feeling Sorry for Celia - Jaclyn Moriarty   *h*   648

Daniel, Daria
Slap Your Sides - M.E. Kerr   *m, h*   489

Deeds, Douglas Allen
The Journal of Douglas Allen Deeds, The Donner Party Expedition, 1846 - Rodman Philbrick   *m*   710

Dunavant, Jamie
Down the Yukon - Will Hobbs   *m, h*   404

Finkelstein, Precious
The Autobiography of Meatball Finkelstein - Ross Venokur   *e, m*   912

Flurp, Philip "Flurp the Town Fool"
Monsieur Eek - David Ives   *m*   443

Hedrick, Dietrich "Dieter"
Soldier Boys - Dean Hughes   *m, h*   434

Iris
Stranger in Dadland - Amy Goldman Koss   *e, m*   519

Kaligaris, Lena
The Sisterhood of the Traveling Pants - Ann Brashares   *m, h*   99

Keely, Kate
A Sea So Far - Jean Thesman   *m, h*   877

LaVaughn, Verna
True Believer - Virginia Euwer Wolff   *m, h*   980

Lawson, Charles Frederick "Chuck"
Takeoffs and Landings - Margaret Peterson Haddix   *m*   367

Lefkowitz, Jake
Night of the Bat - Paul Zindel   *m*   1004

Lesmarais, William
Three Days Off - Susie Morgenstern   *m, h*   647

Liebermann, Rivka
Rivka's Way - Teri Kanefield   *m*   476

Lowell, Carmen Lucille
The Sisterhood of the Traveling Pants - Ann Brashares   *m, h*   99

Lynch, Gabriel
Gabriel's Story - David Anthony Durham   *h, a*   255

Marchand, Paul
Before Wings - Beth Goobie   *m, h*   340

Mason, Deenie
Scorpio's Child - Kezi Matthews   *m*   603

Matthews, Cole
Touching Spirit Bear - Ben Mikaelsen   *m, h*   638

McCully, Eliza Jane
Walk Across the Sea - Susan Fletcher   *m*   294

Mehta, Tara
A Group of One - Rachna Gilmore   *m, h*   332

Miller, Lacey
Sister Split - Sally Warner   *e*   928

Moon, Otis
A Piece of Heaven - Sharon Dennis Wyeth   *m*   989

Murdoch, Callum
The Carved Box - Gillian Chan   *m*   154

Palmer, Kady
Rooster - Beth Nixon Weaver   *m, h*   931

Palmer, Maddie
The Memory Prisoner - Thomas Bloor   *m*   87

Paloma Maria "Dovey Mae"
Get Along, Little Dogies: The Chisholm Trail Diary of Hallie Lou Wells: South Texas, 1878 - Lisa Waller Rogers   *m*   762

Peterson, Chloe
The Courage to Live - Deborah Kent   *m, h*   488

Raskin, Alexander
Ghost Soldier - Elaine Marie Alphin   *m*   13

Raven
Raven's Flight - Diane Silvey   *m, h*   822

Shackleford, Paul
A Hole in the World - Sid Hite   *m*   401

Sheridan, Wakara Windsong "Kara"
Blind Fury - Linda Shands   *m*   815

Shoemaker, Jubal
Slap Your Sides - M.E. Kerr   *m, h*   489

Sophie
What My Mother Doesn't Know - Sonya Sones   *m, h*   839

Tibby
The Sisterhood of the Traveling Pants - Ann Brashares   *m, h*   99

Trager, Olivia "Liv"
Tender - Valerie Hobbs   *h*   403

Vreeland, Bridget
The Sisterhood of the Traveling Pants - Ann Brashares   *m, h*   99

Wood, Adrien
Before Wings - Beth Goobie   *m, h*   340

16-YEAR-OLD

Andreas, Nicholas "Nick"
Breathing Underwater - Alex Flinn   *h*   295

Bennett, Rachel
Last Summer in Agatha - Katherine Holubitsky   *m*   413

Bindart, Cricket
Witches' Key to Terror - Silver RavenWolf   *h*   738

Bindart, Tad
Witches' Key to Terror - Silver RavenWolf   *h*   738

Brandt, Erik
Soldier X - Don Wulffson   *h*   987

Catherine
Destination Gold! - Julie Lawson   *m, h*   538

Colette "Coll"
Love Trilogy - Kate Cann   *h*   136

Cybulski, Sofia
Streets of Gold - Marie Raphael   *m, h*   735

Davies, Battle Hall
Empress of the World - Sara Ryan   *h*   777

Fairchild, Clara
Seeds of Hope: The Gold Rush Diary of Susanna Fairchild, California Territory, 1849 - Kristiana Gregory   *m*   349

Gnedich, Mikhail Sergeyevich "Misha"
Angel on the Square - Gloria Whelan   *m, h*   946

Haldran, Andrew
Focus - Sallie Lowenstein   *m, h*   574

Harley
Razzle - Ellen Wittlinger   *h*   978

Harrington, Dain
The Lobster War - Ethan Howland   *m, h*   430

Hawthorn, Jason
Down the Yukon - Will Hobbs   *m, h*   404

Hurt, Eva Mae
Brides of Eden - Linda Crew   *m, h*   193

17-YEAR-OLD

18-YEAR-OLD

19-YEAR-OLD

1ST GRADER

2ND GRADER

Daniels, Justin
What a Trip, Amber Brown - Paula Danziger
    e   211

Dorfman, Robert
Robert and the Great Pepperoni - Barbara Seuling
    e   811

James, Calliope
Zero Grandparents - Michelle Edwards   e   262

Smith, Howie
Zero Grandparents - Michelle Edwards   e   262

Vang, Pa Lia
Zero Grandparents - Michelle Edwards   e   262

3RD GRADER

Barr, Gordie
Third Grade Stinks! - Colleen O'Shaughnessy
McKenna   e   624

Buckner, Josh
I Was a Third Grade Spy - Mary Jane Auch   e   32

Burrell, Ida
Horrible Harry Goes to Sea - Suzy Kline   e   513

Carlos
Uncle Rain Cloud - Tony Johnston   p   466

Conner, Emily Joy
A Puppy of My Own - Wendy Loggia   e   567

Diaz, Lucy
Third Grade Stinks! - Colleen O'Shaughnessy
McKenna   e   624

Drake, Jake
Jake Drake, Know-It-All - Andrew Clements
    e   166

Hayes, Lamont
Third Grade Stinks! - Colleen O'Shaughnessy
McKenna   e   624

Hopkins, Kaia
A Puppy of My Own - Wendy Loggia   e   567

LaFleur, Sidney
Horrible Harry Goes to Sea - Suzy Kline   e   513

Lewis, Brian
I Was a Third Grade Spy - Mary Jane Auch   e   32

Lewis, Eddie
The Day Eddie Met the Author - Louise Borden
    e   93

Moody, Judy
Judy Moody Gets Famous - Megan McDonald
    e   618

Parker, Lauren
A Puppy of My Own - Wendy Loggia   e   567

Pearl, Frank
Judy Moody Gets Famous - Megan McDonald
    e   618

Robin
Butterfly Buddies - Judy Cox   e   190

Sams, Janie
The Girl with 500 Middle Names - Margaret Peterson
Haddix   e   366

Spooger, Harry
Horrible Harry Goes to Sea - Suzy Kline   e   513

Zoey
Butterfly Buddies - Judy Cox   e   190

4TH GRADER

Anderson, Tamika
Andy Russell, NOT Wanted by the Police - David A.
Adler   e   5

Catherwood, Noreen
*Captain Tweakerbeak's Revenge: A Calliope Day
Adventure* - Charles Haddad   e, m   364

Day, Calliope
*Captain Tweakerbeak's Revenge: A Calliope Day
Adventure* - Charles Haddad   e, m   364

Gecko, Chet
Farewell, My Lunchbag - Bruce Hale   e, m   370

Hatford, Wally
The Boys Return - Phyllis Reynolds Naylor   e,
m   673

Malloy, Caroline
The Boys Return - Phyllis Reynolds Naylor   e,
m   673

Nora
The Days of Summer - Eve Bunting   p   117

Russell, Andy
Andy Russell, NOT Wanted by the Police - David A.
Adler   e   5

5TH GRADER

Baker, Clarice
Belle Teal - Ann M. Martin   e, m   596

Charles
A Book of Coupons - Susie Morgenstern   e, m   646

Coleman, Duane "Denny"
Don't You Know There's a War On? - Avi   m   35

Craig, Darryl
Belle Teal - Ann M. Martin   e, m   596

Crispers, Howard Bellington "Howie"
Don't You Know There's a War On? - Avi   m   35

Doyle, Drake
The Case of the Gasping Garbage - Michele Torrey
    e   887

Fossey, Nell
The Case of the Gasping Garbage - Michele Torrey
    e   887

Harper, Belle Teal
Belle Teal - Ann M. Martin   e, m   596

Hobson, Hoby
Quiet! You're Invisible - Margaret Meacham
    e   629

Kar, Zenon "Zee"
Bobo Crazy - Marilyn Sadler   e   786

Keeperman, Sam
Understanding Buddy - Marc Kornblatt   e   516

Kohler, Alex
Understanding Buddy - Marc Kornblatt   e   516

Maxwell, Simon
No More Nasty - Amy MacDonald   e, m   583

Nebula "Neb"
Bobo Crazy - Marilyn Sadler   e   786

White, Buddy
Understanding Buddy - Marc Kornblatt   e   516

6TH GRADER

Adams, Amy Kate "Buddy"
Buddy Is a Stupid Name for a Girl - Willo Davis
Roberts   e, m   753

Anderson, Wynona
Mama's Way - Helen Ketteman   p, e   492

Bailey, Sistine
The Tiger Rising - Kate DiCamillo   m   231

Belinda
Don't Bug Me! - Pam Zollman   e   1006

Benson, Tony
The Boys Return - Phyllis Reynolds Naylor   e,
m   673

Bettencourt, Charlie
Don't Bug Me! - Pam Zollman   e   1006

Biggs, Kara
How to Be a Real Person (in Just One Day) - Sally
Warner   m   927

Brynn "Brynnie"
Bad Girl Blues - Sally Warner   m   925

Chaikin, Marc
6-321 - Michael Laser   m   533

Chip
My Brother, the Robot - Bonnie Becker   e   65

Connolly, Scott "Beamer"
The Mysterious Matter of I.M. Fine - Diane Stanley
    e   850

Cricklestein, Adam
Frankenbug - Steven Cousins   e, m   185

Emerson, Harrison
Notes from a Liar and Her Dog - Gennifer Choldenko
    m   162

Franny
The Mysterious Matter of I.M. Fine - Diane Stanley
    e   850

Harper, Marguerite
Bad Girl Blues - Sally Warner   m   925

Hollander, Megan
Don't Bug Me! - Pam Zollman   e   1006

Horton, Robert "Rob"
The Tiger Rising - Kate DiCamillo   m   231

Inez
The Beastly Arms - Patrick Jennings   m   453

Jenkins, Judge
A Day for Vincent Chin and Me - Jacqueline Turner
Banks   e   50

Jenkins, Jury
A Day for Vincent Chin and Me - Jacqueline Turner
Banks   e   50

Keet, Perry
Trial by Jury/Journal - Kate Klise   m   514

Knapp, Augie
The Gypsies Never Came - Stephen Roos   m   763

LeClerc, Therese "Tessy"
The Hero of Ticonderoga - Gail Gauthier   m   320

MacPherson, Antonia Jane "Ant"
Notes from a Liar and Her Dog - Gennifer Choldenko
    m   162

McCallister, Jeb
Frankenbug - Steven Cousins   e, m   185

McCarthy, Bugsie
Racing the Past - Sis Deans   m   220

Meisenheimer, Lydie Rose
The Gypsies Never Came - Stephen Roos   m   763

Meredith, Hallie
Spyhole Secrets - Zilpha Keatley Snyder   e, m   837

Miller, Stephanie
How to Be a Real Person (in Just One Day) - Sally
Warner   m   927

Nelson, Nadia
In Ned's Head - Soren Olsson   e   687

Nicholas "Nugget"
In Ned's Head - Soren Olsson   e   687

Nickowsky, Pete
Deep Doo-Doo and the Mysterious E-Mail - Michael
Delaney   e   224

Carillo, Jason
Rainbow Boys - Alex Sanchez   *h*   791

Conan
Love Rules - Marilyn Reynolds   *h*   743

Crutchfield, Bram
Scribbler of Dreams - Mary E. Pearson   *m, h*   703

Dandridge, Katherine "Kit"
Love Rules - Marilyn Reynolds   *h*   743

Dawes, Olivia
Have a Nice Life Series - Scarlett Macdougal   *h*   585

Dennison, Theo
Of Sound Mind - Jean Ferris   *m, h*   286

Draper, Jon
Love, Sara - Mary Beth Lundgren   *m, h*   577

Flanders, Adam
The Intimacy of Indiana - Susan Finch   *h*   287

Glassman, Nelson "Nelly"
Rainbow Boys - Alex Sanchez   *h*   791

Gonzales, Ellie
The Million Dollar Kick - Dan Gutman   *m*   360

Hamilton, Jon
Rooster - Beth Nixon Weaver   *m, h*   931

Hightower, Curtis
Damage - A.M. Jenkins   *h*   451

Jones, The Tao "T.J."
Whale Talk - Chris Crutcher   *h*   199

Macka, Jake
To Live Again - Lurlene McDaniel   *m*   614

Mackenzie, Heather
Damage - A.M. Jenkins   *h*   451

Malone, Kaitlin "Kait"
Scribbler of Dreams - Mary E. Pearson   *m, h*   703

McCafferty, Devin
Shades of Simon Gray - Joyce McDonald   *m, h*   617

Meeks, Kyle
Rainbow Boys - Alex Sanchez   *h*   791

Mitchell, Zola
Have a Nice Life Series - Scarlett Macdougal   *h*   585

Montgomery, Keisha
Darkness Before Dawn - Sharon M. Draper   *h*   249

Radkovitz, Robert A. "Rob"
Seek - Paul Fleischman   *m, h*   290

Reid, Austin
Damage - A.M. Jenkins   *h*   451

Rhonda
To Live Again - Lurlene McDaniel   *m*   614

Rochelle, Dawn
To Live Again - Lurlene McDaniel   *m*   614

Roper, Ivy
Of Sound Mind - Jean Ferris   *m, h*   286

Rycerson, Olivia
The Intimacy of Indiana - Susan Finch   *h*   287

Stephens, Neil A.
The Intimacy of Indiana - Susan Finch   *h*   287

Swensen, Joshua/Larry "Josh"
The Gospel According to Larry - Janet Tashjian   *h*   866

Weinstock, Wilamina "Min"
Have a Nice Life Series - Scarlett Macdougal   *h*   585

Wilder, Sally
Have a Nice Life Series - Scarlett Macdougal   *h*   585

Wilkins, Rob
When Lightning Strikes - Jenny Carroll   *m, h*   142

Wright, Lynn
Love Rules - Marilyn Reynolds   *h*   743

AARDVARK

Read, Arthur
D.W.'s Library Card - Marc Brown   *p*   103

Read, Dora Winifred "D.W."
D.W.'s Library Card - Marc Brown   *p*   103

ABANDONED CHILD

English, Janie "Leshaya"
Born Blue - Han Nolan   *h*   681

ABUSE VICTIM

Greg
One of the Problems of Everett Anderson - Lucille Clifton   *p*   168

Irwin, Jesse
Charlotte's Choice - Cathleen Twomey   *m*   892

Major, Kambia Elaine
Shayla's Double Brown Baby Blues - Lori Aurelia Williams   *m, h*   963

McCourt, Caitlin Alyssa
Breathing Underwater - Alex Flinn   *h*   295

ACCOUNTANT

Macpherson, Duncan
Danger in Disguise - Mary Alice Downie   *m*   245

ACTIVIST

Bell, Noah
Missing from Haymarket Square - Harriette Gillem Robinet   *m*   755

Bott, Miracle
Up a Creek - Laura E. Williams   *m*   962

ACTOR

Eslingen, Philip
Point of Dreams - Melissa Scott   *h, a*   806

Holtz, Jacob "Jake"
A Dance for Emilia - Peter S. Beagle   *h, a*   63

Martinka, Charlie "Paw Paw"
Bo & Mzzz Mad - Sid Fleischman   *m*   291

Pyke, John
A Question of Will - Lynne Kositsky   *m*   517

Willoughby, Perin "Willow"
A Question of Will - Lynne Kositsky   *m*   517

ACTRESS

Dunavant, Jamie
Down the Yukon - Will Hobbs   *m, h*   404

Keyes/Windsor, Lana/Dominique
Sammy Keyes and the Hollywood Mummy - Wendelin Van Draanen   *m*   900

Papillon, Fawn
Trial by Jury/Journal - Kate Klise   *m*   514

ADDICT

Mama Linda
Born Blue - Han Nolan   *h*   681

Marcie
Raven's Flight - Diane Silvey   *m, h*   822

ADMINISTRATOR

Daniels, Robert
Lick Creek - Brad Kessler   *a*   490

Wood, Erin
Before Wings - Beth Goobie   *m, h*   340

ADOPTEE

Abbott, Vidalia "Viddy"
Extra Innings - Robert Newton Peck   *m*   705

David
Jin Woo - Eve Bunting   *p*   119

Jin Woo
Jin Woo - Eve Bunting   *p*   119

Manning, Mariel
All the Way Home - Patricia Reilly Giff   *e*   330

Max
Emma's Yucky Brother - Jean Little   *b*   562

Newton, Dulciana "Dulcie"
Love, Sara - Mary Beth Lundgren   *m, h*   577

Sheridan, Elizabeth "Turtle"
Tides - V.M. Caldwell   *m*   133

Tu Thi
Heart of Mine: A Story of Adoption - Lotta Hojer   *p*   408

Zeel
Rowan and the Travelers - Emily Rodda   *e*   759

ADVENTURER

Strong Jonn
Rowan of Rin - Emily Rodda   *e, m*   760

ADVISOR

Conroy, John
Victoria: May Blossom of Britannia, England, 1829 - Anna Kirwan   *e, m*   509

AGED PERSON

Beezer, Ebenezer
A Plump and Perky Turkey - Teresa Bateman   *p*   62

Blooming Mary
Goin' Someplace Special - Patricia C. McKissack   *p, e*   625

Claude
All the Way Home - Patricia Reilly Giff   *e*   330

David
Pearl - Debbie Atwell   *p, e*   31

Grampa
Heaven Eyes - David Almond   *m*   12

Gran
The Hickory Chair - Lisa Rowe Fraustino   *p*   300

Grandma
See You Soon Moon - Donna Conrad   *p*   179

Grandma Marilyn
Aunt Claire's Yellow Beehive Hair - Deborah Blumenthal   *p*   88

Grandma Soukeye
Bintou's Braids - Sylviane A. Diouf   *p*   235

Grandmother
Ghost Wings - Barbara Joosse   *p*   470

Granny
One More Wednesday - Malika Doray   *p*   242

Great-Aunt Ray
Aunt Claire's Yellow Beehive Hair - Deborah Blumenthal   *p*   88

Jewels, Bentley
The Calling - Cathryn Clinton   *m, h*   169

Lulu
Lulu's Birthday - Elizabeth Fitzgerald Howard   *p*   425

Martinka, Charlie "Paw Paw"
Bo & Mzzz Mad - Sid Fleischman   *m*   291

Master Melwyn
Tree Girl - T.A. Barron   *e, m*   55

Miss Perfidy
Everything on a Waffle - Polly Horvath   *m*   422

Miss Rosemary
The Goose Who Went Off in a Huff - Paul Brett Johnson   *p*   459

Montgomery, Roderick Jackson
Fly! - Christopher Myers   *p, e*   663

Mother Greenwood
The Famous Adventures of Jack - Berlie Doherty   *e*   239

Mother Holly
Mother Holly - John Warren Stewig   *p, e*   858

Mr. Cao
Angelfish - Laurence Yep   *m*   994

Mr. Kang
Happy Birthday Mr. Kang - Susan L. Roth   *p, e*   770

Mr. Putter
Mr. Putter & Tabby Feed the Fish - Cynthia Rylant   *b*   783

Mrs. Brown
Cats, Cats, Cats! - Leslea Newman   *p*   675

Mrs. Diggs
Widget - Lyn Rossiter McFarland   *p*   623

Ms. Witherspoon "Cat Lady"
Just Ask Iris - Lucy Frank   *m*   299

Nana
The Dog Prince - Lauren Mills   *p, e*   642

Nell
The Circus in the Woods - Bill Littlefield   *m, h*   563

Noah
A Stormy Ride on Noah's Ark - Patricia Hooper   *p*   417

Papillon, Fawn
Trial by Jury/Journal - Kate Klise   *m*   514

Pearl
Pearl - Debbie Atwell   *p, e*   31

Pop
Fur-Ever Yours, Booker Jones - Betsy Duffey   *e, m*   252

Preminger, Yoshe
Rivka's First Thanksgiving - Elsa Okon Rael   *p, e*   733

Santa
How Santa Lost His Job - Stephen Krensky   *p*   521
Rover Saves Christmas - Roddy Doyle   *e*   247

Sheba
Rowan of Rin - Emily Rodda   *e, m*   760

Snow
The Circus in the Woods - Bill Littlefield   *m, h*   563

Unnamed Character
Hide & Seek - Brenda Shannon Yee   *p*   993
A Ladder to the Stars - Simon Puttock   *p, e*   729
Meaner than Meanest - Kevin Somers   *p*   838

The Moon Quilt - Sunny Warner   *p, e*   929
The Tin Forest - Helen Ward   *p*   924

Williams, Mattie
One Unhappy Horse - C.S. Adler   *m*   4

AGENT

Baldt, William
Boston Jane: An Adventure - Jennifer L. Holm   *m*   409

Mueller, Max
Sammy Keyes and the Hollywood Mummy - Wendelin Van Draanen   *m*   900

Reisman, Zoe/Zee Zee
The School Story - Andrew Clements   *e, m*   167

ALCOHOLIC

Mr. Olson
Hank's Story - Jane Buchanan   *e*   113

Spraig, Luther
Out of the Night That Covers Me: A Novel - Pat Cunningham Devoto   *a*   229

Turley, Lemm
Shayla's Double Brown Baby Blues - Lori Aurelia Williams   *m, h*   963

Wattley, Charles "Groover"
Groover's Heart - Carole Crowe   *e*   197

ALIEN

Alien
Alien & Possum: Friends No Matter What - Tony Johnston   *b*   463

Baloney, Henry P.
Baloney (Henry P) - Jon Scieszka   *p, e*   804

Bibliogoth
A Matter of Profit - Hilari Bell   *h, a*   67

Blorp
New Pet - Dan Yaccarino   *e*   992

Gemini Jack
Expiration Date: Never - Stephanie Spinner   *e*   844

Horus
Horus's Horrible Day - Shana Corey   *e*   182

Lin
Perdido Street Station - China Mieville   *h, a*   637

Major Quilan
Look to Windward - Iain Banks   *h, a*   49

Miss Bugscuffle
Baloney (Henry P) - Jon Scieszka   *p, e*   804

Norbert
A Nose for Adventure - Richard Scrimger   *m*   808

Tabini
Defender - C.J. Cherryh   *h, a*   155

Uxno
Beatnik Rutabagas from Beyond the Stars - Quentin Dodd   *m, h*   238

Yagharek
Perdido Street Station - China Mieville   *h, a*   637

Ziller, Mahrai
Look to Windward - Iain Banks   *h, a*   49

ALLIGATOR

Claude
Petite Rouge: A Cajun Red Riding Hood - Mike Artell   *p, e*   22

AMNESIAC

Ambriel
Stained Glass - Michael Bedard   *m, h*   66

AMPUTEE

Captain Vince
Dodo Gets Married - Petra Mathers   *p*   601

Woodward, Robert
Finnie Walsh - Steven Galloway   *a*   309

ANALYST

Walker, John
Death Benefits - Thomas Perry   *a*   708

ANGEL

Samuel
The Second Summoning - Tanya Huff   *h, a*   433

Terence, Clarence
Have a Nice Life Series - Scarlett Macdougal   *h*   585

ANIMAL

Tiger
The Tiger Rising - Kate DiCamillo   *m*   231

Toby
Toby, What Are You? - William Steig   *p*   852

ANIMAL LOVER

Albert
Albert - Donna Jo Napoli   *p, e*   668

Beasley/Beastley, Julius
The Beastly Arms - Patrick Jennings   *m*   453

Cricklestein, Adam
Frankenbug - Steven Cousins   *e, m*   185

Dabble, Jimmy
Jimmy Dabble - Frans Vischer   *e*   914

Dill, Nicholas "Nickel"
The Beastly Arms - Patrick Jennings   *m*   453

Elligator, Emily
Reptiles Are My Life - Megan McDonald   *p*   619

Fallon, Brenna
A Feral Darkness - Doranna Durgin   *h, a*   254

Frankenstein, Amanda
Reptiles Are My Life - Megan McDonald   *p*   619

Jonathan
One Dark Night - Hazel Hutchins   *p*   440

Judy
Runaway Radish - Jessie Haas   *e*   363

Kelandry
Squire - Tamora Pierce   *m, h*   712

Maggie
Reptiles Are My Life - Megan McDonald   *p*   619

McIntire, Holly
Hank's Story - Jane Buchanan   *e*   113

Mike
Pugdog - Andrea U'Ren   *p*   895

Montgomery, Roderick Jackson
Fly! - Christopher Myers   *p, e*   663

Mr. Pockets
The Pocket Dogs - Margaret Wild   *p*   954

Mrs. Brown
Cats, Cats, Cats! - Leslea Newman   *p*   675

Mrs. Diggs
Widget - Lyn Rossiter McFarland   *p* 623

Mrs. McTats
Mrs. McTats and Her Houseful of Cats - Alyssa Satin Capucilli   *p* 137

Ms. Witherspoon "Cat Lady"
Just Ask Iris - Lucy Frank   *m* 299

Nina
Runaway Radish - Jessie Haas   *e* 363

Peachwood, "Peachie"
The Summer of Riley - Eve Bunting   *e* 122

Rowan
Rowan of Rin - Emily Rodda   *e, m* 760

Unnamed Character
The Very Kind Rich Lady and Her One Hundred Dogs - Chinlun Lee   *p* 541
You're Growing Up, Pontus! - Ann-Sofie Jeppson   *p, e* 455

ANIMAL TRAINER

Masera, Iban "Gil"
A Feral Darkness - Doranna Durgin   *h, a* 254

Skinner, Johnny
Lady Lollipop - Dick King-Smith   *e* 503

ANTHROPOLOGIST

Boomer, Kinsasha Rosa Parks "Kinchy"
The Transmogrification of Roscoe Wizzle - David Elliott   *e* 272

Dutton, Jim
Dark Inheritance - W. Michael Gear   *a* 322

ANTIQUES DEALER

Trowbridge, Doris "Weird Doris"
Rat Boys: A Dating Experiment - Thom Eberhardt   *m* 258

APPRENTICE

Angelo
Shadows in the Glasshouse - Megan McDonald   *e, m* 620

Collier, Sam
Surviving Jamestown: The Adventures of Young Sam Collier - Gail Langer Karwoski   *m* 479

Peacock, Nathaniel "Nate"
Surviving Jamestown: The Adventures of Young Sam Collier - Gail Langer Karwoski   *m* 479

Rind, William
Maria's Story: 1773 - Joan Lowery Nixon   *e, m* 678

Tree-Ear
A Single Shard - Linda Sue Park   *m* 696

ARCHAEOLOGIST

Jones, Vanessa
The Last Grail Keeper - Pamela Smith Hill   *m* 398

ART DEALER

Pencarreth, Erica
A Lovely Illusion - Tessa Barclay   *a* 54

Townley, Willard
A Lovely Illusion - Tessa Barclay   *a* 54

ARTIFICIAL INTELLIGENCE

Hub
Look to Windward - Iain Banks   *h, a* 49

ARTISAN

Ameyaw, Nana
The Spider Weaver: A Legend of Kente Cloth - Margaret Musgrove   *p, e* 661

Briggs, James
Lord of the Nutcracker Men - Iain Lawrence   *m* 537

Harley
Equinox - Monte Killingsworth   *m* 494

Koragu, Nana
The Spider Weaver: A Legend of Kente Cloth - Margaret Musgrove   *p, e* 661

Marpessa
Troy - Adele Geras   *h, a* 327

Min
A Single Shard - Linda Sue Park   *m* 696

Momma
The Girl with 500 Middle Names - Margaret Peterson Haddix   *e* 366

Unnamed Character
The Moon Quilt - Sunny Warner   *p, e* 929

Will
Freewill - Chris Lynch   *h* 581

ARTIST

Butter, Roland
Skinny Melon and Me - Jean Ure   *m* 894

Castle, Owen
Following Fake Man - Barbara Ware Holmes   *m* 410

Coppercorn, Jilly
The Onion Girl - Charles De Lint   *h, a* 219

Crutchfield, Bram
Scribbler of Dreams - Mary E. Pearson   *m, h* 703

Dennison, Palma
Of Sound Mind - Jean Ferris   *m, h* 286

Emily
Emily's Art - Peter Catalanotto   *p* 149

Feldman, Alexander "Alex"
Desperate Measures - Kate Wilhelm   *a* 959

Forrest
Equinox - Monte Killingsworth   *m* 494

Gugu
Gugu's House - Catherine Stock   *p* 860

Lin
Perdido Street Station - China Mieville   *h, a* 637

Martinka, Juna
Bo & Mzzz Mad - Sid Fleischman   *m* 291

Mead, Francis "El Pintor"
The Summer of El Pintor - Ofelia Dumas Lachtman   *m, h* 525

Nakunte
My Baby - Jeanette Winter   *p* 975

Richards, Rachel
When Dad Killed Mom - Julius Lester   *h* 549

Sophie
Sophie's Masterpiece: A Spider's Tale - Eileen Spinelli   *p* 843

Stenrill, Mirrin
The Sands of Time - Michael Hoeye   *m, h* 406

Unnamed Character
Little Green - Keith Baker   *p* 43
Wait! No Paint! - Bruce Whatley   *p* 943
What's So Scary? - John Stadler   *p, e* 848

Winthrop, Homer Aldrich
Following Fake Man - Barbara Ware Holmes   *m* 410

ASSISTANT

Campbell, Oscar
As Long as She Needs Me - Nicholas Weinstock   *a* 934

Tuway
Out of the Night That Covers Me: A Novel - Pat Cunningham Devoto   *a* 229

ASTHMATIC

Land, Reuben
Peace Like a River - Leif Enger   *h, a* 278

ATHLETE

Angela
Freewill - Chris Lynch   *h* 581

AUNT

Abbott, Vidalia "Viddy"
Extra Innings - Robert Newton Peck   *m* 705

Ada
A Farm of Her Own - Natalie Kinsey-Warnock   *p* 504

Armiger, Aggie
Anna on the Farm - Mary Downing Hahn   *e* 369

Auntie
Altoona Up North - Janie Bynum   *p* 130

Bess
Maggie in the Morning - Elizabeth Van Steenwyk   *e* 904

Beth
Stolen Words - Amy Goldman Koss   *m* 518

Briggs, Ivy
Lord of the Nutcracker Men - Iain Lawrence   *m* 537

Buchanan, Charity
The Secret Road - Robert Nordan   *e, m* 682

Butterfield, Julie
Raising the Shades - Doug Wilhelm   *m* 958

Clara
The Journey - Sarah Stewart   *p, e* 857

Dora
Prairie School - Avi   *b, e* 37

Fleischacker, Euterpe Fuller
Fair Weather - Richard Peck   *m* 704

Florencia
In the Shadow of the Alamo - Sherry Garland   *m* 316

Funk, Vera
Cissy Funk - Kim Taylor   *m* 870

Graham, Cindy
Piper - Natale Ghent   *m* 328

Great-Aunt Ray
Aunt Claire's Yellow Beehive Hair - Deborah Blumenthal   *p* 88

Hubbard, Margaret
Finding Hattie - Sally Warner   *m* 926

Hull, Edna
West of Rehoboth - Alexs D. Pate   *a*   699

Jane
Witch Hill - Marcus Sedgwick   *m, h*   809

Jen
Oliver's Milk Shake - Vivian French   *p*   302

Jordan, Geneva
Welcome to the Great Mysterious - Lorna Landvik   *a*   531

Loretta
A Fish Named Spot - Jennifer P. Goldfinger   *p*   337

Lucy
Elinor and Violet: The Story of Two Naughty Chickens - Patti Beling Murphy   *p*   657

Lulu
Lulu's Birthday - Elizabeth Fitzgerald Howard   *p*   425

Martinka, Juna
Bo & Mzzz Mad - Sid Fleischman   *m*   291

Mary
Hannah's Bookmobile Christmas - Sally Derby   *p, e*   226

Maxwell, Matilda "Aunt Mattie"
No More Nasty - Amy MacDonald   *e, m*   583

McIntosh, Annie
Gwyneth's Secret Grandpa - Annie Morris Williams   *e*   961

Merle
Four Corners - Diane Freund   *a*   304

Miller, Cassie
Buddy Is a Stupid Name for a Girl - Willo Davis Roberts   *e, m*   753

Ostrom, Addie
Buddy Is a Stupid Name for a Girl - Willo Davis Roberts   *e, m*   753

Patterson, Ivy
Moonpie and Ivy - Barbara O'Connor   *m*   683

Quade, Lily
In Spite of Killer Bees - Julie Johnston   *m, h*   462

Shapley, Madeline
On the Street Where You Live - Mary Higgins Clark   *a*   165

Shavani
The Serpent's Shadow - Mercedes Lackey   *h, a*   526

Smythe, Joan
Cherokee - Creina Mansfield   *m*   592

Snodde-Brittle, Frieda
Dial-a-Ghost - Eva Ibbotson   *e, m*   441

Sparrow, Mattie
Moonshiner's Gold - John R. Erickson   *m*   279

Spraig, Nelda
Out of the Night That Covers Me: A Novel - Pat Cunningham Devoto   *a*   229

Tia Lola
How Tia Lola Came to Visit/Stay - Julia Alvarez   *e, m*   15

Viola
Groover's Heart - Carole Crowe   *e*   197

Wilhelm, Georgia
Rain Is Not My Indian Name - Cynthia Leitich Smith   *m*   831

Wood, Erin
Before Wings - Beth Goobie   *m, h*   340

AUTISTIC

McPhee/McGee, Tommy/Timmy
Clay - Colby Rodowsky   *m*   761

BABOON

Auntie
Altoona Up North - Janie Bynum   *p*   130

Baboona, Altoona
Altoona Up North - Janie Bynum   *p*   130

BABY

Anneke
Katje, the Windmill Cat - Gretchen Woelfle   *p*   979

Baby Bert
The Adventures of Bert - Allan Ahlberg   *p*   8

Baby Brenda
Midnight Babies - Margaret Wild   *p*   952

Baby Duck
Baby Duck's New Friend - Frank Asch   *p*   24

Baby Mario
Midnight Babies - Margaret Wild   *p*   952

Danny
Secret in St. Something - Barbara Brooks Wallace   *m*   919

Dolci, Nina
The Orphan Singer - Emily Arnold McCully   *p*   613

Fairchild, Henry
Riddle of the Prairie Bride - Kathryn Reiss   *m*   740

Fox, Gift Marie
Shayla's Double Brown Baby Blues - Lori Aurelia Williams   *m, h*   963

Graham, Grover C.
Grover C. Graham and Me - Mary Quattlebaum   *e, m*   731

Hannah
Come Back, Hannah! - Marisabina Russo   *p*   774

Henry
Henry's First-Moon Birthday - Lenore Look   *p*   570

Jefferson, Smokey
Spellbound - Janet McDonald   *m, h*   616

Jin Woo
Jin Woo - Eve Bunting   *p*   119

Jo
The Other Dog - Madeleine L'Engle   *p*   544

Little Zeb
Naughty! - Caroline Castle   *p*   148

Meri
The Merbaby - Teresa Bateman   *p, e*   61

Strega-Borgia, Damp
Pure Dead Magic - Debi Gliori   *e, m*   335

Tu Thi
Heart of Mine: A Story of Adoption - Lotta Hojer   *p*   408

BABYSITTER

Alice
Emily and Alice Baby-Sit Burton - Joyce Champion   *b, e*   153

Emily
Emily and Alice Baby-Sit Burton - Joyce Champion   *b, e*   153

BACHELOR

Ralph
The Princess and the Pea - Alain Vaes   *p*   897

BADGER

Badger
Coyote and Badger: Desert Hunters of the Southwest - Bruce Hiscock   *p, e*   400

Little Badger
Little Badger, Terror of the Seven Seas - Eve Bunting   *p*   120

Old Badger
Little Badger, Terror of the Seven Seas - Eve Bunting   *p*   120

BAKER

Pikche, Katorna "Kat"
Benno's Bear - N.F. Zucker   *m*   1007

Unnamed Character
Sun Bread - Elisa Kleven   *p*   512

BANKER

Shylock
Shylock's Daughter - Mirjam Pressler   *h*   724

Vance, Bryon "Judge"
Out of the Night That Covers Me: A Novel - Pat Cunningham Devoto   *a*   229

BASEBALL PLAYER

Burke, Coley
Plunking Reggie Jackson - James W. Bennett   *h*   69

Nygerski, Cyrus
Tartabull's Throw - Henry Garfield   *h*   313

Robinson, Jackie
The Journal of Biddy Owens: The Negro Leagues, Birmingham, Alabama, 1948 - Walter Dean Myers   *m*   664

Urbino, Enrique "Ricky"
Playing for Keeps - Joan Lowery Nixon   *m, h*   679

Wall, Cannonball
Till Tomorrow - John Donahue   *m*   240

BASKETBALL PLAYER

Carillo, Jason
Rainbow Boys - Alex Sanchez   *h*   791

Gus
Gus and Grandpa at Basketball - Claudia Mills   *b*   641

Jakarta
Jakarta Missing - Jane Kurtz   *m*   524

BASTARD SON

Apropos
Sir Apropos of Nothing - Peter David   *h, a*   214

BAT

Bat
Bat Loves the Night - Nicola Davies   *p*   216

Batbaby
Batbaby Finds a Home - Robert Quackenbush   *b*   730

Benny
Bunbun at Bedtime - Sharon Pierce McCullough
    p 610

Benson, Tony
The Boys Return - Phyllis Reynolds Naylor   *e*,
    m 673

Berg, Peter
Clara's War - Kathy Kacer   *e, m* 474

Berghoff, Fynnegan "Fynn"
Rain Is Not My Indian Name - Cynthia Leitich Smith
    m 831

Bird, Billy
Billy the Bird - Dick King-Smith   *e* 502

Bolinski, Stefan
Streets of Gold - Marie Raphael   *m, h* 735

Borgia, Lucifer di S'Embowelli
Pure Dead Magic - Debi Gliori   *e, m* 335

Bunbun
Bunbun at Bedtime - Sharon Pierce McCullough
    p 610

Caleb
Gabriel's Story - David Anthony Durham   *h*,
    a 255

Capel, Will
The Dragon Charmer - Jan Siegel   *h, a* 820

Chambers, Seth
Stopping to Home - Lea Wait   *e* 917

Charlie
I Am NOT Sleepy and I Will NOT Go to Bed - Lauren
    Child   *p* 160

Christopher
Mom Pie - Lynne Jonell   *p* 468

Cody
Bluebird Summer - Deborah Hopkinson   *p, e* 418

Dan
Happy Easter, Davy! - Brigitte Weninger   *p* 940

Daniels, Danny
What a Trip, Amber Brown - Paula Danziger
    e 211

Daniels, Ronald
One True Friend - Joyce Hansen   *m* 372

Davy
Happy Easter, Davy! - Brigitte Weninger   *p* 940

Delgado, Juan Pablo
Secrets in the House of Delgado - Gloria D. Miklowitz
    m, h 639

Diaz-Pinkowitz, Freddy
Just Ask Iris - Lucy Frank   *m* 299

Dolci, Antonio
The Orphan Singer - Emily Arnold McCully
    p 613

Dorfman, Robert
Robert and the Great Pepperoni - Barbara Seuling
    e 811

Ebenezer
Sorry - Jean Van Leeuwen   *p, e* 902

Eugene
Bun Bun's Birthday - Richard Scrimger   *p* 807

Flip
Flip and Flop - Dawn Apperley   *p* 17

Flop
Flip and Flop - Dawn Apperley   *p* 17

Folger, David
The Life History of a Star - Kelly Easton   *m*,
    h 257

Franklin
Starring Lucille - Kathryn Lasky   *p* 534

Fred
The Class Artist - G. Brian Karas   *p* 477

Funk, Jonas
Cissy Funk - Kim Taylor   *m* 870

Gates, Marvin
Marvin One Too Many - Katherine Paterson   *b* 701

George
Singing Diggety - Maggie Stern   *b, e* 854

Gibson, Tod
Expiration Date: Never - Stephanie Spinner   *e* 844

Gordon, Matt
Racing the Past - Sis Deans   *m* 220

Grant, Simon
How Many Days Until Tomorrow? - Caroline Janover
    e, m 449

Guzman, Miguel
How Tia Lola Came to Visit/Stay - Julia Alvarez   *e*,
    m 15

Harry
Spookier Than a Ghost - Karen Gray Ruelle   *b* 772

Hatford, Wally
The Boys Return - Phyllis Reynolds Naylor   *e*,
    m 673

Hathaway, Henry
Tub-boo-boo - Margie Palatini   *p* 693

Henry
Henry's First-Moon Birthday - Lenore Look
    p 570

Hollander, Alexander
Don't Bug Me! - Pam Zollman   *e* 1006

Jack
Christmas in Camelot - Mary Pope Osborne   *e* 691

Jacques
*Puss in Boots: The Adventures of That Most
    Enterprising Feline* - Philip Pullman   *p, e* 728

Jake
Super-Completely and Totally the Messiest - Judith
    Viorst   *p, e* 913

Jakie
Rattletrap Car - Phyllis Root   *p* 765

Jeff
A Bus of Our Own - Freddi Williams Evans   *p*,
    e 280

Jones, Ebon
Dad, in Spirit - A. LaFaye   *e, m* 527

Josh
The Merbaby - Teresa Bateman   *p, e* 61

Kane, Ceej
Hole in the Sky - Pete Hautman   *m, h* 383

Leo
Breakout at the Bug Lab - Ruth Horowitz   *b* 421

Leventhal, Daniel
Black Mirror - Nancy Werlin   *h* 941

Little Boy James
*Grandpa Blows His Penny Whistle Until the Angels
    Sing* - Susan L. Roth   *p, e* 769

MacGillyCuddy, Dan
Dancing for Danger: A Meggy Tale - Margot Griffin
    e 352

Madsen, Albert
Sailing Home: A Story of a Childhood at Sea - Gloria
    Rand   *p, e* 734

Marco
Marco's Millions - William Sleator   *m* 829

Max
Bunny Party - Rosemary Wells   *p* 935
Pirates - C. Drew Lamm   *p, e* 530

McDaniel, Coy
Moonshiner's Gold - John R. Erickson   *m* 279

Michael
The Snail House - Allan Ahlberg   *p* 10

Milagros, Domingo de
*Valley of the Moon: The Diary of Maria Rosalia De
    Milagros, Sonoma Valley, Alta California, 1846* -
    Sherry Garland   *m* 317

Moe
A Mountain of Blintzes - Barbara Diamond Goldin
    p 338

Moody, Stink
Judy Moody Gets Famous - Megan McDonald
    e 618

Musa, Abubakari
Mansa Musa: The Lion of Mali - Khephra Burns   *e*,
    m 127

Nebula, Ralph
Fat Camp Commandos - Daniel Pinkwater   *e* 716

Nichols, Michael
The Ghost and Mrs. Hobbs - Cynthia DeFelice   *e*,
    m 221

Obadiah
Sorry - Jean Van Leeuwen   *p, e* 902

Paine, Timmy
Tartabull's Throw - Henry Garfield   *h* 313

Pinky
Pinky and Rex and the Just-Right Pet - James Howe
    b, e 429

Puckett, Tom
Emma Jo's Song - Faye Gibbons   *p* 329

Read, Arthur
D.W.'s Library Card - Marc Brown   *p* 103

Rind, William
Maria's Story: 1773 - Joan Lowery Nixon   *e*,
    m 678

Robbie
Mom Pie - Lynne Jonell   *p* 468

Robin
Robin's Home - Jeannine Atkins   *p* 29

Royce
Mim's Christmas Jam - Andrea Davis Pinkney
    p 715

Samuels, Floyd
*Rose's Journal: The Story of a Girl in the Great
    Depression* - Marissa Moss   *e* 655

Shek
Coolies - Yin   *p, e* 996

Sheridan, Greg
Blind Fury - Linda Shands   *m* 815

Sollis, Nate
Diamond in the Dust - Carla Joinson   *m, h* 467

Squeak
Squeak's Good Idea - Max Eilenberg   *p* 268

Tall One
Stella's Dancing Days - Sandy Asher   *p* 25

Tarron
The Merbaby - Teresa Bateman   *p, e* 61

Tolliver, Willie
Wishes, Kisses, and Pigs - Betsy Gould Hearne
    e 386

Tom
Stop, Drop, and Roll - Margery Cuyler   *p* 202

Unnamed Character
Breakout at the Bug Lab - Ruth Horowitz   *b* 421
Chanukah Lights Everywhere - Michael J. Rosen
    p 767
Ride - Stephen Gammell   *p* 310

Louie
No Kiss for Grandpa - Harriet Ziefert   p   1001

Maurice
Amazing Maurice and His Educated Rodents: A Novel of Discworld - Terry Pratchett   h   723

Molly
Molly and the Magic Wishbone - Barbara McClintock   p   609

Mother
Estelle and Lucy - Anna Alter   p   14

Obaasan
Yoko's Paper Cranes - Rosemary Wells   p   939

Ojiisan
Yoko's Paper Cranes - Rosemary Wells   p   939

Osi
The Spy Wore Shades - Martha Freeman   e, m   301

Patch
You're Growing Up, Pontus! - Ann-Sofie Jeppson   p, e   455

Patches
Pinky and Rex and the Just-Right Pet - James Howe   b, e   429

Penny
One Day at Wood Green Animal Shelter - Patricia Casey   p   146

Perkins
The Cats of Cuckoo Square: Two Stories - Adele Geras   e   326

Phylis
Molly and the Magic Wishbone - Barbara McClintock   p   609

Puss
Puss in Boots: The Adventures of That Most Enterprising Feline - Philip Pullman   p, e   728

Ralph
Rotten Ralph Helps Out - Jack Gantos   b   311

Stella
Stella's Dancing Days - Sandy Asher   p   25

Tabby
Mr. Putter & Tabby Feed the Fish - Cynthia Rylant   b   783

TeJean
Petite Rouge: A Cajun Red Riding Hood - Mike Artell   p, e   22

Unnamed Character
Four Hungry Kittens - Emily Arnold McCully   p   611
The Moon Quilt - Sunny Warner   p, e   929
One Dark Night - Hazel Hutchins   p   440
The Three Pigs - David Wiesner   p, e   950

Yoko
Mama, Don't Go! - Rosemary Wells   b   937

CELESTIAL BODY

Moon
The Day Ocean Came to Visit - Diane Wolkstein   p   981
When Moon Fell Down - Linda Smith   p   832

Sun
The Day Ocean Came to Visit - Diane Wolkstein   p   981

CENTIPEDE

Belinda
Harry the Poisonous Centipede's Big Adventure: Another Story to Make You Squirm - Lynne Reid Banks   e   52

George
Harry the Poisonous Centipede's Big Adventure: Another Story to Make You Squirm - Lynne Reid Banks   e   52

Harry
Harry the Poisonous Centipede's Big Adventure: Another Story to Make You Squirm - Lynne Reid Banks   e   52

CHICKEN

Chicken
The Scarecrow's Hat - Ken Brown   p   102

Christmas
What's Cooking, Jamela? - Niki Daly   p   206

Elinor
Elinor and Violet: The Story of Two Naughty Chickens - Patti Beling Murphy   p   657

Little Hen
Something Wonderful - Jenny Nimmo   p   676

Little Red Hen
With Love, Little Red Hen - Alma Flor Ada   p   2

Lucy
Elinor and Violet: The Story of Two Naughty Chickens - Patti Beling Murphy   p   657

Poulet, Violet
Elinor and Violet: The Story of Two Naughty Chickens - Patti Beling Murphy   p   657

Unnamed Character
Book! Book! Book! - Deborah Bruss   p   111

CHILD

Alex
Loki & Alex: The Adventures of a Dog & His Best Friend - Charles R. Smith Jr.   p   830

Amanda
Pinky and Rex and the Just-Right Pet - James Howe   b, e   429

Amaroq
Nutik & Amaroq Play Ball - Jean Craighead George   p   324

Amber
Amber Was Brave, Essie Was Smart - Vera B. Williams   e   965

Andres
Buzz Buzz Buzz - Veronica Uribe   p   896

Anna
Anna's Goat - Janice Kulyk Keefer   p, e   481

Annabelle
One Monday - Amy Huntington   p   436

Annie
Aunt Claire's Yellow Beehive Hair - Deborah Blumenthal   p   88

Antonella
Antonella and Her Santa Claus - Barbara Augustin   p   34

April
The Reluctant Flower Girl - Lynne Barasch   p   53

Bartlett, Alicia
The Rag and Bone Shop - Robert Cormier   m, h   183

Bean, Clarice
Clarice Bean: Guess Who's Babysitting? - Lauren Child   p, e   159

Beatrice
Clever Beatrice - Margaret Willey   p   960

Beckett, Buster
Fair Weather - Richard Peck   m   704

Beto
Beto and the Bone Dance - Gina Freschet   p   303

Boy
The Shine Man: A Christmas Story - Mary Quattlebaum   p, e   732

Briggs, Johnny
Lord of the Nutcracker Men - Iain Lawrence   m   537

Calhoun, Cooper
Maggie in the Morning - Elizabeth Van Steenwyk   e   904

Chambers, Seth
Stopping to Home - Lea Wait   e   917

Charley
Alphabet Adventure - Audrey Wood   p   982

Charlie
I Am NOT Sleepy and I Will NOT Go to Bed - Lauren Child   p   160

Chester
The Lima Bean Monster - Dan Yaccarino   p   991

Claus, Peter
Peter Claus and the Naughty List - Lawrence David   p   213

Clover
The Other Side - Jacqueline Woodson   p, e   983

Cody
Bluebird Summer - Deborah Hopkinson   p, e   418

Coleman, Maude
Falling Angels - Tracy Chevalier   a   156

Crestman, Zachary
Spyhole Secrets - Zilpha Keatley Snyder   e, m   837

Crosby, Hattie
Hattie's Story - Susan E. Kirby   e   505

Daisy
Meaner than Meanest - Kevin Somers   p   838

Daniel
Daniel's Mystery Egg - Alma Flor Ada   b   1

Daniels, Ronald
One True Friend - Joyce Hansen   m   372

David
Jin Woo - Eve Bunting   p   119

Diamante
Rufferella - Vanessa Gill-Brown   p   331

Didi
Didi and Daddy on the Promenade - Marilyn Singer   p   825

Dougherty, Lorraine "Rainey"
Four Corners - Diane Freund   a   304

Dusty Locks
Dusty Locks and the Three Bears - Susan Lowell   p   573

Eamon
Knockabeg: A Famine Tale - Mary E. Lyons   m   582

Edward
Tattered Sails - Verla Kay   p   480

Eli
Eli's Night Light - Liz Rosenberg   p   768

Elsie
Elsie Times Eight - Natalie Babbitt   p   41

Emily
A Penguin Pup for Pinkerton - Steven Kellogg   p   486
The Sick Day - Patricia MacLachlan   p   587

Essie
Amber Was Brave, Essie Was Smart - Vera B. Williams   e   965

Welcome to Kindergarten - Anne Rockwell *p* 758

Tommy
Bus Stop, Bus Go! - Daniel Kirk *p* 507

'Tricia Ann
Goin' Someplace Special - Patricia C. McKissack *p, e* 625

Tucker, Charlotte
On Tide Mill Lane - Melissa Wiley *e* 957

Unnamed Character
Car Wash - Sandra Steen *p* 851
Car Wash - Sandra Steen *p* 851
Five Creatures - Emily Jenkins *p* 452
Fribbity Ribbit! - Suzanne C. Johnson *p* 461
Ghost Wings - Barbara Joosse *p* 470
A Gift from the Sea - Kate Banks *p* 51
Goodbye Mousie - Robie H. Harris *p* 379
Grandma's Records - Eric Velasquez *p, e* 910
Hungry! Hungry! Hungry! - Malachy Doyle *p* 246
I Lost My Dad - Taro Gomi *p* 339
I Love Going Through This Book - Robert Burleigh *p* 124
I Love You Because You're You - Liza Baker *p* 44
I'm Not Feeling Well Today - Shirley Neitzel *p* 674
Little Green - Keith Baker *p* 43
Love Me, Love You - Susan Heyboer O'Keefe *p* 684
The Magical, Mystical, Marvelous Coat - Catherine Ann Cullen *p* 200
Miss Mouse Takes Off - Jan Ormerod *p* 688
Miss Mouse's Day - Jan Ormerod *p* 689
More Parts - Tedd Arnold *p, e* 20
My Best Friend Bear - Tony Johnston *p* 465
My Dad - Anthony Browne *p* 107
A Safe Place Called Home - Eileen Spinelli *p* 842
Scared Stiff - Katie Davis *p* 217
See You Soon Moon - Donna Conrad *p* 179
The Shark God - Rafe Martin *p* 597
The Shark God - Rafe Martin *p* 597
The Stray Dog - Marc Simont *p* 823
The Stray Dog - Marc Simont *p* 823
Ted - Tony DiTerlizzi *p* 237
Ten Seeds - Ruth Brown *p* 106
We're Going on a Ghost Hunt - Marcia Vaughan *p* 909
We're Going on a Ghost Hunt - Marcia Vaughan *p* 909
When We Go Camping - Margriet Ruurs *p* 775
When We Go Camping - Margriet Ruurs *p* 775
White Water - Jonathan London *p* 569
You're Growing Up, Pontus! - Ann-Sofie Jeppson *p, e* 455

Violet
Shrinking Violet - Cari Best *p, e* 71

Waddell, John Henry
Freedom Summer - Deborah Wiles *p, e* 955

Waterhouse, Lavinia Ermyntrude "Livy"
Falling Angels - Tracy Chevalier *a* 156

Whittingham, Jake
Through the Lock - Carol Otis Hurst *m* 438

Will
Farmer Will - Jane Cowen-Fletcher *p* 188

William
William and the Night Train - Mij Kelly *p* 487

Winifred
Bun Bun's Birthday - Richard Scrimger *p* 807

Yoko
Yoko's Paper Cranes - Rosemary Wells *p* 939

CHILD-CARE GIVER

McLachlan, Flora
Pure Dead Magic - Debi Gliori *e, m* 335

Melissa
Do Try to Speak as We Do: The Diary of an American Au Pair - Marjorie Leet Ford *a* 297

CHILD OF AN ALCOHOLIC

Butterfield, Casey
Raising the Shades - Doug Wilhelm *m* 958

CHILD OF DIVORCED PARENTS

Alex
Two Homes - Claire Masurel *p* 599

Anderson, Elizabeth "Lizzie"
By Lizzie - Mary Eccles *e* 259

Guzman, Juanita
How Tia Lola Came to Visit/Stay - Julia Alvarez *e, m* 15

Guzman, Miguel
How Tia Lola Came to Visit/Stay - Julia Alvarez *e, m* 15

Lavender, Ruby
Love, Ruby Lavender - Deborah Wiles *e, m* 956

Rainie
Loon Summer - Barbara Santucci *p* 793

CHIMPANZEE

Umber
Dark Inheritance - W. Michael Gear *a* 322

CHIPMUNK

Chipmunk
Where Did Bunny Go? - Nancy Tafuri *p* 865

Tentintrotter, Birch
The Sands of Time - Michael Hoeye *m, h* 406

CLASSMATE

Attired, Natalie
Farewell, My Lunchbag - Bruce Hale *e, m* 370

Frances
The Class Artist - G. Brian Karas *p* 477

Frankenstein, Amanda
Reptiles Are My Life - Megan McDonald *p* 619

Julio
Fat Chance Thanksgiving - Patricia Lakin *p, e* 529

Unnamed Character
Circus Girl - Tomek Bogacki *p* 90

Willis, Phil "Willie"
Jake Drake, Know-It-All - Andrew Clements *e* 166

Zoey
Butterfly Buddies - Judy Cox *e* 190

CLERK

Tibby
The Sisterhood of the Traveling Pants - Ann Brashares *m, h* 99

CLOWN

Zuckerman, Jerry
My Guy - Sarah Weeks *e, m* 933

COACH

Hardaway, Jonathan
Darkness Before Dawn - Sharon M. Draper *h* 249

Mr. Simet
Whale Talk - Chris Crutcher *h* 199

COCKROACH

Max
Breakout at the Bug Lab - Ruth Horowitz *b* 421

COLLECTOR

Brian
The Comic Book Kid - Adam Osterweil *e* 692

Paul
The Comic Book Kid - Adam Osterweil *e* 692

Unnamed Character
Rocks in His Head - Carol Otis Hurst *p, e* 437

COMPUTER EXPERT

Carter, Raylene
The Onion Girl - Charles De Lint *h, a* 219

Casey, Mary Catherine "Serena"
Death Benefits - Thomas Perry *a* 708

Gray, Simon
Shades of Simon Gray - Joyce McDonald *m, h* 617

Katrina
Empress of the World - Sara Ryan *h* 777

Kirby, Jess
The Million Dollar Kick - Dan Gutman *m* 360

Salzmann, Eugenia "Byte"
The Protestor's Song - Mark Delaney *m* 223

COMPUTER GAME PLAYER

Lyons, Jessica
Website of the Warped Wizard - Eric A. Kimmel *e* 498

Matthew
Website of the Warped Wizard - Eric A. Kimmel *e* 498

CON ARTIST

Carter, Raylene
The Onion Girl - Charles De Lint *h, a* 219

Daley, Montana Jim
Destination Gold! - Julie Lawson *m, h* 538

Donner, Cornelius
Down the Yukon - Will Hobbs *m, h* 404

Donovan
Stranded - Patricia H. Rushford *m, h* 773

Gardiner, Otis
Coram Boy - Jamila Gavin *m, h* 321

Jan
The Foreigner - Meg Castaldo *a* 147

Jewels, Peter Earl
The Calling - Cathryn Clinton *m, h* 169

Mansfield, Harvey
The Stones of Mourning Creek - Diane Les Becquets *m, h* 546

Morley, Drake
Playing with Fire - Kathleen Karr *m* 478

Patcher, Dick "Patch"
Chipper - James Lincoln Collier *m* 176

Townley, Willard
A Lovely Illusion - Tessa Barclay   a   54

CONSTRUCTION WORKER

Pap
Mim's Christmas Jam - Andrea Davis Pinkney
p   715

CONVICT

Abernathy, J.E. "Brother Mustard Seed"
Pray Hard - Pamela Walker   m   918

Bailey
Scorpio's Child - Kezi Matthews   m   603

Maguire, Jack "Blackjack"
Above and Beyond - Susan Bonners   m   91

COOK

Blakeman, Josh
Lightning Rider - Jacqueline Guest   m, h   355

Carter, Sophie
Black Angels - Rita Murphy   m   658

Cook
Fast Food! Gulp! Gulp! - Bernard Waber   p   915

Doyle, Naomi
The Maiden of Mayfair - Lawana Blackwell   a   82

Momma Chang
The Runaway Rice Cake - Ying Chang Compestine
p   178

Mommy
Mom Pie - Lynne Jonell   p   468

Nana
The Friday Nights of Nana - Amy Hest   p   393

Rosa Maria
Mice and Beans - Pam Munoz Ryan   p   776

Schulz, Goldy
Sticks & Scones - Diane Mott Davidson   a   215

Waddell, Annie Mae
Freedom Summer - Deborah Wiles   p, e   955

COUNSELOR

Furukawa, Mark
The Jasmine Trade - Denise Hamilton   a   371

Miss Honeycutt
Everything on a Waffle - Polly Horvath   m   422

Mrs. Wainwright
Vicky Angel - Jacqueline Wilson   m   972

O'Sullivan, Donna
Fiddleback - Elizabeth Honey   m   414

Snow
The Circus in the Woods - Bill Littlefield   m,
h   563

Vreeland, Bridget
The Sisterhood of the Traveling Pants - Ann Brashares
m, h   99

Wood, Adrien
Before Wings - Beth Goobie   m, h   340

COUSIN

Angelica
Tiger's Fall - Molly Bang   e   48

Annie
The Gawgon and the Boy - Lloyd Alexander   m   11

Emma
A Farm of Her Own - Natalie Kinsey-Warnock
p   504

Findlay, Charles
Above and Beyond - Susan Bonners   m   91

Graham, Cassel
Piper - Natale Ghent   m   328

Gwendolyn "Gwen"
Strike Two - Amy Goldman Koss   e, m   520

Hanley, Liam
*Fiona McGilray's Story: A Voyage from Ireland in
1849* - Clare Pastore   m   698

Hubbard, Sophia "Sophie"
Finding Hattie - Sally Warner   m   926

Jessica
Strike Two - Amy Goldman Koss   e, m   520

Joan
Four Corners - Diane Freund   a   304

Lily
Oliver's Milk Shake - Vivian French   p   302
Summer Party - Cynthia Rylant   e   785

Mabel
Night of the Living Gerbil - Elizabeth Levy   e   553

Mad-Rat, Maggie
The Revenge of Randal Reese-Rat - Tor Seidler
e   810

Miller, Max
Buddy Is a Stupid Name for a Girl - Willo Davis
Roberts   e, m   753

Rita
Raven's Flight - Diane Silvey   m, h   822

Rosie
Summer Party - Cynthia Rylant   e   785

Ruth
Toni's Topsy-Turvy Telephone Day - Laura Ljungkvist
p   566

Salvador
Delfino's Journey - Jo Harper   m, h   375

Seldomridge, Danny
Private Captain: A Novel of Gettysburg - Marty Crisp
m   194

Sheridan, Adam
Tides - V.M. Caldwell   m   133

Smythe, Wesley
Cherokee - Creina Mansfield   m   592

Tess
Summer Party - Cynthia Rylant   e   785

Toni
Toni's Topsy-Turvy Telephone Day - Laura Ljungkvist
p   566

Van Velsor, Araminta
Fire on the Waters - David Poyer   a   722

COW

Cow
And the Dish Ran Away with the Spoon - Janet
Stevens   p   855
When Moon Fell Down - Linda Smith   p   832

Gertrude
The Goose Who Went Off in a Huff - Paul Brett
Johnson   p   459

Minnie
Minnie and Moo Meet Frankenswine - Denys Cazet
b   150

Moo
Minnie and Moo Meet Frankenswine - Denys Cazet
b   150

COWBOY

Caleb
Gabriel's Story - David Anthony Durham   h,
a   255

Hogg, Marshall
Gabriel's Story - David Anthony Durham   h,
a   255

O'Reilly, Ernestine
A Cowboy Named Ernestine - Nicole Rubel   p   771

Texas Teeth
A Cowboy Named Ernestine - Nicole Rubel   p   771

COWGIRL

Rosie
Cowgirl Rosie and Her Five Baby Bison - Stephen
Gulbis   p   356

COYOTE

Coyote
Coyote and Badger: Desert Hunters of the Southwest -
Bruce Hiscock   p, e   400

CRIME SUSPECT

White, Bob
Trial by Jury/Journal - Kate Klise   m   514

CRIME VICTIM

Bishop, John
Green Grow the Victims - Jeanne M. Dams   a   207

Casselman, Alison
Alison, Who Went Away - Vivian Vande Velde
m   906

Chin, Vincent
A Day for Vincent Chin and Me - Jacqueline Turner
Banks   e   50

Dora
Bone House - Betsy Tobin   h, a   885

Driscal, Peter
Touching Spirit Bear - Ben Mikaelsen   m, h   638

Hawkins, Hub
The Boy in the Burning House - Tim Wynne-Jones
m, h   990

Keet, Perry
Trial by Jury/Journal - Kate Klise   m   514

Leventhal, Daniel
Black Mirror - Nancy Werlin   h   941

Lu, Marina
The Jasmine Trade - Denise Hamilton   a   371

Marchand, Gus
Desperate Measures - Kate Wilhelm   a   959

O'Malley
Murphy's Law - Rhys Bowen   a   96

Richards, Rachel
When Dad Killed Mom - Julius Lester   h   549

Shapley, Madeline
On the Street Where You Live - Mary Higgins Clark
a   165

Sizemore, Henry
Sound Tracks - Marcia Simpson   a   824

Ysa
Every Time a Rainbow Dies - Rita Williams-Garcia
h   966

CRIMINAL

Dobbler, Hannah
Shades of Simon Gray - Joyce McDonald   *m,*
h 617

Hogg, Marshall
Gabriel's Story - David Anthony Durham   *h,*
a 255

Matthews, Cole
Touching Spirit Bear - Ben Mikaelsen   *m, h* 638

Unnamed Character
The Bookstore Burglar - Barbara Maitland   *b* 590

Yagharek
Perdido Street Station - China Mieville   *h, a* 637

CROCODILE

Crocodile
Crocodile Listens - April Pulley Sayre   *p* 795

CYBORG

Joseph
The Graveyard Game - Kage Baker   *h, a* 42

Lewis
The Graveyard Game - Kage Baker   *h, a* 42

Mendoza
The Graveyard Game - Kage Baker   *h, a* 42

DANCER

Daisy G.
Blister - Susan Shreve   *e, m* 819

Gillespie, Aimee Anne
Only the Lonely - Laura Dower   *e* 244

La Rue, Dumpy
Dumpy La Rue - Elizabeth Winthrop   *p* 976

LeBec, Leland
Just Imagine - Pat Lowery Collins   *m* 177

Lee, Robin
Angelfish - Laurence Yep   *m* 994

MacGillyCuddy, Meggy
Dancing for Danger: A Meggy Tale - Margot Griffin
e 352

Margaret
Ballet Bug - Christine McDonnell   *e, m* 621

Mr. Cao
Angelfish - Laurence Yep   *m* 994

Nash, Bea
Ballet Bug - Christine McDonnell   *e, m* 621

Piggy
Dancing Class - H.M. Ehrlich   *p* 265

Rebecca
Ballet Bug - Christine McDonnell   *e, m* 621

Stella
Stella's Dancing Days - Sandy Asher   *p* 25

Terry
Ballerina! - Peter Sis   *p* 826

DAUGHTER

Alison "Ali"
Lord of the Deep - Graham Salisbury   *m* 788

Anderson, Wynona
Mama's Way - Helen Ketteman   *p, e* 492

Araceli
Juan Verdades: The Man Who Couldn't Tell a Lie -
Joe Hayes   *p, e* 385

Aziza
One Riddle, One Answer - Lauren Thompson   *p,*
e 881

Beatrice
Beatrice's Goat - Page McBrier   *p* 608
Clever Beatrice - Margaret Willey   *p* 960

Bintou
Bintou's Braids - Sylviane A. Diouf   *p* 235

Blanche
Mother Holly - John Warren Stewig   *p, e* 858

Callahan, Nita
The Wizard's Dilemma - Diane Duane   *m, h* 251

Carla
Fat Chance Thanksgiving - Patricia Lakin   *p,*
e 529

Culhane, Kate
Kate Culhane: A Ghost Story - Michael Hague   *e,*
m 368

Didi
Didi and Daddy on the Promenade - Marilyn Singer
p 825

Elsie
Elsie Times Eight - Natalie Babbitt   *p* 41

Emily
The Sick Day - Patricia MacLachlan   *p* 587

Flora
Flora's Blanket - Debi Gliori   *p* 333

Frost, Emma
Emma's Yucky Brother - Jean Little   *b* 562

Girl
The Christmas Promise - Susan Campbell Bartoletti
p, e 56

Grim, Malicia
*Amazing Maurice and His Educated Rodents: A Novel
of Discworld* - Terry Pratchett   *h* 723

Hannah
Come Back, Hannah! - Marisabina Russo   *p* 774

Harvey, Anne
Heroes of Isle Aux Morts - Alice Walsh   *p, e* 920

Hum, Agapanthus
Agapanthus Hum and Major Bark - Joy Cowley
b 189

Jamela
What's Cooking, Jamela? - Niki Daly   *p* 206

Jo
The Other Dog - Madeleine L'Engle   *p* 544

Junie
Rattletrap Car - Phyllis Root   *p* 765

Kate
Kate Can't Wait - Marilyn Eisenstein   *p* 269
Let's Get a Pup! Said Kate - Bob Graham   *p* 344

Katie
Katie and the Sunflowers - James Mayhew   *p* 604

Kranny, Bertha
Franny B. Kranny, There's a Bird in Your Hair! -
Harriet Lerner   *p* 545

Kranny, Franny B.
Franny B. Kranny, There's a Bird in Your Hair! -
Harriet Lerner   *p* 545

Lily
The Great Good Thing - Roderick Townley   *e,*
m 888
Home before Dark - Ian Beck   *p* 64
Oliver's Milk Shake - Vivian French   *p* 302

Lulu
My Grandmother Is a Singing Yaya - Karen Scourby
D'Arc   *p* 212

Meg
Swollobog - Alastair Taylor   *p* 869

Merriweather, Annie
Minnie Saves the Day - Melodye Benson Rosales
e 766

Merriweather, Hester
Minnie Saves the Day - Melodye Benson Rosales
e 766

Mom
The Days of Summer - Eve Bunting   *p* 117

Petite Rouge Riding Hood
Petite Rouge: A Cajun Red Riding Hood - Mike Artell
p, e 22

Pip
Grandmas Trick-or-Treat - Emily Arnold McCully
b 612

Potter, Hope Penny
Five Smooth Stones: Hope's Diary - Kristiana Gregory
e 348

Rachel
Rachel Captures the Moon - Samuel Tenenbaum   *p,*
e 874

Read, Patty
Snow Mountain Passage - James D. Houston
a 423

Reed, Alyssa "Blister"
Blister - Susan Shreve   *e, m* 819

Rind, Maria
Maria's Story: 1773 - Joan Lowery Nixon   *e,*
m 678

Rusoe, Nim
Nim's Island - Wendy Orr   *e* 690

Sams, Janie
The Girl with 500 Middle Names - Margaret Peterson
Haddix   *e* 366

Sarah
Sweet, Sweet Memory - Jacqueline Woodson   *p,*
e 984

Saraleen
Mim's Christmas Jam - Andrea Davis Pinkney
p 715

Sofia
Mama Does the Mambo - Katherine Leiner   *p,*
e 543

Tabitha
Tabitha's Terrifically Tough Tooth - Charlotte
Middleton   *p* 636

Tilja
The Ropemaker - Peter Dickinson   *m, h* 232

Unnamed Character
The Biggest Fish in the Lake - Margaret Carney   *p,*
e 140
Desser the Best Ever Cat - Maggie Smith   *p* 833
Earthquake - Milly Lee   *p* 542
Five Creatures - Emily Jenkins   *p* 452
The Magical, Mystical, Marvelous Coat - Catherine
Ann Cullen   *p* 200
Miss Mouse Takes Off - Jan Ormerod   *p* 688
Ride - Stephen Gammell   *p* 310
The Singing Hat - Tohby Riddle   *p* 747

Witting, Cassie
Caleb's Story - Patricia MacLachlan   *e, m* 586

Yoko
Yoko's Paper Cranes - Rosemary Wells   *p* 939

Zeel
Rowan and the Travelers - Emily Rodda   *e* 759

DEAF PERSON

Haig-Ereildoun, Claire
Do Try to Speak as We Do: The Diary of an American Au Pair - Marjorie Leet Ford   a 297

DEITY

Kaputano
The Great Canoe: A Karina Legend - Maria Elena Maggi   p, e 589

Kauhuhu
The Shark God - Rafe Martin   p 597

King of Heaven
Jabuti the Tortoise: A Trickster Tale from the Amazon - Gerald McDermott   p 615

DEMON

Unnamed Character
ZigaZak!: A Magical Hanukkah Night - Eric A. Kimmel   p 499
ZigaZak!: A Magical Hanukkah Night - Eric A. Kimmel   p 499

DESIGNER

Bloom, Cleo
What Every Girl (Except Me) Knows - Nora Raleigh Baskin   m 58

Conda, Anna
Trial by Jury/Journal - Kate Klise   m 514

DETECTIVE

Dot
Dot & Jabber and the Great Acorn Mystery - Ellen Stoll Walsh   p 921

Jabber
Dot & Jabber and the Great Acorn Mystery - Ellen Stoll Walsh   p 921

DETECTIVE—AMATEUR

Armstrong, Jake
The Protestor's Song - Mark Delaney   m 223

Braddock, Peter
The Protestor's Song - Mark Delaney   m 223

Collin
4 1/2 Friends and the Secret Cave - Joachim Friedrich   e 305
41/2 Friends and the Disappearing Bio Teacher - Joachim Friedrich   e 306

Doyle, Drake
The Case of the Gasping Garbage - Michele Torrey   e 887

Dulcie
Cat Spitting Mad - Shirley Rousseau Murphy   a 659

Gates, Russell "Rusty"
Mystery from History - Dayle Campbell Gaetz   e, m 307

Gecko, Chet
Farewell, My Lunchbag - Bruce Hale   e, m 370

Jacques, Orville
The Secrets of Code Z - T.M. Murphy   m 660

Jansen, Cam
Cam Jansen and the School Play Mystery - David A. Adler   e 6

Joe Grey
Cat Spitting Mad - Shirley Rousseau Murphy   a 659

Johansson, Hilda
Green Grow the Victims - Jeanne M. Dams   a 207

Keyes, Samantha "Sammy"
Sammy Keyes and the Hollywood Mummy - Wendelin Van Draanen   m 900

Konoike, Seikei
The Demon in the Teahouse - Dorothy Hoobler   m 416

McGrady, Jennie
Stranded - Patricia H. Rushford   m, h 773

Murphy, Molly
Murphy's Law - Rhys Bowen   a 96

Nate the Great
Nate the Great and the Big Sniff - Marjorie Weinman Sharmat   b 816

Norbert
4 1/2 Friends and the Secret Cave - Joachim Friedrich   e 305
41/2 Friends and the Disappearing Bio Teacher - Joachim Friedrich   e 306

Rademacher, Austin "Radish"
4 1/2 Friends and the Secret Cave - Joachim Friedrich   e 305
41/2 Friends and the Disappearing Bio Teacher - Joachim Friedrich   e 306

Rademacher, Stefanie "Steffi"
4 1/2 Friends and the Secret Cave - Joachim Friedrich   e 305
41/2 Friends and the Disappearing Bio Teacher - Joachim Friedrich   e 306

Ramiro, Matthew "Mattie"
The Protestor's Song - Mark Delaney   m 223

Reid, Katie
Mystery from History - Dayle Campbell Gaetz   e, m 307

Salzmann, Eugenia "Byte"
The Protestor's Song - Mark Delaney   m 223

Tantamoq, Hermux
The Sands of Time - Michael Hoeye   m, h 406

Walton, Sheila
Mystery from History - Dayle Campbell Gaetz   e, m 307

Zwake, Finnegan
The Viking Claw - Michael Dahl   m 204

DETECTIVE—POLICE

Bill
The Web Files - Margie Palatini   p, e 694

Ducktective Web
The Web Files - Margie Palatini   p, e 694

Mr. Trent
The Rag and Bone Shop - Robert Cormier   m, h 183

DETECTIVE—PRIVATE

Brown, Bunny
The Case of the Puzzling Possum - Cynthia Rylant   b, e 778
The Case of the Troublesome Turtle - Cynthia Rylant   b, e 779

Jones, Jack
The Case of the Puzzling Possum - Cynthia Rylant   b, e 778
The Case of the Troublesome Turtle - Cynthia Rylant   b, e 779

DINOSAUR

Clyne
Ancient Fire - Mark London Williams   m 964

DIPLOMAT

Alvarez-Shipton, Benita
The Fresco - Sheri S. Tepper   h, a 875

Cameron, Bren
Defender - C.J. Cherryh   h, a 155

DIVER

Montana
Waiting to Dive - Karen Rivers   e, m 750

Samantha
Waiting to Dive - Karen Rivers   e, m 750

Trager, Mark
Tender - Valerie Hobbs   h 403

DIVORCED PERSON

Daddy
Two Homes - Claire Masurel   p 599

Mommy
Two Homes - Claire Masurel   p 599

DOCTOR

Baldt, William
Boston Jane: An Adventure - Jennifer L. Holm   m 409

Dr. Duck
Felix Feels Better - Rosemary Wells   p 936

Dr. Fairchild
Seeds of Hope: The Gold Rush Diary of Susanna Fairchild, California Territory, 1849 - Kristiana Gregory   m 349

Dr. Hodgins
Kit's Law - Donna Morrissey   h, a 651

Minick, Graham
Desperate Measures - Kate Wilhelm   a 959

Richards, Eric
When Dad Killed Mom - Julius Lester   h 549

Rush, Benjamin
Thomas Jefferson: Letters from a Philadelphia Bookworm - Jennifer Armstrong   m 19

Witherspoon, Maya
The Serpent's Shadow - Mercedes Lackey   h, a 526

DOG

Bandit
Delfino's Journey - Jo Harper   m, h 375

Barker, Moffat "Moffie"
Meet the Barkers: Morgan and Moffat Go to School - Tomie DePaola   p 225

Barker, Morgan "Morgie"
Meet the Barkers: Morgan and Moffat Go to School - Tomie DePaola   p 225

Beans
A Fine, Fine School - Sharon Creech   p 191

Biff
The Pocket Dogs - Margaret Wild   p 954

Briquette
Fiddleback - Elizabeth Honey   m 414

GOOSE

Goose
Silly Little Goose! - Nancy Tafuri   *p*   864

Magnolia
The Goose Who Went Off in a Huff - Paul Brett Johnson   *p*   459

GOVERNMENT OFFICIAL

Haig-Ereildoun, Angus
Do Try to Speak as We Do: The Diary of an American Au Pair - Marjorie Leet Ford   *a*   297

Jefferson, Thomas
Thomas Jefferson: Letters from a Philadelphia Bookworm - Jennifer Armstrong   *m*   19

Kennedy, John Fitzgerald
6-321 - Michael Laser   *m*   533

Roosevelt, Theodore
Theodore Roosevelt: Letters from a Young Coal Miner - Jennifer Armstrong   *m*   18

Shapiro, Hank
The Pickup Artist - Terry Bisson   *h, a*   78

GRANDFATHER

Alnor
The Ropemaker - Peter Dickinson   *m, h*   232

Bannister, Armand
Lorenzo's Secret Mission - Lila Guzman   *m*   362

Crawford, William "Cherokee"
Cherokee - Creina Mansfield   *m*   592

Dawson, Abner "Grampy"
Moonshiner's Gold - John R. Erickson   *m*   279

Duncan, Chet
Flipped - Wendelin Van Draanen   *m*   899

Gramps
Bluebird Summer - Deborah Hopkinson   *p, e*   418
Butterfly Buddies - Judy Cox   *e*   190

Grand-Pierre
Zazoo: A Novel - Richard Mosher   *m, h*   653

Grandad Fuller
Fair Weather - Richard Peck   *m*   704

Granddad
A Thanksgiving Turkey - Julian Scheer   *p, e*   799

Grandpa
The Biggest Fish in the Lake - Margaret Carney   *p, e*   140
Grandpa Blows His Penny Whistle Until the Angels Sing - Susan L. Roth   *p, e*   769
Gus and Grandpa at Basketball - Claudia Mills   *b*   641
No Kiss for Grandpa - Harriet Ziefert   *p*   1001
Sweet, Sweet Memory - Jacqueline Woodson   *p, e*   984

Grandpap
Dancing in Cadillac Light - Kimberly Willis Holt   *m*   411

Griffith, Martin
Gwyneth's Secret Grandpa - Annie Morris Williams   *e*   961

Lemon, Silas
The Memory Prisoner - Thomas Bloor   *m*   87

Mead, Francis "El Pintor"
The Summer of El Pintor - Ofelia Dumas Lachtman   *m, h*   525

Mr. Kang
Happy Birthday Mr. Kang - Susan L. Roth   *p, e*   770

Ojiisan
Yoko's Paper Cranes - Rosemary Wells   *p*   939

Pentreath, Thomas "Chips"
A Sailor Returns - Theodore Taylor   *e*   873

Pop
Fur-Ever Yours, Booker Jones - Betsy Duffey   *e, m*   252

Poppa Joe
Little Cliff's First Day of School - Clifton L. Taulbert   *p*   868

Pops
Freewill - Chris Lynch   *h*   581

Stonemason, Abbott Bristol
Extra Innings - Robert Newton Peck   *m*   705

Unnamed Character
Wild Bog Tea - Annette LeBox   *p, e*   540

Wilkes, Hobson
How Many Days Until Tomorrow? - Caroline Janover   *e, m*   449

Williams, Ulysses
Storm Warriors - Elisa Carbone   *m*   138

Witting, John "Grandfather"
Caleb's Story - Patricia MacLachlan   *e, m*   586

GRANDMOTHER

Bott, Lucy "Memaw"
Up a Creek - Laura E. Williams   *m*   962

Bradley, Helen
Stranded - Patricia H. Rushford   *m, h*   773

Bramblewine, Arianna "Grandy"
Witch Twins - Adele Griffin   *e*   351

Bubbeh
Rivka's First Thanksgiving - Elsa Okon Rael   *p, e*   733

Claire
The Great Good Thing - Roderick Townley   *e, m*   888

Crosby, Hattie
Hattie's Story - Susan E. Kirby   *e*   505

Daisy G.
Blister - Susan Shreve   *e, m*   819

Dapplevine, Eula "Miss Eula"
Love, Ruby Lavender - Deborah Wiles   *e, m*   956

GninGnin
Henry's First-Moon Birthday - Lenore Look   *p*   570

Gogo
What's Cooking, Jamela? - Niki Daly   *p*   206

Gram Jennie
Hattie's Story - Susan E. Kirby   *e*   505
Ida Lou's Story - Susan E. Kirby   *e*   506

Gran
Freewill - Chris Lynch   *h*   581
The Hickory Chair - Lisa Rowe Fraustino   *p*   300
Sammy and the Robots - Ian Whybrow   *p*   949

Grand-mere
Petite Rouge: A Cajun Red Riding Hood - Mike Artell   *p, e*   22

Grandma
Bunny Party - Rosemary Wells   *p*   935
Grandma's Records - Eric Velasquez   *p, e*   910
Joining the Boston Tea Party - Diane Stanley   *p, e*   849
Katie and the Sunflowers - James Mayhew   *p*   604
See You Soon Moon - Donna Conrad   *p*   179
The Snail House - Allan Ahlberg   *p*   10
Sweet, Sweet Memory - Jacqueline Woodson   *p, e*   984

Grandma Marilyn
Aunt Claire's Yellow Beehive Hair - Deborah Blumenthal   *p*   88

Grandma Nan
Grandmas Trick-or-Treat - Emily Arnold McCully   *b*   612

Grandma Pinot
The Things I Know Best - Lynne Hinton   *a*   399

Grandma Sal
Grandmas Trick-or-Treat - Emily Arnold McCully   *b*   612

Grandma Soukeye
Bintou's Braids - Sylviane A. Diouf   *p*   235

Grandmere
Princess in the Spotlight - Meg Cabot   *m, h*   131

Grandmother
Ghost Wings - Barbara Joosse   *p*   470

Granny
A Houseful of Christmas - Barbara Joosse   *p*   471
One More Wednesday - Malika Doray   *p*   242
A Penguin Pup for Pinkerton - Steven Kellogg   *p*   486

Granville, Fiona "Gramma"
The Gramma War - Kristin Butcher   *m*   129

Gugu
Gugu's House - Catherine Stock   *p*   860

Jenkins, Pearl
Black Angels - Rita Murphy   *m*   658

Mama Frances
Goin' Someplace Special - Patricia C. McKissack   *p, e*   625

Mama Pearl
Little Cliff's First Day of School - Clifton L. Taulbert   *p*   868

Marstead, Gloria "Glory"
Playing for Keeps - Joan Lowery Nixon   *m, h*   679

Meena
The Ropemaker - Peter Dickinson   *m, h*   232

Mehta, Naniji
A Group of One - Rachna Gilmore   *m, h*   332

Nana
The Friday Nights of Nana - Amy Hest   *p*   393

Obaasan
Yoko's Paper Cranes - Rosemary Wells   *p*   939

Oma
Jimmy Dabble - Frans Vischer   *e*   914

PawPaw
Coolies - Yin   *p, e*   996

Pearl
Pearl - Debbie Atwell   *p, e*   31

Pitman, Lizzy
Kit's Law - Donna Morrissey   *h, a*   651

PoPo
Earthquake - Milly Lee   *p*   542

Rosa Maria
Mice and Beans - Pam Munoz Ryan   *p*   776

Ryan, Rosemary Regina "Mimi"
Rosemary Meets Rosemarie - Barbara Robertson   *e, m*   754

Sheridan, Martha "Grandma"
Tides - V.M. Caldwell   *m*   133

Sprague, Aurelia
Mountain Pose - Nancy Hope Wilson   *m*   973

Yaya
My Grandmother Is a Singing Yaya - Karen Scourby D'Arc   *p*   212

GUARDIAN

Armiger, George
Anna on the Farm - Mary Downing Hahn   e   369

GUIDE

Keeley, Ote
Open Season - C.J. Box   a   97

Smoky
Clarence and the Great Surprise - Jean Ekman Adams   p   3

GUINEA PIG

Felix
Felix Feels Better - Rosemary Wells   p   936

Little Whistle
Little Whistle - Cynthia Rylant   p   781
Little Whistle's Dinner Party - Cynthia Rylant   p   782

Mama
Felix Feels Better - Rosemary Wells   p   936

Patches
Patches Lost and Found - Steven Kroll   p   523

Pee Wee
Lexi's Tale - Johanna Hurwitz   e   439

HAMSTER

Hammy
Bus Stop, Bus Go! - Daniel Kirk   p   507

HANDICAPPED

Apropos
Sir Apropos of Nothing - Peter David   h, a   214

Crane-Man
A Single Shard - Linda Sue Park   m   696

Edward
Bone House - Betsy Tobin   h, a   885

Feldman, Alexander "Alex"
Desperate Measures - Kate Wilhelm   a   959

Gladd, Will
Just Ask Iris - Lucy Frank   m   299

Lupe
Tiger's Fall - Molly Bang   e   48

Miller, Frieda
A Nose for Adventure - Richard Scrimger   m   808

Torgerson, Conrad
Welcome to the Great Mysterious - Lorna Landvik   a   531

HANDYMAN

Marchand, Paul
Before Wings - Beth Goobie   m, h   340

White, Nelson
Uncle Daddy - Ralph Fletcher   e, m   293

HEALER

Blackheart, Lilliana "Lili"
The Queen's Necklace - Teresa Edgerton   h, a   260

Gabriel
Secret Sacrament - Sherryl Jordan   h   472

Hannah
Treasure at the Heart of the Tanglewood - Meredith Ann Pierce   m, h   711

HEALTER

Florencia
In the Shadow of the Alamo - Sherry Garland   m   316

HEALTH CARE PROFESSIONAL

DaCosta, Shayna
Change of Heart - Marcia King-Gamble   a   501

HEIR

Smith, Oliver
Dial-a-Ghost - Eva Ibbotson   e, m   441

HEIRESS

Pied, Piper
Eccentric Circles - Rebecca Lickiss   h, a   556

HERO

Crockett, Davy
Davy Crockett Saves the World - Rosalyn Schanzer   p   798

Findlay, Charles
Above and Beyond - Susan Bonners   m   91

Hook, Robin
Robin Hook, Pirate Hunter! - Eric A. Kimmel   p, e   497

Rowan
Rowan and the Travelers - Emily Rodda   e   759

Sam
Scatterbrain Sam - Ellen Jackson   p, e   444

HEROINE

Mabela
Mabela the Clever - Margaret Read MacDonald   p   584

HIPPOPOTAMUS

Big Hippo
Naughty! - Caroline Castle   p   148

Blinky
New Pet - Dan Yaccarino   e   992

Hip
The Problem with Pumpkins: A Hip & Hop Story - Barney Saltzberg   p   790

Little Hippo
Naughty! - Caroline Castle   p   148

Mr. Paris
The Case of the Troublesome Turtle - Cynthia Rylant   b, e   779

HISTORICAL FIGURE

Adams, John Quincy
John Quincy Adams: Letters from a Southern Planter's Son - Steven Kroll   m   522

Aethelflaed "Flaed"
The Edge on the Sword - Rebecca Tingle   m, h   884

Alcott, Bronson
Becoming Little Women: Louisa May at Fruitlands - Jeannine Atkins   e, m   28
Little Women Next Door - Sheila Solomon Klass   e, m   511

Alcott, Louisa May
Becoming Little Women: Louisa May at Fruitlands - Jeannine Atkins   e, m   28
Little Women Next Door - Sheila Solomon Klass   e, m   511

Alfred
The Edge on the Sword - Rebecca Tingle   m, h   884

Allen, Ethan
The Hero of Ticonderoga - Gail Gauthier   m   320

Banks, John
Through the Wormhole - Robert J. Favole   m   284

Carnegie, Andrew
In Sunlight, in a Beautiful Garden - Kathleen Cambor   a   135

Chin, Vincent
A Day for Vincent Chin and Me - Jacqueline Turner Banks   e   50

Cleghorn, Victoria Kawekiu Lunalilo Kala
Kaiulani: The People's Princess, Hawaii, 1889 - Ellen Emerson White   m   948

Clyman, James
Daniel's Walk - Michael Spooner   m   845

Cody, Buffalo Bill
The Sketchbook of Thomas Blue Eagle - Gay Matthaei   m   602

Columbus, Christopher
Freedom beyond the Sea - Waldtraut Lewin   m, h   554

Coram, Thomas
Coram Boy - Jamila Gavin   m, h   321

de Galvez, Bernardo
Lorenzo's Secret Mission - Lila Guzman   m   362

de Vere, Edward
A Question of Will - Lynne Kositsky   m   517

Edison, Thomas Alva
The Edison Mystery - Dan Gutman   e, m   359

Edward VI
Beware, Princess Elizabeth - Carolyn Meyer   m   634

Elizabeth
Beware, Princess Elizabeth - Carolyn Meyer   m   634

Ethelred of Mercia
The Edge on the Sword - Rebecca Tingle   m, h   884

Frank, Anne
Anne Frank and Me - Cherie Bennett   m   68

General Santa Anna
In the Shadow of the Alamo - Sherry Garland   m   316
Victor Lopez at the Alamo - James Rice   m   745

Haywood, Bill
Rockbuster - Gloria Skurzynski   m, h   827

Hill, Joe
Rockbuster - Gloria Skurzynski   m, h   827

Jack the Ripper
My Grandfather, Jack the Ripper - Claudio Apone   m   16

James, Frank
Horse Sense - Jan Neubert Schultz   e, m   801

James, Jesse
Horse Sense - Jan Neubert Schultz   e, m   801

Jefferson, Thomas
Thomas Jefferson: Letters from a Philadelphia Bookworm - Jennifer Armstrong   m   19

Kennedy, John Fitzgerald
6-321 - Michael Laser   m   533

Mommy
Goodbye Mousie - Robie H. Harris   p   379
Little Bird, Biddle Bird - David Kirk   p   508
Mom Pie - Lynne Jonell   p   468
Two Homes - Claire Masurel   p   599

Mother
Estelle and Lucy - Anna Alter   p   14
The Journey - Sarah Stewart   p, e   857
My Best Friend Bear - Tony Johnston   p   465
Tub-boo-boo - Margie Palatini   p   693

Mother Claus
Peter Claus and the Naughty List - Lawrence David
   p   213

Mrs. Bear
Kiss Good Night - Amy Hest   p   394

Mrs. Bert
The Adventures of Bert - Allan Ahlberg   p   8

Mrs. Gaskitt
The Man Who Wore All His Clothes - Allan Ahlberg
   e   9

Mrs. Haig-Ereildoun
*Do Try to Speak as We Do: The Diary of an American
   Au Pair* - Marjorie Leet Ford   a   297

Mutton, Momma
The Many Adventures of Johnny Mutton - James
   Proimos   e   726

Nakunte
My Baby - Jeanette Winter   p   975

Nelson, Hannah
The School Story - Andrew Clements   e, m   167

Nimue
The Dragon's Son - Sarah L. Thomson   h, a   882

O'Connor, Kathleen
Murphy's Law - Rhys Bowen   a   96

Pitman, Josie
Kit's Law - Donna Morrissey   h, a   651

Rind, Clementina
Maria's Story: 1773 - Joan Lowery Nixon   e,
   m   678

Sarah
A Mountain of Blintzes - Barbara Diamond Goldin
   p   338

Strang, Lorraine
My Guy - Sarah Weeks   e, m   933

Tolliver, Clara
Wishes, Kisses, and Pigs - Betsy Gould Hearne
   e   386

Unnamed Character
Farm Flu - Teresa Bateman   p   59
Five Creatures - Emily Jenkins   p   452
Four Hungry Kittens - Emily Arnold McCully
   p   611
Franny B. Kranny, There's a Bird in Your Hair! -
   Harriet Lerner   p   545
Heart of Mine: A Story of Adoption - Lotta Hojer
   p   408
I Am the King! - Nathalie Dieterle   p   234
I Love You Because You're You - Liza Baker   p   44
Love Me, Love You - Susan Heyboer O'Keefe
   p   684
Miss Mouse Takes Off - Jan Ormerod   p   688
One Dark Night - Hazel Hutchins   p   440
Oranges on Golden Mountain - Elizabeth Partridge
   p, e   697
Sophie's Masterpiece: A Spider's Tale - Eileen Spinelli
   p   843
Welcome to Kindergarten - Anne Rockwell   p   758

Vener, Miriam Starobin
Half a Heart - Rosellen Brown   a   105

Victoire, of Sax
Victoria: May Blossom of Britannia, England, 1829 -
   Anna Kirwan   e, m   509

Waysorta, Elaine Mae
The Truth about Rats, Rules, & Seventh Grade - Linda
   Zinnen   e, m   1005

Winthrop, Catherine
Following Fake Man - Barbara Ware Holmes
   m   410

MOTORCYCLIST

Fournier, Grey
Lightning Rider - Jacqueline Guest   m, h   355

Fournier, January "Jan"
Lightning Rider - Jacqueline Guest   m, h   355

Turner, Jed
Labyrinth - John Herman   m, h   388

Wilkins, Rob
When Lightning Strikes - Jenny Carroll   m, h   142

MOUNTAINEER

Howie
Witch's Fang - Heather Kellerhals-Stewart   m,
   h   484

Leo
Witch's Fang - Heather Kellerhals-Stewart   m,
   h   484

Rushton, Todd
Witch's Fang - Heather Kellerhals-Stewart   m,
   h   484

Stone, Kurt
Witch's Fang - Heather Kellerhals-Stewart   m,
   h   484

MOUSE

Brown, Audrey
The Crystal Prison - Robin Jarvis   m   450

Chitter, Oswald
The Crystal Prison - Robin Jarvis   m   450

Dot
Dot & Jabber and the Great Acorn Mystery - Ellen
   Stoll Walsh   p   921

Jabber
Dot & Jabber and the Great Acorn Mystery - Ellen
   Stoll Walsh   p   921

Louise
Sheila Rae's Peppermint Stick - Kevin Henkes
   p   387

Lucy
Estelle and Lucy - Anna Alter   p   14

Mabela
Mabela the Clever - Margaret Read MacDonald
   p   584

Miss Mouse
Miss Mouse's Day - Jan Ormerod   p   689

Mousie
Goodbye Mousie - Robie H. Harris   p   379

Sheila Rae
Sheila Rae's Peppermint Stick - Kevin Henkes
   p   387

Stenrill, Mirrin
The Sands of Time - Michael Hoeye   m, h   406

Tantamoq, Hermux
The Sands of Time - Michael Hoeye   m, h   406

Unnamed Character
Hide & Seek - Brenda Shannon Yee   p   993

Too Big, Too Small, Just Right - Frances Minters
   p   643

MUSEUM CURATOR

Johnson, Grace
Rocks in His Head - Carol Otis Hurst   p, e   437

MUSICIAN

Armstrong, Jake
The Protestor's Song - Mark Delaney   m   223

Ashbrook, Alexander
Coram Boy - Jamila Gavin   m, h   321

Bruce, Orphelia
The Minstrel's Melody - Eleanora E. Tate   e,
   m   867

Cat
And the Dish Ran Away with the Spoon - Janet
   Stevens   p   855

Crawford, William "Cherokee"
Cherokee - Creina Mansfield   m   592

Davis, Miles
Lookin' for Bird in the Big City - Robert Burleigh
   p, e   125

Freddy
The Case of the Puzzling Possum - Cynthia Rylant
   b, e   778

Hayes, Violet
You Don't Know Me - David Klass   m, h   510

Hill, Joe
Rockbuster - Gloria Skurzynski   m, h   827

Jackson, D'Angola
A Piece of Heaven - Sharon Dennis Wyeth   m   989

John
You Don't Know Me - David Klass   m, h   510

Keith
*Amazing Maurice and His Educated Rodents: A Novel
   of Discworld* - Terry Pratchett   h   723

Lancaster, Nicola "Nic"
Empress of the World - Sara Ryan   h   777

Lionel
Rowan Hood: Outlaw Girl of Sherwood Forest -
   Nancy Springer   e, m   847

MacDougall, Big Murdoch
A Fiddle for Angus - Budge Wilson   p, e   968

O'Neal, James
Welcome to the Great Mysterious - Lorna Landvik
   a   531

Parker, Charlie "Bird"
Lookin' for Bird in the Big City - Robert Burleigh
   p, e   125

Smilin' Jack
Rent Party Jazz - William Miller   p, e   640

Throbber, Nigel
Expiration Date: Never - Stephanie Spinner   e   844

Ziller, Mahrai
Look to Windward - Iain Banks   h, a   49

Zuckerman, Jerry
My Guy - Sarah Weeks   e, m   933

MYTHICAL CREATURE

Aelvarim
Eccentric Circles - Rebecca Lickiss   h, a   556

Aquamarine
Aquamarine - Alice Hoffman   m   407

Dennis
Website of the Warped Wizard - Eric A. Kimmel
   e   498

Golem
Prisoner in Time: A Child of the Holocaust - Pamela
   Melnikoff   m   632

Line, Victoria "Vikki"
Flatterland: Like Flatland, Only More So - Ian Stewart
   h   856

Master Man
Master Man: A Tall Tale of Nigeria - Aaron Shepard
   p, e   817

Meri
The Merbaby - Teresa Bateman   p, e   61

Minotaur
Labyrinth - John Herman   m, h   388

Mogg
The Moon Robber - Dean Morrissey   e   650

Muckle
How Santa Lost His Job - Stephen Krensky   p   521

Nana
The Dog Prince - Lauren Mills   p, e   642

Nuadha's Silver Druid "Druid"
A Feral Darkness - Doranna Durgin   h, a   254

O'Dell, Sean
Harp O' Gold - Teresa Bateman   p, e   60

Santa
How Santa Lost His Job - Stephen Krensky   p   521
Rover Saves Christmas - Roddy Doyle   e   247

Space Hopper
Flatterland: Like Flatland, Only More So - Ian Stewart
   h   856

NARRATOR

Clover
The Other Side - Jacqueline Woodson   p, e   983

Davis, Miles
Lookin' for Bird in the Big City - Robert Burleigh
   p, e   125

Drake, Jake
Jake Drake, Know-It-All - Andrew Clements
   e   166

Echo
Echo - Francesca Lia Block   h   84

Hathaway, Lucy
Tub-boo-boo - Margie Palatini   p   693

Honey
*Grandpa Blows His Penny Whistle Until the Angels
   Sing* - Susan L. Roth   p, e   769

Law, Erin
Heaven Eyes - David Almond   m   12

Madsen, Matilda
Sailing Home: A Story of a Childhood at Sea - Gloria
   Rand   p, e   734

McKinley
The Good Dog - Avi   e, m   36

Olivia
Super-Completely and Totally the Messiest - Judith
   Viorst   p, e   913

Pontus
You're Growing Up, Pontus! - Ann-Sofie Jeppson   p,
   e   455

Unnamed Boy
The Great Whale of Kansas - Richard W. Jennings
   m   454

Unnamed Character
The Biggest Fish in the Lake - Margaret Carney   p,
   e   140
Breakout at the Bug Lab - Ruth Horowitz   b   421

Unnamed character
The Cheese Monkeys: A Novel in Two Semesters -
   Chip Kidd   a   493

Unnamed Character
Circus Girl - Tomek Bogacki   p   90
Desser the Best Ever Cat - Maggie Smith   p   833
Earthquake - Milly Lee   p   542
Ghost Wings - Barbara Joosse   p   470
Hide & Seek - Brenda Shannon Yee   p   993
The Hole - Guy Burt   a   128
I Love Going Through This Book - Robert Burleigh
   p   124
My Best Friend Bear - Tony Johnston   p   465
One More Wednesday - Malika Doray   p   242
Polar Bolero: A Bedtime Dance - Debi Gliori
   p   334
A Thanksgiving Turkey - Julian Scheer   p, e   799
The Whole Night Through: A Lullaby - David
   Frampton   p   298
Wild Bog Tea - Annette LeBox   p, e   540

Unnamed Girl
Bone House - Betsy Tobin   h, a   885

Wise, Poppy
What Pete Ate from A-Z - Maira Kalman   p   475

NEIGHBOR

Brownbear, Morgan
Morgan Plays Soccer - Anne Rockwell   p   757

Cousin Smith
A Bus of Our Own - Freddi Williams Evans   p,
   e   280

de Gaulle, Celeste
McDuff Goes to School - Rosemary Wells   p   938

Gray, Sally
Emma's Yucky Brother - Jean Little   b   562

Jones, Harold "Hammerhead"
Quiet! You're Invisible - Margaret Meacham
   e   629

Julio
Fat Chance Thanksgiving - Patricia Lakin   p,
   e   529

Kohn, Shannon
The Ghost Sitter - Peni R. Griffin   e, m   353

Paul, Annie
The Other Side - Jacqueline Woodson   p, e   983

Rockett, Wes
The Field of the Dogs - Katherine Paterson   e,
   m   700

Taggert, Belinda Jane "B.J."
Dad, in Spirit - A. LaFaye   e, m   527

Watson, Vera
The Jacob Ladder - Gerald Hausman   m   381

NEPHEW

Alex
Maxwell's Magic Mix-Up - Linda Ashman   p   27

Armiger, Theodore
Anna on the Farm - Mary Downing Hahn   e   369

Bidson, Noah
Prairie School - Avi   b, e   37

Carlos
Uncle Rain Cloud - Tony Johnston   p   466

Doyle, William
The Maiden of Mayfair - Lawana Blackwell   a   82

Guzman, Miguel
How Tia Lola Came to Visit/Stay - Julia Alvarez   e,
   m   15

J. Matthew
Lulu's Birthday - Elizabeth Fitzgerald Howard
   p   425

Maxwell, Simon
No More Nasty - Amy MacDonald   e, m   583

Oliver
Oliver's Milk Shake - Vivian French   p   302

Rich
Welcome to the Great Mysterious - Lorna Landvik
   a   531

NIECE

Annie
Aunt Claire's Yellow Beehive Hair - Deborah
   Blumenthal   p   88

Baboona, Altoona
Altoona Up North - Janie Bynum   p   130

Bean, Clarice
Clarice Bean: Guess Who's Babysitting? - Lauren
   Child   p, e   159

Emma
A Farm of Her Own - Natalie Kinsey-Warnock
   p   504

Hannah
Hannah's Bookmobile Christmas - Sally Derby   p,
   e   226

Iris
Stranger in Dadland - Amy Goldman Koss   e,
   m   519

Laurie
Lulu's Birthday - Elizabeth Fitzgerald Howard
   p   425

Orlando, Alexandra Rockangela "Alex"
The Foreigner - Meg Castaldo   a   147

Sherwood, Anna
Anna on the Farm - Mary Downing Hahn   e   369

Tess
Summer Party - Cynthia Rylant   e   785

NOBLEMAN

Beryn
Straw into Gold - Gary D. Schmidt   m   800

Black Bull of Norroway
The Black Bull of Norroway - Charlotte Huck   p,
   e   432

Blackheart, Wilrowan "Wil"
The Queen's Necklace - Teresa Edgerton   h, a   260

Cathan
Heresy - Anselm Audley   h, a   33

de Vere, Edward
A Question of Will - Lynne Kositsky   m   517

deRais, Gilles
The Merlin of the Oak Woods - Ann Chamberlin   h,
   a   151

Dudley, Amy Robsart
The Twylight Tower - Karen Harper   a   376

Dudley, Robert
The Twylight Tower - Karen Harper   a   376

Ethelred of Mercia
The Edge on the Sword - Rebecca Tingle   m,
   h   884

Lorenzo
Shylock's Daughter - Mirjam Pressler   h   724

NOBLEWOMAN

Baranova, Irina Ivanova
Angel on the Square - Gloria Whelan   *m, h* 946

Betriz
The Curse of Chalion - Lois McMaster Bujold   *h, a* 115

NURSE

Leslie
A Face First - Priscilla Cummings   *m* 201

Loretta
All the Way Home - Patricia Reilly Giff   *e* 330

Nell
The Circus in the Woods - Bill Littlefield   *m, h* 563

Tamara
Soldier X - Don Wulffson   *h* 987

Xanthe
Troy - Adele Geras   *h, a* 327

OPOSSUM

Freddy
The Case of the Puzzling Possum - Cynthia Rylant   *b, e* 778

Possum
Alien & Possum: Friends No Matter What - Tony Johnston   *b* 463

ORPHAN

Armiger, Theodore
Anna on the Farm - Mary Downing Hahn   *e* 369

Barnavelt, Lewis
The Tower at the End of the World - Brad Strickland   *m* 862

Carey, Chipper
Chipper - James Lincoln Collier   *m* 176

Carr, January
Heaven Eyes - David Almond   *m* 12

Caterina
The Orphan Singer - Emily Arnold McCully   *p* 613

Crawford, Gene
Cherokee - Creina Mansfield   *m* 592

Curnow, Maggie
A Bushel of Light - Troon Harrison   *m* 380

Curnow, Thomasina
A Bushel of Light - Troon Harrison   *m* 380

Dearborn, Charlotte
Groover's Heart - Carole Crowe   *e* 197

Deeds, Douglas Allen
The Journal of Douglas Allen Deeds, The Donner Party Expedition, 1846 - Rodman Philbrick   *m* 710

Donohue, Hank
Hank's Story - Jane Buchanan   *e* 113

Donohue, Peter "Pete"
Hank's Story - Jane Buchanan   *e* 113

Fortunato, Alexandria Aurora
Goose Chase - Patrice Kindl   *m, h* 500

Gamage, Bo
Bo & Mzzz Mad - Sid Fleischman   *m* 291

Gullane, Mouse
Heaven Eyes - David Almond   *m* 12

Heart's Delight
Larky Mavis - Brock Cole   *p, e* 170

Heaven Eyes
Heaven Eyes - David Almond   *m* 12

Holland, Jeremy
The Hideout - Peg Kehret   *e, m* 482

Hook, Robin
Robin Hook, Pirate Hunter! - Eric A. Kimmel   *p, e* 497

Ingham, Peter
The Story of Tracy Beaker - Jacqueline Wilson   *e, m* 971

Jubela
Jubela - Cristina Kessler   *p* 491

Kaheena
Benny and Omar - Eoin Colfer   *m* 175

Keely, Kate
A Sea So Far - Jean Thesman   *m, h* 877

Keith
Amazing Maurice and His Educated Rodents: A Novel of Discworld - Terry Pratchett   *h* 723

Knowlton, Harriet "Hattie"
Finding Hattie - Sally Warner   *m* 926

Law, Erin
Heaven Eyes - David Almond   *m* 12

Mateo
Thunder on the Sierra - Kathy Balmes   *e, m* 47

McCulloch, Rosalie
Daniel's Walk - Michael Spooner   *m* 845

McMillan, John Gallatin III
Out of the Night That Covers Me: A Novel - Pat Cunningham Devoto   *a* 229

Milagros, Maria Rosalia de
Valley of the Moon: The Diary of Maria Rosalia De Milagros, Sonoma Valley, Alta California, 1846 - Sherry Garland   *m* 317

Murdoch, Callum
The Carved Box - Gillian Chan   *m* 154

Omar Ben Ali
Benny and Omar - Eoin Colfer   *m* 175

Ortega, Felipe
Stolen by the Sea - Anna Myers   *m* 662

Prentice, Etta
Through the Lock - Carol Otis Hurst   *m* 438

Rayburn, Sarah Matthews
The Maiden of Mayfair - Lawana Blackwell   *a* 82

Rowanna "Anna"
Tree Girl - T.A. Barron   *e, m* 55

Sanchez, Maria
Secrets in the House of Delgado - Gloria D. Miklowitz   *m, h* 639

Shipman, Meredith "Merry"
Shadows in the Glasshouse - Megan McDonald   *e, m* 620

Silver, Sarabeth
Girlhearts - Norma Fox Mazer   *m* 606

Skinner, Johnny
Lady Lollipop - Dick King-Smith   *e* 503

Smith, Oliver
Dial-a-Ghost - Eva Ibbotson   *e, m* 441

Tomas, Mikulase "Mikul"
Rivka's Way - Teri Kanefield   *m* 476

Tree-Ear
A Single Shard - Linda Sue Park   *m* 696

Zazoo
Zazoo: A Novel - Richard Mosher   *m, h* 653

OTTER

Deyna/Tagg
Taggerung - Brian Jacques   *m, h* 447

OUTCAST

Larky Mavis
Larky Mavis - Brock Cole   *p, e* 170

OUTLAW

James, Frank
Horse Sense - Jan Neubert Schultz   *e, m* 801

James, Jesse
Horse Sense - Jan Neubert Schultz   *e, m* 801

Robin Hood
Rowan Hood: Outlaw Girl of Sherwood Forest - Nancy Springer   *e, m* 847

PACIFIST

Shoemaker, Efram Elam "Bud"
Slap Your Sides - M.E. Kerr   *m, h* 489

PAGE

Piers/Pierre
Parsifal's Page - Gerald Morris   *m* 649

PAPERBOY

Charlestown Charlie
Joshua's Song - Joan Hiatt Harlow   *m* 373

Harper, Joshua
Joshua's Song - Joan Hiatt Harlow   *m* 373

PARAPLEGIC

Dora
Prairie School - Avi   *b, e* 37

PAROLE OFFICER

Garvey
Touching Spirit Bear - Ben Mikaelsen   *m, h* 638

PARROT

Baby "Captain Tweakerbeak"
Captain Tweakerbeak's Revenge: A Calliope Day Adventure - Charles Haddad   *e, m* 364

Squawk
Captain and Matey Set Sail - Daniel Laurence   *b* 535

PASSENGER

Unnamed Character
Miss Mouse Takes Off - Jan Ormerod   *p* 688

PATIENT

Bannerjee, Ravi
The Year of My Indian Prince - Ella Thorp Ellis   *m, h* 275

Brennan, Kelley Anne
A Face First - Priscilla Cummings   *m* 201

Luchesi, Nancie
The Year of My Indian Prince - Ella Thorp Ellis   *m, h* 275

PREHISTORIC HUMAN

Agon "Axe Man"
Song of the Axe - John R. Dann   a   209

Eena "Spear Woman"
Song of the Axe - John R. Dann   a   209

Ka
Song of the Axe - John R. Dann   a   209

Tessa
The Eye of the Stone - Tom Birdseye   e, m   75

PRESCHOOLER

Bernard
Bernard Goes to School - Joan Elizabeth Goodman
p   342

Bridget
Bridget and the Gray Wolves - Pija Lindenbaum
p   560

Daniel
Don't Go! - Jane Breskin Zalben   p   1000

Emily
Bernard Goes to School - Joan Elizabeth Goodman
p   342

PRINCIPAL

Duncan, "Frog Face"
Frog Face and the Three Boys - Don Trembath   e,
m   889

Lomister, Gilbert
Don't You Know There's a War On? - Avi   m   35

Mahoney, Marty
Owen Foote, Super Spy - Stephanie Greene   e   346

Mr. Bundy
The Frog Principal - Stephanie Calmenson   p   134

Mr. Keene
A Fine, Fine School - Sharon Creech   p   191

Mr. Krupp
*Captain Underpants and the Wrath of the Wicked
    Wedgie Woman* - Dav Pilkey   e   713

Mr. Lincoln
Mr. Lincoln's Way - Patricia Polacco   p, e   719

Mr. Merrick
Mrs. Spitzer's Garden - Edith Pattou   p   702

Perez, Incarnation
A Book of Coupons - Susie Morgenstern   e, m   646

Westlake, Dan "Uncle Daddy"
Uncle Daddy - Ralph Fletcher   e, m   293

PRODUCER

Smith, Grantley
Evan Can Wait - Rhys Bowen   a   95

PROFESSOR

Branden, Michael
Clouds without Rain - P.L. Gaus   a   319

Hambrick, Paige
Ghost Soldier - Elaine Marie Alphin   m   13

Reece, Eljay
Half a Heart - Rosellen Brown   a   105

Richards, Eric
When Dad Killed Mom - Julius Lester   h   549

Solaja, Dele
The Other Side of Truth - Beverley Naidoo   m,
h   666

Sorbeck, Winter
The Cheese Monkeys: A Novel in Two Semesters -
Chip Kidd   a   493

PROSPECTOR

Thurston, Frosty Jack
Destination Gold! - Julie Lawson   m, h   538

Turner, Edward "Ned"
Destination Gold! - Julie Lawson   m, h   538

PROSTITUTE

Dora
Bone House - Betsy Tobin   h, a   885

PSYCHIC

Baby Girl
Sights - Susanna Vance   m, h   905

Duquesne, Camille
Playing with Fire - Kathleen Karr   m   478

Duquesne, Greer
Playing with Fire - Kathleen Karr   m   478

Grandma Pinot
The Things I Know Best - Lynne Hinton   a   399

Ivy, Liddy
The Things I Know Best - Lynne Hinton   a   399

Ivy, Mama Bertie
The Things I Know Best - Lynne Hinton   a   399

Ivy, Tessa Lucille
The Things I Know Best - Lynne Hinton   a   399

Mastriani, Jessica Antonia
When Lightning Strikes - Jenny Carroll   m, h   142

Raymond, Elijah
Flight of the Raven - Stephanie S. Tolan   m, h   886

Voight, Rachel "Rae"
Gifted Touch - Melinda Metz   m, h   633

PUBLISHER

Davis, Dawn
As Long as She Needs Me - Nicholas Weinstock
a   934

QUAKER

Buchanan, Charity
The Secret Road - Robert Nordan   e, m   682

Crandall, Prudence
The Education of Mary: A Little Miss of Color - Ann
    Rinaldi   m   748

Quinn, Sarah
Five Smooth Stones: Hope's Diary - Kristiana Gregory
e   348

RABBIT

Benny
Bunbun at Bedtime - Sharon Pierce McCullough
p   610

Bibi
Bunbun at Bedtime - Sharon Pierce McCullough
p   610

Brown, Bunny
The Case of the Puzzling Possum - Cynthia Rylant
b, e   778
The Case of the Troublesome Turtle - Cynthia Rylant
b, e   779

Bunbun
Bunbun at Bedtime - Sharon Pierce McCullough
p   610

Bunny
Where Did Bunny Go? - Nancy Tafuri   p   865

Buster
Robert and the Great Pepperoni - Barbara Seuling
e   811

Dan
Happy Easter, Davy! - Brigitte Weninger   p   940

Davy
Happy Easter, Davy! - Brigitte Weninger   p   940

Father Rabbit
Happy Easter, Davy! - Brigitte Weninger   p   940

Flora
Flora's Blanket - Debi Gliori   p   333

Grandma
Bunny Party - Rosemary Wells   p   935

Hop
The Problem with Pumpkins: A Hip & Hop Story -
    Barney Saltzberg   p   790

Little Louis
I Am the King! - Nathalie Dieterle   p   234

Louey
The Adventure of Louey and Frank - Carolyn White
p   947

Max
Bunny Party - Rosemary Wells   p   935

Ms. Turner
D.W.'s Library Card - Marc Brown   p   103

Officer Bunny
Irving and Muktuk: Two Bad Bears - Daniel Pinkwater
p   717

Ruby
Bunny Party - Rosemary Wells   p   935

Unnamed Character
How Hungry Are You? - Donna Jo Napoli   p   669
I Am the King! - Nathalie Dieterle   p   234
I Am the King! - Nathalie Dieterle   p   234
Love Me, Love You - Susan Heyboer O'Keefe
p   684
Love Me, Love You - Susan Heyboer O'Keefe
p   684
The Rabbit Who Longed for Home - Lilian Edvall
p   261
Too Big, Too Small, Just Right - Frances Minters
p   643
Too Big, Too Small, Just Right - Frances Minters
p   643

Willa
Tell Me What It's Like to Be Big - Joyce Dunbar
p   253

Willoughby
Tell Me What It's Like to Be Big - Joyce Dunbar
p   253

RACCOON

Jones, Jack
The Case of the Puzzling Possum - Cynthia Rylant
b, e   778
The Case of the Troublesome Turtle - Cynthia Rylant
b, e   779

Timothy
Mama, Don't Go! - Rosemary Wells   b   937

Unnamed Character
Raccoon on His Own - Jim Arnosky   p   21

RACE CAR DRIVER

Janine, Loren
Conflict in California - Ken Stuckey   *m, h*   863

Mann, Orly
Conflict in California - Ken Stuckey   *m, h*   863

RAILROAD WORKER

Jones, John Luther "Casey"
Casey Jones - Allan Drummond   *p*   250

Papa
Minnie Saves the Day - Melodye Benson Rosales
   e   766

Webb, Sim
Casey Jones - Allan Drummond   *p*   250

RANCHER

Daugherty, John
Victor Lopez at the Alamo - James Rice   *m*   745

don Arturo
Juan Verdades: The Man Who Couldn't Tell a Lie -
   Joe Hayes   *p, e*   385

don Ignacio
Juan Verdades: The Man Who Couldn't Tell a Lie -
   Joe Hayes   *p, e*   385

Rosie
Cowgirl Rosie and Her Five Baby Bison - Stephen
   Gulbis   *p*   356

Stennett, Jackson
Jackson's Way - Leslie LaFoy   *h, a*   528

Weathers, Billy Lindsay
Jackson's Way - Leslie LaFoy   *h, a*   528

RAT

Dangerous Beans
*Amazing Maurice and His Educated Rodents: A Novel
   of Discworld* - Terry Pratchett   *h*   723

Dirty Rat
The Web Files - Margie Palatini   *p, e*   694

Mad-Rat, Maggie
The Revenge of Randal Reese-Rat - Tor Seidler
   e   810

Mad-Rat, Montague "Monty"
The Revenge of Randal Reese-Rat - Tor Seidler
   e   810

Moberly-Rat, Isabel
The Revenge of Randal Reese-Rat - Tor Seidler
   e   810

Peaches
*Amazing Maurice and His Educated Rodents: A Novel
   of Discworld* - Terry Pratchett   *h*   723

Reese-Rat, Randal
The Revenge of Randal Reese-Rat - Tor Seidler
   e   810

Scooter
Rat Boys: A Dating Experiment - Thom Eberhardt
   m   258

Spike
Rat Boys: A Dating Experiment - Thom Eberhardt
   m   258

RECLUSE

Albert
Albert - Donna Jo Napoli   *p, e*   668

Forrester, William
Finding Forrester - James W. Ellison   *a, h*   276

REFUGEE

Anna
Anna's Goat - Janice Kulyk Keefer   *p, e*   481

Mama
Anna's Goat - Janice Kulyk Keefer   *p, e*   481
Gleam and Glow - Eve Bunting   *p, e*   118

Urbino, Enrique "Ricky"
Playing for Keeps - Joan Lowery Nixon   *m, h*   679

Wanda
Anna's Goat - Janice Kulyk Keefer   *p, e*   481

REINDEER

Rudolph
Rover Saves Christmas - Roddy Doyle   *e*   247

RELIGIOUS

Caderine, Martyne
Eyes of the Calculor - Sean McMullen   *h, a*   627

Creffield, Franz Edmund
Brides of Eden - Linda Crew   *m, h*   193

Donovan
Stranded - Patricia H. Rushford   *m, h*   773

Eilan/Julia Helena
Priestess of Avalon - Marion Zimmer Bradley   *h,
   a*   98

Eric
Stranded - Patricia H. Rushford   *m, h*   773

Fisher, Eldon
The Boy in the Burning House - Tim Wynne-Jones
   m, h   990

Loewe ben Bezalel, Judah
Prisoner in Time: A Child of the Holocaust - Pamela
   Melnikoff   *m*   632

Lucas
The Crusader - Michael Alexander Eisner   *a*   270

Mompellion, Michael
Year of Wonders - Geraldine Brooks   *h, a*   101

Peters, Oscar Jarvis "O.J."
Between Brothers - C. Kelly Robinson   *a*   756

Preminger, Yoshe
Rivka's First Thanksgiving - Elsa Okon Rael   *p,
   e*   733

Rabbi
ZigaZak!: A Magical Hanukkah Night - Eric A.
   Kimmel   *p*   499

Rabbi Hartman
Death on Sacred Ground - Harriet K. Feder   *m,
   h*   285

Ygnacio
*Valley of the Moon: The Diary of Maria Rosalia De
   Milagros, Sonoma Valley, Alta California, 1846* -
   Sherry Garland   *m*   317

REPTILE

Mrs. Bagoong
Farewell, My Lunchbag - Bruce Hale   *e, m*   370

RESCUER

al-Aya, Tariq
Mansa Musa: The Lion of Mali - Khephra Burns   *e,
   m*   127

Hairy Man
Heroes of Isle Aux Morts - Alice Walsh   *p, e*   920

Harvey, Anne
Heroes of Isle Aux Morts - Alice Walsh   *p, e*   920

Rover, Alex
Nim's Island - Wendy Orr   *e*   690

Skevla, Torstein
The Race of the Birkebeiners - Lise Lunge-Larsen   *p,
   e*   578

Skrukka, Skervald
The Race of the Birkebeiners - Lise Lunge-Larsen   *p,
   e*   578

RESEARCHER

Jones, Luke "Dad"
Dad, in Spirit - A. LaFaye   *e, m*   527

RESISTANCE FIGHTER

Grand-Pierre
Zazoo: A Novel - Richard Mosher   *m, h*   653

Hubener, Helmuth
Brothers in Valor: A Story of Resistance - Michael O.
   Tunnell   *m, h*   890

Ollenik, Rudi
Brothers in Valor: A Story of Resistance - Michael O.
   Tunnell   *m, h*   890

Papa
Gleam and Glow - Eve Bunting   *p, e*   118

Parkinson, Anthony
Brother Enemy - Robert Elmer   *m*   277

Schneider, Karl
Brothers in Valor: A Story of Resistance - Michael O.
   Tunnell   *m, h*   890

Zalinski, Natan
Brother Enemy - Robert Elmer   *m*   277

RESTAURATEUR

Bowzer
Everything on a Waffle - Polly Horvath   *m*   422

Colonel Mane
Fast Food! Gulp! Gulp! - Bernard Waber   *p*   915

REVOLUTIONARY

Gnedich, Mikhail Sergeyevich "Misha"
Angel on the Square - Gloria Whelan   *m, h*   946

Innes
Straw into Gold - Gary D. Schmidt   *m*   800

RHINOCEROS

Jubela
Jubela - Cristina Kessler   *p*   491

Unnamed Character
Jubela - Cristina Kessler   *p*   491

ROBOT

Bobo Dog
Bobo Crazy - Marilyn Sadler   *e*   786

Simon
My Brother, the Robot - Bonnie Becker   *e*   65

ROOMMATE

Johannsen, Mary Jo
Wurst Case Scenario - Catherine Clark   *h*   164

ROOSTER

Arthur
Something Wonderful - Jenny Nimmo   p   676

Bernard
Bernard the Angry Rooster - Mary Wormell   p   985

ROYALTY

Adeline "Addie"
The Two Princesses of Bamarre - Gail Carson Levine
  m   550

Aethelflaed "Flaed"
The Edge on the Sword - Rebecca Tingle   m,
  h   884

Alexandrina Victoria
Victoria: May Blossom of Britannia, England, 1829 -
  Anna Kirwan   e, m   509

Alfred
The Edge on the Sword - Rebecca Tingle   m,
  h   884

Bannerjee, Ravi
The Year of My Indian Prince - Ella Thorp Ellis   m,
  h   275

Bryan
Summers at Castle Auburn - Sharon Shinn   h,
  a   818

Claudio
Goose Chase - Patrice Kindl   m, h   500

Cleghorn, Victoria Kawekiu Lunalilo Kala
Kaiulani: The People's Princess, Hawaii, 1889 - Ellen
  Emerson White   m   948

Connaire
The Destruction of the Inn - Randy Lee Eickhoff   h,
  a   266

Edmund
Goose Chase - Patrice Kindl   m, h   500

Edward VI
Beware, Princess Elizabeth - Carolyn Meyer
  m   634

Elisandra
Summers at Castle Auburn - Sharon Shinn   h,
  a   818

Elizabeth
Beware, Princess Elizabeth - Carolyn Meyer
  m   634

Elizabeth I
The Twylight Tower - Karen Harper   a   376

Entipy
Sir Apropos of Nothing - Peter David   h, a   214

Ettarde "Etty"
Rowan Hood: Outlaw Girl of Sherwood Forest -
  Nancy Springer   e, m   847

Fabien
The War - Anais Vaugelade   p, e   908

Frieda
The Princess and the Pea - Alain Vaes   p   897

Hakon
The Race of the Birkebeiners - Lise Lunge-Larsen   p,
  e   578

Helen
Odysseus in the Serpent Maze - Jane Yolen   m   997

Iselle
The Curse of Chalion - Lois McMaster Bujold   h,
  a   115

Julius
The War - Anais Vaugelade   p, e   908

Liliuokalani
Kaiulani: The People's Princess, Hawaii, 1889 - Ellen
  Emerson White   m   948

Meryl
The Two Princesses of Bamarre - Gail Carson Levine
  m   550

Musa, Abubakari
Mansa Musa: The Lion of Mali - Khephra Burns   e,
  m   127

Musa, Kankan
Mansa Musa: The Lion of Mali - Khephra Burns   e,
  m   127

Nicholaievna, Anastasia
Angel on the Square - Gloria Whelan   m, h   946

Odysseus
Odysseus in the Serpent Maze - Jane Yolen   m   997

Penelope
Lady Lollipop - Dick King-Smith   e   503

Prince
The Dog Prince - Lauren Mills   p, e   642

Ralph
The Princess and the Pea - Alain Vaes   p   897

Redbird
*Lady of Ch'iao Kuo: Warrior of the South, Southern
  China, A.D. 531* - Laurence Yep   m   995

Renaldo, Amelia "Mia"
Princess in the Spotlight - Meg Cabot   m, h   131

Sameth
Lirael: Daughter of the Clayr - Garth Nix   h   677

Sylvie
The Great Good Thing - Roderick Townley   e,
  m   888

Tudor, Mary
Beware, Princess Elizabeth - Carolyn Meyer
  m   634

Unnamed Character
The Apple King - Francesca Bosca   p, e   94
The Storytelling Princess - Rafe Martin   p   598
The Storytelling Princess - Rafe Martin   p   598

Urdo
The King's Name - Jo Walton   h, a   922
The King's Peace - Jo Walton   h, a   923

Victoire, of Sax
Victoria: May Blossom of Britannia, England, 1829 -
  Anna Kirwan   e, m   509

von Highbredde, Opaline "Opal"
The Princess and the Pea - Alain Vaes   p   897

RULER

Romanov, Nicholas Alexandrovitch II
Angel on the Square - Gloria Whelan   m, h   946

RUNAWAY

Buckley, Celia
Feeling Sorry for Celia - Jaclyn Moriarty   h   648

Catherine
Destination Gold! - Julie Lawson   m, h   538

Donohue, Peter "Pete"
Hank's Story - Jane Buchanan   e   113

Dusty Locks
Dusty Locks and the Three Bears - Susan Lowell
  p   573

Gracie
The Great Gracie Chase: Stop That Dog! - Cynthia
  Rylant   p   780

Hammy
Bus Stop, Bus Go! - Daniel Kirk   p   507

Jackson, Johnny
Drummer - George C. Richardson   m   746

James
Gabriel's Story - David Anthony Durham   h,
  a   255

Lynch, Gabriel
Gabriel's Story - David Anthony Durham   h,
  a   255

Radish
Runaway Radish - Jessie Haas   e   363

Tiernan, Brick
All the Way Home - Patricia Reilly Giff   e   330

RUNNER

Alrika
Time Out - David Hill   m, h   397

Kit
Time Out - David Hill   m, h   397

SAILOR

Cringle, Tom
Tom Cringle: The Pirate and the Patriot - Gerald
  Hausman   m   382

Horn
The Buccaneers - Iain Lawrence   m, h   536

Keeler
The Captain's Wife - Douglas Kelley   a   485

Mangrove, Peter
Tom Cringle: The Pirate and the Patriot - Gerald
  Hausman   m   382

Matey
Captain and Matey Set Sail - Daniel Laurence
  b   535

Pentreath, Thomas "Chips"
A Sailor Returns - Theodore Taylor   e   873

Scudder, Jehu
Boston Jane: An Adventure - Jennifer L. Holm
  m   409

Spencer, John
The Buccaneers - Iain Lawrence   m, h   536

SALESWOMAN

Orlando, Alexandra Rockangela "Alex"
The Foreigner - Meg Castaldo   a   147

SALOON KEEPER/OWNER

Dwyer, Jack
Prowlers - Christopher Golden   h   336

SCHOLAR

Bibliogoth
A Matter of Profit - Hilari Bell   h, a   67

SCIENTIST

der Grimnebulin, Isaac Dan
Perdido Street Station - China Mieville   h, a   637

Dr. Lefkowitz
Night of the Bat - Paul Zindel   m   1004

Fossey, Nell
The Case of the Gasping Garbage - Michele Torrey
  e   887

Lander, Joanna
Passage - Connie Willis   h, a   967

O'Flannery, Megan
The Phoenix Code - Catherine Asaro   *h, a*   23

Rusoe, Jack
Nim's Island - Wendy Orr   *e*   690

Sands, Sandusky
Ancient Fire - Mark London Williams   *m*   964

Smith, Gail
In the Company of Others - Julie Czerneda   *h, a*   203

Sundaram, Chandrarajan "Raj"
The Phoenix Code - Catherine Asaro   *h, a*   23

Wright, Richard
Passage - Connie Willis   *h, a*   967

SEA CAPTAIN

Butterfield, Stanley
The Buccaneers - Iain Lawrence   *m, h*   536

Captain
Captain and Matey Set Sail - Daniel Laurence   *b*   535

Captain Vanderdecken
Castaways of the Flying Dutchman - Brian Jacques   *m*   446

Hook, James
Robin Hook, Pirate Hunter! - Eric A. Kimmel   *p, e*   497

Madsen, Mads Albert
Sailing Home: A Story of a Childhood at Sea - Gloria Rand   *p, e*   734

Monks, Bill
Lord of the Deep - Graham Salisbury   *m*   788

Patten, Joshua
The Captain's Wife - Douglas Kelley   *a*   485

Patten, Mary Ann
The Captain's Wife - Douglas Kelley   *a*   485

Romero, Liza
Sound Tracks - Marcia Simpson   *a*   824

Sanchez, Francisco
Secrets in the House of Delgado - Gloria D. Miklowitz   *m, h*   639

Thatch
Robin Hook, Pirate Hunter! - Eric A. Kimmel   *p, e*   497

SEAMSTRESS

Bell, Dinah
Missing from Haymarket Square - Harriette Gillem Robinet   *m*   755

Lovell, Wanda Jo
A Mother's Gift - Britney Spears   *m*   841

Mama
Mama's Way - Helen Ketteman   *p, e*   492

Schaeffer, Olive
Missing from Haymarket Square - Harriette Gillem Robinet   *m*   755

SERVANT

Butler
Artemis Fowl - Eoin Colfer   *m*   174

Foley, Sean
The Star-Spangled Secret - K.M. Kimball   *e, m*   495

Frith, Anna
Year of Wonders - Geraldine Brooks   *h, a*   101

Fumiko
The Yokota Officers Club - Sarah Bird   *h, a*   74

Johansson, Hilda
Green Grow the Victims - Jeanne M. Dams   *a*   207

Luned
The Dragon's Son - Sarah L. Thomson   *h, a*   882

Morales, Silvia
Finn: A Novel - Matthew Olshan   *h*   686

Paloma Maria "Dovey Mae"
Get Along, Little Dogies: The Chisholm Trail Diary of Hallie Lou Wells: South Texas, 1878 - Lisa Waller Rogers   *m*   762

Rafferty, Leo
Playing with Fire - Kathleen Karr   *m*   478

Rafferty, Peg
Playing with Fire - Kathleen Karr   *m*   478

Sanchez, Maria
Secrets in the House of Delgado - Gloria D. Miklowitz   *m, h*   639

Unnamed Girl
Bone House - Betsy Tobin   *h, a*   885

SETTLER

Barker, Elizabeth "Lizzie"
The Starving Time: Elizabeth's Diary - Patricia Hermes   *e*   389

Elizabeth
William's House - Ginger Howard   *p, e*   426

William
William's House - Ginger Howard   *p, e*   426

SHAMAN

Perika, Daisy
Grandmother Spider - James D. Doss   *a*   243

SHAPE-CHANGER

Hunger Monster
The Hungriest Boy in the World - Lensey Namioka   *p*   667

Kauhuhu
The Shark God - Rafe Martin   *p*   597

Ogre
Puss in Boots: The Adventures of That Most Enterprising Feline - Philip Pullman   *p, e*   728

Quicksilver
Ill Met by Moonlight - Sarah Hoyt   *h, a*   431

Sash
Tree Girl - T.A. Barron   *e, m*   55

Unnamed Character
ZigaZak!: A Magical Hanukkah Night - Eric A. Kimmel   *p*   499

Unnamed Character
ZigaZak!: A Magical Hanukkah Night - Eric A. Kimmel   *p*   499

SHEEP

Mutton, Johnny
The Many Adventures of Johnny Mutton - James Proimos   *e*   726

SHEPHERD

Sandoval, Catalina
In the Shadow of the Alamo - Sherry Garland   *m*   316

Unnamed Character
Harley - Star Livingstone   *b*   565

SINGER

Caterina
The Orphan Singer - Emily Arnold McCully   *p*   613

English, Janie "Leshaya"
Born Blue - Han Nolan   *h*   681

Jordan, Geneva
Welcome to the Great Mysterious - Lorna Landvik   *a*   531

Lovell, Holly Faye
A Mother's Gift - Britney Spears   *m*   841

Molly
A Fiddle for Angus - Budge Wilson   *p, e*   968

Ruff/Rufferella
Rufferella - Vanessa Gill-Brown   *p*   331

Yaya
My Grandmother Is a Singing Yaya - Karen Scourby D'Arc   *p*   212

SINGLE FATHER

Daddy
Just the Two of Us - Will Smith   *p*   835

Jenkins, Colin
The Singing Hat - Tohby Riddle   *p*   747

SINGLE MOTHER

Griffin, Kate
A Long Way Home - Nancy Price Graff   *m*   343

Ingram, Aisha
Spellbound - Janet McDonald   *m, h*   616

Jefferson, Raven
Spellbound - Janet McDonald   *m, h*   616

Mama
Mama's Way - Helen Ketteman   *p, e*   492
Rent Party Jazz - William Miller   *p, e*   640

Mom
By Lizzie - Mary Eccles   *e*   259

Patterson, Ruby
Moonpie and Ivy - Barbara O'Connor   *m*   683

White, Anna
Uncle Daddy - Ralph Fletcher   *e, m*   293

SINGLE PARENT

Brown, Bonnie
The Secret Life of Dr. Demented - Dan Gutman   *m*   361

Mama
Fat Chance Thanksgiving - Patricia Lakin   *p, e*   529

Strang, Lorraine
My Guy - Sarah Weeks   *e, m*   933

Waysorta, Elaine Mae
The Truth about Rats, Rules, & Seventh Grade - Linda Zinnen   *e, m*   1005

SISTER

Amanda
Pinky and Rex and the Just-Right Pet - James Howe   *b, e*   429

Amber
Amber Was Brave, Essie Was Smart - Vera B. Williams   *e*   965

Amelia
Oh Boy, Amelia! - Marissa Moss   *e*   654

Phylis
Molly and the Magic Wishbone - Barbara McClintock
p 609

Puckett, Emma Jo
Emma Jo's Song - Faye Gibbons   p 329

Rafferty, Peg
Playing with Fire - Kathleen Karr   m 478

Read, Dora Winifred "D.W."
D.W.'s Library Card - Marc Brown   p 103

Ridley, Sarah Louise
The Calling - Cathryn Clinton   m, h 169

Robin
Butterfly Buddies - Judy Cox   e 190

Root, Kit
The Yokota Officers Club - Sarah Bird   h, a 74

Rosie
Summer Party - Cynthia Rylant   e 785

Ruby
Bunny Party - Rosemary Wells   p 935

Sabri
A Matter of Profit - Hilari Bell   h, a 67

Samuels, Rose
*Rose's Journal: The Story of a Girl in the Great
   Depression* - Marissa Moss   e 655

Saraleen
Mim's Christmas Jam - Andrea Davis Pinkney
   p 715

Severna, Tracey
Brave New Girl - Louisa Luna   h 576

Sheila Rae
Sheila Rae's Peppermint Stick - Kevin Henkes
   p 387

Sophie
Super-Completely and Totally the Messiest - Judith
   Viorst   p, e 913

Stevens, Barbara
The Edison Mystery - Dan Gutman   e, m 359

Stevens, Madison
The Edison Mystery - Dan Gutman   e, m 359

Susannah
Stealing South: A Story of the Underground Railroad -
   Katherine Ayres   m, h 40

Teresa
Delfino's Journey - Jo Harper   m, h 375

Thomas, Tina
Willimena and the Cookie Money - Valerie Wilson
   Wesley   e 942

Thomas, Willimena "Willie"
Willimena and the Cookie Money - Valerie Wilson
   Wesley   e 942

Tillie
A Fine, Fine School - Sharon Creech   p 191

Turner, Sarah
Destination Gold! - Julie Lawson   m, h 538

Unnamed Character
Ride - Stephen Gammell   p 310
The Shark God - Rafe Martin   p 597
The Stray Dog - Marc Simont   p 823
We're Going on a Ghost Hunt - Marcia Vaughan
   p 909
When We Go Camping - Margriet Ruurs   p 775

Verstuyft, Charlotte
The Ghost Sitter - Peni R. Griffin   e, m 353

Volson, Signy
Bloodtide - Melvin Burgess   h, a 123

Walker, Sarah
The Monsters of Morley Manor: A Madcap Adventure
   - Bruce Coville   e, m 187

Wanda
Anna's Goat - Janice Kulyk Keefer   p, e 481

Wheeler, Lila
Swimming - Joanna Hershon   a 391

Willa
Tell Me What It's Like to Be Big - Joyce Dunbar
   p 253

Winifred
Bun Bun's Birthday - Richard Scrimger   p 807

Wise, Poppy
What Pete Ate from A-Z - Maira Kalman   p 475

Xanthe
Troy - Adele Geras   h, a 327

SKIER

Hill, Beaumont "Beau"
Change of Heart - Marcia King-Gamble   a 501

Skevla, Torstein
The Race of the Birkebeiners - Lise Lunge-Larsen   p,
   e 578

Skrukka, Skervald
The Race of the Birkebeiners - Lise Lunge-Larsen   p,
   e 578

SLAVE

Birdsong, Corey
Freedom's Wings: Corey's Diary - Sharon Dennis
   Wyeth   e, m 988

Daddy
Freedom's Wings: Corey's Diary - Sharon Dennis
   Wyeth   e, m 988

Jackson, Johnny
Drummer - George C. Richardson   m 746

Johnny
Daniel's Walk - Michael Spooner   m 845

Liney
If I Just Had Two Wings - Virginia Frances Schwartz
   m 803

Mama
Freedom's Wings: Corey's Diary - Sharon Dennis
   Wyeth   e, m 988

Mangrove, Peter
Tom Cringle: The Pirate and the Patriot - Gerald
   Hausman   m 382

Noah
Stealing South: A Story of the Underground Railroad -
   Katherine Ayres   m, h 40

Phoebe
If I Just Had Two Wings - Virginia Frances Schwartz
   m 803

Rosetta
The Secret Road - Robert Nordan   e, m 682

Susannah
Stealing South: A Story of the Underground Railroad -
   Katherine Ayres   m, h 40

SLOTH

Sparky
Score One for the Sloths - Helen Lester   p 547

SOCCER PLAYER

Gonzales, Ellie
The Million Dollar Kick - Dan Gutman   m 360

Monkey, Nina Jane
Morgan Plays Soccer - Anne Rockwell   p 757

SOCIAL WORKER

Mrs. Walmsley
Cherokee - Creina Mansfield   m 592

SOFTBALL PLAYER

Gwendolyn "Gwen"
Strike Two - Amy Goldman Koss   e, m 520

Jessica
Strike Two - Amy Goldman Koss   e, m 520

SON

Anderson, Everett
One of the Problems of Everett Anderson - Lucille
   Clifton   p 168

Anderson, John Franklin
Mama's Way - Helen Ketteman   p, e 492

Angus
A Fiddle for Angus - Budge Wilson   p, e 968

Baby Bert
The Adventures of Bert - Allan Ahlberg   p 8

Batbaby
Batbaby Finds a Home - Robert Quackenbush
   b 730

Beto
Beto and the Bone Dance - Gina Freschet   p 303

Christopher
Mom Pie - Lynne Jonell   p 468

Claus, Peter
Peter Claus and the Naughty List - Lawrence David
   p 213

Comeaux, Sonny
Rent Party Jazz - William Miller   p, e 640

Dabble, Jimmy
Jimmy Dabble - Frans Vischer   e 914

Davy
The School Trip - Tjibbe Veldkamp   p 911

Duck, Webster J.
Webster J. Duck - Martin Waddell   p 916

Eli
Eli's Night Light - Liz Rosenberg   p 768

Felix
Felix Feels Better - Rosemary Wells   p 936

Froggy
Froggy Eats Out - Jonathan London   p 568

Gus
Gus and Grandpa at Basketball - Claudia Mills
   b 641

Hakon
The Race of the Birkebeiners - Lise Lunge-Larsen   p,
   e 578

Harry
*Harry the Poisonous Centipede's Big Adventure:
   Another Story to Make You Squirm* - Lynne Reid
   Banks   e 52

Herb
Beware of the Storybook Wolves - Lauren Child   p,
   e 158

Jack
The Famous Adventures of Jack - Berlie Doherty
   e 239
Fearless Jack - Paul Brett Johnson   p, e 458

Jakie
Rattletrap Car - Phyllis Root   p 765

Jiro
The Hungriest Boy in the World - Lensey Namioka
   p 667

Jo Lee
Oranges on Golden Mountain - Elizabeth Partridge
p, e   697

Johann "Long Boy"
Bone House - Betsy Tobin   h, a   885

Josh
The Field of the Dogs - Katherine Paterson   e,
m   700

Kostof, Jack
The Good Dog - Avi   e, m   36

Little Louis
I Am the King! - Nathalie Dieterle   p   234

Little Monster
One Day, Daddy - Frances Thomas   p   879

Louie
No Kiss for Grandpa - Harriet Ziefert   p   1001

Madsen, Albert
Sailing Home: A Story of a Childhood at Sea - Gloria
Rand   p, e   734

Max
Max, the Stubborn Little Wolf - Marie-Odile Judes
p   473

Medraud
The Dragon's Son - Sarah L. Thomson   h, a   882

Moe
A Mountain of Blintzes - Barbara Diamond Goldin
p   338

Pig, Preston
Oomph! - Colin McNaughton   p   628

Potter, Ethan
Five Smooth Stones: Hope's Diary - Kristiana Gregory
e   348

Puddicombe, Percival
His Mother's Nose - Peter Maloney   p   591

Robbie
Mom Pie - Lynne Jonell   p   468

Rowan
Rowan and the Travelers - Emily Rodda   e   759

Royce
Mim's Christmas Jam - Andrea Davis Pinkney
p   715

Sam
Happy Birthday Mr. Kang - Susan L. Roth   p,
e   770
Kiss Good Night - Amy Hest   p   394

Sammy
The Lima Bean Monster - Dan Yaccarino   p   991
Sammy and the Robots - Ian Whybrow   p   949

Simon
A Fish Named Spot - Jennifer P. Goldfinger   p   337

Sol
Lemuel the Fool - Myron Uhlberg   p   893

Tahl
The Ropemaker - Peter Dickinson   m, h   232

Tim
Welcome to Kindergarten - Anne Rockwell   p   758

Toby
Toby, What Are You? - William Steig   p   852

Unnamed Character
Farm Flu - Teresa Bateman   p   59
Fribbity Ribbit! - Suzanne C. Johnson   p   461
Goodbye Mousie - Robie H. Harris   p   379
I Lost My Dad - Taro Gomi   p   339
Just the Two of Us - Will Smith   p   835
More Parts - Tedd Arnold   p, e   20
The Rabbit Who Longed for Home - Lilian Edvall
p   261
Ride - Stephen Gammell   p   310
A Safe Place Called Home - Eileen Spinelli   p   842

See You Soon Moon - Donna Conrad   p   179
Ted - Tony DiTerlizzi   p   237
White Water - Jonathan London   p, e   569
Wild Bog Tea - Annette LeBox   p, e   540

White, Rivers
Uncle Daddy - Ralph Fletcher   e, m   293

William
William and the Night Train - Mij Kelly   p   487

Witting, Caleb
Caleb's Story - Patricia MacLachlan   e, m   586

SORCERER

Barnavelt, Jonathan
The Tower at the End of the World - Brad Strickland
m   862

Ragginbone
The Dragon Charmer - Jan Siegel   h, a   820

Rhys
The Two Princesses of Bamarre - Gail Carson Levine
m   550

SORCERESS

Morgan
Christmas in Camelot - Mary Pope Osborne   e   691
I Am Morgan Le Fay - Nancy Springer   h   846

Widder Woman
Scatterbrain Sam - Ellen Jackson   p, e   444

SPACE EXPLORER

Moe
Company's Going - Arthur Yorinks   p, e   998

Shirley
Company's Going - Arthur Yorinks   p, e   998

SPIDER

Madame Octa
Cirque du Freak: A Living Nightmare - Darren Shan
m, h   813

Sophie
Sophie's Masterpiece: A Spider's Tale - Eileen Spinelli
p   843

SPIRIT

Chamblee, Richeson Francis
Ghost Soldier - Elaine Marie Alphin   m   13

Susie
The Ghost Sitter - Peni R. Griffin   e, m   353

Wildemere, Jessup
Shades of Simon Gray - Joyce McDonald   m,
h   617

Wilkinson, Adopta
Dial-a-Ghost - Eva Ibbotson   e, m   441

Wilkinson, Eric
Dial-a-Ghost - Eva Ibbotson   e, m   441

SPOUSE

Armiger, Aggie
Anna on the Farm - Mary Downing Hahn   e   369

Bert
The Adventures of Bert - Allan Ahlberg   p   8
The Great Pig Search - Eileen Christelow   p   163

Blackheart, Wilrowan "Wil"
The Queen's Necklace - Teresa Edgerton   h, a   260

Dad
Let's Get a Pup! Said Kate - Bob Graham   p   344

David
Pearl - Debbie Atwell   p, e   31

Eckert, Angela "Angie"
The Dragon and the Fair Maid of Kent - Gordon
Dickson   h, a   233

Eckert, James "Jim"
The Dragon and the Fair Maid of Kent - Gordon
Dickson   h, a   233

Elizabeth
William's House - Ginger Howard   p, e   426

Essie
Lemuel the Fool - Myron Uhlberg   p   893

Ethel
The Great Pig Search - Eileen Christelow   p   163

Grandma
Grandpa's Overalls - Tony Crunk   p   198

Lemuel
Lemuel the Fool - Myron Uhlberg   p   893

Lena
Katje, the Windmill Cat - Gretchen Woelfle   p   979

Mama Pearl
Little Cliff's First Day of School - Clifton L. Taulbert
p   868

Max
A Mountain of Blintzes - Barbara Diamond Goldin
p   338

Moe
Company's Going - Arthur Yorinks   p, e   998

Mom
Let's Get a Pup! Said Kate - Bob Graham   p   344

Moon
The Day Ocean Came to Visit - Diane Wolkstein
p   981

Mother Claus
Peter Claus and the Naughty List - Lawrence David
p   213

Mrs. Bert
The Adventures of Bert - Allan Ahlberg   p   8

Mrs. Field
Something Wonderful - Jenny Nimmo   p   676

Nico
Katje, the Windmill Cat - Gretchen Woelfle   p   979

Olson, Jo
Hank's Story - Jane Buchanan   e   113

Poppa Joe
Little Cliff's First Day of School - Clifton L. Taulbert
p   868

Preston
A Mile from Ellington Station - Tim Egan   p   264

Ruth
A Mile from Ellington Station - Tim Egan   p   264

Santa Claus
Peter Claus and the Naughty List - Lawrence David
p   213

Sarah
A Mountain of Blintzes - Barbara Diamond Goldin
p   338

Shadusa
Master Man: A Tall Tale of Nigeria - Aaron Shepard
p, e   817

Shettu
Master Man: A Tall Tale of Nigeria - Aaron Shepard
p, e   817

Shirley
Company's Going - Arthur Yorinks   p, e   998

Character Description Index

STUDENT—ELEMENTARY SCHOOL

STUDENT—EXCHANGE

STUDENT—GRADUATE

STUDENT—HIGH SCHOOL

STUDENT—JUNIOR HIGH SCHOOL

STUDENT—MEDICAL SCHOOL

STUDENT—MIDDLE SCHOOL

STUDENT—PRIVATE SCHOOL

Wallace, Jamal
Finding Forrester - James W. Ellison   *a, h*   276

STUFFED ANIMAL

Bear
My Best Friend Bear - Tony Johnston   *p*   465

Blue Kangaroo
Where Are You, Blue Kangaroo? - Emma Chichester Clark   *p*   157

Miss Mouse
Miss Mouse Takes Off - Jan Ormerod   *p*   688
Miss Mouse's Day - Jan Ormerod   *p*   689

Teddy
Home before Dark - Ian Beck   *p*   64

Unnamed Character
The Whole Night Through: A Lullaby - David Frampton   *p*   298

Wilson
Amber Was Brave, Essie Was Smart - Vera B. Williams   *e*   965

SUFFRAGETTE

Black, Caroline
Falling Angels - Tracy Chevalier   *a*   156

Coleman, Kitty
Falling Angels - Tracy Chevalier   *a*   156

SURVIVOR

Pardell, Aaron
In the Company of Others - Julie Czerneda   *h, a*   203

SWIMMER

Coughlin, Chris
Whale Talk - Chris Crutcher   *h*   199

Hammond, Kate
Through the Wormhole - Robert J. Favole   *m*   284

Jones, The Tao "T.J."
Whale Talk - Chris Crutcher   *h*   199

Wright, Keisha
Born in Sin - Evelyn Coleman   *h*   171

TAILOR

Haskel
A Cloak for the Moon - Eric A. Kimmel   *p, e*   496

TAXI DRIVER

Mrs. Gaskitt
The Man Who Wore All His Clothes - Allan Ahlberg   *e*   9

TEACHER

Annie
Freedom School, Yes! - Amy Littlesugar   *p, e*   564

Bidson, Ida
The Secret School - Avi   *e, m*   38

Chambers, Margaret
Esther's Pillow - Marlin Fitzwater   *a*   288

Gossim, Rolanda
Don't You Know There's a War On? - Avi   *m*   35

Graham, Norman
Piper - Natale Ghent   *m*   328

Jackson, D'Angola
A Piece of Heaven - Sharon Dennis Wyeth   *m*   989

MacDougall, Big Murdoch
A Fiddle for Angus - Budge Wilson   *p, e*   968

Master Chen
Lady of Ch'iao Kuo: Warrior of the South, Southern China, A.D. 531 - Laurence Yep   *m*   995

Master Cleary
Dancing for Danger: A Meggy Tale - Margot Griffin   *e*   352

Maxwell, Matilda "Aunt Mattie"
No More Nasty - Amy MacDonald   *e, m*   583

Miss Bindergarten
Miss Bindergarten Takes a Field Trip with Kindergarten - Joseph Slate   *p*   828

Miss Brody
Bernard Goes to School - Joan Elizabeth Goodman   *p*   342

Miss Bugscuffle
Baloney (Henry P) - Jon Scieszka   *p, e*   804

Miss Cherry
Iris and Walter: True Friends - Elissa Haden Guest   *b*   354

Miss Johnette
Anna Casey's Place in the World - Adrian Fogelin   *m*   296

Miss Mackle
Horrible Harry Goes to Sea - Suzy Kline   *e*   513

Miss March
Three Days Off - Susie Morgenstern   *m, h*   647

Miss Stretchberry
Love That Dog - Sharon Creech   *e, m*   192

Miss Wing
Butterfly Buddies - Judy Cox   *e*   190

Mr. Barraclough
Luke's Way of Looking - Nadia Wheatley   *p, e*   944

Mr. Benito
How to Be a Real Person (in Just One Day) - Sally Warner   *m*   927

Mr. Berry
Don't Go! - Jane Breskin Zalben   *p*   1000

Mr. Brockhurst
The Gramma War - Kristin Butcher   *m*   129

Mr. Gianini
Princess in the Spotlight - Meg Cabot   *m, h*   131

Mr. Griswold
Patches Lost and Found - Steven Kroll   *p*   523

Mr. Martin
Stop, Drop, and Roll - Margery Cuyler   *p*   202

Mr. Santangelo
The Hero of Ticonderoga - Gail Gauthier   *m*   320

Mr. Simet
Whale Talk - Chris Crutcher   *h*   199

Mrs.
Junie B. Jones Is a Graduation Girl - Barbara Park   *e*   695

Mrs. Byrd
We Gather Together ... Now Please Get Lost! - Diane DeGroat   *p*   222

Mrs. Gourd
Math Man - Teri Daniels   *p*   208

Mrs. Jardin
Welcome to Kindergarten - Anne Rockwell   *p*   758

Mrs. Jenkins
Mama, Don't Go! - Rosemary Wells   *b*   937

Mrs. Maxwell
Shrinking Violet - Cari Best   *p, e*   71

Mrs. Morrow
The Day Eddie Met the Author - Louise Borden   *e*   93

Mrs. Spitzer
Mrs. Spitzer's Garden - Edith Pattou   *p*   702

Ms. Benson
Cam Jansen and the School Play Mystery - David A. Adler   *e*   6

Ms. Brown
Marvin One Too Many - Katherine Paterson   *b*   701

Ms. Clayton
The School Story - Andrew Clements   *e, m*   167

Ms. Fair
Emily's Art - Peter Catalanotto   *p*   149

Ms. Ribble
Captain Underpants and the Wrath of the Wicked Wedgie Woman - Dav Pilkey   *e*   713

Ms. Shepherd
Meet the Barkers: Morgan and Moffat Go to School - Tomie DePaola   *p*   225

Ms. Snickle
The Secrets of Ms. Snickle's Class - Laurie Miller Hornik   *e*   419

Noel, Hubert
A Book of Coupons - Susie Morgenstern   *e, m*   646

Price, Sarah Jane
My Face to the Wind: The Diary of Sarah Jane Price, a Prairie Teacher, Broken Bow, Nebraska, 1881 - Jim Murphy   *m*   656

Samborsen, Carol "Just Carol"
Notes from a Liar and Her Dog - Gennifer Choldenko   *m*   162

Sarah
Looking Out for Sarah - Glenna Lang   *p*   532

Shabbas, Maureen
Skeleton Man - Joseph Bruchac   *m*   110

Shakespeare, William "Will"
Ill Met by Moonlight - Sarah Hoyt   *h, a*   431

Stan
You Don't Know Me - David Klass   *m, h*   510

Steenwilly, Arthur Flemingham
You Don't Know Me - David Klass   *m, h*   510

Unnamed Character
The Rabbit Who Longed for Home - Lilian Edvall   *p*   261
The Tale of Tricky Fox: A New England Trickster Tale - Jim Aylesworth   *p*   39

Wheeler, Landon "Dr. Demented"
The Secret Life of Dr. Demented - Dan Gutman   *m*   361

Whistle, Penny
The Great Whale of Kansas - Richard W. Jennings   *m*   454

Wiles, Yvette
Black Mirror - Nancy Werlin   *h*   941

TEENAGER

Almayo, Antonia "Toni"
The Summer of El Pintor - Ofelia Dumas Lachtman   *m, h*   525

Baranova, Ekaterina "Katya" Ivanona
Angel on the Square - Gloria Whelan   *m, h*   946

Baumgart, Sylvester "Slick"
Ida Lou's Story - Susan E. Kirby   *e*   506

Blackthorn, Tessa
Blind Beauty - K.M. Peyton   *m, h* 709

Castaneda, Rey
The Jumping Tree - Rene Saldana Jr.   *m* 787

Crawford, Nathaniel "Peewee"
Faraway Home - Marilyn Taylor   *m* 871

d'Arc, Jehanette
The Merlin of the Oak Woods - Ann Chamberlin   *h, a* 151

de Caldicot, Arthur
The Seeing Stone - Kevin Crossley-Holland   *m, h* 196

Eric
Stranded - Patricia H. Rushford   *m, h* 773

Finch, Ian
The Broken Places - Susan Perabo   *a* 707

Hambrick, Nicole
Ghost Soldier - Elaine Marie Alphin   *m* 13

Hornsby, Amelia
Thomas Jefferson: Letters from a Philadelphia Bookworm - Jennifer Armstrong   *m* 19

Jimenez, Francisco
Breaking Through - Francisco Jimenez   *m, h* 456

Jimenez, Roberto
Breaking Through - Francisco Jimenez   *m, h* 456

Kelandry
Squire - Tamora Pierce   *m, h* 712

Lindsay, Barnett
Proud and Angry Dust - Kathryn Mitchell   *a* 644

Line, Victoria "Vikki"
Flatterland: Like Flatland, Only More So - Ian Stewart   *h* 856

Marik
The Beguilers - Kate Thompson   *m, h* 880

McGrady, Jennie
Stranded - Patricia H. Rushford   *m, h* 773

Meisenheimer, Lydie Rose
The Gypsies Never Came - Stephen Roos   *m* 763

Milford, Laura
The Secret Road - Robert Nordan   *e, m* 682

Muller, Karl
Faraway Home - Marilyn Taylor   *m* 871

O'Donnell, Hugh Roe "Red Hugh"
Red Hugh: The Kidnap of Hugh O'Donnell - Deborah Lisson   *m, h* 561

O'Malley, Theodore Roosevelt Bullmoose
Proud and Angry Dust - Kathryn Mitchell   *a* 644

Parkinson, Emily
Brother Enemy - Robert Elmer   *m* 277

Penelope
Odysseus in the Serpent Maze - Jane Yolen   *m* 997

Penney, Razzle
Razzle - Ellen Wittlinger   *h* 978

Pitman, Kit
Kit's Law - Donna Morrissey   *h, a* 651

Renfrow, Sterling
The Things I Know Best - Lynne Hinton   *a* 399

Renifer
For All Time - Caroline B. Cooney   *m, h* 180

Rilka
The Beguilers - Kate Thompson   *m, h* 880

Rodriguez, Arturo "Arthur"
Any Small Goodness: A Novel of the Barrio - Tony Johnston   *m* 464

Ropson, Sidney "Sid"
Kit's Law - Donna Morrissey   *h, a* 651

Simons, Judy
Faraway Home - Marilyn Taylor   *m* 871

Singer, Betsy
Proud and Angry Dust - Kathryn Mitchell   *a* 644

Stratton, Lockwood
For All Time - Caroline B. Cooney   *m, h* 180

Wilder, Chloe/Finn
Finn: A Novel - Matthew Olshan   *h* 686

Young, Florida Louisa "Ida Lou"
Ida Lou's Story - Susan E. Kirby   *e* 506

TERRORIST

Ellie
The Night Is for Hunting - John Marsden   *h* 595

Landis, Charles
Flight of the Raven - Stephanie S. Tolan   *m, h* 886

THIEF

Dirty Rat
The Web Files - Margie Palatini   *p, e* 694

Haggard, Thompson
Daniel's Walk - Michael Spooner   *m* 845

Murieta, Joaquin
Thunder on the Sierra - Kathy Balmes   *e, m* 47

"Snakey" Jake
Cowgirl Rosie and Her Five Baby Bison - Stephen Gulbis   *p* 356

Voler
Nursery Crimes - Arthur Geisert   *p, e* 323

TIGER

Lily
Tiger Trouble! - Diane Goode   *p* 341

Unnamed Character
It's Simple, Said Simon - Mary Ann Hoberman   *p* 405

TIME TRAVELER

Annie
Christmas in Camelot - Mary Pope Osborne   *e* 691

Fred
Sam Samurai - Jon Scieszka   *e, m* 805

Grandma
Joining the Boston Tea Party - Diane Stanley   *p, e* 849

Hampton, Rosemary Rita
Rosemary Meets Rosemarie - Barbara Robertson   *e, m* 754

Jack
Christmas in Camelot - Mary Pope Osborne   *e* 691

Joe
Sam Samurai - Jon Scieszka   *e, m* 805

Jones, Felicity
The Last Grail Keeper - Pamela Smith Hill   *m* 398

le Fey, Morgan
The Last Grail Keeper - Pamela Smith Hill   *m* 398

Lenny
Joining the Boston Tea Party - Diane Stanley   *p, e* 849

Liz
Joining the Boston Tea Party - Diane Stanley   *p, e* 849

Lockwood, Anna Sophia "Annie"
For All Time - Caroline B. Cooney   *m, h* 180

Orflandu, Zircus "Zirc"
Quiet! You're Invisible - Margaret Meacham   *e* 629

Sam
Sam Samurai - Jon Scieszka   *e, m* 805

Sandusky, Eli
Ancient Fire - Mark London Williams   *m* 964

Slade, Sarah
Genius Games - Narinder Dhami   *e* 230

Stratton, Hiram "Strat" Jr.
For All Time - Caroline B. Cooney   *m, h* 180

Willoughby, Perin "Willow"
A Question of Will - Lynne Kositsky   *m* 517

TOAD

Unnamed Character
Dig Wait Listen: A Desert Toad's Tale - April Pulley Sayre   *p* 796

TOURIST

Klopot, Stefan
Lexi's Tale - Johanna Hurwitz   *e* 439

TOY

Big Blue
Max's Starry Night - Ken Wilson-Max   *p* 974

Little Pink
Max's Starry Night - Ken Wilson-Max   *p* 974

TRAVELER

al-Aya, Tariq
Mansa Musa: The Lion of Mali - Khephra Burns   *e, m* 127

Clarence
Clarence and the Great Surprise - Jean Ekman Adams   *p* 3

Haskel
A Cloak for the Moon - Eric A. Kimmel   *p, e* 496

Lisa
Lisa's Airplane Trip - Anne Gutman   *p* 358

Loretta
A Fish Named Spot - Jennifer P. Goldfinger   *p* 337

Oma
Jimmy Dabble - Frans Vischer   *e* 914

TRICKSTER

Cat
Mabela the Clever - Margaret Read MacDonald   *p* 584

Jabuti
Jabuti the Tortoise: A Trickster Tale from the Amazon - Gerald McDermott   *p* 615

Monkey
Monkey King - Ed Young   *p, e* 999

Tricky Fox
The Tale of Tricky Fox: A New England Trickster Tale - Jim Aylesworth   *p* 39

TURKEY

Pete
A Plump and Perky Turkey - Teresa Bateman   *p* 62

TURTLE

Jabuti
Jabuti the Tortoise: A Trickster Tale from the Amazon - Gerald McDermott   p   615

TWIN

Amy
Big Trouble in Little Twinsville - Elizabeth Levy   e   552

Barker, Caleb
The Starving Time: Elizabeth's Diary - Patricia Hermes   e   389

Barker, Moffat "Moffie"
Meet the Barkers: Morgan and Moffat Go to School - Tomie DePaola   p   225

Barker, Morgan "Morgie"
Meet the Barkers: Morgan and Moffat Go to School - Tomie DePaola   p   225

Bindart, Cricket
Witches' Key to Terror - Silver RavenWolf   h   738

Bindart, Tad
Witches' Key to Terror - Silver RavenWolf   h   738

Bundkin, Claire
Witch Twins - Adele Griffin   e   351

Bundkin, Luna
Witch Twins - Adele Griffin   e   351

Gaskitt, Gloria
The Man Who Wore All His Clothes - Allan Ahlberg   e   9

Gaskitt, Gus
The Man Who Wore All His Clothes - Allan Ahlberg   e   9

Gemini Jack
Expiration Date: Never - Stephanie Spinner   e   844

Gibson, Tessa
Expiration Date: Never - Stephanie Spinner   e   844

Gibson, Tod
Expiration Date: Never - Stephanie Spinner   e   844

Lenny
Joining the Boston Tea Party - Diane Stanley   p, e   849

Liz
Joining the Boston Tea Party - Diane Stanley   p, e   849

May
Big Trouble in Little Twinsville - Elizabeth Levy   e   552

Nikolas
Shattered Mirror - Amelia Atwater-Rhodes   h   30

O'Carr, Alex
The Hungry Year - Connie Brummel Crook   m   195

O'Carr, Ryan
The Hungry Year - Connie Brummel Crook   m   195

Rademacher, Austin "Radish"
4 1/2 Friends and the Secret Cave - Joachim Friedrich   e   305
41/2 Friends and the Disappearing Bio Teacher - Joachim Friedrich   e   306

Rademacher, Stefanie "Steffi"
4 1/2 Friends and the Secret Cave - Joachim Friedrich   e   305
41/2 Friends and the Disappearing Bio Teacher - Joachim Friedrich   e   306

Ravena, Christopher
Shattered Mirror - Amelia Atwater-Rhodes   h   30

Rushton, Jess
Witch's Fang - Heather Kellerhals-Stewart   m, h   484

Ruth
When Lightning Strikes - Jenny Carroll   m, h   142

Unnamed Character
Car Wash - Sandra Steen   p   851
Car Wash - Sandra Steen   p   851

UNCLE

Armiger, George
Anna on the Farm - Mary Downing Hahn   e   369

Bailey
Scorpio's Child - Kezi Matthews   m   603

Barnavelt, Jonathan
The Tower at the End of the World - Brad Strickland   m   862

Brown, Rufus
West of Rehoboth - Alexs D. Pate   a   699

Buchanan, Jesse
The Secret Road - Robert Nordan   e, m   682

Dick
Maggie in the Morning - Elizabeth Van Steenwyk   e   904

Dion, Jack
Everything on a Waffle - Polly Horvath   m   422

Ed
The Hideout - Peg Kehret   e, m   482

Edward "Ed"
Groover's Heart - Carole Crowe   e   197

Fourth Uncle
Oranges on Golden Mountain - Elizabeth Partridge   p, e   697

Graham, Norman
Piper - Natale Ghent   m   328

Hubbard, Charles "Charley"
Finding Hattie - Sally Warner   m   926

Jewels, Bentley
The Calling - Cathryn Clinton   m, h   169

Jewels, Peter Earl
The Calling - Cathryn Clinton   m, h   169

Lindsay, Barnett
Proud and Angry Dust - Kathryn Mitchell   a   644

MacBean, Rory
The Carved Box - Gillian Chan   m   154

Maguire, Jack "Blackjack"
Above and Beyond - Susan Bonners   m   91

Maxwell
Maxwell's Magic Mix-Up - Linda Ashman   p   27

Orlando, Anthony Carmine
The Foreigner - Meg Castaldo   a   147

Parkinson, Anthony
Brother Enemy - Robert Elmer   m   277

Quinn, Josh
The Protestor's Song - Mark Delaney   m   223

Sanchez, Francisco
Secrets in the House of Delgado - Gloria D. Miklowitz   m, h   639

Skeleton Man
Skeleton Man - Joseph Bruchac   m   110

Snodde-Brittle, Fulton
Dial-a-Ghost - Eva Ibbotson   e, m   441

Solaja, Dele
The Other Side of Truth - Beverley Naidoo   m, h   666

Sprague, Lyman
Mountain Pose - Nancy Hope Wilson   m   973

Spraig, Luther
Out of the Night That Covers Me: A Novel - Pat Cunningham Devoto   a   229

Sterling, Stoppard
The Viking Claw - Michael Dahl   m   204

Ted
Clarice Bean: Guess Who's Babysitting? - Lauren Child   p, e   159

Tomas
Uncle Rain Cloud - Tony Johnston   p   466

Wattley, Charles "Groover"
Groover's Heart - Carole Crowe   e   197

Westlake, Dan "Uncle Daddy"
Uncle Daddy - Ralph Fletcher   e, m   293

Will
A Farm of Her Own - Natalie Kinsey-Warnock   p   504

UNEMPLOYED

Dickinson, Cam
Run If You Dare - Randy Powell   m, h   721

Mama
Rent Party Jazz - William Miller   p, e   640

Poppa
The Christmas Promise - Susan Campbell Bartoletti   p, e   56

VACATIONER

Hannah
The Journey - Sarah Stewart   p, e   857

Mother
The Journey - Sarah Stewart   p, e   857

VAMPIRE

Crepsley
Cirque du Freak: The Vampire's Assistant - Darren Shan   m, h   814

Mr. Crepsley
Cirque du Freak: A Living Nightmare - Darren Shan   m, h   813

Nikolas
Shattered Mirror - Amelia Atwater-Rhodes   h   30

Ravena, Christopher
Shattered Mirror - Amelia Atwater-Rhodes   h   30

VETERINARIAN

Dr. Simmonds
One Day at Wood Green Animal Shelter - Patricia Casey   p   146

VICTIM

Bartlett, Alicia
The Rag and Bone Shop - Robert Cormier   m, h   183

Carroll, Arthur "Artie"
Prowlers - Christopher Golden   h   336

VINTNER

McNaughton, Alexander "Zan"
A Lovely Illusion - Tessa Barclay   a   54

VOLUNTEER

Annie
Freedom School, Yes! - Amy Littlesugar   p, e   564

WAGONMASTER

Clyman, James
Daniel's Walk - Michael Spooner   m   845

WAITRESS

Quade, Helen
In Spite of Killer Bees - Julie Johnston   m, h   462

WARLOCK

Scott, Peter
The Serpent's Shadow - Mercedes Lackey   h, a   526

WARRIOR

Bran "the Painted Man"
Son of the Shadows - Juliet Marillier   h, a   593

Cazaril
The Curse of Chalion - Lois McMaster Bujold   h, a   115

Dunbar/Dances with Wolves, John
The Holy Road - Michael Blake   a   83

Eckert, James "Jim"
The Dragon and the Fair Maid of Kent - Gordon Dickson   h, a   233

Lord Raoul
Squire - Tamora Pierce   m, h   712

Thomas
I Am Morgan Le Fay - Nancy Springer   h   846

WEALTHY

Andreas, Nicholas "Nick"
Breathing Underwater - Alex Flinn   h   295

Blake, Dorothea
The Maiden of Mayfair - Lawana Blackwell   a   82

Caldecott, Amos
Playing with Fire - Kathleen Karr   m   478

de Montcada, Francisco
The Crusader - Michael Alexander Eisner   a   270

don Ignacio
Juan Verdades: The Man Who Couldn't Tell a Lie - Joe Hayes   p, e   385

Eaker, Micah
Fire on the Waters - David Poyer   a   722

Ed
The Hideout - Peg Kehret   e, m   482

Hamilton, Jon
Rooster - Beth Nixon Weaver   m, h   931

Hyde, Eliot
Sticks & Scones - Diane Mott Davidson   a   215

McNaughton, Alexander "Zan"
A Lovely Illusion - Tessa Barclay   a   54

Mrs. Broder
Fiona McGilray's Story: A Voyage from Ireland in 1849 - Clare Pastore   m   698

Renzi, Nicholas
Kydd - Julian Stockwin   a   861

Sibley, Elizabeth
Chipper - James Lincoln Collier   m   176

Sleat
Danger in Disguise - Mary Alice Downie   m   245

Tyle, Rhett
Trial by Jury/Journal - Kate Klise   m   514

Unnamed Character
The Very Kind Rich Lady and Her One Hundred Dogs - Chinlun Lee   p   541

WEREWOLF

Fang, Lucy
The Werewolf Club Meets Dorkula - Daniel Pinkwater   e   718

Furball, Billy
The Werewolf Club Meets Dorkula - Daniel Pinkwater   e   718

Paine, Cassandra
Tartabull's Throw - Henry Garfield   h   313

WIDOW

Blake, Dorothea
The Maiden of Mayfair - Lawana Blackwell   a   82

Fleischacker, Euterpe Fuller
Fair Weather - Richard Peck   m   704

Griffin, Kate
A Long Way Home - Nancy Price Graff   m   343

Inga
The Race of the Birkebeiners - Lise Lunge-Larsen   p, e   578

Unnamed Character
Oranges on Golden Mountain - Elizabeth Partridge   p, e   697

WIDOW(ER)

Chase, Lydia
Stopping to Home - Lea Wait   e   917

Dapplevine, Eula "Miss Eula"
Love, Ruby Lavender - Deborah Wiles   e, m   956

Frith, Anna
Year of Wonders - Geraldine Brooks   h, a   101

Gramps
Bluebird Summer - Deborah Hopkinson   p, e   418

Lynch, Eliza
Gabriel's Story - David Anthony Durham   h, a   255

Mama
Mama Does the Mambo - Katherine Leiner   p, e   543

Mrs. Hobbs
The Ghost and Mrs. Hobbs - Cynthia DeFelice   e, m   221

Quinn, Sarah
Five Smooth Stones: Hope's Diary - Kristiana Gregory   e   348

WIDOWER

Randall, Kenny
Diamond in the Dust - Carla Joinson   m, h   467

WIDOW(ER)

Rind, Clementina
Maria's Story: 1773 - Joan Lowery Nixon   e, m   678

Widow Tyler
Enemy in the Fort - Sarah Masters Buckey   e, m   114

Winn, Winifred
Castaways of the Flying Dutchman - Brian Jacques   m   446

WIFE

Dudley, Amy Robsart
The Twylight Tower - Karen Harper   a   376

Howard, Kathleen
A Bushel of Light - Troon Harrison   m   380

Nimue
The Dragon's Son - Sarah L. Thomson   h, a   882

Romanov, Alexandra
Angel on the Square - Gloria Whelan   m, h   946

Stands with a Fist
The Holy Road - Michael Blake   a   83

WITCH

Adolpho
The Pillars of the World - Anne Bishop   h, a   77

Ari
The Pillars of the World - Anne Bishop   h, a   77

Blaire, Cal
Book of Shadows - Cate Tiernan   h   883

Bramblewine, Arianna "Grandy"
Witch Twins - Adele Griffin   e   351

Capel, Fernanda "Fern"
The Dragon Charmer - Jan Siegel   h, a   820

Catty
Into the Cold Fire - Lynne Ewing   m, h   281

Cleveland, Vanessa
Into the Cold Fire - Lynne Ewing   m, h   281

Goldfarb, Mavis
Fat Camp Commandos - Daniel Pinkwater   e   716

Green, Sarah
Shattered Mirror - Amelia Atwater-Rhodes   h   30

Jimena
Into the Cold Fire - Lynne Ewing   m, h   281

Killingsworth, Serena
Into the Cold Fire - Lynne Ewing   m, h   281

Mitzi
Hoodwinked - Arthur Howard   p   424

Morgus
The Dragon Charmer - Jan Siegel   h, a   820

Newbury, Mary
Witch Child - Celia Rees   m, h   739

Rowlands, Morgan
Book of Shadows - Cate Tiernan   h   883

Salem, Bethany
Witches' Key to Terror - Silver RavenWolf   h   738

Shavani
The Serpent's Shadow - Mercedes Lackey   h, a   526

Sheba
Rowan of Rin - Emily Rodda   e, m   760

Unnamed Character
Meaner than Meanest - Kevin Somers   p   838
Room on the Broom - Julia Donaldson   p   241

Watson, Vera
The Jacob Ladder - Gerald Hausman   m   381

Witherspoon, Maya
The Serpent's Shadow - Mercedes Lackey   h, a   526

Yann
The Merlin of the Oak Woods - Ann Chamberlin   h, a   151

Zimmerman, Florence
The Tower at the End of the World - Brad Strickland
m 862

WIZARD

Adrian, Jason
The Magickers - Emily Drake m 248

Blackheart, Lilliana "Lili"
The Queen's Necklace - Teresa Edgerton h, a 260

Callahan, Nita
The Wizard's Dilemma - Diane Duane m, h 251

Carolinus
The Dragon and the Fair Maid of Kent - Gordon
Dickson h, a 233

Cathan
Heresy - Anselm Audley h, a 33

Chrestomanci
Mixed Magics: Four Tales of Chrestomanci - Diana
Wynne Jones m, h 469

Faleel
The Ropemaker - Peter Dickinson m, h 232

Hawk
Spellfall - Katherine Roberts m, h 752

Izard, Ishmael
The Tower at the End of the World - Brad Strickland
m 862

Landau, Bailey
The Magickers - Emily Drake m 248

Rodriguez, Kit
The Wizard's Dilemma - Diane Duane m, h 251

WOLF

Big Wolf
Beware of the Storybook Wolves - Lauren Child p,
e 158

Little Wolf
Beware of the Storybook Wolves - Lauren Child p,
e 158

Lupin
The Good Dog - Avi e, m 36

Max
Max, the Stubborn Little Wolf - Marie-Odile Judes
p 473

Mr. Wolf
Oomph! - Colin McNaughton p 628

Nutik
Nutik & Amaroq Play Ball - Jean Craighead George
p 324
Nutik, the Wolf Pup - Jean Craighead George
p 325

Papa Wolf
Max, the Stubborn Little Wolf - Marie-Odile Judes
p 473

Unnamed Character
The Three Little Pigs - Barry Moser p 652
The Three Pigs - David Wiesner p, e 950
Wait! No Paint! - Bruce Whatley p 943

WOODPECKER

Woodpecker
Batbaby Finds a Home - Robert Quackenbush
b 730

WORKER

Dorsey, Charlie
The Star-Spangled Secret - K.M. Kimball e,
m 495

Garth "Math Man"
Math Man - Teri Daniels p 208

Gershon, Joseph
Lick Creek - Brad Kessler a 490

Gray, Hennley
A Hole in the World - Sid Hite m 401

Larry
The Shine Man: A Christmas Story - Mary
Quattlebaum p, e 732

Lateef
Bikes for Rent! - Isaac Olaleye p 685

Mr. Jackson
Falling Angels - Tracy Chevalier a 156

Raymond
Aquamarine - Alice Hoffman m 407

Schaeffer, Ben
Missing from Haymarket Square - Harriette Gillem
Robinet m 755

Walsh, Finnie
Finnie Walsh - Steven Galloway a 309

WRESTLER

Wheeler, Landon "Dr. Demented"
The Secret Life of Dr. Demented - Dan Gutman
m 361

WRITER

Father
The Sick Day - Patricia MacLachlan p 587

Fine, Ida Mae "I.M."
The Mysterious Matter of I.M. Fine - Diane Stanley
e 850

Forrester, William
Finding Forrester - James W. Ellison a, h 276

Haig-Ereildoun, Angus
*Do Try to Speak as We Do: The Diary of an American
Au Pair* - Marjorie Leet Ford a 297

Jack
Love That Dog - Sharon Creech e, m 192

Jones, Walter "Booker"
Fur-Ever Yours, Booker Jones - Betsy Duffey e,
m 252

Kagan, Sam
A Dance for Emilia - Peter S. Beagle h, a 63

Land, Swede
Peace Like a River - Leif Enger h, a 278

Lawson, Cam
The Story of Tracy Beaker - Jacqueline Wilson e,
m 971

Linda
Equinox - Monte Killingsworth m 494

Major, Kambia Elaine
Shayla's Double Brown Baby Blues - Lori Aurelia
Williams m, h 963

Nelson/Day, Natalie/Cassandra
The School Story - Andrew Clements e, m 167

Nickowsky, Pete
Deep Doo-Doo and the Mysterious E-Mail - Michael
Delaney e 224

Ostrom, Addie
Buddy Is a Stupid Name for a Girl - Willo Davis
Roberts e, m 753

Pied, Piper
Eccentric Circles - Rebecca Lickiss h, a 556

Rossi, Emily "Emilia"
A Dance for Emilia - Peter S. Beagle h, a 63

Rover, Alex
Nim's Island - Wendy Orr e 690

Shakespeare, William
A Question of Will - Lynne Kositsky m 517

Sterling, Stoppard
The Viking Claw - Michael Dahl m 204

Unnamed Character
The Day Eddie Met the Author - Louise Borden
e 93

YOUNG MAN

Harold
The Reluctant Flower Girl - Lynne Barasch p 53

Sam
Scatterbrain Sam - Ellen Jackson p, e 444

YOUNG WOMAN

Culhane, Kate
Kate Culhane: A Ghost Story - Michael Hague e,
m 368

Jill
The Famous Adventures of Jack - Berlie Doherty
e 239

Larky Mavis
Larky Mavis - Brock Cole p, e 170

Maizie Mae
Scatterbrain Sam - Ellen Jackson p, e 444

Unnamed Character
Sophie's Masterpiece: A Spider's Tale - Eileen Spinelli
p 843

ZEBRA

Big Zeb
Naughty! - Caroline Castle p 148

Little Zeb
Naughty! - Caroline Castle p 148

Unnamed Character
Kipper's A to Z: An Alphabet Adventure - Mick
Inkpen p 442

Age Index

This index groups books according to the grade levels for which they are most appropriate. Beneath each grade range, book titles are listed alphabetically, with author names and entry numbers included.

Age Index

Age Index

Page Count Index

This index groups books according to their page counts. Beneath each page count range, book titles are listed alphabetically, followed by the author's name, age-level code(s), the exact page count and the entry number. The age-level codes are as follows: *p* Preschool, *b* Beginning Reader, *e* Elementary School (Grades 2-5), *m* Middle School (Grades 5-8), *h* High School (Grades 9-12), and *a* Adult.

LESS THAN 25 PAGES

When Poppy and Max Grow Up - Lindsey Gardiner (20 pages) *p* 312

Ten Seeds - Ruth Brown (22 pages) *p* 106

The Adventure of Louey and Frank - Carolyn White (24 pages) *p* 947

Bun Bun's Birthday - Richard Scrimger (24 pages) *p* 807

Bunbun at Bedtime - Sharon Pierce McCullough (24 pages) *p* 610

Crocodile Listens - April Pulley Sayre (24 pages) *p* 795

D.W.'s Library Card - Marc Brown (24 pages) *p* 103

Daniel's Mystery Egg - Alma Flor Ada (24 pages) *b* 1

Estelle and Lucy - Anna Alter (24 pages) *p* 14

Kate Can't Wait - Marilyn Eisenstein (24 pages) *p* 269

Little Tree - Chris Raschka (24 pages) *p* 736

Lulu's Birthday - Elizabeth Fitzgerald Howard (24 pages) *p* 425

Mom Pie - Lynne Jonell (24 pages) *p* 468

No Kiss for Grandpa - Harriet Ziefert (24 pages) *p* 1001

Sheila Rae's Peppermint Stick - Kevin Henkes (24 pages) *p* 387

25 TO 39 PAGES

Ballerina! - Peter Sis (26 pages) *p* 826

Bear in Sunshine - Stella Blackstone (26 pages) *p* 80

Carlo Likes Reading - Jessica Spanyol (26 pages) *p* 840

Chanukah Lights Everywhere - Michael J. Rosen (26 pages) *p* 767

Dancing Class - H.M. Ehrlich (26 pages) *p* 265

Hungry! Hungry! Hungry! - Malachy Doyle (26 pages) *p* 246

I Love You Because You're You - Liza Baker (26 pages) *p* 44

One of the Problems of Everett Anderson - Lucille Clifton (26 pages) *p* 168

Puss in Boots: The Adventures of That Most Enterprising Feline - Philip Pullman (26 pages) *p, e* 728

Table Manners - Chris Raschka (26 pages) *p, e* 737

Astro Bunnies - Christine Loomis (28 pages) *p* 571

Bunny Party - Rosemary Wells (28 pages) *p* 935

Buzz Buzz Buzz - Veronica Uribe (28 pages) *p* 896

Cats, Cats, Cats! - Leslea Newman (28 pages) *p* 675

Cowgirl Rosie and Her Five Baby Bison - Stephen Gulbis (28 pages) *p* 356

Dim Sum for Everyone! - Grace Lin (28 pages) *p* 558

Farmer Will - Jane Cowen-Fletcher (28 pages) *p* 188

Flip and Flop - Dawn Apperley (28 pages) *p* 17

Heart of Mine: A Story of Adoption - Lotta Hojer (28 pages) *p* 408

I Am the King! - Nathalie Dieterle (28 pages) *p* 234

Katje, the Windmill Cat - Gretchen Woelfle (28 pages) *p* 979

Lisa's Airplane Trip - Anne Gutman (28 pages) *p* 358

Max's Starry Night - Ken Wilson-Max (28 pages) *p* 974

Oliver's Milk Shake - Vivian French (28 pages) *p* 302

One Day, Daddy - Frances Thomas (28 pages) *p* 879

Oomph! - Colin McNaughton (28 pages) *p* 628

The Rabbit Who Longed for Home - Lilian Edvall (28 pages) *p* 261

Rufferella - Vanessa Gill-Brown (28 pages) *p* 331

Sammy and the Robots - Ian Whybrow (28 pages) *p* 949

Something Wonderful - Jenny Nimmo (28 pages) *p* 676

Tell Me What It's Like to Be Big - Joyce Dunbar (28 pages) *p* 253

Webster J. Duck - Martin Waddell (28 pages) *p* 916

You're Growing Up, Pontus! - Ann-Sofie Jeppson (28 pages) *p, e* 455

Bat Loves the Night - Nicola Davies (30 pages) *p* 216

The Adventures of Bert - Allan Ahlberg (32 pages) *p* 8

Albert - Donna Jo Napoli (32 pages) *p, e* 668

Anna's Goat - Janice Kulyk Keefer (32 pages) *p, e* 481

Antonella and Her Santa Claus - Barbara Augustin (32 pages) *p* 34

The Apple King - Francesca Bosca (32 pages) *p, e* 94

Aunt Claire's Yellow Beehive Hair - Deborah Blumenthal (32 pages) *p* 88

Baby Duck's New Friend - Frank Asch (32 pages) *p* 24

Baloney (Henry P) - Jon Scieszka (32 pages) *p, e* 804

Beach Day - Karen Roosa (32 pages) *p* 764

Bernard Goes to School - Joan Elizabeth Goodman (32 pages) *p* 342

Bernard the Angry Rooster - Mary Wormell (32 pages) *p* 985

Beto and the Bone Dance - Gina Freschet (32 pages) *p* 303

Beware of the Storybook Wolves - Lauren Child (32 pages) *p, e* 158

The Biggest Fish in the Lake - Margaret Carney (32 pages) *p, e* 140

Bikes for Rent! - Isaac Olaleye (32 pages) *p* 685

Bluebird Summer - Deborah Hopkinson (32 pages) *p, e* 418

Book! Book! Book! - Deborah Bruss (32 pages) *p* 111

The Bookstore Burglar - Barbara Maitland (32 pages) *b* 590

Bridget and the Gray Wolves - Pija Lindenbaum (32 pages) *p* 560

Bully - Judith Caseley (32 pages) *p, e* 145

The Bus for Us - Suzanne Bloom (32 pages) *p* 86

A Bus of Our Own - Freddi Williams Evans (32 pages) *p, e* 280

Bus Stop, Bus Go! - Daniel Kirk (32 pages) *p* 507

Car Wash - Sandra Steen (32 pages) *p* 851

Casey Jones - Allan Drummond (32 pages) *p* 250

A Castle on Viola Street - DyAnne DiSalvo (32 pages) *p* 236

Castles, Caves, and Honeycombs - Linda Ashman (32 pages) *p, e* 26

The Christmas Cobwebs - Odds Bodkin (32 pages) *p* 89

Circus Girl - Tomek Bogacki (32 pages) *p* 90

Clara Caterpillar - Pamela Duncan Edwards (32 pages) *p* 263

Clarence and the Great Surprise - Jean Ekman Adams (32 pages) *p* 3

Clarice Bean: Guess Who's Babysitting? - Lauren Child (32 pages) *p, e* 159

The Class Artist - G. Brian Karas (32 pages) *p* 477

Clever Beatrice - Margaret Willey (32 pages) *p* 960

A Cloak for the Moon - Eric A. Kimmel (32 pages) *p, e* 496

Come Back, Hannah! - Marisabina Russo (32 pages) *p* 774

151 TO 200 PAGES

Page Count Index

Page Count Index

Illustrator Index

This index lists the illustrators of the featured titles. Illustrators are listed alphabetically, followed by the title, with author names, age-level code(s) and entry numbers also included. The age-level codes are as follows: *p* Preschool, *b* Beginning Reader, *e* Elementary School (Grades 2-5), *m* Middle School (Grades 5-8), *h* High School (Grades 9-12), and *a* Adult.

A

Adams, Jean Ekman
Clarence and the Great Surprise - Jean Ekman Adams *p* 3

Agee, Jon
Milo's Hat Trick - Jon Agee *p* 7

Ajhar, Brian
Rover Saves Christmas - Roddy Doyle *e* 247

Allen, Joy
My Best Friend Bear - Tony Johnston *p* 465

Alter, Anna
Estelle and Lucy - Anna Alter *p* 14

Andersen, Bethanne
Bluebird Summer - Deborah Hopkinson *p, e* 418

Anderson, Wayne
The Tin Forest - Helen Ward *p* 924

Andreasen, Dan
On Tide Mill Lane - Melissa Wiley *e* 957
Tattered Sails - Verla Kay *p* 480

Andrews, Benny
The Hickory Chair - Lisa Rowe Fraustino *p* 300

Apperley, Dawn
Flip and Flop - Dawn Apperley *p* 17

Apple, Margot
Runaway Radish - Jessie Haas *e* 363

Argent, Kerry
Nighty Night - Margaret Wild *p* 953

Arnold, Tedd
More Parts - Tedd Arnold *p, e* 20

Arnosky, Jim
Raccoon on His Own - Jim Arnosky *p* 21

Aruego, Jose
How Chipmunk Got His Stripes: A Tale of Bragging and Teasing - Joseph Bruchac *p* 108

Asch, Frank
Baby Duck's New Friend - Frank Asch *p* 24

Atwell, Debbie
Pearl - Debbie Atwell *p, e* 31

Auch, Herm
I Was a Third Grade Spy - Mary Jane Auch *e* 32

Avendano, Dolores
Jake Drake, Know-It-All - Andrew Clements *e* 166

Azarian, Mary
The Race of the Birkebeiners - Lise Lunge-Larsen *p, e* 578

B

Babbitt, Natalie
Elsie Times Eight - Natalie Babbitt *p* 41

Bachem, Paul
Shadows in the Glasshouse - Megan McDonald *e, m* 620

Baker, Keith
Little Green - Keith Baker *p* 43

Ballard, Robin
My Day, Your Day - Robin Ballard *p* 46

Bang, Molly
Harley - Star Livingstone *b* 565
Tiger's Fall - Molly Bang *e* 48

Barasch, Lynne
The Reluctant Flower Girl - Lynne Barasch *p* 53

Bartlett, Alison
Oliver's Milk Shake - Vivian French *p* 302

Barton, Byron
My Car - Byron Barton *p* 57

Barton, Jill
Lady Lollipop - Dick King-Smith *e* 503
Rattletrap Car - Phyllis Root *p* 765

Bash, Barbara
Dig Wait Listen: A Desert Toad's Tale - April Pulley Sayre *p* 796

Basso, Bill
Night of the Living Gerbil - Elizabeth Levy *e* 553

Bayley, Nicola
Katje, the Windmill Cat - Gretchen Woelfle *p* 979

Beaton, Clare
There's a Cow in the Cabbage Patch - Stella Blackstone *p* 81

Beck, Ian
Home before Dark - Ian Beck *p* 64
Puss in Boots: The Adventures of That Most Enterprising Feline - Philip Pullman *p, e* 728

Beeke, Tiphanie
Book! Book! Book! - Deborah Bruss *p* 111

Benson, Patrick
Squeak's Good Idea - Max Eilenberg *p* 268

Berry, Holly
Joining the Boston Tea Party - Diane Stanley *p, e* 849

Biet, Pascal
Crackers - Becky Bloom *p* 85

Black, Theodor
Ghosts and Golems: Haunting Tales of the Supernatural - Malka Penn *m* 706

Bliss, Harry
A Fine, Fine School - Sharon Creech *p* 191

Bloch, Serge
A Book of Coupons - Susie Morgenstern *e, m* 646

Bloom, Suzanne
The Bus for Us - Suzanne Bloom *p* 86

Bluthenthal, Diana Cain
Meaner than Meanest - Kevin Somers *p* 838

Bogacki, Tomek
Circus Girl - Tomek Bogacki *p* 90
Five Creatures - Emily Jenkins *p* 452

Bollen, Roger
Bobo Crazy - Marilyn Sadler *e* 786

Boon, Debbie
Something Wonderful - Jenny Nimmo *p* 676

Boon, Emilie
No Kiss for Grandpa - Harriet Ziefert *p* 1001

Bourre, Martine
Max, the Stubborn Little Wolf - Marie-Odile Judes *p* 473

Bowers, Tim
Little Whistle - Cynthia Rylant *p* 781
Little Whistle's Dinner Party - Cynthia Rylant *p* 782

Boynton, Sandra
The Heart of Cool - Jamie McEwan *b, e* 622

Brewer, Paul
Robert and the Great Pepperoni - Barbara Seuling *e* 811

Brewster, Patience
Lexi's Tale - Johanna Hurwitz *e* 439
The Merbaby - Teresa Bateman *p, e* 61

Briggs, Raymond
The Adventures of Bert - Allan Ahlberg *p* 8

Illustrator Index

Illustrator Index

Author Index

This index is an alphabetical listing of the authors of books featured in entries and those listed under "Other books by the author" and "Other books you might like." Editors and co-authors are interfiled with author names. For each author, the titles of books written and entry numbers are also provided. Bold numbers indicate a featured main entry; light-face numbers refer to books recommended for further reading.

Author Index

Author Index

Hall, Barbara
Dixie Storms 753
Hall, Donald
Old Home Day 31
Hall, James W.
Blackwater Sound 97
Hall, Lynn
Murder in a Pig's Eye 990
The Soul of the Silver Dog 328
Windsong 122
Hall, Zoe
It's Pumpkin Time! 412
Hallinan, P.K.
Just Open a Book 840
Hamilton, Denise
The Jasmine Trade 371
Hamilton, Jane
The Short History of a Prince 391
Hamilton, Morse
The Garden of Eden Motel 894
Hamilton, Virginia
The House of Dies Drear 307
*A Ring of Tricksters: Animal Tales from
    America, the West Indies, and
    Africa* 39, 615, 741
Hamm, Diane Johnston
Laney's Lost Momma 339
Hanel, Wolfram
Rescue at Sea! 920
Hansard, Peter
Jig, Fig, and Mrs. Pig 858
Hansen, Brooks
Caesar's Antlers 439
Hansen, Joyce
The Heart Calls Home 372
*I Thought My Soul Would Rise and Fly:
    The Diary of Patsy, a Freed
    Girl* 372
One True Friend **372**
Out from This Place 372
Yellow Bird and Me 372
Hardman, Ric Lynden
*Sunshine Rider: The First Vegetarian
    Western* 279, 762
Hardy, Thomas
Far from the Madding Crowd 651
Harlow, Joan Hiatt
Joshua's Song **373**
Star in the Storm 373
Harper, Charise Mericle
When I Grow Up 312
Harper, Dan
Sit, Truman! **374**
Telling Time with Big Mama Cat 374
Harper, Isabelle
My Cats Nick and Nora 25
My Dog Rosie 435
Our New Puppy 344
Harper, Jo
Delfino's Journey **375**
Harper, Karen
Down to the Bone 319, 990
The Poyson Garden 376
The Queen's Cure 376
The Tidal Poole 376
The Twylight Tower **376**
Harrar, George
First Tiger 377
Junk in Space 377

Parents Wanted **377**
Harrell, Beatrice Orcutt
*How Thunder and Lightning Came to
    Be: A Choctaw Legend* 817
Harris, Anne
The Nature of Smoke 42
Harris, Carol Flynn
A Place for Joey 373, **378**, 930
Harris, Jesse
Vampire's Kiss 336
Harris, Robert J.
Odysseus in the Serpent Maze **997**
Harris, Robie H.
Goodbye Mousie **379**, 833
Happy Birth Day! 379
Hi, New Baby! 379
Harrison, Maggie
Lizzie's List 262
Harrison, Sue
Mother Earth, Father Sky 209
Harrison, Troon
A Bushel of Light **380**
Goodbye to Atlantis 380
The Long Weekend 764
Hartley, Karen
Cockroach 421
Haruf, Kent
Plainsong 288
Haugaard, Eric Christian
The Boy and the Samurai 416
Haugaard, Erik Christian
Under the Black Flag 382
Hausman, Gerald
Coyote Bead 381
*Doctor Moledinky's Castle: A
    Hometown Tale* 382
The Jacob Ladder **381**, 382, 586
Night Flight 381, 516
*Tom Cringle: Battle on the High
    Seas* 381, 382, 446, 536
*Tom Cringle: The Pirate and the
    Patriot* 381, **382**
Hautman, Pete
Hole in the Sky **383**
Mr. Was 383
Stone Cold 383
Haviland, Virginia
*Favorite Fairy Tales Told in
    England* 239
*Favorite Fairy Tales Told in
    Norway* 578
Havill, Juanita
Jamaica and Brianna 264
Hawes, Louise
Rosey in the Present Tense 972
Hawks, Robert
This Stranger, My Father 549
Hawxhurst, Joan C.
*Bubbe and Gram: My Two
    Grandmothers* 393
Hayes, Geoffrey
Bear by Himself 384
Patrick and His Grandpa 384
Patrick and Ted 384
Patrick and the Big Bully **384**
Hayes, Joe
*Juan Verdades: The Man Who Couldn't
    Tell a Lie* 385
Little Gold Star/Estrellita de Oro 385
A Spoon for Every Bite 385

Hayles, Marsha
Beach Play 557
Pet of a Pet 146
Hearne, Betsy Gould
*The Canine Connection: Stories about
    Dogs and Humans* 386
Listening for Leroy 386
Seven Brave Women 31
*Who's in the Hall: A Mystery in Four
    Chapters* 159
Wishes, Kisses, and Pigs 386, 912
Heath, Lorraine
The Outlaw and the Lady 528
Heidenreich, Elke
Nero Corleone: A Cat's Story 326
Heinlein, Robert
Between Planets 67
Starship Troopers 139
Heinz, Brian J.
The Monster's Test 448
Heisel, Sharon E.
Eyes of a Stranger 941
Precious Gold, Precious Jade 294
Helldorfer, M.C.
*Jack, Skinny Bones and the Golden
    Pancakes* 458
Helldorfer, Mary-Claire
Moon Trouble 832
Heller, Nicholas
Elwood and the Witch 241
Hemingway, Ernest
The Old Man and the Sea 788
Henderson, Kathy
The Baby Dances 635, 774
Hendry, Diana
Double Vision 367
Hendry, Frances Mary
Quest for a Maid 884
Henkes, Kevin
The Birthday Room 973
Chrysanthemum 161
Jessica 237
Lilly's Purple Plastic Purse 387
Oh! 387
Owen 387
Sheila Rae, the Brave 387, 842
Sheila Rae's Peppermint Stick **387**
Wemberly Worried 387, 937, 1000
Henrietta
*A Mouse in the House: A Real-Life
    Game of Hide and Seek* 993
Henry, Chad
Dogbreath Victorious 361
Henry, Marguerite
*Brown Sunshine of Sawdust
    Valley* 363
Henry, Sue
Murder on the Yukon Quest 824
Herbert, Frank
Dune 472
Herman, John
Deep Waters 340, 388
Labyrinth **388**, 397
Hermes, Patricia
Calling Me Home 390
Cheat the Moon 220
*Nothing but Trouble, Trouble,
    Trouble* 389
On Winter's Wind 389, 390

*Our Strange New Land: Elizabeth's
    Diary* 389
Someone to Count On 819
*The Starving Time: Elizabeth's
    Diary* 389, 390
*Westward to Home: Joshua's
    Diary* 390
Herrick, Ann
The Perfect Guy 978
Herron, Carolivia
Nappy Hair 235
Herschler, Mildred Barger
The Darkest Corner 392, 546
Hershon, Joanna
Swimming 391
Hess, Debra
Wilson Sat Alone 90
Hesse, Karen
Letters from Rifka 476, 735
*A Light in the Storm: The Civil War
    Diary of Amelia Martin* 392
The Music of Dolphins 392
Out of the Dust 201, 392
Sable 811
Stowaway 392, 536
A Time of Angels 392
Witness **392**
Hesser, Terry Spencer
Kissing Doorknobs 927
Hest, Amy
The Friday Nights of Nana **393**
In the Rain with Baby Duck 394
Jamaica Louise James 149, 425
Kiss Good Night **394**
Mabel Dancing 393, 394
Nana's Birthday Party 393, 939
Nannies for Hire 153
Off to School, Baby Duck! 225, 394,
    1000
Rosie's Fishing Trip 140
*When Jessie Came Across the
    Sea* 393
Hewitt, Lorri
Dancer 994
Heynen, Jim
Being Youngest 395, 396
*The Boys' House: New and Selected
    Stories* **395**, 396
*Cosmos Coyote and William the
    Nice* 395, 396
*Fishing for Chickens: Short Stories
    about Rural Youth* 395, **396**
*The One-Room Schoolhouse: Stories
    about the Boys* 395, 396
*Standing Naked: New and Selected
    Poems* 396
Hiatt, Fred
If I Were Queen of the World 234
Hicyilmaz, Gaye
Smiling for Strangers 630
Higginsen, Vy
Mama, I Want to Sing 841
High, Linda Oatman
A Christmas Star 56
Hill, David
See Ya, Simon 397
Take It Easy 397
Time Out **397**
Hill, Donna
Shipwreck Season 138
Hill, Kirkpatrick
The Year of Miss Agnes 646

Hill, Pamela Smith
Ghost Horses 398
The Last Grail Keeper **398**
A Voice from the Border 398, 600

Hilts, Len
Timmy O'Dowd and the Big Ditch: A Story of the Glory Days on the Old Erie Canal 438

Himmelman, John
A Hummingbird's Life 43

Hindley, Judy
The Big Red Bus 507
Mrs. Mary Malarky's Seven Cats 137

Hinds, Uton
The Jacob Ladder **381**

Hines, Anna Grossnickle
What Joe Saw 828

Hinton, Lynne
Friendship Cake 399
Garden of Faith 399
The Things I Know Best **399**

Hinton, S.E.
The Puppy Sister 32

Hippely, Hilary Horder
A Song for Lena 60

Hiscock, Bruce
The Big Storm 400
The Big Tree 400
Coyote and Badger: Desert Hunters of the Southwest **400**
When Will It Snow? 400

Hissey, Jane
Old Bear 782

Hite, Sid
Cecil in Space 401
The Distance of Hope 401
Dither Farm 704
An Even Break 401
A Hole in the World **401**
Stick and Whittle 291, 551
Those Darn Dithers 401, 422, 443, 563

Hoban, Russell
Bedtime for Frances 217, 394, 610, 974
A Birthday for Frances 387, 807, 935

Hobb, Robin
Ship of Magic 33, 116

Hobbie, Holly
Toot & Puddle 402
Toot & Puddle: A Present for Toot 402, 534
Toot & Puddle: I'll Be Home for Christmas **402**
Toot & Puddle: Puddle's ABC 402, 442, 982
Toot & Puddle: You Are My Sunshine 402, 790

Hobbs, Valerie
Carolina Crow Girl 403
Charlie's Run 403
Get It While It's Hot, or Not 403
How Far Would You Have Gotten If I Hadn't Called You Back? 355, 403
Tender **403**

Hobbs, Will
Bearstone 815, 853
Down the Yukon **404**
Far North 404
Ghost Canoe 404
Jason's Gold 347, 404, 538

Wild Man Island 404

Hoberman, Mary Ann
A House Is a House for Me 26
It's Simple, Said Simon **405**
One of Each 405
The Seven Silly Eaters 991
The Two Sillies 8, 405
You Read to Me, I'll Read to You: Very Short Stories to Read Together 405, 579, 607

Hoeye, Michael
The Sands of Time **406**
Time Stops for No Mouse 406

Hoffman, Alice
Aquamarine **407**
Illumination Night 288
Indigo 407
The River King 990

Hojer, Dan
Heart of Mine: A Story of Adoption **408**

Hojer, Lotta
Heart of Mine: A Story of Adoption **408**

Holl, Kristi D.
No Strings Attached 129

Holland, Cecelia
An Ordinary Woman 423

Holland, Isabelle
Paperboy 919

Holm, Jennifer L.
Boston Jane: An Adventure 58, **409**, 899
Our Only Mae Amelia 409

Holman, Felice
Secret City, U.S.A. 289
The Wild Children 946

Holmes, Barbara Ware
Following Fake Man 58, **410**, 1005
Letters to Julia 410

Holt, Kimberly Willis
Dancing in Cadillac Light **411**, 653
Mister and Me 411
My Louisiana Sky 411, 683
When Zachary Beaver Came to Town 411

Holub, Joan
Cinderdog and the Wicked Stepcat 412
The Garden That We Grew **412**
My First Book of Sign Language 412
The Pizza That We Made 412
Scat, Cats! 412, 675

Holubitsky, Katherine
Alone at Ninety Foot 413
Last Summer in Agatha 413

Honey, Elizabeth
45 and 47 Stella Street and Everything That Happened 414
The Book of Little Books 414
Don't Pat the Wombat 414
Fiddleback **414**

Hong, Lily Toy
Two of Everything 41

Hoobler, Dorothy
The 1920s: Luck 415
The 1930s: Directions 415
The 1940s: Secrets **415**, 1003
The 1950s: Music 415
The 1960s: Rebels 415
The 1970s: Arguments 415
The 1980s: Earthsong 415

The 1990s: Families 415
The Demon in the Teahouse **416**, 900
The Ghost in the Tokaido Inn 416
Promise Me the Moon 416
Real American Girls: Tell Their Own Stories 416
Sally Bradford: The Story of a Rebel Girl 416

Hoobler, Thomas
The 1940s: Secrets **415**
The Demon in the Teahouse **416**

Hooks, Bell
Happy to Be Nappy 235

Hooks, William H.
Lo-Jack and the Pirates 535

Hooper, Meredith
River Story 569

Hooper, Patricia
A Bundle of Beasts 417
How the Sky's Housekeeper Wore Her Scarves 417
A Stormy Ride on Noah's Ark **417**

Hoopes, Lynn Littlefield
The Unbeatable Bread 512

Hoover, H.M.
The Dawn Palace: the Story of Medea 327
Orvis 65

Hopkins, Jackie Mims
The Horned Toad Prince 134

Hopkinson, Deborah
A Band of Angels: A Story Inspired by the Jubilee Singers 418, 613
Birdie's Lighthouse 418
Bluebird Summer **418**
Maria's Comet 418
Sweet Clara and the Freedom Quilt 418

Hopkinson, Nalo
Midnight Robber 219, 266

Hopper, Nancy J.
What Happened in Mr. Fisher's Room 533

Hornik, Laurie Miller
The Secrets of Ms. Snickle's Class **419**

Horowitz, Anthony
Death Walks Tonight 420
The Devil and His Boy 420
The Devil's Door-Bell 420
The Night of the Scorpion 420
Point Blank 420
Stormbreaker 174, **420**, 900, 964

Horowitz, Ruth
Bat Time 421, 730
Breakout at the Bug Lab **421**
Crab Moon 421
Mommy's Lap 421

Horvath, Polly
Everything on a Waffle 110, **422**, 443
The Happy Yellow Car 422
The Trolls 422
When the Circus Came to Town 422

Hotze, Sollace
A Circle Unbroken 181

House, James
The San Francisco Earthquake 542

Houston, Gloria
Bright Freedom's Song: A Story of the Underground Railroad 40, 803
Mountain Valor 600

Houston, James D.
Farewell to Manzanar 423
In the Ring of Fire: A Pacific Basin Journey 423
The Last Paradise 423
Snow Mountain Passage **423**, 710

Howard, Arthur
Cosmo Zooms 424, 780
Hoodwinked **424**
When I Was Five 253, 424

Howard, Elizabeth Fitzgerald
Aunt Flossie's Hats (and Crab Cakes Later) 425
Lulu's Birthday **425**
The Train to Lulu's 425
Virgie Goes to School with Us Boys 280, 564, 868
What's in Aunt Mary's Room? 425
When Will Sarah Come? 86

Howard, Ellen
A Different Kind of Courage 871

Howard, Ginger
A Basket of Bangles: How a Business Begins 426
William's House **426**, 480

Howarth, Lesley
Maphead 829
The Pits 75

Howe, James
Bunnicula 428
Bunnicula: A Rabbit Tale of Mystery 718
The Celery Stalks at Midnight 428
The Color of Absence: Twelve Stories about Loss and Hope 427, 428
Dew Drop Dead 427, 428
Harold and Chester in the Fright Before Christmas 247
Horace and Morris but Mostly Dolores 802
The Misfits 427, **428**
The New Nick Kramer, or My Life as a Baby-Sitter 427, 428
Pinky and Rex 210
Pinky and Rex and the Double-Dad Weekend 211
Pinky and Rex and the Just-Right Pet **429**, 895
Pinky and Rex and the New Baby 153, 562
Pinky and Rex and the New Neighbors 429
Pinky and Rex and the Perfect Pumpkin 429
Pinky and Rex and the School Play 429
Pinky and Rex and the Spelling Bee 354
Rabbit-Cadabra! 7
The Watcher 427, 428

Howe, Norma
The Adventures of Blue Avenger 692

Howker, Janni
Isaac Campion 113

Howland, Ethan
The Lobster War **430**

Howland, Naomi
ABCDrive! A Car Trip Alphabet 57
Latkes, Latkes Good to Eat: A Chanukah Story 499

Hoyt, Sarah
Ill Met by Moonlight **431**

Hrdlitschka, Shelley
Disconnected 142

Author Index

Author Index

Walker, Pamela
Pray Hard **918**

Wallace, Barbara Brooks
Cousins in the Castle 919
Ghosts in the Gallery 197, 606, 919
Peppermints in the Palace 919
Secret in St. Something **919**
Sparrows in the Scullery 919
The Twin in the Tavern 919

Wallace, Bill
Aloha Summer 605
Coyote Autumn 122
Never Say Quit 360
Watchdog and the Coyotes 36

Wallace, Ian
Boy of the Deeps 457

Wallace, John
Little Bean's Friend 825
*Tiny Rabbit Goes to a Birthday
    Party* 261

Wallace, Karen
City Pig 3
Imagine You Are a Crocodile 795

Wallace, Nancy Elizabeth
Apples, Apples, Apples 302
Snow 17
Tell-a-Bunny 566, 935

Wallace, Rich
Wrestling Sturbridge 361

Wallace-Brodeur, Ruth
Goodbye, Mitch 379, 833

Wallin, Luke
Ceremony of the Panther 355

Wallner, Alexandra
Since 1920 236

Walsh, Alice
Heroes of Isle Aux Morts **920**
Uncle Farley's Teeth 920

Walsh, Ellen Stoll
*Dot & Jabber and the Great Acorn
    Mystery* **921**
Hop Jump 976
Jack's Tale 158, 848
Mouse Magic 921
Mouse Paint 725
Pip's Magic 560, 921, 974
Samantha 921

Walsh, Jill Paton
Grace 138
A Parcel of Patterns 101

Walter, Virginia
Making Up Megaboy 515

Walters, Catherine
When Will It Be Spring? 269

Walters, Virginia
Are We There Yet, Daddy? 310

Walton, Jo
The King's Name **922**, 923
The King's Peace 922, **923**

Walton, Rick
Bullfrog Pops! 461
That's My Dog! 895

Ward, Helen
The Golden Pear 924
The King of the Birds 924
*The Moonrat and the White
    Turtle* 924
The Tin Forest 924

Wardlaw, Lee
*Punia and the King of Sharks: A
    Hawaiian Folktale* 597
Seventh Grade Weirdo 220

Ware, Cheryl
Catty-Cornered 129, 894

Warner, Gertrude Chandler
*The Boxcar Children Mystery
    Series* 5, 887

Warner, Sally
Bad Girl Blues **925**, 927, 928
Ellie & the Bunheads 621, 926, 994
Finding Hattie 925, **926**, 927, 928
*How to Be a Real Person (in Just One
    Day)* 870, **927**, 928
Sister Split 925, 926, 927, **928**
Some Friend 925
Sort of Forever 750, 925, 926, 927,
    928
This Isn't about the Money 926
Totally Confidential 925, 926, 927,
    928

Warner, Sunny
Madison Finds a Line 929
The Magic Sewing Machine 929
The Moon Quilt **929**

Wartski, Maureen Crane
Candle in the Wind 50

Waters, Kate
Mary Geddy's Day 678
*On the Mayflower: Voyage of the Ship's
    Apprentice and a Passenger
    Girl* 480

Watson, Mary
The Butterfly Seeds 697

Watson, Wendy
Hooray for the Fourth of July 903

Watt, Alan
Diamond Dogs 278, 707

Watt-Evans, Lawrence
Touched By the Gods 115

Watts, Irene N.
*Remember Me: A Search for Refuge in
    Wartime Britain* 871

Watts, Jeri Hanel
Keepers 88, 425

Waugh, Sylvia
Space Race 187

Wax, Wendy
Empire Dreams **930**

Weaver, Beth Nixon
Rooster **931**

Weaver, Will
Farm Team 932
Hard Ball 932
Memory Boy **932**
Striking Out 932

Weeks, Sarah
Guy Time 933
Guy Wire 933
My Guy 361, **933**
Regular Guy 162, 933

Wegman, William
Cinderella 331

Wein, Elizabeth
The Winter Prince 846

Weinstock, Nicholas
As Long as She Needs Me **934**

Weir, Joan
The Brideship 409

Weiss, M. Jerry
From One Experience to Another 427

Weitzmann, Jacqueline Preiss
*You Can't Take a Balloon into the
    Metropolitan Museum* 604

Welch, James
Fool's Crow 83

Wells, Ken
Meely LaBauve 229

Wells, Martha
The Death of the Necromancer 116,
    260, 806

Wells, Rosemary
Be My Valentine 937
Bunny Cakes 935, 936
Bunny Money 935, 939
Bunny Party 782, **935**
Emily's First 100 Days of School 939
Felix Feels Better 936
The Halloween Parade 937
Mama, Don't Go! 937
Mama Don't Go 939
Max Cleans Up 935, 936
Max's Chocolate Chicken 387
McDuff and the Baby 544, 938
McDuff Goes to School **938**
McDuff Moves In 623, 938
McDuff's New Friend 938
Read to Your Bunny 840, 936
The School Play 937
Waiting for the Evening Star 504
Yoko 558, 936, 939
Yoko's Paper Cranes **939**

Weninger, Brigitte
Happy Easter, Davy! **940**
A Letter to Santa Claus 34
Merry Christmas, Davy! 940
What's the Matter, Davy? 333
Where Have You Gone, Davy? 940
Will You Mind the Baby, Davy? 940

Wennick, Elizabeth
Changing Jareth 413

Werlin, Nancy
Are You Alone on Purpose? 941
Black Mirror **941**
The Killer's Cousin 941, 990
Locked Inside 941

Wesley, Valerie Wilson
Willimena and the Cookie Money **942**

West, Dorothy
The Wedding 934

West, Paul
*The Women of Whitechapel and Jack
    the Ripper* 16

Westall, Robert
Futuretrack 5 574
The Promise 972

Weston, Carol
*The Diary of Melanie Martin: Or How
    I Survived Matt the Brat,
    Michelangelo and the Leaning Tower
    of Pizza* 259, 518

Weston, Martha
Space Guys! 571

Whatley, Bruce
*Captain Pajamas: Defender of the
    Universe* 943
*Detective Donut and the Wild Goose
    Chase* 694
My First Nursery Rhymes 943
The Teddy Bear's Picnic 943
Wait! No Paint! 848, **943**

Wheatley, Nadia
Luke's Way of Looking **944**
My Place 944

Whelan, Gerard
The Dream Invader 945
The Guns of Easter **945**
Out of Nowhere 945
A Winter of Spies 945

Whelan, Gloria
Angel on the Square **946**
Friends 946
Homeless Bird 946
Miranda's Last Stand 506, 602, 946
Once on This Island 495, 957
The Wanigan: A Life on the River 946

Whitcher, Susan
Moonfall 832

White, Carolyn
*The Adventure of Louey and
    Frank* **947**
*The Tree House Children: An African
    Folktale* 947
*Whuppity Stoorie: A Scottish
    Folktale* 947

White, E.B.
Charlotte's Web 914

White, Ellen Emerson
*The Journal of Patrick Seamus
    Flaherty: United States Marine
    Corps* 948
*Kaiulani: The People's Princess,
    Hawaii, 1889* **948**
*Voyage on the Great Titanic: The Diary
    of Margaret Ann Brady* 948
*Where Have All the Flowers Gone?:
    The Diary of Molly Mackenzie
    Flaherty* 948

White, Linda Arms
Comes a Wind 436

White, Michael C.
A Dream of Wolves: A Novel 391

White, Ruth
Belle Prater's Boy 683
Memories of Summer 969

Whitmore, Arvella
*Trapped: Between the Lash and the
    Gun* 284

Whybrow, Ian
A Baby for Grace 949
Harry and the Snow King 949
Little Wolf's Book of Badness 503
Sammy and the Dinosaurs 949
Sammy and the Robots **949**

Whyte, Jack
The Singing Sword 922
The Skystone 923

Widman, Christine
The Hummingbird Garden 43

Wieler, Diana
Bad Boy 309

Wiencirz, Gerlinda
Teddy's Easter Secret 940

Wiesner, David
June 29, 1999 950
Sector 7 950
The Three Pigs 848, 943, **950**
Tuesday 950

Wilcox, Brian
Full Moon 496

Title Index

This index alphabetically lists all titles featured in entries and those listed under "Other books by the author" and "Other books you might like." Each title is followed by the author's name and the number of the entry of that title. Bold numbers indicate featured main entries; light-face numbers refer to books recommended for further reading.

A

1st to Die
Patterson, James 165

4 1/2 Friends and the Disappearing Bio Teacher
Friedrich, Joachim 305

4 1/2 Friends and the Secret Cave
Friedrich, Joachim 305, 306, 900

6-321
Laser, Michael **533**

10 Minutes till Bedtime
Rathmann, Peggy 160, 487

The 13th Floor: A Ghost Story
Fleischman, Sid 291

22 Orphans
Veldkamp, Tjibbe 911

41/2 Friends and the Disappearing Bio Teacher
Friedrich, Joachim **306**

41/2 Friends and the Secret Cave
Friedrich, Joachim 307

45 and 47 Stella Street and Everything That Happened
Honey, Elizabeth 414

The $66 Summer
Armistead, John 546

100th Day Worries
Cuyler, Margery 202

999: Twenty-Nine Original Tales of Horror and Suspense
Sarrantonio, Al 45

1609: Winter of the Dead: A Novel about the Founding of Jamestown
Massie, Elizabeth 620

The 1920s: Luck
Hoobler, Dorothy 415

The 1930s: Directions
Hoobler, Dorothy 415

The 1940s: Secrets
Hoobler, Dorothy **415**, 1003

The 1950s: Music
Hoobler, Dorothy 415

The 1960s: Rebels
Hoobler, Dorothy 415

The 1970s: Arguments
Hoobler, Dorothy 415

The 1980s: Earthsong
Hoobler, Dorothy 415

1984
Orwell, George 78

The 1990s: Families
Hoobler, Dorothy 415

A-Boo-C: A Spooky Alphabet Story
Jane, Pamela 448

A Is for Apple, W Is for Witch
Dexter, Catherine 351

A Is for Salad
Lester, Mike 442

Aani and the Tree Huggers
Atkins, Jeannine 29

Abandoned
Rushford, Patricia H. 773

ABC
Reese, Bob 982

ABCDrive! A Car Trip Alphabet
Howland, Naomi 57

Abigail Takes the Wheel
Avi 37

About Face
Wood, June Rae 876

Above and Beyond
Bonners, Susan **91**

Above the Veil
Nix, Garth 677

The Absentminded Fellow
Marshak, Samuel 8

The Accidental Witch
Mazer, Anne 351

Achingly Alice
Naylor, Phyllis Reynolds 672

Ackamarackus: Julius Lester's Sumptuously Silly Fantastically Funny Fables
Lester, Julius **548**

Acorn Magic
Stern, Maggie 854

Across the Blue Mountains
Chichester Clark, Emma 157

Across the Grain
Ferris, Jean 286, 696, 876

Across the Lines
Reeder, Carolyn 682

Across the Steel River
Stenhouse, Ted **853**

Across the Wide Dark Sea: The Mayflower Journey
Van Leeuwen, Jean 480, 902

The Acts of King Arthur and his Noble Knights
Steinbeck, John 266

Adam and Eve and Pinch-Me
Johnston, Julie 462, 577, 731

Addie's Bad Day
Robins, Joan 210, 354

Adem's Cross
Mead, Alice 630

Adopting Pets: How to Choose Your New Best Friend
Gutman, Bill 146

Adventure in the Haunted House
McBrier, Page 608

The Adventure of Louey and Frank
White, Carolyn **947**

The Adventures of Ali Baba Bernstein
Hurwitz, Johanna 346

The Adventures of Bert
Ahlberg, Allan **8**

The Adventures of Blue Avenger
Howe, Norma 692

The Adventures of Hershel of Ostropol
Kimmel, Eric A. 893

The Adventures of Huckleberry Finn
Twain, Mark 229, 278, 686

The Adventures of Snail at School
Stadler, John 848

The Adventures of Super Diaper Baby: The First Graphic Novel
Pilkey, Dav 247

Aenir
Nix, Garth 677

After the Flood
Geisert, Arthur 323, 589

After the Rain
Mazer, Norma Fox 449, 873

After the War
Matas, Carol 600

Agapanthus Hum and Major Bark
Cowley, Joy **189**

Agapanthus Hum and the Eyeglasses
Cowley, Joy 189

Aggie's Home
Nixon, Joan Lowery 678

Airman Mortensen
Blake, Michael 83

Akiak: A Tale from Iditarod
Blake, Robert J. 324

Albert
Napoli, Donna Jo 545, **668**, 669, 747

Albert & Lila
Schami, Rafik 951

Albert's Thanksgiving
Tryon, Leslie 222

Albion's Dream: A Novel of Terror
Norman, Robert 862

Alejandro's Gift
Albert, Richard E. 796

Alex Is My Friend
Russo, Marisabina 774

Alexander, Who Used to Be Rich Last Sunday
Viorst, Judith 913

Title Index

Title Index

Title Index

Title Index

Title Index

Title Index

Title Index

Title Index

Title Index